HARPER COLLINS
FRENCH
DICTIONARY

HARPER COLLINS
FRENCH
DICTIONARY
FRENCH · ENGLISH   ENGLISH · FRENCH

HarperResource
An Imprint of HarperCollinsPublishers

ISBN 0-06-273741-4

The HarperCollins website address is
www.harpercollins.com

The HarperCollins UK website address is
www.fireandwater.com

Harper*Resource*   A Division of HarperCollins*Publishers*
10 East 53rd Street, New York, N.Y. 10022

first published 1990
second edition 2000

First Harper*Resource* printing: 2000

Typeset by Morton Word Processing Ltd, Scarborough
Printed in the United States of America

Harper*Resource* and colophons are trademarks of HarperCollins*Publishers*

TABLE DES MATIÈRES

CONTENTS

Les marques déposées

Les termes qui constituent à notre connaissance une marque déposée ont été désignés comme tels. La présence ou l'absence de cette désignation ne peut toutefois être considérée comme ayant valeur juridique.

Note on trademarks

Words which we have reason to believe constitute trademarks have been designated as such. However, neither the presence nor the absence of such designation should be regarded as affecting the legal status of any trademark.

INTRODUCTION

We are delighted you have decided to buy the Collins French Dictionary and hope you will enjoy and benefit from using it at school, at home, on holiday or at work.

This introduction gives you a few tips on how to get the most out of your dictionary — not simply from its comprehensive wordlist but also from the information provided in each entry. This will help you to read and understand modern French, as well as communicate and express yourself in the language.

The Collins French Dictionary begins by listing the abbreviations used in the text and illustrating the sounds shown by the phonetic symbols. You will find French verb tables and English irregular verbs at the back.

USING YOUR COLLINS DICTIONARY

A wealth of information is presented in the dictionary, using various type-faces, sizes of type, symbols, abbreviations and brackets. The conventions and symbols used are explained in the following sections.

Headwords

The words you look up in a dictionary — "headwords" — are listed alpha-betically. They are printed in **bold type** for rapid identification. The two headwords appearing at the top of each page indicate the first and last word dealt with on the page in question.

Information about the usage or form of certain headwords is given in brackets after the phonetic spelling. This usually appears in abbreviated form and in italics (e.g. (*fam*), (*COMM*)).

Where appropriate, words related to headwords are grouped in the same entry (**ronger, rongeur; accept, acceptance**) in a slightly smaller bold type than the headword.

Common expressions in which the headword appears are shown in a different bold roman type (e.g. **avoir du retard**).

Phonetic spellings

The phonetic spelling of each headword (indicating its pronunciation) is given in square brackets immediately after the headword (e.g. **fumer** [fyme]; **knead** [ni:d]). A list of these symbols is given on page xi.

Translations

Headword translations are given in ordinary type and, where more than one meaning or usage exists, these are separated by a semi-colon. You will often find other words in italics in brackets before the translations. These offer suggested contexts in which the headword might appear (e.g. **rough** (*voice*) or (*weather*)) or provide synonyms (e.g. **rough** (*violent*)).

"Key" words

Special status is given to certain French and English words which are considered as "key" words in each language. They may, for example, occur very frequently or have several types of usage (e.g. **vouloir, plus; get, that**). A combination of lozenges and numbers helps you to distinguish different parts of speech and different meanings. Further helpful information is provided in brackets and in italics in the relevant language for the user.

Grammatical information

Parts of speech are given in abbreviated form in italics after the phonetic spellings of headwords (e.g. *vt, adv, conj*).

Genders of French nouns are indicated as follows: *nm* for a masculine and *nf* for a feminine noun. Feminine and irregular plural forms of nouns are also shown (**directeur, trice; cheval, aux**).

Adjectives are given in both masculine and feminine forms where these forms are different (e.g. **noir, e**). Clear information is provided where adjectives have an irregular feminine or plural form (e.g. **net, nette**).

INTRODUCTION

Nous sommes très heureux que vous ayez décidé d'acheter le dictionnaire anglais de Collins et espérons que vous aimerez l'utiliser et que vous en tirerez profit au lycée, à la maison, en vacances ou au travail.

Cette introduction a pour but de vous donner quelques conseils sur la meilleure façon d'utiliser au mieux votre dictionnaire, en vous référant non seulement à son importante nomenclature mais aussi aux informations contenues dans chaque entrée. Ceci vous aidera à lire et à comprendre, mais aussi à communiquer et à vous exprimer en anglais contemporain.

Le dictionnaire anglais de Collins commence par la liste des abréviations utilisées dans le texte et par la transcription des sons par des symboles phonétiques. À la fin vous trouverez des tables de verbes français ainsi que la liste des verbes irréguliers en anglais.

COMMENT UTILISER VOTRE DICTIONNAIRE COLLINS

Ce dictionnaire offre une masse d'informations et use de divers formes et tailles de caractères, symboles, abréviations, parenthèses et crochets. Les conventions et symboles utilisés sont expliqués dans les sections qui suivent.

Entrées

Les mots que vous cherchez dans le dictionnaire (les 'entrées') sont classés par ordre alphabétique. Ils sont imprimés en **caractères gras** pour pouvoir être repérés rapidement. Les deux entrées figurant en haut de page indiquent le premier et le dernier mot qui apparaissent sur la page en question.

Des informations sur l'usage ou sur la forme de certaines entrées sont données entre parenthèses, après la transcription phonétique. Ces indications apparaissent sous forme abrégée et en italiques (ex (*fam*), (*COMM*)).

Dans les cas appropriés, les mots apparentés aux entrées sont regroupés sous la même entrée (**ronger, rongeur; accept, acceptance**) et apparaissent en caractères gras, légèrement plus petits que ceux de l'entrée.

Les expressions courantes dans lesquelles apparaît l'entrée sont indiquées par des caractères romains gras différents (ex **avoir du retard**).

Transcription phonétique

La transcription phonétique de chaque entrée (indiquant sa prononciation) est indiquée entre crochets immédiatement après l'entrée (ex **fumer** [fyme]; **knead** [ni:d]). Une liste de ces symboles figure à la page xi.

Traductions

Les traductions des entrées apparaissent en caractères ordinaires et, lorsque plusieurs sens ou usages coexistent, ces traductions sont séparées par un point-virgule. Vous trouverez souvent entre parenthèses d'autres mots en italiques qui précèdent les traductions. Ces mots fournissent souvent certains des contextes dans lesquels l'entrée est susceptible d'être utilisée (ex **rough** (*voice*) ou (*weather*)) ou offrent des synonymes (ex **rough** (*violent*)).

'Mots-clés'

Une importance particulière est accordée à certains mots français et anglais qui sont considérés comme des "mots-clés" dans chacune des langues. Cela peut être dû à leur utilisation très fréquente ou au fait qu'ils ont divers types d'usages (ex **vouloir, plus; get, that**). Une combinaison de losanges et de chiffres vous aident à distinguer différentes catégories grammaticales et différents sens. D'autres renseignements utiles apparaissent en italiques et entre parenthèses dans la langue de l'utilisateur.

Données grammaticales

Les catégories grammaticales sont données sous forme abrégée et en italiques après la transcription phonétique des entrées (ex *vt, adv, conj*).

Les genres des noms français sont indiqués de la manière suivante: *nm* pour un nom masculin et *nf* pour un nom féminin. Le féminin et le pluriel irréguliers de certains noms sont également indiqués (**directeur, trice; cheval, aux**).

Le masculin et le féminin des adjectif sont indiqués lorsque ces deux formes sont différentes (ex **noir, e**). Lorsque l'adjectif a un féminin ou un pluriel irrégulier, ces formes sont clairement indiquées (ex **net, nette**). Les pluriels irréguliers des noms, et les formes irrégulières des verbes anglais sont indiqués entre parenthèses, avant la catégorie grammaticale (ex **man** ... (*pl* **men**) *n*; **give** (*pt* **gave**, *pp* **given**) *vt*).

ABRÉVIATIONS

ABBREVIATIONS

abréviation	ab(b)r	abbreviation
adjectif, locution adjective	adj	adjective, adjectival phrase
adverbe, locution adverbiale	adv	adverb, adverbial phrase
administration	ADMIN	administration
agriculture	AGR	agriculture
anatomie	ANAT	anatomy
architecture	ARCHIT	architecture
article défini	art déf	definite article
article indéfini	art indéf	indefinite article
l'automobile	AUT(O)	the motor car and motoring
aviation, voyages aériens	AVIAT	flying, air travel
biologie	BIO(L)	biology
botanique	BOT	botany
anglais de Grande-Bretagne	BRIT	British English
chimie	CHEM	chemistry
commerce, finance, banque	COMM	commerce, finance, banking
comparatif	compar	comparative
informatique	COMPUT	computing
conjonction	conj	conjunction
construction	CONSTR	building
nom utilisé comme adjectif	cpd	compound element
cuisine, art culinaire	CULIN	cookery
article défini	def art	definite article
déterminant: article; adjectif démonstratif ou indéfini etc	dét	determiner: article, demonstrative etc
diminutif	dimin	diminutive
économie	ECON	economics
électricité, électronique	ELEC	electricity, electronics
exclamation, interjection	excl	exclamation, interjection
féminin	f	feminine
langue familière (! emploi vulgaire)	fam (!)	colloquial usage (! particularly offensive)
emploi figuré	fig	figurative use
(verbe anglais) dont la particule est inséparable du verbe	fus	(phrasal verb) where the particle cannot be separated from main verb
généralement	gén, gen	generally
géographie, géologie	GEO	geography, geology
géométrie	GEOM	geometry
impersonnel	impers	impersonal
article indéfini	indef art	indefinite article
langue familière (! emploi vulgaire)	inf(!)	colloquial usage (! particularly offensive)
infinitif	infin	infinitive
informatique	INFORM	computing
invariable	inv	invariable
irrégulier	irrég, irreg	irregular
domaine juridique	JUR	law
grammaire, linguistique	LING	grammar, linguistics
masculin	m	masculine
mathématiques, algèbre	MATH	mathematics, calculus
médecine	MÉD MED	medical term, medicine

ABRÉVIATIONS

ABBREVIATIONS

masculin ou féminin, suivant le sexe	m/f	masculine or feminine depending on sex
domaine militaire, armée	MIL	military matters
musique	MUS	music
nom	n	noun
navigation, nautisme	NAVIG, NAUT	sailing, navigation
adjectif ou nom numérique	num	numeral adjective or noun
	o.s.	oneself
péjoratif	péj, pej	derogatory, pejorative
photographie	PHOT(O)	photography
physiologie	PHYSIOL	physiology
pluriel	pl	plural
politique	POL	politics
participe passé	pp	past participle
préposition	prép, prep	preposition
pronom	pron	pronoun
psychologie, psychiatrie	PSYCH	psychology, psychiatry
temps du passé	pt	past tense
quelque chose	qch	
quelqu'un	qn	
religions, domaine ecclésiastique	REL	religions, church service
	sb	somebody
enseignement, système scolaire et universitaire	SCOL	schooling, schools and universities
singulier	sg	singular
	sth	something
subjonctif	sub	subjunctive
sujet (grammatical)	su(b)j	(grammatical) subject
superlatif	superl	superlative
techniques, technologie	TECH	technical term, technology
télécommunications	TEL	telecommunications
télévision	TV	television
typographie	TYP(O)	typography, printing
anglais des USA	US	American English
verbe (auxiliaire)	vb (aux)	(auxiliary) verb
verbe intransitif	vi	intransitive verb
verbe transitif	vt	transitive verb
zoologie	ZOOL	zoology
marque déposée	®	registered trademark
indique une équivalence culturelle	≃	introduces a cultural equivalent

TRANSCRIPTION PHONÉTIQUE

CONSONNES

CONSONANTS

NB. **p, b, t, d, k, g** sont suivis
d'une aspiration en anglais.

NB. **p, b, t, d, k, g** are not
aspirated in French.

French	Symbol	English
poupée	p	*puppy*
bombe	b	*baby*
tente thermal	t	*tent*
dinde	d	*daddy*
coq qui képi	k	*cork kiss chord*
gag bague	g	*gag guess*
sale ce nation	s	*so rice kiss*
zéro rose	z	*cousin buzz*
tache chat	ʃ	*sheep sugar*
gilet juge	ʒ	*pleasure beige*
	tʃ	*church*
	dʒ	*judge general*
fer phare	f	*farm raffle*
valve	v	*very rev*
	θ	*thin maths*
	ð	*that other*
lent salle	l	*little ball*
rare rentrer	R	
	r	*rat rare* ·
maman femme	m	*mummy comb*
non nonne	n	*no ran*
agneau vigne	ɲ	
	ŋ	*singing bank*
hop!	h	*hat reheat*
yeux paille pied	j	*yet*
nouer oui	w	*wall bewail*
huile lui	ɥ	
	x	*loch*

DIVERS

MISCELLANEOUS

pour l'anglais: le r final se prononce en liaison devant une voyelle	r	in French wordlist: no liaison
pour l'anglais: précède la syllabe accentuée	'	in French transcription: no liaison

PHONETIC TRANSCRIPTION

VOYELLES

NB. La mise en équivalence de certains sons n'indique qu'une ressemblance approximative.

VOWELS

NB. The pairing of some vowe sounds only indicates approx imate equivalence.

ici vie lyre	i i:	*heel bead*
	ɪ	*hit pity*
jouer été	e	
lait jouet merci	ɛ	*set tent*
plat amour	a æ	*bat apple*
bas pâte	ɑ ɑ:	*after car calm*
	ʌ	*fun cousin*
le premier	ə	*over above*
beurre peur	œ	
peu deux	ø ə:	*urn fern work*
or homme	ɔ	*wash pot*
mot eau gauche	o ɔ:	*born cork*
genou roue	u	*full soot*
	u:	*boon lewd*
rue urne	y	

DIPHTONGUES

DIPHTHONGS

	ɪə	*beer tier*
	ɛə	*tear fair there*
	eɪ	*date plaice day*
	aɪ	*life buy cry*
	au	*owl foul now*
	əu	*low no*
	ɔɪ	*boil boy oily*
	uə	*poor tour*

NASALES

NASAL VOWELS

matin plein	ɛ̃
brun	œ̃
sang an dans	ɑ̃
non pont	ɔ̃

FRANÇAIS – ANGLAIS

FRENCH – ENGLISH

A, a

a [a] *vb voir* **avoir**

MOT-CLÉ

à [a] (*à + le* = **au**, *à + les* = **aux**) *prép* **1**
(*endroit, situation*) at, in; **être à Paris/au
Portugal** to be in Paris/Portugal; **être à la
maison/à l'école** to be at home/at school; **à la
campagne** in the country; **c'est à 10 km/à 20
minutes (d'ici)** it's 10 km/20 minutes away
2 (*direction*) to; **aller à Paris/au Portugal** to
go to Paris/Portugal; **aller à la maison/à
l'école** to go home/to school; **à la campagne**
to the country
3 (*temps*): **à 3 heures/minuit** at 3 o'clock/
midnight; **au printemps/mois de juin** in the
spring/the month of June
4 (*attribution, appartenance*) to; **le livre est à
Paul/à lui/à nous** this book is Paul's/his/ours;
donner qch à qn to give sth to sb
5 (*moyen*) with; **se chauffer au gaz** to have
gas heating; **à bicyclette** on *ou* by bicycle;
à la main/machine by hand/machine
6 (*provenance*) from; **boire à la bouteille** to
drink from the bottle
7 (*caractérisation, manière*): **l'homme aux
yeux bleus** the man with the blue eyes; **à la
russe** the Russian way
8 (*but, destination*): **tasse à café** coffee cup;
maison à vendre house for sale
9 (*rapport, évaluation, distribution*): **100 km/
unités à l'heure** 100 km/units per *ou* an hour;
payé à l'heure paid by the hour; **cinq à six**
five to six

---

abaisser [abese] *vt* to lower, bring down;
(*manette*) to pull down; **s'~** *vi* to go down;
(*fig*) to demean o.s.
abandon [abãdɔ̃] *nm* abandoning; giving up;
withdrawal; **être à l'~** to be in a state of
neglect
abandonner [abãdɔne] *vt* (*personne*) to
abandon; (*projet, activité*) to abandon, give
up; (SPORT) to retire *ou* withdraw from;
(*céder*) to surrender; **s'~ à** (*paresse, plaisirs*) to
give o.s. up to
abasourdir [abazurdir] *vt* to stun, stagger
abat-jour [abaʒur] *nm inv* lampshade
abats [aba] *nmpl* (*de bœuf, porc*) offal *sg*; (*de
volaille*) giblets
abattement [abatmɑ̃] *nm*: **~ fiscal** ≈ tax
allowance
abattoir [abatwar] *nm* slaughterhouse
abattre [abatr] *vt* (*arbre*) to cut down, fell;
(*mur, maison*) to pull down; (*avion, personne*)
to shoot down; (*animal*) to shoot, kill; (*fig*)
to wear out, tire out; to demoralize; **s'~** *vi* to
crash down; **ne pas se laisser ~** to keep one's
spirits up, not to let things get one down;
s'~ sur to beat down on; (*fig*) to rain down
on
abbaye [abei] *nf* abbey
abbé [abe] *nm* priest; (*d'une abbaye*) abbot
abcès [apsɛ] *nm* abscess
abdiquer [abdike] *vi* to abdicate
abdominaux [abdɔmino] *nmpl*: **faire des ~**
to do exercises for one's abdominals, do
one's abdominals
abeille [abej] *nf* bee
aberrant, e [aberã, ãt] *adj* absurd
aberration [aberasjɔ̃] *nf* aberration
abêtir [abetir] *vt* to make morons of (*ou a
moron of*)
abime [abim] *nm* abyss, gulf
abimer [abime] *vt* to spoil, damage; **s'~** *vi* to
get spoilt *ou* damaged
ablation [ablasjɔ̃] *nf* removal
aboiement [abwamɑ̃] *nm* bark, barking
abois [abwa] *nmpl*: **aux ~** at bay
abolir [abolir] *vt* to abolish
abominable [abɔminabl] *adj* abominable
abondance [abɔ̃dɑ̃s] *nf* abundance
abondant, e [abɔ̃dã, ãt] *adj* plentiful,
abundant, copious; **abonder** *vi* to abound,
be plentiful; **abonder dans le sens de qn** to
concur with sb
abonné, e [abɔne] *nm/f* subscriber; season
ticket holder
abonnement [abɔnmɑ̃] *nm* subscription;
(*transports, concerts*) season ticket
abonner [abɔne] *vt*: **s'~ à** to subscribe to,
take out a subscription to
abord [abɔr] *nm*: **au premier ~** at first sight,
initially; **~s** *nmpl* (*environs*) surroundings; **d'~**
first
abordable [abɔrdabl] *adj* (*prix*) reasonable;
(*personne*) approachable
aborder [abɔrde] *vi* to land ♦ *vt* (*sujet,
difficulté*) to tackle; (*personne*) to approach;
(*rivage etc*) to reach
aboutir [abutir] *vi* (*négociations etc*) to

succeed; ~ à to end up at; n'~ à rien to come
to nothing

aboyer [abwaje] vi to bark

abréger [abʀeʒe] vt to shorten

abreuver [abʀœve]: s'~ vi to drink;
abreuvoir nm watering place

abréviation [abʀevjasjɔ̃] nf abbreviation

abri [abʀi] nm shelter; **être à l'~** to be under
cover; **se mettre à l'~** to shelter

abricot [abʀiko] nm apricot

abriter [abʀite] vt to shelter; s'~ vt to shelter,
take cover

abrupt, e [abʀypt] adj sheer, steep; (ton)
abrupt

abruti, e [abʀyti] adj stunned, dazed ♦ nm/f
(fam) idiot, moron; ~ **de travail** overworked

absence [apsɑ̃s] nf absence; (MÉD) blackout;
avoir des ~s to have mental blanks

absent, e [apsɑ̃, ɑ̃t] adj absent ♦ nm/f
absentee; **absenter: s'absenter** vi to take
time off work; (sortir) to leave, go out

absolu, e [apsɔly] adj absolute; **absolument** adv absolutely

absorbant, e [apsɔʀbɑ̃, ɑ̃t] adj absorbent

absorber [apsɔʀbe] vt to absorb; (gén MÉD:
manger, boire) to take

abstenir [apstəniʀ] vb: s'~ **de qch/de faire** to
refrain from sth/from doing

abstraction [apstʀaksjɔ̃] nf abstraction

abstrait, e [apstʀɛ, ɛt] adj abstract

absurde [apsyʀd] adj absurd

abus [aby] nm abuse; ~ **de confiance** breach
of trust; **abuser** vi to go too far, overstep the
mark; **abuser de** (duper) to take advantage
of; **abusif, -ive** adj exorbitant; (punition)
excessive

acabit [akabi] nm: **de cet ~** of that type

académie [akademi] nf academy; (SCOL:
circonscription) ≈ regional education authority

acajou [akaʒu] nm mahogany

acariâtre [akaʀjɑtʀ] adj cantankerous

accablant, e [akablɑ̃, ɑ̃t] adj (chaleur)
oppressive; (témoignage, preuve) overwhelming

accablement [akabləmɑ̃] nm despondency

accabler [akable] vt to overwhelm, overcome; ~ **qn d'injures** to heap ou shower
abuse on sb

accalmie [akalmi] nf lull

accaparer [akapaʀe] vt to monopolize; (suj:
travail etc) to take up (all) the time ou
attention of

accéder [aksede]: ~ **à** vt (lieu) to reach;
(accorder: requête) to grant, accede to

accélérateur [akseleʀatœʀ] nm accelerator

accélération [akseleʀasjɔ̃] nf acceleration

accélérer [akseleʀe] vt to speed up ♦ vi to
accelerate

accent [aksɑ̃] nm accent; (PHONÉTIQUE, fig)
stress; **mettre l'~ sur** (fig) to stress; ~ **aigu/
grave/circonflexe** acute/grave/circumflex
accent; **accentuer** vt (LING) to accent; (fig)
to accentuate, emphasize; **s'accentuer** vi to
become more marked ou pronounced

acceptation [akseptasjɔ̃] nf acceptance

accepter [aksepte] vt to accept; ~ **de faire** to
agree to do

accès [aksɛ] nm (à un lieu) access; (MÉD: de
toux) fit; (: de fièvre) bout; **d'~ facile** easily
accessible; **facile d'~** easy to get to; ~ **de
colère** fit of anger; **accessible** adj accessible;
(livre, sujet): **accessible à qn** within the reach
of sb

accessoire [akseswaʀ] adj secondary;
incidental ♦ nm accessory; (THÉÂTRE) prop

accident [aksidɑ̃] nm accident; **par ~** by
chance; ~ **de la route** road accident; ~ **du
travail** industrial injury ou accident;
accidenté, e adj damaged; injured; (relief,
terrain) uneven; hilly; **accidentel, le** adj
accidental

acclamations [aklamasjɔ̃] nfpl cheers

acclamer [aklame] vt to cheer, acclaim

acclimater [aklimate]: s'~ vi (personne) to
adapt (o.s.)

accolade [akɔlad] nf (amicale) embrace;
(signe) brace

accommodant, e [akɔmɔdɑ̃, ɑ̃t] adj
accommodating, easy-going

accommoder [akɔmɔde] vt (CULIN) to
prepare; s'~ **de** vt to put up with; (se
contenter de) to make do with

accompagnateur, -trice [akɔ̃paɲatœʀ,
tʀis] nm/f (MUS) accompanist; (de voyage:
guide) guide; (de voyage organisé) courier

accompagner [akɔ̃paɲe] vt to accompany,
be ou go ou come with; (MUS) to accompany

accompli, e [akɔ̃pli] adj accomplished

accomplir [akɔ̃pliʀ] vt (tâche, projet) to carry
out; (souhait) to fulfil; s'~ vi to be fulfilled

accord [akɔʀ] nm agreement; (entre des
styles, tons etc) harmony; (MUS) chord; **d'~!**
OK!; **se mettre d'~** to come to an agreement;
être d'~ (pour faire qch) to agree (to do sth)

accordéon [akɔʀdeɔ̃] nm (MUS) accordion

accorder [akɔʀde] vt (faveur, délai) to grant;
(harmoniser) to match; (MUS) to tune; s'~ vt
to get on together; to agree

accoster [akɔste] vt (NAVIG) to draw
alongside ♦ vi to berth

accotement [akɔtmɑ̃] nm verge (BRIT),
shoulder

accouchement [akuʃmɑ̃] nm delivery,
(child)birth; labour

accoucher [akuʃe] vi to give birth, have a
baby; ~ **d'un garçon** to give birth to a boy;
accoucheur nm: **(médecin) accoucheur**
obstetrician

accouder [akude]: **s'~** vi to rest one's elbows on/against; **accoudoir** nm armrest

accoupler [akuple] vt to couple; (pour la reproduction) to mate; **s'~** vt to mate

accourir [akuʀiʀ] vi to rush ou run up

accoutrement [akutʀəmɑ̃] (péj) nm (tenue) outfit

accoutumance [akutymɑ̃s] nf (gén) adaptation; (MÉD) addiction

accoutumé, e [akutyme] adj (habituel) customary, usual

accoutumer [akutyme] vt: **s'~ à** to get accustomed ou used to

accréditer [akʀedite] vt (nouvelle) to substantiate

accroc [akʀo] nm (déchirure) tear; (fig) hitch, snag

accrochage [akʀɔʃaʒ] nm (AUTO) collision; (dispute) clash, brush

accrocher [akʀɔʃe] vt (fig) to catch, attract; **s'~** (se disputer) to have a clash ou brush; **~ qch à** (suspendre) to hang sth (up) on; (attacher: remorque) to hitch sth (up) to; **~ qch (à)** (déchirer) to catch sth (on); un passant (heurter) to hit a pedestrian; **s'~ à** (rester prix à) to catch on; (agripper, fig) to hang on ou cling to

accroissement [akʀwasmɑ̃] nm increase

accroître [akʀwatʀ]: **s'~** vi to increase

accroupir [akʀupiʀ]: **s'~** vi to squat, crouch (down)

accru, e [akʀy] pp de **accroître**

accueil [akœj] nm welcome; **comité d'~** reception committee; **accueillir** vt to welcome; (aller chercher) to meet, collect

acculer [akyle] vt: **~ qn à** ou **contre** to drive sb back against

accumuler [akymyle] vt to accumulate, amass; **s'~** vi to accumulate; to pile up

accusation [akyzasjɔ̃] nf (gén) accusation; (JUR) charge; (partie): **l'~** the prosecution

accusé, e [akyze] nm/f accused; defendant; **~ de réception** acknowledgement of receipt

accuser [akyze] vt to accuse; (fig) to emphasize, bring out; to show; **~ qn de** to accuse sb of; (JUR) to charge sb with; **~ réception de** to acknowledge receipt of

acerbe [asɛʀb] adj caustic, acid

acéré, e [aseʀe] adj sharp

acharné, e [aʃaʀne] adj (efforts) relentless; (lutte, adversaire) fierce, bitter

acharner [aʃaʀne] vb: **s'~ contre** to set o.s. against; (suj: malchance) to dog; **s'~ à faire** to try doggedly to do; (persister) to persist in doing

achat [aʃa] nm purchase; **faire des ~s** to do some shopping; **faire l'~ de qch** to purchase sth

acheminer [aʃ(ə)mine] vt (courrier) to forward, dispatch; **s'~ vers** to head for

acheter [aʃ(ə)te] vt to buy, purchase; (soudoyer) to buy; **~ qch à** (marchand) to buy ou purchase sth from; (ami etc: offrir) to buy sth for; **acheteur, -euse** nm/f buyer; shopper; (COMM) buyer

achever [aʃ(ə)ve] vt to complete, finish; (blessé) to finish off; **s'~** vi to end

acide [asid] adj sour, sharp; (CHIMIE) acid(ic) ♦ nm (CHIMIE) acid; **acidulé, e** adj slightly acid

acier [asje] nm steel; **aciérie** nf steelworks sg

acné [akne] nf acne

acolyte [akɔlit] (péj) nm associate

acompte [akɔ̃t] nm deposit

à-côté [akote] nm side-issue; (argent) extra

à-coup [aku] nm: **par ~-~s** by fits and starts

acoustique [akustik] nf (d'une salle) acoustics pl

acquéreur [akeʀœʀ] nm buyer, purchaser

acquérir [akeʀiʀ] vt to acquire

acquis, e [aki, iz] pp de **acquérir** ♦ nm (accumulated) experience; **son aide nous est ~e** we can count on her help

acquit [aki] vb voir **acquérir** ♦ nm (quittance) receipt; **par ~ de conscience** to set one's mind at rest

acquitter [akite] vt (JUR) to acquit; (facture) to pay, settle; **s'~ de** (devoir) to discharge; (promesse) to fulfil

âcre [akʀ] adj acrid, pungent

acrobate [akʀɔbat] nm/f acrobat; **acrobatie** nf acrobatics sg

acte [akt] nm act, action; (THÉÂTRE) act; **prendre ~ de** to note, take note of; **faire ~ de candidature** to apply; **faire ~ de présence** to put in an appearance; **~ de naissance** birth certificate

acteur [aktœʀ] nm actor

actif, -ive [aktif, iv] adj active ♦ nm (COMM) assets pl; (fig): **avoir à son ~** to have to one's credit; **population active** working population

action [aksjɔ̃] nf (gén) action; (COMM) share; **une bonne ~** a good deed; **actionnaire** nm/f shareholder; **actionner** vt (mécanisme) to activate; (machine) to operate

activer [aktive] vt to speed up; **s'~** vi to bustle about; to hurry up

activité [aktivite] nf activity; **en ~** (volcan) active; (fonctionnaire) in active life

actrice [aktʀis] nf actress

actualiser [aktɥalize] vt to bring up to date

actualité [aktɥalite] nf (d'un problème) topicality; (événements): **l'~** current events; **les ~s** nfpl (CINÉMA, TV) the news; **d'~** topical

actuel, le [aktɥɛl] adj (présent) present; (d'actualité) topical; **à l'heure ~le** at the present time; **actuellement** adv at present, at the present time

acuité [akqite] *nf* acuteness
acuponcteur [akypɔ̃ktœʀ] *nm* acupuncturist
acuponcture [akypɔ̃ktyʀ] *nf* acupuncture
adaptateur [adaptatœʀ] *nm* (*ÉLEC*) adapter
adapter [adapte] *vt* to adapt; **s'~ (à)** (*suj: personne*) to adapt (to); **~ qch à** (*approprier*) to adapt sth to (fit); **~ qch sur/dans/à** (*fixer*) to fit sth on/into/to
additif [aditif] *nm* additive
addition [adisjɔ̃] *nf* addition; (*au café*) bill; **additionner** *vt* to add (up)
adepte [adɛpt] *nm/f* follower
adéquat, e [adekwa(t), at] *adj* appropriate, suitable
adhérent, e [aderɑ̃, ɑ̃t] *nm/f* member
adhérer [adeʀe]: **~ à** *vt* (*coller*) to adhere ou stick to; (*se rallier à*) to join; **adhésif, -ive** *adj* adhesive, sticky; **ruban adhésif** sticky ou adhesive tape; **adhésion** *nf* joining; (*fait d'être membre*) membership; (*accord*) support
adieu, x [adjø] *excl* goodbye ♦ *nm* farewell
adjectif [adʒɛktif] *nm* adjective
adjoindre [adʒwɛ̃dʀ] *vt*: **~ qch à** to attach sth to; (*ajouter*) to add sth to; **s'~ vt** (*collaborateur etc*) to take on, appoint; **adjoint, e** *nm/f* assistant; **adjoint au maire** deputy mayor; **directeur adjoint** assistant manager
adjudant [adʒydɑ̃] *nm* (*MIL*) warrant officer
adjuger [adʒyʒe] *vt* (*prix, récompense*) to award; (*lors d'une vente*) to auction (off); **s'~ vt** to take for o.s.
adjurer [adʒyʀe] *vt*: **~ qn de faire** to implore ou beg sb to do
admettre [admɛtʀ] *vt* (*laisser entrer*) to admit; (*candidat: SCOL*) to pass; (*tolérer*) to allow, accept; (*reconnaître*) to admit, acknowledge
administrateur, -trice [administʀatœʀ, tʀis] *nm/f* (*COMM*) director; (*ADMIN*) administrator
administration [administʀasjɔ̃] *nf* administration; **l'A~** ≈ the Civil Service
administrer [administʀe] *vt* (*firme*) to manage, run; (*biens, remède, sacrement etc*) to administer
admirable [admiʀabl] *adj* admirable, wonderful
admirateur, -trice [admiʀatœʀ, tʀis] *nm/f* admirer
admiration [admiʀasjɔ̃] *nf* admiration
admirer [admiʀe] *vt* to admire
admis, e [admi, iz] *pp de* **admettre**
admissible [admisibl] *adj* (*candidat*) eligible; (*comportement*) admissible, acceptable
admission [admisjɔ̃] *nf* admission; acknowledgement; **demande d'~** application

for membership
ADN *sigle m* (= *acide désoxyribonucléique*) DNA
adolescence [adɔlesɑ̃s] *nf* adolescence
adolescent, e [adɔlesɑ̃, ɑ̃t] *nm/f* adolescent, teenager
adonner [adɔne]: **s'~ à** *vt* (*sport*) to devote o.s. to; (*boisson*) to give o.s. over to
adopter [adɔpte] *vt* to adopt; **adoptif, -ive** *adj* (*parents*) adoptive; (*fils, patrie*) adopted
adorable [adɔʀabl] *adj* delightful, adorable
adorer [adɔʀe] *vt* to adore; (*REL*) to worship
adosser [adose] *vt*: **~ qch à** ou **contre** to stand sth against; **s'~ à** ou **contre** to lean with one's back against
adoucir [adusiʀ] *vt* (*goût, température*) to make milder; (*avec du sucre*) to sweeten; (*peau, voix*) to soften; (*caractère*) to mellow
adresse [adʀɛs] *nf* (*domicile*) address; (*dextérité*) skill, dexterity
adresser [adʀese] *vt* (*lettre: expédier*) to send; (: *écrire l'adresse sur*) to address; (*injure, compliments*) to address; **s'~ à** (*parler à*) to speak to, address; (*s'informer auprès de*) to go and see; (: *bureau*) to enquire at; (*suj: livre, conseil*) to be aimed at; **~ la parole à** to speak to, address
adroit, e [adʀwa, wat] *adj* skilful, skilled
adulte [adylt] *nm/f* adult, grown-up ♦ *adj* (*chien, arbre*) fully-grown, mature; (*attitude*) adult, grown-up
adultère [adyltɛʀ] *nm* (*acte*) adultery
advenir [advəniʀ] *vi* to happen
adverbe [advɛʀb] *nm* adverb
adversaire [advɛʀsɛʀ] *nm/f* (*SPORT, gén*) opponent, adversary
adverse [advɛʀs] *adj* opposing
aération [aeʀasjɔ̃] *nf* airing; (*circulation de l'air*) ventilation
aérer [aeʀe] *vt* to air; (*fig*) to lighten; **s'~ vi** to get some (fresh) air
aérien, ne [aeʀjɛ̃, jɛn] *adj* (*AVIAT*) air *cpd*, aerial; (*câble, métro*) overhead; (*fig*) light; **compagnie ~ne** airline
aéro... [aeʀɔ] *préfixe*: **aérobic** *nm* aerobics *sg*; **aérogare** *nf* airport (buildings); (*en ville*) air terminal; **aéroglisseur** *nm* hovercraft; **Aéronavale** *nf* ≈ Fleet Air Arm (*BRIT*), ≈ Naval Air Force (*US*); **aérophagie** *nf* (*MÉD*) wind, aerophagia (*MÉD*); **aéroport** *nm* airport; **aéroporté, e** *adj* airborne, airlifted; **aérosol** *nm* aerosol
affable [afabl] *adj* affable
affaiblir [afeblirʀ]: **s'~ vi** to weaken
affaire [afɛʀ] *nf* (*problème, question*) matter; (*criminelle, judiciaire*) case; (*scandaleuse etc*) affair; (*entreprise*) business; (*marché, transaction*) deal; **business** *no pl*; (*occasion intéressante*) bargain; **~s** *nfpl* (*intérêts publics*)

et privés) affairs; (*activité commerciale*) business *sg*; (*effets personnels*) things, belongings; **ce sont mes ~s** (*cela me concerne*) that's my business; **ça fera l'~** that will do (nicely); **se tirer d'~** to sort it *ou* things out for o.s.; **avoir ~ à** (*être en contact*) to be dealing with; **les A~s étrangères** Foreign Affairs; **affairer: s'affairer** *vi* to busy o.s., bustle about

affaisser [afese]: **s'~** *vi* (*terrain, immeuble*) to subside, sink; (*personne*) to collapse

affaler [afale] *vb*: **s'~ (dans/sur)** to collapse *ou* slump (into/onto)

affamé, e [afame] *adj* starving

affectation [afɛktasjɔ̃] *nf* (*nomination*) appointment; (*manque de naturel*) affectation

affecter [afɛkte] *vt* to affect; **~ qch à** to allocate *ou* allot sth to; **~ qn à** to appoint sb to; (*diplomate*) to post sb to

affectif, -ive [afɛktif, iv] *adj* emotional

affection [afɛksjɔ̃] *nf* affection; (*mal*) ailment; **affectionner** *vt* to be fond of; **affectueux, -euse** *adj* affectionate

affermir [afɛrmir] *vt* to consolidate, strengthen; (*muscles*) to tone up

affichage [afiʃaʒ] *nm* billposting; (*électronique*) display

affiche [afiʃ] *nf* poster; (*officielle*) notice; (*THÉÂTRE*) bill

afficher [afiʃe] *vt* (*affiche*) to put up; (*réunion*) to put up a notice about; (*électroniquement*) to display; (*fig*) to exhibit, display; **"défense d'~"** "stick no bills"

affilée [afile]: **d'~** *adv* at a stretch

affiler [afile] *vt* to sharpen

affilier [afilje]: **s'~ à** *vt* (*club, société*) to join

affiner [afine] *vt* to refine

affirmatif, -ive [afirmatif, iv] *adj* affirmative

affirmation [afirmasjɔ̃] *nf* assertion

affirmer [afirme] *vt* to assert

affligé, e [afliʒe] *adj* distressed, grieved; **~ de** (*maladie, tare*) afflicted with

affliger [afliʒe] *vt* (*peiner*) to distress, grieve

affluence [aflyɑ̃s] *nf* crowds *pl*; **heures d'~** rush hours; **jours d'~** busiest days

affluent [aflyɑ̃] *nm* tributary

affluer [aflye] *vi* (*secours, biens*) to flood in, pour in; (*sang*) to rush, flow

affolant, e [afɔlɑ̃, ɑ̃t] *adj* frightening

affolement [afɔlmɑ̃] *nm* panic

affoler [afɔle] *vt* to throw into a panic; **s'~ vi** to panic

affranchir [afrɑ̃ʃir] *vt* to put a stamp *ou* stamps on; (*à la machine*) to frank (*BRIT*), meter (*US*); (*fig*) to free, liberate; **affranchissement** *nm* postage

affréter [afrete] *vt* to charter

affreux, -euse [afrø, øz] *adj* dreadful, awful

affront [afrɔ̃] *nm* affront; **affrontement** *nm* clash, confrontation

affronter [afrɔ̃te] *vt* to confront, face

affubler [afyble] (*péj*) *vt*: **~ qn de** to rig *ou* deck sb out in

affût [afy] *nm*: **à l'~ (de)** (*gibier*) lying in wait (for); (*fig*) on the look-out (for)

affûter [afyte] *vt* to sharpen, grind

afin [afɛ̃]: **~ que** *conj* so that, in order that; **~ de faire** in order to do, so as to do

africain, e [afrikɛ̃, ɛn] *adj, nm/f* African

Afrique [afrik] *nf*: **l'~** Africa; **l'~ du Sud** South Africa

agacer [agase] *vt* to irritate

âge [ɑʒ] *nm* age; **quel ~ as-tu?** how old are you?; **prendre de l'~** to be getting on (in years); **âgé, e** *adj* old, elderly; **âgé de 10 ans** 10 years old

agence [aʒɑ̃s] *nf* agency, office; (*succursale*) branch; **~ de voyages** travel agency; **~ immobilière** estate (*BRIT*) *ou* real estate (*US*) agent's (office)

agencer [aʒɑ̃se] *vt* to put together, (*local*) to arrange, lay out

agenda [aʒɛ̃da] *nm* diary

agenouiller [aʒ(ə)nuje]: **s'~ vi** to kneel (down)

agent [aʒɑ̃] *nm* (*aussi*: **~ de police**) policeman; (*ADMIN*) official, officer; **~ d'assurances** insurance broker

agglomération [aglɔmerasjɔ̃] *nf* town; built-up area; **l'~ parisienne** the urban area of Paris

aggloméré [aglɔmere] *nm* (*bois*) chipboard

aggraver [agrave]: **s'~ vi** to worsen

agile [aʒil] *adj* agile, nimble

agir [aʒir] *vi* to act; **il s'agit de** (*ça traite de*) it is about; (*il est important de*) it's a matter *ou* question of

agitation [aʒitasjɔ̃] *nf* (hustle and) bustle; (*trouble*) agitation, unrest; (*politique*) unrest, agitation

agité, e [aʒite] *adj* fidgety, restless; (*troublé*) agitated, perturbed; (*mer*) rough

agiter [aʒite] *vt* (*bouteille, chiffon*) to shake; (*bras, mains*) to wave; (*préoccuper, exciter*) to perturb; **s'~ vi** (*enfant, élève*) to fidget

agneau, x [aɲo] *nm* lamb

agonie [agɔni] *nf* mortal agony, death pangs *pl*; (*fig*) death throes *pl*

agrafe [agraf] *nf* (*de vêtement*) hook, fastener; (*de bureau*) staple; **agrafer** *vt* to fasten; to staple; **agrafeuse** *nf* stapler

agrandir [agrɑ̃dir] *vt* to enlarge; **s'~ vi** (*ville, famille*) to grow, expand; (*trou, écart*) to get bigger; **agrandissement** *nm* (*PHOTO*) enlargement

agréable [agreabl] *adj* pleasant, nice

agréé, e [agree] *adj*: **concessionnaire ~** registered dealer

agréer [agree] vt (requête) to accept; ~ à to please, suit; **veuillez** ~ ... (formule épistolaire) yours faithfully

agrégation [agregasjɔ̃] nf highest teaching diploma in France; **agrégé, e** nm/f holder of the agrégation

agrément [agremɑ̃] nm (accord) consent, approval; **agrémenter** vt to embellish, adorn

agresser [agrese] vt to attack; **agresseur** nm aggressor, attacker; (POL, MIL) aggressor; **agressif, -ive** adj aggressive

agricole [agrikɔl] adj agricultural; **agriculteur** nm farmer; **agriculture** nf agriculture, farming

agripper [agripe] vt to grab, clutch; **s'~ à** to cling (on) to, clutch, grip

agroalimentaire [agroalimɑ̃tɛr] nm farm-produce industry

agrumes [agrym] nmpl citrus fruit(s)

aguerrir [agerir] vt to harden

aguets [age] nmpl: **être aux ~** to be on the look out

aguicher [agiʃe] vt to entice

ahuri, e [ayri] adj (stupéfait) flabbergasted

ai [ɛ] vb voir avoir

aide [ɛd] nm/f assistant; carer ♦ nf assistance, help; (secours financier) aid; **à l'~ de** (avec) with the help ou aid of; **appeler (qn) à l'~** to call for help (from sb); ~ **familiale** home help, mother's help; ~ **judiciaire** nf legal aid; ~ **sociale** nf (assistance) state aid; **aide-mémoire** nm inv memoranda pages pl; (key facts) handbook; **aide-soignant, e** nm/f auxiliary nurse

aider [ede] vt to help; **s'~ de** (se servir de) to use, make use of

aie etc [ɛ] vb voir avoir

aïe [aj] excl ouch!

aïeul, e [ajœl] nm/f grandparent, grandfather(-mother)

aïeux [ajø] nmpl grandparents; (ancêtres) forebears, forefathers

aigle [ɛgl] nm eagle

aigre [ɛgr] adj sour, sharp; (fig) sharp, cutting; **aigre-doux, -ce** adj (sauce) sweet and sour; **aigreur** nf sourness; sharpness; **aigreurs d'estomac** heartburn sg; **aigrir** vt (personne) to embitter; (caractère) to sour

aigu, ë [egy] adj (objet, douleur) sharp; (son, voix) high-pitched, shrill; (note) high(-pitched)

aiguille [egɥij] nf needle; (de montre) hand; ~ **à tricoter** knitting needle

aiguiller [egɥije] vt (orienter) to direct; **aiguilleur du ciel** nm air-traffic controller

aiguillon [egɥijɔ̃] nm (d'abeille) sting; **aiguillonner** vt to spur ou goad on

aiguiser [egize] vt to sharpen; (fig) to stimulate; (: sens) to excite

ail [aj, o] nm garlic

aile [ɛl] nf wing; **aileron** nm (de requin) fin; **ailier** nm winger

aille etc [aj] vb voir aller

ailleurs [ajœr] adv elsewhere, somewhere else; **partout/nulle part** ~ everywhere/nowhere else; **d'~** (du reste) moreover, besides; **par** ~ (d'autre part) moreover, furthermore

aimable [ɛmabl] adj kind, nice

aimant [ɛmɑ̃] nm magnet

aimer [eme] vt to love; (d'amitié, affection, par goût) to like; (souhait): **j'~ais** ... I would like ...; **bien** ~ **qn/qch** to like sb/sth; **j'~ais mieux faire** I'd much rather do

aine [ɛn] nf groin

aîné, e [ene] adj elder, older; (le plus âgé) eldest, oldest ♦ nm/f oldest child ou one, oldest boy ou son/girl ou daughter

ainsi [ɛ̃si] adv (de cette façon) like this, in this way, thus; (ce faisant) thus ♦ conj thus, so; ~ **que** (comme) (just) as; (et aussi) as well as; **pour** ~ **dire** so to speak; **et** ~ **de suite** and so on

aïoli [ajɔli] nm garlic mayonnaise

air [ɛr] nm air; (mélodie) tune; (expression) look, air; **prendre l'~** to get some (fresh) air; **avoir l'~** (sembler) to look, appear; **avoir l'~ de** to look like; **avoir l'~ de faire** to look as though one is doing, appear to be doing; **en l'~** (promesses) empty

aisance [ɛzɑ̃s] nf ease; (richesse) affluence

aise [ɛz] nf comfort; **être à l'~ ou à son** ~ to be comfortable; (pas embarrassé) to be at ease; (financièrement) to be comfortably off; **se mettre à l'~** to make o.s. comfortable; **être mal à l'~** to be uncomfortable; (gêné) to be ill at ease; **en faire à son** ~ to do as one likes; **aisé, e** adj easy; (assez riche) well-to-do, well-off

aisselle [ɛsɛl] nf armpit

ait [ɛ] vb voir avoir

ajonc [aʒɔ̃] nm gorse no pl

ajourner [aʒurne] vt (réunion) to adjourn; (décision) to defer, postpone

ajouter [aʒute] vt to add

ajusté, e [aʒyste] adj: **bien** ~ (robe etc) close-fitting

ajuster [aʒyste] vt (régler) to adjust; (vêtement) to alter; (coup de fusil) to aim; (cible) to aim at; (TECH, gén: adapter): ~ **qch à** to fit sth to

alarme [alarm] nf alarm; **donner l'~** to give ou raise the alarm; **alarmer** vt to alarm; **s'alarmer** vi to become alarmed; **alarmiste** adj, nm/f alarmist

album [albɔm] nm album

albumine [albymin] nf albumin; **avoir de l'~**

to suffer from albuminuria

alcool [alkɔl] nm: **l'~** alcohol; **un ~** a spirit, a brandy; **bière sans ~** non-alcoholic ou alcohol-free beer; **~ à brûler** methylated spirits (BRIT), wood alcohol (US); **~ à 90°** surgical spirit; **alcoolique** adj, nm/f alcoholic; **alcoolisé, e** adj alcoholic; **une boisson non alcoolisée** a soft drink; **alcoolisme** nm alcoholism; **alcootest** ® nm Breathalyser ®; (test) breath-test

aléas [alea] nmpl hazards; **aléatoire** adj uncertain; (INFORM) random

alentour [alātur] adv around, round about; **~s** nmpl (environs) surroundings, **aux ~s de** in the vicinity ou neighbourhood of, round about; (temps) round about

alerte [alɛrt] adj agile, nimble; brisk, lively ♦ nf alert; warning; **~ à la bombe** bomb scare; **alerter** vt to alert

algèbre [alʒɛbr] nf algebra

Alger [alʒe] n Algiers

Algérie [alʒeri] nf: **l'~** Algeria; **algérien, ne** adj Algerian ♦ nm/f: **Algérien, ne** Algerian

algue [alg] nf (gén) seaweed no pl; (BOT) alga

alibi [alibi] nm alibi

aliéné, e [aljene] nm/f insane person, lunatic (péj)

aligner [aliɲe] vt to align, line up; (idées, chiffres) to string together; (adapter): **~ qch sur** to bring sth into alignment with; **s'~** (soldats etc) to line up; **s'~ sur** (POL) to align o.s. on

aliment [alimā] nm food; **alimentaire** adj: **denrées alimentaires** foodstuffs; **alimentation** nf (commerce) food trade; (magasin) grocery store; (régime) diet; (en eau etc, de moteur) supplying; (INFORM) feed; **alimenter** vt to feed; (TECH): **alimenter (en)** to supply (with); to feed (with); (fig) to sustain, keep going

alinéa [alinea] nm paragraph

aliter [alite]: **s'~** vi to take to one's bed

allaiter [alete] vt to (breast-)feed, nurse; (suj: animal) to suckle

allant [alā] nm drive, go

alléchant, e [aleʃā, āt] adj (odeur) mouth-watering; (offre) enticing

allécher [aleʃe] vt: **~ qn** to make sb's mouth water; to tempt ou entice sb

allée [ale] nf (de jardin) path; (en ville) avenue, drive; **~s et venues** comings and goings

allégé, e [aleʒe] adj (yaourt etc) low-fat

alléger [aleʒe] vt (voiture) to make lighter; (chargement) to lighten; (souffrance) to alleviate, soothe

allègre [a(l)lɛgr] adj lively, cheerful

alléguer [a(l)lege] vt to put forward (as proof ou an excuse)

Allemagne [alman] nf: **l'~** Germany; **allemand, e** adj German ♦ nm/f: **Allemand, e** German ♦ nm (LING) German

aller [ale] nm (trajet) outward journey; (billet: aussi: **~ simple**) single (BRIT) ou one-way (US) ticket ♦ vi (gén) to go; **~ à** (convenir) to suit; (suj: forme, pointure etc) to fit; **~** (bien) avec (couleurs, style etc) to go (well) with; **je vais y ~/me fâcher** I'm going to go/to get angry; **~ voir** to go and see, go to see; **allez!** come on!; **allons!** come now!; **comment allez-vous?** how are you?; **comment ça va?** how are you?; (affaires etc) how are things?; **il va bien/mal** he's well/not well, he's fine/ill; **ça va bien/mal** (affaires etc) it's going well/not going well; **~ mieux** to be better; **s'en ~** (partir) to be off, go, leave; (disparaître) to go away; **~ retour** return journey (BRIT), round trip; (billet) return (ticket) (BRIT), round trip ticket (US)

allergique [alɛrʒik] adj: **~ à** allergic to

alliage [aljaʒ] nm alloy

alliance [aljɑ̃s] nf (MIL, POL) alliance; (bague) wedding ring

allier [alje] vt (POL, gén) to ally; (fig) to combine; **s'~** to become allies; to combine

allô [alo] excl hullo, hallo

allocation [alɔkasjɔ̃] nf allowance; **~ (de) chômage** unemployment benefit; **~s familiales** ≈ child benefit

allocution [a(l)lɔkysjɔ̃] nf short speech

allonger [alɔ̃ʒe] vt to lengthen, make longer; (étendre: bras, jambe) to stretch (out); **s'~** vi to get longer; (se coucher) to lie down, stretch out; **~ le pas** to hasten one's step(s)

allouer [alwe] vt to allocate, allot

allumage [alymaʒ] nm (AUTO) ignition

allume-cigare [alymsigar] nm inv cigar lighter

allumer [alyme] vt (lampe, phare, radio) to put ou switch on; (pièce) to put ou switch the light(s) on in; (feu) to light; **s'~** vi (lumière, lampe) to come ou go on

allumette [alymɛt] nf match

allure [alyr] nf (vitesse) speed, pace; (démarche) walk; (aspect, air) look; **avoir de l'~** to have style; **à toute ~** at top speed

allusion [a(l)lyzjɔ̃] nf allusion; (sous-entendu) hint; **faire ~ à** to allude ou refer to; to hint at

---

MOT-CLÉ

---

alors [alɔr] adv **1** (à ce moment-là) then, at that time; **il habitait alors à Paris** he lived in Paris at that time

2 (par conséquent) then; **tu as fini? alors je m'en vais** have you finished? I'm going then; **et alors?** so what?

alors que conj **1** (au moment où) when, as; **il est arrivé alors que je partais** he arrived as I

was leaving
2 (*pendant que*) while, when; **alors qu'il était
à Paris, il a visité ...** while *ou* when he was in
Paris, he visited ...
3 (*tandis que*) whereas, while; **alors que son
frère travaillait dur, lui se reposait** while his
brother was working hard, HE would rest

alouette [alwɛt] *nf* (sky)lark
alourdir [aluʀdiʀ] *vt* to weigh down, make
heavy
aloyau [alwajo] *nm* sirloin
Alpes [alp] *nfpl*: **les ~** the Alps
alphabet [alfabɛ] *nm* alphabet; (*livre*) ABC
(book); **alphabétique** *adj* alphabetical;
alphabétiser *vt* to teach to read and write;
(*pays*) to eliminate illiteracy in
alpinisme [alpinism] *nm* mountaineering,
climbing; **alpiniste** *nm/f* mountaineer,
climber
Alsace [alzas] *nf* Alsace; **alsacien, ne** *adj*
Alsatian ♦ *nm/f*: **Alsacien, ne** Alsatian
altérer [alteʀe] *vt* (*vérité*) to distort; **s'~** *vi* to
deteriorate
alternateur [altɛʀnatœʀ] *nm* alternator
alternatif, -ive [altɛʀnatif, iv] *adj*
alternating; **alternative** *nf* (*choix*)
alternative; **alternativement** *adv*
alternately; **alterner** *vi* to alternate
Altesse [altɛs] *nf* Highness
altitude [altityd] *nf* altitude, height
alto [alto] *nm* (*instrument*) viola
aluminium [alyminjɔm] *nm* aluminium
(*BRIT*), aluminum (*US*)
amabilité [amabilite] *nf* kindness
amadouer [amadwe] *vt* to mollify, soothe
amaigrir [amegʀiʀ] *vt* to make thin(ner);
amaigrissant, e *adj* (*régime*) slimming
amalgame [amalgam] (*péj*) *nm* (strange)
mixture
amande [amãd] *nf* (*de l'amandier*) almond;
amandier *nm* almond (tree)
amant [amã] *nm* lover
amarrer [amaʀe] *vt* (*NAVIG*) to moor; (*gén*)
to make fast
amas [ama] *nm* heap, pile; **amasser** *vt* to
amass; **s'amasser** *vi* (*foule*) to gather
amateur [amatœʀ] *nm* amateur; **en ~** (*péj*)
amateurishly; **~ de musique/sport** *etc* music/
sport *etc* lover
amazone [amazon] *nf*: **en ~** sidesaddle
ambassade [ãbasad] *nf* embassy; **l'~ de
France** the French Embassy; **ambassadeur,
-drice** *nm/f* ambassador(-dress)
ambiance [ãbjãs] *nf* atmosphere
ambiant, e [ãbjã, jãt] *adj* (*air, milieu*)
surrounding; (*température*) ambient
ambigu, ë [ãbigy] *adj* ambiguous
ambitieux, -euse [ãbisjø, jøz] *adj*

ambitious
ambition [ãbisjɔ̃] *nf* ambition
ambulance [ãbylãs] *nf* ambulance;
ambulancier, -ière *nm/f* ambulance
man(-woman) (*BRIT*), paramedic (*US*)
ambulant, e [ãbylã, ãt] *adj* travelling,
itinerant
âme [ɑm] *nf* soul
amélioration [ameljɔʀasjɔ̃] *nf* improvement
améliorer [ameljɔʀe] *vt* to improve; **s'~** *vi* to
improve, get better
aménager [amenaʒe] *vt* (*agencer,
transformer*) to fit out; to lay out; (: *quartier,
territoire*) to develop; (*installer*) to fix up, put
in; **ferme aménagée** converted farmhouse
amende [amãd] *nf* fine; **faire ~ honorable** to
make amends
amener [am(ə)ne] *vt* to bring; (*causer*) to
bring about; **s'~** *vi* to show up (*fam*), turn up
amenuiser [amənɥize]: **s'~** *vi* (*chances*) to
grow slimmer, lessen
amer, amère [amɛʀ] *adj* bitter
américain, e [ameʀikɛ̃, ɛn] *adj* American
♦ *nm/f*: **A~, e** American
Amérique [ameʀik] *nf*: **l'~** America;
l'~ centrale/latine Central/Latin America;
l'~ du Nord/du Sud North/South America
amertume [ameʀtym] *nf* bitterness
ameublement [amœbləmã] *nm* furnishing;
(*meubles*) furniture
ameuter [amøte] *vt* (*peuple*) to rouse
ami, e [ami] *nm/f* friend; (*amant/maîtresse*)
boyfriend/girlfriend ♦ *adj*: **pays/groupe ~**
friendly country/group
amiable [amjabl]: **à l'~** *adv* (*JUR*) out of
court; (*gén*) amicably
amiante [amjãt] *nm* asbestos
amical, e, -aux [amikal, o] *adj* friendly;
amicalement *adv* in a friendly way; (*formule
épistolaire*) regards
amidon [amidɔ̃] *nm* starch
amincir [amɛ̃siʀ] *vt*: **~ qn** to make sb thinner
ou slimmer; (*suj: vêtement*) to make sb look
slimmer
amincissant, e [amɛ̃sisã, ãt] *adj*: **régime ~**
(slimming) diet; **crème ~e** slimming cream
amiral, -aux [amiʀal, o] *nm* admiral
amitié [amitje] *nf* friendship; **prendre en ~** to
befriend; **~s, Christèle** best wishes, Christèle;
présenter ses ~s à qn to send sb one's best
wishes
ammoniaque [amɔnjak] *nf* ammonia
(water)
amnistie [amnisti] *nf* amnesty
amoindrir [amwɛ̃dʀiʀ] *vt* to reduce
amollir [amɔliʀ] *vt* to soften
amonceler [amɔ̃s(ə)le] *vt* to pile *ou* heap
up; **s'~** *vi* to pile *ou* heap up; (*fig*) to
accumulate

amont [amɔ̃]: en ~ *adv* upstream

amorce [amɔʀs] *nf* (*sur un hameçon*) bait; (*explosif*) cap; primer; priming; (*fig: début*) beginning(s), start; **amorcer** *vt* to start

amorphe [amɔʀf] *adj* passive, lifeless

amortir [amɔʀtiʀ] *vt* (*atténuer: choc*) to absorb, cushion; (*bruit, douleur*) to deaden; (COMM: *dette*) to pay off; ~ **un achat** to make a purchase pay for itself; **amortisseur** *nm* shock absorber

amour [amuʀ] *nm* love; **faire l'~** to make love; **amouracher: s'amouracher de** (*péj*) *vt* to become infatuated with; **amoureux, -euse** *adj* (*regard, tempérament*) amorous; (*vie, problèmes*) love *cpd*; (*personne*): **amoureux (de qn)** in love (with sb) ♦ *nmpl* courting couple(s); **amour-propre** *nm* self-esteem, pride

amovible [amɔvibl] *adj* removable, detachable

ampère [ɑ̃pɛʀ] *nm* amp(ere)

amphithéâtre [ɑ̃fiteatʀ] *nm* amphitheatre; (*d'université*) lecture hall ou theatre

ample [ɑ̃pl] *adj* (*vêtement*) roomy, ample; (*gestes, mouvement*) broad; (*ressources*) ample; **amplement** *adv*: **c'est amplement suffisant** that's more than enough; **ampleur** *nf* (*de dégâts, problème*) extent

amplificateur [ɑ̃plifikatœʀ] *nm* amplifier

amplifier [ɑ̃plifje] *vt* (*fig*) to expand, increase

ampoule [ɑ̃pul] *nf* (*électrique*) bulb; (*de médicament*) phial; (*aux mains, pieds*) blister; **ampoulé, e** (*péj*) *adj* pompous, bombastic

amputer [ɑ̃pyte] *vt* (MÉD) to amputate; (*fig*) to cut ou reduce drastically

amusant, e [amyzɑ̃, ɑ̃t] *adj* (*divertissant, spirituel*) entertaining, amusing; (*comique*) funny, amusing

amuse-gueule [amyzgœl] *nm inv* appetizer, snack

amusement [amyzmɑ̃] *nm* (*divertissement*) amusement; (*jeu etc*) pastime, diversion

amuser [amyze] *vt* (*divertir*) to entertain, amuse; (*égayer, faire rire*) to amuse; **s'~** *vi* (*jouer*) to play; (*se divertir*) to enjoy o.s., have fun; (*fig*) to mess around

amygdale [amidal] *nf* tonsil

an [ɑ̃] *nm* year; **avoir quinze ~s** to be fifteen (years old); **le jour de l'~, le premier de l'~, le nouvel** ~ New Year's Day

analogique [analɔʒik] *adj* (INFORM, *montre*) analog

analogue [analɔg] *adj*: ~ **(à)** analogous (to), similar (to)

analphabète [analfabɛt] *nm/f* illiterate

analyse [analiz] *nf* analysis; (MÉD) test; **analyser** *vt* to analyse; to test

ananas [anana(s)] *nm* pineapple

anarchie [anaʀʃi] *nf* anarchy

anatomie [anatɔmi] *nf* anatomy

ancêtre [ɑ̃sɛtʀ] *nm/f* ancestor

anchois [ɑ̃ʃwa] *nm* anchovy

ancien, ne [ɑ̃sjɛ̃, jɛn] *adj* old; (*de jadis, de l'antiquité*) ancient; (*précédent, ex-*) former, old; (*par l'expérience*) senior ♦ *nm/f* (*dans une tribu*) elder, **~-combattant** ♦ *nm* war veteran; **anciennement** *adv* formerly; **ancienneté** *nf* (ADMIN) (length of) service; (*privilèges obtenus*) seniority

ancre [ɑ̃kʀ] *nf* anchor; **jeter/lever l'~** to cast/weigh anchor; **ancrer** *vt* (CONSTR: *câble etc*) to anchor; (*fig*) to fix firmly

Andorre [ɑ̃dɔʀ] *nf* Andorra

andouille [ɑ̃duj] *nf* (CULIN) sausage made of chitterlings; (*fam*) clot, nit

âne [ɑn] *nm* donkey, ass; (*péj*) dunce

anéantir [aneɑ̃tiʀ] *vt* to annihilate, wipe out; (*fig*) to obliterate, destroy

anémie [anemi] *nf* anaemia; **anémique** *adj* anaemic

ânerie [ɑnʀi] *nf* stupidity; (*parole etc*) stupid ou idiotic comment *etc*

anesthésie [anɛstezi] *nf* anaesthesia; **faire une ~ locale/générale à qn** to give sb a local/general anaesthetic

ange [ɑ̃ʒ] *nm* angel; **être aux ~s** to be over the moon

angélus [ɑ̃ʒelys] *nm* angelus; (*cloches*) evening bells *pl*

angine [ɑ̃ʒin] *nf* throat infection; ~ **de poitrine** angina

anglais, e [ɑ̃glɛ, ɛz] *adj* English ♦ *nm/f*: A~, e Englishman(-woman) ♦ *nm* (LING) English; **les A~** the English; **filer à l'~e** to take French leave

angle [ɑ̃gl] *nm* angle; (*coin*) corner; ~ **droit** right angle

Angleterre [ɑ̃glətɛʀ] *nf*: **l'~** England

anglo... [ɑ̃glɔ] *préfixe* Anglo-, anglo(-); **anglophone** *adj* English-speaking

angoisse [ɑ̃gwas] *nf* anguish, distress; **angoissé, e** *adj* (*personne*) distressed; **angoisser** *vt* to harrow, cause anguish to ♦ *vi* to worry, fret

anguille [ɑ̃gij] *nf* eel

anicroche [anikʀɔʃ] *nf* hitch, snag

animal, e, -aux [animal, o] *adj, nm* animal

animateur, -trice [animatœʀ, tʀis] *nm/f* (*de télévision*) host; (*de groupe*) leader, organizer

animation [animasjɔ̃] *nf* (*voir animé*) busyness; liveliness; (CINÉMA: *technique*) animation; **~s culturelles** cultural activities

animé, e [anime] *adj* (*lieu*) busy, lively; (*conversation, réunion*) lively, animated

animer [anime] *vt* (*ville, soirée*) to liven up; (*mener*) to lead; **s'~** *vi* to liven up

anis [ani(s)] *nm* (CULIN) aniseed; (BOT) anise

ankyloser [ãkiloze]: **s'~** vi to get stiff

anneau, x [ano] nm (de rideau, bague) ring; (de chaîne) link

année [ane] nf year

annexe [anɛks] adj (problème) related; (document) appended; (salle) adjoining ♦ nf (bâtiment) annex(e); (jointe à une lettre) enclosure

anniversaire [anivɛRsɛR] nm birthday; (d'un événement, bâtiment) anniversary

annonce [anɔ̃s] nf announcement; (signe, indice) sign; (aussi: ~ publicitaire) advertisement; **les petites ~s** the classified advertisements, the small ads

annoncer [anɔ̃se] vt to announce; (être le signe de) to herald; **s'~ bien/difficile** to look promising/difficult; **annonceur, -euse** nm/f (publicitaire) advertiser; (TV, RADIO: speaker) announcer

annuaire [anɥɛR] nm yearbook, annual; **~ téléphonique** (telephone) directory, phone book

annuel, le [anɥɛl] adj annual, yearly

annuité [anɥite] nf annual instalment

annulation [anylasjɔ̃] nf cancellation

annuler [anyle] vt (rendez-vous, voyage) to cancel, call off; (jugement) to quash (BRIT), repeal (US); (MATH, PHYSIQUE) to cancel out

anodin, e [anɔdɛ̃, in] adj (blessure) harmless; (détail) insignificant, trivial

anonymat [anɔnima] nm anonymity

anonyme [anɔnim] adj anonymous; (fig) impersonal

ANPE sigle f (= Agence nationale pour l'emploi) national employment agency

anorak [anɔrak] nm anorak

anorexie [anɔreksi] nf anorexia

anormal, e, -aux [anɔrmal, o] adj abnormal

anse [ãs] nf (de panier, tasse) handle

antan [ãtã]: **d'~** adj of long ago

antarctique [ãtarktik] adj Antarctic ♦ nm: **l'A~** the Antarctic

antécédents [ãtesedã] nmpl (MÉD etc) past history sg

antenne [ãtɛn] nf (de radio) aerial; (d'insecte) antenna, feeler; (poste avancé) outpost; (petite succursale) sub-branch; **passer à l'~** to go on the air

antérieur, e [ãterjœr] adj (d'avant) previous, earlier; (de devant) front

anti... [ãti] préfixe anti...; **antialcoolique** adj anti-alcohol; **antiatomique** adj: **abri antiatomique** fallout shelter; **antibiotique** nm antibiotic; **antibrouillard** adj: **phare antibrouillard** fog lamp (BRIT) ou light (US)

anticipation [ãtisipasjɔ̃] nf: **livre/film d'~** science fiction book/film

anticipé, e [ãtisipe] adj: **avec mes remerciements ~s** thanking you in advance ou anticipation

anticiper [ãtisipe] vt (événement, coup) to anticipate, foresee

anti...: **anticonceptionnel, le** adj contraceptive; **anticorps** nm antibody; **antidote** nm antidote; **antigel** nm antifreeze; **antihistaminique** nm antihistamine

antillais, e [ãtijɛ, ɛz] adj West Indian, Caribbean ♦ nm/f: **A~, e** West Indian, Caribbean

Antilles [ãtij] nfpl: **les ~** the West Indies

antilope [ãtilɔp] nf antelope

anti...: **antimite(s)** adj, nm: **(produit) antimite(s)** mothproofer; moth repellent; **antipathique** adj unpleasant, disagreeable; **antipelliculaire** adj anti-dandruff

antipodes [ãtipɔd] nmpl (fig): **être aux ~ de** to be the opposite extreme of

antiquaire [ãtikɛR] nm/f antique dealer

antique [ãtik] adj antique; (très vieux) ancient, antiquated; **antiquité** nf (objet) antique; **l'Antiquité** Antiquity; **magasin d'antiquités** antique shop

anti...: **antirabique** adj rabies cpd; **antirouille** adj inv anti-rust cpd; **antisémite** adj anti-Semitic; **antiseptique** adj, nm antiseptic; **antivol** adj, nm: **(dispositif) antivol** anti-theft device

antre [ãtR] nm den, lair

anxiété [ãksjete] nf anxiety

anxieux, -euse [ãksjø, jøz] adj anxious, worried

AOC sigle f (= appellation d'origine contrôlée) label guaranteeing the quality of wine

août [u(t)] nm August

apaiser [apeze] vt (colère, douleur) to soothe; (personne) to calm (down), pacify; **s'~** vi (tempête, bruit) to die down, subside; (personne) to calm down

apanage [apanaʒ] nm: **être l'~ de** to be the privilege ou prerogative of

aparté [aparte] nm (entretien) private conversation; **en ~** in an aside

apathique [apatik] adj apathetic

apatride [apatrid] nm/f stateless person

apercevoir [apɛRsəvwaR] vt to see; **s'~ de** vt to notice; **s'~ que** to notice that

aperçu [apɛRsy] nm (vue d'ensemble) general survey

apéritif [aperitif] nm (boisson) aperitif; (réunion) drinks pl

à-peu-près [apøprɛ] (péj) nm inv vague approximation

apeuré, e [apœre] adj frightened, scared

aphte [aft] nm mouth ulcer

apiculture [apikyltyR] nf beekeeping, apiculture

apitoyer [apitwaje] vt to move to pity; **s'~ (sur)** to feel pity (for)

aplanir [aplaniʀ] vt to level; (fig) to smooth away, iron out

aplatir [aplatiʀ] vt to flatten; **s'~** vi to become flatter; (écrasé) to be flattened; **s'~ devant qn** (fig: s'humilier) to crawl to sb

aplomb [aplɔ̃] nm (équilibre) balance, equilibrium; (fig) self-assurance; nerve; **d'~** steady

apogée [apɔʒe] nm (fig) peak, apogee

apologie [apɔlɔʒi] nf vindication, praise

a posteriori [aposteʀjɔʀi] adv after the event

apostrophe [apɔstʀɔf] nf (signe) apostrophe

apostropher [apɔstʀɔfe] vt (interpeller) to shout at, address sharply

apothéose [apɔteoz] nf pinnacle (of achievement); (MUS) grand finale

apôtre [apotʀ] nm apostle

apparaître [apaʀɛtʀ] vi to appear

apparat [apaʀa] nm: **tenue d'~** ceremonial dress

appareil [apaʀɛj] nm (outil, machine) piece of apparatus, device; (électrique, ménager) appliance; (avion) (aero)plane, aircraft inv; (téléphonique) phone; (dentier) brace (BRIT), braces (US); **"qui est à l'~?"** "who's speaking?"; **dans le plus simple ~** in one's birthday suit; **appareiller** vi (NAVIG) to cast off, get under way ♦ vt (assortir) to match up; **appareil(-photo)** nm camera

apparemment [apaʀamɑ̃] adv apparently

apparence [apaʀɑ̃s] nf appearance; **en ~** apparently

apparent, e [apaʀɑ̃, ɑ̃t] adj visible; (évident) obvious; (superficiel) apparent

apparenté, e [apaʀɑ̃te] adj: **~ à** related to; (fig) similar to

apparition [apaʀisjɔ̃] nf appearance; (surnaturelle) apparition

appartement [apaʀtəmɑ̃] nm flat (BRIT), apartment (US)

appartenir [apaʀtəniʀ]: **~ à** vt to belong to; **il lui appartient de** it is his duty to

apparu, e [apaʀy] pp de **apparaître**

appât [apa] nm (PÊCHE) bait; (fig) lure, bait; **appâter** vt to lure

appauvrir [apovʀiʀ] vt to impoverish

appel [apɛl] nm call; (nominal) roll call; (: SCOL) register; (MIL: recrutement) call-up; **faire ~ à** (invoquer) to appeal to; (avoir recours à) to call on; (nécessiter) to call for, require; **faire ~** (JUR) to appeal; **faire l'~** to call the roll; to call the register; **sans ~** (fig) final, irrevocable; **~ d'offres** (COMM) invitation to tender; **faire un ~ de phares** to flash one's headlights; **~ (téléphonique)** (tele)phone call

appelé [ap(ə)le] nm (MIL) conscript

appeler [ap(ə)le] vt to call; (faire venir: médecin etc) to call, send for; **s'~** vi: **elle s'appelle Gabrielle** her name is Gabrielle, she's called Gabrielle; **comment ça s'appelle?** what is it called?; **être appelé à** (fig) to be destined to

appendice [apɛdis] nm appendix; **appendicite** nf appendicitis

appentis [apɑ̃ti] nm lean-to

appesantir [apəzɑ̃tiʀ]: **s'~** vi to grow heavier; **s'~ sur** (fig) to dwell on

appétissant, e [apetisɑ̃, ɑ̃t] adj appetizing, mouth-watering

appétit [apeti] nm appetite; **bon ~!** enjoy your meal!

applaudir [aplodiʀ] vt to applaud ♦ vi to applaud, clap; **applaudissements** nmpl applause sg, clapping sg

application [aplikasjɔ̃] nf application

applique [aplik] nf wall lamp

appliquer [aplike] vt to apply; (loi) to enforce; **s'~** vi (élève etc) to apply o.s.; **s'~ à** to apply to

appoint [apwɛ] nm (extra) contribution ou help; **chauffage d'~** extra heating

appointements [apwɛtmɑ̃] nmpl salary sg

apport [apɔʀ] nm (approvisionnement) supply; (contribution) contribution

apporter [apɔʀte] vt to bring

apposer [apoze] vt (signature) to affix

appréciable [apʀesjabl] adj appreciable

apprécier [apʀesje] vt to appreciate; (évaluer) to estimate, assess

appréhender [apʀeɑ̃de] vt (craindre) to dread; (arrêter) to apprehend; **appréhension** nf apprehension, anxiety

apprendre [apʀɑ̃dʀ] vt to learn; (événement, résultats) to hear of, learn of; **~ qch à qn** (informer) to tell sb (of) sth; (enseigner) to teach sb sth; **~ à faire qch** to learn to do sth; **~ à qn à faire qch** to teach sb to do sth; **apprenti, e** nm/f apprentice; **apprentissage** nm learning; (COMM, SCOL: période) apprenticeship

apprêté, e [apʀɛte] adj (fig) affected

apprêter [apʀɛte] vt: **s'~ à faire qch** to get ready to do sth

appris, e [apʀi, iz] pp de **apprendre**

apprivoiser [apʀivwaze] vt to tame

approbation [apʀɔbasjɔ̃] nf approval

approchant, e [apʀɔʃɑ̃, ɑ̃t] adj similar; **quelque chose d'~** something like that

approche [apʀɔʃ] nf approach

approcher [apʀɔʃe] vi to approach, come near ♦ vt to approach; (rapprocher): **~ qch (de qch)** to bring ou put sth near (to sth); **s'~ de** to approach, go ou come near to; **~ de** (lieu, but) to draw near to; (quantité, moment) to approach

approfondir [apʀɔfɔ̃diʀ] vt to deepen;

(*question*) to go further into

approprié, e [apʀɔpʀije] *adj*: ~ (à) appropriate (to), suited to

approprier [apʀɔpʀije] *vt* to appropriate, take over

approuver [apʀuve] *vt* to agree with; (*trouver louable*) to approve of

approvisionner [apʀɔvizjɔne] *vt* to supply; (*compte bancaire*) to pay funds into; **s'~ en** to stock up with

approximatif, -ive [apʀɔksimatif, iv] *adj* approximate, rough; (*termes*) vague

appt *abr* = **appartement**

appui [apɥi] *nm* support; **prendre ~ sur** to lean on; (*objet*) to rest on; **l'~ de la fenêtre** the windowsill, the window ledge; **appui(e)-tête** *nm inv* headrest

appuyer [apɥije] *vt* (*poser*): ~ **qch sur/contre** to lean ou rest sth on/against; (*soutenir: personne, demande*) to support, back (up) ♦ *vi*: ~ **sur** (*bouton, frein*) to press, push; (*mot, détail*) to stress, emphasize; **s'~ sur** to lean on; (*fig: compter sur*) to rely on

âpre [ɑpʀ] *adj* acrid, pungent; ~ **au gain** grasping

après [apʀe] *prép* after ♦ *adv* afterwards; **2 heures ~** 2 hours later; ~ **qu'il est** ou **soit parti** after he left; ~ **avoir fait** after having done; **d'~** (*selon*) according to; ~ **coup** after the event, afterwards; ~ **tout** (*au fond*) after all; **et (puis) ~?** so what?; **après-demain** *adv* the day after tomorrow; **après-guerre** *nm* post-war years *pl*; **après-midi** *nm ou nf inv* afternoon; **après-rasage** *nm inv* aftershave; **après-shampooing** *nm inv* conditioner; **après-ski** *nm inv* snow boot

à-propos [apʀopo] *nm* (*d'une remarque*) aptness; **faire preuve d'~~** to show presence of mind

apte [apt] *adj* capable; (*MIL*) fit

aquarelle [akwaʀɛl] *nf* watercolour

aquarium [akwaʀjɔm] *nm* aquarium

arabe [aʀab] *adj* Arabic; (*désert, cheval*) Arabian; (*nation, peuple*) Arab ♦ *nm/f*: **A~** Arab ♦ *nm* (*LING*) Arabic

Arabie [aʀabi] *nf*: **l'~ (Saoudite)** Saudi Arabia

arachide [aʀaʃid] *nf* (*plante*) groundnut (plant); (*graine*) peanut, groundnut

araignée [aʀeɲe] *nf* spider

arbitraire [aʀbitʀɛʀ] *adj* arbitrary

arbitre [aʀbitʀ] *nm* (*SPORT*) referee; (: *TENNIS, CRICKET*) umpire; (*fig*) arbiter, judge; (*JUR*) arbitrator; **arbitrer** *vt* to referee; to umpire; to arbitrate

arborer [aʀbɔʀe] *vt* to bear, display

arbre [aʀbʀ] *nm* tree; (*TECH*) shaft; ~ **généalogique** family tree

arbuste [aʀbyst] *nm* small shrub

arc [aʀk] *nm* (*arme*) bow; (*GÉOM*) arc;

(*ARCHIT*) arch; **en ~ de cercle** semi-circular

arcade [aʀkad] *nf* arch(way); **~s** *nfpl* (*série*) arcade *sg*, arches

arcanes [aʀkan] *nmpl* mysteries

arc-boutant [aʀkbutɑ̃] *nm* flying buttress

arceau, x [aʀso] *nm* (*métallique etc*) hoop

arc-en-ciel [aʀkɑ̃sjɛl] *nm* rainbow

arche [aʀʃ] *nf* arch; ~ **de Noé** Noah's Ark

archéologie [aʀkeɔlɔʒi] *nf* arch(a)eology; **archéologue** *nm/f* arch(a)eologist

archet [aʀʃɛ] *nm* bow

archevêque [aʀʃəvɛk] *nm* archbishop

archi... [aʀʃi] (*fam*) *préfixe* tremendously; **archicomble** (*fam*) *adj* chock-a-block; **archiconnu, e** (*fam*) *adj* enormously well-known

archipel [aʀʃipɛl] *nm* archipelago

architecte [aʀʃitɛkt] *nm* architect

architecture [aʀʃitɛktyʀ] *nf* architecture

archives [aʀʃiv] *nfpl* (*collection*) archives

arctique [aʀktik] *adj* Arctic ♦ *nm*: **l'A~** the Arctic

ardemment [aʀdamɑ̃] *adv* ardently, fervently

ardent, e [aʀdɑ̃, ɑ̃t] *adj* (*soleil*) blazing; (*amour*) ardent, passionate; (*prière*) fervent

ardeur [aʀdœʀ] *nf* ardour (*BRIT*), ardor (*US*); (*du soleil*) heat

ardoise [aʀdwaz] *nf* slate

ardu, e [aʀdy] *adj* (*travail*) arduous; (*problème*) difficult

arène [aʀɛn] *nf* arena; **~s** *nfpl* (*amphithéâtre*) bull-ring *sg*

arête [aʀɛt] *nf* (*de poisson*) bone; (*d'une montagne*) ridge

argent [aʀʒɑ̃] *nm* (*métal*) silver; (*monnaie*) money; ~ **de poche** pocket money; ~ **liquide** ready money, (ready) cash; **argenté, e** *adj* (*couleur*) silver, silvery; **en métal argenté** silver-plated; **argenterie** *nf* silverware

argentin, e [aʀʒɑ̃tɛ̃, in] *adj* Argentinian, Argentine

Argentine [aʀʒɑ̃tin] *nf*: **l'~** Argentina, the Argentine

argile [aʀʒil] *nf* clay

argot [aʀgo] *nm* slang; **argotique** *adj* slang *cpd*; (*très familier*) slangy

argument [aʀgymɑ̃] *nm* argument

argumentaire [aʀgymɑ̃tɛʀ] *nm* sales leaflet

argumenter [aʀgymɑ̃te] *vi* to argue

argus [aʀgys] *nm* guide to second-hand car etc prices

aride [aʀid] *adj* arid

aristocratie [aʀistɔkʀasi] *nf* aristocracy; **aristocratique** *adj* aristocratic

arithmétique [aʀitmetik] *adj* arithmetic(al) ♦ *nf* arithmetic

armateur [aʀmatœʀ] *nm* shipowner

armature [aʀmatyʀ] *nf* framework; (*de tente*

etc) frame; **soutien-gorge à/sans ~** underwired/unwired bra

arme [aʀm] *nf* weapon; **~s** *nfpl* (~*ment*) weapons, arms; (*blason*) (coat of) arms; **~ à feu** firearm

armée [aʀme] *nf* army; **~ de l'air** Air Force; **~ de terre** Army

armement [aʀməmɑ̃] *nm* (*matériel*) arms *pl*, weapons *pl*

armer [aʀme] *vt* to arm; (*arme à feu*) to cock; (*appareil-photo*) to wind on; **~ qch de** to reinforce sth with; **s'~ de** to arm o.s. with

armistice [aʀmistis] *nm* armistice; **l'A~ ≈** Remembrance (*BRIT*) *ou* Veterans (*US*) Day

armoire [aʀmwaʀ] *nf* (*tall*) cupboard; (*penderie*) wardrobe (*BRIT*), closet (*US*)

armoiries [aʀmwaʀi] *nfpl* coat *sg* of arms

armure [aʀmyʀ] *nf* armour *no pl*, suit of armour; **armurier** *nm* gunsmith

arnaque [aʀnak] (*fam*) *nf* swindling; **c'est de l'~** it's a rip-off; **arnaquer** (*fam*) *vt* to swindle

aromates [aʀɔmat] *nmpl* seasoning *sg*, herbs (and spices)

aromathérapie [aʀɔmateʀapi] *nf* aromatherapy

aromatisé, e [aʀɔmatize] *adj* flavoured

arôme [aʀom] *nm* aroma

arpenter [aʀpɑ̃te] *vt* (*salle, couloir*) to pace up and down

arpenteur [aʀpɑ̃tœʀ] *nm* surveyor

arqué, e [aʀke] *adj* arched; (*jambes*) bandy

arrache-pied [aʀaʃpje]: **d'~~** *adv* relentlessly

arracher [aʀaʃe] *vt* to pull out; (*page etc*) to tear off, tear out; (*légumes, herbe*) to pull up; (*bras etc*) to tear off; **s'~** *vt* (*article recherché*) to fight over; **~ qch à** to snatch sth from sb; (*fig*) to wring sth out of sb

arraisonner [aʀezɔne] *vt* (*bateau*) to board and search

arrangeant, e [aʀɑ̃ʒɑ̃, ɑ̃t] *adj* accommodating, obliging

arrangement [aʀɑ̃ʒmɑ̃] *nm* agreement, arrangement

arranger [aʀɑ̃ʒe] *vt* (*gén*) to arrange; (*réparer*) to fix, put right; (*régler: différend*) to settle, sort out; (*convenir à*) to suit, be convenient for; **s'~** *vi* (*se mettre d'accord*) to come to an agreement; **je vais m'~** I'll manage; **ça va s'~** it'll sort itself out

arrestation [aʀestasjɔ̃] *nf* arrest

arrêt [aʀe] *nm* stopping; (*de bus etc*) stop; (*JUR*) judgment, decision; **à l'~** stationary; **tomber en ~ devant** to stop short in front of; **sans ~** (*sans interruption*) non-stop; (*très fréquemment*) continually; **~ de travail** stoppage (of work); **~ maladie** sick leave

arrêté [aʀete] *nm* order, decree

arrêter [aʀete] *vt* to stop; (*chauffage etc*) to

turn off, switch off; (*fixer: date etc*) to appoint, decide on; (*criminel, suspect*) to arrest; **s'~** *vi* to stop; **~ de faire** to stop doing

arrhes [aʀ] *nfpl* deposit *sg*

arrière [aʀjɛʀ] *nm* back; (*SPORT*) fullback
♦ *adj inv*: **siège/roue ~** back *ou* rear seat/wheel; **à l'~** behind, at the back; **en ~** behind; (*regarder*) back, behind; (*tomber, aller*) backwards; **arriéré, e** *adj* (*péj*) backward
♦ *nm* (*d'argent*) arrears *pl*; **arrière-goût** *nm* aftertaste; **arrière-grand-mère** *nf* great-grandmother; **arrière-grand-père** *nm* great-grandfather; **arrière-pays** *nm inv* hinterland; **arrière-pensée** *nf* ulterior motive; mental reservation; **arrière-plan** *nm* background; **arrière-saison** *nf* late autumn; **arrière-train** *nm* hindquarters *pl*

arrimer [aʀime] *vt* to secure; (*cargaison*) to stow

arrivage [aʀivaʒ] *nm* consignment

arrivée [aʀive] *nf* arrival; (*ligne d'~*) finish

arriver [aʀive] *vi* to arrive; (*survenir*) to happen, occur; **il arrive à Paris à 8h** he gets to *ou* arrives in Paris at 8; **~ à** (*atteindre*) to reach; **~ à faire qch** to succeed in doing sth; **en ~ à** (*finir par*) to come to; **il arrive que** it happens that; **il lui arrive de faire** he sometimes does; **arriviste** *nm/f* go-getter

arrogance [aʀɔgɑ̃s] *nf* arrogance

arrogant, e [aʀɔgɑ̃, ɑ̃t] *adj* arrogant

arrondir [aʀɔ̃diʀ] *vt* (*forme, objet*) to round; (*somme*) to round off

arrondissement [aʀɔ̃dismɑ̃] *nm* (*ADMIN*) ≈ district

arroser [aʀoze] *vt* to water; (*victoire*) to celebrate (over a drink); (*CULIN*) to baste; **arrosoir** *nm* watering can

arsenal, -aux [aʀsənal, o] *nm* (*NAVIG*) naval dockyard; (*MIL*) arsenal; (*fig*) paraphernalia

art [aʀ] *nm* art

artère [aʀtɛʀ] *nf* (*ANAT*) artery; (*rue*) main road

arthrite [aʀtʀit] *nf* arthritis

artichaut [aʀtiʃo] *nm* artichoke

article [aʀtikl] *nm* article; (*COMM*) item, article; **à l'~ de la mort** at the point of death; **~s de luxe** luxury goods

articulation [aʀtikylasjɔ̃] *nf* articulation; (*ANAT*) joint

articuler [aʀtikyle] *vt* to articulate

artifice [aʀtifis] *nm* device, trick

artificiel, le [aʀtifisjɛl] *adj* artificial

artisan [aʀtizɑ̃] *nm* artisan, (self-employed) craftsman; **artisanal, e, -aux** *adj* of *ou* made by craftsmen; (*péj*) cottage industry *cpd*; **de fabrication artisanale** home-made; **artisanat** *nm* arts and crafts *pl*

artiste [aʀtist] *nm/f* artist; (*de variétés*) entertainer; (*musicien etc*) performer;

artistique [artistik] *adj* artistic

as¹ [a] *vb voir* **avoir**

as² [as] *nm* ace

ascendance [asɑ̃dɑ̃s] *nf* (*origine*) ancestry

ascendant, e [asɑ̃dɑ̃, ɑ̃t] *adj* upward ♦ *nm* influence

ascenseur [asɑ̃sœr] *nm* lift (*BRIT*), elevator (*US*)

ascension [asɑ̃sjɔ̃] *nf* ascent; (*de montagne*) climb; **l'A~** (*REL*) the Ascension

aseptisé, e (*péj*) *adj* sanitized

aseptiser [asɛptize] *vt* (*ustensile*) to sterilize; (*plaie*) to disinfect

asiatique [azjatik] *adj* Asiatic, Asian ♦ *nm/f:* **A~** Asian

Asie [azi] *nf:* **l'~** Asia

asile [azil] *nm* (*refuge*) refuge, sanctuary; (*POL*): **droit d'~** (political) asylum; **~ (de vieillards)** old people's home

aspect [aspɛ] *nm* appearance, look; (*fig*) aspect, side; **à l'~ de** at the sight of

asperge [aspɛrʒ] *nf* asparagus *no pl*

asperger [aspɛrʒe] *vt* to spray, sprinkle

aspérité [asperite] *nf* bump, protruding bit (of rock *etc*)

asphalte [asfalt] *nm* asphalt

asphyxier [asfiksje] *vt* to suffocate, asphyxiate; (*fig*) to stifle

aspirateur [aspiratœr] *nm* vacuum cleaner; **passer l'~** to vacuum

aspirer [aspire] *vt* (*air*) to inhale; (*liquide*) to suck (up); (*suj: appareil*) to suck up; **~ à** to aspire to

aspirine [aspirin] *nf* aspirin

assagir [asaʒir]: **s'~** *vi* to quieten down, settle down

assaillir [asajir] *vt* to assail, attack

assainir [asenir] *vt* (*logements*) to clean up; (*eau, air*) to purify

assaisonnement [asezɔnmɑ̃] *nm* seasoning

assaisonner [asezɔne] *vt* to season

assassin [asasɛ̃] *nm* murderer; assassin; **assassiner** *vt* to murder; (*esp POL*) to assassinate

assaut [aso] *nm* assault, attack; **prendre d'~** to storm, assault; **donner l'~** to attack

assécher [aseʃe] *vt* to drain

assemblage [asɑ̃blaʒ] *nm* (*action*) assembling; (*de couleurs, choses*) collection

assemblée [asɑ̃ble] *nf* (*réunion*) meeting; (*assistance*) gathering; (*POL*) assembly

assembler [asɑ̃ble] *vt* (*joindre, monter*) to assemble, put together; (*amasser*) to gather (together), collect (together); **s'~** *vi* to gather

assener, asséner [asene] *vt:* **~ un coup à qn** to deal sb a blow

assentiment [asɑ̃timɑ̃] *nm* assent, consent

asseoir [aswar] *vt* (*malade, bébé*) to sit up; (*personne debout*) to sit down; (*autorité, réputation*) to establish; **s'~** *vi* to sit (o.s.) down

assermenté, e [asɛrmɑ̃te] *adj* sworn, on oath

asservir [asɛrvir] *vt* to subjugate, enslave

assez [ase] *adv* (*suffisamment*) enough, sufficiently; (*passablement*) rather, quite, fairly; **~ de pain/livres** enough *ou* sufficient bread/books; **vous en avez ~?** have you got enough?; **j'en ai ~!** I've had enough!

assidu, e [asidy] *adj* (*appliqué*) assiduous, painstaking; (*ponctuel*) regular

assied *etc* [asje] *vb voir* **asseoir**

assiéger [asjeʒe] *vt* to besiege

assiérai *etc* [asjere] *vb voir* **asseoir**

assiette [asjɛt] *nf* plate; (*contenu*) plate(ful); **il n'est pas dans son ~** he's not feeling quite himself; **~ à dessert** dessert plate; **~ anglaise** assorted cold meats; **~ creuse** (soup) dish, soup plate; **~ plate** (dinner) plate

assigner [asiɲe] *vt:* **~ qch à** (*poste, part, travail*) to assign sth to

assimiler [asimile] *vt* to assimilate, absorb; (*comparer*): **~ qch/qn à** to liken *ou* compare sth/sb to

assis, e [asi, iz] *pp de* **asseoir** ♦ *adj* sitting (down), seated; **assise** *nf* (*fig*) basis, foundation; **assises** *nfpl* (*JUR*) assizes

assistance [asistɑ̃s] *nf* (*public*) audience; (*aide*) assistance; **enfant de l'A~ publique** child in care

assistant, e [asistɑ̃, ɑ̃t] *nm/f* assistant; (*d'université*) probationary lecturer; **~(e) social(e)** social worker

assisté, e [asiste] *adj* (*AUTO*) power assisted; **~ par ordinateur** computer-assisted

assister [asiste] *vt* (*aider*) to assist; **~ à** (*scène, événement*) to witness; (*conférence, séminaire*) to attend, be at; (*spectacle, match*) to be at, see

association [asɔsjasjɔ̃] *nf* association

associé, e [asɔsje] *nm/f* associate; (*COMM*) partner

associer [asɔsje] *vt* to associate; **s'~** *vi* to join together; **s'~ à qn pour faire** to join (forces) with sb to do; **s'~ à** (*couleurs, qualités*) to be combined with; (*opinions, joie de qn*) to share in; **~ qn à** (*profits*) to give sb a share of; (*affaire*) to make sb a partner in; (*joie, triomphe*) to include sb in; **~ qch à** (*allier à*) to combine sth with

assoiffé, e [aswafe] *adj* thirsty

assombrir [asɔ̃brir] *vt* to darken; (*fig*) to fill with gloom

assommer [asɔme] *vt* (*étourdir, abrutir*) to knock out, stun

Assomption [asɔ̃psjɔ̃] *nf:* **l'~** the Assumption

assorti, e [asɔrti] *adj* matched, matching; (*varié*) assorted; **~ à** matching; **assortiment**

nm assortment, selection

assortir [asɔʀtiʀ] *vt* to match; ~ **qch à** to match sth with; ~ **qch de** to accompany sth with

assoupi, e [asupi] *adj* dozing, sleeping

assoupir [asupiʀ]: **s'~** *vi* to doze off

assouplir [asupliʀ] *vt* to make supple; *(fig)* to relax; **assouplissant** *nm* (fabric) softener

assourdir [asuʀdiʀ] *vt* (*bruit*) to deaden, muffle; (*suj: bruit*) to deafen

assouvir [asuviʀ] *vt* to satisfy, appease

assujettir [asyʒetiʀ] *vt* to subject

assumer [asyme] *vt* (*fonction, emploi*) to assume, take on

assurance [asyʀɑ̃s] *nf* (*certitude*) assurance; (*confiance en soi*) (self-)confidence; (*contrat*) insurance (policy); (*secteur commercial*) insurance; ~ **maladie** health insurance; ~ **tous risques** comprehensive insurance; ~**s sociales** ≈ National Insurance (*BRIT*), ≈ Social Security (*US*); **assurance-vie** *nf* life assurance ou insurance

assuré, e [asyʀe] *adj* (*certain: réussite, échec*) certain, sure; (*air*) assured; (*pas*) steady ♦ *nm/f* insured (person); **assurément** *adv* assuredly, most certainly

assurer [asyʀe] *vt* (*FIN*) to insure; (*victoire etc*) to ensure; (*frontières, pouvoir*) to make secure; (*service*) to provide, operate; **s'~ (contre)** (*COMM*) to insure o.s. (against); **s'~ de/que** (*vérifier*) to make sure of/that; **s'~ (de)** (*aide de qn*) to secure; ~ **à qn que** to assure sb that; ~ **qn de** to assure sb of; **assureur** *nm* insurer

asthmatique [asmatik] *adj, nm/f* asthmatic

asthme [asm] *nm* asthma

asticot [astiko] *nm* maggot

astiquer [astike] *vt* to polish, shine

astre [astʀ] *nm* star

astreignant, e [astʀɛɲɑ̃, ɑ̃t] *adj* demanding

astreindre [astʀɛ̃dʀ] *vt*: ~ **qn à faire** to compel ou force sb to do; **s'~ à faire** to force o.s. to do

astrologie [astʀɔlɔʒi] *nf* astrology

astronaute [astʀonot] *nm/f* astronaut

astronomie [astʀonɔmi] *nf* astronomy

astuce [astys] *nf* shrewdness, astuteness; (*truc*) trick, clever way; **astucieux, -euse** *adj* clever

atelier [atalje] *nm* workshop; (*de peintre*) studio

athée [ate] *adj* atheistic ♦ *nm/f* atheist

Athènes [atɛn] *n* Athens

athlète [atlɛt] *nm/f* (*SPORT*) athlete; **athlétisme** *nm* athletics *sg*

atlantique [atlɑ̃tik] *adj* Atlantic ♦ *nm*: **l'(océan) A~** the Atlantic (Ocean)

atlas [atlas] *nm* atlas

atmosphère [atmɔsfɛʀ] *nf* atmosphere

atome [atom] *nm* atom; **atomique** *adj* atomic, nuclear

atomiseur [atɔmizœʀ] *nm* atomizer

atout [atu] *nm* trump; (*fig*) asset

âtre [ɑtʀ] *nm* hearth

atroce [atʀɔs] *adj* atrocious

attabler [atable]: **s'~** *vi* to sit down at (the) table

attachant, e [ataʃɑ̃, ɑ̃t] *adj* engaging, lovable, likeable

attache [ataʃ] *nf* clip, fastener; (*fig*) tie

attacher [ataʃe] *vt* to tie up; (*étiquette*) to attach, tie on; (*ceinture*) to fasten ♦ *vi* (*poêle, riz*) to stick; **s'~ à** (*par affection*) to become attached to; **s'~ à faire** to endeavour to do; ~ **qch à** to tie ou attach sth to

attaque [atak] *nf* attack; (*cérébrale*) stroke; (*d'épilepsie*) fit; ~ **à main armée** armed attack

attaquer [atake] *vt* to attack; (*en justice*) to bring an action against, sue ♦ *vi* to attack; **s'~ à** ♦ *vt* (*personne*) to attack; (*problème*) to tackle

attardé, e [ataʀde] *adj* (*enfant*) backward; (*passants*) late

attarder [ataʀde]: **s'~** *vi* to linger

atteindre [atɛ̃dʀ] *vt* to reach; (*blesser*) to hit; (*émouvoir*) to affect; **atteint, e** *adj* (*MÉD*): **être atteint de** to be suffering from; **atteinte** *nf*: **hors d'atteinte** out of reach; **porter atteinte à** to strike a blow at

atteler [at(a)le] *vt* (*cheval, bœufs*) to hitch up; **s'~ à** (*travail*) to buckle down to

attelle [atɛl] *nf* splint

attenant, e [at(a)nɑ̃, ɑ̃t] *adj*: ~ **(à)** adjoining

attendant [atɑ̃dɑ̃] *adv*: **en ~** meanwhile, in the meantime

attendre [atɑ̃dʀ] *vt* (*gén*) to wait for; (*être destiné ou réservé à*) to await, be in store for ♦ *vi* to wait; **s'~ à (ce que)** to expect (that); ~ **un enfant** to be expecting a baby; ~ **de faire/d'être** to wait until one does/is; **attendez qu'il vienne** wait until he comes; ~ **qch de** to expect sth of

attendrir [atɑ̃dʀiʀ] *vt* to move (to pity); (*viande*) to tenderize; **attendrissant, e** *adj* moving, touching

attendu, e [atɑ̃dy] *adj* (*visiteur*) expected; (*événement*) long-awaited; ~ **que** considering that, since

attentat [atɑ̃ta] *nm* assassination attempt; ~ **à la bombe** bomb attack; ~ **à la pudeur** indecent assault *no pl*

attente [atɑ̃t] *nf* wait; (*espérance*) expectation

attenter [atɑ̃te]: ~ **à** *vt* (*liberté*) to violate; ~ **à la vie de qn** to make an attempt on sb's life

attentif, -ive [atɑ̃tif, iv] *adj* (*auditeur*) attentive; (*examen*) careful; ~ **à** careful to

attention [atɑ̃sjɔ̃] *nf* attention; (*prévenance*)

attention, thoughtfulness *no pl*; **à l'~ de** for the attention of; **faire ~ (à)** to be careful (of); **faire ~ (à ce) que** to be sure *ou* make sure that; **~!** careful!, watch out!; **attentionné, e** *adj* thoughtful, considerate

atténuer [atenɥe] *vt* (*douleur*) to alleviate, ease; (*couleurs*) to soften

atterrer [atere] *vt* to dismay, appal

atterrir [aterir] *vi* to land; **atterrissage** *nm* landing

attestation [atɛstasjɔ̃] *nf* certificate

attester [atɛste] *vt* to testify to

attirail [atiraj] (*fam*) *nm* gear; (*péj*) paraphernalia

attirant, e [atirɑ̃, ɑ̃t] *adj* attractive, appealing

attirer [atire] *vt* to attract; (*appâter*) to lure, entice; **~ qn dans un coin** to draw sb into a corner; **~ l'attention de qn** to attract sb's attention; **~ l'attention de qn sur** to draw sb's attention to; **s'~ des ennuis** to bring trouble upon o.s., get into trouble

attiser [atize] *vt* (*feu*) to poke (up)

attitré, e [atitre] *adj* (*habituel*) regular, usual; (*agréé*) accredited

attitude [atityd] *nf* attitude; (*position du corps*) bearing

attouchements [atuʃmɑ̃] *nmpl* (*sexuels*) fondling *sg*

attraction [atraksjɔ̃] *nf* (*gén*) attraction; (*de cabaret, cirque*) number

attrait [atrɛ] *nm* appeal, attraction

attrape-nigaud [atrapnigo] (*fam*) *nm* con

attraper [atrape] *vt* (*gén*) to catch; (*habitude, amende*) to get, pick up; (*fam: duper*) to con; **se faire ~** (*fam*) to be told off

attrayant, e [atrejɑ̃, ɑ̃t] *adj* attractive

attribuer [atribɥe] *vt* (*prix*) to award; (*rôle, tâche*) to allocate, assign; (*imputer*): **~ qch à** to attribute sth to; **s'~** *vt* (*s'approprier*) to claim for o.s.; **attribut** *nm* attribute

attrister [atriste] *vt* to sadden

attroupement [atrupmɑ̃] *nm* crowd

attrouper [atrupe]: **s'~** *vi* to gather

au [o] *prép* +*dét* = **à +le**

aubaine [obɛn] *nf* godsend

aube [ob] *nf* dawn, daybreak; **à l'~** at dawn *ou* daybreak

aubépine [obepin] *nf* hawthorn

auberge [obɛrʒ] *nf* inn; **~ de jeunesse** youth hostel

aubergine [obɛrʒin] *nf* aubergine

aubergiste [obɛrʒist] *nm/f* inn-keeper, hotel-keeper

aucun, e [okœ̃, yn] *dét* no, *tournure négative* +any; (*positif*) any ♦ *pron* none, *tournure négative* +any; any(one); **sans ~ doute** without any doubt; **plus qu'~ autre** more than any other; **~ des deux** neither of the

two; **~ d'entre eux** none of them;

aucunement *adv* in no way, not in the least

audace [odas] *nf* daring, boldness; (*péj*) audacity; **audacieux, -euse** *adj* daring, bold

au-delà [od(ə)la] *adv* beyond ♦ *nm*: **l'~~** the hereafter; **~~ de** beyond

au-dessous [odsu] *adv* underneath; below; **~~ de** under(neath); below; (*limite, somme etc*) below, under; (*dignité, condition*) below

au-dessus [odsy] *adv* above; **~~ de** above

au-devant [od(ə)vɑ̃]: **~~ de** *prép*: **aller ~~ de** (*personne, danger*) to go (out) and meet; (*souhaits de qn*) to anticipate

audience [odjɑ̃s] *nf* audience; (*JUR: séance*) hearing

audimat ® [odimat] *nm* (*taux d'écoute*) ratings *pl*

audio-visuel, le [odjovizɥɛl] *adj* audio-visual

auditeur, -trice [oditœr, tris] *nm/f* listener

audition [odisjɔ̃] *nf* (*ouïe, écoute*) hearing; (*JUR: de témoins*) examination; (*MUS, THÉÂTRE: épreuve*) audition

auditoire [oditwar] *nm* audience

auge [oʒ] *nf* trough

augmentation [ɔgmɑ̃tasjɔ̃] *nf* increase; **~ (de salaire)** rise (in salary) (*BRIT*), (pay) raise (*US*)

augmenter [ɔgmɑ̃te] *vt* (*gén*) to increase; (*salaire, prix*) to increase, raise, put up; (*employé*) to increase the salary of ♦ *vi* to increase

augure [ogyr] *nm*: **de bon/mauvais ~** of good/ill omen; **augurer** *vt*: **augurer bien de** to augur well for

aujourd'hui [oʒurdɥi] *adv* today

aumône [omon] *nf inv* alms *sg*; **aumônier** *nm* chaplain

auparavant [oparavɑ̃] *adv* before(hand)

auprès [oprɛ]: **~ de** *prép* next to, close to; (*recourir, s'adresser*) to; (*en comparaison de*) compared with

auquel [okɛl] *prép* +*pron* = **à +lequel**

aurai *etc* [ɔre] *vb voir* **avoir**

auréole [ɔreɔl] *nf* halo; (*tache*) ring

aurons *etc* [ɔrɔ̃] *vb voir* **avoir**

aurore [ɔrɔr] *nf* dawn, daybreak

ausculter [ɔskylte] *vt* to sound (the chest of)

aussi [osi] *adv* (*également*) also, too; (*de comparaison*) as ♦ *conj* therefore, consequently; **~ fort que** as strong as; **moi ~** me too

aussitôt [osito] *adv* straight away, immediately; **~ que** as soon as

austère [ostɛr] *adj* austere

austral, e [ɔstral] *adj* southern

Australie [ostrali] *nf*: **l'~** Australia; **australien, ne** *adj* Australian ♦ *nm/f*: **Australien, ne** Australian

autant [otɑ̃] adv so much; (comparatif): ~ **(que)** as much (as); (nombre) as many (as); ~ **(de)** so much (ou many); as much (ou many); ~ **partir** we (ou you etc) may as well leave; ~ **dire que ...** one might as well say that ...; **pour** ~ for all that; **d'~ plus/mieux (que)** all the more/the better (since)

autel [otɛl] nm altar

auteur [otœʀ] nm author

authenticité [otɑ̃tisite] nf authenticity

authentique [otɑ̃tik] adj authentic, genuine

auto [oto] nf car

auto...: **autobiographie** nf autobiography; **autobus** nm bus; **autocar** nm coach

autochtone [otɔktɔn] nm/f native

auto...: **autocollant, e** adj self-adhesive; (enveloppe) self-seal ♦ nm sticker; **auto-couchettes** adj: **train auto-couchettes** car sleeper train; **autocuiseur** nm pressure cooker; **autodéfense** nf self-defence; **autodidacte** nm/f self-taught person; **auto-école** nf driving school; **autographe** nm autograph

automate [ɔtɔmat] nm (machine) (automatic) machine

automatique [ɔtɔmatik] adj automatic ♦ nm: **l'~** direct dialling; **automatiquement** adv automatically; **automatiser** vt to automate

automne [ɔtɔn] nm autumn (BRIT), fall (US)

automobile [ɔtɔmɔbil] adj motor cpd ♦ nf (motor) car; **automobiliste** nm/f motorist

autonome [ɔtɔnɔm] adj autonomous; **autonomie** nf autonomy; (POL) self-government, autonomy

autopsie [ɔtɔpsi] nf post-mortem (examination), autopsy

autoradio [otɔʀadjo] nm car radio

autorisation [ɔtɔʀizasjɔ̃] nf permission, authorization; (papiers) permit

autorisé, e [ɔtɔʀize] adj (opinion, sources) authoritative

autoriser [ɔtɔʀize] vt to give permission for, authorize; (fig) to allow (of)

autoritaire [ɔtɔʀitɛʀ] adj authoritarian

autorité [ɔtɔʀite] nf authority; **faire ~** to be authoritative

autoroute [otɔʀut] nf motorway (BRIT), highway (US); ~ **de l'information** (INFORM) information superhighway

auto-stop [otostɔp] nm: **faire de l'~~~** to hitch-hike; **prendre qn en ~~~** to give sb a lift; **auto-stoppeur, -euse** nm/f hitch-hiker

autour [otuʀ] adv around; ~ **de** around; **tout ~** all around

MOT-CLÉ

autre [otʀ] adj **1** (différent) other, different; **je préférerais un autre verre** I'd prefer another

ou a different glass
2 (supplémentaire) other; **je voudrais un autre verre d'eau** I'd like another glass of water
3: **autre chose** something else; **autre part** somewhere else; **d'autre part** on the other hand
♦ pron: **un autre** another (one); **nous/vous autres** us/you; **d'autres** others; **l'autre** the other (one); **les autres** the others; (autrui) others; **l'un et l'autre** both of them; **se détester l'un l'autre/les uns les autres** to hate each other ou one another; **d'une semaine à l'autre** from one week to the next; (incessamment) any week now; **entre autres** among other things

autrefois [otʀəfwa] adv in the past

autrement [otʀəmɑ̃] adv differently; (d'une manière différente) in another way; (sinon) otherwise; ~ **dit** in other words

Autriche [otʀiʃ] nf: **l'~** Austria; **autrichien, ne** adj Austrian ♦ nm/f: **Autrichien, ne** Austrian

autruche [otʀyʃ] nf ostrich

autrui [otʀɥi] pron others

auvent [ovɑ̃] nm canopy

aux [o] prép +dét = à +les

auxiliaire [ɔksiljɛʀ] adj, nm/f auxiliary

auxquelles [okɛl] prép +pron = à +lesquelles

auxquels [okɛl] prép +pron = à +lesquels

avachi, e [avaʃi] adj limp, flabby

aval [aval] nm: **en ~** downstream, downriver

avalanche [avalɑ̃ʃ] nf avalanche

avaler [avale] vt to swallow

avance [avɑ̃s] nf (de troupes etc) advance; progress; (d'argent) advance; (sur un concurrent) lead; ~**s** nfpl (amoureuses) advances; **(être) en ~** (to be) early; (sur un programme) (to be) ahead of schedule; **à l'~, d'~** in advance

avancé, e [avɑ̃se] adj advanced; (travail) well on, well under way

avancement [avɑ̃smɑ̃] nm (professionnel) promotion

avancer [avɑ̃se] vi to move forward, advance; (projet, travail) to make progress; (montre, réveil) to be fast; to gain ♦ vt to move forward, advance; (argent) to advance; (montre, pendule) to put forward; **s'~** vi to move forward, advance; (fig) to commit o.s.

avant [avɑ̃] prép, adv before ♦ adj inv: **siège/roue ~** front seat/wheel ♦ nm (d'un véhicule, bâtiment) front; (SPORT: joueur) forward; ~ **qu'il (ne) fasse/de faire** before he does/doing; ~ **tout** (surtout) above all; **à l'~** (dans un véhicule) in (the) front; **en ~** forward(s); **en ~ de** in front of

avantage [avɑ̃taʒ] nm advantage; ~**s sociaux** fringe benefits; **avantager** vt (favoriser) to favour; (embellir) to flatter; **avantageux, -euse** adj (prix) attractive

avant...: **avant-bras** nm inv forearm; **avantcoureur** adj inv: **signe avantcoureur** advance indication ou sign; **avant-dernier, -ière** adj, nm/f next to last, last but one; **avant-goût** nm foretaste; **avant-guerre** nm pre-war years; **avant-hier** adv the day before yesterday; **avant-première** nf (de film) preview; **avant-projet** nm (preliminary) draft; **avant-propos** nm foreword; **avant-veille** nf: **l'avant-veille** two days before

avare [avaʀ] adj miserly, avaricious ♦ nm/f miser; ~ **de** (compliments etc) sparing of

avarié, e [avaʀje] adj (aliment) rotting

avaries [avaʀi] nfpl (NAVIG) damage sg

avec [avɛk] prép with; (à l'égard de) to(wards), with; **et ~ ça?** (dans magasin) anything else?

avenant, e [av(ə)nɑ̃, ɑ̃t] adj pleasant; **à l'~** in keeping

avènement [avɛnmɑ̃] nm (d'un changement) advent, coming

avenir [avniʀ] nm future; **à l'~** in future; **politicien d'~** politician with prospects ou a future

aventure [avɑ̃tyʀ] nf adventure; (amoureuse) affair; **aventurer**: **s'aventurer** vi to venture; **aventureux, -euse** adj adventurous, venturesome; (projet) risky, chancy

avenue [avny] nf avenue

avérer: **s'avérer** vb +attrib to prove (to be)

averse [avɛʀs] nf shower

averti, e [avɛʀti] adj (well-)informed

avertir [avɛʀtiʀ] vt: ~ **qn (de qch/que)** to warn sb (of sth/that); (renseigner) to inform sb (of sth/that); **avertissement** nm warning; **avertisseur** nm horn, siren

aveu, x [avø] nm confession

aveugle [avœgl] adj blind ♦ nm/f blind man/woman; **aveuglément** adv blindly; **aveugler** vt to blind

aviateur, -trice [avjatœʀ, tʀis] nm/f aviator, pilot

aviation [avjasjɔ̃] nf aviation; (sport) flying; (MIL) air force

avide [avid] adj eager; (péj) greedy, grasping

avilir [aviliʀ] vt to debase

avion [avjɔ̃] nm (aero)plane (BRIT), (air)plane (US); **aller (quelque part) en ~** to go (somewhere) by plane, fly (somewhere); **par ~** by airmail; ~ **à réaction** jet (plane)

aviron [aviʀɔ̃] nm oar; (sport): **l'~** rowing

avis [avi] nm opinion; (notification) notice; **à mon ~** in my opinion; **changer d'~** to change one's mind; **jusqu'à nouvel ~** until further notice

avisé, e [avize] adj sensible, wise; **bien/mal ~ de** well-/ill-advised to

aviser [avize] vt (informer): ~ **qn de/que** to advise ou inform sb of/that ♦ vi to think about things, assess the situation; **nous ~ons sur place** we'll work something out once we're there; **s'~ de qch/que** to become suddenly aware of sth/that; **s'~ de faire** to take it into one's head to do

avocat, e [avɔka, at] nm/f (JUR) barrister (BRIT), lawyer ♦ nm (CULIN) avocado (pear); ~ **de la défense** counsel for the defence; ~ **général** assistant public prosecutor

avoine [avwan] nf oats pl

MOT-CLÉ

avoir [avwaʀ] nm assets pl, resources pl; (COMM) credit
♦ vt **1** (posséder) to have; **elle a 2 enfants/une belle maison** she has (got) 2 children/a lovely house; **il a les yeux bleus** he has (got) blue eyes
2 (âge, dimensions) to be; **il a 3 ans** he is 3 (years old); **le mur a 3 mètres de haut** the wall is 3 metres high; voir aussi **faim**; **peur** etc
3 (fam: duper) to do, have; **on vous a eu!** you've been done ou had!
4: **en avoir contre qn** to have a grudge against sb; **en avoir assez** to be fed up; **j'en ai pour une demi-heure** it'll take me half an hour
♦ vb aux **1** to have; **avoir mangé/dormi** to have eaten/slept
2 (avoir +à +infinitif): **avoir à faire qch** to have to do sth; **vous n'avez qu'à lui demander** you only have to ask him
♦ vb impers **1**: **il y a** (+ singulier) there is; (+ pluriel) there are; **qu'y a-t-il?**, **qu'est-ce qu'il y a?** what's the matter?, what is it?; **il doit y avoir une explication** there must be an explanation; **il n'y a qu'à ...** we (ou you etc) will just have to ...
2 (temporel): **il y a 10 ans** 10 years ago; **il y a 10 ans/longtemps que je le sais** I've known it for 10 years/a long time; **il y a 10 ans qu'il est arrivé** it's 10 years since he arrived

---

avoisiner [avwazine] vt to be near ou close to; (fig) to border ou verge on

avortement [avɔʀtəmɑ̃] nm abortion

avorter [avɔʀte] vi (MÉD) to have an abortion; (fig) to fail

avoué, e [avwe] adj avowed ♦ nm (JUR) ≈ solicitor

avouer [avwe] vt (crime, défaut) to confess (to); ~ **avoir fait/que** to admit ou confess to having done/that

avril [avʀil] nm April

axe [aks] nm axis; (de roue etc) axle; (fig) main line; **axer** vt: **axer qch sur** to centre sth on

ayons etc [ejɔ̃] vb voir **avoir**

azote [azɔt] nm nitrogen

B, b

baba [baba] nm: ~ **au rhum** rum baba

babines [babin] nfpl chops

babiole [babjɔl] nf (bibelot) trinket; (vétille) trifle

bâbord [babɔr] nm: **à ~** to port, on the port side

baby-foot [babifut] nm table football

baby-sitting [babisitiŋ] nm: **faire du ~~** to baby-sit

bac [bak] abr m = **baccalauréat** ♦ nm (récipient) tub

baccalauréat [bakalɔrea] nm high school diploma

bâche [baʃ] nf tarpaulin

bachelier, -ière [baʃəlje, jɛr] nm/f holder of the baccalauréat

bâcler [bakle] vt to botch (up)

badaud, e [bado, od] nm/f idle onlooker, stroller

badigeonner [badiʒɔne] vt (barbouiller) to daub

badiner [badine] vi: ~ **avec qch** to treat sth lightly

baffe [baf] (fam) nf slap, clout

baffle [bafl] nm speaker

bafouer [bafwe] vt to deride, ridicule

bafouiller [bafuje] vi, vt to stammer

bâfrer [bafre] (fam) vi to guzzle

bagages [bagaʒ] nmpl luggage sg; **à main** hand-luggage

bagarre [bagar] nf fight, brawl; **bagarrer: se bagarrer** vi to have a fight ou scuffle, fight

bagatelle [bagatɛl] nf trifle

bagne [baɲ] nm penal colony

bagnole [baɲɔl] (fam) nf car

bagout [bagu] nm: **avoir du ~** to have the gift of the gab

bague [bag] nf ring; ~ **de fiançailles** engagement ring

baguette [bagɛt] nf stick, (cuisine chinoise) chopstick; (de chef d'orchestre) baton; (pain) stick of (French) bread; ~ **magique** magic wand

baie [bɛ] nf (GÉO) bay; (fruit) berry; ~ (vitrée) picture window

baignade [bɛɲad] nf bathing; "~ interdite" "no bathing"

baigner [bɛɲe] vt (bébé) to bath; **se ~** vi to have a swim, go swimming ou bathing; **baignoire** nf bath(tub)

bail [baj, bo] (pl baux) nm lease

bâillement [bajmã] nm yawn

bâiller [baje] vi to yawn; (être ouvert) to gape; **bâillonner** vt to gag

bain [bɛ̃] nm bath; **prendre un ~** to have a bath; **se mettre dans le ~** (fig) to get into it ou things; ~ **de soleil: prendre un ~ de soleil** to sunbathe; **~s de mer** sea bathing sg; **bain-marie** nm: **faire chauffer au bain-marie** (boîte etc) to immerse in boiling water

baiser [beze] nm kiss ♦ vt (main, front) to kiss; (fam!) to screw (!)

baisse [bɛs] nf fall, drop; **être en ~** to be falling, be declining

baisser [bese] vt to lower; (radio, chauffage) to turn down ♦ vi to fall, drop, go down; (vue, santé) to fail, dwindle; **se ~** vi to bend down

bal [bal] nm dance; (grande soirée) ball; ~ **costumé** fancy-dress ball

balade [balad] (fam) nf (à pied) walk, stroll; (en voiture) drive; **balader** (fam): **se balader** vi to go for a walk ou stroll; to go for a drive; **baladeur** nm personal stereo, Walkman ®

balafre [balafr] nf (cicatrice) scar

balai [balɛ] nm broom, brush; **balai-brosse** nm (long-handled) scrubbing brush

balance [balãs] nf scales pl; (signe): **la B~** Libra

balancer [balãse] vt to swing; (fam: lancer) to fling, chuck; (: jeter) to chuck out; **se ~** vi to swing, rock; **se ~ de** (fam) not to care about; **balançoire** nf swing; (sur pivot) seesaw

balayer [baleje] vt (feuilles etc) to sweep up, brush up; (pièce) to sweep; (objections) to sweep aside; (suj: radar) to scan; **balayeur, -euse** nm/f roadsweeper

balbutier [balbysje] vi, vt to stammer

balcon [balkɔ̃] nm balcony; (THÉÂTRE) dress circle

baleine [balɛn] nf whale

balise [baliz] nf (NAVIG) beacon; (marker) buoy; (AVIAT) runway light, beacon; (AUTO, SKI) sign, marker; **baliser** vt to mark out (with lights etc)

balivernes [balivɛrn] nfpl nonsense sg

ballant, e [balã, ãt] adj dangling

balle [bal] nf (de fusil) bullet; (de sport) ball; (fam: franc) franc

ballerine [bal(ə)rin] nf (danseuse) ballet dancer; (chaussure) ballet shoe

ballet [balɛ] nm ballet

ballon [balɔ̃] nm (de sport) ball; (jouet, AVIAT) balloon; ~ **de football** football

ballot [balo] nm bundle; (péj) nitwit

ballottage [balɔtaʒ] nm (POL) second ballot

ballotter [balɔte] vt: **être ballotté** to be thrown about

balnéaire [balneɛr] adj seaside cpd; **station ~** seaside resort

balourd, e [balur, urd] adj clumsy

balustrade [balystrad] nf railings pl, handrail

bambin [bɑ̃bɛ̃] nm little child
bambou [bɑ̃bu] nm bamboo
ban [bɑ̃] nm: **mettre au ~ de** to outlaw from;
~s nmpl (de mariage) banns
banal, e [banal] adj banal, commonplace;
(péj) trite; **banalité** nf banality
banane [banan] nf banana; (sac) waist-bag,
bum-bag
banc [bɑ̃] nm seat, bench; (de poissons) shoal;
~ d'essai (fig) testing ground
bancaire [bɑ̃kɛʀ] adj banking; (chèque, carte)
bank cpd
bancal, e [bɑ̃kal] adj wobbly
bandage [bɑ̃daʒ] nm bandage
bande [bɑ̃d] nf (de tissu etc) strip; (MÉD)
bandage; (motif) stripe; (magnétique etc)
tape; (groupe) band; (: péj) bunch; **faire ~ à
part** to keep to o.s.; **~ dessinée** comic strip;
~ sonore sound track
bandeau, x [bɑ̃do] nm headband; (sur les
yeux) blindfold
bander [bɑ̃de] vt (blessure) to bandage; **~ les
yeux à qn** to blindfold sb
banderole [bɑ̃dʀɔl] nf banner, streamer
bandit [bɑ̃di] nm bandit; **banditisme** nm
violent crime, armed robberies pl
bandoulière [bɑ̃duljɛʀ] nf: **en ~** (slung ou
worn) across the shoulder
banlieue [bɑ̃ljø] nf suburbs pl; **lignes/
quartiers de ~** suburban lines/areas; **trains de
~** commuter trains
banlieusard, e [bɑ̃ljøzaʀ, -aʀd(ə)] nm/f
(suburban) commuter
bannière [banjɛʀ] nf banner
bannir [baniʀ] vt to banish
banque [bɑ̃k] nf bank; (activités) banking;
~ d'affaires merchant bank; **banqueroute**
nf bankruptcy
banquet [bɑ̃kɛ] nm dinner; (d'apparat)
banquet
banquette [bɑ̃kɛt] nf seat
banquier [bɑ̃kje] nm banker
banquise [bɑ̃kiz] nf ice field
baptême [batɛm] nm christening; baptism;
~ de l'air first flight
baptiser [batize] vt to baptize, christen
baquet [bakɛ] nm tub, bucket
bar [baʀ] nm bar
baraque [baʀak] nf shed; (fam) house;
baraqué, e [baʀake] (fam) adj well-built, hefty;
baraquements nmpl (provisoires) huts
baratin [baʀatɛ̃] (fam) nm smooth talk,
patter; **baratiner** vt to chat up
barbare [baʀbaʀ] adj barbaric; **barbarie** nf
barbarity
barbe [baʀb] nf beard; **la ~!** (fam) damn it!;
quelle ~! (fam) what a drag ou borel; **à la
~ de qn** under sb's nose; **~ à papa** candy-floss
(BRIT), cotton candy (US)

barbelé [baʀbəle] adj, nm: **(fil de fer) ~**
barbed wire no pl
barber [baʀbe] (fam) vt to bore stiff
barbiturique [baʀbityʀik] nm barbiturate
barboter [baʀbɔte] vi (enfant) to paddle
barbouiller [baʀbuje] vt to daub; **avoir
l'estomac barbouillé** to feel queasy
barbu, e [baʀby] adj bearded
barda [baʀda] (fam) nm kit, gear
barder [baʀde] (fam) vi: **ça va ~** sparks will
fly, things are going to get hot
barème [baʀɛm] nm (SCOL) scale; (table de
référence) table
baril [baʀi(l)] nm barrel; (poudre) keg
bariolé, e [baʀjɔle] adj gaudily-coloured
baromètre [baʀɔmɛtʀ] nm barometer
baron, ne [baʀɔ̃] nm/f baron(ess)
baroque [baʀɔk] adj (ART) baroque; (fig)
weird
barque [baʀk] nf small boat
barquette [baʀkɛt] nf (pour repas) tray;
(pour fruits) punnet
barrage [baʀaʒ] nm dam; (sur route)
roadblock, barricade
barre [baʀ] nf bar; (NAVIG) helm; (écrite) line,
stroke
barreau, x [baʀo] nm bar; (JUR): **le ~** the Bar
barrer [baʀe] vt (route etc) to block; (mot) to
cross out; (chèque) to cross (BRIT); (NAVIG) to
steer; **se ~** (fam) vi to clear off
barrette [baʀɛt] nf (pour cheveux) (hair) slide
(BRIT) ou clip (US)
barricader [baʀikade]: **se ~** vi to barricade o.s.
barrière [baʀjɛʀ] nf fence; (obstacle) barrier;
(porte) gate
barrique [baʀik] nf barrel, cask
bar-tabac [baʀtaba] nm bar (which sells
tobacco and stamps)
bas, basse [bɑ, bɑs] adj low ♦ nm bottom,
lower part; (vêtement) stocking ♦ adv low;
(parler) softly; **au ~ mot** at the lowest
estimate; **en ~** down below; (d'une liste, d'un
mur etc) at/to the bottom; (dans une maison)
downstairs; **en ~ de** at the bottom of; **un
enfant en ~ âge** a young child; **à ~ ...!** down
with ...!; **~ morceaux** nmpl (viande) cheap
cuts
basané, e [bazane] adj tanned
bas-côté [bakote] nm (de route) verge (BRIT),
shoulder (US)
bascule [baskyl] nf: **(jeu de) ~** seesaw;
(balance à) ~ scales pl; **fauteuil à ~** rocking
chair
basculer [baskyle] vi to fall over, topple
(over); (benne) to tip up ♦ vt (contenu) to tip
out; (benne) to tip up
base [bɑz] nf base; (POL) rank and file;
(fondement, principe) basis; **de ~** basic; **à ~ de
café** etc coffee etc -based; **~ de données**

database; **baser** vt to base; **se baser sur** vt (preuves) to base one's argument on
bas-fond [bafɔ̃] nm (NAVIG) shallow; **~-~s** nmpl (fig) dregs
basilic [bazilik] nm (CULIN) basil
basket [baskɛt] nm trainer (BRIT), sneaker (US); (aussi: **~-ball**) basketball
basque [bask] adj, nm/f Basque
basse [bas] adj voir **bas** ♦ nf (MUS) bass; **basse-cour** nf farmyard
bassin [basɛ̃] nm (pièce d'eau) pond, pool; (de fontaine, GÉO) basin; (ANAT) pelvis; (portuaire) dock
bassine [basin] nf (ustensile) basin; (contenu) bowl(ful)
basson [basɔ̃] nm bassoon
bas-ventre [bavɑ̃tʀ] nm (lower part of the) stomach
bat [ba] vb voir **battre**
bataille [bataj] nf (MIL) battle; (rixe) fight; **batailler** vi to fight
bâtard, e [bataʀ, aʀd] nm/f illegitimate child, bastard (péj)
bateau, x [bato] nm boat, ship; **bateau mouche** nm passenger pleasure boat (on the Seine)
bâti, e [bati] adj: **bien ~** well-built
batifoler [batifɔle] vi to frolic about
bâtiment [batimɑ̃] nm building; (NAVIG) ship, vessel; (industrie) building trade
bâtir [batiʀ] vt to build
bâtisse [batis] nf building
bâton [batɔ̃] nm stick; **à ~s rompus** informally
bats [ba] vb voir **battre**
battage [bataʒ] nm (publicité) (hard) plugging
battant [batɑ̃, ɑ̃t] nm: **porte à double ~** double door
battement [batmɑ̃] nm (de cœur) beat; (intervalle) interval (between classes, trains); **10 minutes de ~** 10 minutes to spare
batterie [batʀi] nf (MIL, ÉLEC) battery; (MUS) drums pl, drum kit; **~ de cuisine** pots and pans pl, kitchen utensils pl
batteur [batœʀ] nm (MUS) drummer; (appareil) whisk
battre [batʀ] vt to beat; (blé) to thresh; (passer au peigne fin) to scour; (cartes) to shuffle ♦ vi (cœur) to beat; (volets etc) to bang, rattle; **se ~** vi to fight; **~ la mesure** to beat time; **~ son plein** to be at its height, be going full swing; **~ des mains** to clap one's hands
battue [baty] nf (chasse) beat; (policière etc) search, hunt
baume [bom] nm balm
baux [bo] nmpl de **bail**
bavard, e [bavaʀ, aʀd] adj (very) talkative; gossipy; **bavarder** vi to chatter; (commérer)

to gossip; (divulguer un secret) to blab
bave [bav] nf dribble; (de chien etc) slobber; (d'escargot) slime; **baver** vi to dribble; (chien) to slobber; **en baver** (fam) to have a hard time (of it); **baveux, -euse** adj (omelette) runny; **bavoir** nm bib
bavure [bavyʀ] nf smudge; (fig) hitch; (policière etc) blunder
bayer [baje] vi: **~ aux corneilles** to stand gaping
bazar [bazaʀ] nm general store; (fam) jumble; **bazarder** (fam) vt to chuck out
BCBG sigle adj (= bon chic bon genre) preppy, smart and trendy
BD sigle f = **bande dessinée**
bd abr = **boulevard**
béant, e [beɑ̃, ɑ̃t] adj gaping
béat, e [bea, at] adj: **~ d'admiration** struck dumb with admiration; **béatitude** nf bliss
beau (bel), belle [bo, bɛl] (mpl beaux) adj beautiful, lovely; (homme) handsome; (femme) beautiful ♦ adv: **il fait beau** the weather's fine; **un ~jour** one (fine) day; **de plus belle** more than ever, even more; **on a ~essayer** however hard we try; **bel et bien** well and truly

MOT-CLÉ

beaucoup [boku] adv **1** a lot; **il boit beaucoup** he drinks a lot; **il ne boit pas beaucoup** he doesn't drink much ou a lot
2 (suivi de plus, trop etc) much, a lot, far; **il est beaucoup plus grand** he is much ou a lot ou far taller
3: **beaucoup de** (nombre) many, a lot of; (quantité) a lot of; **beaucoup d'étudiants/de touristes** a lot of ou many students/tourists; **beaucoup de courage** a lot of courage; **il n'a pas beaucoup d'argent** he hasn't got much ou a lot of money
4: **de beaucoup** by far

beau...: **beau-fils** nm son-in-law; (remariage) stepson; **beau-frère** nm brother-in-law; **beau-père** nm father-in-law; (remariage) stepfather
beauté [bote] nf beauty; **de toute ~** beautiful; **finir qch en ~** to complete sth brilliantly
beaux-arts [bozaʀ] nmpl fine arts
beaux-parents [boparɑ̃] nmpl wife's/husband's family, in-laws
bébé [bebe] nm baby
bec [bɛk] nm beak, bill; (de théière) spout; (de casserole) lip; (fam) mouth; **~ de gaz** (street) gaslamp; **~ verseur** pouring lip
bécane [bekan] (fam) nf bike
bec-de-lièvre [bɛkdəljɛvʀ] nm harelip
bêche [bɛʃ] nf spade; **bêcher** vt to dig
bécoter [bekɔte]: **se ~** vi to smooch

becqueter [bɛkte] (fam) vt to eat
bedaine [bədɛn] nf paunch
bedonnant, e [bədɔnã, ãt] adj potbellied
bée [be] adj: **bouche ~** gaping
beffroi [befʀwa] nm belfry
bégayer [begeje] vt, vi to stammer
bègue [bɛg] nm/f: **être ~** to have a stammer
beige [bɛʒ] adj beige
beignet [bɛɲɛ] nm fritter
bel [bɛl] adj voir **beau**
bêler [bele] vi to bleat
belette [bəlɛt] nf weasel
belge [bɛlʒ] adj Belgian ♦ nm/f: **B~** Belgian
Belgique [bɛlʒik] nf: **la ~** Belgium
bélier [belje] nm ram; (signe): **le B~** Aries
belle [bɛl] adj voir **beau** ♦ nf (SPORT) decider;
   belle-fille nf daughter-in-law; (remariage)
   stepdaughter; **belle-mère** nf mother-in-law;
   stepmother; **belle-sœur** nf sister-in-law
belliqueux, -euse [belikø, øz] adj
   aggressive, warlike
belvédère [bɛlvedeʀ] nm panoramic
   viewpoint (or small building there)
bémol [bemɔl] nm (MUS) flat
bénédiction [benediksjɔ̃] nf blessing
bénéfice [benefis] nm (COMM) profit;
   (avantage) benefit; **bénéficier: bénéficier de**
   vt to enjoy; (situation) to benefit by ou from;
   bénéfique adj beneficial
bénévole [benevɔl] adj voluntary, unpaid
bénin, -igne [benɛ̃, iɲ] adj minor, mild;
   (tumeur) benign
bénir [beniʀ] vt to bless; **bénit, e** adj
   consecrated; **eau bénite** holy water
benjamin, e [bɛ̃ʒamɛ̃, in] nm/f youngest
   child
benne [bɛn] nf skip; (de téléphérique) (cable)
   car; **~ basculante** tipper (BRIT), dump truck
   (US)
BEP sigle m (= brevet d'études professionnelles)
   technical school certificate
béquille [bekij] nf crutch; (de bicyclette)
   stand
berceau, x [bɛʀso] nm cradle, crib
bercer [bɛʀse] vt to rock, cradle; (suj: musique
   etc) to lull; **~ qn de** (promesses etc) to delude
   sb with; **berceuse** nf lullaby
béret (basque) [bere (bask(ə))] nm beret
berge [bɛʀʒ] nf bank
berger, -ère [bɛʀʒe, ɛʀ] nm/f shep-
   herd(-ess); **~ allemand** alsatian (BRIT), German
   shepherd
berlingot [bɛʀlɛ̃go] nm (bonbon) boiled
   sweet, humbug (BRIT)
berlue [bɛʀly] nf: **j'ai la ~** I must be seeing
   things
berner [bɛʀne] vt to fool
besogne [bəzɔɲ] nf work no pl, job
besoin [bəzwɛ̃] nm need; **avoir ~ de qch/faire**

qch to need sth/to do sth; **au ~** if need be; **le**
   ~ (pauvreté) need, want; **être dans le ~** to be
   in need ou want; **faire ses ~s** to relieve o.s.
bestiaux [bɛstjo] nmpl cattle
bestiole [bɛstjɔl] nf (tiny) creature
bétail [betaj] nm livestock, cattle pl
bête [bɛt] nf animal; (bestiole) insect, creature
   ♦ adj stupid, silly; **il cherche la petite ~** he's
   being pernickety ou overfussy; **~ noire** pet
   hate
bêtement [bɛtmã] adv stupidly
bêtise [betiz] nf stupidity; (action) stupid
   thing (to say ou do)
béton [betɔ̃] nm concrete; **(en) ~** (alibi,
   argument) cast iron; **~ armé** reinforced
   concrete; **bétonnière** nf cement mixer
betterave [bɛtʀav] nf beetroot (BRIT), beet
   (US); **~ sucrière** sugar beet
beugler [bøgle] vi to low; (radio etc) to blare
   ♦ vt (chanson) to bawl out
Beur [bœʀ] nm/f person of North African origin
   living in France
beurre [bœʀ] nm butter; **beurrer** vt to
   butter; **beurrier** nm butter dish
beuverie [bøvʀi] nf drinking session
bévue [bevy] nf blunder
Beyrouth [beʀut] n Beirut
bi... [bi] préfixe bi-, two-
biais [bjɛ] nm (moyen) device, expedient;
   (aspect) angle; **en ~, de ~** (obliquement) at an
   angle; **par le ~ de** by means of; **biaiser** vi
   (fig) to sidestep the issue
bibelot [biblo] nm trinket, curio
biberon [bibʀɔ̃] nm (feeding) bottle; **nourrir**
   au ~ to bottle-feed
bible [bibl] nf bible
biblio... [biblijo] préfixe: **bibliobus** nm mobile
   library van; **bibliographie** nf bibliography;
   bibliothécaire nm/f librarian; **bibliothèque**
   nf library; (meuble) bookcase
bic ® [bik] nm Biro ®
bicarbonate [bikaʀbɔnat] nm: **~ (de soude)**
   bicarbonate of soda
biceps [bisɛps] nm biceps
biche [biʃ] nf doe
bichonner [biʃɔne] vt to pamper
bicolore [bikɔlɔʀ] adj two-coloured
bicoque [bikɔk] (péj) nf shack
bicyclette [bisiklɛt] nf bicycle
bide [bid] (fam) nm (ventre) belly; (THÉÂTRE)
   flop
bidet [bide] nm bidet
bidon [bidɔ̃] nm can ♦ adj inv (fam) phoney
bidonville [bidɔ̃vil] nm shanty town
bidule [bidyl] (fam) nm thingumajig

MOT-CLÉ

bien [bjɛ̃] nm 1 (avantage, profit): **faire du**
   bien à qn to do sb good; **dire du bien de** to

speak well of; **c'est pour son bien** it's for his own good
2 (*possession, patrimoine*) possession, property; **son bien le plus précieux** his most treasured possession; **avoir du bien** to have property; **biens (de consommation** *etc***)** (*consumer etc*) goods
3 (*moral*): **le bien** good; **distinguer le bien du mal** to tell good from evil
♦ *adv* **1** (*de façon satisfaisante*) well; **elle travaille/mange bien** she works/eats well; **croyant bien faire, je/il ...** thinking I/he was doing the right thing, I/he ...; **c'est bien fait!** it serves him (*ou* her *etc*) right!
2 (*valeur intensive*) quite; **bien jeune** quite young; **bien assez** quite enough; **bien mieux** (very) much better; **j'espère bien y aller** I do hope to go; **je veux bien le faire** (*concession*) I'm quite willing to do it; **il faut bien le faire** it has to be done
3: **bien du temps/des gens** quite a time/a number of people
♦ *adj inv* **1** (*en bonne forme, à l'aise*): **je me sens bien** I feel fine; **je ne me sens pas bien** I don't feel well; **on est bien dans ce fauteuil** this chair is very comfortable
2 (*joli, beau*) good-looking; **tu es bien dans cette robe** you look good in that dress
3 (*satisfaisant*) good; **elle est bien, cette maison/secrétaire** it's a good house/she's a good secretary
4 (*moralement*) right; (*: personne*) good, nice; (*respectable*) respectable; **ce n'est pas bien de ...** it's not right to ...; **elle est bien, cette femme** she's a nice woman, she's a good sort; **des gens biens** respectable people
5 (*en bons termes*): **être bien avec qn** to be on good terms with sb
♦ *préfixe*: **bien-aimé** *adj, nm/f* beloved; **bien-être** *nm* well-being; **bienfaisance** *nf* charity, **bienfaisant, e** *adj* (*chose*) beneficial; **bienfait** *nm* act of generosity, benefaction; (*de la science etc*) benefit; **bienfaiteur, -trice** *nm/f* benefactor/benefactress; **bien-fondé** *nm* soundness; **bien-fonds** *nm* property; **bienheureux, -euse** *adj* happy; (*REL*) blessed, blest; **bien que** *conj* (al)though; **bien sûr** *adv* certainly

bienséant, e [bjẽseã, ãt] *adj* seemly
bientôt [bjẽto] *adv* soon; **à ~** see you soon
bienveillant, e [bjẽvɛjã, ãt] *adj* kindly
bienvenu, e [bjẽvny] *adj* welcome; **bienvenue** *nf*: **souhaiter la bienvenue à** to welcome; **bienvenue à** welcome to
bière [bjɛʀ] *nf* (*boisson*) beer; (*cercueil*) bier; **~ (à la) pression** draught beer; **~ blonde** lager; **~ brune** brown ale
biffer [bife] *vt* to cross out

bifteck [biftɛk] *nm* steak
bifurquer [bifyʀke] *vi* (*route*) to fork; (*véhicule*) to turn off
bigarré, e [bigaʀe] *adj* multicoloured; (*disparate*) motley
bigorneau, x [bigɔʀno] *nm* winkle
bigot, e [bigo, ɔt] (*péj*) *adj* bigoted
bigoudi [bigudi] *nm* curler
bijou, x [biʒu] *nm* jewel; **bijouterie** *nf* jeweller's (shop); **bijoutier, -ière** *nm/f* jeweller
bikini [bikini] *nm* bikini
bilan [bilã] *nm* (*fig*) (net) outcome; (*: de victimes*) toll; (*COMM*) balance sheet(s); **un ~ de santé** a (medical) checkup; **faire le ~ de** to assess, review; **déposer son ~** to file a bankruptcy statement
bile [bil] *nf* bile; **se faire de la ~** (*fam*) to worry o.s. sick
bilieux, -euse [biljø, øz] *adj* bilious; (*fig: colérique*) testy
bilingue [bilɛ̃g] *adj* bilingual
billard [bijaʀ] *nm* (*jeu*) billiards *sg*; (*table*) billiard table; **~ américain** pool
bille [bij] *nf* (*gén*) ball; (*du jeu de ~s*) marble
billet [bijɛ] *nm* (*aussi*: **~ de banque**) (bank)note; (*de cinéma, de bus etc*) ticket; (*courte lettre*) note; **~ Bige** cheap rail ticket for under-26s; **billetterie** *nf* ticket office; (*distributeur*) ticket machine; (*BANQUE*) cash dispenser
billion [biljɔ̃] *nm* billion (*BRIT*), trillion (*US*)
billot [bijo] *nm* block
bimensuel, le [bimãsɥɛl] *adj* bimonthly
binette [binɛt] *nf* hoe
bio... [bjɔ] *préfixe* bio...; **biochimie** *nf* biochemistry; **biodiversité** *nf* biodiversity; **bioéthique** *nf* bioethics *sg*; **biographie** *nf* biography; **biologie** *nf* biology; **biologique** *adj* biological; (*produits, aliments*) organic; **biologiste** *nm/f* biologist
Birmanie [biʀmani] *nf* Burma
bis [bis] *adv*: **12 ~ 12a** *ou* A ♦ *excl, nm* encore
bisannuel, le [bizanɥɛl] *adj* biennial
biscornu, e [biskɔʀny] *adj* twisted
biscotte [biskɔt] *nf* toasted bread (*sold in packets*)
biscuit [biskɥi] *nm* biscuit; **~ de savoie** sponge cake
bise [biz] *nf* (*fam: baiser*) kiss; (*vent*) North wind; **grosses ~s (de)** (*sur lettre*) love and kisses (from)
bisou [bizu] (*fam*) *nm* kiss
bissextile [bisɛkstil] *adj*: **année ~** leap year
bistouri [bisturi] *nm* lancet
bistro(t) [bistro] *nm* bistro, café
bitume [bitym] *nm* asphalt
bizarre [bizaʀ] *adj* strange, odd
blafard, e [blafaʀ, aʀd] *adj* wan

blague [blag] nf (propos) joke; (farce) trick; **sans ~!** no kidding!; **blaguer** vi to joke

blaireau, x [blɛʀo] nm (ZOOL) badger; (brosse) shaving brush

blairer [blɛʀe] (fam) vt: **je ne peux pas le ~ I** can't bear ou stand him

blâme [blɑm] nm blame; (sanction) reprimand; **blâmer** vt to blame

blanc, blanche [blɑ̃, blɑ̃ʃ] adj white; (non imprimé) blank ♦ nm/f white, white man(-woman) ♦ nm (couleur) white; (espace non écrit) blank; (aussi: ~ d'œuf) (egg-)white; (aussi: ~ de poulet) breast, white meat; (aussi: vin ~) white wine; ~ **cassé** off-white; **chèque en ~** blank cheque; **à ~** (chauffer) white-hot; (tirer, charger) with blanks; **blanc-bec** nm greenhorn; **blanche** nf (MUS) minim (BRIT), half-note (US); **blancheur** nf whiteness

blanchir [blɑ̃ʃiʀ] vt (gén) to whiten; (linge) to launder; (CULIN) to blanch; (fig: disculper) to clear ♦ vi to grow white; (cheveux) to go white; **blanchisserie** nf laundry

blason [blazɔ̃] nm coat of arms

blasphème [blasfɛm] nm blasphemy

blazer [blazɛʀ] nm blazer

blé [ble] nm wheat; ~ **noir** buckwheat

bled [blɛd] (péj) nm hole

blême [blɛm] adj pale

blessant, e [blesɑ̃, ɑ̃t] adj (offensant) hurtful

blessé, e [blese] adj injured ♦ nm/f injured person, casualty

blesser [blese] vt to injure; (délibérément: MIL etc) to wound; (offenser) to hurt; **se ~** to injure o.s.; **se ~ au pied** etc to injure one's foot etc; **blessure** nf (accidentelle) injury; (intentionnelle) wound

bleu, e [blø] adj blue; (bifteck) very rare ♦ nm (couleur) blue; (contusion) bruise; (vêtement: aussi: ~s) overalls pl; ~ **marine** navy blue; **bleuet** nm cornflower; **bleuté, e** adj blue-shaded

blinder [blɛ̃de] vt to armour; (fig) to harden

bloc [blɔk] nm (de pierre etc) block; (de papier à lettres) pad; (ensemble) group, block; **serré à ~** tightened right down; **en ~** as a whole; ~ **opératoire** operating ou theatre block; ~ **sanitaire** toilet block; **blocage** nm (des prix) freezing; (PSYCH) hang-up; **bloc-notes** nm note pad

blocus [blɔkys] nm blockade

blond, e [blɔ̃, blɔ̃d] adj fair, blond; (sable, blés) golden; ~ **cendré** ash blond; **blonde** nf (femme) blonde; (bière) lager; (cigarette) Virginia cigarette

bloquer [blɔke] vt (passage) to block; (pièce mobile) to jam; (crédits, compte) to freeze; **se ~** to jam; (PSYCH) to have a mental block

blottir [blɔtiʀ]: **se ~** vi to huddle up

blouse [bluz] nf overall

blouson [bluzɔ̃] nm blouson jacket; ~ **noir** (fig) ≈ rocker

blue-jean [bludʒin] nm (pair of) jeans

bluff [blœf] nm bluff; **bluffer** vi to bluff

bobard [bɔbaʀ] (fam) nm tall story

bobine [bɔbin] nf reel; (ÉLEC) coil

bocal, -aux [bɔkal, o] nm jar

bock [bɔk] nm glass of beer

body [bɔdi] nm body(suit); (SPORT) leotard

bœuf [bœf] nm ox; (CULIN) beef

bof! [bɔf] (fam) excl don't care!; (pas terrible) nothing special

bohème [bɔɛm] adj happy-go-lucky, unconventional; **bohémien, ne** nm/f gipsy

boire [bwaʀ] vt to drink; (s'imprégner de) to soak up; ~ **un coup** (fam) to have a drink

bois [bwa] nm wood; **de ~, en ~** wooden; **boisé, e** adj woody, wooded

boisson [bwasɔ̃] nf drink

boîte [bwat] nf box; (fam: entreprise) firm; **aliments en ~** canned ou tinned (BRIT) foods; ~ **aux lettres** letter box; ~ **d'allumettes** box of matches; (vide) matchbox; ~ **(de conserve)** can ou tin (BRIT) (of food); ~ **de nuit** night club; ~ **de vitesses** gear box; ~ **postale** PO Box

boiter [bwate] vi to limp; (fig: raisonnement) to be shaky

boîtier [bwatje] nm case

boive etc [bwav] vb voir **boire**

bol [bɔl] nm bowl; **un ~ d'air** a breath of fresh air; **j'en ai ras le ~** (fam) I'm fed up with this; **avoir du ~** (fam) to be lucky

bolide [bɔlid] nm racing car; **comme un ~** at top speed, like a rocket

bombardement [bɔ̃baʀdəmɑ̃] nm bombing

bombarder [bɔ̃baʀde] vt to bomb; ~ **qn de** (cailloux, lettres) to bombard sb with

bombe [bɔ̃b] nf bomb; (atomiseur) (aerosol) spray; **bombé, e** adj (forme) rounded; **bomber** vt: **bomber le torse** to swell out one's chest

---

┌─ MOT-CLÉ ─────────────────────┐

bon, bonne [bɔ̃, bɔn] adj **1** (agréable, satisfaisant) good; **un bon repas/restaurant** a good meal/restaurant; **être bon en maths** to be good at maths

2 (charitable): **être bon (envers)** to be good (to)

3 (correct) right; **le bon numéro/moment** the right number/moment

4 (souhaits): **bon anniversaire** happy birthday; **bon voyage** have a good trip; **bonne chance** good luck; **bonne année** happy New Year; **bonne nuit** good night

5 (approprié, apte): **bon à/pour** fit to/for

6: bon enfant adj inv accommodating, easy-going; **bonne femme** (*péj*) woman; **de bonne heure** early; **bon marché** *adj inv* cheap ♦ *adv* cheap; **bon mot** witticism; **bon sens** common sense; **bon vivant** jovial chap; **bonnes œuvres** charitable works, charities

♦ *nm* **1** (*billet*) voucher; (*aussi:* **bon cadeau**) gift voucher; **bon d'essence** petrol coupon; **bon du Trésor** Treasury bond

2: **avoir du bon** to have its good points; **pour de bon** for good

♦ *adv*: **il fait bon** it's *ou* the weather is fine; **sentir bon** to smell good; **tenir bon** to stand firm

♦ *excl* good!; **ah bon?** really?; *voir aussi* **bonne**

---

bonbon [bɔ̃bɔ̃] *nm* (boiled) sweet
bonbonne [bɔ̃bɔn] *nf* demijohn
bond [bɔ̃] *nm* leap; **faire un ~** to leap in the air
bondé, e [bɔ̃de] *adj* packed (full)
bondir [bɔ̃diʀ] *vi* to leap
bonheur [bɔnœʀ] *nm* happiness; **porter ~** (**à qn**) to bring (sb) luck; **au petit ~** haphazardly; **par ~** fortunately
bonhomie [bɔnɔmi] *nf* goodnaturedness
bonhomme [bɔnɔm] (*pl* **bonshommes**) *nm* fellow; **~ de neige** snowman
bonifier [bɔnifje] *vt* to improve
boniment [bɔnimɑ̃] *nm* patter *no pl*
bonjour [bɔ̃ʒuʀ] *excl, nm* hello; (*selon l'heure*) good morning/afternoon; **c'est simple comme ~!** it's easy as pie!
bonne [bɔn] *adj voir* **bon** ♦ *nf* (*domestique*) maid; **bonnement** *adv*: **tout bonnement** quite simply
bonnet [bɔnɛ] *nm* hat; (*de soutien-gorge*) cup; **~ de bain** bathing cap
bonshommes [bɔ̃zɔm] *nmpl de* **bonhomme**
bonsoir [bɔ̃swaʀ] *excl* good evening
bonté [bɔ̃te] *nf* kindness *no pl*
bonus [bɔnys] *nm* no claims bonus
bord [bɔʀ] *nm* (*de table, verre, falaise*) edge; (*de rivière, lac*) bank; (*de route*) side; (**monter**) **à ~** (to go) on board; **jeter par-dessus ~** to throw overboard; **le commandant de/les hommes du ~** the ship's master/crew; **au ~ de la mer** at the seaside; **être au ~ des larmes** to be on the verge of tears
bordeaux [bɔʀdo] *nm* Bordeaux (wine) ♦ *adj inv* maroon
bordel [bɔʀdɛl] *nm* brothel; (*fam!*) bloody mess (*!*)
bordelais, e [bɔʀdəlɛ, ɛz] *adj* of *ou* from Bordeaux
border [bɔʀde] *vt* (*être le long de*) to line; (*qn dans son lit*) to tuck up; (*garnir*): **~ qch de** to edge sth with
bordereau, x [bɔʀdəro] *nm* (*formulaire*) slip
bordure [bɔʀdyʀ] *nf* border; **en ~ de** on the edge of

borgne [bɔʀɲ] *adj* one-eyed
borne [bɔʀn] *nf* boundary stone; (*aussi:* **~ kilométrique**) kilometre-marker; ≈ milestone; **~s** *nfpl* (*fig*) limits; **dépasser les ~s** to go too far
borné, e [bɔʀne] *adj* (*personne*) narrow-minded
borner [bɔʀne] *vt*: **se ~ à faire** (*se contenter de*) to content o.s. with doing; (*se limiter à*) to limit o.s. to doing
bosquet [bɔskɛ] *nm* grove
bosse [bɔs] *nf* (*de terrain etc*) bump; (*enflure*) lump; (*du bossu, du chameau*) hump; **avoir la ~ des maths** *etc* (*fam*) to have a gift for maths *etc*; **il a roulé sa ~** (*fam*) he's been around
bosser [bɔse] (*fam*) *vi* (*travailler*) to work; (*travailler dur*) to slave (away)
bossu, e [bɔsy] *nm/f* hunchback
botanique [bɔtanik] *nf* botany ♦ *adj* botanic(al)
botte [bɔt] *nf* (*soulier*) (high) boot; (*gerbe*): **~ de paille** bundle of straw; **~ de radis** bunch of radishes; **~s de caoutchouc** wellington boots; **botter** *vt*: **ça me botte** (*fam*) I fancy that
bottin [bɔtɛ̃] *nm* directory
bottine [bɔtin] *nf* ankle boot
bouc [buk] *nm* goat; (*barbe*) goatee; **~ émissaire** scapegoat
boucan [bukɑ̃] (*fam*) *nm* din, racket
bouche [buʃ] *nf* mouth; **rester ~ bée** to stand open-mouthed; **le ~ à ~** the kiss of life; **~ d'égout** manhole; **~ d'incendie** fire hydrant; **~ de métro** métro entrance
bouché, e [buʃe] *adj* (*temps, ciel*) overcast; **c'est ~** there's no future in it
bouchée [buʃe] *nf* mouthful; **~s à la reine** chicken vol-au-vents
boucher, ère [buʃe] *nm/f* butcher ♦ *vt* (*trou*) to fill up, (*obstruer*) to block (up), **se ~** *vi* (*tuyau etc*) to block up, get blocked up; **j'ai le nez bouché** my nose is blocked; **se ~ le nez** to hold one's nose; **boucherie** *nf* butcher's (shop), (*fig*) slaughter
bouche-trou [buʃtʀu] *nm* (*fig*) stop-gap
bouchon [buʃɔ̃] *nm* stopper; (*de tube*) top; (*en liège*) cork; (*fig: embouteillage*) holdup; (*PÊCHE*) float
boucle [bukl] *nf* (*forme, figure*) loop; (*objet*) buckle; **~ (de cheveux)** curl; **~ d'oreille** earring
bouclé, e [bukle] *adj* (*cheveux*) curly
boucler [bukle] *vt* (*fermer: ceinture etc*) to fasten; (*terminer*) to finish off; (*fam: enfermer*) to shut away; (*quartier*) to seal off ♦ *vi* to curl
bouclier [buklije] *nm* shield
bouddhiste [budist] *nm/f* Buddhist
bouder [bude] *vi* to sulk ♦ *vt* to stay away

from
boudin [budɛ̃] *nm*: ~ **(noir)** black pudding;
~ **blanc** white pudding
boue [bu] *nf* mud
bouée [bwe] *nf* buoy; ~ **(de sauvetage)**
lifebuoy
boueux, -euse [bwø, øz] *adj* muddy
bouffe [buf] *(fam) nf* grub *(fam)*, food
bouffée [bufe] *nf (de cigarette)* puff; **une**
~ **d'air pur** a breath of fresh air
bouffer [bufe] *(fam) vi* to eat
bouffi, e [bufi] *adj* swollen
bougeoir [buʒwaʀ] *nm* candlestick
bougeotte [buʒɔt] *nf*: **avoir la** ~ *(fam)* to
have the fidgets
bouger [buʒe] *vi* to move; *(dent etc)* to be
loose; *(s'activer)* to get moving ♦ *vt* to move;
les prix/les couleurs n'ont pas bougé prices/
colours haven't changed
bougie [buʒi] *nf* candle; *(AUTO)* spark(ing)
plug
bougon, ne [bugɔ̃, ɔn] *adj* grumpy
bougonner [bugɔne] *vi, vt* to grumble
bouillabaisse [bujabɛs] *nf* type of fish soup
bouillant, e [bujɑ̃, ɑ̃t] *adj (qui bout)* boiling;
(très chaud) boiling (hot)
bouillie [buji] *nf (de bébé)* cereal; **en** ~ *(fig)*
crushed
bouillir [bujiʀ] *vi, vt* to boil; ~ **d'impatience**
to seethe with impatience
bouilloire [bujwaʀ] *nf* kettle
bouillon [bujɔ̃] *nm (CULIN)* stock *no pl*;
bouillonner *vi* to bubble; *(fig: idées)* to
bubble up
bouillotte [bujɔt] *nf* hot-water bottle
boulanger, -ère [bulɑ̃ʒe, ɛʀ] *nm/f* baker;
boulangerie *nf* bakery; **boulangerie-
pâtisserie** *nf* baker's and confectioner's
(shop)
boule [bul] *nf (gén)* ball; ~**s** *nfpl (jeu)* bowls;
se mettre en ~ *(fig: fam)* to fly off the handle,
to blow one's top; **jouer aux** ~**s** to play
bowls; ~ **de neige** snowball
bouleau, x [bulo] *nm* (silver) birch
bouledogue [buldɔg] *nm* bulldog
boulet [bulɛ] *nm (aussi:* ~ **de canon)**
cannonball
boulette [bulɛt] *nf (de viande)* meatball
boulevard [bulvaʀ] *nm* boulevard
bouleversant, e [bulvɛʀsɑ̃, ɑ̃t] *adj (scène,
récit)* deeply moving
bouleversement [bulvɛʀsəmɑ̃] *nm*
upheaval
bouleverser [bulvɛʀse] *vt (émouvoir)* to
overwhelm; *(causer du chagrin)* to distress;
(pays, vie) to disrupt; *(papiers, objets)* to turn
upside down
boulon [bulɔ̃] *nm* bolt
boulot, te [bulo, ɔt] *adj* plump, tubby ♦ *nm*

(fam: travail) work
boum [bum] *nm* bang ♦ *nf (fam)* party
bouquet [bukɛ] *nm (de fleurs)* bunch (of
flowers), bouquet; *(de persil etc)* bunch; **c'est
le** ~! *(fam)* that takes the biscuit!
bouquin [bukɛ̃] *(fam) nm* book; **bouquiner**
(fam) vi to read; **bouquiniste** *nm/f*
bookseller
bourbeux, -euse [buʀbø, øz] *adj* muddy
bourbier [buʀbje] *nm* (quag)mire
bourde [buʀd] *(fam) nf (erreur)* howler;
(gaffe) blunder
bourdon [buʀdɔ̃] *nm* bumblebee;
bourdonner *vi* to buzz
bourg [buʀ] *nm* small market town
bourgeois, e [buʀʒwa, waz] *(péj) adj* ≈
(upper) middle class; **bourgeoisie** *nf* ≈
upper middle classes *pl*
bourgeon [buʀʒɔ̃] *nm* bud
Bourgogne [buʀgɔɲ] *nf*: **la** ~ Burgundy
♦ *nm*: **b~** burgundy (wine)
bourguignon, ne [buʀgiɲɔ̃, ɔn] *adj* of *ou*
from Burgundy, Burgundian
bourlinguer [buʀlɛ̃ge] *(fam) vi* to knock
about a lot, get around a lot
bourrade [buʀad] *nf* shove, thump
bourrage [buʀaʒ] *nm*: ~ **de crâne**
brainwashing; *(SCOL)* cramming
bourrasque [buʀask] *nf* squall
bourratif, -ive [buʀatif, iv] *(fam) adj* filling,
stodgy *(péj)*
bourré, e [buʀe] *adj (fam: ivre)* plastered,
tanked up *(BRIT)*; *(rempli)*: ~ **de** crammed full
of
bourreau, x [buʀo] *nm* executioner; *(fig)*
torturer; ~ **de travail** workaholic
bourrelet [buʀlɛ] *nm* fold *ou* roll (of flesh)
bourrer [buʀe] *vt (pipe)* to fill; *(poêle)* to
pack; *(valise)* to cram (full)
bourrique [buʀik] *nf (âne)* ass
bourru, e [buʀy] *adj* surly, gruff
bourse [buʀs] *nf (subvention)* grant; *(porte-
monnaie)* purse; **la B~** the Stock Exchange
boursier, -ière [buʀsje, jɛʀ] *nm/f (étudiant)*
grant holder
boursoufler [buʀsufle]: **se** ~ *vi* to swell (up)
bous [bu] *vb voir* **bouillir**
bousculade [buskylad] *nf (hâte)* rush;
(cohue) crush; **bousculer** *vt (heurter)* to
knock into; *(fig)* to push, rush
bouse [buz] *nf* dung *no pl*
bousiller [buzije] *(fam) vt (appareil)* to
wreck
boussole [busɔl] *nf* compass
bout [bu] *vb voir* **bouillir** ♦ *nm* bit; *(d'un bâton
etc)* tip; *(d'une ficelle, table, rue, période)* end;
au ~ **de** at the end of, after; **pousser qn à** ~ to
push sb to the limit; **venir à** ~ **de** to manage
to finish

boutade [butad] *nf* quip, sally
boute-en-train [butɑ̃trɛ̃] *nm inv* (*fig*) live wire
bouteille [butɛj] *nf* bottle; (*de gaz butane*) cylinder
boutique [butik] *nf* shop
bouton [butɔ̃] *nm* button; (*sur la peau*) spot; (*BOT*) bud; ~ **d'or** buttercup; **boutonner** *vt* to button up; **boutonnière** *nf* buttonhole; **bouton-pression** *nm* press stud
bouture [butyʀ] *nf* cutting
bovins [bɔvɛ̃] *nmpl* cattle *pl*
bowling [buliŋ] *nm* (tenpin) bowling; (*salle*) bowling alley
box [bɔks] *nm* (*d'écurie*) loose-box; (*JUR*): ~ **des accusés** dock
boxe [bɔks] *nf* boxing; **boxeur** *nm* boxer
boyaux [bwajo] *nmpl* (*viscères*) entrails, guts
BP *abr* = **boîte postale**
bracelet [bʀaslɛ] *nm* bracelet
braconnier [bʀakɔnje] *nm* poacher
brader [bʀade] *vt* to sell off; **braderie** *nf* cut-price shop/stall
braguette [bʀagɛt] *nf* fly ou flies *pl* (*BRIT*), zipper (*US*)
brailler [bʀɑje] *vi* to bawl, yell
braire [bʀɛʀ] *vi* to bray
braise [bʀɛz] *nf* embers *pl*
brancard [bʀɑ̃kaʀ] *nm* (*civière*) stretcher; **brancardier** *nm* stretcher-bearer
branchages [bʀɑ̃ʃaʒ] *nmpl* boughs
branche [bʀɑ̃ʃ] *nf* branch
branché, e [bʀɑ̃ʃe] (*fam*) *adj* trendy
brancher [bʀɑ̃ʃe] *vt* to connect (up); (*en mettant la prise*) to plug in
brandir [bʀɑ̃diʀ] *vt* to brandish
branle [bʀɑ̃l] *nm*: **mettre en ~** to set in motion; **branle-bas** *nm inv* commotion
braquer [bʀake] *vi* (*AUTO*) to turn (the wheel) ♦ *vt* (*révolver etc*): ~ **qch sur** to aim sth at, point sth at; (*mettre en colère*): ~ **qn** to put sb's back up
bras [bʀɑ] *nm* arm; ~ **dessus**, ~ **dessous** arm in arm; **se retrouver avec qch sur les** ~ (*fam*) to be landed with sth; ~ **droit** (*fig*) right hand man; ~ **de fer** arm wrestling
brasier [bʀazje] *nm* blaze, inferno
bras-le-corps [bʀalkɔʀ] *adv*: **à** ~-~-~ (a)round the waist
brassard [bʀasaʀ] *nm* armband
brasse [bʀas] *nf* (*nage*) breast-stroke
brassée [bʀase] *nf* armful
brasser [bʀase] *vt* to mix; ~ **l'argent/les affaires** to handle a lot of money/business
brasserie [bʀasʀi] *nf* (*restaurant*) café-restaurant; (*usine*) brewery
brave [bʀav] *adj* (*courageux*) brave; (*bon, gentil*) good, kind
braver [bʀave] *vt* to defy

bravo [bʀavo] *excl* bravo ♦ *nm* cheer
bravoure [bʀavuʀ] *nf* bravery
break [bʀɛk] *nm* (*AUTO*) estate car
brebis [bʀəbi] *nf* ewe; ~ **galeuse** black sheep
brèche [bʀɛʃ] *nf* breach, gap; **être toujours sur la** ~ (*fig*) to be always on the go
bredouille [bʀəduj] *adj* empty-handed
bredouiller [bʀəduje] *vi, vt* to mumble, stammer
bref, brève [bʀɛf, ɛv] *adj* short, brief ♦ *adv* in short; **d'un ton** ~ sharply, curtly; **en** ~ in short, in brief
Brésil [bʀezil] *nm* Brazil; **brésilien, -ne** *adj* Brazilian ♦ *nm/f*: **Brésilien, ne** Brazilian
Bretagne [bʀətaɲ] *nf* Brittany
bretelle [bʀətɛl] *nf* (*de vêtement, de sac*) strap; (*d'autoroute*) slip road (*BRIT*), entrance/exit ramp (*US*); ~**s** *nfpl* (*pour pantalon*) braces (*BRIT*), suspenders (*US*)
breton, ne [bʀətɔ̃, ɔn] *adj* Breton ♦ *nm/f*: **B~, ne** Breton
breuvage [bʀœvaʒ] *nm* beverage, drink
brève [bʀɛv] *adj voir* **bref**
brevet [bʀəvɛ] *nm* diploma, certificate; ~ (**d'invention**) patent; **breveté, e** *adj* patented
bribes [bʀib] *nfpl* (*de conversation*) snatches; **par** ~ piecemeal
bricolage [bʀikɔlaʒ] *nm*: **le** ~ do-it-yourself
bricole [bʀikɔl] *nf* (*babiole*) trifle
bricoler [bʀikɔle] *vi* (*petits travaux*) to do DIY jobs; (*passe-temps*) to potter about ♦ *vt* (*réparer*) to fix up; **bricoleur, -euse** *nm/f* handyman(-woman), DIY enthusiast
bride [bʀid] *nf* bridle; **tenir qn en** ~ to keep a tight rein on sb
bridé, e [bʀide] *adj*: **yeux** ~**s** slit eyes
bridge [bʀidʒ] *nm* (*CARTES*) bridge
brièvement [bʀijɛvmɑ̃] *adv* briefly
brigade [bʀigad] *nf* (*POLICE*) squad; (*MIL*) brigade, **brigadier** *nm* sergeant
brigandage [bʀigɑ̃daʒ] *nm* robbery
briguer [bʀige] *vt* to aspire to
brillamment [bʀijamɑ̃] *adv* brilliantly
brillant, e [bʀijɑ̃, ɑ̃t] *adj* (*remarquable*) bright; (*luisant*) shiny, shining
briller [bʀije] *vi* to shine
brimer [bʀime] *vt* to bully
brin [bʀɛ̃] *nm* (*de laine, ficelle etc*) strand; (*fig*): **un** ~ **de** a bit of; ~ **d'herbe** blade of grass; ~ **de muguet** sprig of lily of the valley
brindille [bʀɛ̃dij] *nf* twig
brio [bʀijo] *nm*: **avec** ~ with panache
brioche [bʀijɔʃ] *nf* brioche (bun); (*fam: ventre*) paunch
brique [bʀik] *nf* brick; (*de lait*) carton
briquer [bʀike] *vt* to polish up
briquet [bʀikɛ] *nm* (cigarette) lighter
brise [bʀiz] *nf* breeze

briser [bʀize] vt to break; **se ~** vi to break

britannique [bʀitanik] adj British ♦ nm/f: **B~** British person, Briton; **les B~s** the British

brocante [bʀɔkɑ̃t] nf junk, second-hand goods pl; **brocanteur, -euse** nm/f junkshop owner; junk dealer

broche [bʀɔʃ] nf brooch; (CULIN) spit; (MÉD) pin; **à la ~** spit-roasted

broché, e [bʀɔʃe] adj (livre) paper-backed

brochet [bʀɔʃɛ] nm pike inv

brochette [bʀɔʃɛt] nf (ustensile) skewer; (plat) kebab

brochure [bʀɔʃyʀ] nf pamphlet, brochure, booklet

broder [bʀɔde] vt to embroider ♦ vi to embroider the facts; **broderie** nf embroidery

broncher [bʀɔ̃ʃe] vi: **sans ~** without flinching, without turning a hair

bronches [bʀɔ̃ʃ] nfpl bronchial tubes; **bronchite** nf bronchitis

bronze [bʀɔ̃z] nm bronze

bronzer [bʀɔ̃ze] vi to get a tan; **se ~** to sunbathe

brosse [bʀɔs] nf brush; **coiffé en ~** with a crewcut; **~ à cheveux** hairbrush; **~ à dents** toothbrush; **~ à habits** clothesbrush; **brosser** vt (nettoyer) to brush; (fig: tableau etc) to paint; **se brosser les dents** to brush one's teeth

brouette [bʀuɛt] nf wheelbarrow

brouhaha [bʀuaa] nm hubbub

brouillard [bʀujaʀ] nm fog

brouille [bʀuj] nf quarrel

brouiller [bʀuje] vt (œufs, message) to scramble; (idées) to mix up; (rendre trouble) to cloud; (désunir: amis) to set at odds; **se ~** vi (vue) to cloud over; (gens) to fall out

brouillon, ne [bʀujɔ̃, ɔn] adj (sans soin) untidy; (qui manque d'organisation) disorganized ♦ nm draft; **(papier) ~** rough paper

broussailles [bʀusaj] nfpl undergrowth sg; **broussailleux, -euse** adj bushy

brousse [bʀus] nf: **la ~** the bush

brouter [bʀute] vi to graze

broutille [bʀutij] nf trifle

broyer [bʀwaje] vt to crush; **~ du noir** to be down in the dumps

bru [bʀy] nf daughter-in-law

brugnon [bʀynɔ̃] nm (BOT) nectarine

bruiner [bʀɥine] vb impers: **il bruine** it's drizzling, there's a drizzle

bruire [bʀɥiʀ] vi (feuilles) to rustle

bruit [bʀɥi] nm: **un ~** a noise, a sound; (fig: rumeur) a rumour; **le ~** noise; **sans ~** without a sound, noiselessly; **~ de fond** background noise; **bruitage** nm sound effects pl

brûlant, e [bʀylɑ̃, ɑ̃t] adj burning; (liquide) boiling (hot)

brûlé, e [bʀyle] adj (fig: démasqué) blown ♦ nm: **odeur de ~** smell of burning

brûle-pourpoint [bʀylpuʀpwɛ̃]: **à ~~** adv point-blank

brûler [bʀyle] vt to burn; (suj: eau bouillante) to scald; (consommer: électricité, essence) to use; (feu rouge, signal) to go through ♦ vi to burn; (jeu): **tu brûles!** you're getting hot!; **se ~** to burn o.s.; (s'ébouillanter) to scald o.s.

brûlure [bʀylyʀ] nf (lésion) burn; **~s d'estomac** heartburn sg

brume [bʀym] nf mist; **brumisateur** nm atomizer

brun, e [bʀœ̃, bʀyn] adj (gén, bière) brown; (cheveux, tabac) dark; **elle est ~e** she's got dark hair

brunch [bʀœntʃ] nm brunch

brunir [bʀyniʀ] vi to get a tan

brushing [bʀœʃiŋ] nm blow-dry

brusque [bʀysk] adj abrupt; **brusquer** vt to rush

brut, e [bʀyt] adj (minerai, soie) raw; (diamant) rough; (COMM) gross; **(pétrole) ~** crude (oil)

brutal, e, -aux [bʀytal, o] adj brutal; **brutaliser** vt to handle roughly, manhandle

Bruxelles [bʀysɛl] n Brussels

bruyamment [bʀɥijamɑ̃] adv noisily

bruyant, e [bʀɥijɑ̃, ɑ̃t] adj noisy

bruyère [bʀɥijɛʀ] nf heather

BTS sigle m (= brevet de technicien supérieur) vocational training certificate taken at the end of a higher education course

bu, e [by] pp de **boire**

buccal, e, -aux [bykal, o] adj: **par voie ~e** orally

bûche [byʃ] nf log; **prendre une ~** (fig) to come a cropper; **~ de Noël** Yule log

bûcher [byʃe] nm (funéraire) pyre; (supplice) stake ♦ vi (fam) to swot (BRIT), slave (away) ♦ vt (fam) to swot up (BRIT), slave away at; **bûcheron** nm woodcutter; **bûcheur, -euse** (fam) adj hard-working

budget [bydʒɛ] nm budget

buée [bɥe] nf (sur une vitre) mist

buffet [byfɛ] nm (meuble) sideboard; (de réception) buffet; **~ (de gare)** (station) buffet, snack bar

buffle [byfl] nm buffalo

buis [bɥi] nm box tree; (bois) box(wood)

buisson [bɥisɔ̃] nm bush

buissonnière [bɥisɔnjɛʀ] adj: **faire l'école ~** to skip school

bulbe [bylb] nm (BOT, ANAT) bulb

Bulgarie [bylgaʀi] nf Bulgaria

bulle [byl] nf bubble

bulletin [byltɛ̃] nm (communiqué, journal) bulletin; (SCOL) report; **~ d'informations** news bulletin; **~ de salaire** pay-slip; **~ (de vote)**

ballot paper; **~ météorologique** weather
report

bureau, x [byʀo] nm (meuble) desk; (pièce,
service) office; **~ de change** (foreign)
exchange office ou bureau; **~ de poste** post
office; **~ de tabac** tobacconist's (shop); **~ de
vote** polling station; **bureaucratie**
[byʀokʀasi] nf bureaucracy

burin [byʀɛ̃] nm cold chisel; (ART) burin

burlesque [byʀlɛsk] adj ridiculous;
(LITTÉRATURE) burlesque

bus¹ [by] vb voir **boire**

bus² [bys] nm bus

busqué, e [byske] adj (nez) hook(ed)

buste [byst] nm (torse) chest; (seins) bust

but¹ [by] vb voir **boire**

but² [by(t)] nm (cible) target; (fig) goal, aim;
(FOOTBALL etc) goal; **de ~ en blanc** point-
blank; **avoir pour ~ de faire** to aim to do;
dans le ~ de with the intention of

butane [bytan] nm (camping) butane; (usage
domestique) Calor gas ®

buté, e [byte] adj stubborn, obstinate

buter [byte] vi: **~ contre** (cogner) to bump
into; (trébucher) to stumble against; **se ~** vi
to get obstinate, dig in one's heels; **~ contre
une difficulté** (fig) to hit a snag

butin [bytɛ̃] nm booty, spoils pl; (d'un vol)
loot

butiner [bytine] vi (abeilles) to gather nectar

butte [byt] nf mound, hillock; **être en ~ à** to
be exposed to

buvais etc [byve] vb voir **boire**

buvard [byvaʀ] nm blotter

buvette [byvɛt] nf bar

buveur, -euse [byvœʀ, øz] nm/f drinker

C, c

c' [s] dét voir **ce**

CA sigle m = **chiffre d'affaires**

ça [sa] pron (pour désigner) this; (: plus loin)
that; (comme sujet indéfini) it; **comment ~ va?**
how are you?; **~ va?** (d'accord?) OK?, all
right?; **où ~?** where's that?; **pourquoi ~?**
why's that?; **qui ~?** who's that?; **~ alors!** well
really!; **~ fait 10 ans (que)** it's 10 years
(since); **c'est ~** that's right; **~ y est** that's it

çà [sa] adv: **~ et là** here and there

cabane [kaban] nf hut, cabin

cabaret [kabaʀɛ] nm night club

cabas [kaba] nm shopping bag

cabillaud [kabijo] nm cod inv

cabine [kabin] nf (de bateau) cabin; (de
piscine etc) cubicle; (de camion, train) cab;
(d'avion) cockpit; **~ d'essayage** fitting room;
~ (téléphonique) call ou (tele)phone box

cabinet [kabinɛ] nm (petite pièce) closet; (de

médecin) surgery (BRIT), office (US); (de
notaire etc) office; (: clientèle) practice; (POL)
Cabinet; **~s** nmpl (w.-c.) toilet sg; **~ d'affaires**
business consultancy; **~ de toilette** toilet

câble [kabl] nm cable

cabosser [kabɔse] vt to dent

cabrer [kabʀe]: **se ~** vi (cheval) to rear up

cabriole [kabʀijɔl] nf: **faire des ~s** to caper
about

cacahuète [kakaɥɛt] nf peanut

cacao [kakao] nm cocoa

cache [kaʃ] nm mask, card (for masking)

cache-cache [kaʃkaʃ] nm: **jouer à ~~** to play
hide-and-seek

cachemire [kaʃmiʀ] nm cashmere

cache-nez [kaʃne] nm inv scarf, muffler

cacher [kaʃe] vt to hide, conceal; **se ~** vi
(volontairement) to hide; (être caché) to be
hidden ou concealed; **~ qch à qn** to hide ou
conceal sth from sb

cachet [kaʃe] nm (comprimé) tablet; (de la
poste) postmark; (rétribution) fee; (fig) style,
character; **cacheter** vt to seal

cachette [kaʃɛt] nf hiding place; **en ~** on the
sly, secretly

cachot [kaʃo] nm dungeon

cachotterie [kaʃɔtʀi] nf: **faire des ~s** to be
secretive

cactus [kaktys] nm cactus

cadavre [kadavʀ] nm corpse, (dead) body

Caddie ®, **caddy** [kadi] nm (supermarket)
trolley

cadeau, x [kado] nm present, gift; **faire un
~ à qn** to give sb a present ou gift; **faire ~ de
qch à qn** to make a present of sth to sb, give
sb sth as a present

cadenas [kadna] nm padlock

cadence [kadɑ̃s] nf (tempo) rhythm; (de
travail etc) rate; **en ~** rhythmically

cadet, te [kadɛ, ɛt] adj younger; (le plus
jeune) youngest ♦ nm/f youngest child ou
one

cadran [kadʀɑ̃] nm dial; **~ solaire** sundial

cadre [kadʀ] nm frame; (environnement)
surroundings pl ♦ nm/f (ADMIN) managerial
employee, executive; **dans le ~ de** (fig) within
the framework ou context of

cadrer [kadʀe] vi: **~ avec** to tally ou
correspond with ♦ vt to centre

cafard [kafaʀ] nm cockroach; **avoir le ~** (fam)
to be down in the dumps

café [kafe] nm coffee; (bistro) café ♦ adj inv
coffee(-coloured); **~ au lait** white coffee;
~ noir black coffee; **~ tabac** tobacconist's or
newsagent's serving coffee and spirits;
cafetière nf (pot) coffee-pot

cafouiller [kafuje] (fam) vi to get into a
shambles

cage [kaʒ] nf cage; **~ d'escalier** (stair)well;

~ **thoracique** rib cage
cageot [kaʒo] nm crate
cagibi [kaʒibi] (fam) nm (débarass) boxroom
cagnotte [kaɲɔt] nf kitty
cagoule [kagul] nf (passe-montagne) balaclava
cahier [kaje] nm notebook; ~ **de brouillons** roughbook, jotter; ~ **d'exercices** exercise book
cahot [kao] nm jolt, bump
caïd [kaid] nm big chief, boss
caille [kaj] nf quail
cailler [kaje] vi (lait) to curdle; **ça caille** (fam) it's freezing; **caillot** (blood) clot
caillou, x [kaju] nm (little) stone; **caillouteux, -euse** adj (route) stony
Caire [kɛʀ] nm: **le** ~ Cairo
caisse [kɛs] nf box; (tiroir où l'on met la recette) till; (où l'on paye) cash desk (BRIT), check-out; (de banque) cashier's desk; ~ **d'épargne** savings bank; ~ **de retraite** pension fund; ~ **enregistreuse** cash register; **caissier, -ière** nm/f cashier
cajoler [kaʒɔle] vt (câliner) to cuddle; (amadouer) to wheedle, coax
cake [kɛk] nm fruit cake
calandre [kalɑ̃dʀ] nf radiator grill
calanque [kalɑ̃k] nf rocky inlet
calcaire [kalkɛʀ] nm limestone ♦ adj (eau) hard; (GÉO) limestone cpd
calciné, e [kalsine] adj burnt to ashes
calcul [kalkyl] nm calculation; **le** ~ (SCOL) arithmetic; ~ **(biliaire)** (gall)stone; **calculatrice** nf calculator; **calculer** vt to calculate, work out; **calculette** nf pocket calculator
cale [kal] nf (de bateau) hold; (en bois) wedge; ~ **sèche** dry dock
calé, e [kale] (fam) adj clever, bright
caleçon [kalsɔ̃] nm (d'homme) boxer shorts; (de femme) leggings
calembour [kalɑ̃buʀ] nm pun
calendrier [kalɑ̃dʀije] nm calendar; (fig) timetable
calepin [kalpɛ̃] nm notebook
caler [kale] vt to wedge ♦ vi (moteur, véhicule) to stall
calfeutrer [kalføtʀe] vt to (make) draughtproof; **se** ~ vi to make o.s. snug and comfortable
calibre [kalibʀ] nm calibre
califourchon [kalifuʀʃɔ̃]: **à** ~ adv astride
câlin, e [kalɛ̃, in] adj cuddly, cuddlesome; (regard, voix) tender; **câliner** vt to cuddle
calmant [kalmɑ̃] nm tranquillizer, sedative; (pour la douleur) painkiller
calme [kalm] adj calm, quiet ♦ nm calm(ness), quietness; **calmer** vt to calm (down); (douleur, inquiétude) to ease, soothe; **se calmer** vi to calm down

calomnie [kalɔmni] nf slander; (écrite) libel; **calomnier** vt to slander; to libel
calorie [kalɔʀi] nf calorie
calotte [kalɔt] nf (coiffure) skullcap; (fam: gifle) slap; ~ **glaciaire** (GÉO) icecap
calquer [kalke] vt to trace; (fig) to copy exactly
calvaire [kalvɛʀ] nm (croix) wayside cross, calvary; (souffrances) suffering
calvitie [kalvisi] nf baldness
camarade [kamaʀad] nm/f friend, pal; (POL) comrade; **camaraderie** nf friendship
cambouis [kɑ̃bwi] nm dirty oil ou grease
cambrer [kɑ̃bʀe]: **se** ~ vi to arch one's back
cambriolage [kɑ̃bʀijɔlaʒ] nm burglary; **cambrioler** vt to burgle (BRIT), burglarize (US); **cambrioleur, -euse** nm/f burglar
camelote [kamlɔt] (fam) nf rubbish, trash, junk
caméra [kameʀa] nf (CINÉMA, TV) camera; (d'amateur) cine-camera
caméscope ® [kameskɔp] nm camcorder ®
camion [kamjɔ̃] nm lorry (BRIT), truck; ~ **de dépannage** breakdown (BRIT) ou tow (US) truck; **camion-citerne** nm tanker; **camionnette** nf (small) van; **camionneur** nm (chauffeur) lorry (BRIT) ou truck driver; (entrepreneur) haulage contractor (BRIT), trucker (US)
camisole [kamizɔl] nf: ~ **(de force)** straitjacket
camomille [kamɔmij] nf camomile; (boisson) camomile tea
camoufler [kamufle] vt to camouflage; (fig) to conceal, cover up
camp [kɑ̃] nm camp; (fig) side; ~ **de vacances** children's holiday camp (BRIT), summer camp (US)
campagnard, e [kɑ̃paɲaʀ, aʀd] adj country cpd
campagne [kɑ̃paɲ] nf country, countryside; (MIL, POL, COMM) campaign; **à la** ~ in the country
camper [kɑ̃pe] vi to camp ♦ vt to sketch; **se** ~ **devant** to plant o.s. in front of; **campeur, -euse** nm/f camper
camping [kɑ̃piŋ] nm camping; (terrain de) ~ campsite, camping site; **faire du** ~ to go camping; **camping-car** nm caravanette, motorhome (US); **camping-gaz** ® nm inv camp(ing) stove
Canada [kanada] nm: **le** ~ Canada; **canadien, ne** adj Canadian ♦ nm/f: **Canadien, ne** Canadian; **canadienne** nf (veste) fur-lined jacket
canaille [kanaj] (péj) nf scoundrel
canal, -aux [kanal, o] nm canal; (naturel) channel; **canalisation** nf (tuyau) pipe;

canaliser [kanalize] *vt* to canalize; (*fig*) to channel

canapé [kanape] *nm* settee, sofa

canard [kanaʀ] *nm* duck; (*fam: journal*) rag

canari [kanaʀi] *nm* canary

cancans [kãkã] *nmpl* (malicious) gossip *sg*

cancer [kãsɛʀ] *nm* cancer; (*signe*): **le C~** Cancer; **~ de la peau** skin cancer

cancre [kãkʀ] *nm* dunce

candeur [kãdœʀ] *nf* ingenuousness, guilelessness

candidat, e [kãdida, at] *nm/f* candidate; (*à un poste*) applicant, candidate; **candidature** *nf* (*POL*) candidature; (*à poste*) application; **poser sa candidature à un poste** to apply for a job

candide [kãdid] *adj* ingenuous, guileless

cane [kan] *nf* (female) duck

caneton [kantɔ̃] *nm* duckling

canette [kanɛt] *nf* (*de bière*) (flip-top) bottle

canevas [kanva] *nm* (*COUTURE*) canvas

caniche [kaniʃ] *nm* poodle

canicule [kanikyl] *nf* scorching heat

canif [kanif] *nm* penknife, pocket knife

canine [kanin] *nf* canine (tooth)

caniveau, x [kanivo] *nm* gutter

canne [kan] *nf* (walking) stick; **~ à pêche** fishing rod; **~ à sucre** sugar cane

cannelle [kanɛl] *nf* cinnamon

canoë [kanɔe] *nm* canoe; (*sport*) canoeing

canon [kanɔ̃] *nm* (*arme*) gun; (*HISTOIRE*) cannon; (*d'une arme: tube*) barrel; (*fig: norme*) model; (*MUS*) canon

canot [kano] *nm* ding(h)y; **~ de sauvetage** lifeboat; **~ pneumatique** inflatable ding(h)y; **canotier** *nm* boater

cantatrice [kãtatʀis] *nf* (opera) singer

cantine [kãtin] *nf* canteen

cantique [kãtik] *nm* hymn

canton [kãtɔ̃] *nm* district consisting of several communes; (*en Suisse*) canton

cantonade [kãtɔnad]: **à la ~** *adv* to everyone in general

cantonner [kãtɔne]: **se ~ à** *vt* to confine o.s. to

cantonnier [kãtɔnje] *nm* roadmender

canular [kanylaʀ] *nm* hoax

caoutchouc [kautʃu] *nm* rubber

cap [kap] *nm* (*GÉO*) cape; (*promontoire*) headland; (*fig: tournant*) watershed; (*NAVIG*): **changer de ~** to change course; **mettre le ~ sur** to head *ou* steer for

CAP *sigle m* (= *Certificat d'aptitude professionnelle*) vocational training certificate taken at secondary school

capable [kapabl] *adj* able, capable; **~ de qch/faire** capable of sth/doing

capacité [kapasite] *nf* (*compétence*) ability; (*JUR, contenance*) capacity

cape [kap] *nf* cape, cloak; **rire sous ~** to laugh up one's sleeve

CAPES [kapɛs] *sigle m* (= *Certificat d'aptitude pédagogique à l'enseignement secondaire*) teaching diploma

capillaire [kapilɛʀ] *adj* (*soins, lotion*) hair *cpd*; (*vaisseau etc*) capillary

capitaine [kapitɛn] *nm* captain

capital, e, -aux [kapital, o] *adj* (*œuvre*) major; (*question, rôle*) fundamental ♦ *nm* capital; (*fig*) stock; **d'une importance ~e** of capital importance; *voir aussi* **capitaux**; **~ (social)** authorized capital; **capitale** *nf* (*ville*) capital; (*lettre*) capital (letter); **capitalisme** *nm* capitalism; **capitaliste** *adj, nm/f* capitalist; **capitaux** *nmpl* (*fonds*) capital *sg*

capitonné, e [kapitɔne] *adj* padded

caporal, -aux [kapɔral, o] *nm* lance corporal

capot [kapo] *nm* (*AUTO*) bonnet (*BRIT*), hood (*US*)

capote [kapɔt] *nf* (*de voiture*) hood (*BRIT*), top (*US*); (*fam*) condom

capoter [kapɔte] *vi* (*négociations*) to founder

câpre [kɑpʀ] *nf* caper

caprice [kapʀis] *nm* whim, caprice; **faire des ~s** to make a fuss; **capricieux, -euse** *adj* (*fantasque*) capricious, whimsical; (*enfant*) awkward

Capricorne [kapʀikɔʀn] *nm*: **le ~** Capricorn

capsule [kapsyl] *nf* (*de bouteille*) cap; (*BOT etc, spatiale*) capsule

capter [kapte] *vt* (*ondes radio*) to pick up; (*fig*) to win, capture

captivant, e [kaptivã, ãt] *adj* captivating

captivité [kaptivite] *nf* captivity

capturer [kaptyʀe] *vt* to capture

capuche [kapyʃ] *nf* hood

capuchon [kapyʃɔ̃] *nm* hood; (*de stylo*) cap, top

capucine [kapysin] *nf* (*BOT*) nasturtium

caquet [kakɛ] *nm*: **rabattre le ~ à qn** (*fam*) to bring sb down a peg or two

caqueter [kakte] *vi* to cackle

car [kaʀ] *nm* coach ♦ *conj* because, for

carabine [kaʀabin] *nf* rifle

caractère [kaʀaktɛʀ] *nm* (*gén*) character; **avoir bon/mauvais ~** to be good-/ill-natured; **en ~s gras** in bold type; **en petits ~s** in small print; **~s d'imprimerie** (block) capitals; **caractériel, le** *adj* (*traits*) (of) character; (*enfant*) emotionally disturbed

caractérisé, e [kaʀakteʀize] *adj* sheer, downright

caractériser [kaʀakteʀize] *vt* to be characteristic of

caractéristique [kaʀakteʀistik] *adj, nf* characteristic

carafe [kaʀaf] *nf* (*pour eau, vin ordinaire*)

carafe

caraïbe [kaʀaib] *adj* Caribbean ♦ *n*: **les C~s** the Caribbean (Islands)

carambolage [kaʀɑ̃bɔlaʒ] *nm* multiple crash, pileup

caramel [kaʀamɛl] *nm* (*bonbon*) caramel, toffee; (*substance*) caramel

carapace [kaʀapas] *nf* shell

caravane [kaʀavan] *nf* caravan; **caravaning** *nm* caravanning

carbone [kaʀbɔn] *nm* carbon; (*double*) carbon (copy); **carbonique** *adj*: **gaz carbonique** carbon dioxide; **neige carbonique** dry ice; **carbonisé, e** *adj* charred

carburant [kaʀbyʀɑ̃] *nm* (motor) fuel

carburateur [kaʀbyʀatœʀ] *nm* carburettor

carcan [kaʀkɑ̃] *nm* (*fig*) yoke, shackles *pl*

carcasse [kaʀkas] *nf* carcass; (*de véhicule etc*) shell

cardiaque [kaʀdjak] *adj* cardiac, heart *cpd* ♦ *nm/f* heart patient; **être ~** to have heart trouble

cardigan [kaʀdigɑ̃] *nm* cardigan

cardiologue [kaʀdjɔlɔg] *nm/f* cardiologist, heart specialist

carême [kaʀɛm] *nm*: **le C~** Lent

carence [kaʀɑ̃s] *nf* (*manque*) deficiency

caresse [kaʀɛs] *nf* caress

caresser [kaʀese] *vt* to caress; (*animal*) to stroke

cargaison [kaʀgɛzɔ̃] *nf* cargo, freight

cargo [kaʀgo] *nm* cargo boat, freighter

caricature [kaʀikatyʀ] *nf* caricature

carie [kaʀi] *nf*: **la ~ (dentaire)** tooth decay; **une ~** a bad tooth

carillon [kaʀijɔ̃] *nm* (*air, de pendule*) chimes *pl*

caritatif, -ive [kaʀitatif, iv] *adj*: **organisation caritative** charity

carnassier, -ière [kaʀnasje, jɛʀ] *adj* carnivorous

carnaval [kaʀnaval] *nm* carnival

carnet [kaʀnɛ] *nm* (*calepin*) notebook; (*de tickets, timbres etc*) book; **~ de chèques** cheque book; **~ de notes** school report

carotte [kaʀɔt] *nf* carrot

carpette [kaʀpɛt] *nf* rug

carré, e [kaʀe] *adj* square; (*fig: franc*) straightforward ♦ *nm* (*MATH*) square; **mètre/kilomètre ~** square metre/kilometre

carreau, x [kaʀo] *nm* (*par terre*) (floor) tile; (*au mur*) (wall) tile; (*de fenêtre*) (window) pane; (*motif*) check, square; (*CARTES: couleur*) diamonds *pl*; **tissu à ~x** checked fabric

carrefour [kaʀfuʀ] *nm* crossroads *sg*

carrelage [kaʀlaʒ] *nm* (*sol*) (tiled) floor

carrelet [kaʀlɛ] *nm* (*poisson*) plaice

carrément [kaʀemɑ̃] *adv* (*franchement*) straight out, bluntly; (*sans hésiter*) straight;

(*intensif*) completely; **c'est ~ impossible** it's completely impossible

carrière [kaʀjɛʀ] *nf* (*métier*) career; (*de roches*) quarry; **militaire de ~** professional soldier

carrossable [kaʀɔsabl] *adj* suitable for (motor) vehicles

carrosse [kaʀɔs] *nm* (horse-drawn) coach

carrosserie [kaʀɔsʀi] *nf* body, coachwork *no pl*

carrure [kaʀyʀ] *nf* build; (*fig*) stature, calibre

cartable [kaʀtabl] *nm* satchel, (school)bag

carte [kaʀt] *nf* (*de géographie*) map; (*marine, du ciel*) chart; (*d'abonnement, à jouer*) card; (*au restaurant*) menu; (*aussi:* **~ de visite**) (visiting) card; **à la ~** (*au restaurant*) à la carte; **donner ~ blanche à qn** to give sb a free rein; **~ bancaire** cash card; **~ de crédit** credit card; **~ d'identité** identity card; **~ de séjour** residence permit; **~ grise** (*AUTO*) ≈ (car) registration book, logbook; **~ postale** postcard; **~ routière** road map; **~ téléphonique** phonecard

carter [kaʀtɛʀ] *nm* sump

carton [kaʀtɔ̃] *nm* (*matériau*) cardboard; (*boîte*) (cardboard) box; **faire un ~** (*fam*) to score a hit; **~ (à dessin)** portfolio; **carton-pâte** *nm* pasteboard

cartouche [kaʀtuʃ] *nf* cartridge; (*de cigarettes*) carton

cas [kɑ] *nm* case; **ne faire aucun ~ de** to take no notice of; **en aucun ~** on no account; **au ~ où** in case; **en ~ de** in case of, in the event of; **en ~ de besoin** if need be; **en tout ~** in any case, at any rate; **~ de conscience** matter of conscience

casanier, -ière [kazanje, jɛʀ] *adj* stay-at-home

cascade [kaskad] *nf* waterfall, cascade; (*fig*) stream, torrent; **cascadeur, -euse** *nm/f* stuntman(-girl)

case [kɑz] *nf* (*hutte*) hut; (*compartiment*) compartment; (*sur un formulaire, de mots croisés etc*) box

caser [kɑze] (*fam*) *vt* (*placer*) to put (away); (*loger*) to put up; **se ~** *vi* (*se marier*) to settle down; (*trouver un emploi*) to find a (steady) job

caserne [kazɛʀn] *nf* barracks *pl*

cash [kaʃ] *adv*: **payer ~** to pay cash down

casier [kɑzje] *nm* (*pour courrier*) pigeonhole; (*compartiment*) compartment; (*à clef*) locker; **~ judiciaire** police record

casino [kazino] *nm* casino

casque [kask] *nm* helmet; (*chez le coiffeur*) (hair-)drier; (*pour audition*) (head-)phones *pl*, headset

casquette [kaskɛt] *nf* cap

cassant, e [kɑsɑ̃, ɑ̃t] *adj* brittle; (*fig: ton*)

curt, abrupt

cassation [kasasjɔ̃] nf: **cour de ~** final court of appeal

casse [kɑs] (fam) nf (pour voitures): **mettre à la ~** to scrap; (dégâts): **il y a eu de la ~** there were a lot of breakages; **casse-cou** adj inv daredevil, reckless; **casse-croûte** nm inv snack; **casse-noix** nm inv nutcrackers pl; **casse-pieds** (fam) adj inv: **il est casse-pieds** he's a pain in the neck

casser [kase] vt to break; (JUR) to quash; **se ~** vi to break; **~ les pieds à qn** (fam: irriter) to get on sb's nerves; **se ~ la tête** (fam) to go to a lot of trouble

casserole [kasɔl] nf saucepan

casse tête [kastɛt] nm inv (difficultés) headache (fig)

cassette [kaset] nf (bande magnétique) cassette; (coffret) casket

casseur [kasœr] nm hooligan

cassis [kasis] nm blackcurrant

cassoulet [kasulɛ] nm bean and sausage hot-pot

cassure [kasyr] nf break, crack

castor [kastɔr] nm beaver

castrer [kastre] vt (mâle) to castrate; (: cheval) to geld; (femelle) to spay

catalogue [katalɔg] nm catalogue

cataloguer [kataloge] vt to catalogue, to list; (péj) to put a label on

catalyseur [katalizœr] nm catalyst; **catalytique** adj: **pot catalytique** catalytic convertor

catastrophe [katastrɔf] nf catastrophe, disaster; **catastrophé, e** (fam) adj stunned

catch [katʃ] nm (all-in) wrestling

catéchisme [kateʃism] nm catechism

catégorie [kategɔri] nf category; **catégorique** adj categorical

cathédrale [katedral] nf cathedral

catholique [katɔlik] adj, nm/f (Roman) Catholic; **pas très ~** a bit shady ou fishy

catimini [katimini]: **en ~** adv on the sly

cauchemar [koʃmar] nm nightmare

cause [koz] nf cause; (JUR) lawsuit, case; **à ~ de** because of, owing to; **pour ~ de** on account of; **(et) pour ~** and for (a very) good reason; **être en ~** (intérêts) to be at stake; **remettre en ~** to challenge; **causer** vt to cause ♦ vi to chat, talk; **causerie** nf (conférence) talk; **causette** nf: **faire la causette** to have a chat

caution [kosjɔ̃] nf guarantee, security; (JUR) bail (bond); (fig) backing, support; **libéré sous ~** released on bail; **cautionner** vt (répondre de) to guarantee; (soutenir) to support

cavalcade [kavalkad] nf (fig) stampede

cavalier, -ière [kavalje, jɛr] adj (désinvolte) offhand ♦ nm/f rider; (au bal) partner ♦ nm (ÉCHECS) knight

cave [kav] nf cellar

caveau, x [kavo] nm vault

caverne [kavɛrn] nf cave

CCP sigle m = **compte chèques postaux**

CD sigle m (= compact disc) CD

CD-ROM [sederɔm] sigle m CD-ROM

CE n abr (= Communauté Européenne) EC

---

ce, cette [sə, sɛt] (devant nm **cet** + voyelle ou h aspiré; pl **ces**) dét (proximité) this; these pl; (non-proximité) that; those pl; **cette maison(-ci/-là)** this/that house; **cette nuit** (qui vient) tonight; (passée) last night

♦ pron **1**: **c'est** it's ou it is; **c'est un peintre** he's ou he is a painter; **ce sont des peintres** they're ou they are painters; **c'est le facteur** (à la porte) it's the postman; **qui est-ce?** who is it?; (en désignant) who is he/she?; **qu'est-ce?** what is it?

2: **ce qui**, **ce que** what; (chose qui): **il est bête, ce qui me chagrine** he's stupid, which saddens me; **tout ce qui bouge** everything that ou which moves; **tout ce que je sais** all I know; **ce dont j'ai parlé** the thing I talked about; **ce que c'est grand!** it's so big!; voir aussi **-ci**; **est-ce que**; **n'est-ce pas**; **c'est-à-dire**

---

ceci [səsi] pron this

cécité [sesite] nf blindness

céder [sede] vt (donner) to give up ♦ vi (chaise, barrage) to give way; (personne) to give in; **~ à** to yield to, give in to

CEDEX [sedɛks] sigle m (= courrier d'entreprise à distribution exceptionnelle) postal service for bulk users

cédille [sedij] nf cedilla

cèdre [sɛdr] nm cedar

CEI abr m (= Communauté des États Indépendants) CIS

ceinture [sɛ̃tyr] nf belt; (taille) waist; **~ de sécurité** safety ou seat belt

cela [s(ə)la] pron that; (comme sujet indéfini) it; **quand/où ~?** when/where (was that)?

célèbre [selɛbr] adj famous; **célébrer** vt to celebrate

céleri [selri] nm: **~(-rave)** celeriac; **~ (en branche)** celery

célibat [seliba] nm (homme) bachelorhood; (femme) spinsterhood; (prêtre) celibacy; **célibataire** adj single, unmarried ♦ nm bachelor ♦ nf unmarried woman

celle(s) [sɛl] pron voir **celui**

cellier [selje] nm storeroom (for wine)

cellule [selyl] nf (gén) cell

cellulite [selylit] nf excess fat, cellulite

MOT-CLÉ

celui, celle [səlɥi, sɛl] (*mpl* **ceux**, *fpl* **celles**)
pron **1**: **celui-ci/là**, **celle-ci/là** this one/that
one; **ceux-ci**, **celles-ci** these (ones); **ceux-là**,
celles-là those (ones); **celui de mon frère** my
brother's; **celui du salon/du dessous** the one
in (*ou* from) the lounge/below
2: **celui qui bouge** the one which *ou* that
moves; (*personne*) the one who moves; **celui
que je vois** the one (which *ou* that) I see; the
one (whom) I see; **celui dont je parle** the one
I'm talking about
3 (*valeur indéfinie*): **celui qui veut** whoever
wants

cendre [sɑ̃dʀ] *nf* ash; **~s** *nfpl* (*d'un défunt*)
ashes; **sous la ~** (*CULIN*) in (the) embers;
cendrier *nm* ashtray
cène [sɛn] *nf*: **la ~** (Holy) Communion
censé, e [sɑ̃se] *adj*: **être ~ faire** to be
supposed to do
censeur [sɑ̃sœʀ] *nm* (*SCOL*) deputy-head
(*BRIT*), vice-principal (*US*); (*CINÉMA, POL*)
censor
censure [sɑ̃syʀ] *nf* censorship; **censurer** *vt*
(*CINÉMA, PRESSE*) to censor; (*POL*) to censure
cent [sɑ̃] *num* a hundred, one hundred;
centaine *nf*: **une centaine (de)** about a
hundred, a hundred or so; **des centaines (de)**
hundreds (of); **centenaire** *adj* hundred-
year-old ♦ *nm* (*anniversaire*) centenary
centième *num* hundredth; **centigrade** *nm*
centigrade; **centilitre** *nm* centilitre;
centime *nm* centime; **centimètre** *nm*
centimetre; (*ruban*) tape measure, measuring
tape
central, e, -aux [sɑ̃tʀal, o] *adj* central
♦ *nm*: **~ (téléphonique)** (telephone)
exchange; **centrale** *nf* power station
centre [sɑ̃tʀ] *nm* centre; **~ commercial**
shopping centre; **centre-ville** *nm* town
centre, downtown (area) (*US*)
centuple [sɑ̃typl] *nm*: **le ~ de qch** a hundred
times sth; **au ~** a hundredfold
cep [sɛp] *nm* (vine) stock
cèpe [sɛp] *nm* (edible) boletus
cependant [s(ə)pɑ̃dɑ̃] *adv* however
céramique [seʀamik] *nf* ceramics *sg*
cercle [sɛʀkl] *nm* circle; **~ vicieux** vicious circle
cercueil [sɛʀkœj] *nm* coffin
céréale [seʀeal] *nf* cereal; **~s** *nfpl* breakfast
cereal
cérémonie [seʀemɔni] *nf* ceremony; **sans ~**
informally
cerf [sɛʀ] *nm* stag
cerfeuil [sɛʀfœj] *nm* chervil
cerf-volant [sɛʀvɔlɑ̃] *nm* kite
cerise [s(ə)ʀiz] *nf* cherry; **cerisier** *nm* cherry
(tree)
cerne [sɛʀn] *nm*: **avoir des ~s** to have
shadows *ou* dark rings under one's eyes
cerner [sɛʀne] *vt* (*MIL etc*) to surround; (*fig*:
problème) to delimit, define
certain, e [sɛʀtɛ̃, ɛn] *adj* certain ♦ *dét*
certain; **d'un ~ âge** past one's prime, not so
young; **un ~ temps** (quite) some time; **~s**
♦ *pron* some; **certainement** *adv*
(*probablement*) most probably *ou* likely; (*bien
sûr*) certainly, of course
certes [sɛʀt] *adv* (*sans doute*) admittedly;
(*bien sûr*) of course
certificat [sɛʀtifika] *nm* certificate
certifier [sɛʀtifje] *vt*: **~ qch à qn** to assure sb
of sth; **copie certifiée conforme (à l'original)**
certified copy of the original
certitude [sɛʀtityd] *nf* certainty
cerveau, x [sɛʀvo] *nm* brain
cervelas [sɛʀvəla] *nm* saveloy
cervelle [sɛʀvɛl] *nf* (*ANAT*) brain; (*CULIN*)
brains
ces [se] *dét voir* **ce**
CES *sigle m* (= *Collège d'enseignement
secondaire*) ≈ (junior) secondary school (*BRIT*)
cesse [sɛs]: **sans ~** *adv* (*tout le temps*)
continually, constantly; (*sans interruption*)
continuously; **il n'a eu de ~ que** he did not
rest until; **cesser** *vt* to stop ♦ *vi* to stop,
cease; **cesser de faire** to stop doing; **cessez-
le-feu** *nm inv* ceasefire
c'est-à-dire [sɛtadiʀ] *adv* that is (to say)
cet, cette [sɛt] *dét voir* **ce**
ceux [sø] *pron voir* **celui**
CFC *abr* (= *chlorofluorocarbon*) CFC
CFDT *sigle f* (= *Confédération française
démocratique du travail*) French trade union
CGT *sigle f* (= *Confédération générale du
travail*) French trade union
chacun, e [ʃakœ̃, yn] *pron* each; (*indéfini*)
everyone, everybody
chagrin [ʃagʀɛ̃] *nm* grief, sorrow; **avoir du ~**
to be grieved; **chagriner** *vt* to grieve
chahut [ʃay] *nm* uproar; **chahuter** *vt* to rag,
bait ♦ *vi* to make an uproar
chaîne [ʃɛn] *nf* chain; (*RADIO, TV*: *stations*)
channel; **~s** *nfpl* (*AUTO*) (snow) chains; **travail
à la ~** production line work; **~ (de montage)**
production *ou* assembly line; **~ de montagnes**
mountain range; **~ (hi-fi)** hi-fi system; **~ laser**
CD player; **~ (stéréo)** stereo (system);
chaînette *nf* (small) chain
chair [ʃɛʀ] *nf* flesh; **avoir la ~ de poule** to have
goosepimples *ou* gooseflesh; **bien en ~**
plump, well-padded; **en ~ et en os** in the
flesh; **~ à saucisse** sausage meat
chaire [ʃɛʀ] *nf* (*d'église*) pulpit; (*d'université*)
chair
chaise [ʃɛz] *nf* chair; **~ longue** deckchair

châle [ʃal] nm shawl

chaleur [ʃalœr] nf heat; (fig: accueil) warmth; **chaleureux, -euse** adj warm

chaloupe [ʃalup] nf launch; (de sauvetage) lifeboat

chalumeau, x [ʃalymo] nm blowlamp, blowtorch

chalutier [ʃalytje] nm trawler

chamailler [ʃamaje]: **se ~** vi to squabble, bicker

chambouler [ʃābule] (fam) vt to disrupt, turn upside down

chambre [ʃābr] nf bedroom; (POL, COMM) chamber; **faire ~ à part** to sleep in separate rooms; **~ à air** (de pneu) (inner) tube; **~ à coucher** bedroom; **~ à un lit/deux lits** (à l'hôtel) single-/twin-bedded room; **~ d'amis** spare ou guest room; **~ noire** (PHOTO) dark room; **chambrer** vt (vin) to bring to room temperature

chameau, x [ʃamo] nm camel

chamois [ʃamwa] nm chamois

champ [ʃā] nm field; **~ de bataille** battlefield; **~ de courses** racecourse; **~ de tir** rifle range

champagne [ʃāpaɲ] nm champagne

champêtre [ʃāpɛtr] adj country cpd, rural

champignon [ʃāpiɲɔ̃] nm mushroom; (terme générique) fungus; **~ de Paris** button mushroom

champion, ne [ʃāpjɔ̃, jɔn] adj, nm/f champion; **championnat** nm championship

chance [ʃās] nf: **la ~** luck; **~s** nfpl (probabilités) chances; **avoir de la ~** to be lucky; **il a des ~s de réussir** he's got a good chance of passing

chanceler [ʃās(ə)le] vi to totter

chancelier [ʃāsəlje] nm (allemand) chancellor

chanceux, -euse [ʃāsø, øz] adj lucky

chandail [ʃādaj] nm (thick) sweater

Chandeleur [ʃādlœr] nf: **la ~** Candlemas

chandelier [ʃādəlje] nm candlestick

chandelle [ʃādɛl] nf (tallow) candle; **dîner aux ~s** candlelight dinner

change [ʃāʒ] nm (devises) exchange

changement [ʃāʒmā] nm change; **~ de vitesses** gears pl

changer [ʃāʒe] vt (modifier) to change, alter; (remplacer, COMM) to change ♦ vi to change, alter; **se ~** vi to change (o.s.); **~ de** (remplacer: adresse, nom, voiture etc) to change one's; (échanger: place, train etc) to change; **~ d'avis** to change one's mind; **~ de vitesse** to change gear

chanson [ʃāsɔ̃] nf song

chant [ʃā] nm song; (art vocal) singing; (d'église) hymn

chantage [ʃātaʒ] nm blackmail; **faire du ~** to use blackmail

chanter [ʃāte] vt, vi to sing; **si cela lui chante** (fam) if he feels like it; **chanteur, -euse** nm/f singer

chantier [ʃātje] nm (building) site; (sur une route) roadworks pl; **mettre en ~** to put in hand; **~ naval** shipyard

chantilly [ʃātiji] nf voir **crème**

chantonner [ʃātɔne] vi, vt to sing to oneself, hum

chanvre [ʃāvr] nm hemp

chaparder [ʃaparde] (fam) vt to pinch

chapeau, x [ʃapo] nm hat; **~! well done!**

chapelet [ʃaplɛ] nm (REL) rosary

chapelle [ʃapɛl] nf chapel

chapelure [ʃaplyr] nf (dried) breadcrumbs pl

chapiteau, x [ʃapito] nm (de cirque) marquee, big top

chapitre [ʃapitr] nm chapter

chaque [ʃak] dét each, every; (indéfini) every

char [ʃar] nm (MIL): **~ (d'assaut)** tank; **~ à voile** sand yacht

charabia [ʃarabja] (péj) nm gibberish

charade [ʃarad] nf riddle; (mimée) charade

charbon [ʃarbɔ̃] nm coal; **~ de bois** charcoal

charcuterie [ʃarkytri] nf (magasin) pork butcher's shop and delicatessen; (produits) cooked pork meats pl; **charcutier, -ière** nm/f pork butcher

chardon [ʃardɔ̃] nm thistle

charge [ʃarʒ] nf (fardeau) load, burden; (explosif, ÉLEC, MIL, JUR) charge; (rôle, mission) responsibility; **~s** nfpl (du loyer) service charges; **à la ~ de** (dépendant de) dependent upon; (aux frais de) chargeable to; **prendre en ~** to take charge of; (suj: véhicule) to take on; (dépenses) to take care of; **~s sociales** social security contributions

chargé, e [ʃarʒe] adj (emploi du temps, journée) full, heavy

chargement [ʃarʒəmā] nm (objets) load

charger [ʃarʒe] vt (voiture, fusil, caméra) to load; (batterie) to charge ♦ vi (MIL etc) to charge; **se ~ de** vt to see to; **~ qn de (faire) qch** to put sb in charge of (doing) sth

chariot [ʃarjo] nm trolley; (charrette) waggon

charité [ʃarite] nf charity

charmant, e [ʃarmā, āt] adj charming

charme [ʃarm] nm charm; **charmer** vt to charm

charnel, le [ʃarnɛl] adj carnal

charnière [ʃarnjɛr] nf hinge; (fig) turning-point

charnu, e [ʃarny] adj fleshy

charpente [ʃarpāt] nf frame(work); **charpentier** nm carpenter

charpie [ʃarpi] nf: **en ~** (fig) in shreds ou ribbons

charrette [ʃarɛt] nf cart

charrier [ʃarje] vt (entraîner: fleuve) to carry

(along); (*transporter*) to cart, carry

charrue [ʃaʀy] *nf* plough (*BRIT*), plow (*US*)

charter [ʃaʀtɛʀ] *nm* (*vol*) charter flight

chasse [ʃas] *nf* hunting; (*au fusil*) shooting; (*poursuite*) chase; (*aussi:* ~ **d'eau**) flush; ~ **gardée** private hunting grounds *pl*; **prendre en ~ to** give chase to; **tirer la ~ (d'eau)** to flush the toilet, pull the chain; ~ **à courre** hunting; **chasse-neige** *nm inv* snowplough (*BRIT*), snowplow (*US*); **chasser** *vt* to hunt; (*expulser*) to chase away *ou* out, drive away *ou* out; **chasseur, -euse** *nm/f* hunter ♦ *nm* (*avion*) fighter

châssis [ʃasi] *nm* (*AUTO*) chassis; (*cadre*) frame

chat [ʃa] *nm* cat

châtaigne [ʃatɛɲ] *nf* chestnut; **châtaignier** *nm* chestnut (tree)

châtain [ʃatɛ̃] *adj inv* (*cheveux*) chestnut (brown); (*personne*) chestnut-haired

château, x [ʃato] *nm* (*forteresse*) castle; (*résidence royale*) palace; (*manoir*) mansion; ~ **d'eau** water tower; ~ **fort** stronghold, fortified castle

châtier [ʃatje] *vt* to punish; **châtiment** *nm* punishment

chaton [ʃatɔ̃] *nm* (*ZOOL*) kitten

chatouiller [ʃatuje] *vt* to tickle; **chatouilleux, -euse** *adj* ticklish; (*fig*) touchy, over-sensitive

chatoyer [ʃatwaje] *vi* to shimmer

châtrer [ʃatʀe] *vt* (*mâle*) to castrate; (: *cheval*) to geld; (*femelle*) to spay

chatte [ʃat] *nf* (she-)cat

chaud, e [ʃo, ʃod] *adj* (*gén*) warm; (*très ~*) hot; **il fait ~** it's warm; it's hot; **avoir ~** to be warm; to be hot; **ça me tient ~** it keeps me warm; **rester au ~** to stay in the warm

chaudière [ʃodjɛʀ] *nf* boiler

chaudron [ʃodʀɔ̃] *nm* cauldron

chauffage [ʃofaʒ] *nm* heating; ~ **central** central heating

chauffard [ʃofaʀ] *nm* (*péj*) reckless driver

chauffe-eau [ʃofo] *nm inv* water-heater

chauffer [ʃofe] *vt* to heat ♦ *vi* to heat up, warm up; (*trop:* *moteur*) to overheat; **se ~** *vi* (*au soleil*) to warm o.s

chauffeur [ʃofœʀ] *nm* driver; (*privé*) chauffeur

chaume [ʃom] *nm* (*du toit*) thatch; **chaumière** *nf* (thatched) cottage

chaussée [ʃose] *nf* road(way)

chausse-pied [ʃospje] *nm* shoe-horn

chausser [ʃose] *vt* (*bottes, skis*) to put on; (*enfant*) to put shoes on; ~ **du 38/42** to take size 38/42

chaussette [ʃosɛt] *nf* sock

chausson [ʃosɔ̃] *nm* slipper; (*de bébé*) bootee; ~ **(aux pommes)** (apple) turnover

chaussure [ʃosyʀ] *nf* shoe; ~**s à talon** high-heeled shoes; ~**s de marche** walking shoes/ boots; ~**s de ski** ski boots

chauve [ʃov] *adj* bald; **chauve-souris** *nf* bat

chauvin, e [ʃovɛ̃, in] *adj* chauvinistic

chaux [ʃo] *nf* lime; **blanchi à la** ~ whitewashed

chavirer [ʃaviʀe] *vi* to capsize

chef [ʃɛf] *nm* head, leader; (*de cuisine*) chef; ~ **d'accusation** charge; ~ **d'entreprise** company head; ~ **d'état** head of state; ~ **de famille** head of the family; ~ **de gare** station master; ~ **d'orchestre** conductor; ~ **de service** department head; **chef-d'œuvre** *nm* masterpiece; **chef-lieu** *nm* county town

chemin [ʃ(ə)mɛ̃] *nm* path; (*itinéraire, direction, trajet*) way; **en ~** on the way; ~ **de fer** railway (*BRIT*), railroad (*US*); **par ~ de fer** by rail

cheminée [ʃ(ə)mine] *nf* chimney; (*à l'intérieur*) chimney piece, fireplace; (*de bateau*) funnel

cheminement [ʃ(ə)minmã] *nm* progress

cheminot [ʃ(ə)mino] *nm* railwayman

chemise [ʃ(ə)miz] *nf* shirt; (*dossier*) folder; ~ **de nuit** nightdress

chemisier [ʃ(ə)mizje, jɛʀ] *nm* blouse

chenal, -aux [ʃənal, o] *nm* channel

chêne [ʃɛn] *nm* oak (tree); (*bois*) oak

chenil [ʃ(ə)nil] *nm* kennels *pl*

chenille [ʃ(ə)nij] *nf* (*ZOOL*) caterpillar

chèque [ʃɛk] *nm* cheque (*BRIT*), check (*US*); ~ **sans provision** bad cheque; ~ **de voyage** traveller's cheque; **chéquier** [ʃekje] *nm* cheque book

cher, -ère [ʃɛʀ] *adj* (*aimé*) dear; (*coûteux*) expensive, dear ♦ *adv:* **ça coûte ~** it's expensive

chercher [ʃɛʀʃe] *vt* to look for; (*gloire etc*) to seek; **aller ~** to go for, go and fetch; ~ **à faire** to try to do; **chercheur, -euse** *nm/f* researcher, research worker

chère [ʃɛʀ] *adj voir* **cher**

chéri, e [ʃeʀi] *adj* beloved, dear; (**mon**) ~ darling

chérir [ʃeʀiʀ] *vt* to cherish

cherté [ʃɛʀte] *nf:* **la ~ de la vie** the high cost of living

chétif, -ive [ʃetif, iv] *adj* (*enfant*) puny

cheval, -aux [ʃ(ə)val, o] *nm* horse; (*AUTO*): ~ **(vapeur)** horsepower *no pl*; **faire du ~** to ride; **à ~** on horseback; **à ~ sur** astride; (*fig*) overlapping; ~ **de course** racehorse

chevalet [ʃ(ə)valɛ] *nm* easel

chevalier [ʃ(ə)valje] *nm* knight

chevalière [ʃ(ə)valjɛʀ] *nf* signet ring

chevalin, e [ʃ(ə)valɛ̃, in] *adj:* **boucherie ~e** horse-meat butcher's

chevaucher [ʃ(ə)voʃe] *vi* (*aussi:* **se ~**) to overlap (each other) ♦ *vt* to be astride,

straddle
chevaux [ʃəvo] nmpl de **cheval**
chevelu, e [ʃəv(ə)ly] (péj) adj long-haired
chevelure [ʃəv(ə)lyʀ] nf hair no pl
chevet [ʃ(ə)vɛ] nm: **au ~ de qn** at sb's
  bedside; **lampe de ~** bedside lamp
cheveu, x [ʃ(ə)vø] nm hair; **~x** nmpl
  (chevelure) hair sg; **avoir les ~x courts** to have
  short hair
cheville [ʃ(ə)vij] nf (ANAT) ankle; (de bois)
  peg; (pour une vis) plug
chèvre [ʃɛvʀ] nf (she-)goat
chevreau, x [ʃəvʀo] nm kid
chèvrefeuille [ʃɛvʀəfœj] nm honeysuckle
chevreuil [ʃəvʀœj] nm roe deer inv, (CULIN)
  venison
chevronné, e [ʃəvʀɔne] adj seasoned

┌─────────────┐
│ **MOT-CLÉ** │
└─────────────┘

chez [ʃe] prép **1** (à la demeure de) at; (: direction) to; **chez qn** at/to sb's house ou place;
chez moi at home; (direction) home
2 (+profession) at; (: direction) to; **chez le
boulanger/dentiste** at ou to the baker's/
dentist's
3 (dans le caractère, l'œuvre de) in; **chez les
renards/Racine** in foxes/Racine

chez-soi [ʃeswa] nm inv home
chic [ʃik] adj inv chic, smart; (fam: généreux)
  nice, decent ♦ nm stylishness; **~ (alors)!** (fam)
  great!; **avoir le ~ de** to have the knack of
chicane [ʃikan] nf (querelle) squabble;
  chicaner vi (ergoter): **chicaner sur** to quibble
  about
chiche [ʃiʃ] adj niggardly, mean ♦ excl (à un
  défi) you're on!
chichis [ʃiʃi] (fam) nmpl fuss sg
chicorée [ʃikɔʀe] nf (café) chicory; (salade)
  endive
chien [ʃjɛ̃] nm dog; **~ de garde** guard dog;
  chien-loup nm wolfhound
chiendent [ʃjɛ̃dɑ̃] nm couch grass
chienne [ʃjɛn] nf dog, bitch
chier [ʃje] (fam!) vi to crap (!)
chiffon [ʃifɔ̃] nm (piece of) rag; **chiffonner**
  vt to crumple; (fam: tracasser) to concern
chiffre [ʃifʀ] nm (représentant un nombre)
  figure, numeral; (montant, total) total, sum;
  en ~s ronds in round figures; **~ d'affaires**
  turnover; **chiffrer** vt (dépense) to put a
  figure to, assess; (message) to (en)code,
  cipher; **se chiffrer à** to add up to, amount to
chignon [ʃiɲɔ̃] nm chignon, bun
Chili [ʃili] nm: **le ~** Chile; **chilien, ne** adj
  Chilean ♦ nm/f: **Chilien, ne** Chilean
chimie [ʃimi] nf chemistry; **chimique** adj
  chemical; **produits chimiques** chemicals
chimpanzé [ʃɛ̃pɑ̃ze] nm chimpanzee

Chine [ʃin] nf: **la ~** China; **chinois, e** adj
  Chinese ♦ nm/f: **Chinois, e** Chinese ♦ nm
  (LING) Chinese
chiot [ʃjo] nm pup(py)
chiper [ʃipe] (fam) vt to pinch
chipoter [ʃipɔte] (fam) vi (ergoter) to quibble
chips [ʃips] nfpl crisps (BRIT), (potato) chips
  (US)
chiquenaude [ʃiknod] nf flick, flip
chirurgical, e, -aux [ʃiʀyʀʒikal, o] adj
  surgical
chirurgie [ʃiʀyʀʒi] nf surgery; **~ esthétique**
  plastic surgery; **chirurgien, ne** nm/f surgeon
chlore [klɔʀ] nm chlorine
choc [ʃɔk] nm (heurt) impact, shock; (collision)
  crash; (moral) shock; (affrontement) clash
chocolat [ʃɔkɔla] nm chocolate; **~ au lait** milk
  chocolate; **~ (chaud)** hot chocolate
chœur [kœʀ] nm (chorale) choir; (OPÉRA,
  THÉÂTRE) chorus; **en ~** in chorus
choisir [ʃwaziʀ] vt to choose, select
choix [ʃwa] nm choice, selection; **avoir le ~** to
  have the choice; **premier ~** (COMM) class one;
  de ~ choice, selected; **au ~** as you wish
chômage [ʃomaʒ] nm unemployment;
  mettre au ~ to make redundant, put out of
  work; **être au ~** to be unemployed ou out of
  work; **chômeur, -euse** nm/f unemployed
  person
chope [ʃɔp] nf tankard
choper [ʃɔpe] (fam) vt (objet, maladie) to
  catch
choquer [ʃɔke] vt (offenser) to shock; (deuil)
  to shake
chorale [kɔʀal] nf choir
choriste [kɔʀist] nm/f choir member; (OPÉRA)
  chorus member
chose [ʃoz] nf thing; **c'est peu de ~** it's
  nothing (really)
chou, x [ʃu] nm cabbage; **mon petit ~** (my)
  sweetheart; **~ à la crème** choux bun; **~x de
  Bruxelles** Brussels sprouts; **chouchou, te**
  (fam) nm/f darling; (SCOL) teacher's pet;
  choucroute nf sauerkraut
chouette [ʃwɛt] nf owl ♦ adj (fam) great,
  smashing
chou-fleur [ʃuflœʀ] nm cauliflower
choyer [ʃwaje] vt (dorloter) to cherish;
  (: excessivement) to pamper
chrétien, ne [kʀetjɛ̃, jɛn] adj, nm/f Christian
Christ [kʀist] nm: **le ~** Christ; **christianisme**
  nm Christianity
chrome [kʀom] nm chromium; **chromé, e**
  adj chromium-plated
chronique [kʀɔnik] adj chronic ♦ nf (de
  journal) column, page; (historique) chronicle;
  (RADIO, TV): **la ~ sportive** the sports review
chronologique [kʀɔnɔlɔʒik] adj
  chronological

chronomètre [krɔnɔmɛtr] nm stopwatch;
   chronométrer vt to time
chrysanthème [krizɑ̃tem] nm
   chrysanthemum
chuchotement [ʃyʃɔtmɑ̃] nm whisper
chuchoter [ʃyʃɔte] vt, vi to whisper
chut [ʃyt] excl sh!
chute [ʃyt] nf fall; (déchet) scrap; **faire une
   ~ (de 10 m)** to fall (10 m); **~ (d'eau)**
   waterfall; **la ~ des cheveux** hair loss; **~ libre**
   free fall; **~s de pluie/neige** rain/snowfalls
Chypre [ʃipr] nm/f Cyprus
-ci [si] adv voir **par ♦** dét: **ce garçon-~/-là** this/
   that boy; **ces femmes-~/-là** these/those
   women
cible [sibl] nf target
ciboulette [sibulet] nf (small) chive
cicatrice [sikatris] nf scar; **cicatriser** vt to
   heal
ci-contre [sikɔ̃tr] adv opposite
ci-dessous [sidəsu] adv below
ci-dessus [sidəsy] adv above
cidre [sidr] nm cider
Cie abr (= compagnie) Co.
ciel [sjɛl] nm sky; (REL) heaven; **cieux** nmpl
   (REL) heaven sg; **à ~ ouvert** open-air; (mine)
   open-cast
cierge [sjɛrʒ] nm candle
cieux [sjø] nmpl de **ciel**
cigale [sigal] nf cicada
cigare [sigar] nm cigar
cigarette [sigaret] nf cigarette
ci-gît [siʒi] adv +vb here lies
cigogne [sigɔɲ] nf stork
ci-inclus, e [siɛ̃kly, yz] adj, adv enclosed
ci-joint, e [siʒwɛ̃, ɛt] adj, adv enclosed
cil [sil] nm (eye)lash
cime [sim] nf top; (montagne) peak
ciment [simɑ̃] nm cement
cimetière [simtjɛr] nm cemetery; (d'église)
   churchyard
cinéaste [sineast] nm/f film-maker
cinéma [sinema] nm cinema;
   cinématographique adj film cpd, cinema
   cpd
cinglant, e [sɛ̃glɑ̃, ɑ̃t] adj (remarque) biting
cinglé, e [sɛ̃gle] (fam) adj crazy
cinq [sɛ̃k] num five; **cinquantaine** nf: **une
   cinquantaine (de)** about fifty; **avoir la
   cinquantaine** (âge) to be around fifty;
   cinquante num fifty; **cinquantenaire** adj,
   nm/f fifty-year-old; **cinquième** num fifth
cintre [sɛ̃tr] nm coat-hanger
cintré, e [sɛ̃tre] adj (chemise) fitted
cirage [siraʒ] nm (shoe) polish
circonflexe [sirkɔ̃flɛks] adj: **accent ~**
   circumflex accent
circonscription [sirkɔ̃skripsjɔ̃] nf district;
   ~ électorale (d'un député) constituency

circonscrire [sirkɔ̃skrir] vt (sujet) to define,
   delimit; (incendie) to contain
circonstance [sirkɔ̃stɑ̃s] nf circumstance;
   (occasion) occasion; **~s atténuantes**
   mitigating circumstances
circuit [sirkɥi] nm (ÉLEC, TECH) circuit; (trajet)
   tour, (round) trip
circulaire [sirkylɛr] adj, nf circular
circulation [sirkylasjɔ̃] nf circulation;
   (AUTO): **la ~** (the) traffic
circuler [sirkyle] vi (sang, devises) to
   circulate; (véhicules) to drive (along);
   (passants) to walk along; (train, bus) to run;
   faire ~ (nouvelle) to spread (about), circulate;
   (badauds) to move on
cire [sir] nf wax; **ciré** nm oilskin; **cirer** vt to
   wax, polish
cirque [sirk] nm circus; (fig) chaos, bedlam;
   quel ~! what a carry-on!
cisaille(s) [sizaj] nf(pl) (gardening) shears pl
ciseau, x [sizo] nm: **~ (à bois)** chisel; **~x** nmpl
   (paire de ~x) (pair of) scissors
ciseler [siz(ə)le] vt to chisel, carve
citadin, e [sitadɛ̃, in] nm/f city dweller
citation [sitasjɔ̃] nf (d'auteur) quotation; (JUR)
   summons sg
cité [site] nf town; (plus grande) city;
   ~ universitaire students' residences pl
citer [site] vt (un auteur) to quote (from);
   (nommer) to name; (JUR) to summon
citerne [sitɛrn] nf tank
citoyen, ne [sitwajɛ̃, jɛn] nm/f citizen
citron [sitrɔ̃] nm lemon; **~ vert** lime;
   citronnade nf still lemonade
citrouille [sitruj] nf pumpkin
civet [sivɛ] nm: **~ de lapin** rabbit stew
civière [sivjɛr] nf stretcher
civil, e [sivil] adj (mariage, poli) civil; (non
   militaire) civilian; **en ~** in civilian clothes; **dans
   le ~** in civilian life
civilisation [sivilizasjɔ̃] nf civilization
clair, e [klɛr] adj light; (pièce) light, bright;
   (eau, son, fig) clear ♦ adv: **voir ~** to see
   clearly; **tirer qch au ~** to clear sth up, clarify
   sth; **mettre au ~** (notes etc) to tidy up; **~ de
   lune ♦** nm moonlight; **clairement** adv
   clearly
clairière [klɛrjɛr] nf clearing
clairon [klɛrɔ̃] nm bugle; **claironner** vt (fig)
   to trumpet, shout from the rooftops
clairsemé, e [klɛrsəme] adj sparse
clairvoyant, e [klɛrvwajɑ̃, ɑ̃t] adj
   perceptive, clear-sighted
clandestin, e [klɑ̃dɛstɛ̃, in] adj clandestine,
   secret; (mouvement) underground;
   (travailleur) illegal; **passager ~** stowaway
clapier [klapje] nm (rabbit) hutch
clapoter [klapɔte] vi to lap
claque [klak] nf (gifle) slap; **claquer** vi

(*porte*) to bang, slam; (*fam: mourir*) to snuff it ♦ vt (*porte*) to slam, bang; (*doigts*) to snap; (*fam: dépenser*) to blow; **il claquait des dents** his teeth were chattering; **être claqué** (*fam*) to be dead tired; **se claquer un muscle** to pull *ou* strain a muscle; **claquettes** *nfpl* tap-dancing *sg*; (*chaussures*) flip-flops

clarinette [klaʀinɛt] *nf* clarinet

clarté [klaʀte] *nf* (*luminosité*) brightness; (*d'un son, de l'eau*) clearness; (*d'une explication*) clarity

classe [klɑs] *nf* class; (SCOL: *local*) class(room); (: *leçon, élèves*) class; **aller en ~** to go to school; **classement** *nm* (*rang*: SCOL) place; (: SPORT) placing; (*liste*: SCOL) class list (in order of merit); (: SPORT) placings *pl*

classer [klɑse] *vt* (*idées, livres*) to classify; (*papiers*) to file; (*candidat, concurrent*) to grade; (JUR: *affaire*) to close; **se ~ premier/ dernier** to come first/last; (SPORT) to finish first/last; **classeur** *nm* (*cahier*) file

classique [klasik] *adj* classical; (*sobre: coupe etc*) classic(al); (*habituel*) standard, classic

clause [kloz] *nf* clause

clavecin [klav(ə)sɛ̃] *nm* harpsichord

clavicule [klavikyl] *nf* collarbone

clavier [klavje] *nm* keyboard

clé [kle] *nf* key; (MUS) clef; (*de mécanicien*) spanner (BRIT), wrench (US); **prix ~s en main** (*d'une voiture*) on-the-road price; **~ anglaise** (monkey) wrench; **~ de contact** ignition key

clef [kle] *nf* = **clé**

clément, e [klemɑ̃, ɑ̃t] *adj* (*temps*) mild; (*indulgent*) lenient

clerc [klɛʀ] *nm*: **~ de notaire** solicitor's clerk

clergé [klɛʀʒe] *nm* clergy

cliché [kliʃe] *nm* (*fig*) cliché; (*négatif*) negative; (*photo*) print

client, e [klijɑ̃, klijɑ̃t] *nm/f* (*acheteur*) customer, client; (*d'hôtel*) guest, patron; (*du docteur*) patient; (*de l'avocat*) client; **clientèle** *nf* (*du magasin*) customers *pl*, clientèle; (*du docteur, de l'avocat*) practice

cligner [kliɲe] *vi*: **~ des yeux** to blink (one's eyes); **~ de l'œil** to wink; **clignotant** *nm* (AUTO) indicator; **clignoter** *vi* (*étoiles etc*) to twinkle; (*lumière*) to flicker

climat [klima] *nm* climate

climatisation [klimatizasjɔ̃] *nf* air conditioning; **climatisé, e** *adj* air-conditioned

clin d'œil [klɛ̃dœj] *nm* wink; **en un ~** in a flash

clinique [klinik] *nf* private hospital

clinquant, e [klɛ̃kɑ̃, ɑ̃t] *adj* flashy

clip [klip] *nm* (*boucle d'oreille*) clip-on; (**vidéo**) (pop) video

cliqueter [klik(ə)te] *vi* (*ferraille*) to jangle;

(*clés*) to jingle

clochard, e [klɔʃaʀ, aʀd] *nm/f* tramp

cloche [klɔʃ] *nf* (*d'église*) bell; (*fam*) clot; **cloche-pied**: **à cloche-pied** *adv* on one leg, hopping (along); **clocher** *nm* church tower; (*en pointe*) steeple ♦ *vi* (*fam*) to be *ou* go wrong; **de clocher** (*péj*) parochial

cloison [klwazɔ̃] *nf* partition (wall)

cloître [klwatʀ] *nm* cloister; **cloîtrer** *vt*: **se cloîtrer** to shut o.s. up *ou* away

cloque [klɔk] *nf* blister

clore [klɔʀ] *vt* to close; **clos, e** *adj voir* **maison; huis**

clôture [klotyʀ] *nf* closure; (*barrière*) enclosure; **clôturer** *vt* (*terrain*) to enclose; (*débuts*) to close

clou [klu] *nm* nail; **~s** *nmpl* (*passage ~té*) pedestrian crossing; **pneus à ~s** studded tyres; **le ~ du spectacle** the highlight of the show; **~ de girofle** clove; **clouer** *vt* to nail down *ou* up; **clouer le bec à qn** (*fam*) to shut sb up

clown [klun] *nm* clown

club [klœb] *nm* club

CNRS *sigle m* (= *Centre nationale de la recherche scientifique*) ≈ SERC (BRIT), ≈ NSF (US)

coaguler [kɔagyle] *vt, vi* (*aussi*: **se ~**: *sang*) to coagulate

coasser [kɔase] *vi* to croak

cobaye [kɔbaj] *nm* guinea-pig

coca [kɔka] *nm* Coke ®

cocaïne [kɔkain] *nf* cocaine

cocasse [kɔkas] *adj* comical, funny

coccinelle [kɔksinɛl] *nf* ladybird (BRIT), ladybug (US)

cocher [kɔʃe] *vt* to tick off

cochère [kɔʃɛʀ] *adj f*: **porte ~** carriage entrance

cochon, ne [kɔʃɔ̃, ɔn] *nm* pig ♦ *adj* (*fam*) dirty, smutty; **~ d'Inde** guinea pig; **cochonnerie** (*fam*) *nf* (*saleté*) filth; (*marchandise*) rubbish, trash

cocktail [kɔktɛl] *nm* cocktail; (*réception*) cocktail party

coco [kɔko] *nm voir* **noix**

cocorico [kɔkɔriko] *excl, nm* cock-a-doodle-do

cocotier [kɔkɔtje] *nm* coconut palm

cocotte [kɔkɔt] *nf* (*en fonte*) casserole; **~ (minute)** pressure cooker; **ma ~** (*fam*) sweetie (*pie*)

cocu [kɔky] (*fam*) *nm* cuckold

code [kɔd] *nm* code ♦ *adj*: **phares ~s** dipped lights; **se mettre en ~(s)** to dip one's (head)lights; **~ à barres** bar code; **~ civil** Common Law; **~ de la route** highway code; **~ pénal** penal code; **~ postal** (*numéro*) post (BRIT) *ou* zip (US) code

cœur [kœʀ] nm heart; (CARTES: couleur) hearts pl; (: carte) heart; **avoir bon ~** to be kind-hearted; **avoir mal au ~** to feel sick; **en avoir le ~ net** to be clear in one's own mind (about it); **par ~** by heart; **de bon ~** willingly; **cela lui tient à ~** that's (very) close to his heart

coffre [kɔfʀ] nm (meuble) chest; (d'auto) boot (BRIT), trunk (US); **coffre(-fort)** nm safe; **coffret** nm casket

cognac [kɔɲak] nm brandy, cognac

cogner [kɔɲe] vi to knock; **se ~ la tête** to bang one's head

cohérent, e [kɔeʀɑ̃, ɑ̃t] adj coherent, consistent

cohorte [kɔɔʀt] nf troop

cohue [kɔy] nf crowd

coi, coite [kwa, kwat] adj: **rester ~** to remain silent

coiffe [kwaf] nf headdress

coiffé, e [kwafe] adj: **bien/mal ~** with tidy/untidy hair

coiffer [kwafe] vt (fig: surmonter) to cover, top; **se ~** vi to do one's hair; **~ qn** to do sb's hair; **coiffeur, -euse** nm/f hairdresser; **coiffeuse** nf (table) dressing table; **coiffure** nf (cheveux) hairstyle, hairdo; (art): **la coiffure** hairdressing

coin [kwɛ̃] nm corner; (pour ~cer) wedge; **l'épicerie du ~** the local grocer; **dans le ~** (aux alentours) in the area, around about; (habiter) locally; **je ne suis pas du ~** I'm not from here; **au ~ du feu** by the fireside; **regard en ~** sideways glance

coincé, e [kwɛ̃se] adj stuck, jammed; (fig: inhibé) inhibited, hung up (fam)

coincer [kwɛ̃se] vt to jam; (fam: attraper) to pinch

coïncidence [kɔɛ̃sidɑ̃s] nf coincidence

coïncider [kɔɛ̃side] vi to coincide

coing [kwɛ̃] nm quince

col [kɔl] nm (de chemise) collar; (encolure, cou) neck; (de montagne) pass; **~ de l'utérus** cervix; **~ roulé** polo-neck

colère [kɔlɛʀ] nf anger; **une ~** a fit of anger; **(se mettre) en ~** (to get) angry; **coléreux, -euse** adj, **colérique** adj quick-tempered, irascible

colifichet [kɔlifiʃe] nm trinket

colimaçon [kɔlimasɔ̃] nm: **escalier en ~** spiral staircase

colin [kɔlɛ̃] nm hake

colique [kɔlik] nf diarrhoea

colis [kɔli] nm parcel

collaborateur, -trice [kɔ(l)labɔʀatœʀ, tʀis] nm/f (aussi POL) collaborator; (d'une revue) contributor

collaborer [kɔ(l)labɔʀe] vi to collaborate; **~ à** to collaborate on; (revue) to contribute to

collant, e [kɔlɑ̃, ɑ̃t] adj sticky; (robe etc)

clinging, skintight; (péj) clinging ♦ nm (bas) tights pl; (de danseur) leotard

collation [kɔlasjɔ̃] nf light meal

colle [kɔl] nf glue; (à papiers peints) (wallpaper) paste; (fam: devinette) teaser, riddle; (SCOL: fam) detention

collecte [kɔlɛkt] nf collection; **collectif, -ive** adj collective; (visite, billet) group cpd

collection [kɔlɛksjɔ̃] nf collection; (ÉDITION) series; **collectionner** vt to collect; **collectionneur, -euse** nm/f collector

collectivité [kɔlɛktivite] nf group; **~s locales** (ADMIN) local authorities

collège [kɔlɛʒ] nm (école) (secondary) school; (assemblée) body; **collégien** nm schoolboy; **collégienne** nf schoolgirl

collègue [kɔ(l)lɛg] nm/f colleague

coller [kɔle] vt (papier, timbre) to stick (on); (affiche) to stick up; (enveloppe) to stick down; (morceaux) to stick ou glue together; (fam: mettre, fourrer) to stick, shove; (SCOL: fam) to keep in ♦ vi (être collant) to be sticky; (adhérer) to stick; **~ à** to stick to; **être collé à un examen** (fam) to fail an exam

collet [kɔle] nm (piège) snare, noose; (cou): **prendre qn au ~** to grab sb by the throat

collier [kɔlje] nm (bijou) necklace; (de chien, TECH) collar

collimateur [kɔlimatœʀ] nm: **avoir qn/qch dans le ~** (fig) to have sb/sth in one's sights

colline [kɔlin] nf hill

collision [kɔlizjɔ̃] nf collision, crash; **entrer en ~ (avec)** to collide (with)

colloque [kɔ(l)lɔk] nm symposium

collyre [kɔliʀ] nm eye drops

colmater [kɔlmate] vt (fuite) to seal off; (brèche) to plug, fill in

colombe [kɔlɔ̃b] nf dove

Colombie [kɔlɔ̃bi] nf: **la ~** Colombia

colon [kɔlɔ̃] nm settler

colonel [kɔlɔnɛl] nm colonel

colonie [kɔlɔni] nf colony; **~ (de vacances)** holiday camp (for children)

colonne [kɔlɔn] nf column; **se mettre en ~ par deux** to get into twos; **~ (vertébrale)** spine, spinal column

colorant [kɔlɔʀɑ̃, ɑ̃t] nm colouring

colorer [kɔlɔʀe] vt to colour

colorier [kɔlɔʀje] vt to colour (in)

coloris [kɔlɔʀi] nm colour, shade

colporter [kɔlpɔʀte] vt to hawk, peddle

colza [kɔlza] nm rape(seed)

coma [kɔma] nm coma; **être dans le ~** to be in a coma

combat [kɔ̃ba] nm fight, fighting no pl; **~ de boxe** boxing match; **combattant** nm: **ancien combattant** war veteran; **combattre** vt to fight; (épidémie, ignorance) to combat, fight against

combien [kɔ̃bjɛ̃] adv (quantité) how much; (nombre) how many; **~ de** (quantité) how much; (nombre) how many; **~ de temps** how long; **~ ça coûte/pèse?** how much does it cost/weigh?; **on est le ~ aujourd'hui?** (fam) what's the date today?

combinaison [kɔ̃binɛzɔ̃] nf combination; (astuce) device, scheme; (de femme) slip; (de plongée) wetsuit; (bleu de travail) boiler suit (BRIT), coveralls pl (US)

combine [kɔ̃bin] nf trick; (péj) scheme, fiddle (BRIT)

combiné [kɔ̃bine] nm (aussi: **~ téléphonique**) receiver

combiner [kɔ̃bine] vt (grouper) to combine; (plan, horaire) to work out, devise

comble [kɔ̃bl] adj (salle) packed (full) ♦ nm (du bonheur, plaisir) height; **~s** nmpl (CONSTR) attic sg, loft sg; **c'est le ~!** that beats everything!

combler [kɔ̃ble] vt (trou) to fill in; (besoin, lacune) to fill; (déficit) to make good; (satisfaire) to gratify

combustible [kɔ̃bystibl] nm fuel

comédie [kɔmedi] nf comedy; (fig) playacting no pl; **faire la ~** (fam) to make a fuss; **~ musicale** musical; **comédien, ne** nm/f actor(-tress)

comestible [kɔmɛstibl] adj edible

comique [kɔmik] adj (drôle) comical; (THÉÂTRE) comic ♦ nm (artiste) comic, comedian

comité [kɔmite] nm committee; **~ d'entreprise** works council

commandant [kɔmɑ̃dɑ̃] nm (gén) commander, commandant; (NAVIG, AVIAT) captain

commande [kɔmɑ̃d] nf (COMM) order; **~s** nfpl (AVIAT etc) controls; **sur ~** to order; **commandement** nm command; (REL) commandment; **commander** vt (COMM) to order; (diriger, ordonner) to command; **commander à qn de faire** to command ou order sb to do

commando [kɔmɑ̃do] nm commando (squad)

MOT-CLÉ

comme [kɔm] prép 1 (comparaison) like; **tout comme son père** just like his father; **fort comme un bœuf** as strong as an ox; **joli comme tout** ever so pretty

2 (manière) like; **faites-le comme ça** do it like this, do it this way; **comme ci, comme ça** so-so, middling

3 (en tant que) as a; **donner comme prix** to give as a prize; **travailler comme secrétaire** to work as a secretary

♦ conj 1 (ainsi que) as; **elle écrit comme elle parle** she writes as she talks; **comme si** as if

2 (au moment où, alors que) as; **il est parti comme j'arrivais** he left as I arrived

3 (parce que, puisque) as; **comme il était en retard, il ... as** he was late, he ...

♦ adv: **comme il est fort/c'est bon!** he's so strong/it's so good!

commémorer [kɔmemɔre] vt to commemorate

commencement [kɔmɑ̃smɑ̃] nm beginning, start

commencer [kɔmɑ̃se] vt, vi to begin, start; **~ à ou de faire** to begin ou start doing

comment [kɔmɑ̃] adv how; **~?** (que dites-vous?) pardon?

commentaire [kɔmɑ̃tɛr] nm (remarque) comment, remark; (exposé) commentary

commenter [kɔmɑ̃te] vt (jugement, événement) to comment (up)on; (RADIO, TV: match, manifestation) to cover

commérages [kɔmeraʒ] nmpl gossip sg

commerçant, e [kɔmɛrsɑ̃, ɑ̃t] nm/f shopkeeper, trader

commerce [kɔmɛrs] nm (activité) trade, commerce; (boutique) business; **commercial, e, -aux** adj commercial, trading; (péj) commercial; **les commerciaux** the sales people; **commercialiser** vt to market

commère [kɔmɛr] nf gossip

commettre [kɔmɛtr] vt to commit

commis [kɔmi] nm (de magasin) (shop) assistant; (de banque) clerk

commissaire [kɔmisɛr] nm (de police) ~ (police) superintendent; **commissaire-priseur** nm auctioneer; **commissariat** nm police station

commission [kɔmisjɔ̃] nf (comité, pourcentage) commission; (message) message; (course) errand; **~s** nfpl (achats) shopping sg

commode [kɔmɔd] adj (pratique) convenient, handy; (facile) easy; (personne): **pas ~** awkward (to deal with) ♦ nf chest of drawers; **commodité** nf convenience

commotion [kɔmosjɔ̃] nf: **~ (cérébrale)** concussion; **commotionné, e** adj shocked, shaken

commun, e [kɔmœ̃, yn] adj common; (pièce) communal, shared; (effort) joint; **ça sort du ~** it's out of the ordinary; **le ~ des mortels** the common run of people; **en ~** (faire) jointly; **mettre en ~** to pool, share; voir aussi **communs**

communauté [kɔmynote] nf community

commune [kɔmyn] nf (ADMIN) commune, ≈ district; (: urbaine) ≈ borough

communicatif, -ive [kɔmynikatif, iv] adj

(*rire*) infectious; (*personne*) communicative

communication [kɔmynikasjɔ̃] *nf*
communication; ~ **(téléphonique)** (telephone)
call

communier [kɔmynje] *vi* (*REL*) to receive
communion

communion [kɔmynjɔ̃] *nf* communion

communiquer [kɔmynike] *vt* (*nouvelle,
dossier*) to pass on, convey; (*peur etc*) to
communicate ♦ *vi* to communicate; **se ~ à**
(*se propager*) to spread to

communisme [kɔmynism] *nm*
communism; **communiste** *adj, nm/f*
communist

communs [kɔmœ̃] *nmpl* (*bâtiments*)
outbuildings

commutateur [kɔmytatœR] *nm* (*ÉLEC*)
(change-over) switch, commutator

compact, e [kɔ̃pakt] *adj* (*dense*) dense;
(*appareil*) compact

compagne [kɔ̃paɲ] *nf* companion

compagnie [kɔ̃paɲi] *nf* (*firme, MIL*)
company; **tenir ~ à qn** to keep sb company;
fausser ~ à qn to give sb the slip, slip *ou*
sneak away from sb; ~ **aérienne** airline
(company)

compagnon [kɔ̃paɲɔ̃] *nm* companion

comparable [kɔ̃paRabl] *adj*: ~ **(à)**
comparable (to)

comparaison [kɔ̃paRɛzɔ̃] *nf* comparison

comparaître [kɔ̃paRɛtR] *vi*: ~ **(devant)** to
appear (before)

comparer [kɔ̃paRe] *vt* to compare; ~ **qch/qn
à** *ou* **et** (*pour choisir*) to compare sth/sb with
ou and; (*pour établir une similitude*) to
compare sth/sb to

compartiment [kɔ̃paRtimã] *nm*
compartment

comparution [kɔ̃paRysjɔ̃] *nf* (*JUR*)
appearance

compas [kɔ̃pa] *nm* (*GÉOM*) (pair of)
compasses *pl*; (*NAVIG*) compass

compatible [kɔ̃patibl] *adj* compatible

compatir [kɔ̃patiR] *vi* to sympathize

compatriote [kɔ̃patRijɔt] *nm/f* compatriot

compensation [kɔ̃pãsasjɔ̃] *nf* compensation

compenser [kɔ̃pãse] *vt* to compensate for,
make up for

compère [kɔ̃pER] *nm* accomplice

compétence [kɔ̃petãs] *nf* competence

compétent, e [kɔ̃petã, ãt] *adj* (*apte*)
competent, capable

compétition [kɔ̃petisjɔ̃] *nf* (*gén*)
competition; (*SPORT: épreuve*) event; **la
~ automobile** motor racing

complainte [kɔ̃plɛ̃t] *nf* lament

complaire [kɔ̃plER] : **se ~** *vi*: **se ~ dans** to take
pleasure in

complaisance [kɔ̃plɛzãs] *nf* kindness;

pavillon de ~ flag of convenience

complaisant, e [kɔ̃plɛzã, ãt] *adj* (*aimable*)
kind, obliging

complément [kɔ̃plemã] *nm* complement;
(*reste*) remainder; ~ **d'information** (*ADMIN*)
supplementary *ou* further information;
complémentaire *adj* complementary;
(*additionnel*) supplementary

complet, -ète [kɔ̃plɛ, ɛt] *adj* complete;
(*plein: hôtel etc*) full ♦ *nm* (*aussi:* **~-veston**)
suit; **pain ~** wholemeal bread; **complètement** *adv* completely; **compléter** *vt*
(*porter à la quantité voulue*) to complete;
(*augmenter: connaissances, études*) to
complement, supplement; (: *garde-robe*) to
add to; **se compléter** (*caractères*) to
complement one another

complexe [kɔ̃plɛks] *adj, nm* complex;
complexé, e *adj* mixed-up, hung-up

complication [kɔ̃plikasjɔ̃] *nf* complexity,
intricacy; (*difficulté, ennui*) complication

complice [kɔ̃plis] *nm* accomplice;
complicité *nf* complicity

compliment [kɔ̃plimã] *nm* (*louange*)
compliment; **~s** *nmpl* (*félicitations*)
congratulations

compliqué, e [kɔ̃plike] *adj* complicated,
complex; (*personne*) complicated

compliquer [kɔ̃plike] *vt* to complicate; **se ~**
to become complicated

complot [kɔ̃plo] *nm* plot

comportement [kɔ̃pɔRtəmã] *nm* behaviour

comporter [kɔ̃pɔRte] *vt* (*consister en*) to
consist of, comprise; (*inclure*) to have; **se ~** *vi*
to behave

composant [kɔ̃pozã] *nm*, **composante**
[kɔ̃pozãt] *nf* component

composé [kɔ̃poze] *nm* compound

composer [kɔ̃poze] *vt* (*musique, texte*) to
compose; (*mélange, équipe*) to make up;
(*numéro*) to dial; (*constituer*) to make up,
form ♦ *vi* (*transiger*) to come to terms; **se
~ de** to be composed of, be made up of;
compositeur, -trice *nm/f* (*MUS*) composer;
composition *nf* composition; (*SCOL*) test

composter [kɔ̃pɔste] *vt* (*billet*) to punch

compote [kɔ̃pɔt] *nf* stewed fruit *no pl*; ~ **de
pommes** stewed apples

compréhensible [kɔ̃pReãsibl] *adj*
comprehensible; (*attitude*) understandable

compréhensif, -ive [kɔ̃pReãsif, iv] *adj*
understanding

comprendre [kɔ̃pRãdR] *vt* to understand;
(*se composer de*) to comprise, consist of

compresse [kɔ̃pREs] *nf* compress

compression [kɔ̃pResjɔ̃] *nf* compression;
(*de personnes*) reduction

comprimé [kɔ̃pRime] *nm* tablet

comprimer [kɔ̃pRime] *vt* to compress; (*fig:*

crédit etc) to reduce, cut down

compris, e [kɔ̃pri, iz] *pp de* **comprendre**
♦ *adj* (*inclus*) included; ~ **entre** (*situé*)
contained between; **l'électricité ~e/non ~e,**
y/non ~ l'électricité including/excluding
electricity; **100 F tout ~** 100 F all inclusive *ou*
all-in

compromettre [kɔ̃prɔmɛtr] *vt* to
compromise; **compromis** *nm* compromise

comptabilité [kɔ̃tabilite] *nf* (*activité*)
accounting, accountancy; (*comptes*) accounts
pl, books *pl*; (*service*) accounts office

comptable [kɔ̃tabl] *nm/f* accountant

comptant [kɔ̃tɑ̃] *adv*: **payer ~** to pay cash;
acheter ~ to buy for cash

compte [kɔ̃t] *nm* count: (*total, montant*)
count, (right) number; (*bancaire, facture*)
account; **~s** *nmpl* (*FINANCE*) accounts, books;
(*fig*) explanation *sg*; **en fin de ~** all things
considered; **s'en tirer à bon ~** to get off
lightly; **pour le ~ de** on behalf of; **pour son**
propre ~ for one's own benefit; **tenir ~ de** to
take account of; **travailler à son ~** to work for
oneself; **rendre ~ (à qn) de qch** to give (sb)
an account of sth; *voir aussi* **rendre ~ à**
rebours countdown; **~ chèques postaux** Post
Office account; **~ courant** current account;
~ rendu account, report; (*de film, livre*)
review; **compte-gouttes** *nm inv* dropper

compter [kɔ̃te] *vt* to count; (*facturer*) to
charge for; (*avoir à son actif, comporter*) to
have; (*prévoir*) to allow, reckon; (*penser,*
espérer): **~ réussir** to expect to succeed ♦ *vi*
to count; (*être économe*) to economize;
(*figurer*): **~ parmi** to be *ou* rank among; **~**
sur to count (up)on; **~ avec qch/qn** to reckon
with *ou* take account of sth/sb; **sans ~ que**
besides which

compteur [kɔ̃tœr] *nm* meter; **~ de vitesse**
speedometer

comptine [kɔ̃tin] *nf* nursery rhyme

comptoir [kɔ̃twar] *nm* (*de magasin*) counter;
(*bar*) bar

compulser [kɔ̃pylse] *vt* to consult

comte [kɔ̃t] *nm* count; **comtesse** *nf*
countess

con, ne [kɔ̃, kɔn] (*fam!*) *adj* damned *ou*
bloody (*BRIT*) stupid (!)

concéder [kɔ̃sede] *vt* to grant; (*défaite,*
point) to concede

concentré [kɔ̃sɑ̃tre] *adj* (*lait*) condensed
♦ *nm*: **~ de tomates** tomato purée

concentrer [kɔ̃sɑ̃tre] *vt* to concentrate; **se ~**
vi to concentrate

concept [kɔ̃sɛpt] *nm* concept

conception [kɔ̃sɛpsjɔ̃] *nf* conception; (*d'une*
machine etc) design; (*d'un problème, de la*
vie) approach

concerner [kɔ̃sɛrne] *vt* to concern; **en ce**

qui me **concerne** as far as I am concerned

concert [kɔ̃sɛr] *nm* concert; **de ~** (*décider*)
unanimously; **concerter: se concerter** *vi* to
put their *etc* heads together

concession [kɔ̃sesjɔ̃] *nf* concession;
concessionnaire *nm/f* agent, dealer

concevoir [kɔ̃s(ə)vwar] *vt* (*idée, projet*) to
conceive (of); (*comprendre*) to understand;
(*enfant*) to conceive; **bien/mal conçu** well-/
badly-designed

concierge [kɔ̃sjɛrʒ] *nm/f* caretaker

conciliabules [kɔ̃siljabyl] *nmpl* (*private*)
discussions, confabulations

concilier [kɔ̃silje] *vt* to reconcile; **se ~** *vt* to
win over

concis, e [kɔ̃si, iz] *adj* concise

concitoyen, ne [kɔ̃sitwajɛ̃, jɛn] *nm/f* fellow
citizen

concluant, e [kɔ̃klyɑ̃, ɑ̃t] *adj* conclusive

conclure [kɔ̃klyr] *vt* to conclude;
conclusion *nf* conclusion

conçois *etc* [kɔ̃swa] *vb voir* **concevoir**

concombre [kɔ̃kɔ̃br] *nm* cucumber

concorder [kɔ̃kɔrde] *vi* to tally, agree

concourir [kɔ̃kurir] *vi* (*SPORT*) to compete;
~ à (*effet etc*) to work towards

concours [kɔ̃kur] *nm* competition; (*SCOL*)
competitive examination; (*assistance*) aid,
help; **~ de circonstances** combination of
circumstances; **~ hippique** horse show

concret, -ète [kɔ̃krɛ, ɛt] *adj* concrete

concrétiser [kɔ̃kretize] **se ~** *vi* to
materialize

conçu, e [kɔ̃sy] *pp de* **concevoir**

concubinage [kɔ̃kybinaʒ] *nm* (*JUR*)
cohabitation

concurrence [kɔ̃kyrɑ̃s] *nf* competition; **faire**
~ à to be in competition with; **jusqu'à ~ de**
up to

concurrent, e [kɔ̃kyrɑ̃, ɑ̃t] *nm/f* (*SPORT,*
ÉCON etc) competitor; (*SCOL etc*) candidate

condamner [kɔ̃dane] *vt* (*blâmer*) to
condemn; (*JUR*) to sentence; (*porte,*
ouverture) to fill in, block up; **~ qn à 2 ans de**
prison to sentence sb to 2 years' imprisonment

condensation [kɔ̃dɑ̃sasjɔ̃] *nf* condensation

condenser [kɔ̃dɑ̃se] *vt* to condense; **se ~** *vi*
to condense

condisciple [kɔ̃disipl] *nm/f* fellow student

condition [kɔ̃disjɔ̃] *nf* condition; **~s** *nfpl*
(*tarif, prix*) terms; (*circonstances*) conditions;
à ~ de ou que provided that; **conditionnel,**
le *nm* conditional (tense)

conditionnement [kɔ̃disjɔnmɑ̃] *nm*
(*emballage*) packaging

conditionner [kɔ̃disjɔne] *vt* (*déterminer*) to
determine; (*COMM: produit*) to package; **air**
conditionné air conditioning

condoléances [kɔ̃dɔleɑ̃s] nfpl condolences
conducteur, -trice [kɔ̃dyktœʀ, tʀis] nm/f
driver ♦ nm (ÉLEC etc) conductor
conduire [kɔ̃dɥiʀ] vt to drive; (délégation,
troupeau) to lead; **se ~** vi to behave; **~ à** to
lead to; **~ qn quelque part** to take sb
somewhere; to drive sb somewhere
conduite [kɔ̃dɥit] nf (comportement)
behaviour; (d'eau, de gaz) pipe; **sous la ~ de**
led by; **~ à gauche** left-hand drive
cône [kon] nm cone
confection [kɔ̃feksjɔ̃] nf (fabrication) making;
(COUTURE): **la ~** the clothing industry
confectionner [kɔ̃feksjɔne] vt to make
conférence [kɔ̃feʀɑ̃s] nf conference;
(exposé) lecture; **~ de presse** press
conference; **conférencier, -ière** nm/f
speaker, lecturer
confesser [kɔ̃fese] vt to confess; **se ~** vi (REL)
to go to confession; **confession** nf
confession; (culte: catholique etc)
denomination
confiance [kɔ̃fjɑ̃s] nf (en l'honnêteté de qn)
confidence, trust; (en la valeur de qch) faith;
avoir ~ en to have confidence ou faith in,
trust; **faire ~ à qn** to trust sb; **mettre qn en ~**
to win sb's trust; **~ en soi** self-confidence
confiant, e [kɔ̃fjɑ̃, jɑ̃t] adj confident;
trusting
confidence [kɔ̃fidɑ̃s] nf confidence;
confidentiel, le adj confidential
confier [kɔ̃fje] vt: **~ à qn** (objet, travail) to
entrust to sb; (secret, pensée) to confide to
sb; **se ~ à qn** to confide in sb
confins [kɔ̃fɛ̃] nmpl: **aux ~ de** on the borders
of
confirmation [kɔ̃fiʀmasjɔ̃] nf confirmation
confirmer [kɔ̃fiʀme] vt to confirm
confiserie [kɔ̃fizʀi] nf (magasin)
confectioner's ou sweet shop; **~s** nfpl
(bonbons) confectionery sg
confisquer [kɔ̃fiske] vt to confiscate
confit, e [kɔ̃fi, it] adj: **fruits ~s** crystallized
fruits ♦ nm: **~ d'oie** conserve of goose
confiture [kɔ̃fityʀ] nf jam; **~ d'oranges**
(orange) marmalade
conflit [kɔ̃fli] nm conflict
confondre [kɔ̃fɔ̃dʀ] vt (jumeaux, faits) to
confuse, mix up; (témoin, menteur) to
confound; **se ~** vi to merge; **se ~ en excuses**
to apologize profusely; **confondu, e** adj
(stupéfait) speechless, overcome
conforme [kɔ̃fɔʀm] adj: **~ à** (loi, règle) in
accordance with; **conformément** adv:
conformément à in accordance with;
conformer vt: **se conformer à** to conform to
confort [kɔ̃fɔʀ] nm comfort; **tout ~** (COMM)
with all modern conveniences; **confortable**
adj comfortable

confrère [kɔ̃fʀɛʀ] nm colleague
confronter [kɔ̃fʀɔ̃te] vt to confront
confus, e [kɔ̃fy, yz] adj (vague) confused;
(embarrassé) embarrassed; **confusion** nf
(voir confus) confusion; embarrassment; (voir
confondre) confusion, mixing up
congé [kɔ̃ʒe] nm (vacances) holiday; **en ~** on
holiday; **semaine de ~** week off; **prendre ~ de
qn** to take one's leave of sb; **donner son ~ à**
to give in one's notice to; **~ de maladie** sick
leave; **~ de maternité** maternity leave; **~s
payés** paid holiday
congédier [kɔ̃ʒedje] vt to dismiss
congélateur [kɔ̃ʒelatœʀ] nm freezer
congeler [kɔ̃ʒ(ə)le] vt to freeze; **les produits
congelés** frozen foods
congestion [kɔ̃ʒɛstjɔ̃] nf congestion;
~ cérébrale stroke; **congestionner** vt (rue)
to congest; (visage) to flush
congrès [kɔ̃gʀɛ] nm congress
conifère [kɔnifɛʀ] nm conifer
conjecture [kɔ̃ʒɛktyʀ] nf conjecture
conjoint, e [kɔ̃ʒwɛ̃, wɛ̃t] adj joint ♦ nm/f
spouse
conjonction [kɔ̃ʒɔ̃ksjɔ̃] nf (LING) conjunction
conjonctivite [kɔ̃ʒɔ̃ktivit] nf conjunctivitis
conjoncture [kɔ̃ʒɔ̃ktyʀ] nf circumstances pl;
la ~ actuelle the present (economic) situation
conjugaison [kɔ̃ʒygezɔ̃] nf (LING)
conjugation
conjuguer [kɔ̃ʒyge] vt (LING) to conjugate;
(efforts etc) to combine
conjuration [kɔ̃ʒyʀasjɔ̃] nf conspiracy
conjurer [kɔ̃ʒyʀe] vt (sort, maladie) to avert;
(implorer) to beseech, entreat
connaissance [kɔnɛsɑ̃s] nf (savoir)
knowledge no pl; (personne connue)
acquaintance; **être sans ~** to be unconscious;
perdre/reprendre ~ to lose/regain
consciousness; **à ma/sa ~** to (the best of)
my/his knowledge; **faire la ~ de qn** to meet sb
connaisseur [kɔnɛsœʀ, øz] nm connoisseur
connaître [kɔnɛtʀ] vt to know; (éprouver) to
experience; (avoir: succès) to have, enjoy;
~ de nom/vue to know by name/sight; **ils se
sont connus à Genève** they (first) met in
Geneva; **s'y ~ en qch** to know a lot about sth
connecter [kɔnɛkte] vt to connect
connerie [kɔnʀi] (fam!) nf stupid thing (to
do/say)
connu, e [kɔny] adj (célèbre) well-known
conquérir [kɔ̃keʀiʀ] vt to conquer;
conquête nf conquest
consacrer [kɔ̃sakʀe] vt (employer) to devote,
dedicate; (REL) to consecrate
conscience [kɔ̃sjɑ̃s] nf conscience; **avoir/
prendre ~ de** to be/become aware of; **perdre
~** to lose consciousness; **avoir bonne/
mauvaise ~** to have a clear/guilty conscience;

consciencieux, -euse adj conscientious; **conscient, e** adj conscious

conscrit [kɔ̃skri] nm conscript

consécutif, -ive [kɔ̃sekytif, iv] adj consecutive; **~ à** following upon

conseil [kɔ̃sɛj] nm (avis) piece of advice; (assemblée) council; **des ~s** advice; **prendre ~ (auprès de qn)** to take advice (from sb); **~ d'administration** board (of directors); **le ~ des ministres** ≈ the Cabinet; **~ municipal** town council

conseiller, -ère [kɔ̃seje, ɛʀ] nm/f adviser ♦ vt (personne) to advise; (méthode, action) to recommend, advise; **~ à qn de** to advise sb to; **~ municipal** town councillor

consentement [kɔ̃sɑ̃tmɑ̃] nm consent

consentir [kɔ̃sɑ̃tiʀ] vt to agree, consent

conséquence [kɔ̃sekɑ̃s] nf consequence; **en ~** (donc) consequently; (de façon appropriée) accordingly; **conséquent, e** adj logical, rational; (fam: important) substantial; **par conséquent** consequently

conservateur, -trice [kɔ̃sɛʀvatœʀ, tʀis] nm/f (POL) conservative; (de musée) curator ♦ nm (pour aliments) preservative

conservatoire [kɔ̃sɛʀvatwaʀ] nm academy

conserve [kɔ̃sɛʀv] nf (gén pl) canned ou tinned (BRIT) food; **en ~** canned, tinned (BRIT)

conserver [kɔ̃sɛʀve] vt (faculté) to retain, keep; (amis, livres) to keep; (préserver, aussi CULIN) to preserve

considérable [kɔ̃sideʀabl] adj considerable, significant, extensive

considération [kɔ̃sideʀasjɔ̃] nf consideration; (estime) esteem

considérer [kɔ̃sideʀe] vt to consider; **~ qch comme** to regard sth as

consigne [kɔ̃siɲ] nf (de gare) left luggage (office) (BRIT), checkroom (US); (ordre, instruction) instructions pl; **~ (automatique)** left-luggage locker; **consigner** vt (note, pensée) to record; (punir: élève) to put in detention; (COMM) to put a deposit on

consistant, e [kɔ̃sistɑ̃, ɑ̃t] adj (mélange) thick; (repas) solid

consister [kɔ̃siste] vi: **~ en/à faire** to consist of/in doing

consœur [kɔ̃sœʀ] nf (lady) colleague

consoler [kɔ̃sɔle] vt to console

consolider [kɔ̃sɔlide] vt to strengthen; (fig) to consolidate

consommateur, -trice [kɔ̃sɔmatœʀ, tʀis] nm/f (ÉCON) consumer; (dans un café) customer

consommation [kɔ̃sɔmasjɔ̃] nf (boisson) drink; (ÉCON) consumption

consommer [kɔ̃sɔme] vt (suj: personne) to eat ou drink, consume; (: voiture, machine) to use, consume; (mariage) to consummate

♦ vi (dans un café) to (have a) drink

consonne [kɔ̃sɔn] nf consonant

conspirer [kɔ̃spiʀe] vi to conspire

constamment [kɔ̃stamɑ̃] adv constantly

constant, e [kɔ̃stɑ̃, ɑ̃t] adj constant; (personne) steadfast

constat [kɔ̃sta] nm (de police, d'accident) report; **~ (à l'amiable)** jointly-agreed statement for insurance purposes; **~ d'échec** acknowledgement of failure

constatation [kɔ̃statasjɔ̃] nf (observation) (observed) fact, observation

constater [kɔ̃state] vt (remarquer) to note; (ADMIN, JUR: attester) to certify

consterner [kɔ̃stɛʀne] vt to dismay

constipé, e [kɔ̃stipe] adj constipated

constitué, e [kɔ̃stitɥe] adj: **~ de** made up ou composed of

constituer [kɔ̃stitɥe] vt (équipe) to set up; (dossier, collection) to put together; (suj: éléments: composer) to make up, constitute; (représenter, être) to constitute; **se ~ prisonnier** to give o.s. up; **constitution** nf (composition) composition, make-up; (santé, POL) constitution

constructeur [kɔ̃stʀyktœʀ] nm manufacturer, builder

constructif, -ive [kɔ̃stʀyktif, iv] adj constructive

construction [kɔ̃stʀyksjɔ̃] nf construction, building

construire [kɔ̃stʀɥiʀ] vt to build, construct

consul [kɔ̃syl] nm consul; **consulat** nm consulate

consultant, e [kɔ̃syltɑ̃, ɑ̃t] adj, nm consultant

consultation [kɔ̃syltasjɔ̃] nf consultation; **~s** nfpl (POL) talks; **heures de ~** (MÉD) surgery (BRIT) ou office (US) hours

consulter [kɔ̃sylte] vt to consult ♦ vi (médecin) to hold surgery (BRIT), be in (the office) (US); **se ~** vi to confer

consumer [kɔ̃syme] vt to consume; **se ~** vi to burn

contact [kɔ̃takt] nm contact; **au ~ de** (air, peau) on contact with; (gens) through contact with; **mettre/couper le ~** (AUTO) to switch on/off the ignition; **entrer en** ou **prendre ~ avec** to get in touch ou contact with; **contacter** vt to contact, get in touch with

contagieux, -euse [kɔ̃taʒjø, jøz] adj infectious; (par le contact) contagious

contaminer [kɔ̃tamine] vt to contaminate

conte [kɔ̃t] nm tale; **~ de fées** fairy tale

contempler [kɔ̃tɑ̃ple] vt to contemplate, gaze at

contemporain, e [kɔ̃tɑ̃pɔʀɛ̃, ɛn] adj, nm/f contemporary

contenance [kɔ̃t(ə)nɑ̃s] nf (d'un récipient) capacity; (attitude) bearing, attitude; **perdre ~** to lose one's composure

conteneur [kɔ̃t(ə)nœʀ] nm container

contenir [kɔ̃t(ə)niʀ] vt to contain; (avoir une capacité de) to hold; **se ~ vi** to contain o.s.

content, e [kɔ̃tɑ̃, ɑ̃t] adj pleased, glad; **~ de** pleased with; **contenter** vt to satisfy, please; **se contenter de** to content o.s. with

contentieux [kɔ̃tɑ̃sjø] nm (COMM) litigation; (service) litigation department

contenu [kɔ̃t(ə)ny] nm (d'un récipient) contents pl; (d'un texte) content

conter [kɔ̃te] vt to recount, relate

contestable [kɔ̃testabl] adj questionable

contestation [kɔ̃testasjɔ̃] nf (POL) protest

conteste [kɔ̃test]: **sans ~** adv unquestionably, indisputably; **contester** vt to question, contest ♦ vi (POL, gén) to protest, rebel (against established authority)

contexte [kɔ̃tekst] nm context

contigu, ë [kɔ̃tigy] adj: **~ (à)** adjacent (to)

continent [kɔ̃tinɑ̃] nm continent

continu, e [kɔ̃tiny] adj continuous; **faire la journée ~e** to work without taking a full lunch break; **(courant) ~** direct current, DC

continuel, le [kɔ̃tinɥɛl] adj (qui se répète) constant, continual; (continu) continuous

continuer [kɔ̃tinɥe] vt (travail, voyage etc) to continue (with), carry on (with), go on (with); (prolonger: alignement, rue) to continue ♦ vi (vie, bruit) to continue, go on; **~ à ou de faire** to go on ou continue doing

contorsionner [kɔ̃tɔʀsjɔne]: **se ~ vi** to contort o.s., writhe about

contour [kɔ̃tuʀ] nm outline, contour; **contourner** vt to go round; (difficulté) to get round

contraceptif, -ive [kɔ̃tʀaseptif, iv] adj, nm contraceptive; **contraception** nf contraception

contracté, e [kɔ̃tʀakte] adj tense

contracter [kɔ̃tʀakte] vt (muscle etc) to tense, contract; (maladie, dette) to contract; (assurance) to take out; **se ~ vi** (muscles) to contract

contractuel, le [kɔ̃tʀaktɥɛl] nm/f (agent) traffic warden

contradiction [kɔ̃tʀadiksjɔ̃] nf contradiction; **contradictoire** adj contradictory, conflicting

contraignant, e [kɔ̃tʀɛɲɑ̃, ɑ̃t] adj restricting

contraindre [kɔ̃tʀɛ̃dʀ] vt: **~ qn à faire** to compel sb to do; **contrainte** nf constraint

contraire [kɔ̃tʀɛʀ] adj, nm opposite; **~ à** contrary to; **au ~** on the contrary

contrarier [kɔ̃tʀaʀje] vt (personne: irriter) to annoy; (fig: projets) to thwart, frustrate; **contrariété** nf annoyance

contraste [kɔ̃tʀast] nm contrast

contrat [kɔ̃tʀa] nm contract; **~ de travail** employment contract

contravention [kɔ̃tʀavɑ̃sjɔ̃] nf parking ticket

contre [kɔ̃tʀ] prép against; (en échange) (in exchange) for; **par ~** on the other hand

contrebande [kɔ̃tʀəbɑ̃d] nf (trafic) contraband, smuggling; (marchandise) contraband, smuggled goods pl; **faire la ~ de** to smuggle; **contrebandier, -ière** nm/f smuggler

contrebas [kɔ̃tʀəba]: **en ~** adv (down) below

contrebasse [kɔ̃tʀəbas] nf (double) bass

contre...: **contrecarrer** vt to thwart; **contrecœur**: **à contrecœur** adv (be)grudgingly, reluctantly; **contrecoup** nm repercussions pl; **contredire** vt (personne) to contradict; (faits) to refute

contrée [kɔ̃tʀe] nf (région) region; (pays) land

contrefaçon [kɔ̃tʀəfasɔ̃] nf forgery

contrefaire [kɔ̃tʀəfɛʀ] vt (document, signature) to forge, counterfeit

contre...: **contre-indication** (pl contre-indications) nf (MÉD) contra-indication; **"contre-indication en cas d'eczéma"** "should not be used by people with eczema"; **contre-indiqué, e** adj (MÉD) contra-indicated; (déconseillé) unadvisable, ill-advised; **contre-jour**: **à contre-jour** adv against the sunlight

contremaître [kɔ̃tʀəmɛtʀ] nm foreman

contrepartie [kɔ̃tʀəpaʀti] nf: **en ~** in return

contre-pied [kɔ̃tʀəpje] nm: **prendre le ~~ de** (opinion) to take the opposing view of; (action) to take the opposite course to

contre-plaqué [kɔ̃tʀəplake] nm plywood

contrepoids [kɔ̃tʀəpwa] nm counterweight, counterbalance

contrepoison [kɔ̃tʀəpwazɔ̃] nm antidote

contrer [kɔ̃tʀe] vt to counter

contresens [kɔ̃tʀəsɑ̃s] nm (erreur) misinterpretation; (de traduction) mistranslation; **à ~** the wrong way

contretemps [kɔ̃tʀətɑ̃] nm hitch; **à ~** (fig) at an inopportune moment

contrevenir [kɔ̃tʀəv(ə)niʀ]: **~ à** vt to contravene

contribuable [kɔ̃tʀibɥabl] nm/f taxpayer

contribuer [kɔ̃tʀibɥe]: **~ à** vt to contribute towards; **contribution** nf contribution; **contributions directes/indirectes** direct/indirect taxation; **mettre à contribution** to call upon

contrôle [kɔ̃tʀol] nm checking no pl, check; (des prix) monitoring, control; (test) test, examination; **perdre le ~ de** (véhicule) to lose control of; **~ continu** (SCOL) continuous assessment; **~ d'identité** identity check

contrôler [kɔ̃tʀole] vt (*vérifier*) to check; (*surveiller: opérations*) to supervise; (: *prix*) to monitor, control; (*maîtriser: COMM: firme*) to control; **se ~** vi to control o.s.; **contrôleur, -euse** nm/f (*de train*) (ticket) inspector; (*de bus*) (bus) conductor(-tress)

contrordre [kɔ̃tʀɔʀdʀ] nm: **sauf ~** unless otherwise directed

controversé, e [kɔ̃tʀɔvɛʀse] adj (*personnage, question*) controversial

contusion [kɔ̃tyzjɔ̃] nf bruise, contusion

convaincre [kɔ̃vɛ̃kʀ] vt: **~ qn (de qch)** to convince sb (of sth); **~ qn (de faire)** to persuade sb (to do)

convalescence [kɔ̃valesɑ̃s] nf convalescence

convenable [kɔ̃vnabl] adj suitable; (*assez bon, respectable*) decent

convenance [kɔ̃vnɑ̃s] nf: **à ma/votre ~** to my/your liking; **~s** nfpl (*normes sociales*) proprieties

convenir [kɔ̃vniʀ] vi to be suitable; **~ à** to suit; **~ de** (*bien-fondé de qch*) to admit (to), acknowledge; (*date, somme etc*) to agree upon; **~ que** (*admettre*) to admit that; **~ de faire** to agree to do

convention [kɔ̃vɑ̃sjɔ̃] nf convention; **~s** nfpl (*convenances*) convention sg; **~ collective** (*ÉCON*) collective agreement; **conventionné, e** adj (*ADMIN*) applying charges laid down by the state

convenu, e [kɔ̃vny] pp de **convenir** ♦ adj agreed

conversation [kɔ̃vɛʀsasjɔ̃] nf conversation

convertir [kɔ̃vɛʀtiʀ] vt: **~ qn (à)** to convert sb (to); **se ~ (à)** to be converted (to); **~ qch en** to convert sth into

conviction [kɔ̃viksjɔ̃] nf conviction

convienne etc [kɔ̃vjɛn] vb voir **convenir**

convier [kɔ̃vje] vt: **~ qn à** (*dîner etc*) to (cordially) invite sb to

convive [kɔ̃viv] nm/f guest (*at table*)

convivial, e, -aux [kɔ̃vivjal, jo] adj (*INFORM*) user-friendly

convocation [kɔ̃vɔkasjɔ̃] nf (*document*) notification to attend; (: *JUR*) summons sg

convoi [kɔ̃vwa] nm convoy; (*train*) train

convoiter [kɔ̃vwate] vt to covet

convoquer [kɔ̃vɔke] vt (*assemblée*) to convene; (*subordonné*) to summon; (*candidat*) to ask to attend

convoyeur [kɔ̃vwajœʀ] nm: **~ de fonds** security guard

coopération [kɔɔpeʀasjɔ̃] nf co-operation; (*ADMIN*): **la C~** ≈ Voluntary Service Overseas (*BRIT*), ~ Peace Corps (*US*)

coopérer [kɔɔpeʀe] vi: **~ (à)** to co-operate (in)

coordonnées [kɔɔʀdɔne] nfpl: **donnez-moi vos ~** (*fam*) can I have your details please?

coordonner [kɔɔʀdɔne] vt to coordinate

copain [kɔpɛ̃] (*fam*) nm mate, pal; (*petit ami*) boyfriend

copeau, x [kɔpo] nm shaving

copie [kɔpi] nf copy; (*SCOL*) script, paper; **copier** vt, vi to copy; **copier sur** to copy from; **copieur** nm (photo)copier

copieux, -euse [kɔpjø, jøz] adj copious

copine [kɔpin] (*fam*) nf mate, pal; (*petite amie*) girlfriend

copropriété [kɔpʀɔpʀijete] nf co-ownership, joint ownership

coq [kɔk] nm cock, rooster; **coq-à-l'âne** nm inv abrupt change of subject

coque [kɔk] nf (*de noix, mollusque*) shell; (*de bateau*) hull; **à la ~** (*CULIN*) (soft-)boiled

coquelicot [kɔkliko] nm poppy

coqueluche [kɔklyʃ] nf whooping-cough

coquet, te [kɔkɛ, ɛt] adj appearance-conscious, (*logement*) smart, charming

coquetier [kɔk(ə)tje] nm egg-cup

coquillage [kɔkijaʒ] nm (*mollusque*) shellfish inv; (*coquille*) shell

coquille [kɔkij] nf shell; (*TYPO*) misprint; **~ St Jacques** scallop

coquin, e [kɔkɛ̃, in] adj mischievous, roguish; (*polisson*) naughty

cor [kɔʀ] nm (*MUS*) horn; (*MÉD*): **~ (au pied)** corn

corail, -aux [kɔʀaj, o] nm coral no pl

Coran [kɔʀɑ̃] nm: **le ~** the Koran

corbeau, x [kɔʀbo] nm crow

corbeille [kɔʀbɛj] nf basket; **~ à papier** waste paper basket ou bin

corbillard [kɔʀbijaʀ] nm hearse

corde [kɔʀd] nf rope; (*de violon, raquette*) string; **usé jusqu'à la ~** threadbare; **~ à linge** washing ou clothes line; **~ à sauter** skipping rope; **~s vocales** vocal cords

cordée [kɔʀde] nf (*d'alpinistes*) rope, roped party

cordialement [kɔʀdjalmɑ̃] adv (*formule épistolaire*) (kind) regards

cordon [kɔʀdɔ̃] nm cord, string; **~ ombilical** umbilical cord; **~ sanitaire/de police** sanitary/police cordon

cordonnerie [kɔʀdɔnʀi] nf shoe repairer's (shop); **cordonnier** nm shoe repairer

Corée [kɔʀe] nf: **la ~ du Sud/du Nord** South/North Korea

coriace [kɔʀjas] adj tough

corne [kɔʀn] nf horn; (*de cerf*) antler

cornée [kɔʀne] nf cornea

corneille [kɔʀnɛj] nf crow

cornemuse [kɔʀnəmyz] nf bagpipes pl

cornet [kɔʀnɛ] nm (paper) cone; (*de glace*) cornet, cone

corniche [kɔʀniʃ] nf (*route*) coast road

cornichon [kɔʀniʃɔ̃] nm gherkin

Cornouailles [kɔʀnwaj] nf Cornwall

corporation [kɔʀpɔʀasjɔ̃] nf corporate body

corporel, le [kɔʀpɔʀɛl] adj bodily; (punition) corporal

corps [kɔʀ] nm body; **à ~ perdu** headlong; **prendre ~** to take shape; **~ à ~** ♦ adv hand-to-hand ♦ nm clinch; **le ~ électoral** the electorate; **le ~ enseignant** the teaching profession

corpulent, e [kɔʀpylɑ̃, ɑ̃t] adj stout

correct, e [kɔʀɛkt] adj correct; (fam: acceptable: salaire, hôtel) reasonable, decent; **correcteur, -trice** nm/f (SCOL) examiner; **correction** nf (voir corriger) correction; (voir correct) correctness; (coups) thrashing; **correctionnel, le** adj (JUR): **tribunal correctionnel** ≈ criminal court

correspondance [kɔʀɛspɔ̃dɑ̃s] nf correspondence; (de train, d'avion) connection; **de chaque ~** correspondence course; **vente par ~** mail-order business

correspondant, e [kɔʀɛspɔ̃dɑ̃, ɑ̃t] nm/f correspondent; (TÉL) person phoning (ou being phoned)

correspondre [kɔʀɛspɔ̃dʀ] vi to correspond, tally; **~ à** to correspond to; **~ avec qn** to correspond with sb

corrida [kɔʀida] nf bullfight

corridor [kɔʀidɔʀ] nm corridor

corrigé [kɔʀiʒe] nm (SCOL: d'exercice) correct version

corriger [kɔʀiʒe] vt (devoir) to correct; (punir) to thrash; **~ qn de** (défaut) to cure sb of

corroborer [kɔʀɔbɔʀe] vt to corroborate

corrompre [kɔʀɔ̃pʀ] vt to corrupt; (acheter: témoin etc) to bribe

corruption [kɔʀypsjɔ̃] nf corruption; (de témoins) bribery

corsage [kɔʀsaʒ] nm bodice; (chemisier) blouse

corsaire [kɔʀsɛʀ] nm pirate

corse [kɔʀs] adj, nm/f Corsican ♦ nf: **la C~** Corsica

corsé, e [kɔʀse] adj (café) full-flavoured; (sauce) spicy; (problème) tough

corset [kɔʀsɛ] nm corset

cortège [kɔʀtɛʒ] nm procession

cortisone [kɔʀtizɔn] nf cortisone

corvée [kɔʀve] nf chore, drudgery no pl

cosmétique [kɔsmetik] nm beauty care product

cosmopolite [kɔsmɔpɔlit] adj cosmopolitan

cossu, e [kɔsy] adj (maison) opulent(-looking)

costaud, e [kɔsto, od] (fam) adj strong, sturdy

costume [kɔstym] nm (d'homme) suit; (de théâtre) costume; **costumé, e** adj dressed up; **bal costumé** fancy dress ball

cote [kɔt] nf (en Bourse) quotation; **~ d'alerte** danger ou flood level

côte [kot] nf (rivage) coast(line); (pente) hill; (ANAT) rib; (d'un tricot, tissu) rib, ribbing no pl; **~ à ~** side by side; **la C~ (d'Azur)** the (French) Riviera

coté, e [kɔte] adj: **être bien ~** to be highly rated

côté [kote] nm (gén) side; (direction) way, direction; **de chaque ~ (de)** on each side (of); **de tous les ~s** from all directions; **de quel ~ est-il parti?** which way did he go?; **de ce/de l'autre ~** this/the other way; **du ~ de** (provenance) from; (direction) towards; (proximité) near; **de ~** (regarder) sideways; (mettre) aside; **mettre de l'argent de ~** to save some money; **à ~** (right) nearby; (voisins) next door; **à ~ de** beside, next to; (en comparaison) compared to; **être aux ~s de** to be by the side of

coteau, x [kɔto] nm hill

côtelette [kotlɛt] nf chop

côtier, -ière [kotje, jɛʀ] adj coastal

cotisation [kɔtizasjɔ̃] nf subscription, dues pl; (pour une pension) contributions pl

cotiser [kɔtize] vi: **~ (à)** to pay contributions (to); **se ~** vi to club together

coton [kɔtɔ̃] nm cotton; **~ hydrophile** cotton wool (BRIT), absorbent cotton (US); **Coton-Tige** ® nm cotton bud

côtoyer [kotwaje] vt (fréquenter) to rub shoulders with

cou [ku] nm neck

couchant [kuʃɑ̃] adj: **soleil ~** setting sun

couche [kuʃ] nf layer; (de peinture, vernis) coat; (de bébé) nappy (BRIT), diaper (US); **~ d'ozone** ozone layer; **~s sociales** social levels ou strata

couché, e [kuʃe] adj lying down; (au lit) in bed

coucher [kuʃe] nm (du soleil) setting ♦ vt (personne) to put to bed; (: loger) to put up; (objet) to lay on its side ♦ vi to sleep; **se ~** vi (pour dormir) to go to bed; (pour se reposer) to lie down; (soleil) to set; **~ de soleil** sunset

couchette [kuʃɛt] nf couchette; (pour voyageur, sur bateau) berth

coucou [kuku] nm cuckoo

coude [kud] nm (ANAT) elbow; (de tuyau, de la route) bend; **~ à ~** shoulder to shoulder, side by side

coudre [kudʀ] vt (bouton) to sew on ♦ vi to sew

couenne [kwan] nf (de lard) rind

couette [kwɛt] nf duvet, quilt; **~s** nfpl (cheveux) bunches

couffin [kufɛ̃] nm Moses basket

couler [kule] vi to flow, run; (fuir: stylo,

récipient) to leak; (*nez*) to run; (*sombrer: bateau*) to sink ♦ *vt* (*cloche, sculpture*) to cast; (*bateau*) to sink; (*faire échouer: personne*) to bring down

couleur [kulœʀ] *nf* colour (BRIT), color (US); (CARTES) suit; **film/télévision en ~s** colo(u)r film/television

couleuvre [kulœvʀ] *nf* grass snake

coulisse [kulis] *nf*: **~s** ♦ *nfpl* (THÉÂTRE) wings; (*fig*): **dans les ~s** behind the scenes; **coulisser** *vi* to slide, run

couloir [kulwaʀ] *nm* corridor, passage; (*d'avion*) aisle; (*de bus*) gangway; **~ aérien/de navigation** air/shipping lane

coup [ku] *nm* (*heurt, choc*) knock; (*affectif*) blow, shock; (*agressif*) blow; (*avec arme à feu*) shot; (*de l'horloge*) stroke; (*tennis, golf*) stroke; (*boxe*) blow; (*fam: fois*) time; **~ de coude** nudge (with the elbow); **~ de tonnerre** clap of thunder; **~ de sonnette** ring of the bell; **donner un ~ de balai** to give the floor a sweep; **boire un ~** (*fam*) to have a drink; **être dans le ~** to be in on it; **du ~ ...** as a result; **d'un seul ~** (*subitement*) suddenly; (*à la fois*) at one go; **du premier ~** first time; **du même ~** at the same time; **à tous les ~s** (*fam*) every time; **tenir le ~** to hold out; **après ~** afterwards; **à ~ sûr** definitely, without fail; **~ sur ~** in quick succession; **sur le ~** outright; **sous le ~ de** (*surprise etc*) under the influence of; **en ~ de vent** in a tearing hurry; **~ de chance** stroke of luck; **~ de couteau** stab (of a knife); **~ d'État** coup; **~ de feu** shot; **~ de fil** (*fam*) phone call; **~ de frein** (sharp) braking *no pl*; **~ de main**: **donner un ~ de main à qn** to give sb a (helping) hand; **~ d'œil** glance; **~ de pied** kick; **~ de poing** punch; **~ de soleil** sunburn *no pl*; **~ de téléphone** phone call; **~ de tête** (*fig*) (sudden) impulse

coupable [kupabl] *adj* guilty ♦ *nm/f* (*gén*) culprit; (JUR) guilty party

coupe [kup] *nf* (*verre*) goblet; (*à fruits*) dish; (SPORT) cup; (*de cheveux, de vêtement*) cut; (*graphique, plan*) (cross) section

coupe-papier [kuppapje] *nm inv* paper knife

couper [kupe] *vt* to cut; (*retrancher*) to cut (out); (*route, courant*) to cut off; (*appétit*) to take away; (*vin à table*) to dilute ♦ *vi* to cut; (*prendre un raccourci*) to take a short-cut; **se ~** *vi* (*se blesser*) to cut o.s.; **~ la parole à qn** to cut sb short

couple [kupl] *nm* couple

couplet [kuple] *nm* verse

coupole [kupɔl] *nf* dome

coupon [kupɔ̃] *nm* (*ticket*) coupon; (*reste de tissu*) remnant; **coupon-réponse** *nm* reply coupon

coupure [kupyʀ] *nf* cut; (*billet de banque*) note; (*de journal*) cutting; **~ de courant** power cut

cour [kuʀ] *nf* (*de ferme, jardin*) (court)yard; (*d'immeuble*) back yard; (JUR, royale) court; **faire la ~ à qn** to court sb; **~ d'assises** court of assizes; **~ de récréation** playground; **~ martiale** court-martial

courage [kuʀaʒ] *nm* courage, bravery; **courageux, -euse** *adj* brave, courageous

couramment [kuʀamɑ̃] *adv* commonly; (*parler*) fluently

courant, e [kuʀɑ̃, ɑ̃t] *adj* (*fréquent*) common; (COMM, gén: normal) standard; (*en cours*) current ♦ *nm* current; (*fig*) movement; (*: d'opinion*) trend; **être au ~ (de)** (*fait, nouvelle*) to know (about); **mettre qn au ~ (de)** to tell sb (about); (*nouveau travail etc*) to teach sb the basics (of); **se tenir au ~ (de)** (*techniques etc*) to keep o.s. up-to-date (on); **dans le ~ de** (*pendant*) in the course of; **le 10 ~** (COMM) the 10th inst.; **~ d'air** draught; **~ électrique** electric(ity) current, power

courbature [kuʀbatyʀ] *nf* ache

courbe [kuʀb] *adj* curved ♦ *nf* curve; **courber** *vt* to bend; **se courber** *vi* (*personne*) to bend (down), stoop

coureur, -euse [kuʀœʀ, øz] *nm/f* (SPORT) runner (*ou* driver); (*péj*) womanizer manhunter; **~ automobile** racing driver

courge [kuʀʒ] *nf* (CULIN) marrow; **courgette** *nf* courgette (BRIT), zucchini (US)

courir [kuʀiʀ] *vi* to run ♦ *vt* (SPORT: épreuve) to compete in; (*risque*) to run; (*danger*) to face; **~ les magasins** to go round the shops; **le bruit court que** the rumour is going round that

couronne [kuʀɔn] *nf* crown; (*de fleurs*) wreath, circlet

courons *etc* [kuʀɔ̃] *vb voir* **courir**

courrier [kuʀje] *nm* mail, post; (*lettres à écrire*) letters *pl*; **~ électronique** E-mail

courroie [kuʀwa] *nf* strap; (TECH) belt

courrons *etc* [kuʀɔ̃] *vb voir* **courir**

cours [kuʀ] *nm* (*leçon*) class; (*: particulier*) lesson; (*série de leçons, cheminement*) course; (*écoulement*) flow; (COMM: de devises) rate; (*: de denrées*) price; **donner libre ~ à** to give free expression to; **avoir ~** (SCOL) to have a class *ou* lecture; **en ~** (*année*) current; (*travaux*) in progress; **en ~ de route** on the way; **au ~ de** in the course of, during; **~ d'eau** waterway; **~ du soir** night school; **~ intensif** crash course

course [kuʀs] *nf* running; (SPORT: épreuve) race; (*d'un taxi*) journey, trip; (*commission*) errand; **~s** *nfpl* (*achats*) shopping *sg*; **faire des ~s** to do some shopping

court, e [kuʀ, kuʀt(ə)] *adj* short ♦ *adv* short ♦ *nm*: **~ (de tennis)** (tennis) court; **à ~ de** short of; **prendre qn de ~** to catch sb unawares; **court-circuit** *nm* short-circuit

courtier, -ère [kuʀtje, jɛʀ] nm/f broker
courtiser [kuʀtize] vt to court, woo
courtois, e [kuʀtwa, waz] adj courteous;
courtoisie nf courtesy
couru, e [kuʀy] pp de **courir**
cousais etc [kuze] vb voir **coudre**
couscous [kuskus] nm couscous
cousin, e [kuzɛ̃, in] nm/f cousin
coussin [kusɛ̃] nm cushion
cousu, e [kuzy] pp de **coudre**
coût [ku] nm cost; **le ~ de la vie** the cost of
living; **coûtant** adj m: **au prix coûtant** at
cost price
couteau, x [kuto] nm knife
coûter [kute] vt, vi to cost; **combien ça coûte?**
how much is it?, what does it cost?; **coûte
que coûte** at all costs; **coûteux, -euse** adj
costly, expensive
coutume [kutym] nf custom
couture [kutyʀ] nf sewing; (profession)
dressmaking; (points) seam; **couturier** nm
fashion designer; **couturière** nf dressmaker
couvée [kuve] nf brood, clutch
couvent [kuvɑ̃] nm (de sœurs) convent; (de
frères) monastery
couver [kuve] vt to hatch; (maladie) to be
coming down with ♦ vi (feu) to smoulder;
(révolte) to be brewing
couvercle [kuvɛʀkl] nm lid; (de bombe
aérosol etc, qui se visse) cap, top
couvert, e [kuvɛʀ, ɛʀt] pp de **couvrir** ♦ adj
(ciel) overcast ♦ nm place setting; (place à
table) place; **~s** nmpl (ustensiles) cutlery sg;
~ de covered with ou in; **mettre le ~** to lay
the table
couverture [kuvɛʀtyʀ] nf blanket; (de livre,
assurance, fig) cover; (presse) coverage;
~ chauffante electric blanket
couveuse [kuvøz] nf (de maternité)
incubator
couvre-feu [kuvʀəfø] nm curfew
couvre-lit [kuvʀəli] nm bedspread
couvreur [kuvʀœʀ] nm roofer
couvrir [kuvʀiʀ] vt to cover; **se ~** vi
(s'habiller) to cover up; (se coiffer) to put on
one's hat; (ciel) to cloud over
cow-boy [kobɔj] nm cowboy
crabe [kʀɑb] nm crab
cracher [kʀaʃe] vi, vt to spit
crachin [kʀaʃɛ̃] nm drizzle
crack [kʀak] nm (fam: as) ace
craie [kʀɛ] nf chalk
craindre [kʀɛ̃dʀ] vt to fear, be afraid of; (être
sensible à: chaleur, froid) to be easily
damaged by
crainte [kʀɛ̃t] nf fear; **de ~ de/que** for fear of/
that; **craintif, -ive** adj timid
cramoisi, e [kʀamwazi] adj crimson
crampe [kʀɑ̃p] nf cramp

crampon [kʀɑ̃pɔ̃] nm (de chaussure de
football) stud; (de chaussure de course) spike;
(d'alpinisme) crampon; **cramponner** vb: **se
cramponner (à)** to hang ou cling on (to)
cran [kʀɑ̃] nm (entaille) notch; (de courroie)
hole; (fam: courage) guts pl; **~ d'arrêt** safety
catch
crâne [kʀɑn] nm skull
crâner [kʀɑne] (fam) vi to show off
crapaud [kʀapo] nm toad
crapule [kʀapyl] nf villain
craquement [kʀakmɑ̃] nm crack, snap; (du
plancher) creak, creaking no pl
craquer [kʀake] vi (bois, plancher) to creak;
(fil, branche) to snap; (couture) to come
apart; (fig: accusé) to break down; (: fam) to
crack up ♦ vt (allumette) to strike; **j'ai craqué**
(fam) I couldn't resist it
crasse [kʀas] nf grime, filth; **crasseux,
-euse** adj grimy, filthy
cravache [kʀavaʃ] nf (riding) crop
cravate [kʀavat] nf tie
crawl [kʀol] nm crawl; **dos ~é** backstroke
crayon [kʀɛjɔ̃] nm pencil; **~ à bille** ball-point
pen; **~ de couleur** crayon, colouring pencil;
crayon-feutre (pl crayons-feutres) nm felt(-
tip) pen
créancier, -ière [kʀeɑ̃sje, jɛʀ] nm/f creditor
création [kʀeasjɔ̃] nf creation
créature [kʀeatyʀ] nf creature
crèche [kʀɛʃ] nf (de Noël) crib; (garderie)
crèche, day nursery
crédit [kʀedi] nm (gén) credit; **~s** nmpl
(fonds) funds; **payer/acheter à ~** to pay/buy
on credit ou on easy terms; **faire ~ à qn** to
give sb credit; **créditer** vt: **créditer un
compte (de)** to credit an account (with)
crédule [kʀedyl] adj credulous, gullible
créer [kʀee] vt to create
crémaillère [kʀemajɛʀ] nf: **pendre la ~** to
have a house-warming party
crématoire [kʀematwaʀ] adj: **four ~**
crematorium
crème [kʀɛm] nf cream; (entremets) cream
dessert ♦ adj inv cream(-coloured); **un (café)
~ ≈** a white coffee; **~ anglaise** (egg) custard;
~ chantilly whipped cream; **~ fouettée
= crème chantilly**; **crémerie** nf dairy;
crémeux, -euse adj creamy
créneau, x [kʀeno] nm (de fortification)
crenel(le); (dans marché) gap, niche; (AUTO):
faire un ~ to reverse into a parking space
(between two cars alongside the kerb)
crêpe [kʀɛp] nf (galette) pancake ♦ nm (tissu)
crêpe; **crêpé, e** adj (cheveux) backcombed;
crêperie nf pancake shop ou restaurant
crépiter [kʀepite] vi (friture) to sputter,
splutter; (fire) to crackle
crépu, e [kʀepy] adj frizzy, fuzzy

crépuscule [krepyskyl] *nm* twilight, dusk

cresson [kresɔ̃] *nm* watercress

crête [krɛt] *nf* (*de coq*) comb; (*de vague, montagne*) crest

creuser [krøze] *vt* (*trou, tunnel*) to dig; (*sol*) to dig a hole in; (*fig*) to go (deeply) into; **ça creuse** that gives you a real appetite; **se ~ la cervelle** (*fam*) to rack one's brains

creux, -euse [krø, krøz] *adj* hollow ♦ *nm* hollow; **heures creuses** slack periods; (*électricité, téléphone*) off-peak periods; **avoir un ~** (*fam*) to be hungry

crevaison [krəvɛzɔ̃] *nf* puncture

crevasse [krəvas] *nf* (*dans le sol, la peau*) crack; (*de glacier*) crevasse

crevé, e [krəve] (*fam*) *adj* (*fatigué*) all in, exhausted

crever [krəve] *vt* (*ballon*) to burst ♦ *vi* (*pneu*) to burst; (*automobiliste*) to have a puncture (*BRIT*) ou a flat (tire) (*US*); (*fam*) to die

crevette [krəvɛt] *nf*: **~** (*rose*) prawn; **~ grise** shrimp

cri [kri] *nm* cry, shout; (*d'animal: spécifique*) cry, call; **c'est le dernier ~** (*fig*) it's the latest fashion

criant, e [krijɑ̃, krijɑ̃t] *adj* (*injustice*) glaring

criard, e [krijar, krijard] *adj* (*couleur*) garish, loud; (*voix*) yelling

crible [kribl] *nm* riddle; **passer qch au ~** (*fig*) to go over sth with a fine-tooth comb; **criblé, e** *adj*: **criblé de** riddled with; (*de dettes*) crippled with

cric [krik] *nm* (*AUTO*) jack

crier [krije] *vi* (*pour appeler*) to shout, cry (out), (*de douleur etc*) to scream, yell ♦ *vt* (*injure*) to shout (out), yell (out)

crime [krim] *nm* crime; (*meurtre*) murder; **criminel, le** *nm/f* criminal; (*assassin*) murderer

crin [krɛ̃] *nm* (*de cheval*) hair *no pl*

crinière [krinjɛr] *nf* mane

crique [krik] *nf* creek, inlet

criquet [krike] *nm* grasshopper

crise [kriz] *nf* crisis; (*MÉD*) attack; (: *d'épilepsie*) fit; **piquer une ~ de nerfs** to go hysterical; **~ cardiaque** heart attack; **~ de foie** bilious attack

crisper [krispe] *vt* (*poings*) to clench; **se ~ vi** (*visage*) to tense; (*personne*) to get tense

crisser [krise] *vi* (*neige*) to crunch; (*pneu*) to screech

cristal, -aux [kristal, o] *nm* crystal; **cristallin, e** *adj* crystal-clear

critère [kritɛr] *nm* criterion

critiquable [kritikabl] *adj* open to criticism

critique [kritik] *adj* critical ♦ *nm/f* (*de théâtre, musique*) critic ♦ *nf* criticism; (*THÉÂTRE etc*: *article*) review

critiquer [kritike] *vt* (*dénigrer*) to criticize;

(*évaluer*) to assess, examine (critically)

croasser [krɔase] *vi* to caw

Croatie [krɔasi] *nf* Croatia

croc [kro] *nm* (*dent*) fang; (*de boucher*) hook; **croc-en-jambe** *nm*: **faire un croc-en-jambe à qn** to trip sb up

croche [krɔʃ] *nf* (*MUS*) quaver (*BRIT*), eighth note (*US*); **croche-pied** *nm* = **croc-en-jambe**

crochet [krɔʃɛ] *nm* hook; (*détour*) detour; (*TRICOT: aiguille*) crochet hook; (: *technique*) crochet; **vivre aux ~s de qn** to live *ou* sponge off sb

crochu, e [krɔʃy] *adj* (*nez*) hooked; (*doigts*) claw-like

crocodile [krɔkɔdil] *nm* crocodile

croire [krwar] *vt* to believe; **se ~ fort** to think one is strong; **~ que** to believe *ou* think that; **~ à, ~ en** to believe in

croîs [krwa] *vb voir* **croître**

croisade [krwazad] *nf* crusade

croisé, e [krwaze] *adj* (*veste*) doublebreasted

croisement [krwazmɑ̃] *nm* (*carrefour*) crossroads *sg*; (*BIO*) crossing; (: *résultat*) crossbreed

croiser [krwaze] *vt* (*personne, voiture*) to pass; (*route*) to cross, cut across; (*BIO*) to cross; **se ~ vi** (*personnes, véhicules*) to pass each other; (*routes, lettres*) to cross; (*regards*) to meet; **~ les jambes/bras** to cross one's legs/fold one's arms

croisière [krwazjɛr] *nf* cruise

croissance [krwasɑ̃s] *nf* growth

croissant [krwasɑ̃] *nm* (*à manger*) croissant; (*motif*) crescent

croître [krwatr] *vi* to grow

croix [krwa] *nf* cross; **~ gammée** swastika; **la C~ Rouge** the Red Cross

croque-monsieur [krɔkməsjø] *nm inv* toasted ham and cheese sandwich

croquer [krɔke] *vt* (*manger*) to crunch; (: *fruit*) to munch; (*dessiner*) to sketch; **chocolat à ~** plain dessert chocolate

croquis [krɔki] *nm* sketch

cross [krɔs] *nm*: **faire du ~** (*à pied*) to do cross-country running

crosse [krɔs] *nf* (*de fusil*) butt; (*de revolver*) grip

crotte [krɔt] *nf* droppings *pl*; **crotté, e** *adj* muddy, mucky; **crottin** *nm* dung, manure; (*fromage*) (small round) cheese (*made of goat's milk*)

crouler [krule] *vi* (*s'effondrer*) to collapse; (*être délabré*) to be crumbling

croupe [krup] *nf* rump; **en ~** pillion

croupir [krupir] *vi* to stagnate

croustillant, e [krustijɑ̃, ɑ̃t] *adj* crisp

croûte [krut] *nf* crust; (*du fromage*) rind; (*MÉD*) scab; **en ~** (*CULIN*) in pastry

croûton [krut5] nm (CULIN) crouton; (bout du pain) crust, heel

croyable [krwajabl] adj credible

croyant, e [krwajɑ̃, ɑ̃t] nm/f believer

CRS sigle fpl (= Compagnies républicaines de sécurité) state security police force ♦ sigle m member of the CRS

cru, e [kry] pp de croire ♦ adj (non cuit) raw; (lumière, couleur) harsh; (paroles) crude ♦ nm (vignoble) vineyard; (vin) wine; **un grand ~** a great vintage; **jambon ~** Parma ham

crû [kry] pp de croître

cruauté [kryote] nf cruelty

cruche [kryʃ] nf pitcher, jug

crucifix [krysifi] nm crucifix; **crucifixion** nf crucifixion

crudités [krydite] nfpl (CULIN) salads

crue [kry] nf (inondation) flood

cruel, le [kryel] adj cruel

crus etc [kry] vb voir croire; croître

crûs etc [kry] vb voir croître

crustacés [krystase] nmpl shellfish

Cuba [kyba] nf Cuba; **cubain, e** adj Cuban ♦ nm/f: **Cubain, e** Cuban

cube [kyb] nm cube; (jouet) brick; **mètre ~** cubic metre; **2 au ~** 2 cubed

cueillette [kœjet] nf picking; (quantité) crop, harvest

cueillir [kœjir] vt (fruits, fleurs) to pick, gather; (fig) to catch

cuiller [kɥijɛr], **cuillère** [kɥijɛr] nf spoon; **~ à café** coffee spoon; (CULIN) teaspoonful; **~ à soupe** soup-spoon; (CULIN) tablespoonful; **cuillerée** nf spoonful

cuir [kɥir] nm leather; **~ chevelu** scalp

cuire [kɥir] vt (aliments) to cook; (au four) to bake ♦ vi to cook; **bien cuit** (viande) well done; **trop cuit** overdone

cuisant, e [kɥizɑ̃, ɑ̃t] adj (douleur) stinging; (fig: souvenir, échec) bitter

cuisine [kɥizin] nf (pièce) kitchen; (art culinaire) cookery, cooking; (nourriture) cooking, food; **faire la ~** to cook; **cuisiné, e** adj: **plat cuisiné** ready-made meal ou dish; **cuisiner** vt to cook; (fam) to grill ♦ vi to cook; **cuisinier, -ière** nm/f cook; **cuisinière** nf (poêle) cooker

cuisse [kɥis] nf thigh; (CULIN) leg

cuisson [kɥis5] nf cooking

cuit, e [kɥi, kɥit] pp de cuire

cuivre [kɥivr] nm copper; **les ~s** (MUS) the brass

cul [ky] (fam!) nm arse (!)

culbute [kylbyt] nf somersault; (accidentelle) tumble, fall

culminant, e [kylminɑ̃, ɑ̃t] adj: **point ~** highest point

culminer [kylmine] vi to reach its highest point

culot [kylo] (fam) nm (effronterie) cheek

culotte [kylɔt] nf (de femme) knickers pl (BRIT), panties pl

culpabilité [kylpabilite] nf guilt

culte [kylt] nm (religion) religion; (hommage, vénération) worship; (protestant) service

cultivateur, -trice [kyltivatœr, tris] nm/f farmer

cultivé, e [kyltive] adj (personne) cultured, cultivated

cultiver [kyltive] vt to cultivate; (légumes) to grow, cultivate

culture [kyltyr] nf cultivation; (connaissances etc) culture; **les ~s intensives** intensive farming; **~ physique** physical training; **culturel, le** adj cultural; **culturisme** nm body-building

cumin [kymɛ̃] nm cumin

cumuler [kymyle] vt (emplois) to hold concurrently; (salaires) to draw concurrently

cupide [kypid] adj greedy, grasping

cure [kyr] nf (MÉD) course of treatment

curé [kyre] nm parish priest

cure-dent [kyrdɑ̃] nm toothpick

cure-pipe [kyrpip] nm pipe cleaner

curer [kyre] vt to clean out

curieusement [kyrjøzmɑ̃] adv curiously

curieux, -euse [kyrjø, jøz] adj (indiscret) curious, inquisitive; (étrange) strange, curious ♦ nmpl (badauds) onlookers; **curiosité** nf curiosity; (site) unusual feature

curriculum vitae [kyrikylɔmvite] nm inv curriculum vitae

curseur [kyrsœr] nm (INFORM) cursor

cutané, e [kytane] adj skin

cuti-réaction [kytireaksj5] nf (MÉD) skin-test

cuve [kyv] nf vat; (à mazout etc) tank

cuvée [kyve] nf vintage

cuvette [kyvet] nf (récipient) bowl, basin; (GÉO) basin

CV sigle m (AUTO) = cheval vapeur; (COMM) = curriculum vitae

cyanure [sjanyr] nm cyanide

cyclable [siklabl] adj: **piste ~** cycle track

cycle [sikl] nm cycle; **cyclisme** nm cycling; **cycliste** nm/f cyclist ♦ adj cycle cpd; **coureur cycliste** racing cyclist

cyclomoteur [siklomotœr] nm moped

cyclone [siklon] nm hurricane

cygne [siɲ] nm swan

cylindre [silɛ̃dr] nm cylinder; **cylindrée** nf (AUTO) (cubic) capacity

cymbale [sɛ̃bal] nf cymbal

cynique [sinik] adj cynical

cystite [sistit] nf cystitis

D, d

d' [d] *prép voir de*
dactylo [daktilo] *nf (aussi:* ~**graphe**) typist; *(aussi:* ~**graphie**) typing; **dactylographier** *vt* to type (out)
dada [dada] *nm* hobby-horse
daigner [dɛɲe] *vt* to deign
daim [dɛ̃] *nm (fallow)* deer *inv; (cuir suédé)* suede
dalle [dal] *nf* paving stone, slab
daltonien, ne [daltɔnjɛ̃, jɛn] *adj* colour-blind
dam [dã] *nm:* **au grand ~ de** much to the detriment *(ou* annoyance) of
dame [dam] *nf* lady; *(CARTES, ÉCHECS)* queen; **~s** *nfpl (jeu)* draughts *sg (BRIT),* checkers *sg (US)*
damner [dane] *vt* to damn
dancing [dɑ̃siŋ] *nm* dance hall
Danemark [danmark] *nm* Denmark
danger [dɑ̃ʒe] *nm* danger, **dangereux, -euse** *adj* dangerous
danois, e [danwa, waz] *adj* Danish ♦ *nm/f:* D~, e Dane ♦ *nm (LING)* Danish

dans [dã] *prép* **1** *(position)* in; *(à l'intérieur de)* inside; **c'est dans le tiroir/le salon** it's in the drawer/lounge; **dans la boîte** in *ou* inside the box; **marcher dans la ville** to walk about the town
2 *(direction)* into; **elle a couru dans le salon** she ran into the lounge
3 *(provenance)* out of, from; **je l'ai pris dans le tiroir/salon** I took it out of *ou* from the drawer/lounge; **boire dans un verre** to drink out of *ou* from a glass
4 *(temps)* in; **dans 2 mois** in 2 months, in 2 months' time
5 *(approximation)* about; **dans les 20 F** about 20F

danse [dãs] *nf:* **la ~** dancing; **une ~** a dance; **la ~ classique** ballet; **danser** *vi, vt* to dance; **danseur, -euse** *nm/f* ballet dancer; *(au bal etc)* dancer; *(: cavalier)* partner
dard [dar] *nm (d'animal)* sting
date [dat] *nf* date; **de longue ~** longstanding; **~ de naissance** date of birth; **~ de péremption** expiry date; **~ limite** deadline; **dater** *vt, vi* to date; **dater de** to date from; **à dater de** (as) from
datte [dat] *nf* date
dauphin [dofɛ̃] *nm (ZOOL)* dolphin
davantage [davɑ̃taʒ] *adv* more; *(plus longtemps)* longer; **~ de** more

de, d' [də] *(de + le =* **du,** *de + les =* **des**) *prép*
1 *(appartenance)* of; **le toit de la maison** the roof of the house; **la voiture d'Elisabeth/de mes parents** Elizabeth's/my parents' car
2 *(provenance)* from; **il vient de Londres** he comes from London; **elle est sortie du cinéma** she came out of the cinema
3 *(caractérisation, mesure):* **un mur de brique/bureau d'acajou** a brick wall/mahogany desk; **un billet de 50 F** a 50F note; **une pièce de 2 m de large** *ou* **large de 2 m** a room 2m wide, a 2m-wide room; **un bébé de 10 mois** a 10 month old baby; **12 mois de crédit/travail** 12 months' credit/work; **augmenter de 10 F** to increase by 10F; **de 14 à 18** from 14 to 18
♦ *dét* **1** *(phrases affirmatives)* some *(souvent omis);* **du vin, de l'eau, des pommes** (some) wine, (some) water, (some) apples; **des enfants sont venus** some children came; **pendant des mois** for months
2 *(phrases interrogatives et négatives)* any, a-t-il du vin? has he got any wine?; **il n'a pas de pommes/d'enfants** he hasn't (got) any apples/children, he has no apples/children

dé [de] *nm (à jouer)* die *ou* dice; *(aussi:* ~ **à coudre**) thimble
dealer [dilœr] *(fam) nm (drug)* pusher
déambuler [deɑ̃byle] *vi* to stroll about
débâcle [debakl] *nf* rout
déballer [debale] *vt* to unpack
débandade [debɑ̃dad] *nf (dispersion)* scattering
débarbouiller [debarbuje] *vt* to wash; **se ~** *vi* to wash (one's face)
débarcadère [debarkadɛr] *nm* wharf
débardeur [debardœr] *nm (maillot)* tank top
débarquer [debarke] *vt* to unload, land ♦ *vi* to disembark; *(fig: fam)* to turn up
débarras [debara] *nm (pièce)* lumber room; *(placard)* junk cupboard; **bon ~!** good riddance!; **débarrasser** *vt* to clear; **se débarrasser de** *vt* to get rid of; **débarrasser qn de** *(vêtements, paquets)* to relieve sb of
débat [deba] *nm* discussion, debate; **débattre** *vt* to discuss, debate; **se débattre** *vi* to struggle
débaucher [debofe] *vt (licencier)* to lay off, dismiss; *(entraîner)* to lead astray, debauch
débile [debil] *(fam) adj (idiot)* dim-witted
débit [debi] *nm (d'un liquide, fleuve)* flow; *(d'un magasin)* turnover (of goods); *(élocution)* delivery; *(bancaire)* debit; **~ de boissons** drinking establishment; **~ de tabac** tobacconist's; **débiter** *vt (compte)* to debit;

(couper: bois, viande) to cut up; (péj: dire) to churn out; **débiteur, -trice** nm/f debtor ♦ adj in debit; (compte) debit cpd

déblayer [debleje] vt to clear

débloquer [deblɔke] vt (prix, crédits) to free

déboires [debwar] nmpl setbacks

déboiser [debwaze] vt to deforest

déboîter [debwate] vt (AUTO) to pull out; se ~ le genou etc to dislocate one's knee etc

débonnaire [debɔnɛR] adj easy-going, good-natured

débordé, e [debɔrde] adj: être ~ (de) (travail, demandes) to be snowed under (with)

déborder [debɔrde] vi to overflow; (lait etc) to boil over; ~ (de) qch (dépasser) to extend beyond sth

débouché [debuʃe] nm (pour vendre) outlet; (perspective d'emploi) opening

déboucher [debuʃe] vt (évier, tuyau etc) to unblock; (bouteille) to uncork ♦ vi: ~ de to emerge from; ~ sur (études) to lead on to

débourser [deburse] vt to pay out

déboussolé, e [debusɔle] (fam) adj disorientated

debout [d(ə)bu] adv: être ~ (personne) to be standing, stand; (: levé, éveillé) to be up; se mettre ~ to stand up; se tenir ~ to stand; ~! stand up!; (du lit) get up!; cette histoire ne tient pas ~ this story doesn't hold water

déboutonner [debutɔne] vt to undo, unbutton

débraillé, e [debraje] adj slovenly, untidy

débrancher [debrãʃe] vt to disconnect; (appareil électrique) to unplug

débrayage [debrejaʒ] nm (AUTO) clutch; **débrayer** vi (AUTO) to declutch; (cesser le travail) to stop work

débris [debri] nmpl fragments; des ~ de verre bits of glass

débrouillard, e [debrujar, ard] (fam) adj smart, resourceful

débrouiller [debruje] vt to disentangle, untangle; se ~ vi to manage; débrouillez-vous you'll have to sort things out yourself

début [deby] nm beginning, start; ~s nmpl (de carrière) début sg; ~ juin in early June; **débutant, e** nm/f beginner, novice; **débuter** vi to begin, start; (faire ses débuts) to start out

deçà [dəsa] : en ~ de prép this side of

décadence [dekadãs] nf decline

décaféiné, e [dekafeine] adj decaffeinated

décalage [dekalaʒ] nm gap; ~ horaire time difference

décaler [dekale] vt to shift

décalquer [dekalke] vt to trace

décamper [dekãpe] (fam) vi to clear out ou off

décaper [dekape] vt (surface peinte) to strip

décapiter [dekapite] vt to behead; (par accident) to decapitate

décapotable [dekapɔtabl] adj convertible

décapsuleur [dekapsylœr] nm bottle-opener

décarcasser [dekarkase]: se ~ (fam) vi to flog o.s. to death

décédé, e [desede] adj deceased

décéder [desede] vi to die

déceler [des(ə)le] vt (trouver) to discover, detect

décembre [desãbr] nm December

décemment [desamã] adv decently

décennie [deseni] nf decade

décent, e [desã, ãt] adj decent

déception [desɛpsjɔ̃] nf disappointment

décerner [deserne] vt to award

décès [desɛ] nm death

décevant, e [des(ə)vã, ãt] adj disappointing

décevoir [des(ə)vwar] vt to disappoint

déchaîner [deʃene] vt (violence) to unleash; (enthousiasme) to arouse; se ~ (tempête) to rage; (personne) to fly into a rage

déchanter [deʃãte] vi to become disillusioned

décharge [deʃarʒ] nf (dépôt d'ordures) rubbish tip ou dump; (électrique) electrical discharge; **décharger** vt (marchandise, véhicule) to unload; (tirer) to discharge; se **décharger** vi (batterie) to go flat; **décharger** qn de (responsabilité) to release sb from

décharné, e [deʃarne] adj emaciated

déchausser [deʃose] vt (skis) to take off; se ~ vi to take off one's shoes; (dent) to come ou work loose

déchéance [deʃeãs] nf (physique) degeneration; (morale) decay

déchet [deʃɛ] nm (reste) scrap; ~s nmpl (ordures) refuse sg, rubbish sg; ~s nucléaires nuclear waste

déchiffrer [deʃifre] vt to decipher

déchiqueter [deʃik(ə)te] vt to tear ou pull to pieces

déchirant, e [deʃirã, ãt] adj heart-rending

déchirement [deʃirmã] nm (chagrin) wrench, heartbreak; (gén pl: conflit) rift, split

déchirer [deʃire] vt to tear; (en morceaux) to tear up; (arracher) to tear out; (fig: conflit) to tear (apart); se ~ vi to tear, rip; se ~ un muscle to tear a muscle

déchirure [deʃiryr] nf (accroc) tear, rip; ~ musculaire torn muscle

déchoir [deʃwar] vi (personne) to lower o.s., demean o.s.

déchu, e [deʃy] adj (roi) deposed

décidé, e [deside] adj (personne, air) determined; c'est ~ it's decided; **décidément** adv really

décider [deside] vt: ~ **qch** to decide on sth; **se ~ (à faire)** to decide (to do), make up one's mind (to do); **se ~ pour** to decide on ou in favour of; ~ **de faire/que** to decide to do/that; ~ **qn (à faire qch)** to persuade sb (to do sth)

décimal, e, -aux [desimal, o] adj decimal; **décimale** nf decimal

décimètre [desimetʀ] nm decimetre

décisif, -ive [desizif, iv] adj decisive

décision [desizjɔ̃] nf decision

déclaration [deklaʀasjɔ̃] nf declaration; (discours: POL etc) statement; ~ **(d'impôts)** ≈ tax return

déclarer [deklaʀe] vt to declare; (décès, naissance) to register; **se ~** vi (feu) to break out

déclencher [deklɑ̃ʃe] vt (mécanisme etc) to release; (sonnerie) to set off; (attaque, grève) to launch; (provoquer) to trigger off; **se ~** vi (sonnerie) to go off

déclic [deklik] nm (bruit) click

décliner [dekline] vi to decline ♦ vt (invitation) to decline; (nom, adresse) to state

décocher [dekɔʃe] vt (coup de poing) to throw; (flèche, regard) to shoot

décoiffer [dekwafe] vt: ~ **qn** to mess up sb's hair; **je suis toute décoiffée** my hair is in a real mess

déçois etc [deswa] vb voir **décevoir**

décollage [dekɔlaʒ] nm (AVIAT) takeoff

décoller [dekɔle] vt to unstick ♦ vi (avion) to take off; **se ~** vi to come unstuck

décolleté, e [dekɔlte] adj low-cut ♦ nm low neck(line); (plongeant) cleavage

décolorer [dekɔlɔʀe]: **se ~** vi to fade; **se faire ~ les cheveux** to have one's hair bleached

décombres [dekɔ̃bʀ] nmpl rubble sg, debris sg

décommander [dekɔmɑ̃de] vt to cancel; **se ~** vi to cry off

décomposé, e [dekɔ̃poze] adj (pourri) decomposed; (visage) haggard, distorted

décompte [dekɔ̃t] nm deduction; (facture) detailed account

déconcerter [dekɔ̃sɛʀte] vt to disconcert, confound

déconfit, e [dekɔ̃fi, it] adj crestfallen

décongeler [dekɔ̃ʒ(ə)le] vt to thaw

déconner [dekɔne] (fam) vi to talk rubbish

déconseiller [dekɔ̃seje] vt: ~ **qch (à qn)** to advise (sb) against sth; **c'est déconseillé** it's not recommended

décontracté, e [dekɔ̃tʀakte] adj relaxed, laid-back (fam)

décontracter [dekɔ̃tʀakte]: **se ~** vi to relax

déconvenue [dekɔ̃v(ə)ny] nf disappointment

décor [dekɔʀ] nm décor; (paysage) scenery;

~s nmpl (THÉÂTRE) scenery sg, décor sg; (CINÉMA) set sg; **décorateur** nm (interior) decorator; **décoration** nf decoration; **décorer** vt to decorate

décortiquer [dekɔʀtike] vt to shell; (fig: texte) to dissect

découcher [dekuʃe] vi to spend the night away from home

découdre [dekudʀ]: **se ~** vi to come unstitched

découler [dekule] vi: ~ **de** to ensue ou follow from

découper [dekupe] vt (papier, tissu etc) to cut up; (viande) to carve; (article) to cut out; **se ~ sur** to stand out against

décourager [dekuʀaʒe] vt to discourage; **se ~** vi to lose heart, become discouraged

décousu, e [dekuzy] adj unstitched; (fig) disjointed, disconnected

découvert, e [dekuvɛʀ, ɛʀt] adj (tête) bare, uncovered; (lieu) open, exposed ♦ nm (bancaire) overdraft; **découverte** nf discovery; **faire la découverte de** to discover

découvrir [dekuvʀiʀ] vt to discover; (enlever ce qui couvre) to uncover; (dévoiler) to reveal; **se ~** vi (chapeau) to take off one's hat; (vêtement) to take something off; (ciel) to clear

décret [dekʀɛ] nm decree; **décréter** vt to decree

décrié, e [dekʀije] adj disparaged

décrire [dekʀiʀ] vt to describe

décrocher [dekʀɔʃe] vt (détacher) to take down; (téléphone) to take off the hook; (: pour répondre) to lift the receiver; (fam: contrat etc) to get, land ♦ vi (fam: abandonner) to drop out; (: cesser d'écouter) to switch off

décroître [dekʀwatʀ] vi to decrease, decline

décrypter [dekʀipte] vt to decipher

déçu, e [desy] pp de **décevoir**

décupler [dekyple] vt, vi to increase tenfold

dédaigner [dedɛɲe] vt to despise, scorn; (négliger) to disregard, spurn; **dédaigneux, -euse** adj scornful, disdainful; **dédain** nm scorn, disdain

dédale [dedal] nm maze

dedans [dədɑ̃] adv inside; (pas en plein air) indoors, inside ♦ nm inside; **au ~** inside

dédicacer [dedikase] vt: ~ **(à qn)** to sign (for sb), autograph (for sb)

dédier [dedje] vt to dedicate

dédire [dediʀ]: **se ~** vi to go back on one's word, retract

dédommagement [dedɔmaʒmɑ̃] nm compensation

dédommager [dedɔmaʒe] vt: ~ **qn (de)** to compensate sb (for)

dédouaner [dedwane] vt to clear through

customs

dédoubler [deduble] vt (classe, effectifs) to
split (into two)

déduire [deduir] vt: ~ **qch (de)** (ôter) to
deduct sth (from); (conclure) to deduce ou
infer sth (from)

déesse [dees] nf goddess

défaillance [defajɑ̃s] nf (syncope) blackout;
(fatigue) (sudden) weakness no pl;
(technique) fault, failure; ~ **cardiaque** heart
failure

défaillir [defajir] vi to feel faint; (mémoire
etc) to fail

défaire [defɛr] vt to undo; (installation) to
take down, dismantle; **se ~** vi to come
undone; **se ~ de** to get rid of

défait, e [defɛ, ɛt] adj (visage) haggard,
ravaged; **défaite** nf defeat

défalquer [defalke] vt to deduct

défaut [defo] nm (moral) fault, failing, defect;
(tissu) fault, flaw; (manque, carence) de
shortage of; **prendre qn en ~** to catch sb out;
faire ~ (manquer) to be lacking; **à ~ de** for
lack ou want of

défavorable [defavɔrabl] adj unfavourable
(BRIT), unfavorable (US)

défavoriser [defavɔrize] vt to put at a
disadvantage

défection [defɛksjɔ̃] nf defection, failure to
give support

défectueux, -euse [defɛktɥø, øz] adj
faulty, defective

défendre [defɑ̃dr] vt to defend; (interdire) to
forbid; **se ~** vi to defend o.s.; **~ à qn qch/de
faire** to forbid sb sth/to do; **il se défend** (fam:
se débrouille) he can hold his own; **~ de/
contre** (se protéger) to protect o.s. from/
against; **se ~ de** (se garder de) to refrain from

défense [defɑ̃s] nf defence; (d'éléphant etc)
tusk; **"~ de fumer"** "no smoking"

déférer [defere] vt (JUR) to refer; **~ à** (requête,
décision) to defer to

déferler [defɛrle] vi (vagues) to break; (fig:
foule) to surge

défi [defi] nm challenge; **lancer un ~ à qn** to
challenge sb; **sur un ton de ~** defiantly

déficit [defisit] nm (COMM) deficit;
déficitaire adj in deficit

défier [defje] vt (provoquer) to challenge;
(mort, autorité) to defy

défigurer [defigyre] vt to disfigure

défilé [defile] nm (GÉO) (narrow) gorge ou
pass; (soldats) parade; (manifestants)
procession, march; **~ de mode** fashion parade

défiler [defile] vi (troupes) to march past;
(sportifs) to parade; (manifestants) to march;
(visiteurs) to pour, stream; **se ~** vi: **il s'est
défilé** (fam) he wriggled out of it

définir [definir] vt to define

définitif, -ive [definitif, iv] adj (final) final,
definitive; (pour longtemps) permanent,
definitive; (refus) definite; **définitive** nf: **en
définitive** eventually; (somme toute) in fact;
définitivement adv (partir, s'installer) for
good

défoncer [defɔ̃se] vt (porte) to smash in ou
down; **se ~** (fam) vi (travailler) to work like a
dog; (drogué) to get high

déformer [defɔrme] vt to put out of shape;
(pensée, fait) to distort; **se ~** vi to lose its
shape

défouler [defule]: **se ~** vi to unwind, let off
steam

défraîchir [defrɛʃir]: **se ~** vi to fade

défricher [defriʃe] vt to clear (for cultivation)

défunt, e [defœ̃, œ̃t] nm/f deceased

dégagé, e [degaʒe] adj (route, ciel) clear; **sur
un ton ~** casually

dégagement [degaʒmɑ̃] nm: **voie de ~** slip
road

dégager [degaʒe] vt (exhaler) to give off;
(délivrer) to free, extricate; (désencombrer) to
clear; (isoler: idée, aspect) to bring out; **se ~**
vi (passage, ciel) to clear

dégarnir [degarnir] vt (vider) to empty,
clear; **se ~** vi (tempes, crâne) to go bald

dégâts [dega] nmpl damage sg

dégel [deʒɛl] nm thaw; **dégeler** vt to thaw
(out)

dégénérer [deʒenere] vi to degenerate

dégingandé, e [deʒɛ̃gɑ̃de] adj gangling

dégivrer [deʒivre] vt (frigo) to defrost;
(vitres) to de-ice

dégonflé, e [degɔ̃fle] adj (pneu) flat

dégonfler [degɔ̃fle] vt (pneu, ballon) to let
down, deflate; **se ~** vi (fam) to chicken out

dégouliner [deguline] vi to trickle, drip

dégourdi, e [degurdi] adj smart, resourceful

dégourdir [degurdir] vt: **se ~ les jambes** to
stretch one's legs (fig)

dégoût [degu] nm disgust, distaste;
dégoûtant, e adj disgusting; **dégoûté, e**
adj disgusted; **dégoûté de** sick of; **dégoûter**
vt to disgust; **dégoûter qn de qch** to put sb
off sth

dégrader [degrade] vt (MIL: officier) to
degrade; (abîmer) to damage, deface; **se ~** vi
(relations, situation) to deteriorate

dégrafer [degrafe] vt to unclip, unhook

degré [dəgre] nm degree

dégressif, -ive [degresif, iv] adj on a
decreasing scale

dégringoler [degrɛ̃gɔle] vi to tumble
(down)

dégrossir [degrosir] vt (fig: projet) to work
out roughly

déguenillé, e [deg(ə)nije] adj ragged,
tattered

déguerpir [degɛʀpiʀ] vi to clear off
dégueulasse [degœlas] (fam) adj disgusting
dégueuler [degœle] (fam) vi to throw up
déguisement [degizmɑ̃] nm (pour s'amuser)· fancy dress
déguiser [degize]: **se ~** vi (se costumer) to dress up; (pour tromper) to disguise o.s.
dégustation [degystasjɔ̃] nf (de fromages etc) sampling; **~ de vins** wine-tasting session
déguster [degyste] vt (vins) to taste; (fromages etc) to sample; (savourer) to enjoy, savour
dehors [dəɔʀ] adv outside; (en plein air) outdoors ♦ nm outside ♦ nmpl (apparences) appearances; **mettre** ou **jeter ~** (expulser) to throw out; **au ~** outside; **au ~ de** outside; **en ~ de** (hormis) apart from
déjà [deʒa] adv already; (auparavant) before, already
déjeuner [deʒœne] vi to (have) lunch; (le matin) to have breakfast ♦ nm lunch
déjouer [deʒwe] vt (complot) to foil
delà [dəla] adv: **en ~ (de)**, **au ~ (de)** beyond
délabrer [delabʀe]: **se ~** vi to fall into decay, become dilapidated
délacer [delase] vt (chaussures) to undo
délai [dele] nm (attente) waiting period; (sursis) extension (of time); (temps accordé) time limit; **sans ~** without delay; **dans les ~s** within the time limit
délaisser [delese] vt to abandon, desert
délasser [delase] vt to relax; **se ~** vi to relax
délavé, e [delave] adj faded
délayer [deleje] vt (CULIN) to mix (with water etc); (peinture) to thin down
delco [delko] nm (AUTO) distributor
délecter [delɛkte]: **se ~** vi to revel ou delight in
délégué, e [delege] nm/f representative
déléguer [delege] vt to delegate
délibéré, e [delibeʀe] adj (conscient) deliberate
délibérer [delibeʀe] vi to deliberate
délicat, e [delika, at] adj delicate; (plein de tact) tactful; (attention) thoughtful; **délicatement** adv delicately; (avec douceur) gently
délice [delis] nm delight
délicieux, -euse [delisjø, jøz] adj (au goût) delicious; (sensation) delightful
délimiter [delimite] vt (terrain) to delimit, demarcate
délinquance [delɛ̃kɑ̃s] nf criminality; **délinquant, e** adj, nm/f delinquent
délirant, e [deliʀɑ̃, ɑ̃t] adj (fam) adj wild
délirer [deliʀe] vi to be delirious; **tu délires!** (fam) you're crazy!
délit [deli] nm (criminal) offence
délivrer [delivʀe] vt (prisonnier) to (set) free,

release; (passeport) to issue
déloger [deloʒe] vt (objet coincé) to dislodge
déloyal, e, -aux [delwajal, o] adj (ami) disloyal; (procédé) unfair
deltaplane [dɛltaplan] nm hang-glider
déluge [delyʒ] nm (pluie) downpour; (biblique) Flood
déluré, e [delyʀe] (péj) adj forward, pert
demain [d(ə)mɛ̃] adv tomorrow
demande [d(ə)mɑ̃d] nf (requête) request; (revendication) demand; (d'emploi) application; (ÉCON): **la ~** demand; **"~s d'emploi"** (annonces) "situations wanted"; **~ en mariage** proposal (of marriage)
demandé, e [d(ə)mɑ̃de] adj (article etc): **très ~** (very) much in demand
demander [d(ə)mɑ̃de] vt to ask for; (chemin, heure etc) to ask; (nécessiter) to require, demand; **se ~ si/pourquoi** etc to wonder whether/why etc; **~ qch à qn** to ask sb for sth; **~ un service à qn** to ask sb a favour; **~ à qn de faire qch** to ask sb to do sth; **demandeur, -euse** nm/f: **demandeur d'emploi** job-seeker
démangeaison [demɑ̃ʒɛzɔ̃] nf itching; **avoir des ~s** to be itching
démanger [demɑ̃ʒe] vi to itch
démanteler [demɑ̃t(ə)le] vt to break up
démaquillant [demakijɑ̃] nm make-up remover
démaquiller [demakije] vt: **se ~** to remove one's make-up
démarche [demaʀʃ] nf (allure) gait, walk; (intervention) step; (fig: intellectuelle) thought processes pl; **faire les ~s nécessaires (pour obtenir qch)** to take the necessary steps (to obtain sth)
démarcheur, -euse [demaʀʃœʀ, øz] nm/f (COMM) door-to-door salesman(-woman)
démarque [demaʀk] nf (article) markdown
démarrage [demaʀaʒ] nm start
démarrer [demaʀe] vi (conducteur) to start (up); (véhicule) to move off; (travaux) to get moving; **démarreur** nm (AUTO) starter
démêlant [demɛlɑ̃] nm conditioner
démêler [demele] vt to untangle; **démêlés** nmpl problems
déménagement [demenaʒmɑ̃] nm move; **camion de ~** removal van
déménager [demenaʒe] vt (meubles) to (re)move ♦ vi to move (house); **déménageur** nm removal man
démener [dem(ə)ne]: **se ~** vi (se dépenser) to exert o.s.; (pour obtenir qch) to go to great lengths
dément, e [demɑ̃, ɑ̃t] adj (fou) mad, crazy; (fam) brilliant, fantastic
démentiel, le [demɑ̃sjɛl] adj insane
démentir [demɑ̃tiʀ] vt to refute; **~ que** to deny that

démerder [demɛʀde] (*fam*): **se ~** *vi* to sort things out for o.s.

démesuré, e [dem(ə)zyʀe] *adj* immoderate

démettre [demɛtʀ] *vt*: **~ qn de** (*fonction, poste*) to dismiss sb from; **se ~ l'épaule** *etc* to dislocate one's shoulder *etc*

demeurant [d(ə)mœʀɑ̃]: **au ~** *adv* for all that

demeure [d(ə)mœʀ] *nf* residence; **demeurer** *vi* (*habiter*) to live; (*rester*) to remain

demi, e [dəmi] *adj* half ♦ *nm* (*bière*) ≈ half-pint (*0,25 litres*) ♦ *préfixe*: **~...** half-, semi..., demi-; **trois heures/bouteilles et ~es** three and a half hours/bottles, three hours/bottles and a half; **il est 2 heures et ~e/midi et ~** it's half past 2/half past 12; **à ~** half-; **à la ~e** (*heure*) on the half-hour; **demi-cercle** *nm* semicircle; **en demi-cercle** *adj* semicircular ♦ *adv* in a half circle; **demi-douzaine** *nf* half-dozen, half a dozen; **demi-finale** *nf* semifinal; **demi-frère** *nm* half-brother; **demi-heure** *nf* half-hour, half an hour; **demi-journée** *nf* half-day, half a day; **demi-litre** *nm* half-litre, half a litre; **demi-livre** *nf* half-pound, half a pound; **demi-mot** *adv*: **à demi-mot** without having to spell things out; **demi-pension** *nf* (*à l'hôtel*) half-board; **demi-pensionnaire** *nm/f*: **être demi-pensionnaire** to take school lunches; **demi-place** *nf* half-fare

démis, e [demi, iz] *adj* (*épaule* etc) dislocated

demi-sel [dəmisɛl] *adj inv* (*beurre, fromage*) slightly salted

demi-sœur [dəmisœʀ] *nf* half-sister

démission [demisjɔ̃] *nf* resignation; **donner sa ~** to give ou hand in one's notice; **démissionner** *vi* to resign

demi-tarif [dəmitaʀif] *nm* half-price; **voyager à ~~** to travel half-fare

demi-tour [dəmituʀ] *nm* about-turn; **faire ~~** to turn (and go) back

démocratie [demɔkʀasi] *nf* democracy; **démocratique** *adj* democratic

démodé, e [demɔde] *adj* old-fashioned

demoiselle [d(ə)mwazɛl] *nf* (*jeune fille*) young lady; (*célibataire*) single lady, maiden lady; **~ d'honneur** bridesmaid

démolir [demɔliʀ] *vt* to demolish

démon [demɔ̃] *nm* (*enfant turbulent*) devil, demon; **le D~** the Devil

démonstration [demɔ̃stʀasjɔ̃] *nf* demonstration

démonté, e [demɔ̃te] *adj* (*mer*) raging, wild

démonter [demɔ̃te] *vt* (*machine* etc) to take down, dismantle

démontrer [demɔ̃tʀe] *vt* to demonstrate

démordre [demɔʀdʀ] *vi*: **ne pas ~ de** to refuse to give up, stick to

démouler [demule] *vt* to turn out

démuni, e [demyni] *adj* (*sans argent*) impoverished; **~ de** without

démunir [demyniʀ] *vt*: **~ qn de** to deprive sb of; **se ~ de** to part with, give up

dénaturer [denatyʀe] *vt* (*goût*) to alter; (*pensée, fait*) to distort

dénicher [denife] (*fam*) *vt* (*objet*) to unearth; (*restaurant* etc) to discover

dénier [denje] *vt* to deny

dénigrer [denigʀe] *vt* to denigrate, run down

dénivellation [denivelasjɔ̃] *nf* (*pente*) slope

dénombrer [denɔ̃bʀe] *vt* to count

dénomination [denɔminasjɔ̃] *nf* designation, appellation

dénommé, e [denɔme] *adj*: **un ~ Dupont** a certain Mr Dupont

dénoncer [denɔ̃se] *vt* to denounce

dénouement [denumɑ̃] *nm* outcome

dénouer [denwe] *vt* to unknot, undo; **se ~** *vi* (*nœud*) to come undone

dénoyauter [denwajɔte] *vt* to stone

denrée [dɑ̃ʀe] *nf*: **~s (alimentaires)** foodstuffs

dense [dɑ̃s] *adj* dense; **densité** *nf* density

dent [dɑ̃] *nf* tooth; **~ de lait/sagesse** milk/wisdom tooth; **dentaire** *adj* dental

dentelé, e [dɑ̃t(ə)le] *adj* jagged, indented

dentelle [dɑ̃tɛl] *nf* lace *no pl*

dentier [dɑ̃tje] *nm* denture

dentifrice [dɑ̃tifʀis] *nm* toothpaste

dentiste [dɑ̃tist] *nm/f* dentist

dentition [dɑ̃tisjɔ̃] *nf* teeth

dénuder [denyde] *vt* to bare

dénué, e [denye] *adj*: **~ de** devoid of; **dénuement** *nm* destitution

déodorant [deodɔʀɑ̃] *nm* deodorant

déontologie [deɔ̃tɔlɔʒi] *nf* code of practice

dépannage [depanaʒ] *nm*: **service de ~** (*AUTO*) breakdown service

dépanner [depane] *vt* (*voiture, télévision*) to fix, repair; (*fig*) to bail out, help out; **dépanneuse** *nf* breakdown lorry (*BRIT*), tow truck (*US*)

dépareillé, e [depaʀeje] *adj* (*collection, service*) incomplete; (*objet*) odd

départ [depaʀ] *nm* departure; (*SPORT*) start; **au ~** at the start; **la veille de son ~** the day before he leaves/left

départager [depaʀtaʒe] *vt* to decide between

département [depaʀtəmɑ̃] *nm* department

dépassé, e [depase] *adj* superseded, outmoded; **il est complètement ~** he's completely out of his depth, he can't cope

dépasser [depase] *vt* (*véhicule, concurrent*) to overtake; (*endroit*) to pass, go past; (*somme, limite*) to exceed; (*fig: en beauté* etc) to surpass, outshine ♦ *vi* (*jupon* etc) to show

dépaysé, e [depeize] adj disoriented
dépaysement [depeizmã] nm (changement) change of scenery
dépecer [depəse] vt to joint, cut up
dépêche [depɛʃ] nf dispatch
dépêcher [depeʃe]: **se ~** vi to hurry
dépeindre [depɛ̃dʀ] vt to depict
dépendance [depãdãs] nf dependence; (bâtiment) outbuilding
dépendre [depãdʀ]: **~ de** vt to depend on; (financièrement etc) to be dependent on
dépens [depã] nmpl: **aux ~ de** at the expense of
dépense [depãs] nf spending no pl, expense, expenditure no pl; **dépenser** vt to spend; (energie) to expend, use up; **se dépenser** vi to exert o.s.; **dépensier, -ière** adj: il est dépensier he's a spendthrift
dépérir [depeʀiʀ] vi (personne) to waste away; (plante) to wither
dépêtrer [depetʀe] vt: **se ~ de** to extricate o.s. from
dépeupler [depœple]: **se ~** vi to become depopulated
dépilatoire [depilatwaʀ] adj depilatory, hair-removing
dépister [depiste] vt to detect; (voleur) to track down
dépit [depi] nm vexation, frustration; **en ~ de** in spite of; **en ~ du bon sens** contrary to all good sense; **dépité, e** adj vexed, frustrated
déplacé, e [deplase] adj (propos) out of place, uncalled-for
déplacement [deplasmã] nm (voyage) trip, travelling no pl
déplacer [deplase] vt (table, voiture) to move, shift; **se ~** vi to move; (voyager) to travel; **se ~ une vertèbre** to slip a disc
déplaire [deplɛʀ] vt: **ça me déplaît** I don't like this, I dislike this; **se ~** vi to be unhappy; **déplaisant, e** adj disagreeable
dépliant [deplijã] nm leaflet
déplier [deplije] vt to unfold
déplorer [deplɔʀe] vt to deplore
déployer [deplwaje] vt (carte) to open out; (ailes) to spread; (troupes) to deploy
déporter [depɔʀte] vt (exiler) to deport; (dévier) to carry off course
déposer [depoze] vt (gén: mettre, poser) to lay ou put down; (à la banque, à la consigne) to deposit; (passager) to drop (off), set down; (roi) to depose; (plainte) to lodge; (marque) to register; **se ~** vi to settle; **dépositaire** nm/f (COMM) agent; **déposition** nf statement
dépôt [depo] nm (à la banque, sédiment) deposit; (entrepôt) warehouse, store
dépotoir [depɔtwaʀ] nm dumping ground, rubbish dump

dépouiller [depuje] vt (documents) to go through, peruse; **~ qn/qch de** to strip sb/sth of; **~ le scrutin** to count the votes
dépourvu, e [depuʀvy] adj: **~ de** lacking in, without; **prendre qn au ~** to catch sb unprepared
déprécier [depʀesje]: **se ~** vi to depreciate
dépression [depʀesjɔ̃] nf depression; **~ (nerveuse)** (nervous) breakdown
déprimant, e [depʀimã, ãt] adj depressing
déprimer [depʀime] vi to be/get depressed

MOT-CLÉ

---

depuis [dəpɥi] prép **1** (point de départ dans le temps) since; **il habite Paris depuis 1983/l'an dernier** he has been living in Paris since 1983/last year; **depuis quand le connaissez-vous?** how long have you known him?
2 (temps écoulé) for; **il habite Paris depuis 5 ans** he has been living in Paris for 5 years; **je le connais depuis 3 ans** I've known him for 3 years
3 (lieu): **il a plu depuis Metz** it's been raining since Metz, **elle a téléphoné depuis Valence** she rang from Valence
4 (quantité, rang) from; **depuis les plus petits jusqu'aux plus grands** from the youngest to the oldest
♦ adv (temps) since (then); **je ne lui ai pas parlé depuis** I haven't spoken to him since (then) **depuis que** conj (ever) since; **depuis qu'il m'a dit ça** (ever) since he said that to me

---

député, e [depyte] nm/f (POL) ≈ Member of Parliament (BRIT), ≈ Member of Congress (US)
députer [depyte] vt to delegate
déraciner [deʀasine] vt to uproot
dérailler [deʀaje] vi (train) to be derailed; **faire ~** to derail
déraisonner [deʀezɔne] vi to talk nonsense, rave
dérangement [deʀãʒmã] nm (gêne) trouble; (gastrique etc) disorder; **en ~** (téléphone, machine) out of order
déranger [deʀãʒe] vt (personne) to trouble, bother; (projets) to disrupt, upset; (objets, vêtements) to disarrange; **se ~** vi: **surtout ne vous dérangez pas pour moi** please don't put yourself out on my account; **est-ce que cela vous dérange si ...?** do you mind if ...?
déraper [deʀape] vi (voiture) to skid; (personne, semelles) to slip
dérégler [deʀegle] vt (mécanisme) to put out of order; (estomac) to upset
dérider [deʀide]: **se ~** vi to brighten up
dérision [deʀizjɔ̃] nf: **tourner en ~** to deride; **dérisoire** adj derisory

dérive [deʀiv] nf: **aller à la ~** (NAVIG, fig) to drift

dérivé, e [deʀive] nm (TECH) by-product

dériver [deʀive] vt (MATH) to derive; (cours d'eau etc) to divert ♦ vi (bateau) to drift; **~ de** to derive from

dermatologue [dɛʀmatɔlɔg] nm/f dermatologist

dernier, -ière [dɛʀnje, jɛʀ] adj last; (le plus récent) latest, last; **lundi/le mois ~** last Monday/month; **c'est le ~ cri** it's the very latest thing; **en ~** last; **ce ~** the latter; **dernièrement** adv recently

dérobé, e [deʀɔbe] adj: **à la ~e** surreptitiously

dérober [deʀɔbe] vt to steal; **se ~** vi (s'esquiver) to slip away; **se ~ à** (justice, regards) to hide from; (obligation) to shirk

dérogation [deʀɔgasjɔ̃] nf (special) dispensation

déroger [deʀɔʒe]: **~ à** vt to go against, depart from

dérouiller [deʀuje] vt: **se ~ les jambes** to stretch one's legs (fig)

déroulement [deʀulmɑ̃] nm (d'une opération etc) progress

dérouler [deʀule] vt (ficelle) to unwind; **se ~** vi (avoir lieu) to take place; (se passer) to go (off); **tout s'est déroulé comme prévu** everything went as planned

dérouter [deʀute] vt (avion, train) to reroute, divert; (étonner) to disconcert, throw (out)

derrière [dɛʀjɛʀ] adv, prép behind ♦ nm (d'une maison) back; (postérieur) behind, bottom; **les pattes de ~** the back ou hind legs; **par ~** from behind; (fig) behind one's back

des [de] dét voir de ♦ prép +dét = **de +les**

dès [dɛ] prép from; **~ que** as soon as; **~ son retour** as soon as he was (ou is) back

désabusé, e [dezabyze] adj disillusioned

désaccord [dezakɔʀ] nm disagreement; **désaccordé, e** adj (MUS) out of tune

désaffecté, e [dezafɛkte] adj disused

désagréable [dezagʀeabl] adj unpleasant

désagréger [dezagʀeʒe]: **se ~** vi to disintegrate, break up

désagrément [dezagʀemɑ̃] nm annoyance, trouble no pl

désaltérer [dezaltere] vt: **se ~** to quench one's thirst

désapprobateur, -trice [dezapʀɔbatœʀ, tʀis] adj disapproving

désapprouver [dezapʀuve] vt to disapprove of

désarmant, e [dezaʀmɑ̃, ɑ̃t] adj disarming

désarroi [dezaʀwa] nm disarray

désastre [dezastʀ] nm disaster; **désastreux, -euse** adj disastrous

désavantage [dezavɑ̃taʒ] nm disadvantage;

désavantager vt to put at a disadvantage

descendre [desɑ̃dʀ] vt (escalier, montagne) to go (ou come) down; (valise, paquet) to take ou get down; (étagère etc) to lower; (fam: abattre) to shoot down ♦ vi to go (ou come) down; (passager: s'arrêter) to get out, alight; **~ à pied/en voiture** to walk/drive down; **~ du train** to get out of ou get off the train; **~ de cheval** to dismount; **~ à l'hôtel** to stay at a hotel

descente [desɑ̃t] nf descent, going down; (chemin) way down; (SKI) downhill (race); **~ de lit** bedside rug; **~ (de police)** (police) raid

description [dɛskʀipsjɔ̃] nf description

désemparé, e [dezɑ̃paʀe] adj bewildered, distraught

désemplir [dezɑ̃pliʀ] vi: **ne pas ~** to be always full

déséquilibre [dezekilibʀ] nm (position): **en ~** unsteady; (fig: des forces, du budget) imbalance; **déséquilibré, e** nm/f (PSYCH) unbalanced person; **déséquilibrer** vt to throw off balance

désert, e [dezɛʀ, ɛʀt] adj deserted ♦ nm desert; **déserter** vi, vt to desert; **désertique** adj desert cpd

désespéré, e [dezɛspere] adj desperate

désespérer [dezɛspere] vi: **~ (de)** to despair (of); **désespoir** nm despair; **en désespoir de cause** in desperation

déshabiller [dezabije] vt to undress; **se ~** to undress (o.s.)

déshériter [dezerite] vt to disinherit; **déshérités** nmpl: **les déshérités** the underprivileged

déshonneur [dezɔnœʀ] nm dishonour

déshydraté, e [dezidʀate] adj dehydrated

desiderata [deziderata] nmpl requirements

désigner [dezine] vt (montrer) to point out, indicate; (dénommer) to denote; (candidat etc) to name

désinfectant, e [dezɛ̃fɛktɑ̃, ɑ̃t] adj, nm disinfectant

désinfecter [dezɛ̃fɛkte] vt to disinfect

désintégrer [dezɛ̃tegʀe]: **se ~** vi to disintegrate

désintéressé, e [dezɛ̃terese] adj disinterested, unselfish

désintéresser [dezɛ̃terese] vt: **se ~ (de)** to lose interest (in)

désintoxication [dezɛ̃tɔksikasjɔ̃] nf: **faire une cure de ~** to undergo treatment for alcoholism (ou drug addiction)

désinvolte [dezɛ̃vɔlt] adj casual, off-hand; **désinvolture** nf casualness

désir [deziʀ] nm wish; (sensuel) desire; **désirer** vt to want, wish for; (sexuellement) to desire; **je désire ...** (formule de politesse) I would like ...

désister [deziste]: se ~ *vi* to stand down, withdraw

désobéir [dezɔbeiʀ] *vi*: ~ (à qn/qch) to disobey (sb/sth); **désobéissant, e** *adj* disobedient

désobligeant, e [dezɔbliʒɑ̃, ɑ̃t] *adj* disagreeable

désodorisant [dezɔdɔʀizɑ̃] *nm* air freshener, deodorizer

désœuvré, e [dezœvʀe] *adj* idle

désolé, e [dezɔle] *adj* (*paysage*) desolate; **je suis ~** I'm sorry

désoler [dezɔle] *vt* to distress, grieve

désopilant, e [dezɔpilɑ̃, ɑ̃t] *adj* hilarious

désordonné, e [dezɔʀdɔne] *adj* untidy

désordre [dezɔʀdʀ] *nm* disorder(liness), untidiness; (*anarchie*) disorder; **en ~** in a mess, untidy

désorienté, e [dezɔʀjɑ̃te] *adj* disorientated

désormais [dezɔʀmɛ] *adv* from now on

désossé, e [dezɔse] *adj* (*viande*) boned

desquelles [dekɛl] *prép* +*pron* = **de +lesquelles**

desquels [dekɛl] *prép* +*pron* = **de +lesquels**

desséché, e [deseʃe] *adj* dried up

dessécher [deseʃe]: se ~ *vi* to dry out

dessein [desɛ̃] *nm*: **à ~** intentionally, deliberately

desserrer [deseʀe] *vt* to loosen; (*frein*) to release

dessert [desɛʀ] *nm* dessert, pudding

desserte [desɛʀt] *nf* (*table*) side table; (*transport*): **la ~ du village est assurée par autocar** there is a coach service to the village

desservir [desɛʀviʀ] *vt* (*ville, quartier*) to serve; (*débarrasser*): ~ **(la table)** to clear the table

dessin [desɛ̃] *nm* (*œuvre, art*) drawing; (*motif*) pattern, design; ~ **animé** cartoon (film); ~ **humoristique** cartoon,
dessinateur, -trice *nm/f* drawer; (*de bandes dessinées*) cartoonist; (*industriel*) draughtsman(-woman) (*BRIT*), draftsman(-woman) (*US*); **dessiner** *vt* to draw; (*concevoir*) to design

dessous [d(ə)su] *adv* underneath, beneath ♦ *nm* underside ♦ *nmpl* (*sous-vêtements*) underwear *sg*; **en ~, par ~** underneath; **au- ~ (de)** below; (*peu digne de*) beneath; **avoir le ~** to get the worst of it; **les voisins du ~** the downstairs neighbours; **dessous-de-plat** *nm inv* tablemat

dessus [d(ə)sy] *adv* on top; (*collé, écrit*) on it ♦ *nm* top; **en ~** above; **par ~** ♦ *adv* over it ♦ *prép* over; **au-~ (de)** above; **avoir le ~** to get the upper hand; **dessus-de-lit** *nm inv* bedspread

destin [dɛstɛ̃] *nm* fate; (*avenir*) destiny

destinataire [dɛstinatɛʀ] *nm/f* (*POSTES*) addressee; (*d'un colis*) consignee

destination [dɛstinasjɔ̃] *nf* (*lieu*) destination; (*usage*) purpose; **à ~ de** bound for, travelling to

destinée [dɛstine] *nf* fate; (*existence, avenir*) destiny

destiner [dɛstine] *vt*: ~ **qch à qn** (*envisager de donner*) to intend sb to have sth; (*adresser*) to intend sth for sb; **être destiné à** (*usage*) to be meant for

désuet, -ète [dezyɛ, ɛt] *adj* outdated, outmoded

détachant [detaʃɑ̃] *nm* stain remover

détachement [detaʃmɑ̃] *nm* detachment

détacher [detaʃe] *vt* (*enlever*) to detach, remove; (*délier*) to untie; (*ADMIN*): ~ **qn (auprès de** ou **à)** to post sb (to); **se ~** *vi* (*se séparer*) to come off; (: *page*) to come out; (*se défaire*) to come undone; **se ~ sur** to stand out against; **se ~ de** (*se désintéresser*) to grow away from

détail [detaj] *nm* detail; (*COMM*): **le ~** retail; **en ~** in detail, **au ~** (*COMM*) retail, **détaillant** *nm* retailer; **détaillé, e** *adj* (*plan, explications*) detailed; (*facture*) itemized; **détailler** *vt* (*expliquer*) to explain in detail

détaler [detale] (*fam*) *vi* (*personne*) to take off

détartrant [detaʀtʀɑ̃] *nm* scale remover

détaxé, e [detakse] *adj*: **produits ~s** tax-free goods

détecter [detɛkte] *vt* to detect

détective [detɛktiv] *nm*: ~ **(privé)** private detective

déteindre [detɛ̃dʀ] *vi* (*au lavage*) to run, lose its colour

détendre [detɑ̃dʀ] *vt* (*corps, esprit*) to relax; **se ~** *vi* (*ressort*) to lose its tension; (*personne*) to relax

détenir [det(ə)niʀ] *vt* (*record, pouvoir, secret*) to hold; (*prisonnier*) to detain, hold

détente [detɑ̃t] *nf* relaxation

détention [detɑ̃sjɔ̃] *nf* (*d'armes*) possession; (*captivité*) detention; ~ **préventive** custody

détenu, e [det(ə)ny] *nm/f* prisoner

détergent [detɛʀʒɑ̃] *nm* detergent

détériorer [deteʀjɔʀe] *vt* to damage; **se ~** *vi* to deteriorate

déterminé, e [detɛʀmine] *adj* (*résolu*) determined; (*précis*) specific, definite

déterminer [detɛʀmine] *vt* (*fixer*) to determine; **se ~ à faire qch** to make up one's mind to do sth

déterrer [deteʀe] *vt* to dig up

détestable [detɛstabl] *adj* foul, detestable

détester [detɛste] *vt* to hate, detest

détonner [detɔne] *vi* (*fig*) to clash

détour [detuʀ] *nm* detour; (*tournant*) bend,

curve; **ça vaut le ~** it's worth the trip; **sans ~**
(*fig*) plainly

détourné, e [detuʀne] *adj* (*moyen*)
roundabout

détournement [detuʀnəmɑ̃] *nm*: **~ d'avion**
hijacking

détourner [detuʀne] *vt* to divert; (*par la
force*) to hijack; (*yeux, tête*) to turn away; (*de
l'argent*) to embezzle; **se ~** *vi* to turn away

détracteur, -trice [detʀaktœʀ, tʀis] *nm/f*
disparager, critic

détraquer [detʀake] *vt* to put out of order;
(*estomac*) to upset; **se ~** *vi* (*machine*) to go
wrong

détrempé, e [detʀɑ̃pe] *adj* (*sol*) sodden,
waterlogged

détresse [detʀɛs] *nf* distress

détriment [detʀimɑ̃] *nm*: **au ~ de** to the
detriment of

détritus [detʀity(s)] *nmpl* rubbish *sg*, refuse
sg

détroit [detʀwa] *nm* strait

détromper [detʀɔ̃pe] *vt* to disabuse

détruire [detʀɥiʀ] *vt* to destroy

dette [dɛt] *nf* debt

DEUG [dœg] *sigle m* (= *diplôme d'études
universitaires générales*) diploma taken after 2
years at university

deuil [dœj] *nm* (*perte*) bereavement; (*période*)
mourning; **être en ~** to be in mourning

deux [dø] *num* two; **tous les ~** both; **ses
~ mains** both his hands, his two hands; **~ fois**
twice; **deuxième** *num* second;
deuxièmement *adv* secondly; **deux-
pièces** *nm inv* (*tailleur*) two-piece suit; (*de
bain*) two-piece (swimsuit); (*appartement*)
two-roomed flat (*BRIT*) *ou* apartment (*US*);
deux-points *nm inv* colon *sg*; **deux-roues**
nm inv two-wheeled vehicle

devais *etc* [dəvɛ] *vb voir* **devoir**

dévaler [devale] *vt* to hurtle down

dévaliser [devalize] *vt* to rob, burgle

dévaloriser [devalɔʀize] *vt* to depreciate; **se
~** *vi* to depreciate

dévaluation [devalɥasjɔ̃] *nf* devaluation

devancer [d(ə)vɑ̃se] *vt* (*coureur, rival*) to get
ahead of; (*arriver*) to arrive before; (*prévenir:
questions, désirs*) to anticipate

devant [d(ə)vɑ̃] *adv* in front; (*à distance: en
avant*) ahead ♦ *prép* in front of; (*en avant*)
ahead of; (*avec mouvement: passer*) past; (*en
présence de*) before, in front of; (*étant donné*)
in view of ♦ *nm* front; **prendre les ~s** to make
the first move; **les pattes de ~** the front legs,
the forelegs; **par ~** (*boutonner*) at the front;
(*entrer*) the front way; **aller au-~ de qn** to go
out to meet sb; **aller au-~ de** (*désirs de qn*) to
anticipate

devanture [d(ə)vɑ̃tyʀ] *nf* (*étalage*) display;

(*vitrine*) (shop) window

déveine [devɛn] (*fam*) *nf* rotten luck *no pl*

développement [dev(ə)lɔpmɑ̃] *nm*
development; **pays en voie de ~** developing
countries

développer [dev(ə)lɔpe] *vt* to develop; **se ~**
vi to develop

devenir [dəv(ə)niʀ] *vb +attrib* to become;
que sont-ils devenus? what has become of
them?

dévergondé, e [devɛʀgɔ̃de] *adj* wild,
shameless

déverser [devɛʀse] *vt* (*liquide*) to pour (out);
(*ordures*) to tip (out); **se ~ dans** (*fleuve*) to
flow into

dévêtir [devetiʀ]: **se ~** *vi* to undress

devez *etc* [dəve] *vb voir* **devoir**

déviation [devjasjɔ̃] *nf* (*AUTO*) diversion
(*BRIT*), detour (*US*)

devienne *etc* [dəvjɛn] *vb voir* **devenir**

dévier [devje] *vt* (*fleuve, circulation*) to divert;
(*coup*) to deflect ♦ *vi* to veer (off course)

devin [dəvɛ̃] *nm* soothsayer, seer

deviner [d(ə)vine] *vt* to guess; (*apercevoir*) to
distinguish; **devinette** *nf* riddle

devins *etc* [dəvɛ̃] *vb voir* **devenir**

devis [d(ə)vi] *nm* estimate, quotation

dévisager [devizaʒe] *vt* to stare at

devise [dəviz] *nf* (*formule*) motto,
watchword; **~s** *nfpl* (*argent*) currency *sg*

deviser [dəvize] *vi* to converse

dévisser [devise] *vt* to unscrew, undo

dévoiler [devwale] *vt* to unveil

devoir [d(ə)vwaʀ] *nm* duty; (*SCOL*)
homework *no pl*; (: *en classe*) exercise ♦ *vt*
(*argent, respect*): **~ qch (à qn)** to owe (sb)
sth; (+*infin*: *obligation*): **il doit le faire** he has
to do it, he must do it; (: *intention*): **le
nouveau centre commercial doit ouvrir en mai**
the new shopping centre is due to open in
May; (: *probabilité*): **il doit être tard** it must
be late

dévolu [devɔly] *nm*: **jeter son ~ sur** to fix
one's choice on

dévorer [devɔʀe] *vt* to devour

dévot, e [devo, ɔt] *adj* devout, pious;
dévotion *nf* devoutness

dévoué, e [devwe] *adj* devoted

dévouement [devumɑ̃] *nm* devotion

dévouer [devwe]: **se ~** *vi* (*se sacrifier*): **se
~ (pour)** to sacrifice o.s. (for); (*se consacrer*):
se ~ à to devote *ou* dedicate o.s. to

dévoyé, e [devwaje] *adj* delinquent

devrai *etc* [dəvʀe] *vb voir* **devoir**

diabète [djabɛt] *nm* diabetes *sg*; **diabétique**
nm/f diabetic

diable [djabl] *nm* devil

diabolo [djabɔlo] *nm* (*boisson*) lemonade with
fruit cordial

63

diagnostic → discontinu

diagnostic [djagnɔstik] nm diagnosis sg;
  diagnostiquer vt to diagnose
diagonal, e, -aux [djagɔnal, o] adj
  diagonal; **diagonale** nf diagonal; **en
  diagonale** diagonally
diagramme [djagram] nm chart, graph
dialecte [djalɛkt] nm dialect
dialogue [djalɔg] nm dialogue
diamant [djamɑ̃] nm diamond
diamètre [djamɛtr] nm diameter
diapason [djapazɔ̃] nm tuning fork
diaphragme [djafragm] nm diaphragm
diapo [djapo] (fam) nf slide
diapositive [djapozitiv] nf transparency,
  slide
diarrhée [djaʀe] nf diarrhoea
dictateur [diktatœʀ] nm dictator; **dictature**
  nf dictatorship
dictée [dikte] nf dictation
dicter [dikte] vt to dictate
dictionnaire [diksjɔnɛʀ] nm dictionary
dicton [diktɔ̃] nm saying, dictum
dièse [djɛz] nm sharp
diesel [djezɛl] nm diesel ♦ adj inv diesel
diète [djɛt] nf (jeûne) starvation diet; (régime)
  diet; **diététique** adj: **magasin diététique**
  health food shop
dieu, x [djø] nm god; **D~** God; **mon D~!** good
  heavens!
diffamation [difamasjɔ̃] nf slander; (écrite)
  libel
différé [difeʀe] nm (TV): **en ~** (pre-)recorded
différemment [difeʀamɑ̃] adv differently
différence [difeʀɑ̃s] nf difference; **à la ~ de**
  unlike; **différencier** vt to differentiate;
  différend nm difference (of opinion),
  disagreement
différent, e [difeʀɑ̃, ɑ̃t] adj (dissemblable)
  different; **~ de** different from; (divers)
  different, various
différer [difeʀe] vt to postpone, put off ♦ vi:
  ~ (de) to differ (from)
difficile [difisil] adj difficult; (exigeant) hard
  to please; **difficilement** adv with difficulty
difficulté [difikylte] nf difficulty; **en ~**
  (bateau, alpiniste) in difficulties
difforme [difɔrm] adj deformed, misshapen
diffuser [difyze] vt to diffuse;
  (émission, musique) to broadcast; (nouvelle)
  to circulate; (COMM) to distribute
digérer [diʒeʀe] vt to digest; (fam: accepter)
  to stomach, put up with; **digestif** nm (after-
  dinner) liqueur; **digestion** nf digestion
digne [diɲ] adj dignified; **~ de** worthy of;
  ~ de foi trustworthy; **dignité** nf dignity
digue [dig] nf dike, dyke
dilapider [dilapide] vt to squander
dilemme [dilɛm] nm dilemma
dilettante [diletɑ̃t] nm/f: **faire qch en ~** to

dabble in sth
diligence [diliʒɑ̃s] nf stagecoach
diluer [dilye] vt to dilute
diluvien, ne [dilyvjɛ̃, jɛn] adj: **pluie ~ne**
  torrential rain
dimanche [dimɑ̃ʃ] nm Sunday
dimension [dimɑ̃sjɔ̃] nf (grandeur) size; (~s)
  dimensions
diminué, e [diminɥe] adj: **il est très
  ~ depuis son accident** he's not at all the man
  he was since his accident
diminuer [diminɥe] vt to reduce, decrease;
  (ardeur etc) to lessen; (dénigrer) to belittle
  ♦ vi to decrease, diminish; **diminutif** nm
  (surnom) pet name; **diminution** nf
  decreasing, diminishing
dinde [dɛ̃d] nf turkey
dindon [dɛ̃dɔ̃] nm turkey
dîner [dine] nm dinner ♦ vi to have dinner
dingue [dɛ̃g] (fam) adj crazy
dinosaure [dinɔzɔr] nm dinosaur
diplomate [diplɔmat] adj diplomatic ♦ nm
  diplomat; (fig) diplomatist; **diplomatie** nf
  diplomacy
diplôme [diplom] nm diploma; **avoir des ~s**
  to have qualifications; **diplômé, e** adj
  qualified
dire [diʀ] nm: **au ~ de** according to ♦ vt to
  say; (secret, mensonge, heure) to tell; **~ qch à
  qn** to tell sb sth; **~ à qn qu'il fasse** ou **de faire**
  to tell sb to do; **on dit que** they say that; **ceci
  dit** that being said; **si cela lui dit** (plaire) if he
  fancies it; **que dites-vous de** (penser) what do
  you think of; **on dirait que** it looks (ou sounds
  etc) as if; **dis/dites (donc)!** I say!
direct, e [diʀɛkt] adj direct ♦ nm (TV): **en ~**
  live; **directement** adv directly
directeur, -trice [diʀɛktœʀ, tʀis] nm/f
  (d'entreprise) director; (de service)
  manager(-eress); (d'école) head(teacher)
  (BRIT), principal (US)
direction [diʀɛksjɔ̃] nf (sens) direction;
  (d'entreprise) management; (AUTO) steering;
  "toutes ~s" "all routes"
dirent [diʀ] vb voir dire
dirigeant, e [diʀiʒɑ̃, ɑ̃t] adj (classe) ruling
  ♦ nm/f (d'un parti etc) leader
diriger [diʀiʒe] vt (entreprise) to manage,
  run; (véhicule) to steer; (orchestre) to
  conduct; (recherches, travaux) to supervise;
  se ~ vi (s'orienter) to find one's way; **se ~ vers**
  ou **sur** to make ou head for
dis etc [di] vb voir dire
discernement [disɛʀnəmɑ̃] nm (bon sens)
  discernment, judgement
discerner [disɛʀne] vt to discern, make out
discipline [disiplin] nf discipline;
  discipliner vt to discipline
discontinu, e [diskɔ̃tiny] adj intermittent

discontinuer [diskɔ̃tinɥe] vi: **sans ~** without stopping, without a break

discordant, e [diskɔʀdã, ãt] adj discordant

discothèque [diskɔtɛk] nf (boîte de nuit) disco(thèque)

discours [diskuʀ] nm speech

discret, -ète [diskʀɛ, ɛt] adj discreet; (parfum, maquillage) unobtrusive; **discrétion** nf discretion; **à discrétion** as much as one wants

discrimination [diskʀiminasjɔ̃] nf discrimination; **sans ~** indiscriminately

disculper [diskylpe] vt to exonerate

discussion [diskysjɔ̃] nf discussion

discutable [diskytabl] adj debatable

discuté, e [diskyte] adj controversial

discuter [diskyte] vt (débattre) to discuss; (contester) to question, dispute ♦ vi to talk; (protester) to argue; **~ de** to discuss

dise etc [diz] vb voir **dire**

diseuse [dizøz] nf: **~ de bonne aventure** fortuneteller

disgracieux, -euse [disgʀasjø, jøz] adj ungainly, awkward

disjoindre [disʒwɛ̃dʀ] vt to take apart; **se ~** vi to come apart

disjoncteur [disʒɔ̃ktœʀ] nm (ÉLEC) circuit breaker

disloquer [dislɔke]: **se ~** vi (parti, empire) to break up

disons [dizɔ̃] vb voir **dire**

disparaître [dispaʀɛtʀ] vi to disappear; (se perdre: traditions etc) to die out; **faire ~** (tache) to remove; (douleur) to get rid of

disparition [dispaʀisjɔ̃] nf disappearance; **espèce en voie de ~** endangered species

disparu, e [dispaʀy] nm/f missing person ♦ adj: **être porté ~** to be reported missing

dispensaire [dispãsɛʀ] nm community clinic

dispenser [dispãse] vt: **~ qn de** to exempt sb from; **se ~ de** vt (corvée) to get out of

disperser [dispɛʀse] vt to scatter; **se ~** vi to break up

disponibilité [dispɔnibilite] nf availability; **disponible** adj available

dispos [dispo] adj m: (frais et) **~** fresh (as a daisy)

disposé, e [dispoze] adj: **bien/mal ~** (humeur) in a good/bad mood; **~ à** (prêt à) willing ou prepared to

disposer [dispoze] vt to arrange ♦ vi: **vous pouvez ~** you may leave; **~ de** to have (at one's disposal); **se ~ à faire** to prepare to do, be about to do

dispositif [dispozitif] nm device; (fig) system, plan of action

disposition [dispozisjɔ̃] nf (arrangement) arrangement, layout; (humeur) mood; **prendre ses ~s** to make arrangements; **avoir**

des ~s pour la musique etc to have a special aptitude for music etc; **à la ~ de qn** at sb's disposal; **je suis à votre ~** I am at your service

disproportionné, e [dispʀɔpɔʀsjɔne] adj disproportionate, out of all proportion

dispute [dispyt] nf quarrel, argument;
disputer vt (match) to play; (combat) to fight; **se disputer** vi to quarrel

disquaire [diskɛʀ] nm/f record dealer

disqualifier [diskalifje] vt to disqualify

disque [disk] nm (MUS) record; (forme, pièce) disc; (SPORT) discus; **~ compact** compact disc; **~ dur** hard disk; **disquette** nf floppy disk, diskette

disséminer [disemine] vt to scatter

disséquer [diseke] vt to dissect

dissertation [disɛʀtasjɔ̃] nf (SCOL) essay

dissimuler [disimyle] vt to conceal

dissipé, e [disipe] adj (élève) undisciplined, unruly

dissiper [disipe] vt to dissipate; (fortune) to squander; **se ~** vi (brouillard) to clear, disperse

dissolvant [disɔlvã] nm nail polish remover

dissonant, e [disɔnã, ãt] adj discordant

dissoudre [disudʀ] vt to dissolve; **se ~** vi to dissolve

dissuader [disɥade] vt: **~ qn de faire** to dissuade sb from doing; **dissuasion** nf: **force de dissuasion** deterrent power

distance [distãs] nf distance; (fig: écart) gap; **à ~** at ou from a distance; **distancer** vt to outdistance

distant, e [distã, ãt] adj (réservé) distant; **~ de** (lieu) far away from

distendre [distãdʀ]: **se ~** vi to distend

distillerie [distilʀi] nf distillery

distinct, e [distɛ̃(kt), ɛ̃kt] adj distinct; **distinctement** adv distinctly, clearly; **distinctif, -ive** adj distinctive

distingué, e [distɛ̃ge] adj distinguished

distinguer [distɛ̃ge] vt to distinguish

distraction [distʀaksjɔ̃] nf (inattention) absent-mindedness; (passe-temps) distraction, entertainment

distraire [distʀɛʀ] vt (divertir) to entertain, divert; (déranger) to distract; **se ~** vi to amuse ou enjoy o.s.; **distrait, e** adj absent-minded

distrayant, e [distʀɛjã, ãt] adj entertaining

distribuer [distʀibɥe] vt to distribute, hand out; (CARTES) to deal (out); (courrier) to deliver; **distributeur** nm (COMM) distributor; (automatique) (vending) machine; (: de billets) (cash) dispenser; **distribution** nf distribution; (postale) delivery; (choix d'acteurs) casting, cast

dit, e [di, dit] pp de **dire** ♦ adj (fixé): **le jour ~** the arranged day; (surnommé): **X, ~ Pierrot** X, known as Pierrot

dites [dit] *vb voir* **dire**
divaguer [divage] *vi* to ramble; (*fam*) to rave
divan [divɑ̃] *nm* divan
diverger [diverʒe] *vi* to diverge
divers, e [diver, ɛrs] *adj* (*varié*) diverse, varied; (*différent*) different, various; **~es personnes** various *ou* several people
diversifier [diversifje] *vt* to vary
diversité [diversite] *nf* (*variété*) diversity
divertir [divertir]: **se ~** *vi* to amuse *ou* enjoy o.s.; **divertissement** *nm* distraction, entertainment
divin, e [divɛ̃, in] *adj* divine
diviser [divize] *vt* to divide; **division** *nf* division
divorce [divɔrs] *nm* divorce; **divorcé, e** *nm/f* divorcee; **divorcer** *vi* to get a divorce, get divorced
divulguer [divylge] *vt* to divulge, disclose
dix [dis] *num* ten; **dixième** *num* tenth
dizaine [dizɛn] *nf*: **une ~ (de)** about ten, ten or so
do [do] *nm* (*note*) C; (*en chantant la gamme*) do(h)
docile [dɔsil] *adj* docile
dock [dɔk] *nm* dock; **docker** *nm* docker
docteur [dɔktœr] *nm* doctor; **doctorat** *nm* doctorate; **doctoresse** *nf* lady doctor
doctrine [dɔktrin] *nf* doctrine
document [dɔkymɑ̃] *nm* document; **documentaire** *adj, nm* documentary; **documentaliste** *nm/f* (*SCOL*) librarian; **documentation** *nf* documentation, literature; **documenter** *vt*: **se documenter (sur)** to gather information (on)
dodo [dodo] *nm* (*langage enfantin*): **aller faire ~** to go to beddy-byes
dodu, e [dody] *adj* plump
dogue [dɔg] *nm* mastiff
doigt [dwa] *nm* finger; **à deux ~s de** within an inch of; **~ de pied** toe; **doigté** *nm* (*MUS*) fingering; (*fig: habileté*) diplomacy, tact
doit *etc* [dwa] *vb voir* **devoir**
doléances [dɔleɑ̃s] *nfpl* grievances
dollar [dɔlar] *nm* dollar
domaine [dɔmɛn] *nm* estate, property; (*fig*) domain, field
domestique [dɔmɛstik] *adj* domestic ♦ *nm/f* servant, domestic; **domestiquer** *vt* to domesticate
domicile [dɔmisil] *nm* home, place of residence; **à ~** at home; **livrer à ~** to deliver; **domicilié, e** *adj*: "**domicilié à ...**" "address ..."
dominant, e [dɔminɑ̃, ɑ̃t] *adj* (*opinion*) predominant
dominer [dɔmine] *vt* to dominate; (*sujet*) to master; (*surpasser*) to outclass, surpass; (*surplomber*) to tower above, dominate ♦ *vi*

to be in the dominant position; **se ~** *vi* to control o.s.
domino [dɔmino] *nm* domino
dommage [dɔmaʒ] *nm*: **~s** (*dégâts*) damage *no pl*; **c'est ~!** what a shame!; **c'est ~ que** it's a shame *ou* pity that; **dommages-intérêts** *nmpl* damages
dompter [dɔ̃(p)te] *vt* to tame; **dompteur, -euse** *nm/f* trainer
DOM-TOM [dɔmtɔm] *sigle m* (= *départements et territoires d'outre-mer*) *French overseas departments and territories*
don [dɔ̃] *nm* gift; (*charité*) donation; **avoir des ~s pour** to have a gift *ou* talent for; **elle a le ~ de m'énerver** she's got a knack of getting on my nerves
donc [dɔ̃k] *conj* therefore, so; (*après une digression*) so, then
donjon [dɔ̃ʒɔ̃] *nm* keep
donné, e [dɔne] *adj* (*convenu: lieu, heure*) given; (*pas cher: fam*) **c'est ~** it's a gift; **étant ~ ... given ...; données** *nfpl* data
donner [dɔne] *vt* to give; (*vieux habits etc*) to give away; (*spectacle*) to put on; **~ qch à qn** to give sb sth, give sth to sb; **~ sur** (*suj: fenêtre, chambre*) to look (out) onto; **ça donne soif/faim** it makes you (feel) thirsty/hungry; **se ~ à fond** to give one's all; **se ~ du mal** to take (great) trouble; **s'en ~ à cœur joie** (*fam*) to have a great time

---

MOT-CLÉ

dont [dɔ̃] *pron relatif* **1** (*appartenance: objets*) whose, of which; (*appartenance: êtres animés*) whose; **la maison dont le toit est rouge** the house of which the roof is red, the house whose roof is red; **l'homme dont je connais la sœur** the man whose sister I know **2** (*parmi lesquel(le)s*): **2 livres, dont l'un est ...** 2 books, one of which is ...; **il y avait plusieurs personnes, dont Gabrielle** there were several people, among them Gabrielle; **10 blessés, dont 2 grièvement** 10 injured, 2 of them seriously
3 (*complément d'adjectif, de verbe*): **le fils dont il est si fier** the son he's so proud of; **ce dont je parle** what I'm talking about

---

doré, e [dɔre] *adj* golden; (*avec dorure*) gilt, gilded
dorénavant [dɔrenavɑ̃] *adv* henceforth
dorer [dɔre] *vt* to gild; (*faire*) **~** (*CULIN*) to brown
dorloter [dɔrlɔte] *vt* to pamper
dormir [dɔrmir] *vi* to sleep; (*être endormi*) to be asleep
dortoir [dɔrtwar] *nm* dormitory
dorure [dɔryr] *nf* gilding
dos [do] *nm* back; (*de livre*) spine; "**voir au ~**"

"see over"; **de** ~ from the back

dosage [dozaʒ] nm mixture

dose [doz] nf dose; **doser** vt to measure out; **il faut savoir doser ses efforts** you have to be able to pace yourself

dossard [dosaʀ] nm number (worn by competitor)

dossier [dosje] nm (documents) file; (de chaise) back; (PRESSE) feature; **un ~ scolaire** a school report

dot [dɔt] nf dowry

doter [dɔte] vt: ~ **de** to equip with

douane [dwan] nf customs pl; (**droits de**) ~ (customs) duty; **douanier, -ière** adj customs cpd ♦ nm customs officer

double [dubl] adj, adv double ♦ nm (2 fois plus): **le ~ (de)** twice as much (ou many) (as); (autre exemplaire) duplicate, copy; (sosie) double; (TENNIS) doubles sg; **en ~ (exemplaire)** in duplicate; **faire ~ emploi** to be redundant

doubler [duble] vt (multiplier par 2) to double; (vêtement) to line; (dépasser) to overtake, pass; (film) to dub; (acteur) to stand in for ♦ vi to double

doublure [dublyʀ] nf lining; (CINÉMA) stand-in

douce [dus] adj voir **doux**; **douceâtre** adj sickly sweet; **doucement** adv gently; (lentement) slowly; **doucereux, -euse** (péj) adj sugary; **douceur** nf softness; (de quelqu'un) gentleness; (de climat) mildness

douche [duʃ] nf shower; **doucher: se doucher** vi to have ou take a shower

doudoune [dudun] nf padded jacket

doué, e [dwe] adj gifted, talented; **être ~ pour** to have a gift for

douille [duj] nf (ÉLEC) socket

douillet, te [dujɛ, ɛt] adj cosy; (péj: à la douleur) soft

douleur [dulœʀ] nf pain; (chagrin) grief, distress; **douloureux, -euse** adj painful

doute [dut] nm doubt; **sans ~** no doubt; (probablement) probably; **sans aucun ~** without a doubt; **douter** vt to doubt; **douter de** (sincérité de qn) to have (one's) doubts about; (réussite) to be doubtful of; **se douter de qch/que** to suspect sth/that; **je m'en doutais** I suspected as much; **douteux, -euse** adj (incertain) doubtful; (péj) dubious-looking

Douvres [duvʀ] n Dover

doux, douce [du, dus] adj soft; (sucré) sweet; (peu fort: moutarde, clément: climat) mild; (pas brusque) gentle

douzaine [duzɛn] nf (12) dozen; (environ 12): **une ~ (de)** a dozen or so, twelve or so

douze [duz] num twelve; **douzième** num twelfth

doyen, ne [dwajɛ̃, jɛn] nm/f (en âge) most senior member; (de faculté) dean

dragée [dʀaʒe] nf sugared almond

dragon [dʀagɔ̃] nm dragon

draguer [dʀage] vt (rivière) to dredge; (fam) to try to pick up

dramatique [dʀamatik] adj dramatic; (tragique) tragic ♦ nf (TV) (television) drama

dramaturge [dʀamatyʀʒ] nm dramatist, playwright

drame [dʀam] nm drama

drap [dʀa] nm (de lit) sheet; (tissu) woollen fabric

drapeau, x [dʀapo] nm flag

drap-housse [dʀaus] nm fitted sheet

dresser [dʀese] vt (mettre vertical, monter) to put up, erect; (liste) to draw up; (animal) to train; **se ~** vi (obstacle) to stand; (personne) to draw o.s. up; **~ qn contre qn** to set sb against sb; **~ l'oreille** to prick up one's ears

drogue [dʀɔg] nf drug; **la ~** drugs pl; **drogué, e** nm/f drug addict; **droguer** vt (victime) to drug; **se droguer** vi (aux stupéfiants) to take drugs; (péj: de médicaments) to dose o.s. up; **droguerie** nf hardware shop; **droguiste** nm keeper/owner of a hardware shop

droit, e [dʀwa, dʀwat] adj (non courbe) straight; (vertical) upright, straight; (fig: loyal) upright, straight(forward); (opposé à gauche) right, right-hand ♦ adv straight ♦ nm (prérogative) right; (taxe) duty, tax; (: d'inscription) fee; (JUR): **le ~** law; **avoir le ~ de** to be allowed to; **avoir ~ à** to be entitled to; **être dans son ~** to be within one's rights; **à ~e** on the right; (direction) (to the) right; **~s d'auteur** royalties; **~s de l'homme** human rights; **~s d'inscription** enrolment fee; **droite** nf (POL): **la droite** the right (wing); **droitier, -ière** nm/f right-handed person; **droiture** nf uprightness, straightness

drôle [dʀol] adj funny; **une ~ d'idée** a funny idea; **drôlement** (fam) adv (très) terribly, awfully

dromadaire [dʀɔmadɛʀ] nm dromedary

dru, e [dʀy] adj (cheveux) thick, bushy; (pluie) heavy

du [dy] dét voir **de** ♦ prép +dét = **de + le**

dû, due [dy] vb voir **devoir** ♦ adj (somme) owing, owed; (causé par): ~ **à** due to ♦ nm due

duc [dyk] nm duke; **duchesse** nf duchess

dûment [dymɑ̃] adv duly

dune [dyn] nf dune

Dunkerque [dœ̃kɛʀk] n Dunkirk

duo [dɥo] nm (MUS) duet

dupe [dyp] nf dupe ♦ adj: (**ne pas**) **être ~ de** (not) to be taken in by

duplex [dyplɛks] nm (appartement) split-level

apartment, duplex

duplicata [dyplikata] *nm* duplicate

duquel [dykɛl] *prép +pron* = **de +lequel**

dur, e [dyʀ] *adj (pierre, siège, travail, problème)* hard; *(voix, climat)* harsh; *(sévère)* hard, harsh; *(cruel)* hard(-hearted); *(porte, col)* stiff; *(viande)* tough ♦ *adv* hard ♦ *nm (fam: meneur)* tough nut; **~ d'oreille** hard of hearing

durant [dyʀɑ̃] *prép (au cours de)* during; *(pendant)* for; **des mois ~** for months

durcir [dyʀsiʀ] *vt, vi* to harden; **se ~** *vi* to harden

durée [dyʀe] *nf* length; *(d'une pile etc)* life; **de courte ~** *(séjour)* short

durement [dyʀmɑ̃] *adv* harshly

durer [dyʀe] *vi* to last

dureté [dyʀte] *nf* hardness; harshness; stiffness; toughness

durit ® [dyʀit] *nf (car radiator)* hose

dus *etc* [dy] *vb voir* **devoir**

duvet [dyvɛ] *nm* down; *(sac de couchage)* down-filled sleeping bag

dynamique [dinamik] *adj* dynamic; **dynamisme** *nm* dynamism

dynamite [dinamit] *nf* dynamite

dynamo [dinamo] *nf* dynamo

dysenterie [disɑ̃tʀi] *nf* dysentery

dyslexie [disleksi] *nf* dyslexia, word-blindness

E, e

eau, x [o] *nf* water; **~x** *nfpl (MÉD)* waters; **prendre l'~** to leak, let in water; **tomber à l'~** *(fig)* to fall through; **~ courante** running water; **~ de Javel** bleach; **~ de toilette** toilet water; **~ douce** fresh water; **~ gazeuse** sparkling (mineral) water; **~ minérale** mineral water; **~ plate** still water; **~ potable** drinking water; **eau-de-vie** *nf* brandy; **eau-forte** *nf* etching

ébahi, e [ebai] *adj* dumbfounded

ébattre [ebatʀ]: **s'~** *vi* to frolic

ébaucher [eboʃe] *vt* to sketch out, outline; **s'~** *vi* to take shape

ébène [ebɛn] *nf* ebony; **ébéniste** *nm* cabinetmaker

éberlué, e [ebɛʀlɥe] *adj* astounded

éblouir [ebluiʀ] *vt* to dazzle

éborgner [ebɔʀɲe] *vt* to blind in one eye

éboueur [ebwœʀ] *nm* dustman *(BRIT)*, garbageman *(US)*

ébouillanter [ebujɑ̃te] *vt* to scald; *(CULIN)* to blanch

éboulement [ebulmɑ̃] *nm* rock fall

ébouler [ebule]: **s'~** *vi* to crumble, collapse; **éboulis** *nmpl* fallen rocks

ébouriffé, e [ebuʀife] *adj* tousled

ébranler [ebʀɑ̃le] *vt* to shake; *(affaiblir)* to weaken; **s'~** *vi (partir)* to move off

ébrécher [ebʀeʃe] *vt* to chip

ébriété [ebʀijete] *nf*: **en état d'~** in a state of intoxication

ébrouer [ebʀue]: **s'~** *vi* to shake o.s.

ébruiter [ebʀɥite] *vt* to spread, disclose

ébullition [ebylisjɔ̃] *nf* boiling point

écaille [ekaj] *nf (de poisson)* scale; *(matière)* tortoiseshell; **écailler** *vt (poisson)* to scale; **s'écailler** *vi* to flake *ou* peel (off)

écarlate [ekaʀlat] *adj* scarlet

écarquiller [ekaʀkije] *vt*: **~ les yeux** to stare wide-eyed

écart [ekaʀ] *nm* gap; **à l'~** out of the way; **à l'~ de** away from; **faire un ~** *(voiture)* to swerve; **~ de conduite** misdemeanour

écarté, e [ekaʀte] *adj (lieu)* out-of-the-way, remote; *(ouvert)*: **les jambes ~es** legs apart; **les bras ~s** arms outstretched

écarter [ekaʀte] *vt (séparer)* to move apart, separate; *(éloigner)* to push back, move away; *(ouvrir: bras, jambes)* to spread, open; *(: rideau)* to draw (back); *(éliminer: candidat, possibilité)* to dismiss; **s'~** *vi* to part; *(s'éloigner)* to move away; **s'~ de** to wander from

écervelé, e [esɛʀvəle] *adj* scatterbrained, featherbrained

échafaud [eʃafo] *nm* scaffold

échafaudage [eʃafodaʒ] *nm* scaffolding

échafauder [eʃafode] *vt (plan)* to construct

échalote [eʃalɔt] *nf* shallot

échancrure [eʃɑ̃kʀyʀ] *nf (de robe)* scoop neckline

échange [eʃɑ̃ʒ] *nm* exchange; **en ~ de** in exchange *ou* return for; **échanger** *vt*: **échanger qch (contre)** to exchange sth (for); **échangeur** *nm (AUTO)* interchange

échantillon [eʃɑ̃tijɔ̃] *nm* sample

échappement [eʃapmɑ̃] *nm (AUTO)* exhaust

échapper [eʃape]: **~ à** *vt (gardien)* to escape (from); *(punition, péril)* to escape; **s'~** *vi* to escape; **~ à qn** *(détail, sens)* to escape sb; *(objet qu'on tient)* to slip out of sb's hands; **laisser ~** *(cri etc)* to let out; **l'~ belle** to have a narrow escape

écharde [eʃaʀd] *nf* splinter (of wood)

écharpe [eʃaʀp] *nf* scarf; **avoir le bras en ~** to have one's arm in a sling

échasse [eʃas] *nf* stilt

échassier [eʃasje] *nm* wader

échauffer [eʃofe] *vt (moteur)* to overheat; **s'~** *vi (SPORT)* to warm up; *(dans la discussion)* to become heated

échéance [eʃeɑ̃s] *nf (d'un paiement: date)* settlement date; *(fig)* deadline; **à brève ~** in the short term; **à longue ~** in the long run

échéant [eʃeɑ̃]: **le cas ~** *adv* if the case arises

échec [eʃɛk] nm failure; (ÉCHECS): ~ **et mat/au roi** checkmate/check; ~**s** nmpl (jeu) chess sg; **tenir en ~** to hold in check

échelle [eʃɛl] nf ladder; (fig, d'une carte) scale

échelon [eʃ(ə)lɔ̃] nm (d'échelle) rung; (ADMIN) grade; **échelonner** vt to space out

échevelé, e [eʃəv(ə)le] adj tousled, dishevelled

échine [eʃin] nf backbone, spine

échiquier [eʃikje] nm chessboard

écho [eko] nm echo; **échographie** nf: **passer une échographie** to have a scan

échoir [eʃwaʀ] vi (dette) to fall due; (délais) to expire; ~ **à** to fall to

échouer [eʃwe] vi to fail; **s'~** vi to run aground

échu, e [eʃy] pp de **échoir**

éclabousser [eklabuse] vt to splash

éclair [eklɛʀ] nm (d'orage) flash of lightning, lightning no pl; (gâteau) éclair

éclairage [eklɛʀaʒ] nm lighting

éclaircie [eklɛʀsi] nf bright interval

éclaircir [eklɛʀsiʀ] vt to lighten; (fig: mystère) to clear up; (: point) to clarify; **s'~** vi (ciel) to clear; **s'~ la voix** to clear one's throat; **éclaircissement** nm (sur un point) clarification

éclairer [eklɛʀe] vt (lieu) to light (up); (personne) to light the way for; (fig: problème) to shed light on ♦ vi: ~ **mal/bien** to give a poor/good light; **s'~ à la bougie** to use candlelight

éclaireur, -euse [eklɛʀœʀ, øz] nm/f (scout) (boy) scout/(girl) guide ♦ nm (MIL) scout

éclat [ekla] nm (de bombe, de verre) fragment; (du soleil, d'une couleur etc) brightness, brilliance; (d'une cérémonie) splendour; (scandale): **faire un ~** to cause a commotion; ~**s de voix** shouts; ~ **de rire** roar of laughter

éclatant, e [eklatɑ̃, ɑ̃t] adj brilliant

éclater [eklate] vi (pneu) to burst; (bombe) to explode; (guerre) to break out; (groupe, parti) to break up; ~ **en sanglots/de rire** to burst out sobbing/laughing

éclipser [eklipse]: **s'~** vi to slip away

éclore [eklɔʀ] vi (œuf) to hatch; (fleur) to open (out)

écluse [eklyz] nf lock

écœurant, e [ekœrɑ̃, ɑ̃t] adj (gâteau etc) sickly; (fig) sickening

écœurer [ekœre] vt: ~ **qn** (nourriture) to make sb feel sick; (conduite, personne) to disgust sb

école [ekɔl] nf school; **aller à l'~** to go to school; ~ **maternelle/primaire** nursery/primary school; ~ **publique** state school; **écolier, -ière** nm/f schoolboy(-girl)

écologie [ekɔlɔʒi] nf ecology; **écologique** adj environment-friendly; **écologiste** nm/f ecologist

éconduire [ekɔ̃dɥiʀ] vt to dismiss

économe [ekɔnɔm] adj thrifty ♦ nm/f (de lycée etc) bursar (BRIT), treasurer (US)

économie [ekɔnɔmi] nf economy; (gain: d'argent, de temps etc) saving; (science) economics sg; ~**s** nfpl (pécule) savings; **économique** adj (avantageux) economical; (ÉCON) economic; **économiser** vt, vi to save

écoper [ekɔpe] vi to bale out; ~ **de 3 ans de prison** (fig: fam) to get sentenced to 3 years

écorce [ekɔʀs] nf bark; (de fruit) peel

écorcher [ekɔʀʃe] vt: **s'~ le genou/la main** to graze one's knee/one's hand; **écorchure** nf graze

écossais, e [ekɔsɛ, ɛz] adj Scottish ♦ nm/f: É~, e Scot

Écosse [ekɔs] nf: **l'~** Scotland

écosser [ekɔse] vt to shell

écoulement [ekulmɑ̃] nm (d'eau) flow

écouler [ekule] vt (marchandise) to sell; **s'~** vi (eau) to flow (out); (jours, temps) to pass (by)

écourter [ekuʀte] vt to curtail, cut short

écoute [ekut] nf (RADIO, TV): **temps/heure d'~** listening (ou viewing) time/hour; **rester à l'~ (de)** to stay tuned in (to); ~**s téléphoniques** phone tapping sg

écouter [ekute] vt to listen to; **écouteur** nm (TÉL) receiver; (RADIO) headphones pl, headset

écoutille [ekutij] nf hatch

écran [ekrɑ̃] nm screen; **petit ~** television; ~ **total** sunblock

écrasant, e [ekrazɑ̃, ɑ̃t] adj overwhelming

écraser [ekraze] vt to crush; (piéton) to run over; **s'~** vi to crash; **s'~ contre** to crash into

écrémé, e [ekreme] adj (lait) skimmed

écrevisse [ekrəvis] nf crayfish inv

écrier [ekrije]: **s'~** vi to exclaim

écrin [ekrɛ̃] nm case, box

écrire [ekriʀ] vt to write; **s'~** to write to each other; **ça s'écrit comment?** how is it spelt?; **écrit** nm (examen) written paper; **par écrit** in writing

écriteau, x [ekrito] nm notice, sign

écriture [ekrityʀ] nf writing; **l'É~, les É~s** the Scriptures

écrivain [ekrivɛ̃] nm writer

écrou [ekru] nm nut

écrouer [ekrue] vt to imprison

écrouler [ekrule]: **s'~** vi to collapse

écru, e [ekry] adj (couleur) off-white, écru

ECU [eky] sigle m ECU

écueil [ekœj] nm reef; (fig) pitfall

éculé, e [ekyle] adj (chaussure) down-at-heel; (fig: péj) hackneyed

écume [ekym] nf foam; **écumer** vt (CULIN) to skim; **écumoire** nf skimmer

écureuil [ekyʀœj] nm squirrel

écurie [ekyʀi] nf stable

écusson [ekysɔ̃] nm badge

écuyer, -ère [ekɥije, jɛʀ] nm/f rider

eczéma [ɛgzema] nm eczema

édenté, e [edɑ̃te] adj toothless

EDF sigle f (= Électricité de France) national electricity company

édifice [edifis] nm edifice, building

édifier [edifje] vt to build, erect; (fig) to edify

Édimbourg [edɛ̃buʀ] n Edinburgh

éditer [edite] vt (publier) to publish; (annoter) to edit; **éditeur, -trice** nm/f publisher; **édition** nf edition; (industrie du livre) publishing

édredon [edʀədɔ̃] nm elderdown

éducateur, -trice [edykatœʀ, tʀis] nm/f teacher; (in special school) instructor

éducatif, -ive [edykatif, iv] adj educational

éducation [edykasjɔ̃] nf education; (familiale) upbringing; (manières) (good) manners pl; ~ physique physical education

édulcorant [edylkɔʀɑ̃] nm sweetener

éduquer [edyke] vt to educate; (élever) to bring up

effacé, e [efase] adj unassuming

effacer [efase] vt to erase, rub out; **s'~** vi (inscription etc) to wear off; (pour laisser passer) to step aside

effarant, e [efaʀɑ̃, ɑ̃t] adj alarming

effarer [efaʀe] vt to alarm

effaroucher [efaʀuʃe] vt to frighten ou scare away

effectif, -ive [efɛktif, iv] adj real ♦ nm (SCOL) (pupil) numbers pl; (entreprise) staff, workforce; **effectivement** adv (réellement) actually, really; (en effet) indeed

effectuer [efɛktɥe] vt (opération) to carry out; (trajet) to make

efféminé, e [efemine] adj effeminate

effervescent, e [efɛʀvesɑ̃, ɑ̃t] adj effervescent

effet [efɛ] nm effect; (impression) impression; **~s** nmpl (vêtements etc) things; **faire ~** (médicament) to take effect; **faire bon/ mauvais ~ sur qn** to make a good/bad impression on sb; **en ~** indeed; **~ de serre** greenhouse effect

efficace [efikas] adj (personne) efficient; (action, médicament) effective; **efficacité** nf efficiency; effectiveness

effilocher [efilɔʃe] : **s'~** vi to fray

efflanqué, e [eflɑ̃ke] adj emaciated

effleurer [eflœʀe] vt to brush (against); (sujet) to touch upon; (suj: idée, pensée): **ça ne m'a pas effleuré** it didn't cross my mind

effluves [eflyv] nmpl exhalation(s)

effondrer [efɔ̃dʀe] : **s'~** vi to collapse

efforcer [efɔʀse] : **s'~ de** vt : **s'~ de faire** to try hard to do

effort [efɔʀ] nm effort

effraction [efʀaksjɔ̃] nf: **s'introduire par ~ dans** to break into

effrayant, e [efʀɛjɑ̃, ɑ̃t] adj frightening

effrayer [efʀeje] vt to frighten, scare

effréné, e [efʀene] adj wild

effriter [efʀite] : **s'~** vi to crumble

effroi [efʀwa] nm terror, dread no pl

effronté, e [efʀɔ̃te] adj cheeky

effroyable [efʀwajabl] adj horrifying, appalling

effusion [efyzjɔ̃] nf effusion; **sans ~ de sang** without bloodshed

égal, e, -aux [egal, o] adj equal; (constant: vitesse) steady ♦ nm/f equal; **être ~ à** (prix, nombre) to be equal to; **ça lui est ~** it's all the same to him, he doesn't mind; **sans ~** matchless, unequalled; **d'~ à ~** as equals;

également adv equally; (aussi) too, as well;

égaler vt to equal; **égaliser** vt (sol, salaires) to level (out); (chances) to equalize ♦ vi (SPORT) to equalize; **égalité** nf equality; **être à égalité** to be equal

égard [egaʀ] nm: **~s** consideration sg; **à cet ~** in this respect; **par ~ pour** out of consideration for; **à l'~ de** towards

égarement [egaʀmɑ̃] nm distraction

égarer [egaʀe] vt to mislay; **s'~** vi to get lost, lose one's way; (objet) to go astray

égayer [egeje] vt to cheer up; (pièce) to brighten up

églantine [eglɑ̃tin] nf wild ou dog rose

églefin [eglɔtɛ̃] nm haddock

église [egliz] nf church; **aller à l'~** to go to church

égoïsme [egɔism] nm selfishness; **égoïste** adj selfish

égorger [egɔʀʒe] vt to cut the throat of

égosiller [egozije] : **s'~** vi to shout o.s. hoarse

égout [egu] nm sewer

égoutter [egute] vi to drip; **s'~** vi to drip; **égouttoir** nm draining board; (mobile) draining rack

égratigner [egʀatiɲe] vt to scratch; **égratignure** nf scratch

Égypte [eʒipt] nf: **l'~** Egypt; **égyptien, ne** adj Egyptian ♦ nm/f: **Égyptien, ne** Egyptian

eh [e] excl hey!; **~ bien** well

éhonté, e [eɔ̃te] adj shameless, brazen

éjecter [eʒɛkte] vt (TECH) to eject; (fam) to kick ou chuck out

élaborer [elabɔʀe] vt to elaborate; (projet, stratégie) to work out; (rapport) to draft

élan [elɑ̃] nm (ZOOL) elk, moose; (SPORT) run up; (fig: de tendresse etc) surge; **prendre de l'~** to gather speed

élancé, e [elɑ̃se] adj slender

élancement [elɑ̃smɑ̃] nm shooting pain

élancer [elɑ̃se] : **s'~** vi to dash, hurl o.s.

élargir [elaʀʒiʀ] vt to widen; **s'~** vi to widen; (vêtement) to stretch

élastique [elastik] adj elastic ♦ nm (de bureau) rubber band; (pour la couture) elastic no pl

électeur, -trice [elɛktœʀ, tʀis] nm/f elector, voter

élection [elɛksjɔ̃] nf election

électorat [elɛktɔʀa] nm electorate

électricien, ne [elɛktʀisjɛ̃, jɛn] nm/f electrician

électricité [elɛktʀisite] nf electricity; **allumer/éteindre l'~** to put on/off the light

électrique [elɛktʀik] adj electric(al)

électrocuter [elɛktʀɔkyte] vt to electrocute

électroménager [elɛktʀomenaʒe] adj, nm: **appareils ~s, l'~** domestic (electrical) appliances

électronique [elɛktʀɔnik] adj electronic ♦ nf electronics sg

électrophone [elɛktʀɔfɔn] nm record player

élégance [elegɑ̃s] nf elegance

élégant, e [elegɑ̃, ɑ̃t] adj elegant

élément [elemɑ̃] nm element; (pièce) component, part; **~s de cuisine** kitchen units;
élémentaire adj elementary

éléphant [elefɑ̃] nm elephant

élevage [el(ə)vaʒ] nm breeding; (de bovins) cattle rearing; **truite d'~** farmed trout

élévation [elevasjɔ̃] nf (hausse) rise

élevé, e [el(ə)ve] adj high; **bien/mal ~** well-/ ill-mannered

élève [elɛv] nm/f pupil

élever [el(ə)ve] vt (enfant) to bring up, raise; (animaux) to breed; (hausser: taux, niveau) to raise; (édifier: monument) to put up, erect; **s'~** vi (avion) to go up; (niveau, température) to rise; **s'~ à** (suj: frais, dégâts) to amount to, add up to; **s'~ contre qch** to rise up against sth; **~ la voix** to raise one's voice; **éleveur, -euse** nm/f breeder

élimé, e [elime] adj threadbare

éliminatoire [eliminatwaʀ] nf (SPORT) heat

éliminer [elimine] vt to eliminate

élire [eliʀ] vt to elect

elle [ɛl] pron (sujet) she; (: chose) it; (complément) her; it; **~s** (sujet) they; (complément) them; **~-même** herself; itself; **~s-mêmes** themselves; voir aussi **il**

élocution [elɔkysjɔ̃] nf delivery; **défaut d'~** speech impediment

éloge [elɔʒ] nm (gén no pl) praise; **faire l'~ de** to praise; **élogieux, -euse** adj laudatory, full of praise

éloigné, e [elwaɲe] adj distant, far-off; (parent) distant; **éloignement** nm (distance, aussi fig) distance

éloigner [elwaɲe] vt (échéance) to put off, postpone; (soupçons, danger) to ward off;

(objet): **~ qch (de)** to move ou take sth away (from); (personne): **~ qn (de)** to take sb away ou remove sb (from); **s'~ (de)** (personne) to go away (from); (véhicule) to move away (from); (affectivement) to become estranged (from); **ne vous éloignez pas!** don't go far away!

élu, e [ely] pp de **élire** ♦ nm/f (POL) elected representative

éluder [elyde] vt to evade

Élysée [elize] nm: **(le palais de) l'~** the Élysée Palace (the French president's residence)

émacié, e [emasje] adj emaciated

émail, -aux [emaj, o] nm enamel

émaillé, e [emaje] adj (fig): **~ de** dotted with

émanciper [emɑ̃sipe]: **s'~** vi (fig) to become emancipated ou liberated

émaner [emane]: **~ de** vt to come from

emballage [ɑ̃balaʒ] nm (papier) wrapping; (boîte) packaging

emballer [ɑ̃bale] vt to wrap (up); (dans un carton) to pack (up); (fig: fam) to thrill (to bits); **s'~** vi (moteur) to race; (cheval) to bolt; (fig: personne) to get carried away

embarcadère [ɑ̃baʀkadɛʀ] nm wharf, pier

embarcation [ɑ̃baʀkasjɔ̃] nf (small) boat, (small) craft inv

embardée [ɑ̃baʀde] nf: **faire une ~** to swerve

embarquement [ɑ̃baʀkəmɑ̃] nm (de passagers) boarding; (de marchandises) loading

embarquer [ɑ̃baʀke] vt (personne) to embark; (marchandise) to load; (fam) to cart off ♦ vi (passager) to board; **s'~** vi to board; **s'~ dans** (affaire, aventure) to embark upon

embarras [ɑ̃baʀa] nm (gêne) embarrassment; **mettre qn dans l'~** to put sb in an awkward position; **vous n'avez que l'~ du choix** the only problem is choosing

embarrassant, e [ɑ̃baʀasɑ̃, ɑ̃t] adj embarrassing

embarrasser [ɑ̃baʀase] vt (encombrer) to clutter (up); (gêner) to hinder, hamper; **~ qn** to put sb in an awkward position; **s'~ de** to burden o.s. with

embauche [ɑ̃boʃ] nf hiring; **embaucher** vt to take on, hire

embaumer [ɑ̃bome] vt: **~ la lavande** etc to be fragrant with (the scent of) lavender etc

embellie [ɑ̃beli] nf brighter period

embellir [ɑ̃beliʀ] vt to make more attractive; (une histoire) to embellish ♦ vi to grow lovelier ou more attractive

embêtements [ɑ̃bɛtmɑ̃] nmpl trouble sg

embêter [ɑ̃bete] vt to bother; **s'~** vi (s'ennuyer) to be bored

emblée [ɑ̃ble]: **d'~** adv straightaway

embobiner [ɑ̃bɔbine] vt (fam) to get round

emboîter [ɑ̃bwate] vt to fit together;

s'~ (dans) to fit (into); **~ le pas à qn** to follow in sb's footsteps

embonpoint [ãbɔpwɛ̃] nm stoutness

embouchure [ãbuʃyr] nf (GÉO) mouth

embourber [ãburbe]: **s'~** vi to get stuck in the mud

embourgeoiser [ãburʒwaze]: **s'~** vi to become middle-class

embouteillage [ãbutɛjaʒ] nm traffic jam

emboutir [ãbutir] vt (heurter) to crash into, ram

embranchement [ãbrãʃmã] nm (routier) junction

embraser [ãbraze]: **s'~** vi to flare up

embrassades [ãbrasad] nfpl hugging and kissing

embrasser [ãbrase] vt to kiss; (sujet, période) to embrace, encompass; **s'~** to kiss (each other)

embrasure [ãbrazyr] nf: **dans l'~ de la porte** in the door(way)

embrayage [ãbrɛjaʒ] nm clutch

embrayer [ãbreje] vi (AUTO) to let in the clutch

embrocher [ãbrɔʃe] vt to put on a spit

embrouiller [ãbruje] vt to muddle up; (fils) to tangle (up); **s'~** vi (personne) to get in a muddle

embruns [ãbrœ̃] nmpl sea spray sg

embryon [ãbrijɔ̃] nm embryo

embûches [ãbyʃ] nfpl pitfalls, traps

embué, e [ãbɥe] adj misted up

embuscade [ãbyskad] nf ambush

éméché, e [emeʃe] adj tipsy, merry

émeraude [em(ə)rod] nf emerald

émerger [emɛrʒe] vi to emerge; (faire saillie, aussi fig) to stand out

émeri [em(ə)ri] nm: **toile ou papier ~** emery paper

émerveillement [emɛrvɛjmã] nm wonder

émerveiller [emɛrveje] vt to fill with wonder; **s'~ de** to marvel at

émettre [emɛtr] vt (son, lumière) to give out, emit; (message etc: RADIO) to transmit; (billet, timbre, emprunt) to issue; (hypothèse, avis) to voice, put forward ♦ vi to broadcast

émeus etc [emø] vb voir **émouvoir**

émeute [emøt] nf riot

émietter [emjete] vt to crumble

émigrer [emigre] vi to emigrate

émincer [emɛ̃se] vt to cut into thin slices

éminent, e [eminã, ãt] adj distinguished

émission [emisjɔ̃] nf (RADIO, TV) programme, broadcast; (d'un message) transmission; (de timbre) issue

emmagasiner [ãmagazine] vt (amasser) to store up

emmanchure [ãmãʃyr] nf armhole

emmêler [ãmele] vt to tangle (up); (fig) to

muddle up; **s'~** vi to get in a tangle

emménager [ãmenaʒe] vi to move in; **~ dans** to move into

emmener [ãm(ə)ne] vt to take (with one); (comme otage, capture) to take away; **~ qn au cinéma** to take sb to the cinema

emmerder [ãmɛrde] (fam!) vt to bug, bother; **s'~** vi to be bored stiff

emmitoufler [ãmitufle]: **s'~** vi to wrap up (warmly)

émoi [emwa] nm commotion

émotif, -ive [emotif, iv] adj emotional

émotion [emosjɔ̃] nf emotion

émousser [emuse] vt to blunt; (fig) to dull

émouvoir [emuvwar] vt to move; **s'~** vi to be moved; (s'indigner) to be roused

empailler [ãpaje] vt to stuff

empaqueter [ãpakte] vt to parcel up

emparer [ãpare]: **s'~ de** vt (objet) to seize, grab; (comme otage, MIL) to seize; (suj: peur etc) to take hold of

empâter [ãpate]: **s'~** vi to thicken out

empêchement [ãpɛʃmã] nm (unexpected) obstacle, hitch

empêcher [ãpeʃe] vt to prevent; **~ qn de faire** to prevent ou stop sb (from) doing; **il n'empêche que** nevertheless; **il n'a pas pu s'~ de rire** he couldn't help laughing

empereur [ãprœr] nm emperor

empester [ãpɛste] vi to stink, reek

empêtrer [ãpetre] vt: **s'~ dans** (fils etc) to get tangled up in

emphase [ãfaz] nf pomposity, bombast

empiéter [ãpjete] vi: **~ sur** to encroach upon

empiffrer [ãpifre]: **s'~** (fam) vi to stuff o.s

empiler [ãpile] vt to pile (up)

empire [ãpir] nm empire; (fig) influence

empirer [ãpire] vi to worsen, deteriorate

emplacement [ãplasmã] nm site

emplettes [ãplɛt] nfpl shopping sg

emplir [ãplir] vt to fill; **s'~ (de)** to fill (with)

emploi [ãplwa] nm use; (COMM, ÉCON) employment; (poste) job, situation; **mode d'~** directions for use; **~ du temps** timetable, schedule

employé, e [ãplwaje] nm/f employee; **~ de bureau** office employee ou clerk

employer [ãplwaje] vt to use; (ouvrier, main-d'œuvre) to employ; **s'~ à faire** to apply ou devote o.s. to doing; **employeur, -euse** nm/f employer

empocher [ãpɔʃe] vt to pocket

empoigner [ãpwaɲe] vt to grab

empoisonner [ãpwazɔne] vt to poison; (empester: air, pièce) to stink out; (fam): **~ qn** to drive sb mad

emporté, e [ãpɔrte] adj quick-tempered

emporter [ãpɔrte] vt to take (with one); (en dérobant ou enlevant, emmener: blessés, *voyageurs)* to take away; (*entraîner*) to carry away; **s'~** *vi (de colère)* to lose one's temper; **l'~ (sur)** to get the upper hand (of); **plats à ~** take-away meals

empreint, e [ɑ̃pʀɛ̃, ɛ̃t] *adj:* **~ de** *(regret, jalousie)* marked with; **empreinte** *nf:* **empreinte (de pas)** footprint; **empreinte (digitale)** fingerprint

empressé, e [ɑ̃pʀese] *adj* attentive

empressement [ɑ̃pʀɛsmɑ̃] *nm (hâte)* eagerness

empresser [ɑ̃pʀese]: **s'~** *vi:* **s'~ auprès de qn** to surround sb with attentions; **s'~ de faire** *(se hâter)* to hasten to do

emprise [ɑ̃pʀiz] *nf* hold, ascendancy

emprisonnement [ɑ̃pʀizɔnmɑ̃] *nm* imprisonment

emprisonner [ɑ̃pʀizɔne] *vt* to imprison

emprunt [ɑ̃pʀœ̃] *nm* loan

emprunté, e [ɑ̃pʀœ̃te] *adj (fig)* ill-at-ease, awkward

emprunter [ɑ̃pʀœ̃te] *vt* to borrow; (*itinéraire*) to take, follow

ému, e [emy] *pp de* **émouvoir ♦** *adj (gratitude)* touched; *(compassion)* moved

---
MOT-CLÉ
---

en [ɑ̃] *prép* **1** *(endroit, pays)* in; *(direction)* to; **habiter en France/ville** to live in France/town; **aller en France/ville** to go to France/town
2 *(moment, temps)* in; **en été/juin** in summer/June
3 *(moyen)* by; **en avion/taxi** by plane/taxi
4 *(composition)* made of; **c'est en verre** it's (made of) glass; **un collier en argent** a silver necklace
5 *(description, état)*: **une femme (habillée) en rouge** a woman (dressed) in red; **peindre qch en rouge** to paint sth red; **en T/étoile** T/star-shaped; **en chemise/chaussettes** in one's shirt-sleeves/socks; **en soldat** as a soldier; **cassé en plusieurs morceaux** broken into several pieces; **en réparation** being repaired, under repair; **en vacances** on holiday; **en deuil** in mourning; **le même en plus grand** the same but *ou* only bigger
6 *(avec gérondif)* while, on, by; **en dormant** while sleeping, as one sleeps; **en sortant** on going out, as he *etc* went out; **sortir en courant** to run out
♦ *pron* **1** *(indéfini)*: **j'en ai/veux** I have/want some; **en as-tu?** have you got any?; **je n'en veux pas** I don't want any; **j'en ai 2** I've got 2; **combien y en a-t-il?** how many (of them) are there?; **j'en ai assez** I've got enough (of it *ou* them); *(j'en ai marre)* I've had enough
2 *(provenance)* from there; **j'en viens** I've come from there
3 *(cause)*: **il en est malade/perd le sommeil**

he is ill/can't sleep because of it
4 *(complément de nom, d'adjectif, de verbe)*: **j'en connais les dangers** I know its *ou* the dangers; **j'en suis fier/ai besoin** I am proud of it/need it

---

ENA [ena] *sigle f* (= *École Nationale d'Administration*) one of the *Grandes Écoles*

encadrement [ɑ̃kɑdʀəmɑ̃] *nm (cadres)* managerial staff

encadrer [ɑ̃kɑdʀe] *vt (tableau, image)* to frame; *(fig: entourer)* to surround; *(personnel, soldats etc)* to train

encaissé, e [ɑ̃kese] *adj (vallée)* steep-sided; *(rivière)* with steep banks

encaisser [ɑ̃kese] *vt (chèque)* to cash; *(argent)* to collect; *(fam: coup, défaite)* to take

encart [ɑ̃kaʀ] *nm* insert

en-cas [ɑ̃kɑ] *nm* snack

encastré, e [ɑ̃kastʀe] *adj:* **four ~** built-in oven

enceinte [ɑ̃sɛ̃t] *adj f:* **~ (de 6 mois)** (6 months) pregnant **♦** *nf (mur)* wall; *(espace)* enclosure; *(aussi:* **~ acoustique)** (loud)speaker

encens [ɑ̃sɑ̃] *nm* incense

encercler [ɑ̃sɛʀkle] *vt* to surround

enchaîner [ɑ̃ʃene] *vt* to chain up; *(mouvements, séquences)* to link (together) **♦** *vi* to carry on

enchanté, e [ɑ̃ʃɑ̃te] *adj (ravi)* delighted; *(magique)* enchanted; **~ (de faire votre connaissance)** pleased to meet you

enchantement [ɑ̃ʃɑ̃tmɑ̃] *nm* delight; *(magie)* enchantment

enchère [ɑ̃ʃɛʀ] *nf* bid; **mettre/vendre aux ~s** to put up for (sale by)/sell by auction

enchevêtrer [ɑ̃ʃ(ə)vetʀe]: **s'~** *vi* to get in a tangle

enclencher [ɑ̃klɑ̃ʃe] *vt (mécanisme)* to engage; **s'~** *vi* to engage

enclin, e [ɑ̃klɛ̃, in] *adj:* **~ à** inclined *ou* prone to

enclos [ɑ̃klo] *nm* enclosure

enclume [ɑ̃klym] *nf* anvil

encoche [ɑ̃kɔʃ] *nf* notch

encoignure [ɑ̃kɔɲyʀ] *nf* corner

encolure [ɑ̃kɔlyʀ] *nf (cou)* neck

encombrant, e [ɑ̃kɔ̃bʀɑ̃, ɑ̃t] *adj* cumbersome, bulky

encombre [ɑ̃kɔ̃bʀ]: **sans ~** *adv* without mishap *ou* incident; **encombrement** *nm:* **être pris dans un encombrement** to be stuck in a traffic jam

encombrer [ɑ̃kɔ̃bʀe] *vt* to clutter (up); *(gêner)* to hamper; **s'~ de** *(bagages etc)* to load *ou* burden o.s. with

encontre [ɑ̃kɔ̃tʀ]: **à l'~ de** *prép* against,

counter to

encore [ãkɔʀ] adv **1** (*continuation*) still; **il y travaille encore** he's still working on it; **pas encore** not yet
2 (*de nouveau*) again; **j'irai encore demain** I'll go again tomorrow; **encore une fois** (once) again; **encore deux jours** two more days
3 (*intensif*) even, still; **encore plus fort/mieux** even louder/better, louder/better still
4 (*restriction*) even so *ou* then, only; **encore pourrais-je le faire si ...** even so, I might be able to do it if ...; **si encore** if only
encore que *conj* although

encouragement [ãkuʀaʒmã] *nm* encouragement
encourager [ãkuʀaʒe] *vt* to encourage
encourir [ãkuʀiʀ] *vt* to incur
encrasser [ãkʀase] *vt* to make filthy
encre [ãkʀ] *nf* ink; **encrier** *nm* inkwell
encroûter [ãkʀute]: **s'~** (*fam*) *vi* (*tiq*) to get into a rut, get set in one's ways
encyclopédie [ãsiklɔpedi] *nf* encyclopaedia
endetter [ãdete]: **s'~** *vi* to get into debt
endiablé, e [ãdjable] *adj* (*danse*) furious
endimanché, e [ãdimãʃe] *adj* in one's Sunday best
endive [ãdiv] *nf* chicory *no pl*
endoctriner [ãdɔktʀine] *vt* to indoctrinate
endommager [ãdɔmaʒe] *vt* to damage
endormi, e [ãdɔʀmi] *adj* asleep
endormir [ãdɔʀmiʀ] *vt* to put to sleep; (*suj: chaleur etc*) to send to sleep; (*MÉD: dent, nerf*) to anaesthetize; (*fig: soupçons*) to allay; **s'~** *vi* to fall asleep, go to sleep
endosser [ãdose] *vt* (*responsabilité*) to take, shoulder; (*chèque*) to endorse; (*uniforme, tenue*) to put on, don
endroit [ãdʀwa] *nm* place; (*opposé à l'envers*) right side; **à l'~** (*vêtement*) the right way out; (*objet posé*) the right way round
enduire [ãdɥiʀ] *vt* to coat
enduit [ãdɥi] *nm* coating
endurance [ãdyʀãs] *nf* endurance
endurant, e [ãdyʀã, ãt] *adj* tough, hardy
endurcir [ãdyʀsiʀ]: **s'~** *vi* (*physiquement*) to become tougher; (*moralement*) to become hardened
endurer [ãdyʀe] *vt* to endure, bear
énergétique [enɛʀʒetik] *adj* (*aliment*) energy-giving
énergie [enɛʀʒi] *nf* (*PHYSIQUE*) energy; (*TECH*) power; (*morale*) vigour, spirit; **énergique** *adj* energetic, vigorous, (*mesures*) drastic, stringent
énervant, e [enɛʀvã, ãt] *adj* irritating, annoying

énerver [enɛʀve] *vt* to irritate, annoy; **s'~** *vi* to get excited, get worked up
enfance [ãfãs] *nf* childhood
enfant [ãfã] *nm/f* child; **~ de chœur** *nm* (*REL*) altar boy; **enfantillage** (*péj*) *nm* childish behaviour *no pl*; **enfantin, e** *adj* (*puéril*) childlike; (*langage, jeu etc*) children's *cpd*
enfer [ãfɛʀ] *nm* hell
enfermer [ãfɛʀme] *vt* to shut up; (*à clef, interner*) to lock up
enfiévré, e [ãfjevʀe] *adj* feverish
enfiler [ãfile] *vt* (*vêtement*) to slip on, slip into; (*perles*) to string; (*aiguille*) to thread
enfin [ãfɛ̃] *adv* at last; (*en énumérant*) lastly; (*toutefois*) still; (*pour conclure*) in a word; (*somme toute*) after all
enflammer [ãflame]: **s'~** *vi* to catch fire; (*MÉD*) to become inflamed
enflé, e [ãfle] *adj* swollen
enfler [ãfle] *vi* to swell (up)
enfoncer [ãfɔ̃se] *vt* (*clou*) to drive in; (*faire pénétrer*): **~ qch dans** to push (*ou* drive) sth into; (*forcer: porte*) to break open; **s'~** *vi* to sink; **s'~ dans** to sink into; (*forêt, ville*) to disappear into
enfouir [ãfwiʀ] *vt* (*dans le sol*) to bury; (*dans un tiroir etc*) to tuck away
enfourcher [ãfuʀʃe] *vt* to mount
enfreindre [ãfʀɛ̃dʀ] *vt* to infringe, break
enfuir [ãfɥiʀ]: **s'~** *vi* to run away *ou* off
enfumer [ãfyme] *vt* (*pièce*) to fill with smoke
engageant, e [ãgaʒã, ãt] *adj* attractive, appealing
engagement [ãgaʒmã] *nm* commitment
engager [ãgaʒe] *vt* (*embaucher*) to take on; (*: artiste*) to engage; (*commencer*) to start; (*lier*) to bind, commit; (*impliquer*) to involve; (*investir*) to invest, lay out; (*inciter*) to urge; (*introduire: clé*) to insert; **s'~** *vi* (*promettre*) to commit o.s.; (*MIL*) to enlist; (*débuter: conversation etc*) to start (up); **s'~ à faire** to undertake to do; **s'~ dans** (*rue, passage*) to turn into; (*fig: affaire, discussion*) to enter into, embark on
engelures [ãʒlyʀ] *nfpl* chilblains
engendrer [ãʒãdʀe] *vt* to breed, create
engin [ãʒɛ̃] *nm* machine; (*outil*) instrument; (*AUT*) vehicle; (*AVIAT*) aircraft *inv*
englober [ãglɔbe] *vt* to include
engloutir [ãglutiʀ] *vt* to swallow up
engoncé, e [ãgɔ̃se] *adj*: **~ dans** cramped in
engorger [ãgɔʀʒe] *vt* to obstruct, block
engouement [ãgumã] *nm* (*sudden*) passion
engouffrer [ãgufʀe] *vt* to swallow up, devour; **s'~ dans** to rush into
engourdir [ãguʀdiʀ] *vt* to numb; (*fig*) to dull, blunt; **s'~** *vi* to go numb
engrais [ãgʀɛ] *nm* manure; **~ (chimique)**

(chemical) fertilizer

engraisser [ɑ̃gʀese] vt to fatten (up)

engrenage [ɑ̃gʀanaʒ] nm gears pl, gearing; (fig) chain

engueuler [ɑ̃gœle] (fam) vt to bawl at

enhardir [ɑ̃aʀdiʀ]: **s'~** vi to grow bolder

énigme [enigm] nf riddle

enivrer [ɑ̃nivʀe] vt: **s'~** to get drunk

enjambée [ɑ̃ʒɑ̃be] nf stride

enjamber [ɑ̃ʒɑ̃be] vt to stride over

enjeu, x [ɑ̃ʒø] nm stakes pl

enjôler [ɑ̃ʒole] vt to coax, wheedle

enjoliver [ɑ̃ʒolive] vt to embellish; **enjoliveur** nm (AUTO) hub cap

enjoué, e [ɑ̃ʒwe] adj playful

enlacer [ɑ̃lase] vt (étreindre) to embrace, hug

enlaidir [ɑ̃lediʀ] vt to make ugly ♦ vi to become ugly

enlèvement [ɑ̃lɛvmɑ̃] nm (rapt) abduction, kidnapping

enlever [ɑ̃l(ə)ve] vt (ôter: gén) to remove; (: vêtement, lunettes) to take off; (emporter: ordures etc) to take away; (kidnapper) to abduct, kidnap; (obtenir: prix, contrat) to win; (prendre): **~ qch à qn** to take sth (away) from sb

enliser [ɑ̃lize]: **s'~** vi to sink, get stuck

enneigé, e [ɑ̃neʒe] adj (route, maison) snowed-up; (paysage) snowy

ennemi, e [ɛnmi] adj hostile; (MIL) enemy cpd ♦ nm/f enemy

ennui [ɑ̃nɥi] nm (lassitude) boredom; (difficulté) trouble no pl; **avoir des ~s** to have problems; **ennuyer** vt to bother; (lasser) to bore; **s'ennuyer** vi to be bored; **ennuyeux, -euse** adj boring, tedious; (embêtant) annoying

énoncé [enɔ̃se] nm (de problème) terms pl

énoncer [enɔ̃se] vt (faits) to set out, state

enorgueillir [ɑ̃nɔʀgœjiʀ]: **s'~ de** vt to pride o.s. on

énorme [enɔʀm] adj enormous, huge; **énormément** adv enormously; **énormément de neige/gens** an enormous amount of snow/number of people; **énormité** nf (propos) outrageous remark

enquérir [ɑ̃keʀiʀ]: **s'~ de** vt to inquire about

enquête [ɑ̃kɛt] nf (de journaliste, de police) investigation; (judiciaire, administrative) inquiry; (sondage d'opinion) survey; **enquêter** vi to investigate

enquiers etc [ɑ̃kje] vb voir enquérir

enquiquiner [ɑ̃kikine] (fam) vt to annoy, irritate, bother

enraciné, e [ɑ̃ʀasine] adj deep-rooted

enragé, e [ɑ̃ʀaʒe] adj (MÉD) rabid, with rabies; (fig) fanatical

enrageant, e [ɑ̃ʀaʒɑ̃, ɑ̃t] adj infuriating

enrager [ɑ̃ʀaʒe] vi to be in a rage

enrayer [ɑ̃ʀeje] vt to check, stop

enregistrement [ɑ̃ʀ(ə)ʒistʀəmɑ̃] nm recording; **~ des bagages** (à l'aéroport) baggage check-in

enregistrer [ɑ̃ʀ(ə)ʒistʀe] vt (MUS etc) to record; (fig: mémoriser) to make a mental note of; (bagages: à l'aéroport) to check in

enrhumer [ɑ̃ʀyme] vt: **s'~, être enrhumé** to catch a cold

enrichir [ɑ̃ʀiʃiʀ] vt to make rich(er); (fig) to enrich; **s'~** vi to get rich(er)

enrober [ɑ̃ʀɔbe] vt: **~ qch de** to coat sth with

enrôler [ɑ̃ʀole] vt to enlist; **s'~ (dans)** to enlist (in)

enrouer [ɑ̃ʀwe]: **s'~** vi to go hoarse

enrouler [ɑ̃ʀule] vt (fil, corde) to wind (up)

ensanglanté, e [ɑ̃sɑ̃glɑ̃te] adj covered with blood

enseignant, e [ɑ̃sɛɲɑ̃, ɑ̃t] nm/f teacher

enseigne [ɑ̃sɛɲ] nf sign; **~ lumineuse** neon sign

enseignement [ɑ̃sɛɲ(ə)mɑ̃] nm teaching; (ADMIN) education

enseigner [ɑ̃sɛɲe] vt, vi to teach; **~ qch à qn** to teach sb sth

ensemble [ɑ̃sɑ̃bl] adv together ♦ nm (groupement) set; (vêtements) outfit; (totalité): **l'~ du/de la** the whole ou entire; (unité, harmonie) unity; **impression/idée d'~** overall ou general impression/idea; **dans l'~** (en gros) on the whole

ensemencer [ɑ̃s(ə)mɑ̃se] vt to sow

ensevelir [ɑ̃səv(ə)liʀ] vt to bury

ensoleillé, e [ɑ̃sɔleje] adj sunny

ensommeillé, e [ɑ̃sɔmeje] adj drowsy

ensorceler [ɑ̃sɔʀsəle] vt to enchant, bewitch

ensuite [ɑ̃sɥit] adv then, next; (plus tard) afterwards, later

ensuivre [ɑ̃sɥivʀ]: **s'~** vi to follow, ensue; **et tout ce qui s'ensuit** and all that goes with it

entaille [ɑ̃taj] nf cut; (sur un objet) notch

entamer [ɑ̃tame] vt (pain, bouteille) to start; (hostilités, pourparlers) to open

entasser [ɑ̃tase] vt (empiler) to pile up, heap up; **s'~** vi (s'amonceler) to pile up; **s'~ dans** (personnes) to cram into

entendre [ɑ̃tɑ̃dʀ] vt to hear; (comprendre) to understand; (vouloir dire) to mean; **s'~** vi (sympathiser) to get on; (se mettre d'accord) to agree; **j'ai entendu dire que** I've heard (it said) that

entendu, e [ɑ̃tɑ̃dy] adj (réglé) agreed; (au courant: air) knowing; **(c'est) ~** all right, agreed; **bien ~** of course

entente [ɑ̃tɑ̃t] nf understanding; (accord, traité) agreement; **à double ~ (sens)** with a double meaning

entériner [ɑ̃teʀine] vt to ratify, confirm

enterrement [ɑ̃tɛʀmɑ̃] nm (cérémonie)

funeral, burial

enterrer [ãtere] vt to bury

entêtant, e [ãtetã, ãt] adj heady

entêté, e [ãtete] adj stubborn

en-tête [ãtɛt] nm heading; **papier à ~-~** headed notepaper

entêter [ãtete]: **s'~** vi: **s'~ (à faire)** to persist (in doing)

enthousiasme [ãtuzjasm] nm enthusiasm; **enthousiasmer** vt to fill with enthusiasm; **s'enthousiasmer (pour qch)** to get enthusiastic (about sth); **enthousiaste** adj enthusiastic

enticher [ãtiʃe]: **s'~ de** vt to become infatuated with

entier, -ère [ãtje, jɛʀ] adj whole; (total: satisfaction etc) complete; (fig: caractère) unbending ♦ nm (MATH) whole; **en ~** totally; **lait ~** full-cream milk; **entièrement** adv entirely, wholly

entonner [ãtɔne] vt (chanson) to strike up

entonnoir [ãtɔnwaʀ] nm funnel

entorse [ãtɔʀs] nf (MÉD) sprain; (fig): **~ au règlement** infringement of the rule

entortiller [ãtɔʀtije] vt (enrouler) to twist, wind; (fam: cajoler) to get round

entourage [ãtuʀaʒ] nm circle, (famille) circle of family/friends; (ce qui enclôt) surround

entourer [ãtuʀe] vt to surround; (apporter son soutien à) to rally round; **~ de** to surround with

entracte [ãtʀakt] nm interval

entraide [ãtʀɛd] nf mutual aid; **s'~r** vi to help each other

entrain [ãtʀɛ] nm spirit; **avec/sans ~** spiritedly/half-heartedly

entraînement [ãtʀɛnmã] nm training

entraîner [ãtʀɛne] vt (charrier) to carry ou drag along; (TECH) to drive; (emmener: personne) to take (off); (influencer) to lead; (SPORT) to train; (impliquer) to entail; **s'~** vi (SPORT) to train; **s'~ à qch/à faire** to train o.s. for sth/to do; **~ qn à faire** (inciter) to lead sb to do; **entraîneur, -euse** nm/f (SPORT) coach, trainer ♦ nm (HIPPISME) trainer

entraver [ãtʀave] vt (action, progrès) to hinder

entre [ãtʀ] prép between; (parmi) among(st); **l'un d'~ eux/nous** one of them/us; **~ eux** among(st) themselves; **entrebâillé, e** adj half-open, ajar; **entrechoquer: s'entre-choquer** vi to knock ou bang together; **entrecôte** nf entrecôte ou rib steak; **entrecouper** vt: **entrecouper qch de** to interspersе sth with; **entrecroiser: s'entrecroiser** vi to intertwine

entrée [ãtʀe] nf entrance; (accès: au cinéma etc) admission; (billet) (admission) ticket; (CULIN) first course

entre...: **entrefaites: sur ces entrefaites** adv at this juncture; **entrefilet** nm paragraph (short article); **entrejambes** nm crotch; **entrelacer** vt to intertwine; **entremêler: s'entremêler** vi to become entangled; **entremets** nm (cream) dessert; **entremise** nf intervention; **par l'entremise de** through

entreposer [ãtʀəpoze] vt to store, put into storage

entrepôt [ãtʀəpo] nm warehouse

entreprenant, e [ãtʀəpʀənã, ãt] adj (actif) enterprising; (trop galant) forward

entreprendre [ãtʀəpʀãdʀ] vt (se lancer dans) to undertake; (commencer) to begin ou start (upon)

entrepreneur [ãtʀəpʀənœʀ, øz] nm: **~ (en bâtiment)** (building) contractor

entreprise [ãtʀəpʀiz] nf (société) firm, concern; (action) undertaking, venture

entrer [ãtʀe] vi to go (ou come) in, enter ♦ vt (INFORM) to enter, input; (faire) **~ qch dans** to get sth into; **~ dans** (gén) to enter; (pièce) to go (ou come) into, enter; (club) to join; (heurter) to run into; **~ à l'hôpital** to go into hospital; **faire ~** (visiteur) to show in

entresol [ãtʀəsɔl] nm mezzanine

entre-temps [ãtʀətã] adv meanwhile

entretenir [ãtʀət(ə)niʀ] vt to maintain; (famille, maîtresse) to support, keep; **~ qn (de)** to speak to sb (about)

entretien [ãtʀətjɛ] nm maintenance; (discussion) discussion, talk; (pour un emploi) interview

entrevoir [ãtʀəvwaʀ] vt (à peine) to make out; (brièvement) to catch a glimpse of

entrevue [ãtʀəvy] nf (audience) interview

entrouvert, e [ãtʀuvɛʀ, ɛʀt] adj half-open

énumérer [enymeʀe] vt to list, enumerate

envahir [ãvaiʀ] vt to invade; (suj: inquiétude, peur) to come over; **envahissant, e** (péj) adj (personne) interfering, intrusive

enveloppe [ãv(ə)lɔp] nf (de lettre) envelope; (crédits) budget; **envelopper** vt to wrap; (fig) to envelop, shroud

envenimer [ãv(ə)nime] vt to aggravate

envergure [ãvɛʀgyʀ] nf (fig) scope; (personne) calibre

enverrai etc [ãvɛʀe] vb voir **envoyer**

envers [ãvɛʀ] prép towards, to ♦ nm other side; (d'une étoffe) wrong side; **à l'~** (verticalement) upside down; (pull) back to front; (chaussettes) inside out

envie [ãvi] nf (sentiment) envy; (souhait) desire, wish; **avoir ~ de (faire)** to feel like (doing); (plus fort) to want (to do); **avoir ~ que** to wish that; **cette glace me fait ~** I fancy some of that ice cream; **envier** vt to envy; **envieux, -euse** adj envious

environ [ãviʀɔ] adv: **~ 3 h/2 km** (around)

about 3 o'clock/2 km; *voir aussi* **environs**

environnant, e [ãvirɔnã, ãt] *adj* surrounding

environnement [ãvirɔnmã] *nm* environment

environs [ãvirɔ̃] *nmpl* surroundings; **aux ~ de** (round) about

envisager [ãvizaʒe] *vt* to contemplate, envisage; **~ de faire** to consider doing

envoi [ãvwa] *nm* (*paquet*) parcel, consignment; **coup d'~** (SPORT) kick-off

envoler [ãvɔle]: **s'~** *vi* (*oiseau*) to fly away *ou* off; (*avion*) to take off; (*papier, feuille*) to blow away; (*fig*) to vanish (into thin air)

envoûter [ãvute] *vt* to bewitch

envoyé, e [ãvwaje] *nm/f* (POL) envoy; (PRESSE) correspondent

envoyer [ãvwaje] *vt* to send; (*lancer*) to hurl, throw; **~ chercher** to send for; **~ promener qn** (*fam*) to send sb packing

épagneul, e [epaɲœl] *nm/f* spaniel

épais, se [epɛ, ɛs] *adj* thick; **épaisseur** *nf* thickness

épancher [epãʃe]: **s'~** *vi* to open one's heart

épanouir [epanwir]: **s'~** *vi* (*fleur*) to bloom, open out; (*visage*) to light up; (*personne*) to blossom

épargne [eparɲ] *nf* saving

épargner [eparɲe] *vt* to save; (*ne pas tuer ou endommager*) to spare ♦ *vi* to save; **~ qch à qn** to spare sb sth

éparpiller [eparpije] *vt* to scatter; **s'~** *vi* to scatter; (*fig*) to dissipate one's efforts

épars, e [epar, ars] *adj* scattered

épatant, e [epatã, ãt] (*fam*) *adj* super

épater [epate] (*fam*) *vt* (*étonner*) to amaze; (*impressionner*) to impress

épaule [epol] *nf* shoulder

épauler [epole] *vt* (*aider*) to back up, support; (*arme*) to raise (to one's shoulder) ♦ *vi* to (take) aim

épaulette [epolɛt] *nf* (MIL) epaulette; (*rembourrage*) shoulder pad

épave [epav] *nf* wreck

épée [epe] *nf* sword

épeler [ep(ə)le] *vt* to spell

éperdu, e [eperdy] *adj* distraught, overcome; (*amour*) passionate

éperon [eprɔ̃] *nm* spur

épervier [epervje] *nm* sparrowhawk

épi [epi] *nm* (*de blé, d'orge*) ear; (*de maïs*) cob

épice [epis] *nf* spice

épicé, e [epise] *adj* spicy

épicer [epise] *vt* to spice

épicerie [episri] *nf* grocer's shop; (*denrées*) groceries *pl*; **~ fine** delicatessen; **épicier, -ière** *nm/f* grocer

épidémie [epidemi] *nf* epidemic

épiderme [epiderm] *nm* skin

épier [epje] *vt* to spy on, watch closely

épilepsie [epilɛpsi] *nf* epilepsy

épiler [epile] *vt* (*jambes*) to remove the hair from; (*sourcils*) to pluck

épilogue [epilɔg] *nm* (*fig*) conclusion, dénouement; **épiloguer** *vi*: **épiloguer sur** to hold forth on

épinards [epinar] *nmpl* spinach *sg*

épine [epin] *nf* thorn, prickle; (*d'oursin etc*) spine; **~ dorsale** backbone; **épineux, -euse** *adj* thorny

épingle [epɛ̃gl] *nf* pin; **~ à cheveux** hairpin; **~ de nourrice** *ou* **de sûreté** safety pin; **épingler** *vt* (*badge, décoration*): **épingler qch sur** to pin sth on(to); (*fam*) to catch, nick

épique [epik] *adj* epic

épisode [epizɔd] *nm* episode; **film/roman à ~s** serial; **épisodique** *adj* occasional

éploré, e [eplɔre] *adj* tearful

épluche-légumes [eplyʃlegym] *nm inv* (potato) peeler

éplucher [eplyʃe] *vt* (*fruit, légumes*) to peel; (*fig*) to go over with a fine-tooth comb; **épluchures** *nfpl* peelings

éponge [epɔ̃ʒ] *nf* sponge; **éponger** *vt* (*liquide*) to mop up; (*surface*) to sponge; (*fig: déficit*) to soak up

épopée [epɔpe] *nf* epic

époque [epɔk] *nf* (*de l'histoire*) age, era; (*de l'année, la vie*) time; **d'~** (*meuble*) period *cpd*

époumoner [epumɔne]: **s'~** *vi* to shout o.s. hoarse

épouse [epuz] *nf* wife; **épouser** *vt* to marry

épousseter [epuste] *vt* to dust

époustouflant, e [epustuflã, ãt] (*fam*) *adj* staggering, mind-boggling

épouvantable [epuvãtabl] *adj* appalling, dreadful

épouvantail [epuvãtaj] *nm* scarecrow

épouvante [epuvãt] *nf* terror; **film d'~** horror film; **épouvanter** *vt* to terrify

époux [epu] *nm* husband ♦ *nmpl* (married) couple

éprendre [eprãdr]: **s'~ de** *vt* to fall in love with

épreuve [eprœv] *nf* (*d'examen*) test; (*malheur, difficulté*) trial, ordeal; (PHOTO) print; (TYPO) proof; (SPORT) event; **à toute ~** unfailing; **mettre à l'~** to put to the test

épris, e [epri, iz] *pp de* **éprendre**

éprouvant, e [epruvã, ãt] *adj* trying, testing

éprouver [epruve] *vt* (*tester*) to test; (*marquer, faire souffrir*) to afflict, distress; (*ressentir*) to experience

éprouvette [epruvɛt] *nf* test tube

épuisé, e [epɥize] *adj* exhausted; (*livre*) out of print; **épuisement** *nm* exhaustion

épuiser [epɥize] *vt* (*fatiguer*) to exhaust,

wear *ou* tire out; (*stock, sujet*) to exhaust; **s'~**
vi to wear *ou* tire o.s. out, exhaust o.s.

épuisette [epɥizɛt] *nf* shrimping net

épurer [epyʀe] *vt* (*liquide*) to purify; (*parti
etc*) to purge

équateur [ekwatœʀ] *nm* equator; **(la
république de) l'É~** Ecuador

équation [ekwasjɔ̃] *nf* equation

équerre [ekɛʀ] *nf* (*à dessin*) (set) square

équilibre [ekilibʀ] *nm* balance; **garder/perdre
l'~** to keep/lose one's balance; **être en ~** to be
balanced; **équilibré, e** *adj* well-balanced;
équilibrer *vt* to balance; **s'équilibrer** *vi*
(*poids*) to balance; (*fig: défauts etc*) to
balance each other out

équipage [ekipaʒ] *nm* crew

équipe [ekip] *nf* team

équipé, e [ekipe] *adj:* **bien/mal ~** well-/
poorly-equipped; **équipée** *nf* escapade

équipement [ekipmɑ̃] *nm* equipment; **~s**
nmpl (*installations*) amenities, facilities

équiper [ekipe] *vt* to equip; **~ qn/qch de** to
equip sb/sth with

équipier, ière [ekipje, jɛʀ] *nm/f* team
member

équitable [ekitabl] *adj* fair

équitation [ekitasjɔ̃] *nf* (horse-)riding; **faire
de l'~** to go riding

équivalent, e [ekivalɑ̃, ɑ̃t] *adj, nm*
equivalent

équivaloir [ekivalwaʀ]: **~ à** *vt* to be
equivalent to

équivoque [ekivɔk] *adj* equivocal,
ambiguous; (*louche*) dubious ♦ *nf*
(*incertitude*) doubt

érable [eʀabl] *nm* maple

érafler [eʀafle] *vt* to scratch; **éraflure** *nf*
scratch

éraillé, e [eʀaje] *adj* (*voix*) rasping

ère [ɛʀ] *nf* era, en l'an 1050 de notre **~** in the
year 1050 A.D.

érection [eʀɛksjɔ̃] *nf* erection

éreinter [eʀɛ̃te] *vt* to exhaust, wear out;
(*critiquer*) to pull to pieces

ériger [eʀiʒe] *vt* (*monument*) to erect

ermite [ɛʀmit] *nm* hermit

éroder [eʀɔde] *vt* to erode

érotique [eʀɔtik] *adj* erotic

errer [eʀe] *vi* to wander

erreur [eʀœʀ] *nf* mistake, error; **faire ~** to be
mistaken; **par ~** by mistake; **~ judiciaire**
miscarriage of justice

érudit, e [eʀydi, it] *adj* erudite, learned

éruption [eʀypsjɔ̃] *nf* eruption; (*MÉD*) rash

es [ɛ] *vb voir* **être**

ès [ɛs] *prép:* **licencié ~ lettres/sciences** ≈
Bachelor of Arts/Science

escabeau, x [ɛskabo] *nm* (*tabouret*) stool;
(*échelle*) stepladder

escadron [ɛskadʀɔ̃] *nm* squadron

escalade [ɛskalad] *nf* climbing *no pl;* (*POL
etc*) escalation; **escalader** *vt* to climb

escale [ɛskal] *nf* (*NAVIG: durée*) call; (*endroit*)
port of call; (*AVIAT*) stop(over); **faire ~ à**
(*NAVIG*) to put in at; (*AVIAT*) to stop over at;
vol sans ~ nonstop flight

escalier [ɛskalje] *nm* stairs *pl;* **dans l'~** on the
stairs; **~ roulant** escalator

escamoter [ɛskamɔte] *vt* (*esquiver*) to get
round, evade; (*faire disparaître*) to conjure
away

escapade [ɛskapad] *nf:* **faire une ~** to go on
a jaunt; (*s'enfuir*) to run away *ou* off

escargot [ɛskaʀgo] *nm* snail

escarpé, e [ɛskaʀpe] *adj* steep

escarpin [ɛskaʀpɛ̃] *nm* low-fronted shoe,
court shoe (*BRIT*)

escient [esjɑ̃] *nm:* **à bon ~** advisedly

esclaffer [ɛsklafe]: **s'~** *vi* to guffaw

esclandre [ɛsklɑ̃dʀ] *nm* scene, fracas

esclavage [ɛsklavaʒ] *nm* slavery

esclave [ɛsklav] *nm/f* slave

escompte [ɛskɔ̃t] *nm* discount; **escompter**
vt (*fig*) to expect

escorte [ɛskɔʀt] *nf* escort; **escorter** *vt* to
escort

escrime [ɛskʀim] *nf* fencing

escrimer [ɛskʀime]: **s'~** *vi:* **s'~ à faire** to wear
o.s. out doing

escroc [ɛskʀo] *nm* swindler, conman;
escroquer [ɛskʀɔke] *vt:* **escroquer qch (à qn)**
to swindle sth (out of sb); **escroquerie** *nf*
swindle

espace [ɛspas] *nm* space

espacer *vt* to space out; **s'~** *vi* (*visites etc*) to
become less frequent

espadon [ɛspadɔ̃] *nm* swordfish *inv*

espadrille [ɛspadʀij] *nf* rope-soled sandal

Espagne [ɛspaɲ] *nf:* **l'~** Spain; **espagnol, e**
adj Spanish ♦ *nm/f:* **Espagnol, e** Spaniard
♦ *nm* (*LING*) Spanish

escouade [ɛskwad] *nf* squad

espèce [ɛspɛs] *nf* (*BIO, BOT, ZOOL*) species *inv;*
(*gén: sorte*) sort, kind, type; (*péj*): **~ de
maladroit!** you clumsy oaf!; **~s** *nfpl* (*COMM*)
cash *sg;* **en ~** in cash

espérance [ɛspeʀɑ̃s] *nf* hope, **~ de vie** life
expectancy

espérer [ɛspeʀe] *vt* to hope for; **j'espère
(bien)** I hope so; **~ que/faire** to hope that/to
do

espiègle [ɛspjɛgl] *adj* mischievous

espion, ne [ɛspjɔ̃, jɔn] *nm/f* spy;
espionnage *nm* espionage, spying;
espionner *vt* to spy (up)on

esplanade [ɛsplanad] *nf* esplanade

espoir [ɛspwaʀ] *nm* hope

esprit [ɛspʀi] *nm* (*intellect*) mind; (*humour*)

wit; (*mentalité, d'une loi etc, fantôme etc*) spirit; **faire de l'~** to try to be witty; **reprendre ses ~s** to come to; **perdre l'~** to lose one's mind

esquimau, de, x [ɛskimo, od] *adj* Eskimo ♦ *nm/f:* **E~,** de Eskimo ♦ *nm:* **E~** ® ice lolly (*BRIT*), popsicle (*US*)

esquinter [ɛskɛ̃te] (*fam*) *vt* to mess up

esquisse [ɛskis] *nf* sketch; **esquisser** *vt* to sketch; **esquisser un sourire** to give a vague smile

esquiver [ɛskive] *vt* to dodge; **s'~** *vi* to slip away

essai [esɛ] *nm* (*tentative*) attempt, try; (*de produit*) testing; (*RUGBY*) try; (*LITTÉRATURE*) essay; **~s** *nmpl* (*AUTO*) trials; **~ gratuit** (*COMM*) free trial; **à l'~** on a trial basis

essaim [esɛ̃] *nm* swarm

essayer [eseje] *vt* to try; (*vêtement, chaussures*) to try (on); (*méthode, voiture*) to try (out) ♦ *vi* to try; **~ de faire** to try ou attempt to do

essence [esɑ̃s] *nf* (*de voiture*) petrol (*BRIT*), gas(oline) (*US*); (*extrait de plante*) essence; (*espèce: d'arbre*) species *inv*

essentiel, le [esɑ̃sjɛl] *adj* essential; **c'est l'~** (*ce qui importe*) that's the main thing; **l'~ de** the main part of

essieu, x [esjø] *nm* axle

essor [esɔʀ] *nm* (*de l'économie etc*) rapid expansion

essorer [esɔʀe] *vt* (*en tordant*) to wring (out); (*par la force centrifuge*) to spin-dry; **essoreuse** *nf* spin-dryer

essouffler [esufle]: **s'~** *vi* to get out of breath

essuie-glace [esɥiglas] *nm inv* windscreen (*BRIT*) ou windshield (*US*) wiper

essuyer [esɥije] *vt* to wipe; (*fig: échec*) to suffer; **s'~** *vi* (*après le bain*) to dry o.s.; **~ la vaisselle** to dry up

est¹ [ɛ] *vb voir* **être**

est² [ɛst] *nm* east ♦ *adj inv* east; (*région*) east(ern); **à l'~** in the east; (*direction*) to the east, east(wards); **à l'~ de** (to the) east of

estampe [ɛstɑ̃p] *nf* print, engraving

est-ce que [ɛskə] *adv:* **~ c'est cher/c'était bon?** is it expensive/was it good?; **quand est-ce qu'il part?** when does he leave?, when is he leaving?; *voir aussi* **que**

esthéticienne [ɛstetisjɛn] *nf* beautician

esthétique [ɛstetik] *adj* attractive

estimation [ɛstimasjɔ̃] *nf* valuation; (*chiffre*) estimate

estime [ɛstim] *nf* esteem, regard; **estimer** *vt* (*respecter*) to esteem; (*expertiser: bijou etc*) to value; (*évaluer: coût etc*) to assess, estimate; (*penser*): **estimer que/être** to consider that/o.s. to be

estival, e, -aux [ɛstival, o] *adj* summer *cpd*

estivant, e [ɛstivɑ̃, ɑ̃t] *nm/f* (summer) holiday-maker

estomac [ɛstɔma] *nm* stomach

estomaqué, e [ɛstɔmake] (*fam*) *adj* flabbergasted

estomper [ɛstɔ̃pe]: **s'~** *vi* (*sentiments*) to soften; (*contour*) to become blurred

estrade [ɛstʀad] *nf* platform, rostrum

estragon [ɛstʀagɔ̃] *nm* tarragon

estuaire [ɛstɥɛʀ] *nm* estuary

et [e] *conj* and; **~ lui?** what about him?; **~ alors!** so what!

étable [etabl] *nf* cowshed

établi [etabli] *nm* (work)bench

établir [etabliʀ] *vt* (*papiers d'identité, facture*) to make out; (*liste, programme*) to draw up; (*entreprise*) to set up; (*réputation, usage, fait, culpabilité*) to establish; **s'~** *vi* to be established; **s'~** (**à son compte**) to set up in business; **s'~ à/près de** to settle in/near

établissement [etablismɑ̃] *nm* (*entreprise, institution*) establishment; **~ scolaire** school, educational establishment

étage [etaʒ] *nm* (*d'immeuble*) storey, floor; **à l'~** upstairs; **au 2ème ~** on the 2nd (*BRIT*) ou 3rd (*US*) floor

étagère [etaʒɛʀ] *nf* (*rayon*) shelf; (*meuble*) shelves *pl*

étai [etɛ] *nm* stay, prop

étain [etɛ̃] *nm* pewter *no pl*

étais *etc* [etɛ] *vb voir* **être**

étal [etal] *nm* stall

étalage [etalaʒ] *nm* display; (*devanture*) display window; **faire ~ de** to show off, parade

étaler [etale] *vt* (*carte, nappe*) to spread (out); (*peinture*) to spread; (*échelonner: paiements, vacances*) to spread, stagger; (*marchandises*) to display; (*connaissances*) to parade; **s'~** *vi* (*liquide*) to spread out; (*fam*) to fall flat on one's face; **s'~ sur** (*suj: paiements etc*) to be spread out over

étalon [etalɔ̃] *nm* (*cheval*) stallion

étanche [etɑ̃ʃ] *adj* (*récipient*) watertight; (*montre, vêtement*) waterproof; **étancher** *vt:* **étancher sa soif** to quench one's thirst

étang [etɑ̃] *nm* pond

étant [etɑ̃] *vb voir* **être; donné**

étape [etap] *nf* stage; (*lieu d'arrivée*) stopping place; (: *CYCLISME*) staging point

état [eta] *nm* (*POL, condition*) state; **en mauvais ~** in poor condition; **en ~ (de marche)** in (working) order; **remettre en ~** to repair; **hors d'~** out of order; **être en ~/hors d'~ de faire** to be in a/in no fit state to do; **être dans tous ses ~s** to be in a state; **faire ~ de** (*alléguer*) to put forward; **l'É~** the State; **~ civil** civil status; **~ des lieux** inventory of fixtures; **étatiser** *vt* to bring under state control; **état-major** nm (MIL) staff; **États-Unis** nmpl: les États-Unis the United States

étau, x [eto] nm vice (BRIT), vise (US)

étayer [eteje] vt to prop ou shore up

etc. [ɛtsetera] adv etc

et c(a)etera [ɛtsetera] adv et cetera, and so on

été [ete] pp de être ♦ nm summer

éteindre [etɛ̃dʀ] vt (lampe, lumière, radio) to turn ou switch off; (cigarette, feu) to put out, extinguish; s'~ vi (feu, lumière) to go out; (mourir) to pass away; **éteint, e** adj (fig) lacklustre, dull; (volcan) extinct

étendard [etɑ̃daʀ] nm standard

étendre [etɑ̃dʀ] vt (pâte, liquide) to spread; (carte etc) to spread out; (linge) to hang up; (bras, jambes) to stretch out; (fig: agrandir) to extend; s'~ vi (augmenter, se propager) to spread; (terrain, forêt etc) to stretch; (s'allonger) to stretch out; (se coucher) to lie down; (fig: expliquer) to elaborate

étendu, e [etɑ̃dy] adj extensive; **étendue** nf (d'eau, de sable) stretch, expanse; (importance) extent

éternel, le [etɛʀnɛl] adj eternal

éterniser [etɛʀnize]: s'~ vi to last for ages; (visiteur) to stay for ages

éternité [etɛʀnite] nf eternity; ça a duré une ~ it lasted for ages

éternuement [etɛʀnymɑ̃] nm sneeze

éternuer [etɛʀnɥe] vi to sneeze

êtes [ɛt(z)] vb voir être

éthique [etik] adj ethical

ethnie [ɛtni] nf ethnic group

éthylisme [etilism] nm alcoholism

étiez [etje] vb voir être

étinceler [etɛ̃s(ə)le] vi to sparkle

étincelle [etɛ̃sɛl] nf spark

étiqueter [etik(ə)te] vt to label

étiquette [etikɛt] nf label; (protocole): l'~ etiquette

étirer [etiʀe]: s'~ vi (personne) to stretch; (convoi, route): s'~ sur to stretch out over

étoffe [etɔf] nf material, fabric

étoffer [etɔfe] vt to fill out; s'~ vi to fill out

étoile [etwal] nf star; à la belle ~ in the open; ~ de mer starfish; ~ filante shooting star; **étoilé, e** adj starry

étonnant, e [etɔnɑ̃, ɑ̃t] adj amazing

étonnement [etɔnmɑ̃] nm surprise, amazement

étonner [etɔne] vt to surprise, amaze; s'~ que/de to be amazed that/at; cela m'~ait (que) (j'en doute) I'd be very surprised (if)

étouffant, e [etufɑ̃, ɑ̃t] adj stifling

étouffée [etufe]: à l'~ adv (CULIN: légumes) steamed; (: viande) braised

étouffer [etufe] vt to suffocate; (bruit) to muffle; (scandale) to hush up ♦ vi to suffocate; s'~ vi (en mangeant etc) to choke; **on étouffe** it's stifling

étourderie [etuʀdəʀi] nf (caractère) absent-mindedness no pl; (faute) thoughtless blunder

étourdi, e [etuʀdi] adj (distrait) scatterbrained, heedless

étourdir [etuʀdiʀ] vt (assommer) to stun, daze; (griser) to make dizzy ou giddy; **étourdissement** nm dizzy spell

étourneau, x [etuʀno] nm starling

étrange [etʀɑ̃ʒ] adj strange

étranger, ère [etʀɑ̃ʒe, ɛʀ] adj foreign; (pas de la famille, non familier) strange ♦ nm/f foreigner; stranger ♦ nm: à l'~ abroad

étrangler [etʀɑ̃gle] vt to strangle; s'~ vi (en mangeant etc) to choke

---

MOT-CLÉ

être [ɛtʀ] nm being; **être humain** human being
♦ vb +attrib **1** (état, description) to be; **il est instituteur** he is ou he's a teacher; **vous êtes grand/intelligent/fatigué** you are ou you're tall/clever/tired

2 (+à: appartenir) to be; **le livre est à Paul** the book is Paul's ou belongs to Paul; **c'est à moi/eux** it is ou it's mine/theirs

3 (+de: provenance): **il est de Paris** he is from Paris; (: appartenance): **il est des nôtres** he is one of us

4 (date): **nous sommes le 10 janvier** it's the 10th of January (today)
♦ vi to be; **je ne serai pas ici demain** I won't be here tomorrow
♦ vb aux **1** to have; to be; **être arrivé/allé** to have arrived/gone; **il est parti** he has left, he has gone

2 (forme passive) to be; **être fait par** to be made by; **il a été promu** he has been promoted

3 (+à: obligation): **c'est à réparer** it needs repairing; **c'est à essayer** it should be tried
♦ vb impers **1**: **il est** +adjectif it is +adjective, **il est impossible de le faire** it's impossible to do it

2 (heure, date): **il est 10 heures, c'est 10 heures** it is ou it's 10 o'clock

3 (emphatique): **c'est moi** it's me; **c'est à lui de le faire** it's up to him to do it

---

étreindre [etʀɛ̃dʀ] vt to clutch, grip; (amoureusement, amicalement) to embrace; s'~ vi to embrace

étrenner [etʀene] vt to use (ou wear) for the first time; **étrennes** nfpl Christmas box sg

étrier [etʀije] nm stirrup

étriqué, e [etʀike] adj skimpy

étroit, e [etʀwa, wat] adj narrow; (vêtement)

tight; (fig: liens, collaboration) close; à l'~ cramped; ~ d'esprit narrow-minded

étude [etyd] nf studying; (ouvrage, rapport) study; (SCOL: salle de travail) study room; ~s nfpl (SCOL) studies; à l'~ (projet etc) to be under consideration; **faire des ~s (de droit/ médecine)** to study (law/medicine)

étudiant, e [etydjã, jãt] nm/f student

étudier [etydje] vt, vi to study

étui [etɥi] nm case

étuve [etyv] nf steamroom

étuvée [etyve]: à l'~ adv braised

eu, eue [y] pp de **avoir**

euh [ø] excl er

Europe [ørɔp] nf: l'~ Europe; **européen, ne** adj European ♦ nm/f: **Européen, ne** European

eus etc [y] vb voir **avoir**

eux [ø] pron (sujet) they; (objet) them

évacuer [evakɥe] vt to evacuate

évader [evade]: **s'~** vi to escape

évaluer [evalɥe] vt (expertiser) to appraise, evaluate; (juger approximativement) to estimate

évangile [evãʒil] nm gospel

évanouir [evanwiʀ]: **s'~** vi to faint; (disparaître) to vanish, disappear; **évanouissement** nm (syncope) fainting fit

évaporer [evapɔʀe]: **s'~** vi to evaporate

évasé, e [evaze] adj (manches, jupe) flared

évasif, -ive [evazif, iv] adj evasive

évasion [evazjɔ̃] nf escape

évêché [eveʃe] nm bishop's palace

éveil [evɛj] nm awakening; **être en ~** to be alert; **éveillé, e** adj awake; (vif) alert, sharp; **éveiller** vt to (a)waken; (soupçons etc) to arouse; **s'éveiller** vi to (a)waken; (fig) to be aroused

événement [evɛnmã] nm event

éventail [evãtaj] nm fan; (choix) range

éventaire [evãtɛʀ] nm stall, stand

éventer [evãte] vt (secret) to uncover; **s'~** vi (parfum) to go stale

éventualité [evãtɥalite] nf eventuality; possibility; **dans l'~ de** in the event of

éventuel, le [evãtɥɛl] adj possible; **éventuellement** adv possibly

évêque [evɛk] nm bishop

évertuer [evɛʀtɥe]: **s'~** vi: **s'~ à faire** to try very hard to do

éviction [eviksjɔ̃] nf (de locataire) eviction

évidemment [evidamã] adv (bien sûr) of course; (certainement) obviously

évidence [evidãs] nf obviousness; (fait) obvious fact; **de toute ~** quite obviously ou evidently; **être en ~** to be clearly visible; **mettre en ~** (fait) to highlight; (personne) to bring to the fore; **évident, e** adj obvious, evident; **ce n'est pas évident!** (fam) it's not that easy!

évider [evide] vt to scoop out

évier [evje] nm (kitchen) sink

évincer [evɛ̃se] vt to oust

éviter [evite] vt to avoid; **~ de faire** to avoid doing; **~ qch à qn** to spare sb sth

évolué, e [evɔlɥe] adj advanced

évoluer [evɔlɥe] vi (enfant, maladie) to develop; (situation, moralement) to evolve, develop; (aller et venir) to move about; **évolution** nf development, evolution

évoquer [evɔke] vt to call to mind, evoke; (mentionner) to mention

ex... [ɛks] préfixe ex-

exact, e [ɛgza(kt), ɛgzakt] adj exact; (correct) correct; (ponctuel) punctual; **l'heure ~e** the right ou exact time; **exactement** adv exactly

ex aequo [ɛgzeko] adj equally placed; **arriver ~** to finish neck and neck

exagéré, e [ɛgzaʒeʀe] adj (prix etc) excessive

exagérer [ɛgzaʒeʀe] vt to exaggerate ♦ vi to exaggerate; (abuser) to go too far

exalter [ɛgzalte] vt (enthousiasmer) to excite, elate

examen [ɛgzamɛ̃] nm examination; (SCOL) exam, examination; **à l'~** under consideration

examinateur, -trice [ɛgzaminatœʀ, tʀis] nm/f examiner

examiner [ɛgzamine] vt to examine

exaspérant, e [ɛgzaspeʀã, ãt] adj exasperating

exaspérer [ɛgzaspeʀe] vt to exasperate

exaucer [ɛgzose] vt (vœu) to grant

excédent [ɛksedã] nm surplus; **en ~** surplus; **~ de bagages** excess luggage

excéder [ɛksede] vt (dépasser) to exceed; (agacer) to exasperate

excellent, e [ɛksɛlã, ãt] adj excellent

excentrique [ɛksãtʀik] adj eccentric

excepté, e [ɛksɛpte] adj, prép: **les élèves ~s, ~ les élèves** except for the pupils

exception [ɛksɛpsjɔ̃] nf exception; **à l'~ de** except for, with the exception of; **d'~** (mesure, loi) special, exceptional; **exceptionnel, le** adj exceptional; **exceptionnellement** adv exceptionally

excès [ɛksɛ] nm surplus ♦ nmpl excesses; **faire des ~** to overindulge; **~ de vitesse** speeding no pl; **excessif, -ive** adj excessive

excitant, e [ɛksitã, ãt] adj exciting ♦ nm stimulant; **excitation** nf (état) excitement

exciter [ɛksite] vt to excite; (suj: café etc) to stimulate; **s'~** vi to get excited

exclamation [ɛksklamasjɔ̃] nf exclamation

exclamer [ɛksklame]: **s'~** vi to exclaim

exclure [ɛksklyʀ] vt (faire sortir) to expel; (ne pas compter) to exclude, leave out; (rendre impossible) to exclude, rule out; **il est exclu que** it's out of the question that ...; **il n'est pas exclu que ...** it's not impossible that ...;

exclusif, -ive [ɛksklyzif, iv] *adj* exclusive; **exclusion** *nf* exclusion; **à l'exclusion de** with the exclusion *ou* exception of; **exclusivité** *nf* (COMM) exclusive rights *pl*; **film passant en exclusivité à** film showing only at

excursion [ɛkskyʀsjɔ̃] *nf* (*en autocar*) excursion, trip; (*à pied*) walk, hike

excuse [ɛkskyz] *nf* excuse; **~s** *nfpl* (*regret*) apology *sg*, apologies; **excuser** *vt* to excuse; **s'excuser (de)** to apologize (for); **"excusez-moi"** "I'm sorry"; (*pour attirer l'attention*) "excuse me"

exécrable [ɛgzekʀabl] *adj* atrocious

exécuter [ɛgzekyte] *vt* (*tuer*) to execute; (*tâche etc*) to execute, carry out; (MUS: *jouer*) to perform, execute; **s'~** *vi* to comply; **exécutif, -ive** *adj, nm* (POL) executive; **exécution** *nf* execution; **mettre à exécution** to carry out

exemplaire [ɛgzɑ̃plɛʀ] *nm* copy

exemple [ɛgzɑ̃pl] *nm* example; **par ~** for instance, for example; **donner l'~** to set an example

exempt, e [ɛgzɑ̃, ɑ̃(p)t] *adj*: **~ de** (*dispensé de*) exempt from; (*sans*) free from

exercer [ɛgzɛʀse] *vt* (*pratiquer*) to exercise, practise; (*influence, contrôle*) to exert; (*former*) to exercise, train; **s'~** *vi* (*sportif, musicien*) to practise

exercice [ɛgzɛʀsis] *nm* exercise

exhaustif, -ive [ɛgzostif, iv] *adj* exhaustive

exhiber [ɛgzibe] *vt* (*montrer: papiers, certificat*) to present, produce; (*péj*) to display, flaunt; **s'~** *vi* to parade; (*suj: exhibitionniste*) to expose o.s; **exhibitionniste** [ɛgzibisjɔnist] *nm/f* flasher

exhorter [ɛgzɔʀte] *vt* to urge

exigeant, e [ɛgziʒɑ̃, ɑ̃t] *adj* demanding; (*péj*) hard to please

exigence [ɛgziʒɑ̃s] *nf* demand, requirement

exiger [ɛgziʒe] *vt* to demand, require

exigu, ë [ɛgzigy] *adj* cramped, tiny

exil [ɛgzil] *nm* exile; **exiler** *vt* to exile; **s'exiler** *vi* to go into exile

existence [ɛgzistɑ̃s] *nf* existence

exister [ɛgziste] *vi* to exist; **il existe un/des** there is a/are (some)

exonérer [ɛgzɔneʀe] *vt*: **~ de** to exempt from

exorbitant, e [ɛgzɔʀbitɑ̃, ɑ̃t] *adj* exorbitant

exorbité, e [ɛgzɔʀbite] *adj*: **yeux ~s** bulging eyes

exotique [ɛgzɔtik] *adj* exotic; **yaourt aux fruits ~s** tropical fruit yoghurt

expatrier [ɛkspatʀije] *vt*: **s'~** to leave one's country

expectative [ɛkspɛktativ] *nf*: **être dans l'~** to be still waiting

expédient [ɛkspedjɑ̃, jɑ̃t] (*péj*) *nm*: **vivre d'~s** to live by one's wits

expédier [ɛkspedje] *vt* (*lettre, paquet*) to send; (*troupes*) to dispatch; (*fam: travail etc*) to dispose of, dispatch; **expéditeur, -trice** *nm/f* sender; **expédition** *nf* sending; (*scientifique, sportive, MIL*) expedition

expérience [ɛkspeʀjɑ̃s] *nf* (*de la vie*) experience; (*scientifique*) experiment

expérimenté, e [ɛkspeʀimɑ̃te] *adj* experienced

expérimenter [ɛkspeʀimɑ̃te] *vt* to test out, experiment with

expert, e [ɛkspɛʀ, ɛʀt] *adj, nm* expert; **expert-comptable** *nm* ≈ chartered accountant (BRIT), ≈ certified public accountant (US)

expertise [ɛkspɛʀtiz] *nf* (*évaluation*) expert evaluation

expertiser [ɛkspɛʀtize] *vt* (*objet de valeur*) to value; (*voiture accidentée etc*) to assess damage to

expier [ɛkspje] *vt* to expiate, atone for

expirer [ɛkspiʀe] *vi* (*prendre fin, mourir*) to expire; (*respirer*) to breathe out

explicatif, -ive [ɛksplikatif, iv] *adj* explanatory

explication [ɛksplikasjɔ̃] *nf* explanation; (*discussion*) discussion; (*dispute*) argument; **~ de texte** (SCOL) critical analysis

explicite [ɛksplisit] *adj* explicit

expliquer [ɛksplike] *vt* to explain; **s'~** to explain (o.s.); **s'~ avec qn** (*discuter*) to explain o.s. to sb; **son erreur s'explique** one can understand his mistake

exploit [ɛksplwa] *nm* exploit, feat; **exploitant, e** *nm/f*: **exploitant (agricole)** farmer

exploitation *nf* exploitation; (*d'une entreprise*) running; **~ agricole** farming concern; **exploiter** *vt* (*personne, don*) to exploit; (*entreprise, ferme*) to run, operate; (*mine*) to exploit, work

explorer [ɛksplɔʀe] *vt* to explore

exploser [ɛksploze] *vi* to explode, blow up; (*engin explosif*) to go off; (*personne: de colère*) to flare up; **explosif, -ive** *adj, nm* explosive; **explosion** *nf* explosion

exportateur, -trice [ɛkspɔʀtatœʀ, tʀis] *adj* export *cpd*, exporting ♦ *nm* exporter

exportation [ɛkspɔʀtasjɔ̃] *nf* (*action*) exportation; (*produit*) export

exporter [ɛkspɔʀte] *vt* to export

exposant [ɛkspozɑ̃] *nm* exhibitor

exposé, e [ɛkspoze] *nm* talk ♦ *adj*: **~ au sud** facing south

exposer [ɛkspoze] *vt* (*marchandise*) to display; (*peinture*) to exhibit, show; (*parler de*) to explain, set out; (*mettre en danger, orienter, PHOTO*) to expose; **exposition** *nf* (*manifestation*) exhibition; (*PHOTO*) exposure

exprès¹ [ɛkspʀɛ] adv (délibérément) on purpose; (spécialement) specially

exprès², -esse [ɛkspʀɛs] adj (ordre, défense) express, formal ♦ adj inv (PTT) express ♦ adv express

express [ɛkspʀɛs] adj, nm: (café) ~ espresso (coffee); (train) ~ fast train

expressément [ɛkspʀɛsemɑ̃] adv (spécialement) specifically

expressif, -ive [ɛkspʀɛsif, iv] adj expressive

expression [ɛkspʀɛsjɔ̃] nf expression

exprimer [ɛkspʀime] vt (sentiment, idée) to express; (jus, liquide) to press out; **s'~** vi (personne) to express o.s

exproprier [ɛkspʀɔpʀije] vt to buy up by compulsory purchase, expropriate

expulser [ɛkspylse] vt to expel; (locataire) to evict; (SPORT) to send off

exquis, e [ɛkski, iz] adj exquisite

extase [ɛkstɑz] nf ecstasy; **extasier**: **s'extasier sur** vt to go into raptures over

extension [ɛkstɑ̃sjɔ̃] nf (fig) extension

exténuer [ɛkstenɥe] vt to exhaust

extérieur, e [ɛksteʀjœʀ] adj (porte, mur etc) outer, outside; (au dehors: escalier, w.-c.) outside; (commerce) foreign; (influences) external; (apparent: calme, gaieté etc) surface cpd ♦ nm (d'une maison, d'un récipient etc) outside, exterior; (apparence) exterior; **à l'~** outside; (à l'étranger) abroad; **extérieurement** adv on the outside; (en apparence) on the surface

exterminer [ɛkstɛʀmine] vt to exterminate, wipe out

externat [ɛkstɛʀna] nm day school

externe [ɛkstɛʀn] adj external, outer ♦ nm/f (MÉD) non-resident medical student (BRIT), extern (US); (SCOL) day pupil

extincteur [ɛkstɛ̃ktœʀ] nm (fire) extinguisher

extinction [ɛkstɛ̃ksjɔ̃] nf: ~ **de voix** loss of voice

extorquer [ɛkstɔʀke] vt to extort

extra [ɛkstʀa] adj inv first-rate; (fam) fantastic ♦ nm inv extra help

extrader [ɛkstʀade] vt to extradite

extraire [ɛkstʀɛʀ] vt to extract; **extrait** nm extract

extraordinaire [ɛkstʀaɔʀdinɛʀ] adj extraordinary; (POL: mesures etc) special

extravagant, e [ɛkstʀavagɑ̃, ɑ̃t] adj extravagant

extraverti, e [ɛkstʀavɛʀti] adj extrovert

extrême [ɛkstʀɛm] adj, nm extreme; **extrêmement** adv extremely; **extrême-onction** nf last rites pl; **Extrême-Orient** nm Far East

extrémité [ɛkstʀemite] nf end; (situation) straits pl, plight; (geste désespéré) extreme action; **~s** nfpl (pieds et mains) extremities

exubérant, e [ɛgzybeʀɑ̃, ɑ̃t] adj exuberant

exutoire [ɛgzytwaʀ] nm outlet, release

F, f

F abr = **franc**

fa [fa] nm inv (MUS) F; (en chantant la gamme) fa

fable [fɑbl] nf fable

fabricant [fabʀikɑ̃, ɑ̃t] nm manufacturer

fabrication [fabʀikasjɔ̃] nf manufacture

fabrique [fabʀik] nf factory; **fabriquer** vt to make; (industriellement) to manufacture; (fig): **qu'est-ce qu'il fabrique?** (fam) what is he doing?

fabulation [fabylasjɔ̃] nf fantasizing

fac [fak] (fam) abr f (SCOL) = **faculté**

façade [fasad] nf front, façade

face [fas] nf face; (fig: aspect) side ♦ adj: **le côté** ~ heads; **en** ~ **de** opposite; (fig) in front of; **de** ~ (voir) face on; ~ **à** facing; (fig) faced with, in the face of; **faire** ~ **à** to face; ~ **à** ~ adv facing each other ♦ nm inv encounter

fâché, e [fɑʃe] adj angry; (désolé) sorry

fâcher [fɑʃe] vt to anger; **se** ~ vi to get angry; **se** ~ **avec** (se brouiller) to fall out with

fâcheux, -euse [fɑʃø, øz] adj unfortunate, regrettable

facile [fasil] adj easy; (caractère) easy-going; **facilement** adv easily

facilité nf easiness; (disposition, don) aptitude; **facilités de paiement** easy terms; **faciliter** vt to make easier

façon [fasɔ̃] nf (manière) way; (d'une robe etc) making-up, cut; ~**s** nfpl (péj) fuss sg; **de** ~ **à/à ce que** so as to/that; **de toute** ~ anyway, in any case; **façonner** [fasɔne] vt (travailler: matière) to shape, fashion

facteur, -trice [faktœʀ] nm/f postman(-woman) (BRIT), mailman(-woman) (US) ♦ nm (MATH, fig: élément) factor

factice [faktis] adj artificial

faction [faksjɔ̃] nf faction; **être de** ~ to be on guard (duty)

facture [faktyʀ] nf (à payer: gén) bill; invoice; **facturer** vt to invoice

facultatif, -ive [fakyltatif, iv] adj optional

faculté [fakylte] nf (intellectuelle, d'université) faculty; (pouvoir, possibilité) power

fade [fad] adj insipid

fagot [fago] nm bundle of sticks

faible [fɛbl] adj weak; (voix, lumière, vent) faint; (rendement, revenu) low ♦ nm (pour quelqu'un) weakness, soft spot; **faiblesse** nf weakness; **faiblir** vi to weaken; (lumière) to dim; (vent) to drop

faïence [fajɑ̃s] nf earthenware no pl

faignant, e [fɛɲɑ̃, ɑ̃t] nm/f = **fainéant, e**

faille [faj] *vb voir* **falloir** ♦ *nf* (GÉO) fault; (*fig*) flaw, weakness

faillir [fajiʀ] *vi*: **j'ai failli tomber** I almost *ou* very nearly fell

faillite [fajit] *nf* bankruptcy

faim [fɛ̃] *nf* hunger; **avoir ~** to be hungry; **rester sur sa ~** (*aussi fig*) to be left wanting more

fainéant, e [feneã, ãt] *nm/f* idler, loafer

MOT-CLÉ

---

faire [fɛʀ] *vt* **1** (*fabriquer, être l'auteur de*) to make; **faire du vin/une offre/un film** to make wine/an offer/a film; **faire du bruit** to make a noise

2 (*effectuer: travail, opération*) to do; **que faites-vous?** (*quel métier etc*) what do you do?; (*quelle activité: au moment de la question*) what are you doing?; **faire la lessive** to do the washing

3 (*études*) to do; (*sport, musique*) to play; **faire du droit/du français** to do law/French; **faire du rugby/piano** to play rugby/piano

4 (*simuler*): **faire le malade/l'ignorant** to act the invalid/the fool

5 (*transformer, avoir un effet sur*): **faire de qn un frustré/avocat** to make sb frustrated/a lawyer; **ça ne me fait rien** (*m'est égal*) I don't care *ou* mind; (*me laisse froid*) it has no effect on me; **ça ne fait rien** it doesn't matter; **faire que** (*impliquer*) to mean that

6 (*calculs, prix, mesures*): **2 et 2 font 4** 2 and 2 are *ou* make 4, **ça fait 10 m/15 F** it's 10 m/15F; **je vous le fais 10 F** I'll let you have it for 10F

7: **qu'a-t-il fait de sa valise?** what has he done with his case?

8: **ne faire que**: **il ne fait que critiquer** (*sans cesse*) all he (ever) does is criticize; (*seulement*) he's only criticizing

9 (*dire*) to say; **"vraiment?" fit-il** "really?" he said

10 (*maladie*) to have; **faire du diabète** to have diabetes ♦ *vi* **1** (*agir, s'y prendre*) to act, do; **il faut faire vite** we (*ou* you *etc*) must act quickly; **comment a-t-il fait pour?** how did he manage to?; **faites comme chez vous** make yourself at home

2 (*paraître*) to look; **faire vieux/démodé** to look old/old-fashioned; **ça fait bien** it looks good ♦ *vb substitut* to do; **ne le casse pas comme je l'ai fait** don't break it as I did; **je peux le voir? - faites!** can I see it? - please do! ♦ *vb impers* **1**: **il fait beau** *etc* the weather is fine *etc*; *voir aussi* **jour**; **froid** *etc*

2 (*temps écoulé, durée*): **ça fait 2 ans qu'il est parti** it's 2 years since he left; **ça fait 2 ans**

qu'il y est he's been there for 2 years ♦ *vb semi-aux* **1**: **faire +infinitif** (*action directe*) to make; **faire tomber/bouger qch** to make sth fall/move; **faire démarrer un moteur/chauffer de l'eau** to start up an engine/heat some water; **cela fait dormir** it makes you sleep; **faire travailler les enfants** to make the children work *ou* get the children to work

2 (*indirectement, par un intermédiaire*): **faire réparer qch** to get *ou* have sth repaired; **faire punir les enfants** to have the children punished; **se faire** *vi* **1** (*vin, fromage*) to mature

2: **cela se fait beaucoup/ne se fait pas** it's done a lot/not done

3: **se faire +nom** *ou* **pron**: **se faire une jupe** to make o.s. a skirt; **se faire des amis** to make friends; **se faire du souci** to worry; **il ne s'en fait pas** he doesn't worry

4: **se faire +adj** (*devenir*): **se faire vieux** to be getting old; (*délibérément*): **se faire beau** to do o.s. up

5: **se faire à** (*s'habituer*) to get used to; **je n'arrive pas à me faire à la nourriture/au climat** I can't get used to the food/climate

6: **se faire +infinitif**: **se faire examiner la vue/opérer** to have one's eyes tested/to have an operation; **se faire couper les cheveux** to get one's hair cut; **il va se faire tuer/punir** he's going to get himself killed/get (himself) punished; **il s'est fait aider** he got somebody to help him; **il s'est fait aider par Simon** he got Simon to help him; **se faire faire un vêtement** to get a garment made for o.s.

7 (*impersonnel*): **comment se fait-il/faisait-il que?** how is it/was it that?

---

faire-part [fɛʀpaʀ] *nm inv* announcement (*of birth, marriage etc*)

faisable [fəzabl] *adj* feasible

faisan, e [fəzã, an] *nm/f* pheasant; **faisandé, e** *adj* high (*bad*)

faisceau, x [feso] *nm* (*de lumière etc*) beam

faisons [fəzɔ̃] *vb voir* **faire**

fait, e [fɛ, fɛt] *adj* (*mûr: fromage, melon*) ripe ♦ *nm* (*événement*) event, occurrence; (*réalité, donnée*) fact; **être au ~** (**de**) to be informed (of); **au ~** (*à propos*) by the way; **en venir au ~** to get to the point; **du ~ de ceci/qu'il a menti** because of *ou* on account of this/his having lied; **de ce ~** for this reason; **en ~** in fact; **prendre qn sur le ~** to catch sb in the act; **~ divers** news item

faîte [fɛt] *nm* top; (*fig*) pinnacle, height

faites [fɛt] *vb voir* **faire**

faitout [fɛtu] *nm*, **fait-tout** [fɛtu] *nm inv* stewpot

falaise [falɛz] *nf* cliff

falloir [falwaʀ] *vb impers*: **il faut qu'il parte/a**

fallu qu'il parte (*obligation*) he has to *ou* must leave/had to leave; **il a fallu le faire** it had to be done; **il faut faire attention** you have to be careful; **il me faudrait 100 F** I would need 100 F; **il vous faut tourner à gauche après l'église** you have to turn left past the church; **nous avons ce qu'il (nous) faut** we have what we need; **s'en ~: il s'en est fallu de 100 F/5 minutes** we/they *etc* were 100 F short/5 minutes late (*ou* early); **il s'en faut de beaucoup qu'il soit** he is far from being; **il s'en est fallu de peu que cela n'arrive** it very nearly happened

falsifier [falsifje] *vt* to falsify, doctor

famé, e [fame] *adj*: **mal ~** disreputable, of ill repute

famélique [famelik] *adj* half-starved

fameux, -euse [famø, øz] *adj* (*illustre*) famous; (*bon: repas, plat etc*) first-rate, first-class; (*valeur intensive*) real, downright

familial, e, -aux [familjal, jo] *adj* family *cpd*

familiarité [familjarite] *nf* familiarity; **~s** *nfpl* (*privautés*) familiarities

familier, -ère [familje, jɛʀ] *adj* (*connu*) familiar; (*atmosphère*) informal, friendly; (*LING*) informal, colloquial ♦ *nm* regular (visitor)

famille [famij] *nf* family; **il a de la ~ à Paris** he has relatives in Paris

famine [famin] *nf* famine

fanatique [fanatik] *adj* fanatical ♦ *nm/f* fanatic; **fanatisme** *nm* fanaticism

faner [fane]: **se ~** *vi* to fade

fanfare [fɑ̃faʀ] *nf* (*orchestre*) brass band; (*musique*) fanfare

fanfaron, ne [fɑ̃faʀɔ̃, ɔn] *nm/f* braggart

fantaisie [fɑ̃tezi] *nf* (*spontanéité*) fancy, imagination; (*caprice*) whim ♦ *adj*: **bijou ~** costume jewellery; **fantaisiste** (*péj*) *adj* unorthodox, eccentric

fantasme [fɑ̃tasm] *nm* fantasy

fantasque [fɑ̃task] *adj* whimsical, capricious

fantastique [fɑ̃tastik] *adj* fantastic

fantôme [fɑ̃tom] *nm* ghost, phantom

faon [fɑ̃] *nm* fawn

farce [faʀs] *nf* (*viande*) stuffing; (*blague*) (practical) joke; (*THÉÂTRE*) farce; **farcir** *vt* (*viande*) to stuff

fardeau, x [faʀdo] *nm* burden

farder [faʀde]: **se ~** *vi* to make (o.s.) up

farfelu, e [faʀfəly] *adj* hare-brained

farine [faʀin] *nf* flour; **farineux, -euse** *adj* (*sauce, pomme*) floury

farouche [faʀuʃ] *adj* (*timide*) shy, timid

fart [faʀt] *nm* (ski) wax

fascicule [fasikyl] *nm* volume

fascination [fasinasjɔ̃] *nf* fascination

fasciner [fasine] *vt* to fascinate

fascisme [faʃism] *nm* fascism

fasse *etc* [fas] *vb voir* **faire**

faste [fast] *nm* splendour

fastidieux, -euse [fastidjø, jøz] *adj* tedious, tiresome

fastueux, -euse [fastɥø, øz] *adj* sumptuous, luxurious

fatal, e [fatal] *adj* fatal; (*inévitable*) inevitable; **fatalité** *nf* (*destin*) fate; (*coïncidence*) fateful coincidence

fatidique [fatidik] *adj* fateful

fatigant, e [fatigɑ̃, ɑ̃t] *adj* tiring; (*agaçant*) tiresome

fatigue [fatig] *nf* tiredness, fatigue; **fatigué, e** *adj* tired; **fatiguer** *vt* to tire, make tired; (*fig: agacer*) to annoy ♦ *vi* (*moteur*) to labour, strain; **se fatiguer** to get tired

fatras [fatʀɑ] *nm* jumble, hotchpotch

faubourg [fobuʀ] *nm* suburb

fauché, e [foʃe] (*fam*) *adj* broke

faucher [foʃe] *vt* (*herbe*) to cut; (*champs, blés*) to reap; (*fig: véhicule*) to mow down; (*fam: voler*) to pinch

faucille [fosij] *nf* sickle

faucon [fokɔ̃] *nm* falcon, hawk

faudra [fodʀa] *vb voir* **falloir**

faufiler [fofile]: **se ~** *vi*: **se ~ dans** to edge one's way into; **se ~ parmi/entre** to thread one's way among/between

faune [fon] *nf* (*ZOOL*) wildlife, fauna

faussaire [foseʀ] *nm* forger

fausse [fos] *adj voir* **faux**; **faussement** *adv* (*accuser*) wrongly, wrongfully; (*croire*) falsely

fausser [fose] *vt* (*objet*) to bend, buckle; (*fig*) to distort; **~ compagnie à qn** to give sb the slip

faut [fo] *vb voir* **falloir**

faute [fot] *nf* (*erreur*) mistake, error; (*mauvaise action*) misdemeanour; (*FOOTBALL etc*) offence; (*TENNIS*) fault; **c'est de sa/ma ~** it's his/my fault; **être en ~** to be in the wrong; **~ de** (*temps, argent*) for *ou* through lack of; **sans ~** without fail; **~ de frappe** typing error; **~ de goût** error of taste; **~ professionnelle** professional misconduct *no pl*

fauteuil [fotœj] *nm* armchair; **~ roulant** wheelchair

fauteur [fotœʀ] *nm*: **~ de troubles** trouble-maker

fautif, -ive [fotif, iv] *adj* (*responsable*) at fault, in the wrong; (*incorrect*) incorrect, inaccurate; **il se sentait ~** he felt guilty

fauve [fov] *nm* wildcat ♦ *adj* (*couleur*) fawn

faux¹ [fo] *nf* scythe

faux², fausse [fo, fos] *adj* (*inexact*) wrong; (*voix*) out of tune; (*billet*) fake, forged; (*sournois, postiche*) false ♦ *adv* (*MUS*) out of tune ♦ *nm* (*copie*) fake, forgery; (*opposé au vrai*): **le ~** falsehood; **faire ~ bond à qn** to stand sb up; **fausse alerte** false alarm; **fausse**

couche miscarriage; **~ frais** nmpl extras, incidental expenses; **~ pas** tripping no pl; (fig) faux pas; **~ témoignage** (délit) perjury; **faux-filet** nm sirloin; **faux-monnayeur** nm counterfeiter, forger

faveur [favœʀ] nf favour; **traitement de ~** preferential treatment; **en ~ de** in favour of

favorable [favɔʀabl] adj favourable

favori, te [favɔʀi, it] adj, nm/f favourite

favoriser [favɔʀize] vt to favour

fax [faks] nm fax; **faxer** vt to fax

FB abr (= franc belge) BF

fébrile [febʀil] adj feverish, febrile

fécond, e [fekɔ̃, ɔ̃d] adj fertile; **féconder** vt to fertilize; **fécondité** nf fertility

fécule [fekyl] nf potato flour; **féculent** nm starchy food

fédéral, e, -aux [fedeʀal, o] adj federal

fée [fe] nf fairy; **féerique** adj magical, fairytale cpd

feignant, e [fɛɲɑ̃, ɑ̃t] nm/f = **fainéant, e**

feindre [fɛ̃dʀ] vt to feign; **~ de faire** to pretend to do

feinte [fɛ̃t] nf (SPORT) dummy

fêler [fele] vt to crack

félicitations [felisitasjɔ̃] nfpl congratulations

féliciter [felisite] vt: **~ qn (de)** to congratulate sb (on)

félin, e [felɛ̃, in] nm (big) cat

fêlure [felyʀ] nf crack

femelle [fəmɛl] adj, nf female

féminin, e [feminɛ̃, in] adj feminine; (sexe) female; (équipe, vêtements etc) women's ♦ nm (LING) feminine; **féministe** [feminist] adj feminist

femme [fam] nf woman; (épouse) wife; **~ au foyer** housewife; **~ de chambre** chambermaid; **~ de ménage** cleaning lady

fémur [femyʀ] nm femur, thighbone

fendre [fɑ̃dʀ] vt (couper en deux) to split; (fissurer) to crack; (traverser: foule, air) to cleave through; **se ~** vi to crack

fenêtre [f(ə)nɛtʀ] nf window

fenouil [fənuj] nm fennel

fente [fɑ̃t] nf (fissure) crack; (de boîte à lettres etc) slit

féodal, e, -aux [feɔdal, o] adj feudal

fer [fɛʀ] nm iron; **~ à cheval** horseshoe; **~ (à repasser)** iron; **~ forgé** wrought iron

ferai etc [fəʀe] vb voir **faire**

fer-blanc [fɛʀblɑ̃] nm tin(plate)

férié, e [feʀje] adj: **jour ~** public holiday

ferions etc [fəʀjɔ̃] vb voir **faire**

ferme [fɛʀm] adj firm ♦ adv (travailler etc) hard ♦ nf (exploitation) farm; (maison) farmhouse

fermé, e [fɛʀme] adj closed, shut; (gaz, eau etc) off; (fig: milieu) exclusive

fermenter [fɛʀmɑ̃te] vi to ferment

fermer [fɛʀme] vt to close, shut; (cesser l'exploitation de) to close down, shut down; (eau, électricité, robinet) to put off, turn off; (aéroport, route) to close ♦ vi to close, shut; (magasin: définitivement) to close down, shut down; **se ~** vi to close, shut

fermeté [fɛʀməte] nf firmness

fermeture [fɛʀmətyʀ] nf closing; (dispositif) catch; **heures de ~** closing times; **~ éclair** ® zip (fastener) (BRIT), zipper (US)

fermier [fɛʀmje, jɛʀ] nm farmer; **fermière** nf woman farmer; (épouse) farmer's wife

fermoir [fɛʀmwaʀ] nm clasp

féroce [feʀɔs] adj ferocious, fierce

ferons [fəʀɔ̃] vb voir **faire**

ferraille [feʀaj] nf scrap iron; **mettre à la ~** to scrap

ferrer [feʀe] vt (cheval) to shoe

ferronnerie [feʀɔnʀi] nf ironwork

ferroviaire [feʀɔvjɛʀ] adj rail(way) cpd (BRIT), rail(road) cpd (US)

ferry(boat) [feʀe(bot)] nm ferry

fertile [fɛʀtil] adj fertile; **~ en incidents** eventful, packed with incidents

féru, e [feʀy] adj: **~ de** with a keen interest in

fervent, e [fɛʀvɑ̃, ɑ̃t] adj fervent

fesse [fɛs] nf buttock; **fessée** nf spanking

festin [fɛstɛ̃] nm feast

festival [fɛstival] nm festival

festivités [fɛstivite] nfpl festivities

festoyer [fɛstwaje] vi to feast

fêtard [fɛtaʀ, aʀd] (fam) nm high liver, merry-maker

fête [fɛt] nf (religieuse) feast; (publique) holiday; (réception) party; (kermesse) fête, fair; (du nom) feast day, name day; **faire la ~** to live it up; **faire ~ à qn** to give sb a warm welcome; **les ~s (de fin d'année)** the festive season; **la salle des ~s** the village hall; **~ foraine** (fun) fair, **fêter** vt to celebrate; (personne) to have a celebration for

feu, x [fø] nm (gén) fire; (signal lumineux) light; (de cuisinière) ring; **~x** nmpl (AUTO) (traffic) lights; **au ~!** (incendie) fire!; **à ~ doux/vif** over a slow/brisk heat; **à petit ~** (CULIN) over a gentle heat; (fig) slowly; **faire ~** to fire; **prendre ~** to catch fire; **mettre le ~ à** to set fire to; **faire du ~** to make a fire; **avez-vous du ~?** (pour cigarette) have you (got) a light?; **~ arrière** rear light; **~ d'artifice** (spectacle) fireworks pl; **~ de joie** bonfire; **~ rouge/vert/orange** red/green/amber (BRIT) ou yellow (US) light; **~x de brouillard** fog-lamps; **~x de croisement** dipped (BRIT) ou dimmed (US) headlights; **~x de position** sidelights; **~x de route** headlights

feuillage [fœjaʒ] nm foliage, leaves pl

feuille [fœj] nf (d'arbre) leaf; (de papier) sheet; **~ de maladie** medical expenses claim

form; **~ de paie** pay slip
feuillet [fœjɛ] nm leaf
feuilleté, e [fœjte] adj: **pâte ~** flaky pastry
feuilleter [fœjte] vt (livre) to leaf through
feuilleton [fœjtɔ̃] nm serial
feutre [føtʀ] nm felt; (chapeau) felt hat;
(aussi: **stylo-~**) felt-tip pen; **feutré, e** adj
(atmosphère) muffled
fève [fɛv] nf broad bean
février [fevʀije] nm February
FF abr (= franc français) FF
fiable [fjabl] adj reliable
fiançailles [fjɑ̃saj] nfpl engagement sg
fiancé, e [fjɑ̃se] nm/f fiancé(e) ♦ adj: **être
~ (à)** to be engaged (to)
fiancer [fjɑ̃se]: **se ~** vi to become engaged
fibre [fibʀ] nf fibre; **~ de verre** fibreglass, glass
fibre
ficeler [fisle] vt to tie up
ficelle [fisɛl] nf string no pl; (morceau) piece
ou length of string
fiche [fiʃ] nf (pour fichier) (index) card;
(formulaire) form; (ÉLEC) plug
ficher [fiʃe] vt (dans un fichier) to file; (POLICE)
to put on file; (fam: faire) to do; (: donner)
to give; (: mettre) to stick ou shove; **se ~ de**
(fam: se gausser) to make fun of; **fiche-(moi)
le camp** (fam) clear off; **fiche-moi la paix**
(fam) leave me alone; **je m'en fiche!** (fam) I
don't care!
fichier [fiʃje] nm file
fichu, e [fiʃy] pp de **ficher** (fam) ♦ adj (fam:
fini, inutilisable) bust, done for; (: intensif)
wretched, darned ♦ nm (foulard)
(head)scarf; **mal ~** (fam) feeling lousy
fictif, -ive [fiktif, iv] adj fictitious
fiction [fiksjɔ̃] nf fiction; (fait imaginé)
invention
fidèle [fidɛl] adj faithful ♦ nm/f (REL): **les ~s**
(à l'église) the congregation sg; **fidélité** nf
fidelity
fier¹ [fje]: **se ~ à** vt to trust
fier², fière [fjɛʀ] adj proud; **fierté** nf pride
fièvre [fjɛvʀ] nf fever; **avoir de la ~/39 de ~** to
have a high temperature/a temperature of
39°C; **fiévreux, -euse** adj feverish
figé, e [fiʒe] adj (manières) stiff; (société)
rigid; (sourire) set
figer [fiʒe]: **se ~** vi (huile) to congeal;
(personne) to freeze
fignoler [fiɲɔle] (fam) vt to polish up
figue [fig] nf fig; **figuier** nm fig tree
figurant, e [figyʀɑ̃, ɑ̃t] nm/f (THÉÂTRE) walk-
on; (CINÉMA) extra
figure [figyʀ] nf (visage) face; (forme,
personnage) figure; (illustration) picture,
diagram
figuré, e [figyʀe] adj (sens) figurative
figurer [figyʀe] vi to appear ♦ vt to represent;

se ~ que to imagine that
fil [fil] nm (brin, fig: d'une histoire) thread;
(électrique) wire; (d'un couteau) edge; **au
~ des années** with the passing of the years;
au ~ de l'eau with the stream ou current;
coup de ~ (fam) phone call; **~ à coudre**
(sewing) thread; **~ de fer** wire; **~ de fer
barbelé** barbed wire
filament [filamɑ̃] nm (ÉLEC) filament
filandreux, -euse [filɑ̃dʀø, øz] adj stringy
filature [filatyʀ] nf (fabrique) mill; (policière)
shadowing no pl, tailing no pl
file [fil] nf line; (AUTO) lane; **en ~ indienne** in
single file; **à la ~** (d'affilée) in succession;
~ (d'attente) queue (BRIT), line (US)
filer [file] vt (tissu, toile) to spin; (prendre en
filature) to shadow, tail; (fam: donner): **~ qch
à qn** to slip sb sth ♦ vi (bas) to run; (aller
vite) to fly past; (fam: partir) to make ou be
off; **~ doux** to toe the line
filet [filɛ] nm net; (CULIN) fillet; (d'eau, de
sang) trickle; (à provisions) string bag
filiale [filjal] nf (COMM) subsidiary
filière [filjɛʀ] nf (carrière) path; **suivre la ~**
(dans sa carrière) to work one's way up
(through the hierarchy)
filiforme [filifɔʀm] adj spindly
filigrane [filigʀan] nm (d'un billet, timbre)
watermark
fille [fij] nf girl; (opposé à fils) daughter; **vieille
~** old maid; **fillette** nf (little) girl
filleul, e [fijœl] nm/f godchild, godson/
daughter
film [film] nm (pour photo) (roll of) film;
(œuvre) film, picture, movie; **~ d'épouvante**
horror film; **~ policier** thriller
filon [filɔ̃] nm vein, lode; (fig) lucrative line,
money spinner
fils [fis] nm son; **~ à papa** daddy's boy
filtre [filtʀ] nm filter; **filtrer** vt to filter; (fig:
candidats, visiteurs) to screen
fin¹ [fɛ̃] nf end; **~s** nfpl (but) ends; **prendre ~**
to come to an end; **mettre ~ à** to put an end
to; **à la ~** in the end, eventually; **en ~ de
compte** in the end; **sans ~** endless; **~ juin** at
the end of June
fin², e [fɛ̃, fin] adj (papier, couche, fil) thin;
(cheveux, visage) fine; (taille) neat, slim;
(esprit, remarque) subtle ♦ adv (couper)
finely; **~ prêt** quite ready; **~es herbes** mixed
herbs
final, e [final, o] adj final ♦ nm (MUS) finale;
finale nf final; **quarts de finale** quarter finals;
finalement adv finally, in the end; (après
tout) after all
finance [finɑ̃s] nf: **~s** nfpl (situation) finances;
(activités) finance sg; **moyennant ~** for a fee;
financer vt to finance; **financier, -ière** adj
financial

finaud, e [fino, od] *adj* wily

finesse [fines] *nf* thinness; (*raffinement*) fineness; (*subtilité*) subtlety

fini, e [fini] *adj* finished; (*MATH*) finite ♦ *nm* (*d'un objet manufacturé*) finish

finir [finiʀ] *vt* to finish ♦ *vi* to finish, end; **~ par faire** to end up ou finish up doing; **~ de faire** to finish doing; (*cesser*) to stop doing; **il finit par m'agacer** he's beginning to get on my nerves; **en ~ avec** to be ou have done with; **il va mal ~** he will come to a bad end

finition [finisjɔ̃] *nf* (*résultat*) finish

finlandais, e [fɛlɑ̃dɛ, ɛz] *adj* Finnish ♦ *nm/f*: F~, e Finn

Finlande [fɛlɑ̃d] *nf*: **la ~** Finland

fiole [fjɔl] *nf* phial

firme [fiʀm] *nf* firm

fis [fi] *vb voir* faire

fisc [fisk] *nm* tax authorities *pl*; **fiscal, e, -aux** *adj* tax *cpd*, fiscal; **fiscalité** *nf* tax system

fissure [fisyʀ] *nf* crack; **fissurer** *vt* to crack; **se fissurer** *vi* to crack

fiston [fistɔ̃] (*fam*) *nm* son, lad

fit [fi] *vb voir* faire

fixation [fiksasjɔ̃] *nf* (*attache*) fastening; (*PSYCH*) fixation

fixe [fiks] *adj* fixed; (*emploi*) steady, regular ♦ *nm* (*salaire*) basic salary; **à heure ~** at a set time; **menu à prix ~** set menu

fixé, e [fikse] *adj*: **être ~ (sur)** (*savoir à quoi s'en tenir*) to have made up one's mind (about)

fixer [fikse] *vt* (*attacher*): **~ qch (à/sur)** to fix ou fasten sth (to/onto); (*déterminer*) to fix, set; (*regarder*) to stare at; **se ~** *vi* (*s'établir*) to settle down; **se ~ sur** (*suj: attention*) to focus on

flacon [flakɔ̃] *nm* bottle

flageoler [flaʒɔle] *vi* (*jambes*) to sag

flageolet [flaʒɔlɛ] *nm* (*CULIN*) dwarf kidney bean

flagrant, e [flagʀɑ̃, ɑ̃t] *adj* flagrant, blatant; **en ~ délit** in the act

flair [flɛʀ] *nm* sense of smell; (*fig*) intuition; **flairer** *vt* (*humer*) to sniff (at); (*détecter*) to scent

flamand, e [flamɑ̃, ɑ̃d] *adj* Flemish ♦ *nm* (*LING*) Flemish ♦ *nm/f*: F~, e Fleming; **les F~s** the Flemish

flamant [flamɑ̃] *nm* flamingo

flambant [flɑ̃bɑ̃, ɑ̃t] *adv*: **~ neuf** brand new

flambé, e [flɑ̃be] *adj* (*CULIN*) flambé

flambeau, x [flɑ̃bo] *nm* (flaming) torch

flambée [flɑ̃be] *nf* blaze; (*fig: des prix*) explosion

flamber [flɑ̃be] *vi* to blaze (up)

flamboyer [flɑ̃bwaje] *vi* to blaze (up)

flamme [flam] *nf* flame; (*fig*) fire, fervour; **en ~s** on fire, ablaze

flan [flɑ̃] *nm* (*CULIN*) custard tart ou pie

flanc [flɑ̃] *nm* side; (*MIL*) flank

flancher [flɑ̃ʃe] (*fam*) *vi* to fail, pack up

flanelle [flanɛl] *nf* flannel

flâner [flɑne] *vi* to stroll; **flânerie** *nf* stroll

flanquer [flɑ̃ke] *vt* to flank; (*fam: mettre*) to chuck, shove; (: *jeter*): **~ par terre/à la porte** to fling to the ground/chuck out

flaque [flak] *nf* (*d'eau*) puddle; (*d'huile, de sang etc*) pool

flash [flaʃ] (*pl* **~es**) *nm* (*PHOTO*) flash; **~ (d'information)** newsflash

flasque [flask] *adj* flabby

flatter [flate] *vt* to flatter; **se ~ de qch** to pride o.s. on sth; **flatterie** *nf* flattery *no pl*; **flatteur, -euse** *adj* flattering

fléau, x [fleo] *nm* scourge

flèche [flɛʃ] *nf* arrow; (*de clocher*) spire; **monter en ~** (*fig*) to soar, rocket; **partir en ~** to be off like a shot; **fléchette** *nf* dart

fléchir [fleʃiʀ] *vt* (*corps, genou*) to bend; (*fig*) to sway, weaken ♦ *vi* (*fig*) to weaken, flag

flemmard, e [flemaʀ, aʀd] (*fam*) *nm/f* lazybones *sg*, loafer

flemme [flɛm] *nf* (*fam*) laziness; **j'ai la ~ de le faire** I can't be bothered doing it

flétrir [fletʀiʀ]: **se ~** *vi* to wither

fleur [flœʀ] *nf* flower; (*d'un arbre*) blossom; **en ~** (*arbre*) in blossom; **à ~s** flowery

fleuri, e [flœʀi] *adj* (*jardin*) in flower ou bloom; (*tissu, papier*) flowery

fleurir [flœʀiʀ] *vi* (*rose*) to flower; (*arbre*) to blossom; (*fig*) to flourish ♦ *vt* (*tombe*) to put flowers on; (*chambre*) to decorate with flowers

fleuriste [flœʀist] *nm/f* florist

fleuve [flœv] *nm* river

flexible [flɛksibl] *adj* flexible

flic [flik] (*fam: péj*) *nm* cop

flipper [flipœʀ] *nm* pinball (machine)

flirter [flœʀte] *vi* to flirt

flocon [flɔkɔ̃] *nm* flake

flopée [flɔpe] (*fam*) *nf*: **une ~ de** loads of, masses of

floraison [flɔʀɛzɔ̃] *nf* flowering

flore [flɔʀ] *nf* flora

florissant, e [flɔʀisɑ̃, ɑ̃t] *adj* (*économie*) flourishing

flot [flo] *nm* flood, stream; **~s** *nmpl* (*de la mer*) waves; **être à ~** (*NAVIG*) to be afloat; **entrer à ~s** to stream ou pour in

flottant, e [flɔtɑ̃, ɑ̃t] *adj* (*vêtement*) loose

flotte [flɔt] *nf* (*NAVIG*) fleet; (*fam: eau*) water; (: *pluie*) rain

flottement [flɔtmɑ̃] *nm* (*fig*) wavering, hesitation

flotter [flɔte] *vi* to float; (*nuage, odeur*) to drift; (*drapeau*) to fly; (*vêtements*) to hang loose; (*fam: pleuvoir*) to rain; **faire ~** to float;

flotteur nm float

flou, e [flu] adj fuzzy, blurred; (fig) woolly, vague

fluctuation [flyktцasjɔ̃] nf fluctuation

fluet, te [flyɛ, ɛt] adj thin, slight

fluide [flɥid] adj fluid; (circulation etc) flowing freely ♦ nm fluid

fluor [flyɔʀ] nm: **dentifrice au ~** fluoride toothpaste

fluorescent, e [flyɔʀesā, āt] adj fluorescent

flûte [flyt] nf flute; (verre) flute glass; (pain) long loaf; **~!** drat it!; **à bec** recorder

flux [fly] nm incoming tide; (écoulement) flow; **le ~ et le reflux** the ebb and flow

FM sigle f (= fréquence modulée) FM

foc [fɔk] nm jib

foi [fwa] nf faith; **digne de ~** reliable; **être de bonne/mauvaise ~** to be sincere/insincere; **ma ~ ...** well ...

foie [fwa] nm liver; **crise de ~** stomach upset

foin [fwɛ̃] nm hay; **faire du ~** (fig: fam) to kick up a row

foire [fwaʀ] nf fair; (fête foraine) (fun) fair; **faire la ~** (fig: fam) to whoop it up; **~ (exposition)** trade fair

fois [fwa] nf time; **une/deux ~** once/twice; **2 ~ 2** 2 times 2; **une ~** (passé) once; (futur) sometime; **une ~ pour toutes** once and for all; **une ~ que** once; **des ~** (parfois) sometimes; **à la ~** (ensemble) at once

foison [fwazɔ̃] nf: **à ~** in plenty; **foisonner** vi to abound

fol [fɔl] adj voir **fou**

folie [fɔli] nf (d'une décision, d'un acte) madness, folly; (état) madness, insanity; **la ~ des grandeurs** delusions of grandeur; **faire des ~s** (en dépenses) to be extravagant

folklorique [fɔlklɔʀik] adj folk cpd; (fam) weird

folle [fɔl] adj, nf voir **fou**; **follement** adv (très) madly, wildly

foncé, e [fɔ̃se] adj dark

foncer [fɔ̃se] vi to go darker; (fam: aller vite) to tear ou belt along; **~ sur** to charge at

foncier, -ère [fɔ̃sje, jɛʀ] adj (honnêteté etc) basic, fundamental; (COMM) real estate cpd

fonction [fɔ̃ksjɔ̃] nf function; (emploi, poste) post, position; **~s** nfpl (professionnelles) duties; **voiture de ~** company car; **en ~ de** (par rapport à) according to; **faire ~ de** to serve as; **la ~ publique** the state ou civil (BRIT) service; **fonctionnaire** nm/f state employee, local authority employee; (dans l'administration) ≈ civil servant; **fonctionner** vi to work, function

fond [fɔ̃] nm (d'un récipient, trou) bottom; (d'une salle, scène) back; (d'un tableau, décor) background; (opposé à la forme) content; (SPORT): **le ~** long distance (running); **au ~ de**

at the bottom of; at the back of; **à ~** (connaître, soutenir) thoroughly; (appuyer, visser) right down ou home; **à ~ (de train)** (fam) full tilt; **dans le ~, au ~** (en somme) basically, really; **de ~ en comble** from top to bottom; voir aussi **fonds**; **~ de teint** foundation (cream)

fondamental, e, -aux [fɔ̃damātal, o] adj fundamental

fondant, e [fɔ̃dā, āt] adj (neige) melting; (poire) that melts in the mouth

fondateur, -trice [fɔ̃datœʀ, tʀis] nm/f founder

fondation [fɔ̃dasjɔ̃] nf founding; (établissement) foundation; **~s** nfpl (d'une maison) foundations

fondé, e [fɔ̃de] adj (accusation etc) well-founded; **être ~ à** to have grounds for ou good reason to

fondement [fɔ̃dmā] nm: **sans ~** (rumeur etc) groundless, unfounded

fonder [fɔ̃de] vt to found; (fig) to base; **se ~ sur** (suj: personne) to base o.s. on

fonderie [fɔ̃dʀi] nf smelting works sg

fondre [fɔ̃dʀ] vt (aussi: **faire ~**) to melt; (dans l'eau) to dissolve; (fig: mélanger) to merge, blend ♦ vi (à la chaleur) to melt; (dans l'eau) to dissolve; (fig) to melt away; (se précipiter): **~ sur** to swoop down on; **~ en larmes** to burst into tears

fonds [fɔ̃] nm (COMM): **~ (de commerce)** business ♦ nmpl (argent) funds

fondu, e [fɔ̃dy] adj (beurre, neige) melted; (métal) molten; **fondue** nf (CULIN) fondue

font [fɔ̃] vb voir **faire**

fontaine [fɔ̃tɛn] nf fountain; (source) spring

fonte [fɔ̃t] nf melting; (métal) cast iron; **la ~ des neiges** (the spring) thaw

foot [fut] (fam) nm football

football [futbɔl] nm football, soccer; **footballeur** nm footballer

footing [futiŋ] nm jogging; **faire du ~** to go jogging

for [fɔʀ] nm: **dans son ~ intérieur** in one's heart of hearts

forain, e [fɔʀɛ̃, ɛn] adj fairground cpd ♦ nm (marchand) stallholder; (acteur) fairground entertainer

forçat [fɔʀsa] nm convict

force [fɔʀs] nf strength; (PHYSIQUE, MÉCANIQUE) force; **~s** nfpl (physiques) strength sg; (MIL) forces; **à ~ d'insister** by dint of insisting; as he (ou l etc) kept on insisting; **de ~** forcibly, by force; **les ~s de l'ordre** the police

forcé, e [fɔʀse] adj forced; **c'est ~** (fam) it's inevitable; **forcément** adv inevitably; **pas forcément** not necessarily

forcené, e [fɔʀsəne] nm/f maniac

forcer [fɔʀse] vt to force; (voix) to strain ♦ vi

(*SPORT*) to overtax o.s.; **~ la dose** (*fam*) to overdo it; **se ~ (à faire)** to force o.s. (to do)

forcir [fɔʀsiʀ] *vi* (*grossir*) to broaden out

forer [fɔʀe] *vt* to drill, bore

forestier, -ère [fɔʀɛstje, jɛʀ] *adj* forest *cpd*

forêt [fɔʀɛ] *nf* forest

forfait [fɔʀfɛ] *nm* (*COMM*) all-in deal *ou* price; **forfaitaire** *adj* inclusive

forge [fɔʀʒ] *nf* forge, smithy; **forger** *vt* to forge; (*fig: prétexte*) to contrive, make up; **forgeron** *nm* (black)smith

formaliser [fɔʀmalize]: **se ~** *vi*: **se ~ (de)** to take offence (at)

formalité [fɔʀmalite] *nf* formality; **simple ~** mere formality

format [fɔʀma] *nm* size; **formater** *vt* (*disque*) to format

formation [fɔʀmasjɔ̃] *nf* (*développement*) forming; (*apprentissage*) training; **~ permanente** continuing education; **~ professionnelle** vocational training

forme [fɔʀm] *nf* (*gén*) form; (*d'un objet*) shape, form, **~s** *nfpl* (*bonnes manières*) properties; (*d'une femme*) figure *sg*; **être en ~** (*SPORT etc*) to be on form; **en bonne et due ~** in due form

formel, le [fɔʀmɛl] *adj* (*catégorique*) definite, positive; **formellement** *adv* (*absolument*) positively; **formellement interdit** strictly forbidden

former [fɔʀme] *vt* to form; (*éduquer*) to train; **se ~** *vi* to form

formidable [fɔʀmidabl] *adj* tremendous

formulaire [fɔʀmylɛʀ] *nm* form

formule [fɔʀmyl] *nf* (*gén*) formula; (*expression*) phrase; **~ de politesse** polite phrase; (*en fin de lettre*) letter ending; **formuler** *vt* (*émettre: désir*) to formulate

fort, e [fɔʀ, fɔʀt] *adj* strong, (*intensité, rendement*) high, great; (*corpulent*) stout; (*doué*) good, able ♦ *adv* (*serrer, frapper*) hard; (*parler*) loud(ly); (*beaucoup*) greatly, very much; (*très*) very ♦ *nm* (*édifice*) fort; (*point ~*) strong point, forte; **~e tête** rebel; **forteresse** *nf* stronghold

fortifiant [fɔʀtifjɑ̃, jɑ̃t] *nm* tonic

fortifier [fɔʀtifje] *vt* to strengthen, fortify

fortiori [fɔʀsjɔʀi]: **à ~** *adv* all the more so

fortuit, e [fɔʀtɥi, it] *adj* fortuitous, chance *cpd*

fortune [fɔʀtyn] *nf* fortune; **faire ~** to make one's fortune; **de ~** makeshift; **fortuné, e** *adj* wealthy

fosse [fos] *nf* (*grand trou*) pit; (*tombe*) grave

fossé [fose] *nm* ditch; (*fig*) gulf, gap

fossette [fosɛt] *nf* dimple

fossile [fosil] *nm* fossil

fossoyeur [foswajœʀ] *nm* gravedigger

fou (fol), folle [fu, fɔl] *adj* mad; (*déréglé etc*) wild, erratic; (*fam: extrême, très grand*) terrific, tremendous ♦ *nm/f* madman(-woman) ♦ *nm* (*du roi*) jester; **être ~de** to be mad *ou* crazy about; **avoir le ~rire** to have the giggles

foudre [fudʀ] *nf*: **la ~** lightning

foudroyant, e [fudʀwajɑ̃, ɑ̃t] *adj* (*progrès*) lightning *cpd*; (*succès*) stunning; (*maladie, poison*) violent

foudroyer [fudʀwaje] *vt* to strike down; **être foudroyé** to be struck by lightning; **~ qn du regard** to glare at sb

fouet [fwɛ] *nm* whip; (*CULIN*) whisk; **de plein ~** (*se heurter*) head on; **fouetter** *vt* to whip; (*crème*) to whisk

fougère [fuʒɛʀ] *nf* fern

fougue [fug] *nf* ardour, spirit; **fougueux, -euse** *adj* fiery

fouille [fuj] *nf* search; **~s** *nfpl* (*archéologiques*) excavations; **fouiller** *vt* to search; (*creuser*) to dig ♦ *vi* to rummage; **fouillis** *nm* jumble, muddle

fouiner [fwine] (*péj*) *vi*: **~ dans** to nose around *ou* about in

foulard [fulaʀ] *nm* scarf

foule [ful] *nf* crowd; **la ~** crowds *pl*; **une ~ de** masses of

foulée [fule] *nf* stride

fouler [fule] *vt* to press; (*sol*) to tread upon; **se ~ la cheville** to sprain one's ankle; **ne pas se ~** not to overexert o.s.; **il ne se foule pas** he doesn't put himself out; **foulure** *nf* sprain

four [fuʀ] *nm* oven; (*de potier*) kiln; (*THÉÂTRE: échec*) flop

fourbe [fuʀb] *adj* deceitful

fourbu, e [fuʀby] *adj* exhausted

fourche [fuʀʃ] *nf* pitchfork

fourchette [fuʀʃɛt] *nf* fork; (*STATISTIQUE*) bracket, margin

fourgon [fuʀgɔ̃] *nm* van; (*RAIL*) wag(g)on; **fourgonnette** *nf* (small) van

fourmi [fuʀmi] *nf* ant; **~s** *nfpl* (*fig*) pins and needles; **fourmilière** *nf* ant-hill; **fourmiller** *vi* to swarm

fournaise [fuʀnɛz] *nf* blaze; (*fig*) furnace, oven

fourneau, x [fuʀno] *nm* stove

fournée [fuʀne] *nf* batch

fourni, e [fuʀni] *adj* (*barbe, cheveux*) thick; (*magasin*): **bien ~ (en)** well stocked (with)

fournir [fuʀniʀ] *vt* to supply; (*preuve, exemple*) to provide, supply; (*effort*) to put in; **fournisseur, -euse** *nm/f* supplier; **fourniture** *nf* supply(ing); **fournitures scolaires** school stationery

fourrage [fuʀaʒ] *nm* fodder

fourré, e [fuʀe] *adj* (*bonbon etc*) filled; (*manteau etc*) fur-lined ♦ *nm* thicket

fourrer [fuʀe] (*fam*) *vt* to stick, shove; **se**

~ **dans/sous** to get into/under; **fourre-tout** *nm inv* (*sac*) holdall; (*fig*) rag-bag
fourrière [fuʀjɛʀ] *nf* pound
fourrure [fuʀyʀ] *nf* fur; (*sur l'animal*) coat
fourvoyer [fuʀvwaje]: **se ~** *vi* to go astray, stray
foutre [futʀ] (*fam!*) *vt* = **ficher**; **foutu, e** (*fam!*) *adj* = **fichu, e**
foyer [fwaje] *nm* (*maison*) home; (*famille*) family; (*de cheminée*) hearth; (*de jeunes etc*) (social) club; (*résidence*) hostel; (*salon*) foyer; **lunettes à double ~** bi-focal glasses
fracas [fʀaka] *nm* (*d'objet qui tombe*) crash; **fracassant, e** *adj* (*succès*) thundering; **fracasser** *vt* to smash
fraction [fʀaksjɔ̃] *nf* fraction; **fractionner** *vt* to divide (up), split (up)
fracture [fʀaktyʀ] *nf* fracture; **~ du crâne** fractured skull; **fracturer** *vt* (*coffre, serrure*) to break open; (*os, membre*) to fracture
fragile [fʀaʒil] *adj* fragile, delicate; (*fig*) frail; **fragilité** *nf* fragility
fragment [fʀagmɑ̃] *nm* (*d'un objet*) fragment, piece
fraîche [fʀɛʃ] *adj voir* **frais**; **fraîcheur** *nf* coolness; (*d'un aliment*) freshness; **fraîchir** *vi* to get cooler; (*vent*) to freshen
frais, fraîche [fʀɛ, fʀɛʃ] *adj* fresh; (*froid*) cool ♦ *adv* (*récemment*) newly, fresh(ly) ♦ *nm*: **mettre au ~** to put in a cool place ♦ *nmpl* (*gén*) expenses; (*COMM*) costs; **il fait ~** it's cool; **servir ~** serve chilled; **prendre le ~** to take a breath of cool air; **faire des ~** to go to a lot of expense; **~ de scolarité** school fees (*BRIT*), tuition (*US*); **~ généraux** overheads
fraise [fʀɛz] *nf* strawberry; **~ des bois** wild strawberry
framboise [fʀɑ̃bwaz] *nf* raspberry
franc, franche [fʀɑ̃, fʀɑ̃ʃ] *adj* (*personne*) frank, straightforward; (*visage*) open; (*net: refus*) clear; (*: coupure*) clean; (*intensif*) downright ♦ *nm* franc
français, e [fʀɑ̃sɛ, ɛz] *adj* French ♦ *nm/f*: **F~, e** Frenchman(-woman) ♦ *nm* (*LING*) French; **les F~** the French
France [fʀɑ̃s] *nf*: **la ~** France
franche [fʀɑ̃ʃ] *adj voir* **franc**; **franchement** *adv* frankly; (*nettement*) definitely; (*tout à fait: mauvais etc*) downright
franchir [fʀɑ̃ʃiʀ] *vt* (*obstacle*) to clear, get over; (*seuil, ligne, rivière*) to cross; (*distance*) to cover
franchise [fʀɑ̃ʃiz] *nf* frankness; (*douanière*) exemption; (*ASSURANCES*) excess
franc-maçon [fʀɑ̃masɔ̃] *nm* freemason
franco [fʀɑ̃ko] *adv* (*COMM*): **~ (de port)** postage paid
francophone [fʀɑ̃kɔfɔn] *adj* French-speaking
franc-parler [fʀɑ̃paʀle] *nm inv*

outspokenness; **avoir son ~-~** to speak one's mind
frange [fʀɑ̃ʒ] *nf* fringe
frangipane [fʀɑ̃ʒipan] *nf* almond paste
franquette [fʀɑ̃kɛt]: **à la bonne ~** *adv* without any fuss
frappant, e [fʀapɑ̃, ɑ̃t] *adj* striking
frappé, e [fʀape] *adj* iced
frapper [fʀape] *vt* to hit, strike; (*étonner*) to strike; **~ dans ses mains** to clap one's hands; **frappé de stupeur** dumbfounded
frasques [fʀask] *nfpl* escapades
fraternel, le [fʀatɛʀnɛl] *adj* brotherly, fraternal; **fraternité** *nf* brotherhood
fraude [fʀod] *nf* fraud; (*SCOL*) cheating; **passer qch en ~** to smuggle sth in (*ou* out); **~ fiscale** tax evasion; **frauder** *vi, vt* to cheat; **frauduleux, -euse** *adj* fraudulent
frayer [fʀeje] *vt* to open up, clear ♦ *vi* to spawn; **se ~ un chemin dans la foule** to force one's way through the crowd
frayeur [fʀejœʀ] *nf* fright
fredonner [fʀədɔne] *vt* to hum
freezer [fʀizœʀ] *nm* freezing compartment
frein [fʀɛ̃] *nm* brake; **mettre un ~ à** (*fig*) to curb, check; **~ à main** handbrake; **freiner** *vi* to brake ♦ *vt* (*progrès etc*) to check
frêle [fʀɛl] *adj* frail, fragile
frelon [fʀəlɔ̃] *nm* hornet
frémir [fʀemiʀ] *vi* (*de peur, d'horreur*) to shudder; (*de colère*) to shake; (*feuillage*) to quiver
frêne [fʀɛn] *nm* ash
frénétique [fʀenetik] *adj* frenzied, frenetic
fréquemment [fʀekamɑ̃] *adv* frequently
fréquent, e [fʀekɑ̃, ɑ̃t] *adj* frequent
fréquentation [fʀekɑ̃tasjɔ̃] *nf* frequenting; **~s** *nfpl* (*relations*) company *sg*
fréquenté, e [fʀekɑ̃te] *adj*: **très ~** (very) busy; **mal ~** patronized by disreputable elements
fréquenter [fʀekɑ̃te] *vt* (*lieu*) to frequent; (*personne*) to see; **se ~** to see each other
frère [fʀɛʀ] *nm* brother
fresque [fʀɛsk] *nf* (*ART*) fresco
fret [fʀɛ(t)] *nm* freight
frétiller [fʀetije] *vi* (*poisson*) to wriggle
fretin [fʀətɛ̃] *nm*: **menu ~** small fry
friable [fʀijabl] *adj* crumbly
friand, e [fʀijɑ̃, fʀijɑ̃d] *adj*: **~ de** very fond of ♦ *nm*: **~ au fromage** cheese puff
friandise [fʀijɑ̃diz] *nf* sweet
fric [fʀik] (*fam*) *nm* cash, bread
friche [fʀiʃ]: **en ~** *adj, adv* (lying) fallow
friction [fʀiksjɔ̃] *nf* (*massage*) rub, rub-down; (*TECH, fig*) friction; **frictionner** *vt* to rub (down)
frigidaire ® [fʀiʒidɛʀ] *nm* refrigerator
frigide [fʀiʒid] *adj* frigid

frigo [fʀigo] (fam) nm fridge

frigorifié, e [fʀigɔʀifje] (fam) adj: **être ~ to be frozen stiff**

frigorifique [fʀigɔʀifik] adj refrigerating

frileux, -euse [fʀilø, øz] adj sensitive to (the) cold

frime [fʀim] (fam) nf: **c'est de la ~** it's a lot of eyewash, it's all put on; **frimer** (fam) vi to show off

frimousse [fʀimus] nf (sweet) little face

fringale [fʀɛ̃gal] (fam) nf: **avoir la ~** to be ravenous

fringant, e [fʀɛ̃gɑ̃, ɑ̃t] adj dashing

fringues [fʀɛ̃g] (fam) nfpl clothes

fripé, e [fʀipe] adj crumpled

fripon, ne [fʀipɔ̃, ɔn] adj roguish, mischievous ♦ nm/f rascal, rogue

fripouille [fʀipuj] nf scoundrel

frire [fʀiʀ] vt, vi: **faire ~** to fry

frisé, e [fʀize] adj (cheveux) curly; (personne) curly-haired

frisson [fʀisɔ̃] nm (de froid) shiver; (de peur) shudder; **frissonner** vi (de fièvre, froid) to shiver; (d'horreur) to shudder

frit, e [fʀi, fʀit] pp de **frire**; **frite** nf: (pommes) **frites** chips (BRIT), French fries; **friteuse** nf chip pan; **friture** nf (huile) (deep) fat; (plat): **friture (de poissons)** fried fish

frivole [fʀivɔl] adj frivolous

froid, e [fʀwa, fʀwad] adj, nm cold; **il fait ~** it's cold; **avoir/prendre ~** to be/catch cold; **être en ~ avec** to be on bad terms with; **froidement** adv (accueillir) coldly; (décider) coolly

froideur [fʀwadœʀ] nf coldness

froisser [fʀwase] vt to crumple (up), crease; (fig) to hurt, offend; **se ~** vi to crumple, crease; (personne) to take offence; **se ~ un muscle** to strain a muscle

frôler [fʀole] vt to brush against; (suj: projectile) to skim past; (fig) to come very close to

fromage [fʀɔmaʒ] nm cheese; **~ blanc** soft white cheese

froment [fʀɔmɑ̃] nm wheat

froncer [fʀɔ̃se] vt to gather; **~ les sourcils** to frown

frondaisons [fʀɔ̃dɛzɔ̃] nfpl foliage sg

front [fʀɔ̃] nm forehead, brow; (MIL) front; **de ~** (se heurter) head-on; (rouler) together (i.e. 2 or 3 abreast); (simultanément) at once; **faire ~ à** to face up to

frontalier, -ère [fʀɔ̃talje, jɛʀ] adj border cpd, frontier cpd

frontière [fʀɔ̃tjɛʀ] nf frontier, border

frotter [fʀɔte] vi to rub, scrape ♦ vt to rub; (pommes de terre, plancher) to scrub; **~ une allumette** to strike a match

fructifier [fʀyktifje] vi to yield a profit

fructueux, -euse [fʀyktɥø, øz] adj fruitful

frugal, e, -aux [fʀygal, o] adj frugal

fruit [fʀɥi] nm fruit gen no pl; **~ de la passion** passion fruit; **~s de mer** seafood(s); **~s secs** dried fruit sg; **fruité, e** adj fruity; **fruitier, -ère** adj: **arbre fruitier** fruit tree

fruste [fʀyst] adj unpolished, uncultured

frustrer [fʀystʀe] vt to frustrate

FS abr (= franc suisse) SF

fuel(-oil) [fjul(ɔjl)] nm fuel oil; (domestique) heating oil

fugace [fygas] adj fleeting

fugitif, -ive [fyʒitif, iv] adj (fugace) fleeting ♦ nm/f fugitive

fugue [fyg] nf: **faire une ~** to run away, abscond

fuir [fɥiʀ] vt to flee from; (éviter) to shun ♦ vi to run away; (gaz, robinet) to leak

fuite [fɥit] nf flight; (écoulement, divulgation) leak; **être en ~** to be on the run; **mettre en ~** to put to flight

fulgurant, e [fylgyʀɑ̃, ɑ̃t] adj lightning cpd, dazzling

fulminer [fylmine] vi to thunder forth

fumé, e [fyme] adj (CULIN) smoked; (verre) tinted; **fumée** nf smoke

fumer [fyme] vi to smoke; (soupe) to steam ♦ vt to smoke

fûmes etc [fym] vb voir **être**

fumet [fymɛ] nm aroma

fumeur, -euse [fymœʀ, øz] nm/f smoker

fumeux, -euse [fymø, øz] adj (péj) woolly, hazy

fumier [fymje] nm manure

fumiste [fymist] nm/f (péj: paresseux) shirker

funèbre [fynɛbʀ] adj funeral cpd; (fig: atmosphère) gloomy

funérailles [fyneʀɑj] nfpl funeral sg

funeste [fynɛst] adj (erreur) disastrous

fur [fyʀ]: **au ~ et à mesure** adv as one goes along, **au ~ et à mesure que** as

furet [fyʀɛ] nm ferret

fureter [fyʀ(ə)te] (péj) vi to nose about

fureur [fyʀœʀ] nf fury; **être en ~** to be infuriated; **faire ~** to be all the rage

turibond, e [fyʀibɔ̃, ɔ̃d] adj furious

furie [fyʀi] nf fury; (femme) shrew, vixen; **en ~** (mer) raging; **furieux, -euse** adj furious

furoncle [fyʀɔ̃kl] nm boil

furtif, -ive [fyʀtif, iv] adj furtive

fus [fy] vb voir **être**

fusain [fyzɛ̃] nm (ART) charcoal

fuseau, x [fyzo] nm (pour filer) spindle; (pantalon) (ski) pants; **~ horaire** time zone

fusée [fyze] nf rocket; **~ éclairante** flare

fuser [fyze] vi (rires etc) to burst forth

fusible [fyzibl] nm (ÉLEC: fil) fuse wire; (: fiche) fuse

fusil [fyzi] nm (de guerre, à canon rayé) rifle, gun; (de chasse, à canon lisse) shotgun, gun; **fusillade** nf gunfire no pl, shooting no pl; **fusiller** vt to shoot; **fusil-mitrailleur** nm machine gun

fusionner [fyzjɔne] vi to merge

fut [fy] vb voir **être**

fût [fy] vb voir **être** ♦ nm (tonneau) barrel, cask

futé, e [fyte] adj crafty; **Bison ~** ® TV and radio traffic monitoring service

futile [fytil] adj futile; frivolous

futur, e [fytyʀ] adj, nm future

fuyant, e [fɥijɑ̃, ɑ̃t] vb voir **fuir** ♦ adj (regard etc) evasive; (lignes etc) receding

fuyard, e [fɥijaʀ, aʀd] nm/f runaway

G, g

gâcher [ɡɑʃe] vt (gâter) to spoil; (gaspiller) to waste; **gâchis** nm waste no pl

gadoue [ɡadu] nf sludge

gaffe [ɡaf] nf blunder; **faire ~** (fam) to be careful

gage [ɡaʒ] nm (dans un jeu) forfeit; (fig: de fidélité, d'amour) token

gageure [ɡaʒyʀ] nf: **c'est une ~** it's attempting the impossible

gagnant, e [ɡaɲɑ̃, ɑ̃t] nm/f winner

gagne-pain [ɡaɲpɛ̃] nm inv job

gagner [ɡaɲe] vt to win; (somme d'argent, revenu) to earn; (aller vers, atteindre) to reach; (envahir: sommeil, peur) to overcome; (: mal) to spread to ♦ vi to win; (fig) to gain; **~ du temps/de la place** to gain time/ save space; **~ sa vie** to earn one's living

gai, e [ɡe] adj cheerful; (un peu ivre) merry; **gaiement** adv cheerfully; **gaieté** nf cheerfulness; **de gaieté de cœur** with a light heart

gaillard [ɡajaʀ, aʀd] nm (strapping) fellow

gain [ɡɛ̃] nm (revenu) earnings pl; (bénéfice: gén pl) profits pl

gaine [ɡɛn] nf (corset) girdle; (fourreau) sheath

gala [ɡala] nm official reception; **de ~** (soirée etc) gala

galant, e [ɡalɑ̃, ɑ̃t] adj (courtois) courteous, gentlemanly; (entreprenant) flirtatious, gallant; (scène, rendez-vous) romantic

galère [ɡalɛʀ] nf galley; **quelle ~!** (fam) it's a real grind!; **galérer** (fam) vi to slog away, work hard; (rencontrer les difficultés) to have a hassle

galerie [ɡalʀi] nf gallery; (THÉÂTRE) circle; (de voiture) roof rack; (fig: spectateurs) audience; **~ de peinture** (private) art gallery; **~ marchande** shopping arcade

galet [ɡalɛ] nm pebble

galette [ɡalɛt] nf flat cake; **~ des Rois** cake eaten on Twelfth Night

galipette [ɡalipɛt] nf somersault

Galles [ɡal] nfpl: **le pays de ~** Wales; **gallois, e** adj Welsh ♦ nm/f: **Gallois, e** Welshman(-woman) ♦ nm (LING) Welsh

galon [ɡalɔ̃] nm (MIL) stripe; (décoratif) piece of braid

galop [ɡalo] nm gallop; **galoper** vi to gallop

galopin [ɡalɔpɛ̃] nm urchin, ragamuffin

gambader [ɡɑ̃bade] vi (animal, enfant) to leap about

gambas [ɡɑ̃bas] nfpl Mediterranean prawns

gamin, e [ɡamɛ̃, in] nm/f kid ♦ adj childish

gamme [ɡam] nf (MUS) scale; (fig) range

gammé, e [ɡame] adj: **croix ~e** swastika

gang [ɡɑ̃ɡ] nm (de criminels) gang

gant [ɡɑ̃] nm glove; **~ de toilette** face flannel (BRIT), face cloth

garage [ɡaʀaʒ] nm garage; **garagiste** nm/f garage owner; (employé) garage mechanic

garantie [ɡaʀɑ̃ti] nf guarantee; (bon de) **~** guarantee ou warranty slip

garantir [ɡaʀɑ̃tiʀ] vt to guarantee

garce [ɡaʀs] (fam) nf bitch

garçon [ɡaʀsɔ̃] nm boy; (célibataire): **vieux ~** bachelor; (serveur): **~ (de café)** waiter; **~ de courses** messenger; **~ d'honneur** best man; **garçonnière** nf bachelor flat

garde [ɡaʀd(ə)] nm (de prisonnier) guard; (de domaine etc) warden; (soldat, sentinelle) guardsman ♦ nf (soldats) guard; **de ~** on duty; **monter la ~** to stand guard; **mettre en ~** to warn; **prendre ~ (à)** to be careful (of); **~ champêtre** nm rural policeman; **~ du corps** nm bodyguard; **~ des enfants** nf (après divorce) custody of the children; **~ à vue** nf (JUR) ≈ police custody; **garde-à-vous** nm: **être/se mettre au garde-à-vous** to be at/stand to attention; **garde-barrière** nm/f level-crossing keeper; **garde-boue** nm inv mudguard; **garde-chasse** nm gamekeeper; **garde-malade** nf home nurse; **garde-manger** nm inv (armoire) meat safe; (pièce) pantry, larder

garder [ɡaʀde] vt (conserver) to keep; (surveiller: enfants) to look after; (: immeuble, lieu, prisonnier) to guard; **se ~** vi (aliment: se conserver) to keep; **se ~ de faire** to be careful not to do; **~ le lit/la chambre** to stay in bed/ indoors; **pêche/chasse gardée** private fishing/ hunting (ground)

garderie [ɡaʀdəʀi] nf day nursery, crèche

garde-robe [ɡaʀdəʀɔb] nf wardrobe

gardien, ne [ɡaʀdjɛ̃, jɛn] nm/f (garde) guard; (de prison) warder; (de domaine, réserve) warden; (de musée etc) attendant; (de phare, cimetière) keeper; (d'immeuble) caretaker; (fig) guardian; **~ de but**

goalkeeper; ~ de la paix policeman; ~ de nuit
night watchman
gare [gaʀ] nf station; ~ **routière** bus station
garer [gaʀe] vt to park; **se** ~ vi to park
gargariser [gaʀgaʀize]: **se** ~ vi to gargle
gargote [gaʀgɔt] nf cheap restaurant
gargouille [gaʀguj] nf gargoyle
gargouiller [gaʀguje] vi to gurgle
garnement [gaʀnəmɑ̃] nm rascal, scallywag
garni, e [gaʀni] adj (plat) served with
vegetables (and chips or rice etc)
garnison [gaʀnizɔ̃] nf garrison
garniture [gaʀnityʀ] nf (CULIN) vegetables pl;
~ **de frein** brake lining
gars [gɑ] (fam) nm guy
Gascogne [gaskɔɲ] nf Gascony; **le golfe de** ~
the Bay of Biscay
gas-oil [gazɔjl] nm diesel (oid)
gaspiller [gaspije] vt to waste
gastronome [gastʀɔnɔm] nm/f gourmet;
gastronomie nf gastronomy;
gastronomique adj gastronomic
gâteau, x [gɑto] nm cake; ~ **sec** biscuit
gâter [gɑte] vt to spoil, **se** ~ vi (dent, fruit) to
go bad; (temps, situation) to change for the
worse
gâterie [gɑtʀi] nf little treat
gâteux, -euse [gɑtø, øz] adj senile
gauche [goʃ] adj left, left-hand; (maladroit)
awkward, clumsy ♦ nf (POL) left (wing); **le
bras** ~ the left arm; **le côté** ~ the left-hand
side; **à** ~ on the left; (direction) (to the) left;
gaucher, -ère adj left-handed; **gauchiste**
nm/f leftist
gaufre [gofʀ] nf waffle
gaufrette [gofʀɛt] nf wafer
gaulois, e [golwa, waz] adj Gallic ♦ nm/f:
G~, e Gaul
gaver [gave] vt to force-feed; **se** ~ **de** to stuff
o.s. with
gaz [gɑz] nm inv gas
gaze [gɑz] nf gauze
gazer [gɑze] (fam) vi: **ça gaze?** how's things?
gazette [gazɛt] nf news sheet
gazeux, -euse [gɑzø, øz] adj (boisson) fizzy;
(eau) sparkling
gazoduc [gɑzɔdyk] nm gas pipeline
gazon [gɑzɔ̃] nm (herbe) grass; (pelouse) lawn
gazouiller [gazuje] vi to chirp; (enfant) to
babble
geai [ʒɛ] nm jay
géant, e [ʒeɑ̃, ɑ̃t] adj gigantic; (COMM)
giant-size ♦ nm/f giant
geindre [ʒɛ̃dʀ] vi to groan, moan
gel [ʒɛl] nm frost
gélatine [ʒelatin] nf gelatine
gelée [ʒ(ə)le] nf jelly; (gel) frost
geler [ʒ(ə)le] vt, vi to freeze; **il gèle** it's
freezing

gélule [ʒelyl] nf (MÉD) capsule
gelures [ʒəlyʀ] nfpl frostbite sg
Gémeaux [ʒemo] nmpl: **les** ~ Gemini
gémir [ʒemiʀ] vi to groan, moan
gênant, e [ʒenɑ̃, ɑ̃t] adj (irritant) annoying;
(embarrassant) embarrassing
gencive [ʒɑ̃siv] nf gum
gendarme [ʒɑ̃daʀm] nm gendarme;
gendarmerie nf military police force in
countryside and small towns; their police station
or barracks
gendre [ʒɑ̃dʀ] nm son-in-law
gêné, e [ʒene] adj embarrassed
gêner [ʒene] vt (incommoder) to bother;
(encombrer) to be in the way; (embarrasser):
~ **qn** to make sb feel ill-at-ease
général, e, -aux [ʒeneʀal, o] adj, nm
general; **en** ~ usually, in general; **générale**
nf: (répétition) **générale** final dress rehearsal;
généralement adv generally; **généraliser**
vt, vi to generalize; **se généraliser** vi to
become widespread; **généraliste** nm/f
general practitioner, G.P.
génération [ʒeneʀasjɔ̃] nf generation
généreux, -euse [ʒeneʀø, øz] adj generous
générique [ʒeneʀik] nm (CINÉMA) credits pl
générosité [ʒeneʀozite] nf generosity
genêt [ʒ(ə)nɛ] nm broom no pl (shrub)
génétique [ʒenetik] adj genetic
Genève [ʒ(ə)nɛv] n Geneva
génial, e, -aux [ʒenjal, jo] adj of genius;
(fam: formidable) fantastic, brilliant
génie [ʒeni] nm genius; (MIL). **le** ~ the
Engineers pl; ~ **civil** civil engineering
genièvre [ʒənjɛvʀ] nm juniper
génisse [ʒenis] nf heifer
génital, e, -aux [ʒenital, o] adj genital; **les
parties ~es** the genitals
génoise [ʒenwaz] nf sponge cake
genou, x [ʒ(ə)nu] nm knee; **à** ~**x** on one's
knees; **se mettre à** ~**x** to kneel down
genre [ʒɑ̃ʀ] nm kind, type, sort; (LING)
gender; **avoir bon** ~ to look a nice sort; **avoir
mauvais** ~ to be coarse-looking; **ce n'est pas
son** ~ it's not like him
gens [ʒɑ̃] nmpl (f in some phrases) people pl
gentil, le [ʒɑ̃ti, ij] adj kind; (enfant: sage)
good; (endroit etc) nice; **gentillesse** nf
kindness; **gentiment** adv kindly
géographie [ʒeɔgʀafi] nf geography
geôlier [ʒolje, ʒɛʀ] nm jailer
géologie [ʒeɔlɔʒi] nf geology
géomètre [ʒeɔmɛtʀ] nm/f (arpenteur) (land)
surveyor
géométrie [ʒeɔmetʀi] nf geometry;
géométrique adj geometric
géranium [ʒeʀanjɔm] nm geranium
gérant, e [ʒeʀɑ̃, ɑ̃t] nm/f manager(-eress)
gerbe [ʒɛʀb] nf (de fleurs) spray; (de blé)

sheaf

gercé, e [ʒɛʀse] adj chapped

gerçure [ʒɛʀsyʀ] nf crack

gérer [ʒeʀe] vt to manage

germain, e [ʒɛʀmɛ̃, ɛn] adj: **cousin ~** first cousin

germe [ʒɛʀm] nm germ; **germer** vi to sprout; (semence) to germinate

geste [ʒɛst] nm gesture

gestion [ʒɛstjɔ̃] nf management

ghetto [geto] nm ghetto

gibet [ʒibɛ] nm gallows pl

gibier [ʒibje] nm (animaux) game

giboulée [ʒibule] nf sudden shower

gicler [ʒikle] vi to spurt, squirt

gifle [ʒifl] nf slap (in the face); **gifler** vt to slap (in the face)

gigantesque [ʒigɑ̃tɛsk] adj gigantic

gigogne [ʒigɔɲ] adj: **lits ~s** truckle (BRIT) ou trundle beds

gigot [ʒigo] nm leg (of mutton ou lamb)

gigoter [ʒigɔte] vi to wriggle (about)

gilet [ʒilɛ] nm waistcoat; (pull) cardigan; **~ de sauvetage** life jacket

gin [dʒin] nm gin; **~-tonic** gin and tonic

gingembre [ʒɛ̃ʒɑ̃bʀ] nm ginger

girafe [ʒiʀaf] nf giraffe

giratoire [ʒiʀatwaʀ] adj: **sens ~** roundabout

girofle [ʒiʀɔfl] nf: **clou de ~** clove

girouette [ʒiʀwɛt] nf weather vane ou cock

gitan, e [ʒitɑ̃, an] nm/f gipsy

gîte [ʒit] nm (maison) home; (abri) shelter; **~ (rural)** holiday cottage ou apartment

givre [ʒivʀ] nm (hoar) frost; **givré, e** adj covered in frost; (fam: fou) nuts; **orange givrée** orange sorbet (served in peel)

glace [glas] nf ice; (crème glacée) ice cream; (miroir) mirror; (de voiture) window

glacé, e [glase] adj (mains, vent, pluie) freezing; (lac) frozen; (boisson) iced

glacer [glase] vt to freeze; (gâteau) to ice; (fig): **~ qn** (intimider) to chill sb; (paralyser) to make sb's blood run cold

glacial, e [glasjal, jo] adj icy

glacier [glasje] nm (GÉO) glacier; (marchand) ice-cream maker

glacière [glasjɛʀ] nf icebox

glaçon [glasɔ̃] nm icicle; (pour boisson) ice cube

glaïeul [glajœl] nm gladiolus

glaise [glɛz] nf clay

gland [glɑ̃] nm acorn; (décoration) tassel

glande [glɑ̃d] nf gland

glander [glɑ̃de] (fam) vi to fart around (!)

glauque [glok] adj dull blue-green

glissade [glisad] nf (par jeu) slide; (chute) slip; **faire des ~s sur la glace** to slide on the ice

glissant, e [glisɑ̃, ɑ̃t] adj slippery

glissement [glismɑ̃] nm: **~ de terrain** landslide

glisser [glise] vi (avancer) to glide ou slide along; (coulisser, tomber) to slide; (déraper) to slip; (être glissant) to be slippery ♦ vt to slip; **se ~ dans** to slip into

global, e, -aux [global, o] adj overall

globe [glɔb] nm globe

globule [glɔbyl] nm (du sang) corpuscle

globuleux, -euse [glɔbylø, øz] adj: **yeux ~** protruding eyes

gloire [glwaʀ] nf glory; **glorieux, -euse** adj glorious

glousser [gluse] vi to cluck; (rire) to chuckle; **gloussement** nm cluck; chuckle

glouton, ne [glutɔ̃, ɔn] adj gluttonous

gluant, e [glyɑ̃, ɑ̃t] adj sticky, gummy

glucose [glykoz] nm glucose

glycine [glisin] nf wisteria

goal [gol] nm goalkeeper

GO sigle (= grandes ondes) LW

gobelet [gɔblɛ] nm (en étain, verre, argent) tumbler; (d'enfant, de pique-nique) beaker; (à dés) cup

gober [gɔbe] vt to swallow (whole)

godasse [gɔdas] (fam) nf shoe

godet [gɔdɛ] nm pot

goéland [gɔelɑ̃] nm (sea)gull

goélette [gɔelɛt] nf schooner

gogo [gɔgo]: **à ~** adv galore

goguenard, e [gɔg(ə)naʀ, aʀd] adj mocking

goinfre [gwɛ̃fʀ] nm glutton

golf [gɔlf] nm golf; (terrain) golf course

golfe [gɔlf] nm gulf; (petit) bay

gomme [gɔm] nf (à effacer) rubber (BRIT), eraser; **gommer** vt to rub out (BRIT), erase

gond [gɔ̃] nm hinge; **sortir de ses ~s** (fig) to fly off the handle

gondoler [gɔ̃dɔle]: **se ~** vi (planche) to warp; (métal) to buckle

gonflé, e [gɔ̃fle] adj swollen; **il est ~** (fam: courageux) he's got some nerve; (impertinent) he's got a nerve

gonfler [gɔ̃fle] vt (pneu, ballon: en soufflant) to blow up; (: avec une pompe) to pump up; (nombre, importance) to inflate ♦ vi to swell (up); (CULIN: pâte) to rise; **gonfleur** nm pump

gonzesse [gɔ̃zɛs] (fam) nf chick, bird (BRIT)

goret [gɔʀɛ] nm piglet

gorge [gɔʀʒ] nf (ANAT) throat; (vallée) gorge

gorgé, e [gɔʀʒe] adj: **~ de** filled with; (eau) saturated with; **gorgée** nf (petite) sip; (grande) gulp

gorille [gɔʀij] nm gorilla; (fam) bodyguard

gosier [gozje] nm throat

gosse [gɔs] (fam) nm/f kid

goudron [gudʀɔ̃] nm tar; **goudronner** vt to tar(mac) (BRIT), asphalt (US)

gouffre [gufʀ] nm abyss, gulf

goujat [guʒa] nm boor

goulot [gulo] nm neck; **boire au ~** to drink from the bottle

goulu, e [guly] adj greedy

gourd, e [guʀ, guʀd] adj numb (with cold)

gourde [guʀd] nf (récipient) flask; (fam) (clumsy) clot ou oaf ♦ adj oafish

gourdin [guʀdɛ̃] nm club, bludgeon

gourer [guʀe] (fam): **se ~** vi to boob

gourmand, e [guʀmɑ̃, ɑ̃d] adj greedy;

gourmandise [guʀmɑ̃diz] nf greed; (bonbon) sweet

gourmet [guʀme] nm gourmet

gourmette [guʀmet] nf chain bracelet

gousse [gus] nf: **~ d'ail** clove of garlic

goût [gu] nm taste; **avoir bon ~** to taste good; **de bon ~** tasteful; **de mauvais ~** tasteless; **prendre ~ à** to develop a taste ou a liking for

goûter [gute] vt (essayer) to taste; (apprécier) to enjoy ♦ vi to have (afternoon) tea ♦ nm (afternoon) tea

goutte [gut] nf drop; (MÉD) gout; (alcool) brandy; **tomber ~ à ~** to drip; **goutte-à-goutte** nm (MÉD) drip

gouttelette [gutlɛt] nf droplet

gouttière [gutjɛʀ] nf gutter

gouvernail [guvɛʀnaj] nm rudder; (barre) helm, tiller

gouvernante [guvɛʀnɑ̃t] nf governess

gouvernement [guvɛʀnəmɑ̃] nm government

gouverner [guvɛʀne] vt to govern

grabuge [gʀabyʒ] (fam) nm mayhem

grâce [gʀɑs] nf (charme) grace; (faveur) favour; (JUR) pardon; (REL) grace sg; **faire ~ à qn de qch** to spare sb sth; **rendre ~(s) à** to give thanks to; **demander ~** to beg for mercy; **~ à** thanks to; **gracier** vt to pardon; **gracieux, -euse** adj graceful

grade [gʀad] nm rank; **monter en ~** to be promoted

gradin [gʀadɛ̃] nm tier; step; **~s** nmpl (de stade) terracing sg

gradué, e [gʀadye] adj: **verre ~** measuring jug

graduel, le [gʀadyɛl] adj gradual

graduer [gʀadye] vt (effort etc) to increase gradually; (règle, verre) to graduate

graffiti [gʀafiti] nmpl graffiti

grain [gʀɛ̃] nm (gén) grain; (NAVIG) squall; **~ de beauté** beauty spot; **~ de café** coffee bean; **~ de poivre** peppercorn; **~ de poussière** speck of dust; **~ de raisin** grape

graine [gʀɛn] nf seed

graissage [gʀɛsaʒ] nm lubrication, greasing

graisse [gʀɛs] nf fat; (lubrifiant) grease; **graisser** vt to lubricate, grease; (tacher) to make greasy; **graisseux, -euse** adj greasy

grammaire [gʀa(m)mɛʀ] nf grammar; **grammatical, e, -aux** adj grammatical

gramme [gʀam] nm gramme

grand, e [gʀɑ̃, gʀɑ̃d] adj (haut) tall; (gros, vaste, large) big, large; (long) long; (plus âgé) big; (adulte) grown-up; (sens abstraits) great ♦ adv: **~ ouvert** wide open; **au ~ air** in the open (air); **les ~s blessés** the severely injured; **~ ensemble** housing scheme; **~ magasin** department store; **~e personne** grown-up; **~e surface** hypermarket; **~es écoles** prestige schools of university level; **~es lignes** (RAIL) main lines; **~es vacances** summer holidays; **grand-chose** [gʀɑ̃ʃoz] nm/f inv: **pas grand-chose** not much; **Grande-Bretagne** nf (Great) Britain; **grandeur** nf (dimension) size; **grandeur nature** life-size; **grandiose** adj imposing; **grandir** vi to grow ♦ vt: **grandir qn** (suj: vêtement, chaussure) to make sb look taller; **grand-mère** nf grandmother; **grand-messe** nf high mass; **grand-peine**: **à grand-peine** adv with difficulty; **grand-père** nm grandfather; **grand-route** nf main road; **grands-parents** nmpl grandparents

grange [gʀɑ̃ʒ] nf barn

granit(e) [gʀanit] nm granite

graphique [gʀafik] adj graphic ♦ nm graph

grappe [gʀap] nf cluster; **~ de raisin** bunch of grapes

gras, se [gʀɑ, gʀɑs] adj (viande, soupe) fatty; (personne) fat; (surface, main) greasy; (plaisanterie) coarse; (TYPO) bold ♦ nm (CULIN) fat; **faire la ~se matinée** to have a lie-in (BRIT); sleep late (US); **grassement** adv: **grassement payé** handsomely paid; **grassouillet, te** adj podgy, plump

gratifiant, e [gʀatifjɑ̃, jɑ̃t] adj gratifying, rewarding

gratin [gʀatɛ̃] nm (plat) cheese-topped dish; (croûte) cheese topping; **gratiné, e** adj (CULIN) au gratin

gratis [gʀatis] adv free

gratitude [gʀatityd] nf gratitude

gratte-ciel [gʀatsjɛl] nm inv skyscraper

gratte-papier [gʀatpapje] (péj) nm inv penpusher

gratter [gʀate] vt (avec un outil) to scrape; (enlever: avec un outil) to scrape off; (: avec un ongle) to scratch; (enlever avec un ongle) to scratch off ♦ vi (irriter) to be scratchy; (démanger) to itch; **se ~** to scratch (o.s.)

gratuit, e [gʀatɥi, ɥit] adj (entrée, billet) free; (fig) gratuitous

gravats [gʀava] nmpl rubble sg

grave [gʀav] adj (maladie, accident) serious, bad; (sujet, problème) serious, grave; (air) grave, solemn; (voix, son) deep, low-pitched; **gravement** adv seriously; (parler, regarder)

gravely
graver [gʀave] vt to engrave
gravier [gʀavje] nm gravel no pl; **gravillons** nmpl loose chippings ou gravel sg
gravir [gʀaviʀ] vt to climb (up)
gravité [gʀavite] nf (de maladie, d'accident) seriousness; (de sujet, problème) gravity
graviter [gʀavite] vi to revolve
gravure [gʀavyʀ] nf engraving; (reproduction) print
gré [gʀe] nm: **de bon ~** willingly; **contre le ~ de qn** against sb's will; **de son (plein) ~** of one's own free will; **bon ~ mal ~** like it or not; **de ~ ou de force** whether one likes it or not; **savoir ~ à qn de qch** to be grateful to sb for sth
grec, grecque [gʀɛk] adj Greek; (classique: vase etc) Grecian ♦ nm/f: **G~, Grecque** Greek ♦ nm (LING) Greek
Grèce [gʀɛs] nf: **la ~** Greece
greffe [gʀɛf] nf (BOT, MÉD: de tissu) graft; (MÉD: d'organe) transplant; **greffer** vt (BOT, MÉD: tissu) to graft; (MÉD: organe) to transplant
greffier [gʀefje, jɛʀ] nm clerk of the court
grêle [gʀɛl] adj (very) thin ♦ nf hail; **grêler** vb impers: **il grêle** it's hailing; **grêlon** nm hailstone
grelot [gʀəlo] nm little bell
grelotter [gʀələte] vi to shiver
grenade [gʀənad] nf (explosive) grenade; (BOT) pomegranate; **grenadine** nf grenadine
grenat [gʀəna] adj inv dark red
grenier [gʀənje] nm attic; (de ferme) loft
grenouille [gʀənuj] nf frog
grès [gʀɛ] nm sandstone; (poterie) stoneware
grésiller [gʀezije] vi to sizzle; (RADIO) to crackle
grève [gʀɛv] nf (d'ouvriers) strike; (plage) shore; **se mettre en/faire ~** to go on/be on strike; **~ de la faim** hunger strike; **~ du zèle** work-to-rule (BRIT), slowdown (US); **~ sauvage** wildcat strike
gréviste [gʀevist] nm/f striker
gribouiller [gʀibuje] vt to scribble, scrawl
grièvement [gʀijɛvmɑ̃] adv seriously
griffe [gʀif] nf claw; (de couturier) label; **griffer** vt to scratch
griffonner [gʀifɔne] vt to scribble
grignoter [gʀiɲɔte] vt (personne) to nibble at; (souris) to gnaw at ♦ vi to nibble
gril [gʀil] nm steak ou grill pan; **faire cuire au ~** to grill; **grillade** nf (viande etc) grill
grillage [gʀijaʒ] nm (treillis) wire netting; (clôture) wire fencing
grille [gʀij] nf (clôture) wire fence; (portail) (metad) gate; (d'égout) (metad) grate; (fig) grid
grille-pain [gʀijpɛ̃] nm inv toaster

griller [gʀije] vt (pain) to toast; (viande) to grill; (fig: ampoule etc) to blow; **faire ~** to toast; to grill; (châtaignes) to roast; **~ un feu rouge** to jump the lights
grillon [gʀijɔ̃] nm cricket
grimace [gʀimas] nf grimace; (pour faire rire): **faire des ~s** to pull ou make faces
grimper [gʀɛ̃pe] vi, vt to climb
grincer [gʀɛ̃se] vi (objet métallique) to grate; (plancher, porte) to creak; **~ des dents** to grind one's teeth
grincheux, -euse [gʀɛ̃ʃø, øz] adj grumpy
grippe [gʀip] nf flu, influenza; **grippé, e** adj: **être grippé** to have flu
gris, e [gʀi, gʀiz] adj grey; (ivre) tipsy
grisaille [gʀizaj] nf greyness, dullness
griser [gʀize] vt to intoxicate
grisonner [gʀizɔne] vi to be going grey
grisou [gʀizu] nm firedamp
grive [gʀiv] nf thrush
grivois, e [gʀivwa, waz] adj saucy
Groenland [gʀɔɛnlɑ̃d] nm Greenland
grogner [gʀɔɲe] vi to growl; (fig) to grumble; **grognon, ne** adj grumpy
groin [gʀwɛ̃] nm snout
grommeler [gʀɔm(ə)le] vi to mutter to o.s.
gronder [gʀɔ̃de] vi to rumble; (fig: révolte) to be brewing ♦ vt to scold; **se faire ~** to get a telling-off
groom [gʀum] nm bellboy
gros, se [gʀo, gʀos] adj big, large; (obèse) fat; (travaux, dégâts) extensive; (épais) thick; (rhume, averse) heavy ♦ adv: **risquer/gagner ~** to risk/win a lot ♦ nm/f fat man/woman ♦ nm (COMM): **le ~** the wholesale business; **prix de ~** wholesale price; **par ~ temps/grosse mer** in rough weather/heavy seas; **en ~** roughly; (COMM) wholesale; **~ lot** jackpot; **~ mot** coarse word; **~ plan** (PHOTO) close-up; **~ sel** cooking salt; **~ titre** headline; **~se caisse** big drum
groseille [gʀozɛj] nf: **~ (rouge/blanche)** red/white currant; **~ à maquereau** gooseberry
grosse [gʀos] adj voir **gros; grossesse** nf pregnancy; **grosseur** nf size; (tumeur) lump
grossier, -ière [gʀosje, jɛʀ] adj coarse; (insolent) rude; (dessin) rough; (travail) roughly done; (imitation, instrument) crude; (évident: erreur) gross; **grossièrement** adv (sommairement) roughly; (vulgairement) coarsely; **grossièretés** nfpl: **dire des grossièretés** to use coarse language
grossir [gʀosiʀ] vi (personne) to put on weight ♦ vt (exagérer) to exaggerate; (au microscope) to magnify; (suj: vêtement): **~ qn** to make sb look fatter
grossiste [gʀosist] nm/f wholesaler
grosso modo [gʀosomɔdo] adv roughly
grotesque [gʀɔtɛsk] adj (extravagant)

grotesque; (*ridicule*) ludicrous
grotte [gʀɔt] *nf* cave
grouiller [gʀuje] *vi*: ~ **de** to be swarming
with; **se ~** (*fam*) ♦ *vi* to get a move on;
grouillant, e *adj* swarming
groupe [gʀup] *nm* group; **le ~ des 7** Group of
7; ~ **sanguin** blood group; **groupement** *nm*
(*action*) grouping; (*groupe*) group; **grouper**
vt to group; **se grouper** *vi* to gather
grue [gʀy] *nf* crane
grumeaux [gʀymo] *nmpl* lumps
guenilles [gənij] *nfpl* rags
guenon [gənɔ̃] *nf* female monkey
guépard [gepaʀ] *nm* cheetah
guêpe [gɛp] *nf* wasp
guêpier [gepje] *nm* (*fig*) trap
guère [gɛʀ] *adv* (*avec adjectif, adverbe*): **ne ...
~** hardly; (*avec verbe*): **ne ... ~** (*pas beaucoup*)
tournure négative +much; (*pas souvent*) hardly
ever; (*pas longtemps*) tournure négative
i (*very*) long; **il n'y a ~ que/de** there's hardly
anybody (*ou* anything) but/hardly any; **ce
n'est ~ difficile** it's hardly difficult; **nous
n'avons ~ de temps** we have hardly any time
guéridon [gexidɔ̃] *nm* pedestal table
guérilla [gexija] *nf* guerrilla warfare
guérillero [gexijexo] *nm* guerrilla
guérir [gexiʀ] *vt* (*personne, maladie*) to cure;
(*membre, plaie*) to heal ♦ *vi* (*malade, maladie*)
to be cured; (*blessure*) to heal; **guérison** *nf*
(*de maladie*) curing; (*de membre, plaie*)
healing; (*de malade*) recovery; **guérisseur,
-euse** *nm/f* healer
guerre [gɛʀ] *nf* war; ~ **civile** civil war; **en ~** at
war; **faire la ~ à** to wage war against;
guerrier, -ière *adj* warlike ♦ *nm/f* warrior
guet [gɛ] *nm*: **faire le ~** to be on the watch *ou*
look-out; **guet-apens** [gɛtapɑ̃] *nm* ambush;
guetter *vt* (*épier*) to watch (intently);
(*attendre*) to watch (out) for; (*hostilement*) to
be lying in wait for
gueule [gœl] *nf* (*d'animal*) mouth; (*fam:
figure*) face; (: *bouche*) mouth; **ta ~!** (*fam*)
shut up!; ~ **de bois** (*fam*) hangover; **gueuler**
(*fam*) *vi* to bawl; **gueuleton** (*fam*) *nm*
blow-out
gui [gi] *nm* mistletoe
guichet [giʃɛ] *nm* (*de bureau, banque*)
counter; **les ~s** (*à la gare, au théâtre*) the
ticket office *sg*; ~ **automatique** cash dispenser
(*BRIT*), automatic telling machine (*US*)
guide [gid] *nm* guide ♦ *nf* (*éclaireuse*) girl
guide; **guider** *vt* to guide
guidon [gidɔ̃] *nm* handlebars *pl*
guignol [giɲɔl] *nm* ≈ Punch and Judy show;
(*fig*) clown
guillemets [gijmɛ] *nmpl*: **entre ~** in inverted
commas
guillotiner [gijɔtine] *vt* to guillotine

guindé, e [gɛ̃de] *adj* (*personne, air*) stiff,
starchy; (*style*) stilted
guirlande [giʀlɑ̃d] *nf* (*fleurs*) garland; ~ **de
Noël** tinsel garland; ~ **lumineuse** string of fairy
lights; ~ **de papier** paper chain
guise [giz] *nf*: **à votre ~** as you wish *ou*
please; **en ~ de** by way of
guitare [gitaʀ] *nf* guitar
gym [ʒim] *nf* (*exercices*) gym; **gymnase** *nm*
gym(nasium); **gymnaste** *nm/f* gymnast;
gymnastique *nf* gymnastics *sg*; (*au réveil
etc*) keep-fit exercises *pl*
gynécologie [ʒinekɔlɔʒi] *nf* gynaecology;
gynécologique *adj* gynaecological;
gynécologue *nm/f* gynaecologist

H, h

habile [abil] *adj* skilful; (*malin*) clever;
habileté [abilte] *nf* skill, skilfulness;
cleverness
habillé, e [abije] *adj* dressed; (*chic*) dressy
habillement [abijmɑ̃] *nm* clothes *pl*
habiller [abije] *vt* to dress; (*fournir en
vêtements*) to clothe; **s'~** *vi* to dress (o.s.); (*se
déguiser, mettre des vêtements chic*) to dress
up
habit [abi] *nm* outfit; **~s** *nmpl* (*vêtements*)
clothes; ~ (**de soirée**) evening dress; (*pour
homme*) tails *pl*
habitant, e [abitɑ̃, ɑ̃t] *nm/f* inhabitant;
(*d'une maison*) occupant; **loger chez l'~** to
stay with the locals
habitation [abitasjɔ̃] *nf* house, **~s à loyer
modéré** (block of) council flats
habiter [abite] *vt* to live in ♦ *vi*: ~ **à/dans** to
live in
habitude [abityd] *nf* habit; **avoir l'~ de faire**
to be in the habit of doing; (*expérience*) to be
used to doing; **d'~** usually; **comme d'~** as
usual
habitué, e [abitɥe] *nm/f* (*de maison*) regular
visitor; (*de café*) regular (customer)
habituel, le [abitɥɛl] *adj* usual
habituer [abitɥe] *vt*: ~ **qn à** to get sb used
to; **s'~ à** to get used to
'hache [aʃ] *nf* axe
'hacher [aʃe] *vt* (*viande*) to mince; (*persil*) to
chop; **'hachis** *nm* mince *no pl*; **hachis
Parmentier** ≈ shepherd's pie
'hachisch ['aʃiʃ] *nm* hashish
'hachoir ['aʃwaʀ] *nm* (*couteau*) chopper;
(*appareil*) (meat) mincer; (*planche*) chopping
board
'hagard, e ['agaʀ, aʀd] *adj* wild, distraught
'haie ['ɛ] *nf* hedge; (*SPORT*) hurdle
'haillons ['ajɔ̃] *nmpl* rags
'haine ['ɛn] *nf* hatred

'haïr [ˈaiʀ] vt to detest, hate

'hâlé, e [ˈɑle] adj (sun)tanned, sunburnt

haleine [alɛn] nf breath; **hors d'~** out of breath; **tenir en ~** (attention) to hold spellbound; (incertitude) to keep in suspense; **de longue ~** long-term

'haleter [ˈalte] vt to pant

'hall [ˈol] nm hall

'halle [ˈal] nf (covered) market; **~s** nfpl (d'une grande ville) central food market sg

hallucinant, e [alysinɑ̃, ɑ̃t] adj staggering

hallucination [alysinasjɔ̃] nf hallucination

'halte [ˈalt] nf stop, break; (endroit) stopping place ♦ excl stop!; **faire ~** to stop

haltère [altɛʀ] nm dumbbell, barbell; **~s** nmpl: (poids et) **~s** (activité) weightlifting sg; **haltérophilie** nf weightlifting

'hamac [ˈamak] nm hammock

hamburger [ˈɑ̃buʀgœʀ] nm hamburger

'hameau, x [ˈamo] nm hamlet

hameçon [amsɔ̃] nm (fish) hook

'hanche [ˈɑ̃ʃ] nf hip

'hand-ball [ˈɑ̃dbal] nm handball

'handicapé, e [ˈɑ̃dikape] nm/f physically (ou mentally) handicapped person; **~ moteur** spastic

hangar [ˈɑ̃gaʀ] nm shed; (AVIAT) hangar

'hanneton [ˈantɔ̃] nm cockchafer

'hanter [ˈɑ̃te] vt to haunt

'hantise [ˈɑ̃tiz] nf obsessive fear

'happer [ˈape] vt to snatch; (suj: train etc) to hit

'haras [ˈaʀɑ] nm stud farm

'harassant, e [ˈaʀasɑ̃, ɑ̃t] adj exhausting

'harcèlement [ˈaʀsɛlmɑ̃] nm harassment; **~ sexuel** sexual harassment

'harceler [ˈaʀsəle] vt to harass; **~ qn de questions** to plague sb with questions

'hardi, e [ˈaʀdi] adj bold, daring

'hareng [ˈaʀɑ̃] nm herring

'hargne [ˈaʀɲ] nf aggressiveness; **'hargneux, -euse** adj aggressive

'haricot [ˈaʀiko] nm bean; **~ blanc** haricot bean; **~ vert** green bean; **~ rouge** kidney bean

harmonica [aʀmɔnika] nm mouth organ

harmonie [aʀmɔni] nf harmony; **harmonieux, -euse** adj harmonious; (couleurs, couple) well-matched

'harnacher [ˈaʀnaʃe] vt to harness

'harnais [ˈaʀnɛ] nm harness

'harpe [ˈaʀp] nf harp

'harponner [ˈaʀpɔne] vt to harpoon; (fam) to collar

'hasard [ˈazaʀ] nm: **le ~** chance, fate; **un ~ a** coincidence; **au ~** (aller) aimlessly; (choisir) at random; **par ~** by chance; **à tout ~** (en cas de besoin) just in case; (en espérant trouver ce qu'on cherche) on the off chance (BRIT);

'hasarder vt (mot) to venture; **se hasarder à faire** to risk doing

'hâte [ˈɑt] nf haste; **à la ~** hurriedly, hastily; **en ~** posthaste, with all possible speed; **avoir ~ de** to be eager ou anxious to; **'hâter** vt to hasten; **se hâter** vi to hurry; **'hâtif, -ive** adj (travail) hurried; (décision, jugement) hasty

'hausse [ˈos] nf rise, increase; **être en ~** to be going up; **'hausser** vt to raise; **hausser les épaules** to shrug (one's shoulders)

'haut, e [ˈo, ˈot] adj high; (grand) tall ♦ adv high ♦ nm top (part); **de 3 m de ~** 3 m high, 3 m in height; **des ~s et des bas** ups and downs; **en ~ lieu** in high places; **à ~e voix**, **(tout) ~** aloud, out loud; **du ~ de** from the top of; **de ~ en bas** from top to bottom; **plus ~** higher up, further up; (dans un texte) above; (parler) louder; **en ~** (être/aller) at/to the top; (dans une maison) upstairs; **en ~ de** at the top of

'hautain, e [ˈotɛ̃, ɛn] adj haughty

'hautbois [ˈobwɑ] nm oboe

'haut-de-forme [ˈodfɔʀm] nm top hat

'hauteur [ˈotœʀ] nf height; **à la ~ de** (accident) near; (fig: tâche, situation) equal to; **à la ~** (fig) up to it

'haut...: **'haut-fourneau** nm blast ou smelting furnace; **'haut-le-cœur** nm inv retch, heave; **'haut-parleur** nm (loud)speaker

'havre [ˈɑvʀ] nm haven

'Haye [ˈɛ] n: **la ~** the Hague

'hayon [ˈɛjɔ̃] nm hatchback

hebdo [ɛbdo] (fam) nm weekly

hebdomadaire [ɛbdɔmadɛʀ] adj, nm weekly

hébergement [ebɛʀʒəmɑ̃] nm accommodation

héberger [ebɛʀʒe] vt (touristes) to accommodate, lodge; (amis) to put up; (réfugiés) to take in

hébété, e [ebete] adj dazed

hébreu, x [ebʀø] adj m, nm Hebrew

hécatombe [ekatɔ̃b] nf slaughter

hectare [ɛktaʀ] nm hectare

'hein [ˈɛ̃] excl eh?

'hélas [ˈelas] excl alas! ♦ adv unfortunately

'héler [ˈele] vt to hail

hélice [elis] nf propeller

hélicoptère [elikɔptɛʀ] nm helicopter

helvétique [ɛlvetik] adj Swiss

hématome [ematom] nm nasty bruise

hémicycle [emisikl] nm (POL): **l'~** ≈ the benches (of the Commons) (BRIT), ≈ the floor of the House of Representatives) (US)

hémisphère [emisfɛʀ] nm: **l'~ nord/sud** the northern/southern hemisphere

hémorragie [emɔʀaʒi] nf bleeding no pl, haemorrhage

hémorroïdes [emɔʀɔid] nfpl piles, haemorrhoids

'hennir [eniʀ] vi to neigh, whinny; **'hennissement** nm neigh, whinny

hépatite [epatit] nf hepatitis

herbe [ɛʀb] nf grass; (CULIN, MÉD) herb; **~s de Provence** mixed herbs; **en ~** unripe; (fig) budding; **herbicide** nm weed-killer; **herboriste** nm/f herbalist

'hère ['ɛʀ] nm: **pauvre ~** poor wretch

héréditaire [eʀeditɛʀ] adj hereditary

'hérisser ['eʀise] vt: **~ qn** (fig) to ruffle sb; **se ~** vi to bristle, bristle up; **'hérisson** nm hedgehog

héritage [eʀitaʒ] nm inheritance; (coutumes, système) heritage, legacy

hériter [eʀite] vi: **~ de qch (de qn)** to inherit sth (from sb); **héritier, -ière** [eʀitje, jɛʀ] nm/f heir(-ess)

hermétique [ɛʀmetik] adj airtight; watertight; (fig: obscur) abstruse; (: impénétrable) impenetrable

hermine [ɛʀmin] nf ermine

'hornie ['ɛʀni] nf hernia

héroïne [eʀɔin] nf heroine; (drogue) heroin

héroïque [eʀɔik] adj heroic

'héron ['eʀɔ̃] nm heron

'héros ['eʀo] nm hero

hésitant, e [ezitɑ̃, ɑ̃t] adj hesitant

hésitation [ezitasjɔ̃] nf hesitation

hésiter [ezite] vi: **~ (à faire)** to hesitate (to do)

hétéroclite [eteʀɔklit] adj heterogeneous; (objets) sundry

hétérogène [eteʀɔʒɛn] adj heterogeneous

hétérosexuel, le [eteʀɔsɛksɥɛl] adj heterosexual

'hêtre ['ɛtʀ] nm beech

heure [œʀ] nf hour; (SCOL) period; (moment) time; **c'est l'~** it's time; **quelle ~ est-il?** what time is it?; **2 ~s (du matin)** 2 o'clock (in the morning); **être à l'~** to be on time; (montre) to be right; **mettre à l'~** to set right; **à une ~ avancée (de la nuit)** at a late hour of the night; **à toute ~** at any time; **24 ~s sur 24** round the clock, 24 hours a day; **à l'~ qu'il est** at this time (of day); by now; **sur l'~** at once; **~ de pointe** rush hour; (téléphone) peak period; **~ d'affluence** rush hour; **~s creuses** slack periods; (pour électricité, téléphone etc) off-peak periods; **~s supplémentaires** overtime sg

heureusement [œʀøzmɑ̃] adv (par bonheur) fortunately, luckily

heureux, -euse [œʀø, øz] adj happy; (chanceux) lucky, fortunate

'heurter ['œʀte] vt (mur) to strike, hit; (personne) to collide with; **se ~ à** vt (fig) to come up against

'heurts ['œʀ] nmpl (fig) clashes

hexagone [ɛgzagɔn] nm hexagon; (la France) France (because of its shape)

hiberner [ibɛʀne] vi to hibernate

'hibou, x ['ibu] nm owl

'hideux, -euse ['idø, øz] adj hideous

hier [jɛʀ] adv yesterday; **~ soir** last night, yesterday evening; **toute la journée d'~** all day yesterday; **toute la matinée d'~** all yesterday morning

'hiérarchie ['jeʀaʀʃi] nf hierarchy

'hi-fi ['ifi] adj inv hi-fi ♦ nf hi-fi

hilare [ilaʀ] adj mirthful

hindou, e [ɛ̃du] adj Hindu ♦ nm/f: **H~, e** Hindu

hippique [ipik] adj equestrian, horse cpd; **un club ~** a riding centre; **un concours ~** a horse show; **hippisme** nm (horse)riding

hippodrome [ipɔdʀom] nm racecourse

hippopotame [ipɔpɔtam] nm hippopotamus

hirondelle [iʀɔ̃dɛl] nf swallow

hirsute [iʀsyt] adj (personne) shaggy-haired; (barbe) shaggy; (tête) tousled

'hisser ['ise] vt to hoist, haul up; **se ~** vi to heave o.s. up

histoire [istwaʀ] nf (science, événements) history; (anecdote, récit, mensonge) story; (affaire) business no pl; **~s** nfpl (chichis) fuss no pl; (ennuis) trouble sg; **historique** adj historical; (important) historic

'hit-parade ['itpaʀad] nm: **le ~~** the charts

hiver [ivɛʀ] nm winter; **hivernal, e, -aux** adj winter cpd; (glacial) wintry; **hiverner** vi to winter

HLM nm ou f (~ habitation à loyer modéré) council flat; **des HLM** council housing

'hobby ['ɔbi] nm hobby

'hocher ['ɔʃe] vt: **~ la tête** to nod; (signe négatif ou dubitatif) to shake one's head

'hochet ['ɔʃɛ] nm rattle

'hockey ['ɔkɛ] nm: **~ (sur glace/gazon)** (ice/field) hockey

'hold-up ['ɔldœp] nm inv hold-up

'hollandais, e ['ɔlɑ̃dɛ, ɛz] adj Dutch ♦ nm (LING) Dutch ♦ nm/f: **H~, e** Dutchman(-woman); **les H~** the Dutch

'Hollande ['ɔlɑ̃d] nf: **la ~** Holland

'homard ['ɔmaʀ] nm lobster

homéopathique [ɔmeɔpatik] adj homoeopathic

homicide [ɔmisid] nm murder; **~ involontaire** manslaughter

hommage [ɔmaʒ] nm tribute; **~s** nmpl: **présenter ses ~s** to pay one's respects; **rendre ~ à** to pay tribute ou homage to

homme [ɔm] nm man; **~ d'affaires** businessman; **~ d'État** statesman; **~ de main** hired man; **~ de paille** stooge; **~ politique**

politician; **homme-grenouille** nm frogman

homo...: **homogène** adj homogeneous;
homologue nm/f counterpart;
homologué, e adj (SPORT) ratified; (tarif)
authorized; **homonyme** nm (LING)
homonym; (d'une personne) namesake;
homosexuel, le adj homosexual

'Hongrie [ˈɔ̃gRi] nf: **la ~** Hungary;
'hongrois, e adj Hungarian ♦ nm/f:
Hongrois, e Hungarian ♦ nm (LING) Hungarian

honnête [ɔnɛt] adj (intègre) honest; (juste,
satisfaisant) fair; **honnêtement** adv
honestly; **honnêteté** nf honesty

honneur [ɔnœR] nm honour; (mérite) credit;
en l'~ de in honour of; (événement) on the
occasion of; **faire ~ à** (engagements) to
honour; (famille) to be a credit to; (fig: repas
etc) to do justice to

honorable [ɔnɔRabl] adj worthy,
honourable; (suffisant) decent

honoraire [ɔnɔRɛR] adj honorary; **professeur
~** professor emeritus; **honoraires** [ɔnɔRɛR]
nmpl fees pl

honorer [ɔnɔRe] vt to honour; (estimer) to
hold in high regard; (faire honneur à) to do
credit to; **honorifique** [ɔnɔRifik] adj
honorary

'honte [ˈɔ̃t] nf shame; **avoir ~ de** to be
ashamed of; **faire ~ à qn** to make sb (feel)
ashamed; **'honteux, -euse** adj ashamed;
(conduite, acte) shameful, disgraceful

hôpital, -aux [ɔpital, o] nm hospital

'hoquet [ˈɔkɛ] nm: **avoir le ~** to have (the)
hiccoughs; **'hoqueter** vi to hiccough

horaire [ɔRɛR] adj hourly ♦ nm timetable,
schedule; **~s** nmpl (d'employé) hours;
~ souple flexitime

horizon [ɔRizɔ̃] nm horizon

horizontal, e, -aux [ɔRizɔ̃tal, o] adj
horizontal

horloge [ɔRlɔʒ] nf clock; **l'~ parlante** the
speaking clock; **horloger, -ère** nm/f
watchmaker; clockmaker

'hormis [ˈɔRmi] prép save

horoscope [ɔRɔskɔp] nm horoscope

horreur [ɔRœR] nf horror; **quelle ~!** how
awful!; **avoir ~ de** to loathe ou detest;
horrible adj horrible; **horrifier** vt to horrify

horripiler [ɔRipile] vt to exasperate

'hors [ˈɔR] prép: **~ de** out of; **~ pair**
outstanding; **~ de propos** inopportune; **être
~ de soi** to be beside o.s.; **~ d'usage** out of
service; **'hors-bord** nm inv speedboat (with
outboard motor); **'hors-d'œuvre** nm inv hors
d'œuvre; **'hors-jeu** nm inv offside; **'hors-
la-loi** nm inv outlaw; **'hors-taxe** adj
(boutique, articles) duty-free

hortensia [ɔRtɑ̃sja] nm hydrangea

hospice [ɔspis] nm (de vieillards) home

hospitalier, -ière [ɔspitalje, jɛR] adj
(accueillant) hospitable; (MÉD: service, centre)
hospital cpd

hospitaliser [ɔspitalize] vt to take/send to
hospital, hospitalize

hospitalité [ɔspitalite] nf hospitality

hostie [ɔsti] nf host (REL)

hostile [ɔstil] adj hostile; **hostilité** nf hostility

hosto [ɔsto] (fam) nm hospital

hôte [ot] nm (maître de maison) host; (invité)
guest

hôtel [otɛl] nm hotel; **aller à l'~** to stay in a
hotel; **~ de ville** town hall; **~ (particulier)**
(private) mansion; **hôtelier, -ière** adj hotel
cpd ♦ nm/f hotelier; **hôtellerie** nf hotel
business

hôtesse [otes] nf hostess; **~ de l'air** air
stewardess; **~ (d'accueil)** receptionist

'hotte [ˈɔt] nf (panier) basket (carried on the
back); **~ aspirante** cooker hood

'houblon [ˈublɔ̃] nm (BOT) hop; (pour la
bière) hops pl

'houille [ˈuj] nf coal; **~ blanche** hydroelectric
power

'houle [ˈul] nf swell; **'houleux, -euse** adj
stormy

'houligan [ˈuligɑ̃] nm hooligan

'hourra [ˈuRa] excl hurrah!

'houspiller [ˈuspije] vt to scold

'housse [ˈus] nf cover

'houx [ˈu] nm holly

'hublot [ˈyblo] nm porthole

'huche [ˈyʃ] nf: **~ à pain** bread bin

'huer [ˈɥe] vt to boo

huile [ɥil] nf oil; **~ solaire** suntan oil; **huiler** vt
to oil; **huileux, -euse** adj oily

huis [ɥi] nm: **à ~ clos** in camera

huissier [ɥisje] nm usher; (JUR) ≈ bailiff

'huit [ˈɥi(t)] num eight; **samedi en ~** a week
on Saturday; **dans ~ jours** in a week;
'huitaine nf: **une huitaine (de jours)** a week
or so; **'huitième** num eighth

huître [ɥitR] nf oyster

humain, e [ymɛ̃, ɛn] adj human;
(compatissant) humane ♦ nm human
(being); **humanitaire** adj humanitarian;
humanité nf humanity

humble [œ̃bl] adj humble

humecter [ymɛkte] vt to dampen

'humer [ˈyme] vt (plat) to smell; (parfum) to
inhale

humeur [ymœR] nf mood; **de bonne/
mauvaise ~** in a good/bad mood

humide [ymid] adj damp; (main, yeux)
moist; (climat, chaleur) humid; (saison, route)
wet

humilier [ymilje] vt to humiliate

humilité [ymilite] nf humility, humbleness

humoristique [ymɔRistik] adj humorous

humour [ymuʀ] nm humour; **avoir de l'~** to have a sense of humour; **~ noir** black humour

'huppé, e ['ype] (fam) adj posh

'hurlement ['yʀləmɑ̃] nm howling no pl, howl, yelling no pl, yell

'hurler ['yʀle] vi to howl, yell

hurluberlu [yʀlybeʀly] (péj) nm crank

'hutte ['yt] nf hut

hybride [ibʀid] adj, nm hybrid

hydratant, e [idʀatɑ̃, ɑ̃t] adj (crème) moisturizing

hydraulique [idʀolik] adj hydraulic

hydravion [idʀavjɔ̃] nm seaplane

hydrogène [idʀoʒɛn] nm hydrogen

hydroglisseur [idʀoglisœʀ] nm hydroplane

hyène [jɛn] nf hyena

hygiénique [iʒenik] adj hygienic

hymne [imn] nm hymn; **~ national** national anthem

hypermarché [ipeʀmaʀʃe] nm hypermarket

hypermétrope [ipeʀmetʀop] adj long-sighted

hypertension [ipeʀtɑ̃sjɔ̃] nf high blood pressure

hypnose [ipnoz] nf hypnosis; **hypnotiser** vt to hypnotize; **hypnotiseur** nm hypnotist

hypocrisie [ipokʀizi] nf hypocrisy; **hypocrite** adj hypocritical

hypothèque [ipotek] nf mortgage

hypothèse [ipotez] nf hypothesis

hystérique [isteʀik] adj hysterical

I, i

iceberg [ajsbeʀg] nm iceberg

ici [isi] adv here; **jusqu'~** as far as this; (temps) so far; **d'~ demain** by tomorrow; **d'~ là** by then, in the meantime; **d'~ peu** before long

icône [ikon] nf icon

idéal, e, -aux [ideal, o] adj ideal ♦ nm ideal; **idéaliste** adj idealistic ♦ nm/f idealist

idée [ide] nf idea; **avoir dans l'~ que** to have an idea that; **~ fixe** obsession; **~ reçue** generally accepted idea; **~s noires** black ou dark thoughts

identifier [idɑ̃tifje] vt to identify; **s'~ à** (héros etc) to identify with

identique [idɑ̃tik] adj: **~ (à)** identical (to)

identité [idɑ̃tite] nf identity

idiot, e [idjo, idjɔt] adj idiotic ♦ nm/f idiot; **idiotie** nf idiotic thing

idole [idɔl] nf idol

if [if] nm yew

igloo [iglu] nm igloo

ignare [iɲaʀ] adj ignorant

ignifugé, e [iɲifyʒe] adj fireproof

ignoble [iɲɔbl] adj vile

ignorant, e [iɲɔʀɑ̃, ɑ̃t] adj ignorant

ignorer [iɲɔʀe] vt not to know; (personne) to ignore

il [il] pron he; (animal, chose, en tournure impersonnelle) it; **~s** they; voir aussi **avoir**

île [il] nf island; **l'~ Maurice** Mauritius; **les ~s anglo-normandes** the Channel Islands; **les ~s Britanniques** the British Isles

illégal, e, -aux [i(l)legal, o] adj illegal

illégitime [i(l)leʒitim] adj illegitimate

illettré, e [i(l)letʀe] adj, nm/f illiterate

illimité, e [i(l)limite] adj unlimited

illisible [i(l)lizibl] adj illegible; (roman) unreadable

illogique [i(l)lɔʒik] adj illogical

illumination [i(l)lyminasjɔ̃] nf illumination; (idée) flash of inspiration

illuminer [i(l)lymine] vt to light up; (monument, rue: pour une fête) to illuminate; (: au moyen de projecteurs) to floodlight

illusion [i(l)lyzjɔ̃] nf illusion; **se faire des ~s** to delude o.s.; **faire ~** to delude ou fool people; **illusionniste** nm/f conjuror

illustration [i(l)lystʀasjɔ̃] nf illustration

illustre [i(l)lystʀ] adj illustrious

illustré, e [i(l)lystʀe] adj illustrated ♦ nm comic

illustrer [i(l)lystʀe] vt to illustrate; **s'~** to become famous, win fame

îlot [ilo] nm small island, islet

ils [il] pron voir **il**

image [imaʒ] nf (gén) picture; (métaphore) image; **~ de marque** brand image; (fig) public image; **imagé, e** adj (texte) full of imagery; (langage) colourful

imaginaire [imaʒineʀ] adj imaginary

imagination [imaʒinasjɔ̃] nf imagination; **avoir de l'~** to be imaginative

imaginer [imaʒine] vt to imagine; (inventer: expédient) to devise, think up; **s'~** vt (se figurer: scène etc) to imagine, picture; **s'~ que** to imagine that

imbattable [ɛ̃batabl] adj unbeatable

imbécile [ɛ̃besil] adj idiotic ♦ nm/f idiot; **imbécillité** nf idiocy; (action) idiotic thing; (film, livre, propos) rubbish

imbiber [ɛ̃bibe] vt to soak; **s'~ de** to become saturated with

imbu, e [ɛ̃by] adj: **~ de** full of

imbuvable [ɛ̃byvabl] adj undrinkable; (personne: fam) unbearable

imitateur, -trice [imitatœʀ, tʀis] nm/f (gén) imitator; (MUSIC-HALL) impersonator

imitation [imitasjɔ̃] nf imitation; (de personnalité) impersonation

imiter [imite] vt to imitate; (contrefaire) to forge; (ressembler à) to look like

immaculé, e [i(m)makyle] adj (linge, surface, réputation) spotless; (blancheur) immaculate

immangeable [ɛ̃mɑ̃ʒabl] adj inedible

immatriculation [imatʀikylasjɔ̃] nf
registration

immatriculer [imatʀikyle] vt to register;
faire/se faire ~ to register

immédiat, e [imedja, jat] adj immediate
♦ nm: **dans l'~** for the time being;
immédiatement adv immediately

immense [i(m)mɑ̃s] adj immense

immerger [imɛʀʒe] vt to immerse, submerge

immeuble [imœbl] nm building; (à usage
d'habitation) block of flats

immigration [imigʀasjɔ̃] nf immigration

immigré, e [imigʀe] nm/f immigrant

imminent, e [iminɑ̃, ɑ̃t] adj imminent

immiscer [imise]: **s'~** vi: **s'~ dans** to interfere
in ou with

immobile [i(m)mɔbil] adj still, motionless

immobilier, -ière [imɔbilje, jɛʀ] adj
property cpd ♦ nm: **l'~** the property business

immobiliser [imɔbilize] vt (gén) to
immobilize; (circulation, véhicule, affaires) to
bring to a standstill; **s'~** (personne) to stand
still; (machine, véhicule) to come to a halt

immonde [i(m)mɔ̃d] adj foul

immoral, e, -aux [i(m)mɔʀal, o] adj
immoral

immortel, le [imɔʀtɛl] adj immortal

immuable [imɥabl] adj unchanging

immunisé, e [im(m)ynize] adj: **~ contre**
immune to

immunité [imynite] nf immunity

impact [ɛ̃pakt] nm impact

impair, e [ɛ̃pɛʀ] adj odd ♦ nm faux pas,
blunder

impardonnable [ɛ̃paʀdɔnabl] adj
unpardonable, unforgivable

imparfait, e [ɛ̃paʀfɛ, ɛt] adj imperfect

impartial, e, -aux [ɛ̃paʀsjal, jo] adj
impartial, unbiased

impasse [ɛ̃pɑs] nf dead end, cul-de-sac; (fig)
deadlock

impassible [ɛ̃pasibl] adj impassive

impatience [ɛ̃pasjɑ̃s] nf impatience

impatient, e [ɛ̃pasjɑ̃, jɑ̃t] adj impatient;
impatienter: s'impatienter vi to get
impatient

impeccable [ɛ̃pekabl] adj (parfait) perfect;
(propre) impeccable; (fam) smashing

impensable [ɛ̃pɑ̃sabl] adj (événement
hypothétique) unthinkable; (événement qui a
eu lieu) unbelievable

imper [ɛ̃pɛʀ] (fam) nm raincoat

impératif, -ive [ɛ̃peʀatif, iv] adj imperative
♦ nm (LING) imperative; **~s** nmpl (exigences:
d'une fonction, d'une charge) requirements;
(: de la mode) demands

impératrice [ɛ̃peʀatʀis] nf empress

imperceptible [ɛ̃pɛʀsɛptibl] adj
imperceptible

impérial, e, -aux [ɛ̃peʀjal, jo] adj imperial;
impériale nf top deck

impérieux, -euse [ɛ̃peʀjø, jøz] adj
(caractère, ton) imperious; (obligation, besoin)
pressing, urgent

impérissable [ɛ̃peʀisabl] adj undying

imperméable [ɛ̃pɛʀmeabl] adj waterproof;
(fig): **~ à** impervious to ♦ nm raincoat

impertinent, e [ɛ̃pɛʀtinɑ̃, ɑ̃t] adj
impertinent

imperturbable [ɛ̃pɛʀtyʀbabl] adj (personne,
caractère) unperturbable; (sang-froid, gaieté,
sérieux) unshakeable

impétueux, -euse [ɛ̃petɥø, øz] adj
impetuous

impitoyable [ɛ̃pitwajabl] adj pitiless,
merciless

implanter [ɛ̃plɑ̃te]: **s'~** vi to be set up

impliquer [ɛ̃plike] vt to imply; **~ qn (dans)** to
implicate sb (in)

impoli, e [ɛ̃pɔli] adj impolite, rude

impopulaire [ɛ̃pɔpylɛʀ] adj unpopular

importance [ɛ̃pɔʀtɑ̃s] nf importance; **sans ~**
unimportant

important, e [ɛ̃pɔʀtɑ̃, ɑ̃t] adj important; (en
quantité: somme, retard) considerable,
sizeable; (: dégâts) extensive; (péj: airs, ton)
self-important ♦ nm: **l'~** the important thing

importateur, -trice [ɛ̃pɔʀtatœʀ, tʀis] nm/f
importer

importation [ɛ̃pɔʀtasjɔ̃] nf importation;
(produit) import

importer [ɛ̃pɔʀte] vt (COMM) to import;
(maladies, plantes) to introduce ♦ vi (être
important) to matter; **il importe qu'il fasse** it
is important that he should do; **peu
m'importe** (je n'ai pas de préférence) I don't
mind; (je m'en moque) I don't care; **peu
importe (que)** it doesn't matter (if); voir aussi
n'importe

importun, e [ɛ̃pɔʀtœ̃, yn] adj irksome,
importunate; (arrivée, visite) inopportune, ill-
timed ♦ nm intruder; **importuner** vt to
bother

imposable [ɛ̃pozabl] adj taxable

imposant, e [ɛ̃pozɑ̃, ɑ̃t] adj imposing

imposer [ɛ̃poze] vt (taxer) to tax; **s'~** (être
nécessaire) to be imperative; **~ qch à qn** to
impose sth on sb; **en ~ à** to impress;
s'~ comme to emerge as; **s'~ par** to win
recognition through

impossibilité [ɛ̃pɔsibilite] nf impossibility;
être dans l'~ de faire qch to be unable to do
sth

impossible [ɛ̃pɔsibl] adj impossible; **il m'est
~ de le faire** it is impossible for me to do it, I
can't possibly do it; **faire l'~** to do one's
utmost

imposteur [ɛ̃pɔstœʀ] nm impostor

impôt [ɛ̃po] nm tax; **~s** nmpl (contributions) (income) tax sg; **payer 1000 F d'~s** to pay 1,000F in tax; **~ foncier** land tax; **~ sur le chiffre d'affaires** corporation (BRIT) ou corporate (US) tax; **~ sur le revenu** income tax

impotent, e [ɛ̃pɔtɑ̃, ɑ̃t] adj disabled

impraticable [ɛ̃pratikabl] adj (projet) impracticable, unworkable; (piste) impassable

imprécis, e [ɛ̃presi, iz] adj imprecise

imprégner [ɛ̃preɲe] vt (tissu) to impregnate; (lieu, air) to fill; **s'~ de** (fig) to absorb

imprenable [ɛ̃prənabl] adj (forteresse) impregnable; **vue ~** unimpeded outlook

imprésario [ɛ̃presarjo] nm manager

impression [ɛ̃presjɔ̃] nf impression; (d'un ouvrage, tissu) printing; **faire bonne ~** to make a good impression; **impressionnant, e** adj (imposant) impressive; (bouleversant) upsetting; **impressionner** vt (frapper) to impress; (bouleverser) to upset

imprévisible [ɛ̃previzibl] adj unforeseeable

imprévoyant, e [ɛ̃prevwajɑ̃, ɑ̃t] adj lacking in foresight; (en matière d'argent) improvident

imprévu, e [ɛ̃prevy] adj unforeseen, unexpected ♦ nm (incident) unexpected incident; **des vacances pleines d'~** holidays full of surprises; **en cas d'~** if anything unexpected happens; **sauf ~** unless anything unexpected crops up

imprimante [ɛ̃primɑ̃t] nf printer

imprimé [ɛ̃prime] nm (formulaire) printed form; (POSTES) printed matter no pl; (tissu) printed fabric, à fleur floral print

imprimer [ɛ̃prime] vt to print; (publier) to publish; **imprimerie** nf printing; (établissement) printing works sg; **imprimeur** nm printer

Impromptu, e [ɛ̃prɔ̃pty] adj (repas, discours) impromptu; (départ) sudden; (visite) surprise

impropre [ɛ̃prɔpr] adj inappropriate; **~ à** unfit for

improviser [ɛ̃prɔvize] vt, vi to improvise

improviste [ɛ̃prɔvist]: **à l'~** adv unexpectedly, without warning

imprudence [ɛ̃prydɑ̃s] nf (d'une personne, d'une action) carelessness no pl; (d'une remarque) imprudence no pl; **commettre une ~** to do something foolish

imprudent, e [ɛ̃prydɑ̃, ɑ̃t] adj (conducteur, geste, action) careless; (remarque) unwise, imprudent; (projet) foolhardy

impudent, e [ɛ̃pydɑ̃, ɑ̃t] adj impudent

impudique [ɛ̃pydik] adj shameless

impuissant, e [ɛ̃pɥisɑ̃, ɑ̃t] adj helpless; (sans effet) ineffectual; (sexuellement) impotent

impulsif, -ive [ɛ̃pylsif, iv] adj impulsive

impulsion [ɛ̃pylsjɔ̃] nf (ÉLEC, instinct) impulse; (élan, influence) impetus

impunément [ɛ̃pynemɑ̃] adv with impunity

inabordable [inabɔrdabl] adj (cher) prohibitive

inacceptable [inaksɛptabl] adj unacceptable

inaccessible [inaksesibl] adj inaccessible

inachevé, e [inaʃ(ə)ve] adj unfinished

inactif, -ive [inaktif, iv] adj inactive; (remède) ineffective; (BOURSE: marché) slack ♦ nm: **les ~s** the non-working population

inadapté, e [inadapte] adj (gén): **~ à** not adapted to, unsuited to; (PSYCH) maladjusted

inadéquat, e [inadekwa(t), kwat] adj inadequate

inadmissible [inadmisibl] adj inadmissible

inadvertance [inadvɛrtɑ̃s]: **par ~** adv inadvertently

inaltérable [inalterabl] adj (matière) stable; (fig) unfailing; **~ à** unaffected by

inanimé, e [inanime] adj (matière) inanimate; (évanoui) unconscious; (sans vie) lifeless

inanition [inanisjɔ̃] nf: **tomber d'~** to faint with hunger (and exhaustion)

inaperçu, e [inapɛrsy] adj: **passer ~** to go unnoticed

inapte [inapt] adj: **~ à** incapable of; (MIL) unfit for

inattaquable [inatakabl] adj (texte, preuve) irrefutable

inattendu, e [inatɑ̃dy] adj unexpected

inattentif, -ive [inatɑ̃tif, iv] adj inattentive; **~ à** (dangers, détails) heedless of; **inattention** nf: **faute d'inattention** careless mistake

inauguration [inogyrasjɔ̃] nf inauguration

inaugurer [inogyre] vt (monument) to unveil; (exposition, usine) to open; (fig) to inaugurate

inavouable [inavwabl] adj shameful; (bénéfices) undisclosable

incalculable [ɛ̃kalkylabl] adj incalculable

incandescence [ɛ̃kɑ̃desɑ̃s] nf: **porter à ~** to heat white-hot

incapable [ɛ̃kapabl] adj incapable; **~ de faire** incapable of doing; (empêché) unable to do

incapacité [ɛ̃kapasite] nf (incompétence) incapability; (impossibilité) incapacity; **dans l'~ de faire** unable to do

incarcérer [ɛ̃karsere] vt to incarcerate, imprison

incarné, e [ɛ̃karne] adj (ongle) ingrown

incarner [ɛ̃karne] vt to embody, personify; (THÉÂTRE) to play

incassable [ɛ̃kasabl] adj unbreakable

incendiaire [ɛ̃sɑ̃djɛr] adj incendiary; (fig:

discours) inflammatory

incendie [ɛ̃sɑ̃di, ɑ̃t] *nm* fire; ~ **criminel** arson *no pl*; ~ **de forêt** forest fire; **incendier** *vt* (*mettre le feu à*) to set fire to, set alight; (*brûler complètement*) to burn down; **se faire incendier** (*fam*) to get a rocket

incertain, e [ɛ̃sɛʀtɛ̃, ɛn] *adj* uncertain; (*temps*) unsettled; (*imprécis: contours*) indistinct, blurred; **incertitude** *nf* uncertainty

incessamment [ɛ̃sesamɑ̃] *adv* very shortly

incident [ɛ̃sidɑ̃] *nm* incident; ~ **de parcours** minor hitch *ou* setback; ~ **technique** technical difficulties *pl*

incinérer [ɛ̃sineʀe] *vt* (*ordures*) to incinerate; (*mort*) to cremate

incisive [ɛ̃siziv] *nf* incisor

inciter [ɛ̃site] *vt*: ~ **qn à (faire) qch** to encourage sb to do sth; (*à la révolte etc*) to incite sb to do sth

inclinable [ɛ̃klinabl] *adj*: **siège à dossier ~** reclining seat

inclinaison [ɛ̃klinɛzɔ̃] *nf* (*déclivité: d'une route etc*) incline; (: *d'un toit*) slope; (*état penché*) tilt

inclination [ɛ̃klinasjɔ̃] *nf* (*penchant*) inclination; ~ **de (la) tête** nod (of the head); ~ **(de buste)** bow

incliner [ɛ̃kline] *vt* (*pencher*) to tilt ♦ *vi*: ~ **à qch/à faire** to incline towards sth/doing; **s'~** (*devant*) to bow (before); (*céder*) to give in *ou* yield (to); ~ **la tête** to give a slight bow

inclure [ɛ̃klyʀ] *vt* to include; (*joindre à un envoi*) to enclose; **jusqu'au 10 mars inclus** until 10th March inclusive

incognito [ɛ̃kɔɲito] *adv* incognito ♦ *nm*: **garder l'~** to remain incognito

incohérent, e [ɛ̃kɔeʀɑ̃, ɑ̃t] *adj* (*comportement*) inconsistent; (*geste, langage, texte*) incoherent

incollable [ɛ̃kɔlabl] *adj* (*riz*) non-stick; **il est ~** (*fam*) he's got all the answers

incolore [ɛ̃kɔlɔʀ] *adj* colourless

incommoder [ɛ̃kɔmɔde] *vt* (*chaleur, odeur*): ~ **qn** to bother sb

incomparable [ɛ̃kɔ̃paʀabl] *adj* incomparable

incompatible [ɛ̃kɔ̃patibl] *adj* incompatible

incompétent, e [ɛ̃kɔ̃petɑ̃, ɑ̃t] *adj* incompetent

incomplet, -ète [ɛ̃kɔ̃plɛ, ɛt] *adj* incomplete

incompréhensible [ɛ̃kɔ̃pʀeɑ̃sibl] *adj* incomprehensible

incompris, e [ɛ̃kɔ̃pʀi, iz] *adj* misunderstood

inconcevable [ɛ̃kɔ̃s(ə)vabl] *adj* inconceivable

inconciliable [ɛ̃kɔ̃siljabl] *adj* irreconcilable

inconditionnel, le [ɛ̃kɔ̃disjɔnɛl] *adj* unconditional; (*partisan*) unquestioning ♦ *nm/f* (*d'un homme politique*) ardent supporter; (*d'un écrivain, d'un chanteur*)

ardent admirer; (*d'une activité*) fanatic

inconfort [ɛ̃kɔ̃fɔʀ] *nm* discomfort; **inconfortable** *adj* uncomfortable

incongru, e [ɛ̃kɔ̃gʀy] *adj* unseemly

inconnu, e [ɛ̃kɔny] *adj* unknown ♦ *nm/f* stranger ♦ *nm*: **l'~** the unknown; **inconnue** *nf* unknown factor

inconsciemment [ɛ̃kɔ̃sjamɑ̃] *adv* unconsciously

inconscient, e [ɛ̃kɔ̃sjɑ̃, jɑ̃t] *adj* unconscious; (*irréfléchi*) thoughtless, reckless; (*sentiment*) subconscious ♦ *nm* (PSYCH): **l'~** the unconscious; ~ **de** unaware of

inconsidéré, e [ɛ̃kɔ̃sideʀe] *adj* ill-considered

inconsistant, e [ɛ̃kɔ̃sistɑ̃, ɑ̃t] *adj* (*fig*) flimsy, weak

inconsolable [ɛ̃kɔ̃sɔlabl] *adj* inconsolable

incontestable [ɛ̃kɔ̃tɛstabl] *adj* indisputable

incontinent, e [ɛ̃kɔ̃tinɑ̃, ɑ̃t] *adj* incontinent

incontournable [ɛ̃kɔ̃tuʀnabl] *adj* unavoidable

incontrôlable [ɛ̃kɔ̃tʀolabl] *adj* unverifiable; (*irrépressible*) uncontrollable

inconvenant, e [ɛ̃kɔ̃v(ə)nɑ̃, ɑ̃t] *adj* unseemly, improper

inconvénient [ɛ̃kɔ̃venjɑ̃] *nm* disadvantage, drawback; **si vous n'y voyez pas d'~** if you have no objections

incorporer [ɛ̃kɔʀpɔʀe] *vt*: ~ **(à)** to mix in (with); ~ **(dans)** (*paragraphe etc*) to incorporate (in); (MIL: *appeler*) to recruit (into); **il a très bien su s'~ à notre groupe** he was very easily incorporated into our group

incorrect, e [ɛ̃kɔʀɛkt] *adj* (*impropre, inconvenant*) improper; (*défectueux*) faulty; (*inexact*) incorrect; (*impoli*) impolite; (*déloyal*) underhand

incorrigible [ɛ̃kɔʀiʒibl] *adj* incorrigible

incrédule [ɛ̃kʀedyl] *adj* incredulous; (REL) unbelieving

increvable [ɛ̃kʀəvabl] (*fam*) *adj* tireless

incriminer [ɛ̃kʀimine] *vt* (*personne*) to incriminate; (*action, conduite*) to bring under attack; (*bonne foi, honnêteté*) to call into question

incroyable [ɛ̃kʀwajabl] *adj* incredible

incruster [ɛ̃kʀyste] *vt* (ART) to inlay; **s'~** *vi* (*invité*) to take root

inculpé, e [ɛ̃kylpe] *nm/f* accused

inculper [ɛ̃kylpe] *vt*: ~ **(de)** to charge (with)

inculquer [ɛ̃kylke] *vt*: ~ **qch à** to inculcate sth in *ou* instil sth into

inculte [ɛ̃kylt] *adj* uncultivated; (*esprit, peuple*) uncultured

Inde [ɛ̃d] *nf*: **l'~** India

indécent, e [ɛ̃desɑ̃, ɑ̃t] *adj* indecent

indéchiffrable [ɛ̃deʃifʀabl] *adj* indecipherable

indécis, e [ɛ̃desi, iz] *adj* (*par nature*)

indecisive; (*temporairement*) undecided

indéfendable [ɛ̃defɑ̃dabl] *adj* indefensible

indéfini, e [ɛ̃defini] *adj* (*imprécis, incertain*) undefined; (*illimité*, LING) indefinite;
indéfiniment *adv* indefinitely;
indéfinissable *adj* indefinable

indélébile [ɛ̃delebil] *adj* indelible

indélicat, e [ɛ̃delika, at] *adj* tactless

indemne [ɛ̃dɛmn] *adj* unharmed;
indemniser *vt*: **indemniser qn (de)** to compensate sb (for)

indemnité [ɛ̃dɛmnite] *nf* (*dédommagement*) compensation *no pl*; (*allocation*) allowance;
indemnité de licenciement redundancy payment

indépendamment [ɛ̃depɑ̃damɑ̃] *adv* independently; ~ **de** (*abstraction faite de*) irrespective of; (*en plus de*) over and above

indépendance [ɛ̃depɑ̃dɑ̃s] *nf* independence

indépendant, e [ɛ̃depɑ̃dɑ̃, ɑ̃t] *adj* independent; ~ **de** independent of

indescriptible [ɛ̃dɛskʀiptibl] *adj* indescribable

indésirable [ɛ̃dezirabl] *adj* undesirable

indestructible [ɛ̃dɛstʀyktibl] *adj* indestructible

indétermination [ɛ̃detɛʀminasjɔ̃] *nf* (*irrésolution: chronique*) indecision; (: *temporaire*) indecisiveness

indéterminé, e [ɛ̃detɛʀmine] *adj* (*date, cause, nature*) unspecified; (*forme, longueur, quantité*) indeterminate

index [ɛ̃dɛks] *nm* (*doigt*) index finger; (*d'un livre etc*) index; **mettre à l'~** to blacklist;
indexé, e *adj* (ÉCON): **indexé (sur)** index-linked (to)

indic [ɛ̃dik] (*fam*) *nm* (POLICE) grass

indicateur [ɛ̃dikatœʀ] *nm* (POLICE) informer; (TECH) gauge, indicator

indicatif, -ive [ɛ̃dikatif, iv] *adj*: **à titre ~** for (your) information ♦ *nm* (LING) indicative; (RADIO) theme *ou* signature tune; (TÉL) dialling code

indication [ɛ̃dikasjɔ̃] *nf* indication; (*renseignement*) information *no pl*; ~**s** *nfpl* (*directives*) instructions

indice [ɛ̃dis] *nm* (*marque, signe*) indication, sign; (POLICE: *lors d'une enquête*) clue; (JUR: *présomption*) piece of evidence; (SCIENCE, ÉCON, TECH) index

indicible [ɛ̃disibl] *adj* inexpressible

indien, ne [ɛ̃djɛ̃, jɛn] *adj* Indian ♦ *nm/f*: **I~, ne** Indian

indifféremment [ɛ̃difeʀamɑ̃] *adv* (*sans distinction*) equally (well)

indifférence [ɛ̃difeʀɑ̃s] *nf* indifference

indifférent, e [ɛ̃difeʀɑ̃, ɑ̃t] *adj* (*peu intéressé*) indifferent; **ça m'est ~** it doesn't matter to me; **elle m'est ~e** I am indifferent to her

indigence [ɛ̃diʒɑ̃s] *nf* poverty

indigène [ɛ̃diʒɛn] *adj* native, indigenous; (*des gens du pays*) local ♦ *nm/f* native

indigeste [ɛ̃diʒɛst] *adj* indigestible

indigestion [ɛ̃diʒɛstjɔ̃] *nf* indigestion *no pl*

indigne [ɛ̃diɲ] *adj* unworthy

indigner [ɛ̃diɲe] *vt*: **s'~ (de** *ou* **contre)** to get indignant (at)

indiqué, e [ɛ̃dike] *adj* (*date, lieu*) agreed; (*traitement*) appropriate; (*conseillé*) advisable

indiquer [ɛ̃dike] *vt* (*suj: pendule, aiguille*) to show; (: *étiquette, panneau*) to show, indicate; (*renseigner sur*) to point out, tell; (*déterminer: date, lieu*) to give, state; (*signaler, dénoter*) to indicate, point to;
~ **qch/qn à qn** (*montrer du doigt*) to point sth/sb out to sb; (*faire connaître: médecin, restaurant*) to tell sb of sth/sb

indirect, e [ɛ̃diʀɛkt] *adj* indirect

indiscipliné, e [ɛ̃disipline] *adj* undisciplined

indiscret, -ète [ɛ̃diskʀɛ, ɛt] *adj* indiscreet

indiscutable [ɛ̃diskytabl] *adj* indisputable

indispensable [ɛ̃dispɑ̃sabl] *adj* indispensable, essential

indisposé, e [ɛ̃dispoze] *adj* indisposed

indisposer [ɛ̃dispoze] *vt* (*incommoder*) to upset; (*déplaire à*) to antagonize; (*énerver*) to irritate

indistinct, e [ɛ̃distɛ̃(kt), ɛ̃kt] *adj* indistinct;
indistinctement *adv* (*voir, prononcer*) indistinctly; (*sans distinction*) indiscriminately

individu [ɛ̃dividy] *nm* individual; **individuel, le** *adj* (*gén*) individual; (*responsabilité, propriété, liberté*) personal, individual; **chambre individuelle** single room; **maison individuelle** detached house

indolore [ɛ̃dɔlɔʀ] *adj* painless

indomptable [ɛ̃dɔ̃(p)tabl] *adj* untameable; (*fig*) invincible

Indonésie [ɛ̃dɔnezi] *nf* Indonesia

indu, e [ɛ̃dy] *adj*: **à une heure ~e** at some ungodly hour

induire [ɛ̃dɥiʀ] *vt*: ~ **qn en erreur** to lead sb astray, mislead sb

indulgent, e [ɛ̃dylʒɑ̃, ɑ̃t] *adj* (*parent, regard*) indulgent; (*juge, examinateur*) lenient

industrialisé, e [ɛ̃dystʀijalize] *adj* industrialized

industrie [ɛ̃dystʀi] *nf* industry; **industriel, le** *adj* industrial ♦ *nm* industrialist

inébranlable [inebʀɑ̃labl] *adj* (*masse, colonne*) solid; (*personne, certitude, foi*) unshakeable

inédit, e [inedi, it] *adj* (*correspondance, livre*) hitherto unpublished; (*spectacle, moyen*) novel, original; (*film*) unreleased

ineffaçable [inefasabl] *adj* indelible

inefficace [inefikas] *adj* (*remède, moyen*)

ineffective; (*machine, employé*) inefficient

inégal, e, -aux [inegal, o] *adj* unequal; (*irrégulier*) uneven; **inégalable** *adj* matchless; **inégalé, e** *adj* (*record*) unequalled; (*beauté*) unrivalled; **inégalité** *nf* inequality

inépuisable [inepɥizabl] *adj* inexhaustible

inerte [inɛʀt] *adj* (*immobile*) lifeless; (*sans réaction*) passive

inespéré, e [inespeʀe] *adj* unexpected, unhoped-for

inestimable [inestimabl] *adj* priceless; (*fig: bienfait*) invaluable

inévitable [inevitabl] *adj* unavoidable; (*fatal, habituel*) inevitable

inexact, e [inɛgza(kt), akt] *adj* inaccurate

inexcusable [inɛkskyzabl] *adj* unforgivable

inexplicable [inɛksplikabl] *adj* inexplicable

in extremis [inɛkstremis] *adv* at the last minute ♦ *adj* last-minute

infaillible [ɛ̃fajibl] *adj* infallible

infâme [ɛ̃fɑm] *adj* vile

infarctus [ɛ̃faʀktys] *nm*: ~ **(du myocarde)** coronary (thrombosis)

infatigable [ɛ̃fatigabl] *adj* tireless

infect, e [ɛ̃fɛkt] *adj* revolting; (*personne*) obnoxious; (*temps*) foul

infecter [ɛ̃fɛkte] *vt* (*atmosphère, eau*) to contaminate; (*MÉD*) to infect; **s'~** to become infected *ou* septic; **infection** *nf* infection; (*puanteur*) stench

inférieur, e [ɛ̃feʀjœʀ] *adj* lower; (*en qualité, intelligence*) inferior; ~ **à** (*somme, quantité*) less *ou* smaller than; (*moins bon que*) inferior to

infernal, e, -aux [ɛ̃fɛʀnal, o] *adj* (*insupportable: chaleur, rythme*) infernal; (: *enfant*) horrid; (*satanique, effrayant*) diabolical

infidèle [ɛ̃fidɛl] *adj* unfaithful

infiltrer [ɛ̃filtre] *vb*: **s'~ dans** to get into; (*liquide*) to seep through; (*fig: groupe, ennemi*) to infiltrate

infime [ɛ̃fim] *adj* minute, tiny

infini, e [ɛ̃fini] *adj* infinite ♦ *nm* infinity; **à l'~** endlessly; **infiniment** *adv* infinitely; **infinité** *nf*: **une infinité de** an infinite number of

infinitif [ɛ̃finitif, iv] *nm* infinitive

infirme [ɛ̃fiʀm] *adj* disabled ♦ *nm/f* disabled person

infirmerie [ɛ̃fiʀməʀi] *nf* medical room

infirmier, -ière [ɛ̃fiʀmje] *nm/f* nurse; **infirmière chef** sister

infirmité [ɛ̃fiʀmite] *nf* disability

inflammable [ɛ̃flamabl] *adj* (in)flammable

inflation [ɛ̃flasjɔ̃] *nf* inflation

infliger [ɛ̃fliʒe] *vt*: ~ **qch (à qn)** to inflict sth (on sb); (*amende, sanction*) to impose sth (on sb)

influençable [ɛ̃flɥɑ̃sabl] *adj* easily influenced

influence [ɛ̃flɥɑ̃s] *nf* influence; **influencer** *vt* to influence; **influent, e** *adj* influential

informateur, -trice [ɛ̃fɔʀmatœʀ, tʀis] *nm/f* (*POLICE*) informer

informaticien, ne [ɛ̃fɔʀmatisjɛ̃, jɛn] *nm/f* computer scientist

information [ɛ̃fɔʀmasjɔ̃] *nf* (*renseignement*) piece of information; (*PRESSE, TV: nouvelle*) item of news; (*diffusion de renseignements , INFORM*) information; (*JUR*) inquiry, investigation; **~s** *nfpl* (*TV*) news *sg*

informatique [ɛ̃fɔʀmatik] *nf* (*technique*) data processing; (*science*) computer science ♦ *adj* computer *cpd*; **informatiser** *vt* to computerize

informe [ɛ̃fɔʀm] *adj* shapeless

informer [ɛ̃fɔʀme] *vt*: ~ **qn (de)** to inform sb (of); **s'~ (de/si)** to inquire *ou* find out (about/whether *ou* if)

infos [ɛ̃fo] *nfpl*: **les ~** the news *sg*

infraction [ɛ̃fʀaksjɔ̃] *nf* offence; ~ **à** violation *ou* breach of; **être en ~** to be in breach of the law

infranchissable [ɛ̃fʀɑ̃ʃisabl] *adj* impassable; (*fig*) insuperable

infrarouge [ɛ̃fʀaʀuʒ] *adj* infrared

infrastructure [ɛ̃fʀastʀyktyʀ] *nf* (*AVIAT, MIL*) ground installations *pl*; (*ÉCON: touristique etc*) infrastructure

infuser [ɛ̃fyze] *vt, vi* (*thé*) to brew; (*tisane*) to infuse; **infusion** *nf* (*tisane*) herb tea

ingénier [ɛ̃ʒenje]: **s'~** *vi*: **s'~ à faire** to strive to do

ingénierie [ɛ̃ʒeniʀi] *nf* engineering; ~ **génétique** genetic engineering

ingénieur [ɛ̃ʒenjœʀ] *nm* engineer; **ingénieur du son** sound engineer

ingénieux, -euse [ɛ̃ʒenjø, jøz] *adj* ingenious, clever

ingénu, e [ɛ̃ʒeny] *adj* ingenuous, artless

ingérer [ɛ̃ʒeʀe] *vb*: **s'~ dans** to interfere in

ingrat, e [ɛ̃gʀa, at] *adj* (*personne*) ungrateful; (*travail, sujet*) thankless; (*visage*) unprepossessing

ingrédient [ɛ̃gʀedjɑ̃] *nm* ingredient

ingurgiter [ɛ̃gyʀʒite] *vt* to swallow

inhabitable [inabitabl] *adj* uninhabitable

inhabité, e [inabite] *adj* uninhabited

inhabituel, le [inabitɥɛl] *adj* unusual

inhibition [inibisjɔ̃] *nf* inhibition

inhumain, e [inymɛ̃, ɛn] *adj* inhuman

inhumation [inymasjɔ̃] *nf* burial

inhumer [inyme] *vt* to inter, bury

inimaginable [inimaʒinabl] *adj* unimaginable

ininterrompu, e [inɛ̃teʀɔ̃py] *adj* (*file, série*) unbroken; (*flot, vacarme*) uninterrupted, non-stop; (*effort*) unremitting, continuous;

(*suite, ligne*) unbroken

initial, e, -aux [inisjal, jo] *adj* initial;
  initiale *nf* initial; **initialiser** *vt* to initialize

initiation [inisjasjɔ̃] *nf*: ~ **à** introduction to

initiative [inisjativ] *nf* initiative

initier [inisje] *vt*: ~ **qn à** to initiate sb into;
  (*faire découvrir: art, jeu*) to introduce sb to

injecté, e [ɛ̃ʒekte] *adj*: **yeux ~s de sang**
  bloodshot eyes

injecter [ɛ̃ʒekte] *vt* to inject; **injection** *nf*
  injection; **à injection** (*AUTO*) fuel injection
  cpd

injure [ɛ̃ʒyʀ] *nf* insult, abuse *no pl*; **injurier**
  vt to insult, abuse; **injurieux, -euse** *adj*
  abusive, insulting

injuste [ɛ̃ʒyst] *adj* unjust, unfair; **injustice**
  nf injustice

inlassable [ɛ̃lasabl] *adj* tireless

inné, e [i(n)ne] *adj* innate, inborn

innocent, e [inɔsɑ̃, ɑ̃t] *adj* innocent;
  innocenter *vt* to clear, prove innocent

innombrable [i(n)nɔ̃bʀabl] *adj* innumerable

innommable [i(n)nɔmabl] *adj* unspeakable

innover [inɔve] *vi* to break new ground

inoccupé, e [inɔkype] *adj* unoccupied

inodore [inɔdɔʀ] *adj* (*gaz*) odourless; (*fleur*)
  scentless

inoffensif, -ive [inɔfɑ̃sif, iv] *adj* harmless,
  innocuous

inondation [inɔ̃dasjɔ̃] *nf* flood

inonder [inɔ̃de] *vt* to flood; ~ **de** to flood
  with

inopiné, e [inɔpine] *adj* unexpected; (*mort*)
  sudden

inopportun, e [inɔpɔʀtœ̃, yn] *adj* ill-timed,
  untimely

inoubliable [inublijabl] *adj* unforgettable

inouï, e [inwi] *adj* unheard-of, extraordinary

inox [inɔks] *nm* stainless steel

inqualifiable [ɛ̃kalifjabl] *adj* unspeakable

inquiet, -ète [ɛ̃kjɛ, ɛ̃kjɛt] *adj* anxious;
  inquiétant, e *adj* worrying, disturbing;
  inquiéter *vt* to worry; **s'inquiéter** to worry;
  s'inquiéter de to worry about; (*s'enquérir de*)
  to inquire about; **inquiétude** *nf* anxiety

insaisissable [ɛ̃sezisabl] *adj* (*fugitif, ennemi*)
  elusive; (*différence, nuance*) imperceptible

insalubre [ɛ̃salybʀ] *adj* insalubrious

insatisfaisant, e [ɛ̃satisfəzɑ̃, ɑ̃t] *adj*
  unsatisfactory

insatisfait, e [ɛ̃satisfɛ, ɛt] *adj* (*non comblé*)
  unsatisfied; (*mécontent*) dissatisfied

inscription [ɛ̃skʀipsjɔ̃] *nf* inscription;
  (*immatriculation*) enrolment

inscrire [ɛ̃skʀiʀ] *vt* (*marquer: sur son calepin
  etc*) to note ou write down; (: *sur un mur,
  une affiche etc*) to write; (: *dans la pierre, le
  métal*) to inscribe; (*mettre: sur une liste, un
  budget etc*) to put down; **s'~** (*pour une excur-*

sion etc) to put one's name down; **s'~** (**à**)
(*club, parti*) to join; (*université*) to register ou
enrol (at); (*examen, concours*) to register
(for); ~ **qn à** (*club, parti*) to enrol sb at

insecte [ɛ̃sɛkt] *nm* insect; **insecticide** *nm*
  insecticide

insensé, e [ɛ̃sɑ̃se] *adj* mad

insensibiliser [ɛ̃sɑ̃sibilize] *vt* to anaesthetize

insensible [ɛ̃sɑ̃sibl] *adj* (*nerf, membre*)
  numb; (*dur, indifférent*) insensitive

inséparable [ɛ̃sepaʀabl] *adj* inseparable
  ♦ *nm*: **~s** (*oiseaux*) lovebirds

insigne [ɛ̃siɲ] *nm* (*d'un parti, club*) badge;
  (*d'une fonction*) insignia ♦ *adj* distinguished

insignifiant, e [ɛ̃siɲifjɑ̃, jɑ̃t] *adj*
  insignificant; trivial

insinuer [ɛ̃sinɥe] *vt* to insinuate; **s'~ dans**
  (*fig*) to worm one's way into

insipide [ɛ̃sipid] *adj* insipid

insister [ɛ̃siste] *vi* to insist; (*continuer à
  sonner*) to keep on trying; ~ **sur** (*détail, sujet*)
  to lay stress on

insolation [ɛ̃sɔlasjɔ̃] *nf* (*MÉD*) sunstroke *no pl*

insolent, e [ɛ̃sɔlɑ̃, ɑ̃t] *adj* insolent

insolite [ɛ̃sɔlit] *adj* strange, unusual

insomnie [ɛ̃sɔmni] *nf* insomnia *no pl*

insonoriser [ɛ̃sɔnɔʀize] *vt* to soundproof

insouciant, e [ɛ̃susjɑ̃, jɑ̃t] *adj* carefree; ~ **du
  danger** heedless of (the) danger

insoumis, e [ɛ̃sumi, iz] *adj* (*caractère,
  enfant*) rebellious, refractory; (*contrée, tribu*)
  unsubdued

insoupçonnable [ɛ̃supsɔnabl] *adj*
  unsuspected; (*personne*) above suspicion

insoupçonné, e [ɛ̃supsɔne] *adj* unsuspected

insoutenable [ɛ̃sut(ə)nabl] *adj* (*argument*)
  untenable; (*chaleur*) unbearable

inspecter [ɛ̃spɛkte] *vt* to inspect;
  inspecteur, -trice *nm/f* inspector;
  inspecteur d'Académie (regional) director of
  education; **inspecteur des finances** ≈ tax
  inspector (*BRIT*), ≈ Internal Revenue Service
  agent (*US*); **inspection** *nf* inspection

inspirer [ɛ̃spiʀe] *vt* (*gén*) to inspire ♦ *vi*
  (*aspirer*) to breathe in; **s'~ de** (*suj: artiste*) to
  draw one's inspiration from

instable [ɛ̃stabl] *adj* unstable; (*meuble,
  équilibre*) unsteady; (*temps*) unsettled

installation [ɛ̃stalasjɔ̃] *nf* installation; **~s** *nfpl*
  facilities

installer [ɛ̃stale] *vt* (*loger, placer*) to put;
  (*meuble, gaz, électricité*) to put in; (*rideau,
  étagère, tente*) to put up; (*appartement*) to fit
  out; **s'~** (*s'établir: artisan, dentiste etc*) to set
  o.s. up; (*se loger*) to settle; (*emménager*) to
  settle in; (*sur un siège, à un emplacement*) to
  settle (down); (*fig: maladie, grève*) to take a
  firm hold

instance [ɛ̃stɑ̃s] *nf* (*ADMIN: autorité*) authority; **affaire en ~** matter pending; **être en ~ de divorce** to be awaiting a divorce

instant [ɛ̃stɑ̃] *nm* moment, instant; **dans un ~** in a moment; **à l'~** this instant; **pour l'~** for the moment, for the time being

instantané, e [ɛ̃stɑ̃tane] *adj* (*lait, café*) instant; (*explosion, mort*) instantaneous ♦ *nm* snapshot

instar [ɛ̃staʀ]: **à l'~ de** *prép* following the example of, like

instaurer [ɛ̃stɔʀe] *vt* to institute; (*couvre-feu*) to impose

instinct [ɛ̃stɛ̃] *nm* instinct; **instinctivement** *adv* instinctively

instit [ɛ̃stit] (*fam*) *nm/f* (primary school) teacher

instituer [ɛ̃stitɥe] *vt* to establish

institut [ɛ̃stity] *nm* institute; **~ de beauté** beauty salon; **Institut universitaire de technologie** ≈ polytechnic

instituteur, -trice [ɛ̃stitytœʀ, tʀis] *nm/f* (primary school) teacher

institution [ɛ̃stitysjɔ̃] *nf* institution; (*collège*) private school

instructif, -ive [ɛ̃stʀyktif, iv] *adj* instructive

instruction [ɛ̃stʀyksjɔ̃] *nf* (*enseignement, savoir*) education; (*JUR*) (preliminary) investigation and hearing; **~s** *nfpl* (*ordres, mode d'emploi*) instructions; **~ civique** civics *sg*

instruire [ɛ̃stʀɥiʀ] *vt* (*élèves*) to teach; (*recrues*) to train; (*JUR: affaire*) to conduct the investigation for; **s'~** to educate o.s.; **instruit, e** *adj* educated

instrument [ɛ̃stʀymɑ̃] *nm* instrument; **~ à cordes/vent** stringed/wind instrument; **~ de mesure** measuring instrument; **~ de musique** musical instrument; **~ de travail** (working) tool

insu [ɛ̃sy] *nm*: **à l'~ de qn** without sb knowing (it)

insubmersible [ɛ̃sybmɛʀsibl] *adj* unsinkable

insuffisant, e [ɛ̃syfizɑ̃, ɑ̃t] *adj* (*en quantité*) insufficient; (*en qualité*) inadequate; (*sur une copie*) poor

insulaire [ɛ̃sylɛʀ] *adj* island *cpd*; (*attitude*) insular

insuline [ɛ̃sylin] *nf* insulin

insulte [ɛ̃sylt] *nf* insult; **insulter** *vt* to insult

insupportable [ɛ̃sypɔʀtabl] *adj* unbearable

insurger [ɛ̃syʀʒe] *vb*: **s'~ (contre)** to rise up ou rebel (against)

insurmontable [ɛ̃syʀmɔ̃tabl] *adj* (*difficulté*) insuperable; (*aversion*) unconquerable

insurrection [ɛ̃syʀɛksjɔ̃] *nf* insurrection

intact, e [ɛ̃takt] *adj* intact

intangible [ɛ̃tɑ̃ʒibl] *adj* intangible; (*principe*) inviolable

intarissable [ɛ̃taʀisabl] *adj* inexhaustible

intégral, e, -aux [ɛ̃tegʀal, o] *adj* complete; **texte ~** unabridged version; **bronzage ~** all-over suntan; **intégralement** *adv* in full; **intégralité** *nf* whole; **dans son intégralité** in full; **intégrant, e** *adj*: **faire partie intégrante de** to be an integral part of

intègre [ɛ̃tegʀ] *adj* upright

intégrer [ɛ̃tegʀe] *vt*: **bien s'~** to integrate well

intégrisme [ɛ̃tegʀism] *nm* fundamentalism

intellectuel, le [ɛ̃telɛktɥel] *adj* intellectual ♦ *nm/f* intellectual; (*péj*) highbrow

intelligence [ɛ̃teliʒɑ̃s] *nf* intelligence; (*compréhension*): **l'~ de** the understanding of; (*complicité*): **regard d'~** glance of complicity; (*accord*): **vivre en bonne ~ avec qn** to be on good terms with sb

intelligent, e [ɛ̃teliʒɑ̃, ɑ̃t] *adj* intelligent

intelligible [ɛ̃teliʒibl] *adj* intelligible

intempéries [ɛ̃tɑ̃peʀi] *nfpl* bad weather *sg*

intempestif, -ive [ɛ̃tɑ̃pestif, iv] *adj* untimely

intenable [ɛ̃t(ə)nabl] *adj* (*chaleur*) unbearable

intendant, e [ɛ̃tɑ̃dɑ̃] *nm/f* (*MIL*) quartermaster; (*SCOL*) bursar

intense [ɛ̃tɑ̃s] *adj* intense; **intensif, -ive** [ɛ̃tɑ̃sif, iv] *adj* intensive; **un cours intensif** a crash course

intenter [ɛ̃tɑ̃te] *vt*: **~ un procès contre** ou **à** to start proceedings against

intention [ɛ̃tɑ̃sjɔ̃] *nf* intention; (*JUR*) intent; **avoir l'~ de faire** to intend to do; **à l'~ de** for: (*renseignement*) for the benefit of; (*film, ouvrage*) aimed at; **à cette ~** with this aim in view; **intentionné, e** *adj*: **bien intentionné** well-meaning ou -intentioned; **mal intentionné** ill-intentioned

interactif, -ive [ɛ̃teʀaktif, iv] *adj* (*COMPUT*) interactive

intercalaire [ɛ̃teʀkalɛʀ] *nm* divider

intercaler [ɛ̃teʀkale] *vt* to insert

intercepter [ɛ̃teʀsepte] *vt* to intercept; (*lumière, chaleur*) to cut off

interchangeable [ɛ̃teʀʃɑ̃ʒabl] *adj* interchangeable

interclasse [ɛ̃teʀklas] *nm* (*SCOL*) break (between classes)

interdiction [ɛ̃teʀdiksjɔ̃] *nf* ban; **~ de stationner** no parking; **~ de fumer** no smoking

interdire [ɛ̃teʀdiʀ] *vt* to forbid; (*ADMIN*) to ban, prohibit; (: *journal, livre*) to ban; **~ à qn de faire** to forbid sb to do; (*suj: empêchement*) to prevent sb from doing

interdit, e [ɛ̃teʀdi, it] *adj* (*stupéfait*) taken aback

intéressant, e [ɛ̃teʀesɑ̃, ɑ̃t] *adj* interesting; (*avantageux*) attractive

intéressé, e [ɛ̃teʀese] *adj* (*parties*) involved, concerned; (*amitié, motifs*) self-interested

intéresser [ɛ̃teʀese] vt (captiver) to interest; (toucher) to be of interest to; (ADMIN: concerner) to affect, concern; **s'~ à** to be interested in

intérêt [ɛ̃teʀɛ] nm interest; (égoïsme) self-interest; (à accepter) it's in your interest to accept; **tu as ~ à te dépêcher** you'd better hurry

intérieur, e [ɛ̃teʀjœʀ] adj (mur, escalier, poche) inside; (commerce, politique) domestic; (cour, calme, vie) inner; (navigation) inland ♦ nm (d'une maison, d'un récipient etc) inside; (d'un pays, aussi décor, mobilier) interior; **à l'~ (de)** inside; **intérieurement** adv inwardly

intérim [ɛ̃teʀim] nm interim period; **faire de l'~** to temp; **assurer l'~ (de)** to deputize (for); **par ~** interim

intérimaire [ɛ̃teʀimɛʀ] adj (directeur, ministre) acting; (secrétaire, personnel) temporary ♦ nm/f (secrétaire) temporary secretary, temp (BRIT)

interlocuteur, -trice [ɛ̃teʀlɔkytœʀ, tʀis] nm/f speaker; **son ~** the person he was speaking to

interloquer [ɛ̃teʀlɔke] vt to take aback

intermède [ɛ̃teʀmɛd] nm interlude

intermédiaire [ɛ̃teʀmedjɛʀ] adj intermediate; (solution) temporary ♦ nm/f intermediary; (COMM) middleman; **sans ~** directly; **par l'~ de** through

interminable [ɛ̃teʀminabl] adj endless

intermittence [ɛ̃teʀmitɑ̃s] nf: **par ~** sporadically, intermittently

internat [ɛ̃teʀna] nm (SCOL) boarding school

international, e, -aux [ɛ̃teʀnasjɔnal, o] adj, nm/f international

interne [ɛ̃teʀn] adj internal ♦ nm/f (SCOL) boarder; (MÉD) houseman

interner [ɛ̃teʀne] vt (POL) to intern; (MÉD) to confine to a mental institution

Internet [ɛ̃teʀnɛt] nm Internet

interpeller [ɛ̃teʀpəle] vt (appeler) to call out to; (apostropher) to shout at; (POLICE, POL) to question; (concerner) to concern

interphone [ɛ̃teʀfɔn] nm intercom; (d'immeuble) entry phone

interposer [ɛ̃teʀpoze] vt: **s'~** to intervene; **par personnes interposées** through a third party

interprétation [ɛ̃teʀpʀetasjɔ̃] nf interpretation

interprète [ɛ̃teʀpʀɛt] nm/f interpreter; (porte-parole) spokesperson

interpréter [ɛ̃teʀpʀete] vt to interpret; (jouer) to play; (chanter) to sing

interrogateur, -trice [ɛ̃teʀɔgatœʀ, tʀis] adj questioning, inquiring

interrogatif, -ive [ɛ̃teʀɔgatif, iv] adj (LING) interrogative

interrogation [ɛ̃teʀɔgasjɔ̃] nf question; (action) questioning; (SCOL) (written ou oral) test

interrogatoire [ɛ̃teʀɔgatwaʀ] nm (POLICE) questioning no pl; (JUR, aussi fig) cross-examination

interroger [ɛ̃teʀɔʒe] vt to question; (INFORM) to consult; (SCOL) to test

interrompre [ɛ̃teʀɔ̃pʀ] vt (gén) to interrupt; (négociations) to break off; (match) to stop; **s'~** to break off; **interrupteur** nm switch; **interruption** nf interruption; (pause) break; **sans interruption** without stopping

intersection [ɛ̃teʀsɛksjɔ̃] nf intersection

interstice [ɛ̃teʀstis] nm crack; (de volet) slit

interurbain, e [ɛ̃teʀyʀbɛ̃, ɛn] adj (TÉL) long-distance

intervalle [ɛ̃teʀval] nm (espace) space; (de temps) interval; **à deux jours d'~** two days apart

intervenir [ɛ̃teʀvəniʀ] vi (gén) to intervene; **~ auprès de qn** to intervene with sb

intervention [ɛ̃teʀvɑ̃sjɔ̃] nf intervention; (discours) speech; **intervention chirurgicale** (surgical) operation

intervertir [ɛ̃teʀvɛʀtiʀ] vt to invert (the order of), reverse

interview [ɛ̃teʀvju] nf interview

intestin [ɛ̃tɛstɛ̃, in] nm intestine

intime [ɛ̃tim] adj intimate; (vie) private; (conviction) inmost; (dîner, cérémonie) quiet ♦ nm/f close friend; **un journal ~** a diary

intimider [ɛ̃timide] vt to intimidate

intimité [ɛ̃timite] nf: **dans l'~** in private; (sans formalités) with only a few friends, quietly

intitulé, e [ɛ̃tityle] adj entitled

intolérable [ɛ̃tɔleʀabl] adj intolerable

intox [ɛ̃tɔks] (fam) nf brainwashing

intoxication [ɛ̃tɔksikasjɔ̃] nf: **~ alimentaire** food poisoning

intoxiquer [ɛ̃tɔksike] vt to poison; (fig) to brainwash

intraduisible [ɛ̃tʀadɥizibl] adj untranslatable; (fig) inexpressible

intraitable [ɛ̃tʀɛtabl] adj inflexible, uncompromising

intransigeant, e [ɛ̃tʀɑ̃ziʒɑ̃, ɑ̃t] adj intransigent

intransitif, -ive [ɛ̃tʀɑ̃zitif, iv] adj (LING) intransitive

intrépide [ɛ̃tʀepid] adj dauntless

intrigue [ɛ̃tʀig] nf (scénario) plot; **intriguer** vt to puzzle, intrigue

intrinsèque [ɛ̃tʀɛ̃sɛk] adj intrinsic

introduction [ɛ̃tʀɔdyksjɔ̃] nf introduction

introduire [ɛ̃tʀɔdɥiʀ] vt to introduce; (visiteur) to show in; (aiguille, clef): **~ qch dans** to insert ou introduce sth into; **s'~ (dans)** to get in(to); (dans un groupe) to get o.s. accepted (into)

introuvable [ɛ̃tʀuvabl] *adj* which cannot be found; (COMM) unobtainable

introverti, e [ɛ̃tʀɔvɛʀti] *nm/f* introvert

intrus, e [ɛ̃tʀy, yz] *nm/f* intruder

intrusion [ɛ̃tʀyzjɔ̃] *nf* intrusion

intuition [ɛ̃tɥisjɔ̃] *nf* intuition

inusable [inyzabl] *adj* hard-wearing

inusité, e [inyzite] *adj* rarely used

inutile [inytil] *adj* useless; (superflu) unnecessary; **inutilement** *adv* unnecessarily; **inutilisable** *adj* unusable

invalide [ɛ̃valid] *adj* disabled ♦ *nm*: ~ **de guerre** disabled ex-serviceman

invariable [ɛ̃vaʀjabl] *adj* invariable

invasion [ɛ̃vazjɔ̃] *nf* invasion

invectiver [ɛ̃vɛktive] *vt* to hurl abuse at

invendable [ɛ̃vɑ̃dabl] *adj* unsaleable; (COMM) unmarketable; **invendus** *nmpl* unsold goods

inventaire [ɛ̃vɑ̃tɛʀ] *nm* inventory; (COMM: liste) stocklist; (: opération) stocktaking *no pl*

inventer [ɛ̃vɑ̃te] *vt* to invent; (subterfuge) to devise, invent; (histoire, excuse) to make up, invent; **inventeur** *nm* inventor; **inventif, -ive** *adj* inventive; **invention** *nf* invention

inverse [ɛ̃vɛʀs] *adj* opposite ♦ *nm* opposite; **dans l'ordre ~** in the reverse order; **en sens ~** in (ou from) the opposite direction; **dans le sens ~ des aiguilles d'une montre** anticlockwise; **tu t'es trompé, c'est l'~** you've got it wrong, it's the other way round; **inversement** *adv* conversely; **inverser** *vt* to invert, reverse; (ÉLEC) to reverse

investigation [ɛ̃vɛstigasjɔ̃] *nf* investigation

investir [ɛ̃vɛstiʀ] *vt* to invest; **investissement** *nm* investment; **investiture** *nf* nomination

invétéré, e [ɛ̃vetere] *adj* inveterate

invisible [ɛ̃vizibl] *adj* invisible

invitation [ɛ̃vitasjɔ̃] *nf* invitation

invité, e [ɛ̃vite] *nm/f* guest

inviter [ɛ̃vite] *vt* to invite

invivable [ɛ̃vivabl] *adj* unbearable

involontaire [ɛ̃vɔlɔ̃tɛʀ] *adj* (mouvement) involuntary; (insulte) unintentional; (complice) unwitting

invoquer [ɛ̃vɔke] *vt* (Dieu, muse) to call upon, invoke; (prétexte) to put forward (as an excuse); (loi, texte) to refer to

invraisemblable [ɛ̃vʀɛsɑ̃blabl] *adj* (fait, nouvelle) unlikely, improbable; (insolence, habit) incredible

iode [jɔd] *nm* iodine

irai *etc* [iʀe] *vb voir* **aller**

Irak [iʀak] *nm* Iraq; **irakien, ne** *adj* Iraqi ♦ *nm/f*: **Irakien, ne** Iraqi

Iran [iʀɑ̃] *nm* Iran; **iranien, ne** *adj* Iranian ♦ *nm/f*: **Iranien, ne** Iranian

irascible [iʀasibl] *adj* short-tempered

irions *etc* [iʀjɔ̃] *vb voir* **aller**

iris [iʀis] *nm* iris

irlandais, e [iʀlɑ̃dɛ, ɛz] *adj* Irish ♦ *nm/f*: **Irlandais, e** Irishman(-woman); **les Irlandais** the Irish

Irlande [iʀlɑ̃d] *nf* Ireland; **~ du Nord** Northern Ireland; **la République d'~** the Irish Republic

ironie [iʀɔni] *nf* irony; **ironique** *adj* ironical; **ironiser** *vi* to be ironical

irons *etc* [iʀɔ̃] *vb voir* **aller**

irradier [iʀadje] *vt* to irradiate

irraisonné, e [iʀɛzɔne] *adj* irrational

irrationnel, le [iʀasjɔnɛl] *adj* irrational

irréalisable [iʀealizabl] *adj* unrealizable; (projet) impracticable

irrécupérable [iʀekypeʀabl] *adj* beyond repair; (personne) beyond redemption

irréductible [iʀedyktibl] *adj* (volonté) indomitable; (ennemi) implacable

irréel, le [iʀeɛl] *adj* unreal

irréfléchi, e [iʀefleʃi] *adj* thoughtless

irrégularité [iʀegylaʀite] *nf* irregularity; (de travail, d'effort, de qualité) unevenness *no pl*

irrégulier, -ière [iʀegylje, jɛʀ] *adj* irregular; (travail, effort, qualité) uneven; (élève, athlète) erratic

irrémédiable [iʀemedjabl] *adj* irreparable

irremplaçable [iʀɑ̃plasabl] *adj* irreplaceable

irréparable [iʀepaʀabl] *adj* (objet) beyond repair; (dommage etc) irreparable

irréprochable [iʀepʀɔʃabl] *adj* irreproachable, beyond reproach; (tenue) impeccable

irrésistible [iʀezistibl] *adj* irresistible; (besoin, désir, preuve, logique) compelling; (amusant) hilarious

irrésolu, e [iʀezɔly] *adj* (personne) irresolute; (problème) unresolved

irrespectueux, -euse [iʀɛspɛktɥø, øz] *adj* disrespectful

irrespirable [iʀɛspiʀabl] *adj* unbreathable; (fig) oppressive

irresponsable [iʀɛspɔ̃sabl] *adj* irresponsible

irriguer [iʀige] *vt* to irrigate

irritable [iʀitabl] *adj* irritable

irriter [iʀite] *vt* to irritate

irruption [iʀypsjɔ̃] *nf*: **faire ~ (chez qn)** to burst in (on sb)

Islam [islam] *nm* Islam; **islamique** *adj* Islamic; **islamiste** *adj* (militant) Islamic; (mouvement) Islamic fundamentalist ♦ *nm/f* Islamic fundamentalist

Islande [islɑ̃d] *nf* Iceland

isolant, e [izɔlɑ̃, ɑ̃t] *adj* insulating; (insonorisant) soundproofing

isolation [izɔlasjɔ̃] *nf* insulation

isolé, e [izɔle] *adj* isolated; (contre le froid) insulated

isoler [izɔle] vt to isolate; (prisonnier) to put in solitary confinement; (ville) to cut off, isolate; (contre le froid) to insulate; **s'~** vi to isolate o.s.; **isoloir** [izɔlwaʀ] nm polling booth

Israël [israɛl] nm Israel; **israélien, ne** adj Israeli ♦ nm/f: **Israélien, ne** Israeli; **israélite** adj Jewish ♦ nm/f: **Israélite** Jew (Jewess)

issu, e [isy] adj: **~ de** (né de) descended from; (résultant de) stemming from; **issue** nf (ouverture, sortie) exit; (solution) way out, solution; (dénouement) outcome; **à l'issue de** at the conclusion ou close of; **voie sans issue** dead end; **issue de secours** emergency exit

Italie [itali] nf Italy; **italien, ne** adj Italian ♦ nm/f: **Italien, ne** Italian ♦ nm (LING) Italian

italique [italik] nm: **en ~** in italics

itinéraire [itineʀɛʀ] nm itinerary, route; **~ bis** diversion

IUT sigle m = **Institut universitaire de technologie**

IVG sigle f (= interruption volontaire de grossesse) abortion

ivoire [ivwaʀ] nm ivory

ivre [ivʀ] adj drunk, **~ de** (colère, bonheur) wild with; **ivresse** nf drunkenness; **ivrogne** nm/f drunkard

J, j

j' [ʒ] pron voir **je**

jacasser [ʒakase] vi to chatter

jacinthe [ʒasɛ̃t] nf hyacinth

jadis [ʒadis] adv long ago

jaillir [ʒajiʀ] vi (liquide) to spurt out, (cris, responses) to burst forth

jais [ʒɛ] nm jet; (d'un noir) de **~** jet-black

jalousie [ʒaluzi] nf jealousy; (store) slatted blind

jaloux, -ouse [ʒalu, uz] adj jealous

jamais [ʒamɛ] adv never; (sans négation) ever; **ne ... ~** never; **à ~** for ever

jambe [ʒɑ̃b] nf leg

jambon [ʒɑ̃bɔ̃] nm ham; **~ blanc** boiled ou cooked ham; **jambonneau, x** nm knuckle of ham

jante [ʒɑ̃t] nf (wheel) rim

janvier [ʒɑ̃vje] nm January

Japon [ʒapɔ̃] nm Japan; **japonais, e** adj Japanese ♦ nm/f: **Japonais, e** Japanese ♦ nm (LING) Japanese

japper [ʒape] vi to yap, yelp

jaquette [ʒakɛt] nf (de cérémonie) morning coat

jardin [ʒaʀdɛ̃] nm garden; **~ d'enfants** nursery school; **jardinage** nm gardening; **jardiner** vi to do some gardening; **jardinier, -ière** nm/f gardener; **jardinière** nf planter; (de fenêtre) window box; **jardinière de légumes** mixed vegetables

jargon [ʒaʀgɔ̃] nm (baragouin) gibberish; (langue professionnelle) jargon

jarret [ʒaʀɛ] nm back of knee; (CULIN) knuckle, shin

jarretelle [ʒaʀtɛl] nf suspender (BRIT), garter (US)

jarretière [ʒaʀtjɛʀ] nf garter

jaser [ʒaze] vi (médire) to gossip

jatte [ʒat] nf basin, bowl

jauge [ʒoʒ] nf (instrument) gauge; **~ d'essence** petrol gauge; **~ d'huile** (oil) dipstick

jaune [ʒon] adj, nm yellow ♦ adv (fam): **rire ~** to laugh on the other side of one's face; **~ d'œuf** (egg) yolk; **jaunir** vi, vt to turn yellow; **jaunisse** nf jaundice

Javel [ʒavɛl] nf voir **eau**

javelot [ʒavlo] nm javelin

J.-C. abr = **Jésus-Christ**

je, j' [ʒə] pron I

jean [dʒin] nm jeans pl

Jésus-Christ [ʒezykri(st)] n Jesus Christ; **600 avant/après ~-~** ou J.-C. 600 B.C./A.D.

jet¹ [ʒɛ] nm (lancer: action) throwing no pl; (: résultat) throw; (jaillissement: d'eaux) jet; (: de sang) spurt; **~ d'eau** spray

jet² [dʒɛt] nm (avion) jet

jetable [ʒ(ə)tabl] adj disposable

jetée [ʒ(ə)te] nf jetty; (grande) pier

jeter [ʒ(ə)te] vt (gén) to throw; (se défaire de) to throw away ou out; **se ~ dans** (fleuve) to flow into; **~ qch à qn** to throw sth to sb; (de façon agressive) to throw sth at sb; **~ un coup d'œil (à)** to take a look (at); **~ un sort à qn** to cast a spell on sb; **se ~ sur qn** to rush at sb

jeton [ʒ(ə)tɔ̃] nm (au jeu) counter; (de téléphone) token

jette etc [ʒɛt] vb voir **jeter**

jeu, x [ʒø] nm (divertissement, TECH: d'une pièce) play; (TENNIS: partie, FOOTBALL etc: façon de jouer) game; (THÉÂTRE etc) acting; (série d'objets, jouet) set; (CARTES) hand; (au casino): **le ~** gambling; **être en ~** to be at stake; **entrer/mettre en ~** to come/bring into play; **~ de cartes** pack of cards; **~ d'échecs** chess set; **~ de hasard** game of chance; **~ de mots** pun; **~ de société** parlour game; **~ télévisé** television quiz; **~ vidéo** video game

jeudi [ʒødi] nm Thursday

jeun [ʒœ̃]: **à ~** adv on an empty stomach; **être à ~** to have eaten nothing; **rester à ~** not to eat anything

jeune [ʒœn] adj young; **les ~s** young people; **~ fille** girl; **~ homme** young man; **~s mariés** newly-weds

jeûne [ʒøn] nm fast

jeunesse [ʒœnɛs] nf youth; (aspect)

youthfulness

joaillerie [ʒɔajʀi] nf jewellery; (*magasin*) jeweller's; **joaillier, -ière** nm/f jeweller

jogging [dʒɔgin] nm jogging; (*survêtement*) tracksuit; **faire du ~** to go jogging

joie [ʒwa] nf joy

joindre [ʒwɛ̃dʀ] vt to join; (*à une lettre*): **~ qch à** to enclose sth with; (*contacter*) to contact, get in touch with; **se ~ à** to join; **~ les mains** to put one's hands together

joint, e [ʒwɛ̃, ɛ̃t] adj: **pièce ~e** enclosure ♦ nm joint; (*ligne*) join; **~ de culasse** cylinder head gasket; **~ de robinet** washer

joli, e [ʒɔli] adj pretty, attractive; **c'est du ~!** (*ironique*) that's very nice!; **c'est bien ~, mais ...** that's all very well but ...

jonc [ʒɔ̃] nm (bul)rush

jonction [ʒɔ̃ksjɔ̃] nf junction

jongleur, -euse [ʒɔ̃glœʀ, øz] nm/f juggler

jonquille [ʒɔ̃kij] nf daffodil

Jordanie [ʒɔʀdani] nf: **la ~** Jordan

joue [ʒu] nf cheek

jouer [ʒwe] vt to play; (*somme d'argent, réputation*) to stake, wager; (*simuler: sentiment*) to affect, feign ♦ vi to play; (*THÉÂTRE, CINÉMA*) to act; (*au casino*) to gamble; (*bois, porte: se voiler*) to warp; (*clef, pièce: avoir du jeu*) to be loose; **~ sur** (*miser*) to gamble on; **~ de** (*MUS*) to play; **~ à** (*jeu, sport, roulette*) to play; **~ un tour à qn** to play a trick on sb; **~ serré** to play a close game; **~ la comédie** to put on an act; **bien joué!** well done!; **on joue Hamlet au théâtre X** Hamlet is on at the X theatre

jouet [ʒwɛ] nm toy; **être le ~ de** (*illusion etc*) to be the victim of

joueur, -euse [ʒwœʀ, øz] nm/f player; **être beau ~** to be a good loser

joufflu, e [ʒufly] adj chubby-cheeked

joug [ʒu] nm yoke

jouir [ʒwiʀ] vi (*sexe: fam*) to come ♦ vt: **~ de** to enjoy; **jouissance** nf pleasure; (*JUR*) use

joujou [ʒuʒu] (*fam*) nm toy

jour [ʒuʀ] nm day; (*opposé à la nuit*) day, daytime; (*clarté*) daylight; (*fig: aspect*) light; (*ouverture*) gap; **au ~ le ~** from day to day; **de nos ~s** these days; **du ~ au lendemain** overnight; **il fait ~** it's daylight; **au grand ~** (*fig*) in the open; **mettre au ~** to disclose; **mettre à ~** to update; **donner le ~ à** to give birth to; **voir le ~** to be born; **~ férié** public holiday; **~ de fête** holiday; **~ ouvrable** week-day, working day

journal, -aux [ʒuʀnal, o] nm (news)paper; (*spécialisé*) journal; (*intime*) diary; **~ de bord** log; **~ télévisé** television news sg

journalier, -ière [ʒuʀnalje, jɛʀ] adj daily; (*banal*) everyday

journalisme [ʒuʀnalism] nm journalism;

journaliste nm/f journalist

journée [ʒuʀne] nf day; **faire la ~ continue** to work over lunch

journellement [ʒuʀnɛlmã] adv daily

joyau, x [ʒwajo] nm gem, jewel

joyeux, -euse [ʒwajø, øz] adj joyful, merry; **~ Noël!** merry Christmas!; **~ anniversaire!** happy birthday!

jubiler [ʒybile] vi to be jubilant, exult

jucher [ʒyʃe] vt, vi to perch

judas [ʒyda] nm (*trou*) spy-hole

judiciaire [ʒydisjɛʀ] adj judicial

judicieux, -euse [ʒydisjø, jøz] adj judicious

judo [ʒydo] nm judo

juge [ʒyʒ] nm judge; **~ d'instruction** examining (*BRIT*) ou committing (*US*) magistrate; **~ de paix** justice of the peace; **~ de touche** linesman

jugé [ʒyʒe]: **au ~** adv by guesswork

jugement [ʒyʒmã] nm judgment; (*JUR: au pénal*) sentence; (: *au civil*) decision

jugeote [ʒyʒɔt] (*fam*) nf commonsense

juger [ʒyʒe] vt to judge; (*estimer*) to consider; **~ qn/qch satisfaisant** to consider sb/sth (to be) satisfactory; **~ bon de faire** to see fit to do; **~ de** to appreciate

juif, -ive [ʒɥif, ʒɥiv] adj Jewish ♦ nm/f: **J~, ive** Jew (Jewess)

juillet [ʒɥijɛ] nm July

juin [ʒɥɛ̃] nm June

jumeau, -elle, x [ʒymo, ɛl] adj, nm/f twin

jumeler [ʒym(ə)le] vt to twin

jumelle [ʒymɛl] adj, nf voir **jumeau**; **~s** nfpl (*appareil*) binoculars

jument [ʒymã] nf mare

jungle [ʒœ̃gl] nf jungle

jupe [ʒyp] nf skirt

jupon [ʒypɔ̃] nm waist slip

juré, e [ʒyʀe] nm/f juror

jurer [ʒyʀe] vt (*obéissance etc*) to swear, vow ♦ vi (*dire des jurons*) to swear, curse; (*dissoner*): **~ (avec)** to clash (with); **~ de faire/que** to swear to do/that; **~ de qch** (*s'en porter garant*) to swear to sth

juridique [ʒyʀidik] adj legal

juron [ʒyʀɔ̃] nm curse, swearword

jury [ʒyʀi] nm jury; (*ART, SPORT*) panel of judges; (*SCOL*) board of examiners

jus [ʒy] nm juice; (*de viande*) gravy, (meat) juice; **~ de fruit** fruit juice

jusque [ʒysk]: **jusqu'à** prép (*endroit*) as far as, (up) to; (*moment*) until, till; (*limite*) up to; **~ sur/dans** up to; (*y compris*) even on/in; **jusqu'à ce que** until; **jusqu'à présent** so far; **jusqu'où?** how far?

justaucorps [ʒystokɔʀ] nm leotard

juste [ʒyst] adj (*équitable*) just, fair; (*légitime*) just; (*exact*) right; (*pertinent*) apt; (*étroit*) tight; (*insuffisant*) on the short side ♦ adv

rightly, correctly; (*chanter*) in tune;
(*exactement, seulement*) just; **~ assez/au-
dessus** just enough/above; **au ~** exactly; **le
~ milieu** the happy medium; **c'était ~** it was a
close thing; **justement** *adv* justly;
(*précisément*) just, precisely; **justesse** *nf*
(*précision*) accuracy; (*d'une remarque*)
aptness; (*d'une opinion*) soundness; **de
justesse** only just
justice [ʒystis] *nf* (*équité*) fairness, justice;
(ADMIN) justice; **rendre ~ à qn** to do sb
justice; **justicier, -ière** *nm/f* righter of
wrongs
justificatif, -ive [ʒystifikatif, iv] *adj*
(*document*) supporting; **pièce justificative**
written proof
justifier [ʒystifje] *vt* to justify; **~ de** to prove
juteux, -euse [ʒytø, øz] *adj* juicy
juvénile [ʒyvenil] *adj* youthful

K, k

K [ka] *nm* (INFORM) K
kaki [kaki] *adj inv* khaki
kangourou [kãguʀu] *nm* kangaroo
karaté [kaʀate] *nm* karate
karting [kaʀtiŋ] *nm* go-carting, karting
kascher [kaʃɛʀ] *adj* kosher
kayak [kajak] *nm* canoe, kayak; **faire du ~** to
go canoeing
képi [kepi] *nm* kepi
kermesse [kɛʀmɛs] *nf* fair; (*fête de charité*)
bazaar, (charity) fête
kidnapper [kidnape] *vt* to kidnap
kilo [kilo] *nm* = **kilogramme**
kilo...: kilogramme *nm* kilogramme;
kilométrage *nm* number of kilometres
travelled, ≈ mileage; **kilomètre** *nm*
kilometre; **kilométrique** *adj* (*distance*) in
kilometres
kinésithérapeute [kineziteʀapøt] *nm/f*
physiotherapist
kiosque [kjɔsk] *nm* kiosk, stall; **~ à musique**
bandstand
kir [kiʀ] *nm* kir (*white wine with blackcurrant
liqueur*)
kit [kit] *nm*: **en ~** in kit form
kiwi [kiwi] *nm* kiwi
klaxon [klaksɔn] *nm* horn; **klaxonner** *vi, vt*
to hoot (BRIT), honk (US)
km *abr* = **kilomètre**
km/h *abr* (= *kilomètres/heure*) ≈ mph
K.-O. (*fam*) *adj inv* shattered, knackered
k-way ® [kawe] *nm* (lightweight nylon)
cagoule
kyste [kist] *nm* cyst

L, l

l' [l] *art déf voir* **le**
la [la] *art déf voir* **le** ♦ *nm* (MUS) A; (*en
chantant la gamme*) la
là [la] *adv* there; (*ici*) here; (*dans le temps*)
then; **elle n'est pas ~** she isn't here; **c'est
~ que** this is where; **~ où** where; **de ~** (*fig*)
hence; **par ~** (*fig*) by that; *voir aussi* **-ci**; **ce**;
celui; **là-bas** *adv* there
label [label] *nm* stamp, seal
labeur [labœʀ] *nm* toil *no pl*, toiling *no pl*
labo [labo] (*fam*) *nm* (= *laboratoire*) lab
laboratoire [labɔʀatwaʀ] *nm* laboratory;
~ de langues language laboratory
laborieux, -euse [labɔʀjø, jøz] *adj* (*tâche*)
laborious
labour [labuʀ] *nm* ploughing *no pl*; **~s** *nmpl*
(*champs*) ploughed fields; **cheval de ~**
plough- *ou* cart-horse, **labourer** *vt* to plough
labyrinthe [labiʀɛt] *nm* labyrinth, maze
lac [lak] *nm* lake
lacer [lase] *vt* to lace *ou* do up
lacérer [laseʀe] *vt* to tear to shreds
lacet [lasɛ] *nm* (*de chaussure*) lace; (*de route*)
sharp bend; (*piège*) snare
lâche [lɑʃ] *adj* (*poltron*) cowardly; (*desserré*)
loose, slack ♦ *nm/f* coward
lâcher [lɑʃe] *vt* to let go of; (*ce qui tombe,
abandonner*) to drop; (*oiseau, animal: libérer*)
to release, set free; (*fig: mot, remarque*) to let
slip, come out with ♦ *vi* (*freins*) to fail; **~ les
amarres** (NAVIG) to cast off (the moorings);
~ prise to let go
lâcheté [lɑʃte] *nf* cowardice
lacrymogène [lakʀimɔʒɛn] *adj*: **gaz ~**
teargas
lacté, e [lakte] *adj* (*produit, régime*) milk *cpd*
lacune [lakyn] *nf* gap
là-dedans [ladadã] *adv* inside (there), in it;
(*fig*) in that
là-dessous [ladsu] *adv* underneath, under
there; (*fig*) behind that
là-dessus [ladsy] *adv* on there; (*fig: sur ces
mots*) at that point; (: *à ce sujet*) about that
ladite [ladit] *dét voir* **ledit**
lagune [lagyn] *nf* lagoon
là-haut [lao] *adv* up there
laïc [laik] *adj, nm/f* = **laïque**
laid, e [lɛ, lɛd] *adj* ugly; **laideur** *nf* ugliness
no pl
lainage [lɛnaʒ] *nm* (*vêtement*) woollen
garment; (*étoffe*) woollen material
laine [lɛn] *nf* wool
laïque [laik] *adj* lay, civil; (SCOL) state *cpd*
♦ *nm/f* layman(-woman)
laisse [lɛs] *nf* (*de chien*) lead, leash; **tenir en ~**

to keep on a lead *ou* leash

laisser [lese] *vt* to leave ♦ *vb aux*: ~ qn faire to let sb do; **se ~ aller** to let o.s. go; **laisse-toi faire** let me (*ou* him *etc*) do it; **laisser-aller** *nm* carelessness, slovenliness; **laissez-passer** *nm inv* pass

lait [lɛ] *nm* milk; **frère/sœur de ~** foster brother/sister; **~ condensé/concentré** evaporated/condensed milk; **~ démaquillant** cleansing milk; **laitage** *nm* dairy product; **laiterie** [lɛtRi] *nf* dairy; **laitier, -ière** *adj* dairy *cpd* ♦ *nm/f* milkman (dairywoman)

laiton [lɛtɔ̃] *nm* brass

laitue [lety] *nf* lettuce

laïus [lajys] (*péj*) *nm* spiel

lambeau, x [lãbo] *nm* scrap; **en ~x** in tatters, tattered

lambris [lãbRi] *nm* panelling *no pl*

lame [lam] *nf* blade; (*vague*) wave; (*lamelle*) strip; **~ de fond** ground swell *no pl*; **~ de rasoir** razor blade; **lamelle** *nf* thin strip *ou* blade

lamentable [lamãtabl] *adj* appalling

lamenter [lamãte] *vb*: **se ~ (sur)** to moan (over)

lampadaire [lãpadɛR] *nm* (*de salon*) standard lamp; (*dans la rue*) street lamp

lampe [lãp] *nf* lamp; (*TECH*) valve; **~ à souder** blowlamp; **~ de chevet** bedside lamp; **~ de poche** torch (*BRIT*), flashlight (*US*)

lampion [lãpjɔ̃] *nm* Chinese lantern

lance [lãs] *nf* spear; **~ d'incendie** fire hose

lancée [lãse] *nf*: **être/continuer sur sa ~** to be under way/keep going

lancement [lãsmã] *nm* launching

lance-pierres [lãspjɛR] *nm inv* catapult

lancer [lãse] *nm* (*SPORT*) throwing *no pl*, throw ♦ *vt* to throw; (*émettre, projeter*) to throw out, send out; (*produit, fusée, bateau, artiste*) to launch; (*injure*) to hurl, fling; **se ~** *vi* (*prendre de l'élan*) to build up speed; (*se précipiter*): **se ~ sur** *ou* **contre** to rush at; **se ~ dans** (*discussion*) to launch into; (*aventure*) to embark on; **~ qch à qn** to throw sth to sb; (*de façon agressive*) to throw sth at sb; **~ du poids** putting the shot

lancinant, e [lãsinã, ãt] *adj* (*douleur*) shooting

landau [lãdo] *nm* pram (*BRIT*), baby carriage (*US*)

lande [lãd] *nf* moor

langage [lãgaʒ] *nm* language

langouste [lãgust] *nf* crayfish *inv*; **langoustine** *nf* Dublin Bay prawn

langue [lãg] *nf* (*ANAT, CULIN*) tongue; (*LING*) language; **tirer la ~ (à)** to stick out one's tongue (at); **de ~ française** French-speaking; **~ maternelle** native language, mother tongue; **~ vivante/étrangère** modern/foreign language

langueur [lãgœR] *nf* languidness

languir [lãgiR] *vi* to languish; (*conversation*) to flag; **faire ~ qn** to keep sb waiting

lanière [lanjɛR] *nf* (*de fouet*) lash; (*de sac, bretelle*) strap

lanterne [lãtɛRn] *nf* (*portable*) lantern; (*électrique*) light, lamp; (*de voiture*) (side)light

laper [lape] *vt* to lap up

lapidaire [lapidɛR] *adj* (*fig*) terse

lapin [lapɛ̃] *nm* rabbit; (*peau*) rabbitskin; (*fourrure*) cony; **poser un ~ à qn** (*fam*) to stand sb up

Laponie [laponi] *nf* Lapland

laps [laps] *nm*: **~ de temps** space of time, time *no pl*

laque [lak] *nf* (*vernis*) lacquer; (*pour cheveux*) hair spray

laquelle [lakɛl] *pron voir* **lequel**

larcin [laRsɛ̃] *nm* theft

lard [laR] *nm* (*bacon*) (streaky) bacon; (*graisse*) fat

lardon [laRdɔ̃] *nm*: **~s** chopped bacon

large [laRʒ] *adj* wide, broad; (*fig*) generous ♦ *adv*: **calculer/voir ~** to allow extra/think big ♦ *nm* (*largeur*): **5 m de ~** 5 m wide *ou* in width; (*mer*): **le ~** the open sea; **au ~ de** off; **~ d'esprit** broad-minded; **largement** *adv* widely; (*de loin*) greatly; (*au moins*) easily; (*généreusement*) generously; **c'est largement suffisant** that's ample; **largesse** *nf* generosity; **largesses** *nfpl* (*dons*) liberalities; **largeur** *nf* (*qu'on mesure*) width; (*impression visuelle*) wideness, width; (*d'esprit*) broadness

larguer [laRge] *vt* to drop; **~ les amarres** to cast off (the moorings)

larme [laRm] *nf* tear; (*fam: goutte*) drop; **en ~s** in tears; **larmoyer** *vi* (*yeux*) to water; (*se plaindre*) to whimper

larvé, e [laRve] *adj* (*fig*) latent

laryngite [laRɛ̃ʒit] *nf* laryngitis

las, lasse [lɑ, lɑs] *adj* weary

laser [lazɛR] *nm*: **(rayon) ~** laser (beam); **chaîne ~** compact disc (player); **disque ~** compact disc

lasse [lɑs] *adj voir* **las**

lasser [lɑse] *vt* to weary, tire; **se ~ de** *vt* to grow weary *ou* tired of

latéral, e, -aux [lateRal, o] *adj* side *cpd*, lateral

latin, e [latɛ̃, in] *adj* Latin ♦ *nm/f*: **L~, e** Latin ♦ *nm* (*LING*) Latin

latitude [latityd] *nf* latitude

latte [lat] *nf* lath, slat; (*de plancher*) board

lauréat, e [lɔRea, at] *nm/f* winner

laurier [lɔRje] *nm* (*BOT*) laurel; (*CULIN*) bay leaves *pl*

lavable [lavabl] *adj* washable

lavabo [lavabo] nm washbasin; **~s** nmpl
(*toilettes*) toilet sg
lavage [lavaʒ] nm washing no pl, wash; **~ de
cerveau** brainwashing no pl
lavande [lavãd] nf lavender
lave [lav] nf lava no pl
lave-linge [lavliʒ] nm inv washing machine
laver [lave] vt to wash; (*tache*) to wash off; **se
~** vi to have a wash, wash; **se ~ les mains/
dents** to wash one's hands/clean one's teeth;
~ qn de (*accusation*) to clear sb of; **laverie**
nf: **laverie (automatique)** launderette;
lavette nf dish cloth; (*fam*) drip; **laveur,
-euse** nm/f cleaner; **lave-vaisselle** nm inv
dishwasher; **lavoir** nm wash house; (*évier*)
sink
laxatif, -ive [laksatif, iv] adj, nm laxative
layette [lɛjɛt] nf baby clothes

MOT-CLÉ
---

le [lə], **la, l'** (*pl* les) art déf **1** the; **le livre/la
pomme/l'arbre** the book/the apple/the tree;
les étudiants the students
2 (*noms abstraits*): **le courage/l'amour/la
jeunesse** courage/love/youth
3 (*indiquant la possession*): **se casser la jambe**
etc to break one's leg *etc*; **levez la main** put
your hand up; **avoir les yeux gris/le nez rouge**
to have grey eyes/a red nose
4 (*temps*): **le matin/soir** in the morning/
evening; mornings/evenings; **le jeudi** *etc*
(*d'habitude*) on Thursdays *etc*; (*ce jeudi-là etc*)
on (the) Thursday
5 (*distribution, évaluation*) a, an; **10 F le
mètre/kilo** 10F a ou per metre/kilo; **le tiers/
quart de** a third/quarter of
♦ pron **1** (*personne: mâle*) him; (*personne:
femelle*) her; (: *pluriel*) them; **je le/la/les vois**
I can see him/her/them
2 (*animal, chose: singulier*) it; (: *pluriel*)
them; **je le** (*ou* la) **vois** I can see it; **je les vois**
I can see them
3 (*remplaçant une phrase*): **je ne le savais pas**
I didn't know (about it); **il était riche et ne
l'est plus** he was once rich but no longer is

---

lécher [leʃe] vt to lick; (*laper: lait, eau*) to lick
ou lap up; **lèche-vitrines** nm: **faire du
lèche-vitrines** to go window-shopping
leçon [l(ə)sɔ̃] nf lesson; **faire la ~ à** (*fig*) to
give a lecture to; **~s de conduite** driving
lessons
lecteur, -trice [lɛktœʀ, tʀis] nm/f reader;
(*d'université*) foreign language assistant ♦ nm
(*TECH*): **~ de cassettes/CD** cassette/CD player;
~ de disquette disk drive
lecture [lɛktyʀ] nf reading
ledit [lədi], **ladite** (*mpl* lesdits, *fpl* lesdites)
dét the aforesaid

légal, e, -aux [legal, o] adj legal; **légaliser**
vt to legalize; **légalité** nf law
légendaire [leʒãdɛʀ] adj legendary
légende [leʒãd] nf (*mythe*) legend; (*de carte,
plan*) key; (*de dessin*) caption
léger, -ère [leʒe, ɛʀ] adj light; (*bruit, retard*)
slight; (*personne: superficiel*) thoughtless;
(: *volage*) free and easy; **à la légère** (*parler,
agir*) rashly, thoughtlessly; **légèrement** adv
(*s'habiller, bouger*) lightly; (*un peu*) slightly;
manger légèrement to eat a light meal;
légèreté nf lightness; (*d'une remarque*)
flippancy
législatif, -ive [leʒislatif, iv] adj legislative;
législatives nfpl general election sg
légitime [leʒitim] adj (*JUR*) lawful, legitimate;
(*fig*) rightful, legitimate; **en état de ~ défense**
in self-defence
legs [leg] nm legacy
léguer [lege] vt: **~ qch à qn** (*JUR*) to bequeath
sth to sb
légume [legym] nm vegetable
lendemain [lãdmɛ̃] nm: **le ~** the next ou
following day; **le ~ matin/soir** the next ou
following morning/evening; **le ~ de** the day
after
lent, e [lã, lãt] adj slow; **lentement** adv
slowly; **lenteur** nf slowness no pl
lentille [lãtij] nf (*OPTIQUE*) lens sg; (*CULIN*)
lentil
léopard [leɔpaʀ] nm leopard
lèpre [lɛpʀ] nf leprosy

MOT-CLÉ
---

lequel, laquelle [ləkɛl, lakɛl] (*mpl* lesquels,
fpl lesquelles) (*à + lequel = auquel, de + lequel
= duquel etc*) pron **1** (*interrogatif*) which,
which one
2 (*relatif: personne: sujet*) who; (: *objet, après
préposition*) whom; (: *chose*) which
♦ adj: **auquel cas** in which case

---

les [le] dét voir **le**
lesbienne [lɛsbjɛn] nf lesbian
lesdites [ledit], **lesdits** [ledi] dét pl voir
ledit
léser [leze] vt to wrong
lésiner [lezine] vi: **ne pas ~ sur les moyens**
(*pour mariage etc*) to push the boat out
lésion [lezjɔ̃] nf lesion, damage no pl
lesquelles, lesquels [lekɛl] pron pl voir
lequel
lessive [lesiv] nf (*poudre*) washing powder;
(*linge*) washing no pl, wash; **lessiver** vt to
wash; (*fam: fatiguer*) to tire out, exhaust
lest [lɛst] nm ballast
leste [lɛst] adj sprightly, nimble
lettre [lɛtʀ] nf letter; **~s** nfpl (*littérature*)
literature sg; (*SCOL*) arts (subjects); **à la ~**

literally; **en toutes ~s** in full
leucémie [løsemi] *nf* leukaemia

MOT-CLÉ
---

leur [lœʀ] *adj possessif* their; **leur maison** their
house; **leurs amis** their friends
♦ *pron* **1** (*objet indirect*) (to) them; **je leur ai
dit la vérité** I told them the truth; **je le leur ai
donné** I gave it to them, I gave them it
2 (*possessif*): **le(la) leur, les leurs** theirs

---

leurre [lœʀ] *nm* (*fig: illusion*) delusion;
(: *duperie*) deception; **leurrer** *vt* to delude,
deceive
leurs [lœʀ] *adj voir* **leur**
levain [ləvɛ̃] *nm* leaven
levé, e [ləve] *adj*: **être ~** to be up; **levée** *nf*
(*POSTES*) collection
lever [l(ə)ve] *vt* (*vitre, bras etc*) to raise;
(*soulever de terre, supprimer: interdiction,
siège*) to lift; (*impôts, armée*) to levy ♦ *vi* to
rise ♦ *nm*: **au ~ on** getting up; **se ~** *vi* to get
up; (*soleil*) to rise; (*jour*) to break;
(*brouillard*) to lift; **~ de soleil** sunrise; **~ du
jour** daybreak
levier [ləvje] *nm* lever
lèvre [lɛvʀ] *nf* lip
lévrier [levʀije] *nm* greyhound
levure [l(ə)vyʀ] *nf* yeast; **~ chimique** baking
powder
lexique [lɛksik] *nm* vocabulary; (*glossaire*)
lexicon
lézard [lezaʀ] *nm* lizard
lézarde [lezaʀd] *nf* crack
liaison [ljɛzɔ̃] *nf* (*rapport*) connection;
(*transport*) link; (*amoureuse*) affair;
(*PHONÉTIQUE*) liaison; **entrer/être en ~ avec** to
get/be in contact with
liane [ljan] *nf* creeper
liant, e [ljɑ̃, ljɑ̃t] *adj* sociable
liasse [ljas] *nf* wad, bundle
Liban [libɑ̃] *nm*: **le ~** (the) Lebanon;
libanais, e *adj* Lebanese ♦ *nm/f*: **Libanais, e**
Lebanese
libeller [libele] *vt* (*chèque, mandat*): **~ (au
nom de)** to make out (to); (*lettre*) to word
libellule [libelyl] *nf* dragonfly
libéral, e, -aux [liberal, o] *adj, nm/f* liberal;
profession ~e (liberal) profession
libérer [libere] *vt* (*délivrer*) to free, liberate;
(*relâcher: prisonnier*) to discharge, release;
(: *d'inhibitions*) to liberate; (*gaz*) to release;
se ~ *vi* (*de rendez-vous*) to get out of previous
engagements
liberté [libɛʀte] *nf* freedom; (*loisir*) free time;
~s *nfpl* (*privautés*) liberties; **mettre/être en ~**
to set/be free; **en ~ provisoire/surveillée/
conditionnelle** on bail/probation/parole
libraire [libʀɛʀ] *nm/f* bookseller

librairie [libʀeʀi] *nf* bookshop
libre [libʀ] *adj* free; (*route, voie*) clear; (*place,
salle*) free; (*ligne*) not engaged; (*SCOL*) non-
state; **~ de qch/de faire** free from sth/to do;
~ arbitre free will; **libre-échange** *nm* free
trade; **libre-service** *nm* self-service store
Libye [libi] *nf*: **la ~** Libya
licence [lisɑ̃s] *nf* (*permis*) permit; (*diplôme*)
degree; (*liberté*) liberty; **licencié, e** *nm/f*
(*SCOL*): **licencié ès lettres/en droit** ≈ Bachelor
of Arts/Law
licenciement [lisɑ̃simɑ̃] *nm* redundancy
licencier [lisɑ̃sje] *vt* (*débaucher*) to make
redundant, lay off; (*renvoyer*) to dismiss
licite [lisit] *adj* lawful
lie [li] *nf* dregs *pl*, sediment
lié, e [lje] *adj*: **très ~ avec** very friendly with *ou*
close to
liège [ljɛʒ] *nm* cork
lien [ljɛ̃] *nm* (*corde, fig: affectif*) bond;
(*rapport*) link, connection; **~ de parenté**
family tie
lier [lje] *vt* (*attacher*) to tie up; (*joindre*) to link
up; (*fig: unir, engager*) to bind; **se ~ avec** to
make friends with; **~ qch à** to tie *ou* link sth
to; **~ conversation avec** to strike up a
conversation with
lierre [ljɛʀ] *nm* ivy
liesse [ljes] *nf*: **être en ~** to be celebrating *ou*
jubilant
lieu, x [ljø] *nm* place; **~x** *nmpl* (*locaux*)
premises; (*endroit: d'un accident etc*) scene
sg; **en ~ sûr** in a safe place; **en premier ~** in
the first place; **en dernier ~** lastly; **avoir ~** to
take place; **tenir ~ de** to serve as; **donner ~ à**
to give rise to; **au ~ de** instead of; **lieu-dit**
(*pl* **lieux-dits**) *nm* locality
lieutenant [ljøt(ə)nɑ̃] *nm* lieutenant
lièvre [ljɛvʀ] *nm* hare
ligament [ligamɑ̃] *nm* ligament
ligne [liɲ] *nf* (*gén*) line; (*TRANSPORTS: liaison*)
service; (: *trajet*) route; (*silhouette*) figure;
entrer en ~ de compte to come into it
lignée [liɲe] *nf* line, lineage
ligoter [ligɔte] *vt* to tie up
ligue [lig] *nf* league; **liguer** *vt*: **se liguer
contre** (*fig*) to combine against
lilas [lila] *nm* lilac
limace [limas] *nf* slug
limande [limɑ̃d] *nf* dab
lime [lim] *nf* file; **~ à ongles** nail file; **limer** *vt*
to file
limier [limje] *nm* bloodhound; (*détective*)
sleuth
limitation [limitasjɔ̃] *nf*: **~ de vitesse** speed
limit
limite [limit] *nf* (*de terrain*) boundary; (*partie
ou point extrême*) limit; **vitesse/charge ~**
maximum speed/load; **cas ~** borderline case;

date ~ deadline; **limiter** vt (restreindre) to limit, restrict; (délimiter) to border; **limitrophe** adj border cpd

limoger [limɔʒe] vt to dismiss

limon [limɔ̃] nm silt

limonade [limɔnad] nf lemonade

lin [lɛ̃] nm (tissu) linen

linceul [lɛ̃sœl] nm shroud

linge [lɛ̃ʒ] nm (serviettes etc) linen; (lessive) washing; (aussi: ~ de corps) underwear; **lingerie** nf lingerie, underwear

lingot [lɛ̃go] nm ingot

linguistique [lɛ̃gɥistik] adj linguistic ♦ nf linguistics sg

lion, ne [ljɔ̃, ljɔn] nm/f lion (lioness); (signe): le L~ Leo; **lionceau, x** nm lion cub

liqueur [likœr] nf liqueur

liquidation [likidasjɔ̃] nf (vente) sale

liquide [likid] adj liquid ♦ nm liquid; (COMM): en ~ in ready money ou cash; **liquider** vt to liquidate; (COMM: articles) to clear, sell off; **liquidités** nfpl (COMM) liquid assets

lire [lir] nf (monnaie) lira ♦ vt, vi to read

lis [lis] nm = lys

lisible [lizibl] adj legible

lisière [lizjɛr] nf (de forêt) edge

lisons [lizɔ̃] vb voir lire

lisse [lis] adj smooth

liste [list] nf list; **faire la ~ de** to list; ~ **électorale** electoral roll; **listing** nm (INFORM) printout

lit [li] nm bed; **petit ~, lit à une place** single bed; **grand ~, lit à deux places** double bed; **faire son ~** to make one's bed; **aller/se mettre au ~** to go to/get into bed; ~ **de camp** campbed; ~ **d'enfant** cot (BRIT), crib (US)

literie [litri] nf bedding, bedclothes pl

litière [litjɛr] nf litter

litige [litiʒ] nm dispute

litre [litr] nm litre

littéraire [literɛr] adj literary ♦ nm/f arts student; **elle est très ~** (she's very literary)

littéral, e, -aux [literal, o] adj literal

littérature [literatyr] nf literature

littoral, -aux [litɔral, o] nm coast

liturgie [lityrʒi] nf liturgy

livide [livid] adj livid, pallid

livraison [livrɛzɔ̃] nf delivery

livre [livr] nm book ♦ nf (poids, monnaie) pound; ~ **de bord** logbook; ~ **de poche** paperback

livré, e [livre] adj: ~ **à soi-même** left to o.s. ou one's own devices; **livrée** nf livery

livrer [livre] vt (COMM) to deliver; (otage, coupable) to hand over; (secret, information) to give away; **se ~ à** (se confier) to confide in; (se rendre, s'abandonner) to give o.s. up to; (faire: pratiques, actes) to indulge in; (enquête) to carry out

livret [livrɛ] nm booklet; (d'opéra) libretto; ~ **de caisse d'épargne** (savings) bank-book; ~ **de famille** (official) family record book; ~ **scolaire** (school) report book

livreur, -euse [livrœr, øz] nm/f delivery boy ou man/girl ou woman

local, e, -aux [lɔkal] adj local ♦ nm (salle) premises pl; voir aussi **locaux**; **localiser** vt (repérer) to locate, place; (limiter) to confine; **localité** nf locality

locataire [lɔkatɛr] nm/f tenant; (de chambre) lodger

location [lɔkasjɔ̃] nf (par le locataire, le loueur) renting; (par le propriétaire) renting out, letting; (THÉÂTRE) booking office; "~ **de voitures**" "car rental"; **habiter en ~** to live in rented accommodation; **prendre une ~ (pour les vacances)** to rent a house etc (for the holidays)

locaux [lɔko] nmpl premises

locomotive [lɔkɔmɔtiv] nf locomotive, engine

locution [lɔkysjɔ̃] nf phrase

loge [lɔʒ] nf (THÉÂTRE: d'artiste) dressing room; (: de spectateurs) box; (de concierge, francmaçon) lodge

logement [lɔʒmɑ̃] nm accommodation no pl (BRIT), accommodations pl (US); (appartement) flat (BRIT), apartment (US); (hébergement) housing no pl

loger [lɔʒe] vt to accommodate ♦ vi to live; **se ~ dans** (suj: balle, flèche) to lodge itself in; **trouver à se ~** to find accommodation; **logeur, -euse** nm/f landlord(-lady)

logiciel [lɔʒisjɛl] nm software

logique [lɔʒik] adj logical ♦ nf logic

logis [lɔʒi] nm abode, dwelling

logo [lɔgo] nm logo

loi [lwa] nf law; **faire la ~** to lay down the law

loin [lwɛ̃] adv far; (dans le temps: futur) a long way off; (: passé) a long time ago; **plus ~** further; ~ **de** far from; **au ~** far off; **de ~** from a distance; (fig: de beaucoup) by far

lointain, e [lwɛ̃tɛ̃, ɛn] adj faraway, distant; (dans le futur, passé) distant; (cause, parent) remote, distant ♦ nm: **dans le ~** in the distance

loir [lwar] nm dormouse

loisir [lwazir] nm: **heures de ~** spare time; **~s** nmpl (temps libre) leisure sg; (activités) leisure activities; **avoir le ~ de faire** to have the time ou opportunity to do; **à ~** at leisure

londonien, ne [lɔ̃dɔnjɛ̃, jɛn] adj London cpd, of London ♦ nm/f: **L~, ne** Londoner

Londres [lɔ̃dr] n London

long, longue [lɔ̃, lɔ̃g] adj long ♦ adv: **en savoir ~** to know a great deal ♦ nm: **de 3 m de ~** 3 m long, 3 m in length; **ne pas faire ~ feu** not to last long; **(tout) le ~ de** (all) along; **tout au ~ de** (*année, vie*) throughout; **de ~ en large** (*marcher*) to and fro, up and down; *voir aussi* **longue**

longer [lɔ̃ʒe] *vt* to go (*ou* walk *ou* drive) along(side); (*suj: mur, route*) to border

longiligne [lɔ̃ʒiliɲ] *adj* long-limbed

longitude [lɔ̃ʒityd] *nf* longitude

longtemps [lɔ̃tɑ̃] *adv* (for) a long time, (for) long; **avant ~** before long; **pour** *ou* **pendant ~** for a long time; **mettre ~ à faire** to take a long time to do

longue [lɔ̃g] *adj voir* **long** ♦ *nf*: **à la ~** in the end; **longuement** *adv* (*longtemps*) for a long time; (*en détail*) at length

longueur [lɔ̃gœʀ] *nf* length; **~s** *nfpl* (*fig: d'un film etc*) tedious parts; **en ~** lengthwise; **tirer en ~** to drag on; **à ~ de journée** all day long; **~ d'onde** wavelength

longue-vue [lɔ̃gvy] *nf* telescope

look [luk] (*fam*) *nm* look, image

lopin [lɔpɛ̃] *nm*: **~ de terre** patch of land

loque [lɔk] *nf* (*personne*) wreck; **~s** *nfpl* (*habits*) rags

loquet [lɔke] *nm* latch

lorgner [lɔʀɲe] *vt* to eye; (*fig*) to have one's eye on

lors [lɔʀ]: **~ de** *prép* at the time of; during

lorsque [lɔʀsk] *conj* when, as

losange [lɔzɑ̃ʒ] *nm* diamond

lot [lo] *nm* (*part*) share; (*de ~erie*) prize; (*fig: destin*) fate, lot; (*COMM, INFORM*) batch; **le gros ~** the jackpot

loterie [lɔtʀi] *nf* lottery

loti, e [lɔti] *adj*: **bien/mal ~** well-/badly off

lotion [lɔsjɔ̃] *nf* lotion

lotissement [lɔtismɑ̃] *nm* housing development; (*parcelle*) plot, lot

loto [lɔto] *nm* lotto

lotte [lɔt] *nf* monkfish

louable [lwabl] *adj* commendable

louanges [lwɑ̃ʒ] *nfpl* praise *sg*

loubard [lubaʀ] (*fam*) *nm* lout

louche [luʃ] *adj* shady, fishy, dubious ♦ *nf* ladle; **loucher** *vi* to squint

louer [lwe] *vt* (*maison: suj: propriétaire*) to let, rent (out); (*: locataire*) to rent; (*voiture etc: entreprise*) to hire out (*BRIT*), rent (out); (*: locataire*) to hire, rent; (*réserver*) to book; (*faire l'éloge de*) to praise; **"à ~"** "to let" (*BRIT*), "for rent" (*US*)

loup [lu] *nm* wolf

loupe [lup] *nf* magnifying glass

louper [lupe] (*fam*) *vt* (*manquer*) to miss; (*examen*) to flunk

lourd, e [luʀ, luʀd] *adj, adv* heavy; **~ de** (*conséquences, menaces*) charged with; **il fait ~** the weather is close, it's sultry; **lourdaud, e** (*péj*) *adj* clumsy; **lourdement** *adv* heavily; **lourdeur** *nf* weight; **lourdeurs d'estomac**

indigestion

loutre [lutʀ] *nf* otter

louveteau, x [luv(ə)to] *nm* wolf-cub; (*scout*) cub (scout)

louvoyer [luvwaje] *vi* (*fig*) to hedge, evade the issue

loyal, e, -aux [lwajal, o] *adj* (*fidèle*) loyal, faithful; (*fair-play*) fair; **loyauté** *nf* loyalty, faithfulness; fairness

loyer [lwaje] *nm* rent

lu, e [ly] *pp de* **lire**

lubie [lybi] *nf* whim, craze

lubrifiant [lybʀifjɑ̃, jɑ̃t] *nm* lubricant

lubrifier [lybʀifje] *vt* to lubricate

lubrique [lybʀik] *adj* lecherous

lucarne [lykaʀn] *nf* skylight

lucide [lysid] *adj* lucid; (*accidenté*) conscious

lucratif, -ive [lykʀatif, iv] *adj* lucrative, profitable; **à but non ~** non profit-making

lueur [lɥœʀ] *nf* (*pâle*) (faint) light; (*chatoyante*) glimmer *no pl*; (*fig*) glimmer, gleam

luge [lyʒ] *nf* sledge (*BRIT*), sled (*US*)

lugubre [lygybʀ] *adj* gloomy, dismal

┌─────────────────────────────────────┐
│ *MOT-CLÉ* │
└─────────────────────────────────────┘

lui [lɥi] *pron* **1** (*objet indirect: mâle*) (to) him; (*: femelle*) (to) her; (*: chose, animal*) (to) it; **je lui ai parlé** I have spoken to him (*ou* to her); **il lui a offert un cadeau** he gave him (*ou* her) a present

2 (*après préposition, comparatif: personne*) him; (*: chose, animal*) it; **elle est contente de lui** she is pleased with him; **je la connais mieux que lui** I know her better than he does; I know her better than him

3 (*sujet, forme emphatique*) he; **lui, il est à Paris** HE is in Paris

4: **lui-même** himself; itself

---

luire [lɥiʀ] *vi* to shine; (*en rougeoyant*) to glow

lumière [lymjɛʀ] *nf* light; **mettre en ~** (*fig*) to highlight; **~ du jour** daylight

luminaire [lyminɛʀ] *nm* lamp, light

lumineux, -euse [lyminø, øz] *adj* luminous; (*éclairé*) illuminated; (*ciel, couleur*) bright; (*rayon*) of light, light *cpd*; (*fig: regard*) radiant

lunatique [lynatik] *adj* whimsical, temperamental

lundi [lœ̃di] *nm* Monday; **~ de Pâques** Easter Monday

lune [lyn] *nf* moon; **~ de miel** honeymoon

lunette [lynɛt] *nf*: **~s** *nfpl* glasses, spectacles; (*protectrices*) goggles; **~ arrière** (*AUTO*) rear window; **~s de soleil** sunglasses

lus *etc* [ly] *vb voir* **lire**

lustre [lystʀ] *nm* (*de plafond*) chandelier; (*fig:*

éclat) lustre; **lustrer** *vt* to shine

lut [ly] *vb voir* lire

luth [lyt] *nm* lute

lutin [lytɛ̃] *nm* imp, goblin

lutte [lyt] *nf* (*conflit*) struggle; (*sport*) wrestling; **lutter** *vi* to fight, struggle

luxe [lyks] *nm* luxury; **de ~** luxury *cpd*

Luxembourg [lyksɑ̃buʀ] *nm*: **le ~** Luxembourg

luxer [lykse] *vt*: **se ~ l'épaule** to dislocate one's shoulder

luxueux, -euse [lyksɥø, øz] *adj* luxurious

luxure [lyksyʀ] *nf* lust

luxuriant, e [lyksyʀjɑ̃, jɑ̃t] *adj* luxuriant

lycée [lise] *nm* secondary school; **lycéen, ne** *nm/f* secondary school pupil

lyophilisé, e [ljɔfilize] *adj* (*café*) freeze-dried

lyrique [liʀik] *adj* lyrical; (*OPÉRA*) lyric; **artiste ~ opera singer**

lys [lis] *nm* lily

M, m

M *abr* = **Monsieur**

m' [m] *pron voir* me

ma [ma] *adj voir* mon

macaron [makaʀɔ̃] *nm* (*gâteau*) macaroon; (*insigne*) (round) badge

macaronis [makaʀɔni] *nmpl* macaroni *sg*

macédoine [masedwan] *nf*: **~ de fruits** fruit salad; **~ de légumes** mixed vegetables

macérer [maseʀe] *vi, vt* to macerate; (*dans du vinaigre*) to pickle

mâcher [maʃe] *vt* to chew; **ne pas ~ ses mots** not to mince one's words

machin [maʃɛ̃] (*fam*) *nm* thing(umajig)

machinal, e, -aux [maʃinal, o] *adj* mechanical, automatic; **machinalement** *adv* mechanically, automatically

machination [maʃinasjɔ̃] *nf* frame-up

machine [maʃin] *nf* machine; (*locomotive*) engine; **~ à écrire** typewriter; **~ à laver/coudre** washing/sewing machine; **~ à sous** fruit machine

macho [matʃo] (*fam*) *nm* male chauvinist

mâchoire [maʃwaʀ] *nf* jaw

mâchonner [maʃɔne] *vt* to chew (at)

maçon [masɔ̃] *nm* builder; (*poseur de briques*) bricklayer; **maçonnerie** *nf* (*murs*) brickwork; (*pierres*) masonry, stonework

maculer [makyle] *vt* to stain

Madame [madam] (*pl* **Mesdames**) *nf*: **~ X** Mrs X; **occupez-vous de ~/Monsieur/ Mademoiselle** please serve this lady/ gentleman/(*young*) lady; **bonjour ~/ Monsieur/Mademoiselle** good morning; (*ton déférent*) good morning Madam/Sir/Madam; (*le nom est connu*) good morning Mrs/Mr/

Miss X; **~/Monsieur/Mademoiselle!** (*pour appeler*) Madam/Sir/Miss!; **~/Monsieur/ Mademoiselle** (*sur lettre*) Dear Madam/Sir/ Madam; **chère ~/cher Monsieur/chère Mademoiselle** Dear Mrs/Mr/Miss X; **Mesdames** Ladies

madeleine [madlɛn] *nf* madeleine; *small sponge cake*

Mademoiselle [madmwazɛl] (*pl* **Mesdemoiselles**) *nf* Miss; *voir aussi* **Madame**

madère [madɛʀ] *nm* Madeira (wine)

magasin [magazɛ̃] *nm* (*boutique*) shop; (*entrepôt*) warehouse; **en ~** (*COMM*) in stock

magazine [magazin] *nm* magazine

Maghreb [magʀɛb] *nm*: **le ~** North Africa; **maghrébin, e** *adj* North African ♦ *nm/f*: **Maghrébin, e** North African

magicien, ne [maʒisjɛ̃, jɛn] *nm/f* magician

magie [maʒi] *nf* magic; **magique** *adj* magic; (*enchanteur*) magical

magistral, e, -aux [maʒistʀal, o] *adj* (*œuvre, adresse*) masterly; (*ton*) authoritative; **cours ~** lecture

magistrat [maʒistʀa] *nm* magistrate

magnat [magna] *nm* tycoon

magnétique [maɲetik] *adj* magnetic

magnétiser [maɲetize] *vt* to magnetize; (*fig*) to mesmerize, hypnotize

magnétophone [maɲetɔfɔn] *nm* tape recorder; **~ à cassettes** cassette recorder

magnétoscope [maɲetɔskɔp] *nm* video-tape recorder

magnifique [maɲifik] *adj* magnificent

magot [mago] (*fam*) *nm* (*argent*) pile (of money); (*économies*) nest egg

magouille [maguj] (*fam*) *nf* scheming; **magouiller** (*fam*) *vi* to scheme

magret [magʀɛ] *nm*: **~ de canard** duck steaklet

mai [mɛ] *nm* May

maigre [mɛgʀ] *adj* (very) thin, skinny; (*viande*) lean; (*fromage*) low-fat; (*végétation*) thin, sparse; (*fig*) poor, meagre, skimpy; **jours ~s** days of abstinence, fish days; **maigreur** *nf* thinness; **maigrir** *vi* to get thinner, lose weight; **maigrir de 2 kilos** to lose 2 kilos

maille [maj] *nf* stitch; **avoir ~ à partir avec qn** to have a brush with sb; **~ à l'endroit/à l'envers** plain/purl stitch

maillet [majɛ] *nm* mallet

maillon [majɔ̃] *nm* link

maillot [majo] *nm* (*aussi*: **~ de corps**) vest; (*de sportif*) jersey; **~ de bain** swimsuit; (*d'homme*) bathing trunks *pl*

main [mɛ̃] *nf* hand; **à la ~** in one's hand; **se donner la ~** to hold hands; **donner** *ou* **tendre la ~ à qn** to hold out one's hand to sb; **serrer la ~ à qn** to shake hands with sb; **sous la ~** to *ou* at hand; **à remettre en ~s propres** to be delivered personally; **mettre la dernière ~ à** to put the finishing touches to; **se faire/perdre la ~** to get one's hand in/lose one's touch; **avoir qch bien en ~** to have (got) the hang of sth; **main-d'œuvre** *nf* manpower, labour; **main-forte** *nf*: **prêter main-forte à qn** to come to sb's assistance; **mainmise** *nf* (*fig*): **mainmise sur** complete hold on

maint, e [mɛ̃, mɛ̃t] *adj* many a; **~s** many; **à ~es reprises** time and (time) again

maintenant [mɛ̃t(ə)nɑ̃] *adv* now; (*actuellement*) nowadays

maintenir [mɛ̃t(ə)niʀ] *vt* (*retenir, soutenir*) to support; (*contenir: foule etc*) to hold back; (*conserver, affirmer*) to maintain; **se ~** *vi* (*prix*) to keep steady; (*amélioration*) to persist

maintien [mɛ̃tjɛ̃] *nm* (*sauvegarde*) maintenance; (*attitude*) bearing

maire [mɛʀ] *nm* mayor; **mairie** *nf* (*bâtiment*) town hall; (*administration*) town council

mais [mɛ] *conj* but; **~ non!** of course not!; **~ enfin** but after all; (*indignation*) look here!

maïs [mais] *nm* maize (*BRIT*), corn (*US*)

maison [mɛzɔ̃] *nf* house; (*chez-soi*) home; (*COMM*) firm ♦ *adj inv* (*CULIN*) home-made; (*fig*) in-house, own; **à la ~** at home; (*direction*) home; **~ close** *ou* **de passe** brothel; **~ de repos** convalescent home; **~ de santé** mental home; **~ des jeunes** ≈ youth club; **~ mère** parent company; **maisonnée** *nf* household, family; **maisonnette** *nf* small house, cottage

maître, -esse [mɛtʀ, mɛtʀɛs] *nm/f* master (mistress); (*SCOL*) teacher, schoolmaster(-mistress) ♦ *nm* (*peintre etc*) master; (*titre*): **M~** Maître, *term of address gen for a barrister* ♦ *adj* (*principal, essentiel*) main; **être ~ de** (*soi, situation*) to be in control of; **une maîtresse femme** a managing woman; **~ chanteur** blackmailer; **~ d'école** schoolmaster; **~ d'hôtel** (*domestique*) butler; (*d'hôtel*) head waiter; **~ nageur** lifeguard; **maîtresse** *nf* (*amante*) mistress; **maîtresse (d'école)** teacher, (school)mistress; **maîtresse de maison** hostess; (*ménagère*) housewife

maîtrise [mɛtʀiz] *nf* (*aussi:* **~ de soi**) self-control, self-possession; (*habileté*) skill, mastery; (*suprématie*) mastery, command; (*diplôme*) ≈ master's degree; **maîtriser** *vt* (*cheval, incendie*) to (bring under) control; (*sujet*) to master; (*émotion*) to control, master; **se maîtriser** to control o.s.

maizena ® [maizena] *nf* cornflour

majestueux, -euse [maʒɛstɥø, øz] *adj* majestic

majeur, e [maʒœʀ] *adj* (*important*) major; (*JUR*) of age ♦ *nm* (*doigt*) middle finger; **en ~e partie** for the most part; **la ~e partie de** most of

majoration [maʒɔʀasjɔ̃] *nf* rise, increase

majorer [maʒɔʀe] *vt* to increase

majoritaire [maʒɔʀitɛʀ] *adj* majority *cpd*

majorité [maʒɔʀite] *nf* (*gén*) majority; (*parti*) party in power; **en ~** mainly

majuscule [maʒyskyl] *adj, nf*: (**lettre**) **~** capital (letter)

mal [mal, mo] (*pl* **maux**) *nm* (*opposé au bien*) evil; (*tort, dommage*) harm; (*douleur physique*) pain, ache; (*~adie*) illness, sickness *no pl* ♦ *adv* badly ♦ *adj* bad, wrong; **être ~ à l'aise** to be uncomfortable; **être ~ avec qn** to be on bad terms with sb; **il a ~ compris** he misunderstood; **dire/penser du ~ de** to speak/think ill of; **ne voir aucun ~ à** to see no harm in, see nothing wrong in; **faire ~ à qn** to hurt sb; **se faire ~** to hurt o.s.; **se donner du ~ pour faire qch** to go to a lot of trouble to do sth; **ça fait ~** it hurts; **j'ai ~ au dos** my back hurts; **avoir ~ à la tête/à la gorge/aux dents** to have a headache/a sore throat/toothache; **avoir le ~ du pays** to be homesick; *voir aussi* **cœur; maux; ~ de mer** seasickness; **~ en point** in a bad state

malade [malad] *adj* ill, sick; (*poitrine, jambe*) bad; (*plante*) diseased ♦ *nm/f* invalid, sick person; (*à l'hôpital etc*) patient; **tomber ~** to fall ill; **être ~ du cœur** to have heart trouble *ou* a bad heart; **~ mental** mentally sick *ou* ill person; **maladie** *nf* (*spécifique*) disease, illness; (*mauvaise santé*) illness, sickness; **maladif, -ive** *adj* sickly; (*curiosité, besoin*) pathological

maladresse [maladʀɛs] *nf* clumsiness *no pl*; (*gaffe*) blunder

maladroit, e [maladʀwa, wat] *adj* clumsy

malaise [malɛz] *nm* (*MÉD*) feeling of faintness; (*fig*) uneasiness, malaise; **avoir un ~** to feel faint

malaisé, e [maleze] *adj* difficult

malaria [malaʀja] *nf* malaria

malaxer [malakse] *vt* (*pétrir*) to knead; (*mélanger*) to mix

malchance [malʃɑ̃s] *nf* misfortune, ill luck *no pl*; **par ~** unfortunately; **malchanceux, -euse** *adj* unlucky

mâle [mɑl] *adj* (*aussi* ÉLEC, TECH) male; (*viril: voix, traits*) manly ♦ *nm* male

malédiction [malediksjɔ̃] *nf* curse

mal...: malencontreux, -euse *adj* unfortunate, untoward; **mal-en-point** *adj inv* in a sorry state; **malentendant, e** *nm/f*: **les malentendants** the hard of hearing; **malentendu** *nm* misunderstanding; **malfaçon** *nf* fault; **malfaisant, e** *adj* evil, harmful; **malfaiteur** *nm* lawbreaker, criminal; (*voleur*) burglar, thief; **malfamé, e** *adj* disreputable

malgache [malgaʃ] adj Madagascan,
Malagasy ♦ nm/f: **M~** Madagascan, Malagasy
♦ nm (LING) Malagasy

malgré [malgre] prép in spite of, despite;
~ tout all the same

malhabile [malabil] adj clumsy, awkward

malheur [malœr] nm (situation) adversity,
misfortune; (événement) misfortune; (: très
grave) disaster, tragedy; **faire un ~** to be a
smash hit; **malheureusement** adv
unfortunately; **malheureux, -euse** adj
(triste) unhappy, miserable; (infortuné,
regrettable) unfortunate; (malchanceux)
unlucky; (insignifiant) wretched ♦ nm/f poor
soul; **les malheureux** the destitute

malhonnête [malɔnɛt] adj dishonest;
malhonnêteté nf dishonesty

malice [malis] nf mischievousness;
(méchanceté): **par ~** out of malice ou spite;
sans ~ guileless; **malicieux, -euse** adj
mischievous

malin, -igne [malɛ̃, maliɲ] adj (futé: f gén:
~e) smart, shrewd; (MÉD) malignant

malingre [malɛ̃gr] adj puny

malle [mal] nf trunk; **mallette** nf (small)
suitcase; (porte-documents) attaché case

malmener [malməne] vt to manhandle; (fig)
to give a rough handling to

malodorant, e [malɔdɔrɑ̃, ɑ̃t] adj foul- ou
ill-smelling

malotru [malɔtry] nm lout, boor

malpoli, e [malpɔli] adj impolite

malpropre [malprɔpr] adj dirty

malsain, e [malsɛ̃, ɛn] adj unhealthy

malt [malt] nm malt

Malte [malt] nf Malta

maltraiter [maltrete] vt to manhandle, ill-
treat

malveillance [malvejɑ̃s] nf (animosité) ill
will; (intention de nuire) malevolence

malversation [malvɛrsasjɔ̃] nf
embezzlement

maman [mamɑ̃] nf mum(my), mother

mamelle [mamɛl] nf teat

mamelon [mam(ə)lɔ̃] nm (ANAT) nipple

mamie [mami] nf (fam) granny

mammifère [mamifɛr] nm mammal

mammouth [mamut] nm mammoth

manche [mɑ̃ʃ] nf (de vêtement) sleeve; (d'un
jeu, tournoi) round; (GÉO): **la M~** the Channel
♦ nm (d'outil, casserole) handle; (de pelle,
pioche etc) shaft; **à ~s courtes/longues** short-
/long-sleeved

manchette [mɑ̃ʃɛt] nf (de chemise) cuff;
(coup) forearm blow; (titre) headline

manchot [mɑ̃ʃo, ɔt] nm one-armed man;
armless man; (ZOOL) penguin

mandarine [mɑ̃darin] nf mandarin
(orange), tangerine

mandat [mɑ̃da] nm (postal) postal ou money
order; (d'un député etc) mandate;
(procuration) power of attorney, proxy;
(POLICE) warrant; **d'arrêt** warrant for arrest;
mandataire nm/f (représentant)
representative; (JUR) proxy

manège [manɛʒ] nm riding school; (à la
foire) roundabout, merry-go-round; (fig)
game, ploy

manette [manɛt] nf lever, tap; **~ de jeu**
joystick

mangeable [mɑ̃ʒabl] adj edible, eatable

mangeoire [mɑ̃ʒwar] nf trough, manger

manger [mɑ̃ʒe] vt to eat; (ronger: suj: rouille
etc) to eat into ou away ♦ vi to eat; **donner à
~ à** (enfant) to feed; **mangeur, -euse** nm/f
eater; **gros mangeur** big eater

mangue [mɑ̃g] nf mango

maniable [manjabl] adj (outil) handy;
(voiture, voilier) easy to handle

maniaque [manjak] adj finicky, fussy ♦ nm/f
(méticuleux) fusspot; (fou) maniac

manie [mani] nf (tic) odd habit; (obsession)
mania; **avoir la ~ de** to be obsessive about

manier [manje] vt to handle

manière [manjɛr] nf (façon) way, manner;
~s nfpl (attitude) manners; (chichis) fuss sg;
de ~ à so as to; **de cette ~** in this way ou
manner; **d'une certaine ~** in a way; **de toute ~**
in any case

maniéré, e [manjere] adj affected

manif [manif] nf (fam) nf demo

manifestant, e [manifɛstɑ̃, ɑ̃t] nm/f
demonstrator

manifestation [manifɛstasjɔ̃] nf (de joie,
mécontentement) expression, demonstration;
(symptôme) outward sign; (culturelle etc)
event; (POL) demonstration

manifeste [manifɛst] adj obvious, evident
♦ nm manifesto; **manifester** vt (volonté,
intentions) to show, indicate; (joie, peur) to
express, show ♦ vi to demonstrate; **se
manifester** vi (émotion) to show ou express
itself; (difficultés) to arise; (symptômes) to
appear

manigance [manigɑ̃s] nf scheme;
manigancer vt to plot

manipulation [manipylasjɔ̃] nf handling;
(POL, génétique) manipulation

manipuler [manipyle] vt to handle; (fig) to
manipulate

manivelle [manivɛl] nf crank

mannequin [mankɛ̃] nm (COUTURE) dummy;
(MODE) model

manœuvre [manœvr] nf (gén) manoeuvre
(BRIT), maneuver (US) ♦ nm labourer;
manœuvrer vt to manoeuvre (BRIT),
maneuver (US); (levier, machine) to operate
♦ vi to manoeuvre

manoir [manwaʀ] *nm* manor *ou* country house

manque [mãk] *nm* (*insuffisance*): ~ **de** lack of; (*vide*) emptiness, gap; (*MÉD*) withdrawal; **être en état de** ~ to suffer withdrawal symptoms

manqué, e [mãke] *adj* failed; **garçon** ~ tomboy

manquer [mãke] *vi* (*faire défaut*) to be lacking; (*être absent*) to be missing; (*échouer*) to fail ♦ *vt* to miss ♦ *vb impers*: **il (nous) manque encore 100 F** we are still 100 F short; **il manque des pages (au livre)** there are some pages missing (from the book); **il/cela me manque** I miss him/this; ~ **à** (*règles etc*) to be in breach of, fail to observe; ~ **de** to lack; **je ne ~ai pas de le lui dire** I'll be sure to tell him; **il a manqué (de) se tuer** he very nearly got killed

mansarde [mãsaʀd] *nf* attic; **mansardé, e** *adj*: **chambre mansardée** attic room

manteau, x [mãto] *nm* coat

manucure [manykyʀ] *nf* manicurist

manuel, le [manɥɛl] *adj* manual ♦ *nm* (*ouvrage*) manual, handbook

manufacture [manyfaktyʀ] *nf* factory; **manufacturé, e** *adj* manufactured

manuscrit, e [manyskʀi, it] *adj* handwritten ♦ *nm* manuscript

manutention [manytɑ̃sjɔ̃] *nf* (*COMM*) handling

mappemonde [mapmɔ̃d] *nf* (*plane*) map of the world; (*sphère*) globe

maquereau, x [makʀo] *nm* (*ZOOL*) mackerel *inv*; (*fam*) pimp

maquette [makɛt] *nf* (*à échelle réduite*) (scale) model; (*d'une page illustrée*) paste-up

maquillage [makijaʒ] *nm* making up; (*crème etc*) make-up

maquiller [makije] *vt* (*personne, visage*) to make up; (*truquer: passeport, statistique*) to fake; (: *voiture volée*) to do over (*respray etc*); **se** ~ *vi* to make up (one's face)

maquis [maki] *nm* (*GÉO*) scrub; (*MIL*) maquis, underground fighting *no pl*

maraîcher, -ère [maʀeʃe, ɛʀ] *adj*: **cultures maraîchères** market gardening *sg* ♦ *nm/f* market gardener

marais [maʀɛ] *nm* marsh, swamp

marasme [maʀasm] *nm* stagnation, slump

marathon [maʀatɔ̃] *nm* marathon

maraudeur [maʀodœʀ, øz] *nm* prowler

marbre [maʀbʀ] *nm* marble

marc [maʀ] *nm* (*de raisin, pommes*) marc; ~ **de café** coffee grounds *pl ou* dregs *pl*

marchand, e [maʀʃɑ̃, ɑ̃d] *nm/f* shopkeeper, tradesman(-woman); (*au marché*) stallholder; (*de vins, charbon*) merchant ♦ *adj*: **prix/valeur ~(e)** market price/value; **~(e) de fruits** fruiterer

(*BRIT*), fruit seller (*US*); **~(e) de journaux** newsagent; **~(e) de légumes** greengrocer (*BRIT*), produce dealer (*US*); **~(e) de poissons** fishmonger; **marchander** *vi* to bargain, haggle; **marchandise** *nf* goods *pl*, merchandise *no pl*

marche [maʀʃ] *nf* (*d'escalier*) step; (*activité*) walking; (*promenade, trajet, allure*) walk; (*démarche*) walk, gait; (*MIL etc*) march; (*fonctionnement*) running; (*des événements*) course; **dans le sens de la** ~ (*RAIL*) facing the engine; **en** ~ (*monter etc*) while the vehicle is moving *ou* in motion; **mettre en** ~ to start; **se mettre en** ~ (*personne*) to get moving; (*machine*) to start; **être en état de** ~ to be in working order; ~ **à suivre** (*correct*) procedure; ~ **arrière** reverse (gear); **faire** ~ **arrière** to reverse; (*fig*) to backtrack, back-pedal

marché [maʀʃe] *nm* market; (*transaction*) bargain, deal; **faire du** ~ **noir** to buy and sell on the black market; ~ **aux puces** flea market; **M~ commun** Common Market

marchepied [maʀʃəpje] *nm* (*RAIL*) step

marcher [maʀʃe] *vi* to walk; (*MIL*) to march; (*aller: voiture, train, affaires*) to go; (*prospérer*) to go well; (*fonctionner*) to work, run; (*fam: consentir*) to go along, agree; (: *croire naïvement*) to be taken in; **faire** ~ **qn** (*taquiner*) to pull sb's leg; (*tromper*) to lead sb up the garden path; **marcheur, -euse** *nm/f* walker

mardi [maʀdi] *nm* Tuesday; **M~ gras** Shrove Tuesday

mare [maʀ] *nf* pond; (*flaque*) pool

marécage [maʀekaʒ] *nm* marsh, swamp; **marécageux, -euse** *adj* marshy

maréchal, -aux [maʀeʃal, o] *nm* marshal; **maréchal-ferrant** [maʀeʃalfeʀɑ̃, maʀeʃo-] (*pl* **maréchaux-ferrants**) *nm* blacksmith, farrier

marée [maʀe] *nf* tide; (*poissons*) fresh (sea) fish; ~ **haute/basse** high/low tide; ~ **montante/descendante** rising/ebb tide; ~ **noire** oil slick

marelle [maʀɛl] *nf* hopscotch

margarine [maʀgaʀin] *nf* margarine

marge [maʀʒ] *nf* margin; **en** ~ **de** (*fig*) on the fringe of; ~ **bénéficiaire** profit margin

marginal, e, -aux [maʀʒinal, o] *nm/f* (*original*) eccentric; (*déshérité*) dropout

marguerite [maʀgəʀit] *nf* marguerite, (oxeye) daisy; (*d'imprimante*) daisy-wheel

mari [maʀi] *nm* husband

mariage [maʀjaʒ] *nm* marriage; (*noce*) wedding; ~ **civil/religieux** registry office (*BRIT*) *ou* civil/church wedding

marié, e [maʀje] *adj* married ♦ *nm* (bride)groom; **les ~s** the bride and groom; **les (jeunes) ~s** the newly-weds; **mariée** *nf* bride

marier [maʀje] vt to marry; (fig) to blend; **se ~ vr** to get married; **se ~ (avec)** to marry

marin, e [maʀɛ̃, in] adj sea cpd, marine ♦ nm sailor

marine [maʀin] adj voir **marin** ♦ adj inv navy (blue) ♦ nm (MIL) ~ ♦ nf navy; **~ de guerre** navy; **~ marchande** merchant navy

mariner [maʀine] vt: **faire ~** to marinade

marionnette [maʀjɔnɛt] nf puppet

maritalement [maʀitalmɑ̃] adv: **vivre ~** to live as husband and wife

maritime [maʀitim] adj sea cpd, maritime

mark [maʀk] nm mark

marmelade [maʀmalad] nf stewed fruit, compote; **~ d'oranges** marmalade

marmite [maʀmit] nf (cooking-)pot

marmonner [maʀmɔne] vt, vi to mumble, mutter

marmot [maʀmo] (fam) nm kid

marmotter [maʀmɔte] vt to mumble

Maroc [maʀɔk] nm: **le ~** Morocco; **marocain, e** [maʀɔkɛ̃, ɛn] adj Moroccan ♦ nm/f: **Marocain, e** Moroccan

maroquinerie [maʀɔkinʀi] nf (articles) fine leather goods pl; (boutique) shop selling fine leather goods

marquant, e [maʀkɑ̃, ɑ̃t] adj outstanding

marque [maʀk] nf mark; (COMM: de nourriture) brand; (: de voiture, produits manufacturés) make; (de disques) label; **de ~** (produits) high-class; (visiteur etc) distinguished, well-known; **une grande ~ de vin** a well-known brand of wine; **~ de fabrique** trademark; **~ déposée** registered trademark

marquer [maʀke] vt to mark; (inscrire) to write down; (bétail) to brand; (SPORT: but etc) to score; (: joueur) to mark; (accentuer: taille etc) to emphasize; (manifester: refus, intérêt) to show ♦ vi (événement) to stand out, be outstanding; (SPORT) to score

marqueterie [maʀkətʀi] nf inlaid work, marquetry

marquis [maʀki] nm marquis, marquess; **marquise** nf marchioness; (auvent) glass canopy ou awning

marraine [maʀɛn] nf godmother

marrant, e [maʀɑ̃, ɑ̃t] (fam) adj funny

marre [maʀ] (fam) adv: **en avoir ~ de** to be fed up with

marrer [maʀe]: **se ~** (fam) vi to have a (good) laugh

marron [maʀɔ̃] nm (fruit) chestnut ♦ adj inv brown; **~s glacés** candied chestnuts; **marronnier** nm chestnut (tree)

mars [maʀs] nm March

Marseille [maʀsɛj] n Marseilles

marsouin [maʀswɛ̃] nm porpoise

marteau, x [maʀto] nm hammer; **être ~** (fam) to be nuts; **marteau-piqueur** nm pneumatic drill

marteler [maʀtəle] vt to hammer

martien, ne [maʀsjɛ̃, jɛn] adj Martian, of ou from Mars

martyr, e [maʀtiʀ] nm/f martyr; **martyre** nm martyrdom; (fig: sens affaibli) agony, torture; **martyriser** vt (REL) to martyr; (fig) to bully; (enfant) to batter, beat

marxiste [maʀksist] adj, nm/f Marxist

mascara [maskaʀa] nm mascara

masculin, e [maskylɛ̃, in] adj masculine; (sexe, population) male; (équipe, vêtements) men's; (viril) manly ♦ nm masculine; **masculinité** nf masculinity

masochiste [mazɔʃist] adj masochistic

masque [mask] nm mask; **masquer** vt (cacher: paysage, porte) to hide, conceal; (dissimuler: vérité, projet) to mask, obscure

massacre [masakʀ] nm massacre, slaughter; **massacrer** vt to massacre, slaughter; (fam: texte etc) to murder

massage [masaʒ] nm massage

masse [mas] nf mass; (ÉLEC) earth; (maillet) sledgehammer; (péj): **la ~** the masses; **une ~ de** (fam) masses ou loads of; **en ~** adv (acheter) in bulk; (en foule) en masse ♦ adj (exécutions, production) mass cpd

masser [mase] vt (assembler: gens) to gather; (pétrir) to massage; **se ~** vi (foule) to gather; **masseur, -euse** nm/f masseur(-euse)

massif, -ive [masif, iv] adj (porte) solid, massive; (visage) heavy, large; (bois, or) solid; (dose) massive; (déportations etc) mass cpd ♦ nm (montagneux) massif; (de fleurs) clump, bank

massue [masy] nf club, bludgeon

mastic [mastik] nm (pour vitres) putty; (pour fentes) filler

mastiquer [mastike] vt (aliment) to chew, masticate

mat, e [mat] adj (couleur, métal) mat(t); (bruit, son) dull ♦ adj inv (ÉCHECS): **être ~** to be checkmate

mât [ma] nm (NAVIG.) mast; (poteau) pole, post

match [matʃ] nm match; **faire ~ nul** to draw; **~ aller** first leg; **~ retour** second leg, return match

matelas [mat(ə)la] nm mattress; **~ pneumatique** air bed ou mattress; **matelassé, e** adj (vêtement) padded; (tissu) quilted

matelot [mat(ə)lo] nm sailor, seaman

mater [mate] vt (personne) to bring to heel, subdue; (révolte) to put down

matérialiser [mateʀjalize]: **se ~** vi to materialize

matérialiste [mateʀjalist] *adj* materialistic

matériaux [mateʀjo] *nmpl* material(s)

matériel, le [mateʀjɛl] *adj* material ♦ *nm* equipment *no pl*; (*de camping etc*) gear *no pl*; (*INFORM*) hardware

maternel, le [matɛʀnɛl] *adj* (*amour, geste*) motherly, maternal; (*grand-père, oncle*) maternal; **maternelle** *nf* (*aussi*: **école maternelle**) (state) nursery school

maternité [matɛʀnite] *nf* (*établissement*) maternity hospital; (*état de mère*) motherhood, maternity; (*grossesse*) pregnancy; **congé de ~** maternity leave

mathématique [matematik] *adj* mathematical; **mathématiques** *nfpl* (*science*) mathematics *sg*

maths [mat] (*fam*) *nfpl* maths

matière [matjɛʀ] *nf* matter; (*COMM, TECH*) material, matter *no pl*; (*fig: d'un livre etc*) subject matter, material; (*SCOL*) subject; **en ~ de** as regards; **~s grasses** fat content *sg*; **~s premières** raw materials

matin [matɛ̃] *nm, adv* morning; **du ~ au soir** from morning till night; **de bon** *ou* **grand ~** early in the morning; **matinal, e, -aux** *adj* (*toilette, gymnastique*) morning *cpd*; **être matinal** (*personne*) to be up early; to be an early riser; **matinée** *nf* morning; (*spectacle*) matinée

matou [matu] *nm* tom(cat)

matraque [matʀak] *nf* (*de policier*) truncheon (*BRIT*), billy (*US*)

matricule [matʀikyl] *nm* (*MIL*) regimental number; (*ADMIN*) reference number

matrimonial, e, -aux [matʀimɔnjal, jo] *adj* marital, marriage *cpd*

maudire [modiʀ] *vt* to curse; **maudit, e** (*fam*) *adj* (*satané*) blasted, confounded

maugréer [mogʀee] *vi* to grumble

maussade [mosad] *adj* sullen; (*temps*) gloomy

mauvais, e [mɔvɛ, ɛz] *adj* bad; (*faux*): **le ~ numéro/moment** the wrong number/ moment; (*méchant, malveillant*) malicious, spiteful; **il fait ~** the weather is bad; **la mer est ~e** the sea is rough; **~ plaisant** hoaxer; **~e herbe** weed; **~e langue** gossip, scandalmonger (*BRIT*); **~e passe** bad patch

mauve [mov] *adj* mauve

maux [mo] *nmpl de* **mal**; **~ de ventre** stomachache *sg*

maximum [maksimɔm] *adj, nm* maximum; **au ~** (*le plus possible*) as much as one can; (*tout au plus*) at the (very) most *ou* maximum; **faire le ~** to do one's level best

mayonnaise [majɔnɛz] *nf* mayonnaise

mazout [mazut] *nm* (*fuel*) oil

Me *abr* = **Maître**

me, m' [m(ə)] *pron* (*direct: téléphoner,*

attendre etc) me; (*indirect: parler, donner etc*) (*to*) me; (*réfléchi*) myself

mec [mɛk] (*fam*) *nm* bloke, guy

mécanicien, ne [mekanisjɛ̃, jɛn] *nm/f* mechanic; (*RAIL*) (train *ou* engine) driver

mécanique [mekanik] *adj* mechanical ♦ *nf* (*science*) mechanics *sg*; (*mécanisme*) mechanism; **ennui ~** engine trouble *no pl*

mécanisme [mekanism] *nm* mechanism

méchamment [meʃamã] *adv* nastily, maliciously, spitefully

méchanceté [meʃãste] *nf* nastiness, maliciousness; **dire des ~s à qn** to say spiteful things to sb

méchant, e [meʃã, ãt] *adj* nasty, malicious, spiteful; (*enfant: pas sage*) naughty; (*animal*) vicious

mèche [mɛʃ] *nf* (*de cheveux*) lock; (*de lampe, bougie*) wick; (*d'un explosif*) fuse; **de ~ avec** in league with

méchoui [meʃwi] *nm* barbecue of a whole roast sheep

méconnaissable [mekɔnɛsabl] *adj* unrecognizable

méconnaître [mekɔnɛtʀ] *vt* (*ignorer*) to be unaware of; (*mésestimer*) to misjudge

mécontent, e [mekɔ̃tã, ãt] *adj*: **~ (de)** discontented *ou* dissatisfied *ou* displeased (with); (*contrarié*) annoyed (at); **mécontentement** *nm* dissatisfaction, discontent, displeasure; (*irritation*) annoyance

médaille [medaj] *nf* medal

médaillon [medajɔ̃] *nm* (*bijou*) locket

médecin [med(ə)sɛ̃] *nm* doctor; **~ légiste** forensic surgeon

médecine [med(ə)sin] *nf* medicine

média [medja] *nmpl*: **les ~** the media; **médiatique** *adj* media *cpd*; **médiatisé, e** *adj* reported in the media; **ce procès a été très médiatisé** (*péj*) this trial was turned into a media event

médical, e, -aux [medikal, o] *adj* medical; **passer une visite ~e** to have a medical

médicament [medikamã] *nm* medicine, drug

médiéval, e, -aux [medjeval, o] *adj* medieval

médiocre [medjɔkʀ] *adj* mediocre, poor

médire [mediʀ] *vi*: **~ de** to speak ill of; **médisance** *nf* scandalmongering (*BRIT*)

méditer [medite] *vi* to meditate

Méditerranée [mediteʀane] *nf*: **la (mer) ~** the Mediterranean (Sea); **méditerranéen, ne** *adj* Mediterranean ♦ *nm/f*: **Méditerranéen, ne** native *ou* inhabitant of a Mediterranean country

méduse [medyz] *nf* jellyfish

meeting [mitiŋ] *nm* (*POL, SPORT*) rally

méfait [mefɛ] *nm* (*faute*) misdemeanour,

wrongdoing; **~s** *nmpl* (*ravages*) ravages, damage *sg*

méfiance [mefjɑ̃s] *nf* mistrust, distrust

méfiant, e [mefjɑ̃, jɑ̃t] *adj* mistrustful, distrustful

méfier [mefje]: **se ~** *vi* to be wary; to be careful; **se ~ de** to mistrust, be wary of

mégarde [megard] *nf*: **par ~** (*accidentellement*) accidentally; (*par erreur*) by mistake

mégère [meʒɛʀ] *nf* shrew

mégot [mego] (*fam*) *nm* cigarette end

meilleur, e [mɛjœʀ] *adj, adv* better ♦ *nm*: **le ~** the best; **le ~ des deux** the better of the two; **~ marché** (*inv*) cheaper; **meilleure** *nf*: **la meilleure** the best (one)

mélancolie [melɑ̃kɔli] *nf* melancholy, gloom; **mélancolique** *adj* melancholic, melancholy

mélange [melɑ̃ʒ] *nm* mixture; **mélanger** *vt* to mix; (*vins, couleurs*) to blend; (*mettre en désordre*) to mix up, muddle (up)

mélasse [melas] *nf* treacle, molasses *sg*

mêlée [mele] *nf* mêlée, scramble; (*RUGBY*) scrum(mage)

mêler [mele] *vt* (*unir*) to mix; (*embrouiller*) to muddle (up), mix up; **se ~** *vi* to mix, mingle; **se ~ à** (*personne: se joindre*) to join; (: *s'associer à*) to mix with; **se ~ de** (*suj: personne*) to meddle with, interfere in; **mêle-toi de ce qui te regarde!** mind your own business!

mélodie [melɔdi] *nf* melody; **mélodieux, -euse** *adj* melodious

melon [m(ə)lɔ̃] *nm* (*BOT*) (honeydew) melon; (*aussi*: **chapeau ~**) bowler (hat)

membre [mɑ̃bʀ] *nm* (*ANAT*) limb; (*personne, pays, élément*) member ♦ *adj* member *cpd*

mémé [meme] (*fam*) *nf* granny

MOT-CLÉ

même [mɛm] *adj* **1** (*avant le nom*) same; **en même temps** at the same time
2 (*après le nom: renforcement*): **il est la loyauté même** he is loyalty itself; **ce sont ses paroles/celles-là mêmes** they are his very words/the very ones
♦ *pron*: **le(la) même** the same one
♦ *adv* **1** (*renforcement*): **il n'a même pas pleuré** he didn't even cry; **même lui l'a dit** even HE said it; **ici même** at this very place
2: **à même**: **à même la bouteille** straight from the bottle; **à même la peau** next to the skin; **être à même de faire** to be in a position to do, be able to do
3: **de même**: **faire de même** to do likewise; **lui de même** so does (*ou* did *ou* is) he; **de même que** just as; **il en va de même pour** the same goes for

mémo [memo] (*fam*) *nm* memo

mémoire [memwaʀ] *nf* memory ♦ *nm* (*SCOL*) dissertation, paper; **~s** *nmpl* (*souvenirs*) memoirs; **à la ~ de** to the *ou* in memory of; **de ~** from memory; **~ morte/vive** (*INFORM*) ROM/RAM

mémorable [memɔrabl] *adj* memorable, unforgettable

menace [mənas] *nf* threat; **menacer** *vt* to threaten

ménage [menaʒ] *nm* (*travail*) housekeeping, housework; (*couple*) (married) couple; (*famille, ADMIN*) household; **faire le ~** to do the housework; **ménagement** *nm* care and attention; **ménager, -ère** *adj* household *cpd*, domestic ♦ *vt* (*traiter: personne*) to handle with tact; (*utiliser*) to use sparingly; (*prendre soin de*) to take (great) care of, look after; (*organiser*) to arrange; **ménager qch à qn** (*réserver*) to have sth in store for sb; **ménagère** *nf* housewife

mendiant, e [mɑ̃djɑ̃, jɑ̃t] *nm/f* beggar

mendier [mɑ̃dje] *vi* to beg ♦ *vt* to beg (for)

mener [m(ə)ne] *vt* to lead; (*enquête*) to conduct; (*affaires*) to manage ♦ *vi*: **~ à/dans** (*emmener*) to take to/into; **~ qch à bien** to see sth through (to a successful conclusion), complete sth successfully

meneur, -euse [mənœr, øz] *nm/f* leader; (*péj*) agitator

méningite [menɛ̃ʒit] *nf* meningitis *no pl*

ménopause [menopoz] *nf* menopause

menottes [mənɔt] *nfpl* handcuffs

mensonge [mɑ̃sɔ̃ʒ] *nm* lie; (*action*) lying *no pl*; **mensonger, -ère** *adj* false

mensualité [mɑ̃sɥalite] *nf* (*traite*) monthly payment

mensuel, le [mɑ̃sɥɛl] *adj* monthly

mensurations [mɑ̃syrasjɔ̃] *nfpl* measurements

mental, e, -aux [mɑ̃tal, o] *adj* mental; **mentalité** *nf* mentality

menteur, -euse [mɑ̃tœr, øz] *nm/f* liar

menthe [mɑ̃t] *nf* mint

mention [mɑ̃sjɔ̃] *nf* (*annotation*) note, comment; (*SCOL*) grade; **~ bien** *etc* ≈ grade B *etc* (*ou* upper 2nd class *etc*) pass (*BRIT*), ≈ pass with (high) honors (*US*); (*ADMIN*): "**rayer les ~s inutiles**" "delete as appropriate"; **mentionner** *vt* to mention

mentir [mɑ̃tir] *vi* to lie

menton [mɑ̃tɔ̃] *nm* chin

menu, e [məny] *adj* (*personne*) slim, slight; (*frais, difficulté*) minor ♦ *adv* (*couper, hacher*) very fine ♦ *nm* menu; **~ touristique/gastronomique** economy/gourmet's menu

menuiserie [mənɥizri] *nf* (*métier*) joinery, carpentry; (*passe-temps*) woodwork; **menuisier** *nm* joiner, carpenter

méprendre [mepʀɑ̃dʀ]: se ~ vi: se ~ sur to be mistaken (about)

mépris [mepʀi] nm (dédain) contempt, scorn; au ~ de regardless of, in defiance of; **méprisable** adj contemptible, despicable; **méprisant, e** adj scornful; **méprise** nf mistake, error; **mépriser** vt to scorn, despise; (gloire, danger) to scorn, spurn

mer [mɛʀ] nf sea; (marée) tide; en ~ at sea; en haute ou pleine ~ off shore, on the open sea; la ~ du Nord/Rouge the North/Red Sea

mercenaire [mɛʀsənɛʀ] nm mercenary, hired soldier

mercerie [mɛʀsəʀi] nf (boutique) haberdasher's shop (BRIT), notions store (US)

merci [mɛʀsi] excl thank you ♦ nf: à la ~ de qn/qch at sb's mercy/the mercy of sth; ~ beaucoup thank you very much; ~ de thank you for; sans ~ merciless(ly)

mercredi [mɛʀkʀədi] nm Wednesday

mercure [mɛʀkyʀ] nm mercury

merde [mɛʀd] (fam!) nf shit (!) ♦ excl (bloody) hell (!)

mère [mɛʀ] nf mother; ~ célibataire unmarried mother

merguez [mɛʀgɛz] nf merguez sausage (type of spicy sausage from N Africa)

méridional, e, -aux [meʀidjɔnal, o] adj southern ♦ nm/f Southerner

meringue [məʀɛ̃g] nf meringue

mérite [meʀit] nm merit; avoir du ~ (à faire qch) to deserve credit (for doing sth); **mériter** vt to deserve

merlan [mɛʀlɑ̃] nm whiting

merle [mɛʀl] nm blackbird

merveille [mɛʀvɛj] nf marvel, wonder; faire ~ to work wonders; à ~ perfectly, wonderfully; **merveilleux, -euse** adj marvellous, wonderful

mes [me] adj voir mon

mésange [mezɑ̃ʒ] nf tit(mouse)

mésaventure [mezavɑ̃tyʀ] nf misadventure, misfortune

Mesdames [medam] nfpl de Madame

Mesdemoiselles [medmwazɛl] nfpl de Mademoiselle

mesquin, e [mɛskɛ̃, in] adj mean, petty; **mesquinerie** nf meanness; (procédé) mean trick

message [mesaʒ] nm message; **messager, -ère** nm/f messenger

messe [mɛs] nf mass

Messieurs [mesjø] nmpl de Monsieur

mesure [m(ə)zyʀ] nf (évaluation, dimension) measurement; (récipient) measure; (MUS: cadence) time, tempo; (: division) bar; (retenue) moderation; (disposition) measure, step; sur ~ (costume) made-to-measure; dans

la ~ où insofar as, inasmuch as; à ~ que as; être en ~ de to be in a position to; dans une certaine ~ to a certain extent

mesurer [məzyʀe] vt to measure; (juger) to weigh up, assess; (modérer: ses paroles etc) to moderate; se ~ avec to have a confrontation with; il mesure 1 m 80 he's 1 m 80 tall

met [me] vb voir mettre

métal, -aux [metal, o] nm metal; **métallique** adj metallic

météo [meteo] nf (bulletin) weather report

météorologie [meteɔʀɔlɔʒi] nf meteorology

méthode [metɔd] nf method; (livre, ouvrage) manual, tutor

méticuleux, -euse [metikylø, øz] adj meticulous

métier [metje] nm (profession: gén) job; (: manuel) trade; (artisanal) craft; (technique, expérience) (acquired) skill ou technique; (aussi: ~ à tisser) (weaving) loom; avoir du ~ to have practical experience

métis, se [metis] adj, nm/f half-caste, half-breed

métrage [metʀaʒ] nm: long/moyen/court ~ full-length/medium-length/short film

mètre [mɛtʀ] nm metre; (règle) (metre) rule; (ruban) tape measure; **métrique** adj metric

métro [metʀo] nm underground (BRIT), subway

métropole [metʀɔpɔl] nf (capitale) metropolis; (pays) home country

mets [me] nm dish

metteur [metœʀ] nm: ~ en scène (THÉÂTRE) producer; (CINÉMA) director

---

MOT-CLÉ

---

mettre [mɛtʀ] vt 1 (placer) to put; mettre en bouteille/en sac to bottle/put in bags ou sacks; mettre en charge (pour) to charge (with), indict (for)

2 (vêtements: revêtir) to put on; (: porter) to wear; mets ton gilet put your cardigan on; je ne mets plus mon manteau I no longer wear my coat

3 (faire fonctionner: chauffage, électricité) to put on; (: reveil, minuteur) to set; (installer: gaz, eau) to put in, lay on; mettre en marche to start up

4 (consacrer): mettre du temps à faire qch to take time to do sth ou over sth

5 (noter, écrire) to say, put (down); qu'est-ce qu'il a mis sur la carte? what did he say ou write on the card?; mettez au pluriel ... put ... into the plural

6 (supposer): mettons que ... let's suppose ou say that ...

7: y mettre du sien to pull one's weight

se mettre vi 1 (se placer): vous pouvez vous

mettre là you can sit (*ou* stand) there; **où ça se met?** where does it go?; **se mettre au lit** to get into bed; **se mettre au piano** to sit down at the piano; **se mettre de l'encre sur les doigts** to get ink on one's fingers
2 (*s'habiller*): **se mettre en maillot de bain** to get into *ou* put on a swimsuit; **n'avoir rien à se mettre** to have nothing to wear
3: se mettre à to begin, start; **se mettre à faire** to begin *ou* start doing *ou* to do; **se mettre au piano** to start learning the piano; **se mettre au travail/à l'étude** to get down to work/one's studies

meuble [mœbl] *nm* piece of furniture; **des ~s** furniture; **meublé** *nm* furnished flatlet (*BRIT*) *ou* room; **meubler** *vt* to furnish
meugler [møgle] *vi* to low, moo
meule [møl] *nf* (*de foin, blé*) stack; (*de fromage*) round; (*à broyer*) millstone
meunier [mønje, jɛʀ] *nm* miller; **meunière** *nf* miller's wife
meure *etc* [mœʀ] *vb voir* **mourir**
meurtre [mœʀtʀ] *nm* murder; **meurtrier, -ière** *adj* (*arme etc*) deadly; (*fureur, instincts*) murderous ♦ *nm/f* murderer(-eress)
meurtrir [mœʀtʀiʀ] *vt* to bruise; (*fig*) to wound; **meurtrissure** *nf* bruise
meus *etc* [mœ] *vb voir* **mouvoir**
meute [møt] *nf* pack
mexicain, e [mɛksikɛ̃, ɛn] *adj* Mexican ♦ *nm/f* **M~,** e Mexican
Mexico [mɛksiko] *n* Mexico City
Mexique [mɛksik] *nm:* **le ~** Mexico
Mgr *abr* = **Monseigneur**
mi [mi] *nm* (*MUS*) E; (*en chantant la gamme*) mi ♦ *préfixe:* **~...** half(-); mid-; **à la ~-janvier** in mid-January; **à ~-hauteur** halfway up; **mi-bas** *nm inv* knee sock
miauler [mjole] *vi* to mew
miche [miʃ] *nf* round *ou* cob loaf
mi-chemin [miʃmɛ̃]: **à ~-~** *adv* halfway, midway
mi-clos, e [miklo, kloz] *adj* half-closed
micro [mikʀo] *nm* mike, microphone; (*INHUM*) micro
microbe [mikʀɔb] *nm* germ, microbe
micro...: **micro-onde** *nf:* **four à micro-ondes** microwave oven; **micro-ordinateur** *nm* microcomputer; **microscope** *nm* microscope; **microscopique** *adj* microscopic
midi [midi] *nm* midday, noon; (*moment du déjeuner*) lunchtime; (*sud*) south; **à ~** at 12 (o'clock) *ou* midday *ou* noon; **le M~** the South (of France), the Midi
mie [mi] *nf* crumb (*of the loaf*)
miel [mjɛl] *nm* honey; **mielleux, -euse** *adj* (*personne*) unctuous, syrupy
mien, ne [mjɛ̃, mjɛn] *pron:* **le(la) ~(ne), les**
~**(ne)s** mine; **les ~s** my family
miette [mjɛt] *nf* (*de pain, gâteau*) crumb; (*fig: de la conversation etc*) scrap; **en ~s** in pieces *ou* bits

---

MOT-CLÉ

mieux [mjø] *adv* **1** (*d'une meilleure façon*): **mieux (que)** better (than); **elle travaille/ mange mieux** she works/eats better; **elle va mieux** she is better
2 (*de la meilleure façon*) best; **ce que je sais le mieux** what I know best; **les livres les mieux faits** the best made books
3: de mieux en mieux better and better
♦ *adj* **1** (*plus à l'aise, en meilleure forme*) better; **se sentir mieux** to feel better
2 (*plus satisfaisant*) better; **c'est mieux ainsi** it's better like this; **c'est le mieux des deux** it's the better of the two; **le(la) mieux, les mieux** the best; **demandez-lui, c'est le mieux** ask him, it's the best thing
3 (*plus joli*) better looking
4: au mieux at best; **au mieux avec** on the best of terms with; **pour le mieux** for the best
♦ *nm* **1** (*progrès*) improvement
2: de mon/ton mieux as best I/you can (*ou* could); **faire de son mieux** to do one's best

---

mièvre [mjɛvʀ] *adj* mawkish (*BRIT*), sickly sentimental
mignon, ne [miɲɔ̃, ɔn] *adj* sweet, cute
migraine [migʀɛn] *nf* headache; (*MÉD*) migraine
mijoter [miʒɔte] *vt* to simmer; (*préparer avec soin*) to cook lovingly; (*fam: tramer*) to plot, cook up ♦ *vi* to simmer
mil [mil] *num* = **mille**
milieu, x [miljø] *nm* (*centre*) middle; (*BIO, GEO*) environment; (*entourage social*) milieu; (*provenance*) background; (*pègre*): **le ~** the underworld; **au ~ de** in the middle of; **au beau ~ ou en plein ~ (de)** right in the middle (of); **un juste ~** a happy medium
militaire [militɛʀ] *adj* military, army *cpd* ♦ *nm* serviceman
militant, e [militɑ̃, ɑ̃t] *adj, nm/f* militant
militer [milite] *vi* to be a militant
mille [mil] *num* a *ou* one thousand ♦ *nm* (*mesure*): **~ (marin)** nautical mile; **mettre dans le ~** (*fig*) to be bang on target; **millefeuille** *nm* cream *ou* vanilla slice; **millénaire** *nm* millennium ♦ *adj* thousand-year-old; (*fig*) ancient; **mille-pattes** *nm inv* centipede
millésimé, e [milezime] *adj* vintage *cpd*
millet [mijɛ] *nm* millet
milliard [miljaʀ] *nm* milliard, thousand million (*BRIT*), billion (*US*); **milliardaire** *nm/f* multimillionaire (*BRIT*), billionaire (*US*)

millier [milje] *nm* thousand; **un ~ (de)** a thousand or so, about a thousand; **par ~s** in (their) thousands, by the thousand

milligramme [miligʀam] *nm* milligramme

millimètre [milimɛtʀ] *nm* millimetre

million [miljɔ̃] *nm* million; **deux ~s de** two million; **millionnaire** *nm/f* millionaire

mime [mim] *nm/f* (*acteur*) mime(r) ♦ *nm* (*art*) mime, miming; **mimer** *vt* to mime; (*singer*) to mimic, take off

mimique [mimik] *nf* (*grimace*) (funny) face; (*signes*) gesticulations *pl*, sign language *no pl*

minable [minabl] *adj* (*décrépit*) shabby(-looking); (*médiocre*) pathetic

mince [mɛ̃s] *adj* thin; (*personne, taille*) slim, slender; (*fig: profit, connaissances*) slight, small, weak ♦ *excl*: **alors!** drat it!, darn it! (*US*); **minceur** *nf* thinness; (*d'une personne*) slimness, slenderness; **mincir** *vi* to get slimmer

mine [min] *nf* (*physionomie*) expression, look; (*allure*) exterior, appearance; (*de crayon*) lead; (*gisement, explosif, fig: source*) mine; **avoir bonne ~** (*personne*) to look well; (*ironique*) to look an utter idiot; **avoir mauvaise ~** to look unwell *ou* poorly; **faire ~ de faire** to make a pretence of doing; **~ de rien** although you wouldn't think so

miner [mine] *vt* (*saper*) to undermine, erode; (*MIL*) to mine

minerai [minʀe] *nm* ore

minéral, e, -aux [mineʀal, o] *adj, nm* mineral

minéralogique [mineʀalɔʒik] *adj*: **numéro ~** registration number

minet, te [mine, ɛt] *nm/f* (*chat*) pussy-cat; (*péj*) young trendy

mineur, e [minœʀ] *adj* minor ♦ *nm/f* (*JUR*) minor, person under age ♦ *nm* (*travailleur*) miner

miniature [minjatyʀ] *adj, nf* miniature

minibus [minibys] *nm* minibus

mini-cassette [minikaset] *nf* cassette (recorder)

minier, -ière [minje, jɛʀ] *adj* mining

mini-jupe [miniʒyp] *nf* mini-skirt

minime [minim] *adj* minor, minimal

minimiser [minimize] *vt* to minimize; (*fig*) to play down

minimum [minimɔm] *adj, nm* minimum; **au ~** (*au moins*) at the very least

ministère [ministɛʀ] *nm* (*aussi REL*) ministry; (*cabinet*) government

ministre [ministʀ] *nm* (*aussi REL*) minister

Minitel ® [minitel] *nm* videotext terminal and service

minoritaire [minɔʀitɛʀ] *adj* minority

minorité [minɔʀite] *nf* minority; **être en ~** to be in the *ou* a minority

minuit [minɥi] *nm* midnight

minuscule [minyskyl] *adj* minute, tiny ♦ *nf*: **(lettre) ~** small letter

minute [minyt] *nf* minute; **à la ~** (just) this instant; (*faire*) there and then; **minuter** *vt* to time; **minuterie** *nf* time switch

minutieux, -euse [minysjø, jøz] *adj* (*personne*) meticulous; (*travail*) minutely detailed

mirabelle [miʀabel] *nf* (cherry) plum

miracle [miʀakl] *nm* miracle

mirage [miʀaʒ] *nm* mirage

mire [miʀ] *nf*: **point de ~** (*fig*) focal point

miroir [miʀwaʀ] *nm* mirror

miroiter [miʀwate] *vi* to sparkle, shimmer; **faire ~ qch à qn** to paint sth in glowing colours for sb, dangle sth in front of sb's eyes

mis, e [mi, miz] *pp de* **mettre** ♦ *adj*: **bien ~** well-dressed

mise [miz] *nf* (*argent: au jeu*) stake; (*tenue*) clothing, attire; **être de ~** to be acceptable *ou* in season; **~ au point** (*fig*) clarification; **~ de fonds** capital outlay; **~ en examen** charging, indictment; **~ en plis** set; **~ en scène** production

miser [mize] *vt* (*enjeu*) to stake, bet; **~ sur** (*cheval, numéro*) to bet on; (*fig*) to bank *ou* count on

misérable [mizeʀabl] *adj* (*lamentable, malheureux*) pitiful, wretched; (*pauvre*) poverty-stricken; (*insignifiant, mesquin*) miserable ♦ *nm/f* wretch

misère [mizeʀ] *nf* (extreme) poverty, destitution; **~s** *nfpl* (*malheurs*) woes, miseries; (*ennuis*) little troubles; **salaire de ~** starvation wage

missile [misil] *nm* missile

mission [misjɔ̃] *nf* mission; **partir en ~** (*ADMIN, POL*) to go on an assignment; **missionnaire** *nm/f* missionary

mit [mi] *vb voir* **mettre**

mité, e [mite] *adj* moth-eaten

mi-temps [mitɑ̃] *nf inv* (*SPORT: période*) half; (*: pause*) half-time; **à ~~** part-time

miteux, -euse [mitø, øz] *adj* (*lieu*) seedy

mitigé, e [mitiʒe] *adj*: **sentiments ~s** mixed feelings

mitonner [mitɔne] *vt* to cook with loving care; (*fig*) to cook up quietly

mitoyen, ne [mitwajɛ̃, jɛn] *adj* (*mur*) common, party *cpd*

mitrailler [mitʀaje] *vt* to machine-gun; (*fig*) to pelt, bombard; (*: photographier*) to take shot after shot of; **mitraillette** *nf* submachine gun; **mitrailleuse** *nf* machine gun

mi-voix [mivwa]: **à ~~** *adv* in a low *ou* hushed voice

mixage [miksaʒ] *nm* (*CINÉMA*) (sound)

mixing

mixer [miksœʀ] nm (food) mixer

mixte [mikst] adj (gén) mixed; (SCOL) mixed, coeducational

mixture [mikstyʀ] nf mixture; (fig) concoction

Mlle (pl **Mlles**) abr = **Mademoiselle**

MM abr = **Messieurs**

Mme (pl **Mmes**) abr = **Madame**

mobile [mɔbil] adj mobile; (pièce de machine) moving ♦ nm (motif) motive; (œuvre d'art) mobile

mobilier, -ière [mɔbilje, jɛʀ] nm furniture

mobiliser [mɔbilize] vt to mobilize

mocassin [mɔkasɛ̃] nm moccasin

moche [mɔʃ] (fam) adj (laid) ugly; (mauvais) rotten

modalité [mɔdalite] nf form, mode; ~s de paiement methods of payment

mode [mɔd] nf fashion ♦ nm (manière) form, mode; à la ~ fashionable, in fashion; ~ d'emploi directions pl (for use)

modèle [mɔdɛl] adj, nm model; (qui pose) sitter; ~ déposé registered design; ~ réduit small-scale model; **modeler** vt to model

modem [mɔdɛm] nm modem

modéré, e [mɔdeʀe] adj, nm/f moderate

modérer [mɔdeʀe] vt to moderate; se ~ vi to restrain o.s.

moderne [mɔdɛʀn] adj modern ♦ nm (style) modern style; (meubles) modern furniture; **moderniser** vt to modernize

modeste [mɔdɛst] adj modest; **modestie** nf modesty

modifier [mɔdifje] vt to modify, alter; se ~ vi to alter

modique [mɔdik] adj modest

modiste [mɔdist] nf milliner

moelle [mwal] nf marrow; ~ épinière spinal cord

moelleux, -euse [mwalø, øz] adj soft; (gâteau) light and moist

mœurs [mœʀ] nfpl (conduite) morals; (manières) manners; (pratiques sociales, mode de vie) habits

mohair [mɔɛʀ] nm mohair

moi [mwa] pron me; (emphatique): ~, je ... for my part, I ...; I myself ...; à ~ mine; **moi-même** pron myself; (emphatique) I myself

moindre [mwɛ̃dʀ] adj lesser; lower; le(la) ~, les ~s the least, the slightest; **merci** – c'est le ~ des choses! thank you – it's a pleasure!

moine [mwan] nm monk, friar

moineau, x [mwano] nm sparrow

MOT-CLÉ

moins [mwɛ̃] adv **1** (comparatif): **moins (que)** less (than); **moins grand que** less tall than, not as tall as; **moins je travaille, mieux je me** porte the less I work, the better I feel

2 (superlatif): **le moins** (the) least; **c'est ce que j'aime le moins** it's what I like (the) least; **le(la) moins doué(e)** the least gifted; **au moins, du moins** at least; **pour le moins** at the very least

3: **moins de** (quantité) less (than); (nombre) fewer (than); **moins de sable/d'eau** less sand/water; **moins de livres/gens** fewer books/people; **moins de 2 ans** less than 2 years; **moins de midi** not yet midday

4: **de moins, en moins**: **100 F/3 jours de moins** 100F/3 days less; **3 livres en moins** 3 books fewer; **de trop à peu; de l'argent en moins** less money; **le soleil en moins** but for the sun, minus the sun; **de moins en moins** less and less

5: **à moins de, à moins que** unless; **à moins de faire** unless we do (ou he does etc); **à moins que tu ne fasses** unless you do; **à moins d'un accident** barring any accident

♦ prép: **4 moins 2** 4 minus 2; **il est moins 5** it's 5 to; **il fait moins 5** it's 5 (degrees) below (freezing), it's minus 5

mois [mwa] nm month

moisi [mwazi] nm mould, mildew; **odeur de ~** musty smell; **moisir** vi to go mouldy; **moisissure** nf mould no pl

moisson [mwasɔ̃] nf harvest; **moissonner** vt to harvest, reap; **moissonneuse** nf (machine) harvester

moite [mwat] adj sweaty, sticky

moitié [mwatje] nf half; **la ~** half; **la ~ de** half (of); **la ~ du temps** half the time; **à la ~ de** halfway through; **à ~** (avant le verbe) half; (avant l'adjectif) half-; **à ~ prix** (at) half-price; **~ moitié** half and half

moka [mɔka] nm coffee gateau

mol [mɔl] adj voir **mou**

molaire [mɔlɛʀ] nf molar

molester [mɔleste] vt to manhandle, maul (about)

molle [mɔl] adj voir **mou**; **mollement** adv (péj: travailler) sluggishly; (protester) feebly

mollet [mɔlɛ] nm calf ♦ adj m: **œuf ~** soft-boiled egg

molletonné, e [mɔltɔne] adj (gants etc) fleece-lined

mollir [mɔliʀ] vi (fléchir) to relent; (substance) to go soft

mollusque [mɔlysk] nm mollusc

môme [mom] (fam) nm/f (enfant) brat

moment [mɔmɑ̃] nm moment; **ce n'est pas le ~** this is not the (right) time; **pour un bon ~** for a good while; **pour le ~** for the moment, for the time being; **au ~ de** at the time of; **au ~ où** just as; **à tout ~** (peut arriver etc) at any time *ou* moment; (*constamment*) constantly, continually; **en ce ~** at the moment; at present; **sur le ~** at the time; **par ~s** now and then, at times; **du ~ où** *ou que* seeing that, since; **momentané, e** *adj* temporary, momentary; **momentanément** *adv* (*court instant*) for a short while

momie [mɔmi] *nf* mummy

mon, ma [mɔ̃, ma] (*pl* **mes**) *adj* my

Monaco [mɔnako] *nm* Monaco

monarchie [mɔnaʀʃi] *nf* monarchy

monastère [mɔnastɛʀ] *nm* monastery

monceau, x [mɔ̃so] *nm* heap

mondain, e [mɔ̃dɛ̃, ɛn] *adj* (*vie*) society *cpd*

monde [mɔ̃d] *nm* world; (*haute société*): **le ~** (high) society; **il y a du ~** (*beaucoup de gens*) there are a lot of people; (*quelques personnes*) there are some people; **beaucoup/peu de ~** many/few people; **mettre au ~** to bring into the world; **pas le moins du ~** not in the least; **se faire un ~ de qch** to make a great deal of fuss about sth; **mondial, e, -aux** *adj* (*population*) world *cpd*; (*influence*) worldwide; **mondialement** *adv* throughout the world

monégasque [mɔnegask] *adj* Monegasque, of *ou* from Monaco

monétaire [mɔnetɛʀ] *adj* monetary

moniteur, -trice [mɔnitœʀ, tʀis] *nm/f* (*SPORT*) instructor(-tress); (*de colonie de vacances*) supervisor ♦ *nm* (*écran*) monitor

monnaie [mɔnɛ] *nf* (*ÉCON, gén: moyen d'échange*) currency; (*petites pièces*): **avoir de la ~** to have (some) change; **une pièce de ~** a coin; **faire de la ~** to get (some) change; **avoir/faire la ~ de 20 F** to have change of/get change for 20 F; **rendre à qn la ~ (sur 20 F)** to give sb the change (out of *ou* from 20 F); **monnayer** *vt* to convert into cash; (*talent*) to capitalize on

monologue [mɔnɔlɔg] *nm* monologue, soliloquy; **monologuer** *vi* to soliloquize

monopole [mɔnɔpɔl] *nm* monopoly

monotone [mɔnɔtɔn] *adj* monotonous

Monsieur [məsjø] (*pl* **Messieurs**) *titre* Mr ♦ *nm* (*homme quelconque*): **un/le m~** a/the gentleman; **~, ...** (*en tête de lettre*) Dear Sir, ...; *voir aussi* **Madame**

monstre [mɔ̃stʀ] *nm* monster ♦ *adj* (*fam: colossal*) monstrous; **un travail ~** a fantastic amount of work; **monstrueux, -euse** *adj* monstrous

mont [mɔ̃] *nm*: **par ~s et par vaux** up hill and down dale; **le M~ Blanc** Mont Blanc

montage [mɔ̃taʒ] *nm* (*assemblage: d'appareil*) assembly; (*PHOTO*) photomontage; (*CINÉMA*) editing

montagnard, e [mɔ̃taɲaʀ, aʀd] *adj* mountain *cpd* ♦ *nm/f* mountain-dweller

montagne [mɔ̃taɲ] *nf* (*cime*) mountain; (*région*): **la ~** the mountains *pl*; **~s russes** big dipper *sg*, switchback *sg*; **montagneux, -euse** *adj* mountainous; (*basse montagne*) hilly

montant, e [mɔ̃tɑ̃, ɑ̃t] *adj* rising; **pull à col ~** high-necked jumper ♦ *nm* (*somme, total*) (sum) total, (total) amount; (*de fenêtre*) upright; (*de lit*) post

monte-charge [mɔ̃tʃaʀʒ] *nm inv* goods lift, hoist

montée [mɔ̃te] *nf* (*des prix, hostilités*) rise; (*escalade*) climb; (*côte*) hill; **au milieu de la ~** halfway up

monter [mɔ̃te] *vt* (*escalier, côte*) to go (*ou* come) up; (*valise, paquet*) to take (*ou* bring) up; (*étagère*) to raise; (*tente, échafaudage*) to put up; (*machine*) to assemble; (*CINÉMA*) to edit; (*THÉÂTRE*) to put on, stage; (*société etc*) to set up ♦ *vi* to go (*ou* come) up; (*prix, niveau, température*) to go up, rise; (*passager*) to get on; **se ~ à** (*frais etc*) to add up to, come to; **~ à pied** to walk up, go up on foot; **~ dans le train/l'avion** to get into the train/ plane, board the train/plane; **~ sur** to climb up onto; **~ à cheval** (*faire du cheval*) to ride, go riding

montre [mɔ̃tʀ] *nf* watch; **contre la ~** (*SPORT*) against the clock; **montre-bracelet** *nf* wristwatch

montrer [mɔ̃tʀe] *vt* to show; **~ qch à qn** to show sth to sb

monture [mɔ̃tyʀ] *nf* (*cheval*) mount; (*de lunettes*) frame; (*d'une bague*) setting

monument [mɔnymɑ̃] *nm* monument; **~ aux morts** war memorial

moquer [mɔke]: **se ~ de** *vt* to make fun of, laugh at; (*fam: se désintéresser de*) not to care about; (*tromper*): **se ~ de qn** to take sb for a ride; **moquerie** *nf* mockery

moquette [mɔkɛt] *nf* fitted carpet

moqueur, -euse [mɔkœʀ, øz] *adj* mocking

moral, e, -aux [mɔʀal, o] *adj* moral ♦ *nm* morale; **avoir le ~** (*fam*) to be in good spirits; **avoir le ~ à zéro** (*fam*) to be really down; **morale** *nf* (*mœurs*) morals *pl*; (*valeurs*) moral standards *pl*, morality; (*d'une fable etc*) moral; **faire la morale à** to lecture, preach at; **moralité** *nf* morality; (*de fable*) moral

morceau, x [mɔʀso] *nm* piece, bit; (*d'une œuvre*) passage, extract; (*MUS*) piece; (*CULIN: de viande*) cut; (*de sucre*) lump; **mettre en ~x** to pull to pieces *ou* bits; **manger un ~** to have a bite (to eat)

morceler [mɔʀsəle] *vt* to break up, divide up

mordant, e [mɔʀdɑ̃, ɑ̃t] *adj* (*ton, remarque*) scathing, cutting; (*ironie, froid*) biting ♦ *nm* (*style*) bite, punch

mordiller [mɔʀdije] *vt* to nibble at, chew at

mordre [mɔʀdʀ] vt to bite ♦ vi (poisson) to
bite; ~ **sur** (fig) to go over into, overlap into;
~ **à l'hameçon** to bite, rise to the bait

mordu, e [mɔʀdy] (fam) nm/f enthusiast;
un ~ de jazz a jazz fanatic

morfondre [mɔʀfɔ̃dʀ]: **se ~** vi to mope

morgue [mɔʀg] nf (arrogance) haughtiness;
(lieu: de la police) morgue; (: à l'hôpital)
mortuary

morne [mɔʀn] adj dismal, dreary

morose [mɔʀoz] adj sullen, morose

mors [mɔʀ] nm bit

morse [mɔʀs] nm (ZOOL) walrus; (TÉL) Morse
(code)

morsure [mɔʀsyʀ] nf bite

mort¹ [mɔʀ] nf death

mort², e [mɔʀ, mɔʀt] pp de **mourir** ♦ adj
dead ♦ nm/f (défunt) dead man/woman;
(victime): **il y a eu plusieurs ~s** several people
were killed, there were several killed; ~ **de
peur/fatigue** frightened to death/dead tired

mortalité [mɔʀtalite] nf mortality, death rate

mortel, le [mɔʀtɛl] adj (poison etc) deadly,
lethal, (accident, blessure) fatal; (silence,
ennemi) deadly; (péché) mortal; (fam:
ennuyeux) deadly boring

mortier [mɔʀtje] nm (gén) mortar

mort-né, e [mɔʀne] adj (enfant) stillborn

mortuaire [mɔʀtɥɛʀ] adj: **avis ~** death
announcement

morue [mɔʀy] nf (ZOOL) cod inv

mosaïque [mɔzaik] nf mosaic

Moscou [mɔsku] n Moscow

mosquée [mɔske] nf mosque

mot [mo] nm word; (message) line, note; ~
à ~ word for word; ~ **d'ordre** watchword;
~ **de passe** password; **~s croisés** crossword
(puzzle) sg

motard [mɔtaʀ, aʀd] nm biker; (policier)
motorcycle cop

motel [mɔtɛl] nm motel

moteur, -trice [mɔtœʀ, tʀis] adj (ANAT,
PHYSIOL) motor; (TECH) driving, (AUTO): **à 4
roues motrices** 4-wheel drive ♦ nm engine,
motor; **à ~** power-driven, motor cpd

motif [mɔtif] nm (cause) motive; (décoratif)
design, pattern, motif; **sans ~** groundless

motivation [mɔtivasjɔ̃] nf motivation

motiver [mɔtive] vt to motivate; (justifier) to
justify, account for

moto [mɔto] nf (motor)bike; **motocycliste**
nm/f motorcyclist

motorisé, e [mɔtɔʀize] adj (personne)
having transport ou a car

motrice [mɔtʀis] adj voir **moteur**

motte [mɔt] nf: ~ **de terre** lump of earth, clod
(of earth); ~ **de beurre** lump of butter

mou (mol), molle [mu, mɔl] adj soft;
(personne) lethargic; (protestations) weak

♦ nm: **avoir du mou** to be slack

moucharder [muʃaʀde] (fam) vt (SCOL) to
sneak on; (POLICE) to grass on

mouche [muʃ] nf fly

moucher [muʃe]: **se ~** vi to blow one's nose

moucheron [muʃʀɔ̃] nm midge

mouchoir [muʃwaʀ] nm handkerchief,
hanky; ~ **en papier** tissue, paper hanky

moudre [mudʀ] vt to grind

moue [mu] nf pout; **faire la ~** to pout; (fig) to
pull a face

mouette [mwɛt] nf (sea)gull

moufle [mufl] nf (gant) mitt(en)

mouillé, e [muje] adj wet

mouiller [muje] vt (humecter) to wet,
moisten; (tremper): ~ **qn/qch** to make sb/sth
wet ♦ vi (NAVIG) to lie ou be at anchor; **se ~**
to get wet; (fam: prendre des risques) to
commit o.s.

moulant, e [mulã, ãt] adj figure-hugging

moule [mul] nf mussel ♦ nm (CULIN) mould;
~ **à gâteaux** ♦ nm cake tin (BRIT) ou pan (US)

moulent [mul] vb voir **moudre, mouler**

mouler [mule] vt (suj: vêtement) to hug, fit
closely round

moulin [mulɛ̃] nm mill; ~ **à café/à poivre**
coffee/pepper mill; ~ **à légumes** (vegetable)
shredder; ~ **à paroles** (fig) chatterbox; ~ **à
vent** windmill

moulinet [mulinɛ] nm (de canne à pêche)
reel; (mouvement): **faire des ~s avec qch** to
whirl sth around

moulinette ® [mulinɛt] nf (vegetable)
shredder

moulu, e [muly] pp de **moudre**

mourant, e [muʀã, ãt] adj dying

mourir [muʀiʀ] vi to die; (civilisation) to die
out; ~ **de froid/faim** to die of exposure/
hunger; ~ **de faim/d'ennui** (fig) to be
starving/be bored to death; ~ **d'envie de faire**
to be dying to do

mousse [mus] nf (BOT) moss; (de savon)
lather; (écume: sur eau, bière) froth, foam;
(CULIN) mousse ♦ nm (NAVIG) ship's boy; ~ **à
raser** shaving foam

mousseline [muslin] nf muslin; **pommes ~**
mashed potatoes

mousser [muse] vi (bière, détergent) to foam;
(savon) to lather; **mousseux, -euse** adj
frothy ♦ nm: **(vin) mousseux** sparkling wine

mousson [musɔ̃] nf monsoon

moustache [mustaʃ] nf moustache; **~s** nfpl
(du chat) whiskers pl; **moustachu, e** adj
with a moustache

moustiquaire [mustikɛʀ] nf mosquito net

moustique [mustik] nm mosquito

moutarde [mutaʀd] nf mustard

mouton [mutɔ̃] nm sheep inv; (peau)
sheepskin; (CULIN) mutton

mouvement [muvmɑ̃] nm movement; (fig: impulsion) gesture; **avoir un bon ~** to make a nice gesture; **en ~** in motion; on the move; **mouvementé, e** adj (vie, poursuite) eventful; (réunion) turbulent

mouvoir [muvwaʀ]: **se ~** vi to move

moyen, ne [mwajɛ̃, jɛn] adj average; (tailles, prix) medium; (de grandeur moyenne) medium-sized ♦ nm (façon) means sg, way; **~s** nmpl (capacités) means; **très ~** (résultats) pretty poor; **je n'en ai pas les ~s** I can't afford it; **au ~ de** by means of; **par tous les ~s** by every possible means, every possible way; **par ses propres ~s** all by oneself; **~ âge** Middle Ages; **~ de transport** means of transport

moyennant [mwajenɑ̃] prép (somme) for; (service, conditions) in return for; (travail, effort) with

moyenne [mwajen] nf average; (MATH) mean; (SCOL: à l'examen) pass mark; **en ~ on** (an) average; **~ d'âge** average age

Moyen-Orient [mwajenɔʀjɑ̃] nm: **le ~-~** the Middle East

moyeu, x [mwajø] nm hub

MST sigle f (= maladie sexuellement transmissible) STD

mû, mue [my] pp de **mouvoir**

muer [mɥe] vi (oiseau, mammifère) to moult; (serpent) to slough; (jeune garçon): **il mue** his voice is breaking; **se ~ en** to transform into

muet, te [mɥe, mɥet] adj dumb; (fig): **~ d'admiration** etc speechless with admiration etc; (CINÉMA) silent ♦ nm/f mute

mufle [myfl] nm muzzle; (fam: goujat) boor

mugir [myʒiʀ] vi (taureau) to bellow; (vache) to low; (fig) to howl

muguet [myɡɛ] nm lily of the valley

mule [myl] nf (ZOOL) (she-)mule

mulet [mylɛ] nm (ZOOL) (he-)mule

multinationale [myltinasjɔnal] nf multinational

multiple [myltipl] adj multiple, numerous; (varié) many, manifold; **multiplication** nf multiplication; **multiplier** vt to multiply; **se multiplier** vi to multiply

municipal, e, -aux [mynisipal, o] adj (élections, stade) municipal; (conseil) town cpd; **piscine/bibliothèque ~e** public swimming pool/library; **municipalité** nf (ville) municipality; (conseil) town council

munir [myniʀ] vt: **~ qch de** to equip sth with; **se ~ de** to arm o.s. with

munitions [mynisjɔ̃] nfpl ammunition sg

mur [myʀ] nm wall; **~ du son** sound barrier

mûr, e [myʀ] adj ripe; (personne) mature

muraille [myʀɑj] nf (high) wall

mural, e, -aux [myʀal, o] adj wall cpd; (art) mural

mûre [myʀ] nf blackberry

muret [myʀɛ] nm low wall

mûrir [myʀiʀ] vi (fruit, blé) to ripen; (abcès) to come to a head; (fig: idée, personne) to mature ♦ vt (projet) to nurture; (personne) to (make) mature

murmure [myʀmyʀ] nm murmur; **murmurer** vi to murmur

muscade [myskad] nf (aussi: **noix (de) ~**) nutmeg

muscat [myska] nm (raisins) muscat grape; (vin) muscatel (wine)

muscle [myskl] nm muscle; **musclé, e** adj muscular; (fig) strong-arm

museau, x [myzo] nm muzzle; (CULIN) brawn

musée [myze] nm museum; (de peinture) art gallery

museler [myz(ə)le] vt to muzzle; **muselière** nf muzzle

musette [myzɛt] nf (sac) lunchbag

musical, e, -aux [myzikal, o] adj musical

music-hall [myzikol] nm (salle) variety theatre; (genre) variety

musicien, ne [myzisjɛ̃, jɛn] adj musical ♦ nm/f musician

musique [myzik] nf music; **~ d'ambiance** background music

musulman, e [myzylmɑ̃, an] adj, nm/f Moslem, Muslim

mutation [mytasjɔ̃] nf (ADMIN) transfer

muter [myte] vt to transfer, move

mutilé, e [mytile] nm/f disabled person (through loss of limbs)

mutiler [mytile] vt to mutilate, maim

mutin, e [mytɛ̃, in] adj (air, ton) mischievous, impish ♦ nm/f (MIL, NAVIG) mutineer; **mutinerie** nf mutiny

mutisme [mytism] nm silence

mutuel, le [mytɥɛl] adj mutual; **mutuelle** nf voluntary insurance premiums for back-up health cover

myope [mjɔp] adj short-sighted

myosotis [mjɔzɔtis] nm forget-me-not

myrtille [miʀtij] nf bilberry

mystère [mistɛʀ] nm mystery; **mystérieux, -euse** adj mysterious

mystifier [mistifje] vt to fool

mythe [mit] nm myth

mythologie [mitɔlɔʒi] nf mythology

N, n

n' [n] adv voir ne

nacre [nakʀ] nf mother of pearl

nage [naʒ] nf swimming; (manière) style of swimming, stroke; **traverser/s'éloigner à la ~** to swim across/away; **en ~** bathed in sweat; **nageoire** nf fin; **nager** vi to swim; **nageur,**

-euse *nm/f* swimmer

naguère [nagɛʀ] *adv* formerly

naïf, -ïve [naif, naiv] *adj* naïve

nain, e [nɛ̃, nɛn] *nm/f* dwarf

naissance [nesɑ̃s] *nf* birth; **donner ~ à** to give birth to; (*fig*) to give rise to

naître [nɛtʀ] *vi* to be born; (*fig*): **~ de** to arise from, be born out of; **il est né en 1960** he was born in 1960; **faire ~** (*fig*) to give rise to, arouse

naïve [naiv] *adj voir* **naïf**

naïveté [naivte] *nf* naïvety

nana [nana] (*fam*) *nf* (*fille*) chick, bird (*BRIT*)

nantir [nɑ̃tiʀ] *vt*: **~ qn de** to provide sb with; **les nantis** (*péj*) the well-to-do

nappe [nap] *nf* tablecloth; (*de pétrole, gaz*) layer; **~ phréatique** ground water; **napperon** *nm* table-mat

naquit *etc* [naki] *vb voir* **naître**

narcodollars [naʀkodɔlaʀ] *nmpl* drug money *sg*

narguer [naʀge] *vt* to taunt

narine [naʀin] *nf* nostril

narquois, e [naʀkwa, waz] *adj* mocking

natal, e [natal] *adj* native; **natalité** *nf* birth rate

natation [natasjɔ̃] *nf* swimming

natif, -ive [natif, iv] *adj* native

nation [nasjɔ̃] *nf* nation; **national, e, -aux** *adj* national; **nationale** *nf*: (*route*) **nationale** ≈ A road (*BRIT*), ≈ state highway (*US*); **nationaliser** *vt* to nationalize; **nationalisme** *nm* nationalism; **nationalité** *nf* nationality

natte [nat] *nf* (*cheveux*) plait, (*tapis*) mat

naturaliser [natyʀalize] *vt* to naturalize

nature [natyʀ] *nf* nature ♦ *adj, adv* (*CULIN*) plain, without seasoning or sweetening; (*café, thé*) black, without sugar; (*yaourt*) natural; **payer en ~** to pay in kind; **~ morte** still-life; **naturel, le** *adj* (*gén, aussi enfant*) natural ♦ *nm* (*absence d'affectation*) naturalness; (*caractère*) disposition, nature; **naturellement** *adv* naturally; (*bien sûr*) of course

naufrage [nofʀaʒ] *nm* (ship)wreck; **faire ~** to be shipwrecked

nauséabond, e [nozeabɔ̃, ɔ̃d] *adj* foul

nausée [noze] *nf* nausea

nautique [notik] *adj* nautical, water *cpd*; **sports ~s** water sports

naval, e [naval] *adj* naval; (*industrie*) shipbuilding

navet [navɛ] *nm* turnip; (*péj: film*) rubbishy film

navette [navɛt] *nf* shuttle; **faire la ~ (entre)** to go to and fro *ou* shuttle (between)

navigateur [navigatœʀ, tʀis] *nm* (*NAVIG*) seafarer

navigation [navigasjɔ̃] *nf* navigation, sailing

naviguer [navige] *vi* to navigate, sail

navire [naviʀ] *nm* ship

navrer [navʀe] *vt* to upset, distress; **je suis navré** I'm so sorry

ne, n' [n(ə)] *adv voir* **pas**; **plus**; **jamais** *etc*; (*sans valeur négative: non traduit*): **c'est plus loin que je ~ le croyais** it's further than I thought

né, e [ne] *pp* (*voir* **naître**): **~ en 1960** born in 1960; **~e Scott** née Scott

néanmoins [neɑ̃mwɛ̃] *adv* nevertheless

néant [neɑ̃] *nm* nothingness; **réduire à ~** to bring to nought; (*espoir*) to dash

nécessaire [nesesɛʀ] *adj* necessary ♦ *nm* necessary; (*sac*) kit; **je vais faire le ~** I'll see to it; **~ de couture** sewing kit; **nécessité** *nf* necessity; **nécessiter** *vt* to require

nécrologique [nekʀɔlɔʒik] *adj*: **rubrique ~** obituary column

nectar [nɛktaʀ] *nm* nectar

néerlandais, e [neɛʀlɑ̃dɛ, ɛz] *adj* Dutch

nef [nɛf] *nf* (*d'église*) nave

néfaste [nefast] *adj* (*nuisible*) harmful; (*funeste*) ill-fated

négatif, -ive [negatif, iv] *adj* negative ♦ *nm* (*PHOTO*) negative

négligé, e [negliʒe] *adj* (*en désordre*) slovenly ♦ *nm* (*tenue*) negligee

négligeable [negliʒabl] *adj* negligible

négligent, e [negliʒɑ̃, ɑ̃t] *adj* careless, negligent

négliger [negliʒe] *vt* (*tenue*) to be careless about; (*avis, précautions*) to disregard; (*épouse, jardin*) to neglect; **~ de faire** to fail to do, not bother to do

négoce [negɔs] *nm* trade

négociant [negɔsjɑ̃, jɑ̃t] *nm* merchant

négociation [negɔsjasjɔ̃] *nf* negotiation

négocier [negɔsje] *vi, vt* to negotiate

nègre [negʀ] (*péj*) *nm* (*écrivain*) ghost (writer)

neige [nɛʒ] *nf* snow; **neiger** *vi* to snow

nénuphar [nenyfaʀ] *nm* water-lily

néon [neɔ̃] *nm* neon

néo-zélandais, e [neozelɑ̃dɛ, ɛz] *adj* New Zealand *cpd* ♦ *nm/f*: **N~-Z~, e** New Zealander

nerf [nɛʀ] *nm* nerve; **être sur les ~s** to be all keyed up; **allons, du ~!** come on, buck up!; **nerveux, -euse** *adj* nervous; (*irritable*) touchy, nervy; (*voiture*) nippy, responsive; **nervosité** *nf* excitability, tenseness; (*irritabilité passagère*) irritability, nerviness

nervure [nɛʀvyʀ] *nf* vein

n'est-ce pas [nɛspa] *adv* isn't it?, won't you? *etc*, selon le verbe qui précède

net, nette [nɛt] *adj* (*sans équivoque, distinct*) clear; (*évident: amélioration, différence*) marked, distinct; (*propre*) neat, clean;

(COMM: prix, salaire) net ♦ adv (refuser) flatly ♦ nm: **mettre au ~ to** copy out; **s'arrêter ~ to** stop dead; **nettement** adv clearly, distinctly; (incontestablement) decidedly, distinctly; **netteté** nf clearness

nettoyage [netwajaʒ] nm cleaning; **~ à sec** dry cleaning

nettoyer [netwaje] vt to clean

neuf¹ [nœf] num nine

neuf², neuve [nœf, nœv] adj new ♦ nm: **remettre à ~ to** do up (as good as new), refurbish; **quoi de ~?** what's new?

neutre [nøtR] adj neutral; (LING) neuter

neuve [nœv] adj voir **neuf²**

neuvième [nœvjɛm] num ninth

neveu, x [n(ə)vø] nm nephew

névrosé, e [nevRoze] adj, nm/f neurotic

nez [ne] nm nose; **~ à ~ avec** face to face with; **avoir du ~** to have flair

ni [ni] conj: **~ ... ~** neither ... nor; **je n'aime ~ les lentilles ~ les épinards** I like neither lentils nor spinach; **il n'a dit ~ oui ~ non** he didn't say either yes or no; **elles ne sont venues ~ l'une ~ l'autre** neither of them came

niais, e [njɛ, njɛz] adj silly, thick

niche [niʃ] nf (du chien) kennel; (de mur) recess, niche; **nicher** vi to nest

nid [ni] nm nest; **~ de poule** pothole

nièce [njɛs] nf niece

nier [nje] vt to deny

nigaud, e [nigo, od] nm/f booby, fool

Nil [nil] nm: **le ~ the** Nile

n'importe [nɛ̃pɔRt] adv: **~ qui/quoi/où** anybody/anything/anywhere; **~ quand** any time; **~ quel/quelle** any; **~ lequel/laquelle** any (one); **~ comment** (sans soin) carelessly

niveau, x [nivo] nm level; (des élèves, études) standard; **~ de vie** standard of living

niveler [niv(ə)le] vt to level

NN abr (= nouvelle norme) revised standard of hotel classification

noble [nɔbl] adj noble; **noblesse** nf nobility; (d'une action etc) nobleness

noce [nɔs] nf wedding; (gens) wedding party (ou guests pl); **faire la ~** (fam) to go on a binge

nocif, -ive [nɔsif, iv] adj harmful, noxious

nocturne [nɔktyRn] adj nocturnal ♦ nf late-night opening

Noël [nɔɛl] nm Christmas

nœud [nø] nm knot; (ruban) bow; **~ papillon** bow tie

noir, e [nwaR] adj black; (obscur, sombre) dark ♦ nm/f black man/woman ♦ nm: **dans le ~ in** the dark; **travail au ~** moonlighting; **travailler au ~** to work on the side; **noircir** vt, vi to blacken; **noire** nf (MUS) crotchet (BRIT), quarter note (US)

noisette [nwazɛt] nf hazelnut

noix [nwa] nf walnut; (CULIN): **une ~ de beurre** a knob of butter; **~ de cajou** cashew nut; **~ de coco** coconut; **à la ~** (fam) worthless

nom [nɔ̃] nm name; (LING) noun; **~ de famille** surname; **~ de jeune fille** maiden name; **~ déposé** trade name; **~ propre** proper noun

nomade [nɔmad] nm/f nomad

nombre [nɔ̃bR] nm number; **venir en ~** to come in large numbers; **depuis ~ d'années** for many years; **au ~ de mes amis** among my friends; **nombreux, -euse** adj many, numerous; (avec nom sg: foule etc) large; **peu nombreux** few

nombril [nɔ̃bRi(l)] nm navel

nommer [nɔme] vt to name; (élire) to appoint, nominate; **se ~: il se nomme Pascal** his name's Pascal; he's called Pascal

non [nɔ̃] adv (réponse) no; (avec loin, sans, seulement) not; **~ (pas) que** not that; **moi ~ plus** neither do I, I don't either; **c'est bon ~?** (exprimant le doute) it's good, isn't it?

non-alcoolisé, e [nɔ̃alkɔlize] adj non-alcoholic

nonante [nɔnɑ̃t] (BELGIQUE, SUISSE) num ninety

non-fumeur [nɔ̃fymœR, øz] nm non-smoker

non-sens [nɔ̃sɑ̃s] nm absurdity

nonchalant, e [nɔ̃ʃalɑ̃, ɑ̃t] adj nonchalant

nord [nɔR] nm North ♦ adj northern; north; **au ~** (situation) in the north; (direction) to the north; **au ~ de** (to the) north of; **nord-est** nm North-East; **nord-ouest** nm North-West

normal, e, -aux [nɔRmal, o] adj normal; **c'est tout à fait ~** it's perfectly natural; **vous trouvez ça ~?** does it seem right to you?; **normale** nf: **la normale** the norm, the average; **normalement** adv (en général) normally

normand, e [nɔRmɑ̃, ɑ̃d] adj of Normandy

Normandie [nɔRmɑ̃di] nf Normandy

norme [nɔRm] nf norm; (TECH) standard

Norvège [nɔRvɛʒ] nf Norway; **norvégien, ne** adj Norwegian ♦ nm/f: **Norvégien, ne** Norwegian ♦ nm (LING) Norwegian

nos [no] adj voir **notre**

nostalgie [nɔstalʒi] nf nostalgia; **nostalgique** adj nostalgic

notable [nɔtabl] adj (fait) notable, noteworthy; (marqué) noticeable, marked ♦ nm prominent citizen

notaire [nɔtɛR] nm solicitor

notamment [nɔtamɑ̃] adv in particular, among others

note [nɔt] nf (écrite, MUS) note; (SCOL) mark (BRIT), grade; (facture) bill; **~ de service** memorandum

noté, e [nɔte] adj: **être bien/mal ~** (employé etc) to have a good/bad record

noter [nɔte] vt (écrire) to write down;

(*remarquer*) to note, notice; (*devoir*) to mark, grade

notice [nɔtis] *nf* summary, short article; (*brochure*) leaflet, instruction book

notifier [nɔtifje] *vt*: ~ **qch à qn** to notify sb of sth, notify sth to sb

notion [nosjɔ̃] *nf* notion, idea

notoire [nɔtwaʀ] *adj* widely known; (*en mal*) notorious

notre [nɔtʀ] (*pl* **nos**) *adj* our

nôtre [notʀ] *pron*: **le ~, la ~, les ~s ours ♦** *adj* ours; **les ~s ours**; (*alliés etc*) our own people; **soyez des ~s** join us

nouer [nwe] *vt* to tie, knot; (*fig: alliance etc*) to strike up

noueux, -euse [nwø, øz] *adj* gnarled

nouilles [nuj] *nfpl* noodles

nourrice [nuʀis] *nf* (*gardienne*) child-minder

nourrir [nuʀiʀ] *vt* to feed; (*fig: espoir*) to harbour, nurse; **se ~** to eat; **se ~ de** to feed (o.s.) on; **nourrissant, e** *adj* nourishing, nutritious; **nourrisson** *nm* (*unweaned*) infant; **nourriture** *nf* food

nous [nu] *pron* (*sujet*) we; (*objet*) us; **nous-mêmes** *pron* ourselves

nouveau (nouvel), -elle, x [nuvo, nuvɛl] *adj* new ♦ *nm*: **y a-t-il du ~?** is there anything new on this? ♦ *nm/f* new pupil (*ou* employee); **de ~, à ~** again; **~ venu, nouvelle venue** newcomer; **~x mariés** newly-weds; **nouveau-né, e** *nm/f* newborn baby; **nouveauté** *nf* novelty; (*objet*) new thing *ou* article

nouvel [nuvɛl] *adj voir* **nouveau; N~ An** New Year

nouvelle [nuvɛl] *adj voir* **nouveau ♦** *nf* (*piece of*) news *sg*; (*LITTÉRATURE*) short story; **les ~s** the news; **je suis sans ~s de lui** I haven't heard from him; **Nouvelle Calédonie** *nf* New Caledonia; **nouvellement** *adv* recently, newly; **Nouvelle-Zélande** *nf* New Zealand

novembre [nɔvɑ̃bʀ] *nm* November

novice [nɔvis] *adj* inexperienced

noyade [nwajad] *nf* drowning *no pl*

noyau, x [nwajo] *nm* (*de fruit*) stone; (*BIO, PHYSIQUE*) nucleus; (*fig: centre*) core; **noyauter** *vt* (*POL*) to infiltrate

noyer [nwaje] *nm* walnut (tree); (*bois*) walnut ♦ *vt* to drown; (*moteur*) to flood; **se ~** *vi* to be drowned, drown; (*suicide*) to drown o.s.

nu, e [ny] *adj* naked; (*membres*) naked, bare; (*pieds, mains, chambre, fil électrique*) bare ♦ *nm* (*ART*) nude; **tout ~** stark naked; **se mettre ~** to strip; **mettre à ~** to bare

nuage [nɥaʒ] *nm* cloud; **nuageux, -euse** *adj* cloudy

nuance [nɥɑ̃s] *nf* (*de couleur, sens*) shade; **il y a une ~ (entre)** there's a slight difference

(*between*); **nuancer** *vt* (*opinion*) to bring some reservations *ou* qualifications to

nucléaire [nykleɛʀ] *adj* nuclear ♦ *nm*: **le ~** nuclear energy

nudiste [nydist] *nm/f* nudist

nuée [nɥe] *nf*: **une ~ de** a cloud *ou* host *ou* swarm of

nues [ny] *nfpl*: **tomber des ~** to be taken aback; **porter qn aux ~** to praise sb to the skies

nuire [nɥiʀ] *vi* to be harmful; **~ à** to harm, do damage to; **nuisible** *adj* harmful; **animal nuisible** pest

nuit [nɥi] *nf* night; **il fait ~** it's dark; **cette ~** (*hier*) last night; (*aujourd'hui*) tonight; **~ blanche** sleepless night

nul, nulle [nyl] *adj* (*aucun*) no; (*minime*) nil, non-existent; (*non valable*) null; (*péj*) useless, hopeless ♦ *pron* none, no one; **match** *ou* **résultat ~** draw; **~le part** nowhere; **nullement** *adv* by no means; **nullité** *nf* (*personne*) nonentity

numérique [nymeʀik] *adj* numerical; (*affichage*) digital

numéro [nymeʀo] *nm* number; (*spectacle*) act, turn; (*PRESSE*) issue, number; **~ de téléphone** (tele)phone number; **~ vert** ≈ freefone ® number (*BRIT*), ≈ toll-free number (*US*); **numéroter** *vt* to number

nu-pieds [nypje] *adj inv, adv* barefoot

nuque [nyk] *nf* nape of the neck

nu-tête [nytɛt] *adj inv, adv* bareheaded

nutritif, -ive [nytʀitif, iv] *adj* (*besoins, valeur*) nutritional; (*nourrissant*) nutritious

nylon [nilɔ̃] *nm* nylon

O, o

oasis [ɔazis] *nf* oasis

obéir [ɔbeiʀ] *vi* to obey; **~ à** to obey; **obéissance** *nf* obedience; **obéissant, e** *adj* obedient

obèse [ɔbɛz] *adj* obese; **obésité** *nf* obesity

objecter [ɔbʒɛkte] *vt* (*prétexter*) to plead, put forward as an excuse; **~ (à qn) que** to object (to sb) that; **objecteur** *nm*: **objecteur de conscience** conscientious objector

objectif, -ive [ɔbʒɛktif, iv] *adj* objective ♦ *nm* objective; (*PHOTO*) lens *sg*, objective; **objectivité** *nf* objectivity

objection [ɔbʒɛksjɔ̃] *nf* objection

objet [ɔbʒɛ] *nm* object; (*d'une discussion, recherche*) subject; **être** *ou* **faire l'~ de** (*discussion*) to be the subject of; (*soins*) to be given *ou* shown; **sans ~** purposeless; groundless; **~ d'art** objet d'art; **~s trouvés** lost property *sg* (*BRIT*), lost-and-found *sg* (*US*); **~s de valeur** valuables

obligation [ɔbligasjɔ̃] nf obligation; (COMM)
bond, debenture; **obligatoire** adj
compulsory, obligatory; **obligatoirement**
adv necessarily; (fam: sans aucun doute)
inevitably

obligé, e [ɔbliʒe] adj (redevable): être très
~ à qn to be most obliged to sb

obligeance [ɔbliʒɑ̃s] nf: avoir l'~ de ... to be
kind ou good enough to ...; **obligeant, e** adj
(personne) obliging, kind

obliger [ɔbliʒe] vt (contraindre): ~ qn à faire
to force ou oblige sb to do; **je suis bien obligé**
I have to

oblique [ɔblik] adj oblique; **en ~** diagonally;
obliquer vi: **obliquer vers** to turn off towards

oblitérer [ɔblitere] vt (timbre-poste) to cancel

obnubiler [ɔbnybile] vt to obsess

obscène [ɔpsɛn] adj obscene

obscur, e [ɔpskyr] adj dark; (méconnu)
obscure; obscurer ♦ vt (fig) to
obscure; **s'obscurcir** vi to grow dark;
obscurité nf darkness; **dans l'obscurité** in
the dark, in darkness

obsédé, e [ɔpsede] nm/f: **un ~ (sexuel)** a sex
maniac

obséder [ɔpsede] vt to obsess, haunt

obsèques [ɔpsɛk] nfpl funeral sg

observateur, -trice [ɔpsɛrvatœr, tris] adj
observant, perceptive ♦ nm/f observer

observation [ɔpsɛrvasjɔ̃] nf observation;
(d'un règlement etc) observance; (reproche)
reproof; **être en ~** (MÉD) to be under
observation

observatoire [ɔpsɛrvatwar] nm observatory

observer [ɔpsɛrve] vt (regarder) to observe,
watch; (scientifiquement; aussi règlement etc)
to observe; (surveiller) to watch; (remarquer)
to observe, notice; **faire ~ qch à qn** (dire)
to point out sth to sb

obsession [ɔpsesjɔ̃] nf obsession

obstacle [ɔpstakl] nm: obstacle; (ÉQUITATION)
jump, hurdle; **faire ~ à** (projet) to hinder, put
obstacles in the path of

obstiné, e [ɔpstine] adj obstinate

obstiner [ɔpstine]: **s'~** vi to insist, dig one's
heels in; **s'~ à faire** to persist (obstinately) in
doing

obstruer [ɔpstrye] vt to block, obstruct

obtenir [ɔptənir] vt to obtain, get; (résultat)
to achieve, obtain; **~ de pouvoir faire** to
obtain permission to do

obturateur [ɔptyratœr, tris] nm (PHOTO)
shutter

obus [ɔby] nm shell

occasion [ɔkazjɔ̃] nf (aubaine, possibilité)
opportunity; (circonstance) occasion; (COMM:
article non neuf) secondhand buy; (: acqui-
sition avantageuse) bargain; **à plusieurs ~s** on
several occasions; **à l'~** sometimes, on

occasions; **d'~** secondhand; **occasionnel, le**
adj (non régulier) occasional; **occa-
sionnellement** adv occasionally, from time
to time

occasionner [ɔkazjɔne] vt to cause

occident [ɔksidɑ̃] nm: **l'O~** the West;
occidental, e, -aux adj western; (POL)
Western ♦ nm/f Westerner

occupation [ɔkypasjɔ̃] nf occupation

occupé, e [ɔkype] adj (personne) busy;
(place, sièges) taken; (toilettes) engaged;
(ligne) engaged (BRIT), busy (US); (MIL, POL)
occupied

occuper [ɔkype] vt to occupy; (poste) to
hold; **s'~ de** (être responsable de) to be in
charge of; (se charger de: affaire) to take
charge of, deal with; (: clients etc) to attend
to; **s'~ (à qch)** to occupy o.s. ou keep o.s.
busy (with sth)

occurrence [ɔkyrɑ̃s] nf: **en l'~** in this case

océan [ɔseɑ̃] nm ocean

octante [ɔktɑ̃t] adj (regional) eighty

octet [ɔktɛ] nm byte

octobre [ɔktɔbr] nm October

octroyer [ɔktrwaje]: **s'~** vt (vacances etc) to
treat o.s. to

oculiste [ɔkylist] nm/f eye specialist

odeur [ɔdœr] nf smell

odieux, -euse [ɔdjø, jøz] adj hateful

odorant, e [ɔdɔrɑ̃, ɑ̃t] adj sweet-smelling,
fragrant

odorat [ɔdɔra] nm (sense of) smell

œil [œj] (pl **yeux**) nm eye; **à l'œil** (fam) for
free; **à l'œil nu** with the naked eye; **tenir qn à
l'œil** to keep an eye ou a watch on sb; **avoir
l'œil à qch** to keep an eye on; **fermer les yeux
(sur)** (fig) to turn a blind eye (to); **voir qch
d'un bon/mauvais œil** to look on sth
favourably/unfavourably

œillères [œjɛr] nfpl blinkers (BRIT), blinders
(US)

œillet [œjɛ] nm (BOT) carnation

œuf [œf, pl ø] nm egg; **œuf à la coque/sur le
plat/dur** boiled/fried/hard-boiled egg; **œuf de
Pâques** Easter egg; **œufs brouillés** scrambled
eggs

œuvre [œvr] nf (tâche) task, undertaking;
(livre, tableau etc) work; (ensemble de la
production artistique) works pl ♦ nm (CONSTR):
le gros œuvre the shell; **œuvre (de
bienfaisance)** charity; **mettre en œuvre**
(moyens) to make use of; **œuvre d'art** work of
art

offense [ɔfɑ̃s] nf insult; **offenser** vt to
offend, hurt

offert, e [ɔfɛr, ɛrt] pp de offrir

office [ɔfis] nm (agence) bureau, agency;
(REL) service ♦ nm ou nf (pièce) pantry; **faire
~ de** to act as; **d'~** automatically; **~ du**

137

tourisme tourist bureau
officiel, le [ɔfisjɛl] adj, nm/f official
officier [ɔfisje] nm officer
officieux, -euse [ɔfisjø, jøz] adj unofficial
offrande [ɔfʀɑ̃d] nf offering
offre [ɔfʀ] nf offer; (aux enchères) bid;
(ADMIN: soumission) tender; (ÉCON) l'~ et la
demande supply and demand; "~s d'emploi"
"situations vacant"; ~ d'emploi job advertised
offrir [ɔfʀiʀ] vt: ~ (à qn) to offer (to sb); (faire
cadeau de) to give (to sb) s'~ vt (vacances,
voiture) to treat o.s. to; ~ (à qn) de faire qch
to offer to do sth (for sb); ~ à boire à qn
(chez soi) to offer sb a drink
offusquer [ɔfyske] vt to offend
oie [wa] nf (ZOOL) goose
oignon [ɔɲɔ̃] nm onion; (de tulipe etc) bulb
oiseau, x [wazo] nm bird; ~ de proie bird of
prey
oisif, -ive [wazif, iv] adj idle
oléoduc [ɔleɔdyk] nm (oil) pipeline
olive [ɔliv] nf (BOT) olive; **olivier** nm olive
(tree)
OLP sigle f (= Organisation de libération de la
Palestine) PLO
olympique [ɔlɛ̃pik] adj Olympic
ombragé, e [ɔ̃bʀaʒe] adj shaded, shady;
ombrageux, -euse adj (personne) touchy,
easily offended
ombre [ɔ̃bʀ] nf (espace non ensoleillé) shade;
(~ portée, tache) shadow; à l'~ in the shade;
dans l'~ (fig) in the dark; ~ à paupières
eyeshadow; **ombrelle** nf parasol, sunshade
omelette [ɔmlɛt] nf omelette; ~ norvégienne
baked Alaska
omettre [ɔmɛtʀ] vt to omit, leave out
omnibus [ɔmnibys] nm slow ou stopping
train
omoplate [ɔmɔplat] nf shoulder blade

MOT-CLÉ
---

on [ɔ̃] pron **1** (indéterminé) you, one; **on peut
le faire ainsi** you ou one can do it like this, it
can be done like this
2 (quelqu'un): **on les a attaqués** they were
attacked; **on vous demande au téléphone**
there's a phone call for you, you're wanted
on the phone
3 (nous): **on va y aller demain** we're
going tomorrow
4 (les gens) they; **autrefois, on croyait ...** they
used to believe ...
5: on ne peut plus
♦ adv: **on ne peut plus stupide** as stupid as
can be

oncle [ɔ̃kl] nm uncle
onctueux, -euse [ɔ̃ktɥø, øz] adj creamy,
smooth

onde [ɔ̃d] nf wave; **sur les ~s** on the radio; sur
~s courtes on short wave sg; **moyennes/
longues ~s** medium/long wave sg
ondée [ɔ̃de] nf shower
on-dit [ɔ̃di] nm inv rumour
onduler [ɔ̃dyle] vi to undulate; (cheveux) to
wave
onéreux, -euse [ɔneʀø, øz] adj costly
ongle [ɔ̃gl] nm nail
ont [ɔ̃] vb voir avoir
ONU sigle f (= Organisation des Nations Unies)
UN
onze [ɔ̃z] num eleven; **onzième** num
eleventh
OPA sigle f = offre publique d'achat
opaque [ɔpak] adj opaque
opéra [ɔpeʀa] nm opera; (édifice) opera house
opérateur, -trice [ɔpeʀatœʀ, tʀis] nm/f
operator; ~ (de prise de vues) cameraman
opération [ɔpeʀasjɔ̃] nf operation; (COMM)
dealing
opératoire [ɔpeʀatwaʀ] adj (choc etc) post-
operative
opérer [ɔpeʀe] vt (personne) to operate on;
(faire, exécuter) to carry out, make ♦ vi
(remède: faire effet) to act, work; (MÉD) to
operate; **s'~** vi (avoir lieu) to occur, take
place; **se faire ~** to have an operation
opérette [ɔpeʀɛt] nf operetta, light opera
ophtalmologiste [ɔftalmɔlɔʒist] nm/f
ophthalmologist, optician
opiner [ɔpine] vi: ~ de la tête to nod assent
opinion [ɔpinjɔ̃] nf opinion; l'~ (publique)
public opinion
opportun, e [ɔpɔʀtœ̃, yn] adj timely,
opportune; **opportuniste** nm/f opportunist
opposant, e [ɔpozɑ̃, ɑ̃t] nm/f opponent
opposé, e [ɔpoze] adj (direction) opposite;
(faction) opposing; (opinions, intérêt)
conflicting; (contre): ~ à opposed to, against
♦ nm: l'~ the other ou opposite side (ou
direction); (contraire) the opposite; à l'~ (fig)
on the other hand; à l'~ de (fig) contrary to,
unlike
opposer [ɔpoze] vt (personnes, équipes) to
oppose; (couleurs) to contrast; **s'~** vi (équipes)
to confront each other; (opinions) to conflict;
(couleurs, styles) to contrast; **s'~ à** (interdire)
to oppose; ~ qch (comme obstacle, défense)
to set sth against; (comme objection) to put
sth forward against
opposition [ɔpozisjɔ̃] nf opposition; **par ~ à**
as opposed to, in contrast with; **entrer en
~ avec** to come into conflict with; **faire ~ à un
chèque** to stop a cheque
oppressant, e [ɔpʀesɑ̃, ɑ̃t] adj oppressive
oppresser [ɔpʀese] vt to oppress;
oppression nf oppression
opprimer [ɔpʀime] vt to oppress

opter [ɔpte] vi: ~ **pour** to opt for

opticien, ne [ɔptisjɛ̃, jɛn] nm/f optician

optimisme [ɔptimism] nm optimism;
optimiste nm/f optimist ♦ adj optimistic

option [ɔpsjɔ̃] nf option; **matière à ~** (SCOL)
optional subject

optique [ɔptik] adj (nerf) optic; (verres)
optical ♦ nf (fig: manière de voir) perspective

opulent, e [ɔpylɑ̃, ɑ̃t] adj wealthy, opulent;
(formes, poitrine) ample, generous

or [ɔʀ] nm gold ♦ conj now, but; **en ~** (objet)
gold cpd; **une affaire en ~** a real bargain; **il
croyait gagner ~ il a perdu** he was sure he
would win and yet he lost

orage [ɔʀaʒ] nm (thunder)storm; **orageux,
-euse** adj stormy

oral, e, -aux [ɔʀal, o] adj, nm oral; **par voie
~e** (MÉD) orally

orange [ɔʀɑ̃ʒ] nf orange ♦ adj inv orange;
orangeade nf orangeade; **orangé, e** adj
orangey, orange-coloured; **oranger** nm
orange tree

orateur [ɔʀatœʀ, tʀis] nm speaker

orbite [ɔʀbit] nf (ANAT) (eye-)socket;
(PHYSIQUE) orbit

orchestre [ɔʀkɛstʀ] nm orchestra; (de jazz)
band; (places) stalls pl (BRIT), orchestra (US);
orchestrer vt to orchestrate

orchidée [ɔʀkide] nf orchid

ordinaire [ɔʀdinɛʀ] adj ordinary; (qualité)
standard; (péj: commun) common ♦ nm
ordinary; (menus) everyday fare ♦ nf
(essence) ≈ two-star (petrol) (BRIT), ≈ regular
gas (US); **d'~** usually, normally; **comme à l'~**
as usual

ordinateur [ɔʀdinatœʀ] nm computer

ordonnance [ɔʀdɔnɑ̃s] nf (MÉD)
prescription; (MIL) orderly, batman (BRIT)

ordonné, e [ɔʀdɔne] adj tidy, orderly

ordonner [ɔʀdɔne] vt (agencer) to organize,
arrange; (donner un ordre): ~ **à qn de faire** to
order sb to do; (REL) to ordain; (MÉD) to
prescribe

ordre [ɔʀdʀ] nm order; (propreté et soin)
orderliness, tidiness; (nature): **d'~ pratique** of
a practical nature; **~s** nmpl (REL) holy orders;
mettre en ~ to tidy (up), put in order; **à
l'~ de qn** payable to sb; **être aux ~s de qn/
sous les ~s de qn** to be at sb's disposal/under
sb's command; **jusqu'à nouvel ~** until further
notice; **de premier ~** first-rate; **~ du jour**
(d'une réunion) agenda; **à l'~ du jour** (fig)
topical

ordure [ɔʀdyʀ] nf filth no pl; **~s** nfpl
(balayures, déchets) rubbish sg, refuse sg; **~s
ménagères** household refuse

oreille [ɔʀɛj] nf ear; **avoir de l'~** to have a
good ear (for music)

oreiller [ɔʀeje] nm pillow

oreillons [ɔʀɛjɔ̃] nmpl mumps sg

ores [ɔʀ]: **d'~ et déjà** adv already

orfèvrerie [ɔʀfɛvʀəʀi] nf goldsmith's (ou
silversmith's) trade; (ouvrage) gold (ou silver)
plate

organe [ɔʀgan] nm organ; (porte-parole)
representative, mouthpiece

organigramme [ɔʀganigʀam] nm (tableau
hiérarchique) organization chart; (schéma)
flow chart

organique [ɔʀganik] adj organic

organisateur, -trice [ɔʀganizatœʀ, tʀis]
nm/f organizer

organisation [ɔʀganizasjɔ̃] nf organization

organiser [ɔʀganize] vt to organize; (mettre
sur pied: service etc) to set up; **s'~** to get
organized

organisme [ɔʀganism] nm (BIO) organism;
(corps, ADMIN) body

organiste [ɔʀganist] nm/f organist

orgasme [ɔʀgasm] nm orgasm, climax

orge [ɔʀʒ] nf barley

orgue [ɔʀg] nm organ; **~s** nfpl (MUS) organ sg

orgueil [ɔʀgœj] nm pride; **orgueilleux,
-euse** adj proud

Orient [ɔʀjɑ̃] nm: **l'~** the East, the Orient;
oriental, e, -aux adj (langue, produit)
oriental; (frontière) eastern

orientation [ɔʀjɑ̃tasjɔ̃] nf (de recherches)
orientation; (d'une maison etc) aspect; (d'un
journal) leanings pl; **avoir le sens de l'~** to
have a (good) sense of direction;
~ professionnelle careers advisory service

orienté, e [ɔʀjɑ̃te] adj (fig: article, journal)
slanted; **bien/mal ~** (appartement) well/badly
positioned; **~ au sud** facing south, with a
southern aspect

orienter [ɔʀjɑ̃te] vt (tourner: antenne) to
direct, turn; (personne, recherches) to direct;
(fig: élève) to orientate; **s'~** (se repérer) to
find one's bearings; **s'~ vers** (fig) to turn
towards

origan [ɔʀigɑ̃] nm oregano

originaire [ɔʀiʒinɛʀ] adj: **être ~ de** to be a
native of

original, e, -aux [ɔʀiʒinal, o] adj original;
(bizarre) eccentric ♦ nm/f eccentric ♦ nm
(document etc, ART) original

origine [ɔʀiʒin] nf origin; **dès l'~** at ou from
the outset; **à l'~** originally; **originel, le** adj
original

orme [ɔʀm] nm elm

ornement [ɔʀnəmɑ̃] nm ornament

orner [ɔʀne] vt to decorate, adorn

ornière [ɔʀnjɛʀ] nf rut

orphelin, e [ɔʀfəlɛ̃, in] adj orphan(ed)
♦ nm/f orphan; ~ **de père/mère** fatherless/
motherless; **orphelinat** nm orphanage

orteil [ɔʀtɛj] nm toe; **gros ~** big toe

orthographe [ɔʀtɔgraf] nf spelling

ortie [ɔʀti] nf (stinging) nettle

os [ɔs] nm bone; **tomber sur un ~** (fam) to hit a snag

osciller [ɔsile] vi (au vent etc) to rock; (fig): **~ entre** to waver ou fluctuate between

osé, e [oze] adj daring, bold

oseille [ozɛj] nf sorrel

oser [oze] vi, vt to dare; **~ faire** to dare (to) do

osier [ozje] nm willow; **d'~, en ~** wicker(work)

ossature [ɔsatyʀ] nf (ANAT) frame, skeletal structure; (fig) framework

osseux, -euse [ɔsø, øz] adj bony; (tissu, maladie, greffe) bone cpd

ostensible [ɔstãsibl] adj conspicuous

otage [ɔtaʒ] nm hostage; **prendre qn comme ~** to take sb hostage

OTAN sigle f (= Organisation du traité de l'Atlantique Nord) NATO

otarie [ɔtaʀi] nf sea-lion

ôter [ote] vt to remove; (soustraire) to take away, **~ qch à qn** to take sth (away) from sb, **~ qch de** to remove sth from

otite [ɔtit] nf ear infection

ou [u] conj or; **~ ... ~** either ... or; **~ bien** or (else)

MOT-CLÉ

où [u] pron relatif **1** (position, situation) where, that (souvent omis); **la chambre où il était** the room (that) he was in, the room where he was; **la ville où je l'ai rencontré** the town where I met him; **la pièce d'où il est sorti** the room he came out of; **le village d'où je viens** the village I come from; **les villes par où il est passé** the towns he went through

2 (temps, état) that (souvent omis); **le jour où il est parti** the day (that) he left; **au prix où c'est** at the price it is

♦ adv **1** (interrogation) where; **où est-il/va-t-il?** where is he/is he going?; **par où?** which way?; **d'où vient que ...?** how come ...?

2 (position) where; **je sais où il est** I know where he is; **où que l'on aille** wherever you go

---

ouate ['wat] nf cotton wool (BRIT), cotton (US)

oubli [ubli] nm (acte): **l'~ de** forgetting; (trou de mémoire) lapse of memory; (négligence) omission, oversight; **tomber dans l'~** to sink into oblivion

oublier [ublije] vt to forget; (laisser quelque part: chapeau etc) to leave behind; (ne pas voir: erreurs etc) to miss

oubliettes [ublijɛt] nfpl dungeon sg

ouest [wɛst] nm west ♦ adj inv west; (région) western; **à l'~** in the west; (direction) (to the) west, westwards; **à l'~ de** (to the) west of

ouf ['uf] excl phew!

oui ['wi] adv yes

ouï-dire ['widiʀ]: **par ~~** adv by hearsay

ouïe [wi] nf hearing; **~s** nfpl (de poisson) gills

ouille ['uj] excl ouch!

ouragan [uʀagã] nm hurricane

ourlet [uʀlɛ] nm hem

ours [uʀs] nm bear; **~ brun/blanc** brown/polar bear; **~ (en peluche)** teddy (bear)

oursin [uʀsɛ̃] nm sea urchin

ourson [uʀsɔ̃] nm (bear-)cub

ouste [ust] excl hop it!

outil [uti] nm tool; **outiller** vt to equip

outrage [utʀaʒ] nm insult; **~ à la pudeur** indecent conduct no pl; **outrager** vt to offend gravely

outrance [utʀãs]: **à ~** adv excessively, to excess

outre [utʀ] prép besides ♦ adv: **passer ~ à** to disregard, take no notice of; **en ~** besides, moreover; **~ mesure** to excess; (manger, boire) immoderately; **outre-Atlantique** adv across the Atlantic, **outre-Manche** adv across the Channel; **outre-mer** adv overseas; **outrepasser** vt to go beyond, exceed

ouvert, e [uvɛʀ, ɛʀt] pp de **ouvrir** ♦ adj open; (robinet, gaz etc) on; **ouvertement** adv openly; **ouverture** nf opening; (MUS) overture; **ouverture d'esprit** open-mindedness

ouvrable [uvʀabl] adj: **jour ~** working day, weekday

ouvrage [uvʀaʒ] nm (tâche, de tricot etc) work no pl; (texte, livre) work; **ouvragé, e** adj finely embroidered (ou worked ou carved)

ouvre-boîte(s) [uvʀəbwat] nm inv tin (BRIT) ou can opener

ouvre-bouteille(s) [uvʀəbutɛj] nm inv bottle-opener

ouvreuse [uvʀøz] nf usherette

ouvrier, -ière [uvʀije, ijɛʀ] nm/f worker ♦ adj working-class; (conflit) industrial; (mouvement) labour cpd; **classe ouvrière** working class

ouvrir [uvʀiʀ] vt (gén) to open; (brèche, passage, MÉD: abcès) to open up; (commencer l'exploitation de, créer) to open (up); (eau, électricité, chauffage, robinet) to turn on ♦ vi to open; to open up; **s'~** vi to open; **s'~ à qn** to open one's heart to sb; **~ l'appétit à qn** to whet sb's appetite

ovaire [ɔvɛʀ] nm ovary

ovale [ɔval] adj oval

ovni [ɔvni] sigle m (= objet volant non identifié) UFO

oxyder [ɔkside]: **s'~** vi to become oxidized

oxygène [ɔksiʒɛn] nm oxygen

oxygéné, e [ɔksiʒene] adj: **eau ~e** hydrogen peroxide

oxygéner [ɔksiʒene]: **s'~** (fam) vi to get

some fresh air

ozone [ozon] *nf* ozone; **la couche d'~** the ozone layer

P, p

pacifique [pasifik] *adj* peaceful ♦ *nm*: **le P~, l'océan P~** the Pacific (Ocean)

pacotille [pakɔtij] *nf* cheap junk; **bijoux de ~** cheap(-jack) jewellery

pack [pak] *nm* pack

pacte [pakt] *nm* pact, treaty

pagaie [pagɛ] *nf* paddle

pagaille [pagaj] *nf* mess, shambles *sg*

pagayer *vi* to paddle

page [paʒ] *nf* page ♦ *nm* page (boy); **à la ~** (*fig*) up-to-date

paiement [pemɑ̃] *nm* payment

païen, ne [pajɛ̃, pajɛn] *adj, nm/f* pagan, heathen

paillasson [pajasɔ̃] *nm* doormat

paille [paj] *nf* straw

paillettes [pajɛt] *nfpl* (*décoratives*) sequins, spangles

pain [pɛ̃] *nm* (*substance*) bread; (*unité*) loaf (of bread); (*morceau*): **~ de savon** etc bar of soap etc; **~ au chocolat** chocolate-filled pastry; **~ aux raisins** currant bun; **~ bis/complet** brown/wholemeal (*BRIT*) *ou* wholewheat (*US*) bread; **~ d'épice** gingerbread; **~ de mie** sandwich loaf; **~ grillé** toast

pair, e [pɛʀ] *adj* (*nombre*) even ♦ *nm* peer; **aller de ~** to go hand in hand *ou* together; **jeune fille au ~** au pair; **paire** *nf* pair

paisible [pezibl] *adj* peaceful, quiet

paître [pɛtʀ] *vi* to graze

paix [pɛ] *nf* peace; **faire/avoir la ~** to make/ have peace; **fiche-lui la ~!** (*fam*) leave him alone!

Pakistan [pakistɑ̃] *nm*: **le ~** Pakistan

palace [palas] *nm* luxury hotel

palais [palɛ] *nm* palace; (*ANAT*) palate

pâle [pɑl] *adj* pale; **bleu ~** pale blue

Palestine [palestin] *nf*: **la ~** Palestine

palet [palɛ] *nm* disc; (*HOCKEY*) puck

paletot [palto] *nm* (thick) cardigan

palette [palɛt] *nf* (*de peintre*) palette; (*produits*) range

pâleur [pɑlœʀ] *nf* paleness

palier [palje] *nm* (*d'escalier*) landing; (*fig*) level, plateau; **par ~s** in stages

pâlir [pɑliʀ] *vi* to turn *ou* go pale; (*couleur*) to fade

palissade [palisad] *nf* fence

pallier [palje] : **~ à** *vt* to offset, make up for

palmarès [palmaʀɛs] *nm* record (of achievements); (*SPORT*) list of winners

palme [palm] *nf* (*de plongeur*) flipper;

palmé, e *adj* (*pattes*) webbed

palmier [palmje] *nm* palm tree; (*gâteau*) heart-shaped biscuit made of flaky pastry

pâlot, te [pɑlo, ɔt] *adj* pale, peaky

palourde [paluʀd] *nf* clam

palper [palpe] *vt* to feel, finger

palpitant, e [palpitɑ̃, ɑ̃t] *adj* thrilling

palpiter [palpite] *vi* (*cœur, pouls*) to beat; (: *plus fort*) to pound, throb

paludisme [palydism] *nm* malaria

pamphlet [pɑ̃flɛ] *nm* lampoon, satirical tract

pamplemousse [pɑ̃pləmus] *nm* grapefruit

pan [pɑ̃] *nm* section, piece ♦ *excl* bang!

panache [panaʃ] *nm* plume; (*fig*) spirit, panache

panaché, e [panaʃe] *adj*: **glace ~e** mixed-flavour ice cream ♦ *nm* (*bière*) shandy

pancarte [pɑ̃kaʀt] *nf* sign, notice

pancréas [pɑ̃kʀeas] *nm* pancreas

pané, e [pane] *adj* fried in breadcrumbs

panier [panje] *nm* basket; **mettre au ~** to chuck away; **~ à provisions** shopping basket; **panier-repas** *nm* packed lunch

panique [panik] *nf, adj* panic; **paniquer** *vi* to panic

panne [pan] *nf* breakdown; **être/tomber en ~** to have broken down/break down; **être en ~ d'essence** *ou* **sèche** to have run out of petrol (*BRIT*) *ou* gas (*US*); **~ d'électricité** *ou* **de courant** power *ou* electrical failure

panneau, x [pano] *nm* (*écriteau*) sign, notice; **~ d'affichage** notice board; **~ de signalisation** roadsign

panoplie [panɔpli] *nf* (*jouet*) outfit; (*fig*) array

panorama [panɔʀama] *nm* panorama

panse [pɑ̃s] *nf* paunch

pansement [pɑ̃smɑ̃] *nm* dressing, bandage; **~ adhésif** sticking plaster

panser [pɑ̃se] *vt* (*plaie*) to dress, bandage; (*bras*) to put a dressing on, bandage; (*cheval*) to groom

pantalon [pɑ̃talɔ̃] *nm* trousers *pl*, pair of trousers; **~ de ski** ski pants *pl*

panthère [pɑ̃tɛʀ] *nf* panther

pantin [pɑ̃tɛ̃] *nm* puppet

pantois [pɑ̃twa] *adj m*: **rester ~** to be flabbergasted

pantoufle [pɑ̃tufl] *nf* slipper

paon [pɑ̃] *nm* peacock

papa [papa] *nm* dad(dy)

pape [pap] *nm* pope

paperasse [papʀas] (*péj*) *nf* bumf *no pl*, papers *pl*; **paperasserie** (*péj*) *nf* paperwork *no pl*; (*tracasserie*) red tape *no pl*

papeterie [papetʀi] *nf* (*magasin*) stationer's (shop)

papi *nm* (*fam*) granddad

papier [papje] *nm* paper; (*article*) article; **~s**

141   papillon → parer

nmpl (aussi: ~s d'identité) (identity) papers;
~ à lettres writing paper, notepaper;
~ carbone carbon paper; ~ (d')aluminium
aluminium (BRIT) ou aluminum (US) foil,
tinfoil; ~ de verre sandpaper; ~ hygiénique
ou de toilette toilet paper; ~ journal
newspaper; ~ peint wallpaper

papillon [papijɔ̃] nm butterfly; (fam:
contravention) (parking) ticket; ~ de nuit
moth

papillote [papijɔt] nf: en ~ cooked in tinfoil.

papoter [papɔte] vi to chatter

paquebot [pak(ə)bo] nm liner

pâquerette [pakʀɛt] nf daisy

Pâques [pak] nm, nfpl Easter

paquet [pakɛ] nm packet; (colis) parcel; (fig:
tas): ~ de plle ou heap of; **paquet-cadeau**
nm: faites-moi un paquet-cadeau gift-wrap it
for me

par [paʀ] prép by; finir etc ~ to end etc with;
~ amour out of love; passer ~ Lyon/la côte to
go via ou through Lyons/along by the coast;
~ la fenêtre (jeter, regarder) out of the
window; 3 ~ jour/personne 3 a ou per day/
head; 2 ~ 2 in twos; ~ ici this way; (dans le
coin) round here; ~-ci, ~-là here and there;
~ temps de pluie in wet weather

parabolique [paʀabɔlik] adj: antenne ~
parabolic ou dish aerial

parachever [paʀaʃ(ə)ve] vt to perfect

parachute [paʀaʃyt] nm parachute;
parachutiste nm/f parachutist; (MIL)
paratrooper

parade [paʀad] nf (spectacle, défilé) parade;
(ESCRIME, BOXE) parry

paradis [paʀadi] nm heaven, paradise

paradoxe [paʀadɔks] nm paradox

paraffine [paʀafin] nf paraffin

parages [paʀaʒ] nmpl: dans les ~ (de) in the
area ou vicinity (of)

paragraphe [paʀagʀaf] nm paragraph

paraître [paʀɛtʀ] vb +attrib to seem, look,
appear ♦ vi to appear; (être visible) to show;
(PRESSE, ÉDITION) to be published, come out,
appear ♦ vb impers: il paraît que it seems ou
appears that, they say that; **chercher à ~** to
show off

parallèle [paʀalɛl] adj parallel; (non officiel)
unofficial ♦ nm (comparaison): faire un
~ entre to draw a parallel between ♦ nf
parallel (line)

paralyser [paʀalize] vt to paralyse

paramédical, e, -aux [paʀamedikal, o]
adj: **personnel ~** paramedics pl, paramedical
workers pl

paraphrase [paʀafʀɑz] nf paraphrase

parapluie [paʀaplɥi] nm umbrella

parasite [paʀazit] nm parasite; ~s nmpl (TÉL)
interference sg

parasol [paʀasɔl] nm parasol, sunshade

paratonnerre [paʀatɔnɛʀ] nm lightning
conductor

paravent [paʀavɑ̃] nm folding screen

parc [paʀk] nm (public) park, gardens pl; (de
château etc) grounds pl; (d'enfant) playpen;
(ensemble d'unités) stock; (de voitures etc)
fleet; ~ d'attractions theme park; ~ de
stationnement car park

parcelle [paʀsɛl] nf fragment, scrap; (de
terrain) plot, parcel

parce que [paʀskə] conj because

parchemin [paʀʃəmɛ̃] nm parchment

parcmètre [paʀkmɛtʀ] nm parking meter

parcourir [paʀkuʀiʀ] vt (trajet, distance) to
cover; (article, livre) to skim ou glance
through; (lieu) to go all over, travel up and
down; (suj: frisson) to run through

parcours [paʀkuʀ] nm (trajet) journey;
(itinéraire) route

par-derrière [paʀdɛʀjɛʀ] adv round the
back; dire du mal de qn ~~ to speak ill of sb
behind his back

par-dessous [paʀd(ə)su] prép, adv
under(neath)

pardessus [paʀdəsy] nm overcoat

par-dessus [paʀd(ə)sy] prép over (the top
of) ♦ adv over (the top); ~~ le marché on
top of all that; ~~ tout above all; en avoir ~
~ la tête to have had enough

par-devant [paʀd(ə)vɑ̃] adv (passer) round
the front

pardon [paʀdɔ̃] nm forgiveness no pl ♦ excl
sorry!; (pour interpeller etc) excuse me!;
demander ~ à qn (de) to apologize to sb
(for); je vous demande ~ I'm sorry; (pour
interpeller) excuse me; **pardonner** vt to
forgive; **pardonner qch à qn** to forgive sb for
sth

pare...: **pare-balles** adj inv bulletproof;
pare-brise nm inv windscreen (BRIT),
windshield (US); **pare-chocs** nm inv bumper

paré, e [paʀe] adj ready, all set

pareil, le [paʀɛj] adj (identique) the same,
alike; (similaire) similar; (tel): un courage/
livre ~ such courage/a book, courage/a book
like this; de ~s livres such books; ne pas avoir
son(sa) ~(le) to be second to none; ~ à the
same as; (similaire) similar to; sans ~
unparalleled, unequalled

parent, e [paʀɑ̃, ɑ̃t] nm/f: un(e) ~(e) a
relative ou relation; ~s nmpl (père et mère)
parents; **parenté** nf (lien) relationship

parenthèse [paʀɑ̃tɛz] nf (ponctuation)
bracket, parenthesis; (digression) parenthesis,
digression; entre ~s in brackets; (fig)
incidentally

parer [paʀe] vt (adorn) to adorn; (éviter) to ward off;
~ au plus pressé to attend to the most urgent

things first

paresse [paʀɛs] nf laziness; **paresseux, -euse** adj lazy

parfaire [paʀfɛʀ] vt to perfect

parfait, e [paʀfɛ, ɛt] adj perfect ♦ nm (LING) perfect (tense); **parfaitement** adv perfectly ♦ excl (most) certainly

parfois [paʀfwa] adv sometimes

parfum [paʀfœ̃] nm (produit) perfume, scent; (odeur: de fleur) scent, fragrance; (goût) flavour; **parfumé, e** adj (fleur, fruit) fragrant; (femme) perfumed; **parfumé au café** coffee-flavoured; **parfumer** vt (suj: odeur, bouquet) to perfume; (crème, gâteau) to flavour; **parfumerie** nf (produits) perfumes pl; (boutique) perfume shop

pari [paʀi] nm bet; **parier** vt to bet

Paris [paʀi] n Paris; **parisien, ne** adj Parisian; (GÉO, ADMIN) Paris cpd ♦ nm/f: **Parisien, ne** Parisian

parjure [paʀʒyʀ] nm perjury

parking [paʀkiŋ] nm (lieu) car park

parlant, e [paʀlã, ãt] adj (regard) eloquent; (CINÉMA) talking; **les chiffres sont ~s** the figures speak for themselves

parlement [paʀləmã] nm parliament; **parlementaire** adj parliamentary ♦ nm/f member of parliament; **parlementer** vi to negotiate, parley

parler [paʀle] vi to speak, talk; (avouer) to talk; **~ (à qn) de** to talk ou speak (to sb) about; **~ le/en français** to speak French/in French; **~ affaires** to talk business; **sans ~ de** (fig) not to mention, to say nothing of; **tu parles!** (fam: bien sûr) you bet!

parloir [paʀlwaʀ] nm (de prison, d'hôpital) visiting room

parmi [paʀmi] prép among(st)

paroi [paʀwa] nf wall; (cloison) partition; **~ rocheuse** rock face

paroisse [paʀwas] nf parish

parole [paʀɔl] nf (faculté): **la ~** speech; (mot, promesse) word; **~s** nfpl (MUS) words, lyrics; **tenir ~** to keep one's word; **prendre la ~** to speak; **demander la ~** to ask for permission to speak; **je te crois sur ~** I'll take your word for it

parquer [paʀke] vt (voiture, matériel) to park; (bestiaux) to pen (in ou up)

parquet [paʀkɛ] nm (parquet) floor; (JUR): **le ~** the Public Prosecutor's department

parrain [paʀɛ̃] nm godfather; **parrainer** vt (suj: entreprise) to sponsor

pars [paʀ] vb voir **partir**

parsemer [paʀsəme] vt (suj: feuilles, papiers) to be scattered over; **~ qch de** to scatter sth with

part [paʀ] nf (qui revient à qn) share; (fraction, ~ie) part; **prendre ~ à** (débat etc) to take part

in; (soucis, douleur de qn) to share in; **faire ~ de qch à qn** to announce sth to sb, inform sb of sth; **pour ma ~** as for me, as far as I'm concerned; **à ~ entière** full; **de la ~ de** (au nom de) on behalf of; (donné par) from; **de toute(s) ~(s)** from all sides ou quarters; **de ~ et d'autre** on both sides, on either side; **d'une ~ ... d'autre ~** on the one hand ... on the other hand; **d'autre ~** (de plus) moreover; **à ~** ♦ adv (séparément) separately; (de côté) aside ♦ prép apart from, except for; **faire la ~ des choses** to make allowances

partage [paʀtaʒ] nm (fractionnement) dividing up; (répartition) sharing (out) no pl, share-out

partager [paʀtaʒe] vt to share; (distribuer, répartir) to share (out); (morceler, diviser) to divide (up); **se ~** vt (héritage etc) to share between themselves (ou ourselves)

partance [paʀtãs]: **en ~** adv: **en ~ pour** (bound) for

partenaire [paʀtənɛʀ] nm/f partner

parterre [paʀtɛʀ] nm (de fleurs) (flower) bed; (THÉÂTRE) stalls pl

parti [paʀti] nm (POL) party; (décision) course of action; (personne à marier) match; **tirer ~ de** to take advantage of, turn to good account; **prendre ~ (pour/contre)** to take sides ou a stand (for/against); **~ pris** bias

partial, e, -aux [paʀsjal, jo] adj biased, partial

participant, e [paʀtisipã, ãt] nm/f participant; (à un concours) entrant

participation [paʀtisipasjɔ̃] nf participation; (financière) contribution

participer [paʀtisipe]: **~ à** vt (course, réunion) to take part in; (frais etc) to contribute to; (chagrin, succès de qn) to share (in)

particularité [paʀtikylaʀite] nf (distinctive) characteristic

particulier, -ière [paʀtikylje, jɛʀ] adj (spécifique) particular; (spécial) special, particular; (personnel, privé) private; (étrange) peculiar, odd ♦ nm (individu: ADMIN) private individual; **~ à** peculiar to; **en ~** (surtout) in particular, particularly; (en privé) in private; **particulièrement** adv particularly

partie [paʀti] nf (gén) part; (JUR etc: protagonistes) party; (de cartes, tennis etc) game; **une ~ de pêche** a fishing party ou trip; **en ~** partly, in part; **faire ~ de** to be part of; **prendre qn à ~** to take sb to task; **en grande ~** largely, in the main; **~ civile** (JUR) party claiming damages in a criminal case

partiel, le [paʀsjɛl] adj partial ♦ nm (SCOL) class exam

partir [paʀtiʀ] vi (gén) to go; (quitter) to go, leave; (tache) to go, come out; **~ de** (lieu: quitter) to leave; (: commencer à) to start from; à ~ de from

partisan, e [paʀtizɑ̃, an] nm/f partisan
♦ adj: être ~ de qch/de faire to be in favour
of sth/doing

partition [paʀtisjɔ̃] nf (MUS) score

partout [paʀtu] adv everywhere; ~ où il allait
everywhere ou wherever he went

paru [paʀy] pp de paraître

parure [paʀyʀ] nf (bijoux etc) finery no pl;
jewellery no pl; (assortiment) set

parution [paʀysjɔ̃] nf publication

parvenir [paʀvəniʀ]: ~ à vt (atteindre) to
reach; (réussir): ~ à faire to manage to do,
succeed in doing; ~ à ses fins to achieve
one's ends

pas¹ [pɑ] nm (enjambée, DANSE) step; (allure,
mesure) pace; (bruit) (foot)step; (trace)
footprint; ~ à ~ step by step; au ~ at walking
pace; faire les cent ~ to pace up and down;
faire les premiers ~ to make the first move;
sur le ~ de la porte on the doorstep

MOT-CLÉ

pas² [pɑ] adv **1** (en corrélation avec ne, non
etc) not; **il ne pleure pas** he does not ou
doesn't cry; he's not ou isn't crying; **il n'a pas
pleuré/ne pleurera pas** he did not ou didn't/
will not ou won't cry; **ils n'ont pas de
voiture/d'enfants** they haven't got a car/any
children, they have no car/children; **il m'a dit
de ne pas le faire** he told me not to do it; **non
pas que ...** not that ...

2 (employé sans ne etc): **pas moi** not me; not
I, I don't (ou can't etc); **une pomme pas mûre**
an apple which isn't ripe; **pas plus tard
qu'hier** only yesterday; **pas du tout** not at all
3: pas mal not bad; not badly; **pas mal de**
quite a lot of

---

passage [pɑsaʒ] nm (fait de passer) voir
passer; (lieu, prix de la traversée, extrait)
passage; (chemin) way; **de ~** (touristes)
passing through; **~ à niveau** level crossing;
~ clouté pedestrian crossing, "**~ interdit**" "no
entry"; **~ souterrain** subway (BRIT), underpass

passager, -ère [pɑsaʒe, ɛʀ] adj passing
♦ nm/f passenger; **~ clandestin** stowaway

passant, e [pɑsɑ̃, ɑ̃t] adj (rue, endroit) busy
♦ nm/f passer-by; **en ~** in passing

passe¹ [pɑs] nf (SPORT, NAVIG) pass; être en
~ de faire to be on the way to doing; être
dans une mauvaise ~ to be going through a
rough patch

passe² [pɑs] nm (~-partout) master ou
skeleton key

passé, e [pɑse] adj (révolu) past; (dernier:
semaine etc) last; (couleur) faded ♦ prép after
♦ nm past; (LING) past (tense); **~ de mode**
out of fashion; **~ composé** perfect (tense);

~ simple past historic

passe-partout [pɑspaʀtu] nm inv master ou
skeleton key ♦ adj inv all-purpose

passeport [pɑspɔʀ] nm passport

passer [pɑse] vi (aller) to go; (voiture,
piétons: défiler) to pass (by), go by; (facteur,
laitier etc) to come, call; (pour rendre visite) to
call ou drop in; (film, émission) to be on;
(temps, jours) to pass, go by; (couleur) to
fade; (mode) to die out; (douleur) to pass, go
away; (SCOL) to go up (to the next class) ♦ vt
(frontière, rivière etc) to cross; (douane) to go
through; (examen) to sit, take; (visite
médicale etc) to have; (journée, temps) to
spend; (enfiler: vêtement) to slip on; (film,
pièce) to show, put on; (disque) to play, put
on; (marché, accord) to agree on; **se ~** vi
(avoir lieu: scène, action) to take place; (se
dérouler: entretien etc) to go; (s'écouler:
semaine etc) to pass, go by; (arriver): **que
s'est-il passé?** what happened?; **~ qch à qn**
(sel etc) to pass sth to sb; (prêter) to lend sb
sth; (lettre, message) to pass sth on to sb; to
(tolérer) to let sb get away with sth; **~ par** to
go through; **~ avant qch/qn** (fig) to come
before sth/sb; **~ un coup de fil à qn** (fam) to
give sb a ring; **laisser ~** (air, lumière,
personne) to let through; (occasion) to let
slip, miss; (erreur) to overlook; **~ la seconde**
(AUTO) to change into second; **~ le balai/
l'aspirateur** to sweep up/hoover; **je vous
passe M. X** (je vous mets en communication
avec lui) I'm putting you through to Mr X; (je
lui passe l'appareil) here is Mr X, I'll hand you
over to Mr X; **se ~ de** to go ou do without

passerelle [pɑsʀɛl] nf footbridge; (de navire,
avion) gangway

passe-temps [pɑstɑ̃] nm inv pastime

passible [pɑsibl] adj: **~ de** liable to

passif, -ive [pɑsif, iv] adj passive

passion [pɑsjɔ̃] nf passion; **passionnant, e**
adj fascinating; **passionné, e** adj (personne)
passionate; (récit) impassioned; être
passionné de to have a passion for;
passionner vt (personne) to fascinate, grip;
se passionner pour (sport) to have a passion
for

passoire [pɑswaʀ] nf sieve; (à légumes)
colander; (à thé) strainer

pastèque [pɑstɛk] nf watermelon

pasteur [pɑstœʀ] nm (protestant) minister,
pastor

pasteurisé, e [pɑstœʀize] adj pasteurized

pastille [pɑstij] nf (à sucer) lozenge, pastille

patate [patat] nf (fam: pomme de terre) spud;
~ douce sweet potato

patauger [patoʒe] vi to splash about

pâte [pɑt] nf (à tarte) pastry; (à pain) dough;
(à frire) batter; **~s** nfpl (macaroni etc) pasta

sg; **~ à modeler** modelling clay, Plasticine ®
(*BRIT*); **~ brisée** shortcrust pastry; **~ d'amandes**
almond paste; **~ de fruits** crystallized fruit *no*
pl; **~ feuilletée** puff *ou* flaky pastry

pâté [pate] *nm* (*charcuterie*) pâté; (*tache*) ink
blot; (*de sable*) sandpie; **~ de maisons** block
(of houses); **~ en croûte** ≈ pork pie

pâtée [pate] *nf* mash, feed

patente [patɑ̃t] *nf* (*COMM*) trading licence

paternel, le [patɛʀnɛl] *adj* (*amour, soins*)
fatherly; (*ligne, autorité*) paternal

pâteux, -euse [patø, øz] *adj* pasty; (*langue*)
coated

pathétique [patetik] *adj* moving

patience [pasjɑ̃s] *nf* patience

patient, e [pasjɑ̃, jɑ̃t] *adj, nm/f* patient;
patienter *vi* to wait

patin [patɛ̃] *nm* skate; (*sport*) skating; **~s (à**
glace) (ice) skates; **~s à roulettes** roller skates

patinage [patinaʒ] *nm* skating

patiner [patine] *vi* to skate; (*roue, voiture*) to
spin; **se ~** *vi* (*meuble, cuir*) to acquire a sheen;
patineur, -euse *nm/f* skater; **patinoire** *nf*
skating rink, (ice) rink

pâtir [patiʀ]: **~ de** *vt* to suffer because of

pâtisserie [patisʀi] *nf* (*boutique*) cake shop;
(*gâteau*) cake, pastry; (*à la maison*) pastry-
ou cake-making, baking; **pâtissier, -ière**
nm/f pastrycook

patois [patwa, waz] *nm* dialect, patois

patraque [patʀak] (*fam*) *adj* peaky, off-
colour

patrie [patʀi] *nf* homeland

patrimoine [patʀimwan] *nm* (*culture*)
heritage

patriotique [patʀijɔtik] *adj* patriotic

patron, ne [patʀɔ̃, ɔn] *nm/f* boss; (*REL*)
patron saint ♦ *nm* (*COUTURE*) pattern;
patronat *nm* employers *pl*; **patronner** *vt*
to sponsor, support

patrouille [patʀuj] *nf* patrol

patte [pat] *nf* (*jambe*) leg; (*pied: de chien,*
chat) paw; (: *d'oiseau*) foot

pâturage [patyʀaʒ] *nm* pasture

paume [pom] *nf* palm

paumé, e [pome] (*fam*) *nm/f* drop-out

paumer [pome] (*fam*) *vt* to lose

paupière [popjɛʀ] *nf* eyelid

pause [poz] *nf* (*arrêt*) break; (*en parlant, MUS*)
pause

pauvre [povʀ] *adj* poor; **pauvreté** *nf* (*état*)
poverty

pavaner [pavane]: **se ~** *vi* to strut about

pavé, e [pave] *adj* (*cour*) paved; (*chaussée*)
cobbled ♦ *nm* (*bloc*) paving stone;
cobblestone

pavillon [pavijɔ̃] *nm* (*de banlieue*) small
(detached) house; pavilion; (*drapeau*) flag

pavoiser [pavwaze] *vi* (*fig*) to rejoice, exult

pavot [pavo] *nm* poppy

payant, e [pɛjɑ̃, ɑ̃t] *adj* (*spectateurs etc*)
paying; (*fig: entreprise*) profitable; (*effort*)
which pays off; **c'est ~** you have to pay, there
is a charge

paye [pɛj] *nf* pay, wages *pl*

payer [pɛje] *vt* (*créancier, employé, loyer*) to
pay; (*achat, réparations, fig: faute*) to pay for
♦ *vi* to pay; (*métier*) to be well-paid; (*tactique*
etc) to pay off; **il me l'a fait ~ 10 F** he charged
me 10 F for it; **~ qch à qn** to buy sth for sb,
buy sb sth; **se ~ la tête de qn** (*fam*) to take
the mickey out of sb

pays [pei] *nm* country; (*région*) region; **du ~**
local

paysage [peizaʒ] *nm* landscape

paysan, ne [peizɑ̃, an] *nm/f* farmer; (*péj*)
peasant ♦ *adj* (*agricole*) farming; (*rural*)
country

Pays-Bas [peiba] *nmpl*: **les ~-~** the
Netherlands

PC *nm* (*INFORM*) PC ♦ *sigle m* = **parti**
communiste

P.D.G. *sigle m* = **président directeur général**

péage [peaʒ] *nm* toll; (*endroit*) tollgate

peau, x [po] *nf* skin; **gants de ~** fine leather
gloves; **être bien/mal dans sa ~** to be quite at
ease/ill-at-ease; **~ de chamois** (*chiffon*)
chamois leather, shammy; **Peau-Rouge**
nm/f Red Indian, redskin

pêche [pɛʃ] *nf* (*sport, activité*) fishing;
(*poissons pêchés*) catch; (*fruit*) peach; **~ à la**
ligne (*en rivière*) angling

péché [peʃe] *nm* sin

pécher [peʃe] *vi* (*REL*) to sin

pêcher [peʃe] *nm* peach tree ♦ *vi* to go
fishing ♦ *vt* (*attraper*) to catch; (*être pêcheur*
de) to fish for

pécheur, -eresse [peʃœʀ, peʃʀɛs] *nm/f*
sinner

pêcheur [pɛʃœʀ] *nm* fisherman; (*à la ligne*)
angler

pécule [pekyl] *nm* savings *pl*, nest egg

pédagogie [pedagɔʒi] *nf* educational
methods *pl*, pedagogy; **pédagogique** *adj*
educational

pédale [pedal] *nf* pedal

pédalo [pedalo] *nm* pedal-boat

pédant, e [pedɑ̃, ɑ̃t] (*péj*) *adj* pedantic

pédestre [pedɛstʀ] *adj*: **randonnée ~** ramble;
sentier ~ pedestrian footpath

pédiatre [pedjatʀ] *nm/f* paediatrician, child
specialist

pédicure [pedikyʀ] *nm/f* chiropodist

pègre [pɛgʀ] *nf* underworld

peignais *etc* [peɲɛ] *vb voir* **peindre**; **peigner**

peigne [pɛɲ] *nm* comb; **peigner** *vt* to comb
(the hair of); **se peigner** *vi* to comb one's hair

peignoir *nm* dressing gown; **peignoir de bain**

bathrobe
peindre [pɛ̃dʀ] vt to paint; (fig) to portray,
depict
peine [pɛn] nf (affliction) sorrow, sadness no
pl; (mal, effort) trouble no pl, effort;
(difficulté) difficulty; (JUR) sentence; **avoir de
la ~** to be sad; **faire de la ~ à qn** to distress ou
upset sb; **prendre la ~ de faire** to go to the
trouble of doing; **se donner de la ~** to make
an effort; **ce n'est pas la ~ de faire** there's no
point in doing, it's not worth doing; **à ~**
scarcely, hardly, barely; **à ~ ... que** hardly ...
than; **~ capitale** ou **de mort** capital
punishment, death sentence; **peiner** vi
(personne) to work hard; (moteur, voiture) to
labour ♦ vt to grieve, sadden
peintre [pɛ̃tʀ] nm painter; **~ en bâtiment**
house painter
peinture [pɛ̃tyʀ] nf painting; (matière) paint;
(surfaces peintes: aussi: **~s**) paintwork;
"~ fraîche" "wet paint"
péjoratif, ive [peʒɔʀatif, iv] adj pejorative,
derogatory
pelage [pəlaʒ] nm coat, fur
pêle-mêle [pɛlmɛl] adv higgledy-piggledy
peler [pəle] vt, vi to peel
pèlerin [pɛlʀɛ̃] nm pilgrim
pèlerinage [pɛlʀinaʒ] nm pilgrimage
pelle [pɛl] nf shovel; (d'enfant, de terrassier)
spade
pellicule [pelikyl] nf film; **~s** nfpl (MÉD)
dandruff sg
pelote [p(ə)lɔt] nf (de fil, laine) ball
peloton [p(ə)lɔtɔ̃] nm group, squad;
(CYCLISME) pack; **~ d'exécution** firing squad
pelotonner [p(ə)lɔtɔne]: **se ~** vi to curl (o.s.)
up
pelouse [p(ə)luz] nf lawn
peluche [p(ə)lyʃ] nf (animal en) **~** fluffy
animal, soft toy; **chien/lapin en ~** fluffy dog/
rabbit
pelure [p(ə)lyʀ] nf peeling, peel no pl
pénal, e, -aux [penal, o] adj penal;
pénalité nf penalty
penaud, e [pəno, od] adj sheepish, contrite
penchant [pɑ̃ʃɑ̃] nm (tendance) tendency,
propensity; (faible) liking, fondness
pencher [pɑ̃ʃe] vi to tilt, lean over ♦ vt to tilt;
se ~ vi to lean over; (se baisser) to bend
down; **se ~ sur** (fig: problème) to look into;
~ pour to be inclined to favour
pendaison [pɑ̃dɛzɔ̃] nf hanging
pendant [pɑ̃dɑ̃] prép (au cours de) during;
(indique la durée) for; **~ que** while
pendentif [pɑ̃dɑ̃tif] nm pendant
penderie [pɑ̃dʀi] nf wardrobe
pendre [pɑ̃dʀ] vt, vi to hang; **se ~** (se
suicider) to hang o.s.; **~ la crémaillère** to have
a house-warming party

pendule [pɑ̃dyl] nf clock ♦ nm pendulum
pénétrer [penetʀe] vi, vt to penetrate; **~ dans**
to enter
pénible [penibl] adj (travail) hard; (sujet)
painful; (personne) tiresome; **péniblement**
adv with difficulty
péniche [peniʃ] nf barge
pénicilline [penisilin] nf penicillin
péninsule [penɛ̃syl] nf peninsula
pénis [penis] nm penis
pénitence [penitɑ̃s] nf (peine) penance;
(repentir) penitence; **pénitencier** nm
penitentiary
pénombre [penɔ̃bʀ] nf (faible clarté) half-
light; (obscurité) darkness
pensée [pɑ̃se] nf thought; (démarche,
doctrine) thinking no pl; (fleur) pansy; **en ~** in
one's mind
penser [pɑ̃se] vi, vt to think; **~ à** (ami,
vacances) to think of ou about; (réfléchir à:
problème, offre) to think about ou over;
(prévoir) to think of; **faire ~ à** to remind one
of; **~ faire qch** to be thinking of doing sth,
intend to do sth; **pensif, -ive** adj pensive,
thoughtful
pension [pɑ̃sjɔ̃] nf (allocation) pension; (prix
du logement) board and lodgings, bed and
board; (école) boarding school; **~ alimentaire**
(de divorcée) maintenance allowance,
alimony; **~ complète** full board; **~ (de famille)**
boarding house, guesthouse; **pensionnaire**
nm/f (SCOL) boarder; **pensionnat** nm
boarding school
pente [pɑ̃t] nf slope; **en ~** sloping
Pentecôte [pɑ̃tkot] nf: **la ~** Whitsun (BRIT),
Pentecost
pénurie [penyʀi] nf shortage
pépé [pepe] (fam) nm grandad
pépin [pepɛ̃] nm (BOT: graine) pip; (ennui)
snag, hitch
pépinière [pepinjɛʀ] nf nursery
perçant, e [pɛʀsɑ̃, ɑ̃t] adj (cri) piercing,
shrill; (regard) piercing
percée [pɛʀse] nf (trouée) opening; (MIL,
technologique) breakthrough
perce-neige [pɛʀsənɛʒ] nf inv snowdrop
percepteur [pɛʀsɛptœʀ, tʀis] nm tax
collector
perception [pɛʀsɛpsjɔ̃] nf perception;
(bureau) tax office
percer [pɛʀse] vt to pierce; (ouverture etc) to
make; (mystère, énigme) to penetrate ♦ vi to
break through; **perceuse** nf drill
percevoir [pɛʀsəvwaʀ] vt (distinguer) to
perceive, detect; (taxe, impôt) to collect;
(revenu, indemnité) to receive
perche [pɛʀʃ] nf (bâton) pole
percher [pɛʀʃe] vt, vi to perch; **se ~** vi to
perch; **perchoir** nm perch

perçois etc [pɛʀswa] vb voir **percevoir**

percolateur [pɛʀkɔlatœʀ] nm percolator

perçu, e [pɛʀsy] pp de **percevoir**

percussion [pɛʀkysjɔ̃] nf percussion

percuter [pɛʀkyte] vt to strike; (suj: véhicule) to crash into

perdant, e [pɛʀdɑ̃, ɑ̃t] nm/f loser

perdre [pɛʀdʀ] vt to lose; (gaspiller: temps, argent) to waste; (personne: moralement etc) to ruin ♦ vi to lose; (sur une vente etc) to lose out; **se ~** vi (s'égarer) to get lost, lose one's way; (denrées) to go to waste

perdrix [pɛʀdʀi] nf partridge

perdu, e [pɛʀdy] pp de **perdre** ♦ adj (isolé) out-of-the-way; (COMM: emballage) non-returnable; (malade): **il est ~** there's no hope left for him; **à vos moments ~s** in your spare time

père [pɛʀ] nm father; **~ de famille** father; **le ~ Noël** Father Christmas

perfection [pɛʀfɛksjɔ̃] nf perfection; **à la ~** to perfection; **perfectionné, e** adj sophisticated; **perfectionner** vt to improve, perfect

perforatrice [pɛʀfɔʀatʀis] nf (de bureau) punch

perforer [pɛʀfɔʀe] vt (poinçonner) to punch

performant, e [pɛʀfɔʀmɑ̃, ɑ̃t] adj: **très ~** high-performance cpd

perfusion [pɛʀfyzjɔ̃] nf: **faire une ~ à qn** to put sb on a drip

péricliter [peʀiklite] vi to collapse

péril [peʀil] nm peril

périmé, e [peʀime] adj (ADMIN) out-of-date, expired

périmètre [peʀimɛtʀ] nm perimeter

période [peʀjɔd] nf period; **périodique** adj periodic ♦ nm periodical

péripéties [peʀipesi] nfpl events, episodes

périphérique [peʀifeʀik] adj (quartiers) outlying ♦ nm (AUTO) ring road

périple [peʀipl] nm journey

périr [peʀiʀ] vi to die, perish

périssable [peʀisabl] adj perishable

perle [pɛʀl] nf pearl; (de plastique, métal, sueur) bead

permanence [pɛʀmanɑ̃s] nf permanence; (local) (duty) office; **assurer une ~** (service public, bureaux) to operate ou maintain a basic service; **être de ~** to be on call ou duty; **en ~** continuously

permanent, e [pɛʀmanɑ̃, ɑ̃t] adj permanent; (spectacle) continuous; **permanente** nf perm

perméable [pɛʀmeabl] adj (terrain) permeable; **~ à** (fig) receptive ou open to

permettre [pɛʀmɛtʀ] vt to allow, permit; **~ à qn de faire/qch** to allow sb to do/sth; **se ~ de faire** to take the liberty of doing

permis, e [pɛʀmi, iz] nm permit, licence; **~ de chasse** hunting permit; **~ (de conduire)** (driving) licence (BRIT), (driver's) license (US); **~ de construire** planning permission (BRIT), building permit (US); **~ de séjour** residence permit; **~ de travail** work permit

permission [pɛʀmisjɔ̃] nf permission; (MIL) leave; **avoir la ~ de faire** to have permission to do; **en ~** on leave

permuter [pɛʀmyte] vt to change around, permutate ♦ vi to change, swap

Pérou [peʀu] nm Peru

perpétuel, le [pɛʀpetɥɛl] adj perpetual; **perpétuité** nf: **à perpétuité** for life; **être condamné à perpétuité** to receive a life sentence

perplexe [pɛʀplɛks] adj perplexed, puzzled

perquisitionner [pɛʀkizisjɔne] vi to carry out a search

perron [pɛʀɔ̃] nm steps pl (leading to entrance)

perroquet [pɛʀɔke] nm parrot

perruche [pɛʀyʃ] nf budgerigar (BRIT), budgie (BRIT), parakeet (US)

perruque [pɛʀyk] nf wig

persan, e [pɛʀsɑ̃, an] adj Persian

persécuter [pɛʀsekyte] vt to persecute

persévérer [pɛʀseveʀe] vi to persevere

persiennes [pɛʀsjen] nfpl shutters

persil [pɛʀsi] nm parsley

Persique [pɛʀsik] adj: **le golfe ~** the (Persian) Gulf

persistant, e [pɛʀsistɑ̃, ɑ̃t] adj persistent

persister [pɛʀsiste] vi to persist; **~ à faire qch** to persist in doing sth

personnage [pɛʀsɔnaʒ] nm (individu) character, individual; (célébrité) important person; (de roman, film) character; (PEINTURE) figure

personnalité [pɛʀsɔnalite] nf personality; (personnage) prominent figure

personne [pɛʀsɔn] nf person ♦ pron nobody, no one; (avec négation en anglais) anybody, anyone; **~s** nfpl (gens) people pl; **il n'y a ~** there's nobody there, there isn't anybody there; **~ âgée** elderly person; **personnel, le** adj personal; (égoïste) selfish ♦ nm staff, personnel; **personnellement** adv personally

perspective [pɛʀspɛktiv] nf (ART) perspective; (vue) view; (point de vue) viewpoint, angle; (chose envisagée) prospect; **en ~** in prospect

perspicace [pɛʀspikas] adj clear-sighted, gifted with (ou showing) insight; **perspicacité** nf clear-sightedness

persuader [pɛʀsɥade] vt: **~ qn (de faire)** to persuade sb (to do); **persuasif, -ive** adj persuasive

perte [pɛʀt] nf loss; (de temps) waste; (fig:

morale) ruin; **à ~ de vue** as far as the eye can (*ou* could) see; **~s blanches** (vaginal) discharge *sg*

pertinemment [pɛʀtinamɑ̃] *adv* (*savoir*) full well

pertinent, e [pɛʀtinɑ̃, ɑ̃t] *adj* apt, relevant

perturbation [pɛʀtyʀbasjɔ̃] *nf*: **~ (atmosphérique)** atmospheric disturbance

perturber [pɛʀtyʀbe] *vt* to disrupt; (*PSYCH*) to perturb, disturb

pervers, e [pɛʀvɛʀ, ɛʀs] *adj* perverted

pervertir [pɛʀvɛʀtiʀ] *vt* to pervert

pesant, e [pəzɑ̃, ɑ̃t] *adj* heavy; (*fig: présence*) burdensome

pèse-personne [pɛzpɛʀsɔn] *nm* (bathroom) scales *pl*

peser [pəze] *vt* to weigh ♦ *vi* to weigh; (*fig: avoir de l'importance*) to carry weight; **~ lourd** to be heavy

pessimisme [pesimism] *nm* pessimism

pessimiste [pesimist] *adj* pessimistic ♦ *nm/f* pessimist

peste [pɛst] *nf* plague

pester [pɛste] *vi*: **~ contre** to curse

pétale [petal] *nm* petal

pétanque [petɑ̃k] *nf* type of bowls

pétarader [petaʀade] *vi* to backfire

pétard [petaʀ] *nm* banger (*BRIT*), firecracker

péter [pete] *vi* (*fam: casser*) to bust; (*fam!*) to fart (*!*)

pétillant, e [petijɑ̃, ɑ̃t] *adj* (*eau etc*) sparkling

pétiller [petije] *vi* (*feu*) to crackle; (*champagne*) to bubble; (*yeux*) to sparkle

petit, e [p(ə)ti, it] *adj* small; (*avec nuance affective*) little, (*voyage*) short, little, (*bruit etc*) faint, slight; **~s** *nmpl* (*d'un animal*) young *pl*; **les tout-~s** the little ones, the tiny tots; **~ à ~** bit by bit, gradually; **~(e) ami(e)** boyfriend/girlfriend; **~ déjeuner** breakfast; **~ pain** (bread) roll; **les ~es annonces** the small ads; **~s pois** garden peas; **petite-fille** *nf* granddaughter; **petit-fils** *nm* grandson

pétition [petisjɔ̃] *nf* petition

petits-enfants [pətizɑ̃fɑ̃] *nmpl* grandchildren

petit-suisse [pətisɥis] (*pl* **~s-~s**) *nm* small individual pot of cream cheese

pétrin [petʀɛ̃] *nm* (*fig*): **dans le ~** (*fam*) in a jam *ou* fix

pétrir [petʀiʀ] *vt* to knead

pétrole [petʀɔl] *nm* oil; (*pour lampe, réchaud etc*) paraffin (oil); **pétrolier, -ière** *nm* oil tanker

---

MOT-CLÉ

---

peu [pø] *adv* **1** (*modifiant verbe, adjectif, adverbe*): **il boit peu** he doesn't drink (very) much; **il est peu bavard** he's not very

talkative; **peu avant/après** shortly before/afterwards

2 (*modifiant nom*): **peu de: peu de gens/d'arbres** few *ou* not (very) many people/trees; **il a peu d'espoir** he hasn't (got) much hope, he has little hope; **pour peu de temps** for (only) a short while

3: peu à peu little by little; **à peu près** just about, more or less; **à peu près 10 kg/10 F** approximately 10 kg/10F

♦ *nm* **1: le peu de gens qui** the few people who; **le peu de sable qui** what little sand, the little sand which

2: un peu a little; **un petit peu** a little bit; **un peu d'espoir** a little hope

♦ *pron*: **peu le savent** few know (it); **avant** *ou* **sous peu** shortly, before long; **de peu** (only) just

---

peuple [pœpl] *nm* people; **peupler** *vt* (*pays, région*) to populate; (*étang*) to stock; (*suj: hommes, poissons*) to inhabit

peuplier [pøplije] *nm* poplar (tree)

peur [pœʀ] *nf* fear; **avoir ~** (*de/de faire/que*) to be frightened *ou* afraid (of/of doing/that); **faire ~ à** to frighten; **de ~ de/que** for fear of/that; **peureux, -euse** *adj* fearful, timorous

peut [pø] *vb voir* **pouvoir**

peut-être [pøtɛtʀ] *adv* perhaps, maybe; **~-~ que** perhaps, maybe; **~-~ bien qu'il fera/est** he may well do/be

peux *etc* [pø] *vb voir* **pouvoir**

phare [faʀ] *nm* (*en mer*) lighthouse; (*de véhicule*) headlight; **~s de recul** reversing lights

pharmacie [faʀmasi] *nf* (*magasin*) chemist's (*BRIT*), pharmacy; (*de salle de bain*) medicine cabinet; **pharmacien, ne** *nm/f* pharmacist, chemist (*BRIT*)

phénomène [fenɔmɛn] *nm* phenomenon

philatélie [filateli] *nf* philately, stamp collecting

philosophe [filɔzɔf] *nm/f* philosopher ♦ *adj* philosophical

philosophie [filɔzɔfi] *nf* philosophy

phobie [fɔbi] *nf* phobia

phonétique [fɔnetik] *nf* phonetics *sg*

phoque [fɔk] *nm* seal

phosphorescent, e [fɔsfɔʀesɑ̃, ɑ̃t] *adj* luminous

photo [fɔto] *nf* photo(graph); **prendre en ~** to take a photo of; **faire de la ~** to take photos; **~ d'identité** passport photograph; **photocopie** *nf* photocopy; **photocopier** *vt* to photocopy; **photocopieuse** *nf* photocopier; **photographe** *nm/f* photographer; **photographie** *nf* (*technique*) photography; (*cliché*) photograph; **photographier** *vt* to photograph

phrase [fʀɑz] nf sentence
physicien, ne [fizisjɛ̃, jɛn] nm/f physicist
physionomie [fizjɔnɔmi] nf face
physique [fizik] adj physical ♦ nm physique
♦ nf physics sg; **au ~** physically;
physiquement adv physically
piailler [pjaje] vi to squawk
pianiste [pjanist] nm/f pianist
piano [pjano] nm piano; **pianoter** vi to tinkle
away (at the piano)
pic [pik] nm (instrument) pick(axe);
(montagne) peak; (ZOOL) woodpecker; **à ~**
vertically; (fig: tomber, arriver) just at the
right time
pichet [piʃɛ] nm jug
picorer [pikɔʀe] vt to peck
picoter [pikɔte] vt (suj: oiseau) to peck ♦ vi
(irriter) to smart, prickle
pie [pi] nf magpie
pièce [pjɛs] nf (d'un logement) room;
(THÉÂTRE) play; (de machine) part; (de
monnaie) coin; (document) document;
(fragment, de collection) piece; **dix francs ~**
ten francs each; **vendre à la ~** to sell
separately; **travailler à la ~** to do piecework;
un maillot une ~ a one-piece swimsuit; **un
deux-~s cuisine** a two-room(ed) flat (BRIT) ou
apartment (US) with kitchen; **à conviction**
exhibit; **~ d'identité: avez-vous une
~ d'identité?** have you got any (means of)
identification?; **~ montée** tiered cake; **~s
détachées** spares, (spare) parts; **~s
justificatives** supporting documents
pied [pje] nm foot; (de table) leg; (de lampe)
base; **à ~** on foot; **au ~ de la lettre** literally;
avoir ~ to be able to touch the bottom, not
to be out of one's depth; **avoir le ~ marin** to
be a good sailor; **sur ~** (debout, rétabli) up
and about; **mettre sur ~** (entreprise) to set
up; **c'est le ~** (fam) it's brilliant; **mettre les ~s
dans le plat** (fam) to put one's foot in it; **il se
débrouille comme un ~** (fam) he's completely
useless; **pied-noir** nm Algerian-born
Frenchman
piège [pjɛʒ] nm trap; **prendre au ~** to trap;
piéger vt (avec une bombe) to booby-trap;
lettre/voiture piégée letter-/car-bomb
pierre [pjɛʀ] nf stone; **~ précieuse** precious
stone, gem; **~ tombale** tombstone;
pierreries nfpl gems, precious stones
piétiner [pjetine] vi (trépigner) to stamp
(one's foot); (fig) to be at a standstill ♦ vt to
trample on
piéton, ne [pjetɔ̃, ɔn] nm/f pedestrian;
piétonnier, -ière adj: **rue** ou **zone
piétonnière** pedestrian precinct
pieu, x [pjø] nm post; (pointu) stake
pieuvre [pjœvʀ] nf octopus
pieux, -euse [pjø, pjøz] adj pious

piffer [pife] (fam) vt: **je ne peux pas le ~ !**
can't stand him
pigeon [piʒɔ̃] nm pigeon
piger [piʒe] (fam) vi, vt to understand
pigiste [piʒist] nm/f freelance(r)
pignon [piɲɔ̃] nm (de mur) gable
pile [pil] nf (tas) pile; (ÉLEC) battery ♦ adv
(fam: s'arrêter etc) dead; **à deux heures ~** at
two on the dot; **jouer à ~ ou face** to toss up
(for it); **~ ou face?** heads or tails?
piler [pile] vt to crush, pound
pilier [pilje] nm pillar
piller [pije] vt to pillage, plunder, loot
pilote [pilɔt] nm pilot; (de voiture) driver
♦ adj pilot cpd; **~ de course** racing driver;
~ de ligne/d'essai/de chasse airline/test/
fighter pilot; **piloter** vt (avion) to pilot, fly;
(voiture) to drive
pilule [pilyl] nf pill; **prendre la ~** to be on the
pill
piment [pimɑ̃] nm (aussi: **~ rouge**) chilli;
(fig) spice, piquancy; **~ doux** pepper,
capsicum; **pimenté, e** adj (plat) hot, spicy
pimpant, e [pɛ̃pɑ̃, ɑ̃t] adj spruce
pin [pɛ̃] nm pine
pinard [pinaʀ] (fam) nm (cheap) wine, plonk
(BRIT)
pince [pɛ̃s] nf (outil) pliers pl; (de homard,
crabe) pincer, claw; (COUTURE: pli) dart; **~ à
épiler** tweezers pl; **~ à linge** clothes peg (BRIT)
ou pin (US)
pincé, e [pɛ̃se] adj (air) stiff
pinceau, x [pɛ̃so] nm (paint)brush
pincée [pɛ̃se] nf: **une ~ de** a pinch of
pincer [pɛ̃se] vt to pinch; (fam) to nab
pinède [pinɛd] nf pinewood, pine forest
pingouin [pɛ̃gwɛ̃] nm penguin
ping-pong ® [piŋpɔ̃g] nm table tennis
pingre [pɛ̃gʀ] adj niggardly
pinson [pɛ̃sɔ̃] nm chaffinch
pintade [pɛ̃tad] nf guinea-fowl
pioche [pjɔʃ] nf pickaxe; **piocher** vt to dig
up (with a pickaxe); **piocher dans** (le tas, ses
économies) to dig into
pion [pjɔ̃] nm (ÉCHECS) pawn; (DAMES) piece;
(SCOL) supervisor
pionnier [pjɔnje] nm pioneer
pipe [pip] nf pipe; **fumer la ~** to smoke a pipe
pipeau, x [pipo] nm (reed-)pipe
piquant, e [pikɑ̃, ɑ̃t] adj (barbe, rosier etc)
prickly; (saveur, sauce) hot, pungent; (détail)
titillating; (froid) biting ♦ nm (épine) thorn,
prickle; (fig) spiciness, spice
pique [pik] nf pike; (fig) cutting remark ♦ nm
(CARTES) spades pl
pique-nique [piknik] nm picnic; **pique-
niquer** vi to have a picnic
piquer [pike] vt (suj: guêpe, fumée, orties) to
sting; (: moustique) to bite; (: barbe) to

prick; (: *froid*) to bite; (*MÉD*) to give a jab to; (: *chien, chat*) to put to sleep; (*intérêt*) to arouse; (*fam: voler*) to pinch ♦ vi (*avion*) to go into a dive; **se ~** (*avec une aiguille*) to prick o.s.; (*dans les orties*) to get stung; (*suj: toxicomane*) to shoot up; **~ une colère** to fly into a rage

piquet [pikɛ] nm (*pieu*) post, stake; (*de tente*) peg; **~ de grève** (strike-)picket

piqûre [pikyʀ] nf (*d'épingle*) prick; (*d'ortie*) sting; (*de moustique*) bite; (*MÉD*) injection, shot (*US*); **faire une ~ à qn** to give sb an injection

pirate [piʀat] nm, adj pirate; **~ de l'air** hijacker

pire [piʀ] adj worse; (*superlatif*): **le(la) ~** ... the worst ... ♦ nm: **le ~ (de)** the worst (of); **au ~** at (the very) worst

pis [pi] nm (*de vache*) udder; (*pire*): **le ~** the worst ♦ adj, adv worse; **de mal en ~** from bad to worse

piscine [pisin] nf (*swimming*) pool; **~ couverte** indoor (*swimming*) pool

pissenlit [pisāli] nm dandelion

pistache [pistaʃ] nf pistachio (*nut*)

piste [pist] nf (*d'un animal, sentier*) track, trail; (*indice*) lead; (*de skate*) track; (*de cirque*) ring; (*de danse*) floor; (*de patinage*) rink; (*de ski*) run; (*AVIAT*) runway; **~ cyclable** cycle track

pistolet [pistɔlɛ] nm (*arme*) pistol, gun; (*à peinture*) spray gun; **pistolet-mitrailleur** nm submachine gun

piston [pistɔ̃] nm (*TECH*) piston; **avoir du ~** (*fam*) to have friends in the right places; **pistonner** vt (*candidat*) to pull strings for

piteux, -euse [pitø, øz] adj pitiful, sorry (*avant le nom*)

pitié [pitje] nf pity; **il me fait ~** I feel sorry for him; **avoir ~ de** (*compassion*) to pity, feel sorry for; (*merci*) to have pity ou mercy on

pitoyable [pitwajabl] adj pitiful

pitre [pitʀ] nm clown; **pitrerie** nf tomfoolery no pl

pittoresque [pitɔʀɛsk] adj picturesque

pivot [pivo] nm pivot; **pivoter** vi to revolve; (*fauteuil*) to swivel

P.J. sigle f (= *police judiciaire*) ≈ CID (*BRIT*), ≈ FBI (*US*)

placard [plakaʀ] nm (*armoire*) cupboard; (*affiche*) poster, notice

place [plas] nf (*emplacement, classement*) place; (*de ville, village*) square; (*espace libre*) room, space; (*de parking*) space; (*siège: de train, cinéma, voiture*) seat; (*emploi*) job; **en ~** (*mettre*) in its place; **sur ~** on the spot; **faire ~ à** to give way to; **ça prend de la ~** it takes up a lot of room ou space; **à la ~ de** in place of, instead of; **à ta ~** ... if I were you ...; **se mettre à la ~ de qn** to put o.s. in sb's place ou

in sb's shoes

placé, e [plase] adj: **être bien/mal ~** (*spectateur*) to have a good/a poor seat; (*concurrent*) to be in a good/bad position; **il est bien ~ pour le savoir** he is in a position to know

placement [plasmɑ̃] nm (*FINANCE*) investment; **bureau de ~** employment agency

placer [plase] vt to place; (*convive, spectateur*) to seat; (*argent*) to place, invest; **il n'a pas pu ~ un mot** he couldn't get a word in; **se ~ au premier rang** to go and stand (*ou* sit) in the first row

plafond [plafɔ̃] nm ceiling

plage [plaʒ] nf beach

plagiat [plaʒja] nm plagiarism

plaid [plɛd] nm (*tartan*) car rug

plaider [plede] vi (*avocat*) to plead ♦ vt to plead; **~ pour** (*fig*) to speak for; **plaidoyer** nm (*JUR*) speech for the defence; (*fig*) plea

plaie [plɛ] nf wound

plaignant, e [plɛɲɑ̃, ɑ̃t] nm/f plaintiff

plaindre [plɛ̃dʀ] vt to pity, feel sorry for; **se ~** vi (*gémir*) to moan; (*protester*): **se ~ (à qn) (de)** to complain (to sb) (about); (*souffrir*): **se ~ de** to complain of

plaine [plɛn] nf plain

plain-pied [plɛ̃pje] adv: **de ~~ (avec)** on the same level (as)

plainte [plɛ̃t] nf (*gémissement*) moan, groan; (*doléance*) complaint; **porter ~** to lodge a complaint

plaire [plɛʀ] vi to be a success, be successful; **ça plaît beaucoup aux jeunes** it's very popular with young people; **~ à**: **cela me plaît** I like it; **se ~ quelque part** to like being somewhere ou like it somewhere; **j'irai si ça me plaît** I'll go if I feel like it; **s'il vous plaît** please

plaisance [plɛzɑ̃s] nf (*aussi:* **navigation de ~**) (*pleasure*) sailing, yachting

plaisant, e [plɛzɑ̃, ɑ̃t] adj pleasant; (*histoire, anecdote*) amusing

plaisanter [plɛzɑ̃te] vi to joke; **plaisanterie** nf joke

plaise etc [plɛz] vb voir **plaire**

plaisir [plɛziʀ] nm pleasure; **faire ~ à qn** (*délibérément*) to be nice to sb, please sb; **ça me fait ~** I like (doing) it; **j'espère que ça te fera ~** I hope you'll like it; **pour le ~** for pleasure

plaît [plɛ] vb voir **plaire**

plan, e [plɑ̃, an] adj flat ♦ nm plan; (*fig*) level, plane; (*CINÉMA*) shot; **au premier/second ~** in the foreground/middle distance; **à l'arrière ~** in the background; **rester en ~** (*fam*) to be left stranded; **laisser en ~** (*fam: travail*) to drop, abandon; **~ d'eau** lake

planche [plɑ̃ʃ] nf (*pièce de bois*) plank, (*wooden*) board; (*illustration*) plate; **~ à**

repasser ironing board; **~ à roulettes** skateboard; **~ à voile** (*sport*) windsurfing

plancher [plɑ̃ʃe] *nm* floor; floorboards *pl* ♦ *vi* (*fam*) to work hard

planer [plane] *vi* to glide; (*fam: rêveur*) to have one's head in the clouds; **~ sur** (*fig: danger*) to hang over

planète [planɛt] *nf* planet

planeur [planœR] *nm* glider

planification [planifikasjɔ̃] *nf* (economic) planning

planifier [planifje] *vt* to plan

planning [planiŋ] *nm* programme, schedule

planque [plɑ̃k] (*fam*) *nf* (*emploi peu fatigant*) cushy (BRIT) ou easy number; (*cachette*) hiding place

plant [plɑ̃] *nm* seedling, young plant

plante [plɑ̃t] *nf* plant; **~ d'appartement** house ou pot plant; **~ des pieds** sole (of the foot)

planter [plɑ̃te] *vt* (*plante*) to plant; (*enfoncer*) to hammer ou drive in; (*tente*) to put up, pitch; (*fam: personne*) to dump; **se ~** (*fam: se tromper*) to get it wrong

plantureux, -euse [plɑ̃tyRø, øz] *adj* copious, lavish; (*femme*) buxom

plaque [plak] *nf* plate; (*de verglas, d'eczéma*) patch; (*avec inscription*) plaque; **~ chauffante** hotplate; **~ de chocolat** bar of chocolate; **~ (minéralogique ou d'immatriculation)** number (BRIT) ou license (US) plate; **~ tournante** (*fig*) centre

plaqué, e [plake] *adj*: **~ or/argent** gold-/silver-plated

plaquer [plake] *vt* (*aplatir*): **~ qch sur** ou **contre** to make sth stick ou cling to; (RUGBY) to bring down; (*fam: laisser tomber*) to drop

plaquette [plakɛt] *nf* (*de chocolat*) bar; (*beurre*) pack(et); **~ de frein** brake pad

plastique [plastik] *adj, nm* plastic; **plastiquer** *vt* to blow up (*with a plastic bomb*)

plat, e [pla, -at] *adj* flat; (*cheveux*) straight; (*style*) flat, dull ♦ *nm* (*récipient, CULIN*) dish; (*d'un repas*) course; **à ~ ventre** face down; **à ~** (*pneu, batterie*) flat; (*fam: personne*) dead beat; **~ cuisiné** pre-cooked meal; **~ de résistance** main course; **~ du jour** dish of the day

platane [platan] *nm* plane tree

plateau, x [plato] *nm* (*support*) tray; (GÉO) plateau; (CINÉMA) set; **~ de fromages** cheeseboard

plate-bande [platbɑ̃d] *nf* flower bed

plate-forme [platfɔRm] *nf* platform; **~~ de forage/pétrolière** drilling/oil rig

platine [platin] *nm* platinum ♦ *nf* (*d'un tourne-disque*) turntable

plâtre [plɑtR] *nm* (*matériau*) plaster; (*statue*) plaster statue; (MÉD) (plaster) cast; **avoir un**

bras dans le ~ to have an arm in plaster

plein, e [plɛ̃, plɛn] *adj* full ♦ *nm*: **faire le ~ (d'essence)** to fill up (with petrol); **à ~es mains** (*ramasser*) in handfuls; **à ~ temps** full-time; **en ~ air** in the open air; **en ~ soleil** in direct sunlight; **en ~e nuit/rue** in the middle of the night/street; **en ~ jour** in broad daylight

pleurer [plœRe] *vi* to cry; (*yeux*) to water ♦ *vt* to mourn (for); **~ sur** to lament (over), to bemoan

pleurnicher [plœRniʃe] *vi* to snivel, whine

pleurs [plœR] *nmpl*: **en ~** in tears

pleut [plø] *vb voir* **pleuvoir**

pleuvoir [pløvwaR] *vb impers* to rain ♦ *vi* (*coups*) to rain down; (*critiques, invitations*) to shower down; **il pleut** it's raining

pli [pli] *nm* fold; (*de jupe*) pleat; (*de pantalon*) crease; **prendre le ~ de faire** to get into the habit of doing; **un mauvais ~** a bad habit

pliant, e [plijɑ̃, ɑ̃t] *adj* folding

plier [plije] *vt* to fold; (*pour ranger*) to fold up; (*genou, bras*) to bend ♦ *vi* to bend; (*fig*) to yield; **se ~** *vi* to fold; **se ~ à** to submit to

plinthe [plɛ̃t] *nf* skirting board

plisser [plise] *vt* (*jupe*) to put pleats in; (*yeux*) to screw up; (*front*) to crease

plomb [plɔ̃] *nm* (*métal*) lead; (*d'une cartouche*) (lead) shot; (PÊCHE) sinker; (ÉLEC) fuse; **sans ~** (*essence etc*) unleaded

plombage [plɔ̃baʒ] *nm* (*de dent*) filling

plomberie [plɔ̃bRi] *nf* plumbing

plombier [plɔ̃bje] *nm* plumber

plonge [plɔ̃ʒ] *nf* washing-up

plongeant, e [plɔ̃ʒɑ̃, ɑ̃t] *adj* (*vue*) from above; (*décolleté*) plunging

plongée [plɔ̃ʒe] *nf* (SPORT) diving *no pl*; (*sans scaphandre*) skin diving; **~ sous-marine** diving

plongeoir [plɔ̃ʒwaR] *nm* diving board

plongeon [plɔ̃ʒɔ̃] *nm* dive

plonger [plɔ̃ʒe] *vi* to dive ♦ *vt*: **~ qch dans** to plunge sth into; **se ~ dans** (*études, lecture*) to bury ou immerse o.s. in; **plongeur** *nm* diver

ployer [plwaje] *vt, vi* to bend

plu [ply] *pp de* **plaire**; **pleuvoir**

pluie [plɥi] *nf* rain

plume [plym] *nf* feather; (*pour écrire*) (pen) nib; (*fig*) pen

plupart [plypaR]: **la ~** *pron* the majority, most (of them); **la ~ des** most, the majority of; **la ~ du temps/d'entre nous** most of the time/of us; **pour la ~** for the most part, mostly

pluriel [plyRjɛl] *nm* plural

plus¹ [ply] *vb voir* **plaire**

MOT-CLÉ
---

plus² [ply] *adv* **1** (*forme négative*): **ne ... plus** no more, no longer; **je n'ai plus d'argent** I've got no more money ou no money left; **il ne**

travaille plus he's no longer working, he doesn't work any more

2 (comparatif) more, ...+er; (superlatif): **le plus** the most, the ...+est; **plus grand/ intelligent (que)** bigger/more intelligent (than); **le plus grand/intelligent** the biggest/ most intelligent; **tout au plus** at the very most

3 (davantage) more; **il travaille plus (que)** he works more (than); **plus il travaille, plus il est heureux** the more he works, the happier he is; **plus de pain** more bread; **plus de 10 personnes** more than 10 people, over 10 people; **3 heures de plus que** 3 hours more than; **de plus** what's more, moreover; **3 kilos en plus** 3 kilos more; **en plus de** in addition to; **de plus en plus** more and more; **plus ou moins** more or less; **ni plus ni moins** no more, no less

♦ prép: **4 plus 2** 4 plus 2

plusieurs [plyzjœr] dét, pron several; **ils sont ~** there are several of them

plus-value [plyvaly] nf (bénéfice) surplus

plut [ply] vb voir **plaire**

plutôt [plyto] adv rather; **je préfère ~ celui-ci** I'd rather have this one; **~ que (de) faire** rather than ou instead of doing

pluvieux, -euse [plyvjø, jøz] adj rainy, wet

PME sigle f (= petite(s) et moyenne(s) entreprise(s)) small business(es)

PMU sigle m (= Pari mutuel urbain) system of betting on horses; (café) betting agency

PNB sigle m (= produit national brut) GNP

pneu [pnø] nm tyre (BRIT), tire (US)

pneumonie [pnømɔni] nf pneumonia

poche [pɔʃ] nf pocket; (sous les yeux) bag, pouch; **argent de ~** pocket money

pocher [pɔʃe] vt (CULIN) to poach

pochette [pɔʃɛt] nf (d'aiguilles etc) case; (mouchoir) breast pocket handkerchief; (sac à main) clutch bag; **~ de disque** record sleeve

poêle [pwal] nm stove ♦ nf: **~ (à frire)** frying pan

poème [pɔɛm] nm poem

poésie [pɔezi] nf (poème) poem; (art): **la ~** poetry

poète [pɔɛt] nm poet

poids [pwa] nm weight; (SPORT) shot; **vendre au ~** to sell by weight; **prendre du ~** to put on weight; **~ lourd** (camion) lorry (BRIT), truck (US)

poignant, e [pwaɲɑ̃, ɑ̃t] adj poignant

poignard [pwaɲar] nm dagger; **poignarder** vt to stab, knife

poigne [pwaɲ] nf grip; **avoir de la ~** (fig) to rule with a firm hand

poignée [pwaɲe] nf (de sel etc, fig) handful; (de couvercle, porte) handle; **~ de main** handshake

poignet [pwaɲɛ] nm (ANAT) wrist; (de chemise) cuff

poil [pwal] nm (ANAT) hair; (de pinceau, brosse) bristle; (de tapis) strand; (pelage) coat; **à ~** (fam) starkers; **au ~** (fam) hunky-dory; **poilu, e** adj hairy

poinçon [pwɛ̃sɔ̃] nm (marque) hallmark; **poinçonner** [pwɛ̃sɔne] vt (bijou) to hallmark; (billet) to punch

poing [pwɛ̃] nm fist; **coup de ~** punch

point [pwɛ̃] nm (endroit) spot; (marque, signe) dot; (: de ponctuation) full stop, period (US); (COUTURE, TRICOT) stitch ♦ adv = **pas²**; **faire le ~** (fig) to take stock (of the situation); **sur le ~ de faire** (just) about to do; **à tel ~ que** so much so that; **mettre au ~** (procédé) to develop; (affaire) to settle; **à ~** (CULIN: viande) medium; **à ~ (nommé)** just at the right time; **deux ~s** colon; **~ (de côté)** stitch (pain); **~ d'exclamation/d'interrogation** exclamation/question mark; **~ de repère** landmark; (dans le temps) point of reference; **~ de suture** (MÉD) stitch; **~ de vente** retail outlet; **~ de vue** viewpoint; (fig: opinion) point of view; **~ d'honneur: mettre un ~ d'honneur à faire qch** to make it a point of honour to do sth; **~ faible/fort** weak/strong point; **~ noir** blackhead; **~s de suspension** suspension points

pointe [pwɛ̃t] nf point; (clou) tack; (fig): **une ~ de** a hint of; **être à la ~ de** (fig) to be in the forefront of; **sur la ~ des pieds** on tiptoe; **en ~** pointed, tapered; **de ~** (technique etc) leading; **heures de ~** peak hours

pointer [pwɛ̃te] vt (diriger: canon, doigt): **~ sur qch** to point at sth ♦ vi (employé) to clock in

pointillé [pwɛ̃tije] nm (trait) dotted line

pointilleux, euse [pwɛ̃tijø, øz] adj particular, pernickety

pointu, e [pwɛ̃ty] adj pointed; (voix) shrill; (analyse) precise

pointure [pwɛ̃tyr] nf size

point-virgule [pwɛ̃virgyl] nm semi-colon

poire [pwar] nf pear; (fam: péj) mug

poireau, x [pwaro] nm leek

poireauter [pwarote] vi (fam) to be left kicking one's heels

poirier [pwarje] nm pear tree

pois [pwa] nm (BOT) pea; (sur une étoffe) dot, spot; **~ chiche** chickpea; **à ~** (cravate etc) spotted, polka-dot cpd

poison [pwazɔ̃] nm poison

poisse [pwas] (fam) nf rotten luck

poisseux, -euse [pwasø, øz] adj sticky

poisson [pwasɔ̃] nm fish gén inv; **les P~s** (signe) Pisces; **~ d'avril!** April fool!; **~ rouge** goldfish; **poissonnerie** nf fish-shop; **poissonnier, -ière** nm/f fishmonger (BRIT), fish merchant (US)

poitrine [pwatʀin] nf chest; (seins) bust, bosom; (CULIN) breast

poivre [pwavʀ] nm pepper

poivron [pwavʀɔ̃] nm pepper, capsicum

polaire [pɔlɛʀ] adj polar

polar [pɔlaʀ] (fam) nm detective novel

pôle [pol] nm (GÉO, ÉLEC) pole

poli, e [pɔli] adj polite; (lisse) smooth

police [pɔlis] nf police; ~ d'assurance insurance policy; ~ judiciaire ≈ Criminal Investigation Department (BRIT), ≈ Federal Bureau of Investigation (US); ~ secours ≈ emergency services pl (BRIT), ≈ paramedics pl (US); **policier, -ière** adj police cpd ♦ nm policeman; (aussi: roman policier) detective novel

polio [pɔljo] nf polio

polir [pɔliʀ] vt to polish

polisson, ne [pɔlisɔ̃, ɔn] nm/f (enfant) (little) rascal

politesse [pɔlites] nf politeness

politicien, ne [pɔlitisjɛ̃, jɛn] (péj) nm/f politician

politique [pɔlitik] adj political ♦ nf politics sg; (mesures, méthode) policies pl

pollen [pɔlɛn] nm pollen

polluant, e [pɔlɥɑ̃, ɑ̃t] adj polluting; **produit ~** pollutant

polluer [pɔlɥe] vt to pollute; **pollution** nf pollution

polo [pɔlo] nm (chemise) polo shirt

Pologne [pɔlɔɲ] nf: la ~ Poland; **polonais, e** adj Polish ♦ nm/f: **Polonais, e** Pole ♦ nm (LING) Polish

poltron, ne [pɔltʀɔ̃, ɔn] adj cowardly

polycopier [pɔlikɔpje] vt to duplicate

Polynésie [pɔlinezi] nf: la ~ Polynesia

polyvalent, e [pɔlivalɑ̃, ɑ̃t] adj (rôle) varied; (salle) multi-purpose

pommade [pɔmad] nf ointment, cream

pomme [pɔm] nf apple; **tomber dans les ~s** (fam) to pass out; ~ **d'Adam** Adam's apple; ~ **de pin** pine ou fir cone; ~ **de terre** potato

pommeau, x [pɔmo] nm (boule) knob; (de selle) pommel

pommette [pɔmɛt] nf cheekbone

pommier [pɔmje] nm apple tree

pompe [pɔ̃p] nf pump; (faste) pomp (and ceremony); ~ **à essence** petrol pump; ~s **funèbres** funeral parlour sg, undertaker's sg; **pomper** vt to pump; (aspirer) to pump up; (absorber) to soak up

pompeux, -euse [pɔ̃pø, øz] adj pompous

pompier [pɔ̃pje] nm fireman

pompiste [pɔ̃pist] nm/f petrol (BRIT) ou gas (US) pump attendant

poncer [pɔ̃se] vt to sand (down)

ponctuation [pɔ̃ktɥasjɔ̃] nf punctuation

ponctuel, le [pɔ̃ktɥɛl] adj punctual

pondéré, e [pɔ̃deʀe] adj level-headed, composed

pondre [pɔ̃dʀ] vt to lay

poney [pɔne] nm pony

pont [pɔ̃] nm bridge; (NAVIG) deck; **faire le ~** to take the extra day off; ~ **suspendu** suspension bridge; **pont-levis** nm drawbridge

pop [pɔp] adj inv pop

populace [pɔpylas] (péj) nf rabble

populaire [pɔpylɛʀ] adj popular; (manifestation) mass cpd; (milieux, quartier) working-class; (expression) vernacular

popularité [pɔpylaʀite] nf popularity

population [pɔpylasjɔ̃] nf population; ~ **active** working population

populeux, -euse [pɔpylø, øz] adj densely populated

porc [pɔʀ] nm pig; (CULIN) pork

porcelaine [pɔʀsəlɛn] nf porcelain, china; piece of china(ware)

porc-épic [pɔʀkepik] nm porcupine

porche [pɔʀʃ] nm porch

porcherie [pɔʀʃəʀi] nf pigsty

pore [pɔʀ] nm pore

porno [pɔʀno] adj porno ♦ nm porn

port [pɔʀ] nm harbour, port; (ville) port; (de l'uniforme etc) wearing; (pour lettre) postage; (pour colis, aussi: posture) carriage; ~ **de pêche/de plaisance** fishing/sailing harbour

portable [pɔʀtabl] nm (COMPUT) laptop (computer)

portail [pɔʀtaj] nm gate

portant, e [pɔʀtɑ̃, ɑ̃t] adj: **bien/mal ~** in good/poor health

portatif, -ive [pɔʀtatif, iv] adj portable

porte [pɔʀt] nf door; (de ville, jardin) gate; **mettre à la ~** to throw out; ~ **à ~** nm door-to-door selling; ~ **d'entrée** front door; **porte-avions** nm inv aircraft carrier; **porte-bagages** nm inv luggage rack; **porte-bonheur** nm inv lucky charm; **porte-clefs** nm inv key ring; **porte-documents** nm inv attaché ou document case

porté, e [pɔʀte] adj: **être ~ à faire** to be inclined to do; **être ~ sur qch** to be keen on sth; **portée** nf (d'une arme) range; (fig: effet) impact, import; (: capacité) scope, capability; (de chatte etc) litter; (MUS) stave, staff; **à/hors de portée (de)** within/out of reach (of); **à portée de (la) main** within (arm's) reach; **à la portée de qn** (fig) at sb's level, within sb's capabilities

porte...: **porte-fenêtre** nf French window; **portefeuille** nm wallet; **portemanteau, x** nm (cintre) coat hanger; (au mur) coat rack; **porte-monnaie** nm inv purse; **porte-parole** nm inv spokesman

porter [pɔʀte] vt to carry; (sur soi: vêtement, barbe, bague) to wear; (fig: responsabilité etc) to bear, carry; (inscription, nom, fruits) to bear; (coup) to deal; (attention) to turn; (apporter): ~ qch à qn to take sth to sb ♦ vi (voix) to carry; (coup, argument) to hit home; se ~ vi (se sentir): se ~ bien/mal to be well/unwell; ~ sur (recherches) to be concerned with; se faire ~ malade to report sick

porteur, euse [pɔʀtœʀ, øz] nm (de bagages) porter; (de chèque) bearer

porte-voix [pɔʀtəvwa] nm inv megaphone

portier [pɔʀtje] nm doorman

portière [pɔʀtjɛʀ] nf door

portillon [pɔʀtijɔ̃] nm gate

portion [pɔʀsjɔ̃] nf (part) portion, share; (partie) portion, section

porto [pɔʀto] nm port (wine)

portrait [pɔʀtʀɛ] nm (peinture) portrait; (photo) photograph; **portrait-robot** nm Identikit ® ou photo-fit ® picture

portuaire [pɔʀtɥɛʀ] adj port cpd, harbour cpd

portugais, e [pɔʀtygɛ, ɛz] adj Portuguese ♦ nm/f: P~, e Portuguese ♦ nm (LING) Portuguese

Portugal [pɔʀtygal] nm: le ~ Portugal

pose [poz] nf (de moquette) laying; (attitude, d'un modèle) pose; (PHOTO) exposure

posé, e [poze] adj serious

poser [poze] vt to put; (installer: moquette, carrelage) to lay; (rideaux, papier peint) to hang; (question) to ask; (principe, conditions) to lay ou set down; (problème) to formulate; (difficulté) to pose ♦ vi (modèle) to pose, se ~ vi (oiseau, avion) to land; (question) to arise; ~ qch (sur) (déposer) to put sth down (on); ~ qch sur/quelque part (placer) to put sth on/somewhere, ~ sa candidature à un poste to apply for a post

positif, -ive [pozitif, iv] adj positive

position [pozisjɔ̃] nf position; **prendre ~** (fig) to take a stand

posologie [pozɔlɔʒi] nf dosage

posséder [posede] vt to own, possess; (qualité, talent) to have, possess; (sexuellement) to possess; **possession** nf ownership no pl, possession

possibilité [posibilite] nf possibility; **~s** nfpl (potentiel) potential sg

possible [posibl] adj possible; (projet, entreprise) feasible ♦ nm: **faire son ~** to do all one can, do one's utmost; **le plus/moins de livres** ~ as many/few books as possible; **le plus vite** ~ as quickly as possible; **dès que** ~ as soon as possible

postal, e, -aux [pɔstal, o] adj postal

poste [pɔst] nf (service) post, postal service; (administration, bureau) post office ♦ nm (fonction, MIL) post; (TÉL) extension; (de radio etc) set; **mettre à la** ~ to post; ~ **(de police)** nm police station; ~ **de secours** nm first-aid post; ~ **restante** nf poste restante (BRIT), general delivery (US)

poster¹ [pɔste] vt to post

poster² [pɔstɛʀ] nm poster

postérieur, e [pɔsteʀjœʀ] adj (date) later; (partie) back ♦ nm (fam) behind

posthume [pɔstym] adj posthumous

postulant, e [pɔstylɑ̃, ɑ̃t] nm/f applicant

postuler [pɔstyle] vi: ~ **à** ou **pour un emploi** to apply for a job

posture [pɔstyʀ] nf position

pot [po] nm (en verre) jar; (en terre) pot; (en plastique, carton) carton; (en métal) tin; (fam: chance) luck; **avoir du** ~ (fam) to be lucky; **boire** ou **prendre un** ~ (fam) to have a drink; **petit** ~ **(pour bébé)** (jar of) baby food; ~ **catalytique** catalytic converter; ~ **d'échappement** exhaust pipe; ~ **de fleurs** plant pot, flowerpot; (plante) pot plant

potable [pɔtabl] adj: **eau (non)** ~ (non-)drinking water

potage [pɔtaʒ] nm soup; **potager, -ère** adj: (jardin) potager kitchen ou vegetable garden

pot-au-feu [pɔtofø] nm inv (beef) stew

pot-de-vin [pɔdvɛ̃] nm bribe

pote [pɔt] (fam) nm pal

poteau, x [pɔto] nm post; ~ **indicateur** signpost

potelé, e [pɔt(ə)le] adj plump, chubby

potence [pɔtɑ̃s] nf gallows sg

potentiel, le [pɔtɑ̃sjɛl] adj, nm potential

poterie [pɔtʀi] nf pottery; (objet) piece of pottery

potier, ère [pɔtje, jɛʀ] nm potter

potins [pɔtɛ̃] (fam) nmpl gossip sg

potiron [pɔtiʀɔ̃] nm pumpkin

pou, x [pu] nm louse

poubelle [pubɛl] nf (dust)bin

pouce [pus] nm thumb

poudre [pudʀ] nf powder; (fard) (face) powder; (explosif) gunpowder; **en** ~: **café en** ~ instant coffee; **lait en** ~ dried ou powdered milk, **poudreuse** nf powder snow; **poudrier** nm (powder) compact

pouffer [pufe] vi: ~ **(de rire)** to burst out laughing

poulailler [pulaje] nm henhouse

poulain [pulɛ̃] nm foal; (fig) protégé

poule [pul] nf hen; (CULIN) (boiling) fowl

poulet [pulɛ] nm chicken; (fam) cop

poulie [puli] nf pulley

pouls [pu] nm pulse; **prendre le** ~ **de qn** to feel sb's pulse

poumon [pumɔ̃] nm lung

poupe [pup] nf stern; **en** ~ astern

poupée [pupe] nf doll

pouponnière [pupɔnjɛʀ] nf crèche, day nursery

pour [puʀ] prép for ♦ nm: **le ~ et le contre** the pros and cons; **~ faire** (so as) to do, in order to do; **~ avoir fait** for having done; **~ que** so that, in order that; **~ 100 francs d'essence** 100 francs' worth of petrol; **~ cent** per cent; **~ ce qui est de** as for

pourboire [puʀbwaʀ] nm tip

pourcentage [puʀsɑ̃taʒ] nm percentage

pourchasser [puʀʃase] vt to pursue

pourparlers [puʀpaʀle] nmpl talks, negotiations

pourpre [puʀpʀ] adj crimson

pourquoi [puʀkwa] adv, conj why ♦ nm inv: **le ~ (de)** the reason (for)

pourrai etc [puʀe] vb voir **pouvoir**

pourri, e [puʀi] adj rotten

pourrir [puʀiʀ] vi to rot; (fruit) to go rotten ou bad ♦ vt to rot; (fig) to spoil thoroughly; **pourriture** nf rot

pourrons etc [puʀɔ̃] vb voir **pouvoir**

poursuite [puʀsɥit] nf pursuit, chase; **~s** nfpl (JUR) legal proceedings

poursuivre [puʀsɥivʀ] vt to pursue, chase (after); (obséder) to haunt; (JUR) to bring proceedings against, prosecute; (: au civil) to sue; (but) to strive towards; (continuer: études etc) to carry on with, continue; **se ~ vi** to go on, continue

pourtant [puʀtɑ̃] adv yet; **c'est ~ facile** (and) yet it's easy

pourtour [puʀtuʀ] nm perimeter

pourvoir [puʀvwaʀ] vt: **~ qch/qn de** to equip sth/sb with ♦ vi: **~ à** to provide for; **pourvoyeur** nm supplier; **pourvu, e** adj: **pourvu de** equipped with; **pourvu que** (si) provided that, so long as; (espérons que) let's hope (that)

pousse [pus] nf growth; (bourgeon) shoot

poussé, e [puse] adj (études) advanced; exhaustive; **poussée** nf thrust; (d'acné) eruption; (fig: prix) upsurge

pousser [puse] vt to push; (émettre: cri, soupir) to give; (stimuler: élève) to urge on; (poursuivre: études, discussion) to carry on (further) ♦ vi to push; (croître) to grow; **se ~ vi** to move over; **~ qn à** (inciter) to urge ou press sb to; (acculer) to drive sb to; **faire ~** (plante) to grow

poussette [puset] nf push chair (BRIT), stroller (US)

poussière [pusjɛʀ] nf dust; **poussiéreux, -euse** adj dusty

poussin [pusɛ̃] nm chick

poutre [putʀ] nf beam

MOT-CLÉ
---

pouvoir [puvwaʀ] nm power; (POL: dirigeants): **le pouvoir** those in power; **les**

pouvoirs publics the authorities; **pouvoir d'achat** purchasing power

♦ vb semi-aux **1** (être en état de) can, be able to; **je ne peux pas le réparer** I can't ou I am not able to repair it; **déçu de ne pas pouvoir le faire** disappointed not to be able to do it

2 (avoir la permission) can, may, be allowed to; **vous pouvez aller au cinéma** you can ou may go to the pictures

3 (probabilité, hypothèse) may, might, could; **il a pu avoir un accident** he may ou might ou could have had an accident; **il aurait pu le dire!** he might ou could have said (so)!

♦ vb impers may, might, could; **il peut arriver que** it may ou might ou could happen that

♦ vt can, be able to; **j'ai fait tout ce que j'ai pu** I did all I could; **je n'en peux plus** (épuisé) I'm exhausted; (à bout) I can't take any more; **se pouvoir vi: il se peut que** it may ou might be that; **cela se pourrait** that's quite possible

---

prairie [pʀeʀi] nf meadow

praline [pʀalin] nf sugared almond

praticable [pʀatikabl] adj passable, practicable

pratiquant, e [pʀatikɑ̃, ɑ̃t] nm/f (regular) churchgoer

pratique [pʀatik] nf practice ♦ adj practical; **pratiquement** adv (pour ainsi dire) practically, virtually; **pratiquer** vt to practise; (l'équitation, la pêche) to go in for; (le golf, football) to play; (intervention, opération) to carry out

pré [pʀe] nm meadow

préalable [pʀealabl] adj preliminary; **au ~** beforehand

préambule [pʀeɑ̃byl] nm preamble; (fig) prelude; **sans ~** straight away

préau [pʀeo] nm (SCOL) covered playground

préavis [pʀeavi] nm notice

précaution [pʀekosjɔ̃] nf precaution; **avec ~** cautiously; **par ~** as a precaution

précédemment [pʀesedamɑ̃] adv before, previously

précédent, e [pʀesedɑ̃, ɑ̃t] adj previous ♦ nm precedent

précéder [pʀesede] vt to precede

précepteur, -trice [pʀeseptœʀ, tʀis] nm/f (private) tutor

prêcher [pʀeʃe] vt to preach

précieux, -euse [pʀesjø, jøz] adj precious; (aide, conseil) invaluable

précipice [pʀesipis] nm drop, chasm

précipitamment [pʀesipitamɑ̃] adv hurriedly, hastily

précipitation [pʀesipitasjɔ̃] nf (hâte) haste; **~s** nfpl (pluie) rain sg

précipité, e [pʀesipite] adj hurried, hasty
précipiter [pʀesipite] vt (hâter: départ) to hasten; (faire tomber): **~ qn/qch du haut de** to throw ou hurl sb/sth off ou from; **se ~** vi to speed up; **se ~ sur/vers** to rush at/towards
précis, e [pʀesi, iz] adj precise; (mesures) accurate, precise; **à 4 heures ~es** at 4 o'clock sharp; **précisément** adv precisely; **préciser** vt (expliquer) to be more specific about, clarify; (spécifier) to state, specify; **se préciser** vi to become clear(er); **précision** nf precision; (détail) point ou detail; **demander des précisions** to ask for further explanation
précoce [pʀekɔs] adj early; (enfant) precocious
préconçu, e [pʀekɔ̃sy] adj preconceived
préconiser [pʀekɔnize] vt to advocate
prédécesseur [pʀedesesœʀ] nm predecessor
prédilection [pʀedileksjɔ̃] nf: **avoir une ~ pour** to be partial to
prédire [pʀediʀ] vt to predict
prédominer [pʀedɔmine] vi to predominate
préface [pʀefas] nf preface
préfecture [pʀefektyʀ] nf prefecture; **~ de police** police headquarters pl
préférable [pʀefeʀabl] adj preferable
préféré, e [pʀefeʀe] adj, nm/f favourite
préférence [pʀefeʀɑ̃s] nf preference; **de ~** preferably
préférer [pʀefeʀe] vt: **~ qn/qch (à)** to prefer sb/sth (to), like sb/sth better (than); **~ faire** to prefer to do; **je ~ais du thé** I would rather have tea, I'd prefer tea
préfet [pʀefe] nm prefect
préhistorique [pʀeistɔʀik] adj prehistoric
préjudice [pʀeʒydis] nm (matériel) loss; (moral) harm no pl; **porter ~ à** to harm, be detrimental to; **au ~ de** at the expense of
préjugé [pʀeʒyʒe] nm prejudice; **avoir un ~ contre** to be prejudiced ou biased against
préjuger [pʀeʒyʒe]: **~ de** vt to prejudge
prélasser [pʀelase]: **se ~** vi to lounge
prélèvement [pʀelɛvmɑ̃] nm (montant) deduction; **faire un ~ de sang** to take a blood sample
prélever [pʀel(ə)ve] vt (échantillon) to take; **~ (sur)** (montant) to deduct (from); (argent: sur son compte) to withdraw (from)
prématuré, e [pʀematyʀe] adj premature ♦ nm premature baby
premier, -ière [pʀəmje, jɛʀ] adj first; (rang) front; (fig: objectif) basic; **le ~ venu** the first person to come along; **de ~ ordre** first-rate; **P~ Ministre** Prime Minister; **première** nf (SCOL) lower sixth form; (THÉÂTRE) first night; (AUTO) first (gear); (AVIAT, RAIL etc) first class; (CINÉMA) première; (exploit) first; **premièrement** adv firstly

prémonition [pʀemɔnisjɔ̃] nf premonition
prémunir [pʀemyniʀ]: **se ~** vi: **se ~ contre** to guard against
prenant, e [pʀənɑ̃, ɑ̃t] adj absorbing, engrossing
prénatal, e [pʀenatal] adj (MÉD) antenatal
prendre [pʀɑ̃dʀ] vt to take; (repas) to have; (se procurer) to get; (malfaiteur, poisson) to catch; (passager) to pick up; (personnel) to take on; (traiter: personne) to handle; (voix, ton) to put on; (ôter): **~ qch à** to take sth from; (coincer): **se ~ les doigts dans** to get one's fingers caught in ♦ vi (liquide, ciment) to set; (greffe, vaccin) to take; (feu: foyer) to go; (se diriger): **~ à gauche** to turn to (the) left; **~ froid** to catch cold; **se ~ pour** to think one is; **s'en ~ à** to attack; **se ~ d'amitié pour** to befriend; **s'y ~** (procéder) to set about it
preneur [pʀənœʀ, øz] nm: **être/trouver ~** to be willing to buy/find a buyer
preniez [pʀənje] vb voir prendre
prenne etc [pʀɛn] vb voir prendre
prénom [pʀenɔ̃] nm first ou Christian name
préoccupation [pʀeɔkypasjɔ̃] nf (souci) concern; (idée fixe) preoccupation
préoccuper [pʀeɔkype] vt (inquiéter) to worry; (absorber) to preoccupy; **se ~ de** to be concerned with
préparatifs [pʀepaʀatif] nmpl preparations
préparation [pʀepaʀasjɔ̃] nf preparation
préparer [pʀepaʀe] vt to prepare; (café, thé) to make; (examen) to prepare for; (voyage, entreprise) to plan; **se ~** vi (orage, tragédie) to brew, be in the air; **~ qch à qn** (surprise etc) to have sth in store for sb; **se ~ (à qch/faire)** to prepare (o.s.) ou get ready (for sth/to do)
prépondérant, e [pʀepɔ̃deʀɑ̃, ɑ̃t] adj major, dominating
préposé, e [pʀepoze] nm/f employee; (facteur) postman
préposition [pʀepozisjɔ̃] nf preposition
près [pʀɛ] adv near, close; **~ de** near (to), close to; (environ) nearly, almost; **de ~** closely; **à 5 kg ~** to within about 5 kg; **à cela ~ que** apart from the fact that; **il n'est pas à 10 minutes ~** he can spare 10 minutes
présage [pʀezaʒ] nm omen; **présager** vt to foresee
presbyte [pʀesbit] adj long-sighted
presbytère [pʀesbitɛʀ] nm presbytery
prescription [pʀeskʀipsjɔ̃] nf prescription
prescrire [pʀeskʀiʀ] vt to prescribe
présence [pʀezɑ̃s] nf presence; (au bureau, à l'école) attendance
présent, e [pʀezɑ̃, ɑ̃t] adj, nm present; **à ~ (que)** now (that)
présentation [pʀezɑ̃tasjɔ̃] nf presentation; (de nouveau venu) introduction; (allure) appearance; **faire les ~s** to do the

introductions

présenter [prezãte] vt to present; (excuses, condoléances) to offer; (invité, conférencier): ~ **qn (à)** to introduce sb (to) ♦ vi: ~ **bien** to have a pleasing appearance; **se** ~ vi (occasion) to arise; **se** ~ **à** (examen) to sit; (élection) to stand at, run for

préservatif [prezervatif, iv] nm sheath, condom

préserver [prezerve] vt: ~ **de** (protéger) to protect from

président [prezidã] nm (POL) president; (d'une assemblée, COMM) chairman; ~ **directeur général** chairman and managing director; **présidentielles** nfpl presidential elections

présider [prezide] vt to preside over; (dîner) to be the guest of honour at

présomptueux, -euse [prezõptɥø, øz] adj presumptuous

presque [presk] adv almost, nearly; ~ **personne** hardly anyone; ~ **rien** hardly anything; ~ **pas** hardly (at all); ~ **pas (de)** hardly any

presqu'île [preskil] nf peninsula

pressant, e [presã, ãt] adj urgent

presse [pres] nf press; (affluence): **heures de** ~ busy times

pressé, e [prese] adj in a hurry; (travail) urgent; **orange** ~**e** freshly-squeezed orange juice

pressentiment [presãtimã] nm foreboding, premonition

pressentir [presãtir] vt to sense

presse-papiers [prespapje] nm inv paperweight

presser [prese] vt (fruit, éponge) to squeeze; (bouton) to press; (allure) to speed up; (inciter): ~ **qn de faire** to urge ou press sb to do ♦ vi to be urgent; **se** ~ vi (se hâter) to hurry (up); **se** ~ **contre qn** to squeeze up against sb; **rien ne presse** there's no hurry

pressing [presiŋ] nm (magasin) dry-cleaner's

pression [presjõ] nf pressure; (bouton) press stud; (fam: bière) draught beer; **faire** ~ **sur** to put pressure on; ~ **artérielle** blood pressure

prestance [prestãs] nf presence, imposing bearing

prestataire [prestater] nm/f supplier

prestation [prestasjõ] nf (allocation) benefit; (d'une entreprise) service provided; (d'un artiste) performance

prestidigitateur, -trice [prestidiʒitatœr, tris] nm/f conjurer

prestige [prestiʒ] nm prestige; **prestigieux, -euse** adj prestigious

présumer [prezyme] vt: ~ **que** to presume ou assume that

prêt, e [pre, pret] adj ready ♦ nm (somme)

loan; **prêt-à-porter** nm ready-to-wear ou off-the-peg (BRIT) clothes pl

prétendre [pretãdr] vt (affirmer): ~ **que** to claim that; (avoir l'intention de): ~ **faire qch** to mean ou intend to do sth; **prétendu, e** adj (supposé) so-called

prétentieux, -euse [pretãsjø, jøz] adj pretentious

prétention [pretãsjõ] nf claim; (vanité) pretentiousness; ~**s** nfpl (salaire) expected salary

prêter [prete] vt (livres, argent): ~ **qch (à)** to lend sth (to); (supposer): ~ **à qn** (caractère, propos) to attribute to sb; **se** ~ **à** to lend o.s. (ou itself) to; (manigances etc) to go along with; ~ **à** (critique, commentaires etc) to be open to, give rise to; ~ **attention à** to pay attention to; ~ **serment** to take the oath

prétexte [pretekst] nm pretext, excuse; **sous aucun** ~ on no account; **prétexter** vt to give as a pretext ou an excuse

prêtre [pretr] nm priest

preuve [prœv] nf proof; (indice) proof, evidence no pl; **faire** ~ **de** to show; **faire ses** ~**s** to prove o.s. (ou itself)

prévaloir [prevalwar] vi to prevail

prévenant, e [prev(ə)nã, ãt] adj thoughtful, kind

prévenir [prev(ə)nir] vt (éviter: catastrophe etc) to avoid, prevent; (anticiper: désirs, besoins) to anticipate; ~ **qn (de)** (avertir) to warn sb (about); (informer) to tell ou inform sb (about)

préventif, -ive [prevãtif, iv] adj preventive

prévention [prevãsjõ] nf prevention; ~ **routière** road safety

prévenu, e [prev(ə)ny] nm/f (JUR) defendant, accused

prévision [previzjõ] nf: ~**s** predictions; (ÉCON) forecast sg; **en** ~ **de** in anticipation of; ~**s météorologiques** weather forecast sg

prévoir [prevwar] vt (anticiper) to foresee; (s'attendre à) to expect, reckon on; (organiser: voyage etc) to plan; (envisager) to allow; **comme prévu** as planned; **prévoyant, e** adj gifted with (ou showing) foresight; **prévu, e** pp de prévoir

prier [prije] vi to pray ♦ vt (Dieu) to pray to; (implorer) to beg; (demander): ~ **qn de faire** to ask sb to do; **se faire** ~ to need coaxing ou persuading; **je vous en prie** (allez-y) please do; (de rien) don't mention it; **prière** nf prayer; **"prière de ..."** "please ..."

primaire [primer] adj primary ♦ nm (SCOL) primary education

prime [prim] nf (bonus) bonus; (subvention) premium; (COMM: cadeau) free gift; (ASSURANCES, BOURSE) premium ♦ adj: **de** ~ **abord** at first glance; **primer** vt

(*récompenser*) to award a prize to ♦ *vi* to
dominate; to be most important
primeurs [primœr] *nfpl* early fruits and
vegetables
primevère [primver] *nf* primrose
primitif, -ive [primitif, iv] *adj* primitive;
(*originel*) original
primordial, e, -iaux [primɔrdjal, jo] *adj*
essential
prince [prɛ̃s] *nm* prince; **princesse** *nf*
princess
principal, e, -aux [prɛ̃sipal, o] *adj*
principal, main ♦ *nm* (SCOL) principal,
head(master); (*essentiel*) main thing
principe [prɛ̃sip] *nm* principle; **par ~** on
principle; **en ~** (*habituellement*) as a rule;
(*théoriquement*) in principle
printemps [prɛ̃tɑ̃] *nm* spring
priorité [prijɔrite] *nf* priority; (AUTO) right of
way; **~ à droite** right of way to vehicles
coming from the right
pris, e [pri, priz] *pp de* prendre ♦ *adj* (*place*)
taken; (*mains*) full; (*personne*) busy; **avoir le
nez/la gorge ~(e)** to have a stuffy nose/a
hoarse throat; **être ~ de panique** to be panic-
stricken
prise [priz] *nf* (*d'une ville*) capture; (PÊCHE,
CHASSE) catch; (*point d'appui ou pour
empoigner*) hold; (ÉLEC: *fiche*) plug; (: *femelle*)
socket; **être aux ~s avec** to be grappling with;
~ de conscience awareness, realization; **~ de
contact** (*rencontre*) initial meeting, first
contact; **~ de courant** power point; **~ de sang**
blood test; **~ de vue** (*photo*) shot; **~ multiple**
adaptor
priser [prize] *vt* (*estimer*) to prize, value
prison [prizɔ̃] *nf* prison; **aller/être en ~** to go
to/be in prison ou jail; **prisonnier, -ière**
nm/f prisoner ♦ *adj* captive
prit [pri] *vb voir* prendre
privé, e [prive] *adj* private ♦ *nm* (COMM)
private sector; **en ~** in private
priver [prive] *vt*: **~ qn de** to deprive sb of; **se
~ de** to go ou do without
privilège [privilɛʒ] *nm* privilege
prix [pri] *nm* price; (*récompense, SCOL*) prize;
hors de ~ exorbitantly priced; **à aucun ~** not
at any price; **à tout ~** at all costs; **~ d'achat/de
vente/de revient** purchasing/selling/cost price
probable [prɔbabl] *adj* likely, probable;
probablement *adv* probably
probant, e [prɔbɑ̃, ɑ̃t] *adj* convincing
problème [prɔblɛm] *nm* problem
procédé [prɔsede] *nm* (*méthode*) process;
(*comportement*) behaviour *no pl*
procéder [prɔsede] *vi* to proceed;
(*moralement*) to behave; **~ à** to carry out
procès [prɔsɛ] *nm* trial; (*poursuites*)
proceedings *pl*; **être en ~ avec** to be involved

in a lawsuit with
processus [prɔsesys] *nm* process
procès-verbal, -aux [prɔsɛverbal, o] *nm*
(*de réunion*) minutes *pl*; (: *aussi:* P.V.) parking
ticket
prochain, e [prɔʃɛ̃, ɛn] *adj* next; (*proche:
départ, arrivée*) impending ♦ *nm* fellow man;
la ~e fois/semaine ~e next time/week;
prochainement *adv* soon, shortly
proche [prɔʃ] *adj* nearby; (*dans le temps*)
imminent; (*parent, ami*) close; **~s** *nmpl*
(*parents*) close relatives; **être ~ (de)** to be
near, be close (to); **le P~ Orient** the Middle
East
proclamer [prɔklame] *vt* to proclaim
procuration [prɔkyrasjɔ̃] *nf* proxy
procurer [prɔkyre] *vt*: **~ qch à qn** (*fournir*) to
obtain sth for sb; (*causer: plaisir etc*) to bring
sb sth; **se ~** *vt* to get; **procureur** *nm* public
prosecutor
prodige [prɔdiʒ] *nm* marvel, wonder;
(*personne*) prodigy; **prodiguer** *vt* (*soins,
attentions*): **prodiguer qch à qn** to give sb sth
producteur, -trice [prɔdyktœr, tris] *nm/f*
producer
productif, -ive [prɔdyktif, iv] *adj*
productive
production [prɔdyksjɔ̃] *nf* production;
(*rendement*) output
productivité [prɔdyktivite] *nf* productivity
produire [prɔdɥir] *vt*: to produce; **se ~** *vi*
(*événement*) to happen, occur; (*acteur*) to
perform, appear
produit [prɔdɥi] *nm* product; **~ chimique**
chemical; **~ d'entretien** cleaning product;
~ national brut gross national product; **~s
alimentaires** foodstuffs
prof [prɔf] (*fam*) *nm* teacher
profane [prɔfan] *adj* (REL) secular ♦ *nm/f*
layman(-woman)
proférer [prɔfere] *vt* to utter
professeur [prɔfesœr] *nm* teacher; (*de
faculté*) (university) lecturer; (: *titulaire d'une
chaire*) professor
profession [prɔfesjɔ̃] *nf* occupation;
~ libérale (liberal) profession; **sans ~**
unemployed; **professionnel, le** *adj, nm/f*
professional
profil [prɔfil] *nm* profile; **de ~** in profile
profit [prɔfi] *nm* (*avantage*) benefit,
advantage; (COMM, FINANCE) profit; **au ~ de** in
aid of; **tirer ~ de** to profit from; **profitable**
adj (*utile*) beneficial; (*lucratif*) profitable;
profiter *vi*: **profiter de** (*situation, occasion*) to
take advantage of; (*vacances, jeunesse etc*) to
make the most of
profond, e [prɔfɔ̃, ɔ̃d] *adj* deep; (*sentiment,
intérêt*) profound; **profondément** *adv*
deeply; **il dort profondément** he is sound

asleep; **profondeur** nf depth

progéniture [prɔʒenityr] nf offspring inv

programme [prɔgram] nm programme; (SCOL) syllabus, curriculum; (INFORM) program; **programmer** vt (émission) to schedule; (INFORM) to program; **programmeur, -euse** nm/f programmer

progrès [prɔgrɛ] nm progress no pl; **faire des ~** to make progress; **progresser** vi to progress; **progressif, -ive** adj progressive

prohiber [prɔibe] vt to prohibit, ban

proie [prwa] nf prey no pl

projecteur [prɔʒɛktœr] nm (pour film) projector; (de théâtre, cirque) spotlight

projectile [prɔʒɛktil] nm missile

projection [prɔʒɛksjɔ̃] nf projection; (séance) showing

projet [prɔʒɛ] nm plan; (ébauche) draft; **~ de loi** bill; **projeter** vt (envisager) to plan; (film, photos) to project; (ombre, lueur) to throw, cast; (jeter) to throw up (ou off ou out)

prolétaire [prɔleter] adj, nmf proletarian

prolongement [prɔlɔ̃ʒmã] nm extension; **dans le ~ de** running on from

prolonger [prɔlɔ̃ʒe] vt (débat, séjour) to prolong; (délai, billet, rue) to extend; **se ~** vi to go on

promenade [prɔm(ə)nad] nf walk (ou drive ou ride); **faire une ~** to go for a walk; **une ~ en voiture/à vélo** a drive/(bicycle) ride

promener [prɔm(ə)ne] vt (chien) to take out for a walk; (doigts, regard): **~ qch sur** to run sth over; **se ~** vi to go for (ou be out for) a walk

promesse [prɔmɛs] nf promise

promettre [prɔmɛtr] vt to promise ♦ vi to be ou look promising; **~ à qn de faire** to promise sb that one will do

promiscuité [prɔmiskɥite] nf (chambre) lack of privacy

promontoire [prɔmɔ̃twar] nm headland

promoteur, -trice [prɔmɔtœr, tris] nm/f: **~ (immobilier)** property developer (BRIT), real estate promoter (US)

promotion [prɔmosjɔ̃] nf promotion; **en ~** on special offer

promouvoir [prɔmuvwar] vt to promote

prompt, e [prɔ̃(pt), prɔ̃(p)t] adj swift, rapid

prôner [prone] vt (préconiser) to advocate

pronom [prɔnɔ̃] nm pronoun

prononcer [prɔnɔ̃se] vt (dire) to pronounce; (discours) to deliver; **se ~** vi to be pronounced; **se ~ (sur)** (se décider) to reach a decision (on ou about), give a verdict (on); **prononciation** nf pronunciation

pronostic [prɔnɔstik] nm (MÉD) prognosis; (fig: aussi: **~s**) forecast

propagande [prɔpagãd] nf propaganda

propager [prɔpaʒe] vt to spread; **se ~** vi to spread

prophète [prɔfɛt] nm prophet

prophétie [prɔfesi] nf prophecy

propice [prɔpis] adj favourable

proportion [prɔpɔrsjɔ̃] nf proportion; **toute(s) ~(s) gardée(s)** making due allowance(s)

propos [prɔpo] nm (intention) intention, aim; (sujet): **à quel ~?** what about? ♦ nmpl (paroles) talk no pl, remarks; **à ~ de** about, regarding; **à tout ~** for the slightest thing ou reason; **à ~** by the way; (opportunément) at the right moment

proposer [prɔpoze] vt to propose; **~ qch (à qn)** (suggérer) to suggest sth (to sb), propose sth (to sb); (offrir) to offer (sb) sth; **se ~** to offer one's services; **se ~ de faire** to intend ou propose to do; **proposition** nf (suggestion) proposal, suggestion; (LING) clause

propre [prɔpr] adj clean; (net) neat, tidy; (possessif) own; (sens) literal; (particulier): **~ à** peculiar to; (approprié): **~ à** suitable for ♦ nm: **recopier au ~** to make a fair copy of; **proprement** adv (avec propreté) cleanly; **le village proprement dit** the village itself; **à proprement parler** strictly speaking; **propreté** nf cleanliness

propriétaire [prɔprijeter] nm/f owner; (pour le locataire) landlord(-lady)

propriété [prɔprijete] nf property; (droit) ownership

propulser [prɔpylse] vt to propel

proroger [prɔrɔʒe] vt (prolonger) to extend

proscrire [prɔskrir] vt (interdire) to ban, prohibit

prose [proz] nf (style) prose

prospecter [prɔspɛkte] vt to prospect; (COMM) to canvass

prospectus [prɔspɛktys] nm leaflet

prospère [prɔspɛr] adj prosperous; **prospérer** vi to prosper

prosterner [prɔsterne]: **se ~** vi to bow low, prostrate o.s.

prostituée [prɔstitɥe] nf prostitute

prostitution [prɔstitysjɔ̃] nf prostitution

protecteur, -trice [prɔtɛktœr, tris] adj protective; (air, ton: péj) patronizing ♦ nm/f protector

protection [prɔtɛksjɔ̃] nf protection; (d'un personnage influent: aide) patronage

protéger [prɔteʒe] vt to protect; **se ~ de ou contre** to protect o.s. from

protéine [prɔtein] nf protein

protestant, e [prɔtɛstã, ãt] adj, nm/f Protestant

protestation [prɔtɛstasjɔ̃] nf (plainte) protest

protester [prɔtɛste] vi: **~ (contre)** to protest (against ou about); **~ de** (son innocence) to

protest
prothèse [pʀɔtɛz] nf: ~ **dentaire** denture
protocole [pʀɔtɔkɔl] nm (fig) étiquette
proue [pʀu] nf bow(s pl), prow
prouesse [pʀuɛs] nf feat
prouver [pʀuve] vt to prove
provenance [pʀɔv(ə)nɑ̃s] nf origin; **avion en ~ de** plane (arriving) from
provenir [pʀɔv(ə)niʀ]: ~ **de** vt to come from
proverbe [pʀɔvɛʀb] nm proverb
province [pʀɔvɛ̃s] nf province
proviseur [pʀɔvizœʀ] nm ≈ head(teacher) (BRIT), ≈ principal (US)
provision [pʀɔvizjɔ̃] nf (réserve) stock, supply; ~s nfpl (vivres) provisions, food no pl
provisoire [pʀɔvizwaʀ] adj temporary; **provisoirement** adv temporarily
provocant, e [pʀɔvɔkɑ̃, ɑ̃t] adj provocative
provoquer [pʀɔvɔke] vt (défier) to provoke; (causer) to cause, bring about; (inciter): ~ **qn à** to incite sb to
proxénète [pʀɔksenɛt] nm procurer
proximité [pʀɔksimite] nf nearness, closeness; (dans le temps) imminence, closeness; à ~ near ou close by; à ~ **de** near (to), close to
prudemment [pʀydamɑ̃] adv carefully; wisely, sensibly
prudence [pʀydɑ̃s] nf carefulness; **avec ~** carefully; **par ~** as a precaution
prudent, e [pʀydɑ̃, ɑ̃t] adj (pas téméraire) careful; (: en général) safety-conscious; (sage, conseillé) wise, sensible; **c'est plus ~** it's wiser
prune [pʀyn] nf plum
pruneau, x [pʀyno] nm prune
prunelle [pʀynɛl] nf (BOT) sloe; **il y tient comme à la ~ de ses yeux** he treasures ou cherishes it
prunier [pʀynje] nm plum tree
PS sigle m = **parti socialiste**
psaume [psom] nm psalm
pseudonyme [psødɔnim] nm (gén) fictitious name; (d'écrivain) pseudonym, pen name
psychanalyse [psikanaliz] nf psychoanalysis
psychiatre [psikjatʀ] nm/f psychiatrist; **psychiatrique** adj psychiatric
psychique [psiʃik] adj psychological
psychologie [psikɔlɔʒi] nf psychology; **psychologique** adj psychological; **psychologue** nm/f psychologist
P.T.T. sigle fpl = **Postes, Télécommunications et Télédiffusion**
pu [py] pp de **pouvoir**
puanteur [pɥɑ̃tœʀ] nf stink, stench
pub [pyb] nf (fam: annonce) ad, advert; (pratique) advertising
public, -ique [pyblik] adj public; (école, instruction) state cpd ♦ nm public;

(assistance) audience; **en ~** in public
publicitaire [pyblisitɛʀ] adj advertising cpd; (film) publicity cpd
publicité [pyblisite] nf (méthode, profession) advertising; (annonce) advertisement; (révélations) publicity
publier [pyblije] vt to publish
publique [pyblik] adj voir **public**
puce [pys] nf flea; (INFORM) chip; **carte à ~** smart card; ~**s** nfpl (marché) flea market sg
pudeur [pydœʀ] nf modesty; **pudique** adj (chaste) modest; (discret) discreet
puer [pɥe] (péj) vi to stink
puéricultrice [pɥeʀikyltʀis] nf p(a)ediatric nurse
puéril, e [pɥeʀil] adj childish
puis [pɥi] vb voir **pouvoir** ♦ adv then
puiser [pɥize] vt: ~ (**dans**) to draw (from)
puisque [pɥisk] conj since
puissance [pɥisɑ̃s] nf power; **en ~** ♦ adj potential
puissant, e [pɥisɑ̃, ɑ̃t] adj powerful
puisse etc [pɥis] vb voir **pouvoir**
puits [pɥi] nm well
pull(-over) [pyl(ɔvɛʀ)] nm sweater
pulluler [pylyle] vi to swarm
pulpe [pylp] nf pulp
pulvérisateur [pylveʀizatœʀ] nm spray
pulvériser [pylveʀize] vt to pulverize; (liquide) to spray
punaise [pynɛz] nf (ZOOL) bug; (clou) drawing pin (BRIT), thumbtack (US)
punch[1] [pɔ̃ʃ] nm (boisson) punch
punch[2] [pœnʃ] nm (BOXE, fig) punch
punir [pyniʀ] vt to punish; **punition** nf punishment
pupille [pypij] nf (ANAT) pupil ♦ nm/f (enfant) ward
pupitre [pypitʀ] nm (SCOL) desk
pur, e [pyʀ] adj pure; (vin) undiluted; (whisky) neat; **en ~e perte** to no avail; **c'est de la folie ~e** it's sheer madness; **purement** adv purely
purée [pyʀe] nf: ~ (**de pommes de terre**) mashed potatoes pl; ~ **de marrons** chestnut purée
purgatoire [pyʀgatwaʀ] nm purgatory
purger [pyʀʒe] vt (MÉD, POL) to purge; (JUR: peine) to serve
purin [pyʀɛ̃] nm liquid manure
pur-sang [pyʀsɑ̃] nm inv thoroughbred
pus [py] nm pus
putain [pytɛ̃] (fam!) nf whore (!)
puzzle [pœzl] nm jigsaw (puzzle)
P.-V. sigle m = **procès-verbal**
pyjama [piʒama] nm pyjamas pl (BRIT), pajamas pl (US)
pyramide [piʀamid] nf pyramid
Pyrénées [piʀene] nfpl: **les ~** the Pyrenees

Q, q

QI sigle m (= quotient intellectuel) IQ

quadragénaire [k(w)adʀaʒenɛʀ] nm/f man/woman in his/her forties

quadriller [kadʀije] vt (POLICE) to keep under tight control

quadruple [k(ʷw)adʀypl] nm: **le ~ de** four times as much as; **quadruplés, -ées** nm/fpl quadruplets, quads

quai [ke] nm (de port) quay; (de gare) platform; **être à ~** (navire) to be alongside

qualification [kalifikasjɔ̃] nf (aptitude) qualification

qualifié, e [kalifje] adj qualified; (main d'œuvre) skilled

qualifier [kalifje] vt to qualify; **se ~** vi to qualify; **~ qch/qn de** to describe sth/sb as

qualité [kalite] nf quality

quand [kɑ̃] conj, adv when; **~ je serai riche** when I'm rich; **~ même** all the same; **~ même, il exagère!** really, he overdoes it!; **~ bien même** even though

quant [kɑ̃]: **~ à** prép (pour ce qui est de) as for, as to; (au sujet de) regarding; **quant-à-soi** nm: **rester sur son quant-à-soi** to remain aloof

quantité [kɑ̃tite] nf quantity, amount; (grand nombre): **une** ou **des ~(s) de** a great deal of

quarantaine [kaʀɑ̃tɛn] nf (MÉD) quarantine; **avoir la ~** (âge) to be around forty; **une ~ (de)** forty or so, about forty

quarante [kaʀɑ̃t] num forty

quart [kaʀ] nm (fraction) quarter; (surveillance) watch; **un ~ de vin** a quarter litre of wine; **le ~ de** a quarter of; **~ d'heure** quarter of an hour; **~s de finale** quarter finals

quartier [kaʀtje] nm (de ville) district, area; (de bœuf) quarter; (de fruit) piece; **cinéma de ~** local cinema; **avoir ~ libre** (fig) to be free; **~ général** headquarters pl

quartz [kwaʀts] nm quartz

quasi [kazi] adv almost, nearly; **quasiment** adv almost, nearly; **quasiment jamais** hardly ever

quatorze [katɔʀz] num fourteen

quatre [katʀ] num four; **à ~ pattes** on all fours; **se mettre en ~ pour qn** to go out of one's way for sb; **~ à ~** (monter, descendre) four at a time; **quatre-quarts** nm inv pound cake; **quatre-vingt-dix** num ninety; **quatre-vingts** num eighty; **quatre-vingt-un** num eighty-one; **quatrième** num fourth ♦ nf (SCOL) third form ou year

quatuor [kwatɥɔʀ] nm quartet(te)

que [kə] conj 1 (introduisant complétive) that; **il sait que tu es là** he knows (that) you're here; **je veux que tu acceptes** I want you to accept; **il a dit que oui** he said he would (ou it was etc)

2 (reprise d'autres conjonctions): **quand il rentrera et qu'il aura mangé** when he gets back and (when) he has eaten; **si vous y allez ou que vous …** if you go there or if you …

3 (en tête de phrase: hypothèse, souhait etc): **qu'il le veuille ou non** whether he likes it or not; **qu'il fasse ce qu'il voudra!** let him do as he pleases!

4 (après comparatif) than, as; voir aussi **plus; aussi; autant** etc

5 (seulement): **ne … que** only; **il ne boit que de l'eau** he only drinks water

♦ adv (exclamation): **qu'il** ou **qu'est-ce qu'il est bête/court vite!** he's so silly!/he runs so fast!; **que de livres!** what a lot of books!

♦ pron 1 (relatif: personne) whom; (: chose) that, which; **l'homme que je vois** the man (whom) I see; **le livre que tu vois** the book (that ou which) you see; **un jour que j'étais …** a day when I was …

2 (interrogatif) what; **que fais-tu?, qu'est-ce que tu fais?** what are you doing?; **qu'est-ce que c'est?** what is it?, what's that?; **que faire?** what can one do?

Québec [kebɛk] n: **le ~** Quebec

québecois, e [kebekwa, -waz] adj Quebec ♦ nm/f: **Québecois, e** Quebecker ♦ nm (LING) Quebec French

quel, quelle [kɛl] adj 1 (interrogatif: personne) who; (: chose) what; which; **quel est cet homme?** who is this man?; **quel est ce livre?** what is this book?; **quel livre/homme?** what book/man?; (parmi un certain choix) which book/man?; **quels acteurs préférez-vous?** which actors do you prefer?; **dans quels pays êtes-vous allé?** which ou what countries did you go to?

2 (exclamatif): **quelle surprise!** what a surprise!

3: **quel que soit le coupable** whoever is guilty; **quel que soit votre avis** whatever your opinion

quelconque [kɛlkɔ̃k] adj (indéfini): **un ami/ prétexte ~** some friend/pretext or other; (médiocre: repas) indifferent, poor; (laid: personne) plain-looking

---
MOT-CLÉ
---

quelque [kɛlk] *adj* **1** some; a few; (*tournure interrogative*) any; **quelque espoir** some hope; **il a quelques amis** he has a few *ou* some friends; **a-t-il quelques amis?** has he any friends?; **les quelques livres qui** the few books which; **20 kg et quelque(s)** a bit over 20 kg
2: **quelque ... que: quelque livre qu'il choisisse** whatever (*ou* whichever) book he chooses
3: quelque chose something; (*tournure interrogative*) anything; **quelque chose d'autre** something else; anything else; **quelque part** somewhere; anywhere; **en quelque sorte** as it were
♦ *adv* **1** (*environ*): **quelque 100 mètres** some 100 metres
2: quelque peu rather, somewhat

---

quelquefois [kɛlkəfwa] *adv* sometimes
quelques-uns, -unes [kɛlkəzœ̃, yn] *pron a* few, some
quelqu'un [kɛlkœ̃] *pron* someone, somebody; (+*tournure interrogative*) anyone, anybody; ~ **d'autre** someone *ou* somebody else; (+ *tournure interrogative*) anybody else
quémander [kemɑ̃de] *vt* to beg for
qu'en dira-t-on [kɑ̃diʁatɔ̃] *nm inv:* **le ~ ~-~~** gossip, what people say
querelle [kəʁɛl] *nf* quarrel; **quereller: se quereller** *vi* to quarrel
qu'est-ce que [kɛskə] *voir* que
qu'est-ce qui [kɛski] *voir* qui
question [kɛstjɔ̃] *nf* question; (*fig*) matter, issue; **il a été ~ de** we (*ou* they) spoke about; **de quoi est-il ~?** what is it about?; **il n'en est pas ~** there's no question of it; **hors de ~** out of the question; **remettre en ~** to question; **questionner** *vt* to question
quête [kɛt] *nf* collection; (*recherche*) quest, search; **faire la ~** (*à l'église*) to take the collection; (*artiste*) to pass the hat round
quetsche [kwɛtʃ] *nf* kind of dark-red plum
queue [kø] *nf* tail; (*fig: du classement*) bottom; (: *de poêle*) handle; (: *de fruit, feuille*) stalk; (: *de train, colonne, file*) rear; **faire la ~** to queue (up) (*BRIT*), line up (*US*); ~ **de cheval** ponytail; ~ **de poisson** (*AUT*): **faire une ~ de poisson à qn** to cut in front of sb
qui [ki] *pron* (*personne*) who; (+*prép*) whom; (*chose, animal*) which, that; **qu'est-ce ~ est sur la table?** what is on the table?; ~ **est-ce ~?** who?; ~ **est-ce que?** who?; **à ~ est ce sac?** whose bag is this?; **à ~ parlais-tu?** who were you talking to?, to whom were you talking?; **amenez ~ vous voulez** bring who you like; ~ **que ce soit** whoever it may be
quiconque [kikɔ̃k] *pron* (*celui qui*) whoever, anyone who; (*n'importe qui*) anyone,

anybody
quiétude [kjetyd] *nf:* **en toute ~** in complete peace
quille [kij] *nf:* (*jeu de*) ~**s** skittles *sg* (*BRIT*), bowling (*US*)
quincaillerie [kɛ̃kajʁi] *nf* (*ustensiles*) hardware; (*magasin*) hardware shop; **quincaillier, -ière** *nm/f* hardware dealer
quinquagénaire [kɛ̃kaʒenɛʁ] *nm/f* man/ woman in his/her fifties
quintal, -aux [kɛ̃tal, o] *nm* quintal (*100 kg*)
quinte [kɛ̃t] *nf:* ~ (**de toux**) coughing fit
quintuple [kɛ̃typl] *nm:* **le ~ de** five times as much as; **quintuplés, -ées** *nm/fpl* quintuplets, quins
quinzaine [kɛ̃zɛn] *nf:* **une ~ (de)** about fifteen, fifteen or so; **une ~ (de jours)** a fortnight (*BRIT*), two weeks
quinze [kɛ̃z] *num* fifteen; **dans ~ jours** in a fortnight('s time), in two weeks(' time)
quiproquo [kipʁɔko] *nm* misunderstanding
quittance [kitɑ̃s] *nf* (*reçu*) receipt
quitte [kit] *adj:* **être ~ envers qn** to be no longer in sb's debt; (*fig*) to be quits with sb; ~ **à faire** even if it means doing
quitter [kite] *vt* to leave; (*vêtement*) to take off; **se ~** *vi* (*couples, interlocuteurs*) to part; **ne quittez pas** (*au téléphone*) hold the line
qui-vive [kiviv] *nm:* **être sur le ~-~** to be on the alert
quoi [kwa] *pron* (*interrogatif*) what; ~ **de neuf?** what's the news?; **as-tu de ~ écrire?** have you anything to write with?; ~ **qu'il arrive** whatever happens; ~ **qu'il en soit** be that as it may; ~ **que ce soit** anything at all; **"il n'y a pas de ~"** "(please) don't mention it"; **il n'y a pas de ~ rire** there's nothing to laugh about; **à ~ bon?** what's the use?; **en ~ puis-je vous aider?** how can I help you?
quoique [kwak] *conj* (*al*)though
quote-part [kɔtpaʁ] *nf* share
quotidien, ne [kɔtidjɛ̃, jɛn] *adj* daily; (*banal*) everyday ♦ *nm* (*journal*) daily (paper)

R, r

r. *abr* = route; rue
rab [ʁab] (*fam*) *nm* (*nourriture*) extra; **est-ce qu'il y a du ~?** is there any extra (left)?
rabâcher [ʁabaʃe] *vt* to keep on repeating
rabais [ʁabɛ] *nm* reduction, discount; **rabaisser** *vt* (*dénigrer*) to belittle; (*rabattre: prix*) to reduce
rabat-joie [ʁabaʒwa] *nm inv* killjoy
rabattre [ʁabatʁ] *vt* (*couvercle, siège*) to pull down; (*déduire*) to reduce; **se ~** *vi* (*se refermer: couvercle*) to fall shut; (*véhicule, coureur*) to cut in; **se ~ sur** to fall back on

rabbin [Rabɛ̃] nm rabbi

râblé, e [Rɑble] adj stocky

rabot [Rabo] nm plane

rabougri, e [RabugRi] adj stunted

rabrouer [RabRue] vt to snub

racaille [Rakɑj] (péj) nf rabble, riffraff

raccommoder [Rakɔmɔde] vt to mend, repair; **se ~** vi (fam) to make it up

raccompagner [Rakɔ̃paɲe] vt to take ou see back

raccord [RakɔR] nm link; (retouche) touch up; **raccorder** vt to join (up), link up; (suj: pont etc) to connect, link

raccourci [RakuRsi] nm short cut

raccourcir [RakuRsiR] vt to shorten ♦ vi (jours) to grow shorter, draw in

raccrocher [RakRɔʃe] vt (tableau) to hang back up; (récepteur) to put down ♦ vi (TÉL) to hang up, ring off; **se ~ à** vt to cling to, hang on to

race [Ras] nf race; (d'animaux, fig) breed; **de ~** purebred, pedigree

rachat [Raʃa] nm buying; (du même objet) buying back

racheter [Raʃ(ə)te] vt (article perdu) to buy another; (après avoir vendu) to buy back; (d'occasion) to buy; (COMM: part, firme) to buy up; (davantage): **~ du lait/3 œufs** to buy more milk/another 3 eggs ou 3 more eggs; **se ~** vi (fig) to make amends

racial, e, -aux [Rasjal, jo] adj racial

racine [Rasin] nf root; **~ carrée/cubique** square/cube root

raciste [Rasist] adj, nm/f raci(al)ist

racket [Raket] nm racketeering no pl

raclée [Rɑkle] (fam) nf hiding, thrashing

racler [Rɑkle] vt (surface) to scrape; **se ~ la gorge** to clear one's throat

racoler [Rakɔle] vt (suj: prostituée) to solicit; (: parti, marchand) to tout for

racontars [Rakɔ̃taR] nmpl story, lie

raconter [Rakɔ̃te] vt: **~ (à qn)** (décrire) to relate to sb; tell (sb) about; (dire de mauvaise foi) to tell (sb); **~ une histoire** to tell a story

racorni, e [RakɔRni] adj hard(ened)

radar [RadaR] nm radar

rade [Rad] nf (natural) harbour; **rester en ~** (fig) to be left stranded

radeau, x [Rado] nm raft

radiateur [RadjatœR] nm radiator, heater; (AUTO) radiator; **~ électrique/à gaz** electric/gas heater ou fire

radiation [Radjasjɔ̃] nf (PHYSIQUE) radiation

radical, e, -aux [Radikal, o] adj radical

radier [Radje] vt to strike off

radieux, -euse [Radjø, jøz] adj radiant

radin, e [Radɛ̃, in] (fam) adj stingy

radio [Radjo] nf radio; (MÉD) X-ray ♦ nm radio operator; **à la ~** on the radio; **radioactif, -ive** adj radioactive; **radiocassette** nf cassette radio, radio cassette player; **radiodiffuser** vt to broadcast; **radiographie** nf radiography; (photo) X-ray photograph; **radiophonique** adj radio cpd; **radio-réveil** (pl radios-réveils) nm radio alarm clock

radis [Radi] nm radish

radoter [Radɔte] vi to ramble on

radoucir [RadusiR]: **se ~** vi (temps) to become milder; (se calmer) to calm down

rafale [Rafal] nf (vent) gust (of wind); (tir) burst of gunfire

raffermir [RafɛRmiR] vt to firm up; **se ~** vi (fig: autorité, prix) to strengthen

raffiner [Rafine] vt to refine; **raffinerie** nf refinery

raffoler [Rafɔle]: **~ de** vt to be very keen on

rafistoler [Rafistɔle] (fam) vt to patch up

rafle [Rɑfl] nf (de police) raid; **rafler** (fam) vt to swipe, nick

rafraîchir [RafReʃiR] vt (atmosphère, température) to cool (down); (aussi: **mettre à ~**) to chill; (fig: rénover) to brighten up; **se ~** vi (temps) to grow cooler; (en se lavant) to freshen up; (en buvant) to refresh o.s.; **rafraîchissant, e** adj refreshing; **rafraîchissement** nm (boisson) cool drink; **rafraîchissements** nmpl (boissons, fruits etc) refreshments

rage [Raʒ] nf (MÉD): **la ~** rabies; (fureur) rage, fury; **faire ~** to rage; **~ de dents** (raging) toothache

ragot [Rago] (fam) nm malicious gossip no pl

ragoût [Ragu] nm stew

raide [Red] adj stiff; (câble) taut, tight; (escarpé) steep; (droit: cheveux) straight; (fam: sans argent) flat broke; (osé) daring, bold ♦ adv (en pente) steeply; **~ mort** stone dead; **raidir** vt (muscles) to stiffen; **se raidir** vi (tissu) to stiffen; (personne) to tense up; (: se préparer moralement) to brace o.s.; (fig: position) to harden; **raideur** nf (rigidité) stiffness; **avec raideur** (répondre) stiffly, abruptly

raie [Re] nf (ZOOL) skate, ray; (rayure) stripe; (des cheveux) parting

raifort [RefɔR] nm horseradish

rail [Rɑj] nm rail; (chemins de fer) railways pl; **par ~** by rail

railler [Rɑje] vt to scoff at, jeer at

rainure [RenyR] nf groove

raisin [Rezɛ̃] nm (aussi: **~s**) grapes pl; **~s secs** raisins

raison [Rezɔ̃] nf reason; **avoir ~** to be right; **donner ~ à qn** to agree with sb; (événement) to prove sb right; **perdre la ~** to become insane; **~ de plus** all the more reason; **à plus**

forte ~ all the more so; **en** ~ **de** because of; **à** ~ **de** at the rate of; **sans** ~ for no reason; **raisonnable** *adj* reasonable, sensible

raisonnement [REzɔnmɑ̃] *nm* (*façon de réfléchir*) reasoning; (*argumentation*) argument

raisonner [REzɔne] *vi* (*penser*) to reason; (*argumenter, discuter*) to argue ♦ *vt* (*personne*) to reason with

rajeunir [Raʒœniʀ] *vt* (*suj: coiffure, robe*): ~ **qn** to make sb look younger; (*fig: personnel*) to inject new blood into ♦ *vi* to become (*ou* look) younger

rajouter [Raʒute] *vt* to add

rajuster [Raʒyste] *vt* (*vêtement*) to straighten, tidy; (*salaires*) to adjust

ralenti [Ralɑ̃ti] *nm*: **au** ~ (*fig*) at a slower pace; **tourner au** ~ (AUTO) to tick over (AUTO), idle

ralentir [Ralɑ̃tiʀ] *vt* to slow down

râler [ʀɑle] *vi* to groan; (*fam*) to grouse, moan (and groan)

rallier [Ralje] *vt* (*rejoindre*) to rejoin; (*gagner à sa cause*) to win over; **se** ~ **à** (*avis*) to come over *ou* round to

rallonge [Ralɔ̃ʒ] *nf* (*de table*) (extra) leaf

rallonger [Ralɔ̃ʒe] *vt* to lengthen

rallye [Rali] *nm* rally; (POL) march

ramassage [Ramasaʒ] *nm*: ~ **scolaire** school bus service

ramassé, e [Ramase] *adj* (*trapu*) squat

ramasser [Ramase] *vt* (*objet tombé ou par terre, fam*) to pick up; (*recueillir: copies, ordures*) to collect; (*récolter*) to gather; **se** ~ *vi* (*sur soi-même*) to huddle up; **ramassis** (*péj*) *nm* (*de voyous*) bunch; (*d'objets*) jumble

rambarde [ʀɑ̃baʀd] *nf* guardrail

rame [Ram] *nf* (*aviron*) oar; (*de métro*) train; (*de papier*) ream

rameau, x [Ramo] *nm* (small) branch; **les R~x** (REL) Palm Sunday *sg*

ramener [Ram(ə)ne] *vt* to bring back; (*reconduire*) to take back; ~ **qch à** (*réduire à*) to reduce sth to

ramer [Rame] *vi* to row

ramollir [Ramɔliʀ] *vt* to soften; **se** ~ *vi* to go soft

ramoner [Ramɔne] *vt* to sweep

rampe [ʀɑ̃p] *nf* (*d'escalier*) banister(s *pl*); (*dans un garage*) ramp; (THÉÂTRE): **la** ~ the footlights *pl*; ~ **de lancement** launching pad

ramper [ʀɑ̃pe] *vi* to crawl

rancard [ʀɑ̃kaʀ] (*fam*) *nm* (*rendez-vous*) date

rancart [ʀɑ̃kaʀ] *nm*: **mettre au** ~ (*fam*) to scrap

rance [ʀɑ̃s] *adj* rancid

rancœur [ʀɑ̃kœʀ] *nf* rancour

rançon [ʀɑ̃sɔ̃] *nf* ransom

rancune [ʀɑ̃kyn] *nf* grudge, rancour; **garder** ~ **à qn (de qch)** to bear sb a grudge (for sth); **sans** ~! no hard feelings!; **rancunier, -ière** *adj* vindictive, spiteful

randonnée [ʀɑ̃dɔne] *nf* ride; (*pédestre*) walk, ramble; (: *en montagne*) hike, hiking *no pl*

rang [ʀɑ̃] *nm* (*rangée*) row; (*grade, classement*) rank; ~**s** *nmpl* (MIL) ranks; **se mettre en** ~**s** to get into *ou* form rows; **au premier** ~ in the first row; (*fig*) ranking first

rangé, e [ʀɑ̃ʒe] *adj* (*vie*) well-ordered; (*personne*) steady

rangée [ʀɑ̃ʒe] *nf* row

ranger [ʀɑ̃ʒe] *vt* (*mettre de l'ordre dans*) to tidy up; (*classer, grouper*) to order, arrange; (*mettre à sa place*) to put away; (*fig: classer*): ~ **qn/qch parmi** to rank sb/sth among; **se** ~ *vi* (*véhicule, conducteur*) to pull over *ou* in; (*piéton*) to step aside; (*s'assagir*) to settle down; **se** ~ **à** (*avis*) to come round to

ranimer [Ranime] *vt* (*personne*) to bring round; (*douleur, souvenir*) to revive; (*feu*) to rekindle

rap [Rap] *nm* rap (music)

rapace [Rapas] *nm* bird of prey

râpe [ʀɑp] *nf* (CULIN) grater; **râper** *vt* (CULIN) to grate

rapetisser [Rap(ə)tise] *vt* to shorten

rapide [Rapid] *adj* fast; (*prompt: coup d'œil, mouvement*) quick ♦ *nm* express (train); (*de cours d'eau*) rapid; **rapidement** *adv* fast; quickly

rapiécer [Rapjese] *vt* to patch

rappel [Rapel] *nm* (THÉÂTRE) curtain call; (MÉD: *vaccination*) booster; (*deuxième avis*) reminder; **rappeler** *vt* to call back; (*ambassadeur, MIL*) to recall; (*faire se souvenir*): **rappeler qch à qn** to remind sb of sth; **se rappeler** *vt* (*se souvenir de*) to remember, recall

rapport [Rapɔʀ] *nm* (*lien, analogie*) connection; (*compte rendu*) report; (*profit*) yield, return; ~**s** *nmpl* (*entre personnes, pays*) relations; **avoir** ~ **à** to have something to do with; **être/se mettre en** ~ **avec qn** to be/get in touch with sb; **par** ~ **à** in relation to; ~**s (sexuels)** (sexual) intercourse *sg*

rapporter [Rapɔʀte] *vt* (*rendre, ramener*) to bring back; (*bénéfice*) to yield, bring in; (*mentionner, répéter*) to report ♦ *vi* (*investissement*) to give a good return *ou* yield; (: *activité*) to be very profitable; **se** ~ **à** *vt* (*correspondre à*) to relate to; **rapporteur, -euse** *nm/f* (*péj*) telltale ♦ *nm* (GÉOM) protractor

rapprochement [Rapʀɔʃmɑ̃] *nm* (*de nations*) reconciliation; (*rapport*) parallel

rapprocher [Rapʀɔʃe] *vt* (*deux objets*) to bring closer together; (*fig: ennemis, partis etc*) to bring together; (*comparer*) to establish a

parallel between; *(chaise d'une table)*: ~ **qch**
(de) to bring sth closer (to); **se ~** *vi* to draw
closer *ou* nearer; **se ~ de** to come closer to;
(présenter une analogie avec) to be close to

rapt [Rapt] *nm* abduction

raquette [Raket] *nf (de tennis)* racket; *(de
ping-pong)* bat

rare [RɑR] *adj* rare; **se faire ~** to become
scarce; **rarement** *adv* rarely, seldom

ras, e [Rɑ, Rɑz] *adj (poil, herbe)* short; *(tête)*
close-cropped ♦ *adv* short; **en ~e campagne**
in open country; **à ~ bords** to the brim; **en
avoir ~ le bol** *(fam)* to be fed up; **~ du cou**
♦ *adj (pull, robe)* crew-neck

rasade [Razad] *nf* glassful

raser [Raze] *vt (barbe, cheveux)* to shave off;
(menton, personne) to shave; *(fam: ennuyer)*
to bore; *(démolir)* to raze (to the ground);
(frôler) to graze, skim; **se ~** *vi* to shave; *(fam)*
to be bored (to tears); **rasoir** *nm* razor

rassasier [Rasazje] *vt*: **être rassasié** to have
eaten one's fill

rassemblement [Rasɑ̃bləmɑ̃] *nm (groupe)*
gathering; *(POL)* union

rassembler [Rasɑ̃ble] *vt (réunir)* to
assemble, gather; *(documents, notes)* to
gather together, collect; **se ~** *vi* to gather

rassis, e [Rasi, iz] *adj (pain)* stale

rassurer [RasyRe] *vt* to reassure; **se ~** *vi* to
reassure o.s.; **rassure-toi** don't worry

rat [Ra] *nm* rat

rate [Rat] *nf* spleen

raté, e [Rate] *adj (tentative)* unsuccessful,
failed ♦ *nm/f (fam: personne)* failure

râteau, x [Rɑto] *nm* rake

rater [Rate] *vi (affaire, projet etc)* to go wrong,
fail ♦ *vt (fam: cible, train, occasion)* to miss;
(plat) to spoil; *(fam: examen)* to fail

ration [Rasjɔ̃] *nf* ration

ratisser [Ratise] *vt (allée)* to rake; *(feuilles)* to
rake up; *(suj: armée, police)* to comb

RATP *sigle f (= Régie autonome des transports
parisiens)* Paris transport authority

rattacher [Ratɑʃe] *vt (animal, cheveux)* to tie
up again; *(fig: relier)*: **~ qch à** to link sth with

rattrapage [RatRapaʒ] *nm*: **cours de ~**
remedial class

rattraper [RatRape] *vt (fugitif)* to recapture;
(empêcher de tomber) to catch (hold of);
(atteindre, rejoindre) to catch up with;
(réparer: erreur) to make up for; **se ~** *vi* to
make up for it; **se ~ (à)** *(se raccrocher)* to stop
o.s. falling (by catching hold of)

rature [RatyR] *nf* deletion, erasure

rauque [Rok] *adj (voix)* hoarse

ravages [Ravaʒ] *nmpl*: **faire des ~** to wreak
havoc

ravaler [Ravale] *vt (mur, façade)* to restore;
(déprécier) to lower

ravi, e [Ravi] *adj*: **être ~ de/que** to be
delighted with/that

ravigoter [Ravigɔte] *(fam) vt* to buck up

ravin [Ravɛ̃] *nm* gully, ravine

ravir [RaviR] *vt (enchanter)* to delight; **à ~** *adv*
beautifully

raviser: **se ~** *vi* to change one's mind

ravissant, e [Ravisɑ̃, ɑ̃t] *adj* delightful

ravisseur, -euse [RavisœR, øz] *nm/f*
abductor, kidnapper

ravitaillement [Ravitajmɑ̃] *nm (réserves)*
supplies *pl*

ravitailler [Ravitaje] *vt (en vivres,
ammunitions)* to provide with fresh supplies;
(avion) to refuel; **se ~** *vi* to get fresh supplies;
(avion) to refuel

raviver [Ravive] *vt (feu, douleur)* to revive;
(couleurs) to brighten up

rayé, e [Reje] *adj (à rayures)* striped

rayer [Reje] *vt (érafler)* to scratch; *(barrer)* to
cross out; *(d'une liste)* to cross off

rayon [Rejɔ̃] *nm (de soleil etc)* ray; *(GÉOM)*
radius; *(de roue)* spoke; *(étagère)* shelf; *(de
grand magasin)* department; **dans un ~ de**
within a radius of; **~ de soleil** sunbeam; **~s X**
X-rays

rayonnement [Rejɔnmɑ̃] *nm (fig: d'une
culture)* influence

rayonner [Rejɔne] *vi (fig)* to shine forth;
(personne: de joie, de beauté) to be radiant;
(touriste) to go touring *(from one base)*

rayure [RejyR] *nf (motif)* stripe; *(éraflure)*
scratch; **à ~s** striped

raz-de-marée [Radmare] *nm inv* tidal wave

ré [Re] *nm (MUS)* D; *(en chantant la gamme)* re

réacteur [Reaktœr] *nm (d'avion)* jet engine;
(nucléaire) reactor

réaction [Reaksjɔ̃] *nf* reaction

réadapter: **se ~ (à)** *vi* to readjust
(to)

réagir [ReaʒiR] *vi* to react

réalisateur, -trice [RealizatœR, tRis] *nm/f*
(TV, CINÉMA) director

réalisation [Realizasjɔ̃] *nf* realization;
(cinéma) production; **en cours de ~** under
way

réaliser [Realize] *vt (projet, opération)* to carry
out, realize; *(rêve, souhait)* to realize, fulfil;
(exploit) to achieve; *(film)* to produce; *(se
rendre compte de)* to realize; **se ~** *vi* to be
realized

réaliste [Realist] *adj* realistic

réalité [Realite] *nf* reality; **en ~** in (actual)
fact; **dans la ~** in reality

réanimation [Reanimasjɔ̃] *nf* resuscitation;
service de ~ intensive care unit

rébarbatif, -ive [Rebarbatif, iv] *adj*
forbidding

rebattu, e [R(ə)baty] *adj* hackneyed

rebelle [ʀabɛl] nm/f rebel ♦ adj (troupes) rebel; (enfant) rebellious; (mèche etc) unruly

rebeller [ʀ(ə)bele]: se ~ vi to rebel

rebondi, e [ʀ(ə)bɔ̃di] adj (joues) chubby

rebondir [ʀ(ə)bɔ̃diʀ] vi (ballon: au sol) to bounce; (: contre un mur) to rebound; (fig) to get moving again; **rebondissement** nm new development

rebord [ʀ(ə)bɔʀ] nm edge; **le ~ de la fenêtre** the windowsill

rebours [ʀ(ə)buʀ]: **à ~** adv the wrong way

rebrousser [ʀ(ə)bʀuse] vt: **~ chemin** to turn back

rebut [ʀəby] nm: **mettre au ~** to scrap; **rebutant, e** adj off-putting; **rebuter** vt to put off

récalcitrant, e [ʀekalsitʀɑ̃, ɑ̃t] adj refractory

recaler [ʀ(ə)kale] vt (SCOL) to fail; **se faire ~** to fail

récapituler [ʀekapityle] vt to recapitulate, sum up

receler [ʀ(ə)səle] vt (produit d'un vol) to receive; (fig) to conceal; **receleur, euse** nm/f receiver

récemment [ʀesamɑ̃] adv recently

recensement [ʀ(ə)sɑ̃smɑ̃] nm (population) census

recenser [ʀ(ə)sɑ̃se] vt (population) to take a census of; (inventorier) to list

récent, e [ʀesɑ̃, ɑ̃t] adj recent

récépissé [ʀesepise] nm receipt

récepteur [ʀesɛptœʀ, tʀis] nm receiver

réception [ʀesɛpsjɔ̃] nf receiving no pl; (accueil) reception, welcome; (bureau) reception desk; (réunion mondaine) reception, party; **réceptionniste** nm/f receptionist

recette [ʀ(ə)sɛt] nf recipe; (COMM) takings pl; **~s** nfpl (COMM: rentrées) receipts

receveur, -euse [ʀ(ə)səvœʀ, øz] nm/f (des contributions) tax collector; (des postes) postmaster(-mistress)

recevoir [ʀ(ə)səvwaʀ] vt to receive; (client, patient) to see; **être reçu (à un examen)** to pass

rechange [ʀ(ə)ʃɑ̃ʒ]: **de ~** adj (pièces, roue) spare; (fig: solution) alternative; **des vêtements de ~** a change of clothes

réchapper [ʀeʃape]: **~ de ou à** vt (accident, maladie) to come through

recharge [ʀ(ə)ʃaʀʒ] nf refill; **rechargeable** adj (stylo etc) refillable; **recharger** vt (stylo) to refill; (batterie) to recharge

réchaud [ʀeʃo] nm (portable) stove

réchauffer [ʀeʃofe] vt (plat) to reheat; (mains, personne) to warm; **se ~** vi (température) to get warmer; (personne) to warm o.s. (up)

rêche [ʀɛʃ] adj rough

recherche [ʀ(ə)ʃɛʀʃ] nf (action) search; (raffinement) studied elegance; (scientifique etc): **la ~** research; **~s** nfpl (de la police) investigations; (scientifiques) research sg; **la ~ de** the search for; **être à la ~ de qch** to be looking for sth

recherché, e [ʀ(ə)ʃɛʀʃe] adj (rare, demandé) much sought-after; (raffiné: style) mannered; (: tenue) elegant

rechercher [ʀ(ə)ʃɛʀʃe] vt (objet égaré, personne) to look for; (causes, nouveau procédé) to try to find; (bonheur, compliments) to seek

rechigner [ʀ(ə)ʃiɲe] vi: **~ à faire qch** to balk ou jib at doing sth

rechute [ʀ(ə)ʃyt] nf (MÉD) relapse

récidiver [ʀesidive] vi to commit a subsequent offence; (fig) to do it again

récif [ʀesif] nm reef

récipient [ʀesipjɑ̃] nm container

réciproque [ʀesipʀɔk] adj reciprocal

récit [ʀesi] nm story; **récital** nm recital; **réciter** vt to recite

réclamation [ʀeklamasjɔ̃] nf complaint; **~s** nfpl (bureau) complaints department sg

réclame [ʀeklam] nf ad, advert(isement); **en ~** on special offer; **réclamer** vt to ask for; (revendiquer) to claim, demand ♦ vi to complain

réclusion [ʀeklyzjɔ̃] nf imprisonment

recoin [ʀəkwɛ̃] nm nook, corner

reçois etc [ʀəswa] vb voir **recevoir**

récolte [ʀekɔlt] nf harvesting, gathering; (produits) harvest, crop; **récolter** vt to harvest, gather (in); (fig) to collect

recommandé [ʀ(ə)kɔmɑ̃de] nm (POSTES): **en ~** by registered mail

recommander [ʀ(ə)kɔmɑ̃de] vt to recommend; (POSTES) to register

recommencer [ʀ(ə)kɔmɑ̃se] vt (reprendre: lutte, séance) to resume, start again; (refaire: travail, explications) to start afresh, start (over) again ♦ vi to start again; (récidiver) to do it again

récompense [ʀekɔ̃pɑ̃s] nf reward, (prix) award; **récompenser** vt: **récompenser qn (de ou pour)** to reward sb (for)

réconcilier [ʀekɔ̃silje] vt to reconcile; **se ~ (avec)** to be reconciled (with)

reconduire [ʀ(ə)kɔ̃dɥiʀ] vt (raccompagner) to take ou see back; (renouveler) to renew

réconfort [ʀekɔ̃fɔʀ] nm comfort; **réconforter** vt (consoler) to comfort

reconnaissance [ʀ(ə)kɔnɛsɑ̃s] nf (gratitude) gratitude, gratefulness; (action de reconnaître) recognition; (MIL) reconnaissance, recce; **reconnaissant, e** adj grateful

reconnaître [ʀ(ə)kɔnɛtʀ] vt to recognize; (MIL: lieu) to reconnoitre; (JUR: enfant, torts) to acknowledge; **~ que** to admit *ou* acknowledge that; **reconnu, e** *adj* (*indiscuté, connu*) recognized

reconstituant, e [ʀ(ə)kɔ̃stitɥɑ̃, ɑ̃t] *adj* (*aliment, régime*) strength-building

reconstituer [ʀ(ə)kɔ̃stitɥe] *vt* (*événement, accident*) to reconstruct; (*fresque, vase brisé*) to piece together, reconstitute

reconstruction [ʀ(ə)kɔ̃stʀyksjɔ̃] *nf* rebuilding

reconstruire [ʀ(ə)kɔ̃stʀɥiʀ] *vt* to rebuild

reconvertir [ʀ(ə)kɔ̃vɛʀtiʀ]: **se ~ dans** *vr* (*un métier, une branche*) to go into

record [ʀ(ə)kɔʀ] *nm, adj* record

recoupement [ʀ(ə)kupmɑ̃] *nm*: **par ~** by cross-checking

recouper [ʀ(ə)kupe]: **se ~** *vi* (*témoignages*) to tie *ou* match up

recourber [ʀ(ə)kuʀbe]: **se ~** *vi* to curve (up), bend (up)

recourir [ʀ(ə)kuʀiʀ]: **~ à** *vt* (*ami, agence*) to turn *ou* appeal to; (*force, ruse, emprunt*) to resort to

recours [ʀ(ə)kuʀ] *nm*: **avoir ~ à = recourir à**; **en dernier ~** as a last resort

recouvrer [ʀ(ə)kuvʀe] *vt* (*vue, santé etc*) to recover, regain

recouvrir [ʀ(ə)kuvʀiʀ] *vt* (*couvrir à nouveau*) to re-cover; (*couvrir entièrement, aussi fig*) to cover

récréation [ʀekʀeasjɔ̃] *nf* (*SCOL*) break

récrier [ʀekʀije]: **se ~** *vi* to exclaim

récriminations [ʀekʀiminasjɔ̃] *nfpl* remonstrations, complaints

recroqueviller [ʀ(ə)kʀɔk(ə)vije]: **se ~** *vi* (*personne*) to huddle up

recrudescence [ʀ(ə)kʀydesɑ̃s] *nf* fresh outbreak

recrue [ʀəkʀy] *nf* recruit

recruter [ʀ(ə)kʀyte] *vt* to recruit

rectangle [ʀɛktɑ̃gl] *nm* rectangle; **rectangulaire** *adj* rectangular

rectificatif [ʀɛktifikatif, iv] *nm* correction

rectifier [ʀɛktifje] *vt* (*calcul, adresse, paroles*) to correct; (*erreur*) to rectify

rectiligne [ʀɛktiliɲ] *adj* straight

recto [ʀɛkto] *nm* front (of a page); **~ verso** on both sides (of the page)

reçu, e [ʀ(ə)sy] *pp de* **recevoir** ♦ *adj* (*candidat*) successful; (*admis, consacré*) accepted ♦ *nm* (*COMM*) receipt

recueil [ʀəkœj] *nm* collection; **recueillir** *vt* to collect; (*voix, suffrages*) to win; (*accueillir: réfugiés, chat*) to take in; **se recueillir** *vi* to gather one's thoughts, meditate

recul [ʀ(ə)kyl] *nm* (*éloignement*) distance; (*déclin*) decline; **être en ~** to be on the decline; **avec du ~** with hindsight; **avoir un mouvement de ~** to recoil; **prendre du ~** to

stand back; **reculé, e** *adj* remote; **reculer** *vi* to move back, back away; (*AUTO*) to reverse, back (up); (*fig*) to (be on the) decline ♦ *vt* to move back; (*véhicule*) to reverse, back (up); (*date, décision*) to postpone; **reculons**: **à reculons** *adv* backwards

récupérer [ʀekypeʀe] *vt* to recover, get back; (*heures de travail*) to make up; (*déchets*) to salvage ♦ *vi* to recover

récurer [ʀekyʀe] *vt* to scour

récuser [ʀekyze] *vt* to challenge; **se ~** *vi* to decline to give an opinion

reçut [ʀəsy] *vb voir* **recevoir**

recycler [ʀ(ə)sikle] *vt* (*TECH*) to recycle; **se ~** *vi* to retrain

rédacteur, -trice [ʀedaktœʀ, tʀis] *nm/f* (*journaliste*) writer; subeditor; (*d'ouvrage de référence*) editor, compiler; **~ en chef** chief editor

rédaction [ʀedaksjɔ̃] *nf* writing; (*rédacteurs*) editorial staff; (*SCOL: devoir*) essay, composition

redemander [ʀədmɑ̃de] *vt* (*une nouvelle fois*) to ask again for; (*davantage*) to ask for more of

redescendre [ʀ(ə)desɑ̃dʀ] *vi* to go back down ♦ *vt* (*pente etc*) to go down

redevance [ʀ(ə)dəvɑ̃s] *nf* (*TÉL*) rental charge; (*TV*) licence fee

rédiger [ʀediʒe] *vt* to write; (*contrat*) to draw up

redire [ʀ(ə)diʀ] *vt* to repeat; **trouver à ~ à** to find fault with

redonner [ʀ(ə)dɔne] *vt* (*rendre*) to give back; (*resservir: nourriture*) to give more

redoubler [ʀ(ə)duble] *vi* (*tempête, violence*) to intensify; (*SCOL*) to repeat a year; **~ de patience/prudence** to be doubly patient/careful

redoutable [ʀ(ə)dutabl] *adj* formidable, fearsome

redouter [ʀ(ə)dute] *vt* to dread

redressement [ʀ(ə)dʀɛsmɑ̃] *nm* (*économique*) recovery

redresser [ʀ(ə)dʀese] *vt* (*relever*) to set upright; (*pièce tordue*) to straighten out; (*situation, économie*) to put right; **se ~** *vi* (*personne*) to sit (*ou* stand) up (straight); (*économie*) to recover

réduction [ʀedyksjɔ̃] *nf* reduction

réduire [ʀedɥiʀ] *vt* to reduce; (*prix, dépenses*) to cut, reduce; **se ~ à** (*revenir à*) to boil down to; **réduit** *nm* (*pièce*) tiny room

rééducation [ʀeedykasjɔ̃] *nf* (*d'un membre*) re-education; (*de délinquants, d'un blessé*) rehabilitation

réel, le [ʀeɛl] *adj* real; **réellement** *adv* really

réexpédier [ʀeɛkspedje] *vt* (*à l'envoyeur*) to return, send back; (*au destinataire*) to send on, forward

refaire [ʀ(ə)fɛʀ] *vt* to do again; (*faire de nouveau: sport*) to take up again; (*réparer, restaurer*) to do up

réfection [ʀefɛksjɔ̃] *nf* repair

réfectoire [ʀefɛktwaʀ] *nm* refectory

référence [ʀefeʀɑ̃s] *nf* reference; **~s** *nfpl* (*recommandations*) reference *sg*

référer [ʀefeʀe]: **se ~ à** *vt* to refer to

refermer [ʀ(ə)fɛʀme] *vt* to close *ou* shut again; **se ~** *vi* (*porte*) to close *ou* shut (again)

refiler [ʀ(ə)file] *vt* (*fam*) to palm off

réfléchi, e [ʀefleʃi] *adj* (*caractère*) thoughtful; (*action*) well-thought-out; (*LING*) reflexive; **c'est tout ~** my mind's made up

réfléchir [ʀefleʃiʀ] *vt* to reflect ♦ *vi* to think; **~ à** to think about

reflet [ʀ(ə)flɛ] *nm* reflection; (*sur l'eau etc*) sheen *no pl*, glint; **refléter** *vt* to reflect; **se refléter** *vt* to be reflected

réflexe [ʀeflɛks] *nm, adj* reflex

réflexion [ʀeflɛksjɔ̃] *nf* (*de la lumière etc*) reflection; (*fait de penser*) thought; (*remarque*) remark; **~ faite, à la ~** on reflection

refluer [ʀ(ə)flye] *vi* to flow back; (*foule*) to surge back

reflux [ʀəfly] *nm* (*de la mer*) ebb

réforme [ʀefɔʀm] *nf* reform; (*REL*): **la R~** the Reformation; **réformer** *vt* to reform; (*MIL*) to declare unfit for service

refouler [ʀ(ə)fule] *vt* (*envahisseurs*) to drive back; (*larmes*) to force back; (*désir, colère*) to repress

refrain [ʀ(ə)fʀɛ̃] *nm* refrain, chorus

refréner [ʀəfʀene] *vt*, **réfréner** [ʀefʀene] *vt* to curb, check

réfrigérateur [ʀefʀiʒeʀatœʀ] *nm* refrigerator, fridge

refroidir [ʀ(ə)fʀwadiʀ] *vt* to cool; (*fig: personne*) to put off ♦ *vi* to cool (down); **se ~** *vi* (*temps*) to get cooler *ou* colder; (*fig: ardeur*) to cool (off); **refroidissement** *nm* (*grippe etc*) chill

refuge [ʀ(ə)fyʒ] *nm* refuge; **réfugié, e** *adj, nm/f* refugee; **réfugier**: **se réfugier** *vi* to take refuge

refus [ʀ(ə)fy] *nm* refusal; **ce n'est pas de ~** I won't say no, it's welcome; **refuser** *vt* to refuse; (*SCOL: candidat*) to fail; **refuser qch à qn** to refuse sb sth; **se refuser à faire** to refuse to do

réfuter [ʀefyte] *vt* to refute

regagner [ʀ(ə)ɡaɲe] *vt* (*faveur*) to win back; (*lieu*) to get back to

regain [ʀəɡɛ̃] *nm* (*renouveau*): **un ~ de** renewed +*nom*

régal [ʀeɡal] *nm* treat; **régaler**: **se régaler** *vi* to have a delicious meal; (*fig*) to enjoy o.s.

regard [ʀ(ə)ɡaʀ] *nm* (*coup d'œil*) look, glance; (*expression*) look (in one's eye); **au ~ de** (*loi, morale*) from the point of view of; **en ~ de** in comparison with

regardant, e [ʀ(ə)ɡaʀdɑ̃, ɑ̃t] *adj* (*économe*) tight-fisted; **peu ~ (sur)** very free (about)

regarder [ʀ(ə)ɡaʀde] *vt* to look at; (*film, télévision, match*) to watch; (*concerner*) to concern ♦ *vi* to look; **ne pas ~ à la dépense** to spare no expense; **~ qn/qch comme** to regard sb/sth as

régie [ʀeʒi] *nf* (*COMM, INDUSTRIE*) state-owned company; (*THÉÂTRE, CINÉMA*) production; (*RADIO, TV*) control room

regimber [ʀ(ə)ʒɛ̃be] *vi* to balk, jib

régime [ʀeʒim] *nm* (*POL*) régime; (*MÉD*) diet; (*ADMIN: carcéral, fiscal etc*) system; (*de bananes, dattes*) bunch; **se mettre au/suivre un ~** to go on/be on a diet

régiment [ʀeʒimɑ̃] *nm* regiment

région [ʀeʒjɔ̃] *nf* region; **régional, e, -aux** *adj* regional

régir [ʀeʒiʀ] *vt* to govern

régisseur [ʀeʒisœʀ] *nm* (*d'un domaine*) steward; (*CINÉMA, TV*) assistant director; (*THÉÂTRE*) stage manager

registre [ʀəʒistʀ] *nm* register

réglage [ʀeɡlaʒ] *nm* adjustment

règle [ʀɛɡl] *nf* (*instrument*) ruler; (*loi*) rule; **~s** *nfpl* (*menstruation*) period *sg*; **en ~** (*papiers d'identité*) in order; **en ~ générale** as a (general) rule

réglé, e [ʀeɡle] *adj* (*vie*) well-ordered; (*arrangé*) settled

règlement [ʀɛɡləmɑ̃] *nm* (*paiement*) settlement; (*arrêté*) regulation; (*règles, statuts*) regulations *pl*, rules *pl*; **~ de compte(s)** settling of old scores; **réglementaire** *adj* conforming to the regulations; (*tenue*) regulation *cpd*; **réglementation** *nf* (*règles*) regulations; **réglementer** *vt* to regulate

régler [ʀeɡle] *vt* (*conflit, facture*) to settle; (*personne*) to settle up with; (*mécanisme, machine*) to regulate, adjust; (*thermostat etc*) to set, adjust

réglisse [ʀeɡlis] *nf* liquorice

règne [ʀɛɲ] *nm* (*d'un roi etc, fig*) reign; **régner** *vi* (*roi*) to rule, reign; (*fig*) to reign

regorger [ʀ(ə)ɡɔʀʒe] *vi*: **~ de** to overflow with, be bursting with

regret [ʀ(ə)ɡʀɛ] *nm* regret; **à ~** with regret; **sans ~** with no regrets; **regrettable** *adj* regrettable; **regretter** *vt* to regret; (*personne*) to miss; **je regrette mais** ... I'm sorry but ...

regrouper [ʀ(ə)ɡʀupe] *vt* (*grouper*) to group together; (*contenir*) to include, comprise; **se ~** *vi* to gather (together)

régulier, -ière [ʀegylje, jɛʀ] *adj* (*gén*) regular; (*vitesse, qualité*) steady; (*égal: couche, ligne*) even, (*TRANSPORTS: ligne, service*), scheduled, regular; (*légal*) lawful, in order; (*honnête*) straight, on the level; **régulièrement** *adv* regularly; (*uniformément*) evenly

rehausser [ʀaose] *vt* (*relever*) to heighten, raise; (*fig: souligner*) to set off, enhance

rein [ʀɛ̃] *nm* kidney; **~s** *nmpl* (*dos*) back *sg*

reine [ʀɛn] *nf* queen

reine-claude [ʀɛnklod] *nf* greengage

réinsertion [ʀeɛ̃sɛʀsjɔ̃] *nf* (*de délinquant*) reintegration, rehabilitation

réintégrer [ʀeɛ̃tegʀe] *vt* (*lieu*) to return to; (*fonctionnaire*) to reinstate

rejaillir [ʀ(ə)ʒajiʀ] *vi* to splash up; **~ sur** (*fig: scandale*) to rebound on; (: *gloire*) to be reflected on

rejet [ʀaʒɛ] *nm* rejection; **rejeter** *vt* (*relancer*) to throw back; (*écarter*) to reject; (*déverser*) to throw out, discharge; (*vomir*) to bring *ou* throw up; **rejeter la responsabilité de qch sur qn** to lay the responsibility for sth at sb's door

rejoindre [ʀ(ə)ʒwɛ̃dʀ] *vt* (*famille, régiment*) to rejoin, return to; (*lieu*) to get (back) to; (*suj: route etc*) to meet, join; (*rattraper*) to catch up (with); **se ~** *vi* to meet; **je te rejoins à la gare** I'll see *ou* meet you at the station

réjouir [ʀeʒwiʀ] *vt* to delight; **se ~ (de)** *vi* to be delighted (about); **réjouissances** *nfpl* (*fête*) festivities

relâche [ʀəlɑʃ] *nm ou nf*: **sans ~** without respite *ou* a break; **relâché, e** *adj* loose, lax; **relâcher** *vt* (*libérer*) to release; (*desserrer*) to loosen; **se relâcher** *vi* (*discipline*) to become slack *ou* lax; (*élève etc*) to slacken off

relais [ʀ(ə)lɛ] *nm* (*SPORT*): **(course de) ~** relay (race); **prendre le ~ (de)** to take over (from); **~ routier** ≈ transport café (*BRIT*), ≈ truck stop (*US*)

relancer [ʀ(ə)lɑ̃se] *vt* (*balle*) to throw back; (*moteur*) to restart; (*fig*) to boost, revive; (*harceler*): **~ qn** to pester sb

relatif, -ive [ʀ(ə)latif, iv] *adj* relative

relation [ʀ(ə)lasjɔ̃] *nf* (*rapport*) relation(ship); (*connaissance*) acquaintance; **~s** *nfpl* (*rapports*) relations; (*connaissances*) connections; **être/entrer en ~(s) avec** to be/ get in contact with

relaxe [ʀəlaks] (*fam*) *adj* (*tenue*) informal; (*personne*) relaxed; **relaxer**: **se relaxer** *vi* to relax

relayer [ʀ(ə)leje] *vt* (*collaborateur, coureur etc*) to relieve; **se ~** *vi* (*dans une activité*) to take it in turns

reléguer [ʀ(ə)lege] *vt* to relegate

relent(s) [ʀəlɑ̃] *nm(pl)* (foul) smell

relevé, e [ʀəl(ə)ve] *adj* (*manches*) rolled-up;

(*sauce*) highly-seasoned ♦ *nm* (*de compteur*) reading; (*bancaire*) statement

relève [ʀəlɛv] *nf* (*personne*) relief; **prendre la ~** to take over

relever [ʀəl(ə)ve] *vt* (*meuble*) to stand up again; (*personne tombée*) to help up; (*vitre, niveau de vie*) to raise; (*col*) to turn up; (*style*) to elevate; (*plat, sauce*) to season; (*sentinelle, équipe*) to relieve; (*fautes*) to pick out; (*défi*) to accept, take up; (*noter: adresse etc*) to take down, note; (: *plan*) to sketch; (*compteur*) to read; (*ramasser: cahiers*) to collect, take in; **se ~** *vi* (*se remettre debout*) to get up; **~ de** (*maladie*) to be recovering from; (*être du ressort de*) to be a matter for; (*fig*) to pertain to; **~ qn de** (*fonctions*) to relieve sb of

relief [ʀəljɛf] *nm* relief; **mettre en ~** (*fig*) to bring out, highlight

relier [ʀəlje] *vt* to link up; (*livre*) to bind; **~ qch à** to link sth to

religieuse [ʀ(ə)liʒjøz] *nf* nun; (*gâteau*) cream bun

religieux, -euse [ʀ(ə)liʒjø, jøz] *adj* religious ♦ *nm* monk

religion [ʀ(ə)liʒjɔ̃] *nf* religion

relire [ʀ(ə)liʀ] *vt* (*à nouveau*) to reread, read again; (*vérifier*) to read over

reliure [ʀəljyʀ] *nf* binding

reluire [ʀ(ə)lɥiʀ] *vi* to gleam

remanier [ʀ(ə)manje] *vt* to reshape, recast; (*POL*) to reshuffle

remarquable [ʀ(ə)maʀkabl] *adj* remarkable

remarque [ʀ(ə)maʀk] *nf* remark; (*écrite*) note

remarquer [ʀ(ə)maʀke] *vt* (*voir*) to notice; **se ~** *vi* to be noticeable; **faire ~ (à qn) que** to point out (to sb) that; **faire ~ qch (à qn)** to point sth out (to sb); **remarquez, ...** mind you ...; **se faire ~** to draw attention to o.s.

rembourrer [ʀɑ̃buʀe] *vt* to stuff

remboursement [ʀɑ̃buʀsəmɑ̃] *nm* (*de dette, d'emprunt*) repayment; (*de frais*) refund; **rembourser** *vt* to pay back, repay; (*frais, billet etc*) to refund; **se faire rembourser** to get a refund

remède [ʀ(ə)mɛd] *nm* (*médicament*) medicine; (*traitement, fig*) remedy, cure

remémorer [ʀ(ə)memɔʀe]: **se ~** *vt* to recall, recollect

remerciements [ʀəmɛʀsimɑ̃] *nmpl* thanks

remercier [ʀ(ə)mɛʀsje] *vt* to thank; (*congédier*) to dismiss; **~ qn de/d'avoir fait** to thank sb for/for having done

remettre [ʀ(ə)mɛtʀ] *vt* (*replacer*) to put back; (*vêtement*) to put back on; (*ajouter*) to add; (*ajourner*): **~ qch (à)** to postpone sth (until); **se ~** *vi*: **se ~ (de)** to recover (from); **~ qch à qn** (*donner: lettre, clé etc*) to hand over sth to sb; (: *prix, décoration*) to present sb with sth; **se ~ à faire qch** to start doing sth again

remise [R(ə)miz] *nf* (*rabais*) discount; (*local*) shed; **~ de peine** reduction of sentence; **~ en jeu** (FOOTBALL) throw-in

remontant [R(ə)mɔ̃tɑ̃, ɑ̃t] *nm* tonic, pick-me-up

remonte-pente [R(ə)mɔ̃tpɑ̃t] *nm* ski-lift

remonter [R(ə)mɔ̃te] *vi* to go back up; (*prix, température*) to go up again ♦ *vt* (*pente*) to go up; (*fleuve*) to sail (*ou* swim *etc*) up; (*manches, pantalon*) to roll up; (*col*) to turn up; (*niveau, limite*) to raise; (*fig: personne*) to buck up; (*qch de démonté*) to put back together, reassemble; (*montre*) to wind up; **~ le moral à qn** to raise sb's spirits; **~ à** (*dater de*) to date *ou* go back to

remontrance [R(ə)mɔ̃trɑ̃s] *nf* reproof, reprimand

remontrer [R(ə)mɔ̃tre] *vt* (*fig*): **en ~ à** to prove one's superiority over

remords [R(ə)mɔR] *nm* remorse *no pl*; **avoir des ~** to feel remorse

remorque [R(ə)mɔRk] *nf* trailer; **remorquer** *vt* to tow; **remorqueur** *nm* tug(boat)

remous [Rəmu] *nm* (*d'un navire*) (back)wash *no pl*; (*de rivière*) swirl, eddy ♦ *nmpl* (*fig*) stir *sg*

remparts [Rɑ̃paR] *nmpl* walls, ramparts

remplaçant, e [Rɑ̃plasɑ̃, ɑ̃t] *nm/f* replacement, stand-in; (SCOL) supply teacher

remplacement [Rɑ̃plasmɑ̃] *nm* replacement; **faire des ~s** (*professeur*) to do supply teaching; (*secrétaire*) to temp

remplacer [Rɑ̃plase] *vt* to replace, **~ qch/qn par** to replace sth/sb with

rempli, e [Rɑ̃pli] *adj* (*emploi du temps*) full, busy; **~ de** full of, filled with

remplir [Rɑ̃pliR] *vt* to fill (up); (*questionnaire*) to fill out *ou* up; (*obligations, fonction, condition*) to fulfil; **se ~** *vi* to fill up

remporter [Rɑ̃pɔRte] *vt* (*marchandise*) to take away; (*fig*) to win, achieve

remuant, e [Rəmɥɑ̃, ɑ̃t] *adj* restless

remue-ménage [R(ə)mymenaʒ] *nm inv* commotion

remuer [Rəmɥe] *vt* to move; (*café, sauce*) to stir ♦ *vi* to move; **se ~** *vi* to move; (*fam: s'activer*) to get a move on

rémunérer [Remynere] *vt* to remunerate

renard [R(ə)naR] *nm* fox

renchérir [Rɑ̃feriR] *vi* (*fig*): **~ (sur)** (*en paroles*) to add something (to)

rencontre [Rɑ̃kɔ̃tR] *nf* meeting; (*imprévue*) encounter; **aller à la ~ de qn** to go and meet sb; **rencontrer** *vt* to meet; (*mot, expression*) to come across; (*difficultés*) to meet with; **se rencontrer** *vi* to meet

rendement [Rɑ̃dmɑ̃] *nm* (*d'un travailleur,*

d'une machine) output; (*d'un champ*) yield

rendez-vous [Rɑ̃devu] *nm* appointment; (*d'amoureux*) date; (*lieu*) meeting place; **donner ~~ à qn** to arrange to meet sb; **avoir/prendre ~~ (avec)** to have/make an appointment (with)

rendre [Rɑ̃dR] *vt* (*restituer*) to give back, return; (*invitation*) to return, repay; (*vomir*) to bring up; (*exprimer, traduire*) to render; (*faire devenir*): **~ qn célèbre/qch possible** to make sb famous/sth possible; **se ~** *vi* (*capituler*) to surrender, give o.s. up; (*aller*): **se ~ quelque part** to go somewhere; **~ la monnaie à qn** to give sb his change; **se ~ compte de qch** to realize sth

rênes [REn] *nfpl* reins

renfermé, e [Rɑ̃fERme] *adj* (*fig*) withdrawn ♦ *nm*: **sentir le ~** to smell stuffy

renfermer [Rɑ̃fERme] *vt* to contain

renflouer [Rɑ̃flue] *vt* to refloat; (*fig*) to set back on its (*ou* his/her *etc*) feet

renfoncement [Rɑ̃fɔ̃smɑ̃] *nm* recess

renforcer [Rɑ̃fɔRse] *vt* to reinforce; **renfort**: **renforts** *nmpl* reinforcements; **à grand renfort de** with a great deal of

renfrogné, e [Rɑ̃frɔɲe] *adj* sullen

rengaine [Rɑ̃gɛn] (*péj*) *nf* old tune

renier [Rənje] *vt* (*personne*) to disown, repudiate; (*foi*) to renounce

renifler [R(ə)nifle] *vi, vt* to sniff

renne [REn] *nm* reindeer *inv*

renom [Rənɔ̃] *nm* reputation; (*célébrité*) renown; **renommé, e** *adj* celebrated, renowned; **renommée** *nf* fame

renoncer [R(ə)nɔ̃se]: **~ à** *vt* to give up; **~ à faire** to give up the idea of doing

renouer [Rənwe] *vt*: **~ avec** (*habitude*) to take up again

renouvelable [R(ə)nuv(ə)labl] *adj* (*énergie etc*) renewable

renouveler [R(ə)nuv(ə)le] *vt* to renew; (*exploit, méfait*) to repeat; **se ~** *vi* (*incident*) to recur, happen again; **renouvellement** *nm* (*remplacement*) renewal

rénover [Renɔve] *vt* (*immeuble*) to renovate, do up; (*quartier*) to redevelop

renseignement [Rɑ̃sɛɲmɑ̃] *nm* information *no pl*, piece of information; **(bureau des) ~s** information office

renseigner [Rɑ̃seɲe] *vt*: **~ qn (sur)** to give information to sb (about); **se ~** *vi* to ask for information, make inquiries

rentabilité [Rɑ̃tabilite] *nf* profitability

rentable [Rɑ̃tabl] *adj* profitable

rente [Rɑ̃t] *nf* private income; (*pension*) pension

rentrée [Rɑ̃tRe] *nf*: **~ (d'argent)** cash *no pl* coming in; **la ~ (des classes)** the start of the new school year

rentrer [Rɑ̃tRe] vi (revenir chez soi) to go (ou come) (back) home; (entrer de nouveau) to go (ou come) back in; (entrer) to go (ou come) in; (air, clou: pénétrer) to go in; (revenu) to come in ♦ vt to bring in; (mettre à l'abri: animaux etc) to bring in; (: véhicule) to put away; (chemise dans pantalon etc) to tuck in; (griffes) to draw in; ~ **le ventre** to pull in one's stomach; ~ **dans** (heurter) to crash into; ~ **dans l'ordre** to be back to normal; ~ **dans ses frais** to recover one's expenses

renverse [Rɑ̃vɛRs]: **à la** ~ adv backwards

renverser [Rɑ̃vɛRse] vt (faire tomber: chaise, verre) to knock over, overturn; (liquide, contenu) to spill, upset; (piéton) to knock down; (retourner) to turn upside down; (: ordre des mots etc) to reverse; (fig: gouvernement etc) to overthrow; (fam: stupéfier) to bowl over; **se** ~ vi (verre, vase) to fall over; (contenu) to spill

renvoi [Rɑ̃vwa] nm (d'employé) dismissal; (d'élève) expulsion; (référence) cross-reference; (éructation) belch; **renvoyer** vt to send back; (congédier) to dismiss; (élève: définitivement) to expel; (lumière) to reflect; (ajourner): **renvoyer qch (à)** to put sth off ou postpone sth (until)

repaire [R(ə)pɛR] nm den

répandre [Repɑ̃dR] vt (renverser) to spill; (étaler, diffuser) to spread; (odeur) to give off; **se** ~ vi to spill; (se propager) to spread; **répandu, e** adj (opinion, usage) widespread

réparation [RepaRasjɔ̃] nf repair

réparer [Repare] vt to repair; (fig: offense) to make up for, atone for; (: oubli, erreur) to put right

repartie [Reparti] nf retort; **avoir de la** ~ to be quick at repartee

repartir [R(ə)paRtiR] vi to leave again; (voyageur) to set off again; (fig) to get going again; ~ **à zéro** to start from scratch (again)

répartir [RepaRtiR] vt (pour attribuer) to share out; (pour disperser, disposer) to divide up; (poids) to distribute; **se** ~ vt (travail, rôles) to share out between themselves; **répartition** nf (des richesses etc) distribution

repas [R(ə)pɑ] nm meal

repassage [R(ə)pɑsaʒ] nm ironing

repasser [R(ə)pɑse] vi to come (ou go) back ♦ vt (vêtement, tissu) to iron; (examen) to retake, resit; (film) to show again; (leçon: revoir) to go over (again)

repêcher [R(ə)peʃe] vt to fish out; (candidat) to pass (by inflating marks)

repentir [Rapɑ̃tiR] nm repentance; **se** ~ vi to repent; **se** ~ **d'avoir fait qch** (regretter) to regret having done sth

répercussions [RepɛRkysjɔ̃] nfpl (fig)

repercussions

répercuter [RepɛRkyte]: **se** ~ vi (bruit) to reverberate; (fig): **se** ~ **sur** to have repercussions on

repère [R(ə)pɛR] nm mark; (monument, événement) landmark

repérer [R(ə)peRe] vt (fam: erreur, personne) to spot; (: endroit) to locate; **se** ~ vi to find one's way about

répertoire [RepɛRtwaR] nm (liste) (alphabetical) list; (carnet) index notebook; (d'un artiste) repertoire

répéter [Repete] vt to repeat; (préparer: leçon) to learn, go over; (THÉÂTRE) to rehearse; **se** ~ vi (redire) to repeat o.s.; (se reproduire) to be repeated, recur

répétition [Repetisjɔ̃] nf repetition; (THÉÂTRE) rehearsal

répit [Repi] nm respite

replier [R(ə)plije] vt (rabattre) to fold down ou over; **se** ~ vi (troupes, armée) to withdraw, fall back; (sur soi-même) to withdraw into o.s.

réplique [Replik] nf (repartie, fig) reply; (THÉÂTRE) line; (copie) replica; **répliquer** vi to reply; (riposter) to retaliate

répondeur [Repɔ̃dœR, øz] nm: ~ **automatique** (TÉL) answering machine

répondre [Repɔ̃dR] vi to answer, reply; (freins) to respond; ~ **à** to reply to, answer; (affection, salut) to return; (provocation) to respond to; (correspondre à: besoin) to answer; (: conditions) to meet; (: description) to match; (avec impertinence): ~ **à qn** to answer sb back; ~ **de** to answer for

réponse [Repɔ̃s] nf answer, reply; **en** ~ **à** in reply to

reportage [R(ə)pɔRtaʒ] nm report; ~ **en direct** (live) commentary

reporter[1] [RəpɔRtɛR] nm reporter

reporter[2] [RəpɔRte] vt (ajourner): ~ **qch (à)** to postpone sth (until); (transférer): ~ **qch sur** to transfer sth to; **se** ~ **à** (époque) to think back to; (document) to refer to

repos [R(ə)po] nm rest; (tranquillité) peace (and quiet); (MIL): ~! stand at ease!; **ce n'est pas de tout** ~! it's no picnic!

reposant, e [R(ə)pozɑ̃, ɑ̃t] adj restful

reposer [R(ə)poze] vt (verre, livre) to put down; (délasser) to rest ♦ vi: **laisser** ~ (pâte) to leave to stand; **se** ~ vi to rest; **se** ~ **sur qn** to rely on sb; ~ **sur** (fig) to rest on

repoussant, e [R(ə)pusɑ̃, ɑ̃t] adj repulsive

repousser [R(ə)puse] vi to grow again ♦ vt to repel, repulse; (offre) to turn down, reject; (personne) to push back; (différer) to put back

reprendre [R(ə)pRɑ̃dR] vt (objet prêté, donné) to take back; (prisonnier, ville) to recapture; (firme, entreprise) to take over; (le *travail*) to resume; (*emprunter: argument, idée*) to take up, use; (*refaire: article etc*) to go over again; (*vêtement*) to alter; (*réprimander*) to tell off; (*corriger*) to correct; (*chercher*): **je viendrai te ~ à 4 h** I'll come and fetch you at 4; (*se resservir de*): **~ du pain/un œuf** to take (*ou* eat) more bread/another egg ♦ *vi* (*classes, pluie*) to start (up) again; (*activités, travaux, combats*) to resume, start (up) again; (*affaires*) to pick up; (*dire*): **reprit-il** he went on; **se ~** *vi* (*se ressaisir*) to recover; **~ des forces** to recover one's strength; **~ courage** to take new heart; **~ la route** to set off again; **~ haleine** *ou* **son souffle** to get one's breath back

représailles [ʀ(ə)pʀezaj] *nfpl* reprisals

représentant, e [ʀ(ə)pʀezɑ̃tɑ̃, ɑ̃t] *nm/f* representative

représentation [ʀ(ə)pʀezɑ̃tasjɔ̃] *nf* (*symbole, image*) representation; (*spectacle*) performance

représenter [ʀ(ə)pʀezɑ̃te] *vt* to represent; (*donner: pièce, opéra*) to perform; **se ~** *vt* (*se figurer*) to imagine

répression [ʀepʀesjɔ̃] *nf* repression

réprimer [ʀepʀime] *vt* (*émotions*) to suppress; (*peuple etc*) to repress

repris [ʀ(ə)pʀi, iz] *nm*: **~ de justice** ex-prisoner, ex-convict

reprise [ʀ(ə)pʀiz] *nf* (*recommencement*) resumption; (*économique*) recovery; (*TV*) repeat; (*COMM*) trade-in, part exchange; (*raccommodage*) mend, **à plusieurs ~s** on several occasions

repriser [ʀ(ə)pʀize] *vt* (*chaussette, lainage*) to darn, (*tissu*) to mend

reproche [ʀ(ə)pʀɔʃ] *nm* (*remontrance*) reproach; **faire des ~s à qn** to reproach sb; **sans ~(s)** beyond reproach; **reprocher** *vt*: **reprocher qch à qn** to reproach *ou* blame sb for sth; **reprocher qch à** (*critiquer*) to have sth against

reproduction [ʀ(ə)pʀɔdyksjɔ̃] *nf* reproduction

reproduire [ʀ(ə)pʀɔdɥiʀ] *vt* to reproduce; **se ~** *vi* (*BIO*) to reproduce; (*recommencer*) to recur, re-occur

réprouver [ʀepʀuve] *vt* to reprove

reptile [ʀɛptil] *nm* reptile

repu, e [ʀəpy] *adj* satisfied, sated

république [ʀepyblik] *nf* republic

répugnant, e [ʀepyɲɑ̃, ɑ̃t] *adj* disgusting

répugner [ʀepyɲe]: **~ à** *vt*: **~ à qn** to repel *ou* disgust sb; **~ à faire** to be loath *ou* reluctant to do

réputation [ʀepytasjɔ̃] *nf* reputation; **réputé, e** *adj* renowned

requérir [ʀəkeʀiʀ] *vt* (*nécessiter*) to require, call for

requête [ʀəkɛt] *nf* request

requin [ʀəkɛ̃] *nm* shark

requis, e [ʀəki, iz] *adj* required

RER *sigle m* (= *réseau express régional*) Greater Paris high-speed train service

rescapé, e [ʀɛskape] *nm/f* survivor

rescousse [ʀɛskus] *nf*: **aller à la ~ de qn** to go to sb's aid *ou* rescue

réseau, x [ʀezo] *nm* network

réservation [ʀezɛʀvasjɔ̃] *nf* booking, reservation

réserve [ʀezɛʀv] *nf* (*retenue*) reserve; (*entrepôt*) storeroom; (*restriction, d'Indiens*) reservation; (*de pêche, chasse*) preserve; **de ~** (*provisions etc*) in reserve

réservé, e [ʀezɛʀve] *adj* reserved; **chasse/pêche ~e** private hunting/fishing

réserver [ʀezɛʀve] *vt* to reserve; (*chambre, billet etc*) to book, reserve; (*fig: destiner*) to have in store; (*garder*): **~ qch pour/à** to keep *ou* save sth for

réservoir [ʀezɛʀvwaʀ] *nm* tank

résidence [ʀezidɑ̃s] *nf* residence; **~ secondaire** second home; **résidentiel, le** *adj* residential; **résider** *vi*: **résider à/dans/en** to reside in; **résider dans** (*fig*) to lie in

résidu [ʀezidy] *nm* residue *no pl*

résigner [ʀeziɲe]: **se ~** *vi*: **se ~ (à qch/à faire)** to resign o.s. (to sth/to doing)

résilier [ʀezilje] *vt* to terminate

résistance [ʀezistɑ̃s] *nf* resistance; (*de réchaud, bouilloire: fil*) element

résistant, e [ʀezistɑ̃, ɑ̃t] *adj* (*personne*) robust, tough; (*matériau*) strong, hard-wearing

résister [ʀeziste] *vi* to resist; **~ à** (*assaut, tentation*) to resist; (*supporter: gel etc*) to withstand; (*désobéir à*) to stand up to, oppose

résolu, e [ʀezɔly] *pp de* **résoudre** ♦ *adj*: **être ~ à qch/faire** to be set upon sth/doing

résolution [ʀezɔlysjɔ̃] *nf* (*fermeté, décision*) resolution; (*d'un problème*) solution

résolve *etc* [ʀezɔlv] *vb voir* **résoudre**

résonner [ʀezɔne] *vi* (*cloche, pas*) to reverberate, resound; (*salle*) to be resonant

résorber [ʀezɔʀbe]: **se ~** *vi* (*fig: chômage*) to be reduced; (: *déficit*) to be absorbed

résoudre [ʀezudʀ] *vt* to solve; **se ~ à faire** to bring o.s. to do

respect [ʀɛspɛ] *nm* respect; **tenir en ~** to keep at bay; **respecter** *vt* to respect; **respectueux, -euse** *adj* respectful

respiration [ʀɛspiʀasjɔ̃] *nf* breathing *no pl*

respirer [ʀɛspiʀe] *vi* to breathe; (*fig: se détendre*) to get one's breath, (: *se rassurer*) to breathe again ♦ *vt* to breathe (in), inhale; (*manifester: santé, calme etc*) to exude

resplendir [ʀɛsplɑ̃diʀ] *vi* to shine; (*fig*):

~ **(de)** to be radiant (with)

responsabilité [Rɛspɔ̃sabilite] *nf* responsibility; *(légale)* liability

responsable [Rɛspɔ̃sabl] *adj* responsible ♦ *nm/f (coupable)* person responsible; *(personne compétente)* person in charge; *(de parti, syndicat)* official, ~ **de** responsible for

resquiller [Rɛskije] *(fam)* *vt* to get in without paying; *(ne pas faire la queue)* to jump the queue

ressaisir [R(ə)seziʀ]: **se** ~ *vi* to regain one's self-control

ressasser [R(ə)sase] *vt* to keep going over

ressemblance [R(ə)sɑ̃blɑ̃s] *nf* resemblance, similarity, likeness

ressemblant, e [R(ə)sɑ̃blɑ̃, ɑ̃t] *adj (portrait)* lifelike, true to life

ressembler [R(ə)sɑ̃ble]: ~ **à** *vt* to be like, resemble; *(visuellement)* to look like; **se** ~ *vi* to be *(ou* look) alike

ressemeler [R(ə)səm(ə)le] *vt* to (re)sole

ressentiment [R(ə)sɑ̃timɑ̃] *nm* resentment

ressentir [R(ə)sɑ̃tiʀ] *vt* to feel

resserrer [R(ə)seʀe] *vt (nœud, boulon)* to tighten (up); *(fig: liens)* to strengthen

resservir [R(ə)seʀviʀ] *vi* to do *ou* serve again; **se** ~ *vi* to help o.s. again

ressort [R(ə)sɔʀ] *nm (pièce)* spring; *(énergie)* spirit; *(recours)*: **en dernier** ~ as a last resort; *(compétence)*: **être du** ~ **de** to fall within the competence of

ressortir [R(ə)sɔʀtiʀ] *vi* to go *(ou* come) out (again); *(contraster)* to stand out; ~ **de** to emerge from; **faire** ~ *(fig: souligner)* to bring out

ressortissant, e [R(ə)sɔʀtisɑ̃, ɑ̃t] *nm/f* national

ressources [R(ə)suʀs] *nfpl (moyens)* resources

ressusciter [Resysite] *vt (fig)* to revive, bring back ♦ *vi* to rise (from the dead)

restant, e [Rɛstɑ̃, ɑ̃t] *adj* remaining ♦ *nm*: **le ~ (de)** the remainder (of); **un ~ de** *(de trop)* some left-over

restaurant [Rɛstɔʀɑ̃] *nm* restaurant

restauration [Rɛstɔʀasjɔ̃] *nf* restoration; *(hôtellerie)* catering; ~ **rapide** fast food

restaurer [Rɛstɔʀe] *vt* to restore; **se** ~ *vi* to have something to eat

reste [Rɛst] *nm (restant)*: **le ~ (de)** the rest (of); *(de trop)*: **un ~ (de)** some left-over; **~s** *nmpl (nourriture)* left-overs; *(d'une cité etc, dépouille mortelle)* remains; **du ~, au ~** besides, moreover

rester [Rɛste] *vi* to stay, remain; *(subsister)* to remain, be left; *(durer)* to last, live on ♦ *vb impers*: **il reste du pain/2 œufs** there's some bread/there are 2 eggs left (over); **restons-en là** let's leave it at that; **il me reste assez de temps** I have enough time left; **il ne me reste plus qu'à ...** I've just got to ...

restituer [Rɛstitɥe] *vt (objet, somme)*: ~ **qch (à qn)** to return sth (to sb)

restreindre [Rɛstʀɛ̃dʀ] *vt* to restrict, limit

restriction [Rɛstʀiksjɔ̃] *nf* restriction

résultat [Rezylta] *nm* result; *(d'examen, d'élection)* results *pl*

résulter [Rezylte]: ~ **de** *vt* to result from, be the result of

résumé [Rezyme] *nm* summary, résumé

résumer [Rezyme] *vt (texte)* to summarize; *(récapituler)* to sum up

résurrection [RezyRɛksjɔ̃] *nf* resurrection

rétablir [Retabliʀ] *vt* to restore, re-establish; **se** ~ *vi (guérir)* to recover; *(silence, calme)* to return, be restored; **rétablissement** *nm* restoring; *(guérison)* recovery

retaper [R(ə)tape] *(fam)* *vt (maison, voiture etc)* to do up; *(revigorer)* to buck up

retard [R(ə)taʀ] *nm (d'une personne attendue)* lateness *no pl*; *(sur l'horaire, un programme)* delay; *(fig: scolaire, mental etc)* backwardness; **en ~ (de 2 heures)** (2 hours) late; **avoir du** ~ to be late; *(sur un programme)* to be behind (schedule); **prendre du ~** *(train, avion)* to be delayed; **sans** ~ without delay

retardataire [R(ə)taʀdatɛʀ] *nmf* latecomer

retardement [R(ə)taʀdəmɑ̃]: **à** ~ *adj* delayed action *cpd*; **bombe à** ~ time bomb

retarder [R(ə)taʀde] *vt* to delay; *(montre)* to put back ♦ *vi (montre)* to be slow; ~ **qn (d'une heure)** *(sur un horaire)* to delay sb (an hour); ~ **qch (de 2 jours)** *(départ, date)* to put sth back (2 days)

retenir [Rət(ə)niʀ] *vt (garder, retarder)* to keep, detain; *(maintenir: objet qui glisse, fig: colère, larmes)* to hold back; *(se rappeler)* to retain; *(réserver)* to reserve; *(accepter: proposition etc)* to accept; *(fig: empêcher d'agir)*: ~ **qn (de faire)** to hold sb back (from doing); *(prélever)*: ~ **qch (sur)** to deduct sth (from); **se** ~ *vi (se raccrocher)*: **se** ~ **à** to hold onto; *(se contenir)*: **se** ~ **de faire** to restrain o.s. from doing; ~ **son souffle** to hold one's breath

retentir [R(ə)tɑ̃tiʀ] *vi* to ring out; *(salle)*: ~ **de** to ring *ou* resound with; **retentissant, e** *adj* resounding; **retentissement** *nm* repercussion

retenu, e [Rət(ə)ny] *adj (place)* reserved; *(personne: empêché)* held up; **retenue** *nf (prélèvement)* deduction; *(scol)* detention; *(modération)* (self-)restraint

réticence [Retisɑ̃s] *nf* hesitation, reluctance *no pl*; **réticent, e** *adj* hesitant, reluctant

rétine [Retin] *nf* retina

retiré, e [R(ə)tiʀe] *adj (vie)* secluded; *(lieu)*

remote

retirer [ʀ(ə)tiʀe] vt (*vêtement, lunettes*) to take off, remove; (*argent, plainte*) to withdraw; (*reprendre: bagages, billets*) to collect, pick up; (*extraire*): ~ **qch de** to take sth out of, remove sth from

retombées [ʀɔtɔ̃be] nfpl (*radioactives*) fallout sg; (*fig: répercussions*) effects

retomber [ʀ(ə)tɔ̃be] vi (*à nouveau*) to fall again; (*atterrir: après un saut etc*) to land; (*échoir*): ~ **sur qn** to fall on sb

rétorquer [ʀetɔʀke] vt: ~ **(à qn) que** to retort (to sb) that

retouche [ʀ(ə)tuʃ] nf (*sur vêtement*) alteration; **retoucher** vt (*photographie*) to touch up; (*texte, vêtement*) to alter

retour [ʀ(ə)tuʀ] nm return; **au** ~ (*en route*) on the way back; **à mon** ~ when I get/got back; **être de** ~ (**de**) to be back (from); **par** ~ **du courrier** by return of post

retourner [ʀ(ə)tuʀne] vt (*dans l'autre sens: matelas, crêpe etc*) to turn (over); (*sac, vêtement*) to turn inside out; (*fam: bouleverser*) to shake; (*renvoyer, restituer*): ~ **qch à qn** to return sth to sb ♦ vi (*aller, revenir*): ~ **quelque part/à** to go back ou return somewhere/to; **se** ~ vi (*tourner la tête*) to turn round; ~ **à** (*état, activité*) to return to, go back to; **se** ~ **contre** (*fig*) to turn against

retrait [ʀ(ə)tʀɛ] nm (*d'argent*) withdrawal; **en** ~ set back; ~ **du permis (de conduire)** disqualification from driving (*BRIT*), revocation of driver's license (*US*)

retraite [ʀ(ə)tʀɛt] nf (*d'un employé*) retirement; (*revenu*) pension; (*d'une armée, REL*) retreat; **prendre sa** ~ to retire; ~ **anticipée** early retirement; **retraité, e** adj retired ♦ nm/f pensioner

retrancher [ʀ(ə)tʀɑ̃ʃe] vt (*nombre, somme*): ~ **qch de** to take ou deduct sth from; **se** ~ **derrière/dans** to take refuge behind/in

retransmettre [ʀ(ə)tʀɑ̃smɛtʀ] vt (*RADIO*) to broadcast; (*TV*) to show

rétrécir [ʀetʀesiʀ] vt (*vêtement*) to take in ♦ vi to shrink

rétribution [ʀetʀibysjɔ̃] nf payment

rétro [ʀetʀo] adj inv: **la mode** ~ the nostalgia vogue

rétrograde [ʀetʀɔgʀad] adj reactionary, backward-looking

rétroprojecteur [ʀetʀopʀɔʒɛktœʀ] nm overhead projector

rétrospective [ʀetʀɔspɛktiv] nf retrospective exhibition/season; **rétrospectivement** adv in retrospect

retrousser [ʀ(ə)tʀuse] vt to roll up

retrouvailles [ʀ(ə)tʀuvɑj] nfpl reunion sg

retrouver [ʀ(ə)tʀuve] vt (*fugitif, objet perdu*) to find; (*calme, santé*) to regain; (*revoir*) to

see again; (*rejoindre*) to meet (again), join; **se** ~ vi to meet; (*s'orienter*) to find one's way; **se** ~ **quelque part** to find o.s. somewhere; **s'y** ~ (*y voir clair*) to make sense of it; (*rentrer dans ses frais*) to break even

rétroviseur [ʀetʀɔvizœʀ] nm (rear-view) mirror

réunion [ʀeynjɔ̃] nf (*séance*) meeting

réunir [ʀeyniʀ] vt (*rassembler*) to gather together; (*inviter: amis, famille*) to have round, have in; (*cumuler: qualités etc*) to combine; (*rapprocher: ennemis*) to bring together (again), reunite; (*rattacher: parties*) to join (together); **se** ~ vi (*se rencontrer*) to meet

réussi, e [ʀeysi] adj successful

réussir [ʀeysiʀ] vi to succeed, be successful; (*à un examen*) to pass ♦ vt to make a success of; ~ **à faire** to succeed in doing; ~ **à qn** (*être bénéfique à*) to agree with sb; **réussite** nf success; (*CARTES*) patience

revaloir [ʀ(ə)valwaʀ] vt: **je vous revaudrai cela** I'll repay you some day; (*en mal*) I'll pay you back for this

revanche [ʀ(ə)vɑ̃ʃ] nf revenge; (*sport*) revenge match; **en** ~ on the other hand

rêve [ʀɛv] nm dream; **de** ~ dream cpd; **faire un** ~ to have a dream

revêche [ʀəvɛʃ] adj surly, sour-tempered

réveil [ʀevɛj] nm waking up no pl; (*fig*) awakening; (*pendule*) alarm (clock); **au** ~ on waking (up); **réveille-matin** nm inv alarm clock; **réveiller** vt (*personne*) to wake up; (*fig*) to awaken, revive; **se réveiller** vi to wake up

réveillon [ʀevɛjɔ̃] nm Christmas Eve; (*de la Saint-Sylvestre*) New Year's Eve; **réveillonner** vi to celebrate Christmas Eve (ou New Year's Eve)

révélateur, -trice [ʀevelatœʀ, tʀis] adj: ~ **(de qch)** revealing (sth)

révéler [ʀevele] vt to reveal; **se** ~ vi to be revealed, reveal itself ♦ vb +attrib: **se** ~ **difficile/aisé** to prove difficult/easy

revenant, e [ʀ(ə)vənɑ̃, ɑ̃t] nm/f ghost

revendeur, -euse [ʀ(ə)vɑ̃dœʀ, øz] nm/f (*détaillant*) retailer; (*de drogue*) (drug-)dealer

revendication [ʀ(ə)vɑ̃dikasjɔ̃] nf claim, demand

revendiquer [ʀ(ə)vɑ̃dike] vt to claim, demand; (*responsabilité*) to claim

revendre [ʀ(ə)vɑ̃dʀ] vt (*d'occasion*) to resell; (*détailler*) to sell; **à** ~ (*en abondance*) to spare

revenir [ʀəv(ə)niʀ] vi to come back; (*coûter*): ~ **cher/à 100 F (à qn)** to cost (sb) a lot/100 F; ~ **à** (*reprendre: études, projet*) to return to, go back to; (*équivaloir à*) to amount to; ~ **à qn** (*part, honneur*) to go to sb, be sb's; (*souvenir, nom*) to come back to sb; ~ **sur** (*question,* *sujet)* to go back over; *(engagement)* to go back on; ~ **à soi** to come round; **n'en pas ~: je n'en reviens pas** I can't get over it; ~ **sur ses pas** to retrace one's steps; **cela revient à dire que/au même** it amounts to saying that/ the same thing; **faire ~** *(CULIN)* to brown

revenu [ʀəv(ə)ny] *nm* income; **~s** *nmpl* income *sg*

rêver [ʀeve] *vi, vt* to dream; ~ **de/à** to dream of

réverbère [ʀeveʀbɛʀ] *nm* street lamp *ou* light; **réverbérer** *vt* to reflect

révérence [ʀeveʀɑ̃s] *nf* (*salut*) bow; (*: de femme*) curtsey

rêverie [ʀɛvʀi] *nf* daydreaming *no pl*, daydream

revers [ʀ(ə)vɛʀ] *nm* (*de feuille, main*) back; (*d'étoffe*) wrong side; (*de pièce, médaille*) back, reverse; (*TENNIS, PING-PONG*) backhand; (*de veste*) lapel; (*fig: échec*) setback

revêtement [ʀ(ə)vɛtmɑ̃] *nm* (*des sols*) flooring; (*de chaussée*) surface

revêtir [ʀ(ə)vetiʀ] *vt* (*habit*) to don, put on; (*prendre: importance, apparence*) to take on; ~ **qch** to cover sth with

rêveur, -euse [ʀɛvœʀ, øz] *adj* dreamy ♦ *nm/f* dreamer

revient [ʀəvjɛ̃] *vb voir* **revenir**

revigorer [ʀ(ə)vigɔʀe] *vt* (*air frais*) to invigorate, brace up; (*repas, boisson*) to revive, buck up

revirement [ʀ(ə)viʀmɑ̃] *nm* change of mind; (*d'une situation*) reversal

réviser [ʀevize] *vt* to revise; (*machine*) to overhaul, service

révision [ʀevizjɔ̃] *nf* revision; (*de voiture*) servicing *no pl*

revivre [ʀ(ə)vivʀ] *vi* (*reprendre des forces*) to come alive again ♦ *vt* (*épreuve, moment*) to relive

revoir [ʀəvwaʀ] *vt* to see again; (*réviser*) to revise ♦ *nm*: **au ~** goodbye

révoltant, e [ʀevɔltɑ̃, ɑ̃t] *adj* revolting, appalling

révolte [ʀevɔlt] *nf* rebellion, revolt

révolter [ʀevɔlte] *vt* to revolt; **se ~ (contre)** to rebel (against); **ça me révolte (de voir que ...)** I'm revolted *ou* appalled (to see that ...)

révolu, e [ʀevɔly] *adj* past; (*ADMIN*): **âgé de 18 ans ~s** over 18 years of age

révolution [ʀevɔlysjɔ̃] *nf* revolution; **révolutionnaire** *adj, nm/f* revolutionary

revolver [ʀevɔlvɛʀ] *nm* gun; (*à barillet*) revolver

révoquer [ʀevɔke] *vt* (*fonctionnaire*) to dismiss; (*arrêt, contrat*) to revoke

revue [ʀ(ə)vy] *nf* review; (*périodique*) review, magazine; (*de music-hall*) variety show; **passer en ~** (*mentalement*) to go through

rez-de-chaussée [ʀed(ə)ʃose] *nm inv* ground floor

RF *sigle f* = **République française**

Rhin [ʀɛ̃] *nm* Rhine

rhinocéros [ʀinɔseʀɔs] *nm* rhinoceros

Rhône [ʀon] *nm* Rhone

rhubarbe [ʀybaʀb] *nf* rhubarb

rhum [ʀɔm] *nm* rum

rhumatisme [ʀymatism] *nm* rheumatism *no pl*

rhume [ʀym] *nm* cold; ~ **de cerveau** head cold; **le ~ des foins** hay fever

ri [ʀi] *pp de* **rire**

riant, e [ʀ(i)jɑ̃, ʀ(i)jɑ̃t] *adj* smiling, cheerful

ricaner [ʀikane] *vi* (*avec méchanceté*) to snigger; (*bêtement*) to giggle

riche [ʀiʃ] *adj* rich; (*personne, pays*) rich, wealthy; ~ **en** rich in; **richesse** *nf* wealth; (*fig: de sol, musée etc*) richness; **richesses** *nfpl* (*ressources, argent*) wealth *sg*; (*fig: trésors*) treasures

ricochet [ʀikɔʃɛ] *nm*: **faire des ~s** to skip stones; **par ~** (*fig*) as an indirect result

rictus [ʀiktys] *nm* grin

ride [ʀid] *nf* wrinkle

rideau, x [ʀido] *nm* curtain; ~ **de fer** (*boutique*) metal shutter(s)

rider [ʀide] *vt* to wrinkle; **se ~** *vi* to become wrinkled

ridicule [ʀidikyl] *adj* ridiculous ♦ *nm*: **le ~** ridicule; **ridiculiser: se ridiculiser** *vi* to make a fool of o.s.

MOT-CLÉ

rien [ʀjɛ̃] *pron* **1**: (**ne**) ... **rien** nothing; *tournure negative + anything*; **qu'est-ce que vous avez? – rien** what have you got? – nothing; **il n'a rien dit/fait** he said/did nothing; he hasn't said/done anything; **il n'a rien** (*n'est pas blessé*) he's all right; **de rien!** not at all!
2 (*quelque chose*): **a-t-il jamais rien fait pour nous?** has he ever done anything for us?
3: **rien de**: **rien d'intéressant** nothing interesting; **rien d'autre** nothing else; **rien du tout** nothing at all
4: **rien que** just, only; nothing but; **rien que pour lui faire plaisir** only *ou* just to please him; **rien que la vérité** nothing but the truth; **rien que cela** that alone
♦ *nm*: **un petit rien** (*cadeau*) a little something; **des riens** trivia *pl*; **un rien de** a hint of; **en un rien de temps** in no time at all

---

rieur, -euse [ʀ(i)jœʀ, ʀ(i)jøz] *adj* cheerful

rigide [ʀiʒid] *adj* stiff; (*fig*) rigid; strict

rigole [ʀigɔl] *nf* (*conduit*) channel

rigoler [ʀigɔle] *vi* (*fam: rire*) to laugh; (*s'amuser*) to have (some) fun; (*plaisanter*) to be joking *ou* kidding; **rigolo, -ote** (*fam*) *adj* funny ♦ nm/f comic; (péj) fraud, phoney

rigoureusement [ʀiguʀøzmɑ̃] adv (vrai) absolutely; (interdit) strictly

rigoureux, -euse [ʀiguʀø, øz] adj rigorous; (hiver) hard, harsh

rigueur [ʀigœʀ] nf rigour; **être de ~** to be the rule; **à la ~** at a pinch; **tenir ~ à qn de qch** to hold sth against sb

rillettes [ʀijɛt] nfpl potted meat (made from pork or goose)

rime [ʀim] nf rhyme

rinçage [ʀɛ̃saʒ] nm rinsing (out); (opération) rinse

rincer [ʀɛ̃se] vt to rinse; (récipient) to rinse out

ring [ʀiŋ] nm (boxing) ring

ringard, e [ʀɛ̃gaʀ, aʀd] (fam) adj old-fashioned

rions [ʀiɔ̃] vb voir **rire**

riposter [ʀipɔste] vi to retaliate ♦ vt: **~ que** to retort that

rire [ʀiʀ] vi to laugh; (se divertir) to have fun ♦ nm laugh; **le ~** laughter; **~ de** to laugh at; **pour ~** (pas sérieusement) for a joke ou a laugh

risée [ʀize] nf: **être la ~ de** to be the laughing stock of

risible [ʀizibl] adj laughable

risque [ʀisk] nm risk; **le ~** danger; **à ses ~s et périls** at his own risk; **risqué, e** adj risky; (plaisanterie) risqué, daring; **risquer** vt to risk; (allusion, question) to venture, hazard; **ça ne risque rien** it's quite safe; **risquer de: il risque de se tuer** he could get himself killed; **ce qui risque de se produire** what might ou could well happen; **il ne risque pas de recommencer** there's no chance of him doing that again; **se risquer à faire** (tenter) to venture ou dare to do

rissoler [ʀisɔle] vi, vt: **(faire) ~** to brown

ristourne [ʀistuʀn] nf discount

rite [ʀit] nm rite; (fig) ritual

rivage [ʀivaʒ] nm shore

rival, e, -aux [ʀival, o] adj, nm/f rival; **rivaliser** vi: **rivaliser avec** (personne) to rival, vie with; **rivalité** nf rivalry

rive [ʀiv] nf shore; (de fleuve) bank; **riverain, e** nm/f riverside (ou lakeside) resident; (d'une route) local resident

rivet [ʀivɛ] nm rivet

rivière [ʀivjɛʀ] nf river

rixe [ʀiks] nf brawl, scuffle

riz [ʀi] nm rice; **rizière** nf paddy-field, ricefield

RMI sigle m (= revenu minimum d'insertion) ≈ income support (BRIT), welfare (US)

RN sigle f = **route nationale**

robe [ʀɔb] nf dress; (de juge) robe; (pelage) coat; **~ de chambre** dressing gown; **~ de soirée/de mariée** evening/wedding dress

robinet [ʀɔbinɛ] nm tap

robot [ʀɔbo] nm robot

robuste [ʀɔbyst] adj robust, sturdy; **robustesse** nf robustness, sturdiness

roc [ʀɔk] nm rock

rocade [ʀɔkad] nf bypass

rocaille [ʀɔkaj] nf loose stones pl; (jardin) rockery, rock garden

roche [ʀɔʃ] nf rock

rocher [ʀɔʃe] nm rock

rocheux, -euse [ʀɔʃø, øz] adj rocky

rodage [ʀɔdaʒ] nm: **en ~** running in

roder [ʀɔde] vt (AUTO) to run in

rôder [ʀɔde] vi to roam about; (de façon suspecte) to lurk (about ou around); **rôdeur, -euse** nm/f prowler

rogne [ʀɔɲ] (fam) nf: **être en ~** to be in a temper

rogner [ʀɔɲe] vt to clip; **~ sur** (fig) to cut down ou back on

rognons [ʀɔɲɔ̃] nmpl (CULIN) kidneys

roi [ʀwa] nm king; **la fête des R~s, les R~s** Twelfth Night

rôle [ʀol] nm role, part

romain, e [ʀɔmɛ̃, ɛn] adj Roman ♦ nm/f: **R~, e** Roman

roman, e [ʀɔmɑ̃, an] adj (ARCHIT) Romanesque ♦ nm novel; **~ d'espionnage** spy novel ou story; **~ policier** detective story

romance [ʀɔmɑ̃s] nf ballad

romancer [ʀɔmɑ̃se] vt (agrémenter) to romanticize; **romancier, -ière** nm/f novelist; **romanesque** nf (amours, aventures) storybook cpd; (sentimental: personne) romantic

roman-feuilleton [ʀɔmɑ̃fœjtɔ̃] nm serialized novel

romanichel, le [ʀɔmaniʃɛl] (péj) nm/f gipsy

romantique [ʀɔmɑ̃tik] adj romantic

romarin [ʀɔmaʀɛ̃] nm rosemary

rompre [ʀɔ̃pʀ] vt to break; (entretien, fiançailles) to break off ♦ vi (fiancés) to break it off; **se ~** vi to break; **rompu, e** adj (fourbu) exhausted

ronces [ʀɔ̃s] nfpl brambles

ronchonner [ʀɔ̃ʃɔne] (fam) vi to grouse, grouch

rond, e [ʀɔ̃, ʀɔ̃d] adj round; (joues, mollets) well-rounded; (fam: ivre) tight ♦ nm (cercle) ring; (fam: sou): **je n'ai plus un ~** I haven't a penny left; **en ~** (s'asseoir, danser) in a ring; **ronde** nf (gén: de surveillance) rounds pl, patrol; (danse) round (dance); (MUS) semibreve (BRIT), whole note (US); **à la ronde** (alentour): **à 10 km à la ronde** for 10 km round; **rondelet, te** adj plump

rondelle [ʀɔ̃dɛl] nf (tranche) slice, round; (TECH) washer

rondement [ʀɔ̃dmɑ̃] adv (efficacement)

briskly

rondin [ʀɔ̃dɛ̃] *nm* log

rond-point [ʀɔ̃pwɛ̃] *nm* roundabout

ronflant, e [ʀɔ̃flɑ̃, ɑ̃t] *(péj) adj* high-flown, grand

ronflement [ʀɔ̃fləmɑ̃] *nm* snore, snoring

ronfler [ʀɔ̃fle] *vi* to snore; *(moteur, poêle)* to hum

ronger [ʀɔ̃ʒe] *vt* to gnaw (at); *(suj: vers, rouille)* to eat into; **se ~ les ongles** to bite one's nails; **se ~ les sangs** to worry o.s. sick; **rongeur** *nm* rodent

ronronner [ʀɔ̃ʀɔne] *vi* to purr

rosace [ʀozas] *nf (vitrail)* rose window

rosbif [ʀɔsbif] *nm*: **du ~** roasting beef; *(cuit)* roast beef

rose [ʀoz] *nf* rose ♦ *adj* pink

rosé, e [ʀoze] *adj* pinkish; **(vin) ~ rosé**

roseau, x [ʀozo] *nm* reed

rosée [ʀoze] *nf* dew

rosette [ʀozɛt] *nf (nœud)* bow

rosier [ʀozje] *nm* rosebush, rose tree

rosse [ʀɔs] *(fam) adj* nasty, vicious

rossignol [ʀɔsiɲɔl] *nm (ZOOL)* nightingale

rot [ʀo] *nm* belch; *(de bébé)* burp

rotatif, -ive [ʀɔtatif, iv] *adj* rotary

rotation [ʀɔtasjɔ̃] *nf* rotation

roter [ʀɔte] *(fam) vi* to burp, belch

rôti [ʀoti] *nm*: **du ~** roasting meat; *(cuit)* roast meat; **~ de bœuf/porc** joint of beef/pork

rotin [ʀɔtɛ̃] *nm* rattan (cane); **fauteuil en ~** cane (arm)chair

rôtir [ʀotiʀ] *vi, vt (aussi:* **faire ~)** to roast; **rôtisserie** *nf (restaurant)* steakhouse; *(traiteur)* roast meat shop; **rôtissoire** *nf (roasting)* spit

rotule [ʀɔtyl] *nf* kneecap

roturier, -ière [ʀɔtyʀje, jɛʀ] *nm/f* commoner

rouage [ʀwaʒ] *nm* cog(wheel), gearwheel; **les ~s de l'État** the wheels of State

roucouler [ʀukule] *vi* to coo

roue [ʀu] *nf* wheel; **~ de secours** spare wheel

roué, e [ʀwe] *adj* wily

rouer [ʀwe] *vt*: **~ qn de coups** to give sb a thrashing

rouge [ʀuʒ] *adj, nm/f* red ♦ *nm* red; **(vin) ~** red wine; **sur la liste ~** ex-directory *(BRIT)*, unlisted *(US)*; **passer au ~** *(signal)* to go red; *(automobiliste)* to go through a red light; **~ (à lèvres)** lipstick; **rouge-gorge** *nm* robin (redbreast)

rougeole [ʀuʒɔl] *nf* measles *sg*

rougeoyer [ʀuʒwaje] *vi* to glow red

rouget [ʀuʒɛ] *nm* mullet

rougeur [ʀuʒœʀ] *nf* redness; *(MÉD: tache)* red blotch

rougir [ʀuʒiʀ] *vi* to turn red; *(de honte, timidité)* to blush, flush; *(de plaisir, colère)* to

flush

rouille [ʀuj] *nf* rust; **rouillé, e** *adj* rusty; **rouiller** *vt* to rust ♦ *vi* to rust, go rusty; **se rouiller** *vi* to rust

roulant, e [ʀulɑ̃, ɑ̃t] *adj (meuble)* on wheels; *(tapis etc)* moving; **escalier ~** escalator

rouleau, x [ʀulo] *nm* roll; *(à mise en plis, à peinture, vague)* roller; **~ à pâtisserie** rolling pin

roulement [ʀulmɑ̃] *nm (rotation)* rotation; *(bruit)* rumbling *no pl,* rumble; **travailler par ~** to work on a rota *(BRIT)* ou rotation *(US)* basis; **~ (à billes)** ball bearings *pl;* **~ de tambour** drum roll

rouler [ʀule] *vt* to roll; *(papier, tapis)* to roll up; *(CULIN: pâte)* to roll out; *(fam: duper)* to do, con ♦ *vi (bille, boule)* to roll; *(voiture, train)* to go, run; *(automobiliste)* to drive; *(bateau)* to roll; **se ~ dans** *(boue)* to roll in; *(couverture)* to roll o.s. (up) in

roulette [ʀulɛt] *nf (de table, fauteuil)* castor; *(de dentiste)* drill; *(jeu)* roulette; **à ~s** on castors; **ça a marché comme sur des ~s** *(fam)* it went off very smoothly

roulis [ʀuli] *nm* roll(ing)

roulotte [ʀulɔt] *nf* caravan

roumain, e [ʀumɛ̃, ɛn] *adj* Rumanian ♦ *nm/f:* **R~, e** Rumanian

Roumanie [ʀumani] *nf* Rumania

rouquin, e [ʀukɛ̃, in] *(péj) nm/f* redhead

rouspéter [ʀuspete] *(fam) vi* to moan

rousse [ʀus] *adj voir* **roux**

roussir [ʀusiʀ] *vt* to scorch ♦ *vi (CULIN):* **faire ~** to brown

route [ʀut] *nf* road; *(fig: chemin)* way; *(itinéraire, parcours)* route; *(fig: voie)* road, path; **il y a 3h de ~** it's a 3-hour ride ou journey; **en ~** on the way; **mettre en ~** to start up; **se mettre en ~** to set off; **~ nationale** ≈ A road *(BRIT)*, ≈ state highway *(US)*; **routier, -ière** *adj* road *cpd* ♦ *nm (camionneur)* (long-distance) lorry *(BRIT)* ou truck *(US)* driver; *(restaurant)* ≈ transport café *(BRIT)*, ≈ truck stop *(US)*

routine [ʀutin] *nf* routine; **routinier, -ière** *(péj) adj (activité)* humdrum; *(personne)* addicted to routine

rouvrir [ʀuvʀiʀ] *vt, vi* to reopen, open again; **se ~** *vi* to reopen, open again

roux, rousse [ʀu, ʀus] *adj* red; *(personne)* red-haired ♦ *nm/f* redhead

royal, e, -aux [ʀwajal, o] *adj* royal; *(cadeau etc)* fit for a king

royaume [ʀwajom] *nm* kingdom; *(fig)* realm; **le R~-Uni** the United Kingdom

royauté [ʀwajote] *nf (régime)* monarchy

RPR *sigle m*: **Rassemblement pour la République** *French right-wing political party*

ruban [ʀybɑ̃] *nm* ribbon; **~ adhésif** adhesive

tape

rubéole [ʀybeɔl] nf German measles sg, rubella

rubis [ʀybi] nm ruby

rubrique [ʀybʀik] nf (titre, catégorie) heading; (PRESSE: article) column

ruche [ʀyʃ] nf hive

rude [ʀyd] adj (au toucher) rough; (métier, tâche) hard, tough; (climat) severe, harsh; (bourru) harsh, rough; (fruste: manières) rugged, tough; (fam: fameux) jolly good; **rudement** (fam) adv (très) terribly

rudimentaire [ʀydimɑ̃tɛʀ] adj rudimentary, basic

rudiments [ʀydimɑ̃] nmpl: **avoir des ~ d'anglais** to have a smattering of English

rudoyer [ʀydwaje] vt to treat harshly

rue [ʀy] nf street

ruée [ʀɥe] nf rush

ruelle [ʀɥɛl] nf alley(-way)

ruer [ʀɥe] vi (cheval) to kick out; **se ~** vi: **se ~ sur** to pounce on; **se ~ vers/dans/hors de** to rush ou dash towards/into/out of

rugby [ʀygbi] nm rugby (football)

rugir [ʀyʒiʀ] vi to roar

rugueux, -euse [ʀygø, øz] adj rough

ruine [ʀɥin] nf ruin; **ruiner** vt to ruin; **ruineux, -euse** adj ruinous

ruisseau, x [ʀɥiso] nm stream, brook

ruisseler [ʀɥis(ə)le] vi to stream

rumeur [ʀymœʀ] nf (nouvelle) rumour; (bruit confus) rumbling

ruminer [ʀymine] vt (herbe) to ruminate; (fig) to ruminate on ou over, chew over

rupture [ʀyptyʀ] nf (séparation, désunion) break-up, split; (de négociations etc) breakdown; (de contrat) breach; (dans continuité) break

rural, e, -aux [ʀyʀal, o] adj rural, country cpd

ruse [ʀyz] nf: **la ~** cunning, craftiness; (pour tromper) trickery; **une ~** a trick, a ruse; **rusé, e** adj cunning, crafty

russe [ʀys] adj Russian ♦ nm/f: **R~** Russian ♦ nm (LING) Russian

Russie [ʀysi] nf: **la ~** Russia

rustine ® [ʀystin] nf rubber repair patch (for bicycle tyre)

rustique [ʀystik] adj rustic

rustre [ʀystʀ] nm boor

rutilant, e [ʀytilɑ̃, ɑ̃t] adj gleaming

rythme [ʀitm] nm rhythm; (vitesse) rate; (: de la vie) pace, tempo; **rythmé, e** adj rhythmic(al)

S, s

s' [s] pron voir **se**

sa [sa] adj voir **son¹**

SA sigle (= société anonyme) ≈ Ltd (BRIT), ≈ Inc. (US)

sable [sabl] nm sand; **~s mouvants** quicksand(s)

sablé [sable] nm shortbread biscuit

sabler [sable] vt (contre le verglas) to grit; **~ le champagne** to drink champagne

sablier [sablije] nm hourglass; (de cuisine) egg timer

sablonneux, -euse [sablɔnø, øz] adj sandy

saborder [sabɔʀde] vt (navire) to scuttle; (fig: projet) to put paid to, scupper

sabot [sabo] nm clog; (de cheval) hoof; **~ de frein** brake shoe

saboter [sabɔte] vt to sabotage; (bâcler) to make a mess of, botch

sac [sak] nm bag; (à charbon etr) sack; **~ à dos** rucksack; **~ à main** handbag; **~ de couchage** sleeping bag; **~ de voyage** travelling bag; **~ poubelle** bin liner

saccadé, e [sakade] adj jerky; (respiration) spasmodic

saccager [sakaʒe] vt (piller) to sack; (dévaster) to create havoc in

saccharine [sakaʀin] nf saccharin

sacerdoce [sasɛʀdɔs] nm priesthood; (fig) calling, vocation

sache etc [saʃ] vb voir **savoir**

sachet [saʃɛ] nm (small) bag; (de sucre, café) sachet; **du potage en ~** packet soup; **~ de thé** tea bag

sacoche [sakɔʃ] nf (gén) bag; (de bicyclette) saddlebag

sacquer [sake] (fam) vt (employé) to fire; (détester): **je ne peux pas le ~** I can't stand him

sacre [sakʀ] nm (roi) coronation

sacré, e [sakʀe] adj sacred; (fam: satané) blasted; (: fameux): **un ~ toupé** a heck of a cheek

sacrement [sakʀəmɑ̃] nm sacrament

sacrifice [sakʀifis] nm sacrifice; **sacrifier** vt to sacrifice

sacristie [sakʀisti] nf (catholique) sacristy; (protestante) vestry

sadique [sadik] adj sadistic

safran [safʀɑ̃] nm saffron

sage [saʒ] adj wise; (enfant) good

sage-femme [saʒfam] nf midwife

sagesse [saʒɛs] nf wisdom

Sagittaire [saʒitɛʀ] nm: **le ~** Sagittarius

Sahara [saaʀa] nm: **le ~** the Sahara (desert)

saignant, e [sɛɲɑ̃, ɑ̃t] adj (viande) rare

saignée [seɲe] nf (fig) heavy losses pl

saigner [seɲe] vi to bleed ♦ vt to bleed; (animal) to kill (by bleeding); **~ du nez** to have a nosebleed

saillie [saji] nf (sur un mur etc) projection

saillir [sajiʀ] vi to project, stick out; (veine, muscle) to bulge

sain, e [sɛ̃, sɛn] adj healthy; **~ d'esprit** sound in mind, sane; **~ et sauf** safe and sound, unharmed

saindoux [sɛ̃du] nm lard

saint, e [sɛ̃, sɛt] adj holy ♦ nm/f saint; **le S~ Esprit** the Holy Spirit ou Ghost; **la S~e Vierge** the Blessed Virgin; **la S~-Sylvestre** New Year's Eve; **sainteté** nf holiness

sais etc [se] vb voir **savoir**

saisi, e [sezi] adj: **~ de panique** panic-stricken; **être ~** (par le froid) to be struck by the sudden cold

saisie nf seizure; **~e (de données)** (data) capture

saisir [seziʀ] vt to take hold of, grab; (fig: occasion) to seize; (comprendre) to grasp; (entendre) to get, catch; (données) to capture; (CULIN) to fry quickly; (JUR: biens, publication) to seize; **se ~ de** vt to seize; **saisissant, e** adj startling, striking

saison [sɛzɔ̃] nf season; **morte ~** slack season; **saisonnier, -ière** adj seasonal

sait [se] vb voir **savoir**

salade [salad] nf (BOT) lettuce etc; (CULIN) (green) salad; (fam: confusion) tangle, muddle; **~ composée** mixed salad; **~ de fruits** fruit salad; **saladier** nm (salad) bowl

salaire [salɛʀ] nm (annuel, mensuel) salary; (hebdomadaire, journalier) pay, wages pl; **~ minimum interprofessionnel de croissance** index-linked guaranteed minimum wage

salarié, e [salaʀje] nm/f salaried employee; wage-earner

salaud [salo] (fam!) nm sod (!), bastard (!)

sale [sal] adj dirty, filthy; (fam: mauvais) nasty

salé, e [sale] adj (mer, goût) salty; (CULIN: amandes, beurre etc) salted; (: gâteaux) savoury; (fam: grivois) spicy; (: facture) steep

saler [sale] vt to salt

saleté [salte] nf (état) dirtiness; (crasse) dirt, filth; (tache etc) dirt no pl; (fam: méchanceté) dirty trick; (: camelote) rubbish no pl; (: obscénité) filthy thing (to say)

salière [saljɛʀ] nf saltcellar

salin, e [salɛ̃, in] adj saline

salir [saliʀ] vt to (make) dirty; (fig: quelqu'un) to soil the reputation of; **se ~** vi to get dirty; **salissant, e** adj (tissu) which shows the dirt; (travail) dirty, messy

salle [sal] nf room; (d'hôpital) ward; (de restaurant) dining room; (d'un cinéma) auditorium; (: public) audience; **~ à manger**

dining room; **~ d'attente** waiting room; **~ de bain(s)** bathroom; **~ de classe** classroom; **~ de concert** concert hall; **~ d'eau** shower-room; **~ d'embarquement** (à l'aéroport) departure lounge; **~ de jeux** (pour enfants) playroom; **~ d'opération** (d'hôpital) operating theatre; **~ de séjour** living room; **~ des ventes** saleroom

salon [salɔ̃] nm lounge, sitting room; (mobilier) lounge suite; (exposition) exhibition, show; **~ de coiffure** hairdressing salon; **~ de thé** tearoom

salope [salɔp] (fam!) nf bitch (!); **saloperie** (fam!) nf (action) dirty trick; (chose sans valeur) rubbish no pl

salopette [salɔpɛt] nf dungarees pl; (d'ouvrier) overall(s)

salsifis [salsifi] nm salsify

salubre [salybʀ] adj healthy, salubrious

saluer [salɥe] vt (pour dire bonjour, fig) to greet; (pour dire au revoir) to take one's leave; (MIL) to salute

salut [saly] nm (geste) wave; (parole) greeting; (MIL) salute; (sauvegarde) safety; (REL) salvation ♦ excl (fam: bonjour) hi (there); (: au revoir) see you, bye

salutations [salytasjɔ̃] nfpl greetings; **Veuillez agréer, Monsieur, mes ~ distinguées** yours faithfully

samedi [samdi] nm Saturday

SAMU [samy] sigle m (= service d'assistance médicale d'urgence) ≈ ambulance (service) (BRIT), ≈ paramedics pl (US)

sanction [sɑ̃ksjɔ̃] nf sanction; **sanctionner** vt (loi, usage) to sanction; (punir) to punish

sandale [sɑ̃dal] nf sandal

sandwich [sɑ̃dwi(t)ʃ] nm sandwich

sang [sɑ̃] nm blood; **en ~** covered in blood; **se faire du mauvais ~** to fret, get in a state; **sang-froid** nm calm, sangfroid; **de sang-froid** in cold blood; **sanglant, e** adj bloody

sangle [sɑ̃gl] nf strap

sanglier [sɑ̃glije] nm (wild) boar

sanglot [sɑ̃glo] nm sob; **sangloter** vi to sob

sangsue [sɑ̃sy] nf leech

sanguin, e [sɑ̃gɛ̃, in] adj blood cpd; **sanguinaire** adj bloodthirsty

sanitaire [sanitɛʀ] adj health cpd; **~s** nmpl (lieu) bathroom sg

sans [sɑ̃] prép without; **un pull ~ manches** a sleeveless jumper; **~ faute** without fail; **~ arrêt** without a break; **~ ça** (fam) otherwise; **~ qu'il s'en aperçoive** without him ou his noticing; **sans-abri** nmpl homeless; **sans-emploi** nm/f inv unemployed person; **les sans-emploi** the unemployed; **sans-gêne** adj inv inconsiderate

santé [sɑ̃te] nf health; **en bonne ~** in good health; **boire à la ~ de qn** to drink (to) sb's health; **à ta/votre ~!** cheers!

saoudien, ne [saudjɛ̃, jɛn] *adj* Saudi Arabian
♦ *nm/f*: **S~, ne** Saudi Arabian

saoul, e [su, sul] *adj* = **soûl**

saper [sape] *vt* to undermine, sap

sapeur-pompier [sapœʀpɔ̃pje] *nm* fireman

saphir [safiʀ] *nm* sapphire

sapin [sapɛ̃] *nm* fir (tree); (*bois*) fir; **~ de Noël** Christmas tree

sarcastique [saʀkastik] *adj* sarcastic

sarcler [saʀkle] *vt* to weed

Sardaigne [saʀdɛɲ] *nf*: **la ~** Sardinia

sardine [saʀdin] *nf* sardine

sarrasin [saʀazɛ̃] *nm* buckwheat

SARL *sigle f* (= *société à responsabilité limitée*)
≈ plc (*BRIT*), ≈ Inc. (*US*)

sas [sas] *nm* (*de sous-marin, d'engin spatial*)
airlock; (*d'écluse*) lock

satané, e [satane] (*fam*) *adj* confounded

satellite [satelit] *nm* satellite

satin [satɛ̃] *nm* satin

satire [satiʀ] *nf* satire; **satirique** *adj* satirical

satisfaction [satisfaksjɔ̃] *nf* satisfaction

satisfaire [satisfɛʀ] *vt* to satisfy; **~ à**
(*conditions*) to meet; **satisfaisant, e** *adj*
(*acceptable*) satisfactory; **satisfait, e** *adj*
satisfied; **satisfait de** happy *ou* satisfied with

saturer [satyʀe] *vt* to saturate

sauce [sos] *nf* sauce; (*avec un rôti*) gravy;
saucière *nf* sauceboat

saucisse [sosis] *nf* sausage

saucisson [sosisɔ̃] *nm* (slicing) sausage

sauf [sof, sov] *adj* unharmed,
unhurt; (*fig*: *honneur*) intact, saved ♦ *prép*
except; **laisser la vie sauve à qn** to spare sb's
life; **~ si** (*à moins que*) unless; **~ erreur** if I'm
not mistaken; **~ avis contraire** unless you hear
to the contrary

sauge [soʒ] *nf* sage

saugrenu, e [sogʀəny] *adj* preposterous

saule [sol] *nm* willow (tree)

saumon [somɔ̃] *nm* salmon *inv*

saumure [somyʀ] *nf* brine

saupoudrer [sopudʀe] *vt*: **~ qch de** to
sprinkle sth with

saur [sɔʀ] *adj m*: **hareng ~** smoked *ou* red
herring, kipper

saurai *etc* [sɔʀe] *vb voir* **savoir**

saut [so] *nm* jump; (*discipline sportive*)
jumping; **faire un ~ chez qn** to pop over to
sb's (place); **~ à l'élastique** bungee jumping;
~ à la perche pole vaulting; **~ en hauteur/
longueur** high/long jump; **~ périlleux**
somersault

saute [sot] *nf*: **~ d'humeur** sudden change of
mood

sauter [sote] *vi* to jump, leap; (*exploser*) to
blow up, explode; (*: fusibles*) to blow; (*se
détacher*) to pop out (*ou* off) ♦ *vt* to jump

(over), leap (over); (*fig*: *omettre*) to skip,
miss (out); **faire ~** to blow up; (*CULIN*) to
sauté; **~ au cou de qn** to fly into sb's arms;
~ sur une occasion to jump at an
opportunity; **~ aux yeux** to be (quite) obvious

sauterelle [sotʀɛl] *nf* grasshopper

sautiller [sotije] *vi* (*oiseau*) to hop; (*enfant*)
to skip

sauvage [sovaʒ] *adj* (*gén*) wild; (*peuplade*)
savage; (*farouche*: *personne*) unsociable;
(*barbare*) wild, savage; (*non officiel*)
unauthorized, unofficial; **faire du camping ~**
to camp in the wild ♦ *nm/f* savage; (*timide*)
unsociable type

sauve [sov] *adj f voir* **sauf**

sauvegarde [sovgaʀd] *nf* safeguard;
(*INFORM*) backup; **sauvegarder** *vt* to
safeguard; (*INFORM*: *enregistrer*) to save;
(*: copier*) to back up

sauve-qui-peut [sovkipø] *excl* run for your
life!

sauver [sove] *vt* to save; (*porter secours à*) to
rescue; (*récupérer*) to salvage, rescue; **se ~** *vi*
(*s'enfuir*) to run away; (*fam*: *partir*) to be off;
sauvetage *nm* rescue; **sauveteur** *nm*
rescuer; **sauvette**: **à la sauvette** *adv* (*se
marier etc*) hastily, hurriedly; **sauveur** *nm*
saviour (*BRIT*), savior (*US*)

savais *etc* [save] *vb voir* **savoir**

savamment [savamɑ̃] *adv* (*avec érudition*)
learnedly; (*habilement*) skilfully, cleverly

savant, e [savɑ̃, ɑ̃t] *adj* scholarly, learned
♦ *nm* scientist

saveur [savœʀ] *nf* flavour; (*fig*) savour

savoir [savwaʀ] *vt* to know; (*être capable de*):
il sait nager he can swim ♦ *nm* knowledge;
se ~ *vi* (*être connu*) to be known; **à ~** that is,
namely; **faire ~ qch à qn** to let sb know sth;
pas que je sache not as far as I know

savon [savɔ̃] *nm* (*produit*) soap; (*morceau*)
bar of soap; (*fam*): **passer un ~ à qn** to give
sb a good dressing-down; **savonner** *vt* to
soap; **savonnette** *nf* bar of soap

savons [savɔ̃] *vb voir* **savoir**

savourer [savuʀe] *vt* to savour; **savoureux,
-euse** *adj* tasty; (*fig*: *anecdote*) spicy, juicy

saxo(phone) [saksɔ(fɔn)] *nm* sax(ophone)

scabreux, -euse [skabʀø, øz] *adj* risky;
(*indécent*) improper, shocking

scandale [skɑ̃dal] *nm* scandal; (*tapage*): **faire
un ~** to make a scene, create a disturbance;
faire ~ to scandalize people; **scandaleux,
-euse** *adj* scandalous, outrageous

scandinave [skɑ̃dinav] *adj* Scandinavian
♦ *nm/f*: **S~** Scandinavian

Scandinavie [skɑ̃dinavi] *nf* Scandinavia

scaphandre [skafɑ̃dʀ] *nm* (*de plongeur*)
diving suit

scarabée [skaʀabe] *nm* beetle

scarlatine [skaʀlatin] *nf* scarlet fever
scarole [skaʀɔl] *nf* endive
sceau, x [so] *nm* seal
scélérat, e [selera, at] *nm/f* villain
sceller [sele] *vt* to seal
scénario [senarjo] *nm* scenario
scène [sɛn] *nf* (*gén*) scene; (*estrade, fig*: *théâtre*) stage; **entrer en ~** to come on stage; **mettre en ~** (*THÉÂTRE*) to stage; (*CINÉMA*) to direct; **~ de ménage** domestic scene
sceptique [sɛptik] *adj* sceptical
schéma [ʃema] *nm* (*diagramme*) diagram, sketch; **schématique** *adj* diagrammatic(al), schematic; (*fig*) oversimplified
sciatique [sjatik] *nf* sciatica
scie [si] *nf* saw; **~ à métaux** hacksaw
sciemment [sjamā] *adv* knowingly
science [sjãs] *nf* science; (*savoir*) knowledge; **~s naturelles** (*SCOL*) natural science *sg*, biology *sg*; **~s po** political science *ou* studies *pl*; **science-fiction** *nf* science fiction; **scientifique** *adj* scientific ♦ *nm/f* scientist; (*étudiant*) science student
scier [sje] *vt* to saw; (*retrancher*) to saw off; **scierie** *nf* sawmill
scinder [sɛ̃de] *vt* to split up; **se ~** *vi* to split up
scintiller [sɛ̃tije] *vi* to sparkle; (*étoile*) to twinkle
scission [sisjɔ̃] *nf* split
sciure [sjyʀ] *nf*: **~ (de bois)** sawdust
sclérose [skleʀoz] *nf*: **~ en plaques** multiple sclerosis
scolaire [skɔlɛʀ] *adj* school *cpd*; **scolariser** *vt* to provide with schooling/schools; **scolarité** *nf* schooling
scooter [skutœʀ] *nm* (motor) scooter
score [skɔʀ] *nm* score
scorpion [skɔʀpjɔ̃] *nm* (*signe*): **le S~** Scorpio
Scotch ® [skɔtʃ] *nm* adhesive tape
scout, e [skut] *adj, nm* scout
script [skʀipt] *nm* (*écriture*) printing; (*CINÉMA*) (shooting) script
scrupule [skʀypyl] *nm* scruple
scruter [skʀyte] *vt* to scrutinize; (*l'obscurité*) to peer into
scrutin [skʀytɛ̃] *nm* (*vote*) ballot; (*ensemble des opérations*) poll
sculpter [skylte] *vt* to sculpt; (*bois*) to carve; **sculpteur** *nm* sculptor; **sculpture** *nf* sculpture; **sculpture sur bois** wood carving
SDF *sigle m* (= *sans domicile fixe*) homeless person; **les SDF** the homeless

---

MOT-CLÉ

se [sə], **s'** *pron* **1** (*emploi réfléchi*) oneself; (: *masc*) himself; (: *fém*) herself; (: *sujet non humain*) itself; (: *pl*) themselves; **se voir comme l'on est** to see o.s. as one is
2 (*réciproque*) one another, each other; **ils**

s'aiment they love one another *ou* each other
3 (*passif*): **cela se répare facilement** it is easily repaired
4 (*possessif*): **se casser la jambe/laver les mains** to break one's leg/wash one's hands

---

séance [seɑ̃s] *nf* (*d'assemblée*) meeting, session; (*de tribunal*) sitting, session; (*musicale, CINÉMA, THÉÂTRE*) performance; **~ tenante** forthwith
seau, x [so] *nm* bucket, pail
sec, sèche [sɛk, sɛʃ] *adj* dry; (*raisins, figues*) dried; (*cœur: insensible*) hard, cold ♦ *nm*: **tenir au ~** to keep in a dry place ♦ *adv* hard; **je le bois ~** I drink it straight *ou* neat; **à ~** (*puits*) dried up
sécateur [sekatœʀ] *nm* secateurs *pl* (*BRIT*), shears *pl*
sèche [sɛʃ] *adj f voir* **sec**; **sèche-cheveux** *nm inv* hair-drier; **sèche-linge** *nm inv* tumble dryer; **sèchement** *adv* (*répondre*) drily
sécher [seʃe] *vt* to dry; (*dessécher: peau, blé*) to dry (out); (: *étang*) to dry up; (*fam: cours*) to skip ♦ *vi* to dry; to dry out; to dry up; (*fam: candidat*) to be stumped; **se ~** (*après le bain*) to dry o.s.; **sécheresse** *nf* dryness; (*absence de pluie*) drought; **séchoir** *nm* drier
second, e [s(ə)gɔ̃, ɔ̃d] *adj* second ♦ *nm* (*assistant*) second in command; (*NAVIG*) first mate; **voyager en ~e** to travel second-class; **secondaire** *adj* secondary; **seconde** *nf* second; **seconder** *vt* to assist
secouer [s(ə)kwe] *vt* to shake; (*passagers*) to rock; (*traumatiser*) to shake (up); **se ~** *vi* (*fam: faire un effort*) to shake o.s. up; (: *se dépêcher*) to get a move on
secourir [s(ə)kuʀiʀ] *vt* (*venir en aide à*) to assist, aid; **secourisme** *nm* first aid; **secouriste** *nmf* first-aid worker
secours [s(ə)kuʀ] *nm* help, aid, assistance ♦ *nmpl* aid *sg*; **au ~!** help!; **appeler au ~** to shout *ou* call for help; **porter ~ à qn** to give sb assistance, help sb; **les premiers ~** first aid *sg*
secousse [s(ə)kus] *nf* jolt, bump; (*électrique*) shock; (*fig: psychologique*) jolt, shock; **~ sismique** earth tremor
secret, -ète [səkʀɛ, ɛt] *adj* secret; (*fig: renfermé*) reticent, reserved ♦ *nm* secret; (*discrétion absolue*): **le ~** secrecy
secrétaire [s(ə)kʀetɛʀ] *nm/f* secretary ♦ *nm* (*meuble*) writing desk; **~ de direction** private *ou* personal secretary; **~ d'État** junior minister; **~ général** (*COMM*) company secretary; **secrétariat** *nm* (*profession*) secretarial work; (*bureau*) office; (: *d'organisation internationale*) secretariat
secteur [sɛktœʀ] *nm* sector; (*zone*) area; (*ÉLEC*): **branché sur ~** plugged into the mains

(supply)

section [sɛksjɔ̃] nf section; (de parcours d'autobus) fare stage; (MIL: unité) platoon; **sectionner** vt to sever

Sécu [seky] abr f = **sécurité sociale**

séculaire [sekylɛʀ] adj (très vieux) age-old

sécuriser [sekyʀize] vt to give (a feeling of) security to

sécurité [sekyʀite] nf (absence de danger) safety; (absence de troubles) security; **système de ~** security system; **être en ~** to be safe; **la ~ routière** road safety; **la ~ sociale** ≈ (the) Social Security (BRIT), ≈ Welfare (US)

sédentaire [sedɑ̃tɛʀ] adj sedentary

séduction [sedyksjɔ̃] nf seduction; (charme, attrait) appeal, charm

séduire [seduiʀ] vt to charm; (femme: abuser de) to seduce, **séduisant, e** adj (femme) seductive; (homme, offre) very attractive

ségrégation [segʀegasjɔ̃] nf segregation

seigle [sɛɡl] nm rye

seigneur [sɛɲœʀ] nm lord

sein [sɛ̃] nm breast; (entrailles) womb; **au ~ de** (équipe, institution) within

séisme [seism] nm earthquake

seize [sɛz] num sixteen; **seizième** num sixteenth

séjour [seʒuʀ] nm stay; (pièce) living room; **séjourner** vi to stay

sel [sɛl] nm salt; (fig: piquant) spice

sélection [selɛksjɔ̃] nf selection; **sélectionner** vt to select

self-service [selfsɛʀvis] adj, nm self-service

selle [sɛl] nf saddle; **~s** nfpl (MÉD) stools; **seller** vt to saddle

sellette [selɛt] nf: **être sur la ~** to be in the hot seat

selon [s(ə)lɔ̃] prép according to; (en se conformant à) in accordance with; **~ que** according to whether; **~ moi** as I see it

semaine [s(ə)mɛn] nf week; **en ~** during the week, on weekdays

semblable [sɑ̃blabl] adj similar; (de ce genre): **de ~s mésaventures** such mishaps ♦ nm fellow creature ou man, **~ à** similar to, like

semblant [sɑ̃blɑ̃] nm: **un ~ de ...** a semblance of ...; **faire ~ (de faire)** to pretend (to do)

sembler [sɑ̃ble] vb +attrib to seem ♦ vb impers: **il semble (bien) que/inutile de** it (really) seems ou appears that/useless to; **il me semble que** it seems to me that; **comme bon lui semble** as he sees fit

semelle [s(ə)mɛl] nf sole; (intérieure) insole, inner sole

semence [s(ə)mɑ̃s] nf (graine) seed

semer [s(ə)me] vt to sow; (fig: éparpiller) to scatter; (: confusion) to spread; (fam:

poursuivants) to lose, shake off; **semé de** (difficultés) riddled with

semestre [s(ə)mɛstʀ] nm half-year; (SCOL) semester

séminaire [seminɛʀ] nm seminar

semi-remorque [səmiʀəmɔʀk] nm articulated lorry (BRIT), semi(trailer) (US)

semoule [s(ə)mul] nf semolina

sempiternel, le [sɑ̃pitɛʀnɛl] adj eternal, never-ending

sénat [sena] nm senate; **sénateur** nm senator

sens [sɑ̃s] nm (PHYSIOL, instinct) sense; (signification) meaning, sense; (direction) direction; **à mon ~** to my mind; **dans le ~ des aiguilles d'une montre** clockwise; **~ dessus dessous** upside down; **~ interdit** one-way street; **~ unique** one-way street

sensation [sɑ̃sasjɔ̃] nf sensation; **à ~** (péj) sensational; **faire ~** to cause ou create a sensation; **sensationnel, le** adj (fam) fantastic, terrific

sensé, e [sɑ̃se] adj sensible

sensibiliser [sɑ̃sibilize] vt: **~ qn à** to make sb sensitive to

sensibilité [sɑ̃sibilite] nf sensitivity

sensible [sɑ̃sibl] adj sensitive; (aux sens) perceptible; (appréciable: différence, progrès) appreciable, noticeable; **sensiblement** adv (à peu près): **ils sont sensiblement du même âge** they are approximately the same age; **sensiblerie** nf sentimentality

sensuel, le [sɑ̃sɥɛl] adj (personne) sensual; (musique) sensuous

sentence [sɑ̃tɑ̃s] nf (jugement) sentence

sentier [sɑ̃tje] nm path

sentiment [sɑ̃timɑ̃] nm feeling; **sentimental, e, -aux** adj sentimental; (vie, aventure) love cpd

sentinelle [sɑ̃tinɛl] nf sentry

sentir [sɑ̃tiʀ] vt (par l'odorat) to smell; (par le goût) to taste; (au toucher, fig) to feel; (répandre une odeur de) to smell of; (: ressemblance) to smell like ♦ vi to smell: **~ mauvais** to smell bad; **se ~ bien** to feel good; **se ~ mal** (être indisposé) to feel unwell ou ill; **se ~ le courage/la force de faire** to feel brave/strong enough to do; **il ne peut pas le ~** (fam) he can't stand him

séparation [sepaʀasjɔ̃] nf separation; (cloison) division, partition

séparé, e [sepaʀe] adj (distinct) separate; (époux) separated; **séparément** adv separately

séparer [sepaʀe] vt to separate; (désunir) to drive apart; (détacher): **~ qch de** to pull sth (off) from; **se ~** vi (époux, amis) to separate, part; (se diviser: route etc) to divide; **se ~ de** (époux) to separate ou part from; (employé, *objet personnel*) to part with

sept [sɛt] *num* seven; **septante** (*BELGIQUE, SUISSE*) *adj inv* seventy

septembre [sɛptɑ̃br] *nm* September

septennat [sɛptena] *nm* seven year term of office (*of French President*)

septentrional, e, -aux [sɛptɑ̃trijɔnal, o] *adj* northern

septicémie [sɛptisemi] *nf* blood poisoning, septicaemia

septième [sɛtjɛm] *num* seventh

septique [sɛptik] *adj*: **fosse ~** septic tank

sépulture [sepyltyr] *nf* (*tombeau*) burial place, grave

séquelles [sekɛl] *nfpl* after-effects; (*fig*) aftermath *sg*

séquestrer [sekɛstre] *vt* (*personne*) to confine illegally; (*biens*) to impound

serai *etc* [səre] *vb voir* **être**

serein, e [sərɛ̃, ɛn] *adj* serene

serez [səre] *vb voir* **être**

sergent [sɛrʒɑ̃] *nm* sergeant

série [seri] *nf* series *inv*; (*de clés, casseroles, outils*) set; (*catégorie: SPORT*) rank; **en ~** in quick succession; (*COMM*) mass *cpd*; **hors ~** (*COMM*) custom-built

sérieusement [serjøzmɑ̃] *adv* seriously

sérieux, -euse [serjø, jøz] *adj* serious; (*élève, employé*) reliable, responsible; (*client, maison*) reliable, dependable ♦ *nm* seriousness; (*d'une entreprise etc*) reliability; **garder son ~** *etc* to keep a straight face; **prendre qch/qn au ~** to take sth/sb seriously

serin [s(ə)rɛ̃] *nm* canary

seringue [s(ə)rɛ̃g] *nf* syringe

serions [sərjɔ̃] *vb voir* **être**

serment [sɛrmɑ̃] *nm* (*juré*) oath; (*promesse*) pledge, vow

sermon [sɛrmɔ̃] *nm* sermon

séronégatif, -ive [seronegatif, iv] *adj* (*MÉD*) HIV negative

séropositif, -ive [seropozitif, iv] *adj* (*MÉD*) HIV positive

serpent [sɛrpɑ̃] *nm* snake; **serpenter** *vi* to wind

serpillière [sɛrpijɛr] *nf* floorcloth

serre [sɛr] *nf* (*AGR*) greenhouse; **~s** *nfpl* (*griffes*) claws, talons

serré, e [sere] *adj* (*habits*) tight; (*fig: lutte, match*) tight, close-fought; (*passagers etc*) (tightly) packed; (*réseau*) dense; **avoir le cœur ~** to have a heavy heart

serrer [sere] *vt* (*tenir*) to grip *ou* hold tight; (*comprimer, coincer*) to squeeze; (*poings, mâchoires*) to clench; (*suj: vêtement*) to be too tight for; (*ceinture, nœud, vis*) to tighten ♦ *vi*: **~ à droite** to keep *ou* get over to the right; **se ~** *vi* (*se rapprocher*) to squeeze up; **se ~ contre qn** to huddle up to sb; **~ la main**

à qn to shake sb's hand; **~ qn dans ses bras** to hug sb, clasp sb in one's arms

serrure [seryr] *nf* lock; **serrurier** *nm* locksmith

sert *etc* [sɛr] *vb voir* **servir**

servante [sɛrvɑ̃t] *nf* (*maid*)servant

serveur, -euse [sɛrvœr, øz] *nm/f* waiter (waitress)

serviable [sɛrvjabl] *adj* obliging, willing to help

service [sɛrvis] *nm* service; (*assortiment de vaisselle*) set, service; (*bureau: de la vente etc*) department, section; (*travail*) duty; **premier ~** (*série de repas*) first sitting; **être de ~** to be on duty; **faire le ~** to serve; **rendre un ~ à qn** to do sb a favour; (*objet: s'avérer utile*) to come in useful *ou* handy for sb; **mettre en ~** to put into service *ou* operation; **~ compris/non compris** service included/not included; **hors ~** out of order; **~ après-vente** after-sales service; **~ d'ordre** police (*ou* stewards) in charge of maintaining order; **~ militaire** military service; **~s secrets** secret service *sg*

serviette [sɛrvjɛt] *nf* (*de table*) (table) napkin, serviette; (*de toilette*) towel; (*porte-documents*) briefcase; **~ hygiénique** sanitary towel

servir [sɛrvir] *vt* to serve; (*au restaurant*) to wait on; (*au magasin*) to serve, attend to ♦ *vi* (*TENNIS*) to serve; (*CARTES*) to deal; **se ~** *vi* (*prendre d'un plat*) to help o.s.; **vous êtes servi?** are you being served?; **~ à qn** (*diplôme, livre*) to be of use to sb; **~ à qch/faire** (*outil etc*) to be used for sth/doing; **ça ne sert à rien** it's no use; **~ (à qn) de** to serve as (for sb); **se ~ de** (*plat*) to help o.s. to; (*voiture, outil, relations*) to use

serviteur [sɛrvitœr] *nm* servant

ses [se] *adj voir* **son**[1]

set [sɛt] *nm*: **~ (de table)** tablemat, place mat

seuil [sœj] *nm* doorstep; (*fig*) threshold

seul, e [sœl] *adj* (*sans compagnie*) alone; (*unique*): **un ~ livre** only one book, a single book ♦ *adv* (*vivre*) alone, on one's own ♦ *nm, nf*: **il en reste un(e) ~(e)** there's only one left; **le ~ livre** the only book; **parler tout ~** to talk to oneself; **faire qch (tout) ~** to do sth (all) on one's own *ou* (all) by oneself; **à lui (tout) ~** single-handed, on his own; **se sentir ~** to feel lonely; **seulement** *adv* only; **non seulement ... mais aussi** *ou* **encore** not only ... but also

sève [sɛv] *nf* sap

sévère [sever] *adj* severe

sévices [sevis] *nmpl* (physical) cruelty *sg*, ill treatment *sg*

sévir [sevir] *vi* (*punir*) to use harsh measures, crack down; (*suj: fléau*) to rage, be rampant

sevrer [səvre] *vt* (*enfant etc*) to wean

sexe [sɛks] nm sex; (*organes génitaux*) genitals, sex organs; **sexuel, le** adj sexual

seyant, e [sejɑ̃, ɑ̃t] adj becoming

shampooing [ʃɑ̃pwɛ̃] nm shampoo

short [ʃɔʀt] nm (pair of) shorts pl

MOT-CLÉ
---

si [si] nm (*MUS*) B; (*en chantant la gamme*) ti
♦ adv **1** (*oui*) yes
2 (*tellement*) so; **si gentil/rapidement** so kind/fast; **(tant et) si bien que** so much so that; **si rapide qu'il soit** however fast he may be
♦ conj if; **si tu veux** if you want; **je me demande si** I wonder if ou whether; **si seulement** if only

---

Sicile [sisil] nf: **la ~** Sicily

SIDA [sida] sigle m (= *syndrome immuno déficitaire acquis*) AIDS sg

sidéré, e [sidere] adj staggered

sidérurgie [sideʀyʀʒi] nf steel industry

siècle [sjɛkl] nm century

siège [sjɛʒ] nm seat; (*d'entreprise*) head office; (*d'organisation*) headquarters pl; (*MIL*) siege; **~ social** registered office; **siéger** vi to sit

sien, ne [sjɛ̃, sjɛn] pron: **le(la) ~(ne)**, **les ~(ne)s** (*homme*) his; (*femme*) hers; (*chose, animal*) its; **les ~s** (*sa famille*) one's family; **faire des ~nes** (*fam*) to be up to one's (*usual*) tricks

sieste [sjɛst] nf (afternoon) snooze ou nap; **faire la ~** to have a snooze ou nap

sifflement [siflamɑ̃] nm: **un ~ a** whistle

siffler [sifle] vi (*gén*) to whistle; (*en respirant*) to wheeze; (*serpent, vapeur*) to hiss ♦ vt (*chanson*) to whistle; (*chien etc*) to whistle for; (*fille*) to whistle at; (*pièce, orateur*) to hiss, boo; (*fin du match, départ*) to blow one's whistle for; (*fam: verre*) to guzzle

sifflet [siflɛ] nm whistle; **coup de ~** whistle

siffloter [siflɔte] vi, vt to whistle

sigle [sigl] nm acronym

signal, -aux [sinal, o] nm signal; (*indice, écriteau*) sign; **donner le ~ de** to give the signal for; **~ d'alarme** alarm signal; **signaux (lumineux)** (*AUTO*) traffic signals; **signalement** nm description, particulars pl

signaler [sinale] vt to indicate; (*personne: faire un signe*) to signal; (*vol, perte*) to report; (*faire remarquer*): **~ qch à qn/(à qn)** que to point out sth to sb/(to sb) that; **se ~ (par)** to distinguish o.s. (by)

signature [sinatyʀ] nf signature; (*action*) signing

signe [sin] nm sign; (*TYPO*) mark; **faire un ~ de la main** to give a sign with one's hand; **faire ~ à qn** (*fig: contacter*) to get in touch with sb; **faire ~ à qn d'entrer** to motion (to)

sb to come in; **signer** vt to sign; **se signer** vi to cross o.s.

significatif, -ive [sinifikatif, iv] adj significant

signification [sinifikasjɔ̃] nf meaning

signifier [sinifje] vt (*vouloir dire*) to mean; (*faire connaître*): **~ qch (à qn)** to make sth known (to sb)

silence [silɑ̃s] nm silence; (*MUS*) rest; **garder le ~** to keep silent, say nothing; **silencieux, -euse** adj quiet, silent ♦ nm silencer

silex [silɛks] nm flint

silhouette [silwɛt] nf outline, silhouette; (*lignes, contour*) outline; (*allure*) figure

silicium [silisjɔm] nm silicon

sillage [sijaʒ] nm wake

sillon [sijɔ̃] nm furrow; (*de disque*) groove; **sillonner** vt to criss-cross

simagrées [simagre] nfpl fuss sg

similaire [similɛʀ] adj similar; **similicuir** nm imitation leather; **similitude** nf similarity

simple [sɛ̃pl] adj simple; (*non multiple*) single; **~ messieurs** nm (*TENNIS*) men's singles sg; **~ soldat** private

simplicité [sɛ̃plisite] nf simplicity

simplifier [sɛ̃plifje] vt to simplify

simulacre [simylakʀ] nm (*péj*): **un ~ de a** pretence of

simuler [simyle] vt to sham, simulate

simultané, e [simyltane] adj simultaneous

sincère [sɛ̃sɛʀ] adj sincere; **sincèrement** adv sincerely; (*pour parler franchement*) honestly, really; **sincérité** nf sincerity

sine qua non [sinekwanɔn] adj: **condition ~** indispensable condition

singe [sɛ̃ʒ] nm monkey; (*de grande taille*) ape; **singer** vt to ape, mimic; **singeries** nfpl antics

singulariser [sɛ̃gylaʀize]: **se ~** vi to call attention to o.s.

singularité [sɛ̃gylaʀite] nf peculiarity

singulier, -ière [sɛ̃gylje, jɛʀ] adj remarkable, singular ♦ nm singular

sinistre [sinistʀ] adj sinister ♦ nm (*incendie*) blaze; (*catastrophe*) disaster; (*ASSURANCES*) damage (*giving rise to a claim*); **sinistré, e** adj disaster-stricken ♦ nm/f disaster victim

sinon [sinɔ̃] conj (*autrement, sans quoi*) otherwise, or else; (*sauf*) except, other than; (*si ce n'est*) if not

sinueux, -euse [sinuø, øz] adj winding

sinus [sinys] nm (*ANAT*) sinus; (*GÉOM*) sine; **sinusite** nf sinusitis

siphon [sifɔ̃] nm (*tube, d'eau gazeuse*) siphon; (*d'évier etc*) U-bend

sirène [siʀɛn] nf siren; **~ d'alarme** fire alarm; (*en temps de guerre*) air-raid siren

sirop [siʀo] nm (*à diluer: de fruit etc*) syrup; (*pharmaceutique*) syrup, mixture; **~ pour la**

toux cough mixture

siroter [siʀɔte] vt to sip

sismique [sismik] adj seismic

site [sit] nm (paysage, environnement) setting; (d'une ville etc: emplacement) site; ~ (pittoresque) beauty spot; ~s touristiques places of interest

sitôt [sito] adv: ~ parti as soon as he etc had left; ~ que as soon as; pas de ~ not for a long time

situation [situasjɔ̃] nf situation; (d'un édifice, d'une ville) position, location; ~ de famille marital status

situé, e [situe] adj situated

situer [situe] vt to site, situate; (en pensée) to set, place; se ~ vi to be situated

six [sis] num six; **sixième** num sixth ♦ nf (SCOL) first form

Skaï ® [skaj] nm Leatherette ®

ski [ski] nm (objet) ski; (sport) skiing; **faire du** ~ to ski; ~ **de fond** cross-country skiing; ~ **nautique** water-skiing; ~ **de piste** downhill skiing; ~ **de randonnée** cross-country skiing; **skier** vi to ski; **skieur, -euse** nm/f skier

slip [slip] nm (sous-vêtement) pants pl, briefs pl; (de bain: d'homme) trunks pl; (: du bikini) (bikini) briefs pl

slogan [slɔgɑ̃] nm slogan

SMIC [smik] sigle m = **salaire minimum interprofessionnel de croissance**

smicard, e [smikaʀ, aʀd] (fam) nm/f minimum wage earner

smoking [smɔkiŋ] nm dinner ou evening suit

SNCF sigle f (= Société nationale des chemins de fer français) French railways

snob [snɔb] adj snobbish ♦ nm/f snob; **snobisme** nm snobbery, snobbishness

sobre [sɔbʀ] adj (personne) temperate, abstemious; (élégance, style) sober

sobriquet [sɔbʀikɛ] nm nickname

social, e, -aux [sɔsjal, jo] adj social

socialisme [sɔsjalism] nm socialism; **socialiste** nm/f socialist

société [sɔsjete] nf society; (sportive) club; (COMM) company; **la ~ de consommation** the consumer society; ~ **anonyme** ≈ limited (BRIT) ou incorporated (US) company

sociologie [sɔsjɔlɔʒi] nf sociology

socle [sɔkl] nm (de colonne, statue) plinth, pedestal; (de lampe) base

socquette [sɔkɛt] nf ankle sock

sœur [sœʀ] nf sister; (religieuse) nun, sister

soi [swa] pron oneself; **en** ~ (intrinsèquement) in itself; **cela va de** ~ that ou it goes without saying; **soi-disant** adj inv so-called ♦ adv supposedly

soie [swa] nf silk; **soierie** nf (tissu) silk

soif [swaf] nf thirst; **avoir** ~ to be thirsty; **donner** ~ **à qn** to make sb thirsty

soigné, e [swaɲe] adj (tenue) well-groomed, neat; (travail) careful, meticulous

soigner [swaɲe] vt (malade, maladie: suj: docteur) to treat; (suj: infirmière, mère) to nurse, look after; (travail, détails) to take care over; (jardin, invités) to look after; **soigneux, -euse** adj (propre) tidy, neat; (appliqué) painstaking, careful

soi-même [swamɛm] pron oneself

soin [swɛ̃] nm (application) care; (propreté, ordre) tidiness, neatness; ~s nmpl (à un malade, blessé) treatment sg, medical attention sg; (hygiène) care sg; **prendre** ~ **de** to take care of, look after; **prendre** ~ **de faire** to take care to do; **les premiers** ~s first aid sg

soir [swaʀ] nm evening; **ce** ~ this evening, tonight; **demain** ~ tomorrow evening, tomorrow night; **soirée** nf evening; (réception) party

soit [swa] vb voir **être** ♦ conj (à savoir) namely; (ou): ~ ... ~ either ... or ♦ adv so be it, very well; ~ **que** ... ~ **que** ou **ou que** whether ... or whether

soixantaine [swasɑ̃tɛn] nf: **une** ~ (**de**) sixty or so, about sixty; **avoir la** ~ (âge) to be around sixty

soixante [swasɑ̃t] num sixty; **soixante-dix** num seventy

soja [sɔʒa] nm soya; (graines) soya beans pl; **germes de** ~ beansprouts

sol [sɔl] nm ground; (de logement) floor; (AGR) soil; (MUS) G; (: en chantant la gamme) so(h)

solaire [sɔlɛʀ] adj (énergie etc) solar; (crème etc) sun cpd

soldat [sɔlda] nm soldier

solde [sɔld] nf pay ♦ nm (COMM) balance; ~s nm ou f pl (articles) sale goods; (vente) sales; **en** ~ at sale price; **solder** vt (marchandise) to sell at sale price, sell off; **se solder par** (fig) to end in; **article soldé (à) 10 F** item reduced to 10 F

sole [sɔl] nf sole inv (fish)

soleil [sɔlɛj] nm sun; (lumière) sun(light); (temps ensoleillé) sun(shine); **il fait du** ~ it's sunny; **au** ~ in the sun

solennel, le [sɔlanɛl] adj solemn

solfège [sɔlfɛʒ] nm musical theory

solidaire [sɔlidɛʀ] adj: **être** ~s to show solidarity, stand ou stick together; **être** ~ **de** (collègues) to stand by; **solidarité** nf solidarity; **par solidarité (avec)** in sympathy (with)

solide [sɔlid] adj solid; (mur, maison, meuble) solid, sturdy; (connaissances, argument) sound; (personne, estomac) robust, sturdy ♦ nm solid

soliste [sɔlist] nm/f soloist

solitaire [sɔlitɛʀ] adj (sans compagnie) solitary, lonely; (lieu) lonely ♦ nm/f (ermite) recluse; (fig: ours) loner

solitude [sɔlityd] nf loneliness; (tranquillité) solitude

solive [sɔliv] nf joist

solliciter [sɔlisite] vt (personne) to appeal to; (emploi, faveur) to seek

sollicitude [sɔlisityd] nf concern

soluble [sɔlybl] adj soluble

solution [sɔlysjɔ̃] nf solution; ~ de facilité easy way out

solvable [sɔlvabl] adj solvent

sombre [sɔ̃br] adj dark; (fig) gloomy; **sombrer** vi (bateau) to sink; **sombrer dans** (misère, désespoir) to sink into

sommaire [sɔmɛr] adj (simple) basic; (expéditif) summary ♦ nm summary

sommation [sɔmasjɔ̃] nf (JUR) summons sg; (avant de faire feu) warning

somme [sɔm] nf (MATH) sum; (quantité) amount; (argent) sum, amount ♦ nm: **faire un ~** to have a (short) nap; **en ~** all in all, ~ **toute** all in all

sommeil [sɔmɛj] nm sleep; **avoir ~** to be sleepy, **sommeiller** vi to doze

sommer [sɔme] vt: ~ **qn de faire** to command ou order sb to do

sommes [sɔm] vb voir **être**

sommet [sɔmɛ] nm top; (d'une montagne) summit, top; (fig: de la perfection, gloire) height

sommier [sɔmje] nm (bed) base

somnambule [sɔmnɑ̃byl] nm/f sleepwalker

somnifère [sɔmnifɛr] nm sleeping drug no pl (ou pill)

somnoler [sɔmnɔle] vi to doze

somptueux, euse [sɔ̃ptɥø, øz] adj sumptuous

son¹, sa [sɔ̃, sa] (pl **ses**) adj (antécédent humain: mâle) his; (: femelle) her; (: valeur indéfinie) one's, his/her; (antécédent non humain) its

son² [sɔ̃] nm sound; (de blé) bran

sondage [sɔ̃daʒ] nm: ~ **(d'opinion)** (opinion) poll

sonde [sɔ̃d] nf (NAVIG) lead ou sounding line; (MÉD) probe; (TECH: de forage) borer, driller

sonder [sɔ̃de] vt (NAVIG) to sound; (TECH) to bore, drill; (fig: personne) to sound out; ~ **le terrain** (fig) to test the ground

songe [sɔ̃ʒ] nm dream; **songer** vi: **songer à** (penser à) to think over; (envisager) to consider, think of; **songer que** to think that; **songeur, -euse** adj pensive

sonnant, e [sɔnɑ̃, ɑ̃t] adj: **à 8 heures ~es** on the stroke of 8

sonné, e [sɔne] adj (fam) cracked; **il est midi ~** it's gone twelve

sonner [sɔne] vi to ring ♦ vt (cloche) to ring; (glas, tocsin) to sound; (portier, infirmière) to

ring for; ~ **faux** (instrument) to sound out of tune; (rire) to ring false

sonnerie [sɔnri] nf (son) ringing; (sonnette) bell; ~ **d'alarme** alarm bell

sonnette [sɔnɛt] nf bell; ~ **d'alarme** alarm bell

sono [sɔno] abr f = **sonorisation**

sonore [sɔnɔr] adj (voix) sonorous, ringing; (salle) resonant; (film, signal) sound cpd; **sonorisation** nf (équipement: de salle de conférences) public address system, P.A. system; (: de discothèque) sound system; **sonorité** nf (de piano, violon) tone; (d'une salle) acoustics pl

sont [sɔ̃] vb voir **être**

sophistiqué, e [sɔfistike] adj sophisticated

sorbet [sɔrbɛ] nm water ice, sorbet

sorcellerie [sɔrsɛlri] nf witchcraft no pl

sorcier [sɔrsje] nm sorcerer; **sorcière** nf witch ou sorceress

sordide [sɔrdid] adj (lieu) squalid; (action) sordid

sornettes [sɔrnɛt] nfpl twaddle sg

sort [sɔr] nm (destinée) fate; (condition) lot; (magique) curse, spell; **tirer au ~** to draw lots

sorte [sɔrt] nf sort, kind; **de la ~** in that way; **de (telle) ~ que** so that; **en quelque ~** in a way; **faire en ~ que** to see to it that

sortie [sɔrti] nf (issue) way out, exit; (remarque drôle) sally; (promenade) outing; (le soir: au restaurant etc) night out; (COMM: d'un disque) release; (: d'un livre) publication; (: d'un modèle) launching; **~s** nfpl (COMM: somme) items of expenditure, outgoings; ~ **de bain** (vêtement) bathrobe; ~ **de secours** emergency exit

sortilège [sɔrtilɛʒ] nm (magic) spell

sortir [sɔrtir] vi (gén) to come out; (partir, se promener, aller au spectacle) to go out; (numéro gagnant) to come up ♦ vt (gén) to take out; (produit, modèle) to bring out; (fam: dire) to come out with; ~ **avec qn** to be going out with sb; **s'en ~** (malade) to pull through; (d'une difficulté etc) to get through; ~ **de** (endroit) to go (ou come) out of, leave; (provenir de) to come from; (compétence) to be outside

sosie [sozi] nm double

sot, sotte [so, sɔt] adj silly, foolish ♦ nm/f fool; **sottise** nf (caractère) silliness, foolishness; (action) silly ou foolish thing

sou [su] nm: **près de ses ~s** tight-fisted; **sans le ~** penniless

soubresaut [subrəso] nm start; (cahot) jolt

souche [suʃ] nf (d'arbre) stump; (de carnet) counterfoil (BRIT), stub

souci [susi] nm (inquiétude) worry; (préoccupation) concern; (BOT) marigold; **se faire du ~** to worry; **soucier: se soucier de** vt

to care about; **soucieux, -euse** adj
concerned, worried

soucoupe [sukup] nf saucer; ~ **volante** flying
saucer

soudain, e [sudɛ̃, ɛn] adj (douleur, mort)
sudden ♦ adv suddenly, all of a sudden

soude [sud] nf soda

souder [sude] vt (avec fil à ~) to solder; (par
soudure autogène) to weld; (fig) to bind
together

soudoyer [sudwaje] (péj) vt to bribe

soudure [sudyʀ] nf soldering; welding;
(joint) soldered joint; weld

souffert, e [sufɛʀ, ɛʀt] pp de **souffrir**

souffle [sufl] nm (en expirant) breath; (en
soufflant) puff, blow; (respiration) breathing;
(d'explosion, de ventilateur) blast; (du vent)
blowing; **être à bout de ~** to be out of breath;
un ~ d'air a breath of air

soufflé, e [sufle] adj (fam: stupéfié)
staggered ♦ nm (CULIN) soufflé

souffler [sufle] vi (gén) to blow; (haleter) to
puff (and blow) ♦ vt (feu, bougie) to blow
out; (chasser: poussière etc) to blow away;
(TECH: verre) to blow; (dire): ~ **qch à qn** to
whisper sth to sb; **soufflet** nm (instrument)
bellows pl; (gifle) slap (in the face);
souffleur nm (THÉÂTRE) prompter

souffrance [sufʀɑ̃s] nf suffering; **en ~**
(affaire) pending

souffrant, e [sufʀɑ̃, ɑ̃t] adj unwell

souffre-douleur [sufʀədulœʀ] nm inv butt,
underdog

souffrir [sufʀiʀ] vi to suffer, be in pain ♦ vt to
suffer, endure; (supporter) to bear, stand;
~ **de** (maladie, froid) to suffer from; **elle ne
peut pas le ~** she can't stand ou bear him

soufre [sufʀ] nm sulphur

souhait [swɛ] nm wish; **tous nos ~s de** good
wishes ou our best wishes for; **à vos ~s!** bless
you!; **souhaitable** adj desirable

souhaiter [swete] vt to wish for; ~ **la bonne
année à qn** to wish sb a happy New Year;
~ **que** to hope that

souiller [suje] vt to dirty, soil; (fig: réputation
etc) to sully, tarnish

soûl, e [su, sul] adj drunk ♦ nm: **tout son ~** to
one's heart's content

soulagement [sulaʒmɑ̃] nm relief

soulager [sulaʒe] vt to relieve

soûler [sule] vt: ~ **qn** to get sb drunk; (suj:
boisson) to make sb drunk; (fig) to make sb's
head spin ou reel; **se ~** vi to get drunk

soulever [sul(ə)ve] vt to lift; (poussière) to
send up; (enthousiasme) to arouse; (question,
débat) to raise; **se ~** vi (peuple) to rise up;
(personne couchée) to lift o.s. up

soulier [sulje] nm shoe

souligner [suliɲe] vt to underline; (fig) to

emphasize, stress

soumettre [sumɛtʀ] vt (pays) to subject,
subjugate; (rebelle) to put down, subdue; **se
~ (à)** to submit (to); ~ **qch à qn** (projet etc) to
submit sth to sb

soumis, e [sumi, iz] adj submissive;
soumission nf submission

soupape [supap] nf valve

soupçon [supsɔ̃] nm suspicion; (petite
quantité): **un ~ de** a hint ou touch of;
soupçonner vt to suspect; **soupçonneux,
-euse** adj suspicious

soupe [sup] nf soup

souper [supe] vi to have supper ♦ nm supper

soupeser [supəze] vt to weigh in one's
hand(s); (fig) to weigh up

soupière [supjɛʀ] nf (soup) tureen

soupir [supiʀ] nm sigh; **pousser un ~ de
soulagement** to heave a sigh of relief

soupirail, -aux [supiʀaj, o] nm (small)
basement window

soupirer [supiʀe] vi to sigh

souple [supl] adj supple; (fig: règlement,
caractère) flexible; (: démarche, taille) lithe,
supple; **souplesse** nf suppleness; (de
caractère) flexibility

source [suʀs] nf (point d'eau) spring; (d'un
cours d'eau, fig) source; **de bonne ~** on good
authority

sourcil [suʀsi] nm (eye)brow; **sourciller** vi:
sans sourciller without turning a hair ou
batting an eyelid

sourd, e [suʀ, suʀd] adj deaf; (bruit)
muffled; (douleur) dull ♦ nm/f deaf person;
faire la ~e oreille to turn a deaf ear;
sourdine nf (MUS) mute; **en sourdine** softly,
quietly; **sourd-muet, sourde-muette** adj
deaf-and-dumb ♦ nm/f deaf-mute

souriant, e [suʀjɑ̃, jɑ̃t] adj cheerful

souricière [suʀisjɛʀ] nf mousetrap; (fig) trap

sourire [suʀiʀ] nm smile ♦ vi to smile; ~ **à qn**
to smile at sb; (fig: plaire à) to appeal to sb;
(suj: chance) to smile on sb; **garder le ~** to
keep smiling

souris [suʀi] nf mouse

sournois, e [suʀnwa, waz] adj deceitful,
underhand

sous [su] prép under; ~ **la pluie** in the rain;
~ **terre** underground; ~ **peu** shortly, before
long; **sous-bois** nm inv undergrowth

souscrire [suskʀiʀ]: ~ **à** vt to subscribe to

sous...: **sous-directeur, -trice** nm/f
assistant manager(-manageress); **sous-
entendre** vt to imply, infer; **sous-entendu,
e** adj implied ♦ nm innuendo, insinuation;
sous-estimer vt to underestimate; **sous-
jacent, e** adj underlying; **sous-louer** vt to
sublet; **sous-marin, e** adj (flore, faune)
submarine; (pêche) underwater ♦ nm

submarine; **sous-officier** *nm* ≈ non-commissioned officer (N.C.O.); **sous-produit** *nm* by-product; **sous-pull** *nm* thin poloneck jersey; **soussigné, e** *adj*: je soussigné I the undersigned; **sous-sol** *nm* basement; **sous-titre** *nm* subtitle

soustraction [sustraksjɔ̃] *nf* subtraction

soustraire [sustrɛr] *vt* to subtract, take away; (*dérober*) : ~ qch à qn to remove sth from sb; **se ~ à** (*autorité etc*) to elude, escape from

sous...: **sous-traitant** *nm* sub-contractor; **sous-traiter** *vt* to sub-contract; **sous-vêtements** *nmpl* underwear *sg*

soutane [sutan] *nf* cassock, soutane

soute [sut] *nf* hold

soutenir [sut(ə)niʀ] *vt* to support; (*assaut, choc*) to stand up to, withstand; (*intérêt, effort*) to keep up; (*assurer*): ~ que to maintain that; **soutenu, e** *adj* (*efforts*) sustained, unflagging; (*style*) elevated

souterrain, e [sutɛʀɛ̃, ɛn] *adj* underground ♦ *nm* underground passage

soutien [sutjɛ̃] *nm* support; **soutien-gorge** *nm* bra

soutirer [sutiʀe] *vt*: ~ qch à qn to squeeze *ou* get sth out of sb

souvenir [suv(ə)niʀ] *nm* (*réminiscence*) memory; (*objet*) souvenir ♦ *vb*: **se ~ de** ♦ *vt* to remember; **se ~ que** to remember that; **en ~ de** in memory *ou* remembrance of

souvent [suvɑ̃] *adv* often; **peu ~** seldom, infrequently

souverain, e [suv(ə)ʀɛ̃, ɛn] *nm/f* sovereign, monarch

soyeux, euse [swajø, øz] *adj* silky

soyons *etc* [swajɔ̃] *vb voir* **être**

spacieux, -euse [spasjø, jøz] *adj* spacious, roomy

spaghettis [spageti] *nmpl* spaghetti *sg*

sparadrap [spaʀadʀa] *nm* sticking plaster (*BRIT*), Bandaid ® (*US*)

spatial, e, -aux [spasjal, jo] *adj* (*AVIAT*) space *cpd*

speaker, ine [spikœʀ, kʀin] *nm/f* announcer

spécial, e, -aux [spesjal, jo] *adj* special; (*bizarre*) peculiar; **spécialement** *adv* especially, particularly; (*tout exprès*) specially; **spécialiser: se spécialiser** *vi* to specialize; **spécialiste** *nm/f* specialist; **spécialité** *nf* speciality; (*branche*) special field

spécifier [spesifje] *vt* to specify, state

spécimen [spesimɛn] *nm* specimen

spectacle [spɛktakl] *nm* (*scène*) sight; (*représentation*) show; (*industrie*) show business; **spectaculaire** *adj* spectacular

spectateur, -trice [spɛktatœʀ, tʀis] *nm/f* (*CINÉMA etc*) member of the audience; (*SPORT*) spectator; (*d'un événement*) onlooker, witness

spéculer [spekyle] *vi* to speculate

spéléologie [speleɔlɔʒi] *nf* potholing

sperme [spɛʀm] *nm* semen, sperm

sphère [sfɛʀ] *nf* sphere

spirale [spiʀal] *nf* spiral

spirituel, le [spiʀitɥɛl] *adj* spiritual; (*fin, piquant*) witty

splendide [splɑ̃did] *adj* splendid

sponsoriser [spɔ̃sɔʀize] *vt* to sponsor

spontané, e [spɔ̃tane] *adj* spontaneous; **spontanéité** *nf* spontaneity

sport [spɔʀ] *nm* sport ♦ *adj inv* (*vêtement*) casual; **faire du ~** to do sport; **~s d'hiver** winter sports; **sportif, -ive** *adj* (*journal, association, épreuve*) sports *cpd*; (*allure, démarche*) athletic; (*attitude, esprit*) sporting

spot [spɔt] *nm* (*lampe*) spot(light); (*annonce*): ~ (*publicitaire*) commercial (break)

square [skwaʀ] *nm* public garden(s)

squelette [skəlɛt] *nm* skeleton; **squelettique** *adj* scrawny

stabiliser [stabilize] *vt* to stabilize

stable [stabl] *adj* stable, steady

stade [stad] *nm* (*SPORT*) stadium; (*phase, niveau*) stage

stage [staʒ] *nm* (*cours*) training course; ~ de formation (professionnelle) vocational (training) course; ~ de perfectionnement advanced training course; **stagiaire** *nm/f, adj* trainee

stagner [stagne] *vi* to stagnate

stalle [stal] *nf* stall, box

stand [stɑ̃d] *nm* (*d'exposition*) stand; (*de foire*) stall; ~ de tir (à la foire, *SPORT*) shooting range

standard [stɑ̃daʀ] *adj inv* standard ♦ *nm* switchboard; **standardiste** *nm/f* switchboard operator

standing [stɑ̃diŋ] *nm* standing; de grand luxury

starter [staʀtɛʀ] *nm* (*AUTO*) choke

station [stasjɔ̃] *nf* station; (*de bus*) stop; (*de villégiature*) resort; ~ balnéaire seaside resort; ~ de ski ski resort; ~ de taxis taxi rank (*BRIT*) *ou* stand (*US*); **stationnement** *nm* parking; **stationner** *vi* to park; **station-service** *nf* service station

statistique [statistik] *nf* (*science*) statistics *sg*; (*rapport, étude*) statistic ♦ *adj* statistical

statue [staty] *nf* statue

statu quo [statykwo] *nm* status quo

statut [staty] *nm* status; ~s *nmpl* (*JUR, ADMIN*) statutes; **statutaire** *adj* statutory

Sté *abr* = société

steak [stɛk] *nm* steak; ~ haché hamburger

sténo(dactylo) [steno(daktilo)] *nf* shorthand typist (*BRIT*), stenographer (*US*)

sténo(graphie) [steno(gʀafi)] *nf* shorthand

stéréo [steʀeo] *adj* stereo

stérile [steʀil] *adj* sterile

stérilet [steʀilɛ] *nm* coil, loop

stériliser [steʀilize] *vt* to sterilize

stigmates [stigmat] *nmpl* scars, marks

stimulant [stimylɑ̃] *nm* (*fig*) stimulus, incentive; (*physique*) stimulant

stimuler [stimyle] *vt* to stimulate

stipuler [stipyle] *vt* to stipulate

stock [stɔk] *nm* stock; **stocker** *vt* to stock

stop [stɔp] *nm* (AUTO: *écriteau*) stop sign; (: *feu arrière*) brake-light; **faire du ~** (*fam*) to hitch(hike); **stopper** *vt, vi* to stop, halt

store [stɔʀ] *nm* blind; (*de magasin*) shade, awning

strabisme [strabism] *nm* squinting

strapontin [strapɔ̃tɛ̃] *nm* jump *ou* foldaway seat

stratégie [strateʒi] *nf* strategy; **stratégique** *adj* strategic

stress [stres] *nm* stress; **stressant, e** *adj* stressful; **stresser** *vt*: **stresser qn** to make sb (feel) tense

strict, e [strikt] *adj* strict; (*tenue, décor*) severe, plain; **le ~ nécessaire/minimum** the bare essentials/minimum

strident, e [stridɑ̃, ɑ̃t] *adj* shrill, strident

strophe [strɔf] *nf* verse, stanza

structure [stryktyr] *nf* structure

studieux, -euse [stydjø, jøz] *adj* studious

studio [stydjo] *nm* (*logement*) (one-roomed) flatlet (BRIT) *ou* apartment (US); (*d'artiste, TV etc*) studio

stupéfait, e [stypefɛ, ɛt] *adj* astonished

stupéfiant, e [stypefjɑ̃, jɑ̃t] *adj* (*étonnant*) stunning, astounding ♦ *nm* (MÉD) drug, narcotic

stupéfier [stypefje] *vt* (*étonner*) to stun, astonish

stupeur [stypœʀ] *nf* astonishment

stupide [stypid] *adj* stupid; **stupidité** *nf* stupidity; (*parole, acte*) stupid thing (to do *ou* say)

style [stil] *nm* style

stylé, e [stile] *adj* well-trained

styliste [stilist] *nm/f* designer

stylo [stilo] *nm*: **~ (à encre)** (fountain) pen; **~ (à) bille** ball-point pen; **~-feutre** felt-tip pen

su, e [sy] *pp de* savoir ♦ *nm*: **au ~ de** with the knowledge of

suave [sɥav] *adj* sweet

subalterne [sybaltɛʀn] *adj* (*employé, officier*) junior; (*rôle*) subordinate, subsidiary ♦ *nm/f* subordinate

subconscient [sypkɔ̃sjɑ̃] *nm* subconscious

subir [sybiʀ] *vt* (*affront, dégâts*) to suffer; (*opération, châtiment*) to undergo

subit, e [sybi, it] *adj* sudden; **subitement** *adv* suddenly, all of a sudden

subjectif, -ive [sybʒɛktif, iv] *adj* subjective

subjonctif [sybʒɔ̃ktif] *nm* subjunctive

subjuguer [sybʒyge] *vt* to captivate

submerger [sybmɛʀʒe] *vt* to submerge; (*fig*) to overwhelm

subordonné, e [sybɔʀdɔne] *adj, nm/f* subordinate

subrepticement [sybʀɛptismɑ̃] *adv* surreptitiously

subside [sybzid] *nm* grant

subsidiaire [sybzidjɛʀ] *adj*: **question ~** deciding question

subsister [sybziste] *vi* (*rester*) to remain, subsist; (*survivre*) to live on

substance [sypstɑ̃s] *nf* substance

substituer [sypstitɥe] *vt*: **~ qn/qch à** to substitute sb/sth for; **se ~ à qn** (*évincer*) to substitute o.s. for sb

substitut [sypstity] *nm* (*succédané*) substitute

subterfuge [sybtɛʀfyʒ] *nm* subterfuge

subtil, e [syptil] *adj* subtle

subtiliser [syptilize] *vt*: **~ qch (à qn)** to spirit sth away (from sb)

subvenir [sybvəniʀ] : **~ à** *vt* to meet

subvention [sybvɑ̃sjɔ̃] *nf* subsidy, grant; **subventionner** *vt* to subsidize

suc [syk] *nm* (BOT) sap; (*de viande, fruit*) juice

succédané [syksedane] *nm* substitute

succéder [syksede] : **~ à** *vt* to succeed; **se ~** *vi* (*accidents, années*) to follow one another

succès [syksɛ] *nm* success; **avoir du ~** to be a success, be successful; **à ~** successful; **~ de librairie** bestseller; **~ (féminins)** conquests

successif, -ive [syksesif, iv] *adj* successive

successeur [syksesœʀ] *nm* successor

succession [syksesjɔ̃] *nf* (*série, POL*) succession; (JUR: *patrimoine*) estate, inheritance

succomber [sykɔ̃be] *vi* to die, succumb; (*fig*): **~ à** to succumb to

succulent, e [sykylɑ̃, ɑ̃t] *adj* (*repas, mets*) delicious

succursale [sykyʀsal] *nf* branch

sucer [syse] *vt* to suck; **sucette** *nf* (*bonbon*) lollipop; (*de bébé*) dummy (BRIT), pacifier (US)

sucre [sykʀ] *nm* (*substance*) sugar; (*morceau*) lump of sugar, sugar lump *ou* cube; **~ d'orge** barley sugar; **~ en morceaux/en poudre** lump/caster sugar; **~ glace/roux** icing/brown sugar; **sucré, e** *adj* (*produit alimentaire*) sweetened; (*au goût*) sweet; **sucrer** *vt* (*thé, café*) to sweeten, put sugar in; **sucreries** *nfpl* (*bonbons*) sweets, sweet things; **sucrier** *nm* (*récipient*) sugar bowl

sud [syd] *nm*: **le ~** the south ♦ *adj inv* south; (*côte*) south, southern; **au ~** (*situation*) in the south; (*direction*) to the south; **au ~ de** (to the) south of; **sud-africain, e** *adj* South

African ♦ nm/f: **Sud-Africain, e** South African;
sud-américain, e adj South American
♦ nm/f: **Sud-Américain, e** South American;
sud-est nm, adj inv south-east; **sud-ouest**
nm, adj inv south-west
Suède [sɥɛd] nf: la ~ Sweden; **suédois, e**
adj Swedish ♦ nm/f: **Suédois, e** Swede ♦ nm
(LING) Swedish
suer [sɥe] vi to sweat; (suinter) to ooze;
sueur nf sweat; **en sueur** sweating, in a
sweat; **donner des sueurs froids à qn** to put
sb in(to) a cold sweat
suffire [syfir] vi (être assez): ~ (à qn/pour
qch/pour faire) to be enough ou sufficient
(for sb/for sth/to do); **il suffit d'une
négligence** ... it only takes one act of
carelessness ...; **il suffit qu'on oublie pour que**
... one only needs to forget for ...; **ça suffit!**
that's enough!
suffisamment [syfizamɑ̃] adv sufficiently,
enough; ~ **de** sufficient, enough
suffisant, e [syfizɑ̃, ɑ̃t] adj sufficient;
(résultats) satisfactory; (vaniteux) self-
important, bumptious
suffixe [syfiks] nm suffix
suffoquer [syfɔke] vt to choke, suffocate;
(stupéfier) to stagger, astound ♦ vi to choke,
suffocate
suffrage [syfraʒ] nm (POL: voix) vote
suggérer [syɡʒere] vt to suggest;
suggestion nf suggestion
suicide [sɥisid] nm suicide; **suicider: se
suicider** vi to commit suicide
suie [sɥi] nf soot
suinter [sɥɛ̃te] vi to ooze
suis [sɥi] vb voir **être; suivre**
suisse [sɥis] adj Swiss ♦ nm: **S~** Swiss pl inv
♦ nf: **la S~** Switzerland; **la S~ romande/
allemande** French-speaking/German-speaking
Switzerland; **Suissesse** nf Swiss (woman ou
girl)
suite [sɥit] nf (continuation: d'énumération
etc) rest, remainder; (: de feuilleton)
continuation; (: film etc sur le même thème)
sequel; (série) series, succession;
(conséquence) result; (ordre, liaison logique)
coherence; (appartement, MUS) suite;
(escorte) retinue, suite; ~s nfpl (d'une maladie
etc) effects; **prendre la ~ de** (directeur etc) to
succeed, take over from; **donner ~ à** (requête,
projet) to follow up; **faire ~ à** to follow;
(faisant) ~ à votre lettre du ... further to your
letter of the ...; **de ~** (d'affilée) in succession;
(immédiatement) at once; **par la ~** afterwards,
subsequently; **à la ~** one after the other; **à la
~ de** (derrière) behind; (en conséquence de)
following
suivant, e [sɥivɑ̃, ɑ̃t] adj next, following
♦ prép (selon) according to; **au ~!** next!

suivi, e [sɥivi] adj (effort, qualité) consistent;
(cohérent) coherent; **très/peu ~** (cours) well-/
poorly-attended
suivre [sɥivr] vt (gén) to follow; (SCOL: cours)
to attend; (comprendre) to keep up with;
(COMM: article) to continue to stock ♦ vi to
follow; (élève: assimiler) to keep up; **se ~** vi
(accidents etc) to follow one after the other;
faire ~ (lettre) to forward; **"à ~"** "to be
continued"
sujet, te [syʒɛ, ɛt] adj: **être ~ à** (vertige etc)
to be liable ou subject to ♦ nm/f (d'un
souverain) subject ♦ nm subject; **au ~ de**
about; ~ **de conversation** topic ou subject of
conversation; ~ **d'examen** (SCOL) examination
question
summum [sɔ(m)mɔm] nm: **le ~ de** the
height of
super [sypɛr] (fam) adj inv terrific, great,
fantastic, super
superbe [sypɛrb] adj magnificent, superb
super(carburant) [sypɛr(karbyrɑ̃)] nm ≈
4-star petrol (BRIT), ≈ high-octane gasoline
(US)
supercherie [sypɛrʃəri] nf trick
supérette [sypɛrɛt] nf (COMM) minimarket,
superette (US)
superficie [sypɛrfisi] nf (surface) area
superficiel, le [sypɛrfisjɛl] adj superficial
superflu, e [sypɛrfly] adj superfluous
supérieur, e [sypɛrjœr] adj (lèvre, étages,
classes) upper; (plus élevé: température,
niveau, enseignement): ~ **(à)** higher (than);
(meilleur: qualité, produit): ~ **(à)** superior (to);
(excellent, hautain) superior ♦ nm, nf
superior; **supériorité** nf superiority
superlatif [sypɛrlatif] nm superlative
supermarché [sypɛrmarʃe] nm supermarket
superposer [sypɛrpoze] vt (faire chevaucher)
to superimpose; **lits superposés** bunk beds
superproduction [sypɛrprɔdyksjɔ̃] nf
(film) spectacular
superpuissance [sypɛrpɥisɑ̃s] nf superpower
superstitieux, -euse [sypɛrstisjø, jøz] adj
superstitious
superviser [sypɛrvize] vt to supervise
supplanter [syplɑ̃te] vt to supplant
suppléance [sypleɑ̃s] nf: **faire des ~s**
(professeur) to do supply teaching;
suppléant, e adj (professeur) supply cpd;
(juge, fonctionnaire) deputy cpd ♦ nm/f
(professeur) supply teacher
suppléer [syplee] vt (ajouter: mot manquant
etc) to supply, provide; (compenser: lacune)
to fill in; ~ **à** to make up for
supplément [syplemɑ̃] nm supplement; (de
frites etc) extra portion; **un ~ de travail** extra
ou additional work; **payer un ~** to pay an

additional charge; **le vin est en ~** wine is extra; **supplémentaire** adj additional, further; (train, bus) relief cpd, extra

supplications [syplikasjɔ̃] nfpl pleas, entreaties

supplice [syplis] nm torture no pl

supplier [syplije] vt to implore, beseech

support [sypɔr] nm support; (publicitaire) medium; (audio-visuel) aid

supportable [sypɔrtabl] adj (douleur) bearable

supporter[1] [sypɔrtɛr] nm supporter, fan

supporter[2] [sypɔrte] vt (conséquences, épreuve) to bear, endure; (défauts, personne) to put up with; (suj: chose: chaleur etc) to withstand; (: personne: chaleur, vin) to be able to take

supposer [sypoze] vt to suppose; (impliquer) to presuppose; **à ~ que** supposing (that)

suppositoire [sypozitwar] nm suppository

suppression [sypresjɔ̃] nf (voir supprimer) cancellation; removal; deletion

supprimer [syprime] vt (congés, service d'autobus etc) to cancel; (emplois, privilèges, témoin gênant) to do away with; (cloison, cause, anxiété) to remove; (clause, mot) to delete

suprême [syprɛm] adj supreme

MOT-CLÉ
---

sur [syr] prép 1 (position) on; (par-dessus) over; (au-dessus) above; **pose-le sur la table** put it on the table; **je n'ai pas d'argent sur moi** I haven't any money on me

2 (direction) towards; **en allant sur Paris** going towards Paris; **sur votre droite** on ou to your right

3 (à propos de) on, about; **un livre/une conférence sur Balzac** a book/lecture on ou about Balzac

4 (proportion, mesures) out of, by; **un sur 10** one in 10; (SCOL) one out of 10; **4 m sur 2 4** m by 2

sur ce adv hereupon

---

sûr, e [syr] adj sure, certain; (digne de confiance) reliable; (sans danger) safe; (diagnostic, goût) reliable; **le plus ~ est de** the safest thing is to; **~ de soi** self-confident; **~ et certain** absolutely certain

surcharge [syrʃarʒ] nf (de passagers, marchandises) excess load; **surcharger** vt to overload

surchoix [syrʃwa] adj inv top-quality

surclasser [syrklase] vt to outclass

surcroît [syrkrwa] nm: **un ~ de** additional +nom; **par ou de ~** moreover; **en ~** in addition

surdité [syrdite] nf deafness

surélever [syrel(ə)ve] vt to raise, heighten

sûrement [syrmɑ̃] adv (certainement) certainly; (sans risques) safely

surenchère [syrɑ̃ʃɛr] nf (aux enchères) higher bid; **surenchérir** vi to bid higher; (fig) to try and outbid each other

surent [syr] vb voir savoir

surestimer [syrɛstime] vt to overestimate

sûreté [syrte] nf (sécurité) safety; (exactitude: de renseignements etc) reliability; (d'un geste) steadiness; **mettre en ~** to put in a safe place; **pour plus de ~** as an extra precaution, to be on the safe side

surf [sœrf] nm surfing

surface [syrfas] nf surface; (superficie) surface area; **une grande ~** a supermarket; **faire ~** to surface; **en ~** near the surface; (fig) superficially

surfait, e [syrfɛ, ɛt] adj overrated

surgelé, e [syrʒəle] adj (deep-)frozen ♦ nm: **les ~s** (deep-)frozen food

surgir [syrʒir] vi to appear suddenly; (fig: problème, conflit) to arise

sur...: surhumain, e adj superhuman; **sur-le-champ** adv immediately; **surlendemain** nm: **le surlendemain (soir)** two days later (in the evening); **le surlendemain de** two days after; **surmenage** nm overwork(ing); **surmener: se surmener** vi to overwork

surmonter [syrmɔ̃te] vt (vaincre) to overcome; (être au-dessus de) to top

surnaturel, le [syrnatyrɛl] adj, nm supernatural

surnom [syrnɔ̃] nm nickname

surnombre [syrnɔ̃br] nm: **être en ~** to be too many (ou one too many)

surpeuplé, e [syrpœple] adj overpopulated

sur-place [syrplas] nm: **faire du ~~** to mark time

surplomber [syrplɔ̃be] vt, vi to overhang

surplus [syrply] nm (COMM) surplus; (reste): **~ de bois** wood left over

surprenant, e [syrprǝnɑ̃, ɑ̃t] adj amazing

surprendre [syrprɑ̃dr] vt (étonner) to surprise; (tomber sur: intrus etc) to catch; (entendre) to overhear

surpris, e [syrpri, iz] adj: **~ (de/que)** surprised (at/that); **surprise** nf surprise; **faire une surprise à qn** to give sb a surprise; **surprise-partie** nf party

surréservation [syrrezɛrvasjɔ̃] nf double booking, overbooking

sursaut [syrso] nm start, jump; **~ de** (énergie, indignation) sudden fit ou burst of; **en ~** with a start; **sursauter** vi to (give a) start, jump

sursis [syrsi] nm (JUR: gén) suspended sentence; (fig) reprieve

surtaxe [syrtaks] nf surcharge

surtout [syrtu] adv (avant tout, d'abord) above all; (spécialement, particulièrement)

especially; **~, ne dites rien!** whatever you do
don't say anything!; **~ pas!** certainly ou
definitely not!; **~ que ...** especially as ...
surveillance [syʀvɛjɑ̃s] nf watch; (POLICE,
MIL) surveillance; **sous ~ médicale** under
medical supervision
surveillant, e [syʀvɛjɑ̃, ɑ̃t] nm/f (de prison)
warder; (SCOL) monitor
surveiller [syʀveje] vt (enfant, élèves,
bagages) to watch, keep an eye on;
(prisonnier, suspect) to keep (a) watch on;
(territoire, bâtiment) to (keep) watch over;
(travaux, cuisson) to supervise; (SCOL:
examen) to invigilate; **~ son langage/sa ligne**
to watch one's language/figure
survenir [syʀvəniʀ] vi (incident, retards) to
occur, arise; (événement) to take place
survêt(ement) [syʀvɛt(mɑ̃)] nm tracksuit
survie [syʀvi] nf survival; **survivant, e** nm/f
survivor; **survivre** vi to survive; **survivre à**
(accident etc) to survive
survoler [syʀvɔle] vt to fly over; (fig: livre) to
skim through
survolté, e [syʀvɔlte] adj (fig) worked up
sus |sy(s)|: **en ~ de** prép in addition to, over
and above; **en ~** in addition
susceptible [syseptibl] adj touchy, sensitive;
~ de faire (hypothèse) liable to do
susciter [sysite] vt (admiration) to arouse;
(ennuis): **~ (à qn)** to create (for sb)
suspect, e [syspɛ(kt), ɛkt] adj suspicious;
(témoignage, opinions) suspect ♦ nm/f
suspect; **suspecter** vt to suspect; (honnêteté
de qn) to question, have one's suspicions
about
suspendre [syspɑ̃dʀ] vt (accrocher:
vêtement): **~ qch (à)** to hang sth up (on);
(interrompre, démettre) to suspend; **se ~ à** to
hang from
suspendu, e [syspɑ̃dy] adj (accroché): **~ à**
hanging on (ou from); (perché): **~ au-dessus**
de suspended over
suspens [syspɑ̃]: **en ~** adv (affaire) in
abeyance; **tenir en ~** to keep in suspense
suspense [syspɛns, syspɑ̃s] nm suspense
suspension [syspɑ̃sjɔ̃] nf suspension, (lustre)
light fitting ou fitment
sut [sy] vb voir savoir
suture [sytyʀ] nf (MÉD): **point de ~** stitch
svelte [svɛlt] adj slender, svelte
SVP abr (= s'il vous plaît) please
sweat-shirt [switʃœʀt] (pl **~~s**) nm
sweatshirt
syllabe [si(l)lab] nf syllable
symbole [sɛ̃bɔl] nm symbol; **symbolique**
adj symbolic(al); (geste, offrande) token cpd;
symboliser vt to symbolize
symétrique [simetʀik] adj symmetrical
sympa [sɛ̃pa] (fam) adj inv nice; **sois ~,**

prête-le moi be a pal and lend it to me
sympathie [sɛ̃pati] nf (inclination) liking;
(affinité) friendship; (condoléances) sympathy;
j'ai beaucoup de ~ pour lui I like him a lot;
sympathique adj nice, friendly
sympathisant, e [sɛ̃patizɑ̃, ɑ̃t] nm/f
sympathizer
sympathiser [sɛ̃patize] vi (voisins etc:
s'entendre) to get on (BRIT) ou along (US)
(well)
symphonie [sɛ̃fɔni] nf symphony
symptôme [sɛ̃ptom] nm symptom
synagogue [sinagɔg] nf synagogue
syncope [sɛ̃kɔp] nf (MÉD) blackout; **tomber
en ~** to faint, pass out
syndic [sɛ̃dik] nm (d'immeuble) managing
agent
syndical, e, -aux [sɛ̃dikal, o] adj (trade)
union cpd; **syndicaliste** nm/f trade unionist
syndicat [sɛ̃dika] nm (d'ouvriers, employés)
(trade) union; **~ d'initiative** tourist office;
syndiqué, e adj belonging to a (trade)
union; **syndiquer: se syndiquer** vi to form a
trade union; (adhérer) to join a trade union
synonyme [sinɔnim] adj synonymous ♦ nm
synonym; **~ de** synonymous with
syntaxe [sɛ̃taks] nf syntax
synthèse [sɛ̃tɛz] nf synthesis
synthétique [sɛ̃tetik] adj synthetic
Syrie [siʀi] nf: **la ~** Syria
systématique [sistematik] adj systematic
système [sistɛm] nm system; **~ D** (fam)
resourcefulness

T, t

t' [t] pron voir **te**
ta Ital adi voir **ton¹**
tabac [taba] nm tobacco; (magasin)
tobacconist's (shop); **~ blond/brun** light/dark
tobacco
tabagisme [tabaʒism] nm: **~ passif** passive
smoking
tabasser [tabase] (fam) vt to beat up
table [tabl] nf table, **à ~!** dinner etc is ready!;
se mettre à ~ to sit down to eat; **mettre la ~**
to lay the table; **faire ~ rase de** to make a
clean sweep of; **~ à repasser** ironing board;
~ de cuisson (à l'électricité) hotplate; (au gaz)
gas ring; **~ de nuit** ou **de chevet** bedside
table; **~ des matières** (table of) contents pl;
~ d'orientation viewpoint indicator; **~ roulante**
trolley
tableau, x [tablo] nm (peinture) painting;
(reproduction, fig) picture; (panneau) board;
(schéma) table, chart; **~ d'affichage** notice
board; **~ de bord** dashboard; (AVIAT)
instrument panel; **~ noir** blackboard

tabler [table] vi: ~ **sur** to bank on
tablette [tablɛt] nf (planche) shelf; ~ **de chocolat** bar of chocolate
tableur [tablœR] nm spreadsheet
tablier [tablije] nm apron
tabou [tabu] nm taboo
tabouret [tabuRɛ] nm stool
tac [tak] nm: **il m'a répondu du ~ au ~** he answered me right back
tache [taʃ] nf (saleté) stain, mark; (ART, de couleur, lumière) spot; ~ **de rousseur** freckle
tâche [taʃ] nf task
tacher [taʃe] vt to stain, mark
tâcher [taʃe] vi: ~ **de faire** to try ou endeavour to do
tacheté, e [taʃte] adj spotted
tacot [tako] nm (péj) banger (BRIT), (old) heap
tact [takt] nm tact; **avoir du ~** to be tactful
tactique [taktik] adj tactical ♦ nf (technique) tactics sg; (plan) tactic
taie [tɛ] nf: ~ **(d'oreiller)** pillowslip, pillowcase
taille [taj] nf cutting; (d'arbre etc) pruning; (milieu du corps) waist; (hauteur) height; (grandeur) size; **de ~ à faire** capable of doing; **de ~** sizeable; **taille-crayon(s)** nm pencil sharpener
tailler [taje] vt (pierre, diamant) to cut; (arbre, plante) to prune; (vêtement) to cut out; (crayon) to sharpen
tailleur [tajœR] nm (couturier) tailor; (vêtement) suit; **en ~** (assis) cross-legged
taillis [taji] nm copse
taire [tɛR] vi: **faire ~ qn** to make sb be quiet; **se ~** vi to be silent ou quiet
talc [talk] nm talc, talcum powder
talent [talɑ̃] nm talent
talkie-walkie [tokiwoki] nm walkie-talkie
taloche [talɔʃ] (fam) nf clout, cuff
talon [talɔ̃] nm heel; (de chèque, billet) stub, counterfoil (BRIT); ~**s plats/aiguilles** flat/stiletto heels
talonner [talɔne] vt (suivre) to follow hot on the heels of; (harceler) to hound
talus [taly] nm embankment
tambour [tɑ̃buR] nm (MUS, aussi) drum; (musicien) drummer; (porte) revolving door(s pl); **tambourin** nm tambourine; **tambouriner** vi to drum; **tambouriner à/sur** to drum on
tamis [tami] nm sieve
Tamise [tamiz] nf: **la ~** the Thames
tamisé, e [tamize] adj (fig) subdued, soft
tampon [tɑ̃pɔ̃] nm (de coton, d'ouate) wad, pad; (amortisseur) buffer; (bouchon) plug, stopper; (cachet, timbre) stamp; (mémoire) ~ (INFORM) buffer; ~ **hygiénique** tampon; **tamponner** vt (timbres) to stamp; (heurter) to crash ou ram into; **tamponneuse** adj f:

autos tamponneuses dodgems
tandem [tɑ̃dɛm] nm tandem
tandis [tɑ̃di]: ~ **que** conj while
tanguer [tɑ̃ge] vi to pitch (and toss)
tanière [tanjɛR] nf lair, den
tanné, e [tane] adj weather-beaten
tanner [tane] vt to tan; (fam: harceler) to badger
tant [tɑ̃] adv so much; ~ **de** (sable, eau) so much; (gens, livres) so many; ~ **que** as long as; (autant que) as much as; ~ **mieux** that's great; (avec une certaine réserve) so much the better; ~ **pis** too bad; (conciliant) never mind
tante [tɑ̃t] nf aunt
tantôt [tɑ̃to] adv (parfois): ~ ... ~ now ... now; (cet après-midi) this afternoon
taon [tɑ̃] nm horsefly
tapage [tapaʒ] nm uproar, din
tapageur, -euse [tapaʒœR, øz] adj noisy; (voyant) loud, flashy
tape [tap] nf slap
tape-à-l'œil [tapalœj] adj inv flashy, showy
taper [tape] vt (porte) to bang, slam; (enfant) to slap; (dactylographier) to type (out); (fam: emprunter): ~ **qn de 10 F** to touch sb for 10 F ♦ vi (soleil) to beat down; **se ~** vt (repas) to put away; (fam: corvée) to get landed with; ~ **sur qn** to thump sb; (fig) to run sb down; ~ **sur un clou** to hit a nail; ~ **sur la table** to bang on the table; ~ **à** (porte etc) to knock on; ~ **dans** (se servir) to dig into; ~ **des mains/pieds** to clap one's hands/stamp one's feet; ~ **(à la machine)** to type; **se ~ un travail** (fam) to land o.s. a job
tapi, e [tapi] adj (blotti) crouching; (caché) hidden away
tapis [tapi] nm carpet; (petit) rug; **mettre sur le ~** (fig) to bring up for discussion; ~ **de bain** bath mat; ~ **de sol** (de tente) groundsheet; ~ **roulant** (pour piétons) moving walkway; (pour bagages) carousel
tapisser [tapise] vt (avec du papier peint) to paper; (recouvrir): ~ **qch (de)** to cover sth (with); **tapisserie** nf (tenture, broderie) tapestry; (papier peint) wallpaper; **tapissier, -ière** nm/f: **tapissier-décorateur** interior decorator
tapoter [tapɔte] vt (joue, main) to pat; (objet) to tap
taquin, e [takɛ̃, in] adj teasing; **taquiner** vt to tease
tarabiscoté, e [taRabiskɔte] adj over-ornate, fussy
tard [taR] adv late; **plus ~** later (on); **au plus ~** at the latest; **sur le ~** late in life
tarder [taRde] vi (chose) to be a long time coming; (personne): ~ **à faire** to delay doing; **il me tarde d'être** I am longing to be; **sans (plus) ~** without (further) delay

tardif, -ive [taʀdif, iv] *adj* late
taré, e [taʀe] *nm/f* cretin
tarif [taʀif] *nm*: ~ **des consommations** price list; **~s postaux/douaniers** postal/customs rates; ~ **des taxis** taxi fares; ~ **plein/réduit** (*train*) full/reduced fare; (*téléphone*) peak/off-peak rate
tarir [taʀiʀ] *vi* to dry up, run dry
tarte [taʀt] *nf* tart; ~ **aux fraises** strawberry tart; ~ **Tatin** ≈ apple upside-down tart
tartine [taʀtin] *nf* slice of bread; ~ **de miel** slice of bread and honey; **tartiner** *vt* to spread; **fromage à tartiner** cheese spread
tartre [taʀtʀ] *nm* (*des dents*) tartar; (*de bouilloire*) fur, scale
tas [tɑ] *nm* heap, pile; (*fig*): **un ~ de** heaps of, lots of; **en ~** in a heap *ou* pile; **formé sur le ~** trained on the job
tasse [tɑs] *nf* cup; ~ **à café** coffee cup
tassé, e [tɑse] *adj*: **bien ~** (*café etc*) strong
tasser [tɑse] *vt* (*terre, neige*) to pack down; (*entasser*): ~ **qch dans** to cram sth into; **se ~** *vi* (*se serrer*) to squeeze up; (*s'affaisser*) to settle; (*fig*) to settle down
tata [tata] *nf* auntie
tâter [tɑte] *vt* to feel; (*fig*) to try out; **se ~** (*hésiter*) to be in two minds; ~ **de** (*prison etc*) to have a taste of
tatillon, ne [tatijɔ̃, ɔn] *adj* pernickety
tâtonnement [tɑtɔnmɑ̃] *nm*: **par ~s** (*fig*) by trial and error
tâtonner [tɑtɔne] *vi* to grope one's way along
tâtons [tatɔ̃]: **à ~** *adv*: **chercher/avancer à ~** to grope around for/grope one's way forward
tatouage [tatwaʒ] *nm* tattoo
tatouer [tatwe] *vt* to tattoo
taudis [todi] *nm* hovel, slum
taule [tol] (*fam*) *nf* nick (*fam*), prison
taupe [top] *nf* mole
taureau, x [tɔʀo] *nm* bull; (*signe*): **le T~** Taurus
tauromachie [tɔʀɔmaʃi] *nf* bullfighting
taux [to] *nm* rate; (*d'alcool*) level; ~ **de change** exchange rate; ~ **d'intérêt** interest rate
taxe [taks] *nf* tax; (*douanière*) duty, **toutes ~s comprises** inclusive of tax; **la boutique hors ~s** the duty free shop; ~ **à la valeur ajoutée** value added tax
taxer [takse] *vt* (*personne*) to tax; (*produit*) to put a tax on, tax
taxi [taksi] *nm* taxi; (*chauffeur: fam*) taxi driver
Tchécoslovaquie [tʃekɔslɔvaki] *nf* Czechoslovakia; **tchèque** *adj* Czech ♦ *nm/f*: **Tchèque** Czech ♦ *nm* (*LING*) Czech; **la République tchèque** the Czech Republic
te, t' [tə] *pron* you; (*réfléchi*) yourself
technicien, ne [tɛknisjɛ̃, jɛn] *nm/f* technician

technico-commercial, e, -aux [tɛknikokɔmɛʀsjal, jo] *adj*: **agent ~~** sales technician
technique [tɛknik] *adj* technical ♦ *nf* technique; **techniquement** *adv* technically
technologie [tɛknɔlɔʒi] *nf* technology; **technologique** *adj* technological
teck [tɛk] *nm* teak
tee-shirt [tiʃœʀt] *nm* T-shirt, tee-shirt
teignais *etc* [tɛɲɛ] *vb voir* **teindre**
teindre [tɛ̃dʀ] *vt* to dye; **se ~ les cheveux** to dye one's hair; **teint, e** *adj* dyed ♦ *nm* (*du visage*) complexion; (*momentané*) colour ♦ *nf* shade; **grand teint** colourfast
teinté, e [tɛ̃te] *adj*: ~ **de** (*fig*) tinged with
teinter [tɛ̃te] *vt* (*verre, papier*) to tint; (*bois*) to stain
teinture [tɛ̃tyʀ] *nf* dye; ~ **d'iode** tincture of iodine; **teinturerie** *nf* dry cleaner's; **teinturier** *nm* dry cleaner
tel, telle [tɛl] *adj* (*pareil*) such; (*comme*): ~ **un/des ...** like a/like ...; (*indéfini*) such-and-such a; (*intensif*): **un ~/de tels ...** such (a)/ such ...; **rien de ~** nothing like it; ~ **que** like, such as; ~ **quel** as it is *ou* stands (*ou* was *etc*); **venez ~ jour** come on such-and-such a day
télé [tele] (*fam*) *nf* TV
télé...: **télécabine** *nf* (*benne*) cable car; **télécarte** *nf* phonecard; **télécommande** *nf* remote control; **télécopie** *nf* fax; **envoyer qch par télécopie** to fax sth; **télécopieur** *nm* fax machine; **télédistribution** *nf* cable TV; **téléférique** *nm* = **téléphérique**; **télégramme** *nm* telegram; **télégraphier** *vt* to telegraph, cable; **téléguider** *vt* to radio-control; **télématique** *nf* telematics *sg*; **téléobjectif** *nm* telephoto lens *sg*; **télépathie** *nf* telepathy; **téléphérique** *nm* cable car
téléphone [telefɔn] *nm* telephone; **avoir le ~** to be on the (tele)phone; **au ~** on the phone; ~ **mobile** mobile phone; ~ **rouge** hot line; ~ **sans fil** cordless (tele)phone; ~ **de voiture** car phone; **téléphoner** *vi* to make a phone call; **téléphoner à** to phone, call up; **téléphonique** *adj* (tele)phone *cpd*
télescope [teleskɔp] *nm* telescope
télescoper [teleskɔpe] *vt* to smash up; **se ~** (*véhicules*) to concertina
télé...: **téléscripteur** *nm* teleprinter; **télésiège** *nm* chairlift; **téléski** *nm* ski-tow; **téléspectateur, -trice** *nm/f* (television) viewer; **télévente** *nf* telesales; **téléviseur** *nm* television set; **télévision** *nf* television; **à la télévision** on television
télex [teleks] *nm* telex
telle [tɛl] *adj voir* **tel**; **tellement** *adv* (*tant*) so much; (*si*) so; **tellement de** (*sable, eau*) so much; (*gens, livres*) so many; **il s'est endormi**

tellement il était fatigué he was so tired (that) he fell asleep; **pas tellement** not (all) that much; not (all) that +*adjectif*

téméraire [temeʀɛʀ] *adj* reckless, rash; **témérité** *nf* recklessness, rashness

témoignage [temwaɲaʒ] *nm* (*JUR: déclaration*) testimony *no pl*, evidence *no pl*; (*rapport, récit*) account; (*fig: d'affection etc: cadeau*) token, mark; (: *geste*) expression

témoigner [temwaɲe] *vt* (*intérêt, gratitude*) to show ♦ *vi* (*JUR*) to testify, give evidence; **~ de** to bear witness to, testify to

témoin [temwɛ̃] *nm* witness ♦ *adj*: **appartement ~** show flat (*BRIT*); **être ~ de** to witness; **~ oculaire** eyewitness

tempe [tɑ̃p] *nf* temple

tempérament [tɑ̃peʀamɑ̃] *nm* temperament, disposition; **à ~** (*vente*) on deferred (payment) terms; (*achat*) by instalments, hire purchase *cpd*

température [tɑ̃peʀatyʀ] *nf* temperature; **avoir** *ou* **faire de la ~** to be running *ou* have a temperature

tempéré, e [tɑ̃peʀe] *adj* temperate

tempête [tɑ̃pɛt] *nf* storm; **~ de sable/neige** sand/snowstorm

temple [tɑ̃pl] *nm* temple; (*protestant*) church

temporaire [tɑ̃pɔʀɛʀ] *adj* temporary

temps [tɑ̃] *nm* (*atmosphérique*) weather; (*durée*) time; (*époque*) time, times *pl*; (*LING*) tense; (*MUS*) beat; (*TECH*) stroke; **un ~ de chien** (*fam*) rotten weather; **quel ~ fait-il?** what's the weather like?; **il fait beau/mauvais ~** the weather is fine/bad; **avoir le ~/tout son ~** to have time/plenty of time; **en ~ de paix/ guerre** in peacetime/wartime; **en ~ utile** *ou* **voulu** in due time *ou* course; **ces derniers ~** lately; **dans quelque ~** in a (little) while; **de ~ en ~, de ~ à autre** from time to time; **à ~** (*partir, arriver*) in time; **à ~ complet, à plein ~** full-time; **à ~ partiel** part-time; **dans le ~** at one time; **~ d'arrêt** pause, halt; **~ mort** (*COMM*) slack period

tenable [t(ə)nabl] *adj* bearable

tenace [tənas] *adj* persistent

tenailler [tənaje] *vt* (*fig*) to torment

tenailles [tənaj] *nfpl* pincers

tenais *etc* [t(ə)nɛ] *vb voir* **tenir**

tenancier, -ière [tənɑ̃sje] *nm/f* manager/ manageress

tenant, e [tənɑ̃, ɑ̃t] *nm/f* (*SPORT*): **~ du titre** title-holder

tendance [tɑ̃dɑ̃s] *nf* tendency; (*opinions*) leanings *pl*, sympathies *pl*; (*évolution*) trend; **avoir ~ à** to have a tendency to, tend to

tendeur [tɑ̃dœʀ] *nm* (*attache*) elastic strap

tendre [tɑ̃dʀ] *adj* tender; (*bois, roche, couleur*) soft ♦ *vt* (*élastique, peau*) to stretch; (*corde*) to tighten; (*muscle*) to tense; (*fig:*

piège) to set, lay; (*donner*): **~ qch à qn** to hold sth out to sb; (*offrir*) to offer sb sth; **se ~** *vi* (*corde*) to tighten; (*relations*) to become strained; **~ à qch/à faire** to tend towards sth/ to do; **~ l'oreille** to prick up one's ears; **~ la main/le bras** to hold out one's hand/stretch out one's arm; **tendrement** *adv* tenderly; **tendresse** *nf* tenderness

tendu, e [tɑ̃dy] *pp de* **tendre** ♦ *adj* (*corde*) tight; (*muscles*) tensed; (*relations*) strained

ténèbres [tenɛbʀ] *nfpl* darkness *sg*

teneur [tənœʀ] *nf* content; (*d'une lettre*) terms *pl*, content

tenir [t(ə)niʀ] *vt* to hold; (*magasin, hôtel*) to run; (*promesse*) to keep ♦ *vi* to hold; (*neige, gel*) to last; **se ~** *vi* (*avoir lieu*) to be held, take place; (*être: personne*) to stand; **~ à** (*personne, objet*) to be attached to; (*réputation*) to care about; **~ à faire** to be determined to do; **~ de** (*ressembler à*) to take after; **ça ne tient qu'à lui** it is entirely up to him; **~ qn pour** to regard sb as; **~ qch de qn** (*histoire*) to have heard *ou* learnt sth from sb; (*qualité, défaut*) to have inherited *ou* got sth from sb; **~ dans** to fit into; **~ compte de qch** to take sth into account; **~ les comptes** to keep the books; **~ bon** to stand fast; **~ le coup** to hold out; **~ au chaud** to keep hot; **tiens/ tenez, voilà le stylo** there's the pen!; **tiens, voilà Alain!** look, here's Alain!; **tiens?** (*surprise*) really?; **se ~ droit** to stand (*ou* sit) up straight; **bien se ~** to behave well; **se ~ à qch** to hold on to sth; **s'en ~ à qch** to confine o.s. to sth

tennis [tenis] *nm* tennis; (*court*) tennis court ♦ *nm ou f pl* (*aussi*: **chaussures de ~**) tennis *ou* gym shoes; **~ de table** table tennis; **tennisman** *nm* tennis player

tension [tɑ̃sjɔ̃] *nf* tension; (*MÉD*) blood pressure; **avoir de la ~** to have high blood pressure

tentation [tɑ̃tasjɔ̃] *nf* temptation

tentative [tɑ̃tativ] *nf* attempt

tente [tɑ̃t] *nf* tent

tenter [tɑ̃te] *vt* (*éprouver, attirer*) to tempt; (*essayer*): **~ qch/de faire** to attempt *ou* try sth/to do; **~ sa chance** to try one's luck

tenture [tɑ̃tyʀ] *nf* hanging

tenu, e [t(ə)ny] *pp de* **tenir** ♦ *adj* (*maison, comptes*): **bien ~** well-kept; (*obligé*): **~ de faire** obliged to do ♦ *nf* (*vêtements*) clothes *pl*; (*comportement*) (good) manners *pl*, good behaviour; (*d'une maison*) upkeep; **en petite ~e** scantily dressed *ou* clad; **~e de route** (*AUTO*) road-holding; **~e de soirée** evening dress

ter [tɛʀ] *adj*: **16 ~ 16b** *ou* **B**

térébenthine [teʀebɑ̃tin] *nf*: **(essence de) ~** (oil of) turpentine

Tergal ® [tɛʀgal] nm Terylene ®
terme [tɛʀm] nm term; (fin) end; **à court/
long ~ ♦** adj short-/long-term ♦ adv in the
short/long term; **avant ~** (MÉD) prematurely;
mettre un ~ à to put an end ou a stop to; **en
bons ~s** on good terms
terminaison [tɛʀminɛzɔ̃] nf (LING) ending
terminal, o nm terminal;
terminale nf (SCOL) ≈ sixth form ou year
(BRIT), ≈ twelfth grade (US)
terminer [tɛʀmine] vt to finish; **se ~** vi to
end
terne [tɛʀn] adj dull
ternir [tɛʀniʀ] vt to dull; (fig) to sully, tarnish;
se ~ vi to become dull
terrain [tɛʀɛ̃] nm (sol, fig) ground; (COMM:
étendue de terre) land no pl; (parcelle) plot (of
land); (à bâtir) site; **sur le ~** (fig) on the
field; **~ d'aviation** airfield; **~ de camping**
campsite; **~ de football/rugby** football/rugby
pitch (BRIT) ou field (US); **~ de golf** golf
course; **~ de jeu** games field; (pour les petits)
playground; **~ de sport** sports ground;
~ vague waste ground no pl
terrasse [tɛʀas] nf terrace, **à la ~** (café)
outside; **terrasser** vt (adversaire) to floor;
(suj: maladie etc) to strike down
terre [tɛʀ] nf (gén, aussi ÉLEC) earth;
(substance) soil, earth; (opposé à mer) land
no pl; (contrée) land; **~s** nfpl (terrains) lands,
land sg; **en ~** (pipe, poterie) clay cpd; **à ~** ou
par ~ (mettre, être, s'asseoir) on the ground
(ou floor); (jeter, tomber) to the ground,
down; **~ à ~** adj inv down-to-earth; **~ cuite**
terracotta; **la ~ ferme** dry land; **~ glaise** clay
terreau [tɛʀo] nm compost
terre-plein [tɛʀplɛ̃] nm platform; (sur
chaussée) central reservation
terrer [tɛʀe]: **se ~** vi to hide away
terrestre [tɛʀɛstʀ] adj (surface) earth's, of
the earth; (BOT, ZOOL, MIL) land cpd; (REL)
earthly
terreur [tɛʀœʀ] nf terror no pl
terrible [tɛʀibl] adj terrible, dreadful; (fam)
terrific; **pas ~** nothing special
terrien, ne [tɛʀjɛ̃, jɛn] adj: **propriétaire ~**
landowner ♦ nm/f (non martien etc) earthling
terrier [tɛʀje] nm burrow, hole; (chien) terrier
terrifier [tɛʀifje] vt to terrify
terrine [tɛʀin] nf (récipient) terrine; (CULIN)
pâté
territoire [tɛʀitwaʀ] nm territory
terroir [tɛʀwaʀ] nm: **accent du ~** country
accent
terroriser [tɛʀɔʀize] vt to terrorize
terrorisme [tɛʀɔʀism] nm terrorism;
terroriste nm/f terrorist
tertiaire [tɛʀsjɛʀ] adj tertiary ♦ nm (ÉCON)
service industries pl

tertre [tɛʀtʀ] nm hillock, mound
tes [te] adj voir **ton**[1]
tesson [tesɔ̃] nm: **~ de bouteille** piece of
broken bottle
test [tɛst] nm test
testament [tɛstamɑ̃] nm (JUR) will; (REL)
Testament; (fig) legacy
tester [tɛste] vt to test
testicule [tɛstikyl] nm testicle
tétanos [tetanos] nm tetanus
têtard [tɛtaʀ] nm tadpole
tête [tɛt] nf head; (cheveux) hair no pl;
(visage) face; **de ~** adj (wagon etc) front cpd
♦ adv (calculer) in one's head, mentally; **tenir
~ à qn** to stand up to sb; **la ~ en bas** with
one's head down; **la ~ la première** (tomber)
headfirst; **faire une ~** (FOOTBALL) to head the
ball; **faire la ~** (fig) to sulk; **en ~** at the front;
(SPORT) in the lead; **à la ~ de** at the head of;
à ~ reposée in a more leisurely moment; **n'en
faire qu'à sa ~** to do as one pleases; **en avoir
par-dessus la ~** to be fed up; **en ~ à ~** in
private, alone together; **de la ~ aux pieds**
from head to toe; **~ de lecture** (playback)
head; **~ de liste** (POL) chief candidate; **~ de
série** (TENNIS) seeded player, seed; **tête-à-
queue** nm inv: **faire un tête-à-queue** to spin
round
téter [tete] vt: **~ (sa mère)** to suck at one's
mother's breast, feed
tétine [tetin] nf teat; (sucette) dummy (BRIT),
pacifier (US)
têtu, e [tety] adj stubborn, pigheaded
texte [tɛkst] nm text; (morceau choisi) passage
textile [tɛkstil] adj textile cpd ♦ nm textile; **le
~** the textile industry
texto [tɛksto] (fam) adj word for word
texture [tɛkstyʀ] nf texture
thaïlandais, e [tajlɑ̃dɛ, ɛz] adj Thai ♦ nm/f:
T~, e Thai
Thaïlande [tajlɑ̃d] nf Thailand
TGV sigle m (= train à grande vitesse) high-
speed train
thé [te] nm tea; **~ au citron** lemon tea; **~ au
lait** tea with milk; **prendre le ~** to have tea;
faire le ~ to make the tea
théâtral, e, -aux [teatʀal, o] adj theatrical
théâtre [teatʀ] nm theatre; (péj: simulation)
playacting; (fig: lieu): **le ~ de** the scene of;
faire du ~ to act
théière [tejɛʀ] nf teapot
thème [tɛm] nm theme; (SCOL: traduction)
prose (composition)
théologie [teɔlɔʒi] nf theology
théorie [teɔʀi] nf theory; **théorique** adj
theoretical
thérapie [teʀapi] nf therapy
thermal, e, -aux [tɛʀmal, o] adj: **station ~e**
spa; **cure ~e** water cure

thermes [tɛʀm] *nmpl* thermal baths
thermomètre [tɛʀmɔmɛtʀ] *nm* thermometer
thermos ® [tɛʀmos] *nm ou nf*: (**bouteille**) ~ vacuum *ou* Thermos ® flask
thermostat [tɛʀmɔsta] *nm* thermostat
thèse [tɛz] *nf* thesis
thon [tɔ̃] *nm* tuna (fish)
thym [tɛ̃] *nm* thyme
tibia [tibja] *nm* shinbone, tibia; (*partie antérieure de la jambe*) shin
tic [tik] *nm* tic, (nervous) twitch; (*de langage etc*) mannerism
ticket [tikɛ] *nm* ticket; ~ **de caisse** receipt; ~ **de quai** platform ticket
tic-tac [tiktak] *nm* ticking; **faire ~~** to tick
tiède [tjɛd] *adj* lukewarm; (*vent, air*) mild, warm; **tiédir** *vi* to cool; (*se réchauffer*) to grow warmer
tien, ne [tjɛ̃, tjɛn] *pron*: **le(la) ~(ne), les ~(ne)s** yours; **à la ~ne!** cheers!
tiens [tjɛ̃] *vb, excl voir* **tenir**
tierce [tjɛʀs] *adj voir* **tiers**
tiercé [tjɛʀse] *nm* system of forecast betting giving first 3 horses
tiers, tierce [tjɛʀ, tjɛʀs] *adj* third ♦ *nm* (*JUR*) third party; (*fraction*) third; **le ~ monde** the Third World
tifs [tif] (*fam*) *nmpl* hair
tige [tiʒ] *nf* stem; (*baguette*) rod
tignasse [tiɲas] (*péj*) *nf* mop of hair
tigre [tigʀ] *nm* tiger; **tigresse** *nf* tigress; **tigré, e** *adj* (*rayé*) striped; (*tacheté*) spotted; (*chat*) tabby
tilleul [tijœl] *nm* lime (tree), linden (tree); (*boisson*) lime(-blossom) tea
timbale [tɛ̃bal] *nf* (metal) tumbler; **~s** *nfpl* (*MUS*) timpani, kettledrums
timbre [tɛ̃bʀ] *nm* (*tampon*) stamp; (*aussi*: **~ poste**) (postage) stamp; (*MUS: de voix, instrument*) timbre, tone
timbré, e [tɛ̃bʀe] (*fam*) *adj* cracked
timide [timid] *adj* shy; (*timoré*) timid; **timidement** *adv* shyly; timidly; **timidité** *nf* shyness; timidity
tins *etc* [tɛ̃] *vb voir* **tenir**
tintamarre [tɛ̃tamaʀ] *nm* din, uproar
tinter [tɛ̃te] *vi* to ring, chime; (*argent, clefs*) to jingle
tique [tik] *nf* (*parasite*) tick
tir [tiʀ] *nm* (*sport*) shooting; (*fait ou manière de ~er*) firing *no pl*; (*rafale*) fire; (*stand*) shooting gallery; ~ **à l'arc** archery; ~ **au pigeon** clay pigeon shooting
tirage [tiʀaʒ] *nm* (*action*) printing; (*PHOTO*) print; (*de journal*) circulation; (*de livre: nombre d'exemplaires*) (print) run; (: *édition*) edition; (*de loterie*) draw; **par ~ au sort** by drawing lots

tirailler [tiʀaje] *vt*: **être tiraillé entre** to be torn between
tire [tiʀ] *nf*: **vol à la ~** pickpocketing
tiré, e [tiʀe] *adj* (*traits*) drawn; ~ **par les cheveux** far-fetched
tire-au-flanc [tiʀoflɑ̃] (*péj*) *nm inv* skiver
tire-bouchon [tiʀbuʃɔ̃] *nm* corkscrew
tirelire [tiʀliʀ] *nf* moneybox
tirer [tiʀe] *vt* (*gén*) to pull; (*extraire*): ~ **qch de** to take *ou* pull sth out of; (*trait, rideau, carte, conclusion, chèque*) to draw; (*langue*) to stick out; (*en faisant feu: balle, coup*) to fire; (: *animal*) to shoot; (*journal, livre, photo*) to print; (*FOOTBALL: corner etc*) to take ♦ *vi* (*faire feu*) to fire; (*faire du tir , FOOTBALL*) to shoot; **se ~** *vi* (*fam*) to push off; **s'en ~** (*éviter le pire*) to get off; (*survivre*) to pull through; (*se débrouiller*) to manage; ~ **sur** (*corde*) to pull on *ou* at; (*faire feu sur*) to shoot *ou* fire at; (*pipe*) to draw on; (*approcher de: couleur*) to verge *ou* border on; ~ **qn de** (*embarras etc*) to help *ou* get sb out of; ~ **à l'arc/la carabine** to shoot with a bow and arrow/with a rifle; ~ **à sa fin** to be drawing to a close; ~ **qch au clair** to clear sth up; ~ **au sort** to draw lots; ~ **parti de** to take advantage of; ~ **profit de** to profit from
tiret [tiʀɛ] *nm* dash
tireur [tiʀœʀ] *nm* gunman; ~ **d'élite** marksman
tiroir [tiʀwaʀ] *nm* drawer; **tiroir-caisse** *nm* till
tisane [tizan] *nf* herb tea
tisonnier [tizɔnje] *nm* poker
tisser [tise] *vt* to weave; **tisserand** *nm* weaver
tissu [tisy] *nm* fabric, material, cloth *no pl*; (*ANAT, BIO*) tissue; **tissu-éponge** *nm* (terry) towelling *no pl*
titre [titʀ] *nm* (*gén*) title; (*de journal*) headline; (*diplôme*) qualification; (*COMM*) security; **en ~** (*champion*) official; **à juste ~** rightly; **à quel ~?** on what grounds?; **à aucun ~** on no account; **au même ~ (que)** in the same way (as); **à ~ d'information** for (your) information; **à ~ gracieux** free of charge; **à ~ d'essai** on a trial basis; **à ~ privé** in a private capacity; ~ **de propriété** title deed; ~ **de transport** ticket
tituber [titybe] *vi* to stagger (along)
titulaire [titylɛʀ] *adj* (*ADMIN*) with tenure ♦ *nm/f* (*de permis*) holder
toast [tost] *nm* slice *ou* piece of toast; (*de bienvenue*) (welcoming) toast; **porter un ~ à qn** to propose *ou* drink a toast to sb
toboggan [tɔbɔgɑ̃] *nm* slide; (*AUTO*) flyover
toc [tɔk] *excl*: ~, **toc** knock knock ♦ *nm*: **en ~** fake
tocsin [tɔksɛ̃] *nm* alarm (bell)

toge [tɔʒ] nf toga; (de juge) gown

tohu-bohu [tɔybɔy] nm hubbub

toi [twa] pron you

toile [twal] nf (tableau) canvas; **de** ou **en ~** (pantalon) cotton; (sac) canvas; **~ cirée** oilcloth; **~ d'araignée** cobweb; **~ de fond** (fig) backdrop

toilette [twalɛt] nf (habits) outfit; **~s** nfpl (w.-c.) toilet sg; **faire sa ~** to have a wash, get washed; **articles de ~** toiletries

toi-même [twamɛm] pron yourself

toiser [twaze] vt to eye up and down

toison [twazɔ̃] nf (de mouton) fleece

toit [twa] nm roof; **~ ouvrant** sunroof

toiture [twatyʀ] nf roof

tôle [tol] nf (plaque) steel ou iron sheet; **~ ondulée** corrugated iron

tolérable [tɔleʀabl] adj tolerable

tolérant, e [tɔleʀɑ̃, ɑ̃t] adj tolerant

tolérer [tɔleʀe] vt to tolerate; (ADMIN: hors taxe etc) to allow

tollé [tɔ(l)le] nm outcry

tomate [tɔmat] nf tomato; **~s farcies** stuffed tomatoes

tombe [tɔ̃b] nf (sépulture) grave; (avec monument) tomb

tombeau, x [tɔ̃bo] nm tomb

tombée [tɔ̃be] nf: **à la ~ de la nuit** at nightfall

tomber [tɔ̃be] vi to fall; (fièvre, vent) to drop; **laisser ~** (objet) to drop; (personne) to let down; (activité) to give up; **laisse ~!** forget it!; **faire ~** to knock over; **~ sur** (rencontrer) to bump into; **~ de fatigue/sommeil** to drop from exhaustion/be falling asleep on one's feet; **ça tombe bien** that's come at the right time; **il est bien tombé** he's been lucky; **~ à l'eau** (projet) to fall through; **~ en panne** to break down

tombola [tɔ̃bɔla] nf raffle

tome [tɔm] nm volume

ton¹, ta [tɔ̃, ta] (pl **tes**) adj your

ton² [tɔ̃] nm (gén) tone; (couleur) shade, tone; **de bon ~** in good taste

tonalité [tɔnalite] nf (au téléphone) dialling tone

tondeuse [tɔ̃døz] nf (à gazon) (lawn) mower; (du coiffeur) clippers pl; (pour les moutons) shears pl

tondre [tɔ̃dʀ] vt (pelouse, herbe) to mow; (haie) to cut, clip; (mouton, toison) to shear; (cheveux) to crop

tongs [tɔ̃g] nfpl flip-flops

tonifier [tɔnifje] vt (peau, organisme) to tone up

tonique [tɔnik] adj fortifying ♦ nm tonic

tonne [tɔn] nf metric ton, tonne

tonneau, x [tɔno] nm (à vin, cidre) barrel; **faire des ~x** (voiture, avion) to roll over

tonnelle [tɔnɛl] nf bower, arbour

tonner [tɔne] vi to thunder; **il tonne** it is thundering, there's some thunder

tonnerre [tɔnɛʀ] nm thunder

tonton [tɔ̃tɔ̃] nm uncle

tonus [tɔnys] nm energy

top [tɔp] nm: **au 3ème ~** at the 3rd stroke

topinambour [tɔpinɑ̃buʀ] nm Jerusalem artichoke

topo [tɔpo] (fam) nm rundown; **c'est le même ~** it's the same old story

toque [tɔk] nf (de fourrure) fur hat; **~ de cuisinier** chef's hat; **~ de jockey/juge** jockey's/judge's cap

toqué, e [tɔke] (fam) adj cracked

torche [tɔʀʃ] nf torch

torchon [tɔʀʃɔ̃] nm cloth; (à vaisselle) tea towel ou cloth

tordre [tɔʀdʀ] vt (chiffon) to wring; (barre, fig: visage) to twist; **se ~** vi: **se ~ le poignet/la cheville** to twist one's wrist/ankle; **se ~ de douleur/rire** to be doubled up with pain/laughter; **tordu, e** adj bent; (fig) crazy

tornade [tɔʀnad] nf tornado

torpille [tɔʀpij] nf torpedo

torréfier [tɔʀefje] vt to roast

torrent [tɔʀɑ̃] nm mountain stream

torsade [tɔʀsad] nf: **un pull à ~s** a cable sweater

torse [tɔʀs] nm chest; (ANAT, SCULPTURE) torso; **~ nu** stripped to the waist

tort [tɔʀ] nm (défaut) fault; **~s** nmpl (JUR) fault sg; **avoir ~** to be wrong; **être dans son ~** to be in the wrong; **donner ~ à qn** to lay the blame on sb; **causer du ~ à** to harm; **à ~** wrongly; **à ~ et à travers** wildly

torticolis [tɔʀtikɔli] nm stiff neck

tortiller [tɔʀtije] vt to twist; (moustache) to twirl; **se ~** vi to wriggle; (en dansant) to wiggle

tortionnaire [tɔʀsjɔnɛʀ] nm torturer

tortue [tɔʀty] nf tortoise; (d'eau douce) terrapin; (d'eau de mer) turtle

tortueux, -euse [tɔʀtɥø, øz] adj (rue) twisting; (fig) tortuous

torture [tɔʀtyʀ] nf torture; **torturer** vt to torture; (fig) to torment

tôt [to] adv early; **~ ou tard** sooner or later; **si ~** so early; (déjà) so soon; **plus ~** earlier; **au plus ~** at the earliest; **il eut ~ fait de faire** he soon did

total, e, -aux [tɔtal, o] adj, nm total; **au ~** in total; (fig) on the whole; **faire le ~** to work out the total; **totalement** adv totally; **totaliser** vt to total; **totalitaire** adj totalitarian; **totalité** nf: **la totalité de** all (of); the whole +sg; **en totalité** entirely

toubib [tubib] (fam) nm doctor

touchant, e [tuʃɑ̃, ɑ̃t] adj touching

touche [tuʃ] nf (de piano, de machine à écrire)

key; (*de téléphone*) button; (*PEINTURE etc*)
stroke, touch; (*fig: de nostalgie*) touch;
(*FOOTBALL: aussi*: **remise en ~**) throw-in;
(*aussi:* **ligne de ~**) touch-line

toucher [tuʃe] *nm* touch ♦ *vt* to touch;
(*palper*) to feel; (*atteindre: d'un coup de feu
etc*) to hit; (*concerner*) to concern, affect;
(*contacter*) to reach, contact; (*recevoir:
récompense*) to receive, get; (: *salaire*) to
draw, get; (: *chèque*) to cash; **se ~** (*être en
contact*) to touch; **au ~** to the touch; **~ à** to
touch; (*concerner*) to have to do with,
concern; **je vais lui en ~ un mot** I'll have a
word with him about it; **~ à sa fin** to be
drawing to a close

touffe [tuf] *nf* tuft

touffu, e [tufy] *adj* thick, dense

toujours [tuʒuʀ] *adv* always; (*encore*) still;
(*constamment*) forever; **~ plus** more and
more; **pour ~** forever; **~ est-il que** the fact
remains that; **essaie ~** (you can) try anyway

toupet [tupɛ] (*fam*) *nm* cheek

toupie [tupi] *nf* (spinning) top

tour [tuʀ] *nf* tower; (*immeuble*) high-rise block
(*BRIT*) *ou* building (*US*); (*ÉCHECS*) castle, rook
♦ *nm* (*excursion*) trip; (*à pied*) stroll, walk;
(*en voiture*) run, ride; (*SPORT: aussi:* **~ de
piste**) lap; (*d'être servi ou de jouer etc*) turn;
(*de roue etc*) revolution; (*POL: aussi:* **~ de
scrutin**) ballot; (*ruse, de prestidigitation*) trick;
(*de potier*) wheel; (*à bois, métaux*) lathe;
(*circonférence*): **de 3 m** ≃ 3 m round, with
a circumference *ou* girth of 3 m; **faire le ~ de**
to go round; (*à pied*) to walk round; **c'est au
~ de Renée** it's Renée's turn; **à ~ de rôle**, **à ~
de main** in turn; **~ de chant** *nm* song recital; **~ de
contrôle** *nf* control tower; **~ d'horizon** *nm* (*fig*) general survey;
~ de garde *nm* spell
of duty; **~ de taille/tête** *nm* waist/head measurement;
un 33 ~s an LP; **un 45 ~s** a single

tourbe [tuʀb] *nf* peat

tourbillon [tuʀbijɔ̃] *nm* whirlwind; (*d'eau*)
whirlpool; (*fig*) whirl, swirl; **tourbillonner** *vi*
to whirl (round)

tourelle [tuʀɛl] *nf* turret

tourisme [tuʀism] *nm* tourism; **agence de ~**
tourist agency; **faire du ~** to go touring; (*en
ville*) to go sightseeing; **touriste** *nm/f*
tourist; **touristique** *adj* tourist *cpd*; (*région*)
touristic

tourment [tuʀmɑ̃] *nm* torment; **tourmenter** *vt* to torment; **se tourmenter** *vi*
to fret, worry o.s.

tournage [tuʀnaʒ] *nm* (*CINÉMA*) shooting

tournant [tuʀnɑ̃] *nm* (*de route*) bend; (*fig*)
turning point

tournebroche [tuʀnəbʀɔʃ] *nm* roasting spit

tourne-disque [tuʀnədisk] *nm* record
player

tournée [tuʀne] *nf* (*du facteur etc*) round;
(*d'artiste, politicien*) tour; (*au café*) round (of
drinks)

tournemain [tuʀnəmɛ̃]: **en un ~** *adv* (as)
quick as a flash

tourner [tuʀne] *vt* to turn; (*sauce, mélange*)
to stir; (*CINÉMA: faire les prises de vues*) to
shoot; (: *produire*) to make ♦ *vi* to turn;
(*moteur*) to run; (*taximètre*) to tick away;
(*lait etc*) to turn (sour); **se ~** *vi* to turn round;
mal ~ to go wrong; **~ autour de** to go round;
(*péj*) to hang round; **~ à/en** to turn into; **~ à
gauche/droite** to turn left/right; **~ le dos à** to
turn one's back on; to have one's back to;
~ de l'œil to pass out; **se ~ vers** to turn
towards; (*fig*) to turn to

tournesol [tuʀnəsɔl] *nm* sunflower

tournevis [tuʀnəvis] *nm* screwdriver

tourniquet [tuʀnikɛ] *nm* (*pour arroser*)
sprinkler; (*portillon*) turnstile; (*présentoir*)
revolving stand

tournoi [tuʀnwa] *nm* tournament

tournoyer [tuʀnwaje] *vi* to swirl (round)

tournure [tuʀnyʀ] *nf* (*LING*) turn of phrase;
(*évolution*): **la ~ de qch** the way sth is
developing; **~ d'esprit** turn *ou* cast of mind;
la ~ des événements the turn of events

tourte [tuʀt] *nf* pie

tourterelle [tuʀtəʀɛl] *nf* turtledove

tous [tu] *adj, pron voir* **tout**

Toussaint [tusɛ̃] *nf*: **la ~** All Saints' Day

tousser [tuse] *vi* to cough

MOT-CLÉ

---

tout, e [tu, tut] (*mpl* **tous**, *fpl* **toutes**) *adj* **1**
(*avec article singulier*) all; **tout le lait** all the
milk; **toute la nuit** all night, the whole night;
tout le livre the whole book; **tout un pain** a
whole loaf; **tout le temps** all the time; the
whole time; **c'est tout le contraire** it's quite
the opposite
2 (*avec article pluriel*) every, all; **tous les livres**
all the books; **toutes les nuits** every night;
toutes les fois every time; **toutes les trois/
deux semaines** every third/other *ou* second
week, every three/two weeks; **tous les deux**
both *ou* each of us (*ou* them *ou* you); **toutes
les trois** all three of us (*ou* them *ou* you)
3 (*sans article*): **à tout âge** at any age; **pour
toute nourriture, il avait ...** his only food
was ...
♦ *pron* everything, all; **il a tout fait** he's done
everything; **je les vois tous** I can see them all
ou all of them; **nous y sommes tous allés** all
of us went, we all went; **en tout** in all; **tout ce
qu'il sait** all he knows
♦ *nm* whole; **le tout** all of it (*ou* them); **le
tout est de ...** the main thing is to ...; **pas du
tout** not at all

♦ *adv* **1** (*très, complètement*) very; **tout près** very near; **le tout premier** the very first; **tout seul** all alone; **le livre tout entier** the whole book; **tout en haut** right at the top; **tout droit** straight ahead

2: **tout en** while; **tout en travaillant** while working, as he *etc* works

3: **tout d'abord** first of all; **tout à coup** suddenly; **tout à fait** absolutely; **tout à l'heure** a short while ago; (*futur*) in a short while, shortly; **à tout à l'heure!** see you later!; **tout de même** all the same; **tout le monde** everybody; **tout de suite** immediately, straight away; **tout terrain** *ou* **tous terrains** all-terrain

toutefois [tutfwa] *adv* however

toutes [tut] *adj, pron voir* **tout**

toux [tu] *nf* cough

toxicomane [tɔksikɔman] *nm/f* drug addict

toxique [tɔksik] *adj* toxic

trac [tʀak] *nm* (*au théâtre, en public*) stage fright; (*aux examens*) nerves *pl*; **avoir le ~** (*au théâtre, en public*) to have stage fright; (*aux examens*) to be feeling nervous

tracasser [tʀakase] *vt* to worry, bother; **se ~** to worry

trace [tʀas] *nf* (*empreintes*) tracks *pl*; (*marques, aussi fig*) mark; (*quantité infime, indice, vestige*) trace; **~s de pas** footprints

tracé [tʀase] *nm* (*parcours*) line; (*plan*) layout

tracer [tʀase] *vt* to draw; (*piste*) to open up

tract [tʀakt] *nm* tract, pamphlet

tractations [tʀaktasjɔ̃] *nfpl* dealings, bargaining *sg*

tracteur [tʀaktœʀ] *nm* tractor

traction [tʀaksjɔ̃] *nf*: **~ avant/arrière** front-wheel/rear-wheel drive

tradition [tʀadisjɔ̃] *nf* tradition; **traditionnel, le** *adj* traditional

traducteur, -trice [tʀadyktœʀ, tʀis] *nm/f* translator

traduction [tʀadyksjɔ̃] *nf* translation

traduire [tʀadɥiʀ] *vt* to translate; (*exprimer*) to convey; **~ qn en justice** to bring sb before the courts

trafic [tʀafik] *nm* traffic; **~ d'armes** arms dealing; **trafiquant, e** *nm/f* trafficker; (*d'armes*) dealer; **trafiquer** (*péj*) *vt* (*vin*) to doctor; (*moteur, document*) to tamper with

tragédie [tʀaʒedi] *nf* tragedy; **tragique** *adj* tragic

trahir [tʀaiʀ] *vt* to betray; **trahison** *nf* betrayal; (*JUR*) treason

train [tʀɛ̃] *nm* (*RAIL*) train; (*allure*) pace; **être en ~ de faire qch** to be doing sth; **mettre qn en ~** to put sb in good spirits; **se sentir en ~** to feel in good form; **~ d'atterrissage** undercarriage; **~ de vie** style of living; **~ électrique** (*jouet*) (electric) train set; **~-**

autos-couchettes car-sleeper train

traîne [tʀɛn] *nf* (*de robe*) train; **être à la ~** to lag behind

traîneau, x [tʀɛno] *nm* sleigh, sledge

traînée [tʀɛne] *nf* trail; (*sur un mur, dans le ciel*) streak; (*péj*) slut

traîner [tʀɛne] *vt* (*remorque*) to pull; (*enfant, chien*) to drag *ou* trail along ♦ *vi* (*robe, manteau*) to trail; (*être en désordre*) to lie around; (*aller lentement*) to dawdle (along); (*vagabonder, agir lentement*) to hang about; (*durer*) to drag on; **se ~** *vi* to drag o.s. along; **~ les pieds** to drag one's feet

train-train [tʀɛ̃tʀɛ̃] *nm* humdrum routine

traire [tʀɛʀ] *vt* to milk

trait [tʀɛ] *nm* (*ligne*) line; (*de dessin*) stroke; (*caractéristique*) feature, trait; **~s** *nmpl* (*du visage*) features; **d'un ~** (*boire*) in one gulp; **de ~** (*animal*) draught; **avoir ~ à** to concern; **~ d'union** hyphen

traitant, e [tʀɛtɑ̃, ɑ̃t] *adj* (*shampooing*) medicated; **votre médecin ~** your usual *ou* family doctor

traite [tʀɛt] *nf* (*COMM*) draft; (*AGR*) milking; **d'une ~** without stopping; **la ~ des noirs** the slave trade

traité [tʀɛte] *nm* treaty

traitement [tʀɛtmɑ̃] *nm* treatment; (*salaire*) salary; **~ de données** data processing; **~ de texte** word processing; (*logiciel*) word processing package

traiter [tʀɛte] *vt* to treat; (*qualifier*): **~ qn d'idiot** to call sb a fool ♦ *vi* to deal; **~ de** to deal with

traiteur [tʀɛtœʀ] *nm* caterer

traître, -esse [tʀɛtʀ, tʀɛtʀɛs] *adj* (*dangereux*) treacherous ♦ *nm* traitor

trajectoire [tʀaʒɛktwaʀ] *nf* path

trajet [tʀaʒɛ] *nm* (*parcours, voyage*) journey; (*itinéraire*) route; (*distance à parcourir*) distance

trame [tʀam] *nf* (*de tissu*) weft; (*fig*) framework; **usé jusqu'à la ~** threadbare

tramer [tʀame] *vt*: **il se trame quelque chose** there's something brewing

trampoline [tʀɑ̃pɔlin] *nm* trampoline

tramway [tʀamwɛ] *nm* tram(way); (*voiture*) tram(car) (*BRIT*), streetcar (*US*)

tranchant, e [tʀɑ̃ʃɑ̃, ɑ̃t] *adj* sharp; (*fig*) peremptory ♦ *nm* (*d'un couteau*) cutting edge; (*de la main*) edge; **à double ~** double-edged

tranche [tʀɑ̃ʃ] *nf* (*morceau*) slice; (*arête*) edge; **~ d'âge/de salaires** age/wage bracket

tranché, e [tʀɑ̃ʃe] *adj* (*couleurs*) distinct; (*opinions*) clear-cut; **tranchée** *nf* trench

trancher [tʀɑ̃ʃe] *vt* to cut, sever ♦ *vi* to take a decision; **~ avec** to contrast sharply with

tranquille [tʀɑ̃kil] *adj* quiet; (*rassuré*) easy in

one's mind, with one's mind at rest; **se tenir ~** (*enfant*) to be quiet; **laisse-moi/laisse-ça ~** leave me/it alone; **avoir la conscience ~** to have a clear conscience; **tranquillisant** *nm* tranquillizer; **tranquillité** *nf* peace (and quiet); (*d'esprit*) peace of mind

transat [trãzat] *nm* deckchair

transborder [trãsbɔrde] *vt* to tran(s)ship

transcription [trãskripsjɔ̃] *nf* transcription; (*copie*) transcript

transférer [trãsfere] *vt* to transfer; **transfert** *nm* transfer

transformation [trãsfɔrmasjɔ̃] *nf* change; transformation; alteration; (*RUGBY*) conversion

transformer [trãsfɔrme] *vt* to change; (*radicalement*) to transform; (*vêtement*) to alter; (*matière première, appartement, RUGBY*) to convert; (**se**) **~ en** to turn into

transfusion [trãsfyzjɔ̃] *nf*: **~ sanguine** blood transfusion

transgresser [trãsgrese] *vt* to contravene

transi, e [trãzi] *adj* numb (with cold), chilled to the bone

transiger [trãziʒe] *vi* to compromise

transit [trãzit] *nm* transit; **transiter** *vi* to pass in transit

transitif, -ive [trãzitif, iv] *adj* transitive

transition [trãzisjɔ̃] *nf* transition; **transitoire** *adj* transitional

translucide [trãslysid] *adj* translucent

transmettre [trãsmɛtr] *vt* (*passer*): **~ qch à qn** to pass sth on to sb; (*TECH, TÉL, MÉD*) to transmit; (*TV, RADIO: retransmettre*) to broadcast; **transmission** *nf* transmission

transparent, e [trãsparã, ãt] *adj* transparent

transpercer [trãsperse] *vt* (*froid, pluie*) to go through, pierce; (*balle*) to go through

transpiration [trãspirasjɔ̃] *nf* perspiration

transpirer [trãspire] *vi* to perspire

transplanter [trãsplãte] *vt* (*MÉD, BOT*) to transplant; **transplantation** *nf* (*MÉD*) transplant

transport [trãspɔr] *nm* transport; **~s en commun** public transport *sg*; **transporter** *vt* to carry, move; (*COMM*) to transport, convey; **transporteur** *nm* haulage contractor (*BRIT*), trucker (*US*)

transvaser [trãsvaze] *vt* to decant

transversal, e, -aux [trãsversal, o] *adj* (*rue*) which runs across; **coupe ~e** cross section

trapèze [trapɛz] *nm* (*au cirque*) trapeze

trappe [trap] *nf* trap door

trapu, e [trapy] *adj* squat, stocky

traquenard [traknar] *nm* trap

traquer [trake] *vt* to track down; (*harceler*) to hound

traumatiser [tromatize] *vt* to traumatize

travail, -aux [travaj] *nm* (*gén*) work; (*tâche, métier*) work *no pl*, job; (*ÉCON, MÉD*) labour; **être sans ~** (*employé*) to be out of work *ou* unemployed; *voir aussi* **travaux**; **~ (au) noir** moonlighting

travailler [travaje] *vi* to work; (*bois*) to warp ♦ *vt* (*bois, métal*) to work; (*objet d'art, discipline*) to work on; **cela le travaille** it is on his mind; **travailleur, -euse** *adj* hardworking ♦ *nm/f* worker; **travailliste** *adj* ≈ Labour *cpd*

travaux [travo] *nmpl* (*de réparation, agricoles etc*) work *sg*; (*sur route*) roadworks *pl*; (*de construction*) building (work); **travaux des champs** farmwork *sg*; **travaux dirigés** (*SCOL*) tutorial; **travaux forcés** hard labour *sg*; **travaux manuels** (*SCOL*) handicrafts; **travaux ménagers** housework *sg*; **travaux pratiques** (*SCOL*) practical work; (*en laboratoire*) lab work

travers [traver] *nm* fault, failing; **en ~ (de)** across; **au ~ (de)/à ~** through; **de ~** (*nez, bouche*) crooked; (*chapeau*) askew; **comprendre de ~** to misunderstand; **regarder de ~** (*fig*) to look askance at

traverse [travers] *nf* (*de voie ferrée*) sleeper; **chemin de ~** shortcut

traversée [traverse] *nf* crossing

traverser [traverse] *vt* (*gén*) to cross; (*ville, tunnel, aussi: percer, fig*) to go through; (*suj: ligne, trait*) to run across

traversin [traversɛ̃] *nm* bolster

travesti [travesti] *nm* transvestite

trébucher [trebyʃe] *vi*: **~ (sur)** to stumble (over), trip (against)

trèfle [trefl] *nm* (*BOT*) clover; (*CARTES: couleur*) clubs *pl*; (*: carte*) club

treille [trej] *nf* vine arbour

treillis [treji] *nm* (*métallique*) wire-mesh

treize [trez] *num* thirteen; **treizième** *num* thirteenth

tréma [trema] *nm* diaeresis

tremblement [trãbləmã] *nm*: **~ de terre** earthquake

trembler [trãble] *vi* to tremble, shake; **~ de** (*froid, fièvre*) to shiver *ou* tremble with; (*peur*) to shake *ou* tremble with; **~ pour qn** to fear for sb

trémousser [tremuse]: **se ~** *vi* to jig about, wriggle about

trempe [trãp] *nf* (*fig*): **de cette/sa ~** of this/his calibre

trempé, e [trãpe] *adj* soaking (wet), drenched; (*TECH*) tempered

tremper [trãpe] *vt* to soak, drench; (*aussi: faire ~, mettre à ~*) to soak; (*plonger*): **~ qch dans** to dip sth in(to) ♦ *vi* to soak; (*fig*): **~ dans** to be involved *ou* have a hand in; **se ~** *vi* to have a quick dip; **trempette** *nf*: **faire**

trempette to go paddling

tremplin [trɑ̃plɛ̃] nm springboard; (SKI) ski-jump

trentaine [trɑ̃tɛn] nf: une ~ (de) thirty or so, about thirty; **avoir la ~** (âge) to be around thirty

trente [trɑ̃t] num thirty; **être/se mettre sur son ~ et un** to be wearing/put on one's Sunday best; **trentième** num thirtieth

trépidant, e [trepidɑ̃, ɑ̃t] adj (fig: rythme) pulsating; (: vie) hectic

trépied [trepje] nm tripod

trépigner [trepiɲe] vi to stamp (one's feet)

très [trɛ] adv very; much +pp, highly +pp

trésor [trezɔr] nm treasure; T~ **(public)** public revenue; **trésorerie** nf (gestion) accounts pl; (bureaux) accounts department; **difficultés de trésorerie** cash problems, shortage of cash ou funds; **trésorier, -ière** nm/f treasurer

tressaillir [tresajir] vi to shiver, shudder

tressauter [tresote] vi to start, jump

tresse [trɛs] nf braid, plait; **tresser** vt (cheveux) to braid, plait; (fil, jonc) to plait; (corbeille) to weave, (corde) to twist

tréteau, x [treto] nm trestle

treuil [trœj] nm winch

trêve [trɛv] nf (MIL, POL) truce; (fig) respite; ~ **de** ... enough of this ...

tri [tri] nm: **faire le ~ (de)** to sort out; **le (bureau de) ~** (POSTES) the sorting office

triangle [trijɑ̃gl] nm triangle; **triangulaire** adj triangular

tribord [tribɔr] nm: **à ~** starboard, on the starboard side

tribu [triby] nf tribe

tribunal, -aux [tribynal, o] nm (JUR) court, (MIL) tribunal

tribune [tribyn] nf (estrade) platform, rostrum; (débat) forum; (d'église, de tribunal) gallery; (de stade) stand

tribut [triby] nm tribute

tributaire [tribytɛr] adj: **être ~ de** to be dependent on

tricher [trije] vi to cheat; **tricheur, -euse** nm/f cheat(er)

tricolore [trikɔlɔr] adj three-coloured; (français) red, white and blue

tricot [triko] nm (technique, ouvrage) knitting no pl; (vêtement) jersey, sweater; ~ **de peau** vest; **tricoter** vt to knit

trictrac [triktrak] nm backgammon

tricycle [trisikl] nm tricycle

triennal, e, -aux [trijenal, o] adj three-year

trier [trije] vt to sort out; (POSTES, fruits) to sort

trimestre [trimɛstr] nm (SCOL) term; (COMM) quarter; **trimestriel, le** adj quarterly; (SCOL) end-of-term

tringle [trɛ̃gl] nf rod

trinquer [trɛ̃ke] vi to clink glasses

triomphe [trijɔ̃f] nm triumph; **triompher** vi to triumph, win; **triompher de** to triumph over, overcome

tripes [trip] nfpl (CULIN) tripe sg

triple [tripl] adj triple ♦ nm: **le ~ (de)** (comparaison) three times as much (as); **en ~ exemplaire** in triplicate; **tripler** vi, vt to triple, treble

triplés, -ées [triple] nm/fpl triplets

tripoter [tripɔte] vt to fiddle with

triste [trist] adj sad; (couleur, temps, journée) dreary; (péj): ~ **personnage/affaire** sorry individual/affair; **tristesse** nf sadness

trivial, e, -aux [trivjal, o] adj coarse, crude; (commun) mundane

troc [trɔk] nm barter

troène [trɔɛn] nm privet

trognon [trɔɲɔ̃] nm (de fruit) core; (de légume) stalk

trois [trwa] num three; **troisième** num third; **trois quarts** nmpl: **les trois quarts de** three-quarters of

trombe [trɔ̃b] nf: **des ~s d'eau** a downpour; **en ~** like a whirlwind

trombone [trɔ̃bɔn] nm (MUS) trombone; (de bureau) paper clip

trompe [trɔ̃p] nf (d'éléphant) trunk; (MUS) trumpet, horn

tromper [trɔ̃pe] vt to deceive; (vigilance, poursuivants) to elude; **se ~** vi to make a mistake, be mistaken; **se ~ de voiture/jour** to take the wrong car/get the day wrong; **se ~ de 3 cm/20 F** to be out by 3 cm/20 F; **tromperie** nf deception, trickery no pl

trompette [trɔ̃pɛt] nf trumpet; **en ~** (nez) turned-up

trompeur, -euse [trɔ̃pœr, øz] adj deceptive

tronc [trɔ̃] nm (BOT, ANAT) trunk; (d'église) collection box

tronçon [trɔ̃sɔ̃] nm section; **tronçonner** vt to saw up

trône [tron] nm throne

trop [tro] adv (+vb) too much; (+adjectif, adverbe) too; ~ **(nombreux)** too many, ~ **peu (nombreux)** too few; ~ **(souvent)** too often; ~ **(longtemps)** (for) too long; ~ **de** (nombre) too many; (quantité) too much; **de ~, en ~: des livres en ~** a few books too many; **du lait en ~** too much milk; **3 livres/3 F de ~** 3 books too many/3 F too much

tropical, e, -aux [trɔpikal, o] adj tropical

tropique [trɔpik] nm tropic

trop-plein [troplɛ̃] nm (tuyau) overflow ou outlet (pipe); (liquide) overflow

troquer [trɔke] vt: ~ **qch contre** to barter ou trade sth for; (fig) to swap sth for

trot [tro] nm trot; **trotter** vi to trot

trotteuse [tʀɔtøz] nf (sweep) second hand
trottinette [tʀɔtinɛt] nf (child's) scooter
trottoir [tʀɔtwaʀ] nm pavement; **faire le ~**
(péj) to walk the streets; **~ roulant** moving
walkway, travellator
trou [tʀu] nm hole; (fig) gap; (COMM) deficit;
~ d'air air pocket; **~ d'ozone** ozone hole; **le
~ de la serrure** the keyhole; **~ de mémoire**
blank, lapse of memory
troublant, e [tʀublã, ãt] adj disturbing
trouble [tʀubl] adj (liquide) cloudy; (image,
photo) blurred; (affaire) shady, murky ♦ nm
agitation; **~s** nmpl (POL) disturbances,
troubles, unrest sg; (MÉD) trouble sg,
disorders; **trouble-fête** nm spoilsport
troubler [tʀuble] vt to disturb; (liquide) to
make cloudy; (intriguer) to bother; **se ~** vi
(personne) to become flustered ou confused
trouer [tʀue] vt to make a hole (ou holes) in
trouille [tʀuj] (fam) nf: **avoir la ~** to be
scared to death
troupe [tʀup] nf troop; **~ (de théâtre)**
(theatrical) company
troupeau, x [tʀupo] nm (de moutons) flock;
(de vaches) herd
trousse [tʀus] nf case, kit; (d'écolier) pencil
case; **aux ~s de** (fig) on the heels ou tail of;
~ à outils toolkit; **~ de toilette** toilet bag
trousseau, x [tʀuso] nm (de mariée)
trousseau; **~ de clefs** bunch of keys
trouvaille [tʀuvaj] nf find
trouver [tʀuve] vt to find; (rendre visite):
aller/venir ~ qn to go/come and see sb; **se ~**
vi (être) to be; **je trouve que** I find ou think
that; **~ à boire/critiquer** to find something to
drink/criticize; **se ~ bien** to feel well; **se ~ mal**
to pass out
truand [tʀyã] nm gangster; **truander** vt: **se
faire truander** to be swindled
truc [tʀyk] nm (astuce) way, trick; (de cinéma,
prestidigitateur) trick, effect; (chose) thing,
thingumajig; **avoir le ~** to have the knack
truelle [tʀyɛl] nf trowel
truffe [tʀyf] nf truffle; (nez) nose
truffé, e [tʀyfe] adj: **~ de** (fig) peppered
with; (fautes) riddled with; (pièges) bristling
with
truie [tʀɥi] nf sow
truite [tʀɥit] nf trout inv
truquage [tʀykaʒ] nm special effects
truquer [tʀyke] vt (élections, serrure, dés) to
fix
TSVP sigle (= tournez svp) PTO
TTC sigle (= toutes taxes comprises) inclusive of
tax
tu¹ [ty] pron you
tu², e [ty] pp de **taire**
tuba [tyba] nm (MUS) tuba; (SPORT) snorkel
tube [tyb] nm tube; (chanson) hit

tuberculose [tybɛʀkyloz] nf tuberculosis
tuer [tɥe] vt to kill; **se ~** vi to be killed;
(suicide) to kill o.s.; **tuerie** nf slaughter no pl
tue-tête [tytɛt]: **à ~~** adv at the top of one's
voice
tueur [tɥœʀ] nm killer; **~ à gages** hired killer
tuile [tɥil] nf tile; (fam) spot of bad luck, blow
tulipe [tylip] nf tulip
tuméfié, e [tymefje] adj puffed-up, swollen
tumeur [tymœʀ] nf growth, tumour
tumulte [tymylt] nm commotion;
tumultueux, -euse adj stormy, turbulent
tunique [tynik] nf tunic
Tunisie [tynizi] nf: **la ~** Tunisia; **tunisien, ne**
adj Tunisian ♦ nm/f: **Tunisien, ne** Tunisian
tunnel [tynɛl] nm tunnel; **le ~ sous la Manche**
the Channel Tunnel
turbulences [tyʀbylãs] nfpl (AVIAT)
turbulence sg
turbulent, e [tyʀbylã, ãt] adj boisterous,
unruly
turc, turque [tyʀk] adj Turkish ♦ nm/f: **T~,
-que** Turk/Turkish woman ♦ nm (LING) Turkish
turf [tyʀf] nm racing; **turfiste** nm/f racegoer
Turquie [tyʀki] nf: **la ~** Turkey
turquoise [tyʀkwaz] nf turquoise ♦ adj inv
turquoise
tus etc [ty] vb voir **taire**
tutelle [tytɛl] nf (JUR) guardianship; (POL)
trusteeship; **sous la ~ de** (fig) under the
supervision of
tuteur [tytœʀ] nm (JUR) guardian; (de plante)
stake, support
tutoyer [tytwaje] vt: **~ qn** to address sb as
"tu"
tuyau, x [tɥijo] nm pipe; (flexible) tube;
(fam) tip; **~ d'arrosage** hosepipe;
~ d'échappement exhaust pipe; **tuyauterie**
nf piping no pl
TVA sigle f (= taxe à la valeur ajoutée) VAT
tympan [tɛ̃pã] nm (ANAT) eardrum
type [tip] nm type; (fam) chap, guy ♦ adj
typical, classic
typé, e [tipe] adj ethnic
typique [tipik] adj typical
tyran [tiʀã] nm tyrant; **tyrannique** adj
tyrannical
tzigane [dzigan] adj gipsy, tzigane

U, u

UEM sigle f (= union économique et monétaire)
EMU
ulcère [ylsɛʀ] nm ulcer; **ulcérer** vt (fig) to
sicken, appal
ultérieur, e [ylteʀjœʀ] adj later, subsequent;
remis à une date ~e postponed to a later
date; **ultérieurement** adv later,

subsequently
ultime [yltim] *adj* final
ultra... [yltʀa] *préfixe*: **~moderne/-rapide**
ultra-modern/-fast

MOT-CLÉ
---

un, une [œ̃, yn] *art indéf* a; (*devant voyelle*)
an; **un garçon/vieillard** a boy/an old man;
une fille a girl
♦ *pron* one; **l'un des meilleurs** one of the
best; **l'un ..., l'autre** (the) one ..., the other;
les uns ..., les autres some ..., others; **l'un et
l'autre** both (of them); **l'un ou l'autre** either
(of them); **l'un l'autre, les uns les autres** each
other, one another; **pas un seul** not a single
one; **un par un** one by one
♦ *num* one; **une pomme seulement** one apple
only

unanime [ynanim] *adj* unanimous;
unanimité *nf*: **à l'unanimité** unanimously
uni, e [yni] *adj* (*ton, tissu*) plain; (*surface*)
smooth, even; (*famille*) close(-knit); (*pays*)
united
unifier [ynifje] *vt* to unite, unify
uniforme [ynifɔʀm] *adj* uniform; (*surface,
ton*) even ♦ *nm* uniform; **uniformiser** *vt*
(*systèmes*) to standardize
union [ynjɔ̃] *nf* union; **~ de consommateurs**
consumers' association; **U~ européenne**
European Union; **U~ soviétique** Soviet Union
unique [ynik] *adj* (*seul*) only; (*exceptionnel*)
unique; (*le même*): **un prix/système ~** a single
price/system; **fils/fille ~** only son/daughter,
only child; **sens ~** one-way street;
uniquement *adv* only, solely; (*juste*) only,
merely
unir [yniʀ] *vt* (*notions*) to unite; (*en mariage*)
to unite, join together; **s'~** *vi* to unite; (*en
mariage*) to be joined together
unitaire [ynitɛʀ] *adj*: **prix ~** unit price
unité [ynite] *nf* unit; (*harmonie, cohésion*)
unity
univers [ynivɛʀ] *nm* universe; **universel, le**
adj universal
universitaire [ynivɛʀsitɛʀ] *adj* university
cpd; (*diplôme, études*) academic, university
cpd ♦ *nm/f* academic
université [ynivɛʀsite] *nf* university
urbain, e [yʀbɛ̃, ɛn] *adj* urban, city *cpd*, town
cpd; **urbanisme** *nm* town planning
urgence [yʀʒɑ̃s] *nf* urgency; (*MÉD etc*)
emergency; **d'~** *adj* emergency *cpd* ♦ *adv* as a
matter of urgency; (**service des**) **~s** casualty
urgent, e [yʀʒɑ̃, ɑ̃t] *adj* urgent
urine [yʀin] *nf* urine; **urinoir** *nm* (public)
urinal
urne [yʀn] *nf* (*électorale*) ballot box; (*vase*)
urn

urticaire [yʀtikɛʀ] *nf* nettle rash
us [ys] *nmpl*: **~ et coutumes** (habits and)
customs
USA *sigle mpl*: **les USA** the USA
usage [yzaʒ] *nm* (*emploi, utilisation*) use;
(*coutume*) custom; **à l'~** with use; **à l'~ de**
(*pour*) for (use of); **hors d'~** out of service; **à
~ interne** (*MÉD*) to be taken; **à ~ externe**
(*MÉD*) for external use only; **usagé, e** *adj*
(*usé*) worn; **usager, -ère** *nm/f* user
usé, e [yze] *adj* worn; (*banal: argument etc*)
hackneyed
user [yze] *vt* (*outil*) to wear down; (*vêtement*)
to wear out; (*matière*) to wear away;
(*consommer: charbon etc*) to use; **s'~** *vi* (*tissu,
vêtement*) to wear out; **~ de** (*moyen, procédé*)
to use, employ; (*droit*) to exercise
usine [yzin] *nf* factory
usité, e [yzite] *adj* common
ustensile [ystɑ̃sil] *nm* implement; **~ de
cuisine** kitchen utensil
usuel, le [yzɥɛl] *adj* everyday, common
usure [yzyʀ] *nf* wear
utérus [yteʀys] *nm* uterus, womb
utile [ytil] *adj* useful
utilisation [ytilizasjɔ̃] *nf* use
utiliser [ytilize] *vt* to use
utilitaire [ytilitɛʀ] *adj* utilitarian
utilité [ytilite] *nf* usefulness *no pl*; **de peu d'~**
of little use *ou* help
utopie [ytɔpi] *nf* utopia

V, v

va [va] *vb voir* aller
vacance [vakɑ̃s] *nf* (*ADMIN*) vacancy; **~s** *nfpl*
holiday(s *pl*), vacation *sg*; **les grandes ~s** the
summer holidays; **prendre des/ses ~s** to take
a holiday/one's holiday(s); **aller en ~s** to go
on holiday; **vacancier, -ière** *nm/f* holiday-
maker
vacant, e [vakɑ̃, ɑ̃t] *adj* vacant
vacarme [vakaʀm] *nm* (*bruit*) racket
vaccin [vaksɛ̃] *nm* vaccine; (*opération*)
vaccination; **vaccination** *nf* vaccination;
vacciner *vt* to vaccinate; **être vacciné contre
qch** (*fam*) to be cured of sth
vache [vaʃ] *nf* (*ZOOL*) cow; (*cuir*) cowhide
♦ *adj* (*fam*) rotten, mean; **vachement** (*fam*)
adv (*très*) really; (*pleuvoir, travailler*) a hell of
a lot; **vacherie** *nf* (*action*) dirty trick;
(*remarque*) nasty remark
vaciller [vasije] *vi* to sway, wobble; (*bougie,
lumière*) to flicker; (*fig*) to be failing, falter
va-et-vient [vaevjɛ̃] *nm inv* (*de personnes,
véhicules*) comings and goings *pl*, to-ings and
fro-ings *pl*
vagabond [vagabɔ̃] *nm* (*rôdeur*) tramp,

vagrant; (*voyageur*) wanderer; **vagabonder**
vi to roam, wander

vagin [vaʒɛ̃] *nm* vagina

vague [vag] *nf* wave ♦ *adj* vague; (*regard*)
faraway; (*manteau, robe*) loose(-fitting);
(*quelconque*): **un ~ bureau/cousin** some
office/cousin or other; **~ de fond** ground
swell; **~ de froid** cold spell

vaillant, e [vajɑ̃, ɑ̃t] *adj* (*courageux*) gallant;
(*robuste*) hale and hearty

vaille [vaj] *vb voir* **valoir**

vain, e [vɛ̃, vɛn] *adj* vain; **en ~** in vain

vaincre [vɛ̃kʀ] *vt* to defeat; (*fig*) to conquer,
overcome; **vaincu, e** *nm/f* defeated party;
vainqueur *nm* victor; (*SPORT*) winner

vais [vɛ] *vb voir* **aller**

vaisseau, x [vɛso] *nm* (*ANAT*) vessel; (*NAVIG*)
ship, vessel; **~ spatial** spaceship

vaisselier [vɛsəlje] *nm* dresser

vaisselle [vɛsɛl] *nf* (*service*) crockery; (*plats
etc à laver*) (dirty) dishes *pl*; **faire la ~** to do
the washing-up (*BRIT*) *ou* the dishes

val [val, vo] (*pl* **vaux** *ou* **~s**) *nm* valley

valable [valabl] *adj* valid; (*acceptable*)
decent, worthwhile

valent *etc* [val] *vb voir* **valoir**

valet [valɛ] *nm* manservant; (*CARTES*) jack

valeur [valœʀ] *nf* (*gén*) value; (*mérite*) worth,
merit; (*COMM: titre*) security; **mettre en ~**
(*détail*) to highlight; (*objet décoratif*) to show
off to advantage; **avoir de la ~** to be valuable;
sans ~ worthless; **prendre de la ~** to go up *ou*
gain in value

valide [valid] *adj* (*en bonne santé*) fit;
(*valable*) valid; **valider** *vt* to validate

valions [valjɔ̃] *vb voir* **valoir**

valise [valiz] *nf* (*suit*)case; **faire ses ~s** to pack
one's bags

vallée [vale] *nf* valley

vallon [valɔ̃] *nm* small valley; **vallonné, e** *adj*
hilly

valoir [valwaʀ] *vi* (*être valable*) to hold, apply
♦ *vt* (*prix, valeur, effort*) to be worth;
(*causer*): **~ qch à qn** to earn sb sth; **se ~** *vi* to
be of equal merit; (*péj*) to be two of a kind;
faire ~ (*droits, prérogatives*) to assert; **faire
~ que** to point out that; **à ~ sur** to be
deducted from; **vaille que vaille** somehow *ou*
other; **cela ne me dit rien qui vaille** I don't like
the look of it at all; **ce climat ne me vaut rien**
this climate doesn't suit me; **~ le coup** *ou* **la
peine** to be worth the trouble *ou* worth it;
~ mieux: il vaut mieux se taire it's better to
say nothing; **ça ne vaut rien** it's worthless;
que vaut ce candidat? how good is this
applicant?

valse [vals] *nf* waltz

valu, e [valy] *pp de* **valoir**

vandalisme [vɑ̃dalism] *nm* vandalism

vanille [vanij] *nf* vanilla

vanité [vanite] *nf* vanity; **vaniteux, -euse**
adj vain, conceited

vanne [van] *nf* gate; (*fig*) joke

vannerie [vanʀi] *nf* basketwork

vantard, e [vɑ̃taʀ, aʀd] *adj* boastful

vanter [vɑ̃te] *vt* to speak highly of, praise; **se
~** *vi* to boast, brag; **se ~ de** to pride o.s. on;
(*péj*) to boast of

vapeur [vapœʀ] *nf* steam; (*émanation*)
vapour, fumes *pl*; **~s** *nfpl* (*bouffées*) vapours;
à ~ steam-powered, steam *cpd*; **cuit à la ~**
steamed; **vaporeux, -euse** *adj* (*flou*) hazy,
misty; (*léger*) filmy; **vaporisateur** *nm* spray;
vaporiser *vt* (*parfum etc*) to spray

varappe [vaʀap] *nf* rock climbing

vareuse [vaʀøz] *nf* (*blouson*) pea jacket;
(*d'uniforme*) tunic

variable [vaʀjabl] *adj* variable; (*temps,
humeur*) changeable; (*divers: résultats*) varied,
various

varice [vaʀis] *nf* varicose vein

varicelle [vaʀisɛl] *nf* chickenpox

varié, e [vaʀje] *adj* varied; (*divers*) various

varier [vaʀje] *vi* to vary; (*temps, humeur*) to
change ♦ *vt* to vary; **variété** *nf* variety;
variétés *nfpl*: **spectacle/émission de variétés**
variety show

variole [vaʀjɔl] *nf* smallpox

vas [va] *vb voir* **aller**

vase [vaz] *nm* vase ♦ *nf* silt, mud; **vaseux,
-euse** *adj* silty, muddy; (*fig: confus*) woolly,
hazy; (: *fatigué*) woozy

vasistas [vazistɑs] *nm* fanlight

vaste [vast] *adj* vast, immense

vaudrai *etc* [vodʀe] *vb voir* **valoir**

vaurien, ne [voʀjɛ̃, jɛn] *nm/f* good-for-
nothing

vaut [vo] *vb voir* **valoir**

vautour [votuʀ] *nm* vulture

vautrer [votʀe] *vb*: **se ~ dans/sur** to wallow
in/sprawl on

vaux [vo] *nmpl de* **val** ♦ *vb voir* **valoir**

va-vite [vavit]: **à la ~~** *adv* in a rush *ou* hurry

veau, x [vo] *nm* (*ZOOL*) calf; (*CULIN*) veal;
(*peau*) calfskin

vécu, e [veky] *pp de* **vivre**

vedette [vədɛt] *nf* (*artiste etc*) star; (*canot*)
motor boat; (*police*) launch

végétal, e, -aux [veʒetal, o] *adj* vegetable
♦ *nm* vegetable, plant; **végétalien, ne** *adj,
nm/f* vegan

végétarien, ne [veʒetaʀjɛ̃, jɛn] *adj, nm/f*
vegetarian

végétation [veʒetasjɔ̃] *nf* vegetation; **~s** *nfpl*
(*MÉD*) adenoids

véhicule [veikyl] *nm* vehicle; **~ utilitaire**
commercial vehicle

veille [vɛj] *nf* (*état*) wakefulness; (*jour*): **la**

~ **(de)** the day before; **la ~ au soir** the previous evening; **à la ~ de** on the eve of; **la ~ de Noël** Christmas Eve; **la ~ du jour de l'An** New Year's Eve

veillée [veje] *nf* (*soirée*) evening; (*réunion*) evening gathering; **~ (funèbre)** wake

veiller [veje] *vi* to stay up ♦ *vt* (*malade, mort*) to watch over, sit up with; **~ à** to attend to, see to; **~ à ce que** to make sure that; **~ sur** to watch over; **veilleur** *nm*: **veilleur de nuit** night watchman; **veilleuse** *nf* (*lampe*) night light; (*AUTO*) sidelight; (*flamme*) pilot light

veinard, e [venar, ard] *nm/f* lucky devil

veine [ven] *nf* (*ANAT, du bois etc*) vein; (*filon*) vein, seam; (*fam: chance*): **avoir de la ~** to be lucky

véliplanchiste [veliplɑ̃ʃist] *nm/f* windsurfer

vélo [velo] *nm* bike, cycle; **faire du ~** to go cycling; **~ tout-terrain** mountain bike; **vélomoteur** *nm* moped

velours [v(ə)luʀ] *nm* velvet; **~ côtelé** corduroy; **velouté, e** *adj* velvety ♦ *nm*: **velouté de tomates** cream of tomato soup

velu, e [vəly] *adj* hairy

venais *etc* [vəne] *vb voir* **venir**

venaison [vənezɔ̃] *nf* venison

vendange [vɑ̃dɑ̃ʒ] *nf* (*aussi:* **~s**) grape harvest; **vendanger** *vi* to harvest the grapes

vendeur, -euse [vɑ̃dœʀ, øz] *nm/f* shop assistant ♦ *nm* (*JUR*) vendor, seller; **~ de journaux** newspaper seller

vendre [vɑ̃dʀ] *vt* to sell; **~ qch à qn** to sell sb sth; **"à ~"** "for sale"

vendredi [vɑ̃dʀədi] *nm* Friday; **V~ saint** Good Friday

vénéneux, -euse [venenø, øz] *adj* poisonous

vénérien, ne [veneʀjɛ̃, jɛn] *adj* venereal

vengeance [vɑ̃ʒɑ̃s] *nf* vengeance *no pl*, revenge *no pl*

venger [vɑ̃ʒe] *vt* to avenge; **se ~** *vi* to avenge o.s.; **se ~ de qch** to avenge o.s. for sth, take one's revenge for sth; **se ~ de qn** to take revenge on sb; **se ~ sur** to take revenge on

venimeux, -euse [vənimø, øz] *adj* poisonous, venomous; (*fig: haineux*) venomous, vicious

venin [vənɛ̃] *nm* venom, poison

venir [v(ə)niʀ] *vi* to come; **~ de** to come from; **~ de faire: je viens d'y aller/de le voir** I've just been there/seen him; **s'il vient à pleuvoir** if it should rain; **j'en viens à croire que** I have come to believe that; **faire ~** (*docteur, plombier*) to call (out)

vent [vɑ̃] *nm* wind; **il y a du ~** it's windy; **c'est du ~** it's all hot air; **au ~** to windward; **sous le ~** to leeward; **avoir le ~ debout/arrière** to head into the wind/have the wind astern; **dans le ~** (*fam*) trendy

vente [vɑ̃t] *nf* sale; **la ~** (*activité*) selling; (*secteur*) sales *pl*; **mettre en ~** (*produit*) to put on sale; (*maison, objet personnel*) to put up for sale; **~ aux enchères** auction sale; **~ de charité** jumble sale

venteux, -euse [vɑ̃tø, øz] *adj* windy

ventilateur [vɑ̃tilatœʀ] *nm* fan

ventiler [vɑ̃tile] *vt* to ventilate

ventouse [vɑ̃tuz] *nf* (*de caoutchouc*) suction pad

ventre [vɑ̃tʀ] *nm* (*ANAT*) stomach; (*légèrement péj*) belly; (*utérus*) womb; **avoir mal au ~** to have stomach ache (*BRIT*) *ou a* stomach ache (*US*)

ventriloque [vɑ̃tʀilɔk] *nm/f* ventriloquist

venu, e [v(ə)ny] *pp de* **venir** ♦ *adj*: **bien ~** timely; **mal ~** out of place; **être mal ~ à ou de faire** to have no grounds for doing, be in no position to do

ver [vɛʀ] *nm* worm; (*des fruits etc*) maggot; (*du bois*) woodworm *no pl*; *voir aussi* **vers**; **~ à soie** silkworm; **~ de terre** earthworm; **~ luisant** glow-worm; **~ solitaire** tapeworm

verbaliser [vɛʀbalize] *vi* (*POLICE*) to book *ou* report an offender

verbe [vɛʀb] *nm* verb

verdâtre [vɛʀdɑtʀ] *adj* greenish

verdict [vɛʀdik(t)] *nm* verdict

verdir [vɛʀdiʀ] *vi, vt* to turn green; **verdure** *nf* greenery

véreux, -euse [veʀø, øz] *adj* worm-eaten; (*malhonnête*) shady, corrupt

verge [vɛʀʒ] *nf* (*ANAT*) penis

verger [vɛʀʒe] *nm* orchard

verglacé, e [vɛʀglase] *adj* icy, iced-over

verglas [vɛʀgla] *nm* (black) ice

vergogne [vɛʀgɔɲ]: **sans ~** *adv* shamelessly

véridique [veʀidik] *adj* truthful

vérification [veʀifikasjɔ̃] *nf* (*action*) checking *no pl*; (*contrôle*) check

vérifier [veʀifje] *vt* to check; (*corroborer*) to confirm, bear out

véritable [veʀitabl] *adj* real; (*ami, amour*) true

vérité [veʀite] *nf* truth; **en ~** really, actually

vermeil, le [vɛʀmɛj] *adj* ruby red

vermine [vɛʀmin] *nf* vermin *pl*

vermoulu, e [vɛʀmuly] *adj* worm-eaten

verni, e [vɛʀni] *adj* (*fam*) lucky; **cuir ~** patent leather

vernir [vɛʀniʀ] *vt* (*bois, tableau, ongles*) to varnish; (*poterie*) to glaze

vernis *nm* (*enduit*) varnish; glaze; (*fig*) veneer; **~ à ongles** nail polish *ou* varnish; **vernissage** *nm* (*d'une exposition*) preview

vérole [veʀɔl] *nf* (*variole*) smallpox

verrai *etc* [veʀe] *vb voir* **voir**

verre [vɛʀ] *nm* glass; (*de lunettes*) lens *sg*; **boire** *ou* **prendre un ~** to have a drink;

~ **dépoli** frosted glass; ~s **de contact** contact lenses; **verrerie** nf (fabrique) glassworks sg; (activité) glass-making; (objets) glassware; **verrière** nf (paroi vitrée) glass wall; (toit vitré) glass roof

verrons etc [vɛʀɔ̃] vb voir **voir**

verrou [veʀu] nm (targette) bolt; **mettre qn sous les ~s** to put sb behind bars; **verrouillage** nm locking; **verrouillage centralisé** central locking; **verrouiller** vt (porte) to bolt; (ordinateur) to lock

verrue [veʀy] nf wart

vers [vɛʀ] nm line ♦ nmpl (poésie) verse sg ♦ prép (en direction de) toward(s); (près de) around (about); (temporel) about, around

versant [vɛʀsɑ̃] nm slopes pl, side

versatile [vɛʀsatil] adj fickle, changeable

verse [vɛʀs]: à ~ adv: **il pleut à ~** it's pouring (with rain)

Verseau [vɛʀso] nm: **le ~** Aquarius

versement [vɛʀsəmɑ̃] nm payment; **en 3 ~s** in 3 instalments

verser [vɛʀse] vt (liquide, grains) to pour; (larmes, sang) to shed; (argent) to pay ♦ vi (véhicule) to overturn; (fig): ~ **dans** to lapse into

verset [vɛʀse] nm verse

version [vɛʀsjɔ̃] nf version; (SCOL) translation (into the mother tongue); **film en ~ originale** film in the original language

verso [vɛʀso] nm back; **voir au ~** see over(leaf)

vert, e [vɛʀ, vɛʀt] adj green; (vin) young; (vigoureux) sprightly ♦ nm green

vertèbre [vɛʀtɛbʀ] nf vertebra

vertement [vɛʀtəmɑ̃] adv (réprimander) sharply

vertical, e, -aux [vɛʀtikal, o] adj vertical; **verticale** nf vertical; **à la verticale** vertically; **verticalement** adv vertically

vertige [vɛʀtiʒ] nm (peur du vide) vertigo; (étourdissement) dizzy spell; (fig) fever; **vertigineux, -euse** adj breathtaking

vertu [vɛʀty] nf virtue; **en ~ de** in accordance with; **vertueux, -euse** adj virtuous

verve [vɛʀv] nf witty eloquence; **être en ~** to be in brilliant form

verveine [vɛʀvɛn] nf (BOT) verbena, vervain; (infusion) verbena tea

vésicule [vezikyl] nf vesicle; ~ **biliaire** gall-bladder

vessie [vesi] nf bladder

veste [vɛst] nf jacket; ~ **droite/croisée** single-/double-breasted jacket

vestiaire [vɛstjɛʀ] nm (au théâtre etc) cloakroom; (de stade etc) changing-room (BRIT), locker-room (US)

vestibule [vɛstibyl] nm hall

vestige [vɛstiʒ] nm relic; (fig) vestige; ~s

nmpl (de ville) remains

vestimentaire [vɛstimɑ̃tɛʀ] adj (détail) of dress; (élégance) sartorial; **dépenses ~s** clothing expenditure

veston [vɛstɔ̃] nm jacket

vêtement [vɛtmɑ̃] nm garment, item of clothing; ~s nmpl clothes

vétérinaire [veteʀinɛʀ] nm/f vet, veterinary surgeon

vêtir [vetiʀ] vt to clothe, dress

veto [veto] nm veto; **opposer un ~ à** to veto

vêtu, e [vety] pp de **vêtir**

vétuste [vetyst] adj ancient, timeworn

veuf, veuve |vœf, vœv] adj widowed ♦ nm widower

veuille [vœj] vb voir **vouloir**

veuillez [vœje] vb voir **vouloir**

veule [vøl] adj spineless

veuve [vœv] nf widow

veux [vø] vb voir **vouloir**

vexant, e [vɛksɑ̃, ɑ̃t] adj (contrariant) annoying; (blessant) hurtful

vexation [vɛksasjɔ̃] nf humiliation

vexer [vɛkse] vt: ~ **qn** to hurt sb's feelings; **se ~** vi to be offended

viable [vjabl] adj viable; (économie, industrie etc) sustainable

viaduc [vjadyk] nm viaduct

viager, -ère [vjaʒe, ɛʀ] adj: **rente viagère** life annuity

viande [vjɑ̃d] nf meat

vibrer [vibʀe] vi to vibrate; (son, voix) to be vibrant; (fig) to be stirred; **faire ~** to (cause to) vibrate; (fig) to stir, thrill

vice [vis] nm vice; (défaut) fault ♦ préfixe: ~... vice-; ~ **de forme** legal flaw ou irregularity

vichy [viʃi] nm (toile) gingham

vicié, e [visje] adj (air) polluted, tainted; (JUR) invalidated

vicieux, -euse [visjø, jøz] adj (pervers) lecherous; (rétif) unruly ♦ nm/f lecher

vicinal, e, -aux [visinal, o] adj: **chemin ~** by-road, byway

victime [viktim] nf victim; (d'accident) casualty

victoire [viktwaʀ] nf victory

victuailles [viktɥɑj] nfpl provisions

vidange [vidɑ̃ʒ] nf (d'un fossé, réservoir) emptying; (AUTO) oil change; (de lavabo: bonde) waste outlet; ~s nfpl (matières) sewage sg; **vidanger** vt to empty

vide [vid] adj empty ♦ nm (PHYSIQUE) vacuum; (espace) (empty) space, gap; (futilité, néant) void; **avoir peur du ~** to be afraid of heights; **emballé sous ~** vacuum packed; **à ~** (sans occupants) empty; (sans charge) unladen

vidéo [video] nf video ♦ adj: **cassette ~** video cassette; **jeu ~** video game; **vidéoclip** nm music video; **vidéoclub** nm video shop

vide-ordures [vidɔʀdyʀ] nm inv (rubbish) chute

vidéothèque [videɔtɛk] nf video library

vide-poches [vidpɔʃ] nm inv tidy; (AUTO) glove compartment

vider [vide] vt to empty; (CULIN: volaille, poisson) to gut, clean out; **se ~** vi to empty; **~ les lieux** to quit ou vacate the premises; **videur** nm (de boîte de nuit) bouncer

vie [vi] nf life; **être en ~** to be alive; **sans ~** lifeless; **à ~** for life

vieil [vjɛj] adj m voir **vieux**; **vieillard** nm old man; **les vieillards** old people, the elderly; **vieille** adj, nf voir **vieux**; **vieilleries** nfpl old things; **vieillesse** nf old age; **vieillir** vi (prendre de l'âge) to grow old; (population, vin) to age; (doctrine, auteur) to become dated ♦ vt to age; **vieillissement** nm growing old; ageing

Vienne [vjɛn] nf Vienna

viens [vjɛ̃] vb voir **venir**

vierge [vjɛʀʒ] adj virgin; (page) clean, blank ♦ nf virgin; (signe): **la V~** Virgo

Vietnam, Viet-Nam [vjɛtnam] nm Vietnam; **vietnamien, ne** adj Vietnamese ♦ nm/f: **Vietnamien, ne** Vietnamese

vieux (vieil), vieille [vjø, vjɛj] adj old ♦ nm/f old man (woman) ♦ nmpl old people; **mon ~/ma vieille** (fam) old man/girl; **prendre un coup de ~** to put years on; **vieille fille** spinster; **~ garçon** bachelor; **~ jeu** adj inv old-fashioned

vif, vive [vif, viv] adj (animé) lively, (alerte, brusque, aigu) sharp; (lumière, couleur) bright, (air) crisp; (vent, émotion) keen; (fort: regret, déception) great, deep; (vivant): **brûlé ~** burnt alive; **de vive voix** personally; **avoir l'esprit ~** to be quick-witted; **piquer qn au ~** to cut sb to the quick; **à ~** (plaie) open; **avoir les nerfs à ~** to be on edge

vigne [viɲ] nf (plante) vine; (plantation) vineyard; **vigneron** nm wine grower

vignette [viɲɛt] nf (ADMIN) ≈ (road) tax disc (BRIT), ≈ license plate sticker (US); (de médicament) price label (used for reimbursement)

vignoble [viɲɔbl] nm (plantation) vineyard; (vignes d'une région) vineyards pl

vigoureux, -euse [viguʀø, øz] adj vigorous, robust

vigueur [vigœʀ] nf vigour; **entrer en ~** to come into force; **en ~** current

vil, e [vil] adj vile, base

vilain, e [vilɛ̃, ɛn] adj (laid) ugly; (affaire, blessure) nasty; (pas sage: enfant) naughty

villa [vila] nf (detached) house; **~ en multipropriété** time-share villa

village [vilaʒ] nm village; **villageois, e** adj village cpd ♦ nm/f villager

ville [vil] nf town; (importante) city; (administration): **la ~** ≈ the Corporation; ≈ the (town) council; **~ d'eaux** spa

villégiature [vi(l)leʒjatyʀ] nf holiday; **(lieu de) ~** (holiday) resort

vin [vɛ̃] nm wine; **avoir le ~ gai** to get happy after a few drinks; **~ d'honneur** reception (with wine and snacks); **~ de pays** local wine; **~ ordinaire** table wine

vinaigre [vinɛgʀ] nm vinegar; **vinaigrette** nf vinaigrette, French dressing

vindicatif, -ive [vɛ̃dikatif, iv] adj vindictive

vineux, -euse [vinø, øz] adj win(e)y

vingt [vɛ̃] num twenty; **vingtaine** nf: **une vingtaine (de)** about twenty, twenty or so; **vingtième** num twentieth

vinicole [vinikɔl] adj wine cpd, wine-growing

vins etc [vɛ̃] vb voir **venir**

vinyle [vinil] nm vinyl

viol [vjɔl] nm (d'une femme) rape; (d'un lieu sacré) violation

violacé, e [vjɔlase] adj purplish, mauvish

violemment [vjɔlamɑ̃] adv violently

violence [vjɔlɑ̃s] nf violence

violent, e [vjɔlɑ̃, ɑ̃t] adj violent; (remède) drastic

violer [vjɔle] vt (femme) to rape; (sépulture, loi, traité) to violate

violet, te [vjɔlɛ, ɛt] adj, nm purple, mauve; **violette** nf (fleur) violet

violon [vjɔlɔ̃] nm violin; (fam: prison) lock-up; **~ d'Ingres** hobby; **violoncelle** nm cello; **violoniste** nm/f violinist

vipère [vipɛʀ] nf viper, adder

virage [viʀaʒ] nm (d'un véhicule) turn; (d'une route, piste) bend

virée [viʀe] nf trip; (à pied) walk; (longue) walking tour; (dans les cafés) tour

virement [viʀmɑ̃] nm (COMM) transfer

virent [viʀ] vb voir **voir**

virer [viʀe] vt (COMM): **~ qch (sur)** to transfer sth (into); (fam: expulser): **~ qn** to kick sb out ♦ vi to turn; (CHIMIE) to change colour; **~ de bord** to tack

virevolter [viʀvɔlte] vi to twirl around

virgule [viʀgyl] nf comma; (MATH) point

viril, e [viʀil] adj (propre à l'homme) masculine; (énergique, courageux) manly, virile

virtuel, le [viʀtɥɛl] adj potential; (théorique) virtual

virtuose [viʀtɥoz] nm/f (MUS) virtuoso; (gén) master

virus [viʀys] nm virus

vis¹ [vi] vb voir **voir; vivre**

vis² [vis] nf screw

visa [viza] nm (sceau) stamp; (validation de passeport) visa

visage [vizaʒ] nm face

vis-à-vis [vizavi] *prép*: **~-~-~ de qn** to(wards) sb; **en ~-~-~** facing each other

viscéral, e, -aux [viseʀal, o] *adj* (*fig*) deep-seated, deep-rooted

visées [vize] *nfpl* (*intentions*) designs

viser [vize] *vi* to aim ♦ *vt* to aim at; (*concerner*) to be aimed *ou* directed at; (*apposer un visa sur*) to stamp, visa; **~ à qch/faire** to aim at sth/at doing *ou* to do; **viseur** *nm* (*d'arme*) sights *pl*; (*PHOTO*) viewfinder

visibilité [vizibilite] *nf* visibility

visible [vizibl] *adj* visible; (*disponible*): **est-il ~?** can he see me?, will he see visitors?

visière [vizjɛʀ] *nf* (*de casquette*) peak; (*qui s'attache*) eyeshade

vision [vizjɔ̃] *nf* vision; (*sens*) (eye)sight, vision; (*fait de voir*): **la ~ de** the sight of; **visionneuse** *nf* viewer

visite [vizit] *nf* visit; **~ médicale** medical examination; **~ accompagnée** *ou* **guidée** guided tour; **faire une ~ à qn** to call on sb, pay sb a visit; **rendre ~ à qn** to visit sb, pay sb a visit; **être en ~** (**chez qn**) to be visiting (sb); **avoir de la ~** to have visitors; **heures de ~** (*hôpital, prison*) visiting hours

visiter [vizite] *vt* to visit; **visiteur, -euse** *nm/f* visitor

vison [vizɔ̃] *nm* mink

visser [vise] *vt*: **~ qch** (*fixer, serrer*) to screw sth on

visuel, le [vizɥɛl] *adj* visual

vit [vi] *vb voir* **voir**; **vivre**

vital, e, -aux [vital, o] *adj* vital

vitamine [vitamin] *nf* vitamin

vite [vit] *adv* (*rapidement*) quickly, fast; (*sans délai*) quickly; (*sous peu*) soon; **~!** quick!; **faire ~** to be quick; **le temps passe ~** time flies

vitesse [vites] *nf* speed; (*AUTO: dispositif*) gear; **prendre de la ~** to pick up *ou* gather speed; **à toute ~** at full *ou* top speed; **en ~** (*rapidement*) quickly; (*en hâte*) in a hurry

viticole [vitikɔl] *adj* wine *cpd*, wine-growing; **viticulteur** *nm* wine grower

vitrage [vitraʒ] *nm*: **double ~** double glazing

vitrail, -aux [vitraj, o] *nm* stained-glass window

vitre [vitʀ] *nf* (window) pane; (*de portière, voiture*) window; **vitré, e** *adj* glass *cpd*; **vitrer** *vt* to glaze; **vitreux, -euse** *adj* (*terne*) glassy

vitrine [vitʀin] *nf* (shop) window; (*petite armoire*) display cabinet; **en ~** in the window; **~ publicitaire** display case, showcase

vivable [vivabl] *adj* (*personne*) livable-with; (*maison*) fit to live in

vivace [vivas] *adj* (*arbre, plante*) hardy; (*fig*) indestructible, inveterate

vivacité [vivasite] *nf* liveliness, vivacity

vivant, e [vivã, ãt] *adj* (*qui vit*) living, alive;

(*animé*) lively; (*preuve, exemple*) living ♦ *nm*: **du ~ de qn** in sb's lifetime; **les ~s** the living

vive [viv] *adj voir* **vif** ♦ *vb voir* **vivre** ♦ *excl*: **~ le roi!** long live the king!; **vivement** *adv* deeply ♦ *excl*: **vivement les vacances!** roll on the holidays!

vivier [vivje] *nm* (*étang*) fish tank; (*réservoir*) fishpond

vivifiant, e [vivifjã, jãt] *adj* invigorating

vivions [vivjɔ̃] *vb voir* **vivre**

vivoter [vivɔte] *vi* (*personne*) to scrape a living, get by; (*fig: affaire etc*) to struggle along

vivre [vivʀ] *vi, vt* to live; (*période*) to live through; **~ de** to live on; **il vit encore** he is still alive; **se laisser ~** to take life as it comes; **ne plus ~** (*être anxieux*) to live on one's nerves; **il a vécu** (*eu une vie aventureuse*) he has seen life; **être facile à ~** to be easy to get on with; **faire ~ qn** (*pourvoir à sa subsistance*) to provide (a living) for sb; **vivres** *nmpl* provisions, food supplies

vlan [vlã] *excl* wham!, bang!

VO [veo] *nf*: **film en ~** film in the original version; **en ~ sous-titrée** in the original version with subtitles

vocable [vɔkabl] *nm* term

vocabulaire [vɔkabylɛʀ] *nm* vocabulary

vocation [vɔkasjɔ̃] *nf* vocation, calling

vociférer [vɔsifeʀe] *vi, vt* to scream

vœu, x [vø] *nm* wish; (*promesse*) vow; **faire ~ de** to take a vow of; **tous nos ~x de bonne année, meilleurs ~x** best wishes for the New Year

vogue [vɔg] *nf* fashion, vogue

voguer [vɔge] *vi* to sail

voici [vwasi] *prép* (*pour introduire, désigner*) here is +*sg*, here are +*pl*; **et ~ que ...** and now it (*ou* he) ...; *voir aussi* **voilà**

voie [vwa] *nf* way; (*RAIL*) track, line; (*AUTO*) lane; **être en bonne ~** to be going well; **mettre qn sur la ~** to put sb on the right track; **pays en ~ de développement** developing country; **être en ~ d'achèvement/de rénovation** to be nearing completion/in the process of renovation; **par ~ buccale** *ou* **orale** orally; **à ~ étroite** narrow-gauge; **~ d'eau** (*NAVIG*) leak; **~ de garage** (*RAIL*) siding; **~ ferrée** track; railway line; **la ~ publique** the public highway

voilà [vwala] *prép* (*en désignant*) there is +*sg*, there are +*pl*; **les ~** *ou* **voici** here *ou* there they are; **en ~** *ou* **voici un** here's one, there's one; **voici mon frère et ~ ma sœur** this is my brother and that's my sister; **~** *ou* **voici deux ans** two years ago; **~** *ou* **voici deux ans que** it's two years since; **et ~!** there we are!; **~ tout** that's all; **~** *ou* **voici** (*en offrant etc*) there *ou* here you are; **tiens! ~ Paul** look!

there's Paul

voile [vwal] nm veil; (*tissu léger*) net ♦ nf sail; (*sport*) sailing; **voiler** vt to veil; (*fausser: roue*) to buckle; (: *bois*) to warp; **se voiler** vi (*lune, regard*) to mist over; (*voix*) to become husky; (*roue, disque*) to buckle; (*planche*) to warp; **voilier** nm sailing ship; (*de plaisance*) sailing boat; **voilure** nf (*de voilier*) sails pl

voir [vwaʀ] vi, vt to see; **se ~** vt (*être visible*) to show; (*se fréquenter*) to see each other; (*se produire*) to happen; **se ~ critiquer/ transformer** to be criticized/transformed; **cela se voit** (*c'est visible*) that's obvious, it shows; **faire ~ qch à qn** to show sb sth; **en faire ~ à qn** (*fig*) to give sb a hard time; **ne pas pouvoir ~ qn** not to be able to stand sb; **voyons!** let's see now; (*indignation etc*) come on!; **avoir quelque chose à ~ avec** to have something to do with

voire [vwaʀ] adv even

voisin, e [vwazɛ̃, in] adj (*proche*) neighbouring; (*contigu*) next; (*ressemblant*) connected ♦ nm/f neighbour; **voisinage** nm (*proximité*) proximity; (*environs*) vicinity; (*quartier, voisins*) neighbourhood

voiture [vwatyʀ] nf car; (*wagon*) coach, carriage; **~ de course** racing car; **~ de sport** sports car

voix [vwa] nf voice; (*POL*) vote; **à haute ~** aloud; **à ~ basse** in a low voice; **à 2/4 ~** (*MUS*) in 2/4 parts; **avoir ~ au chapitre** to have a say in the matter

vol [vɔl] nm (*d'oiseau, d'avion*) flight; (*larcin*) theft; **~ régulier** scheduled flight; **à ~ d'oiseau** as the crow flies; **au ~: attraper qch au ~** to catch sth as it flies past; **en ~** in flight; **~ à main armée** armed robbery; **~ à voile** gliding; **~ libre** hang-gliding

volage [vɔlaʒ] adj fickle

volaille [vɔlaj] nf (*oiseaux*) poultry pl; (*viande*) poultry no pl; (*oiseau*) fowl

volant, e [vɔlɑ̃, ɑ̃t] adj voir **feuille** etc ♦ nm (*d'automobile*) steering wheel; (*de commande*) wheel; (*objet lancé*) shuttlecock; (*bande de tissu*) flounce

volcan [vɔlkɑ̃] nm volcano

volée [vɔle] nf (*TENNIS*) volley; **à la ~: rattraper à la ~** to catch in mid-air; **à toute ~** (*sonner les cloches*) vigorously; (*lancer un projectile*) with full force; **~ de coups/de flèches** volley of blows/arrows

voler [vɔle] vi (*avion, oiseau, fig*) to fly; (*voleur*) to steal ♦ vt (*objet*) to steal; (*personne*) to rob; **~ qch à qn** to steal sth from sb; **il ne l'a pas volé!** he asked for it!

volet [vɔlɛ] nm (*de fenêtre*) shutter, (*de feuillet, document*) section

voleur, -euse [vɔlœʀ, øz] nm/f thief ♦ adj thieving; **"au ~!"** "stop thief!"

volière [vɔljɛʀ] nf aviary

volley [vɔlɛ] nm volleyball

volontaire [vɔlɔ̃tɛʀ] adj (*acte, enrôlement, prisonnier*) voluntary; (*oubli*) intentional; (*caractère, personne: décidé*) self-willed ♦ nm/f volunteer

volonté [vɔlɔ̃te] nf (*faculté de vouloir*) will; (*énergie, fermeté*) will(power); (*souhait, désir*) wish; **à ~** as much as one likes; **bonne ~** goodwill, willingness; **mauvaise ~** lack of goodwill, unwillingness

volontiers [vɔlɔ̃tje] adv (*avec plaisir*) willingly, gladly; (*habituellement, souvent*) readily, willingly; **voulez-vous boire quelque chose? - ~!** would you like something to drink? - yes, please!

volt [vɔlt] nm volt

volte-face [vɔltəfas] nf inv: **faire ~~** to turn round

voltige [vɔltiʒ] nf (*ÉQUITATION*) trick riding; (*au cirque*) acrobatics sg; **voltiger** vi to flutter (about)

volubile [vɔlybil] adj voluble

volume [vɔlym] nm volume; (*GÉOM: solide*) solid; **volumineux, -euse** adj voluminous, bulky

volupté [vɔlypte] nf sensual delight ou pleasure

vomi [vɔmi] nm vomit; **vomir** vi to vomit, be sick ♦ vt to vomit, bring up; (*fig*) to belch out, spew out; (*exécrer*) to loathe, abhor; **vomissements** nmpl: **être pris de vomissements** to (suddenly) start vomiting

vont [vɔ̃] vb voir **aller**

vorace [vɔʀas] adj voracious

vos [vo] adj voir **votre**

vote [vɔt] nm vote; **~ par correspondance/ procuration** postal/proxy vote; **voter** vi to vote ♦ vt (*projet de loi*) to vote for; (*loi, réforme*) to pass

votre [vɔtʀ] (pl **vos**) adj your

vôtre [votʀ] pron: **le ~, la ~, les ~s** yours; **les ~s** (*fig*) your family ou folks; **à la ~** (*toast*) your (good) health!

voudrai etc [vudʀe] vb voir **vouloir**

voué, e [vwe] adj: **~ à** doomed to

vouer [vwe] vt: **~ qch à** (*Dieu, un saint*) to dedicate sth to; **~ sa vie à** (*étude, cause etc*) to devote one's life to; **~ une amitié éternelle à qn** to vow undying friendship to sb

---

MOT-CLÉ

---

vouloir [vulwaʀ] nm: **le bon vouloir de qn** sb's goodwill; sb's pleasure
♦ vt **1** (*exiger, désirer*) to want; **vouloir faire/ que qn fasse** to want to do/sb to do; **voulez-vous du thé?** would you like ou do you want some tea?; **que me veut-il?** what does he want with me?; **sans le vouloir**

(*involontairement*) without meaning to, unintentionally; **je voudrais ceci/faire** I would *ou* I'd like this/to do

2 (*consentir*): **je veux bien** (*bonne volonté*) I'll be happy to; (*concession*) fair enough, that's fine; **oui, si on veut** (*en quelque sorte*) yes, if you like; **veuillez attendre** please wait; **veuillez agréer ...** (*formule épistolaire*) yours faithfully

3: **en vouloir à qn** to bear sb a grudge; **s'en vouloir (de)** to be annoyed with o.s. (for); **il en veut à mon argent** he's after my money

4: **vouloir de: l'entreprise ne veut plus de lui** the firm doesn't want him any more; **elle ne veut pas de son aide** she doesn't want his help

5: **vouloir dire** to mean

voulu, e [vuly] *adj* (*requis*) required, requisite; (*délibéré*) deliberate, intentional; *voir aussi* **vouloir**

vous [vu] *pron* you; (*objet indirect*) (to) you; (*réfléchi: sg*) yourself; (*: pl*) yourselves; (*réciproque*) each other; **~-même** yourself; **~-mêmes** yourselves

voûte [vut] *nf* vault; **voûter: se voûter** *vi* (*dos, personne*) to become stooped

vouvoyer [vuvwaje] *vt*: **~ qn** to address sb as "vous"

voyage [vwajaʒ] *nm* journey, trip; (*fait de ~r*): **le ~** travel(ling); **partir/être en ~** to go off/be away on a journey *ou* trip; **faire bon ~** to have a good journey; **~ d'agrément/ d'affaires** pleasure/business trip; **~ de noces** honeymoon; **~ organisé** package tour

voyager [vwajaʒe] *vi* to travel; **voyageur, -euse** *nm/f* traveller; (*passager*) passenger

voyant, e [vwajɑ̃, ɑ̃t] *adj* (*couleur*) loud, gaudy ♦ *nm* (*signal*) (warning) light; **voyante** *nf* clairvoyant

voyelle [vwajɛl] *nf* vowel

voyons *etc* [vwajɔ̃] *vb voir* **voir**

voyou [vwaju] *nm* hooligan

vrac [vʀak]: **en ~** *adv* (*au détail*) loose; (*en gros*) in bulk; (*en désordre*) in a jumble

vrai, e [vʀɛ] *adj* (*véridique: récit, faits*) true; (*non factice, authentique*) real; **à ~ dire** to tell the truth; **vraiment** *adv* really; **vraisemblable** *adj* likely; (*excuse*) convincing; **vraisemblablement** *adj* probably; **vraisemblance** *nf* likelihood; (*romanesque*) verisimilitude

vrille [vʀij] *nf* (*de plante*) tendril; (*outil*) gimlet; (*spirale*) spiral; (*AVIAT*) spin

vrombir [vʀɔ̃biʀ] *vi* to hum

VRP *sigle m* (= *voyageur, représentant, placier*) sales rep (*fam*)

VTT *sigle m* (= *vélo tout-terrain*) mountain bike

vu, e [vy] *pp de* **voir** ♦ *adj*: **bien/mal ~** (*fig: personne*) popular/unpopular; (*: chose*) approved/disapproved of ♦ *prép* (*en raison de*) in view of; **~ que** in view of the fact that

vue [vy] *nf* (*fait de voir*): **la ~ de** the sight of; (*sens, faculté*) (eye)sight; (*panorama, image, photo*) view; **~s** *nfpl* (*idées*) views; (*dessein*) designs; **hors de ~** out of sight; **avoir en ~** to have in mind; **tirer à ~** to shoot on sight; **à ~ d'œil** visibly; **de ~** by sight; **perdre de ~** to lose sight of; **en ~** (*visible*) in sight; (*célèbre*) in the public eye; **en ~ de faire** with a view to doing

vulgaire [vylgɛʀ] *adj* (*grossier*) vulgar, coarse; (*ordinaire*) commonplace, mundane; (*péj: quelconque*): **de ~s touristes** common tourists; (*BOT, ZOOL: non latin*) common; **vulgariser** *vt* to popularize

vulnérable [vylneʀabl] *adj* vulnerable

W, w

wagon [vagɔ̃] *nm* (*de voyageurs*) carriage; (*de marchandises*) truck, wagon; **wagon-lit** *nm* sleeper, sleeping car; **wagon-restaurant** *nm* restaurant *ou* dining car

wallon, ne [walɔ̃, ɔn] *adj* Walloon

waters [watɛʀ] *nmpl* toilet *sg*

watt [wat] *nm* watt

WC *sigle mpl* (= *water-closet(s)*) toilet

week-end [wikɛnd] *nm* weekend

western [wɛstɛʀn] *nm* western

whisky [wiski] (*pl* **whiskies**) *nm* whisky

X, x

xénophobe [gzenɔfɔb] *adj* xenophobic ♦ *nm/f* xenophobe

xérès [gzeʀɛs] *nm* sherry

xylophone [gzilɔfɔn] *nm* xylophone

Y, y

y [i] *adv* (*à cet endroit*) there; (*dessus*) on it (*ou* them); (*dedans*) in it (*ou* them) ♦ *pron* (about *ou* on *ou* of) it (*d'après le verbe employé*); **j'~ pense** I'm thinking about it; **ça ~ est!** that's it!; *voir aussi* **aller**; **avoir**

yacht [jɔt] *nm* yacht

yaourt [jauʀt] *nm* yoghourt; **~ nature/aux fruits** plain/fruit yogurt

yeux [jø] *nmpl de* **œil**

yoga [jɔga] *nm* yoga

yoghourt [jɔguʀt] *nm* = **yaourt**

yougoslave [jugɔslav] (*HISTOIRE*) *adj* Yugoslav(ian) ♦ *nm/f*: **Y~** Yugoslav

Yougoslavie [jugɔslavi] (*HISTOIRE*)
   nf Yugoslavia

Z, z

zapper [zape] *vi* to zap

zapping [zapiŋ] *nm*: **faire du ~** to flick
   through the channels

zèbre [zɛbʀ(ə)] *nm* (*ZOOL*) zebra; **zébré, e**
   adj striped, streaked

zèle [zɛl] *nm* zeal; **faire du ~** (*péj*) to be over-
   zealous; **zélé, e** *adj* zealous

zéro [zeʀo] *nm* zero, nought (*BRIT*); **au-
   dessous de ~** below zero (Centigrade) *ou*
   freezing; **partir de ~** to start from scratch;
   trois (buts) à ~ 3 (goals to) nil

zeste [zɛst] *nm* peel, zest

zézayer [zezeje] *vi* to have a lisp

zigzag [zigzag] *nm* zigzag; **zigzaguer** *vi* to
   zigzag

zinc [zɛ̃g] *nm* (*CHIMIE*) zinc

zizanie [zizani] *nf*: **semer la ~** to stir up ill-
   feeling

zizi [zizi] *nm* (*langage enfantin*) willy

zodiaque [zɔdjak] *nm* zodiac

zona [zona] *nm* shingles *sg*

zone [zon] *nf* zone, area; **~ bleue** ≈ restricted parking area; **~ industrielle** industrial
   estate

zoo [zo(o)] *nm* zoo

zoologie [zɔɔlɔʒi] *nf* zoology; **zoologique**
   adj zoological

zut [zyt] *excl* dash (it)! (*BRIT*), nuts! (*US*)

ENGLISH – FRENCH
ANGLAIS – FRANÇAIS

A, a

A [eɪ] *n* (MUS) la *m*

a [eɪ, ə] (*before vowel or silent h: an*) *indef art* **1** un(e); **a book** un livre; **an apple** une pomme; **she's a doctor** elle est médecin
2 (*instead of the number "one"*) un(e); **a year ago** il y a un an; **a hundred/thousand** *etc* **pounds** cent/mille *etc* livres
3 (*in expressing ratios, prices etc*): **3 a day/week** 3 par jour/semaine; **10 km an hour** 10 km à l'heure; **30p a kilo** 30p le kilo

A.A. *n abbr* – Alcoholics Anonymous; (BRIT: *Automobile Association*) ≈ TCF *m*
A.A.A. (US) *n abbr* (= *American Automobile Association*) ≈ TCF *m*
aback [ə'bæk] *adv*: **to be taken ~** être stupéfait(e), être décontenancé(e)
abandon [ə'bændən] *vt* abandonner
abate [ə'beɪt] *vi* s'apaiser, se calmer
abbey ['æbɪ] *n* abbaye *f*
abbot ['æbət] *n* père supérieur
abbreviation [əbriːvɪ'eɪʃən] *n* abréviation *f*
abdicate ['æbdɪkeɪt] *vt, vi* abdiquer
abdomen ['æbdəmen] *n* abdomen *m*
abduct [æb'dʌkt] *vt* enlever
aberration [æbə'reɪʃən] *n* anomalie *f*
abide [ə'baɪd] *vt*: **I can't ~ it/him** je ne peux pas le souffrir or supporter; **~ by** *vt fus* observer, respecter
ability [ə'bɪlɪtɪ] *n* compétence *f*; capacité *f*; (*skill*) talent *m*
abject ['æbdʒekt] *adj* (*poverty*) sordide; (*apology*) plat(e)
ablaze [ə'bleɪz] *adj* en feu, en flammes
able ['eɪbl] *adj* capable, compétent(e); **to be ~ to do sth** être capable de faire qch, pouvoir faire qch; **~-bodied** *adj* robuste; **ably** *adv* avec compétence or talent, habilement
abnormal [æb'nɔːməl] *adj* anormal(e)
aboard [ə'bɔːd] *adv* à bord ♦ *prep* à bord de
abode [ə'bəud] *n* (LAW): **of no fixed ~** sans domicile fixe
abolish [ə'bɔlɪʃ] *vt* abolir
aborigine [æbə'rɪdʒɪnɪ] *n* aborigène *m/f*
abort [ə'bɔːt] *vt* faire avorter; **~ion** *n* avortement *m*; **to have an ~ion** se faire avorter; **~ive** [ə'bɔːtɪv] *adj* manqué(e)

about [ə'baut] *adv* **1** (*approximately*) environ, à peu près; **about a hundred/thousand** *etc* environ cent/mille *etc*, une centaine/un millier *etc*; **it takes about 10 hours** ça prend environ or à peu près 10 heures; **at about 2 o'clock** vers 2 heures; **I've just about finished** j'ai presque fini
2 (*referring to place*) çà et là, de côté et d'autre; **to run about** courir çà et là; **to walk about** se promener, aller et venir
3: **to be about to do sth** être sur le point de faire qch
♦ *prep* **1** (*relating to*) au sujet de, à propos de; **a book about London** un livre sur Londres; **what is it about?** de quoi s'agit-il?; **we talked about it** nous en avons parlé; **what or how about doing this?** et si nous faisions ceci?
2 (*referring to place*) dans; **to walk about the town** se promener dans la ville

about-face [ə'baut'feɪs] *n* demi-tour *m*
about-turn [ə'baut'tɜːn] *n* (MIL) demi-tour *m*; (*fig*) volte-face *f*
above [ə'bʌv] *adv* au-dessus ♦ *prep* au-dessus de; (*more*) plus de; **mentioned ~** mentionné ci-dessus; **~ all** par-dessus tout, surtout; **~board** *adj* franc (franche); honnête
abrasive [ə'breɪzɪv] *adj* abrasif(-ive); (*fig*) caustique, agressif(-ive)
abreast [ə'brest] *adv* de front; **to keep ~ of** se tenir au courant de
abroad [ə'brɔːd] *adv* à l'étranger
abrupt [ə'brʌpt] *adj* (*steep, blunt*) abrupt(e); (*sudden, gruff*) brusque; **~ly** *adv* (*speak, end*) brusquement
abscess ['æbsɪs] *n* abcès *m*
absence ['æbsəns] *n* absence *f*
absent ['æbsənt] *adj* absent(e); **~ee** [æbsən'tiː] *n* absent(e); (*habitual*) absentéiste *m/f*; **~-minded** *adj* distrait(e)
absolute ['æbsəluːt] *adj* absolu(e); **~ly** [æbsə'luːtlɪ] *adv* absolument
absolve [əb'zɔlv] *vt*: **to ~ sb (from)** (*blame, responsibility, sin*) absoudre qn (de)
absorb [əb'zɔːb] *vt* absorber; **to be ~ed in a book** être plongé(e) dans un livre; **~ent cotton** (US) *n* coton *m* hydrophile

abstain [əb'steɪn] vi: to ~ (from) s'abstenir (de)

abstract ['æbstrækt] adj abstrait(e)

absurd [əb'sɔːd] adj absurde

abundant [ə'bʌndənt] adj abondant(e)

abuse [n ə'bjuːs, vb ə'bjuːz] n abus m; (insults) insultes fpl, injures fpl ♦ vt abuser de; (insult) insulter; **abusive** [ə'bjuːsɪv] adj grossier(-ère), injurieux(-euse)

abysmal [ə'bɪzməl] adj exécrable; (ignorance etc) sans bornes

abyss [ə'bɪs] n abîme m, gouffre m

AC abbr (= alternating current) courant alternatif

academic [ækə'demɪk] adj universitaire; (person: scholarly) intellectuel(le); (pej: issue) oiseux(-euse), purement théorique ♦ n universitaire m/f; ~ **year** n année f universitaire

academy [ə'kædəmɪ] n (learned body) académie f; (school) collège m; ~ **of music** conservatoire m

accelerate [æk'seləreɪt] vt, vi accélérer; **accelerator** n accélérateur m

accent ['æksənt] n accent m

accept [ək'sept] vt accepter; ~**able** adj acceptable; ~**ance** n acceptation f

access ['ækses] n accès m; (LAW: in divorce) droit m de visite; ~**ible** [æk'sesəbl] adj accessible

accessory [æk'sesərɪ] n accessoire m

accident ['æksɪdənt] n accident m; (chance) hasard m; **by** ~ accidentellement; par hasard; ~**al** [æksɪ'dentl] adj accidentel(le); ~**ally** [æksɪ'dentəlɪ] adv accidentellement; ~ **insurance** n assurance f accident; ~-**prone** adj sujet(te) aux accidents

acclaim [ə'kleɪm] n acclamations fpl ♦ vt acclamer

accommodate [ə'kɔmədeɪt] vt loger, recevoir; (oblige, help) obliger; (car etc) contenir; **accommodating** adj obligeant(e), arrangeant(e); **accommodation** [əkɔmə'deɪʃən] (US **accommodations**) n logement m

accompany [ə'kʌmpənɪ] vt accompagner

accomplice [ə'kʌmplɪs] n complice m/f

accomplish [ə'kʌmplɪʃ] vt accomplir; ~**ment** n accomplissement m; réussite f; (skill: gen pl) talent m

accord [ə'kɔːd] n accord m ♦ vt accorder; **of his own** ~ de son plein gré; ~**ance** [ə'kɔːdəns] n: **in** ~**ance with** conformément à; ~**ing**: ~**ing to** prep selon; ~**ingly** adv en conséquence

accordion [ə'kɔːdɪən] n accordéon m

account [ə'kaunt] n (COMM) compte m; (report) compte rendu; récit m; ~**s** npl (COMM) comptabilité f, comptes; **of no** ~ sans

importance; **on** ~ en acompte; **on no** ~ en aucun cas; **on** ~ **of** à cause de; **to take into** ~, **take** ~ **of** tenir compte de; ~ **for** vt fus expliquer, rendre compte de; ~**able** adj: ~**able (to)** responsable (devant); ~**ancy** n comptabilité f; ~**ant** n comptable m/f; ~ **number** n (at bank etc) numéro m de compte

accrued interest [ə'kruːd-] n intérêt m cumulé

accumulate [ə'kjuːmjuleɪt] vt accumuler, amasser ♦ vi s'accumuler, s'amasser

accuracy ['ækjurəsɪ] n exactitude f, précision f

accurate ['ækjurɪt] adj exact(e), précis(e); ~**ly** adv avec précision

accusation [ækju'zeɪʃən] n accusation f

accuse [ə'kjuːz] vt: to ~ **sb (of sth)** accuser qn (de qch); the ~**d** l'accusé(e)

accustom [ə'kʌstəm] vt accoutumer, habituer; ~**ed** adj (usual) habituel(le); (in the habit): ~**ed to** habitué(e) or accoutumé(e) à

ace [eɪs] n as m

ache [eɪk] n mal m, douleur f ♦ vi (yearn): to ~ **to do sth** mourir d'envie de faire qch; **my head** ~**s** j'ai mal à la tête

achieve [ə'tʃiːv] vt (aim) atteindre; (victory, success) remporter, obtenir; ~**ment** n exploit m, réussite f

acid ['æsɪd] adj acide ♦ n acide m; ~ **rain** n pluies fpl acides

acknowledge [ək'nɔlɪdʒ] vt (letter: also: ~ **receipt of**) accuser réception de; (fact) reconnaître; ~**ment** n (of letter) accusé m de réception

acne ['æknɪ] n acné f

acorn ['eɪkɔːn] n gland m

acoustic [ə'kuːstɪk] adj acoustique; ~**s** n, npl acoustique f

acquaint [ə'kweɪnt] vt: to ~ **sb with sth** mettre qn au courant de qch; to be ~**ed with** connaître; ~**ance** n connaissance f

acquire [ə'kwaɪə*] vt acquérir

acquit [ə'kwɪt] vt acquitter; to ~ **o.s. well** bien se comporter, s'en tirer très honorablement

acre ['eɪkə*] n acre f (= 4047 m²)

acrid ['ækrɪd] adj âcre

acrobat ['ækrəbæt] n acrobate m/f

across [ə'krɔs] prep (on the other side) de l'autre côté de; (crosswise) en travers de ♦ adv de l'autre côté; en travers; **to run/swim** ~ traverser en courant/à la nage; ~ **from** en face de

acrylic [ə'krɪlɪk] adj acrylique

act [ækt] n acte m, action f; (of play) acte; (in music-hall etc) numéro m; (LAW) loi f ♦ vi agir; (THEATRE) jouer; (pretend) jouer la comédie ♦ vt (part) jouer, tenir; **in the** ~ **of** en train de; **to** ~ **as** servir de; ~**ing** adj suppléant(e), par intérim ♦ n (activity): **to do some ~ing** faire du théâtre (or du cinéma)

action ['ækʃən] n action f; (MIL) combat(s) m(pl); **out of ~** hors de combat; (machine) hors d'usage; **to take ~** agir, prendre des mesures; **~ replay** n (TV) ralenti m

activate ['æktɪveɪt] vt (mechanism) actionner, faire fonctionner

active ['æktɪv] adj actif(-ive); (volcano) en activité; **~ly** adv activement; **activity** [æk'tɪvɪtɪ] n activité f; **activity holiday** n vacances actives

actor ['æktə] n acteur m

actress ['æktrɪs] n actrice f

actual ['æktjuəl] adj réel(le), véritable; **~ly** adv (really) réellement, véritablement; (in fact) en fait

acute [ə'kjuːt] adj aigu(ë); (mind, observer) pénétrant(e), perspicace

ad [æd] n abbr = **advertisement**

A.D. adv abbr (= anno Domini) ap. J.-C.

adamant ['ædəmənt] adj inflexible

adapt [ə'dæpt] vt adapter ♦ vi: **to ~ (to)** s'adapter (à); **~able** adj (device) adaptable; (person) qui s'adapte facilement; **~er, ~or** n (ELEC) adaptateur m

add [æd] vt ajouter; (figures: also: **to ~ up**) additionner ♦ vi: **to ~ to** (increase) ajouter à, accroître

adder ['ædə] n vipère f

addict ['ædɪkt] n intoxiqué(e); (fig) fanatique m/f; **~ed** [ə'dɪktɪd] adj: **to be ~ed to** (drugs, drink etc) être adonné(e) à; (fig: football etc) être un(e) fanatique de; **~ion** n (MED) dépendance f; **~ive** adj qui crée une dépendance

addition [ə'dɪʃən] n addition f; (thing added) ajout m; **in ~** de plus; de surcroît; **in ~ to** en plus de; **~al** adj supplémentaire

additive ['ædɪtɪv] n additif m

address [ə'drɛs] n adresse f; (talk) discours m, allocution f ♦ vt adresser; (speak to) s'adresser à; **to ~ (o.s. to) a problem** s'attaquer à un problème

adept ['ædɛpt] adj: **~ at** expert(e) à or en

adequate ['ædɪkwɪt] adj adéquat(e); suffisant(e)

adhere [əd'hɪə] vi: **to ~ to** adhérer à; (fig: rule, decision) se tenir à

adhesive [əd'hiːzɪv] n adhésif m; **~ tape** n (BRIT) ruban adhésif; (US: MED) sparadrap m

ad hoc [æd'hɔk] adj improvisé(e), ad hoc

adjacent [ə'dʒeɪsənt] adj: **~ (to)** adjacent (à)

adjective ['ædʒɛktɪv] n adjectif m

adjoining [ə'dʒɔɪnɪŋ] adj voisin(e), adjacent(e), attenant(e)

adjourn [ə'dʒəːn] vt ajourner ♦ vi suspendre la séance; clore la session

adjust [ə'dʒʌst] vt (machine) ajuster, régler;

(prices, wages) rajuster ♦ vi: **to ~ (to)** s'adapter (à); **~able** adj réglable; **~ment** n (PSYCH) adaptation f; (to machine) ajustage m, réglage m; (of prices, wages) rajustement m

ad-lib [æd'lɪb] vt, vi improviser; **ad lib** adv à volonté, à loisir

administer [əd'mɪnɪstə] vt administrer; (justice) rendre; **administration** [ədmɪnɪs'treɪʃən] n administration f; **administrative** [əd'mɪnɪstrətɪv] adj administratif(-ive)

admiral ['ædmərəl] n amiral m; **A~ty** ['ædmərəltɪ] n (BRIT) n: **the A~ty** le ministère m de la Marine

admire [əd'maɪə] vt admirer

admission [əd'mɪʃən] n admission f; (to exhibition, night club etc) entrée f; (confession) aveu m; **~ charge** n droits mpl d'admission

admit [əd'mɪt] vt laisser entrer; admettre; (agree) reconnaître, admettre; **~ to** vt fus reconnaître, avouer; **~tance** n admission f, (droit m d')entrée f; **~tedly** adv il faut en convenir

ado [ə'duː] n: **without (any) more ~** sans plus de cérémonies

adolescence [ædəu'lɛsns] n adolescence f; **adolescent** adj, n adolescent(e)

adopt [ə'dɔpt] vt adopter; **~ed** adj adoptif(-ive), adopté(e); **~ion** n adoption f

adore [ə'dɔː] vt adorer

adorn [ə'dɔːn] vt orner

Adriatic (Sea) [eɪdrɪ'ætɪk-] n Adriatique f

adrift [ə'drɪft] adv à la dérive

adult ['ædʌlt] n adulte m/f ♦ adj adulte; (literature, education) pour adultes

adultery [ə'dʌltərɪ] n adultère m

advance [əd'vɑːns] n avance f ♦ adj: **~ booking** réservation f ♦ vt avancer ♦ vi avancer, s'avancer; **~ notice** avertissement m; **to make ~s (to sb)** faire des propositions (à qn); (amorously) faire des avances (à qn); **in ~** à l'avance, d'avance; **~d** adj avancé(e); (SCOL: studies) supérieur(e)

advantage [əd'vɑːntɪdʒ] n (also TENNIS) avantage m; **to take ~ of** (person) exploiter

advent ['ædvənt] n avènement m, venue f; **A~** Avent m

adventure [əd'vɛntʃə] n aventure f

adverb ['ædvəːb] n adverbe m

adverse ['ædvəːs] adj défavorable, contraire

advert ['ædvəːt] (BRIT) n abbr = **advertisement**

advertise ['ædvətaɪz] vi, vt faire de la publicité (pour); (in classified ads etc) mettre une annonce (pour vendre); **to ~ for** (staff, accommodation) faire paraître une annonce pour trouver; **~ment** [əd'vəːtɪsmənt] n (COMM) réclame f, publicité f; (in classified ads) annonce f; **advertising** n publicité f

advice [ǝd'vaɪs] n conseils mpl; (notification) avis m; **piece of ~** conseil; **to take legal ~** consulter un avocat

advisable [ǝd'vaɪzǝbl] adj conseillé(e), indiqué(e)

advise [ǝd'vaɪz] vt conseiller; **to ~ sb of sth** aviser or informer qn de qch; **to ~ against sth/doing sth** déconseiller qch/conseiller de ne pas faire qch; **~r, advisor** n conseiller(-ère); **advisory** adj consultatif(-ive)

advocate [n 'ædvǝkɪt, vb 'ædvǝkeɪt] n (upholder) défenseur m, avocat(e); (LAW) avocat(e) ♦ vt recommander, prôner

Aegean (Sea) [iː'dʒiːǝn-] n (mer f) Égée f

aerial ['ɛǝrɪǝl] n antenne f ♦ adj aérien(ne)

aerobics [ɛǝ'rǝubɪks] n aérobic m

aeroplane ['ɛǝrǝpleɪn] n (BRIT) n avion m

aerosol ['ɛǝrǝsɔl] n aérosol m

aesthetic [iːs'θɛtɪk] adj esthétique

afar [ǝ'fɑː] adv: **from ~** de loin

affair [ǝ'fɛǝ] n affaire f; (also: **love ~**) liaison f; aventure f

affect [ǝ'fɛkt] vt affecter; (disease) atteindre; **~ed** adj affecté(e); **~ion** n affection f; **~ionate** adj affectueux(-euse)

affinity [ǝ'fɪnɪtɪ] n (bond, rapport): **to have an ~ with/for** avoir une affinité avec/pour

afflict [ǝ'flɪkt] vt affliger

affluence ['æfluǝns] n abondance f, opulence f

affluent ['æfluǝnt] adj (person, family, surroundings) aisé(e), riche; **the ~ society** la société d'abondance

afford [ǝ'fɔːd] vt se permettre; (provide) fournir, procurer

afloat [ǝ'flǝut] adj, adv à flot; **to stay ~** surnager

afoot [ǝ'fut] adv: **there is something ~** il se prépare quelque chose

afraid [ǝ'freɪd] adj effrayé(e); **to be ~ of** or **to** avoir peur de; **I am ~ that ...** je suis désolé(e), mais ...; **I am ~ so/not** hélas oui/non

Africa ['æfrɪkǝ] n Afrique f; **~n** adj africain(e) ♦ n Africain(e)

after ['ɑːftǝ] prep, adv après ♦ conj après que, après avoir or être +pp; **what/who are you ~?** que/qui cherchez-vous?; **~ he left/having done** après qu'il fut parti/après avoir fait; **ask ~ him** demandez de ses nouvelles; **to name sb ~ sb** donner à qn le nom de qn; **twenty ~ eight** (US) huit heures vingt; **~ all** après tout; **~ you!** après vous, Monsieur (or Madame etc); **~effects** npl (of disaster, radiation, drink etc) répercussions fpl; (of illness) séquelles fpl, suites fpl; **~math** n conséquences fpl, suites fpl; **~noon** n après-midi m or f; **~s** (inf) n (dessert) dessert m; **~-sales service** (BRIT) n (for car, washing machine etc) service m après-vente; **~-shave**

(lotion) n after-shave m; **~sun** n après-soleil m inv; **~thought** n: **I had an ~thought** il m'est venu une idée après coup; **~wards** (US **afterward**) adv après

again [ǝ'gɛn] adv de nouveau; encore (une fois); **to do sth ~** refaire qch; **not ... ~** ne ... plus; **~ and ~** à plusieurs reprises

against [ǝ'gɛnst] prep contre; (compared to) par rapport à

age [eɪdʒ] n âge m ♦ vt, vi vieillir; **it's been ~s since** ça fait une éternité que ... ne; **he is 20 years of ~** il a 20 ans; **to come of ~** atteindre sa majorité; **~d** [adj eɪdʒd, npl 'eɪdʒɪd] adj: **~d 10** âgé(e) de 10 ans ♦ npl: **the ~d** les personnes âgées; **~ group** n tranche f d'âge; **~ limit** n limite f d'âge

agency ['eɪdʒǝnsɪ] n agence f; (government body) organisme m, office m

agenda [ǝ'dʒɛndǝ] n ordre m du jour

agent ['eɪdʒǝnt] n agent m, représentant m; (firm) concessionnaire m

aggravate ['ægrǝveɪt] vt aggraver; (annoy) exaspérer

aggressive [ǝ'grɛsɪv] adj agressif(-ive)

agitate ['ædʒɪteɪt] vt (person) agiter, émouvoir, troubler ♦ vi: **to ~ for/against** faire campagne pour/contre

AGM n abbr (= annual general meeting) AG f

ago [ǝ'gǝu] adv: **2 days ~** il y a deux jours; **not long ~** il n'y a pas longtemps; **how long ~?** il y a combien de temps (de cela)?

agony ['ægǝnɪ] n (pain) douleur f atroce; **to be in ~** souffrir le martyre

agree [ǝ'griː] vt (price) convenir de ♦ vi: **to ~ with** (person) être d'accord avec; (statements etc) concorder avec; (LING) s'accorder avec; **to ~ to do** accepter de or consentir à faire; **to ~ to sth** consentir à qch; **to ~ that** (admit) convenir or reconnaître que; **garlic doesn't ~ with me** je ne supporte pas l'ail; **~able** adj agréable; (willing) consentant(e), d'accord; **~d** adj (time, place) convenu(e); **~ment** n accord m; **in ~ment** d'accord

agricultural [ægrɪ'kʌltʃǝrǝl] adj agricole

agriculture ['ægrɪkʌltʃǝ] n agriculture f

aground [ǝ'graund] adv: **to run ~** échouer, s'échouer

ahead [ǝ'hɛd] adv (in front: of position, place) devant; (: at the head) en avant; (look, plan, think) en avant; **~ of** devant; (fig: schedule etc) en avance sur; **~ of time** en avance; **go right** or **straight ~** allez tout droit; **go ~!** (fig: permission) allez-y!

aid [eɪd] n aide f; (device) appareil m ♦ vt aider; **in ~ of** en faveur de; see also **hearing**

aide [eɪd] n (person) aide mf, assistant(e)

AIDS [eɪdz] n abbr (= acquired immune deficiency syndrome) SIDA m; **AIDS-related**

adj associé(e) au sida

aim [eɪm] *vt*: to ~ sth (at) (*gun, camera*) braquer *or* pointer qch (sur); (*missile*) lancer qch (à *or* contre *or* en direction de); (*blow*) allonger qch (à); (*remark*) destiner *or* adresser qch (à) ♦ *vi* (*also*: to take ~) viser ♦ n but *m*; (*skill*): his ~ **is bad** il vise mal; **to ~ at** viser (à); (*fig*) viser (à); **to ~ to do** avoir l'intention de faire; **~less** *adj* sans but

ain't [eɪnt] (*inf*) = am not; aren't; isn't

air [ɛə'] *n* air *m* ♦ *vt* (*room, bed, clothes*) aérer; (*grievances, views, ideas*) exposer, faire connaître ♦ *cpd* (*currents, attack etc*) aérien(ne); **to throw sth into the ~** jeter qch en l'air; **by ~** (*travel*) par avion; **to be on the ~** (*RADIO, TV: programme*) être diffusé(e); (: *station*) diffuser; **~bed** *n* matelas *m* pneumatique; **~-conditioned** *adj* climatisé(e); **~ conditioning** *n* climatisation *f*; **~craft** *n inv* avion *m*; **~craft carrier** *n* porte-avions *m inv*; **~field** *n* terrain *m* d'aviation; **A~ Force** *n* armée *f* de l'air; **~ freshener** *n* désodorisant *m*; **~gun** *n* fusil *m* à air comprimé; **~ hostess** *n* (*BRIT*) hôtesse *f* de l'air; **~ letter** *n* (*BRIT*) aérogramme *m*; **~lift** *n* pont aérien; **~line** *n* ligne aérienne, compagnie *f* d'aviation; **~liner** *n* avion *m* de ligne; **~mail** *n*: **by ~mail** par avion; **~ mile** *n* mile aérien; **~plane** *n* (*US*) avion *m*; **~port** *n* aéroport *m*; **~ raid** *n* attaque *or* raid aérien(ne); **~sick** *adj*: **to be ~sick** avoir le mal de l'air; **~tight** *adj* hermétique; **~ traffic controller** *n* aiguilleur *m* du ciel; **~y** *adj* bien aéré(e); (*manners*) dégagé(e)

aisle [aɪl] *n* (*of church*) allée centrale; nef latérale; (*of theatre etc*) couloir *m*, passage *m*, allée; **~ seat** *n* place *f* côté couloir

ajar [ə'dʒɑː'] *adj* entrouvert(e)

akin [ə'kɪn] *adj*: ~ **to** (*similar*) qui tient de *or* ressemble à

alarm [ə'lɑːm] *n* alarme *f* ♦ *vt* alarmer; ~ **call** *n* coup de fil *m* pour réveiller; ~ **clock** *n* réveille-matin *m inv*, réveil *m*

alas [ə'læs] *excl* hélas!

album [ˈælbəm] *n* album *m*

alcohol [ˈælkəhɔl] *n* alcool *m*; **~-free** *adj* sans alcool; **~ic** [ælkəˈhɔlɪk] *adj* alcoolique ♦ *n* alcoolique *m/f*; **A~ics Anonymous** Alcooliques anonymes

ale [eɪl] *n* bière *f*

alert [ə'lɜːt] *adj* alerte, vif (vive); vigilant(e) ♦ *n* alerte *f* ♦ *vt* alerter; **on the ~** sur le qui-vive; (*MIL*) en état d'alerte

algebra [ˈældʒɪbrə] *n* algèbre *f*

Algeria [ælˈdʒɪərɪə] *n* Algérie *f*

alias [ˈeɪlɪəs] *adv* alias ♦ *n* faux nom, nom d'emprunt; (*writer*) pseudonyme *m*

alibi [ˈælɪbaɪ] *n* alibi *m*

alien [ˈeɪlɪən] *n* étranger(-ère); (*from outer space*) extraterrestre *mf* ♦ *adj*: ~ (**to**) étranger(-ère) (à)

alight [ə'laɪt] *adj, adv* en feu ♦ *vi* mettre pied à terre; (*passenger*) descendre

alike [ə'laɪk] *adj* semblable, pareil(le) ♦ *adv* de même; **to look ~** se ressembler

alimony [ˈælɪmənɪ] *n* (*payment*) pension *f* alimentaire

alive [ə'laɪv] *adj* vivant(e); (*lively*) plein(e) de vie

KEYWORD

all [ɔːl] *adj* (*singular*) tout(e); (*plural*) tous (toutes); **all day** toute la journée; **all night** toute la nuit; **all men** tous les hommes; **all five** tous les cinq; **all the food** toute la nourriture; **all the books** tous les livres; **all the time** tout le temps; **all his life** toute sa vie

♦ *pron* **1** tout; **I ate it all, I ate all of it** j'ai tout mangé; **all of us went** nous y sommes tous allés; **all of the boys went** tous les garçons y sont allés

2 (*in phrases*): **above all** surtout, par-dessus tout; **after all** après tout; **not at all** (*in answer to question*) pas du tout; (*in answer to thanks*) je vous en prie!; **I'm not at all tired** je ne suis pas du tout fatigué(e); **anything at all will do** n'importe quoi fera l'affaire; **all in all** tout bien considéré, en fin de compte

♦ *adv*: **all alone** tout(e) seul(e); **it's not as hard as all that** ce n'est pas si difficile que ça; **all the more/the better** d'autant plus/mieux; **all but** presque, pratiquement; **the score is 2 all** le score est de 2 partout

---

allege [ə'ledʒ] *vt* alléguer, prétendre; **~dly** [ə'ledʒɪdlɪ] *adv* à ce que l'on prétend, paraît-il

allegiance [ə'liːdʒəns] *n* allégeance *f*, fidélité *f*, obéissance *f*

allergic [ə'lɜːdʒɪk] *adj*: ~ **to** allergique à

allergy [ˈælədʒɪ] *n* allergie *f*

alleviate [ə'liːvɪeɪt] *vt* soulager, adoucir

alley [ˈælɪ] *n* ruelle *f*

alliance [ə'laɪəns] *n* alliance *f*

allied [ˈælaɪd] *adj* allié(e)

all-in [ˈɔːlɪn] (*BRIT*) *adj* (*also adv*: *charge*) tout compris

all-night [ˈɔːlnaɪt] *adj* ouvert(e) *or* qui dure toute la nuit

allocate [ˈæləkeɪt] *vt* (*share out*) répartir, distribuer; **to ~ sth to** (*duties*) assigner *or* attribuer qch à; (*sum, time*) allouer qch à

allot [ə'lɔt] *vt*: **to ~ (to)** (*money*) répartir (entre), distribuer (à); (*time*) allouer (à); **~ment** *n* (*share*) part *f*; (*garden*) lopin *m* de terre (*loué à la municipalité*)

all-out [ˈɔːlaut] *adj* (*effort etc*) total(e) ♦ *adv*: **all out** à fond

allow [ə'lau] vt (*practice, behaviour*) permettre, autoriser; (*sum to spend etc*) accorder; allouer; (*sum, time estimated*) compter, prévoir; (*claim, goal*) admettre; (*concede*): **to ~ that** convenir que; **to ~ sb to do** permettre à qn de faire, autoriser qn à faire; **he is ~ed to ...** on lui permet de ...; **~ for** vt fus tenir compte de; **~ance** [ə'lauəns] n (*money received*) allocation f; subside m; indemnité f; (*TAX*) somme f déductible du revenu imposable, abattement m; **to make ~ances for** tenir compte de

alloy ['ælɔɪ] n alliage m

all: **~ right** adv (*feel, work*) bien; (*as answer*) d'accord; **~-rounder** n: **to be a good ~-rounder** être doué(e) en tout; **~-time** adj (*record*) sans précédent, absolu(e)

ally [n 'ælaɪ, vb ə'laɪ] n allié m ♦ vt: **to ~ o.s. with** s'allier avec

almighty [ɔːl'maɪtɪ] adj tout-puissant, (*tremendous*) énorme

almond ['ɑːmənd] n amande f

almost ['ɔːlməust] adv presque

alone [ə'ləun] adj, adv seul(e); **to leave sb ~** laisser qn tranquille; **to leave sth ~** ne pas toucher à qch; **let ~ ...** sans parler de ...; encore moins ...

along [ə'lɔŋ] prep le long de ♦ adv: **is he coming ~ with us?** vient-il avec nous?; **he was hopping/limping ~** il avançait en sautillant/boitant; **~ with** (*together with: person*) en compagnie de; (: *thing*) avec, en plus de; **all ~** (*all the time*) depuis le début; **~side** prep le long de; à côté de ♦ adv bord à bord

aloof [ə'luːf] adj distant(e) ♦ adv: **to stand ~** se tenir à distance or à l'écart

aloud [ə'laud] adv à haute voix

alphabet ['ælfəbet] n alphabet m; **~ical** [ælfə'betɪkl] adj alphabétique

alpine ['ælpaɪn] adj alpin(e), alpestre

Alps [ælps] npl: **the ~** les Alpes fpl

already [ɔːl'redɪ] adv déjà

alright ['ɔːl'raɪt] (*BRIT*) adv = **all right**

Alsatian [æl'seɪʃən] (*BRIT*) n (*dog*) berger allemand

also ['ɔːlsəu] adv aussi

altar ['ɔltər] n autel m

alter ['ɔltər] vt, vi changer

alternate [adj ɔl'tɜːnɪt, vb 'ɔltɜːneɪt] adj alterné(e), alternant(e), alternatif(-ive) ♦ vi alterner; **on ~ days** un jour sur deux, tous les deux jours; **alternating current** n courant alternatif

alternative [ɔl'tɜːnətɪv] adj (*solutions*) possible, au choix; (*plan*) autre, de rechange; (*lifestyle etc*) parallèle ♦ n (*choice*) alternative f; (*other possibility*) solution f de remplacement or de rechange, autre possibilité f; **an ~ comedian** un nouveau

comique; **~ medicine** médicines fpl parallèles or douces; **~ly** adv: **~ly one could** une autre or l'autre solution serait de, on pourrait aussi

alternator ['ɔltɜːneɪtər] n (*AUT*) alternateur m

although [ɔːl'ðəu] conj bien que +sub

altitude ['æltɪtjuːd] n altitude f

alto ['æltəu] n (*female*) contralto m; (*male*) haute-contre f

altogether [ɔːltə'geðər] adv entièrement, tout à fait; (*on the whole*) tout compte fait; (*in all*) en tout

aluminium [ælju'mɪnɪəm] (*BRIT*), **aluminum** [ə'luːmɪnəm] (*US*) n aluminium m

always ['ɔːlweɪz] adv toujours

Alzheimer's (disease) ['æltshaɪməz-] n maladie f d'Alzheimer

am [æm] vb see **be**

a.m. adv abbr (= *ante meridiem*) du matin

amalgamate [ə'mælgəmeɪt] vt, vi fusionner

amateur ['æmətər] n amateur m; **~ish** (*pej*) adj d'amateur

amaze [ə'meɪz] vt stupéfier; **to be ~d (at)** être stupéfait(e) (de); **~ment** n stupéfaction f, stupeur f; **amazing** adj étonnant(e); exceptionnel(le)

ambassador [æm'bæsədər] n ambassadeur m

amber ['æmbər] n ambre m; **at ~** (*BRIT: AUT*) à l'orange

ambiguous [æm'bɪgjuəs] adj ambigu(ë)

ambition [æm'bɪʃən] n ambition f; **ambitious** adj ambitieux(-euse)

ambulance ['æmbjuləns] n ambulance f

ambush ['æmbuʃ] n embuscade f ♦ vt tendre une embuscade à

amenable [ə'miːnəbl] adj: **~ to** (*advice etc*) disposé(e) à écouter

amend [ə'mend] vt (*law*) amender; (*text*) corriger; **to make ~s** réparer ses torts, faire amende honorable

amenities [ə'miːnɪtɪz] npl aménagements mpl, équipements mpl

America [ə'merɪkə] n Amérique f; **~n** adj américain(e) ♦ n Américain(e)

amiable ['eɪmɪəbl] adj aimable, affable

amicable ['æmɪkəbl] adj amical(e); (*LAW*) à l'amiable

amid(st) [ə'mɪd(st)] prep parmi, au milieu de

amiss [ə'mɪs] adj, adv: **there's something ~** il y a quelque chose qui ne va pas or qui cloche; **to take sth ~** prendre qch mal or de travers

ammonia [ə'məunɪə] n (*gas*) ammoniac m; (*liquid*) ammoniaque f

ammunition [æmju'nɪʃən] n munitions fpl

amok [ə'mɔk] adv: **to run ~** être pris(e) d'un accès de folie furieuse

among(st) [ə'mʌŋ(st)] prep parmi, entre

amorous ['æmərəs] adj amoureux(-euse)

amount [ə'maunt] n (sum) somme f,
montant m; (quantity) quantité f, nombre m
♦ vi: **to ~ to** (total) s'élever à; (be same as)
équivaloir à, revenir à

amp(ere) ['æmp(εə')] n ampère m

ample ['æmpl] adj ample; spacieux(-euse);
(enough): **this is ~** c'est largement suffisant;
to have ~ time/room avoir bien assez de
temps/place

amplifier ['æmplɪfaɪə'] n amplificateur m

amuse [ə'mju:z] vt amuser, divertir; **~ment** n
amusement m; **~ment arcade** n salle f de
jeu; **~ment park** n parc m d'attractions

an [æn, ən] indef art see **a**

anaemic [ə'ni:mɪk] (US anemic) adj
anémique

anaesthetic [ænɪs'θetɪk] (US anesthetic) n
anesthésique m

analog(ue) ['ænəlɒg] adj (watch, computer)
analogique

analyse ['ænəlaɪz] (US analyze) vt analyser;
analysis [ə'næləsɪs] (pl **analyses**) n analyse f;
analyst ['ænəlɪst] n (POL etc) spécialiste m/f;
(US) psychanalyste m/f

analyze ['ænəlaɪz] (US) vt = **analyse**

anarchist ['ænəkɪst] n anarchiste m/f

anarchy ['ænəkɪ] n anarchie f

anatomy [ə'nætəmɪ] n anatomie f

ancestor ['ænsɪstə'] n ancêtre m, aïeul m

anchor ['æŋkə'] n ancre f ♦ vi (also: **to drop
~**) jeter l'ancre, mouiller ♦ vt mettre à l'ancre;
(fig): **to ~ sth to** fixer qch à

anchovy ['æntʃəvɪ] n anchois m

ancient ['eɪnʃənt] adj ancien(ne), antique;
(person) d'un âge vénérable; (car)
antédiluvien(ne)

ancillary [æn'sɪlərɪ] adj auxiliaire

and [ænd] conj et; **~ so on** et ainsi de suite; **try
~ come** tâchez de venir; **he talked ~ talked** il
n'a pas arrêté de parler; **better ~ better** de
mieux en mieux

anew [ə'nju:] adv à nouveau

angel ['eɪndʒəl] n ange m

anger ['æŋgə'] n colère f

angina [æn'dʒaɪnə] n angine f de poitrine

angle ['æŋgl] n angle m; **from their ~** de leur
point de vue

angler ['æŋglə'] n pêcheur(-euse) à la ligne

Anglican ['æŋglɪkən] adj, n anglican(e)

angling ['æŋglɪŋ] n pêche f à la ligne

Anglo- ['æŋgləu] prefix anglo(-)

angrily ['æŋgrɪlɪ] adv avec colère

angry ['æŋgrɪ] adj en colère, furieux(-euse);
(wound) enflammé(e); **to be ~ with sb/at sth**
être furieux contre qn/de qch; **to get ~** se
fâcher, se mettre en colère

anguish ['æŋgwɪʃ] n (mental) angoisse f

animal ['ænɪməl] n animal m ♦ adj animal(e)

animate [vb 'ænɪmeɪt, adj 'ænɪmɪt] vt animer

aniseed ['ænɪsi:d] n anis m

ankle ['æŋkl] n cheville f; **~ sock** n socquette
f

annex [n 'æneks, vb ə'neks] n (BRIT: ~e)
annexe f ♦ vt annexer

anniversary [ænɪ'vɜ:sərɪ] n anniversaire m

announce [ə'nauns] vt annoncer; (birth,
death) faire part de; **~ment** n annonce f; (for
births etc: in newspaper) avis m de faire-part;
(: letter, card) faire-part m; **~r** n (RADIO, TV:
between programmes) speaker(ine)

annoy [ə'nɔɪ] vt agacer, ennuyer, contrarier;
don't get ~ed! ne vous fâchez pas!; **~ance** n
mécontentement m, contrariété f; **~ing** adj
agaçant(e), contrariant(e)

annual ['ænjuəl] adj annuel(le) ♦ n (BOT)
plante annuelle; (children's book) album m

annul [ə'nʌl] vt annuler

annum ['ænəm] n see **per**

anonymous [ə'nɒnɪməs] adj anonyme

anorak ['ænəræk] n anorak m

anorexia [ænə'reksɪə] n (also: ~ **nervosa**)
anorexie f

another [ə'nʌðə'] adj: ~ **book** (one more) un
autre livre, encore un livre, un livre de plus;
(a different one) un autre livre ♦ pron un(e)
autre, encore un(e), un(e) de plus; see also
one

answer ['ɑ:nsə'] n réponse f; (to problem)
solution f ♦ vi répondre ♦ vt (reply to)
répondre à; (problem) résoudre; (prayer)
exaucer; **in ~ to your letter** en réponse à votre
lettre; **to ~ the phone** répondre (au téléphone); **to ~ the bell** or **the door** aller or venir
ouvrir (la porte); **~ back** vi répondre,
répliquer; **~ for** vt fus (person) répondre de,
se porter garant de; (crime, one's actions) être
responsable de; **~ to** vt fus (description)
répondre or correspondre à; **~able** adj: **~able
(to sb/for sth)** responsable (devant qn/de
qch); **~ing machine** n répondeur m
automatique

ant [ænt] n fourmi f

antagonism [æn'tægənɪzəm] n antagonisme
m

antagonize [æn'tægənaɪz] vt éveiller
l'hostilité de, contrarier

Antarctic [ænt'ɑ:ktɪk] n: **the ~** l'Antarctique
m

antenatal ['æntɪ'neɪtl] adj prénatal(e);
~ clinic n service m de consultation prénatale

anthem ['ænθəm] n: **national ~** hymne
national

anti: **~-aircraft** adj (missile) anti-aérien(ne);
~biotic ['æntɪbaɪ'ɒtɪk] n antibiotique m;
~body n anticorps m

anticipate [æn'tɪsɪpeɪt] vt s'attendre à;
prévoir; (wishes, request) aller au devant de,

devancer

anticipation [æntɪsɪ'peɪʃən] n attente f; **in ~** par anticipation, à l'avance

anticlimax ['æntɪ'klaɪmæks] n déception f, douche froide (fam)

anticlockwise ['æntɪ'klɔkwaɪz] adj, adv dans le sens inverse des aiguilles d'une montre

antics ['æntɪks] npl singeries fpl

antifreeze ['æntɪfriːz] n antigel m

antihistamine ['æntɪ'hɪstəmɪn] n antihistaminique m

antiquated ['æntɪkweɪtɪd] adj vieilli(e), suranné(e), vieillot(te)

antique [æn'tiːk] n objet m d'art ancien, meuble ancien or d'époque, antiquité f ♦ adj ancien(ne); **~ dealer** n antiquaire m; **~ shop** n magasin m d'antiquités

anti- : **~-Semitism** ['æntɪ'semɪtɪzəm] n antisémitisme m; **~septic** [æntɪ'septɪk] n antiseptique m; **~social** ['æntɪ'səuʃəl] adj peu liant(e), sauvage, insociable; (against society) antisocial(e)

antlers ['æntləz] npl bois mpl, ramure f

anvil ['ænvɪl] n enclume f

anxiety [æŋ'zaɪətɪ] n anxiété f; (keenness): **~ to do** grand désir or impatience f de faire

anxious ['æŋkʃəs] adj anxieux(-euse), angoissé(e); (worrying: time, situation) inquiétant(e); (keen): **~ to do/that** qui tient beaucoup à faire/à ce que; impatient(e) de faire/que

KEYWORD

any ['enɪ] adj **1** (in questions etc: singular) du, de l', de la; (: plural) des; **have you any butter/children/ink?** avez-vous du beurre/des enfants/de l'encre?

2 (with negative) de, d'; **I haven't any money/books** je n'ai pas d'argent/de livres

3 (no matter which) n'importe quel(le); **choose any book you like** vous pouvez choisir n'importe quel livre

4 (in phrases): **in any case** de toute façon; **any day now** d'un jour à l'autre; **at any moment** à tout moment, d'un instant à l'autre; **at any rate** en tout cas

♦ pron **1** (in questions etc) en; **have you got any?** est-ce que vous en avez?; **can any of you sing?** est-ce que parmi vous il y en a qui savent chanter?

2 (with negative) en; **I haven't any (of them)** je n'en ai pas, je n'en ai aucun

3 (no matter which one(s)) n'importe lequel (or laquelle); **take any of those books (you like)** vous pouvez prendre n'importe lequel de ces livres

♦ adv **1** (in questions etc): **do you want any more soup/sandwiches?** voulez-vous encore de la soupe/des sandwichs?; **are you feeling any better?** est-ce que vous vous sentez mieux?

2 (with negative): **I can't hear him any more** je ne l'entends plus; **don't wait any longer** n'attendez pas plus longtemps

any- : **~body** pron n'importe qui; (in interrogative sentences) quelqu'un; (in negative sentences): **I don't see ~body** je ne vois personne; **~how** adv (at any rate) de toute façon, quand même; (haphazard) n'importe comment; **~one** pron = anybody; **~thing** pron n'importe quoi, quelque chose, ne ... rien; **~way** adv de toute façon; **~where** adv n'importe où, quelque part; **I don't see him ~where** je ne le vois nulle part

apart [ə'pɑːt] adv (to one side) à part; de côté; à l'écart; (separately) séparément; **10 miles ~** à 10 miles l'un de l'autre; **to take ~** démonter; **~ from** à part, excepté

apartheid [ə'pɑːteɪt] n apartheid m

apartment [ə'pɑːtmənt] n (US) appartement m, logement m; (room) chambre f; **~ building** (US) n immeuble m; (divided house) maison divisée en appartements

ape [eɪp] n (grand) singe ♦ vt singer

apéritif [ə'perɪtiːf] n apéritif m

aperture ['æpətʃuər] n orifice m, ouverture f; (PHOT) ouverture (du diaphragme)

APEX ['eɪpeks] n abbr (AVIAT) (= advance purchase excursion) APEX m

apologetic [əpɔlə'dʒetɪk] adj (tone, letter) d'excuse; (person): **to be ~** s'excuser

apologize [ə'pɔlədʒaɪz] vi: **to ~ (for sth to sb)** s'excuser (de qch auprès de qn), présenter des excuses (à qn pour qch)

apology [ə'pɔlədʒɪ] n excuses fpl

apostle [ə'pɔsl] n apôtre m

apostrophe [ə'pɔstrəfɪ] n apostrophe f

appalling [ə'pɔːlɪŋ] adj épouvantable; (stupidity) consternant(e)

apparatus [æpə'reɪtəs] n appareil m, dispositif m; (in gymnasium) agrès mpl; (of government) dispositif m

apparel [ə'pærəl] (US) n habillement m

apparent [ə'pærənt] adj apparent(e); **~ly** adv apparemment

appeal [ə'piːl] vi (LAW) faire or interjeter appel ♦ n appel m; (request) prière f; appel m; (charm) attrait m, charme m; **to ~ for** lancer un appel pour; **to ~ to** (beg) faire appel à; (be attractive) plaire à; **it doesn't ~ to me** cela ne m'attire pas; **~ing** adj (attractive) attrayant(e)

appear [ə'pɪər] vi apparaître, se montrer; (LAW) comparaître; (publication) paraître, sortir, être publié(e); (seem) paraître, sembler; **it would ~ that** il semble que; **to ~ in**

Hamlet jouer dans Hamlet; **to ~ on TV** passer à la télé; **~ance** n apparition f; parution f; (*look, aspect*) apparence f, aspect m

ppease [əˈpiːz] vt apaiser, calmer

ppendicitis [əpendɪˈsaɪtɪs] n appendicite f

ppendix [əˈpendɪks] (*pl* **appendices**) n appendice m

petite [ˈæpɪtaɪt] n appétit m; **appetizer** n amuse-gueule m; (*drink*) apéritif m

pplaud [əˈplɔːd] vt, vi applaudir

pplause [əˈplɔːz] n applaudissements mpl

pple [ˈæpl] n pomme f; **~ tree** n pommier m

ppliance [əˈplaɪəns] n appareil m

pplicable [əˈplɪkəbl] adj (*relevant*): **to be ~ to** valoir pour

pplicant [ˈæplɪkənt] n: **~ (for)** candidat(e) (à)

pplication [æplɪˈkeɪʃən] n application f; (*for a job, a grant etc*) demande f; candidature f; **~ form** n formulaire m de demande

pplied [əˈplaɪd] adj appliqué(e)

pply [əˈplaɪ] vt: **to ~ (to)** (*paint, ointment*) appliquer (sur); (*law etc*) appliquer (à) ♦ vi: **tu ~ tu** (*be suitable for, relevant to*) s'appliquer à; (*ask*) s'adresser à; **to ~ (for)** (*permit, grant*) faire une demande (en vue d'obtenir); (*job*) poser sa candidature (pour), faire une demande d'emploi (concernant); **to ~ o.s. to** s'appliquer à

ppoint [əˈpɔɪnt] vt nommer, engager; **~ed** adj: **at the ~ed time** à l'heure dite; **~ment** n nomination f; (*meeting*) rendez-vous m; **to make an ~ment (with)** prendre rendez-vous (avec)

ppraisal [əˈpreɪzl] n évaluation f

pprociate [əˈpriːʃieɪt] vt (*like*) apprécier; (*be grateful for*) être reconnaissant(e) de; (*understand*) comprendre; se rendre compte de ♦ vi (*FINANCE*) prendre de la valeur

ppreciation [əpriːʃiˈeɪʃən] n appréciation f; (*gratitude*) reconnaissance f; (*COMM*) hausse f, valorisation f

ppreciative [əˈpriːʃɪətɪv] adj (*person*) sensible; (*comment*) élogieux(-euse)

pprehensive [æprɪˈhensɪv] adj in-quiet(-ète), appréhensif(ive)

pprentice [əˈprentɪs] n apprenti m; **~ship** n apprentissage m

pproach [əˈprəʊtʃ] vi approcher ♦ vt (*come near*) approcher de; (*ask, apply to*) s'adresser à; (*situation, problem*) aborder ♦ n approche f; (*access*) accès m; **~able** adj accessible

ppropriate [adj əˈprəʊprɪɪt, vb əˈprəʊprɪeɪt] adj (*moment, remark*) opportun(e); (*tool etc*) approprié(e) ♦ vt (*take*) s'approprier

pproval [əˈpruːvəl] n approbation f; **on ~** (*COMM*) à l'examen

pprove [əˈpruːv] vt approuver; **~ of** vt fus approuver

approximate [adj əˈprɔksɪmɪt, vb əˈprɔksɪmeɪt] adj approximatif(-ive) ♦ vt se rapprocher de, être proche de; **~ly** adv approximativement

apricot [ˈeɪprɪkɔt] n abricot m

April [ˈeɪprəl] n avril m; **~ Fool's Day** le premier avril

apron [ˈeɪprən] n tablier m

apt [æpt] adj (*suitable*) approprié(e); (*likely*): **~ to do** susceptible de faire; qui a tendance à faire

Aquarius [əˈkweərɪəs] n le Verseau

Arab [ˈærəb] adj arabe ♦ n Arabe m/f; **~ian** [əˈreɪbɪən] adj arabe; **~ic** adj arabe ♦ n arabe m

arbitrary [ˈɑːbɪtrərɪ] adj arbitraire

arbitration [ɑːbɪˈtreɪʃən] n arbitrage m

arcade [ɑːˈkeɪd] n arcade f; (*passage with shops*) passage m, galerie marchande; (*with video games*) salle f de jeu

arch [ɑːtʃ] n arc m; (*of foot*) cambrure f, voûte f plantaire ♦ vt arquer, cambrer

archaeologist [ɑːkɪˈɔlədʒɪst] n archéologue m/f

archaeology [ɑːkɪˈɔlədʒɪ] n archéologie f

archbishop [ɑːtʃˈbɪʃəp] n archevêque m

archeology etc (*US*) [ɑːkɪˈɔlədʒɪ] = **archaeology** etc

archery [ˈɑːtʃərɪ] n tir m à l'arc

architect [ˈɑːkɪtekt] n architecte m; **~ure** n architecture f

archives [ˈɑːkaɪvz] npl archives fpl

Arctic [ˈɑːktɪk] adj arctique ♦ n Arctique m

ardent [ˈɑːdənt] adj fervent(e)

are [ɑːʳ] vb see **be**

area [ˈeərɪə] n (*GEOM*) superficie f; (*zone*) région f; (: *smaller*) secteur m, partie f; (*in room*) coin m; (*knowledge, research*) domaine m; **~ code** (*US*) n (*TEL*) indicatif m téléphonique

aren't [ɑːnt] = **are not**

Argentina [ɑːdʒənˈtiːnə] n Argentine f; **Argentinian** [ɑːdʒənˈtɪnɪən] adj argentin(e) ♦ n Argentin(e)

arguably [ˈɑːɡjuəblɪ] adv: **it is ~** on peut soutenir que c'est ...

argue [ˈɑːɡjuː] vi (*quarrel*) se disputer; (*reason*) argumenter; **to ~ that** objecter or alléguer que

argument [ˈɑːɡjumənt] n (*reasons*) argument m; (*quarrel*) dispute f; **~ative** [ɑːɡjuˈmentətɪv] adj ergoteur(-euse), raisonneur(-euse)

Aries [ˈeərɪz] n le Bélier

arise [əˈraɪz] (*pt* **arose**, *pp* **arisen**) vi survenir, se présenter

aristocrat [ˈærɪstəkræt] n aristocrate m/f

arithmetic [əˈrɪθmətɪk] n arithmétique f

ark [ɑːk] n: **Noah's A~** l'Arche f de Noé

arm [ɑ:m] n bras m ♦ vt armer; **~s** npl (weapons, HERALDRY) armes fpl; **~ in ~** bras dessus bras dessous

armaments ['ɑ:məmənts] npl armement m

armchair ['ɑ:mtʃeə'] n fauteuil m

armed [ɑ:md] adj armé(e); **~ robbery** n vol m à main armée

armour ['ɑ:mə'] (US **armor**) n armure f; (MIL: tanks) blindés mpl; **~ed car** n véhicule blindé

armpit ['ɑ:mpɪt] n aisselle f

armrest ['ɑ:mrest] n accoudoir m

army ['ɑ:mɪ] n armée f

A road (BRIT) (AUT) route nationale

aroma [ə'rəumə] n arôme m; **~therapy** n aromathérapie f

arose [ə'rəuz] pt of arise

around [ə'raund] adv autour; (nearby) dans les parages ♦ prep autour de; (near) près de; (fig: about) environ; (: date, time) vers

arouse [ə'rauz] vt (sleeper) éveiller; (curiosity, passions) éveiller, susciter; (anger) exciter

arrange [ə'reɪndʒ] vt arranger; **to ~ to do sth** prévoir de faire qch; **~ment** n arrangement m; **~ments** npl (plans etc) arrangements mpl, dispositions fpl

array [ə'reɪ] n: **~ of** déploiement m or étalage m de

arrears [ə'rɪəz] npl arriéré m; **to be in ~ with one's rent** devoir un arriéré de loyer

arrest [ə'rest] vt arrêter; (sb's attention) retenir, attirer ♦ n arrestation f; **under ~** en état d'arrestation

arrival [ə'raɪvl] n arrivée f; **new ~** nouveau venu, nouvelle venue; (baby) nouveau-né(e)

arrive [ə'raɪv] vi arriver

arrogant ['ærəgənt] adj arrogant(e)

arrow ['ærəu] n flèche f

arse [ɑ:s] (BRIT: inf!) n cul m (!)

arson ['ɑ:sn] n incendie criminel

art [ɑ:t] n art m; **A~s** npl (SCOL) les lettres fpl

artery ['ɑ:tərɪ] n artère f

art gallery n musée m d'art; (small and private) galerie f de peinture

arthritis [ɑ:'θraɪtɪs] n arthrite f

artichoke ['ɑ:tɪtʃəuk] n (also: **globe ~**) artichaut m; (also: **Jerusalem ~**) topinambour m

article ['ɑ:tɪkl] n article m; **~s** npl (BRIT: LAW: training) ≈ stage m; **~ of clothing** vêtement m

articulate [adj ɑ:'tɪkjulɪt, vb ɑ:'tɪkjuleɪt] adj (person) qui s'exprime bien; (speech) bien articulé(e), prononcé(e) clairement ♦ vt exprimer; **~d lorry** (BRIT) n (camion m) semi-remorque m

artificial [ɑ:tɪ'fɪʃəl] adj artificiel(le); **~ respiration** n respiration artificielle

artist ['ɑ:tɪst] n artiste m/f; **~ic** [ɑ:'tɪstɪk] adj artistique; **~ry** n art m, talent m

art school n ≈ école f des beaux-arts

KEYWORD

as [æz, əz] conj **1** (referring to time) comme, alors que; à mesure que; **he came in as I was leaving** il est arrivé comme je partais; **as the years went by** à mesure que les années passaient; **as from tomorrow** à partir de demain

2 (in comparisons): **as big as** aussi grand que; **twice as big as** deux fois plus grand que; **as much or many as** autant que; **as much money/many books** autant d'argent/de livres que; **as soon as** dès que

3 (since, because) comme, puisque; **as he had to be home by 10** ... comme il or puisqu'il devait être de retour avant 10 h ...

4 (referring to manner, way) comme; **do as you wish** faites comme vous voudrez

5 (concerning): **as for or to that** quant à cela, pour ce qui est de cela

6: **as if or though** comme si; **he looked as if he was ill** il avait l'air d'être malade; see also **long**; **such**; **well**

♦ prep: **he works as a driver** il travaille comme chauffeur; **as chairman of the company, he** ... en tant que président de la société, il ...; **dressed up as a cowboy** déguisé en cowboy; **he gave me it as a present** il me l'a offert, il m'en a fait cadeau

---

a.s.a.p. abbr (= as soon as possible) dès que possible

asbestos [æz'bestəs] n amiante m

ascend [ə'send] vt gravir; (throne) monter sur

ascertain [æsə'teɪn] vt vérifier

ash [æʃ] n (dust) cendre f; (also: **~ tree**) frêne m

ashamed [ə'ʃeɪmd] adj honteux(-euse), confus(e); **to be ~ of** avoir honte de

ashore [ə'ʃɔ:'] adv à terre

ashtray ['æʃtreɪ] n cendrier m

Ash Wednesday n mercredi m des cendres

Asia ['eɪʃə] n Asie f; **~n** n Asiatique m/f ♦ adj asiatique

aside [ə'saɪd] adv de côté; à l'écart ♦ n aparté m

ask [ɑ:sk] vt demander; (invite) inviter; **to ~ sb sth/to do sth** demander qch à qn/à qn de faire qch; **to ~ sb about sth** questionner qn sur qch; se renseigner auprès de qn sur qch; **to ~ (sb) a question** poser une question (à qn); **to ~ sb out to dinner** inviter qn au restaurant; **~ after** vt fus demander des nouvelles de; **~ for** vt fus demander; (trouble) chercher

asking price ['ɑ:skɪŋ-] n: **the ~** le prix de départ

asleep [ə'sli:p] adj endormi(e); **to fall ~** s'endormir

asparagus [əsˈpærəgəs] n asperges fpl
aspect [ˈæspekt] n aspect m; (direction in which a building etc faces) orientation f, exposition f
aspire [əsˈpaɪəʳ] vi: **to ~ to** aspirer à
aspirin [ˈæsprɪn] n aspirine f
ass [æs] n âne m; (inf) imbécile m/f; (US: inf!) cul m (!)
assailant [əˈseɪlənt] n agresseur m; assaillant m
assassinate [əˈsæsɪneɪt] vt assassiner; **assassination** [əsæsɪˈneɪʃən] n assassinat m
assault [əˈsɔːlt] n (MIL) assaut m; (gen: attack) agression f ♦ vt attaquer; (sexually) violenter
assemble [əˈsembl] vt assembler ♦ vi s'assembler, se rassembler; **assembly** n assemblée f, réunion f; (institution) assemblée; (construction) assemblage m; **assembly line** n chaîne f de montage
assent [əˈsent] n assentiment m, consentement m
assert [əˈsɜːt] vt affirmer, déclarer; (one's authority) faire valoir; (one's innocence) protester
assess [əˈses] vt évaluer; (tax, payment) établir or fixer le montant de; (property etc: for tax) calculer la valeur imposable de; (person) juger la valeur de; **~ment** n évaluation f, fixation f, calcul m de la valeur imposable de, jugement m; **~or** n expert m (impôt et assurance)
asset [ˈæset] n avantage m, atout m; **~s** npl (FINANCE) capital m; avoir(s) m(pl); actif m
assign [əˈsaɪn] vt (date) fixer; (task) assigner à; (resources) affecter à; **~ment** n tâche f, mission f
assist [əˈsɪst] vt aider, assister; **~ance** n aide f, assistance f; **~ant** n assistant(e), adjoint(e); (RRIT: also: **shop ~ant**) vendeur(-euse)
associate [n, adj əˈsəʊʃɪt, vb əˈsəʊʃɪeɪt] adj, n associé(e) ♦ vt associer ♦ vi: **to ~ with sb** fréquenter qn; **association** [əsəʊsɪˈeɪʃən] n association f
assorted [əˈsɔːtɪd] adj assorti(e)
assortment [əˈsɔːtmənt] n assortiment m
assume [əˈsjuːm] vt supposer; (responsibilities etc) assumer; (attitude, name) prendre, adopter; **assumption** [əˈsʌmpʃən] n supposition f, hypothèse f; (of power) assomption f, prise f
assurance [əˈʃuərəns] n assurance f
assure [əˈʃuəʳ] vt assurer
asthma [ˈæsmə] n asthme m
astonish [əˈstɒnɪʃ] vt étonner, stupéfier; **~ment** n étonnement m
astound [əˈstaund] vt stupéfier, sidérer
astray [əˈstreɪ] adv: **to go ~** s'égarer; (fig) quitter le droit chemin; **to lead ~** détourner du droit chemin
astride [əˈstraɪd] prep à cheval sur
astrology [əsˈtrɒlədʒɪ] n astrologie f
astronaut [ˈæstrənɔːt] n astronaute m/f
astronomy [əsˈtrɒnəmɪ] n astronomie f
asylum [əˈsaɪləm] n asile m

KEYWORD
---

at [æt] prep **1** (referring to position, direction) à; **at the top** au sommet; **at home/school** à la maison or chez soi/à l'école; **at the baker's** à la boulangerie, chez le boulanger; **to look at sth** regarder qch
2 (referring to time): **at 4 o'clock** à 4 heures; **at Christmas** à Noël; **at night** la nuit; **at times** par moments, parfois
3 (referring to rates, speed etc) à; **at £1 a kilo** une livre le kilo; **two at a time** deux à la fois; **at 50 km/h** à 50 km/h
4 (referring to manner): **at a stroke** d'un seul coup; **at peace** en paix
5 (referring to activity): **to be at work** être au travail, travailler; **to play at cowboys** jouer aux cowboys; **to be good at sth** être bon en qch
6 (referring to cause): **shocked/surprised/annoyed at sth** choqué par/étonné de/agacé par qch; **I went at his suggestion** j'y suis allé sur son conseil

---

ate [eɪt] pt of eat
atheist [ˈeɪθɪɪst] n athée m/f
Athens [ˈæθɪnz] n Athènes
athlete [ˈæθliːt] n athlète m/f; **athletic** [æθˈletɪk] adj athlétique; **athletics** n athlétisme m
Atlantic [atˈlæntɪk] adj atlantique ♦ n: **the ~ (Ocean)** l'(océan m) Atlantique m
atlas [ˈætləs] n atlas m
ATM n abbr (= automated telling machine) guichet m automatique
atmosphere [ˈætməsfɪəʳ] n atmosphère f
atom [ˈætəm] n atome m; **~ic** [əˈtɒmɪk] adj atomique; **~(ic) bomb** n bombe f atomique; **~izer** n atomiseur m
atone [əˈtaun] vi: **to ~ for** expier, racheter
atrocious [əˈtrəʊʃəs] adj (very bad) atroce, exécrable
attach [əˈtætʃ] vt attacher; (document, letter) joindre; **to be ~ed to sb/sth** être attaché à qn/qch
attaché case [əˈtæʃeɪ] n mallette f, attaché-case m
attachment [əˈtætʃmənt] n (tool) accessoire m; (love): **~ (to)** affection f (pour), attachement m (à)
attack [əˈtæk] vt attaquer; (task etc) s'attaquer à ♦ n attaque f; (also: **heart ~**) crise f cardiaque
attain [əˈteɪn] vt (also: **to ~ to**) parvenir à,

atteindre; (: *knowledge*) acquérir
attempt [ə'tɛmpt] *n* tentative *f* ♦ *vt* essayer, tenter; **to make an ~ on sb's life** attenter à la vie de qn; **~ed** *adj*: **~ed murder/suicide** tentative *f* de meurtre/suicide
attend [ə'tɛnd] *vt* (*course*) suivre; (*meeting, talk*) assister à; (*school, church*) aller à, fréquenter; (*patient*) soigner, s'occuper de; **~ to** *vt fus* (*needs, affairs etc*) s'occuper de; (*customer, patient*) s'occuper de; **~ance** *n* (*being present*) présence *f*; (*people present*) assistance *f*; **~ant** *n* employé(e) ♦ *adj* (*dangers*) inhérent(e), concomitant(e)
attention [ə'tɛnʃən] *n* attention *f*; **~!** (*MIL*) garde-à-vous!; **for the ~ of** (*ADMIN*) à l'attention de
attentive [ə'tɛntɪv] *adj* attentif(-ive); (*kind*) prévenant(e)
attest [ə'tɛst] *vi*: **to ~ to** (*demonstrate*) démontrer; (*confirm*) témoigner
attic ['ætɪk] *n* grenier *m*
attitude ['ætɪtjuːd] *n* attitude *f*; pose *f*, maintien *m*
attorney [ə'təːnɪ] *n* (*US: lawyer*) avoué *m*; **A~ General** *n* (*BRIT*) ≈ procureur général; (*US*) ≈ garde *m* des Sceaux, ministre *m* de la Justice
attract [ə'trækt] *vt* attirer; **~ion** *n* (*gen pl: pleasant things*) attraction *f*, attrait *m*; (*PHYSICS*) attraction *f*; (*fig: towards sb or sth*) attirance *f*; **~ive** *adj* attrayant(e); (*person*) séduisant(e)
attribute [*n* 'ætrɪbjuːt, *vb* ə'trɪbjuːt] *n* attribut *m* ♦ *vt*: **to ~ sth to** attribuer qch à
attrition [ə'trɪʃən] *n*: **war of ~** guerre *f* d'usure
aubergine ['əubəʒiːn] *n* aubergine *f*
auction ['ɔːkʃən] *n* (*also*: **sale by ~**) vente *f* aux enchères ♦ *vt* (*also*: **sell by ~**) vendre aux enchères ♦ (*also*: **put up for ~**) mettre aux enchères; **~eer** [ɔːkʃə'nɪər] *n* commissaire-priseur *m*
audience ['ɔːdɪəns] *n* (*people*) assistance *f*; public *m*; spectateurs *mpl*; (*interview*) audience *f*
audiovisual ['ɔːdɪəu'vɪzjuəl] *adj* audiovisuel(le); **~ aids** *npl* supports or moyens audiovisuels
audit ['ɔːdɪt] *vt* vérifier
audition [ɔː'dɪʃən] *n* audition *f*
auditor ['ɔːdɪtər] *n* vérificateur *m* des comptes
augur ['ɔːgər] *vi*: **it ~s well** c'est bon signe or de bon augure
August ['ɔːgəst] *n* août *m*
aunt [ɑːnt] *n* tante *f*; **~ie, ~y** ['ɑːntɪ] *n dimin* of **aunt**
au pair ['əu'pɛər] *n* (*also*: **~ girl**) jeune fille *f* au pair
auspicious [ɔːs'pɪʃəs] *adj* de bon augure,

propice
Australia [ɔs'treɪlɪə] *n* Australie *f*; **~n** *adj* australien(ne) ♦ *n* Australien(ne)
Austria ['ɔstrɪə] *n* Autriche *f*; **~n** *adj* autrichien(ne) ♦ *n* Autrichien(ne)
authentic [ɔː'θɛntɪk] *adj* authentique
author ['ɔːθər] *n* auteur *m*
authoritarian [ɔːθɔrɪ'tɛərɪən] *adj* autoritaire
authoritative [ɔː'θɔrɪtətɪv] *adj* (*account*) digne de foi; (*study, treatise*) qui fait autorité; (*person, manner*) autoritaire
authority [ɔː'θɔrɪtɪ] *n* autorité *f*; (*permission*) autorisation (formelle); **the authorities** *npl* (*ruling body*) les autorités *fpl*, l'administration *f*
authorize ['ɔːθəraɪz] *vt* autoriser
auto ['ɔːtəu] (*US*) *n* auto *f*, voiture *f*
auto: ~biography [ɔːtəbɪ'ɔgrafɪ] *n* autobiographie *f*; **~graph** ['ɔːtəgrɑːf] *n* autographe *m* ♦ *vt* signer, dédicacer; **~mated** ['ɔːtəmeɪtɪd] *adj* automatisé(e), automatique; **~matic** [ɔːtə'mætɪk] *adj* automatique ♦ *n* (*gun*) automatique *m*; (*washing machine*) machine *f* à laver automatique; (*BRIT: AUT*) voiture *f* à transmission automatique; **~matically** *adv* automatiquement; **~mation** [ɔːtə'meɪʃən] *n* automatisation *f* (électronique); **~mobile** ['ɔːtəməbiːl] (*US*) *n* automobile *f*; **~nomy** [ɔː'tɔnəmɪ] *n* autonomie *f*
autumn ['ɔːtəm] *n* automne *m*; **in ~** en automne
auxiliary [ɔːg'zɪlɪərɪ] *adj* auxiliaire ♦ *n* auxiliaire *m/f*
avail [ə'veɪl] *vt*: **to ~ o.s. of** profiter de ♦ *n*: **to no ~** sans résultat, en vain, en pure perte
availability [əveɪlə'bɪlɪtɪ] *n* disponibilité *f*
available [ə'veɪləbl] *adj* disponible
avalanche ['ævəlɑːnʃ] *n* avalanche *f*
Ave *abbr* = **avenue**
avenge [ə'vɛndʒ] *vt* venger
avenue ['ævənjuː] *n* avenue *f*; (*fig*) moyen *m*
average ['ævərɪdʒ] *n* moyenne *f*; (*fig*) moyen *m* ♦ *adj* moyen(ne) ♦ *vt* (*a certain figure*) atteindre or faire *etc* en moyenne; **on ~** en moyenne; **~ out** *vi*: **to ~ out at** représenter en moyenne, donner une moyenne de
averse [ə'vəːs] *adj*: **to be ~ to sth/doing sth** éprouver une forte répugnance envers qch/à faire qch
avert [ə'vəːt] *vt* (*danger*) prévenir, écarter; (*one's eyes*) détourner
aviary ['eɪvɪərɪ] *n* volière *f*
avocado [ævə'kɑːdəu] *n* (*BRIT: ~ pear*) avocat *m*
avoid [ə'vɔɪd] *vt* éviter
await [ə'weɪt] *vt* attendre
awake [ə'weɪk] (*pt* **awoke**, *pp* **awoken**) *adj* éveillé(e) ♦ *vt* éveiller ♦ *vi* s'éveiller; **~ to**

(*dangers, possibilities*) conscient(e) de; **to be ~** être réveillé(e); **he was still ~** il ne dormait pas encore; **~ning** *n* réveil *m*

award [ə'wɔːd] *n* récompense *f*, prix *m*; (*LAW: damages*) dommages-intérêts *mpl* ♦ *vt* (*prize*) décerner; (*LAW: damages*) accorder

aware [ə'wɛəʳ] *adj*: **~ (of)** (*conscious*) conscient(e) (de); (*informed*) au courant (de); **to become ~ of/that** prendre conscience de/que; se rendre compte de/que; **~ness** *n* conscience *f*, connaissance *f*

away [ə'weɪ] *adj, adv* (au) loin; absent(e); **two kilometres ~** à (une distance de) deux kilomètres, à deux kilomètres de distance; **two hours ~ by car** à deux heures de voiture *or* de route; **the holiday was two weeks ~** il restait deux semaines jusqu'aux vacances; **~ from** loin de; **he's ~ for a week** il est parti (pour) une semaine; **to pedal/work/laugh ~** être en train de pédaler/travailler/rire; **to fade ~** (*sound*) s'affaiblir; (*colour*) s'estomper; **to wither ~** (*plant*) se dessécher; **to take ~** emporter; (*subtract*) enlever; **~ game** *n* (*SPORT*) match *m* à l'extérieur

awe [ɔː] *n* respect mêlé de crainte; **~-inspiring** ['ɔːɪnspaɪərɪŋ] *adj* impressionnant(e)

awful ['ɔːfəl] *adj* affreux(-euse); **an ~ lot (of)** un nombre incroyable (de); **~ly** *adv* (*very*) terriblement, vraiment

awkward ['ɔːkwəd] *adj* (*clumsy*) gauche, maladroit(e); (*inconvenient*) peu pratique; (*embarrassing*) gênant(e), délicat(e)

awning ['ɔːnɪŋ] *n* (*of tent*) auvent *m*; (*of shop*) store *m*; (*of hotel etc*) marquise *f*

awoke [ə'wəuk] *pt of* **awake**; **~n** [ə'wəukən] *pp of* **awake**

axe [æks] (*US* **ax**) *n* hache *f* ♦ *vt* (*project etc*) abandonner; (*jobs*) supprimer

axes¹ ['æksɪz] *npl of* **axe**

axes² ['æksiːz] *npl of* **axis**

axis ['æksɪs] (*pl* **axes**) *n* axe *m*

axle ['æksl] *n* (*also:* **~-tree**: *AUT*) essieu *m*

ay(e) [aɪ] *excl* (*yes*) oui

B, b

B [biː] *n* (*MUS*) si *m*; **~ road** (*BRIT*) route départementale

B.A. *abbr* = **Bachelor of Arts**

babble ['bæbl] *vi* bredouiller; (*baby, stream*) gazouiller

baby ['beɪbɪ] *n* bébé *m*; (*US: inf: darling*): **come on, ~!** viens ma belle/mon gars!; **~ carriage** (*US*) *n* voiture *f* d'enfant; **~ food** *n* aliments *mpl* pour bébé(s); **~-sit** *vi* garder les enfants; **~-sitter** *n* baby-sitter *m/f*; **~ wipe** *n* lingette *f* (*pour bébé*)

bachelor ['bætʃələʳ] *n* célibataire *m*; **B~ of Arts/Science** ≈ licencié(e) ès *or* en lettres/sciences

back [bæk] *n* (*of person, horse, book*) dos *m*; (*of hand*) dos, revers *m*; (*of house*) derrière *m*; (*of car, train*) arrière *m*; (*of chair*) dossier *m*; (*of page*) verso *m*; (*of room, audience*) fond *m*; (*SPORT*) arrière *m* ♦ *vt* (*candidate: also:* **~ up**) soutenir, appuyer; (*horse: at races*) parier *or* miser sur; (*car*) (faire) reculer ♦ *vi* (*also:* **~ up**) reculer; (*car: also:* **~ up**: *car etc*) faire marche arrière ♦ *adj* (*in compounds*) de derrière, à l'arrière ♦ *adv* (*not forward*) en arrière; (*returned*): **he's ~** il est rentré, il est de retour; (*restitution*): **throw the ball ~** renvoie la balle; (*again*): **he called ~** il a rappelé; **~ seat/wheels** *mpl/roues fpl* arrière; **~ payments/rent** arriéré *m* de paiements/loyer; **he ran ~** il est revenu en courant; **~ down** *vi* rabattre de ses prétentions; **~ out** *vi* (*of promise*) se dédire; **~ up** *vt* (*candidate etc*) soutenir, appuyer; (*COMPUT*) sauvegarder; **~ache** *n* mal *m* de dos; **~bencher** (*BRIT*) *n* membre du parlement sans portefeuille; **~bone** *n* colonne vertébrale, épine dorsale; **~date** *vt* (*letter*) antidater; **~dated pay rise** augmentation *f* avec effet rétroactif; **~fire** *vi* (*AUT*) pétarader; (*plans*) mal tourner; **~ground** *n* arrière-plan *m*; (*of events*) situation *f*, conjoncture *f*; (*basic knowledge*) éléments *mpl* de base; (*experience*) formation *f*; **family ~ground** milieu familial; **~hand** (*TENNIS: also:* **~hand stroke**) revers *m*; **~hander** (*BRIT*) *n* (*bribe*) pot-de-vin *m*; **~ing** *n* (*fig*) soutien *m*, appui *m*; **~lash** *n* contre-coup *m*, répercussion *f*; **~log** *n*: **~log of work** travail *m* en retard; **~ number** *n* (*of magazine etc*) vieux numéro; **~pack** *n* sac *m* à dos; **~packer** *n* randonneur(-euse); **~ pain** *n* mal *m* de dos; **~ pay** *n* rappel *m* de salaire; **~side** (*inf*) *n* derrière *m*, postérieur *m*; **~stage** *adv* ♦ *n* derrière la scène, dans la coulisse; **~stroke** *n* dos crawlé; **~up** *adj* (*train, plane*) supplémentaire, de réserve; (*COMPUT*) de sauvegarde ♦ *n* (*support*) appui *m*, soutien *m*; (*also:* **~up disk/file**) sauvegarde *f*; **~ward** *adj* (*movement*) en arrière; (*person, country*) arriéré(e); attardé(e); **~wards** *adv* (*move, go*) en arrière; (*read a list*) à l'envers, à rebours; (*fall*) à la renverse; (*walk*) à reculons; **~water** *n* (*fig*) coin reculé; bled perdu (*péj*); **~yard** *n* arrière-cour *f*

bacon ['beɪkən] *n* bacon *m*, lard *m*

bacteria [bæk'tɪərɪə] *npl* bactéries *fpl*

bad [bæd] *adj* mauvais(e); (*child*) vilain(e); (*mistake, accident etc*) grave; (*meat, food*) gâté(e), avarié(e); **his ~ leg** sa jambe malade; **to go ~** (*meat, food*) se gâter

badge [bædʒ] n insigne m; (of policeman) plaque f

badger ['bædʒər] n blaireau m

badly ['bædlɪ] adv (work, dress etc) mal; ~ **wounded** grièvement blessé; **he needs it** ~ il en a absolument besoin; ~ **off** adj, adv dans la gêne

badminton ['bædmɪntən] n badminton m

bad-tempered ['bæd'tempəd] adj (person: by nature) ayant mauvais caractère; (: on one occasion) de mauvaise humeur

baffle ['bæfl] vt (puzzle) déconcerter

bag [bæg] n sac m ♦ vt (inf: take) empocher; s'approprier; ~s **of** (inf: lots of) des masses de; ~**gage** n bagages mpl; ~**gage allowance** n franchise f de bagages; ~**gage reclaim** n livraison f de bagages; ~**gy** adj avachi(e), qui fait des poches; ~**pipes** npl cornemuse f

bail [beɪl] n (payment) caution f; (release) mise f en liberté sous caution ♦ vt (prisoner: also: **grant** ~ **to**) mettre en liberté sous caution; (boat: also: ~ **out**) écoper; **on** ~ (prisoner) sous caution; see also **bale**; ~ **out** vt (prisoner) payer la caution de

bailiff ['beɪlɪf] n (BRIT) ≈ huissier m, huissier-audiencier m; (US) ≈

bait [beɪt] n appât m ♦ vt appâter; (fig: tease) tourmenter

bake [beɪk] vt (faire) cuire au four ♦ vi (bread etc) cuire (au four); (make cakes etc) faire de la pâtisserie; ~**d beans** npl haricots blancs à la sauce tomate; ~**d potato** n pomme de terre en robe des champs; ~**r** n boulanger m; ~**ry** n boulangerie f; boulangerie industrielle; **baking** n cuisson f; **baking powder** n levure f (chimique)

balance ['bæləns] n équilibre m; (COMM: sum) solde m; (remainder) reste m; (scales) balance f ♦ vt mettre or faire tenir en équilibre; (pros and cons) peser; (budget) équilibrer; (account) balancer; ~ **of trade/ payments** balance commerciale/des comptes or paiements; ~**d** adj (personality, diet) équilibré(e); (report) objectif(-ive); ~ **sheet** n bilan m

balcony ['bælkənɪ] n balcon m; (in theatre) deuxième balcon

bald [bɔːld] adj chauve; (tyre) lisse

bale [beɪl] n balle f, ballot m; ~ **out** vi (of a plane) sauter en parachute

ball [bɔːl] n boule f; (football) ballon m; (for tennis, golf) balle f; (of wool) pelote f; (of string) bobine f; (dance) bal m; **to play** ~ **(with sb)** (fig) coopérer (avec qn)

ballast ['bæləst] n lest m

ball bearings npl roulement m à billes

ballerina [bælə'riːnə] n ballerine f

ballet ['bæleɪ] n ballet m; (art) danse f

(classique); ~ **dancer** n danceur(-euse) m/f de ballet; ~ **shoe** n chausson m de danse

balloon [bə'luːn] n ballon m; (in comic strip) bulle f

ballot ['bælət] n scrutin m; ~ **paper** n bulletin m de vote

ballpoint (pen) ['bɔːlpɔɪnt(-)] n stylo m à bille

ballroom ['bɔːlrum] n salle f de bal

ban [bæn] n interdiction f ♦ vt interdire

banana [bə'nɑːnə] n banane f

band [bænd] n bande f; (at a dance) orchestre m; (MIL) musique f, fanfare f; ~ **together** vi se liguer

bandage ['bændɪdʒ] n bandage m, pansement m ♦ vt bander

Bandaid ® ['bændeɪd] (US) n pansement adhésif

bandit ['bændɪt] n bandit m

bandy-legged ['bændɪ'legɪd] adj aux jambes arquées

bang [bæŋ] n détonation f; (of door) claquement m; (blow) coup (violent) ♦ vt frapper (violemment); (door) claquer ♦ vi détoner; claquer ♦ excl pan!; ~**s** (US) npl (fringe) frange f

banish ['bænɪʃ] vt bannir

banister(s) ['bænɪstə(z)] n(pl) rampe f (d'escalier)

bank [bæŋk] n banque f; (of river, lake) bord m, rive f; (of earth) talus m, remblai m ♦ vi (AVIAT) virer sur l'aile; ~ **on** vt fus miser or tabler sur; ~ **account** n compte m en banque; ~ **card** n carte f d'identité bancaire; ~**er's card** (BRIT) n = bank card; ~ **holiday** (BRIT) n jour férié (les banques sont fermées); ~**ing** n opérations fpl bancaires; profession f de banquier; ~**note** n billet m de banque; ~ **rate** n taux m de l'escompte

bankrupt ['bæŋkrʌpt] adj en faillite; **to go** ~ faire faillite; ~**cy** n faillite f

bank statement n relevé m de compte

banner ['bænər] n bannière f

bannister(s) ['bænɪstə(z)] n(pl) = banister(s)

baptism ['bæptɪzəm] n baptême m

bar [bɑːr] n (pub) bar m; (counter: in pub) comptoir m, bar; (rod: of metal etc) barre f; (on window etc) barreau m; (of chocolate) tablette f, plaque f; (fig) obstacle m; (prohibition) mesure f d'exclusion; (MUS) mesure f ♦ vt (road) barrer; (window) munir de barreaux; (person) exclure; (activity) interdire; ~ **of soap** savonnette f; **the B**~ (LAW) le barreau; **behind** ~**s** (prisoner) sous les verrous; ~ **none** sans exception

barbaric [bɑː'bærɪk] adj barbare

barbecue ['bɑːbɪkjuː] n barbecue m

barbed wire ['bɑ:bd-] n fil m de fer barbelé

barber ['bɑ:bəʳ] n coiffeur m (pour hommes)

bar code n (on goods) code m à barres

bare [beəʳ] adj nu(e) ♦ vt mettre à nu, dénuder; (teeth) montrer; **the ~ necessities** le strict nécessaire; **~back** adv à cru, sans selle; **~faced** adj impudent(e), effronté(e); **~foot** adj, adv nu-pieds, (les) pieds nus; **~ly** adv à peine

bargain ['bɑ:gɪn] n (transaction) marché m; (good buy) affaire f, occasion f ♦ vi (haggle) marchander; (negotiate): **to ~ (with sb)** négocier (avec qn), traiter (avec qn); **into the ~** par-dessus le marché; **~ for** vt fus: **he got more than he ~ed for** il ne s'attendait pas à un coup pareil

barge [bɑ:dʒ] n péniche f; **~ in** vi (walk in) faire irruption; (interrupt talk) intervenir mal à propos

bark [bɑ:k] n (of tree) écorce f; (of dog) aboiement m ♦ vi aboyer

barley ['bɑ:lɪ] n orge f, **~ sugar** n sucre m d'orge

bar: ~maid n serveuse f de bar, barmaid f; **~man** (irreg) n barman m; **~ meal** n repas m de bistrot; **to go for a ~ meal** aller manger au bistrot

barn [bɑ:n] n grange f

barometer [bə'rɒmɪtəʳ] n baromètre m

baron ['bærən] n baron m; **~ess** ['bærənɪs] n baronne f

barracks ['bærəks] npl caserne f

barrage [bæ'rɑ:ʒ] n (MIL) tir m de barrage; (dam) barrage m; (fig) pluie f

barrel ['bærəl] n tonneau m; (of oil) baril m; (of gun) canon m

barren ['bærən] adj stérile

barricade [bærɪ'keɪd] n barricade f

barrier ['bærɪəʳ] n barrière f; (fig: to progress etc) obstacle m

barring ['bɑ:rɪŋ] prep sauf

barrister ['bærɪstəʳ] (BRIT) n avocat (plaidant)

barrow ['bærəu] n (wheelbarrow) charrette f à bras

bartender ['bɑ:tendəʳ] (US) n barman m

barter ['bɑ:təʳ] vt: **to ~ sth for** échanger qch contre

base [beɪs] n base f; (of tree, post) pied m ♦ vt: **to ~ sth on** baser or fonder qch sur ♦ adj vil(e), bas(se)

baseball ['beɪsbɔ:l] n base-ball m

basement ['beɪsmənt] n sous-sol m

bases[1] ['beɪsɪz] npl of **base**

bases[2] ['beɪsi:z] npl of **basis**

bash [bæʃ] (inf) vt frapper, cogner

bashful ['bæʃful] adj timide; modeste

basic ['beɪsɪk] adj fondamental(e), de base; (minimal) rudimentaire; **~ally** adv fondamentalement, à la base; (in fact) en fait,

au fond; **~s** npl: **the ~s** l'essentiel m

basil ['bæzl] n basilic m

basin ['beɪsn] n (vessel, also GEO) cuvette f, bassin m; (also: **washbasin**) lavabo m

basis ['beɪsɪs] (pl **bases**) n base f; **on a trial ~** à titre d'essai; **on a part-time ~** à temps partiel

bask [bɑ:sk] vi: **to ~ in the sun** se chauffer au soleil

basket ['bɑ:skɪt] n corbeille f; (with handle) panier m; **~ball** n basket-ball m

bass [beɪs] n (MUS) basse f; **~ drum** n grosse caisse f

bassoon [bə'su:n] n (MUS) basson m

bastard ['bɑ:stəd] n enfant naturel(le), bâtard(e); (inf!) salaud m (!)

bat [bæt] n chauve-souris f; (for baseball etc) batte f; (BRIT: for table tennis) raquette f ♦ vt: **he didn't ~ an eyelid** il n'a pas sourcillé or bronché

batch [bætʃ] n (of bread) fournée f; (of papers) liasse f

bated ['beɪtɪd] adj: **with ~ breath** en retenant son souffle

bath [bɑ:θ] n bain m; (~tub) baignoire f ♦ vt baigner, donner un bain à; **to have a ~** prendre un bain; see also **baths**

bathe [beɪð] vi se baigner ♦ vt (wound) laver; **bathing** n baignade f; **bathing costume**, **bathing suit** (US) n maillot m (de bain)

bath: ~robe n peignoir m de bain; **~room** n salle f de bains; **~s** npl (also: **swimming ~s**) piscine f; **~ towel** n serviette f de bain

baton ['bætən] n bâton m; (MUS) baguette f; (club) matraque f

batter ['bætəʳ] vt battre ♦ n pâte f à frire; **~ed** ['bætəd] adj (hat, pan) cabossé(e)

battery ['bætərɪ] n batterie f; (of torch) pile f; **~ farming** n élevage f en batterie

battle ['bætl] n bataille f, combat m ♦ vi se battre, lutter; **~field** n champ m de bataille; **~ship** n cuirassé m

Bavaria [bə'veərɪə] n Bavière f

bawl [bɔ:l] vi hurler; (child) brailler

bay [beɪ] n (of sea) baie f; **to hold sb at ~** tenir qn à distance or en échec; **~ leaf** n laurier m; **~ window** n baie vitrée

bazaar [bə'zɑ:ʳ] n bazar m; vente f de charité

B & B n abbr = **bed and breakfast**

BBC n abbr (= British Broadcasting Corporation) office de la radiodiffusion et télévision britannique

B.C. adv abbr (= before Christ) av. J.-C.

KEYWORD

---

be [bi:] (pt **was**, **were**, pp **been**) aux vb 1 (with present participle: forming continuous tenses): **what are you doing?** que faites-vous?; **they're coming tomorrow** ils viennent demain; **I've been waiting for you for 2 hours** je t'attends depuis 2 heures

2 (*with pp: forming passives*) être; **to be killed** être tué(e); **he was nowhere to be seen** on ne le voyait nulle part

3 (*in tag questions*): **it was fun, wasn't it?** c'était drôle, n'est-ce pas?; **she's back, is she?** elle est rentrée, n'est-ce pas or alors?

4 (*+to +infinitive*): **the house is to be sold** la maison doit être vendue; **he's not to open it** il ne doit pas l'ouvrir

♦ *vb + complement* **1** (*gen*) être; **I'm English** je suis anglais(e); **I'm tired** je suis fatigué(e); **I'm hot/cold** j'ai chaud/froid; **he's a doctor** il est médecin; **2 and 2 are 4** 2 et 2 font 4

2 (*of health*) aller; **how are you?** comment allez-vous?; **he's fine now** il va bien maintenant; **he's very ill** il est très malade

3 (*of age*) avoir; **how old are you?** quel âge avez-vous?; **I'm sixteen (years old)** j'ai seize ans

4 (*cost*) coûter; **how much was the meal?** combien a coûté le repas?; **that'll be £5, please** ça fera 5 livres, s'il vous plaît

♦ *vi* **1** (*exist, occur etc*) être, exister; **the prettiest girl that ever was** la fille la plus jolie qui ait jamais existé; **be that as it may** quoi qu'il en soit; **so be it** soit

2 (*referring to place*) être, se trouver; **I won't be here tomorrow** je ne serai pas là demain; **Edinburgh is in Scotland** Édimbourg est *or* se trouve en Écosse

3 (*referring to movement*) aller; **where have you been?** où êtes-vous allé(s)?

♦ *impers vb* **1** (*referring to time, distance*) être; **it's 5 o'clock** il est 5 heures; **it's the 28th of April** c'est le 28 avril; **it's 10 km to the village** le village est à 10 km

2 (*referring to the weather*) faire; **it's too hot/ cold** il fait trop chaud/froid; **it's windy** il y a du vent

3 (*emphatic*): **it's me/the postman** c'est moi/ le facteur

beach [biːtʃ] *n* plage *f* ♦ *vt* échouer
beacon ['biːkən] *n* (*lighthouse*) fanal *m*; (*marker*) balise *f*
bead [biːd] *n* perle *f*
beak [biːk] *n* bec *m*
beaker ['biːkər] *n* gobelet *m*
beam [biːm] *n* poutre *f*; (*of light*) rayon *m*
♦ *vi* rayonner
bean [biːn] *n* haricot *m*; (*of coffee*) grain *m*; **runner ~** haricot *m* (à rames); **broad ~** fève *f*; **~sprouts** *npl* germes *mpl* de soja
bear [bɛər] (*pt* bore, *pp* borne) *n* ours *m* ♦ *vt* porter; (*endure*) supporter ♦ *vi*: **to ~ right/ left** obliquer à droite/gauche, se diriger vers la droite/gauche; **~ out** *vt* corroborer, confirmer; **~ up** (*person*) tenir le coup

beard [bɪəd] *n* barbe *f*; **~ed** *adj* barbu(e)
bearer ['bɛərər] *n* porteur *m*; (*of passport*) titulaire *m/f*
bearing ['bɛərɪŋ] *n* maintien *m*, allure *f*; (*connection*) rapport *m*; **~s** *npl* (*also*: **ball ~s**) roulement *m* (à billes); **to take a ~** faire le point
beast [biːst] *n* bête *f*; (*inf: person*) brute *f*; **~ly** *adj* infect(e)
beat [biːt] (*pt* beat, *pp* beaten) *n* battement *m*; (*MUS*) temps *m*, mesure *f*; (*of policeman*) ronde *f* ♦ *vt, vi* battre; **off the ~en track** hors des chemins *or* sentiers battus; **~ it!** (*inf*) fiche(-moi) le camp!; **~ off** *vt* repousser; **~ up** *vt* (*inf: person*) tabasser; (*eggs*) battre; **~ing** *n* raclée *f*
beautiful ['bjuːtɪful] *adj* beau (belle); **~ly** *adv* admirablement
beauty ['bjuːtɪ] *n* beauté *f*; **~ salon** *n* institut *m* de beauté; **~ spot** *n* (*BRIT*) (*TOURISM*) site naturel (d'une grande beauté)
beaver ['biːvər] *n* castor *m*
because [bɪ'kɔz] *conj* parce que; **~ of** *prep* à cause de
beck [bɛk] *n*: **to be at sb's ~ and call** être à l'entière disposition de qn
beckon ['bɛkən] *vt* (*also*: **~ to**) faire signe (de venir) à
become [bɪ'kʌm] (*irreg*: *like* come) *vi* devenir; **to ~ fat/thin** grossir/maigrir; **becoming** *adj* (*behaviour*) convenable, bienséant(e); (*clothes*) seyant(e)
bed [bɛd] *n* lit *m*; (*of flowers*) parterre *m*; (*of coal, clay*) couche *f*; (*of sea*) fond *m*; **to go to ~** aller se coucher; **~ and breakfast** *n* (*terms*) chambre et petit déjeuner; (*place*) ≈ chambre *f* d'hôte; **~clothes** *npl* couvertures *fpl* et draps *mpl*; **~ding** *n* literie *f*; **~ linen** *n* draps *mpl* de lit (et taies *fpl* d'oreillers), literie *f*
bedraggled [bɪ'dræɡld] *adj* (*person, clothes*) débraillé(e); (*hair: wet*) trempé(e)
bed: **~ridden** *adj* cloué(e) au lit; **~room** *n* chambre *f* (à coucher); **~side** *n*: **at sb's ~side** au chevet de qn; **~sit(ter)** *n* (*BRIT*) chambre meublée, studio *m*; **~spread** *n* couvre-lit *m*, dessus-de-lit *m inv*; **~time** *n* heure *f* du coucher
bee [biː] *n* abeille *f*
beech [biːtʃ] *n* hêtre *m*
beef [biːf] *n* bœuf *m*; **roast ~** rosbif *m*; **~burger** *n* hamburger *m*; **~eater** *n* hallebardier de la Tour de Londres
bee: **~hive** *n* ruche *f*; **~line** *n*: **to make a ~line for** se diriger tout droit vers
been [biːn] *pp of* be
beer [bɪər] *n* bière *f*
beet [biːt] *n* (*vegetable*) betterave *f*; (*US: also*: **red ~**) betterave (potagère)

beetle ['bi:tl] n scarabée m

beetroot ['bi:tru:t] (BRIT) n betterave f

before [bɪ'fɔ:r] prep (in time) avant; (in space) devant ♦ conj avant que +sub; avant de ♦ adv avant; devant; ~ going avant de partir; ~ she goes avant qu'elle ne parte; the week ~ la semaine précédente or d'avant; I've seen it ~ je l'ai déjà vu; ~hand adv au préalable, à l'avance

beg [beg] vi mendier ♦ vt mendier; (forgiveness, mercy etc) demander; (entreat) supplier; see also **pardon**

began [bɪ'gæn] pt of **begin**

beggar ['begər] n mendiant(e)

begin [bɪ'gɪn] (pt began, pp begun) vt, vi commencer; to ~ doing or to do sth commencer à or de faire qch; ~ner n débutant(e); ~ning n commencement m, début m

behalf [bɪ'hɑ:f] n: on ~ of, (US) in ~ of (representing) de la part de; (for benefit of) pour le compte de; on my/his ~ pour moi/lui

behave [bɪ'heɪv] vi se conduire, se comporter; (well: also: ~ o.s.) se conduire bien or comme il faut; **behaviour** (US **behavior**) [bɪ'heɪvjər] n comportement m, conduite f

behead [bɪ'hed] vt décapiter

behind [bɪ'haɪnd] prep derrière; (time, progress) en retard sur; (work, studies) en retard dans ♦ adv derrière ♦ n derrière m; to be ~ (schedule) avoir du retard; ~ the scenes dans les coulisses

behold [bɪ'həʊld] (irreg: like **hold**) vt apercevoir, voir

beige [beɪʒ] adj beige

Beijing ['beɪ'dʒɪŋ] n Beijing, Pékin

being ['bi:ɪŋ] n être m

Beirut [beɪ'ru:t] n Beyrouth

Belarus [bɛlɑ'rus] n Bélarus f

belated [bɪ'leɪtɪd] adj tardif(-ive)

belch [beltʃ] vi avoir un renvoi, roter ♦ vt (also: ~ out: smoke etc) vomir, cracher

Belgian ['beldʒən] adj belge, de Belgique ♦ n Belge m/f

Belgium ['beldʒəm] n Belgique f

belie [bɪ'laɪ] vt démentir

belief [bɪ'li:f] n (opinion) conviction f; (trust, faith) foi f

believe [bɪ'li:v] vt, vi croire; to ~ in (God) croire en; (method, ghosts) croire à; ~r n (in idea, activity): ~r in partisan(e) de; (REL) croyant(e)

belittle [bɪ'lɪtl] vt déprécier, rabaisser

bell [bel] n cloche f; (small) clochette f, grelot m; (on door) sonnette f; (electric) sonnerie f

belligerent [bɪ'lɪdʒərənt] adj (person, attitude) agressif(-ive)

bellow ['beləʊ] vi (bull) meugler; (person) brailler

belly ['belɪ] n ventre m

belong [bɪ'lɒŋ] vi: to ~ to appartenir à; (club etc) faire partie de; this book ~s here ce livre va ici; ~ings npl affaires fpl, possessions fpl

beloved [bɪ'lʌvɪd] adj (bien-)aimé(e)

below [bɪ'ləʊ] prep sous, au-dessous de ♦ adv en dessous; see ~ voir plus bas or plus loin or ci-dessous

belt [belt] n ceinture f; (of land) région f; (TECH) courroie f ♦ vt (thrash) donner une raclée à; ~way n (US) (AUT) route f de ceinture; (: motorway) périphérique m

bemused [bɪ'mju:zd] adj stupéfié(e)

bench [bentʃ] n (gen, also BRIT: POL) banc m; (in workshop) établi m; the B~ (LAW: judge) le juge; (: judges collectively) la magistrature, la Cour

bend [bend] (pt, pp bent) vt courber; (leg, arm) plier ♦ vi se courber ♦ n (BRIT: in road) virage m, tournant m; (in pipe, river) coude m; ~ down vi se baisser; ~ over vi se pencher

beneath [bɪ'ni:θ] prep sous, au-dessous de; (unworthy of) indigne de ♦ adv dessous, au-dessous, en bas

benefactor ['benɪfæktər] n bienfaiteur m

beneficial [benɪ'fɪʃəl] adj salutaire; avantageux(-euse); ~ to the health bon(ne) pour la santé

benefit ['benɪfɪt] n avantage m, profit m; (allowance of money) allocation f ♦ vt faire du bien à, profiter à ♦ vi: he'll ~ from it cela lui fera du bien, il y gagnera or s'en trouvera bien

Benelux ['benɪlʌks] n Bénélux m

benevolent [bɪ'nevələnt] adj bienveillant(e); (organization) bénévole

benign [bɪ'naɪn] adj (person, smile) bienveillant(e), affable; (MED) bénin(-igne)

bent [bent] pt, pp of **bend** ♦ n inclination f, penchant m; to be ~ on être résolu(e) à

bequest [bɪ'kwest] n legs m

bereaved [bɪ'ri:vd] n: the ~ la famille du disparu

beret ['bereɪ] n béret m

Berlin [bə:'lɪn] n Berlin

berm [bə:m] (US) n (AUT) accotement m

Bermuda [bə:'mju:də] n Bermudes fpl

berry ['berɪ] n baie f

berserk [bə'sə:k] adj: to go ~ (madman, crowd) se déchaîner

berth [bə:θ] n (bed) couchette f; (for ship) poste m d'amarrage, mouillage m ♦ vi (in harbour) venir à quai; (at anchor) mouiller

beseech [bɪ'si:tʃ] (pt, pp besought) vt implorer, supplier

beset [bɪ'set] (pt, pp beset) vt assaillir

beside [bɪ'saɪd] prep à côté de; to be ~ o.s. (with anger) être hors de soi; that's ~ the point cela n'a rien à voir; **~s** *adv* en outre, de plus; (*in any case*) d'ailleurs ♦ *prep* (*as well as*) en plus de

besiege [bɪˈsiːdʒ] *vt* (*town*) assiéger; (*fig*) assaillir

best [bɛst] *adj* meilleur(e) ♦ *adv* le mieux; **the ~ part of** (*quantity*) le plus clair de, la plus grande partie de; **at ~** au mieux; **to make the ~ of sth** s'accommoder de qch (du mieux que l'on peut); **to do one's ~** faire de son mieux; **to the ~ of my knowledge** pour autant que je sache; **to the ~ of my ability** du mieux que je pourrai; **~ before date** *n* date *f* de limite d'utilisation *or* de consommation; **~ man** *n* garçon *m* d'honneur

bestow [bɪˈstəʊ] *vt*: **to ~ sth on sb** accorder qch à qn; (*title*) conférer qch à qn

bet [bɛt] (*pt, pp* **bet** *or* **betted**) *n* pari *m* ♦ *vt, vi* parier

betray [bɪˈtreɪ] *vt* trahir

better [ˈbɛtəʳ] *adj* meilleur(e) ♦ *adv* mieux ♦ *vt* améliorer ♦ *n*: **to get the ~ of** triompher de, l'emporter sur; **you had ~ do it** vous feriez mieux de le faire; **he thought ~ of it** il s'est ravisé; **to get ~** aller mieux; s'améliorer; **~ off** *adj* plus à l'aise financièrement; (*fig*): **you'd be ~ off this way** vous vous en trouveriez mieux ainsi

betting [ˈbɛtɪŋ] *n* paris *mpl*; **~ shop** (*BRIT*) *n* bureau *m* de paris

between [bɪˈtwiːn] *prep* entre ♦ *adv*: (**in**) **~** au milieu; dans l'intervalle; (*in time*) dans l'intervalle

beverage [ˈbɛvərɪdʒ] *n* boisson *f* (*gén sans alcool*)

beware [bɪˈwɛəʳ] *vi*: **to ~ (of)** prendre garde (à); "**~ of the dog**" "(attention) chien méchant"

bewildered [bɪˈwɪldəd] *adj* dérouté(e), ahuri(e)

beyond [bɪˈjɒnd] *prep* (*in space, time*) au-delà de; (*exceeding*) au-dessus de ♦ *adv* au-delà; **~ doubt** hors de doute; **~ repair** irréparable

bias [ˈbaɪəs] *n* (*prejudice*) préjugé *m*, parti pris; **~(s)ed** *adj* partial(e), montrant un parti pris

bib [bɪb] *n* bavoir *m*, bavette *f*

Bible [ˈbaɪbl] *n* Bible *f*

bicarbonate of soda [baɪˈkɑːbənɪt-] *n* bicarbonate *m* de soude

bicker [ˈbɪkəʳ] *vi* se chamailler

bicycle [ˈbaɪsɪkl] *n* bicyclette *f*

bid [bɪd] (*pt* **bid** *or* **bade**, *pp* **bid(den)**) *n* offre *f*; (*at auction*) enchère *f*; (*attempt*) tentative *f* ♦ *vi* faire une enchère *or* offre ♦ *vt* faire une enchère *or* offre de; **to ~ sb good day** souhaiter le bonjour à qn; **~der** *n*: **the highest ~der** le plus offrant; **~ding** *n* enchères *fpl*

bide [baɪd] *vt*: **to ~ one's time** attendre son

heure

bifocals [baɪˈfəʊklz] *npl* verres *mpl* à double foyer, lunettes bifocales

big [bɪɡ] *adj* grand(e); gros(se); **~headed** *adj* prétentieux(-euse)

bigot [ˈbɪɡət] *n* fanatique *m/f*, sectaire *m/f*; **~ed** *adj* fanatique, sectaire; **~ry** *n* fanatisme *m*, sectarisme *m*

big top *n* grand chapiteau

bike [baɪk] *n* vélo *m*, bécane *f*

bikini [bɪˈkiːnɪ] *n* bikini ® *m*

bilingual [baɪˈlɪŋɡwəl] *adj* bilingue

bill [bɪl] *n* note *f*, facture *f*; (*POL*) projet *m* de loi; (*US: banknote*) billet *m* (de banque); (*of bird*) bec *m*; (*THEATRE*): **on the ~** à l'affiche; "**post no ~s**" "défense d'afficher"; **to fit** *or* **fill the ~** (*fig*) faire l'affaire; **~board** *n* panneau *m* d'affichage

billet [ˈbɪlɪt] *n* cantonnement *m* (chez l'habitant)

billfold [ˈbɪlfəʊld] (*US*) *n* portefeuille *m*

billiards [ˈbɪljədz] *n* (jeu *m* de) billard *m*

billion [ˈbɪljən] *n* (*BRIT*) billion *m* (*million de millions*); (*US*) milliard *m*

bimbo [ˈbɪmbəʊ] (*inf*) *n* ravissante idiote *f*, potiche *f*

bin [bɪn] *n* boîte *f*; (*also:* **dustbin**) poubelle *f*; (*for coal*) coffre *m*

bind [baɪnd] (*pt, pp* **bound**) *vt* attacher; (*book*) relier; (*oblige*) obliger, contraindre ♦ *n* (*inf: nuisance*) scie *f*; **~ing** *adj* (*contract*) constituant une obligation

binge [bɪndʒ] (*inf*) *n*: **to go on a/the ~** aller faire la bringue

bingo [ˈbɪŋɡəʊ] *n* jeu de loto pratiqué dans des établissements publics

binoculars [bɪˈnɒkjuləz] *npl* jumelles *fpl*

bio *prefix*: **~chemistry** *n* biochimie *f*; **~degradable** *adj* biodégradable; **~graphy** *n* biographie *f*; **~logical** *adj* biologique; **~logy** *n* biologie *f*

birch [bɜːtʃ] *n* bouleau *m*

bird [bɜːd] *n* oiseau *m*; (*BRIT: inf: girl*) nana *f*; **~'s-eye view** *n* vue *f* à vol d'oiseau; (*fig*) vue d'ensemble *or* générale; **~-watcher** *n* ornithologue *m/f* amateur

Biro ® [ˈbaɪərəʊ] *n* stylo *m* à bille

birth [bɜːθ] *n* naissance *f*; **to give ~ to** (*subj: woman*) donner naissance à; (: *animal*) mettre bas; **~ certificate** *n* acte *m* de naissance; **~ control** *n* (*policy*) limitation *f* des naissances; (*method*) méthode(s) contraceptive(s); **~day** *n* anniversaire *m* ♦ *cpd* d'anniversaire; **~place** *n* lieu *m* de naissance; (*fig*) berceau *m*; **~ rate** *n* (taux *m* de) natalité *f*

biscuit [ˈbɪskɪt] *n* (*BRIT*) biscuit *m*; (*US*) petit pain au lait

bisect [baɪˈsɛkt] *vt* couper *or* diviser en deux

bishop ['bɪʃəp] n évêque m; (CHESS) fou m

bit [bɪt] pt of **bite** ♦ n morceau m; (of tool) mèche f; (of horse) mors m; (COMPUT) élément m binaire; **a ~ of** un peu de; **a ~ mad** un peu fou; **~ by ~** petit à petit

bitch [bɪtʃ] n (dog) chienne f; (inf!) salope f (!), garce f

bite [baɪt] (pt **bit**, pp **bitten**) vt, vi mordre; (insect) piquer ♦ n (insect ~) piqûre f; (mouthful) bouchée f; **let's have a ~ (to eat)** (inf) mangeons un morceau; **to ~ one's nails** se ronger les ongles

bitter ['bɪtər] adj amer(-ère); (weather, wind) glacial(e); (criticism) cinglant(e); (struggle) acharné(e) ♦ n (BRIT: beer) bière f (forte); **~ness** n amertume f; (taste) goût amer

black [blæk] adj noir(e); (in colour) noir m; (person): B~ noir(e) ♦ vt (BRIT: INDUSTRY) boycotter; **to give sb a ~ eye** pocher l'œil à qn, faire un œil au beurre noir à qn; **~ and blue** couvert(e) de bleus; **to be in the ~** (in credit) être créditeur(-trice); **~berry** n mûre f; **~bird** n merle m; **~board** n tableau noir; **~ coffee** n café noir; **~currant** n cassis m; **~en** vt noircir; **~ ice** n verglas m; **~leg** (BRIT) n briseur m de grève, jaune m; **~list** n liste noire; **~mail** n chantage m ♦ vt faire chanter, soumettre au chantage; **~ market** n marché noir; **~out** n panne f d'électricité; (TV etc) interruption f d'émission; (fainting) syncope f; **~ pudding** n boudin (noir); **B~ Sea** n: **the B~ Sea** la mer Noire; **~ sheep** n brebis galeuse; **~smith** n forgeron m; **~ spot** (AUT) n point noir

bladder ['blædər] n vessie f

blade [bleɪd] n lame f; (of propeller) pale f; **~ of grass** brin m d'herbe

blame [bleɪm] n faute f, blâme m ♦ vt: **to ~ sb/sth for sth** attribuer à qn/qch la responsabilité de qch; reprocher qch à qn/ qch; **who's to ~?** qui est le fautif or coupable or responsable?

bland [blænd] adj (taste, food) doux (douce), fade

blank [blæŋk] adj blanc (blanche); (look) sans expression, dénué(e) d'expression ♦ n espace m vide, blanc m; (cartridge) cartouche f à blanc; **his mind was a ~** il avait la tête vide; **~ cheque** chèque m en blanc

blanket ['blæŋkɪt] n couverture f; (of snow, cloud) couche f

blare [blɛər] vi beugler

blast [blɑːst] n souffle m; (of explosive) explosion f ♦ vt faire sauter or exploser; **~- off** n (SPACE) lancement m

blatant ['bleɪtənt] adj flagrant(e), criant(e)

blaze [bleɪz] n (fire) incendie m; (fig) flamboiement m ♦ vi (fire) flamber; (fig: eyes) flamboyer; (: guns) crépiter ♦ vt: **to ~ a trail**

(fig) montrer la voie

blazer ['bleɪzər] n blazer m

bleach [bliːtʃ] n (also: **household ~**) eau f de Javel ♦ vt (linen etc) blanchir; **~ed** adj (hair) oxygéné(e), décoloré(e)

bleak [bliːk] adj morne, (countryside) désolé(e)

bleat [bliːt] vi bêler

bleed [bliːd] (pt, pp **bled**) vt, vi saigner; **my nose is ~ing** je saigne du nez

bleeper ['bliːpər] n (device) bip m

blemish ['blemɪʃ] n défaut m; (on fruit, reputation) tache f

blend [blend] n mélange m ♦ vt mélanger ♦ vi (colours etc: also: **~ in**) se mélanger, se fondre; **~er** n mixeur m

bless [bles] (pt, pp **blessed** or **blest**) vt bénir; **~ you!** (after sneeze) à vos souhaits!; **~ing** n bénédiction f; (godsend) bienfait m

blew [bluː] pt of **blow**

blight [blaɪt] vt (hopes etc) anéantir; (life) briser

blimey ['blaɪmɪ] (BRIT: inf) excl mince alors!

blind [blaɪnd] adj aveugle ♦ n (for window) store m ♦ vt aveugler; **~ alley** n impasse f; **~ corner** (BRIT) n virage m sans visibilité; **~fold** n bandeau m ♦ adj, adv les yeux bandés ♦ vt bander les yeux à; **~ly** adv aveuglément; **~ness** n cécité f; **~ spot** n (AUT etc) angle mort; **that is her ~ spot** (fig) elle refuse d'y voir clair sur ce point

blink [blɪŋk] vi cligner des yeux; (light) clignoter; **~ers** npl œillères fpl

bliss [blɪs] n félicité f, bonheur m sans mélange

blister ['blɪstər] n (on skin) ampoule f, cloque f; (on paintwork, rubber) boursouflure f ♦ vi (paint) se boursoufler, se cloquer

blizzard ['blɪzəd] n blizzard m, tempête f de neige

bloated ['bləʊtɪd] adj (face) bouffi(e); (stomach, person) gonflé(e)

blob [blɒb] n (drop) goutte f; (stain, spot) tache f

block [blɒk] n bloc m; (in pipes) obstruction f; (toy) cube m; (of buildings) pâté m (de maisons) ♦ vt bloquer; (fig) faire obstacle à; **~ of flats** (BRIT) immeuble (locatif); **mental ~** trou m de mémoire; **~ade** [blɒ'keɪd] n blocus m; **~age** n obstruction f; **~buster** n (film, book) grand succès; **~ letters** npl majuscules fpl

bloke [bləʊk] n (BRIT: inf) n type m

blond(e) [blɒnd] adj, n blond(e)

blood [blʌd] n sang m; **~ donor** n donneur(-euse) de sang; **~ group** n groupe sanguin; **~hound** n limier m; **~ poisoning** n empoisonnement m du sang; **~ pressure** n tension f (artérielle); **~shed** n effusion f de

sang, carnage m; ~ **sports** npl sports mpl
sanguinaires; ~**shot** adj: ~**shot eyes** yeux
injectés de sang; ~**stream** n sang m,
système sanguin; ~ **test** n prise f de sang;
~**thirsty** adj sanguinaire; ~ **vessel** n
vaisseau sanguin; ~**y** adj sanglant(e); (nose)
en sang; (BRIT: infl): **this** ~**y** ... ce foutu ... (!),
ce putain de ... (!); ~**y strong/good**
vachement or sacrément fort/bon; ~**y-
minded** (BRIT: inf) adj contrariant(e),
obstiné(e)

bloom [bluːm] n fleur f ♦ vi être en fleur

blossom ['blɔsəm] n fleur(s) f(pl) ♦ vi être
en fleurs; (fig) s'épanouir; **to ~ into** devenir

blot [blɔt] n tache f ♦ vt tacher; ~ **out** vt
(memories) effacer; (view) cacher, masquer

blotchy ['blɔtʃi] adj (complexion) couvert(e)
de marbrures

blotting paper ['blɔtɪŋ-] n buvard m

blouse [blauz] n chemisier m, corsage m

blow [bləu] (pt **blew**, pp **blown**) n coup m
♦ vi souffler ♦ vt souffler; (fuse) faire sauter;
(instrument) jouer de; **to ~ one's nose** se
moucher; **to ~ a whistle** siffler; ~ **away** vt
chasser, faire s'envoler; ~ **down** vt faire
tomber, renverser; ~ **off** vt emporter; ~ **out**
vi (fire, flame) s'éteindre; ~ **over** vi s'apaiser;
~ **up** vi faire sauter; (tyre) gonfler; (PHOT)
agrandir ♦ vi exploser, sauter; ~**-dry** n
brushing m; ~**lamp** (BRIT) n chalumeau m;
~**-out** n (of tyre) éclatement m; ~**-torch** n
= blowlamp

blue [bluː] adj bleu(e); (fig) triste; ~**s** n
(MUS): **the ~s** le blues; ~ **film/joke** film m/
histoire f pornographique; **to come out of the
~** (fig) être complètement inattendu; ~**bell** n
jacinthe f des bois; ~**bottle** n mouche f à
viande; ~**print** n (fig) projet m, plan
directeur

bluff [blʌf] vi bluffer ♦ n bluff m; **to call sb's ~**
mettre qn au défi d'exécuter ses menaces

blunder ['blʌndər] n gaffe f, bévue f ♦ vi faire
une gaffe or une bévue

blunt [blʌnt] adj (person) brusque, ne
mâchant pas ses mots; (knife) émoussé(e),
peu tranchant(e); (pencil) mal taillé

blur [bləːr] n tache or masse floue or confuse
♦ vt brouiller

blush [blʌʃ] vi rougir ♦ n rougeur f

blustery ['blʌstəri] adj (weather) à
bourrasques

boar [bɔːr] n sanglier m

board [bɔːd] n planche f; (on wall) panneau
m; (for chess) échiquier m; (cardboard)
carton m; (committee) conseil m, comité m;
(in firm) conseil d'administration; (NAUT,
AVIAT): **on ~** à bord ♦ vt (ship) monter à bord
de; (train) monter dans; **full ~** (BRIT) pension
complète; **half ~** demi-pension f; ~ **and**

lodging chambre f avec pension; **which goes
by the ~** (fig) qu'on laisse tomber, qu'on
abandonne; ~ **up** vt (door, window) boucher;
~**er** n (SCOL) interne m/f; ~ **game** n jeu m
de société; ~**ing card** n
= **boarding pass**; ~**ing house** n pension f;
~**ing pass** n (AVIAT, NAUT) carte f
d'embarquement; ~**ing school** n internat m,
pensionnat m; ~ **room** n salle f du conseil
d'administration

boast [bəust] vi: **to ~ (about** or **of)** se vanter
(de)

boat [bəut] n bateau m; (small) canot m;
barque f; ~ **train** n train m (qui assue
correspondance avec le ferry)

bob [bɔb] vi (boat, cork on water: also: ~ **up
and down)** danser, se balancer

bobby ['bɔbi] (BRIT: inf) n ≈ agent m (de
police)

bobsleigh ['bɔbslei] n bob m

bode [bəud] vi: **to ~ well/ill (for)** être de bon/
mauvais augure (pour)

bodily ['bɔdili] adj corporel(le) ♦ adv dans ses
bras

body ['bɔdi] n corps m; (of car) carrosserie f;
(of plane) fuselage m; (fig: society) organe m,
organisme m; (: quantity) ensemble m, masse
f; (of wine) corps m; ~**-building** n culturisme
m; ~**guard** n garde m du corps; ~**work** n
carrosserie f

bog [bɔg] n tourbière f ♦ vt: **to get ~ged down**
(fig) s'enliser

bog-standard (inf) adj tout à fait ordinaire

bogus ['bəugəs] adj bidon inv; fantôme

boil [bɔil] vt (faire) bouillir ♦ vi bouillir ♦ n
(MED) furoncle m; **to come to the** (BRIT) ~ **or**
a (US) ~ bouillir; ~ **down to** vt fus (fig) se
réduire or ramener à; ~ **over** vi déborder;
~**ed egg** n œuf m à la coque; ~**ed
potatoes** npl pommes fpl à l'anglaise or à
l'eau; ~**er** n chaudière f; ~**ing point** n point
m d'ébullition

boisterous ['bɔistərəs] adj bruyant(e),
tapageur(-euse)

bold [bəuld] adj hardi(e), audacieux(-euse);
(peh) effronté(e); (outline, colour) franc
(franche), tranché(e), marqué(e); (pattern)
grand(e)

bollard ['bɔləd] (BRIT) n (AUT) borne
lumineuse or de signalisation

bolt [bəult] n (lock) verrou m; (with nut)
boulon m ♦ adv: ~ **upright** droit(e) comme
un piquet ♦ vt verrouiller; (TECH: also: ~ **on,
~ together)** boulonner; (food) engloutir ♦ vi
(horse) s'emballer

bomb [bɔm] n bombe f ♦ vt bombarder;
~**ing** n (by terrorist) attentat m à la bombe;
~ **disposal unit** n section f de déminage;
~**er** n (AVIAT) bombardier m; ~**shell** n (fig)

bombe f

bond [bɔnd] n lien m; (binding promise)
engagement m, obligation f; (COMM)
obligation; **in ~** (of goods) en douane

bondage ['bɔndɪdʒ] n esclavage m

bone [bəun] n os m; (of fish) arête f ♦ vt
désosser; ôter les arêtes de; **~ dry** adj
complètement sec (sèche); **~ idle** adj
fainéant(e); **~ marrow** n moelle f osseuse

bonfire ['bɔnfaɪər] n feu m (de joie); (for
rubbish) feu

bonnet ['bɔnɪt] n bonnet m; (BRIT: of car)
capot m

bonus ['bəunəs] n prime f, gratification f

bony ['bəunɪ] adj (arm, face, MED: tissue)
osseux(-euse); (meat) plein(e) d'os; (fish)
plein d'arêtes

boo [bu:] excl hou!, peuh! ♦ vt huer

booby trap ['bu:bɪ-] n engin piégé

book [buk] n livre m; (of stamps, tickets)
carnet m ♦ vt (ticket) prendre; (seat, room)
réserver; (driver) dresser un procès-verbal à;
(football player) prendre le nom de; **~s** npl
(accounts) comptes mpl, comptabilité f;
~case n bibliothèque f (meuble); **~ing
office** (BRIT) n bureau m de location; **~-
keeping** n comptabilité f; **~let** n brochure f;
~maker n bookmaker m; **~seller** n libraire
m/f; **~shelf** n (single) étagère f (à livres);
~shop n librairie f; **~store** n librairie f

boom [bu:m] n (noise) grondement m; (in
prices, population) forte augmentation ♦ vi
gronder; prospérer

boon [bu:n] n bénédiction f, grand avantage

boost [bu:st] n stimulant m, remontant m
♦ vt stimuler; **~er** n (MED) rappel m

boot [bu:t] n botte f; (for hiking) chaussure f
(de marche); (for football etc) soulier m;
(BRIT: of car) coffre m ♦ vt (COMPUT) amorcer,
initialiser; **to ~** (in addition) par-dessus le
marché

booth [bu:ð] n (at fair) baraque (foraine);
(telephone etc) cabine f; (also: **voting ~**)
isoloir m

booze [bu:z] (inf) n boissons fpl alcooliques,
alcool m

border ['bɔ:dər] n bordure f; bord m; (of a
country) frontière f ♦ vt border; (also: **~ on:**
country) être limitrophe de; **B~s** n (GEO): **the
B~s** la région frontière entre l'Écosse et
l'Angleterre; **~ on** vt fus être voisin(e) de,
toucher à; **~line** n (fig) ligne f de
démarcation; **~line case** cas m limite

bore [bɔ:r] pt of bear ♦ vt (hole) percer; (oil
well, tunnel) creuser; (person) ennuyer, raser
♦ n raseur(-euse); (of gun) calibre m; **to be
~d** s'ennuyer; **~dom** n ennui m; **boring** adj
ennuyeux(-euse)

born [bɔ:n] adj: **to be ~** naître; **I was ~ in 1960**

je suis né en 1960

borne [bɔ:n] pp of bear

borough ['bʌrə] n municipalité f

borrow ['bɔrəu] vt: **to ~ sth (from sb)**
emprunter qch (à qn)

Bosnia (and) Herzegovina
['bɔznɪə(ənd)hə:tsəgəu'vi:nə] n Bosnie-
Herzégovine f; **Bosnian** adj bosniaque,
bosnien(ne) ♦ n Bosniaque m/f

bosom ['buzəm] n poitrine f; (fig) sein m

boss [bɔs] n patron(ne) f ♦ vt (also: **~ around/
about**) mener à la baguette; **~y** adj
autoritaire

bosun ['bəusn] n maître m d'équipage

botany ['bɔtənɪ] n botanique f

botch [bɔtʃ] vt (also: **~ up**) saboter, bâcler

both [bəuθ] adj les deux, l'un(e) et l'autre
♦ pron: **~** (of them) les deux, tous (toutes)
(les) deux, l'un(e) et l'autre; **they sell ~ the
fabric and the finished curtains** ils vendent
(et) le tissu et les rideaux (finis), ils vendent à
la fois le tissu et les rideaux (finis); **~ of us
went, we ~ went** nous y sommes allés (tous)
les deux

bother ['bɔðər] vt (worry) tracasser; (disturb)
déranger ♦ vi (also: **~ o.s.**) se tracasser, se
faire du souci ♦ n: **it is a ~ to have to do** c'est
vraiment ennuyeux d'avoir à faire; **it's no ~**
aucun problème; **to ~ doing** prendre la peine
de faire

bottle ['bɔtl] n bouteille f; (baby's) biberon m
♦ vt mettre en bouteille(s); **~d beer** bière f en
canette; **~d water** eau minérale; **~ up** vt
refouler, contenir; **~ bank** n conteneur m à
verre; **~neck** n étranglement m; **~-opener** n
ouvre-bouteille m

bottom ['bɔtəm] n (of container, sea etc) fond
m; (buttocks) derrière m; (of page, list) bas m
♦ adj du fond; du bas; **the ~ of the class** le
dernier de la classe

bough [bau] n branche f, rameau m

bought [bɔ:t] pt, pp of buy

boulder ['bəuldər] n gros rocher

bounce [bauns] vi (ball) rebondir; (cheque)
être refusé (étant sans provision) ♦ vt faire
rebondir ♦ n (rebound) rebond m; **~r** (inf) n
(at dance, club) videur m

bound [baund] pt, pp of bind ♦ n (gen pl)
limite f; (leap) bond m ♦ vi (leap) bondir ♦ vt
(limit) borner ♦ adj: **to be ~ to do sth**
(obliged) être obligé(e) or avoir obligation de
faire qch; **he's ~ to fail** (likely) il est sûr
d'échouer, son échec est inévitable or assuré;
~ by (law, regulation) engagé(e) par; **~ for** à
destination de; **out of ~s** dont l'accès est
interdit

boundary ['baundrɪ] n frontière f

bout [baut] n période f; (of malaria etc) accès
m, crise f, attaque f; (BOXING etc) combat m,

match m

bow¹ [bəu] n nœud m; (weapon) arc m; (MUS) archet m

bow² [bau] n (with body) révérence f, inclination f (du buste or corps); (NAUT: also: ~s) proue f ♦ vi faire une révérence, s'incliner; (yield): **to ~ to** or **before** s'incliner devant, se soumettre à

bowels ['bauəlz] npl intestins mpl; (fig) entrailles fpl

bowl [bəul] n (for eating) bol m; (ball) boule f ♦ vi (CRICKET, BASEBALL) lancer (la balle)

bow-legged ['bəu'lɛgɪd] adj aux jambes arquées

bowler ['bəulə*] n (CRICKET, BASEBALL) lanceur m (de la balle); (BRIT: also: ~ hat) (chapeau m) melon m

bowling ['bəulɪŋ] n (game) jeu m de boules; jeu m de quilles; ~ **alley** n bowling m; ~ **green** n terrain m de boules (gazonné et carré)

bowls [bəulz] n (game) (jeu m de) boules fpl

bow tie [bəu-] n nœud m papillon

box [bɔks] n boîte f; (also: **cardboard ~**) carton m; (THEATRE) loge f ♦ vt mettre en boîte; (SPORT) boxer avec ♦ vi boxer, faire de la boxe; ~**er** n (person) boxeur m; ~**er shorts** npl caleçon msg; ~**ing** n (SPORT) boxe f; **B~ing Day** (BRIT) n le lendemain de Noël; ~**ing gloves** npl gants mpl de box; ~**ing ring** n ring m; ~ **office** n bureau m de location; ~**room** n débarras m; chambrette f

boy [bɔɪ] n garçon m

boycott ['bɔɪkɔt] n boycottage m ♦ vt boycotter

boyfriend ['bɔɪfrɛnd] n (petit) ami

boyish ['bɔɪɪʃ] adj (behaviour) de garçon; (girl) garçonnier(-ière)

BR n abbr = British Rail

bra [brɑ:] n soutien-gorge m

brace [breɪs] n (on teeth) appareil m (dentaire); (tool) vilbrequin m ♦ vt (knees, shoulders) appuyer; ~**s** npl (BRIT: for trousers) bretelles fpl; **to ~ o.s.** (lit) s'arc-bouter; (fig) se préparer mentalement

bracelet ['breɪslɪt] n bracelet m

bracing ['breɪsɪŋ] adj tonifiant(e), tonique

bracket ['brækɪt] n (TECH) tasseau m, support m; (group) classe f, tranche f; (also: **brace ~**) accolade f; (also: **round ~**) parenthèse f; (also: **square ~**) crochet m ♦ vt mettre entre parenthèse(s); (fig: also: ~ **together**) regrouper

brag [bræg] vi se vanter

braid [breɪd] n (trimming) galon m; (of hair) tresse f

brain [breɪn] n cerveau m; ~**s** npl (intellect, CULIN) cervelle f; **he's got ~s** il est intelligent; ~**wash** vt faire subir un lavage de cerveau à;

~**wave** n idée géniale; ~**y** adj intelligent(e), doué(e)

braise [breɪz] vt braiser

brake [breɪk] n (on vehicle, also fig) frein m ♦ vi freiner; ~ **light** n feu m de stop

bran [bræn] n son m

branch [brɑ:ntʃ] n branche f; (COMM) succursale f ♦ vi bifurquer; ~ **out** vi (fig): **to ~ out into** étendre ses activités à

brand [brænd] n marque (commerciale) ♦ vt (cattle) marquer (au fer rouge); ~-**new** adj tout(e) neuf (neuve), flambant neuf (neuve)

brandy ['brændɪ] n cognac m, fine f

brash [bræʃ] adj effronté(e)

brass [brɑ:s] n cuivre m (jaune), laiton m; **the ~** (MUS) les cuivres; ~ **band** n fanfare f

brat [bræt] (peh) n mioche m/f, môme m/f

brave [breɪv] adj courageux(-euse), brave ♦ n guerrier indien ♦ vt braver, affronter; ~**ry** n bravoure f, courage m

brawl [brɔ:l] n rixe f, bagarre f

brazen ['breɪzn] adj impudent(e), effronté(e) ♦ vt: **to ~ it out** payer d'effronterie, crâner

brazier ['breɪzɪə*] n brasero m

Brazil [brə'zɪl] n Brésil m

breach [bri:tʃ] vt ouvrir une brèche dans ♦ n (gap) brèche f; (breaking): ~ **of contract** rupture f de contrat; ~ **of the peace** attentat m à l'ordre public

bread [brɛd] n pain m; ~ **and butter** n tartines (beurrées); (fig) subsistance f; ~**bin** (BRIT) n boîte f à pain; (bigger) huche f à pain; ~**crumbs** npl miettes fpl de pain; (CULIN) chapelure f, panure f; ~**line** n: **to be on the ~line** être sans le sou or dans l'indigence

breadth [brɛtθ] n largeur f; (fig) ampleur f

breadwinner ['brɛdwɪnə*] n soutien m de famille

break [breɪk] (pt **broke**, pp **broken**) vt casser, briser; (promise) rompre; (law) violer ♦ vi (se) casser, se briser; (weather) tourner; (story, news) se répandre; (day) se lever ♦ n (gap) brèche f; (fracture) cassure f; (pause, interval) interruption f, arrêt m; (: short) pause f; (: at school) récréation f; (chance) chance f, occasion f favorable; **to ~ one's leg** etc se casser la jambe etc; **to ~ a record** battre un record; **to ~ the news to sb** annoncer la nouvelle à qn; ~ **even** rentrer dans ses frais; ~ **free** or **loose** se dégager, s'échapper; ~ **open** (door etc) forcer, fracturer; ~ **down** vt (figures, data) décomposer, analyser ♦ vi s'effondrer; (MED) faire une dépression (nerveuse); (AUT) tomber en panne; ~ **in** vt (horse etc) dresser ♦ vi (burglar) entrer par effraction; (interrupt) interrompre; ~ **into** vt fus (house) s'introduire or pénétrer par effraction dans; ~ **off** vi (speaker)

s'interrompre; (*branch*) se rompre; **~ out** *vi*
éclater, se déclarer; (*prisoner*) s'évader; **to
~ out in spots** *or* **a rash** avoir une éruption de
boutons; **~ up** *vi* (*ship*) se disloquer; (*crowd,
meeting*) se disperser, se séparer; (*marriage*)
se briser; (*SCOL*) entrer en vacances ♦ *vt*
casser; (*fight etc*) interrompre, faire cesser;
~age *n* casse *f*; **~down** *n* (*AUT*) panne *f*; (*in
communications, marriage*) rupture *f*; (*MED:
also:* **nervous ~down**) dépression (nerveuse);
(*of statistics*) ventilation *f*; **~down van** (*BRIT*)
n dépanneuse *f*; **~er** *n* brisant *m*

breakfast ['brɛkfəst] *n* petit déjeuner

break: ~-in *n* cambriolage *m*; **~ing and
entering** *n* (*LAW*) effraction *f*; **~through** *n*
percée *f*; **~water** *n* brise-lames *m inv*, digue *f*

breast [brɛst] *n* (*of woman*) sein *m*; (*chest, of
meat*) poitrine *f*; **~-feed** (*irreg: like* **feed**) *vt,
vi* allaiter; **~stroke** *n* brasse *f*

breath [brɛθ] *n* haleine *f*, souffle *m*; **out of ~** à bout de
souffle, essoufflé(e); **B~alyser** ®
['brɛθəlaɪzə'] *n* Alcootest ® *m*

breathe [briːð] *vt, vi* respirer; **~ in** *vt, vi*
aspirer, inspirer; **~ out** *vt, vi* expirer; **~r** *n*
moment *m* de repos *or* de répit; **breathing**
n respiration *f*

breathless ['brɛθlɪs] *adj* essoufflé(e),
haletant(e)

breathtaking ['brɛθteɪkɪŋ] *adj* stupéfiant(e)

breed [briːd] (*pt,pp* **bred**) *vt* élever, faire
l'élevage de ♦ *vi* se reproduire ♦ *n* race *f*,
variété *f*; **~ing** *n* (*upbringing*) éducation *f*

breeze [briːz] *n* brise *f*; **breezy** *adj* frais
(fraîche); aéré(e); (*manner etc*) désinvolte,
jovial(e)

brevity ['brɛvɪtɪ] *n* brièveté *f*

brew [bruː] *vt* (*tea*) faire infuser; (*beer*)
brasser ♦ *vi* (*fig*) se préparer, couver; **~ery** *n*
brasserie *f* (*fabrique*)

bribe [braɪb] *n* pot-de-vin *m* ♦ *vt* acheter;
soudoyer; **~ry** *n* corruption *f*

brick [brɪk] *n* brique *f*; **~layer** *n* maçon *m*

bridal ['braɪdl] *adj* nuptial(e)

bride [braɪd] *n* mariée *f*, épouse *f*; **~groom** *n*
marié *m*, époux *m*; **~smaid** *n* demoiselle *f*
d'honneur

bridge [brɪdʒ] *n* pont *m*; (*NAUT*) passerelle *f*
(de commandement); (*of nose*) arête *f*;
(*CARDS, DENTISTRY*) bridge *m* ♦ *vt* (*fig: gap,
gulf*) combler

bridle ['braɪdl] *n* bride *f*; **~ path** *n* piste *or*
allée cavalière

brief [briːf] *adj* bref (brève) ♦ *n* (*LAW*) dossier
m, cause *f*; (*gen*) tâche *f* ♦ *vt* mettre au
courant; **~s** *npl* (*undergarment*) slip *m*; **~case**
n serviette *f*, porte-documents *m inv*; **~ly** *adv*
brièvement

bright [braɪt] *adj* brillant(e); (*room, weather*)
clair(e); (*clever: person, idea*) intelligent(e);

(*cheerful: colour, person*) vif (vive)

brighten ['braɪtn] (*also:* **~ up**) *vt* (*room*)
éclaircir, égayer; (*event*) égayer ♦ *vi*
s'éclaircir; (*person*) retrouver un peu de sa
gaieté; (*face*) s'éclairer; (*prospects*)
s'améliorer

brilliance ['brɪljəns] *n* éclat *m*

brilliant ['brɪljənt] *adj* brillant(e); (*sunshine,
light*) éclatant(e); (*inf: holiday etc*) super

brim [brɪm] *n* bord *m*

brine [braɪn] *n* (*CULIN*) saumure *f*

bring [brɪŋ] (*pt, pp* **brought**) *vt* apporter;
(*person*) amener; **~ about** *vt* provoquer,
entraîner; **~ back** *vt* rapporter; ramener;
(*restore: hanging*) réinstaurer; **~ down** *vt*
(*price*) faire baisser; (*enemy plane*) descendre;
(*government*) faire tomber; **~ forward** *vt*
avancer; **~ off** *vt* (*task, plan*) réussir, mener à
bien; **~ out** *vt* (*meaning*) faire ressortir;
(*book*) publier; (*object*) sortir; **~ round** *vt*
(*unconscious person*) ranimer; **~ up** *vt* (*child*)
élever, (*carry up*) monter, (*question*)
soulever; (*food: vomit*) vomir, rendre

brink [brɪŋk] *n* bord *m*

brisk [brɪsk] *adj* vif (vive)

bristle ['brɪsl] *n* poil *m* ♦ *vi* se hérisser

Britain ['brɪtən] *n* (*also:* **Great ~**) Grande-
Bretagne *f*

British ['brɪtɪʃ] *adj* britannique ♦ *npl:* **the ~** les
Britanniques *mpl*; **~ Isles** *npl:* **the ~ Isles** les
îles *fpl* Britanniques; **~ Rail** *n* compagnie
ferroviaire britannique

Briton ['brɪtən] *n* Britannique *m/f*

Brittany ['brɪtənɪ] *n* Bretagne *f*

brittle ['brɪtl] *adj* cassant(e), fragile

broach [brəʊtʃ] *vt* (*subject*) aborder

broad [brɔːd] *adj* large; (*general: outlines*)
grand(e); (: *distinction*) général(e); (*accent*)
prononcé(e); **in ~ daylight** en plein jour;
~cast (*pt, pp* **broadcast**) *n* émission *f* ♦ *vt*
radiodiffuser; téléviser ♦ *vi* émettre; **~en** *vt*
élargir ♦ *vi* s'élargir; **to ~en one's mind** élargir
ses horizons; **~ly** *adv* en gros, généralement;
~-minded *adj* large d'esprit

broccoli ['brɒkəlɪ] *n* brocoli *m*

brochure ['brəʊʃjʊə'] *n* prospectus *m*,
dépliant *m*

broil [brɔɪl] *vt* griller

broke [brəʊk] *pt of* **break** ♦ *adj* (*inf*)
fauché(e)

broken ['brəʊkn] *pp of* **break** ♦ *adj* cassé(e);
(*machine: also:* **~ down**) fichu(e); **in
~ English/French** dans un anglais/français
approximatif *or* hésitant; **~ leg** *etc* jambe *etc*
cassée; **~-hearted** *adj* (ayant) le cœur brisé

broker ['brəʊkə'] *n* courtier *m*

brolly ['brɒlɪ] (*BRIT: inf*) *n* pépin *m*, parapluie
m

bronchitis [brɒŋ'kaɪtɪs] *n* bronchite *f*

bronze [brɔnz] *n* bronze *m*

brooch [brəutʃ] *n* broche *f*

brood [bru:d] *n* couvée *f* ♦ *vi* (*person*) méditer (sombrement), ruminer

broom [brum] *n* balai *m*; (*BOT*) genêt *m*; **~stick** *n* manche *m* à balai

Bros. *abbr* = **Brothers**

broth [brɔθ] *n* bouillon *m* de viande et de légumes

brothel ['brɔθl] *n* maison close, bordel *m*

brother ['brʌðəʳ] *n* frère *m*; **~-in-law** *n* beau-frère *m*

brought [brɔ:t] *pt, pp of* **bring**

brow [brau] *n* front *m*; (*eyebrow*) sourcil *m*; (*of hill*) sommet *m*

brown [braun] *adj* brun(e), marron *inv*; (*hair*) châtain *inv*, (*eyes*) marron *inv*; (*tanned*) bronzé(e) ♦ *n* (*colour*) brun *m* ♦ *vt* (*CULIN*) faire dorer; **~ bread** *n* pain *m* bis; **B~ie** *n* (*also*: **B~ie Guide**) jeannette *f*, éclaireuse (cadette); **~ie** (*US*) *n* (*cake*) gâteau *m* au chocolat et aux noix; **~ paper** *n* papier *m* d'emballage; **~ sugar** *n* cassonade *f*

browse [brauz] *vi* (*among books*) bouquiner, feuilleter les livres; **to ~ through a book** feuilleter un livre

browser ['brauzəʳ] *n* (*COMPUT*) navigateur *m*

bruise [bru:z] *n* bleu *m*, contusion *f* ♦ *vt* contusionner, meurtrir

brunette [bru:'net] *n* (femme) brune

brunt [brʌnt] *n*: **the ~ of** (*attack, criticism etc*) le plus gros de

brush [brʌʃ] *n* brosse *f*; (*painting*) pinceau *m*; (*shaving*) blaireau *m*; (*quarrel*) accrochage *m*, prise *f* de bec ♦ *vt* brosser; (*also*: **~ against**) effleurer, frôler; **~ aside** *vt* écarter, balayer; **~ up** *vt* (*knowledge*) rafraîchir, réviser; **~wood** *n* broussailles *fpl*, taillis *m*

Brussels ['brʌslz] *n* Bruxelles; **~ sprout** *n* chou *m* de Bruxelles

brutal ['bru:tl] *adj* brutal(e)

brute [bru:t] *n* brute *f* ♦ *adj*: **by ~ force** par la force

BSc *abbr* = **Bachelor of Science**

BSE *n abbr* (= *bovine spongiform encephalopathy*) ESB *f*, BSE *f*

bubble ['bʌbl] *n* bulle *f* ♦ *vi* bouillonner, faire des bulles; (*sparkle*) pétiller; **~ bath** *n* bain moussant; **~ gum** *n* bubblegum *m*

buck [bʌk] *n* mâle *m* (*d'un lapin, daim etc*); (*US*: *inf*) dollar *m* ♦ *vi* ruer, lancer une ruade; **to pass the ~ (to sb)** se décharger de la responsabilité (sur qn); **~ up** *vi* (*cheer up*) reprendre du poil de la bête, se remonter

bucket ['bʌkɪt] *n* seau *m*

buckle ['bʌkl] *n* boucle *f* ♦ *vt* (*belt etc*) boucler, attacher ♦ *vi* (*warp*) tordre, gauchir; (*: wheel*) se voiler; se déformer

bud [bʌd] *n* bourgeon *m*; (*of flower*) bouton *m* ♦ *vi* bourgeonner; (*flower*) éclore

Buddhism ['budɪzəm] *n* bouddhisme *m*

Buddhist *adj* bouddhiste ♦ *n* Bouddhiste *m/f*

budding ['bʌdɪŋ] *adj* (*poet etc*) en herbe; (*passion etc*) naissant(e)

buddy ['bʌdɪ] (*US*) *n* copain *m*

budge [bʌdʒ] *vt* faire bouger; (*fig*: *person*) faire changer d'avis ♦ *vi* bouger; changer d'avis

budgerigar ['bʌdʒərɪgɑ:ʳ] (*BRIT*) *n* perruche *f*

budget ['bʌdʒɪt] *n* budget *m* ♦ *vi*: **to ~ for sth** inscrire qch au budget

budgie ['bʌdʒɪ] (*BRIT*) *n* = **budgerigar**

buff [bʌf] *adj* (couleur *f*) chamois *m* ♦ *n* (*inf*: *enthusiast*) mordu(e); **he's a ... ~** c'est un mordu de ...

buffalo ['bʌfələu] (*pl* **~** *or* **~es**) *n* buffle *m*; (*US*) bison *m*

buffer ['bʌfəʳ] *n* tampon *m*; (*COMPUT*) mémoire *f* tampon

buffet¹ ['bʌfɪt] *vt* secouer, ébranler

buffet² ['bufeɪ] *n* (*food, BRIT*: *bar*) buffet *m*; **~ car** (*BRIT*) *n* (*RAIL*) voiture-buffet *f*

bug [bʌg] *n* (*insect*) punaise *f*; (: *gen*) insecte *m*, bestiole *f*; (*fig*: *germ*) virus *m*, microbe *m*; (*COMPUT*) erreur *f*; (*fig*: *spy device*) dispositif *m* d'écoute (électronique) ♦ *vt* garnir de dispositifs d'écoute; (*inf*: *annoy*) embêter; **~ged** *adj* sur écoute

bugle ['bju:gl] *n* clairon *m*

build [bɪld] (*pt, pp* **built**) *n* (*of person*) carrure *f*, charpente *f* ♦ *vt* construire, bâtir; **~ up** *vt* accumuler, amasser; accroître; **~er** *n* entrepreneur *m*; **~ing** *n* (*trade*) construction *f*; (*house, structure*) bâtiment *m*, construction *f*; (*offices, flats*) immeuble *m*; **~ing society** (*BRIT*) *n* société *f* de crédit immobilier

built [bɪlt] *pt, pp of* **build**; **~-in** ['bɪltɪn] *adj* (*cupboard, oven*) encastré(e); (*device*) incorporé(e); intégré(e); **~-up area** ['bɪltʌp-] *n* zone urbanisée

bulb [bʌlb] *n* (*BOT*) bulbe *m*, oignon *m*; (*ELEC*) ampoule *f*

Bulgaria [bʌl'gɛərɪə] *n* Bulgarie *f*

bulge [bʌldʒ] *n* renflement *m*, gonflement *m* ♦ *vi* (*pocket, file etc*) être plein(e) à craquer; (*cheeks*) être gonflé(e)

bulk [bʌlk] *n* masse *f*, volume *m*; (*of person*) corpulence *f*; **in ~** (*COMM*) en vrac; **the ~ of** la plus grande *or* grosse partie de; **~y** *adj* volumineux(-euse), encombrant(e)

bull [bul] *n* taureau *m*; (*male elephant/whale*) mâle *m*; **~dog** *n* bouledogue *m*

bulldozer ['buldəuzəʳ] *n* bulldozer *m*

bullet ['bulɪt] *n* balle *f* (*de fusil etc*)

bulletin ['bulɪtɪn] *n* bulletin *m*, communiqué *m*; (*news* ~) (bulletin d')informations *fpl*

bulletproof ['bulɪtpru:f] *adj* (*car*) blindé(e); (*vest etc*) pare-balles *inv*

bullfight ['bulfaɪt] n corrida f, course f de taureaux; **~er** n torero m; **~ing** n tauromachie f

bullion ['buljən] n or m or argent m en lingots

bullock ['bulək] n bœuf m

bullring ['bulrɪŋ] n arènes fpl

bull's-eye ['bulzaɪ] n centre m (de la cible)

bully ['bulɪ] n brute f, tyran m ♦ vt tyranniser, rudoyer

bum [bʌm] n (inf: backside) derrière m; (esp US: tramp) vagabond(e), traîne-savates m/f inv

bumblebee ['bʌmblbɪ:] n bourdon m

bump [bʌmp] n (in car: minor accident) accrochage m; (jolt) cahot m; (on road etc, on head) bosse f ♦ vt heurter, cogner; **~ into** vt fus rentrer dans, tamponner; (meet) tomber sur; **~er** n pare-chocs m inv ♦ adj: **~er crop/harvest** récolte/moisson exceptionnelle; **~er cars** (US) npl autos tamponneuses; **~y** adj cahoteux(-euse)

bun [bʌn] n petit pain au lait; (of hair) chignon m

bunch [bʌntʃ] n (of flowers) bouquet m; (of keys) trousseau m; (of bananas) régime m; (of people) groupe m; **~es** npl (in hair) couettes fpl; **~ of grapes** grappe f de raisin

bundle ['bʌndl] n paquet m ♦ vt (also: **~ up**) faire un paquet de; (put): **to ~ sth/sb into** fourrer ou enfourner qch/qn dans

bungalow ['bʌŋgələu] n bungalow m

bungle ['bʌŋgl] vt bâcler, gâcher

bunion ['bʌnjən] n oignon m (au pied)

bunk [bʌŋk] n couchette f; **~ beds** npl lits superposés

bunker ['bʌŋkə'] n (coal store) soute f à charbon; (MIL, GOLF) bunker m

bunting ['bʌntɪŋ] n pavoisement m, drapeaux mpl

buoy [bɔɪ] n bouée f; **~ up** vt faire flotter; (fig) soutenir, épauler; **~ant** adj capable de flotter; (carefree) gai(e), plein(e) d'entrain; (economy) ferme, actif

burden ['bɜ:dn] n fardeau m ♦ vt (trouble) accabler, surcharger

bureau ['bjuərəu] (pl **~x**) n (BRIT: writing desk) bureau m, secrétaire m; (US: chest of drawers) commode f; (office) bureau, office m; **~cracy** [bjuə'rɔkrəsɪ] n bureaucratie f

burglar ['bɜ:glə'] n cambrioleur m; **~ alarm** n sonnerie f d'alarme; **~y** n cambriolage m

Burgundy ['bɜ:gəndɪ] n Bourgogne f

burial ['berɪəl] n enterrement m

burly ['bɜ:lɪ] adj de forte carrure, costaud(e)

Burma ['bɜ:mə] n Birmanie f

burn [bɜ:n] (pt, pp burned or burnt) vt, vi brûler ♦ n brûlure f; **~ down** vt incendier, détruire par le feu; **~er** n brûleur m; **~ing**

adj brûlant(e); (house) en flammes; (ambition) dévorant(e)

burrow ['bʌrəu] n terrier m ♦ vt creuser

bursary ['bɜ:sərɪ] (BRIT) n bourse f (d'études)

burst [bɜ:st] (pt,pp burst) vt crever; faire éclater; (subj: river: banks etc) rompre ♦ vi éclater; (tyre) crever ♦ n (of gunfire) rafale f (de tir); (also: **~ pipe**) rupture f; fuite f; **a ~ of enthusiasm/energy** un accès d'enthousiasme/ d'énergie; **to ~ into flames** s'enflammer soudainement; **to ~ out laughing** éclater de rire; **to ~ into tears** fondre en larmes; **to be ~ing with** être plein (à craquer) de; (fig) être débordant(e) de; **~ into** vt fus (room etc) faire irruption dans

bury ['berɪ] vt enterrer

bus [bʌs] (pl **~es**) n autobus m

bush [buʃ] n buisson m; (scrubland) brousse f; **to beat about the ~** tourner autour du pot; **~y** adj broussailleux(-euse), touffu(e)

busily ['bɪzɪlɪ] adv activement

business ['bɪznɪs] n (matter, firm) affaire f; (trading) affaires fpl; (job, duty) travail m; **to be away on ~** être en déplacement d'affaires; **it's none of my ~** cela ne me regarde pas, ce ne sont pas mes affaires; **he means ~** il ne plaisante pas, il est sérieux; **~like** adj (firm) sérieux(-euse); (method) efficace; **~man** (irreg) n homme m d'affaires; **~ trip** n voyage m d'affaires; **~woman** (irreg) n femme f d'affaires

busker ['bʌskə'] (BRIT) n musicien ambulant

bus: **~ shelter** n abribus m; **~ station** n gare routière; **~ stop** n arrêt m d'autobus

bust [bʌst] n buste m; (measurement) tour m de poitrine ♦ adj (inf: broken) fichu(e), fini(e); **to go ~** faire faillite

bustle ['bʌsl] n remue-ménage m, affairement m ♦ vi s'affairer, se démener; **bustling** adj (town) bruyant(e), affairé(e)

busy ['bɪzɪ] adj occupé(e), (shop, street) très fréquenté(e) ♦ vt: **to ~ o.s.** s'occuper; **~body** n mouche f du coche, âme f charitable; **~ signal** (US) n (TEL) tonalité f occupé inv

---

KEYWORD

but [bʌt] conj mais; **I'd love to come, but I'm busy** j'aimerais venir mais je suis occupé ♦ prep (apart from, except) sauf, excepté; **we've had nothing but trouble** nous n'avons eu que des ennuis; **no-one but him can do it** lui seul peut le faire; **but for you/your help** sans toi/ton aide; **anything but that** tout sauf or excepté ça, tout mais pas ça ♦ adv (just, only) ne ... que; **she's but a child** elle n'est qu'une enfant; **had I but known** si seulement j'avais su; **all but finished** pratiquement terminé

butcher ['bʊtʃə'] n boucher m ♦ vt
massacrer; (cattle etc for meat) tuer; ~'s
(shop) n boucherie f

butler ['bʌtlə'] n maître m d'hôtel

butt [bʌt] n (large barrel) gros tonneau; (of
gun) crosse f; (of cigarette) mégot m; (BRIT:
fig: target) cible f ♦ vt donner un coup de
tête à; ~ in vi (interrupt) s'immiscer dans la
conversation

butter ['bʌtə'] n beurre m ♦ vt beurrer; ~cup
n bouton m d'or

butterfly ['bʌtəflaɪ] n papillon m; (SWIMMING:
also: ~ stroke) brasse f papillon

buttocks ['bʌtəks] npl fesses fpl

button ['bʌtn] n bouton m; (US: badge) pin
m ♦ vt (also: ~ up) boutonner ♦ vi se
boutonner

buttress ['bʌtrɪs] n contrefort m

buy [baɪ] (pt, pp bought) vt acheter ♦ n achat
m; to ~ sb sth/sth from sb acheter qch à qn;
to ~ sb a drink offrir un verre or à boire à qn;
~er n acheteur(-euse)

buzz [bʌz] n bourdonnement m; (inf: phone
call): to give sb a ~ passer un coup m de fil à
qn ♦ vi bourdonner; ~er n timbre m
électrique; ~ word n (inf) mot m à la mode

KEYWORD

by [baɪ] prep 1 (referring to cause, agent) par,
de; killed by lightning tué par la foudre;
surrounded by a fence entouré d'une barrière;
a painting by Picasso un tableau de Picasso
2 (referring to method, manner, means): by
bus/car en autobus/voiture; by train par le or
en train; to pay by cheque payer par chèque;
by saving hard, he ... à force d'économiser,
il ...
3 (via, through) par; we came by Dover nous
sommes venus par Douvres
4 (close to, past) à côté de; the house by the
school la maison à côté de l'école; a holiday
by the sea des vacances au bord de la mer;
she sat by his bed elle était assise à son
chevet; she went by me elle est passée à côté
de moi; I go by the post office every day je
passe devant la poste tous les jours
5 (with time: not later than) avant; (: during):
by daylight à la lumière du jour; by night la
nuit, de nuit; by 4 o'clock avant 4 heures; by
this time tomorrow d'ici demain à la même
heure; by the time I got here it was too late
lorsque je suis arrivé il était déjà trop tard
6 (amount) à; by the kilo/metre au kilo/au
mètre; paid by the hour payé à l'heure
7 (MATH, measure): to divide/multiply by 3
diviser/multiplier par 3; a room 3 metres by 4
une pièce de 3 mètres sur 4; it's broader by a
metre c'est plus large d'un mètre; one by one
un à un; little by little petit à petit, peu à peu

8 (according to) d'après, selon; it's 3 o'clock
by my watch il est 3 heures à ma montre; it's
all right by me je n'ai rien contre
9: (all) by oneself etc tout(e) seul(e)
10: by the way au fait, à propos
♦ adv 1 see go; pass etc
2: by and by un peu plus tard, bientôt; by
and large dans l'ensemble

bye(-bye) ['baɪ('baɪ)] excl au revoir!, salut!

bye(e)-law ['baɪlɔ:] n arrêté municipal

by: ~-election (BRIT) n élection (législative)
partielle; ~gone adj passé(e) ♦ n: let ~gones
be ~gones passons l'éponge, oublions le
passé; ~pass n (route f de) contournement
m; (MED) pontage m ♦ vt éviter; ~-product
n sous-produit m, dérivé m; (fig)
conséquence f secondaire, retombée f;
~stander n spectateur(-trice), badaud(e)

byte [baɪt] n (COMPUT) octet m

byword ['baɪwə:d] n: to be a ~ for être
synonyme de (fig)

C, c

C [si:] n (MUS) do m

CA abbr = chartered accountant

cab [kæb] n taxi m; (of train, truck) cabine f

cabaret ['kæbəreɪ] n (show) spectacle m de
cabaret

cabbage ['kæbɪdʒ] n chou m

cabin ['kæbɪn] n (house) cabane f, hutte f;
(on ship) cabine f; (on plane) compartiment
m; ~ crew n (AVIAT) équipage m; ~ cruiser
n cruiser m

cabinet ['kæbɪnɪt] n (POL) cabinet m;
(furniture) petit meuble à tiroirs et rayons;
(also: display ~) vitrine f, petite armoire vitrée

cable ['keɪbl] n câble m ♦ vt câbler,
télégraphier; ~-car n téléphérique m;
~ television n télévision f par câble

cache [kæʃ] n stock m

cackle ['kækl] vi caqueter

cactus ['kæktəs] (pl cacti) n cactus m

cadet [kə'det] n (MIL) élève m officier

cadge [kædʒ] (inf) vt: to ~ (from or off) se
faire donner (par)

Caesarian [sɪ'zeərɪən] n (also: ~ section)
césarienne f

café ['kæfeɪ] n ≈ café(-restaurant) m (sans
alcool)

cage [keɪdʒ] n cage f

cagey ['keɪdʒɪ] (inf) adj réticent(e);
méfiant(e)

cagoule [kə'gu:l] n K-way ® m

Cairo ['kaɪərəu] n le Caire

cajole [kə'dʒəul] vt couvrir de flatteries or de
gentillesses

cake [keɪk] n gâteau m; **~d** adj: **~d with raidi(e)** par, couvert(e) d'une croûte de

calculate ['kælkjuleɪt] vt calculer; (estimate: chances, effect) évaluer; **calculation** n calcul m; **calculator** n machine f à calculer, calculatrice f; (pocket) calculette f

calendar ['kæləndər] n calendrier m; **~ year** n année civile

calf [kɑːf] (pl **calves**) n (of cow) veau m; (of other animals) petit m; (also: **~skin**) veau m, vachette f; (ANAT) mollet m

calibre ['kælɪbər] (US **caliber**) n calibre m

call [kɔːl] vt appeler; (meeting) convoquer ♦ vi appeler; (also: also: **~ in, ~ round**) passer ♦ n (shout) appel m, cri m; (also: **telephone ~**) coup m de téléphone; (visit) visite f; **she's ~ed** Suzanne elle s'appelle Suzanne; **to be on ~** être de permanence; **~ back** vi (return) repasser; (TEL) rappeler; **~ for** vt fus (demand) demander; (fetch) passer prendre; **~ off** vt annuler; **~ on** vt fus (visit) rendre visite à, passer voir; (request): **to ~ on sb to do** inviter qn à faire; **~ out** vi pousser un cri ou des cris; **~ up** vt (MIL) appeler, mobiliser; (TEL) appeler; **~box** n (BRIT) (TEL) cabine f téléphonique; **~ centre** n centre m d'appels; **~er** n personne f qui appelle; (visitor) visiteur m; **~ girl** n call-girl f; **~-in** (US) n (RADIO, TV: phone-in) programme m à ligne ouverte; **~ing** n vocation f; (trade, occupation) état m; **~ing card** (US) n carte f de visite

callous ['kæləs] adj dur(e), insensible

calm [kɑːm] adj calme ♦ n calme m ♦ vt calmer, apaiser; **~ down** vi se calmer ♦ vt calmer, apaiser

Calor gas ⓡ ['kælər-] n butane m, butagaz m ⓡ

calorie ['kælərɪ] n calorie f

calves [kɑːvz] npl of **calf**

camber ['kæmbər] n (of road) bombement m

Cambodia [kæm'bəudɪə] n Cambodge m

camcorder ['kæmkɔːdər] n caméscope m

came [keɪm] pt of **come**

camel ['kæməl] n chameau m

camera ['kæmərə] n (PHOT) appareil-photo m; (also: **cine-~, movie ~**) caméra f; **in ~** à huis clos; **~man** (irreg) n caméraman m

camouflage ['kæməflɑːʒ] n camouflage m ♦ vt camoufler

camp [kæmp] n camp m ♦ vi camper ♦ adj (man) efféminé(e)

campaign [kæm'peɪn] n (MIL, POL etc) campagne f ♦ vi faire campagne

camp: **~bed** (BRIT) n lit m de camp; **~er** n campeur(-euse); (vehicle) camping-car m; **~ing** n camping m; **to go ~ing** faire du camping; **~ing gas** ⓡ n butane m; **~site** n campement m, (terrain m de) camping m

campus ['kæmpəs] n campus m

can¹ [kæn] n (of milk, oil, water) bidon m; (tin) boîte f de conserve ♦ vt mettre en conserve

can² [kæn] (negative **cannot, can't**, conditional and pt **could**) aux vb **1** (be able to) pouvoir; **you can do it if you try** vous pouvez le faire si vous essayez; **I can't hear you** je ne t'entends pas

2 (know how to) savoir; **I can swim/play tennis/drive** je sais nager/jouer au tennis/conduire; **can you speak French?** parlez-vous français?

3 (may) pouvoir; **can I use your phone?** puis-je me servir de votre téléphone?

4 (expressing disbelief, puzzlement etc): **it can't be true!** ce n'est pas possible!; **what CAN he want?** qu'est-ce qu'il peut bien vouloir?

5 (expressing possibility, suggestion etc): **he could be in the library** il est peut être dans la bibliothèque; **she could have been delayed** il se peut qu'elle ait été retardée

Canada ['kænədə] n Canada m; **Canadian** [kə'neɪdɪən] adj canadien(ne) ♦ n Canadien(ne)

canal [kə'næl] n canal m

canapé ['kænəpeɪ] n canapé m

canary [kə'neərɪ] n canari m, serin m

cancel ['kænsəl] vt annuler; (train) supprimer; (party, appointment) décommander; (cross out) barrer, rayer; **~lation** [kænsə'leɪʃən] n annulation f; suppression f

cancer ['kænsər] n (MED) cancer m; **C~** (ASTROLOGY) le Cancer

candid ['kændɪd] adj (très) franc (franche), sincère

candidate ['kændɪdeɪt] n candidat(e)

candle ['kændl] n bougie f; (of tallow) chandelle f; (in church) cierge m; **~light** n: **by ~light** à la lumière d'une bougie; (dinner) aux chandelles; **~stick** n (also: **~ holder**) bougeoir m; (bigger, ornate) chandelier m

candour ['kændər] (US **candor**) n (grande) franchise or sincérité

candy ['kændɪ] n sucre candi; (US) bonbon m; **~-floss** (BRIT) n barbe f à papa

cane [keɪn] n canne f; (for furniture, baskets etc) rotin m ♦ vt (BRIT: SCOL) administrer des coups de bâton à

canister ['kænɪstər] n boîte f; (of gas, pressurized substance) bombe f

cannabis ['kænəbɪs] n (drug) cannabis m

canned [kænd] adj (food) en boîte, en conserve

cannon ['kænən] (pl **~ or ~s**) n (gun) canon m

cannot ['kænɔt] = **can not**

canoe [kə'nu:] n pirogue f; (SPORT) canoë m; **~ing** n: to go **~ing** faire du canoë

canon ['kænən] n (clergyman) chanoine m; (standard) canon m

can-opener ['kænəupnə'] n ouvre-boîte m

canopy ['kænəpı] n baldaquin m; dais m

can't [kænt] = **cannot**

canteen [kæn'ti:n] n cantine f; (BRIT: of cutlery) ménagère f

canter ['kæntə'] vi (horse) aller au petit galop

canvas ['kænvəs] n toile f

canvass ['kænvəs] vi (POL): to **~ for** faire campagne pour ♦ vt (investigate: opinions etc) sonder

canyon ['kænjən] n cañon m, gorge (profonde)

cap [kæp] n casquette f; (of pen) capuchon m; (of bottle) capsule f; (contraceptive: also: Dutch **~**) diaphragme m; (for toy gun) amorce f ♦ vt (outdo) surpasser; (put limit on) plafonner

capability [keɪpə'bılıtı] n aptitude f, capacité f

capable ['keɪpəbl] adj capable

capacity [kə'pæsıtı] n capacité f; (capability) aptitude f; (of factory) rendement m

cape [keɪp] n (garment) cape f; (GEO) cap m

caper ['keɪpə'] n (CULIN: gen pl) câpre f; (prank) farce f

capital ['kæpıtl] n (also: **~ city**) capitale f; (money) capital m; (also: **~ letter**) majuscule f; **~ gains tax** n (COMM) impôt m sur les plus-values; **~ism** n capitalisme m; **~ist** adj capitaliste ♦ n capitaliste m/f; **~ize** ['kæpıtəlaız] vi: to **~ize on** tirer parti de; **~ punishment** n peine capitale

Capricorn ['kæprıkɔ:n] n le Capricorne

capsize [kæp'saız] vt faire chavirer ♦ vi chavirer

capsule ['kæpsju:l] n capsule f

captain ['kæptın] n capitaine m

caption ['kæpʃən] n légende f

captive ['kæptıv] adj, n captif(-ive)

capture ['kæptʃə'] vt capturer, prendre; (attention) capter; (COMPUT) saisir ♦ n capture f; (data **~**) saisie f de données

car [kɑ:'] n voiture f, auto f; (RAIL) wagon m, voiture

caramel ['kærəməl] n caramel m

caravan ['kærəvæn] n caravane f; **~ning** n: to go **~ning** faire du caravaning; **~ site** (BRIT) n camping m pour caravanes

carbohydrate [kɑ:bəu'haıdreıt] n hydrate m de carbone; (food) féculent m

carbon ['kɑ:bən] n carbone m; **~ dioxide** n gaz m carbonique; **~ monoxide** n oxyde m de carbone; **~ paper** n papier m carbone

car boot sale n marché aux puces où les particuliers vendent des objets entreposés dans le coffre de leur voiture

carburettor [kɑ:bju'retə'] (US **carburetor**) n carburateur m

card [kɑ:d] n carte f; (material) carton m; **~board** n carton m; **~ game** n jeu m de cartes

cardiac ['kɑ:dıæk] adj cardiaque

cardigan ['kɑ:dıgən] n cardigan m

cardinal ['kɑ:dınl] adj cardinal(e) ♦ n cardinal m

card index n fichier m

cardphone n téléphone m à carte

care [kɛə'] n soin m, attention f; (worry) souci m; (charge) charge f, garde f ♦ vi: to **~ about** se soucier de, s'intéresser à; (person) être attaché(e) à; **~ of** chez, aux bons soins de; **in sb's ~** à la garde de qn, confié(e) à qn; **to take ~ (to do)** faire attention (à faire); **to take ~ of** s'occuper de; **I don't ~** ça m'est bien égal; **I couldn't ~ less** je m'en fiche complètement (inf); **~ for** vt fus s'occuper de; (like) aimer

career [kə'rıə'] n carrière f ♦ vi (also: **~ along**) aller à toute allure; **~ woman** (irreg) n femme ambitieuse

care: ~-free adj sans souci, insouciant(e); **~ful** adj (thorough) soigneux(-euse); (cautious) prudent(e); **(be) ~ful!** (fais) attention!; **~fully** adv avec soin, soigneusement; prudemment; **~less** adj négligent(e); (heedless) insouciant(e); **~r** n (MED) aide f

caress [kə'rɛs] n caresse f ♦ vt caresser

caretaker ['kɛəteɪkə'] n gardien(ne), concierge m/f

car-ferry ['kɑ:fɛrı] n (on sea) ferry(-boat) m

cargo ['kɑ:gəu] (pl **~es**) n cargaison f, chargement m

car hire n location f de voitures

Caribbean [kærı'bi:ən] adj: the **~ (Sea)** la mer des Antilles or Caraïbes

caring ['kɛərıŋ] adj (person) bienveillant(e); (society, organization) humanitaire

carnation [kɑ:'neɪʃən] n œillet m

carnival ['kɑ:nıvl] n (public celebration) carnaval m; (US: funfair) fête foraine

carol ['kærəl] n: **(Christmas) ~** chant m de Noël

carp [kɑ:p] n (fish) carpe f

car park (BRIT) n parking m, parc m de stationnement

carpenter ['kɑ:pıntə'] n charpentier m; **carpentry** n menuiserie f

carpet ['kɑ:pıt] n tapis m ♦ vt recouvrir d'un tapis; **~ sweeper** n balai m mécanique

car phone n (TEL) téléphone m de voiture

car rental n location f de voitures

carriage ['kærıdʒ] n voiture f; (of goods) transport m; (: cost) port m; **~way** (BRIT) n (*part of road*) chaussée f

carrier ['kærɪəʳ] n transporteur m, camionneur m; (*company*) entreprise f de transport; (MED) porteur(-euse); **~ bag** (BRIT) n sac m (en papier ou en plastique)

carrot ['kærət] n carotte f

carry ['kærɪ] vt (*subj: person*) porter; (: vehicle) transporter; (: involve: responsibilities etc) comporter, impliquer ♦ vi (*sound*) porter; **to get carried away** (fig) s'emballer, s'enthousiasmer; **~ on** vi: **to ~ on with sth/doing** continuer qch/de faire ♦ vt poursuivre; **~ out** vt (*orders*) exécuter; (*investigation*) mener; **~cot** (BRIT) n porte-bébé m; **~-on** (*inf*) n (*fuss*) histoires fpl

cart [kɑːt] n charrette f ♦ vt (*inf*) transporter, trimballer (*inf*)

carton ['kɑːtən] n (*box*) carton m; (*of yogurt*) pot m; (*of cigarettes*) cartouche f

cartoon [kɑː'tuːn] n (PRESS) dessin m (humoristique), caricature f; (BRIT: comic strip) bande dessinée; (CINEMA) dessin animé

cartridge ['kɑːtrɪdʒ] n cartouche f

carve [kɑːv] vt (*meat*) découper; (*wood, stone*) tailler, sculpter; **~ up** vt découper; (*fig: country*) morceler; **carving** n sculpture f; **carving knife** n couteau m à découper

car wash n station f de lavage (de voitures)

case [keɪs] n cas m; (LAW) affaire f, procès m; (*box*) caisse f, boîte f, étui m; (BRIT: also: suitcase) valise f; **in ~ of** en cas de; **in ~ he ...** au cas où il ...; **just in ~** à tout hasard; **in any ~** en tout cas, de toute façon

cash [kæʃ] n argent m; (COMM) argent liquide, espèces fpl ♦ vt encaisser; **to pay (in) ~** payer comptant; **~ on delivery** payable ou paiement à la livraison; **~-book** n livre m de caisse; **~ card** (BRIT) n carte f de retrait; **~ desk** (BRIT) n caisse f; **~ dispenser** (BRIT) n distributeur m automatique de billets, billeterie f

cashew [kæ'ʃuː] n (*also:* **~ nut**) noix f de cajou

cashier [kæ'ʃɪəʳ] n caissier(-ère)

cashmere ['kæʃmɪəʳ] n cachemire m

cash register n caisse (enregistreuse)

casing ['keɪsɪŋ] n revêtement (protecteur), enveloppe (protectrice)

casino [kə'siːnəu] n casino m

casket ['kɑːskɪt] n coffret m; (US: coffin) cercueil m

casserole ['kæsərəul] n (*container*) cocotte f; (*food*) ragoût m (en cocotte)

cassette [kæ'set] n cassette f, musicassette f; **~ player** n lecteur m de cassettes; **~ recorder** n magnétophone m à cassettes

cast [kɑːst] (pt, pp cast) vt (*throw*) jeter; (*shed*) perdre; se dépouiller de; (*statue*) mouler; (THEATRE): **to ~ sb as Hamlet** attribuer

à qn le rôle de Hamlet ♦ n (THEATRE) distribution f; (*also:* **plaster ~**) plâtre m; **to ~ one's vote** voter; **~ off** vi (NAUT) larguer les amarres; (KNITTING) arrêter les mailles; **~ on** vi (KNITTING) monter les mailles

castaway ['kɑːstəweɪ] n naufragé(e)

caster sugar ['kɑːstə-] (BRIT) n sucre m semoule

casting vote (BRIT) n voix prépondérante (*pour départager*)

cast iron n fonte f

castle ['kɑːsl] n château (fort); (CHESS) tour f

castor ['kɑːstəʳ] n (*wheel*) roulette f; **~ oil** n huile f de ricin

castrate [kæs'treɪt] vt châtrer

casual ['kæʒjul] adj (*by chance*) de hasard, fait(e) au hasard, fortuit(e); (*irregular: work etc*) temporaire; (*unconcerned*) désinvolte; **~ly** adv avec désinvolture, négligemment; (*dress*) de façon décontractée

casualty ['kæʒjultɪ] n accidenté(e), blessé(e); (*dead*) victime f, mort(e); (MED: department) urgences fpl

casual wear n vêtements mpl décontractés

cat [kæt] n chat m

catalogue ['kætəlɒg] (US catalog) n catalogue m ♦ vt cataloguer

catalyst ['kætəlɪst] n catalyseur m

catalytic converter [kætə'lɪtɪk kən'vɜːtəʳ] n pot m catalytique

catapult ['kætəpʌlt] (BRIT) n (*sling*) lance-pierres m inv, fronde m

catarrh [kə'tɑːʳ] n rhume m chronique, catarrhe m

catastrophe [kə'tæstrəfɪ] n catastrophe f

catch [kætʃ] (pt, pp caught) vt attraper; (*person: by surprise*) prendre, surprendre; (*understand, hear*) saisir ♦ vi (*fire*) prendre; (*become trapped*) se prendre, s'accrocher ♦ n prise f; (*trick*) attrape f; (*of lock*) loquet m; **to ~ sb's attention or eye** attirer l'attention de qn; **to ~ one's breath** retenir son souffle; **to ~ fire** prendre feu; **to ~ sight of** apercevoir; **~ on** vi saisir; (*grow popular*) prendre; **~ up** vi se rattraper, combler son retard ♦ vt (*also:* **~ up with**) rattraper; **~ing** adj (MED) contagieux(-euse); **~ment area** ['kætʃmənt-] (BRIT) n (SCOL) secteur m de recrutement; (*of hospital*) circonscription hospitalière; **~ phrase** n slogan m; expression f (à la mode); **~y** adj (*tune*) facile à retenir

category ['kætɪɡərɪ] n catégorie f

cater ['keɪtəʳ] vi (*provide food*): **to ~ (for)** préparer des repas (pour), se charger de la restauration (pour); **~ for** vt fus (*needs*) satisfaire, pourvoir à; (*readers, consumers*) s'adresser à, pourvoir aux besoins de; **~er** n traiteur m; fournisseur m; **~ing** n restauration f; approvisionnement m, ravitaillement m

caterpillar ['kætəpɪlər] n chenille f

cathedral [kə'θi:drəl] n cathédrale f

catholic ['kæθəlɪk] adj (tastes) éclectique, varié(e); **C~** adj catholique ♦ n catholique m/f

Catseye ® ['kæts'aɪ] (BRIT) n (AUT) catadioptre m

cattle ['kætl] npl bétail m

catty ['kætɪ] adj méchant(e)

caucus ['kɔ:kəs] n (POL: group) comité local d'un parti politique; (US: POL) comité électoral (pour désigner des candidats)

caught [kɔ:t] pt, pp of **catch**

cauliflower ['kɔlɪflauər] n chou-fleur m

cause [kɔ:z] n cause f ♦ vt causer

caution ['kɔ:ʃən] n prudence f; (warning) avertissement m ♦ vt avertir, donner un avertissement à; **cautious** adj prudent(e)

cavalry ['kævəlrɪ] n cavalerie f

cave [keɪv] n caverne f, grotte f; **~ in** vi (roof etc) s'effondrer; **~man** ['keɪvmæn] (irreg) n homme m des cavernes

caviar(e) ['kævɪɑ:r] n caviar m

CB n abbr (= Citizens' Band (Radio)) CB f

CBI n abbr (= Confederation of British Industries) groupement du patronat

cc abbr = **carbon copy**; **cubic centimetres**

CD n abbr (= compact disc (player)) CD m; **CDI** n abbr (= Compact Disk Interactive) CD-I m; **CD player** n platine f laser; **CD-ROM** [si:di:'rɒm] n abbr (= compact disc read-only memory) CD-Rom m

cease [si:s] vt, vi cesser; **~fire** n cessez-le-feu m; **~less** adj incessant(e), continuel(le)

cedar ['si:dər] n cèdre m

ceiling ['si:lɪŋ] n plafond m

celebrate ['selɪbreɪt] vt, vi célébrer; **~d** adj célèbre; **celebration** [selɪ'breɪʃən] n célébration f; **celebrity** [sɪ'lebrɪtɪ] n célébrité f

celery ['selərɪ] n céleri m (à côtes)

cell [sel] n cellule f; (ELEC) élément m (de pile)

cellar ['selər] n cave f

cello ['tʃeləu] n violoncelle m

cellphone ['selfəun] n téléphone m cellulaire

Celt [kelt, selt] n Celte m/f; **~ic** adj celte

cement [sə'ment] n ciment m; **~ mixer** n bétonnière f

cemetery ['semɪtrɪ] n cimetière m

censor ['sensər] n censeur m ♦ vt censurer; **~ship** n censure f

censure ['senʃər] vt blâmer, critiquer

census ['sensəs] n recensement m

cent [sent] n (US etc: coin) cent m (= un centième du dollar); see also **per**

centenary [sen'ti:nərɪ] n centenaire m

center ['sentər] (US) n = **centre**

centigrade ['sentɪɡreɪd] adj centigrade

centimetre ['sentɪmi:tər] (US **centimeter**) n centimètre m

centipede ['sentɪpi:d] n mille-pattes m inv

central ['sentrəl] adj central(e); **C~ America** n Amérique centrale; **~ heating** n chauffage central; **~ reservation** (BRIT) n (AUT) terre-plein central

centre ['sentər] (US **center**) n centre m ♦ vt centrer; **~-forward** n (SPORT) avant-centre m; **~-half** n (SPORT) demi-centre m

century ['sentjurɪ] n siècle m; **20th ~** XXe siècle

ceramic [sɪ'ræmɪk] adj céramique

cereal ['si:rɪəl] n céréale f

ceremony ['serɪmənɪ] n cérémonie f; **to stand on ~** faire des façons

certain ['sɜ:tən] adj certain(e); **for ~** certainement, sûrement; **~ly** adv certainement; **~ty** n certitude f

certificate [sə'tɪfɪkɪt] n certificat m

certified ['sɜ:tɪfaɪd] adj: **by ~ mail** (US) en recommandé, avec avis de réception; **~ public accountant** (US) expert-comptable m

certify ['sɜ:tɪfaɪ] vt certifier; (award diploma to) conférer un diplôme etc à; (declare insane) déclarer malade mental(e)

cervical ['sɜ:vɪkl] adj: **~ cancer** cancer m du col de l'utérus; **~ smear** frottis vaginal

cervix ['sɜ:vɪks] n col m de l'utérus

cf. abbr (= compare) cf., voir

CFC n abbr (= chlorofluorocarbon) CFC m (gen pl)

ch. abbr (= chapter) chap

chafe [tʃeɪf] vt irriter, frotter contre

chain [tʃeɪn] n chaîne f ♦ vt (also: **~ up**) enchaîner, attacher (avec une chaîne); **~ reaction** n réaction f en chaîne; **~-smoke** vi fumer cigarette sur cigarette; **~ store** n magasin m à succursales multiples

chair [tʃeər] n chaise f; (armchair) fauteuil m; (of university) chaire f; (of meeting, committee) présidence f ♦ vt (meeting) présider; **~lift** n télésiège m; **~man** (irreg) n président m

chalet ['ʃæleɪ] n chalet m

chalk [tʃɔ:k] n craie f

challenge ['tʃælɪndʒ] n défi m ♦ vt défier; (statement, right) mettre en question, contester; **~ sb to do** mettre qn au défi de faire; **challenging** adj (tone, look) de défi, provocateur(-trice); (task, career) qui représente un défi or une gageure

chamber ['tʃeɪmbər] n chambre f; **~ of commerce** chambre de commerce; **~maid** n femme f de chambre; **~ music** n musique f de chambre

champagne [ʃæm'peɪn] n champagne m

champion ['tʃæmpɪən] n champion(ne); **~ship** n championnat m

243

chance [tʃɑːns] n (opportunity) occasion f, possibilité f; (hope, likelihood) chance f; (risk) risque m ♦ vt: to ~ it risquer (le coup), essayer ♦ adj fortuit(e), de hasard; to take a ~ prendre un risque; by ~ par hasard

chancellor ['tʃɑːnsələʳ] n chancelier m; C~ of the Exchequer (BRIT) n chancelier m de l'Échiquier, ≈ ministre m des Finances

chandelier [ʃændə'lɪəʳ] n lustre m

change [tʃeɪndʒ] vt (alter, replace, COMM: money) changer; (hands, trains, clothes, one's name) changer de; (transform): to ~ sb into changer or transformer qn en ♦ vi (gen) changer; (one's clothes) se changer; (be transformed): to ~ into se changer or transformer en ♦ n changement m; (money) monnaie f; to ~ gear (AUT) changer de vitesse; to ~ one's mind changer d'avis; a ~ of clothes des vêtements de rechange, for a ~ pour changer; ~able adj (weather) variable; ~ machine n distributeur m de monnaie; ~over n (to new system) changement m, passage m; **changing** adj changeant(e); **changing room** n (BRIT: in shop) salon m d'essayage; (SPORT) vestiaire m

channel ['tʃænl] n (TV) chaîne f; (navigable passage) chenal m; (irrigation) canal m ♦ vt canaliser; the (English) C~ la Manche; the C~ Islands les îles de la Manche, les îles Anglo-Normandes; the C~ Tunnel le tunnel sous la Manche; ~-hopping n (TV) zapping m

chant [tʃɑːnt] n chant m; (REL) psalmodie f ♦ vt chanter, scander

chaos ['keɪɒs] n chaos m

chap [tʃæp] (BRIT: inf) n (man) type m

chapel ['tʃæpl] n chapelle f; (BRIT: nonconformist ~) église f

chaplain ['tʃæplɪn] n aumônier m

chapped [tʃæpt] adj (skin, lips) gercé(e)

chapter ['tʃæptəʳ] n chapitre m

char [tʃɑːʳ] vt (burn) carboniser

character ['kærɪktəʳ] n caractère m; (in novel, film) personnage m; (eccentric) numéro m, phénomène m; ~istic [kærɪktə'rɪstɪk] adj caractéristique ♦ n caractéristique f

charcoal ['tʃɑːkəul] n charbon m de bois; (for drawing) charbon m

charge [tʃɑːdʒ] n (cost) prix (demandé); (accusation) accusation f; (LAW) inculpation f ♦ vt: to ~ sb (with) inculper qn (de); (battery, enemy) charger; (customer, sum) faire payer ♦ vi foncer; ~s npl (costs) frais mpl; to reverse the ~s (TEL) téléphoner en P.C.V.; to take ~ of se charger de; to be in ~ of être responsable de, s'occuper de; how much do you ~? combien prenez-vous?; to ~ an expense (up) to sb mettre une dépense sur le compte de qn; ~ card n carte f de client

charity ['tʃærɪtɪ] n charité f; (organization) institution f charitable or de bienfaisance, œuvre f (de charité)

charm [tʃɑːm] n charme m; (on bracelet) breloque f ♦ vt charmer, enchanter; ~ing adj charmant(e)

chart [tʃɑːt] n tableau m, diagramme m; graphique m; (map) carte marine ♦ vt dresser or établir la carte de; ~s npl (hit parade) hit-parade m

charter ['tʃɑːtəʳ] vt (plane) affréter ♦ n (document) charte f; ~ed accountant (BRIT) n expert-comptable m; ~ flight n charter m

chase [tʃeɪs] vt poursuivre, pourchasser; (also: ~ away) chasser ♦ n poursuite f, chasse f

chasm ['kæzəm] n gouffre m, abîme m

chat [tʃæt] vi (also: have a ~) bavarder, causer ♦ n conversation f; ~ show n (BRIT) causerie f télévisée

chatter ['tʃætəʳ] vi (person) bavarder; (animal) jacasser ♦ n bavardage m; jacassement m; my teeth are ~ing je claque des dents; ~box n (inf) moulin m à paroles

chatty ['tʃætɪ] adj (style) familier(-ère); (person) bavard(e)

chauffeur ['ʃəufəʳ] n chauffeur m (de maître)

chauvinist ['ʃəuvɪnɪst] n (male ~) phallocrate m; (nationalist) chauvin(e)

cheap [tʃiːp] adj bon marché inv, pas cher (chère); (joke) facile, d'un goût douteux; (poor quality) à bon marché, de qualité médiocre ♦ adv à bon marché, pour pas cher; ~ day return billet m d'aller et retour réduit (valable pour la journée); ~er adj moins cher (chère); ~ly adv à bon marché, à bon compte

cheat [tʃiːt] vi tricher ♦ vt tromper, duper; (rob): to ~ sb out of sth escroquer qch à qn ♦ n tricheur(-euse); escroc m

check [tʃek] vt vérifier; (passport, ticket) contrôler; (halt) arrêter; (restrain) maîtriser ♦ n vérification f; contrôle m; (curb) frein m; (US: bill) addition f; (pattern: gen pl) carreaux mpl; (US) = cheque ♦ adj (pattern, cloth) à carreaux; ~ in vi (in hotel) remplir sa fiche (d'hôtel); (at airport) se présenter à l'enregistrement ♦ vt (luggage) (faire) enregistrer; ~ out vi (in hotel) régler sa note; ~ up vi: to ~ up (on sth) vérifier (qch); to ~ up on sb se renseigner sur le compte de qn; ~ered adj (US) = chequered; ~ers (US) npl jeu m de dames; ~-in (desk) n enregistrement m; ~ing account (US) n (current account) compte courant; ~mate n échec et mat m; ~out n (in shop) caisse f; ~point n contrôle m; ~room (US) n (left-luggage office) consigne f; ~up n (MED) examen médical, check-up m

cheek [tʃiːk] n joue f; (impudence) toupet m, culot m; **~bone** n pommette f; **~y** adj effronté(e), culotté(e)

cheep [tʃiːp] vi piauler

cheer [tʃɪəʳ] vt acclamer, applaudir; (gladden) réjouir, réconforter ♦ vi applaudir ♦ n (gen pl) acclamations fpl, applaudissements mpl; bravos mpl, hourras mpl; **~s!** à la vôtre!; **~ up** vi se dérider, reprendre courage ♦ vt remonter le moral à or de, dérider; **~ful** adj gai(e), joyeux(-euse)

cheerio [tʃɪərɪˈəu] (BRIT) excl salut!, au revoir!

cheese [tʃiːz] n fromage m; **~board** n plateau m de fromages

cheetah [ˈtʃiːtə] n guépard m

chef [ʃef] n chef (cuisinier)

chemical [ˈkemɪkl] adj chimique ♦ n produit m chimique

chemist [ˈkemɪst] n (BRIT: pharmacist) pharmacien(ne); (scientist) chimiste m/f; **~ry** n chimie f; **~'s (shop)** n pharmacie f

cheque [tʃek] (BRIT) n chèque m; **~book** n chéquier m, carnet m de chèques; **~ card** n carte f (d'identité) bancaire

chequered [ˈtʃekəd] (US **checkered**) adj (fig) varié(e)

cherish [ˈtʃerɪʃ] vt chérir

cherry [ˈtʃerɪ] n cerise f; (also: **~ tree**) cerisier m

chess [tʃes] n échecs mpl; **~board** n échiquier m

chest [tʃest] n poitrine f; (box) coffre m, caisse f; **~ of drawers** n commode f

chestnut [ˈtʃesnʌt] n châtaigne f; (also: **~ tree**) châtaignier m

chew [tʃuː] vt mâcher; **~ing gum** n chewing-gum m

chic [ʃiːk] adj chic inv, élégant(e)

chick [tʃɪk] n poussin m; (inf) nana f

chicken [ˈtʃɪkɪn] n poulet m; (inf: coward) poule mouillée; **~ out** (inf) vi se dégonfler; **~pox** n varicelle f

chicory [ˈtʃɪkərɪ] n (for coffee) chicorée f; (salad) endive f

chief [tʃiːf] n chef ♦ adj principal(e); **~ executive** (US **chief executive officer**) n directeur(-trice) général(e); **~ly** adv principalement, surtout

chiffon [ˈʃɪfɔn] n mousseline f de soie

chilblain [ˈtʃɪlbleɪn] n engelure f

child [tʃaɪld] (pl **~ren**) n enfant m/f; **~birth** n accouchement m; **~hood** n enfance f; **~ish** adj puéril(e), enfantin(e); **~like** adj d'enfant, innocent(e); **~ minder** (BRIT) n garde f d'enfants; **~ren** [ˈtʃɪldrən] npl of **child**

Chile [ˈtʃɪlɪ] n Chili m

chill [tʃɪl] n (of water) froid m; (of air) fraîcheur f; (MED) refroidissement m, coup m de froid ♦ vt (person) faire frissonner; (CULIN)

mettre au frais, rafraîchir

chil(l)i [ˈtʃɪlɪ] n piment m (rouge)

chilly [ˈtʃɪlɪ] adj froid(e), glacé(e); (sensitive to cold) frileux(-euse); **to feel ~** avoir froid

chime [tʃaɪm] n carillon m ♦ vi carillonner, sonner

chimney [ˈtʃɪmnɪ] n cheminée f; **~ sweep** n ramoneur m

chimpanzee [tʃɪmpænˈziː] n chimpanzé m

chin [tʃɪn] n menton m

China [ˈtʃaɪnə] n Chine f

china [ˈtʃaɪnə] n porcelaine f; (crockery) (vaisselle f en) porcelaine

Chinese [tʃaɪˈniːz] adj chinois(e) ♦ n inv (person) Chinois(e); (LING) chinois m

chink [tʃɪŋk] n (opening) fente f, fissure f; (noise) tintement m

chip [tʃɪp] n (gen pl: CULIN: BRIT) frite f; (: US: potato ~) chip m; (of wood) copeau m; (of glass, stone) éclat m; (also: **microchip**) puce f ♦ vt (cup, plate) ébrécher

chiropodist [kɪˈrɔpədɪst] (BRIT) n pédicure m/f

chirp [tʃəːp] vi pépier, gazouiller

chisel [ˈtʃɪzl] n ciseau m

chit [tʃɪt] n mot m, note f

chitchat [ˈtʃɪttʃæt] n bavardage m

chivalry [ˈʃɪvəlrɪ] n esprit m chevaleresque, galanterie f

chives [tʃaɪvz] npl ciboulette f, civette f

chock-a-block [ˈtʃɔkəˈblɔk], **chock-full** [tʃɔkˈful] adj plein(e) à craquer

chocolate [ˈtʃɔklɪt] n chocolat m

choice [tʃɔɪs] n choix m ♦ adj de choix

choir [ˈkwaɪəʳ] n chœur m, chorale f; **~boy** n jeune choriste m

choke [tʃəuk] vi étouffer ♦ vt étrangler; étouffer ♦ n (AUT) starter m; **street ~d with traffic** rue engorgée or embouteillée

cholesterol [kəˈlestərɔl] n cholestérol m

choose [tʃuːz] (pt **chose**, pp **chosen**) vt choisir; **to ~ to do** décider de faire, juger bon de faire; **choosy** adj: (to be) **choosy** (faire le/la) difficile

chop [tʃɔp] vt (wood) couper (à la hache); (CULIN: also: **~ up**) couper (fin), émincer, hacher (en morceaux) ♦ n (CULIN) côtelette f; **~s** npl (jaws) mâchoires fpl

chopper [ˈtʃɔpəʳ] n (helicopter) hélicoptère m, hélico m

choppy [ˈtʃɔpɪ] adj (sea) un peu agité(e)

chopsticks [ˈtʃɔpstɪks] npl baguettes fpl

chord [kɔːd] n (MUS) accord m

chore [tʃɔːʳ] n travail m de routine; **household ~s** travaux mpl du ménage

chortle [ˈtʃɔːtl] vi glousser

chorus [ˈkɔːrəs] n chœur m; (repeated part of song: also fig) refrain m

chose [tʃəuz] pt of **choose**; **~n** pp of **choose**

chowder ['tʃaudə] n soupe f de poisson
Christ [kraɪst] n Christ m
christen ['krɪsn] vt baptiser
christening n baptême m
Christian ['krɪstɪən] adj, n chrétien(ne); **~ity** [krɪstɪ'ænɪtɪ] n christianisme m; **~ name** n prénom m
Christmas ['krɪsməs] n Noël m or f; **Happy or Merry ~!** joyeux Noël!; **~ card** n carte f de Noël; **~ Day** n le jour de Noël; **~ Eve** n la veille de Noël; la nuit de Noël; **~ tree** n arbre m de Noël
chrome [krəum] n chrome m
chromium ['krəumɪəm] n chrome m
chronic ['krɔnɪk] adj chronique
chronicle ['krɔnɪkl] n chronique f
chronological [krɔnə'lɔdʒɪkl] adj chronologique
chrysanthemum [krɪ'sænθəməm] n chrysanthème m
chubby ['tʃʌbɪ] adj potelé(e), rondelet(te)
chuck [tʃʌk] (inf) vt (throw) lancer, jeter; (BRIT: person) plaquer; (: also: **~ up**: job) lâcher; **~ out** vt flanquer dehors or à la porte; (rubbish) jeter
chuckle ['tʃʌkl] vi glousser
chug [tʃʌg] vi faire teuf-teuf; (also: **~ along**) avancer en faisant teuf-teuf
chum [tʃʌm] n copain (copine)
chunk [tʃʌŋk] n gros morceau
church [tʃəːtʃ] n église f; **~yard** n cimetière m
churn [tʃəːn] n (for butter) baratte f; (also: **milk ~**) (grand) bidon à lait; **~ out** vt débiter
chute [ʃuːt] n glissoire f; (also: **rubbish ~**) vide-ordures m inv
chutney ['tʃʌtnɪ] n condiment m à base de fruits au vinaigre
CIA n abbr (= Central Intelligence Agency) CIA f
CID (BRIT) n abbr (= Criminal Investigation Department) P.J. f
cider ['saɪdə] n cidre m
cigar [sɪ'gɑː] n cigare m
cigarette [sɪgə'rɛt] n cigarette f; **~ case** n étui m à cigarettes; **~ end** n mégot m
Cinderella [sɪndə'rɛlə] n Cendrillon
cinders ['sɪndəz] npl cendres fpl
cine-camera ['sɪnɪ'kæmərə] (BRIT) n caméra f
cinema ['sɪnəmə] n cinéma m
cinnamon ['sɪnəmən] n cannelle f
circle ['səːkl] n cercle m; (in cinema, theatre) balcon m ♦ vi faire or décrire des cercles ♦ vt (move round) faire le tour de, tourner autour de; (surround) entourer, encercler
circuit ['səːkɪt] n circuit m, **~ous** [səː'kjuɪtəs] adj indirect(e), qui fait un détour
circular ['səːkjulə] adj circulaire ♦ n circulaire f

circulate ['səːkjuleɪt] vi circuler ♦ vt faire circuler; **circulation** [səːkju'leɪʃən] n circulation f; (of newspaper) tirage m
circumflex ['səːkəmflɛks] n (also: **~ accent**) accent m circonflexe
circumstances ['səːkəmstənsɪz] npl circonstances fpl; (financial condition) moyens mpl, situation financière
circus ['səːkəs] n cirque m
CIS n abbr (= Commonwealth of Independent States) CEI f
cistern ['sɪstən] n réservoir m (d'eau); (in toilet) réservoir de la chasse d'eau
citizen ['sɪtɪzn] n citoyen(ne); (resident): **the ~s of this town** les habitants de cette ville; **~ship** n citoyenneté f
citrus fruit ['sɪtrəs-] n agrume m
city ['sɪtɪ] n ville f, cité f; **the C~** la Cité de Londres (centre des affaires); **~ technology college** n établissement m d'enseignement technologique
civic ['sɪvɪk] adj civique; (authorities) municipal(e); **~ centre** (BRIT) n centre administratif (municipal)
civil ['sɪvɪl] adj civil(e); (polite) poli(e), courtois(e); (disobedience, defence) passif(-ive); **~ engineer** n ingénieur m des travaux publics; **~ian** [sɪ'vɪlɪən] adj, n civil(e)
civilization [sɪvɪlaɪ'zeɪʃən] n civilisation f
civilized ['sɪvɪlaɪzd] adj civilisé(e); (fig) où règnent les bonnes manières
civil: ~ law n code civil; (study) droit civil; **~ servant** n fonctionnaire m/f; **C~ Service** n fonction publique, administration f; **~ war** n guerre civile
clad [klæd] adj: **~ (in)** habillé(e) (de)
claim [kleɪm] vt revendiquer; (rights, inheritance) demander, prétendre à; (assert) déclarer, prétendre ♦ vi (for insurance) faire une déclaration de sinistre ♦ n revendication f; demande f; prétention f, déclaration f; (right) droit m, titre m; **~ant** n (ADMIN, LAW) requérant(e)
clairvoyant [klɛə'vɔɪənt] n voyant(e), extra-lucide m/f
clam [klæm] n palourde f
clamber ['klæmbə] vi grimper, se hisser
clammy ['klæmɪ] adj humide (et froid(e)), moite
clamour ['klæmə] (US **clamor**) vi: **to ~ for** réclamer à grands cris
clamp [klæmp] n agrafe f, crampon m ♦ vt serrer; (sth to sth) fixer; (wheel) mettre un sabot à; **~ down on** vt fus sévir or prendre des mesures draconiennes contre
clan [klæn] n clan m
clang [klæŋ] vi émettre un bruit or fracas métallique
clap [klæp] vi applaudir; **~ping** n

applaudissements *mpl*

claret ['klærət] *n* (vin *m* de) bordeaux *m* (rouge)

clarinet [klærɪ'nɛt] *n* clarinette *f*

clarity ['klærɪtɪ] *n* clarté *f*

clash [klæʃ] *n* choc *m*; (*fig*) conflit *m* ♦ *vi* se heurter; être *or* entrer en conflit; (*colours*) jurer; (*two events*) tomber en même temps

clasp [klɑːsp] *n* (*of necklace, bag*) fermoir *m*; (*hold, embrace*) étreinte *f* ♦ *vt* serrer, étreindre

class [klɑːs] *n* classe *f* ♦ *vt* classer, classifier

classic ['klæsɪk] *adj* classique ♦ *n* (*author, work*) classique *m*; **~al** *adj* classique

classified ['klæsɪfaɪd] *adj* (*information*) secret(-ète); **~ advertisement** *n* petite annonce

classmate ['klɑːsmeɪt] *n* camarade *m/f* de classe

classroom ['klɑːsrum] *n* (salle *f* de) classe *f*

clatter ['klætər] *n* cliquetis *m* ♦ *vi* cliqueter

clause [klɔːz] *n* clause *f*; (*LING*) proposition *f*

claw [klɔː] *n* griffe *f*; (*of bird of prey*) serre *f*; (*of lobster*) pince *f*

clay [kleɪ] *n* argile *f*

clean [kliːn] *adj* propre; (*clear, smooth*) net(te); (*record, reputation*) sans tache; (*joke, story*) correct(e) ♦ *vt* nettoyer; **~ out** *vt* nettoyer (à fond); **~ up** *vt* nettoyer; (*fig*) remettre de l'ordre dans; **~-cut** *adj* (*person*) net(te), soigné(e); **~er** *n* (*person*) nettoyeur(-euse), femme *f* de ménage; (*product*) détachant *m*; **~er's** *n* (*also:* **dry ~er's**) teinturier *m*; **~ing** *n* nettoyage *m*; **~liness** ['klɛnlɪnɪs] *n* propreté *f*

cleanse [klɛnz] *vt* nettoyer; (*purify*) purifier; **~r** *n* (*for face*) démaquillant *m*

clean-shaven ['kliːn'ʃeɪvn] *adj* rasé(e) de près

cleansing department ['klɛnzɪŋ-] (*BRIT*) *n* service *m* de voirie

clear [klɪər] *adj* clair(e); (*glass, plastic*) transparent(e); (*road, way*) libre, dégagé(e); (*conscience*) net(te) ♦ *vt* (*room*) débarrasser; (*of people*) faire évacuer; (*cheque*) compenser; (*LAW: suspect*) innocenter; (*obstacle*) franchir *or* sauter sans heurter ♦ *vi* (*weather*) s'éclaircir; (*fog*) se dissiper ♦ *adv*: **~ of** à distance de, à l'écart de; **to ~ the table** débarrasser la table, desservir; **~ up** *vt* ranger, mettre en ordre; (*mystery*) éclaircir, résoudre; **~ance** *n* (*removal*) déblaiement *m*; (*permission*) autorisation *f*; **~-cut** *adj* clair(e), nettement défini(e); **~ing** *n* (*in forest*) clairière *f*; **~ing bank** (*BRIT*) *n* banque qui appartient à une chambre de compensation; **~ly** *adv* clairement; (*evidently*) de toute évidence; **~way** (*BRIT*) *n* route *f* à stationnement interdit

clef [klɛf] *n* (*MUS*) clé *f*

cleft [klɛft] *n* (*in rock*) crevasse *f*, fissure *f*

clementine ['klɛməntaɪn] *n* clémentine *f*

clench [klɛntʃ] *vt* serrer

clergy ['klɜːdʒɪ] *n* clergé *m*; **~man** (*irreg*) *n* ecclésiastique *m*

clerical ['klɛrɪkl] *adj* de bureau, d'employé de bureau; (*REL*) clérical(e), du clergé

clerk [klɑːk, (*US*) klɜːrk] *n* employé(e) de bureau; (*US: salesperson*) vendeur(-euse)

clever ['klɛvər] *adj* (*mentally*) intelligent(e); (*deft, crafty*) habile, adroit(e); (*device, arrangement*) ingénieux(-euse), astucieux(-euse)

click [klɪk] *vi* faire un bruit sec *or* un déclic

client ['klaɪənt] *n* client(e)

cliff [klɪf] *n* falaise *f*

climate ['klaɪmɪt] *n* climat *m*

climax ['klaɪmæks] *n* apogée *m*, point culminant; (*sexual*) orgasme *m*

climb [klaɪm] *vi* grimper, monter ♦ *vt* gravir, escalader, monter sur ♦ *n* montée *f*, escalade *f*; **~-down** *n* reculade *f*, dérobade *f*; **~er** *n* (*mountaineer*) grimpeur(-euse), varappeur(-euse); (*plant*) plante grimpante; **~ing** *n* (*mountaineering*) escalade *f*, varappe *f*

clinch [klɪntʃ] *vt* (*deal*) conclure, sceller

cling [klɪŋ] (*pt, pp* **clung**) *vi*: **to ~ (to)** se cramponner (à), s'accrocher (à); (*of clothes*) coller (à)

clinic ['klɪnɪk] *n* centre médical; **~al** *adj* clinique; (*attitude*) froid(e), détaché(e)

clink [klɪŋk] *vi* tinter, cliqueter

clip [klɪp] *n* (*for hair*) barrette *f*; (*also:* **paper ~**) trombone *m* ♦ *vt* (*fasten*) attacher; (*hair, nails*) couper; (*hedge*) tailler; **~pers** *npl* (*for hedge*) sécateur *m*; (*also:* **nail ~pers**) coupe-ongles *m inv*; **~ping** *n* (*from newspaper*) coupure *f* de journal

cloak [kləuk] *n* grande cape ♦ *vt* (*fig*) masquer, cacher; **~room** *n* (*for coats etc*) vestiaire *m*; (*BRIT: WC*) toilettes *fpl*

clock [klɔk] *n* (*large*) horloge *f*; (*small*) pendule *f*; **~ in** (*BRIT*) *vi* pointer (en arrivant); **~ off** (*BRIT*) *vi* pointer (en partant); **~ on** (*BRIT*) *vi* = **clock in**; **~ out** (*BRIT*) *vi* = **clock off**; **~wise** *adv* dans le sens des aiguilles d'une montre; **~work** *n* rouages *mpl*, mécanisme *m*; (*of clock*) mouvement *m* (d'horlogerie) ♦ *adj* mécanique

clog [klɔg] *n* sabot *m* ♦ *vt* boucher ♦ *vi* (*also:* **~ up**) se boucher

cloister ['klɔɪstər] *n* cloître *m*

close¹ [kləus] *adj* (*near*) près, proche; (*contact, link*) étroit(e); (*contest*) très serré(e); (*watch*) étroit(e), strict(e); (*examination*) attentif(-ive), minutieux(-euse); (*weather*) lourd(e), étouffant(e) ♦ *adv* près, à proximité; **~ to** près de, proche de; **~ by** *adj* proche ♦ adv tout(e) près; ~ **at hand** = **close by**; **a ~ friend** un ami intime; **to have a ~ shave** (fig) l'échapper belle

close² [kləuz] vt fermer ♦ vi (shop etc) fermer; (lid, door etc) se fermer; (end) se terminer, se conclure ♦ n (end) conclusion f, fin f; **~ down** vt, vi fermer (définitivement); **~d** adj fermé(e); **~d shop** n organisation f qui n'admet que des travailleurs syndiqués

close-knit ['kləus'nɪt] adj (family, community) très uni(e)

closely ['kləuslɪ] adv (examine, watch) de près

closet ['klɔzɪt] n (cupboard) placard m, réduit m

close-up ['kləusʌp] n gros plan

closure ['kləuʒə'] n fermeture f

clot [klɔt] n (gen: blood ~) caillot m; (inf: person) ballot m ♦ vi (blood) se coaguler; **~ted cream** crème fraîche très épaisse

cloth [klɔθ] n (material) tissu m, étoffe f; (also: **teacloth**) torchon m; lavette f

clothe [kləuð] vt habiller, vêtir; **~s** npl vêtements mpl, habits mpl; **~s brush** n brosse f à habits; **~s line** n corde f (à linge); **~s peg** (US **clothes pin**) n pince f à linge; **clothing** n = **clothes**

cloud [klaud] n nuage m; **~burst** n grosse averse; **~y** adj nuageux(-euse), couvert(e); (liquid) trouble

clout [klaut] vt flanquer une taloche à

clove [kləuv] n (CULIN: spice) clou m de girofle; **~ of garlic** gousse f d'ail

clover ['kləuvə'] n trèfle m

clown [klaun] n clown m ♦ vi (also: ~ **about**, ~ **around**) faire le clown

cloying ['klɔɪɪŋ] adj (taste, smell) écœurant(e)

club [klʌb] n (society, place; also: **golf** ~) club m; (weapon) massue f, matraque f ♦ vt matraquer ♦ vi: **to ~ together** s'associer; **~s** npl (CARDS) trèfle m; **~ class** n (AVIAT) classe f club; **~house** n club m

cluck [klʌk] vi glousser

clue [klu:] n indice m; (in crosswords) définition f; **I haven't a ~** je n'en ai pas la moindre idée

clump [klʌmp] n: **~ of trees** bouquet m d'arbres

clumsy ['klʌmzɪ] adj gauche, maladroit(e)

clung [klʌŋ] pt, pp of **cling**

cluster ['klʌstə'] n (of people) (petit) groupe; (of flowers) grappe f; (of stars) amas m ♦ vi se rassembler

clutch [klʌtʃ] n (grip, grasp) étreinte f, prise f; (AUT) embrayage m ♦ vt (grasp) agripper; (hold tightly) serrer fort; (hold on to) se cramponner à

clutter ['klʌtə'] vt (also: ~ **up**) encombrer

CND n abbr (= Campaign for Nuclear Disarmament) mouvement pour le désarmement nucléaire

Co. abbr = **county; company**

c/o abbr (= care of) c/o, aux bons soins de

coach [kəutʃ] n (bus) autocar m; (horse-drawn) diligence f; (of train) voiture f, wagon m; (SPORT: trainer) entraîneur(-euse); (SCOL: tutor) répétiteur(-trice) ♦ vt entraîner; (student) faire travailler; **~ trip** n excursion f en car

coal [kəul] n charbon m; **~ face** n front m de taille; **~field** n bassin houiller

coalition [kəuə'lɪʃən] n coalition f

coalman ['kəulmən] (irreg) n charbonnier m, marchand m de charbon

coalmine ['kəulmaɪn] n mine f de charbon

coarse [kɔ:s] adj grossier(-ère), rude

coast [kəust] n côte f ♦ vi (car, cycle etc) descendre en roue libre; **~al** adj côtier(-ère); **~guard** n garde-côte m; (service) gendarmerie f maritime; **~line** n côte f, littoral m

coat [kəut] n manteau m; (of animal) pelage m, poil m; (of paint) couche f ♦ vt couvrir; **~ hanger** n cintre m; **~ing** n couche f, revêtement m; **~ of arms** n blason m, armoiries fpl

coax [kəuks] vt persuader par des cajoleries

cobbler ['kɔblə'] n cordonnier m

cobbles ['kɔblz] (also: **~tones**) npl pavés (ronds)

cobweb ['kɔbwɛb] n toile f d'araignée

cocaine [kə'keɪn] n cocaïne f

cock [kɔk] n (rooster) coq m; (male bird) mâle m ♦ vt (gun) armer; **~erel** n jeune coq m

cockle ['kɔkl] n coque f

cockney ['kɔknɪ] n cockney m, habitant des quartiers populaires de l'East End de Londres, ≈ faubourien(ne)

cockpit ['kɔkpɪt] n (in aircraft) poste m de pilotage, cockpit m

cockroach ['kɔkrəutʃ] n cafard m

cocktail ['kɔkteɪl] n cocktail m; (fruit ~ etc) salade f; **~ cabinet** n (meuble-)bar m; **~ party** n cocktail m

cocoa ['kəukəu] n cacao m

coconut ['kəukənʌt] n noix f de coco

COD abbr = **cash on delivery**

cod [kɔd] n morue fraîche, cabillaud m

code [kəud] n code m

cod-liver oil n huile f de foie de morue

coercion [kəu'ə:ʃən] n contrainte f

coffee ['kɔfɪ] n café m; **~ bar** (BRIT) n café m; **~ bean** n grain m de café; **~ break** n pause-café f; **~pot** n cafetière f; **~ table** n (petite) table basse

coffin ['kɔfɪn] n cercueil m

cog [kɔg] n dent f (d'engrenage); (wheel)

roue dentée

cogent ['kəudʒənt] adj puissant(e), convaincant(e)

coil [kɔil] n rouleau m, bobine f; (contraceptive) stérilet m ♦ vt enrouler

coin [kɔin] n pièce f de monnaie ♦ vt (word) inventer; **~age** n monnaie f, système m monétaire; **~ box** (BRIT) n cabine f téléphonique

coincide [kəuin'said] vi coïncider; **~nce** [kəu'insidəns] n coïncidence f

Coke ® [kəuk] n coca m

coke [kəuk] n coke m

colander ['kɔləndə'] n passoire f

cold [kəuld] adj froid(e) ♦ n froid m; (MED) rhume m; **it's ~** il fait froid; **to be** or **feel ~** (person) avoir froid; **to catch ~** prendre or attraper froid; **to catch a ~** attraper un rhume; **in ~ blood** de sang-froid; **~-shoulder** vt se montrer froid(e) envers, snober; **~ sore** n bouton m de fièvre

coleslaw ['kəulslɔ:] n sorte de salade de chou cru

colic ['kɔlik] n colique(s) f(pl)

collapse [kə'læps] vi s'effondrer, s'écrouler ♦ n effondrement m, écroulement m; **collapsible** adj pliant(e); télescopique

collar ['kɔlə'] n (of coat, shirt) col m; (for animal) collier m; **~bone** n clavicule f

collateral [kə'lætərl] n nantissement m

colleague ['kɔli:g] n collègue m/f

collect [kə'lekt] vt rassembler; ramasser; (as a hobby) collectionner; (BRIT: call and pick up) (passer) prendre; (mail) faire la levée de, ramasser; (money owed) encaisser; (donations, subscriptions) recueillir ♦ vi (people) se rassembler; (things) s'amasser; **to call ~** (US: TEL) téléphoner en P.C.V.; **~ion** n collection f; (of mail) levée f; (for money) collecte f, quête f; **~or** n collectionneur m

college ['kɔlidʒ] n collège m

collide [kə'laid] vi entrer en collision

colliery ['kɔliəri] (BRIT) n mine f de charbon, houillère f

collision [kə'liʒən] n collision f

colloquial [kə'ləukwiəl] adj familier(-ère)

colon ['kəulən] n (sign) deux-points m inv; (MED) côlon m

colonel ['kə:nl] n colonel m

colony ['kɔləni] n colonie f

colour ['kʌlə'] (US color) n couleur f ♦ vt (paint) peindre; (dye) teindre; (news) fausser, exagérer ♦ vi (blush) rougir; **~s** npl (of party, club) couleurs fpl; **~ in** vt colorier; **~ bar** n discrimination raciale (dans un établissement); **~-blind** adj daltonien(ne); **~ed** adj (person) de couleur; (illustration) en couleur; **~ film** n (for camera) pellicule f (en) couleur; **~ful** adj coloré(e), vif(-vive); (personality) pittoresque,

haut(e) en couleurs; **~ing** n colorant m; (complexion) teint m; **~ scheme** n combinaison f de(s) couleurs; **~ television** n télévision f (en) couleur

colt [kəult] n poulain m

column ['kɔləm] n colonne f; **~ist** ['kɔləmnist] n chroniqueur(-euse)

coma ['kəumə] n coma m

comb [kəum] n peigne m ♦ vt (hair) peigner; (area) ratisser, passer au peigne fin

combat ['kɔmbæt] n combat m ♦ vt combattre, lutter contre

combination [kɔmbi'neiʃən] n combinaison f

combine [vb kəm'bain, n 'kɔmbain] vt: **to ~ sth with sth** combiner qch avec qch; (one quality with another) joindre or allier qch à qch ♦ vi s'associer; (CHEM) se combiner ♦ n (ECON) trust m; **~ (harvester)** (CHEM) moissonneuse-batteuse(-lieuse) f

come [kʌm] (pt came, pp come) vi venir, arriver; **to ~ to** (decision etc) parvenir or arriver à; **to ~ undone/loose** se défaire/ desserrer; **~ about** vi se produire, arriver; **~ across** vt fus rencontrer par hasard, tomber sur; **~ along** vi = come on; **~ away** vi partir, s'en aller, se détacher; **~ back** vi revenir; **~ by** vt fus (acquire) obtenir, se procurer; **~ down** vi descendre; (prices) baisser; (buildings) s'écrouler, être démoli(e); **~ forward** vi s'avancer, se présenter, s'annoncer; **~ from** vt fus être originaire de, venir de; **~ in** vi entrer; **~ in for** vi (criticism etc) être l'objet de; **~ into** vt fus (money) hériter de; **~ off** vi (button) se détacher; (stain) s'enlever; (attempt) réussir; **~ on** vi (pupil, work, project) faire des progrès, s'avancer; (lights, electricity) s'allumer; (central heating) se mettre en marche; **~ on!** viens!, allons!, allez!; **~ out** vi sortir; (book) paraître; (strike) cesser le travail, se mettre en grève; **~ round** vi (after faint, operation) revenir à soi, reprendre connaissance; **~ to** vi revenir à soi; **~ up** vi monter; **~ up against** vt fus (resistance, difficulties) rencontrer; **~ up with** vt fus: **he came up with an idea** il a eu une idée, il a proposé quelque chose; **~ upon** vt fus tomber sur; **~back** n (THEATRE etc) rentrée f

comedian [kə'mi:diən] n (in music hall etc) comique m; (THEATRE) comédien m

comedy ['kɔmidi] n comédie f

comeuppance [kʌm'ʌpəns] n: **to get one's ~** recevoir ce qu'on mérite

comfort ['kʌmfət] n confort m, bien-être m; (relief) soulagement m, réconfort m ♦ vt consoler, réconforter; **the ~s of home** les commodités fpl de la maison; **~able** adj confortable; (person) à l'aise; (patient) dont

l'état est stationnaire; (walk etc) facile; **~ably**
adv (sit) confortablement; (live) à l'aise;
~ station (US) n toilettes fpl
comic ['kɒmɪk] adj (also: ~al) comique ♦ n
comique m; (BRIT: magazine) illustré m;
~ strip n bande dessinée
coming ['kʌmɪŋ] n arrivée f ♦ adj
prochain(e), à venir; **~(s) and going(s)**
n(pl) va-et-vient m inv
comma ['kɒmə] n virgule f
command [kə'mɑːnd] n ordre m,
commandement m; (MIL: authority)
commandement; (mastery) maîtrise f ♦ vt
(troops) commander; **to ~ sb to do** ordonner
à qn de faire; **~eer** [kɒmən'dɪə] vt
réquisitionner; **~er** n (MIL) commandant m
commando [kə'mɑːndəu] n commando m;
membre m d'un commando
commemorate [kə'meməreɪt] vt
commémorer
commence [kə'mens] vt, vi commencer
commend [kə'mend] vt louer; (recommend)
recommander
commensurate [kə'menʃərɪt] adj: **~ with or
to** en proportion de, proportionné(e) à
comment ['kɒment] n commentaire m ♦ vi:
to ~ (on) faire des remarques (sur); **"no ~"**
"je n'ai rien à dire"; **~ary** ['kɒməntərɪ] n
commentaire m; (SPORT) reportage m (en
direct); **~ator** ['kɒmənteɪtə] n
commentateur m; reporter m
commerce ['kɒmɜːs] n commerce m
commercial [kə'mɜːʃəl] adj commercial(e)
♦ n (TV, RADIO) annonce f publicitaire, spot m
(publicitaire)
commiserate [kə'mɪzəreɪt] vi: **to ~ with sb**
témoigner de la sympathie pour qn
commission [kə'mɪʃən] n (order for work)
commande f; (committee, fee) commission f
♦ vt (work of art) commander, charger un
artiste de l'exécution de; **out of ~** (not
working) hors service; **~aire** [kəmɪʃə'neə]
(BRIT) n (at shop, cinema etc) portier m (en
uniforme); **~er** n (POLICE) préfet m (de
police)
commit [kə'mɪt] vt (act) commettre;
(resources) consacrer; (to sb's care) confier
(à); **to ~ o.s. (to do)** s'engager (à faire); **to
~ suicide** se suicider; **~ment** n engagement
m; (obligation) responsabilité(s) f(pl)
committee [kə'mɪtɪ] n comité m
commodity [kə'mɒdɪtɪ] n produit m,
marchandise f, article m
common ['kɒmən] adj commun(e); (usual)
courant(e) ♦ n terrain communal; **the C~s**
(BRIT) npl la chambre des Communes; **in ~** en
commun; **~er** n roturier(-ière); **~ law** n droit
coutumier; **~ly** adv communément,
généralement; couramment; **C~ Market** n

Marché commun; **~place** adj banal(e),
ordinaire; **~ room** n salle commune;
~ sense n bon sens; **C~wealth** (BRIT) n
Commonwealth m
commotion [kə'məuʃən] n désordre m,
tumulte m
communal ['kɒmjuːnl] adj (life)
communautaire; (for common use)
commun(e)
commune [n 'kɒmjuːn, vb kə'mjuːn] n
(group) communauté f ♦ vi: **to ~ with**
communier avec
communicate [kə'mjuːnɪkeɪt] vt, vi
communiquer; **communication**
[kəmjuːnɪ'keɪʃən] n communication f;
communication cord (BRIT) n sonnette f
d'alarme
communion [kə'mjuːnɪən] n (also: Holy C~)
communion f
communism ['kɒmjunɪzəm] n communisme
m; **communist** adj communiste ♦ n
communiste m/f
community [kə'mjuːnɪtɪ] n communauté f;
~ centre n centre m de loisirs; **~ chest** (US)
n fonds commun
commutation ticket [kɒmjuː'teɪʃən-] (US)
n carte f d'abonnement
commute [kə'mjuːt] vi faire un trajet
journalier pour se rendre à son travail ♦ vt
(LAW) commuer; **~r** n banlieusard(e) (qui fait
un trajet journalier pour se rendre à son travail)
compact [adj kəm'pækt, n 'kɒmpækt] adj
compact(e) ♦ n (also: powder ~) poudrier m;
~ disc n disque compact; **~ disc player** n
lecteur m de disque compact
companion [kəm'pænjən] n compagnon
(compagne); **~ship** n camaraderie f
company ['kʌmpənɪ] n compagnie f; **to keep
sb ~** tenir compagnie à qn; **~ secretary**
(BRIT) n (COMM) secrétaire général (d'une
société)
comparative [kəm'pærətɪv] adj (study)
comparatif(-ive); (relative) relatif(-ive); **~ly**
adv (relatively) relativement
compare [kəm'peə] vt: **to ~ sth/sb with/to**
comparer qch/qn avec or et/à ♦ vi: **to
~ (with)** se comparer (à); être comparable
(à); **comparison** [kəm'pærɪsn] n
comparaison f
compartment [kəm'pɑːtmənt] n
compartiment m
compass ['kʌmpəs] n boussole f; **~es** npl
(GEOM: also: pair of ~es) compas m
compassion [kəm'pæʃən] n compassion f;
~ate adj compatissant(e)
compatible [kəm'pætɪbl] adj compatible
compel [kəm'pel] vt contraindre, obliger
compensate ['kɒmpenseɪt] vt indemniser,
dédommager ♦ vi: **to ~ for** compenser;

compensation [kɔmpən'seɪʃən] n compensation f; (money) dédommagement m, indemnité f

compère ['kɔmpeər] n (TV) animateur(-trice)

compete [kəm'piːt] vi: **to ~ (with)** rivaliser (avec), faire concurrence (à)

competent ['kɔmpɪtənt] adj compétent(e), capable

competition [kɔmpɪ'tɪʃən] n (contest) compétition f, concours m; (ECON) concurrence f

competitive [kəm'petɪtɪv] adj (ECON) concurrentiel(le); (sport) de compétition; (person) qui a l'esprit de compétition;

competitor n concurrent(e)

complacency [kəm'pleɪsnsɪ] n suffisance f, vaine complaisance

complain [kəm'pleɪn] vi: **to ~ (about)** se plaindre (de); (in shop etc) réclamer (au sujet de); **to ~ of** (pain) se plaindre de; **~t** n plainte f; réclamation f; (MED) affection f

complement [n 'kɔmplɪmənt, vb 'kɔmplɪment] n complément m; (especially of ship's crew etc) effectif complet ♦ vt (enhance) compléter; **~ary** [kɔmplɪ'mentərɪ] adj complémentaire

complete [kəm'pliːt] adj complet(-ète) ♦ vt achever, parachever; (set, group) compléter; (a form) remplir; **~ly** adv complètement; **completion** n achèvement m; (of contract) exécution f

complex ['kɔmpleks] adj complexe ♦ n complexe m

complexion [kəm'plekʃən] n (of face) teint m

compliance [kəm'plaɪəns] n (submission) docilité f; (agreement): **~ with** le fait de se conformer à; **in ~ with** en accord avec

complicate ['kɔmplɪkeɪt] vt compliquer; **~d** adj compliqué(e); **complication** [kɔmplɪ'keɪʃən] n complication f

compliment [n 'kɔmplɪmənt, vb 'kɔmplɪment] n compliment m ♦ vt complimenter; **~s** npl (respects) compliments mpl, hommages mpl; **to pay sb a ~** faire or adresser un compliment à qn; **~ary** [kɔmplɪ'mentərɪ] adj flatteur(-euse); (free) (offert(e)) à titre gracieux; **~ary ticket** n billet m de faveur

comply [kəm'plaɪ] vi: **to ~ with** se soumettre à, se conformer à

component [kəm'pəunənt] n composant m, élément m

compose [kəm'pəuz] vt composer; (form): **to be ~d of** se composer de; **to ~ o.s.** se calmer, se maîtriser; prendre une contenance; **~d** adj calme, posé(e); **~r** n (MUS) compositeur m; **composition** [kɔmpə'zɪʃən] n composition f; **composure** [kəm'pəuʒər] n

calme m, maîtrise f de soi

compound ['kɔmpaund] n composé m; (enclosure) enclos m, enceinte f; **~ fracture** n fracture compliquée; **~ interest** n intérêt composé

comprehend [kɔmprɪ'hend] vt comprendre; **comprehension** n compréhension f

comprehensive [kɔmprɪ'hensɪv] adj (très) complet(-ète); **~ policy** n (INSURANCE) assurance f tous risques; **~ school** n (BRIT) école secondaire polyvalente; ≈ C.E.S. m

compress [vb kəm'pres, n 'kɔmpres] vt comprimer; (text, information) condenser ♦ n (MED) compresse f

comprise [kəm'praɪz] vt (also: **be ~d of**) comprendre; (constitute) constituer, représenter

compromise ['kɔmprəmaɪz] n compromis m ♦ vt compromettre ♦ vi transiger, accepter un compromis

compulsion [kəm'pʌlʃən] n contrainte f, force f

compulsive [kəm'pʌlsɪv] adj (PSYCH) compulsif(-ive); (book, film etc) captivant(e)

compulsory [kəm'pʌlsərɪ] adj obligatoire

computer [kəm'pjuːtər] n ordinateur m; **~ game** n jeu m vidéo; **~-generated** adj de synthèse; **~ize** vt informatiser; **~ programmer** n programmeur(-euse); **~ programming** n programmation f; **~ science** n informatique f; **computing** n = computer science

comrade ['kɔmrɪd] n camarade m/f

con [kɔn] vt duper; (cheat) escroquer ♦ n escroquerie f

conceal [kən'siːl] vt cacher, dissimuler

conceit [kən'siːt] n vanité f, suffisance f, prétention f; **~ed** adj vaniteux(-euse), suffisant(e)

conceive [kən'siːv] vt, vi concevoir

concentrate ['kɔnsəntreɪt] vi se concentrer ♦ vt concentrer; **concentration** n concentration f; **concentration camp** n camp m de concentration

concept ['kɔnsept] n concept m

concern [kən'səːn] n affaire f; (COMM) entreprise f, firme f; (anxiety) inquiétude f, souci m ♦ vt concerner; **to be ~ed (about)** s'inquiéter (de), être inquiet(-ète) (au sujet de); **~ing** prep en ce qui concerne, à propos de

concert ['kɔnsət] n concert m; **~ed** [kən'səːtɪd] adj concerté(e); **~ hall** n salle f de concert

concerto [kən'tʃəːtəu] n concerto m

concession [kən'seʃən] n concession f; **tax ~** dégrèvement fiscal

conclude [kən'kluːd] vt conclure; **conclusion** [kən'kluːʒən] n conclusion f;

conclusive [kən'kluːsɪv] adj concluant(e), définitif(-ive)

concoct [kən'kɔkt] vt confectionner, composer; (fig) inventer; **~ion** n mélange m

concourse ['kɔŋkɔːs] n (hall) hall m, salle f des pas perdus

concrete ['kɔŋkriːt] n béton m ♦ adj concret(-ète); (floor etc) en béton

concur [kən'kəːr] vi (agree) être d'accord

concurrently [kən'kʌrntlɪ] adv simultanément

concussion [kən'kʌʃən] n (MED) commotion (cérébrale)

condemn [kən'dem] vt condamner

condensation [kɔnden'seɪʃən] n condensation f

condense [kən'dens] vi se condenser ♦ vt condenser; **~d milk** n lait concentré (sucré)

condition [kən'dɪʃən] n condition f; (MED) état m ♦ vt déterminer, conditionner; **on ~ that** à condition que +sub, à condition de; **~al** adj conditionnel(le); **~er** n (for hair) baume après shampooing m; (for fabrics) assouplissant m

condolences [kən'dəulənsɪz] npl condoléances fpl

condom ['kɔndəm] n préservatif m

condominium [kɔndə'mɪnɪəm] n (US) (building) immeuble m (en copropriété)

condone [kən'dəun] vt fermer les yeux sur, approuver (tacitement)

conducive [kən'djuːsɪv] adj: **~ to** favorable à, qui contribue à

conduct [n 'kɔndʌkt, vb kən'dʌkt] n conduite f ♦ vt conduire; (MUS) diriger; **to ~ o.s.** se conduire, se comporter, **~ed tour** n voyage organisé; (of building) visite guidée; **~or** n (of orchestra) chef m d'orchestre; (on bus) receveur m; (US: on train) chef m de train; (ÉLEC) conducteur m; **~ress** n (on bus) receveuse f

cone [kəun] n cône m; (for ice-cream) cornet m; (BOT) pomme f de pin, cône

confectioner [kən'fekʃənər] n confiseur(-euse); **~'s (shop)** n confiserie f; **~y** n confiserie f

confer [kən'fəːr] vt: **to ~ sth on** conférer qch à ♦ vi conférer, s'entretenir

conference ['kɔnfərəns] n conférence f

confess [kən'fes] vt confesser, avouer ♦ vi se confesser; **~ion** n confession f

confetti [kən'fetɪ] n confettis mpl

confide [kən'faɪd] vi: **to ~ in** se confier à

confidence ['kɔnfɪdns] n confiance f; (also: **self-~**) assurance f, confiance en soi; (secret) confidence f; **in ~** (speak, write) en confidence, confidentiellement; **~ trick** n escroquerie f; **confident** adj sûr(e), assuré(e); **confidential** [kɔnfɪ'denʃəl] adj confidentiel(le)

confine [kən'faɪn] vt limiter, borner; (shut up) confiner, enfermer; **~d** adj (space) restreint(e), réduit(e); **~ment** n emprisonnement m, détention f; **~s** ['kɔnfaɪnz] npl confins mpl, bornes fpl

confirm [kən'fəːm] vt confirmer; (appointment) ratifier; **~ation** [kɔnfə'meɪʃən] n confirmation f; **~ed** adj invétéré(e), incorrigible

confiscate ['kɔnfɪskeɪt] vt confisquer

conflict [n 'kɔnflɪkt, vb kən'flɪkt] n conflit m, lutte f ♦ vi être ou entrer en conflit; (opinions) s'opposer, se heurter; **~ing** adj contradictoire

conform [kən'fɔːm] vi: **to ~ (to)** se conformer (à)

confound [kən'faund] vt confondre

confront [kən'frʌnt] vt confronter, mettre en présence; (enemy, danger) affronter, faire face à; **~ation** [kɔnfrən'teɪʃən] n confrontation f

confuse [kən'fjuːz] vt (person) troubler; (situation) embrouiller; (one thing with another) confondre; **~d** adj (person) dérouté(e), désorienté(e); **confusing** adj peu clair(e), déroutant(e); **confusion** [kən'fjuːʒən] n confusion f

congeal [kən'dʒiːl] vi (blood) se coaguler; (oil etc) se figer

congenial [kən'dʒiːnɪəl] adj sympathique, agréable

congested [kən'dʒestɪd] adj (MED) congestionné(e); (area) surpeuplé(e); (road) bloqué(e); **congestion** n congestion f; (fig) encombrement m

congratulate [kən'grætjuleɪt] vt: **to ~ sb (on)** féliciter qn (de); **congratulations** [kəngrætju'leɪʃənz] npl félicitations fpl

congregate ['kɔngrɪgeɪt] vi se rassembler, se réunir; **congregation** [kɔngrɪ'geɪʃən] n assemblée f (des fidèles)

congress ['kɔngres] n congrès m; **~man** (irreg) (US) n membre m du Congrès

conjunction [kən'dʒʌŋkʃən] n (LING) conjonction f

conjunctivitis [kəndʒʌŋktɪ'vaɪtɪs] n conjonctivite f

conjure ['kʌndʒər] vi faire des tours de passe-passe; **~ up** vt (ghost, spirit) faire apparaître; (memories) évoquer; **~r** n prestidigitateur m, illusionniste m/f

con man (irreg) n escroc m

connect [kə'nekt] vt joindre, relier; (ELEC) connecter; (TEL: caller) mettre en connection (with avec); (: new subscriber) brancher; (fig) établir un rapport entre, faire un rapprochement entre ♦ vi (train): **to ~ with** assurer la correspondance avec; **to be ~ed with** (fig) avoir un rapport avec, avoir des rapports avec, être en relation avec; **~ion** *n* relation *f*, lien *m*; (*ELEC*) connexion *f*; (*train, plane etc*) correspondance *f*; (*TEL*) branchement *m*, communication *f*

connive [kə'naɪv] *vi*: **to ~ at** se faire le complice de

conquer ['kɒŋkəʳ] *vt* conquérir; (*feelings*) vaincre, surmonter; **conquest** ['kɒŋkwest] *n* conquête *f*

cons [kɒnz] *npl see* **convenience; pro**

conscience ['kɒnʃəns] *n* conscience *f*; **conscientious** [kɒnʃɪ'enʃəs] *adj* consciencieux(-euse)

conscious ['kɒnʃəs] *adj* conscient(e); **~ness** *n* conscience *f*; (*MED*) connaissance *f*

conscript ['kɒnskrɪpt] *n* conscrit *m*

consent [kən'sent] *n* consentement *m* ♦ *vi*: **to ~ (to)** consentir (à)

consequence ['kɒnsɪkwəns] *n* conséquence *f*, suites *fpl*; (*significance*) importance *f*; **consequently** *adv* par conséquent, donc

conservation [kɒnsə'veɪʃən] *n* préservation *f*, protection *f*

conservative [kən'sə:vətɪv] *adj* conservateur(-trice); **at a ~ estimate** au bas mot; **C~** (*BRIT*) *adj*, *n* (*POL*) conservateur(-trice)

conservatory [kən'sə:vətrɪ] *n* (*greenhouse*) serre *f*

conserve [kən'sə:v] *vt* conserver, préserver; (*supplies, energy*) économiser ♦ *n* confiture *f*

consider [kən'sɪdəʳ] *vt* (*study*) considérer, réfléchir à; (*take into account*) penser à, prendre en considération; (*regard, judge*) considérer, estimer; **to ~ doing sth** envisager de faire qch; **~able** *adj* considérable; **~ably** *adv* nettement; **~ate** *adj* prévenant(e), plein(e) d'égards; **~ation** [kənsɪdə'reɪʃən] *n* considération *f*; **~ing** *prep* étant donné

consign [kən'saɪn] *vt* expédier; (*to sb's care*) confier; (*fig*) livrer; **~ment** *n* arrivage *m*, envoi *m*

consist [kən'sɪst] *vi*: **to ~ of** consister en, se composer de

consistency [kən'sɪstənsɪ] *n* consistance *f*; (*fig*) cohérence *f*

consistent [kən'sɪstənt] *adj* logique, cohérent(e)

consolation [kɒnsə'leɪʃən] *n* consolation *f*

console¹ [kən'səul] *vt* consoler

console² ['kɒnsəul] *n* (*COMPUT*) console *f*

consonant ['kɒnsənənt] *n* consonne *f*

conspicuous [kən'spɪkjuəs] *adj* voyant(e), qui attire l'attention

conspiracy [kən'spɪrəsɪ] *n* conspiration *f*, complot *m*

constable ['kʌnstəbl] (*BRIT*) *n* ≈ agent *m* de police, gendarme *m*; **chief ~** ≈ préfet *m* de police; **constabulary** [kən'stæbjulərɪ] (*BRIT*)

n ≈ police *f*, gendarmerie *f*

constant ['kɒnstənt] *adj* constant(e); incessant(e); **~ly** *adv* constamment, sans cesse

constipated ['kɒnstɪpeɪtɪd] *adj* constipé(e); **constipation** [kɒnstɪ'peɪʃən] *n* constipation *f*

constituency [kən'stɪtjuənsɪ] *n* circonscription électorale

constituent [kən'stɪtjuənt] *n* (*POL*) électeur(-trice); (*part*) élément constitutif, composant *m*

constitution [kɒnstɪ'tju:ʃən] *n* constitution *f*; **~al** *adj* constitutionnel(le)

constraint [kən'streɪnt] *n* contrainte *f*

construct [kən'strʌkt] *vt* construire; **~ion** *n* construction *f*; **~ive** *adj* constructif(-ive); **~ive dismissal** démission forcée

consul ['kɒnsl] *n* consul *m*; **~ate** ['kɒnsjulɪt] *n* consulat *m*

consult [kən'sʌlt] *vt* consulter; **~ant** *n* (*MED*) médecin consultant; (*other specialist*) consultant *m*, (expert-)conseil *m*; **~ing room** (*BRIT*) *n* cabinet *m* de consultation

consume [kən'sju:m] *vt* consommer; **~r** *n* consommateur(-trice); **~r goods** *npl* biens *mpl* de consommation; **~r society** *n* société *f* de consommation

consummate ['kɒnsʌmeɪt] *vt* consommer

consumption [kən'sʌmpʃən] *n* consommation *f*

cont. *abbr* (= *continued*) suite

contact ['kɒntækt] *n* contact *m*; (*person*) connaissance *f*, relation *f* ♦ *vt* contacter, se mettre en contact *or* en rapport avec; **~ lenses** *npl* verres *mpl* de contact, lentilles *fpl*

contagious [kən'teɪdʒəs] *adj* contagieux(-euse)

contain [kən'teɪn] *vt* contenir; **to ~ o.s.** se contenir, se maîtriser; **~er** *n* récipient *m*; (*for shipping etc*) container *m*

contaminate [kən'tæmɪneɪt] *vt* contaminer

cont'd *abbr* (= *continued*) suite

contemplate ['kɒntəmpleɪt] *vt* contempler; (*consider*) envisager

contemporary [kən'tempərərɪ] *adj* contemporain(e); (*design, wallpaper*) moderne ♦ *n* contemporain(e)

contempt [kən'tempt] *n* mépris *m*, dédain *m*; **~ of court** (*LAW*) outrage *m* à l'autorité de la justice; **~uous** [kən'temptjuəs] *adj* dédaigneux(-euse), méprisant(e)

contend [kən'tend] *vt*: **to ~ that** soutenir *or* prétendre que ♦ *vi*: **to ~ with** (*compete*) rivaliser avec; (*struggle*) lutter avec; **~er** *n* concurrent(e); (*POL*) candidat(e)

content [*adj, vb* kən'tent, *n* 'kɒntent] *adj* content(e), satisfait(e) ♦ *vt* contenter, satisfaire ♦ *n* contenu *m*; (*of fat, moisture*) teneur f; **~s** npl (of container etc) contenu m; **(table of) ~s** table f des matières; **~ed** adj content(e), satisfait(e)

contention [kən'tenʃən] n dispute f, contestation f; (argument) assertion f, affirmation f

contest [n 'kɔntest, vb kən'test] n combat m, lutte f; (competition) concours m ♦ vt (decision, statement) contester, discuter; (compete for) disputer; **~ant** [kən'testənt] n concurrent(e); (in fight) adversaire m/f

context ['kɔntekst] n contexte m

continent ['kɔntinənt] n continent m; **the C~** (BRIT) l'Europe continentale; **~al** [kɔntɪ'nentl] adj continental(e); **~al breakfast** n petit déjeuner m à la française; **~al quilt** (BRIT) n couette f

contingency [kən'tɪndʒənsɪ] n éventualité f, événement imprévu

continual [kən'tɪnjuəl] adj continuel(le)

continuation [kəntɪnju'eɪʃən] n continuation f; (after interruption) reprise f, (of story) suite f

continue [kən'tɪnju:] vi, vt continuer; (after interruption) reprendre, poursuivre; **continuity** [kɔntɪ'nju:ɪtɪ] n continuité f; (TV etc) enchaînement m; **continuous** [kən'tɪnjuəs] adj continu(e); (LING) progressif(-ive)

contort [kən'tɔ:t] vt tordre, crisper

contour ['kɔntuə'] n contour m, profil m; (on map: also: **~ line**) courbe f de niveau

contraband ['kɔntrəbænd] n contrebande f

contraceptive [kɔntrə'septɪv] adj contraceptif(-ive), anticonceptionnel(le) ♦ n contraceptif m

contract [n 'kɔntrækt, vb kən'trækt] n contrat m ♦ vi (become smaller) se contracter, se resserrer; (COMM): **to ~ to do sth** s'engager (par contrat) à faire qch; **~ion** [kən'trækʃən] n contraction f; **~or** [kən'træktə'] n entrepreneur m

contradict [kɔntrə'dɪkt] vt contredire

contraflow ['kɔntrəfləu] n (AUT): **~ lane** voie f à contresens; **there's a ~ system in operation on ...** une voie a été mise en sens inverse sur ...

contraption [kən'træpʃən] (pej) n machin m, truc m

contrary¹ ['kɔntrərɪ] adj contraire, opposé(e) ♦ n contraire m; **on the ~** au contraire; **unless you hear to the ~** sauf avis contraire

contrary² [kən'treərɪ] adj (perverse) contrariant(e), entêté(e)

contrast [n 'kɔntrɑ:st, vb kən'trɑ:st] n contraste m ♦ vt mettre en contraste, contraster; **in ~ to** or **with** contrairement à

contravene [kɔntrə'vi:n] vt enfreindre, violer, contrevenir à

contribute [kən'trɪbju:t] vi contribuer ♦ vt: **to ~ £10/an article to** donner 10 livres/un article à; **to ~ to** contribuer à; (newspaper) collaborer à; **contribution** [kɔntrɪ'bju:ʃən] n contribution f; **contributor** [kən'trɪbjutə'] n (to newspaper) collaborateur(-trice)

contrive [kən'traɪv] vi: **to ~ to do** s'arranger pour faire, trouver le moyen de faire

control [kən'trəul] vt maîtriser, commander; (check) contrôler ♦ n contrôle m, autorité f; maîtrise f; **~s** npl (of machine etc) commandes fpl; (on radio, TV) boutons mpl de réglage; **~led substance** narcotique m; **everything is under ~** tout va bien, j'ai (or il a etc) la situation en main; **to be in ~ of** être maître de, maîtriser; **the car went out of ~** j'ai (or il a etc) perdu le contrôle du véhicule; **~ panel** n tableau m de commande; **~ room** n salle f des commandes; **~ tower** n (AVIAT) tour f de contrôle

controversial [kɔntrə'və:ʃl] adj (topic) discutable, controversé(e), (person) qui fait beaucoup parler de lui; **controversy** ['kɔntrəvə:sɪ] n controverse f, polémique f

convalesce [kɔnvə'les] vi relever de maladie, se remettre (d'une maladie)

convector [kən'vektə'] n (heater) radiateur m (à convexion)

convene [kən'vi:n] vt convoquer, assembler ♦ vi se réunir, s'assembler

convenience [kən'vi:nɪəns] n commodité f; **at your ~** quand or comme cela vous convient; **all modern ~s**, (BRIT) **all mod cons** avec tout le confort moderne, tout confort

convenient [kən'vi:nɪənt] adj commode

convent ['kɔnvənt] n couvent m; **~ school** n couvent m

convention [kən'venʃən] n convention f; **~al** adj conventionnel(le)

conversant [kən'və:snt] adj: **to be ~ with** s'y connaître en; être au courant de

conversation [kɔnvə'seɪʃən] n conversation f

converse [n 'kɔnvə:s, vb kən'və:s] n contraire m, inverse m ♦ vi s'entretenir; **~ly** [kɔn'və:slɪ] adv inversement, réciproquement

convert [vb kən'və:t, n 'kɔnvə:t] vt (REL, COMM) convertir; (alter) transformer; (house) aménager ♦ n converti(e); **~ible** [kən'və:təbl] n (voiture f) décapotable f

convey [kən'veɪ] vt transporter; (thanks) transmettre; (idea) communiquer; **~or belt** n convoyeur m, tapis roulant

convict [vb kən'vɪkt, n 'kɔnvɪkt] vt déclarer (or reconnaître) coupable ♦ n forçat m, détenu m; **~ion** n (LAW) condamnation f; (belief) conviction f

convince [kən'vɪns] vt convaincre, persuader; **convincing** adj persuasif(-ive), convaincant(e)

convoluted [ˈkɒnvəluːtɪd] adj (argument) compliqué(e)

convulse [kənˈvʌls] vt: **to be ~d with laughter/pain** se tordre de rire/douleur

cook [kuk] vt (faire) cuire ♦ vi cuire; (person) faire la cuisine ♦ n cuisinier(-ière); **~book** n livre m de cuisine; **~er** n cuisinière f; **~ery** n cuisine f; **~ery book** (BRIT) n = **cookbook**; **~ie** (US) n biscuit m, petit gâteau sec; **~ing** n cuisine f

cool [kuːl] adj frais (fraîche) m; (calm, unemotional) calme; (unfriendly) froid(e) ♦ vt, vi rafraîchir, refroidir

coop [kuːp] n poulailler m; (for rabbits) clapier m ♦ vt: **to ~ up** (fig) cloîtrer, enfermer

cooperate [kəuˈɒpəreɪt] vi coopérer, collaborer; **cooperation** [kəuɒpəˈreɪʃən] n coopération f, collaboration f; **cooperative** [kəuˈɒpərətɪv] adj coopératif(-ive) ♦ n coopérative f

coordinate [vb kəuˈɔːdɪneɪt, n kəuˈɔːdɪnət] vt (efforts) coordonner ♦ n (MATH) coordonnée f; **~s** npl (clothes) ensemble m, coordonnés mpl

co-ownership [kəuˈəunəʃɪp] n co-propriété f

cop [kɒp] (inf) n flic m

cope [kəup] vi: **to ~ with** faire face à; (solve) venir à bout de

copper [ˈkɒpəʳ] n cuivre m; (BRIT: inf: policeman) flic m; **~s** npl (coins) petite monnaie

copy [ˈkɒpɪ] n copie f; (of book etc) exemplaire m ♦ vt copier; **~right** n droit m d'auteur, copyright m

coral [ˈkɒrəl] n corail m

cord [kɔːd] n corde f; (fabric) velours côtelé; (ELEC) cordon m, fil m

cordial [ˈkɔːdɪəl] adj cordial(e), chaleureux(-euse) ♦ n cordial m

cordon [ˈkɔːdn] n cordon m; **~ off** vt boucler (par cordon de police)

corduroy [ˈkɔːdərɔɪ] n velours côtelé

core [kɔːʳ] n noyau m; (of fruit) trognon m, cœur m; (of building, problem) cœur ♦ vt enlever le trognon or le cœur de

cork [kɔːk] n liège m; (of bottle) bouchon m; **~screw** n tire-bouchon m

corn [kɔːn] n (BRIT: wheat) blé m; (US: maize) maïs m; (on foot) cor m; **~ on the cob** (CULIN) épi m de maïs; **~ed beef** n corned-beef m

corner [ˈkɔːnəʳ] n coin m; (AUT) tournant m, virage m; (FOOTBALL: also: ~ **kick**) corner m ♦ vt acculer, mettre au pied du mur; coincer; (COMM: market) accaparer ♦ vi prendre un virage; **~stone** n pierre f angulaire

cornet [ˈkɔːnɪt] n (MUS) cornet m à pistons; (BRIT: of ice-cream) cornet (de glace)

cornflakes [ˈkɔːnfleɪks] npl corn-flakes mpl

cornflour [ˈkɔːnflauəʳ] (BRIT), **cornstarch** [ˈkɔːnstɑːtʃ] (US) n farine f de maïs, maïzena f ®

Cornwall [ˈkɔːnwəl] n Cornouailles f

corny [ˈkɔːnɪ] (inf) adj rebattu(e)

coronary [ˈkɒrənərɪ] n (also: ~ **thrombosis**) infarctus m (du myocarde), thrombose f coronarienne

coronation [kɒrəˈneɪʃən] n couronnement m

coroner [ˈkɒrənəʳ] n officiel chargé de déterminer les causes d'un décès

corporal [ˈkɔːpərl] n caporal m, brigadier m ♦ adj: ~ **punishment** châtiment corporel

corporate [ˈkɔːpərɪt] adj en commun, collectif(-ive); (COMM) de l'entreprise

corporation [kɔːpəˈreɪʃən] n (of town) municipalité f, conseil municipal; (COMM) société f

corps [kɔːʳ] (pl ~) n corps m

corpse [kɔːps] n cadavre m

correct [kəˈrekt] adj (accurate) correct(e), exact(e); (proper) correct, convenable ♦ vt corriger; **~ion** n correction f

correspond [kɒrɪsˈpɒnd] vi correspondre; **~ence** n correspondance f; **~ence course** n cours m par correspondance; **~ent** n correspondant(e)

corridor [ˈkɒrɪdɔːʳ] n couloir m, corridor m

corrode [kəˈrəud] vt corroder, ronger ♦ vi se corroder

corrugated [ˈkɒrəgeɪtɪd] adj plissé(e); ondulé(e); ~ **iron** n tôle ondulée

corrupt [kəˈrʌpt] adj corrompu(e) ♦ vt corrompre; **~ion** n corruption f

Corsica [ˈkɔːsɪkə] n Corse f

cosmetic [kɒzˈmetɪk] n produit m de beauté, cosmétique m

cost [kɒst] (pt, pp cost) n coût m ♦ vi coûter ♦ vt établir or calculer le prix de revient de; **~s** npl (COMM) frais mpl; (LAW) dépens mpl; **it ~s £5/too much** cela coûte cinq livres/c'est trop cher; **at all ~s** coûte que coûte, à tout prix

co-star [ˈkəustɑːʳ] n partenaire m/f

cost: ~-effective adj rentable; **~ly** adj coûteux(-euse); **~-of-living** adj: **~-of-living allowance** indemnité f de vie chère; **~-of-living index** index m du coût de la vie; ~ **price** (BRIT) n prix coûtant or de revient

costume [ˈkɒstjuːm] n costume m; (lady's suit) tailleur m; (BRIT: also: **swimming ~**) maillot m (de bain); ~ **jewellery** n bijoux mpl fantaisie

cosy [ˈkəuzɪ] (US **cozy**) adj douillet(te); (person) à l'aise, au chaud

cot [kɒt] n (BRIT: child's) lit m d'enfant, petit lit; (US: campbed) lit de camp

cottage [ˈkɒtɪdʒ] n petite maison (à la campagne), cottage m; ~ **cheese** n fromage blanc (*maigre*)

cotton ['kɔtn] n coton m; ~ **on** (*inf*) vi: to ~ **on to** piger; ~ **candy** (*US*) n barbe f à papa; ~ **wool** (*BRIT*) n ouate f, coton m hydrophile

couch [kautʃ] n canapé m; divan m

couchette [kuːˈʃet] n couchette f

cough [kɔf] vi tousser ♦ n toux f; ~ **sweet** n pastille f pour or contre la toux

could [kud] pt of **can²**; **~n't** = **could not**

council ['kaunsl] n conseil m; **city** or **town** ~ conseil municipal; ~ **estate** (*BRIT*) n (zone f de) logements loués à/par la municipalité; ~ **house** (*BRIT*) n maison f (à loyer modéré) louée par la municipalité; **~lor** n conseiller(-ère)

counsel ['kaunsl] n (*lawyer*) avocat(e); (*advice*) conseil m, consultation f; **~lor** n conseiller(-ère); (*US: lawyer*) avocat(e)

count [kaunt] vt, vi compter ♦ n compte m; (*nobleman*) comte m; ~ **on** vt fus compter sur; **~down** n compte m à rebours

countenance ['kauntinəns] n expression f ♦ vt approuver

counter ['kauntə'] n comptoir m; (*in post office, bank*) guichet m; (*in game*) jeton m ♦ vt aller à l'encontre de, opposer ♦ adv: ~ **to** contrairement à; **~act** vt neutraliser, contrebalancer; **~feit** n faux m, contrefaçon f ♦ vt contrefaire ♦ adj faux (fausse); **~foil** n talon m, souche f; **~part** n (*of person etc*) homologue m/f

countess ['kauntis] n comtesse f

countless ['kauntlis] adj innombrable

country ['kʌntri] n pays m; (*native land*) patrie f; (*as opposed to town*) campagne f; (*region*) région f, pays; ~ **dancing** (*BRIT*) n danse f folklorique; ~ **house** n manoir m, (petit) château; **~man** (*irreg*) n (*compatriot*) compatriote m; (*country dweller*) habitant m de la campagne, campagnard m; **~side** n campagne f

county ['kaunti] n comté m

coup [kuː] (pl **~s**) n beau coup; (*also*: ~ **d'état**) coup d'État

couple ['kʌpl] n couple m; **a ~ of** deux; (*a few*) quelques

coupon ['kuːpɔn] n coupon m, bon-prime m, bon-réclame f; (*COMM*) coupon

courage ['kʌridʒ] n courage m

courier ['kuriə'] n messager m, courrier m; (*for tourists*) accompagnateur(-trice), guide m/f

course [kɔːs] n cours m; (*of ship*) route f; (*for golf*) terrain m; (*part of meal*) plat m; **first ~** entrée f, **of ~** bien sûr; **~ of action** parti m, ligne f de conduite; **~ of treatment** (*MED*) traitement m

court [kɔːt] n cour f; (*LAW*) cour, tribunal m; (*TENNIS*) court m ♦ vt (*woman*) courtiser, faire la cour à; **to take to ~** actionner or poursuivre en justice

courteous ['kɔːtiəs] adj courtois(e), poli(e); **courtesy** ['kɔːtəsi] n courtoisie f, politesse f; **(by) courtesy of** avec l'aimable autorisation de; **courtesy bus** or **coach** n navette gratuite

court: **~house** (*US*) n palais m de justice; **~ier** n courtisan m, dame f de la cour; ~ **martial** (*pl* **courts martial**) n cour martiale, conseil m de guerre; **~room** n salle f de tribunal; **~yard** n cour f

cousin ['kʌzn] n cousin(e); **first ~** cousin(e) germain(e)

cove [kəuv] n petite baie, anse f

covenant ['kʌvənənt] n engagement m

cover ['kʌvə'] vt couvrir ♦ n couverture f; (*of pan*) couvercle m; (*over furniture*) housse f; (*shelter*) abri m; **to take ~** se mettre à l'abri; **under ~** à l'abri; **under ~ of darkness** à la faveur de la nuit; **under separate ~** (*COMM*) sous pli séparé; **to ~ up for sb** couvrir qn; **~age** n (*TV, PRESS*) reportage m; ~ **charge** n couvert m (*supplément à payer*); **~ing** n couche f; **~ing letter** (*US* **cover letter**) n lettre explicative; ~ **note** n (*INSURANCE*) police f provisoire

covert ['kʌvət] adj (*threat*) voilé(e), caché(e); (*glance*) furtif(-ive)

cover-up ['kʌvərʌp] n tentative f pour étouffer une affaire

covet ['kʌvit] vt convoiter

cow [kau] n vache f ♦ vt effrayer, intimider

coward ['kauəd] n lâche m/f; **~ice** n lâcheté f; **~ly** adj lâche

cowboy ['kaubɔi] n cow-boy m

cower ['kauə'] vi se recroqueviller

coy [kɔi] adj faussement effarouché(e) or timide

cozy ['kəuzi] (*US*) adj = **cosy**

CPA (*US*) n abbr = **certified public accountant**

crab [kræb] n crabe m; ~ **apple** n pomme f sauvage

crack [kræk] n (*split*) fente f, fissure f; (*in cup, bone etc*) fêlure f; (*in wall*) lézarde f; (*noise*) craquement m, coup (sec); (*drug*) crack m ♦ vt fendre, fissurer; fêler; lézarder; (*whip*) faire claquer; (*nut*) casser; (*code*) déchiffrer; (*problem*) résoudre ♦ adj (*athlete*) de première classe, d'élite; ~ **down on** vt fus mettre un frein à; ~ **up** vi être au bout du rouleau, s'effondrer; **~ed** adj (*cup, bone*) fêlé(e); (*broken*) cassé(e); (*wall*) lézardé(e); (*surface*) craquelé(e); (*inf: mad*) cinglé(e); **~er** n (*Christmas cracker*) pétard m; (*biscuit*) biscuit (salé)

crackle ['krækl] vi crépiter, grésiller

cradle ['kreidl] n berceau m

craft [krɑːft] n métier (artisanal); (pl inv: boat) embarcation f, barque f; (: plane) appareil m; **~sman** (irreg) n artisan m, ouvrier (qualifié); **~smanship** n travail m; **~y** adj rusé(e), malin(-igne)

crag [kræg] n rocher escarpé

cram [kræm] vt (fill): to ~ sth with bourrer qch de; (put): to ~ sth into fourrer qch dans ♦ vi (for exams) bachoter

cramp [kræmp] n crampe f ♦ vt gêner, entraver; **~ed** adj à l'étroit, très serré(e)

cranberry ['krænbəri] n canneberge f

crane [krein] n grue f

crank [kræŋk] n manivelle f; (person) excentrique m/f

cranny ['kræni] n see nook

crash [kræʃ] n fracas m; (of car) collision f; (of plane) accident m ♦ vt avoir un accident avec ♦ vi (plane) s'écraser; (two cars) se percuter, s'emboutir; (COMM) s'effondrer; to ~ into se jeter or se fracasser contre; **~ course** n cours intensif; **~ helmet** n casque (protecteur); **~ landing** n atterrissage forcé or en catastrophe

crate [kreit] n cageot m; (for bottles) caisse f

cravat(e) [krə'væt] n foulard (noué autour du cou)

crave [kreiv] vt, vi: to ~ (for) avoir une envie irrésistible de

crawl [krɔːl] vi ramper; (vehicle) avancer au pas ♦ n (SWIMMING) crawl m

crayfish ['kreifiʃ] n inv (freshwater) écrevisse f; (saltwater) langoustine f

crayon ['kreiən] n crayon m (de couleur)

craze [kreiz] n engouement m

crazy ['kreizi] adj fou (folle)

creak [kriːk] vi grincer; craquer

cream [kriːm] n crème f ♦ adj (colour) crème inv; **~ cake** n (petit) gâteau à la crème; **~ cheese** n fromage m à la crème, fromage blanc; **~y** adj crémeux(-euse)

crease [kriːs] n pli m ♦ vt froisser, chiffonner ♦ vi se froisser, se chiffonner

create [kriː'eit] vt créer; **creation** n création f; **creative** adj (artistic) créatif(-ive); (ingenious) ingénieux(-euse)

creature ['kriːtʃər] n créature f

crèche [krɛʃ] n garderie f, crèche f

credence ['kriːdns] n: to lend or give ~ to ajouter foi à

credentials [krɪ'denʃlz] npl (references) références fpl; (papers of identity) pièce f d'identité

credit ['kredɪt] n crédit m; (recognition) honneur m ♦ vt (COMM) créditer; (believe: also: **give ~ to**) ajouter foi à, croire; **~s** npl (CINEMA, TV) générique m; to be in ~ (person, bank account) être créditeur(-trice); to ~ sb with (fig) prêter or attribuer à qn; ~ card n

carte f de crédit; **~or** n créancier(-ière)

creed [kriːd] n croyance f; credo m

creek [kriːk] n crique f, anse f; (US: stream) ruisseau m, petit cours d'eau

creep [kriːp] (pt, pp crept) vi ramper; **~er** n plante grimpante; **~y** adj (frightening) qui fait frissonner, qui donne la chair de poule

cremate [krɪ'meit] vt incinérer; **crematorium** [kremə'tɔːriəm] (pl **crematoria**) n four m crématoire

crêpe [kreip] n crêpe m; ~ **bandage** (BRIT) n bande f Velpeau ®

crept [krept] pt, pp of **creep**

crescent ['kresnt] n croissant m; (street) rue f (en arc de cercle)

cress [kres] n cresson m

crest [krest] n crête f; **~fallen** adj déconfit(e), découragé(e)

Crete [kriːt] n Crète f

crevice ['krevis] n fissure f, lézarde f, fente f

crew [kruː] n équipage m; (CINEMA) équipe f; **~-cut** n: to have a **~-cut** avoir les cheveux en brosse; **~-neck** n col ras du cou

crib [krib] n lit m d'enfant; (for baby) berceau m ♦ vt (inf) copier

crick [krik] n: ~ **in the neck** torticolis m; ~ **in the back** tour m de reins

cricket ['krikit] n (insect) grillon m, cri-cri m inv; (game) cricket m

crime [kraim] n crime m; **criminal** ['krimɪnl] adj, n criminel(le)

crimson ['krimzn] adj cramoisi(e)

cringe [krindʒ] vi avoir un mouvement de recul

crinkle ['kriŋkl] vt froisser, chiffonner

cripple ['kripl] n boiteux(-euse), infirme m/f ♦ vt estropier

crisis ['kraisis] (pl **crises**) n crise f

crisp [krisp] adj croquant(e); (weather) vif (vive); (manner etc) brusque; **~s** (BRIT) npl (pommes) chips fpl

crisscross ['kriskrɔs] adj entrecroisé(e)

criterion [krai'tiəriən] (pl **criteria**) n critère m

critic ['kritik] n critique m; **~al** adj critique; **~ally** adv (examine) d'un œil critique; (speak etc) sévèrement; **~ally ill** gravement malade; **~ism** ['kritisizəm] n critique f; **~ize** ['kritisaiz] vt critiquer

croak [krəuk] vi (frog) coasser; (raven) croasser; (person) parler d'une voix rauque

Croatia [krəu'eiʃə] n Croatie f

crochet ['krəuʃei] n travail m au crochet

crockery ['krɔkəri] n vaisselle f

crocodile ['krɔkədail] n crocodile m

crocus ['krəukəs] n crocus m

croft [krɔft] (BRIT) n petite ferme f

crony ['krəuni] (inf: pej) n copain (copine)

crook [kruk] n escroc m; (of shepherd) houlette f; **~ed** ['krukid] adj courbé(e), tordu(e); (action) malhonnête

crop [krɔp] n (produce) culture f; (amount produced) récolte f; (riding ~) cravache f ♦ vt (hair) tondre; ~ **up** vi surgir, se présenter, survenir

cross [krɔs] n croix f; (BIO etc) croisement m ♦ vt (street etc) traverser; (arms, legs, BIO) croiser; (cheque) barrer ♦ adj en colère, fâché(e); ~ **out** vt barrer, biffer; ~ **over** vi traverser; ~**bar** n barre (transversale); ~-**country (race)** n cross(-country) m; ~-**examine** vt (LAW) faire subir un examen contradictoire à; ~-**eyed** adj qui louche; ~**fire** n feux croisés; ~**ing** n (sea passage) traversée f; (also: **pedestrian** ~**ing**) passage clouté; ~**ing guard** (US) n contractuel qui fait traverser la rue aux enfants; ~ **purposes** npl: **to be at** ~ **purposes with sb** comprendre qn de travers; ~-**reference** n renvoi m, référence f; ~**roads** n carrefour m; ~ **section** n (of object) coupe transversale; (in population) échantillon m; ~**walk** (US) n passage clouté; ~**wind** n vent m de travers; ~**word** n mots mpl croisés

crotch [krɔtʃ] n (ANAT, of garment) entre-jambes m inv

crouch [krautʃ] vi s'accroupir; se tapir

crow [krəu] n (bird) corneille f; (of cock) chant m du coq, cocorico m ♦ vi (cock) chanter

crowbar ['krəubɑːʳ] n levier m

crowd [kraud] n foule f ♦ vt remplir ♦ vi affluer, s'attrouper, s'entasser; **to** ~ **in** entrer en foule; ~**ed** adj bondé(e), plein(e)

crown [kraun] n couronne f; (of head) sommet m de la tête; (of hill) sommet ♦ vt couronner; ~ **jewels** npl joyaux mpl de la Couronne

crow's-feet ['krəuzfiːt] npl pattes fpl d'oie

crucial ['kruːʃ] adj crucial(e), décisif(-ive)

crucifix ['kruːsɪfɪks] n (REL) crucifix m; ~**ion** [kruːsɪ'fɪkʃən] n (REL) crucifixion f

crude [kruːd] adj (materials) brut(e); non raffiné(e); (fig: basic) rudimentaire, sommaire; (: vulgar) cru(e), grossier(-ère); ~ **(oil)** n (pétrole) brut m

cruel ['kruəl] adj cruel(le); ~**ty** n cruauté f

cruise [kruːz] n croisière f ♦ vi (ship) croiser; (car) rouler; ~**r** n croiseur m; (motorboat) yacht m de croisière

crumb [krʌm] n miette f

crumble ['krʌmbl] vt émietter ♦ vi (plaster etc) s'effriter; (land, earth) s'ébouler; (building) s'écrouler, crouler; (fig) s'effondrer; **crumbly** adj friable

crumpet ['krʌmpɪt] n petite crêpe (épaisse)

crumple ['krʌmpl] vt froisser, friper

crunch [krʌntʃ] vt croquer; (underfoot) faire craquer or crisser, écraser ♦ n (fig) instant m

or moment m critique, moment de vérité; ~**y** adj croquant(e), croustillant(e)

crusade [kruː'seɪd] n croisade f

crush [krʌʃ] n foule f, cohue f; (love): **to have a** ~ **on sb** avoir le béguin pour qn (inf); (drink): **lemon** ~ citron pressé ♦ vt écraser; (crumple) froisser; (fig: hopes) anéantir

crust [krʌst] n croûte f

crutch [krʌtʃ] n béquille f

crux [krʌks] n point crucial

cry [kraɪ] vi pleurer; (shout: also: ~ **out**) crier ♦ n cri m; ~ **off** (inf) vi se dédire; se décommander

cryptic ['krɪptɪk] adj énigmatique

crystal ['krɪstl] n cristal m; ~-**clear** adj clair(e) comme de l'eau de roche

CSA n abbr (= Child Support Agency) organisme pour la protection des enfants de parents séparés, qui contrôle le versement des pensions alimentaires

CTC n abbr = **city technology college**

cub [kʌb] n petit m (d'un animal); (also: **C~ scout**) louveteau m

Cuba ['kjuːbə] n Cuba m

cube [kjuːb] n cube m ♦ vt (MATH) élever au cube; **cubic** adj cubique; **cubic metre** etc mètre m etc cube; **cubic capacity** n cylindrée f

cubicle ['kjuːbɪkl] n (in hospital) box m; (at pool) cabine f

cuckoo ['kuku:] n coucou m; ~ **clock** n (pendule f à) coucou m

cucumber ['kjuːkʌmbəʳ] n concombre m

cuddle ['kʌdl] vt câliner, caresser ♦ vi se blottir l'un contre l'autre

cue [kjuː] n (snooker ~) queue f de billard; (THEATRE etc) signal m

cuff [kʌf] n (BRIT: of shirt, coat etc) poignet m, manchette f; (US: of trousers) revers m; (blow) tape f; **off the** ~ à l'improviste; ~ **links** npl boutons mpl de manchette

cul-de-sac ['kʌldəsæk] n cul-de-sac m, impasse f

cull [kʌl] vt sélectionner ♦ n (of animals) massacre m

culminate ['kʌlmɪneɪt] vi: **to** ~ **in** finir or se terminer par; (end in) mener à; **culmination** [kʌlmɪ'neɪʃən] n point culminant

culottes [kjuː'lɒts] npl jupe-culotte f

culprit ['kʌlprɪt] n coupable m/f

cult [kʌlt] n culte m

cultivate ['kʌltɪveɪt] vt cultiver; **cultivation** [kʌltɪ'veɪʃən] n culture f

cultural ['kʌltʃərəl] adj culturel(le)

culture ['kʌltʃəʳ] n culture f; ~**d** adj (person) cultivé(e)

cumbersome ['kʌmbəsəm] adj encombrant(e), embarrassant(e)

cunning ['kʌnɪŋ] n ruse f, astuce f ♦ adj

rusé(e), malin(-igne); (*device, idea*)
astucieux(-euse)

cup [kʌp] *n* tasse *f*; (*as prize*) coupe *f*; (*of bra*)
bonnet *m*

cupboard ['kʌbəd] *n* armoire *f*; (*built-in*)
placard *m*

cup tie (BRIT) *n* match *m* de coupe

curate ['kjuərit] *n* vicaire *m*

curator [kjuə'reitəʳ] *n* conservateur *m* (*d'un
musée etc*)

curb [kə:b] *vt* refréner, mettre un frein à ♦ *n*
(*fig*) frein *m*, restriction *f*; (*US: kerb*) bord *m*
du trottoir

curdle ['kə:dl] *vi* se cailler

cure [kjuəʳ] *vt* guérir; (CULIN: *salt*) saler;
(: *smoke*) fumer; (: *dry*) sécher ♦ *n* remède *m*

curfew ['kə:fju:] *n* couvre-feu *m*

curiosity [kjuəri'ɔsiti] *n* curiosité *f*

curious ['kjuəriəs] *adj* curieux(-euse)

curl [kə:l] *n* boucle *f* (de cheveux) ♦ *vt, vi*
boucler; (*tightly*) friser; **~ up** *vi* s'enrouler;
se pelotonner; **~er** *n* bigoudi *m*, rouleau *m*;
~y *adj* bouclé(e); frisé(e)

currant ['kʌrnt] *n* (*dried*) raisin *m* de
Corinthe, raisin sec; (*bush*) groseiller *m*;
(*fruit*) groseille *f*

currency ['kʌrnsi] *n* monnaie *f*; **to gain ~**
(*fig*) s'accréditer

current ['kʌrnt] *n* courant *m* ♦ *adj*
courant(e); **~ account** (BRIT) *n* compte
courant; **~ affairs** *npl* (questions *fpl*
d'actualité *f*; **~ly** *adv* actuellement

curriculum [kə'rikjuləm] (*pl* **~s** or **curricula**)
n programme *m* d'études; **~ vitae** *n*
curriculum vitae *m*

curry ['kʌri] *n* curry *m* ♦ *vt*: **to ~ favour with**
chercher à s'attirer les bonnes grâces de

curse [kə:s] *vi* jurer, blasphémer ♦ *vt* maudire
♦ *n* (*spell*) malédiction *f*; (*problem, scourge*)
fléau *m*; (*swearword*) juron *m*

cursor ['kə:səʳ] *n* (COMPUT) curseur *m*

cursory ['kə:səri] *adj* superficiel(le), hâtif(-ive)

curt [kə:t] *adj* brusque, sec (sèche)

curtail [kə:'teil] *vt* (*visit etc*) écourter;
(*expenses, freedom etc*) réduire

curtain ['kə:tn] *n* rideau *m*

curts(e)y ['kə:tsi] *vi* faire une révérence

curve [kə:v] *n* courbe *f*; (*in the road*) tournant
m, virage *m* ♦ *vi* se courber; (*road*) faire une
courbe

cushion ['kuʃən] *n* coussin *m* ♦ *vt* (*fall,
shock*) amortir

custard ['kʌstəd] *n* (*for pouring*) crème
anglaise

custody ['kʌstədi] *n* (*of child*) garde *f*; **to
take sb into ~** (*suspect*) placer qn en
détention préventive

custom ['kʌstəm] *n* coutume *f*, usage *m*;
(COMM) clientèle *f*; **~ary** *adj* habituel(le)

customer ['kʌstəməʳ] *n* client(e)

customized ['kʌstəmaizd] *adj* (*car etc*)
construit(e) sur commande

custom-made ['kʌstəm'meid] *adj* (*clothes*)
fait(e) sur mesure; (*other goods*) hors série,
fait(e) sur commande

customs ['kʌstəmz] *npl* douane *f*; **~ officer**
n douanier(-ière)

cut [kʌt] (*pt, pp* **cut**) *vt* couper; (*meat*)
découper; (*reduce*) réduire ♦ *vi* couper ♦ *n*
coupure *f*; (*of clothes*) coupe *f*; (*in salary etc*)
réduction *f*; (*of meat*) morceau *m*; **to ~ one's
hand** se couper la main; **to ~ a tooth** percer
une dent; **~ down** *vt fus* (*tree etc*) couper,
abattre; (*consumption*) réduire; **~ off** *vt*
couper; (*fig*) isoler; **~ out** *vt* découper;
(*stop*) arrêter; (*remove*) ôter; **~ up** *vt* (*paper,
meat*) découper; **~back** *n* réduction *f*

cute [kju:t] *adj* mignon(ne), adorable

cutlery ['kʌtləri] *n* couverts *mpl*

cutlet ['kʌtlit] *n* côtelette *f*

cut: ~out *n* (*switch*) coupe-circuit *m inv*;
(*cardboard cutout*) découpage *m*; **~-price** (US
cut-rate) *adj* au rabais, à prix réduit; **~-
throat** *n* assassin *m* ♦ *adj* acharné(e); **~ting**
adj tranchant(e), coupant(e); (*fig*)
cinglant(e), mordant(e) ♦ *n* (BRIT: *from
newspaper*) coupure *f* (de journal); (*from
plant*) bouture *f*

CV *n abbr* = **curriculum vitae**

cwt *abbr* = **hundredweight(s)**

cyanide ['saiənaid] *n* cyanure *m*

cybercafé ['saibəkæfei] *n* cybercafé *m*

cyberspace ['saibəspeis] *n* cyberspace *m*

cycle ['saikl] *n* cycle *m*; (*bicycle*) bicyclette *f*,
vélo *m* ♦ *vi* faire de la bicyclette; **~ hire** *n*
location *f* de vélos; **~ lane** or **path** *n* piste *f*
cyclable; **cycling** *n* cyclisme *m*; **cyclist**
['saiklist] *n* cycliste *m/f*

cygnet ['sɪgnit] *n* jeune cygne *m*

cylinder ['sɪlindəʳ] *n* cylindre *m*; **~-head
gasket** *n* joint *m* de culasse

cymbals ['sɪmblz] *npl* cymbales *fpl*

cynic ['sɪnik] *n* cynique *m/f*; **~al** *adj* cynique;
~ism ['sɪnisizəm] *n* cynisme *m*

Cypriot ['sɪpriət] *adj* cypriote, chypriote ♦ *n*
Cypriote *m/f*, Chypriote *m/f*

Cyprus ['saiprəs] *n* Chypre *f*

cyst [sist] *n* kyste *m*

cystitis [sis'taitis] *n* cystite *f*

czar [za:ʳ] *n* tsar *m*

Czech [tʃek] *adj* tchèque ♦ *n* Tchèque *m/f*;
(LING) tchèque *m*

Czechoslovak [tʃekə'sləuvæk] *adj*
tchécoslovaque ♦ *n* Tchécoslovaque *m/f*

Czechoslovakia [tʃekəslə'vækiə] *n*
Tchécoslovaquie *f*

D, d

D [di:] n (MUS) ré m

dab [dæb] vt (eyes, wound) tamponner; (paint, cream) appliquer (par petites touches or rapidement)

dabble ['dæbl] vi: **to ~ in** faire or se mêler or s'occuper un peu de

dad [dæd] n, **daddy** [dædɪ] n papa m

daffodil ['dæfədɪl] n jonquille f

daft [dɑ:ft] adj idiot(e), stupide

dagger ['dægə'] n poignard m

daily ['deɪlɪ] adj quotidien(ne), journalier(-ère) ♦ n quotidien m ♦ adv tous les jours

dainty ['deɪntɪ] adj délicat(e), mignon(ne)

dairy ['dɛərɪ] n (BRIT: produce) crémerie f, laiterie f; (on farm) laiterie f; **~ products** npl produits laitiers; **~ store** n (US) crémerie f, laiterie f

daisy ['deɪzɪ] n pâquerette f

dale [deɪl] n vallon m

dam [dæm] n barrage m ♦ vt endiguer

damage ['dæmɪdʒ] n dégâts mpl, dommages mpl; (fig) tort m ♦ vt endommager, abîmer; (fig) faire du tort à; **~s** npl (LAW) dommages-intérêts mpl

damn [dæm] vt condamner; (curse) maudire ♦ n (inf): **I don't give a ~** je m'en fous ♦ adj (inf: also: **~ed**): **this ~** ... ce sacré or foutu ...; **~ (it)!** zut!; **~ing** adj accablant(e)

damp [dæmp] adj humide ♦ n humidité f ♦ vt (also: **~en**: cloth, rag) humecter; (: enthusiasm) refroidir

damson ['dæmzən] n prune f de Damas

dance [dɑ:ns] n danse f; (social event) bal m ♦ vi danser; **~ hall** n salle f de bal, dancing m; **~r** n danseur(-euse); **dancing** n danse f

dandelion ['dændɪlaɪən] n pissenlit m

dandruff ['dændrʌf] n pellicules fpl

Dane [deɪn] n Danois(e)

danger ['deɪndʒə'] n danger m; **there is a ~ of fire** il y a (un) risque d'incendie; **in ~** en danger; **he was in ~ of falling** il risquait de tomber; **~ous** adj dangereux(-euse)

dangle ['dæŋgl] vt balancer ♦ vi pendre

Danish ['deɪnɪʃ] adj danois(e) ♦ n (LING) danois m

dare [dɛə'] vt: **to ~ sb to do** défier qn de faire ♦ vi: **to ~ (to) do sth** oser faire qch; **I ~ say** (I suppose) il est probable (que); **daring** adj hardi(e), audacieux(-euse); (dress) osé(e) ♦ n audace f, hardiesse f

dark [dɑ:k] adj (night, room) obscur(e), sombre; (colour, complexion) foncé(e), sombre ♦ n: **in the ~** dans le noir; **in the ~ about** (fig) ignorant tout de; **after ~** après la tombée de la nuit; **~en** vt obscurcir, assombrir ♦ vi s'obscurcir, s'assombrir;

~ glasses npl lunettes noires; **~ness** n obscurité f; **~room** n chambre noire

darling ['dɑ:lɪŋ] adj chéri(e) ♦ n chéri(e); (favourite): **to be the ~ of** être la coqueluche de

darn [dɑ:n] vt repriser, raccommoder

dart [dɑ:t] n fléchette f; (sewing) pince f ♦ vi: **to ~ towards** (also: **make a ~ towards**) se précipiter or s'élancer vers; **to ~ along/away** partir/passer comme une flèche; **~board** n cible f (de jeu de fléchettes); **~s** n (jeu m de) fléchettes fpl

dash [dæʃ] n (sign) tiret m; (small quantity) goutte f, larme f ♦ vt (missile) jeter or lancer violemment; (hopes) anéantir ♦ vi: **to ~ towards** (also: **make a ~ towards**) se précipiter or se ruer vers; **~ away** vi partir à toute allure, filer; **~ off** vi = **dash away**

dashboard ['dæʃbɔ:d] n (AUT) tableau m de bord

dashing ['dæʃɪŋ] adj fringant(e)

data ['deɪtə] npl données fpl; **~base** n (COMPUT) base f de données; **~ processing** n traitement m de données

date [deɪt] n date f; (with sb) rendez-vous m; (fruit) datte f ♦ vt dater; (person) sortir avec; **~ of birth** date de naissance; **to ~** (until now) à ce jour; **out of ~** (passport) périmé(e); (theory etc) dépassé(e); (clothes etc) démodé(e); **up to ~** moderne; (news) très récent; **~d** ['deɪtɪd] adj démodé(e); **~ rape** n viol m (à l'issue d'un rendez-vous galant)

daub [dɔ:b] vt barbouiller

daughter ['dɔ:tə'] n fille f, **~-in-law** n belle-fille f, bru f

daunting ['dɔ:ntɪŋ] adj décourageant(e)

dawdle ['dɔ:dl] vi traîner, lambiner

dawn [dɔ:n] n aube f, aurore f ♦ vi (day) se lever, poindre; (fig): **it ~ed on him that ...** il lui vint à l'esprit que ...

day [deɪ] n jour m; (as duration) journée f; (period of time, age) époque f, temps m; **the ~ before** la veille, le jour précédent; **the ~ after, the following ~** le lendemain, le jour suivant; **the ~ after tomorrow** après-demain; **the ~ before yesterday** avant-hier; **by ~** de jour; **~break** n point m du jour; **~dream** vi rêver (tout éveillé); **~light** n (lumière f du) jour m; **~ return** (BRIT) n billet m d'aller-retour (valable pour la journée); **~time** n jour m, journée f; **~-to-~** adj quotidien(ne); (event) journalier(-ère)

daze [deɪz] vt (stun) étourdir ♦ n: **in a ~** étourdi(e), hébété(e)

dazzle ['dæzl] vt éblouir, aveugler

DC abbr (= direct current) courant continu

D-day ['di:deɪ] n le jour J

dead [ded] adj mort(e); (numb) engourdi(e), insensible; (battery) à plat; (telephone): **the**

line is ~ la ligne est coupée ♦ *adv* absolument, complètement ♦ *npl*: **the ~** les morts; **he was shot ~** il a été tué d'un coup de revolver; **~ on time** à l'heure pile; **~ tired** éreinté(e), complètement fourbu(e); **to stop ~** s'arrêter pile *or* net; **~en** *vt* (*blow, sound*) amortir; (*pain*) calmer; **~ end** *n* impasse f; **~ heat** *n* (SPORT): **to finish in a ~ heat** terminer ex-æquo; **~line** *n* date f *or* heure f limite; **~lock** (*fig*) *n* impasse f; **~ loss** *n*: **to be a ~ loss** (*inf*: *person*) n'être bon(ne) à rien; **~ly** *adj* mortel(le); (*weapon*) meurtrier(-ère); (*accuracy*) extrême; **~pan** *adj* impassible; **D~ Sea** *n*: **the D~ Sea** la mer Morte

deaf [def] *adj* sourd(e); **~en** *vt* rendre sourd; **~ening** *adj* assourdissant(e); **~-mute** *n* sourd(e)-muet(te); **~ness** *n* surdité f

deal [di:l] (*pt, pp* dealt) *n* affaire f, marché m ♦ *vt* (*blow*) porter; (*cards*) donner, distribuer; **a great ~ (of)** beaucoup (de); **~ in** *vt fus* faire le commerce de; **~ with** *vt fus* (*person, problem*) s'occuper *or* se charger de; (*be about: book etc*) traiter de; **~er** *n* marchand m; **~ings** *npl* (COMM) transactions *fpl*; (*relations*) relations *fpl*, rapports *mpl*

dean [di:n] *n* (REL, BRIT: SCOL) doyen m; (US: SCOL) conseiller(-ère) (principal(e)) d'éducation

dear [dɪəʳ] *adj* cher (chère); (*expensive*) cher, coûteux(-euse) ♦ *n*: **my ~** mon cher/ma chère; **~ me!** mon Dieu!; **D~ Sir/Madam** (*in letter*) Monsieur/Madame; **D~ Mr/Mrs X** Cher Monsieur/Chère Madame; **~ly** *adv* (*love*) tendrement; (*pay*) cher

death [deθ] *n* mort f; (*fatality*) mort m; (ADMIN) décès m; **~ certificate** *n* acte m de décès; **~ly** *adj* de mort; **~ penalty** *n* peine f de mort; **~ rate** *n* (taux m de) mortalité f; **~ toll** *n* nombre m de morts

debase [dɪ'beɪs] *vt* (*value*) déprécier, dévaloriser

debatable [dɪ'beɪtəbl] *adj* discutable

debate [dɪ'beɪt] *n* discussion f, débat m ♦ *vt* discuter, débattre

debit [ˈdebɪt] *n* débit m ♦ *vt*: **to ~ a sum to sb** *or* **to sb's account** porter une somme au débit de qn, débiter qn d'une somme; *see also* **direct**

debt [det] *n* dette f; **to be in ~** avoir des dettes, être endetté(e); **~or** *n* débiteur(-trice)

decade [ˈdekeɪd] *n* décennie f, décade f

decadence [ˈdekədəns] *n* décadence f

decaff [ˈdiːkæf] (*inf*) *n* déca m

decaffeinated [dɪ'kæfɪneɪtɪd] *adj* décaféiné(e)

decanter [dɪ'kæntəʳ] *n* carafe f

decay [dɪ'keɪ] *n* (*of building*) délabrement m; (*also:* **tooth ~**) carie f (dentaire) ♦ *vi* (*rot*) se décomposer, pourrir; (: *teeth*) se carier

deceased [dɪ'siːst] *n* défunt(e)

deceit [dɪ'siːt] *n* tromperie f, supercherie f; **~ful** *adj* trompeur(-euse); **deceive** *vt* tromper

December [dɪ'sembəʳ] *n* décembre m

decent [ˈdiːsənt] *adj* décent(e), convenable

deception [dɪ'sepʃən] *n* tromperie f

deceptive [dɪ'septɪv] *adj* trompeur(-euse)

decide [dɪ'saɪd] *vt* (*person*) décider; (*question, argument*) décider; **to ~ to do/that** décider de faire/que; **to ~ on** décider, se décider pour; **~d** *adj* (*resolute*) résolu(e), décidé(e); (*clear, definite*) net(te), marqué(e); **~dly** *adv* résolument; (*distinctly*) incontestablement, nettement

deciduous [dɪ'sɪdjuəs] *adj* à feuilles caduques

decimal [ˈdesɪməl] *adj* décimal(e) ♦ *n* décimale f; **~ point** *n* ≈ virgule f

decipher [dɪ'saɪfəʳ] *vt* déchiffrer

decision [dɪ'sɪʒən] *n* décision f

decisive [dɪ'saɪsɪv] *adj* décisif(-ive); (*person*) décidé(e)

deck [dek] *n* (NAUT) pont m; (*of bus*): **top ~** impériale f; (*of cards*) jeu m; (*record ~*) platine f; **~chair** *n* chaise longue

declare [dɪ'kleəʳ] *vt* déclarer

decline [dɪ'klaɪn] *n* (*decay*) déclin m; (*lessening*) baisse f ♦ *vt* refuser, décliner ♦ *vi* décliner; (*business*) baisser

decoder [di:'kəudəʳ] *n* (TV) décodeur m

decorate [ˈdekəreɪt] *vt* (*adorn, give a medal to*) décorer; (*paint and paper*) peindre et tapisser; **decoration** [dekə'reɪʃən] *n* (*medal etc, adornment*) décoration f; **decorator** *n* peintre-décorateur m

decoy [ˈdiːkɔɪ] *n* piège m; (*person*) compère m

decrease [*n* ˈdiːkriːs, *vb* diːˈkriːs] *n*: **~ (in)** diminution f (de) ♦ *vt, vi* diminuer

decree [dɪ'kriː] *n* (POL, REL) décret m; (LAW) arrêt m, jugement m; **~ nisi** [-'naɪsaɪ] *n* jugement m provisoire de divorce

dedicate [ˈdedɪkeɪt] *vt* consacrer; (*book etc*) dédier; **~d** *adj* (*person*) dévoué(e); (COMPUT) spécialisé(e), dédié(e); **dedication** [dedɪ'keɪʃən] *n* (*devotion*) dévouement m; (*in book*) dédicace f

deduce [dɪ'djuːs] *vt* déduire, conclure

deduct [dɪ'dʌkt] *vt*: **to ~ sth (from)** déduire qch (de), retrancher qch (de); **~ion** *n* (*deducting, deducing*) déduction f; (*from wage etc*) prélèvement m, retenue f

deed [di:d] *n* action f, acte m; (LAW) acte notarié, contrat m

deep [di:p] *adj* profond(e); (*voice*) grave ♦ *adv*: **spectators stood 20 ~** il y avait 20 rangs de spectateurs; **4 metres ~** de 4 mètres de profondeur; **~ end** (*of swimming pool*)

grand bain; **~en** vt approfondir ♦ vi (fig)
s'épaissir; **~freeze** vt congélateur m; **~-fry** vt
faire frire (en friteuse); **~ly** adv profondément; (interested) vivement; **~-sea
diver** n sous-marin(e); **~-sea diving** n
plongée sous-marine; **~-sea fishing** n
grande pêche; **~-seated** adj profond(e),
profondément enraciné(e)

deer [dɪəʳ] n inv: (red) ~ cerf m, biche f;
(fallow) ~ daim m; (roe) ~ chevreuil m; **~skin**
n daim

deface [dɪ'feɪs] vt dégrader; (notice, poster)
barbouiller

default [dɪ'fɔːlt] n (COMPUT: also: ~ value)
valeur f par défaut; **by** ~ (LAW) par défaut, par
contumace; (SPORT) par forfait

defeat [dɪ'fiːt] n défaite f ♦ vt (team,
opponents) battre

defect [n 'diːfɛkt, vb dɪ'fɛkt] n défaut m ♦ vi:
to ~ **to the enemy** passer à l'ennemi; **~ive**
[dɪ'fɛktɪv] adj défectueux(-euse)

defence [dɪ'fɛns] (US **defense**) n défense f;
~less adj sans défense

defend [dɪ'fɛnd] vt défendre; **~ant** n
défendeur(-deresse); (in criminal case)
accusé(e), prévenu(e); **~er** n défenseur m

defer [dɪ'fɜːʳ] vt (postpone) différer, ajourner

defiance [dɪ'faɪəns] n défi m; **in** ~ **of** au
mépris de; **defiant** adj provocant(e), de défi;
(person) rebelle, intraitable

deficiency [dɪ'fɪʃənsɪ] n insuffisance f,
déficience f; **deficient** adj (inadequate)
insuffisant(e); **to be deficient in** manquer de

deficit ['dɛfɪsɪt] n déficit m

define [dɪ'faɪn] vt définir

definite ['dɛfɪnɪt] adj (fixed) défini(e), (bien)
déterminé(e); (clear, obvious) net(te),
manifeste; (certain) sûr(e); **he was ~ about it**
il a été catégorique; **~ly** adv sans aucun
doute

definition [dɛfɪ'nɪʃən] n définition f;
(clearness) netteté f

deflate [diː'fleɪt] vt dégonfler

deflect [dɪ'flɛkt] vt détourner, faire dévier

deformed [dɪ'fɔːmd] adj difforme

defraud [dɪ'frɔːd] vt frauder; **to** ~ **sb of sth**
escroquer qch à qn

defrost [diː'frɔst] vt dégivrer; (food)
décongeler; **~er** (US) n (demister) dispositif m
anti-buée inv

deft [dɛft] adj adroit(e), preste

defunct [dɪ'fʌŋkt] adj défunt(e)

defuse [diː'fjuːz] vt désamorcer

defy [dɪ'faɪ] vt défier; (efforts etc) résister à

degenerate [vb dɪ'dʒɛnəreɪt, adj dɪ'dʒɛnərɪt]
vi dégénérer ♦ adj dégénéré(e)

degree [dɪ'griː] n degré m; (SCOL) diplôme m
(universitaire); **a (first)** ~ **in maths** une licence
en maths; **by ~s** (gradually) par degrés; **to**

some ~, **to a certain** ~ jusqu'à un certain
point, dans une certaine mesure

dehydrated [diːhaɪ'dreɪtɪd] adj
déshydraté(e); (milk, eggs) en poudre

de-ice ['diː'aɪs] vt (windscreen) dégivrer

deign [deɪn] vi: **to** ~ **to do** daigner faire

dejected [dɪ'dʒɛktɪd] adj abattu(e),
déprimé(e)

delay [dɪ'leɪ] vt retarder ♦ vi s'attarder ♦ n
délai m, retard m; **to be ~ed** être en retard

delectable [dɪ'lɛktəbl] adj délicieux(-euse)

delegate [n 'dɛlɪgɪt, vb 'dɛlɪgeɪt] n délé-
gué(e) ♦ vt déléguer

delete [dɪ'liːt] vt rayer, supprimer

deliberate [adj dɪ'lɪbərɪt, vb dɪ'lɪbəreɪt] adj
(intentional) délibéré(e); (slow) mesuré(e)
♦ vi délibérer, réfléchir; **~ly** [dɪ'lɪbərɪtlɪ] adv
(on purpose) exprès, délibérément

delicacy ['dɛlɪkəsɪ] n délicatesse f; (food)
mets fin or délicat, friandise f

delicate ['dɛlɪkɪt] adj délicat(e)

delicatessen [dɛlɪkə'tɛsn] n épicerie fine

delicious [dɪ'lɪʃəs] adj délicieux(-euse)

delight [dɪ'laɪt] n (grande) joie, grand plaisir
♦ vt enchanter; **to take (a)** ~ **in** prendre
grand plaisir à; **~ed** adj: **~ed (at or with/to
do)** ravi(e) (de/de faire); **~ful** adj (person)
adorable; (meal, evening) merveilleux(-euse)

delinquent [dɪ'lɪŋkwənt] adj, n délin-
quant(e)

delirious [dɪ'lɪrɪəs] adj: **to be** ~ délirer

deliver [dɪ'lɪvəʳ] vt (mail) distribuer; (goods)
livrer; (message) remettre; (speech)
prononcer; (MED: baby) mettre au monde;
~y n distribution f; livraison f; (of speaker)
élocution f; (MED) accouchement m; **to take
~y of** prendre livraison de

delude [dɪ'luːd] vt tromper, leurrer; **delusion**
n illusion f

demand [dɪ'mɑːnd] vt réclamer, exiger ♦ n
exigence f; (claim) revendication f; (ECON)
demande f; **in** ~ demandé(e), recherché(e);
on ~ sur demande; **~ing** adj (person)
exigeant(e); (work) astreignant(e)

demean [dɪ'miːn] vt: **to** ~ **o.s.** s'abaisser

demeanour [dɪ'miːnəʳ] (US **demeanor**) n
comportement m; maintien m

demented [dɪ'mɛntɪd] adj dément(e), fou
(folle)

demise [dɪ'maɪz] n mort f

demister [diː'mɪstəʳ] (BRIT) n (AUT) dispositif
m anti-buée inv

demo ['dɛməu] (inf) n abbr (= demonstration)
manif f

democracy [dɪ'mɔkrəsɪ] n démocratie f;
democrat ['dɛməkræt] n démocrate m/f;
democratic [dɛmə'krætɪk] adj démocratique

demolish [dɪ'mɔlɪʃ] vt démolir

demonstrate ['dɛmənstreɪt] vt démontrer,

prouver; (*show*) faire une démonstration de
♦ *vi*: **to ~ (for/against)** manifester (en faveur
de/contre); **demonstration**
[deman'streɪʃən] *n* démonstration f,
manifestation f; **demonstrator** *n* (*POL*)
manifestant(e)

demote [dɪ'məut] *vt* rétrograder

demure [dɪ'mjuəʳ] *adj* sage, réservé(e)

den [dɛn] *n* tanière f, antre m

denial [dɪ'naɪəl] *n* démenti m; (*refusal*)
dénégation f

denim ['dɛnɪm] *n* jean m; **~s** *npl* (*jeans*)
(blue-)jean(s) m(pl)

Denmark ['dɛnmɑːk] *n* Danemark m

denomination [dɪnɔmɪ'neɪʃən] *n* (*of
money*) valeur f; (*REL*) confession f

denounce [dɪ'nauns] *vt* dénoncer

dense [dɛns] *adj* dense; (*stupid*) obtus(e),
bouché(e); **~ly** *adv*: **~ly populated** à forte
densité de population; **density** ['dɛnsɪtɪ] *n*
densité f; **double/high-density diskette**
disquette f double densité/haute densité

dent [dɛnt] *n* bosse f ♦ *vt* (*also*: **make a ~ in**)
cabosser

dental [dɛntl] *adj* dentaire; **~ surgeon** *n*
(chirurgien(ne)) dentiste

dentist ['dɛntɪst] *n* dentiste m/f

dentures ['dɛntʃəz] *npl* dentier m sg

deny [dɪ'naɪ] *vt* nier; (*refuse*) refuser

deodorant [diː'əudərənt] *n* déodorant m,
désodorisant m

depart [dɪ'pɑːt] *vi* partir; **to ~ from** (*fig*: *differ
from*) s'écarter de

department [dɪ'pɑːtmənt] *n* (*COMM*) rayon
m; (*SCOL*) section f; (*POL*) ministère m,
département m; **~ store** *n* grand magasin

departure [dɪ'pɑːtʃəʳ] *n* départ m; **a new ~**
une nouvelle voie; **~ lounge** *n* (*at airport*)
salle f d'embarquement

depend [dɪ'pɛnd] *vi*: **to ~ on** dépendre de;
(*rely on*) compter sur; **it ~s** cela dépend; **~ing
on the result** selon le résultat; **~able** *adj*
(*person*) sérieux(-euse), sûr(e); (*car, watch*)
solide, fiable; **~ant** *n* personne f à charge;
~ent *adj*: **to be ~ent (on)** dépendre (de) ♦ *n*
= **dependant**

depict [dɪ'pɪkt] *vt* (*in picture*) représenter; (*in
words*) (dé)peindre, décrire

depleted [dɪ'pliːtɪd] *adj* (considérablement)
réduit(e) or diminué(e)

deport [dɪ'pɔːt] *vt* expulser

deposit [dɪ'pɔzɪt] *n* (*CHEM, COMM, GEO*) dépôt
m; (*of ore, oil*) gisement m; (*part payment*)
arrhes fpl, acompte m; (*on bottle etc*)
consigne f; (*for hired goods etc*)
cautionnement m, garantie f ♦ *vt* déposer;
~ account *n* compte m sur livret

depot ['dɛpəu] *n* dépôt m; (*US: RAIL*) gare f

depress [dɪ'prɛs] *vt* déprimer; (*press down*)

appuyer sur, abaisser; (*prices, wages*) faire
baisser; **~ed** *adj* (*person*) déprimé(e); (*area*)
en déclin, touché(e) par le sous-emploi; **~ing**
adj déprimant(e); **~ion** *n* dépression f;
(*hollow*) creux m

deprivation [dɛprɪ'veɪʃən] *n* privation f;
(*loss*) perte f

deprive [dɪ'praɪv] *vt*: **to ~ sb of** priver qn de;
~d *adj* déshérité(e)

depth [dɛpθ] *n* profondeur f; **in the ~s of
despair** au plus profond du désespoir; **to be
out of one's ~** avoir perdu pied, nager

deputize ['dɛpjutaɪz] *vi*: **to ~ for** assurer
l'intérim de

deputy ['dɛpjutɪ] *adj* adjoint(e) ♦ *n* (*second
in command*) adjoint(e); (*US: also*: **~ sheriff**)
shérif adjoint; **~ head** directeur adjoint, sous-
directeur m

derail [dɪ'reɪl] *vt*: **to be ~ed** dérailler

deranged [dɪ'reɪndʒd] *adj*: **to be (mentally) ~**
avoir le cerveau dérangé

derby ['dɑːbɪ] (*US*) *n* (*bowler hat*) (chapeau
m) melon m

derelict ['dɛrɪlɪkt] *adj* abandonné(e), à
l'abandon

derisory [dɪ'raɪsərɪ] *adj* (*sum*) dérisoire;
(*smile, person*) moqueur(-euse)

derive [dɪ'raɪv] *vt*: **to ~ sth from** tirer qch de;
trouver qch dans ♦ *vi*: **to ~ from** provenir de,
dériver de

derogatory [dɪ'rɔgətərɪ] *adj* désobligeant(e);
péjoratif(-ive)

descend [dɪ'sɛnd] *vt, vi* descendre; **to ~ from**
descendre de, être issu(e) de; **to ~ to (doing)
sth** s'abaisser à (faire) qch; **descent** *n*
descente f; (*origin*) origine f

describe [dɪs'kraɪb] *vt* décrire; **description**
[dɪs'krɪpʃən] *n* description f; (*sort*) sorte f,
espèce f

desecrate ['dɛsɪkreɪt] *vt* profaner

desert [*n* 'dɛzət, *vb* dɪ'zəːt] *n* désert m ♦ *vt*
déserter, abandonner ♦ *vi* (*MIL*) déserter; **~s**
npl: **to get one's just ~s** n'avoir que ce qu'on
mérite; **~er** [dɪ'zəːtəʳ] *n* déserteur m; **~ion**
[dɪ'zəːʃən] *n* (*MIL*) désertion f; (*LAW: of
spouse*) abandon m du domicile conjugal;
~ island *n* île déserte

deserve [dɪ'zəːv] *vt* mériter; **deserving** *adj*
(*person*) méritant(e); (*action, cause*) méritoire

design [dɪ'zaɪn] *n* (*sketch*) plan m, dessin m;
(*layout, shape*) conception f, ligne f; (*pattern*)
dessin m, motif(s) m(pl); (*COMM, art*) design
m, stylisme m; (*intention*) dessein m ♦ *vt*
dessiner; élaborer; **~er** *n* (*TECH*) concepteur-
projeteur m; (*ART*) dessinateur(-trice),
designer m; (*fashion*) styliste m/f

desire [dɪ'zaɪəʳ] *n* désir m ♦ *vt* désirer

desk [dɛsk] *n* (*in office*) bureau m; (*for pupil*)
pupitre m; (*BRIT: in shop, restaurant*) caisse f;

(*in hotel, at airport*) réception f; **~-top publishing** n publication assistée par ordinateur, PAO f

desolate ['desəlɪt] adj désolé(e); (*person*) affligé(e)

despair [dɪs'pɛəʳ] n désespoir m ♦ vi: **to ~ of** désespérer de

despatch [dɪs'pætʃ] n, vt = **dispatch**

desperate ['despərɪt] adj désespéré(e); (*criminal*) prêt(e) à tout; **to be ~ for sth/to do sth** avoir désespérément besoin de qch/de faire qch; **~ly** adv désespérément; (*very*) terriblement, extrêmement; **desperation** [despə'reɪʃən] n désespoir m; **in (sheer) desperation** en désespoir de cause

despicable [dɪs'pɪkəbl] adj méprisable

despise [dɪs'paɪz] vt mépriser

despite [dɪs'paɪt] prep malgré, en dépit de

despondent [dɪs'pɔndənt] adj découragé(e), abattu(e)

dessert [dɪ'zə:t] n dessert m; **~spoon** n cuiller f à dessert

destination [destɪ'neɪʃən] n destination f

destined ['destɪnd] adj: **to be ~ to do/for sth** être destiné(e) à faire/à qch

destiny ['destɪnɪ] n destinée f, destin m

destitute ['destɪtju:t] adj indigent(e)

destroy [dɪs'trɔɪ] vt détruire; (*injured horse*) abattre; (*dog*) faire piquer; **~er** n (NAUT) contre-torpilleur m

destruction [dɪs'trʌkʃən] n destruction f

detach [dɪ'tætʃ] vt détacher; **~ed** adj (*attitude, person*) détaché(e); **~ed house** n pavillon m, maison(nette) (individuelle); **~ment** n (MIL) détachement m; (*fig*) détachement, indifférence f

detail ['di:teɪl] n détail m ♦ vt raconter en détail, énumérer; **in ~** en détail; **~ed** adj détaillé(e)

detain [dɪ'teɪn] vt retenir; (*in captivity*) détenir; (*in hospital*) hospitaliser

detect [dɪ'tekt] vt déceler, percevoir; (MED, POLICE) dépister; (MIL, RADAR, TECH) détecter; **~ion** n découverte f; **~ive** n agent m de la sûreté, policier m; **private ~ive** détective privé; **~ive story** n roman policier

detention [dɪ'tenʃən] n détention f; (SCOL) retenue f, consigne f

deter [dɪ'tə:ʳ] vt dissuader

detergent [dɪ'tə:dʒənt] n détergent m, détersif m

deteriorate [dɪ'tɪərɪəreɪt] vi se détériorer, se dégrader

determine [dɪ'tə:mɪn] vt déterminer; **to ~ to do** se résoudre de faire, se déterminer à faire; **~d** adj (*person*) déterminé(e), décidé(e)

deterrent [dɪ'terənt] n effet m de dissuasion; force f de dissuasion

detest [dɪ'test] vt détester, avoir horreur de

detonate ['detəneɪt] vt faire détoner or exploser

detour ['di:tuəʳ] n détour m; (US: AUT: *diversion*) déviation f

detract [dɪ'trækt] vt: **to ~ from** (*quality, pleasure*) diminuer; (*reputation*) porter atteinte à

detriment ['detrɪmənt] n: **to the ~ of** au détriment de, au préjudice de; **~al** [detrɪ'mentl] adj: **~al to** préjudiciable or nuisible à

devaluation [dɪvælju'eɪʃən] n dévaluation f

devastate ['devəsteɪt] vt dévaster; **~d** adj (*fig*) anéanti(e); **devastating** adj dévastateur(-trice); (*news*) accablant(e)

develop [dɪ'veləp] vt (*gen*) développer; (*disease*) commencer à souffrir de; (*resources*) mettre en valeur, exploiter ♦ vi se développer; (*situation, disease: evolve*) évoluer; (*facts, symptoms: appear*) se manifester, se produire; **~ing country** pays m en voie de développement; **the machine has ~ed a fault** un problème s'est manifesté dans cette machine; **~er** n (*also: property ~er*) promoteur m; **~ment** [dɪ'veləpmənt] n développement m; (*of affair, case*) rebondissement m, fait(s) nouveau(x)

device [dɪ'vaɪs] n (*apparatus*) engin m, dispositif m

devil ['devl] n diable m; démon m

devious ['di:vɪəs] adj (*person*) sournois(e), dissimulé(e)

devise [dɪ'vaɪz] vt imaginer, concevoir

devoid [dɪ'vɔɪd] adj: **~ of** dépourvu(e) de, dénué(e) de

devolution [di:və'lu:ʃən] n (POL) décentralisation f

devote [dɪ'vəut] vt: **to ~ sth to** consacrer qch à; **~d** [dɪ'vəutɪd] adj dévoué(e); **to be ~d to** (*book etc*) être consacré(e) à; (*person*) être très attaché(e) à; **~e** [devəu'ti:] n (REL) adepte m/f; (MUS, SPORT) fervent(e); **devotion** n dévouement m, attachement m; (REL) dévotion f, piété f

devour [dɪ'vauəʳ] vt dévorer

devout [dɪ'vaut] adj pieux(-euse), dévot(e)

dew [dju:] n rosée f

diabetes [daɪə'bi:ti:z] n diabète m; **diabetic** [daɪə'betɪk] adj diabétique ♦ n diabétique m/f

diabolical [daɪə'bɔlɪkl] (*inf*) adj (*weather*) atroce; (*behaviour*) infernal(e)

diagnosis [daɪəg'nəusɪs] (*pl* **diagnoses**) n diagnostic m

diagonal [daɪ'ægənl] adj diagonal(e) ♦ n diagonale f

diagram ['daɪəgræm] n diagramme m, schéma m

dial ['daɪəl] n cadran m ♦ vt (*number*) faire, composer

dialect ['daɪəlekt] n dialecte m

dialling code ['daɪəlɪŋ-] (BRIT) n indicatif m (téléphonique)

dialling tone (BRIT) n tonalité f

dialogue ['daɪəlɒg] n dialogue m

dial tone (US) n = **dialling tone**

diameter [daɪ'æmɪtə'] n diamètre m

diamond ['daɪəmənd] n diamant m; (shape) losange m; ~s npl (CARDS) carreau m

diaper ['daɪəpə'] (US) n couche f

diaphragm ['daɪəfræm] n diaphragme m

diarrhoea [daɪə'riːə] (US **diarrhea**) n diarrhée f

diary ['daɪərɪ] n (daily account) journal m; (book) agenda m

dice [daɪs] n inv dé m ♦ vt (CULIN) couper en dés or en cubes

dictate [dɪk'teɪt] vt dicter; **dictation** n dictée f

dictator [dɪk'teɪtə'] n dictateur m; ~**ship** n dictature f

dictionary ['dɪkʃənrɪ] n dictionnaire m

did [dɪd] pt of do; ~**n't** = **did not**

die [daɪ] vi mourir; **to be dying for sth** avoir une envie folle de qch; **to be dying to do sth** mourir d'envie de faire qch; ~ **away** vi s'éteindre; ~ **down** vi se calmer, s'apaiser; ~ **out** vi disparaître

diesel ['diːzl] n (vehicle) diesel m; (also: ~ oil) carburant m diesel, gas-oil m; ~ **engine** n moteur m diesel

diet ['daɪət] n alimentation f; (restricted food) régime m ♦ vi (also: **be on a ~**) suivre un régime

differ ['dɪfə'] vi (be different): **to ~ (from)** être différent (de); différer (de); (disagree): **to ~ (from sb over sth)** ne pas être d'accord (avec qn au sujet de qch); ~**ence** n différence f; (quarrel) différend m, désaccord m; ~**ent** adj différent(e); ~**entiate** [dɪfə'renʃɪeɪt] vi: **to ~entiate (between)** faire une différence (entre)

difficult ['dɪfɪkəlt] adj difficile; ~**y** n difficulté f

diffident ['dɪfɪdənt] adj qui manque de confiance or d'assurance

dig [dɪg] (pt, pp **dug**) vt (hole) creuser; (garden) bêcher ♦ n (prod) coup m de coude; (fig) coup de griffe or de patte; (archeological) fouilles fpl; ~ **in** vi (MIL: also: ~ **o.s. in**) se retrancher; ~ **into** vt fus (savings) puiser dans; **to ~ one's nails into sth** enfoncer ses ongles dans qch; ~ **up** vt déterrer

digest [vb daɪ'dʒest, n 'daɪdʒest] vt digérer ♦ n sommaire m, résumé m; ~**ion** [dɪ'dʒestʃən] n digestion f

digit ['dɪdʒɪt] n (number) chiffre m; (finger) doigt m; ~**al** adj digital(e), à affichage numérique or digital; ~**al computer** calculateur m numérique; ~**al TV** n télévision f numérique; ~**al watch** montre f à affichage numérique

dignified ['dɪgnɪfaɪd] adj digne

dignity ['dɪgnɪtɪ] n dignité f

digress [daɪ'gres] vi: **to ~ from** s'écarter de, s'éloigner de

digs [dɪgz] (BRIT: inf) npl piaule f, chambre meublée

dilapidated [dɪ'læpɪdeɪtɪd] adj délabré(e)

dilemma [daɪ'lemə] n dilemme m

diligent ['dɪlɪdʒənt] adj appliqué(e), assidu(e)

dilute [daɪ'luːt] vt diluer

dim [dɪm] adj (light) faible; (memory, outline) vague, indécis(e); (figure) vague, indistinct(e); (room) sombre; (stupid) borné(e), obtus(e) ♦ vt (light) réduire, baisser; (US: AUT) mettre en code

dime [daɪm] (US) n = **10 cents**

dimension [daɪ'menʃən] n dimension f

diminish [dɪ'mɪnɪʃ] vt, vi diminuer

diminutive [dɪ'mɪnjutɪv] adj minuscule, tout(e) petit(e)

dimmers ['dɪməz] (US) npl (AUT) phares mpl code inv; feux mpl de position

dimple ['dɪmpl] n fossette f

din [dɪn] n vacarme m

dine [daɪn] vi dîner; ~**r** n (person) dîneur(-euse); (US: restaurant) petit restaurant

dinghy ['dɪŋgɪ] n youyou m; (also: **rubber ~**) canot m pneumatique; (also: **sailing ~**) voilier m, dériveur m

dingy ['dɪndʒɪ] adj miteux(-euse), minable

dining car (BRIT) n wagon-restaurant m

dining room n salle f à manger

dinner ['dɪnə'] n dîner m; (lunch) déjeuner m; (public) banquet m; ~ **jacket** n smoking m; ~ **party** n dîner m; ~ **time** n heure f du dîner; (midday) heure du déjeuner

dinosaur ['daɪnəsɔː'] n dinosaure m

dip [dɪp] n déclivité f; (in sea) baignade f, bain m; (CULIN) ≈ sauce f ♦ vt tremper, plonger; (BRIT: AUT: lights) mettre en code, baisser ♦ vi plonger

diploma [dɪ'pləumə] n diplôme m

diplomacy [dɪ'pləuməsɪ] n diplomatie f

diplomat ['dɪpləmæt] n diplomate m; ~**ic** [dɪplə'mætɪk] adj diplomatique

dipstick ['dɪpstɪk] n (AUT) jauge f de niveau d'huile

dipswitch ['dɪpswɪtʃ] (BRIT) n (AUT) interrupteur m de lumière réduite

dire [daɪə'] adj terrible, extrême, affreux(-euse)

direct [daɪ'rekt] adj direct(e) ♦ vt diriger, orienter; (letter, remark) adresser; (film, programme) réaliser; (play) mettre en scène; (order): **to ~ sb to do sth** ordonner à qn de

faire qch ♦ *adv* directement; **can you ~ me to
...?** pouvez-vous m'indiquer le chemin de ...?;
~ debit (*BRIT*) *n* prélèvement *m* automatique
direction [dı'rɛkʃən] *n* direction *f*; **~s** *npl*
(*advice*) indications *fpl*; **sense of ~** sens *m* de
l'orientation; **~s for use** mode *m* d'emploi
directly [dı'rɛktlı] *adv* (*in a straight line*)
directement, tout droit; (*at once*) tout de
suite, immédiatement
director [dı'rɛktə*] *n* directeur *m*; (*THEATRE*)
metteur *m* en scène; (*CINEMA, TV*)
réalisateur(-trice)
directory [dı'rɛktərı] *n* annuaire *m*; (*COMPUT*)
répertoire *m*; **~ enquiries** (*US* **directory
assistance**) *n* renseignements *mpl*
dirt [də:t] *n* saleté *f*; crasse *f*; (*earth*) terre *f*,
boue *f*; **~-cheap** *adj* très bon marché *inv*;
~y *adj* sale ♦ *vt* salir; **~y trick** coup tordu
disability [dısə'bılıtı] *n* invalidité *f*, infirmité *f*
disabled [dıs'eıbld] *adj* infirme, invalide
♦ *npl*: **the ~** les handicapés
disadvantage [dısəd'va:ntıdʒ] *n*
désavantage *m*, inconvénient *m*
disagree [dısə'gri:] *vi* (*be different*) ne pas
concorder; (*be against, think otherwise*): **to
~ (with)** ne pas être d'accord (avec); **~able**
adj désagréable; **~ment** *n* désaccord *m*,
différend *m*
disallow ['dısə'lau] *vt* rejeter
disappear [dısə'pıə*] *vi* disparaître; **~ance** *n*
disparition *f*
disappoint [dısə'pɔınt] *vt* décevoir; **~ed** *adj*
déçu(e); **~ing** *adj* décevant(e); **~ment** *n*
déception *f*
disapproval [dısə'pru:vəl] *n* désapprobation
f
disapprove [dısə'pru:v] *vi*: **to ~ (of)**
désapprouver
disarmament [dıs'ɑ:məmənt] *n*
désarmement *m*
disarray [dısə'reı] *n*: **in ~** (*army*) en déroute;
(*organization*) en désarroi; (*hair, clothes*) en
désordre
disaster [dı'zɑ:stə*] *n* catastrophe *f*, désastre
m; **disastrous** *adj* désastreux(-euse)
disband [dıs'bænd] *vt* démobiliser; disperser
♦ *vi* se séparer; se disperser
disbelief ['dısbə'li:f] *n* incrédulité *f*
disc [dısk] *n* disque *m*; (*COMPUT*) = **disk**
discard [dıs'kɑ:d] *vt* (*old things*) se
débarrasser de; (*fig*) écarter, renoncer à
discern [dı'sə:n] *vt* discerner, distinguer;
~ing *adj* perspicace
discharge [*vb* dıs'tʃɑ:dʒ, *n* 'dıstʃɑ:dʒ] *vt*
décharger; (*duties*) s'acquitter de; (*patient*)
renvoyer (chez lui); (*employee*) congédier,
licencier; (*soldier*) rendre à la vie civile,
réformer; (*defendant*) relaxer, élargir ♦ *n*
décharge *f*; (*dismissal*) renvoi *m*; licenciement

m; élargissement *m*; (*MED*) écoulement *m*
discipline ['dısıplın] *n* discipline *f*
disc jockey *n* disc-jockey *m*
disclaim [dıs'kleım] *vt* nier
disclose [dıs'kləuz] *vt* révéler, divulguer;
disclosure *n* révélation *f*
disco ['dıskəu] *n abbr* = **discotheque**
discomfort [dıs'kʌmfət] *n* malaise *m*, gêne *f*;
(*lack of comfort*) manque *m* de confort
disconcert [dıskən'sə:t] *vt* déconcerter
disconnect [dıskə'nɛkt] *vt* (*ELEC, RADIO, pipe*)
débrancher; (*TEL, water*) couper
discontent [dıskən'tɛnt] *n* mécontentement
m; **~ed** *adj* mécontent(e)
discontinue [dıskən'tınju:] *vt* cesser,
interrompre; **"~d"** (*COMM*) "fin de série"
discord ['dıskɔ:d] *n* discorde *f*, dissension *f*;
(*MUS*) dissonance *f*
discotheque ['dıskəutɛk] *n* discothèque *f*
discount [*n* 'dıskaunt, *vb* dıs'kaunt] *n* remise
f, rabais *m* ♦ *vt* (*sum*) faire une remise de;
(*fig*) ne pas tenir compte de
discourage [dıs'kʌrıdʒ] *vt* décourager
discover [dıs'kʌvə*] *vt* découvrir; **~y** *n*
découverte *f*
discredit [dıs'krɛdıt] *vt* (*idea*) mettre en
doute; (*person*) discréditer
discreet [dıs'kri:t] *adj* discret(-ète)
discrepancy [dıs'krɛpənsı] *n* divergence *f*,
contradiction *f*
discretion [dıs'krɛʃən] *n* discrétion *f*; **use
your own ~** à vous de juger
discriminate [dıs'krımıneıt] *vi*: **to
~ between** établir une distinction entre, faire
la différence entre; **to ~ against** pratiquer une
discrimination contre; **discriminating** *adj*
qui a du discernement; **discrimination**
[dıskrımı'neıʃən] *n* discrimination *f*;
(*judgment*) discernement *m*
discuss [dıs'kʌs] *vt* discuter de; (*debate*)
discuter; **~ion** *n* discussion *f*
disdain [dıs'deın] *n* dédain *m*
disease [dı'zi:z] *n* maladie *f*
disembark [dısım'bɑ:k] *vi* débarquer
disentangle [dısın'tæŋgl] *vt* (*wool, wire*)
démêler, débrouiller; (*from wreckage*)
dégager
disfigure [dıs'fıgə*] *vt* défigurer
disgrace [dıs'greıs] *n* honte *f*; (*disfavour*)
disgrâce *f* ♦ *vt* déshonorer, couvrir de honte;
~ful *adj* scandaleux(-euse), honteux(-euse)
disgruntled [dıs'grʌntld] *adj* mécontent(e)
disguise [dıs'gaız] *n* déguisement *m* ♦ *vt*
déguiser; **in ~** déguisé(e)
disgust [dıs'gʌst] *n* dégoût *m*, aversion *f* ♦ *vt*
dégoûter, écœurer; **~ing** *adj* dégoûtant(e);
révoltant(e)
dish [dıʃ] *n* plat *m*; **to do** *or* **wash the ~es** faire
la vaisselle; **~ out** *vt* servir, distribuer; **~ up**

dishearten → dissipate

266

vt servir; **~cloth** n (for washing) lavette f

dishearten [dɪsˈhɑːtn] vt décourager

dishevelled [dɪˈʃɛvəld] (US **disheveled**) adj ébouriffé(e); décoiffé(e); débraillé(e)

dishonest [dɪsˈɔnɪst] adj malhonnête

dishonour [dɪsˈɔnəʳ] (US **dishonor**) n déshonneur m; **~able** adj (behaviour) déshonorant(e); (person) peu honorable

dishtowel [ˈdɪʃtauəl] (US) n torchon m

dishwasher [ˈdɪʃwɔʃəʳ] n lave-vaisselle m

disillusion [dɪsɪˈluːʒən] vt désabuser, désillusionner

disinfect [dɪsɪnˈfɛkt] vt désinfecter; **~ant** n désinfectant m

disintegrate [dɪsˈɪntɪgreɪt] vi se désintégrer

disinterested [dɪsˈɪntrəstɪd] adj désintéressé(e)

disjointed [dɪsˈdʒɔɪntɪd] adj décousu(e), incohérent(e)

disk [dɪsk] n (COMPUT) disque m; (: floppy ~) disquette f; **single-/double-sided ~** disquette simple/double face; **~ drive** n lecteur m de disquettes; **~ette** [dɪsˈkɛt] n disquette f, disque m souple

dislike [dɪsˈlaɪk] n aversion f, antipathie f ♦ vt ne pas aimer

dislocate [ˈdɪsləkeɪt] vt disloquer; déboîter

dislodge [dɪsˈlɔdʒ] vt déplacer, faire bouger

disloyal [dɪsˈlɔɪəl] adj déloyal(e)

dismal [ˈdɪzml] adj lugubre, maussade

dismantle [dɪsˈmæntl] vt démonter

dismay [dɪsˈmeɪ] n consternation f

dismiss [dɪsˈmɪs] vt congédier, renvoyer; (soldiers) faire rompre les rangs à; (idea) écarter; (LAW): **to ~ a case** rendre une fin de non-recevoir; **~al** n renvoi m

dismount [dɪsˈmaunt] vi mettre pied à terre, descendre

disobedient [dɪsəˈbiːdɪənt] adj désobéissant(e)

disobey [dɪsəˈbeɪ] vt désobéir à

disorder [dɪsˈɔːdəʳ] n désordre m; (rioting) désordres mpl; (MED) troubles mpl; **~ly** adj en désordre; désordonné(e)

disorientated [dɪsˈɔːrɪenteɪtɪd] adj désorienté(e)

disown [dɪsˈaun] vt renier

disparaging [dɪsˈpærɪdʒɪŋ] adj désobligeant(e)

dispassionate [dɪsˈpæʃənət] adj calme, froid(e); impartial(e), objectif(-ive)

dispatch [dɪsˈpætʃ] vt expédier, envoyer ♦ n envoi m, expédition f; (MIL, PRESS) dépêche f

dispel [dɪsˈpɛl] vt dissiper, chasser

dispense [dɪsˈpɛns] vt distribuer, administrer; **~ with** vt fus se passer de; **~r** n (machine) distributeur m; **dispensing chemist** (BRIT) n pharmacie f

disperse [dɪsˈpəːs] vt disperser ♦ vi se disperser

dispirited [dɪsˈpɪrɪtɪd] adj découragé(e), déprimé(e)

displace [dɪsˈpleɪs] vt déplacer

display [dɪsˈpleɪ] n étalage m; déploiement m; affichage m; (screen) écran m, visuel m; (of feeling) manifestation f ♦ vt montrer; (goods) mettre à l'étalage, exposer; (results, departure times) afficher; (pej) faire étalage de

displease [dɪsˈpliːz] vt mécontenter, contrarier; **~d** adj: **~d with** mécontent(e) de; **displeasure** [dɪsˈplɛʒəʳ] n mécontentement m

disposable [dɪsˈpauzəbl] adj (pack etc) jetable, à jeter; (income) disponible; **~ nappy** (BRIT) n couche f à jeter, couche-culotte f

disposal [dɪsˈpauzl] n (of goods for sale) vente f; (of property) disposition f, cession f; (of rubbish) enlèvement m; destruction f; **at one's ~** à sa disposition

dispose [dɪsˈpauz] vt disposer; **~ of** vt fus (unwanted goods etc) se débarrasser de, se défaire de; (problem) expédier; **~d** adj: **to be ~d to do sth** être disposé(e) à faire qch; **disposition** [dɪspəˈzɪʃən] n disposition f; (temperament) naturel m

disprove [dɪsˈpruːv] vt réfuter

dispute [dɪsˈpjuːt] n discussion f; (also: **industrial ~**) conflit m ♦ vt contester; (matter) discuter; (victory) disputer

disqualify [dɪsˈkwɔlɪfaɪ] vt (SPORT) disqualifier; **to ~ sb for sth/from doing** rendre qn inapte à qch/à faire

disquiet [dɪsˈkwaɪət] n inquiétude f, trouble m

disregard [dɪsrɪˈgɑːd] vt ne pas tenir compte de

disrepair [ˈdɪsrɪˈpɛəʳ] n: **to fall into ~** (building) tomber en ruine

disreputable [dɪsˈrɛpjutəbl] adj (person) de mauvaise réputation; (behaviour) déshonorant(e)

disrespectful [dɪsrɪˈspɛktful] adj irrespectueux(-euse)

disrupt [dɪsˈrʌpt] vt (plans) déranger; (conversation) interrompre

dissatisfied [dɪsˈsætɪsfaɪd] adj: **~ (with)** insatisfait(e) (de)

dissect [dɪˈsɛkt] vt disséquer

dissent [dɪˈsɛnt] n dissentiment m, différence f d'opinion

dissertation [dɪsəˈteɪʃən] n mémoire m

disservice [dɪsˈsəːvɪs] n: **to do sb a ~** rendre un mauvais service à qn

dissimilar [dɪˈsɪmɪləʳ] adj: **~ (to)** dissemblable (à), différent(e) (de)

dissipate [ˈdɪsɪpeɪt] vt dissiper; (money, efforts) disperser

dissolute ['dɪsəlu:t] adj débauché(e), dissolu(e)

dissolve [dɪ'zɔlv] vt dissoudre ♦ vi se dissoudre, fondre; **to ~ in(to) tears** fondre en larmes

distance ['dɪstns] n distance f; **in the ~** au loin

distant ['dɪstnt] adj lointain(e), éloigné(e); (manner) distant(e), froid(e)

distaste [dɪs'teɪst] n dégoût m; **~ful** adj déplaisant(e), désagréable

distended [dɪs'tendɪd] adj (stomach) dilaté(e)

distil [dɪs'tɪl] (US **distill**) vt distiller; **~lery** n distillerie f

distinct [dɪs'tɪŋkt] adj distinct(e); (clear) marqué(e); **as ~ from** par opposition à; **~ion** n distinction f; (in exam) mention f très bien; **~ive** adj distinctif(-ive)

distinguish [dɪs'tɪŋgwɪʃ] vt distinguer; **~ed** adj (eminent) distingué(e); **~ing** adj (feature) distinctif(-ive), caractéristique

distort [dɪs'tɔ:t] vt déformer

distract [dɪs'trækt] vt distraire, déranger; **~ed** adj distrait(e); (anxious) éperdu(e), égaré(e); **~ion** n distraction f; égarement m

distraught [dɪs'trɔ:t] adj éperdu(e)

distress [dɪs'tres] n détresse f ♦ vt affliger; **~ing** adj douloureux(-euse), pénible

distribute [dɪs'trɪbju:t] vt distribuer; **distribution** n distribution f; **distributor** n distributeur m

district ['dɪstrɪkt] n (of country) région f; (of town) quartier m; (ADMIN) district m; **~ attorney** (US) n ~ procureur m de la République; **~ nurse** (BRIT) n infirmière visiteuse

distrust [dɪs'trʌst] n méfiance f ♦ vt se méfier de

disturb [dɪs'tə:b] vt troubler; (inconvenience) déranger; **~ance** n dérangement m; (violent event, political etc) troubles mpl; (of a worried, upset) agité(e), troublé(e); **to be emotionally ~ed** avoir des problèmes affectifs; **~ing** adj troublant(e), inquiétant(e)

disuse [dɪs'ju:s] n: **to fall into ~** tomber en désuétude; **~d** [dɪs'ju:zd] adj désaffecté(e)

ditch [dɪtʃ] n fossé m; (irrigation) rigole f ♦ vt (inf) abandonner; (person) plaquer

dither ['dɪðər] vi hésiter

ditto ['dɪtəu] adv idem

dive [daɪv] n plongeon m; (of submarine) plongée f ♦ vi plonger; **to ~ into** (bag, drawer etc) plonger la main dans; (shop, car etc) se précipiter dans; **~r** n plongeur m

diversion [daɪ'və:ʃən] n (BRIT: AUT) déviation f; (distraction, MIL) diversion f

divert [daɪ'və:t] vt (funds, BRIT: traffic) dévier; (river, attention) détourner

divide [dɪ'vaɪd] vt diviser; (separate) séparer ♦ vi se diviser; **~d highway** (US) n route f à quatre voies

dividend ['dɪvɪdend] n dividende m

divine [dɪ'vaɪn] adj divin(e)

diving ['daɪvɪŋ] n plongée (sous-marine); **~ board** n plongeoir m

divinity [dɪ'vɪnɪtɪ] n divinité f; (SCOL) théologie f

division [dɪ'vɪʒən] n division f

divorce [dɪ'vɔ:s] n divorce m ♦ vt divorcer d'avec; (dissociate) séparer; **~d** adj divorcé(e); **~e** n divorcé(e)

D.I.Y. (BRIT) n abbr = **do-it-yourself**

dizzy ['dɪzɪ] adj: **to make sb ~** donner le vertige à qn; **to feel ~** avoir la tête qui tourne

DJ n abbr = **disc jockey**

DNA fingerprinting [-'fɪŋgəprɪntɪŋ] n technique f des empreintes génétiques

---
KEYWORD
---

do [du:] (pt **did**, pp **done**) n (inf: party etc) soirée f, fête f

♦ vb **1** (in negative constructions) non traduit; **I don't understand** je ne comprends pas

2 (to form questions) non traduit; **didn't you know?** vous ne le saviez pas?; **why didn't you come?** pourquoi n'êtes-vous pas venu?

3 (for emphasis, in polite expressions): **she does seem rather late** je trouve qu'elle est bien en retard; **do sit down/help yourself** asseyez-vous/servez-vous je vous en prie

4 (used to avoid repeating vb): **she swims better than I do** elle nage mieux que moi; **do you agree? - yes, I do/no, I don't** vous êtes d'accord? - oui/non; **she lives in Glasgow - so do I** elle habite Glasgow - moi aussi; **who broke it? - I did** qui l'a cassé? - c'est moi

5 (in question tags): **he laughed, didn't he?** il a ri, n'est-ce pas?; **I don't know him, do I?** je ne crois pas le connaître

♦ vt (gen: carry out, perform etc) faire; **what are you doing tonight?** qu'est-ce que vous faites ce soir?; **to do the cooking/washing up** faire la cuisine/la vaisselle; **to do one's teeth/hair/nails** se brosser les dents/se coiffer/se faire les ongles; **the car was doing 100** ≈ la voiture faisait du 160 (à l'heure)

♦ vi **1** (act, behave) faire; **do as I do** faites comme moi

2 (get on, fare) marcher; **the firm is doing well** l'entreprise marche bien; **how do you do?** comment allez-vous?; (on being introduced) enchanté(e)!

3 (suit) aller; **will it do?** est-ce que ça ira?

4 (be sufficient) suffire, aller; **will £10 do?** est-ce que 10 livres suffiront?; **that'll do** ça suffit, ça ira; **that'll do!** (in annoyance) ça va or suffit comme ça!; **to make do (with)** se contenter (de)

do away with vt fus supprimer

do up vt (laces, dress) attacher; (buttons) boutonner; (zip) fermer; (renovate: room) refaire; (: house) remettre à neuf

do with vt fus (need): **I could do with a drink/some help** quelque chose à boire/un peu d'aide ne serait pas de refus; (be connected): **that has nothing to do with you** cela ne vous concerne pas; **I won't have anything to do with it** je ne veux pas m'en mêler

do without vi s'en passer ♦ vt fus se passer de

---

dock [dɔk] n dock m; (LAW) banc m des accusés ♦ vi se mettre à quai; (SPACE) s'arrimer; **~er** n docker m; **~yard** n chantier m de construction navale

doctor ['dɔktə'] n médecin m, docteur m; (PhD etc) docteur ♦ vt (drink) frelater; **D~ of Philosophy** n (degree) doctorat m; (person) Docteur m en Droit or Lettres etc, titulaire m/f d'un doctorat

document ['dɔkjumənt] n document m; **~ary** [dɔkju'mentərɪ] adj documentaire ♦ n documentaire m

dodge [dɔdʒ] n truc m; combine f ♦ vt esquiver, éviter

dodgems ['dɔdʒəmz] (BRIT) npl autos tamponneuses

doe [dəu] n (deer) biche f; (rabbit) lapine f

does [dʌz] vb see do; **~n't = does not**

dog [dɔg] n chien(ne) ♦ vt suivre de près; poursuivre, harceler; **~ collar** n collier m de chien; (fig) faux-col m d'ecclésiastique; **~-eared** adj corné(e); **~ged** ['dɔgɪd] adj obstiné(e), opiniâtre; **~sbody** n bonne f à tout faire, tâcheron m

doings ['duɪŋz] npl activités fpl

do-it-yourself ['du:ɪtjɔ:'self] n bricolage m

doldrums ['dɔldrəmz] npl: **to be in the ~** avoir le cafard; (business) être dans le marasme

dole [dəul] n (BRIT: payment) allocation f de chômage; **on the ~** au chômage; **~ out** vt donner au compte-goutte

doll [dɔl] n poupée f

dollar ['dɔlə'] n dollar m

dolled up [dɔld-] (inf) adj: **(all) ~** sur son trente et un

dolphin ['dɔlfɪn] n dauphin m

dome [dəum] n dôme m

domestic [də'mestɪk] adj (task, appliances) ménager(-ère); (of country: trade, situation etc) intérieur(e); (animal) domestique; **~ated** adj (animal) domestiqué(e); (husband) pantouflard(e)

dominate ['dɔmɪneɪt] vt dominer

domineering [dɔmɪ'nɪərɪŋ] adj dominateur(-trice), autoritaire

dominion [də'mɪnɪən] n (territory) territoire m; **to have ~ over** contrôler

domino ['dɔmɪnəu] (pl **~es**) n domino m; **~es** n (game) dominos mpl

don [dɔn] (BRIT) n professeur m d'université

donate [də'neɪt] vt faire don de, donner

done [dʌn] pp of do

donkey ['dɔŋkɪ] n âne m

donor ['dəunə'] n (of blood etc) donneur(-euse); (to charity) donateur(-trice); **~ card** n carte f de don d'organes

don't [dəunt] vb = do not

donut ['dəunʌt] (US) n = doughnut

doodle ['du:dl] vi griffonner, gribouiller

doom [du:m] n destin m ♦ vt: **to be ~ed (to failure)** être voué(e) à l'échec

door [dɔ:'] n porte f; (RAIL, car) portière f; **~bell** n sonnette f; **~handle** n poignée f de la porte; (car) poignée de portière; **~man** (irreg) n (in hotel) portier m; **~mat** n paillasson m; **~step** n pas m de (la) porte, seuil m; **~way** n (embrasure f de la) porte f

dope [dəup] n (inf: drug) drogue f; (: person) andouille f ♦ vt (horse etc) doper

dormant ['dɔ:mənt] adj assoupi(e), en veilleuse

dormitory ['dɔ:mɪtrɪ] n dortoir m; (US: building) résidence f universitaire

dormouse ['dɔ:maus] (pl **dormice**) n loir m

DOS [dɔs] n abbr (= disk operating system) DOS

dose [dəus] n dose f

dosh [dɔʃ] (inf) n fric m

doss house ['dɔs-] (BRIT) n asile m de nuit

dot [dɔt] n point m; (on material) pois m ♦ vt: **~ted with** parsemé(e) de; **on the ~** à l'heure tapante or pile; **~ted line** n pointillé(s) m(pl)

double ['dʌbl] adj double ♦ adv (twice): **to cost ~ (sth)** coûter le double (de qch) or deux fois plus (que qch) ♦ n double m ♦ vt doubler; (fold) plier en deux ♦ vi doubler; **~s** n (TENNIS) double m; **on** or (BRIT) **at the ~** au pas de course; **~ bass** (BRIT) n contrebasse f; **~ bed** n grand lit; **~ bend** (BRIT) n virage m en S; **~-breasted** adj croisé(e); **~-cross** vt doubler, trahir; **~-decker** n autobus m à impériale; **~ glazing** (BRIT) n double vitrage m; **~ room** n chambre f pour deux personnes; **doubly** adv doublement, deux fois plus

doubt [daut] n doute m ♦ vt douter de; **to ~ that** douter que; **~ful** adj douteux(-euse); (person) incertain(e); **~less** adv sans doute, sûrement

dough [dəu] n pâte f; **~nut** (US **donut**) n beignet m

dove [dʌv] n colombe f

Dover ['dəuvəʳ] n Douvres

dovetail ['dʌvteɪl] vi (fig) concorder

dowdy ['daudɪ] adj démodé(e); mal fagoté(e) (inf)

down [daun] n (soft feathers) duvet m ♦ adv en bas, vers le bas; (on the ground) par terre ♦ prep en bas de; (along) le long de ♦ vt (inf: drink, food) s'envoyer; ~ **with X!** à bas X!; ~-**and-out** n clochard(e); ~-**at-heel** adj éculé(e); (fig) miteux(-euse); ~**cast** adj démoralisé(e); ~**fall** n chute f; ruine f; ~**hearted** adj découragé(e); ~**hill** adv: to go ~**hill** descendre; (fig) péricliter; ~ **payment** n acompte m; ~**pour** n pluie torrentielle, déluge m; ~**right** adj (lie etc) effronté(e); (refusal) catégorique; ~**size** vt (ECON) réduire ses effectifs

Down's syndrome [daunz-] n (MED) trisomie f

down: ~**stairs** adv au rez-de-chaussée; à l'étage inférieur; ~**stream** adv en aval; ~-**to-earth** adj terre à terre inv; ~**town** adv en ville; ~ **under** n en Australie/Nouvelle-Zélande; ~**ward** adj, adv vers le bas; ~**wards** adv vers le bas

dowry ['dauri] n dot f

doz. abbr = **dozen**

doze [dəuz] vi sommeiller; ~ **off** vi s'assoupir

dozen ['dʌzn] n douzaine f; a ~ **books** une douzaine de livres; ~**s of** des centaines de

Dr. abbr = **doctor**; **drive**

drab [dræb] adj terne, morne

draft [drɑːft] n ébauche f, (of letter, essay etc) brouillon m; (COMM) traite f; (US: call-up) conscription f ♦ vt faire le brouillon or un projet de; (MIL: send) détacher; see also **draught**

draftsman ['drɑːftsmən] (irreg) (US) n **draughtsman**

drag [dræg] vt traîner; (river) draguer ♦ vi traîner ♦ n (inf) casse-pieds m/f; (women's clothing): **in** ~ (en) travesti; ~ **on** vi s'éterniser

dragon ['drægn] n dragon m

dragonfly ['drægənflaɪ] n libellule f

drain [dreɪn] n égout m, canalisation f; (on resources) saignée f ♦ vt (land, marshes etc) drainer, assécher; (vegetables) égoutter; (glass) vider ♦ vi (water) s'écouler; ~**age** n drainage m; système m d'égouts or de canalisations; ~**ing board** (US **drain board**) n égouttoir m; ~**pipe** n tuyau m d'écoulement

drama ['drɑːmə] n (art) théâtre m, art m dramatique; (play) pièce f (de théâtre); (event) drame m; ~**tic** [drə'mætɪk] adj dramatique; spectaculaire; ~**tist** ['dræmətɪst] n auteur m dramatique; ~**tize** ['dræmətaɪz] vt (events) dramatiser; (adapt: for TV/cinema) adapter pour la télévision/pour l'écran

drank [dræŋk] pt of **drink**

drape [dreɪp] vt draper; ~**s** (US) npl rideaux mpl

drastic ['dræstɪk] adj sévère; énergique; (change) radical(e)

draught [drɑːft] (US **draft**) n courant m d'air; (NAUT) tirant m d'eau; on ~ (beer) à la pression; ~**board** (BRIT) n damier m; ~**s** (BRIT) n (jeu m de) dames fpl

draughtsman ['drɑːftsmən] (irreg) n dessinateur(-trice) (industriel(le))

draw [drɔː] (pt drew, pp drawn) vt tirer; (tooth) arracher, extraire; (attract) attirer; (picture) dessiner; (line, circle) tracer; (money) retirer; (wages) toucher ♦ vi (SPORT) faire match nul ♦ n match nul; (lottery) tirage m au sort; loterie f; to ~ **near** s'approcher; ~ **out** vi (lengthen) s'allonger ♦ vt (money) retirer; ~ **up** vi (stop) s'arrêter ♦ vt (chair) approcher; (document) établir, dresser; ~**back** n inconvénient m, désavantage m; ~**bridge** n pont-levis m

drawer [drɔːʳ] n tiroir m

drawing ['drɔːɪŋ] n dessin m; ~ **board** n planche f à dessin; ~ **pin** (BRIT) n punaise f; ~ **room** n salon m

drawl [drɔːl] n accent traînant

drawn [drɔːn] pp of **draw**

dread [drɛd] n terreur f, effroi m ♦ vt redouter, appréhender; ~**ful** adj affreux(-euse)

dream [driːm] (pt, pp dreamed or dreamt) n rêve m ♦ vt, vi rêver; ~**y** adj rêveur(-euse); (music) langoureux(-euse)

dreary ['drɪərɪ] adj morne; monotone

dredge [drɛdʒ] vt draguer

dregs [drɛgz] npl lie f

drench [drɛntʃ] vt tremper

dress [drɛs] n robe f; (no pl: clothing) habillement m, tenue f ♦ vi s'habiller ♦ vt habiller; (wound) panser; to get ~**ed** s'habiller; ~ **up** vi s'habiller; (in fancy ~) se déguiser; ~ **circle** (BRIT) n (THEATRE) premier balcon; ~**er** n (furniture) vaisselier m; (: US) coiffeuse f, commode f; ~**ing** n (MED) pansement m; (CULIN) sauce f, assaisonnement m; ~**ing gown** (BRIT) n robe f de chambre; ~**ing room** n (THEATRE) loge f; (SPORT) vestiaire m; ~**ing table** n coiffeuse f; ~**maker** n couturière f; ~ **rehearsal** n (répétition f) générale f

drew [druː] pt of **draw**

dribble ['drɪbl] vi (baby) baver ♦ vt (ball) dribbler

dried [draɪd] adj (fruit, beans) sec (sèche); (eggs, milk) en poudre

drier ['draɪəʳ] n = **dryer**

drift [drɪft] n (of current etc) force f; direction f, mouvement m; (of snow) rafale f; (: on

ground) congère f; (general meaning) sens
(général) ♦ vi (boat) aller à la dérive, dériver;
(sand, snow) s'amonceler, s'entasser; **~wood**
n bois flotté

drill [drɪl] n perceuse f; (~ bit) foret m, mèche
f; (of dentist) roulette f, fraise f; (MIL) exercice
m ♦ vt percer; (troops) entraîner ♦ vi (for oil)
faire un or des forage(s)

drink [drɪŋk] (pt drank, pp drunk) n boisson f;
(alcoholic) verre m ♦ vt, vi boire; **to have a ~**
boire quelque chose, boire un verre; prendre
l'apéritif; **a ~ of water** un verre d'eau; **~er** n
buveur(-euse); **~ing water** n eau f potable

drip [drɪp] n goutte f; (MED) goutte-à-goutte
m inv, perfusion f ♦ vi tomber goutte à
goutte; (tap) goutter; **~-dry** adj (shirt) sans
repassage; **~ping** n graisse f (de rôti)

drive [draɪv] (pt drove, pp driven) n
promenade f or trajet m en voiture; (also:
~way) allée f; (energy) dynamisme m, énergie
f; (push) effort (concerté), campagne f; (also:
disk ~) lecteur m de disquettes ♦ vt conduire;
(push) chasser, pousser; (TECH: motor, wheel)
faire fonctionner; entraîner; (nail, stake etc):
to ~ sth into sth enfoncer qch dans qch ♦ vi
(AUT: at controls) conduire; (: travel) aller en
voiture; **left-/right-hand ~** conduite f à
gauche/droite; **to ~ sb mad** rendre qn fou
(folle); **to ~ sb home/to the airport**
reconduire qn chez lui/conduire qn à
l'aéroport; **~-by shooting** n (tentative
d')assassinat par coups de feu tirés d'un voiture

drivel ['drɪvl] (inf) n idioties fpl

driver ['draɪvər] n conducteur(-trice); (of taxi,
bus) chauffeur m; **~'s license** (US) n permis
m de conduire

driveway ['draɪvweɪ] n allée f

driving ['draɪvɪŋ] n conduite f; **~ instructor**
n moniteur m d'auto-école; **~ lesson** n leçon
f de conduite; **~ licence** (BRIT) n permis m
de conduire; **~ school** n auto-école m; **~ test**
n examen m du permis de conduire

drizzle ['drɪzl] n bruine f, crachin m

drool [druːl] vi baver

droop [druːp] vi (shoulders) tomber; (head)
pencher; (flower) pencher la tête

drop [drɔp] n goutte f; (fall) baisse f; (also:
parachute ~) saut m ♦ vt laisser tomber;
(voice, eyes, price) baisser; (set down from car)
déposer ♦ vi tomber; **~s** npl (MED) gouttes;
~ off vi (sleep) s'assoupir ♦ vt (passenger)
déposer; **~ out** vi (withdraw) se retirer;
(student etc) abandonner, décrocher; **~out** n
marginal(e); **~per** n compte-gouttes m inv;
~pings npl crottes fpl

drought [draut] n sécheresse f

drove [drəuv] pt of **drive**

drown [draun] vt noyer ♦ vi se noyer

drowsy ['drauzɪ] adj somnolent(e)

drug [drʌg] n médicament m; (narcotic)
drogue f ♦ vt droguer; **to be on ~s** se
droguer; **~ addict** n toxicomane m/f; **~gist**
(US) n pharmacien(ne)-droguiste; **~store**
(US) n pharmacie-droguerie f, drugstore m

drum [drʌm] n tambour m; (for oil, petrol)
bidon m; **~s** npl (kit) batterie f; **~mer** n
(joueur m de) tambour m

drunk [drʌŋk] pp of **drink** ♦ adj ivre, soûl(e)
♦ n (also: **~ard**) ivrogne m/f; **~en** adj
(person) ivre, soûl(e); (rage, stupor) ivrogne,
d'ivrogne

dry [draɪ] adj sec (sèche); (day) sans pluie;
(humour) pince-sans-rire inv; (lake, riverbed,
well) à sec ♦ vt sécher; (clothes) faire sécher
♦ vi sécher; **~ up** vi tarir; **~-cleaner's** n
teinturerie f; **~er** n séchoir m; (spin-dryer)
essoreuse f; **~ness** n sécheresse f; **~ rot** n
pourriture sèche (du bois)

DSS n abbr (= Department of Social Security) ≈
Sécurité sociale

DTP n abbr (= desk-top publishing) PAO f

dual ['djuəl] adj double; **~ carriageway**
(BRIT) n route f à quatre voies or à chaussées
séparées; **~-purpose** adj à double usage

dubbed [dʌbd] adj (CINEMA) doublé(e)

dubious ['djuːbɪəs] adj hésitant(e),
incertain(e); (reputation, company)
douteux(-euse)

duchess ['dʌtʃɪs] n duchesse f

duck [dʌk] n canard m ♦ vi se baisser
vivement, baisser subitement la tête; **~ling**
['dʌklɪŋ] n caneton m

duct [dʌkt] n conduite f, canalisation f; (ANAT)
conduit m

dud [dʌd] n (object, tool): **it's a ~** c'est de la
camelote, ça ne marche pas ♦ adj: **~ cheque**
(BRIT) chèque sans provision

due [djuː] adj dû (due); (expected)
attendu(e); (fitting) qui convient ♦ n: **to give
sb his** (or **her**) **~** être juste envers qn ♦ adv:
~ north droit vers le nord; **~s** npl (for club,
union) cotisation f; (in harbour) droits mpl (de
port); **in ~ course** en temps utile or voulu;
finalement; **~ to** dû (due) à; causé(e) par;
he's ~ to finish tomorrow normalement il doit
finir demain

duet [djuː'et] n duo m

duffel bag ['dʌfl-] n sac m marin

duffel coat n duffel-coat m

dug [dʌg] pt, pp of **dig**

duke [djuːk] n duc m

dull [dʌl] adj terne, morne; (boring)
ennuyeux(-euse); (sound, pain) sourd(e);
(weather, day) gris(e), maussade ♦ vt (pain,
grief) atténuer; (mind, senses) engourdir

duly ['djuːlɪ] adv (on time) en temps voulu;
(as expected) comme il se doit

dumb [dʌm] adj muet(te); (stupid) bête;

~founded *adj* sidéré(e)

dummy ['dʌmɪ] *n* (*tailor's model*) mannequin *m*; (*mock-up*) factice *m*, maquette *f*; (BRIT: *for baby*) tétine *f* ♦ *adj* faux (fausse), factice

dump [dʌmp] *n* (*also:* **rubbish ~**) décharge (publique); (*pej*) trou *m* ♦ *vt* (*put down*) déposer; déverser; (*get rid of*) se débarrasser de; (COMPUT: *data*) vider, transférer

dumpling ['dʌmplɪŋ] *n* boulette *f* (de pâte)

dumpy ['dʌmpɪ] *adj* boulot(te)

dunce [dʌns] *n* âne *m*, cancre *m*

dune [dju:n] *n* dune *f*

dung [dʌŋ] *n* fumier *m*

dungarees [dʌŋgə'ri:z] *npl* salopette *f*; bleu(s) *m(pl)*

dungeon ['dʌndʒən] *n* cachot *m*

duplex ['dju:pleks] (US) *n* maison jumelée; (*apartment*) duplex *m*

duplicate [*n* 'dju:plɪkət, *vb* 'dju:plɪkeɪt] *n* double *m* ♦ *vt* faire un double de; (*on machine*) polycopier; photocopier; **in ~** en deux exemplaires

durable ['djuərəbl] *adj* durable; (*clothes, metal*) résistant(e), solide

duration [djuə'reɪʃən] *n* durée *f*

during ['djuərɪŋ] *prep* pendant, au cours de

dusk [dʌsk] *n* crépuscule *m*

dust [dʌst] *n* poussière *f* ♦ *vt* (*furniture*) épousseter, essuyer; (*cake etc*) **to ~ with** saupoudrer de; **~bin** (BRIT) *n* poubelle *f*; **~er** *n* chiffon *m*; **~man** (BRIT) (*irreg*) *n* boueux *m*, éboueur *m*; **~y** *adj* poussiéreux(-euse)

Dutch [dʌtʃ] *adj* hollandais(e), néerlandais(e) ♦ *n* (LING) hollandais *m* ♦ *adv* (*inf*): **to go ~** partager les frais; **the ~** *npl* (*people*) les Hollandais; **~man** (*irreg*) *n* Hollandais; **~woman** (*irreg*) *n* Hollandaise *f*

duty ['dju:tɪ] *n* devoir *m*; (*tax*) droit *m*, taxe *f*; **on ~** de service; (*at night etc*) de garde; **off ~** libre, pas de service or de garde; **~-free** *adj* exempté(e) de douane, hors taxe *inv*

duvet ['du:veɪ] (BRIT) *n* couette *f*

dwarf [dwɔ:f] (*pl* **dwarves**) *n* nain(e) ♦ *vt* écraser

dwell [dwel] (*pt, pp* **dwelt**) *vi* demeurer; **~ on** *vt fus* s'appesantir sur

dwindle ['dwɪndl] *vi* diminuer, décroître

dye [daɪ] *n* teinture *f* ♦ *vt* teindre

dying ['daɪɪŋ] *adj* mourant(e), agonisant(e)

dyke [daɪk] (BRIT) *n* digue *f*

dynamic [daɪ'næmɪk] *adj* dynamique

dynamite ['daɪnəmaɪt] *n* dynamite *f*

dynamo ['daɪnəməu] *n* dynamo *f*

dyslexia [dɪs'leksɪə] *n* dyslexie *f*

E, e

E [i:] *n* (MUS) mi *m*

each [i:tʃ] *adj* chaque ♦ *pron* chacun(e); **~ other** l'un(e) l'autre; **they hate ~ other** ils se détestent (mutuellement); **you are jealous of ~ other** vous êtes jaloux l'un de l'autre; **they have 2 books ~** ils ont 2 livres chacun

eager ['i:gər] *adj* (*keen*) avide; **to be ~ to do sth** avoir très envie de faire qch; **to be ~ for** désirer vivement, être avide de

eagle ['i:gl] *n* aigle *m*

ear [ɪər] *n* oreille *f*; (*of corn*) épi *m*; **~ache** *n* mal aux oreilles; **~drum** *n* tympan *m*

earl [ə:l] (BRIT) *n* comte *m*

earlier ['ə:lɪər] *adj* (*date etc*) plus rapproché(e); (*edition, fashion etc*) plus ancien(ne), antérieur(e) ♦ *adv* plus tôt

early ['ə:lɪ] *adv* tôt, de bonne heure; (*ahead of time*) en avance; (*near the beginning*) au début ♦ *adj* qui se manifeste (or se fait) tôt or de bonne heure; (*work*) de jeunesse; (*settler, Christian*) premier(-ère); (*reply*) rapide; (*death*) prématuré(e); **to have an ~ night** se coucher tôt or de bonne heure; **in the ~** or **~ in the spring/19th century** au début du printemps/19ème siècle; **~ retirement** *n*: **to take ~ retirement** prendre sa retraite anticipée

earmark ['ɪəmɑ:k] *vt*: **to ~ sth for** réserver or destiner qch à

earn [ə:n] *vt* gagner; (COMM: *yield*) rapporter

earnest ['ə:nɪst] *adj* sérieux(-euse); **in ~** ♦ *adv* sérieusement

earnings ['ə:nɪŋz] *npl* salaire *m*; (*of company*) bénéfices *mpl*

ear: **~phones** *npl* écouteurs *mpl*; **~ring** *n* boucle *f* d'oreille; **~shot** *n*: **within ~shot** à portée de voix

earth [ə:θ] *n* (*gen, also* BRIT: ELEC) terre *f* ♦ *vt* relier à la terre; **~enware** *n* poterie *f*; faïence *f*; **~quake** *n* tremblement *m* de terre, séisme *m*; **~y** *adj* (*vulgar: humour*) truculent(e)

ease [i:z] *n* facilité *f*, aisance *f*; (*comfort*) bien-être *m* ♦ *vt* (*soothe*) calmer; (*loosen*) relâcher, détendre; **to ~ sth in/out** faire pénétrer/sortir qch délicatement or avec douceur; faciliter la pénétration/la sortie de qch; **at ~!** (MIL) repos!; **~ off** or **up** *vi* diminuer; (*slow down*) ralentir

easel ['i:zl] *n* chevalet *m*

easily ['i:zɪlɪ] *adv* facilement

east [i:st] *n* est *m* ♦ *adj* (*wind*) d'est; (*side*) est *inv* ♦ *adv* à l'est, vers l'est; **the E~** l'Orient *m*; les pays *mpl* de l'Est

Easter ['i:stər] *n* Pâques *fpl*; **~ egg** *n* œuf *m* de Pâques

east: **~erly** ['i:stəlɪ] *adj* (*wind*) d'est;

(*direction*) est *inv*; (*point*) à l'est; **~ern**
['iːstən] *adj* de l'est, oriental(e); **~ward(s)**
['iːstwəd(z)] *adv* vers l'est, à l'est

easy ['iːzɪ] *adj* facile; (*manner*) aisé(e) ♦ *adv*:
to take it *or* **things ~** ne pas se fatiguer; (*not
worry*) ne pas (trop) s'en faire; **~ chair** *n*
fauteuil *m*; **~-going** *adj* accommodant(e),
facile à vivre

eat [iːt] (*pt* **ate**, *pp* **eaten**) *vt*, *vi* manger;
~ away at, **~ into** *vt fus* ronger, attaquer;
(*savings*) entamer

eaves [iːvz] *npl* avant-toit *m*

eavesdrop ['iːvzdrɔp] *vi*: **to ~ (on a
conversation)** écouter (une conversation) de
façon indiscrète

ebb [eb] *n* reflux *m* ♦ *vi* refluer; (*fig: also:*
~ away) décliner

ebony ['ebənɪ] *n* ébène *f*

EC *n abbr* (= *European Community*) C.E. *f*

ECB *n abbr* (= *European Central Bank*) BCE *f*

eccentric [ɪk'sentrɪk] *adj* excentrique ♦ *n*
excentrique *m/f*

echo ['ekəʊ] (*pl* **~es**) *n* écho *m* ♦ *vt* répéter
♦ *vi* résonner, faire écho

eclipse [ɪ'klɪps] *n* éclipse *f*

ecology [ɪ'kɔlədʒɪ] *n* écologie *f*

economic [iːkə'nɔmɪk] *adj* économique;
(*business etc*) rentable; **~ refugee** réfugié *m*
économique

economical [iːkə'nɔmɪkl] *adj* économique;
(*person*) économe

economics [iːkə'nɔmɪks] *n* économie *f*
politique ♦ *npl* (*of project, situation*) aspect *m*
financier

economize [ɪ'kɔnəmaɪz] *vi* économiser, faire
des économies

economy [ɪ'kɔnəmɪ] *n* économie *f*; **~ class**
n classe *f* touriste; **~ size** *n* format *m*
économique

ecstasy ['ekstəsɪ] *n* extase *f* (*drogue aussi*);
ecstatic [eks'tætɪk] *adj* extatique

ECU ['eɪkjuː] *n abbr* (= *European Currency
Unit*) ECU *m*

eczema ['eksɪmə] *n* eczéma *m*

edge [edʒ] *n* bord *m*; (*of knife etc*) tranchant
m, fil *m* ♦ *vt* border; **on ~** (*fig*) crispé(e),
tendu(e); **to ~ away from** s'éloigner
furtivement de; **~ways** *adv*: **he couldn't get
a word in ~ways** il ne pouvait pas placer un
mot

edgy ['edʒɪ] *adj* crispé(e), tendu(e)

edible ['edɪbl] *adj* comestible

Edinburgh ['edɪnbərə] *n* Édimbourg

edit ['edɪt] *vt* (*text, book*) éditer; (*report*)
préparer; (*film*) monter; (*broadcast*) réaliser;
~ion [ɪ'dɪʃən] *n* édition *f*; **~or** *n* (*of column*)
rédacteur(-trice); (*of newspaper*) rédac-
teur(-trice) en chef; (*of sb's work*) édi-
teur(-trice); **~orial** [edɪ'tɔːrɪəl] *adj* de la

rédaction, éditorial(e) ♦ *n* éditorial *m*

educate ['edjukeɪt] *vt* (*teach*) instruire;
(*instruct*) éduquer; **~d** *adj* (*person*) cultivé(e);
education [edju'keɪʃən] *n* éducation *f*;
(*studies*) études *fpl*; (*teaching*) enseignement
m, instruction *f*; **educational** *adj* (*experience,
toy*) pédagogique; (*institution*) scolaire;
(*policy*) d'éducation

eel [iːl] *n* anguille *f*

eerie ['ɪərɪ] *adj* inquiétant(e)

effect [ɪ'fekt] *n* effet *m* ♦ *vt* effectuer; **to take
~** (*law*) entrer en vigueur, prendre effet;
(*drug*) agir, faire son effet; **in ~** en fait; **~ive**
[ɪ'fektɪv] *adj* efficace; (*actual*) véritable;
~ively *adv* efficacement; (*in reality*)
effectivement; **~iveness** *n* efficacité *f*

effeminate [ɪ'femɪnɪt] *adj* efféminé(e)

effervescent [efə'vesnt] *adj* (*drink*)
gazeux(-euse)

efficiency [ɪ'fɪʃənsɪ] *n* efficacité *f*; (*of
machine*) rendement *m*

efficient [ɪ'fɪʃənt] *adj* efficace; (*machine*) qui
a un bon rendement

effort ['efət] *n* effort *m*; **~less** *adj* (*style*)
aisé(e); (*achievement*) facile

effusive [ɪ'fjuːsɪv] *adj* chaleureux(-euse)

e.g. *adv abbr* (= *exempli gratia*) par exemple,
p. ex.

egg [eg] *n* œuf *m*; **hard-boiled/soft-boiled ~**
œuf dur/à la coque; **~ on** *vt* pousser; **~cup** *n*
coquetier *m*; **~plant** *n* (*esp US*) aubergine *f*;
~shell *n* coquille *f* d'œuf

ego ['iːgəʊ] *n* (*self-esteem*) amour-propre *m*

egotism ['egəʊtɪzəm] *n* égotisme *m*

egotist ['egəʊtɪst] *n* égocentrique *m/f*

Egypt ['iːdʒɪpt] *n* Égypte *f*; **~ian** [ɪ'dʒɪpʃən]
adj égyptien(ne) ♦ *n* Égyptien(ne)

eiderdown ['aɪdədaʊn] *n* édredon *m*

Eiffel Tower ['aɪfəl-] *n* tour *f* Eiffel

eight [eɪt] *num* huit; **~een** [eɪ'tiːn] *num* dix-
huit; **~h** [eɪtθ] *num* huitième; **~y** ['eɪtɪ] *num*
quatre-vingt(s)

Eire ['ɛərə] *n* République *f* d'Irlande

either ['aɪðər] *adj* l'un ou l'autre; (*both, each*)
chaque ♦ *pron*: **~ (of them)** l'un ou l'autre
♦ *adv* non plus ♦ *conj*: **~ good or bad** ou bon
ou mauvais, soit bon soit mauvais; **on ~ side**
de chaque côté; **I don't like ~** je n'aime ni l'un
ni l'autre; **no, I don't ~** moi non plus

eject [ɪ'dʒekt] *vt* (*tenant etc*) expulser; (*object*)
éjecter

elaborate [*adj* ɪ'læbərɪt, *vb* ɪ'læbəreɪt] *adj*
compliqué(e), recherché(e) ♦ *vt* élaborer
♦ *vi*: **to ~ (on)** entrer dans les détails (de)

elastic [ɪ'læstɪk] *adj* élastique ♦ *n* élastique *m*;
~ band *n* élastique *m*

elated [ɪ'leɪtɪd] *adj* transporté(e) de joie

elation [ɪ'leɪʃən] *n* allégresse *f*

elbow ['elbəʊ] *n* coude *m*

elder ['ɛldəʳ] adj aîné(e) ♦ n (tree) sureau m; **one's ~s** ses aînés; **~ly** adj âgé(e) ♦ npl: **the ~ly** les personnes âgées

eldest ['ɛldɪst] adj, n: **the ~ (child)** l'aîné(e) (des enfants)

elect [ɪ'lɛkt] vt élire ♦ adj: **the president ~** le président désigné; **to ~ to do** choisir de faire; **~ion** n élection f; **~ioneering** [ɪlɛkʃə'nɪərɪŋ] n propagande électorale, manœuvres électorales; **~or** n électeur(-trice); **~orate** n électorat m

electric [ɪ'lɛktrɪk] adj électrique; **~al** adj électrique; **~ blanket** n couverture chauffante; **~ fire** (BRIT) n radiateur m électrique; **~ian** [ɪlɛk'trɪʃən] n électricien m; **~ity** [ɪlɛk'trɪsɪtɪ] n électricité f; **electrify** [ɪ'lɛktrɪfaɪ] vt (RAIL, fence) électrifier; (audience) électriser

electronic [ɪlɛk'trɔnɪk] adj électronique; **~ mail** n courrier m électronique; **~s** n électronique f

elegant ['ɛlɪgənt] adj élégant(e)

element ['ɛlɪmənt] n (gen) élément m; (of heater, kettle etc) résistance f; **~ary** [ɛlɪ'mɛntərɪ] adj élémentaire; (school, education) primaire

elephant ['ɛlɪfənt] n éléphant m

elevation [ɛlɪ'veɪʃən] n (raising, promotion) avancement m, promotion f; (height) hauteur f

elevator ['ɛlɪveɪtəʳ] n (in warehouse etc) élévateur m, monte-charge m inv; (US: lift) ascenseur m

eleven [ɪ'lɛvn] num onze; **~ses** [ɪ'lɛvnzɪz] npl ≈ pause-café f; **~th** num onzième

elicit [ɪ'lɪsɪt] vt: **to ~ (from)** obtenir (de), arracher (à)

eligible ['ɛlɪdʒəbl] adj: **to be ~ for** remplir les conditions requises pour; **an ~ young man/ woman** un beau parti

elm [ɛlm] n orme m

elongated ['iːlɔŋgeɪtɪd] adj allongé(e)

elope [ɪ'ləup] vi (lovers) s'enfuir (ensemble)

eloquent ['ɛləkwənt] adj éloquent(e)

else [ɛls] adv d'autre; **something ~** quelque chose d'autre, autre chose; **somewhere ~** ailleurs, autre part; **everywhere ~** partout ailleurs; **nobody ~** personne d'autre; **where ~?** à quel autre endroit?; **little ~** pas grand-chose d'autre; **~where** adv ailleurs, autre part

elude [ɪ'luːd] vt échapper à

elusive [ɪ'luːsɪv] adj insaisissable

emaciated [ɪ'meɪsɪeɪtɪd] adj émacié(e), décharné(e)

e-mail ['iːmeɪl] n courrier m électronique ♦ vt (person) envoyer un message électronique à

emancipate [ɪ'mænsɪpeɪt] vt émanciper

embankment [ɪm'bæŋkmənt] n (of road, railway) remblai m, talus m; (of river) berge f,

quai m

embark [ɪm'baːk] vi embarquer; **to ~ on** (journey) entreprendre; (fig) se lancer or s'embarquer dans; **~ation** [ɛmbaː'keɪʃən] n embarquement m

embarrass [ɪm'bærəs] vt embarrasser, gêner; **~ed** adj gêné(e); **~ing** adj gênant(e), embarrassant(e); **~ment** n embarras m, gêne f

embassy ['ɛmbəsɪ] n ambassade f

embedded [ɪm'bɛdɪd] adj enfoncé(e)

embellish [ɪm'bɛlɪʃ] vt orner, décorer; (fig: account) enjoliver

embers ['ɛmbəz] npl braise f

embezzle [ɪm'bɛzl] vt détourner; **~ment** n détournement m de fonds

embitter [ɪm'bɪtəʳ] vt (person) aigrir; (relations) envenimer

embody [ɪm'bɔdɪ] vt (features) réunir, comprendre; (ideas) formuler, exprimer

embossed [ɪm'bɔst] adj (metal) estampé(e); (leather) frappé(e); **~ wallpaper** papier gaufré

embrace [ɪm'breɪs] vt embrasser, étreindre; (include) embrasser ♦ vi s'étreindre, s'embrasser ♦ n étreinte f

embroider [ɪm'brɔɪdəʳ] vt broder; **~y** n broderie f

emerald ['ɛmərəld] n émeraude f

emerge [ɪ'məːdʒ] vi apparaître; (from room, car) surgir; (from sleep, imprisonment) sortir

emergency [ɪ'məːdʒənsɪ] n urgence f; **in an ~** en cas d'urgence; **~ cord** n sonnette f d'alarme; **~ exit** n sortie f de secours; **~ landing** n atterrissage forcé; **~ services** npl: **the ~ services** (fire, police, ambulance) les services mpl d'urgence

emery board ['ɛmərɪ-] n lime f à ongles (en carton émerisé)

emigrate ['ɛmɪgreɪt] vi émigrer

eminent ['ɛmɪnənt] adj éminent(e)

emissions [ɪ'mɪʃənz] npl émissions fpl

emit [ɪ'mɪt] vt émettre

emotion [ɪ'məuʃən] n émotion f; **~al** adj (person) émotif(-ive), très sensible; (needs, exhaustion) affectif(-ive); (scene) émouvant(e), (tone, speech) qui fait appel aux sentiments; **~ive** adj chargé(e) d'émotion; (subject) sensible

emperor ['ɛmpərəʳ] n empereur m

emphasis ['ɛmfəsɪs] (pl -ases) n (stress) accent m; (importance) insistance f

emphasize ['ɛmfəsaɪz] vt (syllable, word, point) appuyer or insister sur; (feature) souligner, accentuer

emphatic [ɛm'fætɪk] adj (strong) énergique, vigoureux(-euse); (unambiguous, clear) catégorique

empire ['ɛmpaɪəʳ] n empire m

employ [ɪm'plɔɪ] vt employer; **~ee** n

employé(e); **~er** *n* employeur(-euse);
~ment *n* emploi *m*; **~ment agency** *n*
agence *f* ou bureau *m* de placement

empower [ɪmˈpauər] *vt*: **to ~ sb to do**
autoriser ou habiliter qn à faire

empress [ˈɛmprɪs] *n* impératrice *f*

emptiness [ˈɛmptɪnɪs] *n* (*of area, region*)
aspect *m* désertique; (*of life*) vide *m*,
vacuité *f*

empty [ˈɛmptɪ] *adj* vide; (*threat, promise*) en
l'air, vain(e) ♦ *vt* vider ♦ *vi* se vider; (*liquid*)
s'écouler; **~-handed** *adj* les mains vides

EMU *n abbr* (= *economic and monetary union*)
UME *f*

emulate [ˈɛmjuleɪt] *vt* rivaliser avec, imiter

emulsion [ɪˈmʌlʃən] *n* émulsion *f*; (*also:*
~ paint) peinture mate

enable [ɪˈneɪbl] *vt*: **to ~ sb to do** permettre à
qn de faire

enamel [ɪˈnæməl] *n* émail *m*; (*also: ~ paint*)
peinture laquée

enchant [ɪnˈtʃɑːnt] *vt* enchanter; **~ing** *adj*
ravissant(e), enchanteur(-teresse)

encl. *abbr* = **enclosed**

enclose [ɪnˈkləuz] *vt* (*land*) clôturer; (*space,
object*) entourer; (*letter etc*): **to ~** (**with**)
joindre (à); **please find ~d** veuillez trouver ci-
joint; **enclosure** *n* enceinte *f*

encompass [ɪnˈkʌmpəs] *vt* (*include*)
contenir, inclure

encore [ɔŋˈkɔːr] *excl* bis ♦ *n* bis *m*

encounter [ɪnˈkauntər] *n* rencontre ♦ *vt*
rencontrer

encourage [ɪnˈkʌrɪdʒ] *vt* encourager;
~ment *n* encouragement *m*

encroach [ɪnˈkrəutʃ] *vi*: **to ~ (up)on** empiéter
sur

encyclop(a)edia [ɛnsaɪkləuˈpiːdɪə] *n*
encyclopédie *f*

end [ɛnd] *n* (*gen, also: aim*) fin *f*; (*of table,
street, rope etc*) bout *m*, extrémité *f* ♦ *vt*
terminer; (*also:* **bring to an ~, put an ~ to**)
mettre fin à ♦ *vi* se terminer, finir; **in the ~**
finalement; **on ~** (*object*) debout, dressé(e);
to stand on ~ (*hair*) se dresser sur la tête; **for
hours on ~** pendant des heures et des heures;
~ up *vi*: **to ~ up in** (*condition*) finir *or* se
terminer par; (*place*) finir *or* aboutir à

endanger [ɪnˈdeɪndʒər] *vt* mettre en danger;
an ~ed species une espèce en voie de
disparition

endearing [ɪnˈdɪərɪŋ] *adj* attachant(e)

endeavour [ɪnˈdɛvər] (*US* **endeavor**) *n*
tentative *f*, effort *m* ♦ *vi*: **to ~ to do** tenter *or*
s'efforcer de faire

ending [ˈɛndɪŋ] *n* dénouement *m*, fin *f*;
(*LING*) terminaison *f*

endive [ˈɛndaɪv] *n* chicorée *f*; (*smooth*)
endive *f*

endless [ˈɛndlɪs] *adj* sans fin, interminable

endorse [ɪnˈdɔːs] *vt* (*cheque*) endosser;
(*approve*) appuyer, approuver, sanctionner;
~ment *n* (*approval*) appui *m*, aval *m*; (*BRIT:
on driving licence*) contravention portée au
permis de conduire

endure [ɪnˈdjuər] *vt* supporter, endurer ♦ *vi*
durer

enemy [ˈɛnəmɪ] *adj, n* ennemi(e)

energetic [ɛnəˈdʒɛtɪk] *adj* énergique;
(*activity*) qui fait se dépenser (physiquement)

energy [ˈɛnədʒɪ] *n* énergie *f*

enforce [ɪnˈfɔːs] *vt* (*law*) appliquer, faire
respecter

engage [ɪnˈɡeɪdʒ] *vt* engager; (*attention etc*)
retenir ♦ *vi* (*TECH*) s'enclencher, s'engrener;
to ~ in se lancer dans; **~d** *adj* (*BRIT: busy, in
use*) occupé(e); (*betrothed*) fiancé(e); **to get
~d** se fiancer; **~d tone** *n* (*TEL*) tonalité *f*
occupé *inv or* pas libre; **~ment** *n* obligation
f, engagement *m*; rendez-vous *m inv*; (*to
marry*) fiançailles *fpl*; **~ment ring** *n* bague *f*
de fiançailles; **engaging** *adj* engageant(e),
attirant(e)

engine [ˈɛndʒɪn] *n* (*AUT*) moteur *m*; (*RAIL*)
locomotive *f*; **~ driver** *n* mécanicien *m*

engineer [ɛndʒɪˈnɪər] *n* ingénieur *m*; (*BRIT:
repairer*) dépanneur *m*; (*NAVY, US RAIL*)
mécanicien *m*; **~ing** *n* engineering *m*,
ingénierie *f*; (*of bridges, ships*) génie *m*; (*of
machine*) mécanique *f*

England [ˈɪŋɡlənd] *n* Angleterre *f*; **English**
adj anglais(e) ♦ *n* (*LING*) anglais *m*; the
English *npl* (*people*) les Anglais; the **English
Channel** la Manche; **Englishman** (*irreg*) *n*
Anglais; **Englishwoman** (*irreg*) *n* Anglaise *f*

engraving [ɪnˈɡreɪvɪŋ] *n* gravure *f*

engrossed [ɪnˈɡrəust] *adj*: **~ in** absorbé(e)
par, plongé(e) dans

engulf [ɪnˈɡʌlf] *vt* engloutir

enhance [ɪnˈhɑːns] *vt* rehausser, mettre en
valeur

enjoy [ɪnˈdʒɔɪ] *vt* aimer, prendre plaisir à;
(*have: health, fortune*) jouir de; (*: success*)
connaître; **to ~ o.s.** s'amuser; **~able** *adj*
agréable; **~ment** *n* plaisir *m*

enlarge [ɪnˈlɑːdʒ] *vt* accroître; (*PHOT*)
agrandir ♦ *vi*: **to ~ on** (*subject*) s'étendre sur;
~ment *n* (*PHOT*)
agrandissement *m*

enlighten [ɪnˈlaɪtn] *vt* éclairer; **~ed** *adj*
éclairé(e); **~ment** *n*: **the E~ment** (*HISTORY*) ≈
le Siècle des lumières

enlist [ɪnˈlɪst] *vt* recruter; (*support*) s'assurer
♦ *vi* s'engager

enmity [ˈɛnmɪtɪ] *n* inimitié *f*

enormous [ɪˈnɔːməs] *adj* énorme

enough [ɪˈnʌf] *adj, pron*: **~ time/books** assez
or suffisamment de temps/livres ♦ *adv*: **big ~**

assez or suffisamment grand; **have you got ~?** en avez-vous assez?; **he has not worked ~** il n'a pas assez or suffisamment travaillé; **~ to eat** assez à manger; **~!** assez!, ça suffit!; **that's ~, thanks** cela suffit or c'est assez, merci; **I've had ~ of him** j'en ai assez de lui; **... which, funnily or oddly ~** ... qui, chose curieuse

enquire [ɪn'kwaɪəᵊ] vt, vi = **inquire**

enrage [ɪn'reɪdʒ] vt mettre en fureur or en rage, rendre furieux(-euse)

enrol [ɪn'rəul] (US **enroll**) vt inscrire ♦ vi s'inscrire; **~ment** (US **enrollment**) n inscription f

en suite ['ɔnswiːt] adj: **with ~ bathroom** avec salle de bains en attenante

ensure [ɪn'ʃuəᵊ] vt assurer; garantir; **to ~ that** s'assurer que

entail [ɪn'teɪl] vt entraîner, occasionner

entangled [ɪn'tæŋgld] adj: **to become ~ (in)** s'empêtrer (dans)

enter ['entəᵊ] vt (room) entrer dans, pénétrer dans; (club, army) entrer à; (competition) s'inscrire à or pour; (sb for a competition) (faire) inscrire; (write down) inscrire, noter; (COMPUT) entrer, introduire ♦ vi entrer; **~ for** vt fus s'inscrire à, se présenter pour or à; **~ into** vt fus (explanation) se lancer dans; (discussion, negotiations) entamer; (agreement) conclure

enterprise ['entəpraɪz] n entreprise f; (initiative) (esprit m d')initiative f; **free ~** libre entreprise; **private ~** entreprise privée; **enterprising** adj entreprenant(e), dynamique; (scheme) audacieux(-euse)

entertain [entə'teɪn] vt amuser, distraire; (invite) recevoir (à dîner); (idea, plan) envisager; **~er** n artiste m/f de variétés; **~ing** adj amusant(e), distrayant(e); **~ment** n (amusement) divertissement m, amusement m; (show) spectacle m

enthralled [ɪn'θrɔːld] adj captivé(e)

enthusiasm [ɪn'θuːziæzəm] n enthousiasme m

enthusiast [ɪn'θuːziæst] n enthousiaste m/f; **~ic** [ɪnθuːzi'æstɪk] adj enthousiaste; **to be ~ic about** être enthousiasmé(e) par

entire [ɪn'taɪəᵊ] adj (tout) entier(-ère); **~ly** adv entièrement, complètement; **~ty** [ɪn'taɪərətɪ] n: **in its ~ty** dans sa totalité

entitle [ɪn'taɪtl] vt: **to ~ sb to sth** donner droit à qch à qn; **~d** [ɪn'taɪtld] adj (book) intitulé(e); **to be ~d to do** avoir le droit de or être habilité à faire

entrance [n 'entrns, vb ɪn'trɑːns] n entrée f ♦ vt enchanter, ravir; **to gain ~ to** (university etc) être admis à; **~ examination** n examen m d'entrée; **~ fee** n (to museum etc) prix m d'entrée; (to join club etc) droit m d'inscription; **~ ramp** (US) n (AUT) bretelle f

d'accès; **entrant** n participant(e); concurrent(e); (BRIT: in exam) candidat(e)

entrenched [en'trentʃt] adj retranché(e); (ideas) arrêté(e)

entrepreneur ['ɔntrəprə'nəːʳ] n entrepreneur m

entrust [ɪn'trʌst] vt: **to ~ sth to** confier qch à

entry ['entrɪ] n entrée f; (in register) inscription f; **no ~** défense d'entrer, entrée interdite; (AUT) sens interdit; **~ form** n feuille f d'inscription; **~ phone** (BRIT) n interphone m

envelop [ɪn'vɛləp] vt envelopper

envelope ['envələup] n enveloppe f

envious ['envɪəs] adj envieux(-euse)

environment [ɪn'vaɪərnmənt] n environnement m; (social, moral) milieu m; **~al** [ɪnvaɪərn'mɛntl] adj écologique; du milieu; **~-friendly** adj écologique

envisage [ɪn'vɪzɪdʒ] vt (foresee) prévoir

envoy ['envɔɪ] n (diplomat) ministre m plénipotentiaire

envy ['envɪ] n envie f ♦ vt envier; **to ~ sb sth** envier qch à qn

epic ['epɪk] n épopée f ♦ adj épique

epidemic [epɪ'demɪk] n épidémie f

epilepsy ['epɪlepsɪ] n épilepsie f; **epileptic** n épileptique m/f

episode ['epɪsəud] n épisode m

epitome [ɪ'pɪtəmɪ] n modèle m; **epitomize** vt incarner

equal ['iːkwl] adj égal(e) ♦ n égal(e) ♦ vt égaler; **~ to** (task) à la hauteur de; **~ity** [iː'kwɔlɪtɪ] n égalité f; **~ize** vi (SPORT) égaliser; **~ly** adv également; (just as) tout aussi

equanimity [ekwə'nɪmɪtɪ] n égalité f d'humeur

equate [ɪ'kweɪt] vt: **to ~ sth with** comparer qch à; assimiler qch à; **equation** n (MATH) équation f

equator [ɪ'kweɪtəᵊ] n équateur m

equilibrium [iːkwɪ'lɪbrɪəm] n équilibre m

equip [ɪ'kwɪp] vt: **to ~ (with)** équiper (de); **to be well ~ped** être bien équipé(e); **~ment** n équipement m; (electrical etc) appareillage m, installation f

equities ['ekwɪtɪz] (BRIT) npl (COMM) actions cotées en Bourse

equivalent [ɪ'kwɪvələnt] adj: **~ (to)** équivalent(e) (à) ♦ n équivalent m

era ['ɪərə] n ère f, époque f

eradicate [ɪ'rædɪkeɪt] vt éliminer

erase [ɪ'reɪz] vt effacer; **~r** n gomme f

erect [ɪ'rekt] adj droit(e) ♦ vt construire; (monument) ériger, élever; (tent etc) dresser; **~ion** n érection f

ERM n abbr (= Exchange Rate Mechanism) MTC m

erode [ɪ'rəud] vt éroder; (metal) ronger

erotic [ɪ'rɔtɪk] adj érotique

errand ['ɛrənd] n course f, commission f

erratic [ɪ'rætɪk] adj irrégulier(-ère); inconstant(e)

error ['ɛrə'] n erreur f

erupt [ɪ'rʌpt] vi entrer en éruption; (fig) éclater; **~ion** n éruption f

escalate ['ɛskəleɪt] vi s'intensifier

escalator ['ɛskəleɪtə'] n escalier roulant

escapade [ɛskə'peɪd] n (misdeed) fredaine f; (adventure) équipée f

escape [ɪs'keɪp] n fuite f; (from prison) évasion f ♦ vi s'échapper, fuir; (from jail) s'évader; (fig) s'en tirer; (leak) s'échapper ♦ vt échapper à; **to ~ from** (person) échapper à; (place) s'échapper de; (fig) fuir; **escapism** n (fig) évasion f

escort [n 'ɛskɔ:t, vb ɪs'kɔ:t] n escorte f ♦ vt escorter

Eskimo ['ɛskɪməu] n Esquimau(de)

especially [ɪs'pɛʃlɪ] adv (particularly) particulièrement; (above all) surtout

espionage ['ɛspɪɑnɑːʒ] n espionnage m

Esquire [ɪs'kwaɪə'] n: **J Brown, ~** Monsieur J. Brown

essay ['ɛseɪ] n (SCOL) dissertation f; (LITERATURE) essai m

essence ['ɛsns] n essence f

essential [ɪ'sɛnʃl] adj essentiel(le); (basic) fondamental(e) ♦ n: **~s** éléments essentiels; **~ly** adv essentiellement

establish [ɪs'tæblɪʃ] vt établir; (business) fonder, créer; (one's power etc) asseoir, affermir; **~ed** adj bien établi(e); **~ment** n établissement m; (founding) création f

estate [ɪs'teɪt] n (land) domaine m, propriété f; (LAW) biens mpl, succession f; (BRIT: also: **housing ~**) lotissement m, cité f; **~ agent** n agent immobilier; **~ car** (BRIT) n break m

esteem [ɪs'ti:m] n estime f

esthetic [ɪs'θɛtɪk] (US) adj = **aesthetic**

estimate [n 'ɛstɪmət, vb 'ɛstɪmeɪt] n estimation f; (COMM) devis m ♦ vt estimer; **estimation** [ɛstɪ'meɪʃən] n opinion f; (calculation) estimation f

estranged [ɪs'treɪndʒd] adj séparé(e); dont on s'est séparé(e)

etc. abbr (= et cetera) etc

eternal [ɪ'tə:nl] adj éternel(le)

eternity [ɪ'tə:nɪtɪ] n éternité f

ethical ['ɛθɪkl] adj moral(e); **ethics** n éthique f ♦ npl moralité f

Ethiopia [i:θɪ'əupɪə] n Éthiopie f

ethnic ['ɛθnɪk] adj ethnique; (music etc) folklorique; **~ minority** minorité f ethnique

ethos ['i:θɔs] n génie m

etiquette ['ɛtɪkɛt] n convenances fpl, étiquette f

EU n abbr (= European Union) UE f

euro ['juərəu] n (currency) euro m

Euroland ['juərəulænd] n Eurolande f

Eurocheque ['juərəutʃɛk] n eurochèque m

Europe ['juərəp] n Europe f; **~an** n [juərə'pi:ən] adj européen(ne) ♦ n Européen(ne); **~an Community** Communauté européenne

evacuate [ɪ'vækjueɪt] vt évacuer

evade [ɪ'veɪd] vt échapper à; (question etc) éluder; (duties) se dérober à; **to ~ tax** frauder le fisc

evaporate [ɪ'væpəreɪt] vi s'évaporer; **~d milk** n lait condensé non sucré

evasion [ɪ'veɪʒən] n dérobade f; **tax ~** fraude fiscale

eve [i:v] n: **on the ~ of** à la veille de

even ['i:vn] adj (level, smooth) régulier(-ère); (equal) égal(e); (number) pair(e) ♦ adv même; **~ if** même si +indic; **~ though** alors même que +cond; **~ more** encore plus; **~ so** quand même; **not ~** pas même; **to get ~ with sb** prendre sa revanche sur qn

evening ['i:vnɪŋ] n soir m; (as duration, event) soirée f; **in the ~** le soir; **~ class** n cours m du soir; **~ dress** n tenue f de soirée

event [ɪ'vɛnt] n événement m; (SPORT) épreuve f; **in the ~ of** en cas de; **~ful** adj mouvementé(e)

eventual [ɪ'vɛntʃuəl] adj final(e); **~ity** [ɪvɛntʃu'ælɪtɪ] n possibilité f, éventualité f; **~ly** adv finalement

ever ['ɛvə'] adv jamais; (at all times) toujours; **the best ~** le meilleur qu'on ait jamais vu; **have you ~ seen it?** l'as-tu déjà vu?, as-tu eu l'occasion or t'est-il arrivé de le voir?; **why ~ not?** mais enfin, pourquoi pas?; **~ since** adv depuis ♦ conj depuis que; **~green** n arbre m à feuilles persistantes; **~lasting** adj éternel(le)

every ['ɛvrɪ] adj chaque; **~ day** tous les jours, chaque jour; **~ other/third day** tous les deux/ trois jours; **~ other car** une voiture sur deux; **~ now and then** de temps en temps; **~body** pron tout le monde, tous pl; **~day** adj quotidien(ne), de tous les jours; **~one** pron = **everybody**; **~thing** pron tout; **~where** adv partout

evict [ɪ'vɪkt] vt expulser; **~ion** n expulsion f

evidence ['ɛvɪdns] n (proof) preuve(s) f(pl); (of witness) témoignage m; (sign): **to show ~ of** présenter des signes de; **to give ~** témoigner, déposer

evident ['ɛvɪdnt] adj évident(e); **~ly** adv de toute évidence; (apparently) apparemment

evil [ɪ'vi:l] adj mauvais(e) ♦ n mal m

evoke [ɪ'vəuk] vt évoquer

evolution [i:və'lu:ʃən] n évolution f

evolve [ɪ'vɔlv] vt élaborer ♦ vi évoluer

ewe [ju:] n brebis f

ex- [εks] *prefix* ex-

exact [ɪɡ'zækt] *adj* exact(e) ♦ *vt*: **to ~ sth (from)** extorquer qch (à); exiger qch (de); **~ing** *adj* exigeant(e); (*work*) astreignant(e); **~ly** *adv* exactement

exaggerate [ɪɡ'zædʒəreɪt] *vt*, *vi* exagérer; **exaggeration** [ɪɡzædʒə'reɪʃən] *n* exagération *f*

exalted [ɪɡ'zɔːltɪd] *adj* (*prominent*) élevé(e); (: *person*) haut placé(e)

exam [ɪɡ'zæm] *n abbr* (*SCOL*) = **examination**

examination [ɪɡzæmɪ'neɪʃən] *n* (*SCOL*, *MED*) examen *m*

examine [ɪɡ'zæmɪn] *vt* (*gen*) examiner; (*SCOL: person*) interroger; **~r** *n* examinateur(-trice)

example [ɪɡ'zɑːmpl] *n* exemple *m*; **for ~** par exemple

exasperate [ɪɡ'zɑːspəreɪt] *vt* exaspérer; **exasperation** [ɪɡzɑːspə'reɪʃən] *n* exaspération *f*, irritation *f*

excavate ['εkskəveɪt] *vt* excaver; **excavation** [εkskə'veɪʃən] *n* fouilles *fpl*

exceed [ɪk'siːd] *vt* dépasser; (*one's powers*) outrepasser; **~ingly** *adv* extrêmement

excellent ['εksələnt] *adj* excellent(e)

except [ɪk'sεpt] *prep* (*also*: **~ for**, **~ing**) sauf, excepté ♦ *vt* excepter; **~ if/when** sauf si/quand; **~ that** sauf que, si ce n'est que; **~ion** *n* exception *f*; **to take ~ion to** s'offusquer de; **~ional** *adj* exceptionnel(le)

excerpt ['εksəːpt] *n* extrait *m*

excess [ɪk'sεs] *n* excès *m*; **~ baggage** *n* excédent *m* de bagages; **~ fare** (*BRIT*) *n* supplément *m*; **~ive** *adj* excessif(-ive)

exchange [ɪks'tʃeɪndʒ] *n* échange *m*; (*also*: **telephone ~**) central *m* ♦ *vt*: **to ~ (for)** échanger (contre); **~ rate** *n* taux *m* de change

Exchequer [ɪks'tʃεkəʳ] (*BRIT*) *n*: **the ~** l'Échiquier *m*, ≈ le ministère des Finances

excise [*n* 'εksaɪz, *vb* εk'saɪz] *n* taxe *f* ♦ *vt* exciser

excite [ɪk'saɪt] *vt* exciter; **to get ~d** s'exciter; **~ment** *n* excitation *f*; **exciting** *adj* passionnant(e)

exclaim [ɪks'kleɪm] *vi* s'exclamer; **exclamation** [εksklə'meɪʃən] *n* exclamation *f*; **exclamation mark** *n* point *m* d'exclamation

exclude [ɪks'kluːd] *vt* exclure; **exclusion zone** *n* zone interdite; **exclusive** *adj* exclusif(-ive); (*club*, *district*) sélect(e); (*item of news*) en exclusivité; **exclusive of VAT** TVA non comprise; **mutually exclusive** qui s'excluent l'un(e) l'autre

excruciating [ɪks'kruːʃieɪtɪŋ] *adj* atroce

excursion [ɪks'kəːʃən] *n* excursion *f*

excuse [*n* ɪks'kjuːs, *vb* ɪks'kjuːz] *n* excuse *f*

♦ *vt* excuser; **to ~ sb from** (*activity*) dispenser qn de; **~ me!** excusez-moi!, pardon!; **now if you will ~ me,** ... maintenant, si vous (le) permettez ...

ex-directory ['εksdɪ'rεktərɪ] (*BRIT*) *adj* sur la liste rouge

execute ['εksɪkjuːt] *vt* exécuter; **execution** *n* exécution *f*

executive [ɪɡ'zεkjutɪv] *n* (*COMM*) cadre *m*; (*of organization, political party*) bureau *m* ♦ *adj* exécutif(-ive)

exemplify [ɪɡ'zεmplɪfaɪ] *vt* illustrer; (*typify*) incarner

exempt [ɪɡ'zεmpt] *adj*: **~ from** exempté(e) or dispensé(e) de ♦ *vt*: **to ~ sb from** exempter or dispenser qn de

exercise ['εksəsaɪz] *n* exercice *m* ♦ *vt* exercer; (*patience etc*) faire preuve de; (*dog*) promener ♦ *vi* prendre de l'exercice; **~ book** *n* cahier *m*

exert [ɪɡ'zəːt] *vt* exercer, employer; **to ~ o.s.** se dépenser; **~ion** *n* effort *m*

exhale [εks'heɪl] *vt* exhaler ♦ *vi* expirer

exhaust [ɪɡ'zɔːst] *n* (*also*: **~ fumes**) gaz *mpl* d'échappement; (*also*: **~ pipe**) tuyau *m* d'échappement ♦ *vt* épuiser; **~ed** *adj* épuisé(e); **~ion** *n* épuisement *m*; **nervous ~ion** fatigue nerveuse; surmenage mental; **~ive** *adj* très complet(-ète)

exhibit [ɪɡ'zɪbɪt] *n* (*ART*) pièce exposée, objet exposé; (*LAW*) pièce à conviction ♦ *vt* exposer; (*courage, skill*) faire preuve de; **~ion** [εksɪ'bɪʃən] *n* exposition *f*; (*of ill-temper, talent etc*) démonstration *f*

exhilarating [ɪɡ'zɪləreɪtɪŋ] *adj* grisant(e), stimulant(e)

ex-husband *n* ex-mari *m*

exile ['εksaɪl] *n* exil *m*; (*person*) exilé(e) ♦ *vt* exiler

exist [ɪɡ'zɪst] *vi* exister; **~ence** *n* existence *f*; **~ing** *adj* actuel(le)

exit ['εksɪt] *n* sortie *f* ♦ *vi* (*COMPUT*, *THEATRE*) sortir; **~ poll** *n* sondage *m* (fait à la sortie de l'isoloir); **~ ramp** *n* (*AUT*) bretelle *f* d'accès

exodus ['εksədəs] *n* exode *m*

exonerate [ɪɡ'zɔnəreɪt] *vt*: **to ~ from** disculper de

exotic [ɪɡ'zɔtɪk] *adj* exotique

expand [ɪks'pænd] *vt* agrandir; accroître ♦ *vi* (*trade etc*) se développer, s'accroître; (*gas, metal*) se dilater

expanse [ɪks'pæns] *n* étendue *f*

expansion [ɪks'pænʃən] *n* développement *m*, accroissement *m*

expect [ɪks'pεkt] *vt* (*anticipate*) s'attendre à, s'attendre à ce que +*sub*; (*count on*) compter sur, escompter; (*require*) demander, exiger; (*suppose*) supposer; (*await, also baby*) attendre ♦ *vi*: **to be ~ing** être enceinte;

~ancy *n* (*anticipation*) attente *f*; **life ~ancy** espérance *f* de vie; **~ant mother** *n* future maman; **~ation** [ɛkspek'teɪʃən] *n* attente *f*; espérance(s) *f(pl)*

expedient [ɪks'piːdɪənt] *adj* indiqué(e), opportun(e) ♦ *n* expédient *m*

expedition [ɛkspə'dɪʃən] *n* expédition *f*

expel [ɪks'pɛl] *vt* chasser, expulser; (*SCOL*) renvoyer

expend [ɪks'pɛnd] *vt* consacrer; (*money*) dépenser; **~iture** [ɪks'pɛndɪtʃər] *n* dépense *f*; dépenses *fpl*

expense [ɪks'pɛns] *n* dépense *f*, frais *mpl*; (*high cost*) coût *m*; **~s** *npl* (*COMM*) frais *mpl*; **at the ~ of** aux dépens de; **~ account** *n* (note *f* de) frais *mpl*; **expensive** *adj* cher (chère), coûteux(-euse); **to be expensive** coûter cher

experience [ɪks'pɪərɪəns] *n* expérience *f* ♦ *vt* connaître, faire l'expérience de; (*feeling*) éprouver; **~d** *adj* expérimenté(e)

experiment [ɪks'pɛrɪmənt] *n* expérience *f* ♦ *vi* faire une expérience; **to ~ with** expérimenter

expert ['ɛkspəːt] *adj* expert(e) ♦ *n* expert *m*; **~ise** [ɛkspəː'tiːz] *n* (grande) compétence

expire [ɪks'paɪər] *vi* expirer; **expiry** *n* expiration *f*

explain [ɪks'pleɪn] *vt* expliquer; **explanation** [ɛksplə'neɪʃən] *n* explication *f*; **explanatory** [ɪks'plænətrɪ] *adj* explicatif(-ive)

explicit [ɪks'plɪsɪt] *adj* explicite; (*definite*) formel(le)

explode [ɪks'pləud] *vi* exploser

exploit [*n* 'ɛksplɔɪt, *vb* ɪks'plɔɪt] *n* exploit *m* ♦ *vt* exploiter; **~ation** [ɛksplɔɪ'teɪʃən] *n* exploitation *f*

exploratory [ɪks'plɔrətrɪ] *adj* (*expedition*) d'exploration; (*fig: talks*) préliminaire

explore [ɪks'plɔːr] *vt* explorer; (*possibilities*) étudier, examiner; **~r** *n* explorateur(-trice)

explosion [ɪks'pləuʒən] *n* explosion *f*; **explosive** *adj* explosif(-ive) ♦ *n* explosif *m*

exponent [ɪks'pəunənt] *n* (*of school of thought etc*) interprète *m*, représentant *m*

export [*vb* ɛks'pɔːt, *n* 'ɛkspɔːt] *vt* exporter ♦ *n* exportation *f* ♦ *cpd* d'exportation; **~er** *n* exportateur *m*

expose [ɪks'pəuz] *vt* exposer; (*unmask*) démasquer, dévoiler; **~d** *adj* (*position, house*) exposé(e); **exposure** *n* exposition *f*; (*publicity*) couverture *f*; (*PHOT*) (temps *m* de) pose *f*; (: *shot*) pose; **to die from exposure** (*MED*) mourir de froid; **exposure meter** *n* posemètre *m*

express [ɪks'prɛs] *adj* (*definite*) formel(le), exprès(-esse); (*BRIT: letter etc*) exprès *inv* ♦ *n* (*train*) rapide *m*; (*bus*) car *m* express ♦ *vt* exprimer; **~ion** *n* expression *f*; **~ly** *adv*

expressément, formellement; **~way** (*US*) *n* (*urban motorway*) voie *f* express (à plusieurs files)

exquisite [ɛks'kwɪzɪt] *adj* exquis(e)

extend [ɪks'tɛnd] *vt* (*visit, street*) prolonger; (*building*) agrandir; (*offer*) présenter, offrir; (*hand, arm*) tendre ♦ *vi* s'étendre;

extension *n* prolongation *f*; agrandissement *m*; (*building*) annexe *f*; (*to wire, table*) rallonge *f*; (*telephone: in offices*) poste *m*; (: *in private house*) téléphone *m* supplémentaire; **extensive** *adj* étendu(e), vaste; (*damage, alterations*) considérable; (*inquiries*) approfondi(e); **extensively** *adv*: **he's travelled extensively** il a beaucoup voyagé

extent [ɪks'tɛnt] *n* étendue *f*; **to some ~** dans une certaine mesure; **to what ~?** dans quelle mesure?, jusqu'à quel point?; **to the ~ of** ... au point de ...; **to such an ~ that** ... à tel point que ...

extenuating [ɪks'tɛnjueɪtɪŋ] *adj*: **~ circumstances** circonstances atténuantes

exterior [ɛks'tɪərɪər] *adj* extérieur(e) ♦ *n* extérieur *m*; dehors *m*

external [ɛks'təːnl] *adj* externe

extinct [ɪks'tɪŋkt] *adj* éteint(e)

extinguish [ɪks'tɪŋgwɪʃ] *vt* éteindre

extort [ɪks'tɔːt] *vt*: **to ~ sth (from)** extorquer qch (à); **~ionate** *adj* exorbitant(e)

extra ['ɛkstrə] *adj* supplémentaire, de plus ♦ *adv* (*in addition*) en plus ♦ *n* supplément *m*; (*perk*) à-côté *m*; (*THEATRE*) figurant(e) ♦ *prefix* extra...

extract [*vb* ɪks'trækt, *n* 'ɛkstrækt] *vt* extraire; (*tooth*) arracher; (*money, promise*) soutirer ♦ *n* extrait *m*

extracurricular ['ɛkstrəkə'rɪkjulər] *adj* parascolaire

extradite ['ɛkstrədaɪt] *vt* extrader

extra...: ~marital ['ɛkstrə'mærɪtl] *adj* extra-conjugal(e); **~mural** ['ɛkstrə'mjuərl] *adj* hors faculté *inv*; (*lecture*) public(-que); **~ordinary** [ɪks'trɔːdnrɪ] *adj* extraordinaire

extravagance [ɪks'trævəgəns] *n* prodigalités *fpl*; (*thing bought*) folie *f*, dépense excessive; **extravagant** *adj* extravagant(e); (*in spending: person*) prodigue, dépensier(-ère); (: *tastes*) dispendieux(-euse)

extreme [ɪks'triːm] *adj* extrême ♦ *n* extrême *m*; **~ly** *adv* extrêmement; **extremist** *adj*, *n* extrémiste *m/f*

extricate ['ɛkstrɪkeɪt] *vt*: **to ~ sth (from)** dégager qch (de)

extrovert ['ɛkstrəvəːt] *n* extraverti(e)

ex-wife *n* ex-femme *f*

eye [aɪ] *n* œil *m* (*pl* yeux); (*of needle*) trou *m*, chas *m* ♦ *vt* examiner; **to keep an ~ on** surveiller; **~brow** *n* sourcil *m*; **~drops** *npl* gouttes *fpl* pour les yeux; **~lash** *n* cil *m*; **~lid** *n* paupière *f*; **~liner** *n* eye-liner *m*; **~-opener** *n* révélation *f*; **~shadow** *n* ombre *f* à paupières; **~sight** *n* vue *f*; **~sore** *n* horreur *f*; **~ witness** *n* témoin *m* oculaire

F, f

F [ɛf] *n* (*MUS*) fa *m*
fable ['feɪbl] *n* fable *f*
fabric ['fæbrɪk] *n* tissu *m*
fabulous ['fæbjuləs] *adj* fabuleux(-euse); (*inf: super*) formidable
face [feɪs] *n* visage *m*, figure *f*; (*expression*) expression *f*; (*of clock*) cadran *m*; (*of cliff*) paroi *f*; (*of mountain*) face *f*; (*of building*) façade *f* ♦ *vt* faire face à; **~ down** (*person*) à plat ventre; (*card*) face en dessous; **to lose/save ~** perdre/sauver la face; **to make** *or* **pull a ~** faire une grimace; **in the ~ of** (*difficulties etc*) face à, devant; **on the ~ of it** à première vue; **~ to ~** face à face; **~ up to** *vt fus* faire face à, affronter; **~ cloth** (*BRIT*) *n* gant *m* de toilette; **~ cream** *n* crème *f* pour le visage; **~ lift** *n* lifting *m*; (*of building etc*) ravalement *m*, retapage *m*; **~ powder** *n* poudre *f* de riz; **~ value** *n* (*of coin*) valeur nominale; **to take sth at ~ value** (*fig*) prendre qch pour argent comptant
facilities [fə'sɪlɪtɪz] *npl* installations *fpl*, équipement *m*; **credit ~** facilités *fpl* de paiement
facing ['feɪsɪŋ] *prep* face à, en face de
facsimile [fæk'sɪmɪlɪ] *n* (*exact replica*) fac-similé *m*; (*fax*) télécopie *f*
fact [fækt] *n* fait *m*; **in ~** en fait
factor ['fæktər] *n* facteur *m*
factory ['fæktərɪ] *n* usine *f*, fabrique *f*
factual ['fæktjuəl] *adj* basé(e) sur les faits
faculty ['fækəltɪ] *n* faculté *f*; (*US: teaching staff*) corps enseignant
fad [fæd] *n* (*craze*) engouement *m*
fade [feɪd] *vi* se décolorer, passer; (*light, sound*) s'affaiblir; (*flower*) se faner
fag [fæg] (*BRIT: inf*) *n* (*cigarette*) sèche *f*
fail [feɪl] *vt* (*exam*) échouer à; (*candidate*) recaler; (*subj: courage, memory*) faire défaut à ♦ *vi* échouer; (*brakes*) lâcher; (*eyesight, health, light*) baisser, s'affaiblir; **to ~ to do sth** (*neglect*) négliger de faire qch; (*be unable*) ne pas parvenir *or* parvenir à faire qch; **without ~** à coup sûr; sans faute; **~ing** *n* défaut *m* ♦ *prep* faute de; **~ure** *n* échec *m*; (*person*) raté(e); (*mechanical etc*) défaillance *f*
faint [feɪnt] *adj* faible; (*recollection*) vague; (*mark*) à peine visible ♦ *n* évanouissement *m* ♦ *vi* s'évanouir; **to feel ~** défaillir
fair [feər] *adj* équitable, juste, impartial(e);

(*hair*) blond(e); (*skin, complexion*) pâle, blanc (blanche); (*weather*) beau (belle); (*good enough*) assez bon(ne); (*sizeable*) considérable ♦ *adv*: **to play ~** jouer franc-jeu ♦ *n* foire *f*; (*BRIT: funfair*) fête (foraine); **~ly** *adv* équitablement; (*quite*) assez; **~ness** *n* justice *f*, équité *f*, impartialité *f*
fairy ['fɛərɪ] *n* fée *f*; **~ tale** *n* conte *m* de fées
faith [feɪθ] *n* foi *f*; (*trust*) confiance *f*; (*specific religion*) religion *f*; **~ful** *adj* fidèle; **~fully** *adv see* yours
fake [feɪk] *n* (*painting etc*) faux *m*; (*person*) imposteur *m* ♦ *adj* faux (fausse) ♦ *vt* simuler; (*painting*) faire un faux de
falcon ['fɔːlkən] *n* faucon *m*
fall [fɔːl] (*pt* fell, *pp* fallen) *n* chute *f*; (*US: autumn*) automne *m* ♦ *vi* tomber; (*price, temperature, dollar*) baisser; **~s** *npl* (*waterfall*) chute *f* d'eau, cascade *f*; **to ~ flat** (*on one's face*) tomber de tout son long, s'étaler; (*joke*) tomber à plat; (*plan*) échouer; **~ back** *vi* reculer, se retirer; **~ back on** *vt fus* se rabattre sur; **~ behind** *vi* prendre du retard; **~ down** *vi* (*person*) tomber; (*building*) s'effondrer, s'écrouler; **~ for** *vt fus* (*trick, story etc*) se laisser prendre à; (*person*) tomber amoureux de; **~ in** *vi* s'effondrer; (*MIL*) se mettre en rangs; **~ off** *vi* tomber; (*diminish*) baisser, diminuer; **~ out** *vi* (*hair, teeth*) tomber; (*MIL*) rompre les rangs; (*friends etc*) se brouiller; **~ through** *vi* (*plan, project*) tomber à l'eau
fallacy ['fæləsɪ] *n* erreur *f*, illusion *f*
fallout ['fɔːlaut] *n* retombées (radioactives)
fallow ['fæləu] *adj* en jachère; en friche
false [fɔːls] *adj* faux (fausse); **~ alarm** *n* fausse alerte; **~ pretences** *npl*: **under ~ pretences** sous un faux prétexte; **~ teeth** (*BRIT*) *npl* fausses dents
falter ['fɔːltər] *vi* chanceler, vaciller
fame [feɪm] *n* renommée *f*, renom *m*
familiar [fə'mɪlɪər] *adj* familier(-ère); **to be ~ with** (*subject*) connaître
family ['fæmɪlɪ] *n* famille *f* ♦ *cpd* (*business, doctor etc*) de famille; **has he any ~?** (*children*) a-t-il des enfants?
famine ['fæmɪn] *n* famine *f*
famished ['fæmɪʃt] (*inf*) *adj* affamé(e)
famous ['feɪməs] *adj* célèbre; **~ly** *adv* (*get on*) fameusement, à merveille
fan [fæn] *n* (*folding*) éventail *m*; (*ELEC*) ventilateur *m*; (*of person*) fan *m*, admirateur(-trice); (*of team, sport etc*) supporter *m/f* ♦ *vt* éventer; (*fire, quarrel*) attiser
fanatic [fə'nætɪk] *n* fanatique *m/f*
fan belt *n* courroie *f* de ventilateur
fancy ['fænsɪ] *n* fantaisie *f*, envie *f*; imagination *f* ♦ *adj* (de) fantaisie *inv* ♦ *vt* (*feel*

like, want) avoir envie de; (*imagine, think*) imaginer; **to take a ~ to** se prendre d'affection pour; s'enticher de; **he fancies her** (*inf*) elle lui plaît; **~ dress** n déguisement m, travesti m; **~-dress ball** n bal masqué or costumé

fang [fæŋ] n croc m; (*of snake*) crochet m

fantastic [fæn'tæstɪk] adj fantastique

fantasy ['fæntəsɪ] n imagination f, fantaisie f; (*dream*) chimère f

far [fɑːʳ] adj lointain(e), éloigné(e) ♦ adv loin; **~ away** or **off** au loin, dans le lointain; **at the ~ side/end** à l'autre côté/bout; **~ better** beaucoup mieux; **~ from** loin de; **by ~** de loin, de beaucoup; **go as ~ as the farm** allez jusqu'à la ferme; **as ~ as I know** pour autant que je sache; **how ~ is it to ...?** combien y a-t-il jusqu'à ...?; **how ~ have you got?** où en êtes-vous?; **~away** ['fɑːrəweɪ] adj lointain(e); (*look*) distrait(e)

farce [fɑːs] n farce f

fare [fɛəʳ] n (*on trains, buses*) prix m du billet; (*in taxi*) prix de la course; (*food*) table f, chère f; **half ~** demi-tarif; **full ~** plein tarif

Far East n Extrême-Orient m

farewell [fɛə'wɛl] excl adieu ♦ n adieu m

farm [fɑːm] n ferme f ♦ vt cultiver; **~er** n fermier(-ère); cultivateur(-trice); **~hand** n ouvrier(-ère) agricole; **~house** n (maison f de) ferme f; **~ing** n agriculture f; (*of animals*) élevage m; **~land** n terres cultivées; **~ worker** n = **farmhand**; **~yard** n cour f de ferme

far-reaching ['fɑː'riːtʃɪŋ] adj d'une grande portée

fart [fɑːt] (*inf!*) vi péter

farther ['fɑːðəʳ] adv plus loin ♦ adj plus éloigné(e), plus lointain(e)

farthest ['fɑːðɪst] superl of **far**

fascinate ['fæsɪneɪt] vt fasciner; **fascinating** adj fascinant(e)

fascism ['fæʃɪzəm] n fascisme m

fashion ['fæʃən] n mode f; (*manner*) façon f, manière f ♦ vt façonner; **in ~** à la mode; **out of ~** démodé(e); **~able** adj à la mode; **~ show** n défilé m de mannequins or de mode

fast [fɑːst] adj rapide; (*clock*): **to be ~** avancer; (*dye, colour*) grand or bon teint inv ♦ adv vite, rapidement; (*stuck, held*) solidement ♦ n jeûne m ♦ vi jeûner; **~ asleep** profondément endormi

fasten ['fɑːsn] vt attacher, fixer; (*coat*) attacher, fermer ♦ vi se fermer, s'attacher; **~er, ~ing** n attache f

fast food n fast food m, restauration f rapide

fastidious [fæs'tɪdɪəs] adj exigeant(e), difficile

fat [fæt] adj gros(se) ♦ n graisse f; (*on meat*) gras m; (*for cooking*) matière f grasse

fatal ['feɪtl] adj (*injury etc*) mortel(le); (*mistake*) fatal(e); **~ity** [fə'tælɪtɪ] n (*road death etc*) victime f, décès m

fate [feɪt] n destin m; (*of person*) sort m; **~ful** adj fatidique

father ['fɑːðəʳ] n père m; **~-in-law** n beau-père m; **~ly** adj paternel(le)

fathom ['fæðəm] n brasse f (= 1828 mm) ♦ vt (*mystery*) sonder, pénétrer

fatigue [fə'tiːg] n fatigue f

fatten ['fætn] vt, vi engraisser

fatty ['fætɪ] adj (*food*) gras(se) ♦ n (*inf*) gros(se)

fatuous ['fætjuəs] adj stupide

faucet ['fɔːsɪt] (*US*) n robinet m

fault [fɔːlt] n faute f; (*defect*) défaut m; (*GEO*) faille f ♦ vt trouver des défauts à; **it's my ~** c'est de ma faute; **to find ~ with** trouver à redire or à critiquer à; **at ~** fautif(-ive), coupable; **~y** adj défectueux(-euse)

fauna ['fɔːnə] n faune f

favour ['feɪvəʳ] (*US* favor) n faveur f; (*help*) service m ♦ vt (*proposition*) être en faveur de; (*pupil etc*) favoriser; (*team, horse*) donner gagnant; **to do sb a ~** rendre un service à qn; **to find ~ with** trouver grâce aux yeux de; **in ~ of** en faveur de; **~able** adj favorable; **~ite** ['feɪvrɪt] adj, n favori(te)

fawn [fɔːn] n faon m ♦ adj (*colour*) fauve ♦ vi: **to ~ (up)on** flatter servilement

fax [fæks] n (*document*) télécopie f; (*machine*) télécopieur m ♦ vt envoyer par télécopie

FBI n abbr (*US*: = *Federal Bureau of Investigation*) F.B.I. m

fear [fɪəʳ] n crainte f, peur f ♦ vt craindre; **for ~ of** de peur que +sub, de peur de +infin; **~ful** adj craintif(-ive); (*sight, noise*) affreux (-euse), épouvantable; **~less** adj intrépide

feasible ['fiːzəbl] adj faisable, réalisable

feast [fiːst] n festin m, banquet m; (*REL: also*: **~ day**) fête f ♦ vi festoyer

feat [fiːt] n exploit m, prouesse f

feather ['fɛðəʳ] n plume f

feature ['fiːtʃəʳ] n caractéristique f; (*article*) chronique f, rubrique f ♦ vt (*subj: film*) avoir pour vedette(s) ♦ vi: **to ~ in** figurer (en bonne place) dans; (*in film*) jouer dans; **~s** npl (*of face*) traits mpl; **~ film** n long métrage

February ['fɛbruərɪ] n février m

fed [fɛd] pt, pp of **feed**

federal ['fɛdərəl] adj fédéral(e)

fed up adj: **to be ~** en avoir marre, en avoir plein le dos

fee [fiː] n rémunération f; (*of doctor, lawyer*) honoraires mpl; (*for examination*) droits mpl; **school ~s** frais mpl de scolarité

feeble ['fiːbl] adj faible; (*pathetic: attempt, excuse*) pauvre; (: *joke*) piteux(-euse)

feed [fiːd] (*pt, pp* fed) n (*of animal*) fourrage

m; pâture f; (*on printer*) mécanisme m
d'alimentation ♦ vt (*person*) nourrir; (*BRIT:*
baby) allaiter; (: *with bottle*) donner le
biberon à; (*horse etc*) donner à manger à;
(*machine*) alimenter; (*data, information*): to
~ **sth into** fournir qch à; ~ **on** vt fus se nourrir
de; **~back** n feed-back m inv

feel [fi:l] (*pt, pp* felt) n sensation f;
(*impression*) impression f ♦ vt toucher;
(*explore*) tâter, palper; (*cold, pain*) sentir;
(*grief, anger*) ressentir, éprouver; (*think,*
believe) trouver; to ~ **hungry/cold** avoir faim/
froid; to ~ **lonely/better** se sentir seul/mieux; I
don't ~ well je ne me sens pas bien; **it ~s soft**
c'est doux (douce) au toucher; **to ~ like**
(*want*) avoir envie de; ~ **about** vi fouiller,
tâtonner; **~er** n (*of insect*) antenne f; **~ing** n
(*physical*) sensation f; (*emotional*) sentiment
m

feet [fi:t] npl of foot

feign [feɪn] vt feindre, simuler

fell [fɛl] pt of fall ♦ vt (*tree, person*) abattre

follow ['fɛləu] n type m; (*comrade*)
compagnon m; (*of learned society*) membre
m ♦ cpd: their **~ prisoners/students** leurs
camarades prisonniers/d'étude; ~ **citizen** n
concitoyen(ne) m/f; ~ **countryman** (*irreg*) n
compatriote m; ~ **men** npl semblables mpl;
~ship n (*society*) association f; (*comradeship*)
amitié f, camaraderie f; (*grant*) sorte de bourse
universitaire

felony ['fɛlənɪ] n crime m, forfait m

felt [fɛlt] pt, pp of feel ♦ n feutre m; **~-tip**
pen n stylo-feutre m

female ['fi:meɪl] n (*ZOOL*) femelle f; (*pej:*
woman) bonne femme ♦ adj (*BIO*) femelle;
(*sex, character*) féminin(e); (*vote etc*) des
femmes

feminine ['fɛmɪnɪn] adj féminin(e)

feminist ['fɛmɪnɪst] n féministe m/f

fence [fɛns] n barrière f ♦ vt (*also:* ~ **in**)
clôturer ♦ vi faire de l'escrime; **fencing** n
escrime m

fend [fɛnd] vi: **to ~ for o.s.** se débrouiller
(tout seul); ~ **off** vt (*attack etc*) parer

fender ['fɛndər] n garde-feu m inv; (*on boat*)
défense f; (*US: of car*) aile f

ferment [vb fə'mɛnt, n 'fə:mɛnt] vi fermenter
♦ n agitation f, effervescence f

fern [fə:n] n fougère f

ferocious [fə'rəuʃəs] adj féroce

ferret ['fɛrɪt] n furet m

ferry ['fɛrɪ] n (*small*) bac m; (*large: also:*
~boat) ferry(-boat) m ♦ vt transporter

fertile ['fə:taɪl] adj fertile; (*BIO*) fécond(e);

fertilizer ['fə:tɪlaɪzər] n engrais m

fester ['fɛstər] vi suppurer

festival ['fɛstɪvəl] n (*REL*) fête f; (*ART, MUS*)
festival m

festive ['fɛstɪv] adj de fête; **the ~ season**
(*BRIT: Christmas*) la période des fêtes;
festivities npl réjouissances fpl

festoon [fɛs'tu:n] vt: **to ~ with** orner de

fetch [fɛtʃ] vt aller chercher; (*sell for*) se
vendre

fête [feɪt] n fête f, kermesse f

feud [fju:d] n dispute f, dissension f

fever ['fi:vər] n fièvre f; **~ish** adj fiévreux(-euse), fébrile

few [fju:] adj (*not many*) peu de; **a ~** adj
quelques ♦ pron quelques-uns(-unes); **~er**
['fju:ər] adj moins de; moins (nombreux);
~est ['fju:ɪst] adj le moins (de)

fiancé [fɪ'ɑ:nseɪ] n fiancé(e) m/f

fib [fɪb] n bobard m

fibre ['faɪbər] (*US* fiber) n fibre f; **~glass**
['faɪbəglɑ:s] (**Fiberglass** ® *US*) n fibre de verre

fickle ['fɪkl] adj inconstant(e), volage,
capricieux(-euse)

fiction ['fɪkʃən] n romans mpl, littérature f
romanesque; (*invention*) fiction f; **~al** adj
fictif(-ive)

fictitious [fɪk'tɪʃəs] adj fictif(-ive), imaginaire

fiddle ['fɪdl] n (*MUS*) violon m; (*cheating*)
combine f; escroquerie f ♦ vt (*BRIT: accounts*)
falsifier, maquiller; ~ **with** vt fus tripoter

fidget ['fɪdʒɪt] vi se trémousser, remuer

field [fi:ld] n champ m; (*fig*) domaine m,
champ; (*SPORT: ground*) terrain m; **~work** n
travaux mpl pratiques (sur le terrain)

fiend [fi:nd] n démon m

fierce [fɪəs] adj (*look, animal*) féroce, sauvage;
(*wind, attack, person*) (très) violent(e);
(*fighting, enemy*) acharné(e)

fiery ['faɪərɪ] adj ardent(e), brûlant(e);
(*temperament*) fougueux(-euse)

fifteen [fɪf'ti:n] num quinze

fifth [fɪfθ] num cinquième

fifty ['fɪftɪ] num cinquante; **~-fifty** adj: **a ~-**
fifty chance etc une chance etc sur deux ♦ adv
moitié-moitié

fig [fɪg] n figue f

fight [faɪt] (*pt, pp* fought) n (*MIL*) combat m;
(*between persons*) bagarre f; (*against cancer*
etc) lutte f ♦ vt se battre contre; (*cancer,*
alcoholism, emotion) combattre, lutter contre;
(*election*) se présenter à ♦ vi se battre; **~er** n
(*fig*) lutteur m; (*plane*) chasseur m; **~ing** n
combats mpl; (*brawl*) bagarres fpl

figment ['fɪgmənt] n: **a ~ of the imagination**
une invention

figurative ['fɪgjurətɪv] adj figuré(e)

figure ['fɪgər] n figure f; (*number, cipher*)
chiffre m; (*body, outline*) silhouette f; (*shape*)
ligne f, formes fpl ♦ vt (*think: esp US*)
supposer ♦ vi (*appear*) figurer; ~ **out** vt
(*work out*) calculer; **~head** n (*NAUT*) figure f
de proue; (*pej*) prête-nom m; ~ **of speech**

figure f de rhétorique

file [faɪl] n (dossier) dossier m; (folder) dossier, chemise f; (: with hinges) classeur m; (COMPUT) fichier m; (row) file f; (tool) lime f ♦ vt (nails, wood) limer; (papers) classer; (LAW: claim) faire enregistrer; déposer ♦ vi: to ~ in/out entrer/sortir l'un derrière l'autre; to ~ for divorce faire une demande en divorce; **filing cabinet** n classeur m (meuble)

fill [fɪl] vt remplir; (need) répondre à ♦ n: to eat one's ~ manger à sa faim; to ~ with remplir de; ~ **in** vt (hole) boucher; (form) remplir; ~ **up** vt remplir; ~ **it up, please** (AUT) le plein, s'il vous plaît

fillet ['fɪlɪt] n filet m; ~ **steak** n filet m de bœuf, tournedos m

filling ['fɪlɪŋ] n (CULIN) garniture f, farce f; (for tooth) plombage m; ~ **station** n station-service f

film [fɪlm] n film m; (PHOT) pellicule f, film; (of powder, liquid) couche f, pellicule ♦ vt (scene) filmer ♦ vi tourner; ~ **star** n vedette f de cinéma

filter ['fɪltəʳ] n filtre m ♦ vt filtrer; ~ **lane** n (AUT) voie f de sortie; ~-**tipped** adj à bout filtre

filth [fɪlθ] n saleté f; ~**y** adj sale, dégoûtant(e); (language) ordurier(-ère)

fin [fɪn] n (of fish) nageoire f

final ['faɪnl] adj final(e); (definitive) définitif(-ive) ♦ n (SPORT) finale f; ~**s** npl (SCOL) examens mpl de dernière année; ~**e** [fɪ'nɑːlɪ] n finale m; ~**ist** n finaliste m/f; ~**ize** vt mettre au point; ~**ly** adv (eventually) enfin, finalement; (lastly) en dernier lieu

finance [faɪ'næns] n finance f ♦ vt financer; ~**s** npl (financial position) finances fpl; **financial** [faɪ'nænʃəl] adj financier(-ère)

find [faɪnd] (pt, pp found) vt trouver; (lost object) retrouver ♦ n trouvaille f, découverte f; to ~ **sb guilty** (LAW) déclarer qn coupable; ~ **out** vt (truth, secret) découvrir; (person) démasquer ♦ vi: to ~ **out about** (make enquiries) se renseigner; (by chance) apprendre; ~**ings** npl (LAW) conclusions fpl, verdict m; (of report) conclusions

fine [faɪn] adj (excellent) excellent(e); (thin, not coarse, subtle) fin(e); (weather) beau (belle) ♦ adv (well) très bien ♦ n (LAW) amende f; contravention f ♦ vt (LAW) condamner à une amende; donner une contravention à; to be ~ (person) aller bien; (weather) être beau; ~ **arts** npl beaux-arts mpl; ~**ry** n parure f

finger ['fɪŋgəʳ] n doigt m ♦ vt palper, toucher; **little** ~ auriculaire m, petit doigt; **index** ~ index m; ~**nail** n ongle m (de la main); ~**print** n empreinte digitale; ~**tip** n bout m du doigt

finish ['fɪnɪʃ] n fin f; (SPORT) arrivée f; (polish etc) finition f ♦ vt finir, terminer ♦ vi finir, se terminer; to ~ **doing sth** finir de faire qch; to ~ **third** arriver or terminer troisième; ~ **off** vt finir, terminer; (kill) achever; ~ **up** vi, vt finir; ~**ing line** n ligne f d'arrivée

finite ['faɪnaɪt] adj fini(e); (verb) conjugué(e)

Finland ['fɪnlənd] n Finlande f; **Finn** [fɪn] n Finlandais(e); **Finnish** adj finlandais(e) ♦ n (LING) finnois m

fir [fəːʳ] n sapin m

fire ['faɪəʳ] n feu m; (accidental) incendie m; (heater) radiateur m ♦ vt (fig) enflammer, animer; (inf: dismiss) mettre à la porte, renvoyer; (discharge): to ~ **a gun** tirer un coup de feu ♦ vi (shoot) tirer, faire feu; **on** ~ en feu; ~ **alarm** n avertisseur m d'incendie; ~**arm** n arme f à feu; ~ **brigade** n (sapeurs-)pompiers mpl; ~ **department** (US) n = **fire brigade**; ~ **engine** n (vehicle) voiture f des pompiers; ~ **escape** n escalier m de secours; ~ **extinguisher** n extincteur m; ~**man** n pompier m; ~**place** n cheminée f; ~**side** n foyer m, coin du feu m; ~ **station** n caserne f de pompiers; ~**wood** n bois m de chauffage; ~**works** npl feux mpl d'artifice; (display) feu(x) d'artifice

firing squad ['faɪərɪŋ-] n peloton m d'exécution

firm [fəːm] adj ferme ♦ n compagnie f, firme f

first [fəːst] adj premier(-ère) ♦ adv (before all others) le premier, la première; (before all other things) en premier, d'abord; (when listing reasons etc) en premier lieu, premièrement ♦ n (person: in race) premier(-ère); (BRIT: SCOL) mention f très bien; (AUT) première f; **at** ~ au commencement, au début; ~ **of all** tout d'abord, pour commencer; ~ **aid** n premiers secours or soins; ~-**aid kit** n trousse f à pharmacie; ~-**class** adj de première classe; (excellent) excellent(e), exceptionnel(le); ~-**hand** adj de première main; ~ **lady** (US) n femme f du président; ~**ly** adv premièrement, en premier lieu; ~ **name** n prénom m; ~-**rate** adj excellent(e)

fish [fɪʃ] n inv poisson m ♦ vt, vi pêcher; **to go** ~**ing** aller à la pêche; ~**erman** n pêcheur m; ~ **farm** n établissement m piscicole; ~ **fingers** (BRIT) npl bâtonnets de poisson (congelés); ~**ing boat** n barque f or bateau m de pêche; ~**ing line** n ligne f (de pêche); ~**ing rod** n canne f à pêche; ~**ing tackle** n attirail m de pêche; ~**monger's (shop)** n poissonnerie f; ~ **slice** n pelle f à poisson; ~ **sticks** (US) npl = **fish fingers**; ~**y** (inf) adj suspect(e), louche

fist [fɪst] n poing m

fit [fɪt] adj (healthy) en (bonne) forme;

(*proper*) convenable; approprié(e) ♦ vt (*subj: clothes*) aller à; (*put in, attach*) installer, poser; adapter; (*equip*) équiper, garnir, munir; (*suit*) convenir à ♦ vi (*clothes*) aller; (*parts*) s'adapter; (*in space, gap*) entrer, s'adapter ♦ n (*MED*) accès m, crise f; (*of anger*) accès; (*of hysterics, jealousy*) crise; **~ to** en état de; **~ for** digne de; apte à; **~ of coughing** quinte f de toux; **a ~ of giggles** le fou rire; **this dress is a good ~** cette robe (me) va très bien; **by ~s and starts** par à-coups; **~ in** vi s'accorder; s'adapter; **~ful** adj (*sleep*) agité(e); **~ment** n meuble encastré, élément m; **~ness** n (*MED*) forme f physique; **~ted carpet** n moquette f; **~ted kitchen** (*BRIT*) n cuisine équipée; **~ter** n monteur m; **~ting** adj approprié(e) ♦ n (*of dress*) essayage m; (*of piece of equipment*) pose f, installation f; **~tings** npl (*in building*) installations fpl; **~ting room** n cabine f d'essayage

five [faɪv] num cinq; **~r** (*inf*) n (*BRIT*) billet m de cinq livres; (*US*) billet de cinq dollars

fix [fɪks] vt (*date, amount etc*) fixer; (*organize*) arranger; (*mend*) réparer; (*meal, drink*) préparer ♦ n: **to be in a ~** être dans le pétrin; **~ up** vt (*meeting*) arranger; **to ~ sb up with sth** faire avoir qch à qn; **~ation** [fɪk'seɪʃən] n (*PSYCH*) fixation f; (*fig*) obsession f; **~ed** adj (*prices etc*) fixe; (*smile*) figé(e); **~ture** n installation f (fixe); (*SPORT*) rencontre f (au programme)

fizzy ['fɪzɪ] adj pétillant(e); gazeux(euse)

flabbergasted ['flæbəɡɑːstɪd] adj sidéré(e), ahuri(e)

flabby ['flæbɪ] adj mou (molle)

flag [flæɡ] n drapeau m; (*also: ~stone*) dalle f ♦ vi faiblir, fléchir; **~ down** vt héler, faire signe (de s'arrêter) à; **~pole** n mât m; **~ship** n vaisseau m amiral; (*fig*) produit m vedette

flair [fleə'] n flair m

flak [flæk] n (*MIL*) tir antiaérien; (*inf: criticism*) critiques fpl

flake [fleɪk] n (*of rust, paint*) écaille f; (*of snow, soup powder*) flocon m ♦ vi (*also: ~ off*) s'écailler

flamboyant [flæm'bɔɪənt] adj flamboyant(e), éclatant(e); (*person*) haut(e) en couleur

flame [fleɪm] n flamme f

flamingo [flə'mɪŋɡəu] n flamant m (rose)

flammable ['flæməbl] adj inflammable

flan [flæn] (*BRIT*) n tarte f

flank [flæŋk] n flanc m ♦ vt flanquer

flannel ['flænl] n (*fabric*) flanelle f; (*BRIT: also: ~ face*) gant m de toilette

flap [flæp] n (*of pocket, envelope*) rabat m ♦ vt (*wings*) battre (de) ♦ vi (*sail, flag*) claquer; (*inf: also: be in a ~*) paniquer

flare [fleə'] n (*signal*) signal lumineux; (*in skirt etc*) évasement m; **~ up** vi s'embraser; (*fig: person*) se mettre en colère, s'emporter; (: *revolt etc*) éclater

flash [flæʃ] n éclair m; (*also: news ~*) flash m (d'information); (*PHOT*) flash ♦ vt (*light*) projeter; (*send: message*) câbler; (*look*) jeter; (*smile*) lancer ♦ vi (*light*) clignoter; **a ~ of lightning** un éclair; **in a ~** en un clin d'œil; **to ~ one's headlights** faire un appel de phares; **to ~ by** or **past** (*person*) passer (devant) comme un éclair; **~bulb** n ampoule f de flash; **~cube** n cube-flash m; **~light** n lampe f de poche; **~y** (*pej*) adj tape-à-l'œil inv, tapageur(-euse)

flask [flɑːsk] n flacon m, bouteille f; (*also: vacuum ~*) thermos ® m or f

flat [flæt] adj plat(e); (*tyre*) dégonflé(e), à plat; (*beer*) éventé(e); (*denial*) catégorique; (*MUS*) bémol inv; (: *voice*) faux (fausse); (*fee, rate*) fixe ♦ n (*BRIT: apartment*) appartement m; (*AUT*) crevaison f; (*MUS*) bémol m; **to work ~ out** travailler d'arrache-pied; **~ly** adv catégoriquement; **~ten** vt (*also: ~ten out*) aplatir; (*crop*) coucher; (*building(s)*) raser

flatter ['flætə'] vt flatter; **~ing** adj flatteur(-euse); **~y** n flatterie f

flaunt [flɔːnt] vt faire étalage de

flavour ['fleɪvə'] (*US* flavor) n goût m, saveur f; (*of ice cream etc*) parfum m ♦ vt parfumer; **vanilla-~ed** à l'arôme de vanille, à la vanille; **~ing** n arôme m

flaw [flɔː] n défaut m; **~less** adj sans défaut

flax [flæks] n lin m

flea [fliː] n puce f

fleck [flek] n tacheture f; moucheture f

flee [fliː] (*pt, pp* fled) vt fuir ♦ vi fuir, s'enfuir

fleece [fliːs] n toison f ♦ vt (*inf*) voler, filouter

fleet [fliːt] n flotte f; (*of lorries etc*) parc m, convoi m

fleeting ['fliːtɪŋ] adj fugace, fugitif(-ive); (*visit*) très bref (brève)

Flemish ['flemɪʃ] adj flamand(e)

flesh [fleʃ] n chair f; **~ wound** n blessure f superficielle

flew [fluː] pt of fly

flex [fleks] n fil m or câble m électrique ♦ vt (*knee*) fléchir; (*muscles*) tendre; **~ible** adj flexible

flick [flɪk] n petite tape; chiquenaude f; (*of duster*) petit coup ♦ vt donner un petit coup à; (*switch*) appuyer sur; **~ through** vt fus feuilleter

flicker ['flɪkə'] vi (*light*) vaciller; **his eyelids ~ed** il a cillé

flier ['flaɪə'] n aviateur m

flight [flaɪt] n vol m; (*escape*) fuite f; (*also: ~ of steps*) escalier m; **~ attendant** (*US*) n steward m, hôtesse f de l'air; **~ deck** n

(AVIAT) poste m de pilotage; (NAUT) pont m d'envol

flimsy ['flɪmzɪ] adj peu solide; (clothes) trop léger(-ère); (excuse) pauvre, mince

flinch [flɪntʃ] vi tressaillir; **to ~ from** se dérober à, reculer devant

fling [flɪŋ] (pt, pp **flung**) vt jeter, lancer

flint [flɪnt] n silex m; (in lighter) pierre f (à briquet)

flip [flɪp] vt (throw) lancer (d'une chiquenaude); **to ~ sth over** retourner qch

flippant ['flɪpənt] adj désinvolte, irrévérencieux(-euse)

flipper ['flɪpər] n (of seal etc) nageoire f; (for swimming) palme f

flirt [flɜːt] vi flirter ♦ n flirteur(-euse) m/f

float [fləut] n flotteur m; (in procession) char m; (money) réserve f ♦ vi flotter

flock [flɔk] n troupeau m; (of birds) vol m; (REL) ouailles fpl ♦ vi: **to ~ to** se rendre en masse à

flog [flɔg] vt fouetter

flood [flʌd] n inondation f; (of letters, refugees etc) flot m ♦ vt inonder ♦ vi (people): **to ~ into** envahir; **~ing** n inondation f; **~light** n projecteur m

floor [flɔːr] n sol m; (storey) étage m; (of sea, valley) fond m ♦ vt (subj: question) déconcerter; (: blow) terrasser; **on the ~** par terre; **ground ~**, (US) **first ~** rez-de-chaussée m inv; **first ~**, (US) **second ~** premier étage; **~board** n planche f (du plancher); **~ show** n spectacle m de variétés

flop [flɔp] n fiasco m ♦ vi être un fiasco; (fall: into chair) s'affaler, s'effondrer; **~py** adj lâche, flottant(e) ♦ n (COMPUT: also: **~py disk**) disquette f

flora ['flɔːrə] n flore f

floral ['flɔːrl] adj (dress) à fleurs

florid ['flɔrɪd] adj (complexion) coloré(e); (style) plein(e) de fioritures

florist ['flɔrɪst] n fleuriste m/f; **~'s (shop)** n magasin m or boutique f de fleuriste

flounder ['flaundər] vi patauger ♦ n (ZOOL) flet m

flour ['flauər] n farine f

flourish ['flʌrɪʃ] vi prospérer ♦ n (gesture) moulinet m

flout [flaut] vt se moquer de, faire fi de

flow [fləu] n (ELEC, of river) courant m; (of blood in veins) circulation f; (of tide) flux m; (of orders, data) flot m ♦ vi couler; (traffic) s'écouler; (robes, hair) flotter; **the ~ of traffic** l'écoulement m de la circulation; **~ chart** n organigramme m

flower ['flauər] n fleur f ♦ vi fleurir; **~ bed** n plate-bande f; **~pot** n pot m (de fleurs); **~y** adj fleuri(e)

flown [fləun] pp of **fly**

flu [fluː] n grippe f

fluctuate ['flʌktjueɪt] vi varier, fluctuer

fluent ['fluːənt] adj (speech) coulant(e), aisé(e); **he speaks ~ French, he's ~ in French** il parle couramment le français

fluff [flʌf] n duvet m; (on jacket, carpet) peluche f; **~y** adj duveteux(-euse); (toy) en peluche

fluid ['fluːɪd] adj fluide ♦ n fluide m

fluke [fluːk] (inf) n (luck) coup m de veine

flung [flʌŋ] pt, pp of **fling**

fluoride ['fluəraɪd] n fluorure f; **~ toothpaste** dentifrice m au fluor

flurry ['flʌrɪ] n (of snow) rafale f, bourrasque f; **~ of activity/excitement** affairement m/ excitation f soudain(e)

flush [flʌʃ] n (on face) rougeur f; (fig: of youth, beauty etc) éclat m ♦ vt nettoyer à grande eau ♦ vi rougir ♦ adj: **~ with** au ras de, de niveau avec; **to ~ the toilet** tirer la chasse (d'eau); **~ed** adj (tout(e)) rouge

flustered ['flʌstəd] adj énervé(e)

flute [fluːt] n flûte f

flutter ['flʌtər] n (of panic, excitement) agitation f; (of wings) battement m ♦ vi (bird) battre des ailes, voleter

flux [flʌks] n: **in a state of ~** fluctuant sans cesse

fly [flaɪ] (pt **flew**, pp **flown**) n (insect) mouche f; (on trousers: also: **flies**) braguette f ♦ vt piloter; (passengers, cargo) transporter (par avion); (distances) parcourir ♦ vi voler; (passengers) aller en avion; (escape) s'enfuir, fuir; (flag) se déployer; **~ away** vi (bird, insect) s'envoler; **~ off** vi = **fly away**; **~-drive** n formule f avion plus voiture; **~ing** n (activity) aviation f; (action) vol m ♦ adj: **a ~ing visit** une visite éclair; **with ~ing colours** haut la main; **~ing saucer** n soucoupe volante; **~ing start** n: **to get off to a ~ing start** prendre un excellent départ; **~over** (BRIT) n (bridge) saut-de-mouton m; **~sheet** n (for tent) double toit m

foal [fəul] n poulain m

foam [fəum] n écume f; (on beer) mousse f; (also: **~ rubber**) caoutchouc mousse m ♦ vi (liquid) écumer; (soapy water) mousser

fob [fɔb] vt: **to ~ sb off** se débarrasser de qn

focal point ['fəukl-] n (fig) point central

focus ['fəukəs] (pl **~es**) n foyer m; (of interest) centre m ♦ vt (field glasses etc) mettre au point ♦ vi: **to ~ (on)** (with camera) régler la mise au point (sur); (person) fixer son regard (sur); **out of/in ~** (picture) flou(e)/net(te); (camera) pas au point/au point

fodder ['fɔdər] n fourrage m

foe [fəu] n ennemi m

fog [fɔg] n brouillard m; **~gy** adj: **it's ~gy** il y a du brouillard; **~ lamp** (US **fog light**) n (AUT) phare *m* antibrouillard

foil [fɔɪl] *vt* déjouer, contrecarrer ♦ *n* feuille *f* de métal; (*kitchen* ~) papier *m* alu(minium); (*complement*) repoussoir *m*

fold [fəuld] *n* (*bend, crease*) pli *m*; (*AGR*) parc *m* à moutons; (*fig*) bercail *m* ♦ *vt* plier; (*arms*) croiser; ~ **up** *vi* (*map, table etc*) se plier; (*business*) fermer boutique ♦ *vt* (*map, clothes*) plier; ~**er** *n* (*for papers*) chemise *f*; (: *with hinges*) classeur *m*; ~**ing** *adj* (*chair, bed*) pliant(e)

foliage ['fəulɪdʒ] *n* feuillage *m*

folk [fəuk] *npl* gens *mpl* ♦ *cpd* folklorique; ~**s** (*inf*) *npl* (*parents*) parents *mpl*; ~**lore** ['fəuklɔːʳ] *n* folklore *m*; ~ **song** *n* chanson *f* folklorique

follow ['fɔləu] *vt* suivre ♦ *vi* suivre; (*result*) s'ensuivre; **to ~ suit** (*fig*) faire de même; ~ **up** *vt* (*letter, offer*) donner suite à; (*case*) suivre; ~**er** *n* disciple *m/f*, partisan(e); ~**ing** *adj* suivant(e) ♦ *n* partisans *mpl*, disciples *mpl*

folly ['fɔlɪ] *n* inconscience *f*; folie *f*

fond [fɔnd] *adj* (*memory, look*) tendre; (*hopes, dreams*) un peu fou (folle); **to be ~ of** aimer beaucoup

fondle ['fɔndl] *vt* caresser

font [fɔnt] *n* (*in church: for baptism*) fonts baptismaux; (*TYP*) fonte *f*

food [fuːd] *n* nourriture *f*; ~ **mixer** *n* mixer *m*; ~ **poisoning** *n* intoxication *f* alimentaire; ~ **processor** *n* robot *m* de cuisine; ~**stuffs** *npl* denrées *fpl* alimentaires

fool [fuːl] *n* idiot(e); (*CULIN*) mousse *f* de fruits ♦ *vt* berner, duper ♦ *vi* faire l'idiot *or* l'imbécile; ~**hardy** *adj* téméraire, imprudent(e); ~**ish** *adj* idiot(e), stupide; (*rash*) imprudent(e); insensé(e); ~**proof** *adj* (*plan etc*) infaillible

foot [fut] (*pl* **feet**) *n* pied *m*; (*of animal*) patte *f*; (*measure*) pied (= 30,48 cm; 12 inches) ♦ *vt* (*bill*) payer; **on ~** à pied; ~**age** *n* (*CINEMA: length*) ≈ métrage *m*; (: *material*) séquences *fpl*; ~**ball** *n* ballon *m* (de football); (*sport: BRIT*) football *m*, foot *m*; (: *US*) football américain; ~**ball player** (*BRIT*) *n* (*also:* ~**baller**) joueur *m* de football; ~**brake** *n* frein *m* à pédale; ~**bridge** *n* passerelle *f*; ~**hills** *npl* contreforts *mpl*; ~**hold** *n* prise *f* (de pied); ~**ing** *n* (*fig*) position *f*; **to lose one's ~ing** perdre pied; ~**lights** *npl* rampe *f*; ~**note** *n* note *f* (en bas de page); ~**path** *n* sentier *m*; (*in street*) trottoir *m*; ~**print** *n* trace *f* (de pas); ~**step** *n* pas *m*; ~**wear** *n* chaussure(s) *f(pl)*

KEYWORD

for [fɔːʳ] *prep* **1** (*indicating destination, intention, purpose*) pour; **the train for London** le train pour *or* (à destination) de Londres; **he**

went for the paper il est allé chercher le journal; **it's time for lunch** c'est l'heure du déjeuner; **what's it for?** ça sert à quoi?; **what for?** (*why*) pourquoi?

2 (*on behalf of, representing*) pour; **the MP for Hove** le député de Hove; **to work for sb/sth** travailler pour qn/qch; **G for George** G comme Georges

3 (*because of*) pour; **for this reason** pour cette raison; **for fear of being criticized** de peur d'être critiqué

4 (*with regard to*) pour; **it's cold for July** il fait froid pour juillet; **a gift for languages** un don pour les langues

5 (*in exchange for*): **I sold it for £5** je l'ai vendu 5 livres; **to pay 50 pence for a ticket** payer un billet 50 pence

6 (*in favour of*) pour; **are you for or against us?** êtes-vous pour ou contre nous?

7 (*referring to distance*) pendant, sur; **there are roadworks for 5 km** il y a des travaux sur 5 km; **we walked for miles** nous avons marché pendant des kilomètres

8 (*referring to time*) pendant; depuis; pour; **he was away for 2 years** il a été absent pendant 2 ans; **she will be away for a month** elle sera absente (pendant) un mois; **I have known her for years** je la connais depuis des années; **can you do it for tomorrow?** est-ce que tu peux le faire pour demain?

9 (*with infinitive clauses*): **it is not for me to decide** ce n'est pas à moi de décider; **it would be best for you to leave** le mieux serait que vous partiez; **there is still time for you to do it** vous avez encore le temps de le faire; **for this to be possible ...** pour que cela soit possible ...

10 (*in spite of*): **for all his work/efforts** malgré tout son travail/tous ses efforts; **for all his complaints, he's very fond of her** il a beau se plaindre, il l'aime beaucoup

♦ *conj* (*since, as: rather formal*) car

forage ['fɔrɪdʒ] *vi* fourrager

foray ['fɔreɪ] *n* incursion *f*

forbid [fə'bɪd] (*pt* **forbad(e)**, *pp* **forbidden**) *vt* défendre, interdire; **to ~ sb to do** défendre *or* interdire à qn de faire; ~**ding** *adj* sévère, sombre

force [fɔːs] *n* force *f* ♦ *vt* forcer; (*push*) pousser (de force); **the F~s** *npl* (*MIL*) l'armée *f*; **in ~** en vigueur; ~**-feed** *vt* nourrir de force; ~**ful** *adj* énergique, volontaire; **forcibly** *adv* par la force, de force; (*express*) énergiquement

ford [fɔːd] *n* gué *m*

fore [fɔːʳ] *n*: **to come to the ~** se faire remarquer; ~**arm** *n* avant-bras *m* inv; ~**boding** *n* pressentiment *m* (néfaste); ~**cast** (*irreg: like* **cast**) *n* prévision *f* ♦ *vt* prévoir;

~court n (of garage) devant m; **~finger** n index m; **~front** n: **in the ~front of** au premier rang or plan de

foregone ['fɔ:gɒn] adj: **it's a ~ conclusion** c'est couru d'avance

foreground ['fɔ:graund] n premier plan

forehead ['fɒrɪd] n front m

foreign ['fɒrɪn] adj étranger(-ère); (trade) extérieur(-e); **~er** n étranger(-ère); **~ exchange** n change m; **F~ Office** (BRIT) n ministère m des affaires étrangères; **F~ Secretary** (BRIT) n ministre m des affaires étrangères

fore: **~leg** n (of cat, dog) patte f de devant; (of horse) jambe antérieure; **~man** (irreg) n (of factory, building site) contremaître m, chef m d'équipe; **~most** adj le (la) plus en vue; premier(-ère) ♦ adv: **first and ~most** avant tout, tout d'abord

forensic [fə'rensɪk] adj: **~ medicine** médecine légale; **~ scientist** médecin m légiste

fore: **~runner** n précurseur m; **~see** (irreg: like **see**) vt prévoir; **~seeable** adj prévisible; **~shadow** vt présager, annoncer, laisser prévoir; **~sight** n prévoyance f

forest ['fɒrɪst] n forêt f; **~ry** n sylviculture f

foretaste ['fɔ:teɪst] n avant-goût m

foretell [fɔ:'tel] (irreg: like **tell**) vt prédire

forever [fə'revər] adv pour toujours; (fig) continuellement

foreword ['fɔ:wɜ:d] n avant-propos m inv

forfeit ['fɔ:fɪt] vt (lose) perdre

forgave [fə'geɪv] pt of **forgive**

forge [fɔ:dʒ] n forge f ♦ vt (signature) contrefaire; (wrought iron) forger; **to ~ money** (BRIT) fabriquer de la fausse monnaie; **~ ahead** vi pousser de l'avant, prendre de l'avance; **~d** adj faux (fausse); **~r** n faussaire m; **~ry** n faux m, contrefaçon f

forget [fə'get] (pt forgot, pp forgotten) vt, vi oublier; **~ful** adj distrait(e), étourdi(e); **~-me-not** n myosotis m

forgive [fə'gɪv] (pt forgave, pp forgiven) vt pardonner; **to ~ sb sth/for doing sth** pardonner qch à qn/à qn de faire qch; **~ness** n pardon m

forgo [fɔ:'gəu] (pt forwent, pp forgone) vt renoncer à

fork [fɔ:k] n (for eating) fourchette f; (for gardening) fourche f; (of roads) bifurcation f; (of railways) embranchement m ♦ vi (road) bifurquer; **~ out** vt (inf) allonger; **~-lift truck** n chariot élévateur

forlorn [fə'lɔ:n] adj (deserted) abandonné(e); (attempt, hope) désespéré(e)

form [fɔ:m] n forme f; (SCOL) classe f; (questionnaire) formulaire m ♦ vt former; (habit) contracter; **in top ~** en pleine forme

formal ['fɔ:məl] adj (offer, receipt) en bonne et due forme; (person) cérémonieux(-euse); (dinner) officiel(le); (clothes) de soirée; (garden) à la française; (education) à proprement parler; **~ly** adv officiellement; cérémonieusement

format ['fɔ:mæt] n format m ♦ vt (COMPUT) formater

formation [fɔ:'meɪʃən] n formation f

formative ['fɔ:mətɪv] adj: **~ years** années fpl d'apprentissage or de formation

former ['fɔ:mər] adj ancien(ne) (before n), précédent(e); **the ~ ... the latter** le premier ... le second, celui-là ... celui-ci; **~ly** adv autrefois

formidable ['fɔ:mɪdəbl] adj redoutable

formula ['fɔ:mjulə] (pl ~s or ~e) n formule f

forsake [fə'seɪk] (pt forsook, pp forsaken) vt abandonner

fort [fɔ:t] n fort m

forte ['fɔ:tɪ] n (point) fort m

forth [fɔ:θ] adv en avant; **to go back and ~** aller et venir; **and so ~** et ainsi de suite; **~coming** adj (event) qui va avoir lieu prochainement; (character) ouvert(e), communicatif(-ive); (available) disponible; **~right** adj franc (franche), direct(e); **~with** adv sur-le-champ

fortify ['fɔ:tɪfaɪ] vt fortifier

fortitude ['fɔ:tɪtju:d] n courage m

fortnight ['fɔ:tnaɪt] (BRIT) n quinzaine f, quinze jours mpl; **~ly** (BRIT) adj bimensuel(le) ♦ adv tous les quinze jours

fortunate ['fɔ:tʃənɪt] adj heureux(-euse); (person) chanceux(-euse); **it is ~ that** c'est une chance que; **~ly** adv heureusement

fortune ['fɔ:tʃən] n chance f; (wealth) fortune f; **~-teller** n diseuse f de bonne aventure

forty ['fɔ:tɪ] num quarante

forward ['fɔ:wəd] adj (ahead of schedule) en avance; (movement, position) en avant, vers l'avant; (not shy) direct(e); effronté(e) ♦ n (SPORT) avant m ♦ vt (letter) faire suivre; (parcel, goods) expédier; (fig) promouvoir, favoriser; **~(s)** adv en avant; **to move ~** avancer

fossil ['fɒsl] n fossile m

foster ['fɒstər] vt encourager, favoriser; (child) élever (sans obligation d'adopter); **~ child** n enfant adoptif(-ive)

fought [fɔ:t] pt, pp of **fight**

foul [faul] adj (weather, smell, food) infect(e); (language) ordurier(-ère) ♦ n (SPORT) faute f ♦ vt (dirty) salir, encrasser; **he's got a ~ temper** il a un caractère de chien; **~ play** n (LAW) acte criminel

found [faund] pt, pp of **find** ♦ vt (establish) fonder; **~ation** [faun'deɪʃən] n (act) fondation f; (base) fondement m; (also: **~ation cream**) fond m de teint; **~ations** npl (of *building*) fondations *fpl*

founder ['faundə^r] *n* fondateur *m* ♦ *vi* couler, sombrer

foundry ['faundrɪ] *n* fonderie *f*

fountain ['fauntɪn] *n* fontaine *f*; ~ **pen** *n* stylo *m* (à encre)

four [fɔː^r] *num* quatre; **on all ~s** à quatre pattes; **~-poster** *n* (*also*: **~-poster bed**) lit *m* à baldaquin; **~teen** *num* quatorze; **~th** *num* quatrième

fowl [faul] *n* volaille *f*

fox [fɔks] *n* renard *m* ♦ *vt* mystifier

foyer ['fɔɪeɪ] *n* (*hotel*) hall *m*; (THEATRE) foyer *m*

fraction ['frækʃən] *n* fraction *f*

fracture ['fræktʃə^r] *n* fracture *f*

fragile ['frædʒaɪl] *adj* fragile

fragment ['frægmənt] *n* fragment *m*

fragrant ['freɪgrənt] *adj* parfumé(e), odorant(e)

frail [freɪl] *adj* fragile, délicat(e)

frame [freɪm] *n* charpente *f*, (*of picture, bicycle*) cadre *m*, (*of door, window*) encadrement *m*, chambranle *m*; (*of spectacles: also*: **~s**) monture *f* ♦ *vt* encadrer; **~ of mind** disposition *f* d'esprit; **~work** *n* structure *f*

France [frɑːns] *n* France *f*

franchise ['fræntʃaɪz] *n* (POL) droit *m* de vote; (COMM) franchise *f*

frank [fræŋk] *adj* franc (franche) ♦ *vt* (*letter*) affranchir; **~ly** *adv* franchement

frantic ['fræntɪk] *adj* (*hectic*) frénétique; (*distraught*) hors de soi

fraternity [frə'tɜːnɪtɪ] *n* (*spirit*) fraternité *f*; (*club*) communauté *f*, confrérie *f*

fraud [frɔːd] *n* supercherie *f*, fraude *f*, tromperie *f*; (*person*) imposteur *m*

fraught [frɔːt] *adj*: ~ **with** chargé(e) de, plein(e) de

fray [freɪ] *vi* s'effilocher

freak [friːk] *n* (*also cpd*) phénomène *m*, créature ou événement exceptionnel par sa rareté

freckle ['frɛkl] *n* tache *f* de rousseur

free [friː] *adj* libre; (*gratis*) gratuit(e) ♦ *vt* (*prisoner etc*) libérer; (*jammed object or person*) dégager; ~ (**of charge**), **for** ~ gratuitement; **~dom** *n* liberté *f*; **F~fone** ® *n* numéro vert; **~-for-all** *n* mêlée générale; ~ **gift** *n* prime *f*; **~hold** *n* propriété foncière libre; ~ **kick** *n* coup franc; **~lance** *adj* indépendant(e); **~ly** *adv* librement; (*liberally*) libéralement; **F~mason** *n* franc-maçon *m*; **F~post** ® *n* port payé; **~-range** *adj* (*hen, eggs*) de ferme; ~ **trade** *n* libre-échange *m*; **~way** (US) *n* autoroute *f*; ~ **will** *n* libre arbitre *m*; **of one's own** ~ **will** de son plein gré

freeze [friːz] (*pt* **froze**, *pp* **frozen**) *vi* geler ♦ *vt* geler; (*food*) congeler; (*prices, salaries*) bloquer, geler ♦ *n* gel *m*; (*fig*) blocage *m*; **~-dried** *adj* lyophilisé(e); **~r** *n* congélateur *m*;

freezing *adj*: **freezing (cold)** (*weather, water*) glacial(e) ♦ *n*: **3 degrees below freezing** 3 degrés au-dessous de zéro; **freezing point** *n* point *m* de congélation

freight [freɪt] *n* (*goods*) fret *m*, cargaison *f*; (*money charged*) fret, prix *m* du transport; ~ **train** *n* train *m* de marchandises

French [frɛntʃ] *adj* français(e) ♦ *n* (LING) français *m*; **the ~** *npl* (*people*) les Français; ~ **bean** *n* haricot vert; ~ **fried (potatoes)** (*US* ~ **fries**) *npl* (pommes de terre *fpl*) frites *fpl*; ~ **horn** *n* (MUS) cor *m* (d'harmonie); ~ **kiss** *n* baiser profond; ~ **loaf** *n* baguette *f*; **~man** (*irreg*) *n* Français *m*; ~ **window** *n* porte-fenêtre *f*; **~woman** (*irreg*) *n* Française *f*

frenzy ['frɛnzɪ] *n* frénésie *f*

frequency ['friːkwənsɪ] *n* fréquence *f*

frequent [*adj* 'friːkwənt, *vb* frɪ'kwɛnt] *adj* fréquent(e) ♦ *vt* fréquenter; **~ly** *adv* fréquemment

fresh [frɛʃ] *adj* frais (fraîche); (*new*) nouveau (nouvelle); (*cheeky*) familier(-ère), culotté(e); **~en** *vi* (*wind, air*) fraîchir; **~en up** *vi* faire un brin de toilette; **~er** (BRIT: *inf*) *n* (SCOL) bizuth *m*, étudiant(e) de 1ère année; **~ly** *adv* nouvellement, récemment; **~man** (*US*) (*irreg*) *n* = **fresher**; **~ness** *n* fraîcheur *f*; **~water** *adj* (*fish*) d'eau douce

fret [frɛt] *vi* s'agiter, se tracasser

friar ['fraɪə^r] *n* moine *m*, frère *m*

friction ['frɪkʃən] *n* friction *f*

Friday ['fraɪdɪ] *n* vendredi *m*

fridge [frɪdʒ] (BRIT) *n* frigo *m*, frigidaire ® *m*

fried [fraɪd] *adj* frit(e); ~ **egg** œuf *m* sur le plat

friend [frɛnd] *n* ami(e); **~ly** *adj* amical(e); gentil(le); (*place*) accueillant(e); **they were killed by ~ly fire** ils sont morts sous les tirs de leur propre camp; **~ship** *n* amitié *f*

frieze [friːz] *n* frise *f*

fright [fraɪt] *n* peur *f*, effroi *m*; **to take** ~ prendre peur, s'effrayer; **~en** *vt* effrayer, faire peur à; **~ened** *adj*: **to be ~ened (of)** avoir peur (de); **~ening** *adj* effrayant(e); **~ful** *adj* affreux(-euse)

frigid ['frɪdʒɪd] *adj* frigide

frill [frɪl] *n* (*on dress*) volant *m*; (*on shirt*) jabot *m*

fringe [frɪndʒ] *n* (BRIT: *of hair*) frange *f*; (*edge*: *of forest etc*) bordure *f*; ~ **benefits** *npl* avantages sociaux *or* en nature

Frisbee ® ['frɪzbɪ] *n* Frisbee ® *m*

frisk [frɪsk] *vt* fouiller

fritter ['frɪtə^r] *n* beignet *m*; ~ **away** *vt* gaspiller

frivolous ['frɪvələs] *adj* frivole

frizzy ['frɪzɪ] *adj* crépu(e)

fro [frəu] *adv*: **to go to and ~** aller et venir

frock [frɔk] *n* robe *f*

frog [frɔg] *n* grenouille *f*; **~man** *n* homme-grenouille *m*

frolic ['frɔlɪk] *vi* folâtrer, batifoler

KEYWORD

from [frɔm] *prep* **1** (*indicating starting place, origin etc*) de; **where do you come from?, where are you from?** d'où venez-vous?; **from London to Paris** de Londres à Paris; **a letter from my sister** une lettre de ma sœur; **to drink from the bottle** boire à (même) la bouteille

2 (*indicating time*) (à partir) de; **from one o'clock to** *or* **until** *or* **till two** d'une heure à deux heures; **from January (on)** à partir de janvier

3 (*indicating distance*) de; **the hotel is one kilometre from the beach** l'hôtel est à un kilomètre de la plage

4 (*indicating price, number etc*) de; **the interest rate was increased from 9% to 10%** le taux d'intérêt est passé de 9 à 10%

5 (*indicating difference*) de; **he can't tell red from green** il ne peut pas distinguer le rouge du vert

6 (*because of, on the basis of*): **from what he says** d'après ce qu'il dit; **weak from hunger** affaibli par la faim

front [frʌnt] *n* (*of house, dress*) devant *m*; (*of coach, train*) avant *m*; (*promenade: also*: **sea ~**) bord *m* de mer; (*MIL, METEOROLOGY*) front *m*; (*fig: appearances*) contenance *f*, façade *f* ♦ *adj* de devant; (*seat*) avant *inv*; **in ~ (of)** devant; **~age** *n* (*of building*) façade *f*; **~ door** *n* porte *f* d'entrée; (*of car*) portière *f* avant; **~ier** ['frʌntɪə'] *n* frontière *f*; **~ page** *n* première page; **~ room** (*BRIT*) *n* pièce *f* de devant, salon *m*; **~-wheel drive** *n* traction *f* avant

frost [frɔst] *n* gel *m*, gelée *f*; (*also*: **hoarfrost**) givre *m*; **~bite** *n* gelures *fpl*; **~ed** *adj* (*glass*) dépoli(e); **~y** *adj* (*weather, welcome*) glacial(e)

froth [frɔθ] *n* mousse *f*; écume *f*

frown [fraun] *vi* froncer les sourcils

froze [frəuz] *pt of* **freeze**

frozen ['frəuzn] *pp of* **freeze**

fruit [fru:t] *n inv* fruit *m*; **~erer** *n* fruitier *m*, marchand(e) de fruits; **~ful** *adj* (*fig*) fructueux(-euse); **~ion** [fru:'ɪʃən] *n*: **to come to ~ion** se réaliser; **~ juice** *n* jus *m* de fruit; **~ machine** (*BRIT*) *n* machine *f* à sous; **~ salad** *n* salade *f* de fruits

frustrate [frʌs'treɪt] *vt* frustrer

fry [fraɪ] (*pt, pp* **fried**) *vt* (faire) frire; *see also* **small**; **~ing pan** *n* poêle *f* (à frire)

ft. *abbr* = **foot**; **feet**

fudge [fʌdʒ] *n* (*CULIN*) caramel *m*

fuel ['fjuəl] *n* (*for heating*) combustible *m*; (*for propelling*) carburant *m*; **~ oil** *n* mazout *m*; **~ tank** *n* (*in vehicle*) réservoir *m*

fugitive ['fju:dʒɪtɪv] *n* fugitif(-ive)

fulfil [ful'fil] (*US* **fulfill**) *vt* (*function, condition*) remplir; (*order*) exécuter; (*wish, desire*) satisfaire, réaliser; **~ment** (*US* **fulfillment**) *n* (*of wishes etc*) réalisation *f*; (*feeling*) contentement *m*

full [ful] *adj* plein(e); (*details, information*) complet(-ète); (*skirt*) ample, large ♦ *adv*: **to know ~ well that** savoir fort bien que; **I'm ~ (up)** j'ai bien mangé; **a ~ two hours** deux bonnes heures; **at ~ speed** à toute vitesse; **in ~** (*reproduce, quote*) intégralement; (*write*) en toutes lettres; **~ employment** plein emploi; **to pay in ~** tout payer; **~-length** *adj* (*film*) long métrage; (*portrait, mirror*) en pied; (*coat*) long(ue); **~ moon** *n* pleine lune; **~-scale** *adj* (*attack, war*) complet(-ète), total(e); (*model*) grandeur nature *inv*; **~ stop** *n* point *m*; **~-time** *adj, adv* (*work*) à plein temps; **~y** *adv* entièrement, complètement; (*at least*) au moins; **~y licensed** (*hotel, restaurant*) autorisé(e) à vendre des boissons alcoolisées; **~y-fledged** *adj* (*barrister etc*) diplômé(e); (*citizen, member*) à part entière

fumble ['fʌmbl] *vi*: **~ with** tripoter

fume [fju:m] *vi* rager; **~s** *npl* vapeurs *fpl*, émanations *fpl*, gaz *mpl*

fun [fʌn] *n* amusement *m*, divertissement *m*; **to have ~** s'amuser; **for ~** pour rire; **to make ~ of** se moquer de

function ['fʌŋkʃən] *n* fonction *f*; (*social occasion*) cérémonie *f*, soirée officielle ♦ *vi* fonctionner; **~al** *adj* fonctionnel(le)

fund [fʌnd] *n* caisse *f*, fonds *m*; (*source, store*) source *f*, mine *f*; **~s** *npl* (*money*) fonds *mpl*

fundamental [fʌndə'mentl] *adj* fondamental(e)

funeral ['fju:nərəl] *n* enterrement *m*, obsèques *fpl*; **~ parlour** *n* entreprise *f* de pompes funèbres; **~ service** *n* service *m* funèbre

funfair ['fʌnfeə'] (*BRIT*) *n* fête (foraine)

fungi ['fʌŋgaɪ] *npl of* **fungus**

fungus ['fʌŋgəs] (*pl* **fungi**) *n* champignon *m*; (*mould*) moisissure *f*

funnel ['fʌnl] *n* entonnoir *m*; (*of ship*) cheminée *f*

funny ['fʌnɪ] *adj* amusant(e), drôle; (*strange*) curieux(-euse), bizarre

fur [fə:'] *n* fourrure *f*; (*BRIT: in kettle etc*) (dépôt *m* de) tartre *m*

furious ['fjuərɪəs] *adj* furieux(-euse); (*effort*) acharné(e)

furlong ['fəːlɔŋ] n = 201,17 m

furnace ['fəːnɪs] n fourneau m

furnish ['fəːnɪʃ] vt meubler; (supply): **to ~ sb with sth** fournir qch à qn; **~ings** npl mobilier m, ameublement m

furniture ['fəːnɪtʃə'] n meubles mpl, mobilier m; **piece of ~** meuble m

furrow ['fʌrəʊ] n sillon m

furry ['fəːrɪ] adj (animal) à fourrure; (toy) en peluche

further ['fəːðə'] adj (additional) supplémentaire, autre; nouveau (nouvelle) ♦ adv plus loin; (more) davantage; (moreover) de plus ♦ vt faire avancer or progresser, promouvoir; **~ education** n enseignement m postscolaire; **~more** adv de plus, en outre

furthest ['fəːðɪst] superl of **far**

fury ['fjʊərɪ] n fureur f

fuse [fjuːz] (US **fuze**) n fusible m; (for bomb etc) amorce f, détonateur m ♦ vt, vi (metal) fondre; **to ~ the lights** (BRIT) faire sauter les plombs; **~ box** n boîte f à fusibles

fuss [fʌs] n (excitement) agitation f; (complaining) histoire(s) f(pl); **to make a ~** faire des histoires; **to make a ~ of sb** être aux petits soins pour qn; **~y** adj (person) tatillon(ne), difficile; (dress, style) tarabiscoté(e)

future ['fjuːtʃə'] adj futur(e) ♦ n avenir m; (LING) futur m; **in ~** à l'avenir

fuze [fjuːz] (US) n, vt, vi = **fuse**

fuzzy ['fʌzɪ] adj (PHOT) flou(e); (hair) crépu(e)

G, g

G [dʒiː] n (MUS) sol m

G8 n abbr (= Group of 8) le groupe des 8

gabble ['gæbl] vi bredouiller

gable ['geɪbl] n pignon m

gadget ['gædʒɪt] n gadget m

Gaelic ['geɪlɪk] adj gaélique ♦ n (LING) gaélique m

gag [gæg] n (on mouth) bâillon m; (joke) gag m ♦ vt bâillonner

gaiety ['geɪɪtɪ] n gaieté f

gain [geɪn] n (improvement) gain m; (profit) gain, profit m; (increase): **~ (in)** augmentation f (de) ♦ vt gagner ♦ vi (watch) avancer; **to ~ 3 lbs (in weight)** prendre 3 livres; **to ~ on sb** (catch up) rattraper qn; **to ~ from/by** gagner de/à

gal. abbr = **gallon**

gale [geɪl] n coup m de vent

gallant ['gælənt] adj vaillant(e), brave; (towards ladies) galant

gall bladder ['gɔːl-] n vésicule f biliaire

gallery ['gælərɪ] n galerie f; (also: **art ~**) musée m; (: private) galerie

gallon ['gæln] n gallon m (BRIT = 4,5 l; US = 3,8 l)

gallop ['gæləp] n galop m ♦ vi galoper

gallows ['gæləʊz] n potence f

gallstone ['gɔːlstəʊn] n calcul m biliaire

galore [gə'lɔː'] adv en abondance, à gogo

Gambia ['gæmbɪə] n: (**The**) ~ la Gambie

gambit ['gæmbɪt] n (fig): (**opening**) ~ manœuvre f stratégique

gamble ['gæmbl] n pari m, risque calculé ♦ vt, vi jouer; **to ~ on** (fig) miser sur; **~r** n joueur m; **gambling** n jeu m

game [geɪm] n jeu m; (match) match m; (strategy, scheme) plan m; projet m; (HUNTING) gibier m ♦ adj (willing): **to be ~ (for)** être prêt(e) (à or pour); **big ~** gros gibier; **~keeper** n garde-chasse m

gammon ['gæmən] n (bacon) quartier m de lard fumé; (ham) jambon fumé

gamut ['gæmət] n gamme f

gang [gæŋ] n bande f, (of workmen) équipe f, **~ up** vi: **to ~ up on sb** se liguer contre qn; **~ster** n gangster m; **~way** ['gæŋweɪ] n passerelle f; (BRIT: of bus, plane) couloir central; (: in cinema) allée centrale

gaol [dʒeɪl] (BRIT) n = **jail**

gap [gæp] n trou m; (in time) intervalle m; (difference): ~ **between** écart m entre

gape [geɪp] vi (person) être ou rester bouche bée; (hole, shirt) être ouvert(e); **gaping** adj (hole) béant(e)

garage ['gærɑːʒ] n garage m

garbage ['gɑːbɪdʒ] n (US: rubbish) ordures fpl, détritus mpl; (inf: nonsense) foutaises fpl; ~ **can** (US) n poubelle f, boîte f à ordures

garbled ['gɑːbld] adj (account, message) embrouillé(e)

garden ['gɑːdn] n jardin m; **~s** npl jardin public; **~er** n jardinier m; **~ing** n jardinage m

gargle ['gɑːgl] vi se gargariser

garish ['gɛərɪʃ] adj criard(e), voyant(e); (light) cru(e)

garland ['gɑːlənd] n guirlande f; couronne f

garlic ['gɑːlɪk] n ail m

garment ['gɑːmənt] n vêtement m

garrison ['gærɪsn] n garnison f

garter ['gɑːtə'] n jarretière f; (US) jarretelle f

gas [gæs] n gaz m; (US: gasoline) essence f ♦ vt asphyxier; ~ **cooker** (BRIT) n cuisinière f à gaz; ~ **cylinder** n bouteille f de gaz; ~ **fire** (BRIT) n radiateur m à gaz

gash [gæʃ] n entaille f; (on face) balafre f

gasket ['gæskɪt] n (AUT) joint m de culasse

gas mask n masque m à gaz

gas meter n compteur m à gaz

gasoline ['gæsəliːn] (US) n essence f

gasp [gɑːsp] vi haleter

gas: ~ **ring** n brûleur m; ~ **station** (US) n
station-service f; ~ **tap** n bouton m (de
cuisinière à gaz); (on pipe) robinet m à gaz

gastric ['gæstrɪk] adj gastrique; ~ **flu** grippe f
intestinale

gate [geɪt] n (of garden) portail m; (of field)
barrière f; (at airport) porte f

gateau ['gætəʊ] n (pl ~x) (gros) gâteau à la
crème

gatecrash vt s'introduire sans invitation dans

gateway n porte f

gather ['gæðə'] vt (flowers, fruit) cueillir; (pick
up) ramasser; (assemble) rassembler, réunir;
recueillir; (understand) comprendre; (SEWING)
froncer ♦ vi (assemble) se rassembler; **to**
~ **speed** prendre de la vitesse; ~**ing** n
rassemblement m

gaudy ['gɔːdɪ] adj voyant(e)

gauge [geɪdʒ] n (instrument) jauge f ♦ vt
jauger

gaunt [gɔːnt] adj (thin) décharné(e); (grim,
desolate) désolé(e)

gauntlet ['gɔːntlɪt] n (glove) gant m

gauze [gɔːz] n gaze f

gave [geɪv] pt of **give**

gay [geɪ] adj (homosexual) homosexuel(le);
(cheerful) gai(e), réjoui(e); (colour etc) gai,
vif (vive)

gaze [geɪz] n regard m fixe ♦ vi: **to** ~ **at** fixer
du regard

gazump [gə'zʌmp] (BRIT) vi revenir sur une
promesse de vente (pour accepter une offre plus
intéressante)

GB abbr = **Great Britain**

GCE n abbr (BRIT) = **General Certificate of
Education**

GCSE n abbr (BRIT) = **General Certificate of
Secondary Education**

gear [gɪə'] n matériel m, équipement m;
attirail m; (TECH) engrenage m; (AUT) vitesse
f ♦ vt (fig: adapt): **to** ~ **sth** to adapter qch à;
top or (US) **high** ~ quatrième (or cinquième)
vitesse; **low** ~ première vitesse; **in** ~ en prise;
~ **box** n boîte f de vitesses; ~ **lever** (US **gear
shift**) n levier m de vitesse

geese [giːs] npl of **goose**

gel [dʒɛl] n gel m

gem [dʒɛm] n pierre précieuse

Gemini ['dʒɛmɪnaɪ] n les Gémeaux mpl

gender ['dʒɛndə'] n genre m

gene [dʒiːn] n gène m

general ['dʒɛnərl] n général m ♦ adj
général(e); **in** ~ en général; ~ **delivery** n
poste restante; ~ **election** n élection(s)
législative(s); ~ **knowledge** n connaissances
générales; ~**ly** adv généralement;
~ **practitioner** n généraliste m/f

generate ['dʒɛnəreɪt] vt engendrer;
(electricity etc) produire; **generation** n

génération f; (of electricity etc) production f;
generator n générateur m

generosity [dʒɛnə'rɒsɪtɪ] n générosité f

generous ['dʒɛnərəs] adj généreux(-euse);
(copious) copieux(-euse)

genetic [dʒɪ'nɛtɪk] adj: ~ **engineering**
ingénierie f génétique; ~ **fingerprinting**
système m d'empreinte génétique

genetics [dʒɪ'nɛtɪks] n génétique f

Geneva [dʒɪ'niːvə] n Genève

genial ['dʒiːnɪəl] adj cordial(e), chaleu-
reux(-euse)

genitals ['dʒɛnɪtlz] npl organes génitaux

genius ['dʒiːnɪəs] n génie m

genteel [dʒɛn'tiːl] adj de bon ton,
distingué(e)

gentle ['dʒɛntl] adj doux (douce)

gentleman ['dʒɛntlmən] n monsieur m;
(well-bred man) gentleman m

gently ['dʒɛntlɪ] adv doucement

gentry ['dʒɛntrɪ] n inv: **the** ~ la petite
noblesse

gents [dʒɛnts] n W.-C. mpl (pour hommes)

genuine ['dʒɛnjuɪn] adj véritable,
authentique; (person) sincère

geographical [dʒɪə'græfɪkl] adj
géographique

geography [dʒɪ'ɔgrəfɪ] n géographie f

geology [dʒɪ'ɔlədʒɪ] n géologie f

geometric(al) [dʒɪə'mɛtrɪk(l)] adj
géométrique

geometry [dʒɪ'ɔmətrɪ] n géométrie f

geranium [dʒɪ'reɪnɪəm] n géranium m

geriatric [dʒɛrɪ'ætrɪk] adj gériatrique

germ [dʒəːm] n (MED) microbe m

German ['dʒəːmən] adj allemand(e) ♦ n
Allemand(e); (LING) allemand m; ~ **measles**
(BRIT) n rubéole f

Germany ['dʒəːmənɪ] n Allemagne f

gesture ['dʒɛstjə'] n geste m

┌─────────────┐
│ KEYWORD   │
└─────────────┘

get [gɛt] (pt, pp **got**, pp **gotten** (US)) vi **1**
(become, be) devenir; **to get old/tired** devenir
vieux/fatigué, vieillir/se fatiguer; **to get drunk**
s'enivrer; **to get killed** se faire tuer; **when do I
get paid?** quand est-ce que je serai payé?; **it's
getting late** il se fait tard

2 (go): **to get to/from** aller à/de; **to get home**
rentrer chez soi; **how did you get here?**
comment es-tu arrivé ici?

3 (begin) commencer or se mettre à; **I'm
getting to like him** je commence à l'apprécier;
let's get going or **started** allons-y

4 (modal aux vb): **you've got to do it** il faut
que vous le fassiez; **I've got to tell the police**
je dois le dire à la police

♦ vt **1**: **to get sth done** (do) faire qch; (have
done) faire faire qch; **to get one's hair cut** se

faire couper les cheveux; **to get sb to do sth**
faire faire qch à qn; **to get sb drunk** enivrer
qn
2 (obtain: money, permission, results) obtenir,
avoir; (find: job, flat) trouver; (fetch: person,
doctor, object) aller chercher; **to get sth for sb**
procurer qch à qn; **get me Mr Jones, please**
(on phone) passez-moi Mr Jones, s'il vous
plaît; **can I get you a drink?** est-ce que je peux
vous servir à boire?
3 (receive: present, letter) recevoir, avoir;
(acquire: reputation) avoir; (: prize) obtenir;
what did you get for your birthday? qu'est-ce
que tu as eu pour ton anniversaire?
4 (catch) prendre, saisir, attraper; (hit: target
etc) atteindre; **to get sb by the arm/throat**
prendre or saisir or attraper qn par le bras/à la
gorge; **get him!** arrête-le!
5 (take, move) faire parvenir; **do you think**
we'll get it through the door? on arrivera à le
faire passer par la porte?; **I'll get you there**
somehow je me débrouillerai pour t'y
emmener
6 (catch, take: plane, bus etc) prendre
7 (understand) comprendre, saisir; (hear)
entendre; **I've got it!** j'ai compris!, je saisis!; **I**
didn't get your name je n'ai pas entendu
votre nom
8 (have, possess): **to have got** avoir; **how**
many have you got? vous en avez combien?
get about vi se déplacer; (news) se répandre
get along vi (agree) s'entendre; (depart)
s'en aller; = **get by**
get at vt fus (attack) s'en prendre à; (reach)
attraper, atteindre
get away vi partir, s'en aller; (escape)
s'échapper
get away with vt fus en être quitte pour; se
faire passer or pardonner
get back vi (return) rentrer ♦ vt récupérer,
recouvrer
get by vi (pass) passer; (manage) se
débrouiller
get down vi, vt fus descendre ♦ vt
descendre; (depress) déprimer
get down to vt fus (work) se mettre à
(faire)
get in vi rentrer; (train) arriver
get into vt fus entrer dans; (car, train etc)
monter dans; (clothes) mettre, enfiler,
endosser; **to get into bed/a rage** se mettre au
lit/en colère
get off vi (from train etc) descendre; (depart:
person, car) s'en aller; (escape) s'en tirer ♦ vt
(remove: clothes, stain) enlever ♦ vt fus (train,
bus) descendre de
get on vi (at exam etc) se débrouiller;
(agree): **to get on (with)** s'entendre (avec)
♦ vt fus monter dans; (horse) monter sur

get out vi sortir; (of vehicle) descendre ♦ vt
sortir
get out of vt fus sortir de; (duty etc)
échapper à, se soustraire à
get over vt fus (illness) se remettre de
get round vt fus contourner; (fig: person)
entortiller
get through vi (TEL) avoir la
communication; **to get through to sb**
atteindre qn
get together vi se réunir ♦ vt assembler
get up vi (rise) se lever ♦ vt fus monter
get up to vt fus (reach) arriver à; (prank etc)
faire

getaway ['getəweɪ] n: **to make one's ~** filer
geyser ['giːzəʳ] n (GEO) geyser m; (BRIT: water
heater) chauffe-eau m inv
Ghana ['gɑːnə] n Ghana m
ghastly ['gɑːstlɪ] adj atroce, horrible; (pale)
livide, blême
gherkin ['gɜːkɪn] n cornichon m
ghetto blaster ['getəu'blɑːstəʳ] n stéréo f
portable
ghost [gəust] n fantôme m, revenant m
giant ['dʒaɪənt] n géant(e) ♦ adj géant(e),
énorme
gibberish ['dʒɪbərɪʃ] n charabia m
giblets ['dʒɪblɪts] npl abats mpl
Gibraltar [dʒɪ'brɔːltəʳ] n Gibraltar
giddy ['gɪdɪ] adj (dizzy): **to be** or **feel ~** avoir
le vertige
gift [gɪft] n cadeau m; (donation, ability) don
m; **~ed** adj doué(e); **~ shop** n boutique f de
cadeaux; **~ token** n chèque-cadeau m
gigantic [dʒaɪ'gæntɪk] adj gigantesque
giggle ['gɪgl] vi pouffer (de rire), rire
sottement
gill [dʒɪl] n (measure) = 0.25 pints (BRIT
= 0.15 l, US = 0.12 l)
gills [gɪlz] npl (of fish) ouïes fpl, branchies fpl
gilt [gɪlt] adj doré(e) ♦ n dorure f; **~-edged**
adj (COMM) de premier ordre
gimmick ['gɪmɪk] n truc m
gin [dʒɪn] n (liquor) gin m
ginger ['dʒɪndʒəʳ] n gingembre m; **~ ale**,
~ beer n boisson gazeuse au gingembre;
~bread n pain m d'épices
gingerly ['dʒɪndʒəlɪ] adv avec précaution
gipsy ['dʒɪpsɪ] n = **gypsy**
giraffe [dʒɪ'rɑːf] n girafe f
girder ['gɜːdəʳ] n poutrelle f
girl [gɜːl] n fille f, fillette f; (young unmarried
woman) jeune fille; (daughter) fille; **an**
English ~ une jeune Anglaise; **~friend** n (of
girl) amie f; (of boy) petite amie; **~ish** adj de
petite or de jeune fille; (for a boy)
efféminé(e)
giro ['dʒaɪrəu] n (bank ~) virement m

bancaire; (*post office ~*) mandat *m*; (*BRIT: welfare cheque*) mandat *m* d'allocation chômage

gist [dʒɪst] *n* essentiel *m*

give [gɪv] (*pt* **gave**, *pp* **given**) *vt* donner ♦ *vi* (*break*) céder; (*stretch: fabric*) se prêter; **to ~ sb sth, ~ sth to sb** donner qch à qn; **to ~ a cry/sigh** pousser un cri/un soupir; **~ away** *vt* donner; (*~ free*) faire cadeau de; (*betray*) donner, trahir; (*disclose*) révéler; (*bride*) conduire à l'autel; **~ back** *vt* rendre; **~ in** *vi* céder ♦ *vt* donner; **~ off** *vt* dégager; **~ out** *vt* distribuer; annoncer; **~ up** *vi* renoncer ♦ *vt* renoncer à; **to ~ up smoking** arrêter de fumer; **to ~ o.s. up** se rendre; **~ way** (*BRIT*) *vi* céder; (*AUT*) céder la priorité

glacier [ˈglæsɪəʳ] *n* glacier *m*

glad [glæd] *adj* content(e); **~ly** *adv* volontiers

glamorous [ˈglæmərəs] *adj* (*person*) séduisant(e); (*job*) prestigieux(-euse)

glamour [ˈglæməʳ] *n* éclat *m*, prestige *m*

glance [glɑːns] *n* coup *m* d'œil ♦ *vi*: **to ~ at** jeter un coup d'œil à; **glancing** *adj* (*blow*) oblique

gland [glænd] *n* glande *f*

glare [glɛəʳ] *n* (*of anger*) regard furieux; (*of light*) lumière éblouissante; (*of publicity*) feux *mpl* ♦ *vi* briller d'un éclat aveuglant; **to ~ at** lancer un regard furieux à; **glaring** *adj* (*mistake*) criant(e), qui saute aux yeux

glass [glɑːs] *n* verre *m*; **~es** *npl* (*spectacles*) lunettes *fpl*; **~house** (*BRIT*) *n* (*for plants*) serre *f*; **~ware** *n* verrerie *f*

glaze [gleɪz] *vt* (*door, window*) vitrer; (*pottery*) vernir ♦ *n* (*on pottery*) vernis *m*; **~d** *adj* (*pottery*) verni(e); (*eyes*) vitreux(-euse)

glazier [ˈgleɪzɪəʳ] *n* vitrier *m*

gleam [gliːm] *vi* luire, briller

glean [gliːn] *vt* (*information*) glaner

glee [gliː] *n* joie *f*

glib [glɪb] *adj* (*person*) qui a du bagou; (*response*) désinvolte, facile

glide [glaɪd] *vi* glisser; (*AVIAT, birds*) planer; **~r** *n* (*AVIAT*) planeur *m*; **gliding** *n* (*SPORT*) vol *m* à voile

glimmer [ˈglɪməʳ] *n* lueur *f*

glimpse [glɪmps] *n* vision passagère, aperçu *m* ♦ *vt* entrevoir, apercevoir

glint [glɪnt] *vi* étinceler

glisten [ˈglɪsn] *vi* briller, luire

glitter [ˈglɪtəʳ] *vi* scintiller, briller

gloat [gləut] *vi*: **to ~ (over)** jubiler (à propos de)

global [ˈgləubl] *adj* mondial(e); **~ warming** réchauffement *m* de la planète

globe [gləub] *n* globe *m*

gloom [gluːm] *n* obscurité *f*; (*sadness*) tristesse *f*, mélancolie *f*; **~y** *adj* sombre, triste, lugubre

glorious [ˈglɔːrɪəs] *adj* glorieux(-euse); splendide

glory [ˈglɔːrɪ] *n* gloire *f*; splendeur *f*

gloss [glɔs] *n* (*shine*) brillant *m*, vernis *m*; **~ over** *vt fus* glisser sur

glossary [ˈglɔsərɪ] *n* glossaire *m*

glossy [ˈglɔsɪ] *adj* brillant(e); **~ magazine** magazine *m* de luxe

glove [glʌv] *n* gant *m*; **~ compartment** *n* (*AUT*) boîte *f* à gants, vide-poches *m inv*

glow [gləu] *vi* rougeoyer; (*face*) rayonner; (*eyes*) briller

glower [ˈglauəʳ] *vi*: **to ~ (at)** lancer des regards mauvais (à)

glucose [ˈgluːkəus] *n* glucose *m*

glue [gluː] *n* colle *f* ♦ *vt* coller

glum [glʌm] *adj* sombre, morne

glut [glʌt] *n* surabondance *f*

glutton [ˈglʌtn] *n* glouton(ne); **a ~ for work** un bourreau de travail; **a ~ for punishment** un masochiste (*fig*)

GM *abbr* (= *genetically modified*) génétiquement modifé(e)

gnat [næt] *n* moucheron *m*

gnaw [nɔː] *vt* ronger

go [gəu] (*pt* **went**, *pp* **gone**, *pl* **~es**) *vi* aller; (*depart*) partir, s'en aller; (*work*) marcher; (*break etc*) céder; (*be sold*): **to ~ for £10** se vendre 10 livres; (*fit, suit*): **to ~ with** aller avec; (*become*): **to ~ pale/mouldy** pâlir/moisir ♦ *n*: **to have a ~ (at)** essayer (de faire); **to be on the ~** être en mouvement; **whose ~ is it?** à qui est-ce de jouer?; **he's ~ing to do** il va faire, il est sur le point de faire; **to ~ for a walk** aller se promener; **to ~ dancing** aller danser; **how did it ~?** comment est-ce que ça s'est passé?; **to ~ round the back/by the shop** passer par derrière/devant le magasin; **~ about** *vi* (*rumour*) se répandre ♦ *vt fus*: **how do I ~ about this?** comment dois-je m'y prendre (pour faire ceci)?; **~ after** *vt fus* (*pursue*) poursuivre, courir après; (*job, record etc*) essayer d'obtenir; **~ ahead** *vi* (*make progress*) avancer; (*get going*) y aller; **~ along** *vi* aller, avancer ♦ *vt fus* longer, parcourir; **~ away** *vi* partir, s'en aller; **~ back** *vi* rentrer; revenir; (*~ again*) retourner; **~ back on** *vt fus* (*promise*) revenir sur; **~ by** *vi* (*years, time*) passer, s'écouler ♦ *vt fus* s'en tenir à; en croire; **~ down** *vi* descendre; (*ship*) couler; (*sun*) se coucher ♦ *vt fus* descendre; **~ for** *vt fus* (*fetch*) aller chercher; (*like*) aimer; (*attack*) s'en prendre à, attaquer; **~ in** *vi* entrer; **~ in for** *vt fus* (*competition*) se présenter à; (*like*) aimer; **~ into** *vt fus* entrer dans; (*investigate*) étudier, examiner; (*embark on*) se lancer dans; **~ off** *vi* partir, s'en aller; (*food*) se gâter; (*explode*) sauter; (*event*) se dérouler

♦ *vt fus* ne plus aimer; **the gun went off** le coup est parti; **~ on** *vi* continuer; (*happen*) se passer; **to ~ on doing** continuer à faire; **~ out** *vi* sortir; (*fire, light*) s'éteindre; **~ over** *vt fus* (*check*) revoir, vérifier; **~ past** *vt fus:* **to ~ past sth** passer devant qch; **~ round** *vi* (*circulate: news, rumour*) circuler; (*revolve*) tourner; (*suffice*) suffire (pour tout le monde); **to ~ round** to sb's (*visit*) passer chez qn; **to ~ round (by)** (*make a detour*) faire un détour (par); **~ through** *vt fus* (*town etc*) traverser; **~ up** *vi* monter; (*price*) augmenter ♦ *vt fus* gravir; **~ with** *vt fus* (*suit*) aller avec; **~ without** *vt fus* se passer de

goad [gəud] *vt* aiguillonner

go-ahead ['gəuəhɛd] *adj* dynamique, entreprenant(e) ♦ *n* feu vert

goal [gəul] *n* but *m*; **~keeper** *n* gardien *m* de but; **~post** *n* poteau *m* de but

goat [gəut] *n* chèvre *f*

gobble ['gɔbl] *vt* (*also:* **~ down**, **~ up**) engloutir

go-between ['gəubɪtwi:n] *n* intermédiaire *m/f*

god [gɔd] *n* dieu *m*; **G~** *n* Dieu *m*; **~child** *n* filleul(e); **~daughter** *n* filleule *f*; **~dess** *n* déesse *f*; **~father** *n* parrain *m*; **~-forsaken** *adj* maudit(e); **~mother** *n* marraine *f*; **~send** *n* aubaine *f*; **~son** *n* filleul *m*

goggles ['gɔglz] *npl* (*for skiing etc*) lunettes protectrices

going ['gəuɪŋ] *n* (*conditions*) état *m* du terrain ♦ *adj:* **the ~ rate** le tarif (en vigueur)

gold [gəuld] *n* or *m* ♦ *adj* en or; (*reserves*) d'or; **~en** *adj* (*made of gold*) en or; (*gold in colour*) doré(e); **~fish** *n* poisson *m* rouge; **~-plated** *adj* plaqué(e) or *inv*, **~smith** *n* orfèvre *m*

golf [gɔlf] *n* golf *m*; **~ ball** *n* balle *f* de golf; (*on typewriter*) boule *m*; **~ club** *n* club *m* de golf; (*stick*) club *m*, crosse *f* de golf; **~ course** *n* (terrain *m* de) golf *m*; **~er** *n* joueur(-euse) de golf

gone [gɔn] *pp of* **go**

gong [gɔŋ] *n* gong *m*

good [gud] *adj* bon(ne); (*kind*) gentil(le); (*child*) sage *n* bien *m*; **~s** *npl* (*COMM*) marchandises *fpl*, articles *mpl*; **~!** bon!, très bien!; **to be ~ at** être bon en; **to be ~ for** bon pour; **would you be ~ enough to ...?** auriez-vous la bonté *or* l'amabilité de ...?; **a ~ deal (of)** beaucoup (de); **a ~ many** beaucoup (de); **to make ~** *vi* (*succeed*) faire son chemin, réussir ♦ *vt* (*deficit*) combler; (*losses*) compenser; **it's no ~ complaining** cela ne sert à rien de se plaindre; **for ~** pour de bon, une fois pour toutes; **~ morning/afternoon!** bonjour!; **~ evening!** bonsoir!; **~ night!** bonsoir!; (*on going to bed*) bonne

nuit!; **~bye** *excl* au revoir!; **G~ Friday** *n* Vendredi saint; **~-looking** *adj* beau (belle), bien *inv*; **~-natured** *adj* (*person*) qui a un bon naturel; **~ness** *n* (*of person*) bonté *f*; **for ~ness sake!** je vous en prie!; **~ness gracious!** mon Dieu!; **~s train** (*BRIT*) *n* train *m* de marchandises; **~will** *n* bonne volonté *f*

goose [gu:s] (*pl* **geese**) *n* oie *f*

gooseberry ['guzbərɪ] *n* groseille *f* à maquereau; **to play ~** (*BRIT*) tenir la chandelle

gooseflesh ['gu:sflɛʃ] *n*, **goose pimples** *npl* chair *f* de poule

gore [gɔ:ʳ] *vt* encorner ♦ *n* sang *m*

gorge [gɔ:dʒ] *n* gorge *f* ♦ *vt:* **to ~ o.s. (on)** se gorger (de)

gorgeous ['gɔ:dʒəs] *adj* splendide, superbe

gorilla [gə'rɪlə] *n* gorille *m*

gorse [gɔ:s] *n* ajoncs *mpl*

gory ['gɔ:rɪ] *adj* sanglant(e); (*details*) horrible

go-slow ['gəu'sləu] (*BRIT*) *n* grève perlée

gospel ['gɔspl] *n* évangile *m*

gossip ['gɔsɪp] *n* (*chat*) bavardages *mpl*, commérage *m*, cancans *mpl*; (*person*) commère *f* ♦ *vi* bavarder; (*maliciously*) cancaner, faire des commérages

got [gɔt] *pt, pp of* **get**; **~ten** (*US*) *pp of* **get**

gout [gaut] *n* goutte *f*

govern ['gʌvən] *vt* gouverner; **~ess** *n* gouvernante *f*; **~ment** *n* gouvernement *m*; (*BRIT: ministers*) ministère *m*; **~or** *n* (*of state, bank*) gouverneur *m*; (*of school, hospital*) ≈ membre *m/f* du conseil d'établissement; (*BRIT: of prison*) directeur(-trice)

gown [gaun] *n* robe *f*; (*of teacher, BRIT: of judge*) toge *f*

GP *n abbr* = **general practitioner**

grab [græb] *vt* saisir, empoigner ♦ *vi:* **to ~ at** essayer de saisir

grace [greɪs] *n* grâce *f* ♦ *vt* honorer; (*adorn*) orner; **5 days' ~** cinq jours de répit; **~ful** *adj* gracieux(-euse), élégant(e); **gracious** ['greɪʃəs] *adj* bienveillant(e)

grade [greɪd] *n* (*COMM*) qualité *f*; (*in hierarchy*) catégorie *f*, grade *m*, échelon *m*; (*SCOL*) note *f*; (*US: school class*) classe *f* ♦ *vt* classer; **~ crossing** (*US*) *n* passage *m* à niveau; **~ school** (*US*) *n* école *f* primaire

gradient ['greɪdɪənt] *n* inclinaison *f*, pente *f*

gradual ['grædjuəl] *adj* graduel(le), progressif(-ive); **~ly** *adv* peu à peu, graduellement

graduate [*n* 'grædjuɪt, *vb* 'grædjueɪt] *n* diplômé(e), licencié(e); (*US: of high school*) bachelier(-ère) ♦ *vi* obtenir son diplôme; (*US*) obtenir son baccalauréat; **graduation** [grædju'eɪʃən] *n* (cérémonie *f* de) remise *f* des diplômes

graffiti [grə'fi:tɪ] *npl* graffiti *mpl*

graft [grɑ:ft] *n* (*AGR, MED*) greffe *f*; (*bribery*)

corruption f ♦ vt greffer; **hard ~** (BRIT: inf)
boulot acharné
grain [greɪn] n grain m
gram [græm] n gramme m
grammar ['græmə'] n grammaire f;
~ school (BRIT) n ≈ lycée m; **grammatical**
[grə'mætɪkl] adj grammatical(e)
gramme [græm] n = **gram**
grand [grænd] adj magnifique, splendide;
(gesture etc) noble; **~children** npl petits-
enfants mpl; **~dad** (inf) n grand-papa m;
~daughter n petite-fille f; **~father** n grand-
père m; **~ma** (inf) n grand-maman f;
~mother n grand-mère f; **~pa** (inf) n
= **grandad**; **~parents** npl grands-parents
mpl; **~ piano** n piano m à queue; **~son** n
petit-fils m; **~stand** n (SPORT) tribune f
granite ['grænɪt] n granit m
granny ['grænɪ] (inf) n grand-maman f
grant [grɑ:nt] vt accorder; (a request) accéder
à; (admit) concéder ♦ n (SCOL) bourse f;
(ADMIN) subside m, subvention f; **to take it for
~ed that** trouver tout naturel que +sub; **to
take sb for ~ed** considérer qn comme faisant
partie du décor
granulated sugar ['grænjuleɪtɪd-] n sucre
m en poudre
grape [greɪp] n raisin m
grapefruit ['greɪpfru:t] n pamplemousse m
graph [grɑ:f] n graphique m; **~ic** ['græfɪk] adj
graphique; (account, description) vivant(e);
~ics n arts mpl graphiques; graphisme m
♦ npl représentations fpl graphiques
grapple ['græpl] vi: **to ~ with** être aux prises
avec
grasp [grɑ:sp] vt saisir ♦ n (grip) prise f;
(understanding) compréhension f,
connaissance f; **~ing** adj cupide
grass [grɑ:s] n herbe f; (lawn) gazon m;
~hopper n sauterelle f; **~-roots** adj de la
base, du peuple
grate [greɪt] n grille f de cheminée ♦ vi
grincer ♦ vt (CULIN) râper
grateful ['greɪtful] adj reconnaissant(e)
grater ['greɪtə'] n râpe f
gratifying ['grætɪfaɪɪŋ] adj agréable
grating ['greɪtɪŋ] n (iron bars) grille f ♦ adj
(noise) grinçant(e)
gratitude ['grætɪtju:d] n gratitude f
gratuity [grə'tju:ɪtɪ] n pourboire m
grave [greɪv] n tombe f ♦ adj grave,
sérieux(-euse)
gravel ['grævl] n gravier m
gravestone ['greɪvstəun] n pierre tombale
graveyard ['greɪvjɑ:d] n cimetière m
gravity ['grævɪtɪ] n (PHYSICS) gravité f;
pesanteur f; (seriousness) gravité
gravy ['greɪvɪ] n jus m (de viande); sauce f
gray [greɪ] (US) adj = **grey**

graze [greɪz] vi paître, brouter ♦ vt (touch
lightly) frôler, effleurer; (scrape) écorcher ♦ n
écorchure f
grease [gri:s] n (fat) graisse f; (lubricant)
lubrifiant m ♦ vt graisser; lubrifier; **~proof
paper** (BRIT) n papier sulfurisé; **greasy** adj
gras(se), graisseux(-euse)
great [greɪt] adj grand(e); (inf) formidable;
G~ Britain n Grande-Bretagne f; **~-
grandfather** n arrière-grand-père m; **~-
grandmother** n arrière-grand-mère f; **~ly**
adv très, grandement; (with verbs) beaucoup;
~ness n grandeur f
Greece [gri:s] n Grèce f
greed [gri:d] n (also: **~iness**) avidité f; (for
food) gourmandise f, gloutonnerie f; **~y** adj
avide; gourmand(e), glouton(ne)
Greek [gri:k] adj grec (grecque) ♦ n Grec
(Grecque); (LING) grec m
green [gri:n] adj vert(e); (inexperienced)
(bien) jeune, naïf (naïve); (POL) vert(e),
écologiste; (ecological) écologique ♦ n vert
m; (stretch of grass) pelouse f; **~s** npl
(vegetables) légumes verts; (POL): **the G~s** les
Verts mpl; **the G~ Party** (BRIT: POL) le parti
écologiste; **~ belt** n (round town) ceinture
verte; **~ card** n (AUT) carte verte; (US) permis
m de travail; **~ery** n verdure f; **~grocer's**
(BRIT) n marchand m de fruits et légumes;
~house n serre f; **~house effect** n effet m
de serre; **~house gas** n gas m à effet de
serre; **~ish** adj verdâtre
Greenland ['gri:nlənd] n Groenland m
greet [gri:t] vt accueillir; **~ing** n salutation f;
~ing(s) card n carte f de vœux
gregarious [grə'geərɪəs] adj (person) sociable
grenade [grə'neɪd] n grenade f
grew [gru:] pt of **grow**
grey [greɪ] (US **gray**) adj gris(e); (dismal)
sombre; **~-haired** adj grisonnant(e);
~hound n lévrier m
grid [grɪd] n grille f; (ELEC) réseau m; **~lock** n
(traffic jam) embouteillage m; **~locked** adj:
to be ~locked (roads) être bloqué par un
embouteillage; (talks etc) être suspendu
grief [gri:f] n chagrin m, douleur f
grievance ['gri:vəns] n doléance f, grief m
grieve [gri:v] vi avoir du chagrin; se désoler
♦ vt faire de la peine à, affliger; **to ~ for sb**
(dead person) pleurer qn; **grievous** adj
(LAW): **grievous bodily harm** coups mpl et
blessures fpl
grill [grɪl] n (on cooker) gril m; (food: also
mixed ~) grillade(s) f(pl) ♦ vt (BRIT) griller;
(inf: question) cuisiner
grille [grɪl] n grille f, grillage m; (AUT)
calandre f
grim [grɪm] adj sinistre, lugubre; (serious,
stern) sévère

grimace [grɪ'meɪs] n grimace f ♦ vi grimacer, faire une grimace

grime [graɪm] n crasse f, saleté f

grin [grɪn] n large sourire m ♦ vi sourire

grind [graɪnd] (pt, pp ground) vt écraser; (coffee, pepper etc) moudre; (US: meat) hacher; (make sharp) aiguiser ♦ n (work) corvée f

grip [grɪp] n (hold) prise f, étreinte f; (control) emprise f; (grasp) connaissance f; (handle) poignée f; (holdall) sac m de voyage ♦ vt saisir, empoigner; **to come to ~s with** en venir aux prises avec; **~ping** adj prenant(e), palpitant(e)

grisly ['grɪzlɪ] adj sinistre, macabre

gristle ['grɪsl] n cartilage m

grit [grɪt] n gravillon m; (courage) cran m ♦ vt (road) sabler; **to ~ one's teeth** serrer les dents

groan [grəun] n (of pain) gémissement m ♦ vi gémir

grocer ['grəusə'] n épicier m; **~ies** npl provisions fpl, **~'s (shop)** n épicerie f

groin [grɔɪn] n aine f

groom [gru:m] n palefrenier m; (also: **bridegroom**) marié m ♦ vt (horse) panser; (fig): **to ~ sb for** former qn pour; **well-~ed** adj très soigné(e)

groove [gru:v] n rainure f

grope [grəup] vi: **to ~ for** chercher à tâtons

gross [grəus] adj grossier(-ère); (COMM) brut(e); **~ly** adv (greatly) très, grandement

grotto ['grɔtəu] n grotte f

grotty ['grɔtɪ] (inf) adj minable, affreux(-euse)

ground [graund] pt, pp of **grind** ♦ n sol m, terre f; (land) terrain m, terres fpl; (SPORT) terrain m; (US: also: **~ wire**) terre; (reason: gen pl) raison f (vt (plane) empêcher de décoller, retenir au sol; (US: ELEC) équiper d'une prise de terre; **~s** npl (of coffee etc) marc m; (gardens etc) parc m, domaine m; **on the ~, to the ~** par terre; **to gain/lose ~** gagner/perdre du terrain; **~ cloth** (US) n = **groundsheet**; **~ing** n (in education) connaissances fpl de base; **~less** adj sans fondement; **~sheet** (BRIT) n tapis m de sol; **~ staff** n personnel m au sol; **~work** n préparation f

group [gru:p] n groupe m ♦ vt (also: **~ together**) grouper ♦ vi se grouper

grouse [graus] n inv (bird) grouse f ♦ vi (complain) rouspéter, râler

grove [grəuv] n bosquet m

grovel ['grɔvl] vi (fig) ramper

grow [grəu] (pt grew, pp grown) vi pousser, croître; (person) grandir; (increase) augmenter, se développer; (become): **to ~ rich/weak** s'enrichir/s'affaiblir; (develop): **he's ~n out of his jacket** sa veste est

(devenue) trop petite pour lui ♦ vt cultiver, faire pousser; (beard) laisser pousser; **he'll ~ out of it!** ça lui passera!; **~ up** vi grandir; **~er** n producteur m; **~ing** adj (fear, amount) croissant(e), grandissant(e)

growl [graul] vi grogner

grown [grəun] pp of **grow**; **~-up** n adulte m/f, grande personne

growth [grəuθ] n croissance f, développement m; (what has grown) pousse f; poussée f; (MED) grosseur f, tumeur f

grub [grʌb] n larve f; (inf: food) bouffe f

grubby ['grʌbɪ] adj crasseux(-euse)

grudge [grʌdʒ] n rancune f ♦ vt: **to ~ sb sth** (in giving) donner qch à qn à contre-cœur; (resent) reprocher qch à qn; **to bear sb a ~ (for)** garder rancune or en vouloir à qn (de)

gruelling ['gruəlɪŋ] (US **grueling**) adj exténuant(e)

gruesome ['gru:səm] adj horrible

gruff [grʌf] adj bourru(e)

grumble ['grʌmbl] vi rouspéter, ronchonner

grumpy ['grʌmpɪ] adj grincheux(-euse)

grunt [grʌnt] vi grogner

G-string ['dʒi:strɪŋ] n (garment) cache-sexe m inv

guarantee [gærən'ti:] n garantie f ♦ vt garantir

guard [gɑ:d] n garde f; (one man) garde m; (BRIT: RAIL) chef m de train; (on machine) dispositif m de sûreté; (also: **fireguard**) garde-feu m ♦ vt garder, surveiller; (protect): **to ~ (against or from)** protéger (contre); **~ against** vt (prevent) empêcher, se protéger de; **~ed** adj (fig) prudent(e); **~ian** n gardien(ne); (of minor) tuteur(-trice); **~'s van** (BRIT) n (RAIL) fourgon m

guerrilla [gə'rɪlə] n guérillero m

guess [ges] vt deviner; (estimate) évaluer; (US) croire, penser ♦ vi deviner ♦ n supposition f, hypothèse f; **to take** or **have a ~** essayer de deviner; **~work** n hypothèse f

guest [gest] n invité(e); (in hotel) client(e); **~house** n pension f; **~ room** n chambre f d'amis

guffaw [gʌ'fɔ:] vi pouffer de rire

guidance ['gaɪdəns] n conseils mpl

guide [gaɪd] n (person, book etc) guide m; (BRIT: also: **girl ~**) guide f ♦ vt guider; **~book** n guide m; **~ dog** n chien m d'aveugle; **~lines** npl (fig) instructions (générales), conseils mpl

guild [gɪld] n corporation f; cercle m, association f

guillotine ['gɪləti:n] n guillotine f

guilt [gɪlt] n culpabilité f; **~y** adj coupable

guinea pig ['gɪnɪ-] n cobaye m

guise [gaɪz] n aspect m, apparence f

guitar [gɪ'tɑ:'] n guitare f

gulf [gʌlf] n golfe m; (abyss) gouffre m

gull [gʌl] n mouette f; (larger) goéland m

gullible ['gʌlɪbl] adj crédule

gully ['gʌlɪ] n ravin m; ravine f; couloir m

gulp [gʌlp] vi avaler sa salive ♦ vt (also: ~ **down**) avaler

gum [gʌm] n (ANAT) gencive f; (glue) colle f; (sweet: also ~drop) boule f de gomme; (also: chewing ~) chewing-gum m ♦ vt coller; ~**boots** npl (BRIT) bottes fpl en caoutchouc

gun [gʌn] n (small) revolver m, pistolet m; (rifle) fusil m, carabine f; (cannon) canon m; ~**boat** n canonnière f; ~**fire** n fusillade f; ~**man** n bandit armé; ~**point** n: **at ~point** sous la menace du pistolet (or fusil); ~**powder** n poudre f à canon; ~**shot** n coup m de feu

gurgle ['gə:gl] vi gargouiller; (baby) gazouiller

gush [gʌʃ] vi jaillir; (fig) se répandre en effusions

gust [gʌst] n (of wind) rafale f; (of smoke) bouffée f

gusto ['gʌstəu] n enthousiasme m

gut [gʌt] n intestin m, boyau m; ~**s** npl (inf: courage) cran m

gutter ['gʌtə'] n (in street) caniveau m; (of roof) gouttière f

guy [gaɪ] n (inf: man) type m; (also: ~**rope**) corde f; (BRIT: figure) effigie de Guy Fawkes (brûlée en plein air le 5 novembre)

guzzle ['gʌzl] vt avaler gloutonnement

gym [dʒɪm] n (also: ~**nasium**) gymnase m; (also: ~**nastics**) gym f; ~**nast** n gymnaste m/f; ~**nastics** [dʒɪm'næstɪks] n, npl gymnastique f; ~ **shoes** npl chaussures fpl de gym; ~**slip** n (BRIT) n tunique f (d'écolière)

gynaecologist [gaɪnɪ'kɔlədʒɪst] (US **gynecologist**) n gynécologue m/f

gypsy ['dʒɪpsɪ] n gitan(e), bohémien(ne)

H, h

haberdashery [hæbə'dæʃərɪ] (BRIT) n mercerie f

habit ['hæbɪt] n habitude f; (REL: costume) habit m; ~**ual** adj habituel(le); (drinker, liar) invétéré(e)

hack [hæk] vt hacher, tailler ♦ n (pej: writer) nègre m; ~**er** n (COMPUT) pirate m (informatique); (: enthusiast) passionné(e) m/f des ordinateurs

hackneyed ['hæknɪd] adj usé(e), rebattu(e)

had [hæd] pt, pp of **have**

haddock ['hædək] (pl ~ or ~**s**) n églefin m; **smoked ~** haddock m

hadn't ['hædnt] = **had not**

haemorrhage ['hemərɪdʒ] (US **hemorrhage**) n hémorragie f

haemorrhoids ['hemərɔɪdz] (US **hemorrhoids**) npl hémorroïdes fpl

haggle ['hægl] vi marchander

Hague [heɪg] n: **The ~** La Haye

hail [heɪl] n grêle f ♦ vt (call) héler; (acclaim) acclamer ♦ vi grêler; ~**stone** n grêlon m

hair [heə'] n cheveux mpl; (of animal) pelage m; (single ~: on head) cheveu m; (: on body; of animal) poil m; **to do one's ~** se coiffer; ~**brush** n brosse f à cheveux; ~**cut** n coupe f (de cheveux); ~**do** n coiffure f; ~**dresser** n coiffeur(-euse); ~**dresser's** n salon m de coiffure, coiffeur m; ~ **dryer** n sèche-cheveux m; ~ **gel** n gel m pour cheveux; ~**grip** n pince f à cheveux; ~**net** n filet m à cheveux; ~**piece** n perruque f; ~**pin** n épingle f à cheveux; ~**pin bend** (US **hairpin curve**) n virage m en épingle à cheveux; ~**-raising** adj à (vous) faire dresser les cheveux sur la tête; ~ **removing cream** n crème f dépilatoire; ~ **spray** n laque f (pour les cheveux); ~**style** n coiffure f; ~**y** adj poilu(e); (inf: fig) effrayant(e)

hake [heɪk] (pl ~ or ~**s**) n colin m, merlu m

half [hɑ:f] (pl **halves**) n moitié f; (of beer: also: ~ **pint**) ≈ demi m; (RAIL, bus: also: ~ **fare**) demi-tarif m ♦ adj demi(e) ♦ adv (à) moitié, à demi; ~ **a dozen** une demi-douzaine; ~ **a pound** une demi-livre, ≈ 250 g; **two and a ~** deux et demi; **to cut sth in ~** couper qch en deux; ~**-caste** ['hɑ:fkɑ:st] n métis(se); ~**-hearted** adj tiède, sans enthousiasme; ~**-hour** n demi-heure f; ~**-mast** n: **at ~-mast** adv (flag) en berne; ~**penny** (BRIT) n demi-penny m; ~**-price** adj, adv: (**at**) ~**-price** à moitié prix; ~ **term** (BRIT) n (SCOL) congé m de demi-trimestre; ~**-time** n mi-temps f; ~**way** adv à mi-chemin

hall [hɔ:l] n salle f; (entrance way) hall m, entrée f

hallmark ['hɔ:lmɑ:k] n poinçon m; (fig) marque f

hallo [hə'ləu] excl = **hello**

hall of residence (BRIT) (pl **halls of residence**) n résidence f universitaire

Hallowe'en ['hæləu'i:n] n veille f de la Toussaint

hallucination [həlu:sɪ'neɪʃən] n hallucination f

hallway ['hɔ:lweɪ] n vestibule m

halo ['heɪləu] n (of saint etc) auréole f

halt [hɔ:lt] n halte f, arrêt m ♦ vt (progress etc) interrompre ♦ vi faire halte, s'arrêter

halve [hɑ:v] vt (apple etc) partager or diviser en deux; (expense) réduire de moitié; ~**s** npl of **half**

ham [hæm] n jambon m

hamburger ['hæmbə:gə'] n hamburger m

hamlet ['hæmlɪt] n hameau m

hammer ['hæmə^r] n marteau m ♦ vt (nail) enfoncer; (fig) démolir ♦ vi (on door) frapper à coups redoublés; **to ~ an idea into sb** faire entrer de force une idée dans la tête de qn

hammock ['hæmək] n hamac m

hamper ['hæmpə^r] vt gêner ♦ n panier m (d'osier)

hamster ['hæmstə^r] n hamster m

hand [hænd] n main f; (of clock) aiguille f; (~writing) écriture f; (worker) ouvrier(-ère); (at cards) jeu m ♦ vt passer, donner; **to give or lend sb a ~** donner un coup de main à qn; **at ~** à portée de la main; **in ~** (time) à disposition; (job, situation) en main; **to be on ~** (person) être disponible; (emergency services) se tenir prêt(e) (à intervenir); **to ~** (information etc) sous la main, à portée de la main, **on the one ~ ...**, **on the other ~** d'une part ..., d'autre part; **~ in** vt remettre; **~ out** vt distribuer; **~ over** vt transmettre; céder; **~bag** n sac m à main; **~book** n manuel m; **~brake** n frein m à main; **~cuffs** npl menottes fpl; **~ful** n poignée f

handicap ['hændɪkæp] n handicap m ♦ vt handicaper; **mentally/physically ~ped** handicapé(e) mentalement/physiquement

handicraft ['hændɪkrɑ:ft] n (travail m d')artisanat m, technique artisanale; (object) objet artisanal

handiwork ['hændɪwə:k] n ouvrage m

handkerchief ['hæŋkətʃɪf] n mouchoir m

handle ['hændl] n (of door etc) poignée f; (of cup etc) anse f; (of knife etc) manche m; (of saucepan) queue f; (for winding) manivelle f ♦ vt toucher, manier; (deal with) s'occuper de; (treat: people) prendre; **"~ with care"** "fragile"; **to fly off the ~** s'énerver; **~bar(s)** n(pl) guidon m

hand: **~-luggage** n bagages mpl à main; **~made** adj fait(e) à la main; **~out** n (from government, parents) aide f, don m; (leaflet) documentation f, prospectus m; (summary of lecture) polycopié m; **~rail** n rampe f, main courante f; **~set** n (TEL) combiné m; **please replace the ~** raccrochez s'il vous plaît; **~shake** n poignée f de main

handsome ['hænsəm] adj beau (belle); (profit, return) considérable

handwriting ['hændraɪtɪŋ] n écriture f

handy ['hændɪ] adj (person) adroit(e); (close at hand) sous la main; (convenient) pratique

hang [hæŋ] (pt, pp hung) vt accrocher; (criminal: pt, pp: ~ed) pendre ♦ vi pendre; (hair, drapery) tomber; **to get the ~ of (doing) sth** (inf) attraper le coup pour faire qch; **~ about** vi traîner; **~ around** vi = hang about; **~ on** vi (wait) attendre; **~ up** vi (TEL): **to ~ up (on sb)** raccrocher (au nez de qn) ♦ vt (coat, painting etc) accrocher, suspendre

hangar ['hæŋə^r] n hangar m

hanger ['hæŋə^r] n cintre m, portemanteau m; **~-on** n parasite m

hang: **~-gliding** n deltaplane m, vol m libre; **~over** n (after drinking) gueule f de bois; **~-up** n complexe m

hanker ['hæŋkə^r] vi: **to ~ after** avoir envie de

hankie, hanky ['hæŋkɪ] n abbr = handkerchief

haphazard [hæp'hæzəd] adj fait(e) au hasard, fait(e) au petit bonheur

happen ['hæpən] vi arriver; se passer, se produire; **it so ~s that** il se trouve que; **as it ~s** justement; **~ing** n événement m

happily ['hæpɪlɪ] adv heureusement; (cheerfully) joyeusement

happiness ['hæpɪnɪs] n bonheur m

happy ['hæpɪ] adj heureux(-euse); **~ with** (arrangements etc) satisfait(e) de; **to be ~ to do** faire volontiers; **~ birthday!** bon anniversaire!; **~-go-lucky** adj insouciant(e); **~ hour** n heure pendant laquelle les consommations sont à prix réduit

harass ['hærəs] vt accabler, tourmenter; **~ment** n tracasseries fpl

harbour ['hɑ:bə^r] (US harbor) n port m ♦ vt héberger, abriter; (hope, fear etc) entretenir

hard [hɑ:d] adj dur(e); (question, problem) difficile, dur(e); (facts, evidence) concret(-ète) ♦ adv (work) dur; (think, try) sérieusement; **to look ~ at** regarder fixement; (thing) regarder de près; **no ~ feelings!** sans rancune!; **to be ~ of hearing** être dur(e) d'oreille; **to be ~ done by** être traité(e) injustement; **~back** n livre relié; **~ cash** n espèces fpl; **~ disk** n (COMPUT) disque dur; **~en** vt durcir; (fig) endurcir ♦ vi durcir; **~-headed** adj réaliste; décidé(e); **~ labour** n travaux forcés

hardly ['hɑ:dlɪ] adv (scarcely, no sooner) à peine; **~ anywhere/ever** presque nulle part/ jamais

hard: **~ship** n épreuves fpl; **~ shoulder** (BRIT) n (AUT) accotement stabilisé; **~ up** (inf) adj fauché(e); **~ware** n quincaillerie f; (COMPUT, MIL) matériel m; **~ware shop** n quincaillerie f; **~-wearing** adj solide; **~-working** adj travailleur(-euse)

hardy ['hɑ:dɪ] adj robuste; (plant) résistant(e) au gel

hare [hɛə^r] n lièvre m; **~-brained** adj farfelu(e)

harm [hɑ:m] n mal m; (wrong) tort m ♦ vt (person) faire du mal or du tort à; (thing) endommager; **out of ~'s way** à l'abri du danger, en lieu sûr; **~ful** adj nuisible; **~less** adj inoffensif(-ive); sans méchanceté

harmony ['hɑ:mənɪ] n harmonie f

harness ['hɑ:nɪs] n harnais m; (safety ~)

harnais de sécurité ♦ vt (horse) harnacher; (resources) exploiter

harp [hɑːp] n harpe f ♦ vi: to ~ on about rabâcher

harrowing ['hærəʊɪŋ] adj déchirant(e), très pénible

harsh [hɑːʃ] adj (hard) dur(e); (severe) sévère; (unpleasant: sound) discordant(e); (: light) cru(e)

harvest ['hɑːvɪst] n (of corn) moisson f; (of fruit) récolte f; (of grapes) vendange f ♦ vt moissonner; récolter; vendanger

has [hæz] vb see have

hash [hæʃ] n (CULIN) hachis m; (fig: mess) gâchis m

hasn't ['hæznt] = has not

hassle ['hæsl] n (inf: bother) histoires fpl, tracas mpl

haste [heɪst] n hâte f; précipitation f; **~n** ['heɪsn] vt hâter, accélérer ♦ vi se hâter, s'empresser; **hastily** adv à la hâte; précipitamment; **hasty** adj hâtif(-ive); précipité(e)

hat [hæt] n chapeau m

hatch [hætʃ] n (NAUT: also: ~way) écoutille f; (also: service ~) passe-plats m inv ♦ vi éclore; **~back** n (AUT) modèle m avec hayon arrière

hatchet ['hætʃɪt] n hachette f

hate [heɪt] vt haïr, détester ♦ n haine f; **~ful** adj odieux(-euse), détestable; **hatred** ['heɪtrɪd] n haine f

haughty ['hɔːtɪ] adj hautain(e), arrogant(e)

haul [hɔːl] vt traîner, tirer ♦ n (of fish) prise f; (of stolen goods etc) butin m; **~age** n transport routier; (costs) frais mpl de transport; **~ier** ['hɔːlɪə*] (US hauler) n (company) transporteur (routier); (driver) camionneur m

haunch [hɔːntʃ] n hanche f; (of meat) cuissot m

haunt [hɔːnt] vt (subj: ghost, fear) hanter; (: person) fréquenter ♦ n repaire m

KEYWORD

have [hæv] (pt, pp had) aux vb **1** (gen) avoir; être; **to have arrived/gone** être arrivé(e)/ allé(e); **to have eaten/slept** avoir mangé/ dormi; **he has been promoted** il a eu une promotion

2 (in tag questions): **you've done it, haven't you?** vous l'avez fait, n'est-ce pas?

3 (in short answers and questions): **no I haven't/yes we have!** mais non!/mais si!; **so I have!** ah oui, c'est vrai!; **I've been there before, have you?** j'y suis déjà allé, et vous?

♦ modal aux vb (be obliged): **to have (got) to do sth** devoir faire qch; être obligé(e) de faire qch; **she has (got) to do it** elle doit le faire, il faut qu'elle le fasse; **you haven't to tell her**

vous ne devez pas le lui dire

♦ vt **1** (possess, obtain) avoir; **he has (got) blue eyes/dark hair** il a les yeux bleus/les cheveux bruns; **may I have your address?** puis-je avoir votre adresse?

2 (+noun: take, hold etc): **to have breakfast/a bath/a shower** prendre le petit déjeuner/un bain/une douche; **to have dinner/lunch** dîner/déjeuner; **to have a swim** nager; **to have a meeting** se réunir; **to have a party** organiser une fête

3: **to have sth done** faire faire qch; **to have one's hair cut** se faire couper les cheveux; **to have sb do sth** faire faire qch à qn

4 (experience, suffer) avoir; **to have a cold/flu** avoir un rhume/la grippe; **to have an operation** se faire opérer

5 (inf: dupe) avoir; **he's been had** il s'est fait avoir ou rouler

have out vt: **to have it out with sb** (settle a problem etc) s'expliquer (franchement) avec qn

haven ['heɪvn] n port m; (fig) havre m

haven't ['hævnt] = have not

havoc ['hævək] n ravages mpl

hawk [hɔːk] n faucon m

hay [heɪ] n foin m; **~ fever** n rhume m des foins; **~stack** n meule f de foin

haywire ['heɪwaɪə*] (inf) adj: **to go ~** (machine) se détraquer; (plans) mal tourner

hazard ['hæzəd] n (danger) danger m, risque m ♦ vt risquer, hasarder; **~ (warning) lights** npl (AUT) feux mpl de détresse

haze [heɪz] n brume f

hazelnut ['heɪzlnʌt] n noisette f

hazy ['heɪzɪ] adj brumeux(-euse); (idea) vague

he [hiː] pron il; **it is ~ who ...** c'est lui qui ...

head [hɛd] n tête f; (leader) chef m; (of school) directeur(-trice) ♦ vt (list) être en tête de; (group) être à la tête de; **~s (or tails)** pile (ou face); **~ first** la tête la première; **~ over heels in love** follement or éperdument amoureux(-euse); **to ~ a ball** faire une tête; **~ for** vt fus se diriger vers; **~ache** n mal de tête; **~dress** (BRIT) n (of Red Indian etc) coiffure f; **~ing** n titre m; **~lamp** (BRIT) n = headlight; **~land** n promontoire m, cap m; **~light** n phare m; **~line** n titre m; **~long** adv (fall) la tête la première; (rush) tête baissée; **~master** n directeur m; **~mistress** n directrice f; **~ office** n bureau central, siège m; **~-on** adj (collision) de plein fouet; (confrontation) en face à face; **~phones** npl casque m (à écouteurs); **~quarters** npl bureau ou siège central; (MIL) quartier général; **~rest** n appui-tête m; **~room** n (in car) hauteur f de plafond; (under bridge) hauteur limite; **~scarf** n foulard m; **~strong** adj têtu(e), entêté(e); **~ teacher** n directeur(-trice); (of secondary school) proviseur m; **~ waiter** n maître m d'hôtel; **~way** n: **to make ~way** avancer, faire des progrès; **~wind** n vent m contraire; (NAUT) vent debout; **~y** adj capiteux(-euse); enivrant(e); (experience) grisant(e)

heal [hi:l] vt, vi guérir

health [hɛlθ] n santé f; **~ food** n aliment(s) naturel(s); **~ food shop** n magasin m diététique; **H~ Service** (BRIT) n: **the H~ Service** ≈ la Sécurité sociale; **~y** adj (person) en bonne santé; (climate, food, attitude etc) sain(e), bon(ne) pour la santé

heap [hi:p] n tas m ♦ vt: **to ~ (up)** entasser, amonceler; **she ~ed her plate with cakes** elle a chargé son assiette de gâteaux

hear [hɪəʳ] (pt, pp heard) vt entendre; (news) apprendre ♦ vi entendre; **to ~ about** entendre parler de; avoir des nouvelles de; **to ~ from sb** recevoir or avoir des nouvelles de qn; **~d** [hɜːd] pt, pp of hear; **~ing** n (sense) ouïe f; (of witness) audition f; (of a case) audience f; **~ing aid** n appareil m acoustique; **~say: by ~say** adv par ouï-dire m

hearse [hɜːs] n corbillard m

heart [hɑːt] n cœur m; **~s** npl (CARDS) cœur m; **to lose/take ~** perdre/prendre courage; **at ~** au fond; **by ~** (learn, know) par cœur; **~ attack** n crise f cardiaque; **~beat** n battement m du cœur; **~breaking** adj déchirant(e), qui fend le cœur; **~broken** adj: **to be ~broken** avoir beaucoup de chagrin or le cœur brisé; **~burn** n brûlures fpl d'estomac; **~ failure** n arrêt m du cœur; **~felt** adj sincère

hearth [hɑːθ] n foyer m, cheminée f

heartily [hɑːtɪlɪ] adv chaleureusement; (laugh) de bon cœur; (eat) de bon appétit; **to agree ~** être entièrement d'accord

hearty [hɑːtɪ] adj chaleureux(-euse); (appetite) robuste; (dislike) cordial(e)

heat [hi:t] n chaleur f; (fig) feu m, agitation f; (SPORT: also: qualifying ~) éliminatoire f ♦ vt chauffer; **~ up** vi (water) chauffer; (room) se réchauffer ♦ vt réchauffer; **~ed** adj chauffé(e); (fig) passionné(e), échauffé(e); **~er** n appareil m de chauffage; radiateur m; (in car) chauffage m; (water heater) chauffe-eau m

heath [hi:θ] (BRIT) n lande f

heather [hɛðəʳ] n bruyère f

heating [hi:tɪŋ] n chauffage m

heatstroke [hi:tstrəuk] n (MED) coup m de chaleur

heat wave n vague f de chaleur

heave [hi:v] vt soulever (avec effort); (drag) traîner ♦ vi se soulever; (retch) avoir un haut-le-cœur; **to ~ a sigh** pousser un soupir

heaven [hɛvn] n ciel m, paradis m; (fig) paradis; **~ly** adj céleste, divin(e)

heavily [hɛvɪlɪ] adv lourdement; (drink, smoke) beaucoup; (sleep, sigh) profondément

heavy [hɛvɪ] adj lourd(e); (work, sea, rain, eater) gros(se); (snow) beaucoup de; (drinker, smoker) grand(e); (breathing) bruyant(e); (schedule, week) chargé(e); **~ goods vehicle** n poids lourd; **~weight** n (SPORT) poids lourd

Hebrew [hi:bru:] adj hébraïque ♦ n (LING) hébreu m

Hebrides [hɛbrɪdiːz] npl: **the ~** les Hébrides fpl

heckle [hɛkl] vt interpeller (un orateur)

hectic [hɛktɪk] adj agité(e), trépidant(e)

he'd [hi:d] = he would; he had

hedge [hɛdʒ] n haie f ♦ vi se dérober; **to ~ one's bets** (fig) se couvrir

hedgehog [hɛdʒhɔg] n hérisson m

heed [hi:d] vt (also: take ~ of) tenir compte de; **~less** adj insouciant(e)

heel [hi:l] n talon m ♦ vt retalonner

hefty [hɛftɪ] adj (person) costaud(e); (parcel) lourd(e); (profit) gros(se)

heifer [hɛfəʳ] n génisse f

height [haɪt] n (of person) taille f, grandeur f; (of object) hauteur f; (of plane, mountain) altitude f; (high ground) hauteur f, éminence f; (fig: of glory) sommet m; (: of luxury, stupidity) comble m; **~en** vt (fig) augmenter

heir [ɛəʳ] n héritier m; **~ess** n héritière f; **~loom** n héritage m, meuble m (or bijou m or tableau m) de famille

held [hɛld] pt, pp of hold

helicopter [hɛlɪkɔptəʳ] n hélicoptère m

hell [hɛl] n enfer m; **~!** (inf!) merde!

he'll [hi:l] = he will; he shall

hellish [hɛlɪʃ] (inf) adj infernal(e)

hello [hə'ləu] excl bonjour!; (to attract attention) hé!; (surprise) tiens!

helm [hɛlm] n (NAUT) barre f

helmet [hɛlmɪt] n casque m

help [hɛlp] n aide f; (charwoman) femme f de ménage ♦ vt aider; **~!** au secours!; **~ yourself** servez-vous; **he can't ~ it** il ne peut pas s'en empêcher; **~er** n aide m/f, assistant(e); **~ful** adj serviable, obligeant(e); (useful) utile; **~ing** n portion f; **~less** adj impuissant(e); (defenceless) faible

hem [hɛm] n ourlet m ♦ vt ourler; **~ in** vt cerner

hemorrhage [hɛmərɪdʒ] (US) n = haemorrhage

hemorrhoids [hɛmərɔɪdz] (US) npl = haemorrhoids

hen [hɛn] n poule f

hence [hɛns] adv (therefore) d'où, de là; **2 years ~** d'ici 2 ans, dans 2 ans; **~forth** adv dorénavant

her [hɜːʳ] pron (direct) la, l'; (indirect) lui; (stressed, after prep) elle ♦ adj son (sa), ses pl; see also **me**; **my**

herald ['herəld] n héraut m ♦ vt annoncer; **~ry** n (study) héraldique f; (coat of arms) blason m

herb [hɜːb] n herbe f

herd [hɜːd] n troupeau m

here [hɪəʳ] adv ici; (time) alors ♦ excl tiens!, tenez!; **~!** présent!; **~ is, ~ are** voici; **~ he/she is!** le/la voici!; **~ after** adv après, plus tard; **~by** adv (formal: in letter) par la présente

hereditary [hɪˈredɪtrɪ] adj héréditaire

heresy ['herəsɪ] n hérésie f

heritage ['herɪtɪdʒ] n (of country) patrimoine m

hermit ['hɜːmɪt] n ermite m

hernia ['hɜːnɪə] n hernie f

hero ['hɪərəʊ] (pl ~es) n héros m

heroin ['herəʊɪn] n héroïne f

heroine ['herəʊɪn] n héroïne f

heron ['herən] n héron m

herring ['herɪŋ] n hareng m

hers [hɜːz] pron le (la) sien(ne), les siens (siennes); see also **mine**[1]

herself [hɜːˈself] pron (reflexive) se; (emphatic) elle-même; (after prep) elle; see also **oneself**

he's [hiːz] = he is; he has

hesitant ['hezɪtənt] adj hésitant(e), indécis(e)

hesitate ['hezɪteɪt] vi hésiter; **hesitation** [hezɪˈteɪʃən] n hésitation f

heterosexual ['hetərəʊˈseksjʊəl] adj, n hétérosexuel(le)

heyday ['heɪdeɪ] n: **the ~ of** l'âge m d'or de, les beaux jours de

HGV n abbr = **heavy goods vehicle**

hi [haɪ] excl salut!; (to attract attention) hé!

hiatus [haɪˈeɪtəs] n (gap) lacune f; (interruption) pause f

hibernate ['haɪbəneɪt] vi hiberner

hiccough, hiccup ['hɪkʌp] vi hoqueter; **~s** npl hoquet m

hide [haɪd] (pt hid, pp hidden) n (skin) peau f ♦ vt cacher ♦ vi: **to ~ (from sb)** se cacher (de qn); **~-and-seek** n cache-cache m

hideous ['hɪdɪəs] adj hideux(-euse)

hiding ['haɪdɪŋ] n (beating) correction f, volée f de coups; **to be in ~** (concealed) se tenir caché(e)

hierarchy ['haɪərɑːkɪ] n hiérarchie f

hi-fi ['haɪfaɪ] n hi-fi f inv ♦ adj hi-fi inv

high [haɪ] adj haut(e); (speed, respect, number) grand(e); (price) élevé(e); (wind) fort(e), violent(e); (voice) aigu (aiguë) ♦ adv haut; **20 m ~** haut(e) de 20 m; **~brow** adj, n intellectuel(le); **~chair** n (child's) chaise

haute; **~er education** n études supérieures; **~-handed** adj très autoritaire; très cavalier(-ère); **~-heeled** adj à hauts talons; **~ jump** n (SPORT) saut m en hauteur; **~lands** npl Highlands mpl; **~light** n (fig: of event) point culminant ♦ vt faire ressortir, souligner; **~lights** npl (in hair) reflets mpl; **~ly** adv très, fort, hautement; **to speak/think ~ly of sb** dire/penser beaucoup de bien de qn; **~ly paid** adj très bien payé(e); **~ly strung** adj nerveux(-euse), toujours tendu(e); **~ness** n: **Her (or His) H~ness** Son Altesse f; **~-pitched** adj aigu (aiguë); **~-rise** adj: **~-rise block, ~-rise flats** tour f (d'habitation); **~ school** n lycée m; (US) établissement m d'enseignement supérieur; **~ season** (BRIT) n haute saison; **~ street** (BRIT) n grand-rue f; **~way** n route nationale; **H~way Code** (BRIT) n code m de la route

hijack ['haɪdʒæk] vt (plane) détourner; **~er** n pirate m de l'air

hike [haɪk] vi aller or faire des excursions à pied ♦ n excursion f à pied, randonnée f; **~r** n promeneur(-euse), excursionniste m/f; **hiking** n excursions fpl à pied

hilarious [hɪˈleərɪəs] adj (account, event) désopilant(e)

hill [hɪl] n colline f; (fairly high) montagne f; (on road) côte f; **~side** n (flanc m de) coteau m; **~-walking** n randonnée f de basse montagne; **~y** adj vallonné(e); montagneux(-euse)

hilt [hɪlt] n (of sword) garde f; **to the ~** (fig: support) à fond

him [hɪm] pron (direct) le, l'; (stressed, indirect, after prep) lui; see also **me**; **~self** pron (reflexive) se; (emphatic) lui-même; (after prep) lui; see also **oneself**

hinder ['hɪndəʳ] vt gêner; (delay) retarder; **hindrance** n gêne f, obstacle m

hindsight ['haɪndsaɪt] n: **with ~** avec du recul, rétrospectivement

Hindu ['hɪnduː] adj hindou(e)

hinge [hɪndʒ] n charnière f ♦ vi (fig): **to ~ on** dépendre de

hint [hɪnt] n allusion f; (advice) conseil m ♦ vt: **to ~ that** insinuer que ♦ vi: **to ~ at** faire une allusion à

hip [hɪp] n hanche f

hippie ['hɪpɪ] n hippie m/f

hippo ['hɪpəʊ] (pl ~s), **hippopotamus** [hɪpəˈpɔtəməs] (pl ~potamuses or ~potami) n hippopotame m

hire ['haɪəʳ] vt (BRIT: car, equipment) louer; (worker) embaucher, engager ♦ n location f; **for ~** à louer; (taxi) libre; **~(d) car** n voiture f de location; **~ purchase** (BRIT) n achat m (or vente f) à tempérament or crédit

his [hɪz] pron le (la) sien(ne), les siens

(siennes) ♦ *adj* son (sa), ses *pl*; *see also* **my; mine**[1]

hiss [hɪs] *vi* siffler

historic [hɪˈstɒrɪk] *adj* historique; **~al** *adj* historique

history [ˈhɪstərɪ] *n* histoire *f*

hit [hɪt] (*pt, pp* hit) *vt* frapper; (*reach: target*) atteindre, toucher; (*collide with: car*) entrer en collision avec, heurter; (*fig: affect*) toucher ♦ *n* coup *m*; (*success*) succès *m*; (*: song*) tube *m*; **to ~ it off with sb** bien s'entendre avec qn; **~-and-run driver** *n* chauffard *m* (coupable du délit de fuite)

hitch [hɪtʃ] *vt* (*fasten*) accrocher, attacher; (*also: ~ up*) remonter d'une saccade ♦ *n* (*difficulty*) anicroche *f*, contretemps *m*; **to ~ a lift** faire du stop; **~hike** *vi* faire de l'auto-stop; **~hiker** *n* auto-stoppeur(-euse)

hi-tech [ˈhaɪˈtɛk] *adj* de pointe

hitherto [hɪðəˈtuː] *adv* jusqu'ici

hit man *n* tueur *m* à gages

HIV *n abbr*: **~-negative/ positive** *adj* séronégatif(-ive)/-positif(-ive)

hive [haɪv] *n* ruche *f*

HMS *abbr* = Her/His Majesty's Ship

hoard [hɔːd] *n* (*of food*) provisions *fpl*, réserves *fpl*; (*of money*) trésor *m* ♦ *vt* amasser; **~ing** (*BRIT*) *n* (*for posters*) panneau *m* d'affichage or publicitaire

hoarse [hɔːs] *adj* enroué(e)

hoax [həʊks] *n* canular *m*

hob [hɒb] *n* plaque (chauffante)

hobble [ˈhɒbl] *vi* boitiller

hobby [ˈhɒbɪ] *n* passe-temps favori

hobo [ˈhəʊbəʊ] (*US*) *n* vagabond *m*

hockey [ˈhɒkɪ] *n* hockey *m*

hog [hɒg] *n* porc (châtré) ♦ *vt* (*fig*) accaparer; **to go the whole ~** aller jusqu'au bout

hoist [hɔɪst] *n* (*apparatus*) palan *m* ♦ *vt* hisser

hold [həʊld] (*pt, pp* held) *vt* tenir; (*contain*) contenir; (*believe*) considérer; (*possess*) avoir; (*detain*) détenir ♦ *vi* (*withstand pressure*) tenir (bon); (*be valid*) valoir ♦ *n* (*also fig*) prise *f*; (*NAUT*) cale *f*; **~ the line!** (*TEL*) ne quittez pas!; **to ~ one's own** (*fig*) (bien) se défendre; **to catch** or **get (a) ~ of** saisir; **to get ~ of** (*fig*) trouver; **~ back** *vt* retenir; (*secret*) taire; **~ down** *vt* (*person*) maintenir à terre; (*job*) occuper; **~ off** *vt* tenir à distance; **~ on** *vi* tenir bon; (*wait*) attendre; **~ on!** (*TEL*) ne quittez pas!; **~ on to** *vt fus* se cramponner à; (*keep*) conserver, garder; **~ out** *vt* offrir ♦ *vi* (*resist*) tenir bon; **~ up** *vt* (*raise*) lever; (*support*) soutenir; (*delay*) retarder; (*rob*) braquer; **~all** (*BRIT*) *n* fourre-tout *m inv*; **~er** *n* (*of ticket, record*) détenteur(-trice); (*of office, title etc*) titulaire *m/f*; (*container*) support *m*; **~ing** *n* (*share*) intérêts *mpl*; (*farm*) ferme *f*; **~-up** *n* (*robbery*) hold-up *m*;

(*delay*) retard *m*; (*BRIT: in traffic*) bouchon *m*

hole [həʊl] *n* trou *m*; **~-in-the-wall** *n* (*cash dispenser*) distributeur *m* de billets

holiday [ˈhɒlɪdeɪ] *n* vacances *fpl*; (*day off*) jour *m* de congé; (*public*) jour férié; **on ~** en congé; **~ camp** *n* (*also: ~ centre*) camp *m* de vacances; **~-maker** (*BRIT*) *n* vacancier(-ère); **~ resort** *n* centre *m* de villégiature or de vacances

Holland [ˈhɒlənd] *n* Hollande *f*

hollow [ˈhɒləʊ] *adj* creux(-euse) ♦ *n* creux *m* ♦ *vt*: **to ~ out** creuser, évider

holly [ˈhɒlɪ] *n* houx *m*

holocaust [ˈhɒləkɔːst] *n* holocauste *m*

holster [ˈhəʊlstə] *n* étui *m* de revolver

holy [ˈhəʊlɪ] *adj* saint(e); (*bread, water*) bénit(e); (*ground*) sacré(e); **H~ Ghost** *n* Saint-Esprit *m*

homage [ˈhɒmɪdʒ] *n* hommage *m*; **to pay ~ to** rendre hommage à

home [həʊm] *n* foyer *m*, maison *f*; (*country*) pays natal, patrie *f*; (*institution*) maison ♦ *adj* de famille; (*ECON, POL*) national(e), intérieur(e); (*SPORT: game*) sur leur (or notre) terrain; (*team*) qui reçoit ♦ *adv* chez soi, à la maison; au pays natal; (*right in: nail etc*) à fond; **at ~** chez soi, à la maison; **make yourself at ~** faites comme chez vous; **~ address** *n* domicile permanent; **~land** *n* patrie *f*; **~less** *adj* sans foyer; sans abri; **~ly** *adj* (*plain*) simple, sans prétention; **~-made** *adj* fait(e) à la maison; **~ match** *n* match *m* à domicile; **H~ Office** (*BRIT*) *n* ministère *m* de l'Intérieur; **~ page** *n* (*COMPUT*) page *f* d'accueil; **~ rule** *n* autonomie *f*; **H~ Secretary** (*BRIT*) *n* ministre *m* de l'Intérieur; **~sick** *adj*: **to be ~sick** avoir le mal du pays; s'ennuyer de sa famille; **~ town** *n* ville natale; **~ward** *adj* (*journey*) du retour; **~work** *n* devoirs *mpl*

homoeopathic [həʊmɪəʊˈpæθɪk] (*US* **homeopathic**) *adj* (*medicine, methods*) homéopathique; (*doctor*) homéopathe

homogeneous [hɒməʊˈdʒiːnɪəs] *adj* homogène

homosexual [hɒməʊˈsɛksjuəl] *adj, n* homosexuel(le)

honest [ˈɒnɪst] *adj* honnête; (*sincere*) franc (franche); **~ly** *adv* honnêtement; franchement; **~y** *n* honnêteté *f*

honey [ˈhʌnɪ] *n* miel *m*; **~comb** *n* rayon *m* de miel; **~moon** *n* lune *f* de miel, voyage *m* de noces; **~suckle** (*BOT*) *n* chèvrefeuille *m*

honk [hɒŋk] *vi* (*AUT*) klaxonner

honorary [ˈɒnərərɪ] *adj* honoraire; (*duty, title*) honorifique

honour [ˈɒnə] (*US* **honor**) *vt* honorer ♦ *n* honneur *m*; **hono(u)rable** *adj* honorable; **hono(u)rs degree** *n* (*SCOL*) licence avec

mention
hood [hud] *n* capuchon *m*; (*of cooker*) hotte *f*; (*AUT: BRIT*) capote *f*; (: *US*) capot *m*
hoof [hu:f] (*pl* **hooves**) *n* sabot *m*
hook [huk] *n* crochet *m*; (*on dress*) agrafe *f*; (*for fishing*) hameçon *m* ♦ *vt* accrocher; (*fish*) prendre
hooligan ['hu:lɪɡən] *n* voyou *m*
hoop [hu:p] *n* cerceau *m*
hooray [hu:'reɪ] *excl* hourra
hoot [hu:t] *vi* (*AUT*) klaxonner; (*siren*) mugir; (*owl*) hululer; **~er** *n* (*BRIT: AUT*) klaxon *m*; (*NAUT, factory*) sirène *f*
Hoover ® ['hu:vər] (*BRIT*) *n* aspirateur *m* ♦ *vt*: **h~** passer l'aspirateur dans or sur
hooves [hu:vz] *npl of* **hoof**
hop [hɔp] *vi* (*on one foot*) sauter à cloche-pied; (*bird*) sautiller
hope [həup] *vt, vi* espérer ♦ *n* espoir *m*; **I ~ so** je l'espère; **I ~ not** j'espère que non; **~ful** *adj* (*person*) plein(e) d'espoir; (*situation*) prometteur(-euse), encourageant(e); **~fully** *adv* (*expectantly*) avec espoir, avec optimisme; (*one hopes*) avec un peu de chance; **~less** *adj* désespéré(e); (*useless*) nul(le)
hops [hɔps] *npl* houblon *m*
horizon [hə'raɪzn] *n* horizon *m*; **~tal** [hɔrɪ'zɔntl] *adj* horizontal(e)
horn [hɔ:n] *n* corne *f*; (*MUS: also:* **French ~**) cor *m*; (*AUT*) klaxon *m*
hornet ['hɔ:nɪt] *n* frelon *m*
horoscope ['hɔrəskəup] *n* horoscope *m*
horrendous [hə'rendəs] *adj* horrible, affreux(-euse)
horrible ['hɔrɪbl] *adj* horrible, affreux(-euse)
horrid ['hɔrɪd] *adj* épouvantable
horrify ['hɔrɪfaɪ] *vt* horrifier
horror ['hɔrər] *n* horreur *f*; **~ film** *n* film *m* d'épouvante
hors d'oeuvre [ɔ:'də:vrə] *n* (*CULIN*) hors-d'œuvre *m inv*
horse [hɔ:s] *n* cheval *m*; **~back** *n*: **on ~back** à cheval; **~ chestnut** *n* marron *m* (d'Inde); **~man** (*irreg*) *n* cavalier *m*; **~power** *n* puissance *f* (en chevaux); **~-racing** *n* courses *fpl* de chevaux; **~radish** *n* raifort *m*; **~shoe** *n* fer *m* à cheval
hose [həuz] *n* (*also:* **~pipe**) tuyau *m*; (*also:* **garden ~**) tuyau d'arrosage
hospitable ['hɔspɪtəbl] *adj* hospitalier(-ère)
hospital ['hɔspɪtl] *n* hôpital *m*; **in ~** à l'hôpital
hospitality [hɔspɪ'tælɪtɪ] *n* hospitalité *f*
host [həust] *n* hôte *m*; (*TV, RADIO*) animateur(-trice); (*REL*) hostie *f*; (*large number*): **a ~ of** une foule de
hostage ['hɔstɪdʒ] *n* otage *m*
hostel ['hɔstl] *n* foyer *m*; (*also:* **youth ~**) auberge *f* de jeunesse
hostess ['həustɪs] *n* hôtesse *f*; (*TV, RADIO*) animatrice *f*
hostile ['hɔstaɪl] *adj* hostile; **hostility** [hɔ'stɪlɪtɪ] *n* hostilité *f*
hot [hɔt] *adj* chaud(e); (*as opposed to only warm*) très chaud; (*spicy*) fort(e); (*contest etc*) acharné(e); (*temper*) passionné(e); **to be ~** (*person*) avoir chaud; (*object*) être (très) chaud; **it is ~** (*weather*) il fait chaud; **~bed** *n* (*fig*) foyer *m*, pépinière *f*; **~ dog** *n* hot-dog *m*
hotel [həu'tel] *n* hôtel *m*
hot: ~house *n* serre (chaude); **~line** *n* (*POL*) téléphone *m* rouge, ligne directe; **~ly** *adv* passionnément, violemment; **~plate** *n* (*on cooker*) plaque chauffante; **~pot** (*BRIT*) *n* ragoût *m*; **~-water bottle** *n* bouillotte *f*
hound [haund] *vt* poursuivre avec acharnement ♦ *n* chien courant
hour ['auər] *n* heure *f*; **~ly** *adj, adv* toutes les heures; (*rate*) horaire
house [*n* haus, *vb* hauz] *n* maison *f*; (*POL*) chambre *f*; (*THEATRE*) salle *f*; auditoire *m* ♦ *vt* (*person*) loger, héberger; (*objects*) abriter; **on the ~** (*fig*) aux frais de la maison; **~ arrest** *n* assignation *f* à résidence; **~boat** *n* bateau *m* (aménagé en habitation); **~bound** *adj* confiné(e) chez soi; **~breaking** *n* cambriolage *m* (avec effraction); **~hold** *n* (*persons*) famille *f*, maisonnée *f*; (*ADMIN etc*) ménage *m*; **~keeper** *n* gouvernante *f*; **~keeping** *n* (*work*) ménage *m*; **~keeping** (*money*) argent *m* du ménage; **~warming (party)** *n* pendaison *f* de crémaillère; **~wife** (*irreg*) *n* ménagère *f*; femme *f* au foyer; **~work** *n* (travaux *mpl* du) ménage *m*
housing ['hauzɪŋ] *n* logement *m*; **~ development, ~ estate** *n* lotissement *m*
hovel ['hɔvl] *n* taudis *m*
hover ['hɔvər] *vi* planer; **~craft** *n* aéroglisseur *m*
how [hau] *adv* comment; **~ are you?** comment allez-vous?; **~ do you do?** bonjour; enchanté(e); **~ far is it to?** combien y a-t-il jusqu'à ...?; **~ long have you been here?** depuis combien de temps êtes-vous là?; **~ lovely!** que or comme c'est joli!; **~ many/much?** combien?; **~ many people/much milk?** combien de gens/lait?; **~ old are you?** quel âge avez-vous?
however [hau'evər] *adv* de quelque façon or manière que +*subj*; (+*adj*) quelque or si ... que +*subj*; (*in questions*) comment ♦ *conj* pourtant, cependant
howl [haul] *vi* hurler
H.P. *abbr* = **hire purchase**
h.p. *abbr* = **horsepower**
HQ *abbr* = **headquarters**
hub [hʌb] *n* (*of wheel*) moyeu *m*; (*fig*) centre

m, foyer m; **~cap** n enjoliveur m

huddle ['hʌdl] vi: **to ~ together** se blottir les uns contre les autres

hue [hju:] n teinte f, nuance f

huff [hʌf] n: **in a ~** fâché(e)

hug [hʌg] vt serrer dans ses bras; (shore, kerb) serrer

huge [hju:dʒ] adj énorme, immense

hulk [hʌlk] n (ship) épave f; (car, building) carcasse f; (person) mastodonte m

hull [hʌl] n coque f

hullo [hə'ləu] excl = hello

hum [hʌm] vt (tune) fredonner ♦ vi fredonner; (insect) bourdonner; (plane, tool) vrombir

human ['hju:mən] adj humain(e) ♦ n: **~ being** être humain; **~e** [hju:'meɪn] adj humain(e), humanitaire; **~itarian** [hju:mænɪ'teərɪən] adj humanitaire; **~ity** [hju:'mænɪtɪ] n humanité f

humble ['hʌmbl] adj humble, modeste ♦ vt humilier

humdrum ['hʌmdrʌm] adj monotone, banal(e)

humid ['hju:mɪd] adj humide

humiliate [hju:'mɪlɪeɪt] vt humilier; **humiliation** [hju:mɪlɪ'eɪʃən] n humiliation f

humorous ['hju:mərəs] adj humoristique; (person) plein(e) d'humour

humour ['hju:mə*] (US **humor**) n humour m; (mood) humeur f ♦ vt (person) faire plaisir à; se prêter aux caprices de

hump [hʌmp] n bosse f

hunch [hʌntʃ] n (premonition) intuition f; **~back** n bossu(e); **~ed** adj voûté(e)

hundred ['hʌndrəd] num cent; **~s of** des centaines de; **~weight** n (BRIT) 50.8 kg, 112 lb; (US) 45.3 kg, 100 lb

hung [hʌŋ] pt, pp of **hang**

Hungary ['hʌŋgərɪ] n Hongrie f

hunger ['hʌŋgə*] n faim f ♦ vi: **to ~ for** avoir faim de, désirer ardemment

hungry ['hʌŋgrɪ] adj affamé(e); (keen): **~ for** avide de; **to be ~** avoir faim

hunk [hʌŋk] n (of bread etc) gros morceau

hunt [hʌnt] vt chasser; (criminal) pourchasser ♦ vi chasser; (search): **~ for** chercher (partout) ♦ n chasse f; **~er** n chasseur m; **~ing** n chasse f

hurdle ['hɜ:dl] n (SPORT) haie f; (fig) obstacle m

hurl [hɜ:l] vt lancer (avec violence); (abuse, insults) lancer

hurrah [hu'rɑ:] excl = hooray

hurray [hu'reɪ] excl = hooray

hurricane ['hʌrɪkən] n ouragan m

hurried ['hʌrɪd] adj pressé(e), précipité(e); (work) fait(e) à la hâte; **~ly** adv précipitamment, à la hâte

hurry ['hʌrɪ] (vb: also: **~ up**) n hâte f, précipitation f ♦ vi se presser, se dépêcher ♦ vt (person) faire presser, faire se dépêcher; (work) presser; **to be in a ~** être pressé(e); **to do sth in a ~** faire qch en vitesse; **to ~ in/out** entrer/sortir précipitamment

hurt [hɜ:t] (pt, pp **hurt**) vt (cause pain to) faire mal à; (injure, fig) blesser ♦ vi faire mal ♦ adj blessé(e); **~ful** adj (remark) blessant(e)

hurtle ['hɜ:tl] vi: **to ~ past** passer en trombe; **to ~ down** dégringoler

husband ['hʌzbənd] n mari m

hush [hʌʃ] n calme m, silence m ♦ vt faire taire; **~!** chut!; **~ up** vt (scandal) étouffer

husk [hʌsk] n (of wheat) balle f; (of rice, maize) enveloppe f

husky ['hʌskɪ] adj rauque ♦ n chien m esquimau or de traîneau

hustle ['hʌsl] vt pousser, bousculer ♦ n: **~ and bustle** tourbillon m (d'activité)

hut [hʌt] n hutte f; (shed) cabane f

hutch [hʌtʃ] n clapier m

hyacinth ['haɪəsɪnθ] n jacinthe f

hydrant ['haɪdrənt] n (also: **fire ~**) bouche f d'incendie

hydraulic [haɪ'drɔ:lɪk] adj hydraulique

hydroelectric ['haɪdrəu'lektrɪk] adj hydro-électrique

hydrofoil ['haɪdrəfɔɪl] n hydrofoil m

hydrogen ['haɪdrədʒən] n hydrogène m

hyena [haɪ'i:nə] n hyène f

hygiene ['haɪdʒi:n] n hygiène f; **hygienic** adj hygiénique

hymn [hɪm] n hymne m; cantique m

hype [haɪp] (inf) n battage m publicitaire

hypermarket ['haɪpəmɑ:kɪt] (BRIT) n hypermarché m

hypertext ['haɪpətekst] n (COMPUT) hypertexte m

hyphen ['haɪfn] n trait m d'union

hypnotize ['hɪpnətaɪz] vt hypnotiser

hypocrisy [hɪ'pɒkrɪsɪ] n hypocrisie f; **hypocrite** ['hɪpəkrɪt] n hypocrite m/f; **hypocritical** adj hypocrite

hypothesis [haɪ'pɒθɪsɪs] (pl **hypotheses**) n hypothèse f

hysterical [hɪ'sterɪkl] adj hystérique; (funny) hilarant(e); **~ laughter** fou rire m

hysterics [hɪ'sterɪks] npl: **to be in/have ~** (anger, panic) avoir une crise de nerfs; (laughter) attraper un fou rire

I, i

I [aɪ] pron je; (before vowel) j'; (stressed) moi

ice [aɪs] n glace f; (on road) verglas m ♦ vt (cake) glacer ♦ vi (also: **~ over**, **~ up**) geler; (window) se givrer; **~berg** n iceberg m;

~box n (US) réfrigérateur m; (BRIT) compartiment m à glace; (insulated box) glacière f; ~ cream n glace f; ~ cube n glaçon m; ~d adj glacé(e); ~ hockey n hockey m sur glace; **Iceland** n Islande f; ~ lolly n (BRIT) esquimau m (glace); ~ rink n patinoire f; ~-skating n patinage m (sur glace)

icicle ['aɪsɪkl] n glaçon m (naturel)

icing ['aɪsɪŋ] n (CULIN) glace f; ~ sugar (BRIT) n sucre m glace

icy ['aɪsɪ] adj glacé(e); (road) verglacé(e); (weather, temperature) glacial(e)

I'd [aɪd] = I would; I had

idea [aɪ'dɪə] n idée f

ideal [aɪ'dɪəl] n idéal m ♦ adj idéal(e)

identical [aɪ'dɛntɪkl] adj identique

identification [aɪdɛntɪfɪ'keɪʃən] n identification f; **means of ~** pièce f d'identité

identify [aɪ'dɛntɪfaɪ] vt identifier

Identikit picture ® [aɪ'dɛntɪkɪt-] n portrait-robot m

identity [aɪ'dɛntɪtɪ] n identité f; ~ card n carte f d'identité

ideology [aɪdɪ'ɔlədʒɪ] n idéologie f

idiom ['ɪdɪəm] n expression f idiomatique; (style) style m

idiosyncrasy [ɪdɪəu'sɪŋkrəsɪ] n (of person) particularité f, petite manie

idiot ['ɪdɪət] n idiot(e), imbécile m/f; ~ic [ɪdɪ'ɔtɪk] adj idiot(e), bête, stupide

idle ['aɪdl] adj sans occupation, désœuvré(e); (lazy) oisif(-ive), paresseux(-euse); (unemployed) au chômage; (question, pleasures) vain(e), futile ♦ vi (engine) tourner au ralenti; **to lie ~** être arrêté(e), ne pas fonctionner

idol ['aɪdl] n idole f; ~ize vt idolâtrer, adorer

i.e. adv abbr (= id est) c'est-à-dire

if [ɪf] conj si; ~ **so** si c'est le cas; ~ **not** sinon; ~ **only** si seulement

ignite [ɪg'naɪt] vt mettre le feu à, enflammer ♦ vi s'enflammer; **ignition** n (AUT) allumage m; **to switch on/off the ignition** mettre/couper le contact; **ignition key** n clé f de contact

ignorant ['ɪgnərənt] adj ignorant(e); **to be ~ of** (subject) ne rien connaître à; (events) ne pas être au courant de

ignore [ɪg'nɔːɾ] vt ne tenir aucun compte de; (person) faire semblant de ne pas reconnaître, ignorer; (fact) méconnaître

ill [ɪl] adj (sick) malade; (bad) mauvais(e) ♦ n mal m ♦ adv: **to speak/think ~ of** dire/penser du mal de; ~s npl (misfortunes) maux mpl, malheurs mpl; **to be taken ~** tomber malade; ~-**advised** adj (decision) peu judicieux(-euse); (person) malavisé(e); ~-**at-ease** adj mal à l'aise

I'll [aɪl] = I will; I shall

illegal [ɪ'liːgl] adj illégal(e)

illegible [ɪ'lɛdʒɪbl] adj illisible

illegitimate [ɪlɪ'dʒɪtɪmət] adj illégitime

ill-fated [ɪl'feɪtɪd] adj malheureux(-euse); (day) néfaste

ill feeling n ressentiment m, rancune f

illiterate [ɪ'lɪtərət] adj illettré(e); (letter) plein(e) de fautes

ill: ~-**mannered** adj (child) mal élevé(e); ~**ness** n maladie f; ~-**treat** vt maltraiter

illuminate [ɪ'luːmɪneɪt] vt (room, street) éclairer; (for special effect) illuminer; **illumination** [ɪluːmɪ'neɪʃən] n éclairage m; illumination f

illusion [ɪ'luːʒən] n illusion f

illustrate ['ɪləstreɪt] vt illustrer; **illustration** [ɪlə'streɪʃən] n illustration f

ill will n malveillance f

I'm [aɪm] = I am

image ['ɪmɪdʒ] n image f; (public face) image de marque; ~**ry** n images fpl

imaginary [ɪ'mædʒɪnərɪ] adj imaginaire

imagination [ɪmædʒɪ'neɪʃən] n imagination f

imaginative [ɪ'mædʒɪnətɪv] adj imaginatif(-ive); (person) plein(e) d'imagination

imagine [ɪ'mædʒɪn] vt imaginer, s'imaginer; (suppose) imaginer, supposer

imbalance [ɪm'bæləns] n déséquilibre m

imitate ['ɪmɪteɪt] vt imiter; **imitation** [ɪmɪ'teɪʃən] n imitation f

immaculate [ɪ'mækjulət] adj impeccable; (REL) immaculé(e)

immaterial [ɪmə'tɪərɪəl] adj sans importance, insignifiant(e)

immature [ɪmə'tjuəɾ] adj (fruit) (qui n'est) pas mûr(e); (person) qui manque de maturité

immediate [ɪ'miːdɪət] adj immédiat(e); ~**ly** adv (at once) immédiatement; ~**ly next to** juste à côté de

immense [ɪ'mɛns] adj immense; énorme

immerse [ɪ'məːs] vt immerger, plonger; **immersion heater** (BRIT) n chauffe-eau m électrique

immigrant ['ɪmɪgrənt] n immigrant(e); immigré(e); **immigration** [ɪmɪ'greɪʃən] n immigration f

imminent ['ɪmɪnənt] adj imminent(e)

immoral [ɪ'mɔrl] adj immoral(e)

immortal [ɪ'mɔːtl] adj, n immortel(le)

immune [ɪ'mjuːn] adj: ~ (to) immunisé(e) (contre); (fig) à l'abri de; **immunity** n immunité f

impact ['ɪmpækt] n choc m, impact m; (fig) impact

impair [ɪm'pɛəɾ] vt détériorer, diminuer

impart [ɪm'pɑːt] vt communiquer, transmettre; (flavour) donner

impartial [ɪmˈpɑːʃl] adj impartial(e)

impassable [ɪmˈpɑːsəbl] adj infranchissable; (road) impraticable

impassive [ɪmˈpæsɪv] adj impassible

impatience [ɪmˈpeɪʃəns] n impatience f

impatient [ɪmˈpeɪʃənt] adj impatient(e); **to get** or **grow ~** s'impatienter; **~ly** adv avec impatience

impeccable [ɪmˈpɛkəbl] adj impeccable, parfait(e)

impede [ɪmˈpiːd] vt gêner; **impediment** n obstacle m; (also: **speech impediment**) défaut m d'élocution

impending [ɪmˈpɛndɪŋ] adj imminent(e)

imperative [ɪmˈpɛrətɪv] adj (need) urgent(e), pressant(e); (tone) impérieux(-euse) ♦ n (LING) impératif m

imperfect [ɪmˈpəːfɪkt] adj imparfait(e); (goods etc) défectueux(-euse)

imperial [ɪmˈpɪərɪəl] adj impérial(e); (BRIT: measure) légal(e)

impersonal [ɪmˈpəːsənl] adj impersonnel(le)

impersonate [ɪmˈpəːsəneɪt] vt se faire passer pour; (THEATRE) imiter

impertinent [ɪmˈpəːtɪnənt] adj impertinent(e), insolent(e)

impervious [ɪmˈpəːvɪəs] adj (fig): **~ to** insensible à

impetuous [ɪmˈpɛtjuəs] adj impétueux(-euse), fougueux(-euse)

impetus [ˈɪmpətəs] n impulsion f; (of runner) élan m

impinge [ɪmˈpɪndʒ]: **to ~ on** vt fus (person) affecter, toucher; (rights) empiéter sur

implement [n ˈɪmplɪmənt, vb ˈɪmplɪmɛnt] n outil m, instrument m; (for cooking) ustensile m ♦ vt exécuter

implicit [ɪmˈplɪsɪt] adj implicite; (complete) absolu(e), sans réserve

imply [ɪmˈplaɪ] vt suggérer, laisser entendre; indiquer, supposer

impolite [ɪmpəˈlaɪt] adj impoli(e)

import [vb ɪmˈpɔːt, n ˈɪmpɔːt] vt importer ♦ n (COMM) importation f

importance [ɪmˈpɔːtns] n importance f

important [ɪmˈpɔːtənt] adj important(e)

importer [ɪmˈpɔːtər] n importateur(-trice)

impose [ɪmˈpəuz] vt imposer ♦ vi: **to ~ on sb** abuser de la gentillesse de qn; **imposing** adj imposant(e), impressionnant(e); **imposition** [ɪmpəˈzɪʃən] n (of tax etc) imposition f; **to be an imposition on** (person) abuser de la gentillesse or la bonté de

impossible [ɪmˈpɔsɪbl] adj impossible

impotent [ˈɪmpətənt] adj impuissant(e)

impound [ɪmˈpaund] vt confisquer, saisir

impoverished [ɪmˈpɔvərɪʃt] adj appauvri(e), pauvre

impractical [ɪmˈpræktɪkl] adj pas pratique;

(person) qui manque d'esprit pratique

impregnable [ɪmˈprɛgnəbl] adj (fortress) imprenable

impress [ɪmˈprɛs] vt impressionner, faire impression sur; (mark) imprimer, marquer; **to ~ sth on sb** faire bien comprendre qch à qn; **~ed** adj impressionné(e)

impression [ɪmˈprɛʃən] n impression f; (of stamp, seal) empreinte f; (imitation) imitation f; **to be under the ~ that** avoir l'impression que; **~ist** n (ART) impressioniste m/f; (entertainer) imitateur(-trice) m/f

impressive [ɪmˈprɛsɪv] adj impressionnant(e)

imprint [ˈɪmprɪnt] n (outline) marque f, empreinte f

imprison [ɪmˈprɪzn] vt emprisonner, mettre en prison

improbable [ɪmˈprɔbəbl] adj improbable; (excuse) peu plausible

improper [ɪmˈprɔpər] adj (unsuitable) déplacé(e), de mauvais goût; indécent(e); (dishonest) malhonnête

improve [ɪmˈpruːv] vt améliorer ♦ vi s'améliorer; (pupil etc) faire des progrès; **~ment** n amélioration f (in de); progrès m

improvise [ˈɪmprəvaɪz] vt, vi improviser

impudent [ˈɪmpjudnt] adj impudent(e)

impulse [ˈɪmpʌls] n impulsion f; **on ~** impulsivement, sur un coup de tête; **impulsive** adj impulsif(-ive)

KEYWORD

---

in [ɪn] prep **1** (indicating place, position) dans; **in the house/the fridge** dans la maison/le frigo; **in the garden** dans le or au jardin; **in town** en ville; **in the country** à la campagne; **in school** à l'école; **in here/there** ici/là
2 (with place names: of town, region, country): **in London** à Londres; **in England** en Angleterre; **in Japan** au Japon; **in the United States** aux États Unis
3 (indicating time: during): **in spring** au printemps; **in summer** en été, **in May/1992** en mai/1992; **in the afternoon** (dans) l'après-midi; **at 4 o'clock in the afternoon** à 4 heures de l'après-midi
4 (indicating time: in the space of) en; (: future) dans; **I did it in 3 hours/days** je l'ai fait en 3 heures/jours; **I'll see you in 2 weeks** or **in 2 weeks' time** je te verrai dans 2 semaines
5 (indicating manner etc) à; **in a loud/soft voice** à voix haute/basse; **in pencil** au crayon; **in French** en français; **the boy in the blue shirt** le garçon à or avec la chemise bleue
6 (indicating circumstances): **in the sun** au soleil; **in the shade** à l'ombre; **in the rain** sous la pluie
7 (indicating mood, state): **in tears** en larmes;

in anger sous le coup de la colère; **in despair** au désespoir; **in good condition** en bon état; **to live in luxury** vivre dans le luxe
8 (with ratios, numbers): **1 in 10 (households)**, **1 (household) in 10** 1 (ménage) sur 10; **20 pence in the pound** 20 pence par livre sterling; **they lined up in twos** ils se mirent en rangs (deux) par deux; **in hundreds** par centaines
9 (referring to people, works) chez; **the disease is common in children** c'est une maladie courante chez les enfants; **in (the works of) Dickens** chez Dickens, dans (l'œuvre de) Dickens
10 (indicating profession etc) dans; **to be in teaching** être dans l'enseignement
11 (after superlative) de; **the best pupil in the class** le meilleur élève de la classe
12 (with present participle): **in saying this** en disant ceci
♦ adv: **to be in** (person: at home, work) être là; (train, ship, plane) être arrivé(e); (in fashion) être à la mode; **to ask sb in** inviter qn à entrer; **to run/limp etc in** entrer en courant/boitant etc
♦ n: **the ins and outs (of)** (of proposal, situation etc) les tenants et aboutissants (de)

in. abbr = **inch**
inability [ɪnə'bɪlɪtɪ] n incapacité f
inaccurate [ɪn'ækjʊrət] adj inexact(e); (person) qui manque de précision
inadequate [ɪn'ædɪkwət] adj insuffisant(e), inadéquat(e)
inadvertently [ɪnəd'vɜːtntlɪ] adv par mégarde
inadvisable [ɪnəd'vaɪzəbl] adj (action) à déconseiller
inane [ɪ'neɪn] adj inepte, stupide
inanimate [ɪn'ænɪmət] adj inanimé(e)
inappropriate [ɪnə'prəʊprɪət] adj inopportun(e), mal à propos; (word, expression) impropre
inarticulate [ɪnɑː'tɪkjʊlət] adj (person) qui s'exprime mal; (speech) indistinct(e)
inasmuch as [ɪnəz'mʌtʃ-] adv (insofar as) dans la mesure où; (seeing that) attendu que
inauguration [ɪnɔːɡjʊ'reɪʃən] n inauguration f; (of president) investiture f
inborn [ɪn'bɔːn] adj (quality) inné(e)
inbred [ɪn'bred] adj inné(e), naturel(le); (family) consanguin(e)
Inc. abbr = **incorporated**
incapable [ɪn'keɪpəbl] adj incapable
incapacitate [ɪnkə'pæsɪteɪt] vt: **to ~ sb from doing** rendre qn incapable de faire
incense [n 'ɪnsens, vb ɪn'sens] n encens m
♦ vt (anger) mettre en colère
incentive [ɪn'sentɪv] n encouragement m,

raison f de se donner de la peine
incessant [ɪn'sesnt] adj incessant(e); **~ly** adv sans cesse, constamment
inch [ɪntʃ] n pouce m (= 25 mm; 12 in a foot); **within an ~ of** à deux doigts de; **he didn't give an ~** (fig) il n'a pas voulu céder d'un pouce
incident ['ɪnsɪdnt] n incident m; **~al** [ɪnsɪ'dentl] adj (additional) accessoire; **~al to** qui accompagne; **~ally** adv (by the way) à propos
inclination [ɪnklɪ'neɪʃən] n (fig) inclination f
incline [n 'ɪnklaɪn, vb ɪn'klaɪn] n pente f ♦ vt incliner ♦ vi (surface) s'incliner; **to be ~d to do** avoir tendance à faire
include [ɪn'kluːd] vt inclure, comprendre; **including** prep y compris; **inclusive** adj inclus(e), compris(e); **inclusive of tax etc** taxes etc comprises
income ['ɪnkʌm] n revenu m; **~ tax** n impôt m sur le revenu
incoming ['ɪnkʌmɪŋ] adj qui arrive; (president) entrant(e); **~ mail** courrier m du jour; **~ tide** marée montante
incompetent [ɪn'kɒmpɪtnt] adj incompétent(e), incapable
incomplete [ɪnkəm'pliːt] adj incomplet(-ète)
incongruous [ɪn'kɒŋɡrʊəs] adj incongru(e)
inconsiderate [ɪnkən'sɪdərət] adj (person) qui manque d'égards; (action) inconsidéré(e)
inconsistency [ɪnkən'sɪstənsɪ] n (of actions etc) inconséquence f; (of work) irrégularité f; (of statement etc) incohérence f
inconsistent [ɪnkən'sɪstnt] adj inconséquent(e); irrégulier(-ère); peu cohérent(e); **~ with** incompatible avec
inconspicuous [ɪnkən'spɪkjʊəs] adj qui passe inaperçu(e); (colour, dress) discret(-ète)
inconvenience [ɪnkən'viːnjəns] n inconvénient m; (trouble) dérangement m ♦ vt déranger
inconvenient [ɪnkən'viːnjənt] adj (house) malcommode; (time, place) mal choisi(e), qui ne convient pas; (visitor) importun(e)
incorporate [ɪn'kɔːpəreɪt] vt incorporer; (contain) contenir; **~d company** (US) n ≈ société f anonyme
incorrect [ɪnkə'rekt] adj incorrect(e)
increase [n 'ɪnkriːs, vb ɪn'kriːs] n augmentation f ♦ vi, vt augmenter; **increasing** adj (number) croissant(e); **increasingly** adv de plus en plus
incredible [ɪn'kredɪbl] adj incroyable
incubator ['ɪnkjʊbeɪtə'] n (for babies) couveuse f
incumbent [ɪn'kʌmbənt] n (president) président m en exercice; (REL) titulaire m/f ♦ adj: **it is ~ on him to ...** il lui incombe or

appartient de ...

incur [ɪn'kəːʳ] vt (expenses) encourir; (anger, risk) s'exposer à; (debt) contracter; (loss) subir

indebted [ɪn'dɛtɪd] adj: **to be ~ to sb (for)** être redevable à qn (de)

indecent [ɪn'diːsnt] adj indécent(e), inconvenant(e); **~ assault** (BRIT) n attentat m à la pudeur; **~ exposure** n outrage m (public) à la pudeur

indecisive [ɪndɪ'saɪsɪv] adj (person) indécis(e)

indeed [ɪn'diːd] adv vraiment; en effet; (furthermore) d'ailleurs; **yes ~!** certainement!

indefinitely [ɪn'dɛfɪnɪtlɪ] adv (wait) indéfiniment

indemnity [ɪn'dɛmnɪtɪ] n (safeguard) assurance f, garantie f; (compensation) indemnité f

independence [ɪndɪ'pɛndns] n indépendance f

independent [ɪndɪ'pɛndnt] adj indépendant(e); (school) privé(e); (radio) libre

index ['ɪndɛks] n (pl: ~es: in book) index m; (: in library etc) catalogue m; (pl: indices: ratio, sign) indice m; **~ card** n fiche f; **~ finger** n index m; **~-linked** adj indexé(e) (sur le coût de la vie etc)

India ['ɪndɪə] n Inde f; **~n** adj indien(ne) ♦ n Indien(ne); (**American**) **~n** Indien(ne) (d'Amérique); **~n Ocean** n océan Indien

indicate ['ɪndɪkeɪt] vt indiquer; **indication** [ɪndɪ'keɪʃən] n indication f, signe m; **indicative** [ɪn'dɪkətɪv] adj: **indicative of** symptomatique de ♦ n (LING) indicatif m; **indicator** n (sign) indicateur m; (AUT) clignotant m

indices ['ɪndɪsiːz] npl of **index**

indictment [ɪn'daɪtmənt] n accusation f

indifferent [ɪn'dɪfrənt] adj indifférent(e); (poor) médiocre, quelconque

indigenous [ɪn'dɪdʒɪnəs] adj indigène

indigestion [ɪndɪ'dʒɛstʃən] n indigestion f, mauvaise digestion

indignant [ɪn'dɪgnənt] adj: **~ (at sth/with sb)** indigné(e) (de qch/contre qn)

indignity [ɪn'dɪgnɪtɪ] n indignité f, affront m

indirect [ɪndɪ'rɛkt] adj indirect(e)

indiscreet [ɪndɪs'kriːt] adj indiscret(-ète); (rash) imprudent(e)

indiscriminate [ɪndɪs'krɪmɪnət] adj (person) qui manque de discernement; (killings) commis(e) au hasard

indisputable [ɪndɪs'pjuːtəbl] adj incontestable, indiscutable

individual [ɪndɪ'vɪdjuəl] n individu m ♦ adj individuel(le); (characteristic) particulier(-ère), original(e)

indoctrination [ɪndɔktrɪ'neɪʃən] n endoctrinement m

Indonesia [ɪndə'niːzɪə] n Indonésie f

indoor ['ɪndɔːʳ] adj (plant) d'appartement; (swimming pool) couvert(e); (sport, games) pratiqué(e) en salle; **~s** adv à l'intérieur

induce [ɪn'djuːs] vt (persuade) persuader; (bring about) provoquer; **~ment** n (incentive) récompense f; (pej: bribe) pot-de-vin m

indulge [ɪn'dʌldʒ] vt (whim) céder à, satisfaire; (child) gâter ♦ vi: **to ~ in sth** (luxury) se permettre qch; (fantasies etc) se livrer à qch; **~nce** n fantaisie f (que l'on s'offre); (leniency) indulgence f; **~nt** adj indulgent(e)

industrial [ɪn'dʌstrɪəl] adj industriel(le); (injury) du travail; **~ action** n action revendicative; **~ estate** (BRIT) n zone industrielle; **~ist** n industriel m; **~ park** (US) n = **industrial estate**

industrious [ɪn'dʌstrɪəs] adj travailleur(-euse)

industry ['ɪndəstrɪ] n industrie f; (diligence) zèle m, application f

inebriated [ɪ'niːbrɪeɪtɪd] adj ivre

inedible [ɪn'ɛdɪbl] adj immangeable; (plant etc) non comestible

ineffective [ɪnɪ'fɛktɪv], **ineffectual** [ɪnɪ'fɛktjuəl] adj inefficace

inefficient [ɪnɪ'fɪʃənt] adj inefficace

inequality [ɪnɪ'kwɔlɪtɪ] n inégalité f

inescapable [ɪnɪ'skeɪpəbl] adj inéluctable, inévitable

inevitable [ɪn'ɛvɪtəbl] adj inévitable; **inevitably** adv inévitablement

inexpensive [ɪnɪk'spɛnsɪv] adj bon marché inv

inexperienced [ɪnɪk'spɪərɪənst] adj inexpérimenté(e)

infallible [ɪn'fælɪbl] adj infaillible

infamous ['ɪnfəməs] adj infâme, abominable

infancy ['ɪnfənsɪ] n petite enfance, bas âge

infant ['ɪnfənt] n (baby) nourrisson m; (young child) petit(e) enfant; **~ school** (BRIT) n classes fpl préparatoires (entre 5 et 7 ans)

infatuated [ɪn'fætjueɪtɪd] adj: **~ with** entiché(e) de; **infatuation** [ɪnfætju'eɪʃən] n engouement m

infect [ɪn'fɛkt] vt infecter, contaminer; **~ion** n infection f; (contagion) contagion f; **~ious** adj infectieux(-euse); (also fig) contagieux(-euse)

infer [ɪn'fəːʳ] vt conclure, déduire

inferior [ɪn'fɪərɪəʳ] adj inférieur(e); (goods) de qualité inférieure ♦ n inférieur(e); (in rank) subalterne m/f; **~ity** [ɪnfɪərɪ'ɔrɪtɪ] n infériorité f

infertile [ɪn'fəːtaɪl] adj stérile

infighting ['ɪnfaɪtɪŋ] n querelles fpl internes

infinite ['ɪnfɪnɪt] *adj* infini(e)
infinitive [ɪn'fɪnɪtɪv] *n* infinitif *m*
infinity [ɪn'fɪnɪtɪ] *n* infinité *f*; (*also* MATH)
infini *m*
infirmary [ɪn'fə:mərɪ] *n* (*hospital*) hôpital *m*
inflamed [ɪn'fleɪmd] *adj* enflammé(e)
inflammable [ɪn'flæməbl] (*BRIT*) *adj*
inflammable
inflammation [ɪnflə'meɪʃən] *n* inflammation
f
inflatable [ɪn'fleɪtəbl] *adj* gonflable
inflate [ɪn'fleɪt] *vt* (*tyre, balloon*) gonfler;
(*price*) faire monter; **inflation** *n* (ECON)
inflation *f*; **inflationary** *adj* inflationniste
inflict [ɪn'flɪkt] *vt*: **to ~ on** infliger à ♦ *vt*
influence ['ɪnfluəns] *n* influence *f* ♦ *vt*
influencer; **under the ~ of alcohol** en état
d'ébriété; **influential** [ɪnflu'ɛnʃl] *adj*
influent(e)
influenza [ɪnflu'ɛnzə] *n* grippe *f*
influx ['ɪnflʌks] *n* afflux *m*
infomercial ['ɪnfəuməːʃl] (US) *n* (*for product*)
publi-information *f*; (POL) émission où un
candidat présente son programme électoral
inform [ɪn'fɔ:m] *vt*: **to ~ sb (of)** informer or
avertir qn (de) ♦ *vi*: **to ~ on sb** dénoncer qn
informal [ɪn'fɔ:ml] *adj* (*person, manner,
party*) simple; (*visit, discussion*) dénué(e) de
formalités; (*announcement, invitation*) non
officiel(le); (*colloquial*) familier(-ère); **~ity**
[ɪnfɔ:'mælɪtɪ] *n* simplicité *f*, absence *f* de
cérémonie; caractère non officiel
informant [ɪn'fɔ:mənt] *n* informateur(-trice)
information [ɪnfə'meɪʃən] *n* information *f*;
renseignements *mpl*; (*knowledge*)
connaissances *fpl*; **a piece of ~** un
renseignement; **~ desk** *n* accueil *m*; **~ office**
n bureau *m* de renseignements
informative [ɪn'fɔ:mətɪv] *adj* instructif(-ive)
informer [ɪn'fɔ:məʳ] *n* (*also:* **police ~**)
indicateur(-trice)
infringe [ɪn'frɪndʒ] *vt* enfreindre ♦ *vi*: **to ~ on**
empiéter sur; **~ment** *n*: **~ment (of)** infraction
f (à)
infuriating [ɪn'fjuərɪeɪtɪŋ] *adj* exaspérant(e)
ingenious [ɪn'dʒi:njəs] *adj* ingénieux(-euse);
ingenuity [ɪndʒɪ'nju:ɪtɪ] *n* ingéniosité *f*
ingenuous [ɪn'dʒɛnjuəs] *adj* naïf (naïve),
ingénu(e)
ingot ['ɪŋgət] *n* lingot *m*
ingrained [ɪn'greɪnd] *adj* enraciné(e)
ingratiate [ɪn'greɪʃɪeɪt] *vt*: **to ~ o.s. with**
s'insinuer dans les bonnes grâces de, se faire
bien voir de
ingredient [ɪn'gri:dɪənt] *n* ingrédient *m*;
(*fig*) élément *m*
inhabit [ɪn'hæbɪt] *vt* habiter; **~ant** *n*
habitant(e)
inhale [ɪn'heɪl] *vt* respirer; (*smoke*) avaler ♦ *vi*

aspirer; (*in smoking*) avaler la fumée
inherent [ɪn'hɪərənt] *adj*: **~ (in or to)**
inhérent(e) (à)
inherit [ɪn'hɛrɪt] *vt* hériter (de); **~ance** *n*
héritage *m*
inhibit [ɪn'hɪbɪt] *vt* (PSYCH) inhiber; (*growth*)
freiner; **~ion** [ɪnhɪ'bɪʃən] *n* inhibition *f*
inhuman [ɪn'hju:mən] *adj* inhumain(e)
initial [ɪ'nɪʃl] *adj* initial(e) ♦ *n* initiale *f* ♦ *vt*
parafer; **~s** *npl* (*letters*) initiales *fpl*; (*as
signature*) parafe *m*; **~ly** *adv* initialement, au
début
initiate [ɪ'nɪʃɪeɪt] *vt* (*start*) entreprendre,
amorcer; (*entreprise*) lancer; (*person*) initier;
to ~ proceedings against sb intenter une
action à qn; **initiative** *n* initiative *f*
inject [ɪn'dʒɛkt] *vt* injecter; (*person*): **to ~ sb
with sth** faire une piqûre de qch à qn; **~ion**
n injection *f*, piqûre *f*
injure ['ɪndʒəʳ] *vt* blesser; (*reputation etc*)
compromettre; **~d** *adj* blessé(e); **injury** *n*
blessure *f*; **~ time** *n* (SPORT) arrêts *mpl* de jeu
injustice [ɪn'dʒʌstɪs] *n* injustice *f*
ink [ɪŋk] *n* encre *f*
inkling ['ɪŋklɪŋ] *n*: **to have an/no ~ of** avoir
une (vague) idée de/n'avoir aucune idée de
inlaid ['ɪnleɪd] *adj* incrusté(e); (*table etc*)
marqueté(e)
inland [*adj* 'ɪnlənd, *adv* ɪn'lænd] *adj*
intérieur(e) ♦ *adv* à l'intérieur, dans les terres;
Inland Revenue (BRIT) *n* fisc *m*
in-laws ['ɪnlɔ:z] *npl* beaux-parents *mpl*; belle
famille
inlet ['ɪnlɛt] *n* (GEO) crique *f*
inmate ['ɪnmeɪt] *n* (*in prison*) détenu(e); (*in
asylum*) interné(e)
inn [ɪn] *n* auberge *f*
innate [ɪ'neɪt] *adj* inné(e)
inner ['ɪnəʳ] *adj* intérieur(e); **~ city** *n* centre
m de zone urbaine; **~ tube** *n* (*of tyre*)
chambre *f* à air
innings ['ɪnɪŋz] *n* (CRICKET) tour *m* de batte
innocent ['ɪnəsnt] *adj* innocent(e)
innocuous [ɪ'nɔkjuəs] *adj* inoffensif(-ive)
innuendo [ɪnju'ɛndəu] (*pl* **~es**) *n* insinuation
f, allusion (malveillante)
innumerable [ɪ'nju:mrəbl] *adj* innombrable
inpatient ['ɪnpeɪʃnt] *n* malade hospitalisé(e)
input ['ɪnput] *n* (*resources*) ressources *fpl*;
(COMPUT) entrée *f* (de données); (: *data*)
données *fpl*
inquest ['ɪnkwɛst] *n* enquête *f*; (*coroner's*) ~
enquête judiciaire
inquire [ɪn'kwaɪəʳ] *vi* demander ♦ *vt*
demander; **to ~ about** se renseigner sur;
~ into *vt fus* faire une enquête sur; **inquiry**
n demande *f* de renseignements;
(*investigation*) enquête *f*, investigation *f*;
inquiries *npl*: **the inquiries** (RAIL *etc*) les

renseignements; **inquiry** or **inquiries office** (BRIT) n bureau m des renseignements

inquisitive [ɪnˈkwɪzɪtɪv] adj curieux(-euse)

ins abbr = **inches**

insane [ɪnˈseɪn] adj fou (folle); (MED) aliéné(e); **Insanity** [ɪnˈsænɪtɪ] n folie f; (MED) aliénation (mentale)

inscription [ɪnˈskrɪpʃən] n inscription f; (in book) dédicace f

inscrutable [ɪnˈskruːtəbl] adj impénétrable; (comment) obscur(e)

insect [ˈɪnsekt] n insecte m; **~icide** [ɪnˈsektɪsaɪd] n insecticide m; **~ repellent** n crème f anti-insecte

insecure [ɪnsɪˈkjuər] adj peu solide; peu sûr(e); (person) anxieux(-euse)

insensitive [ɪnˈsensɪtɪv] adj insensible

insert [ɪnˈsɜːt] vt insérer; **~ion** n insertion f

in-service [ˈɪnˈsɜːvɪs] adj (training) continu(e), en cours d'emploi; (course) de perfectionnement; de recyclage

inshore [ˈɪnˈʃɔː] adj côtier(-ère) ♦ adv près de la côte, (move) vers la côte

inside [ˈɪnˈsaɪd] n intérieur m ♦ adj intérieur(e) ♦ adv à l'intérieur, dedans ♦ prep à l'intérieur de; (of time): **~ 10 minutes** en moins de 10 minutes; **~s** npl (inf) intestins mpl; **~ information** n renseignements obtenus à la source; **~ lane** n (AUT: in Britain) voie f de gauche; (: in US, Europe etc) voie de droite; **~ out** adv à l'envers; (know) à fond; **~r dealing, ~r trading** n (St Ex) délit m d'initié

insight [ˈɪnsaɪt] n perspicacité f; (glimpse, idea) aperçu m

insignificant [ɪnsɪgˈnɪfɪknt] adj insignifiant(e)

insincere [ɪnsɪnˈsɪər] adj hypocrite

insinuate [ɪnˈsɪnjueɪt] vt insinuer

insist [ɪnˈsɪst] vi insister; **to ~ on doing** insister pour faire; **to ~ on sth** exiger qch; **to ~ that** insister pour que; (claim) maintenir or soutenir que; **~ent** adj insistant(e), pressant(e); (noise, action) ininterrompu(e)

insole [ˈɪnsəul] n (removable) semelle intérieure

insolent [ˈɪnsələnt] adj insolent(e)

insolvent [ɪnˈsɔlvənt] adj insolvable

insomnia [ɪnˈsɔmnɪə] n insomnie f

inspect [ɪnˈspekt] vt inspecter; (ticket) contrôler; **~ion** n inspection f; contrôle m; **~or** n inspecteur(-trice); (BRIT: on buses, trains) contrôleur(-euse)

inspire [ɪnˈspaɪər] vt inspirer

install [ɪnˈstɔːl] vt installer; **~ation** [ɪnstəˈleɪʃən] n installation f

instalment [ɪnˈstɔːlmənt] (US **installment**) n acompte m, versement partiel; (of TV serial etc) épisode m; **in ~s** (pay) à tempérament;

(receive) en plusieurs fois

instance [ˈɪnstəns] n exemple m; **for ~** par exemple; **in the first ~** tout d'abord, en premier lieu

instant [ˈɪnstənt] n instant m ♦ adj immédiat(e); (coffee, food) instantané(e), en poudre; **~ly** adv immédiatement, tout de suite

instead [ɪnˈsted] adv au lieu de cela; **~ of** au lieu de; **~ of sb** à la place de qn

instep [ˈɪnstep] n cou-de-pied m; (of shoe) cambrure f

instigate [ˈɪnstɪgeɪt] vt (rebellion) fomenter, provoquer; (talks etc) promouvoir

instil [ɪnˈstɪl] vt: **to ~ (into)** inculquer (à); (courage) insuffler (à)

instinct [ˈɪnstɪŋkt] n instinct m

institute [ˈɪnstɪtjuːt] n institut m ♦ vt instituer, établir; (inquiry) ouvrir; (proceedings) entamer

institution [ɪnstɪˈtjuːʃən] n institution f; (educational) établissement m (scolaire); (mental home) établissement m (psychiatrique)

instruct [ɪnˈstrʌkt] vt: **to ~ sb in sth** enseigner qch à qn; **to ~ sb to do** charger qn or ordonner à qn de faire; **~ion** n instruction f; **~ions** npl (orders) directives fpl; **~ions (for use)** mode m d'emploi; **~or** n professeur m; (for skiing, driving) moniteur m

instrument [ˈɪnstrumənt] n instrument m; **~al** [ɪnstrʊˈmentl] adj: **to be ~al in** contribuer à; **~ panel** n tableau m de bord

insufficient [ɪnsəˈfɪʃənt] adj insuffisant(e)

insular [ˈɪnsjulər] adj (outlook) borné(e); (person) aux vues étroites

insulate [ˈɪnsjuleɪt] vt isoler; (against sound) insonoriser; **insulation** [ɪnsjuˈleɪʃən] n isolation f; insonorisation f

insulin [ˈɪnsjulɪn] n insuline f

insult [n ˈɪnsʌlt, vb ɪnˈsʌlt] n insulte f, affront m ♦ vt insulter, faire affront à

insurance [ɪnˈʃuərəns] n assurance f; **fire/life ~** assurance-incendie/-vie; **~ policy** n police f d'assurance

insure [ɪnˈʃuər] vt assurer; **to ~ (o.s.) against** (fig) parer à

intact [ɪnˈtækt] adj intact(e)

intake [ˈɪnteɪk] n (of food, oxygen) consommation f; (BRIT: SCOL): **an ~ of 200 a year** 200 admissions fpl par an

integral [ˈɪntɪgrəl] adj (part) intégrant(e)

integrate [ˈɪntɪgreɪt] vt intégrer ♦ vi s'intégrer

intellect [ˈɪntəlekt] n intelligence f; **~ual** [ɪntəˈlektjuəl] adj, n intellectuel(le)

intelligence [ɪnˈtelɪdʒəns] n intelligence f; (MIL etc) informations fpl, renseignements mpl; **~ service** n services secrets; **intelligent** adj intelligent(e)

intend [ɪn'tɛnd] vt (gift etc): **to ~ sth for** destiner qch à; **to ~ to do** avoir l'intention de faire

intense [ɪn'tɛns] adj intense; (person) véhément(e); **~ly** adv intensément; profondément

intensive [ɪn'tɛnsɪv] adj intensif(-ive); **~ care unit** n service m de réanimation

intent [ɪn'tɛnt] n intention f ♦ adj attentif(-ive); (absorbed): **~ (on)** absorbé(e) (par); **to all ~s and purposes** en fait, pratiquement; **to be ~ on doing sth** être (bien) décidé à faire qch; **~ion** n intention f; **~ional** adj intentionnel(le), délibéré(e); **~ly** adv attentivement

interact [ɪntər'ækt] vi avoir une action réciproque; (people) communiquer; **~ive** adj (COMPUT) interactif(-ive)

interchange [n 'ɪntətfeɪndʒ, vb ɪntə'tfeɪndʒ] n (exchange) échange m; (on motorway) échangeur m; **~able** adj interchangeable

intercom ['ɪntəkɔm] n interphone m

intercourse ['ɪntəkɔːs] n (sexual) rapports mpl

interest ['ɪntrɪst] n intérêt m; (pastime): **my main ~** ce qui m'intéresse le plus; (COMM) intérêts mpl ♦ vt intéresser; **to be ~ed in sth** s'intéresser à qch; **I am ~ed in going** ça m'intéresse d'y aller; **~ing** adj intéressant(e); **~ rate** n taux m d'intérêt

interface ['ɪntəfeɪs] n (COMPUT) interface f

interfere [ɪntə'fɪər] vi: **to ~ in** (quarrel) s'immiscer dans; (other people's business) se mêler de; **to ~ with** (object) toucher à; (plans) contrecarrer; (duty) être en conflit avec; **~nce** n (in affairs) ingérance f; (RADIO, TV) parasites mpl

interim ['ɪntərɪm] adj provisoire ♦ n: **in the ~** dans l'intérim, entre-temps

interior [ɪn'tɪərɪər] n intérieur m ♦ adj intérieur(e); (minister, department) de l'Intérieur; **~ designer** n styliste m/f, designer m/f

interjection [ɪntə'dʒɛkʃən] n (interruption) interruption f; (LING) interjection f

interlock [ɪntə'lɔk] vi s'enclencher

interlude ['ɪntəluːd] n intervalle m; (THEATRE) intermède m

intermediate [ɪntə'miːdɪət] adj intermédiaire; (SCOL: course, level) moyen(ne)

intermission [ɪntə'mɪʃən] n pause f; (THEATRE, CINEMA) entracte m

intern [vb ɪn'tɜːn, n 'ɪntɜːn] vt interner ♦ n (US) interne m/f

internal [ɪn'tɜːnl] adj interne; (politics) intérieur(e); **~ly** adv: **"not to be taken ~ly"** "pour usage externe"; **I~ Revenue Service** (US) n fisc m

international [ɪntə'næʃənl] adj

international(e)

Internet ['ɪntənɛt] n Internet m

interplay ['ɪntəpleɪ] n effet m réciproque, interaction f

interpret [ɪn'tɜːprɪt] vt interpréter ♦ vi servir d'interprète; **~er** n interprète m/f

interrelated [ɪntərɪ'leɪtɪd] adj en corrélation, en rapport étroit

interrogate [ɪn'tɛrəɡeɪt] vt interroger; (suspect etc) soumettre à un interrogatoire; **interrogation** [ɪntɛrəu'ɡeɪʃən] n interrogation f; interrogatoire m

interrupt [ɪntə'rʌpt] vt, vi interrompre; **~ion** n interruption f

intersect [ɪntə'sɛkt] vi (roads) se croiser, se couper; **~ion** n (of roads) croisement m

intersperse [ɪntə'spɜːs] vt: **to ~ with** parsemer de

intertwine [ɪntə'twaɪn] vi s'entrelacer

interval ['ɪntəvl] n intervalle m; (BRIT: THEATRE) entracte m; (: SPORT) mi-temps f; **at ~s** par intervalles

intervene [ɪntə'viːn] vi (person) intervenir; (event) survenir; (time) s'écouler (entre-temps); **intervention** n intervention f

interview ['ɪntəvjuː] n (RADIO, TV etc) interview f; (for job) entrevue f ♦ vt interviewer; accorder une entrevue avec; **~er** n (RADIO, TV) interviewer m

intestine [ɪn'tɛstɪn] n intestin m

intimacy ['ɪntɪməsɪ] n intimité f

intimate [adj 'ɪntɪmət, vb 'ɪntɪmeɪt] adj intime; (friendship) profond(e); (knowledge) approfondi(e) ♦ vt (hint) suggérer, laisser entendre

into ['ɪntu] prep dans; **~ pieces/French** en morceaux/français

intolerant [ɪn'tɔlərnt] adj: **~ (of)** intolérant(e) (de)

intoxicated [ɪn'tɔksɪkeɪtɪd] adj (drunk) ivre

intractable [ɪn'træktəbl] adj (child) indocile, insoumis(e); (problem) insoluble

intranet ['ɪntrənɛt] n intranet m

intransitive [ɪn'trænsɪtɪv] adj intransitif(-ive)

intravenous [ɪntrə'viːnəs] adj intraveineux(-euse)

in-tray ['ɪntreɪ] n courrier m "arrivée"

intricate ['ɪntrɪkət] adj complexe, compliqué(e)

intrigue [ɪn'triːɡ] n intrigue f ♦ vt intriguer; **intriguing** adj fascinant(e)

intrinsic [ɪn'trɪnsɪk] adj intrinsèque

introduce [ɪntrə'djuːs] vt introduire; (TV show, people to each other) présenter; **to ~ sb to** (pastime, technique) initier qn à; **introduction** n introduction f; (of person) présentation f; (to new experience) initiation f; **introductory** adj préliminaire, d'introduction; **introductory offer** n

(COMM) offre f de lancement

intrude [ɪnˈtruːd] vi (person) être importun(e); **to ~ on** (conversation etc) s'immiscer dans; **~r** n intrus(e)

intuition [ɪntjuːˈɪʃən] n intuition f

inundate [ˈɪnʌndeɪt] vt: **to ~ with** inonder de

invade [ɪnˈveɪd] vt envahir

invalid [n ˈɪnvəlɪd, adj ɪnˈvælɪd] n malade m/f; (with disability) invalide m/f ♦ adj (not valid) non valide or valable

invaluable [ɪnˈvæljuəbl] adj inestimable, inappréciable

invariably [ɪnˈvɛərɪəblɪ] adv invariablement; toujours

invent [ɪnˈvɛnt] vt inventer; **~ion** n invention f; **~ive** adj inventif(-ive); **~or** n inventeur(-trice)

inventory [ˈɪnvəntrɪ] n inventaire m

invert [ɪnˈvɜːt] vt intervertir; (cup, object) retourner; **~ed commas** (BRIT) npl guillemets mpl

invest [ɪnˈvɛst] vt investir ♦ vi: **to ~ in sth** placer son argent dans qch; (fig) s'offrir qch

investigate [ɪnˈvɛstɪgeɪt] vt (crime etc) faire une enquête sur; **investigation** [ɪnvɛstɪˈgeɪʃən] n (of crime) enquête f

investment [ɪnˈvɛstmənt] n investissement m, placement m

investor [ɪnˈvɛstər] n investisseur m; actionnaire m/f

invigilator [ɪnˈvɪdʒɪleɪtər] n surveillant(e)

invigorating [ɪnˈvɪgəreɪtɪŋ] adj vivifiant(e); (fig) stimulant(e)

invisible [ɪnˈvɪzɪbl] adj invisible

invitation [ɪnvɪˈteɪʃən] n invitation f

invite [ɪnˈvaɪt] vt inviter; (opinions etc) demander; **inviting** adj engageant(e), attrayant(e)

invoice [ˈɪnvɔɪs] n facture f

involuntary [ɪnˈvɔləntrɪ] adj involontaire

involve [ɪnˈvɔlv] vt (entail) entraîner, nécessiter; (concern) concerner; (associate): **to ~ sb (in)** impliquer qn (dans), mêler qn (à); faire participer qn (à); **~d** adj (complicated) complexe; **to be ~d in** participer à; **~ment** n: **~ment (in)** participation f (à); rôle m (dans); (enthusiasm) enthousiasme m (pour)

inward [ˈɪnwəd] adj (thought, feeling) profond(e), intime; (movement) vers l'intérieur; **~(s)** adv vers l'intérieur

I/O abbr (COMPUT) (= input/output) E/S

iodine [ˈaɪədiːn] n iode m

iota [aɪˈəutə] n (fig) brin m, grain m

IOU n abbr (= I owe you) reconnaissance f de dette

IQ n abbr (= intelligence quotient) Q.I. m

IRA n abbr (= Irish Republican Army) IRA m

Iran [ɪˈrɑːn] n Iran m

Iraq [ɪˈrɑːk] n Irak m

irate [aɪˈreɪt] adj courroucé(e)

Ireland [ˈaɪələnd] n Irlande f

iris [ˈaɪrɪs] n (pl **~es**) n iris m

Irish [ˈaɪrɪʃ] adj irlandais(e) ♦ npl: **the ~** les Irlandais; **~man** (irreg) n Irlandais m; **~ Sea** n mer f d'Irlande; **~woman** (irreg) n Irlandaise f

iron [ˈaɪən] n fer m; (for clothes) fer m à repasser ♦ cpd de or en fer; (fig) de fer ♦ vt (clothes) repasser; **~ out** vt aplanir; faire disparaître

ironic(al) [aɪˈrɔnɪk(l)] adj ironique

ironing [ˈaɪənɪŋ] n repassage m; **~ board** n planche f à repasser

ironmonger's (shop) [ˈaɪənmʌŋgəz-] n quincaillerie f

irony [ˈaɪrənɪ] n ironie f

irrational [ɪˈræʃənl] adj irrationnel(le)

irregular [ɪˈregjulər] adj irrégulier(-ère); (surface) inégal(e)

irrelevant [ɪˈreləvənt] adj sans rapport, hors de propos

irresistible [ɪrɪˈzɪstɪbl] adj irrésistible

irrespective [ɪrɪˈspɛktɪv]: **~ of** prep sans tenir compte de

irresponsible [ɪrɪˈspɔnsɪbl] adj (act) irréfléchi(e); (person) irresponsable, inconscient(e)

irrigate [ˈɪrɪgeɪt] vt irriguer; **irrigation** [ɪrɪˈgeɪʃən] n irrigation f

irritate [ˈɪrɪteɪt] vt irriter

irritating [ˈɪrɪteɪtɪŋ] adj irritant(e); **irritation** [ɪrɪˈteɪʃən] n irritation f

IRS n abbr = **Internal Revenue Service**

is [ɪz] vb see **be**

Islam [ˈɪzlɑːm] n Islam m, **~ic** adj islamique; **~ic fundamentalists** intégristes mpl musulmans

island [ˈaɪlənd] n île f; **~er** n habitant(e) d'une île, insulaire m/f

isle [aɪl] n île f

isn't [ˈɪznt] = **is not**

isolate [ˈaɪsəleɪt] vt isoler; **~d** adj isolé(e); **isolation** n isolation f

Israel [ˈɪzreɪl] n Israël m; **~i** [ɪzˈreɪlɪ] adj israélien(ne) ♦ n Israélien(ne)

issue [ˈɪʃuː] n question f, problème m; (of book) publication f, parution f; (of banknotes etc) émission f; (of newspaper etc) numéro m ♦ vt (rations, equipment) distribuer; (statement) publier, faire; (banknotes etc) émettre, mettre en circulation; **at ~** en jeu, en cause; **to take ~ with sb (over)** exprimer son désaccord avec qn (sur); **to make an ~ of sth** faire une montagne de qch

---

KEYWORD

it [ɪt] pron **1** (specific: subject) il (elle); (: direct object) le (la) (l'); (: indirect object) lui; **it's**

on the table c'est or il (or elle) est sur la table; **about/from/of it** en; **I spoke to him about it** je lui en ai parlé; **what did you learn from it?** qu'est-ce que vous en avez retiré?; **I'm proud of it** j'en suis fier; **in/to it** y; **put the book in it** mettez-y le livre; **he agreed to it** il y a consenti; **did you go to it?** (party, concert etc) est-ce que vous y êtes allé(s)?

2 (impersonal) il; ce; **it's raining** il pleut; **it's Friday tomorrow** demain c'est vendredi or nous sommes vendredi; **it's 6 o'clock** il est 6 heures; **who is it? - it's me** qui est-ce? - c'est moi

Italian [ɪ'tæljən] adj italien(ne) ♦ n Italien(ne); (LING) italien m

italics [ɪ'tælɪks] npl italiques fpl

Italy ['ɪtəlɪ] n Italie f

itch [ɪtʃ] n démangeaison f ♦ vi (person) éprouver des démangeaisons; (part of body) démanger; **I'm ~ing to do** l'envie me démange de faire; **~y** adj qui démange; **to be ~y** avoir des démangeaisons

it'd ['ɪtd] = it would; it had

item ['aɪtəm] n article m; (on agenda) question f, point m; (also: **news ~**) nouvelle f; **~ize** vt détailler, faire une liste de

itinerary [aɪ'tɪnərərɪ] n itinéraire m

it'll ['ɪtl] = it will; it shall

its [ɪts] adj son (sa), ses pl

it's [ɪts] = it is; it has

itself [ɪt'sɛlf] pron (reflexive) se; (emphatic) lui-même (elle-même)

ITV n abbr (BRIT: Independent Television) chaîne privée

IUD n abbr (= intra-uterine device) DIU m, stérilet m

I've [aɪv] = I have

ivory ['aɪvərɪ] n ivoire m

ivy ['aɪvɪ] n lierre m

J, j

jab [dʒæb] vt: **to ~ sth into** enfoncer or planter qch dans ♦ n (inf: injection) piqûre f

jack [dʒæk] n (AUT) cric m; (CARDS) valet m; **~ up** vt soulever (au cric)

jackal ['dʒækl] n chacal m

jacket ['dʒækɪt] n veste f, veston m; (of book) jaquette f, couverture f; **~ potato** n pomme f de terre en robe des champs

jack: ~knife vi: **the lorry ~knifed** la remorque (du camion) s'est mise en travers; **~ plug** n (ELEC) prise jack mâle f; **~pot** n gros lot

jaded ['dʒeɪdɪd] adj éreinté(e), fatigué(e)

jagged ['dʒægɪd] adj dentelé(e)

jail [dʒeɪl] n prison f ♦ vt emprisonner, mettre en prison

jam [dʒæm] n confiture f; (also: **traffic ~**) embouteillage m ♦ vt (passage etc) encombrer, obstruer; (mechanism, drawer etc) bloquer, coincer; (RADIO) brouiller ♦ vi se coincer, se bloquer; (gun) s'enrayer; **to be in a ~** (inf) être dans le pétrin; **to ~ sth into** entasser qch dans; enfoncer qch dans

Jamaica [dʒə'meɪkə] n Jamaïque f

jam: ~ jar n pot m à confiture; **~med** adj (window etc) coincé(e); **~-packed** adj: **~-packed (with)** bourré(e) (de)

jangle ['dʒæŋgl] vi cliqueter

janitor ['dʒænɪtəʳ] n concierge m

January ['dʒænjuərɪ] n janvier m

Japan [dʒə'pæn] n Japon m; **~ese** [dʒæpə'ni:z] adj japonais(e) ♦ n inv Japonais(e); (LING) japonais m

jar [dʒɑːʳ] n (stone, earthenware) pot m; (glass) bocal m ♦ vi (sound discordant) produire un son grinçant or discordant; (colours etc) jurer

jargon ['dʒɑːgən] n jargon m

jaundice ['dʒɔːndɪs] n jaunisse f

javelin ['dʒævlɪn] n javelot m

jaw [dʒɔː] n mâchoire f

jay [dʒeɪ] n geai m; **~walker** n piéton indiscipliné

jazz [dʒæz] n jazz m; **~ up** vt animer, égayer

jealous ['dʒɛləs] adj jaloux(-ouse); **~y** n jalousie f

jeans [dʒiːnz] npl jean m

jeer [dʒɪəʳ] vi: **to ~ (at)** se moquer cruellement (de), railler

Jehovah's Witness [dʒɪ'həʊvəz-] n témoin m de Jéhovah

jelly ['dʒɛlɪ] n gelée f; **~fish** ['dʒɛlɪfɪʃ] n méduse f

jeopardy ['dʒɛpədɪ] n: **to be in ~** être en danger or péril

jerk [dʒɜːk] n secousse f; saccade f; sursaut m; spasme m; (inf: idiot) pauvre type m ♦ vt (pull) tirer brusquement ♦ vi (vehicles) cahoter

jersey ['dʒɜːzɪ] n (pullover) tricot m; (fabric) jersey m

Jesus ['dʒiːzəs] n Jésus

jet [dʒɛt] n (gas, liquid) jet m; (AVIAT) avion m à réaction, jet m; **~-black** adj (d'un noir) de jais; **~ engine** n moteur m à réaction; **~ lag** n (fatigue due au) décalage m horaire

jettison ['dʒɛtɪsn] vt jeter par-dessus bord

jetty ['dʒɛtɪ] n jetée f, digue f

Jew [dʒuː] n Juif m

jewel ['dʒuːəl] n bijou m, joyau m; (in watch) rubis m; **~ler** (US **jeweler**) n bijoutier(-ère), joaillier m; **~ler's (shop)** n bijouterie f, joaillerie f; **~lery** (US **jewelry**) n bijoux mpl

Jewess ['dʒuːɪs] n Juive f

Jewish ['dʒu:ɪʃ] *adj* juif (juive)

jibe [dʒaɪb] *n* sarcasme *m*

jiffy ['dʒɪfɪ] (*inf*) *n*: **in a ~** en un clin d'œil

jigsaw ['dʒɪgsɔː] *n* (*also*: ~ **puzzle**) puzzle *m*

jilt [dʒɪlt] *vt* laisser tomber, plaquer

jingle ['dʒɪŋgl] *n* (*for advert*) couplet *m* publicitaire ♦ *vi* cliqueter, tinter

jinx [dʒɪŋks] (*inf*) *n* (*mauvais*) sort

jitters ['dʒɪtəz] (*inf*) *npl*: **to get the ~** (*inf*) avoir la trouille *or* la frousse

job [dʒɔb] *n* (*chore, task*) travail *m*, tâche *f*; (*employment*) emploi *m*, poste *m*, place *f*; **it's a good ~ that** ... c'est heureux *or* c'est une chance que ...; **just the ~!** (c'est) juste *or* exactement ce qu'il faut!; **~ centre** (*BRIT*) *n* agence *f* pour l'emploi; **~less** *adj* sans travail, au chômage

jockey ['dʒɔkɪ] *n* jockey *m* ♦ *vi*: **to ~ for position** manœuvrer pour être bien placé

jog [dʒɔg] *vt* secouer ♦ *vi* (*SPORT*) faire du jogging; **to ~ sb's memory** rafraîchir la mémoire de qn; **~ along** *vi* cheminer; trotter; **~ging** *n* jogging *m*

join [dʒɔɪn] *vt* (*put together*) unir, assembler; (*become member of*) s'inscrire à; (*meet*) rejoindre, retrouver; (*queue*) se joindre à ♦ *vi* (*roads, rivers*) se rejoindre, se rencontrer ♦ *n* raccord *m*; **~ in** *vi* se mettre de la partie, participer ♦ *vt fus* participer à, se mêler à; **~ up** *vi* (*meet*) se rejoindre; (*MIL*) s'engager

joiner ['dʒɔɪnə'] (*BRIT*) *n* menuisier *m*

joint [dʒɔɪnt] *n* (*TECH*) jointure *f*; joint *m*; (*ANAT*) articulation *f*, jointure, (*BRIT: CULIN*) rôti *m*; (*inf: place*) boîte *f*; (: *of cannabis*) joint *m* ♦ *adj* commun(e); **~ account** *n* (*with bank etc*) compte joint

joke [dʒəuk] *n* plaisanterie *f*; (*also*: **practical ~**) farce *f* ♦ *vi* plaisanter; **to play a ~ on** jouer un tour à, faire une farce à; **~r** *n* (*CARDS*) joker *m*

jolly ['dʒɔlɪ] *adj* gai(e), enjoué(e); (*enjoyable*) amusant(e), plaisant(e) ♦ *adv* (*BRIT: inf*) rudement, drôlement

jolt [dʒəult] *n* cahot *m*, secousse *f*; (*shock*) choc *m* ♦ *vt* cahoter, secouer

Jordan ['dʒɔːdən] *n* (*country*) Jordanie *f*

jostle ['dʒɔsl] *vt* bousculer, pousser

jot [dʒɔt] *n*: **not one ~** pas un brin; **~ down** *vt* noter; **~ter** (*BRIT*) *n* cahier *m* (de brouillon); (*pad*) bloc-notes *m*

journal ['dʒɔːnl] *n* journal *m*; **~ism** *n* journalisme *m*; **~ist** *n* journaliste *m/f*

journey ['dʒɔːnɪ] *n* voyage *m*; (*distance covered*) trajet *m*

joy [dʒɔɪ] *n* joie *f*; **~ful** *adj* joyeux(-euse); **~rider** *n* personne qui fait une virée dans une voiture volée; **~stick** *n* (*AVIAT, COMPUT*) manche *m* à balai

JP *n abbr* = **Justice of the Peace**

Jr *abbr* = **junior**

jubilant ['dʒuːbɪlnt] *adj* triomphant(e); réjoui(e)

judge [dʒʌdʒ] *n* juge *m* ♦ *vt* juger; **judg(e)ment** *n* jugement *m*

judicial [dʒuː'dɪʃl] *adj* judiciaire; **judiciary** *n* (*pouvoir m*) judiciaire *n*

judo ['dʒuːdəu] *n* judo *m*

jug [dʒʌg] *n* pot *m*, cruche *f*

juggernaut ['dʒʌgənɔːt] (*BRIT*) *n* (*huge truck*) énorme poids lourd

juggle ['dʒʌgl] *vi* jongler; **~r** *n* jongleur *m*

juice [dʒuːs] *n* jus *m*; **juicy** *adj* juteux(-euse)

jukebox ['dʒuːkbɔks] *n* juke-box *m*

July [dʒuːˈlaɪ] *n* juillet *m*

jumble ['dʒʌmbl] *n* fouillis *m* ♦ *vt* (*also*: ~ **up**) mélanger, brouiller; **~ sale** (*BRIT*) *n* vente *f* de charité

jumbo (jet) ['dʒʌmbəu-] *n* jumbo-jet *m*, gros porteur

jump [dʒʌmp] *vi* sauter, bondir; (*start*) sursauter; (*increase*) monter en flèche ♦ *vt* sauter, franchir ♦ *n* saut *m*, bond *m*, sursaut *m*; **to ~ the queue** (*BRIT*) passer avant son tour

jumper ['dʒʌmpə'] *n* (*BRIT: pullover*) pull-over *m*; (*US: dress*) robe-chasuble *f*

jumper cables (*US*), **jump leads** (*BRIT*) *npl* câbles *mpl* de démarrage

jumpy ['dʒʌmpɪ] *adj* nerveux(-euse), agité(e)

Jun. *abbr* = **junior**

junction ['dʒʌŋkʃən] (*BRIT*) *n* (*of roads*) carrefour *m*; (*of rails*) embranchement *m*

juncture ['dʒʌŋktʃə'] *n*: **at this ~** à ce moment-là, sur ces entrefaites

June [dʒuːn] *n* juin *m*

jungle ['dʒʌŋgl] *n* jungle *f*

junior ['dʒuːnɪə'] *adj*, *n*: **he's ~ to me (by 2 years)**, **he's my ~ (by 2 years)** il est mon cadet (de 2 ans), il est plus jeune que moi (de 2 ans); **he's ~ to me (seniority)** il est en dessous de moi (dans la hiérarchie), j'ai plus d'ancienneté que lui; **~ school** (*BRIT*) *n* ≈ école *f* primaire

junk [dʒʌŋk] *n* (*rubbish*) camelote *f*; (*cheap goods*) bric à brac *m inv*; **~ food** *n* aliments *mpl* sans grande valeur nutritive; **~ mail** *n* prospectus *mpl* (non sollicités); **~ shop** *n* (boutique *f* de) brocanteur *m*

Junr *abbr* = **junior**

juror ['dʒuərə'] *n* juré *m*

jury ['dʒuərɪ] *n* jury *m*

just [dʒʌst] *adj* juste ♦ *adv*: **he's ~ done it/left** il vient de le faire/partir; **~ right/two o'clock** exactement *or* juste ce qu'il faut/deux heures; **she's ~ as clever as you** elle est tout aussi intelligente que vous; **it's ~ as well (that)** ... heureusement que ...; **~ as he was leaving** au moment or à l'instant précis où il partait; **~ before/enough/here** juste avant/assez/ici; **it's ~ me/a mistake** ce n'est que moi/(rien)

qu'une erreur; **~ missed/caught** manqué/
attrapé de justesse; **~ listen to this!** écoutez
un peu ça!
justice ['dʒʌstɪs] n justice f; (US: judge) juge
m de la Cour suprême; **J~ of the Peace** n
juge m de paix
justify ['dʒʌstɪfaɪ] vt justifier
jut [dʒʌt] vi (also: ~ out) dépasser, faire saillie
juvenile ['dʒuːvənaɪl] adj juvénile; (court,
books) pour enfants ♦ n adolescent(e)

K, k

K abbr (= one thousand) K; (= kilobyte) Ko
kangaroo [kæŋgə'ruː] n kangourou m
karate [kə'rɑːtɪ] n karaté m
kebab [kə'bæb] n kébab m
keel [kiːl] n quille f; **on an even ~** (fig) à flot
keen [kiːn] adj (eager) plein(e)
d'enthousiasme; (interest, desire, competition)
vif (vive); (eye, intelligence) pénétrant(e);
(edge) effilé(e); **to be ~ to do** or **on doing sth**
désirer vivement faire qch, tenir beaucoup à
faire qch; **to be ~ on sth/sb** aimer beaucoup
qch/qn
keep [kiːp] (pt, pp kept) vt (retain, preserve)
garder; (detain) retenir; (shop, accounts,
diary, promise) tenir; (house) avoir; (support)
entretenir; (chickens, bees etc) élever ♦ vi
(remain) rester; (food) se conserver ♦ n (of
castle) donjon m; (food etc): **enough for his ~**
assez pour (assurer) sa subsistance; (inf): **for
~s** pour de bon, pour toujours; **to ~ doing sth**
ne pas arrêter de faire qch; **to ~ sb from
doing** empêcher qn de faire or que qn ne
fasse; **to ~ sb happy/a place tidy** faire que qn
soit content/qu'un endroit reste propre; **to ~
sth to o.s.** garder qch pour soi, tenir qch
secret; **to ~ sth (back) from sb** cacher qch à
qn; **to ~ time** (clock) être à l'heure, ne pas
retarder; **well kept** bien entretenu(e); **~ on**
vi: **to ~ on doing** continuer à faire; **don't ~ on
about it!** arrête (d'en parler)!; **~ out** vt
empêcher d'entrer; **"~ out"** "défense
d'entrer"; **~ up** vt continuer, maintenir ♦ vi:
to ~ up with sb (in race etc) aller aussi vite
que qn; (in work etc) se maintenir au niveau
de qn; **~er** n gardien(ne); **~-fit** n
gymnastique f d'entretien; **~ing** n (care)
garde f; **in ~ing with** en accord avec; **~sake**
n souvenir m
kennel ['kɛnl] n niche f; **~s** npl (boarding ~s)
chenil m
kerb [kəːb] (BRIT) n bordure f du trottoir
kernel ['kəːnl] n (of nut) amande f; (fig)
noyau m
kettle ['kɛtl] n bouilloire f; **~drum** n timbale f
key [kiː] n (gen, MUS) clé f; (of piano,

typewriter) touche f ♦ cpd clé ♦ vt (also: ~ in)
introduire (au clavier), saisir; **~board** n
clavier m; **~ed up** adj (person) surexcité(e);
~hole n trou m de la serrure; **~hole
surgery** n chirurgie très minutieuse où
l'incision est minimale; **~note** n (of speech)
note dominante; (MUS) tonique f; **~ ring** n
porte-clés m
khaki ['kɑːkɪ] n kaki m
kick [kɪk] vt donner un coup de pied à ♦ vi
(horse) ruer ♦ n coup m de pied; (thrill): **he
does it for ~s** il le fait parce que ça l'excite, il
le fait pour le plaisir; **to ~ the habit** (inf)
arrêter; **~ off** vi (SPORT) donner le coup
d'envoi
kid [kɪd] n (inf: child) gamin(e), gosse m/f;
(animal, leather) chevreau m ♦ vi (inf)
plaisanter, blaguer
kidnap ['kɪdnæp] vt enlever, kidnapper; **~per**
n ravisseur(-euse); **~ping** n enlèvement m
kidney ['kɪdnɪ] n (ANAT) rein m; (CULIN)
rognon m
kill [kɪl] vt tuer ♦ n mise f à mort; **~er** n
tueur(-euse); meurtrier(-ère); **~ing** n meurtre
m; (of group of people) tuerie f, massacre m;
to make a ~ing (inf) réussir un beau coup (de
filet); **~joy** n rabat-joie m/f
kiln [kɪln] n four m
kilo ['kiːləu] n kilo m; **~byte** n (COMPUT) kilo-
octet m; **~gram(me)** n kilogramme m;
~metre (US **kilometer**) n kilomètre m; **~watt**
n kilowatt m
kilt [kɪlt] n kilt m
kin [kɪn] n see next
kind [kaɪnd] adj gentil(le), aimable ♦ n sorte f,
espèce f, genre m; **to be two of a ~** se
ressembler; **in ~** (COMM) en nature
kindergarten ['kɪndəgɑːtn] n jardin m
d'enfants
kind-hearted [kaɪnd'hɑːtɪd] adj bon
(bonne)
kindle ['kɪndl] vt allumer, enflammer
kindly ['kaɪndlɪ] adj bienveillant(e), plein(e)
de gentillesse ♦ adv avec bonté; **will you ~ ...!**
auriez-vous la bonté or l'obligeance de ...?
kindness ['kaɪndnɪs] n bonté f, gentillesse f
king [kɪŋ] n roi m; **~dom** n royaume m;
~fisher n martin-pêcheur m; **~-size bed** n
grand lit (de 1,95 m de large); **~-size(d)** adj
format géant inv; (cigarettes) long (longue)
kiosk ['kiːɔsk] n kiosque m; (BRIT: TEL) cabine f
(téléphonique)
kipper ['kɪpə'] n hareng fumé et salé
kiss [kɪs] n baiser m ♦ vt embrasser; **to ~ (each
other)** s'embrasser; **~ of life** (BRIT) n bouche
à bouche m
kit [kɪt] n équipement m, matériel m; (set of
tools etc) trousse f; (for assembly) kit m
kitchen ['kɪtʃɪn] n cuisine f; **~ sink** n évier m

kite [kaɪt] n (toy) cerf-volant m
kitten ['kɪtn] n chaton m, petit chat
kitty ['kɪtɪ] n (money) cagnotte f
km abbr = **kilometre**
knack [næk] n: **to have the ~ of doing** avoir le coup pour faire
knapsack ['næpsæk] n musette f
knead [niːd] vt pétrir
knee [niː] n genou m; **~cap** n rotule f
kneel [niːl] (pt, pp knelt) vi (also: ~ **down**) s'agenouiller
knew [njuː] pt of **know**
knickers ['nɪkəz] (BRIT) npl culotte f (de femme)
knife [naɪf] (pl knives) n couteau m ♦ vt poignarder, frapper d'un coup de couteau
knight [naɪt] n chevalier m; (CHESS) cavalier m; **~hood** (BRIT) n (title): **to get a ~hood** être fait chevalier
knit [nɪt] vt tricoter ♦ vi tricoter; (broken bones) se ressouder; **to ~ one's brows** froncer les sourcils; **~ting** n tricot m; **~ting needle** n aiguille f à tricoter; **~wear** n tricots mpl, lainages mpl
knives [naɪvz] npl of **knife**
knob [nɔb] n bouton m
knock [nɔk] vt frapper; (bump into) heurter; (inf) dénigrer ♦ vi (at door etc): **to ~ at** or **on** frapper à ♦ n coup m; **~ down** vt renverser; **~ off** vi (inf: finish) s'arrêter (de travailler) ♦ vt (from price) faire un rabais de; (inf: steal) piquer; **~ out** vt assommer; (BOXING) mettre k.-o.; (defeat) éliminer; **~ over** vt renverser, faire tomber; **~er** n (on door) heurtoir m; **~out** n (BOXING) knock-out m, K.-O. m; **~out competition** compétition f avec épreuves éliminatoires
knot [nɔt] n (gen) nœud m ♦ vt nouer
know [nəu] (pt knew, pp known) vt savoir; (person, place) connaître; **to ~ how to do** savoir (comment) faire; **to ~ how to swim** savoir nager; **to ~ about** or **of sth** être au courant de qch; **to ~ about** or **of sb** avoir entendu parler de qn; **~-all** n (pej) je-sais-tout m/f; **~-how** n savoir-faire m; **~ing** adj (look etc) entendu(e); **~ingly** adv sciemment; (smile, look) d'un air entendu
knowledge ['nɔlɪdʒ] n connaissance f; (learning) connaissances, savoir m; **~able** adj bien informé(e)
knuckle ['nʌkl] n articulation f (des doigts), jointure f
Koran [kɔ'rɑːn] n Coran m
Korea [kə'rɪə] n Corée f
kosher ['kəuʃər] adj kascher inv

L, l

L abbr (= lake, large) L; (= left) g; (BRIT: AUT: learner) signale un conducteur débutant
lab [læb] n abbr (= laboratory) labo m
label ['leɪbl] n étiquette f ♦ vt étiqueter
labor etc ['leɪbər] (US) = **labour** etc
laboratory [lə'bɔrətərɪ] n laboratoire m
labour ['leɪbər] (US **labor**) n (work) travail m; (workforce) main-d'œuvre f ♦ vi: **to ~ (at)** travailler dur (à), peiner (sur) ♦ vt: **to ~ a point** insister sur un point; **in ~** (MED) en travail, en train d'accoucher; **L~, the L~ party** (BRIT) le parti travailliste, les travaillistes mpl; **~ed** ['leɪbəd] adj (breathing) pénible, difficile; **~er** n manœuvre m; **farm ~er** ouvrier m agricole
lace [leɪs] n dentelle f; (of shoe etc) lacet m ♦ vt (shoe: also: ~ **up**) lacer
lack [læk] n manque m ♦ vt manquer de; **through** or **for ~ of** faute de, par manque de; **to be ~ing** manquer, faire défaut; **to be ~ing in** manquer de
lacquer ['lækər] n laque f
lad [læd] n garçon m, gars m
ladder ['lædər] n échelle f; (BRIT: in tights) maille filée
laden ['leɪdn] adj: ~ (**with**) chargé(e) (de)
ladle ['leɪdl] n louche f
lady ['leɪdɪ] n dame f; (in address): **ladies and gentlemen** Mesdames (et) Messieurs; **young ~** jeune fille f; (married) jeune femme f; **the ladies' (room)** les toilettes fpl (pour dames); **~bird** (US **ladybug**) n coccinelle f; **~like** adj distingué(e); **~ship** n: **your ~ship** Madame la comtesse/la baronne etc
lag [læg] n retard m ♦ vi (also: ~ **behind**) rester en arrière, traîner; (fig) rester en traîne ♦ vt (pipes) calorifuger
lager ['lɑːgər] n bière blonde
lagoon [lə'guːn] n lagune f
laid [leɪd] pt, pp of **lay**; **~-back** (inf) adj relaxe, décontracté(e); **~ up** adj alité(e)
lain [leɪn] pp of **lie**
lake [leɪk] n lac m
lamb [læm] n agneau m; **~ chop** n côtelette f d'agneau
lame [leɪm] adj boiteux(-euse)
lament [lə'ment] n lamentation f ♦ vt pleurer, se lamenter sur
laminated ['læmɪneɪtɪd] adj laminé(e); (windscreen) (en verre) feuilleté
lamp [læmp] n lampe f; **~post** (BRIT) n réverbère m; **~shade** n abat-jour m inv
lance [lɑːns] vt (MED) inciser
land [lænd] n (as opposed to sea) terre f (ferme); (soil) terre; terrain m; (estate)

terre(s), domaine(s) m(pl); (country) pays m
♦ vi (AVIAT) atterrir; (fig) (re)tomber ♦ vt
(passengers, goods) débarquer; **to ~ sb with
sth** (inf) coller qch à qn; **~ up** vi atterrir,
(finir par) se retrouver; **~fill site** n décharge
f; **~ing** n (AVIAT) atterrissage m; (of staircase)
palier m; (of troops) débarquement m; **~ing
strip** n piste f d'atterrissage; **~lady** n
propriétaire f, logeuse f; (of pub) patronne f;
~locked adj sans littoral; **~lord** n
propriétaire m, logeur m; (of pub etc) patron
m; **~mark** n (point m de) repère m; **to be a
~mark** (fig) faire date or époque; **~owner** n
propriétaire foncier or terrien; **~scape** n
paysage m; **~scape gardener** n jardin-
ier(-ère) paysagiste; **~slide** n (GEO)
glissement m (de terrain); (fig: POL) raz-de-
marée (électoral)

lane [leɪn] n (in country) chemin m; (AUT) voie
f; file f; (in race) couloir m; **"get in ~"** (AUT)
"mettez-vous dans or sur la bonne file"

language ['læŋgwɪdʒ] n langue f; (way one
speaks) langage m; **bad ~** grossièretés fpl,
langage grossier; **~ laboratory** n laboratoire
m de langues

lank [læŋk] adj (hair) raide et terne

lanky ['læŋkɪ] adj grand(e) et maigre,
efflanqué(e)

lantern ['læntən] n lanterne f

lap [læp] n (of track) tour m (de piste); (of
body): **in** or **on one's ~** sur les genoux ♦ vt
(also: **~ up**) laper ♦ vi (waves) clapoter; **~ up**
vt (fig) accepter béatement, gober

lapel [lə'pɛl] n revers m

Lapland ['læplænd] n Laponie f

lapse [læps] n défaillance f; (in behaviour)
écart m de conduite ♦ vi (LAW) cesser d'être
en vigueur; (contract) expirer; **to ~ into bad
habits** prendre de mauvaises habitudes; **~ of
time** laps m de temps, intervalle m

laptop (computer) ['læptɔp(-)] n portable
m

larceny ['lɑːsənɪ] n vol m

larch [lɑːtʃ] n mélèze m

lard [lɑːd] n saindoux m

larder ['lɑːdəʳ] n garde-manger m inv

large [lɑːdʒ] adj grand(e); (person, animal)
gros(se); **at ~** (free) en liberté; (generally) en
général; see also **by**; **~ly** adv en grande
partie; (principally) surtout; **~-scale** adj
(action) d'envergure; (map) à grande échelle

lark [lɑːk] n (bird) alouette f; (joke) blague f,
farce f

laryngitis [lærɪn'dʒaɪtɪs] n laryngite f

laser ['leɪzəʳ] n laser m; **~ printer** n
imprimante f laser

lash [læʃ] n coup m de fouet; (also: **eyelash**)
cil m ♦ vt fouetter; (tie) attacher; **~ out** vi: **to
~ out at** or **against** attaquer violemment

lass [læs] (BRIT) n (jeune) fille f

lasso [læ'suː] n lasso m

last [lɑːst] adj dernier(-ère) ♦ adv en dernier;
(finally) finalement ♦ vi durer; **~ week** la
semaine dernière; **~ night** (evening) hier soir;
(night) la nuit dernière; **at ~** enfin; **~ but one**
avant-dernier(-ère); **~-ditch** adj (attempt)
ultime, désespéré(e); **~ing** adj durable; **~ly**
adv en dernier lieu, pour finir; **~-minute** adj
de dernière minute

latch [lætʃ] n loquet m

late [leɪt] adj (not on time) en retard; (far on
in day etc) tardif(-ive); (edition, delivery)
dernier(-ère); (former) ancien(ne) ♦ adv tard;
(behind time, schedule) en retard; **of ~**
dernièrement; **in ~ May** vers la fin (du mois)
de mai, fin mai; **the ~ Mr X** feu M. X;
~comer n retardataire m/f; **~ly** adv
récemment; **~r** adj (date etc) ultérieur(e);
(version etc) plus récent(e) ♦ adv plus tard; **~r
on** plus tard; **~st** adj tout(e) dernier(-ère); **at
the ~st** au plus tard

lathe [leɪð] n tour m

lather ['lɑːðəʳ] n mousse f (de savon) ♦ vt
savonner

Latin ['lætɪn] n latin m ♦ adj latin(e);
~ America n Amérique latine; **~ American**
adj latino-américain(e)

latitude ['lætɪtjuːd] n latitude f

latter ['lætəʳ] adj deuxième, dernier(-ère) ♦ n:
the ~ ce dernier, celui-ci; **~ly** adv
dernièrement, récemment

laudable ['lɔːdəbl] adj louable

laugh [lɑːf] n rire m ♦ vi rire; **~ at** vt fus se
moquer de; rire de; **~ off** vt écarter par une
plaisanterie or par une boutade; **~able** adj
risible, ridicule; **~ing stock** n: **the ~ing stock
of** la risée de; **~ter** n rire m; rires mpl

launch [lɔːntʃ] n lancement m; (motorboat)
vedette f ♦ vt lancer; **~ into** vt fus se lancer
dans

Launderette ® [lɔːn'drɛt] (BRIT),
Laundromat ® ['lɔːndrəmæt] (US) n laverie
f (automatique)

laundry ['lɔːndrɪ] n (clothes) linge m;
(business) blanchisserie f; (room) buanderie f

laurel ['lɔrl] n laurier m

lava ['lɑːvə] n lave f

lavatory ['lævətərɪ] n toilettes fpl

lavender ['lævəndəʳ] n lavande f

lavish ['lævɪʃ] adj (amount) copieux(-euse);
(person): **~ with** prodigue de ♦ vt: **to ~ sth
on sb** prodiguer qch à qn; (money) dépenser
qch sans compter pour qn/qch

law [lɔː] n loi f; (science) droit m; **~-abiding**
adj respectueux(-euse) des lois; **~ and order**
n l'ordre public; **~ court** n tribunal m, cour f
de justice; **~ful** adj légal(e); **~less** adj
(action) illégal(e)

lawn [lɔ:n] n pelouse f; **~mower** n tondeuse f à gazon; **~ tennis** n tennis m

law school (US) n faculté f de droit

lawsuit ['lɔ:su:t] n procès m

lawyer ['lɔ:jəʳ] n (consultant, with company) juriste m; (for sales, wills etc) notaire m; (partner, in court) avocat m

lax [læks] adj relâché(e)

laxative ['læksətɪv] n laxatif m

lay [leɪ] (pt, pp laid) pt of lie ♦ adj laïque; (not expert) profane ♦ vt poser, mettre; (eggs) pondre; **to ~ the table** mettre la table; **~ aside** vt mettre de côté; **~ by** vt = lay aside; **~ down** vt poser; **to ~ down the law** faire la loi; **to ~ down one's life** sacrifier sa vie; **~ off** vt (workers) licencier; **~ on** vt (provide) fournir; **~ out** vt (display) disposer, étaler; **~about** (inf) n fainéant(e); **~-by** (BRIT) n aire f de stationnement (sur le bas-côté)

layer ['leɪəʳ] n couche f

layman ['leɪmən] (irreg) n profane m

layout ['leɪaut] n disposition f, plan m, agencement m; (PRESS) mise f en page

laze [leɪz] vi (also: **~ about**) paresser

lazy ['leɪzɪ] adj paresseux(-euse)

lb abbr = **pound** (weight)

lead[1] [li:d] (pt, pp led) n (distance, time ahead) avance f; (clue) piste f; (THEATRE) rôle principal; (ELEC) fil m; (for dog) laisse f ♦ vt mener, conduire; (be ~er of) être à la tête de ♦ vi (street etc) mener, conduire; (SPORT) mener, être en tête; **in the ~** en tête; **to ~ the way** montrer le chemin; **~ away** vt emmener; **~ back** vt: **to ~ back to** ramener à; **~ on** vt (tease) faire marcher; **~ to** vt fus mener à; conduire à; **~ up to** vt fus conduire à

lead[2] [led] n (metal) plomb m; (in pencil) mine f; **~ed petrol** n essence f au plomb; **~en** adj (sky, sea) de plomb

leader ['li:dəʳ] n chef m; dirigeant(e), leader m; (SPORT: in league) leader; (: in race) coureur m de tête, **~ship** n direction f; (quality) qualités fpl de chef

lead-free ['ledfri:] adj (petrol) sans plomb

leading ['li:dɪŋ] adj principal(e); de premier plan; (in race) de tête; **~ lady** n (THEATRE) vedette (féminine); **~ light** n (person) vedette f, sommité f; **~ man** (irreg) n vedette (masculine)

lead singer [li:d-] n (in pop group) (chanteur m) vedette f

leaf [li:f] (pl leaves) n feuille f ♦ vi: **to ~ through** feuilleter; **to turn over a new ~** changer de conduite or d'existence

leaflet ['li:flɪt] n prospectus m, brochure f; (POL, REL) tract m

league [li:g] n ligue f; (FOOTBALL)

championnat m; **to be in ~ with** avoir partie liée avec, être de mèche avec

leak [li:k] n fuite f ♦ vi (pipe, liquid etc) fuir; (shoes) prendre l'eau; (ship) faire eau ♦ vt (information) divulguer

lean [li:n] (pt, pp leaned or leant) adj maigre ♦ vt: **to ~ sth on sth** appuyer qch sur qch ♦ vi (slope) pencher; (rest): **to ~ against** s'appuyer contre; être appuyé(e) contre; **to ~ on** s'appuyer sur; **to ~ back/forward** se pencher en arrière/avant; **~ out** vi se pencher au dehors; **~ over** vi se pencher; **~ing** n: **~ing (towards)** tendance f (à), penchant m (pour); **~t** [lent] pt, pp of lean

leap [li:p] (pt, pp leaped or leapt) n bond m, saut m ♦ vi bondir, sauter; **~frog** n saute-mouton m; **~t** [lept] pt, pp of leap; **~ year** n année f bissextile

learn [lə:n] (pt, pp learned or learnt) vt, vi apprendre; **to ~ to do sth** apprendre à faire qch; **to ~ about or of sth** (hear, read) apprendre qch; **~ed** ['lə:nɪd] adj érudit(e), savant(e); **~er** (BRIT) n (also: **~er driver**) (conducteur(-trice)) débutant(e); **~ing** n (knowledge) savoir m; **~t** pt, pp of learn

lease [li:s] n bail m ♦ vt louer à bail

leash [li:ʃ] n laisse f

least [li:st] adj: **the ~** (+noun) le (la) plus petit(e), le (la) moindre; (: smallest amount of) le moins de ♦ adv (+verb) le moins; (+adj): **the ~** le (la) moins; **at ~** au moins; (or rather) du moins, **not in the ~** pas le moins du monde

leather ['leðəʳ] n cuir m

leave [li:v] (pt, pp left) vt laisser; (go away from) quitter; (forget) oublier ♦ vi partir, s'en aller ♦ n (time off) congé m; (MIL also: consent) permission f; **to be left** rester; **there's some milk left over** il en reste du lait; **on ~** en permission; **~ behind** vt (person, object) laisser; (forget) oublier; **~ out** vt oublier, omettre; **~ of absence** n congé exceptionnel; (MIL) permission spéciale

leaves [li:vz] npl of leaf

Lebanon ['lɛbənən] n Liban m

lecherous ['lɛtʃərəs] (pej) adj lubrique

lecture ['lɛktʃəʳ] n conférence f; (SCOL) cours m ♦ vi donner des cours; enseigner ♦ vt (scold) sermonner, réprimander; **to give a ~** on faire une conférence sur; donner un cours sur; **~r** (BRIT) n (at university) professeur m (d'université)

led [led] pt, pp of lead[1]

ledge [ledʒ] n (of window, on wall) rebord m; (of mountain) saillie f, corniche f

ledger ['ledʒəʳ] n (COMM) registre m, grand livre

leech [li:tʃ] n (also fig) sangsue f

leek [li:k] n poireau m

leer [lɪəʳ] vi: **to ~ at sb** regarder qn d'un air mauvais or concupiscent

leeway ['liːweɪ] n (fig): **to have some ~** avoir une certaine liberté d'action

left [left] pt, pp of **leave ♦** adj (not right) gauche **♦** n gauche f **♦** adv à gauche; **on the ~, to the ~** à gauche; **the L~** (POL) la gauche; **~-handed** adj gaucher(-ère); **~-hand side** n gauche f; **~-luggage locker** n (casier m à) consigne f automatique; **~-luggage (office)** (BRIT) n consigne f; **~overs** npl restes mpl; **~-wing** adj (POL) de gauche

leg [leg] n jambe f; (of animal) patte f; (of furniture) pied m; (CULIN: of chicken, pork) cuisse f; (: of lamb) gigot m; (of journey) étape f; **1st/2nd ~** (SPORT) match m aller/retour

legacy ['legəsɪ] n héritage m, legs m

legal ['liːgl] adj légal(e); **~ holiday** (US) n jour férié; **~ tender** n monnaie légale

legend ['ledʒənd] n légende f

leggings ['legɪŋz] npl caleçon m

legible ['ledʒəbl] adj lisible

legislation [ledʒɪs'leɪʃən] n législation f; **legislature** ['ledʒɪslətʃəʳ] n (corps m) législatif m

legitimate [lɪ'dʒɪtɪmət] adj légitime

leg-room ['legruːm] n place f pour les jambes

leisure ['leʒəʳ] n loisir m, temps m libre; loisirs mpl; **at ~** (tout) à loisir; à tête reposée; **~ centre** n centre m de loisirs; **~ly** adj tranquille; fait(e) sans se presser

lemon ['lemən] n citron m; **~ade** [lemə'neɪd] n limonade f; **~ tea** n thé m au citron

lend [lend] (pt, pp lent) vt: **to ~ sth (to sb)** prêter qch (à qn)

length [leŋθ] n longueur f; (section: of road, pipe etc) morceau m, bout m; (of time) durée f; **at ~** (at last) enfin, à la fin; (~ily) longuement; **~en** vt allonger, prolonger **♦** vi s'allonger; **~ways** adv dans le sens de la longueur, en long; **~y** adj (très) long (longue)

lenient ['liːnɪənt] adj indulgent(e), clément(e)

lens [lenz] n lentille f; (of spectacles) verre m; (of camera) objectif m

Lent [lent] n carême m

lent [lent] pt, pp of **lend**

lentil ['lentɪl] n lentille f

Leo ['liːəu] n le Lion

leotard ['liːətɑːd] n maillot m (de danseur etc), collant m

leprosy ['leprəsɪ] n lèpre f

lesbian ['lezbɪən] n lesbienne f

less [les] adj moins de **♦** pron, adv moins **♦** prep moins; **~ than that/you** moins que cela/vous; **~ than half** moins de la moitié; **~ than ever** moins que jamais; **~ and ~** de

moins en moins; **the ~ he works ...** moins il travaille ...; **~en** vi diminuer, s'atténuer **♦** vt diminuer, réduire, atténuer; **~er** adj moindre; **to a ~er extent** à un degré moindre

lesson ['lesn] n leçon f; **to teach sb a ~** (fig) donner une bonne leçon à qn

let [let] (pt, pp let) vt laisser; (BRIT: lease) louer; **to ~ sb do sth** laisser qn faire qch; **to ~ sb know sth** faire savoir qch à qn, prévenir qn de qch; **~'s go** allons-y; **~ him come** qu'il vienne; **"to ~"** "à louer"; **~ down** vt (tyre) dégonfler; (person) décevoir, faire faux bond à; **~ go** vi lâcher prise **♦** vt lâcher; **~ in** vt laisser entrer; (visitor etc) faire entrer; **~ off** vt (culprit) ne pas punir; (firework etc) faire partir; **~ on** (inf) vi dire; **~ out** vt laisser sortir; (scream) laisser échapper; **~ up** vi diminuer; (cease) s'arrêter

lethal ['liːθl] adj mortel(le), fatal(e)

letter ['letəʳ] n lettre f; **~ bomb** n lettre piégée; **~box** (BRIT) n boîte f aux or à lettres; **~ing** n lettres fpl; caractères mpl

lettuce ['letɪs] n laitue f, salade f

let-up ['letʌp] n répit m, arrêt m

leukaemia [luː'kiːmɪə] (US **leukemia**) n leucémie f

level ['levl] adj plat(e), plan(e), uni(e); horizontal(e) **♦** n niveau m **♦** vt niveler, aplanir; **to be ~ with** être au même niveau que; **to draw ~ with** (person, vehicle) arriver à la hauteur de; **"A" ~s** (BRIT) ≈ baccalauréat m; **"O" ~s** (BRIT) ≈ B.E.P.C.; **on the ~** (fig: honest) régulier(-ère); **~ off** vi (prices etc) se stabiliser; **~ out** vi = level off; **~ crossing** (BRIT) n passage m à niveau; **~-headed** adj équilibré(e)

lever ['liːvəʳ] n levier m; **~age** n: **~age (on** or **with)** prise f (sur)

levy ['levɪ] n taxe f, impôt m **♦** vt prélever, imposer; percevoir

lewd [luːd] adj obscène, lubrique

liability [laɪə'bɪlətɪ] n responsabilité f; (handicap) handicap m; **liabilities** npl (on balance sheet) passif m

liable ['laɪəbl] adj (subject): **~ to** sujet(te) à; passible de; (responsible): **~ (for)** responsable (de); (likely): **~ to do** susceptible de faire

liaise [liː'eɪz] vi: **to ~ (with)** assurer la liaison avec; **liaison** n liaison f

liar ['laɪəʳ] n menteur(-euse)

libel ['laɪbl] n diffamation f; (document) écrit m diffamatoire **♦** vt diffamer

liberal ['lɪbərl] adj libéral(e); (generous): **~ with** prodigue de, généreux(-euse) avec; **the L~ Democrats** (BRIT) le parti libéral-démocrate

liberation [lɪbə'reɪʃən] n libération f

liberty ['lɪbətɪ] n liberté f; **to be at ~ to do** être libre de faire

Libra ['li:brə] n la Balance
librarian [laɪ'brɛərɪən] n bibliothécaire m/f
library ['laɪbrərɪ] n bibliothèque f
libretto [lɪ'brɛtəʊ] n livret m
Libya ['lɪbɪə] n Libye f
lice [laɪs] npl of **louse**
licence ['laɪsns] (US **license**) n autorisation f, permis m; (RADIO, TV) redevance f; **driving ~**, (US) **driver's license** permis m (de conduire); **~ number** n numéro m d'immatriculation; **~ plate** n plaque f minéralogique
license ['laɪsns] n (US) = **licence** ♦ vt donner une licence à; **~d** adj (car) muni(e) de la vignette; (to sell alcohol) patenté(e) pour la vente des spiritueux, qui a une licence de débit de boissons
lick [lɪk] vt lécher; (inf: defeat) écraser; **to ~ one's lips** (fig) se frotter les mains
licorice ['lɪkərɪs] (US) n = **liquorice**
lid [lɪd] n couvercle m; (eyelid) paupière f
lie [laɪ] (pt lay, pp lain) vi (rest) être étendu(e) or allongé(e) or couché(e); (in grave) être enterré(e), reposer; (be situated) se trouver, être; (be untruthful: pt, pp ~d) mentir ♦ n mensonge m; **to ~ low** (fig) se cacher; **~ about** vi traîner; **~ around** vi = lie about; **~-down** (BRIT) n: **to have a ~-down** s'allonger, se reposer; **~-in** (BRIT) n: **to have a ~-in** faire la grasse matinée
lieutenant [lɛf'tɛnənt, (US) lu:'tɛnənt] n lieutenant m
life [laɪf] (pl lives) n vie f; **to come to ~** (fig) s'animer; **~ assurance** (BRIT) n = **life insurance**; **~belt** (BRIT) n bouée f de sauvetage; **~boat** n canot m or chaloupe f de sauvetage; **~buoy** n bouée f de sauvetage; **~guard** n surveillant m de baignade; **~ insurance** n assurance-vie f; **~ jacket** n gilet m or ceinture f de sauvetage; **~less** adj sans vie, inanimé(e); (dull) qui manque de vie or de vigueur; **~like** adj qui semble vrai(e) or vivant(e); (painting) réaliste; **~long** adj de toute une vie, de toujours; **~ preserver** (US) n = **lifebelt**; **life jacket**; **~-saving** n sauvetage m; **~ sentence** n condamnation f à perpétuité; **~-size(d)** adj grandeur nature inv; **~ span** n (durée f de) vie f; **~style** n style m or mode m de vie; **~-support system** n (MED) respirateur artificiel; **~time** n vie f; **in his ~time** de son vivant
lift [lɪft] vt soulever, lever; (end) supprimer, lever ♦ vi (fog) se lever ♦ n (BRIT: elevator) ascenseur m; **to give sb a ~** (BRIT: AUT) emmener or prendre qn en voiture; **~-off** n décollage m
light [laɪt] (pt, pp lit) n lumière f; (lamp) lampe f; (AUT: rear) ~) feu m; (: headlight) phare m; (for cigarette etc): **have you got a ~?**

avez-vous du feu? ♦ vt (candle, cigarette, fire) allumer; (room) éclairer ♦ adj (room, colour) clair(e); (not heavy) léger(-ère); (not strenuous) peu fatigant(e); **~s** npl (AUT: traffic ~s) feux mpl; **to come to ~** être dévoilé(e) or découvert(e), **~ up** vi (face) s'éclairer ♦ vt (illuminate) éclairer, illuminer; **~ bulb** n ampoule f; **~en** vt (make less heavy) alléger; **~er** n (also: **cigarette ~er**) briquet m; **~-headed** adj étourdi(e); (excited) grisé(e); **~-hearted** adj gai(e), joyeux(-euse), enjoué(e); **~house** n phare m; **~ing** n (on road) éclairage m; (in theatre) éclairages; **~ly** adv légèrement; **to get off ~ly** s'en tirer à bon compte; **~ness** n (in weight) légèreté f
lightning ['laɪtnɪŋ] n éclair m, foudre f; **~ conductor** (US **lightning rod**) n paratonnerre m
light pen n crayon m optique
lightweight ['laɪtweɪt] adj (suit) léger(-ère) ♦ n (BOXING) poids léger
like [laɪk] vt aimer (bien) ♦ prep comme ♦ adj semblable, pareil(le) ♦ n: **and the ~** et d'autres du même genre; **his ~s and dislikes** ses goûts mpl or préférences fpl; **I would ~, I'd ~** je voudrais, j'aimerais; **would you ~ a coffee?** voulez-vous du café?; **to be/look ~ sb/sth** ressembler à qn/qch; **what does it look ~?** de quoi est-ce que ça a l'air?; **what does it taste ~?** quel goût est-ce que ça a?; **that's just ~ him** c'est bien de lui, ça lui ressemble; **do it ~ this** fais-le comme ceci; **it's nothing ~ ...** ... ce n'est pas du tout comme ...; **~able** adj sympathique, agréable
likelihood ['laɪklɪhʊd] n probabilité f
likely ['laɪklɪ] adj probable; plausible; **he's ~ to leave** il va sûrement partir, il risque fort de partir; **not ~!** (inf) pas de danger!
likeness ['laɪknɪs] n ressemblance f; **that's a good ~** c'est très ressemblant
likewise ['laɪkwaɪz] adv de même, pareillement
liking ['laɪkɪŋ] n (for person) affection f; (for thing) penchant m, goût m
lilac ['laɪlək] n lilas m
lily ['lɪlɪ] n lis m; **~ of the valley** n muguet m
limb [lɪm] n membre m
limber ['lɪmbə*] : **~ up** vi se dégourdir, faire des exercices d'assouplissement
limbo ['lɪmbəʊ] n: **to be in ~** (fig) être tombé(e) dans l'oubli
lime [laɪm] n (tree) tilleul m; (fruit) lime f, citron vert; (GEO) chaux f
limelight ['laɪmlaɪt] n: **in the ~** (fig) en vedette, au premier plan
limerick ['lɪmərɪk] n poème m humoristique (de 5 vers)
limestone ['laɪmstəʊn] n pierre f à chaux; (GEO) calcaire m

limit ['lɪmɪt] n limite f ♦ vt limiter; **~ed** adj limité(e), restreint(e); **to be ~ed to** se limiter à, ne concerner que; **~ed (liability) company** (BRIT) n ≈ société f anonyme

limousine ['lɪməzi:n] n limousine f

limp [lɪmp] n: **to have a ~** boiter ♦ vi boiter ♦ adj mou (molle)

limpet ['lɪmpɪt] n patelle f

line [laɪn] n ligne f; (stroke) trait m; (wrinkle) ride f; (rope) corde f; (wire) fil m; (of poem) vers m; (row, series) rangée f; (of people) file f, queue f; (railway track) voie f; (COMM: series of goods) article(s) m(pl); (work) métier m, type m d'activité; (attitude, policy) position f ♦ vt (subj: trees, crowd) border; **in a ~** aligné(e); **in his ~ of business** dans sa partie, dans son rayon; **in ~ with** en accord avec; **to ~ (with)** (clothes) doubler (de); (box) garnir or tapisser (de); **~ up** vi s'aligner, se mettre en rang(s) ♦ vt aligner; (event) prévoir, préparer; **~d** adj (face) ridé(e), marqué(e); (paper) réglé(e)

linen ['lɪnɪn] n linge m (de maison); (cloth) lin m

liner ['laɪnər] n paquebot m (de ligne); (for bin) sac m à poubelle

linesman ['laɪnzmən] (irreg) n juge m de touche; (TENNIS) juge m de ligne

line-up ['laɪnʌp] n (US: queue) file f; (SPORT) (composition f de l')équipe f

linger ['lɪŋgər] vi s'attarder; traîner; (smell, tradition) persister

linguist ['lɪŋgwɪst] n: **to be a good ~** être doué(e) par les langues; **~ics** [lɪŋ'gwɪstɪks] n linguistique f

lining ['laɪnɪŋ] n doublure f

link [lɪŋk] n lien m, rapport m; (of a chain) maillon m ♦ vt relier, lier, unir; **~s** npl (GOLF) (terrain m de) golf m; **~ up** vt relier ♦ vi se rejoindre; s'associer

lino ['laɪnəu] n = **linoleum**

linoleum [lɪ'nəuliəm] n linoléum m

lion ['laɪən] n lion m; **~ess** n lionne f

lip [lɪp] n lèvre f

liposuction ['lɪpəusʌkʃən] n liposuccion f

lip: ~-read vi lire sur les lèvres; **~ salve** n pommade f rosat or pour les lèvres; **~ service** n: **to pay ~ service to sth** ne reconnaître que le mérite de qch que pour la forme; **~stick** n rouge m à lèvres

liqueur [lɪ'kjuər] n liqueur f

liquid ['lɪkwɪd] adj liquide ♦ n liquide m; **~ize** vt (CULIN) passer au mixer; **~izer** n mixer m

liquor ['lɪkər] (US) n spiritueux m, alcool m

liquorice ['lɪkərɪs] (BRIT) n réglisse f

liquor store (US) n magasin m de vins et spiritueux

lisp [lɪsp] vi zézayer

list [lɪst] n liste f ♦ vt (write down) faire une or la liste de; (mention) énumérer; **~ed building** (BRIT) n monument classé

listen ['lɪsn] vi écouter; **to ~ to** écouter; **~er** n auditeur(-trice)

listless ['lɪstlɪs] adj indolent(e), apathique

lit [lɪt] pt, pp of **light**

liter ['li:tər] (US) n = **litre**

literacy ['lɪtərəsɪ] n degré m d'alphabétisation, fait m de savoir lire et écrire

literal ['lɪtərəl] adj littéral(e); **~ly** adv littéralement; (really) réellement

literary ['lɪtərərɪ] adj littéraire

literate ['lɪtərət] adj qui sait lire et écrire, instruit(e)

literature ['lɪtrɪtʃər] n littérature f; (brochures etc) documentation f

lithe [laɪð] adj agile, souple

litigation [lɪtɪ'geɪʃən] n litige m; contentieux m

litre ['li:tər] (US **liter**) n litre m

litter ['lɪtər] n (rubbish) détritus mpl, ordures fpl; (young animals) portée f; **~ bin** (BRIT) n boîte f à ordures, poubelle f; **~ed** adj: **~ed with** jonché(e) de, couvert(e) de

little ['lɪtl] adj (small) petit(e) ♦ adv peu; **~ milk/time** peu de lait/temps; **a ~** un peu (de); **a ~ bit** un peu; **~ by ~** petit à petit, peu à peu

live¹ [laɪv] adj (animal) vivant(e), en vie; (wire) sous tension; (bullet, bomb) non explosé(e); (broadcast) en direct; (performance) en public

live² [lɪv] vi vivre; (reside) vivre, habiter; **~ down** vt faire oublier (avec le temps); **~ on** vt fus (food, salary) vivre de; **~ together** vi vivre ensemble, cohabiter; **~ up to** vt fus se montrer à la hauteur de

livelihood ['laɪvlɪhud] n moyens mpl d'existence

lively ['laɪvlɪ] adj vif (vive), plein(e) d'entrain; (place, book) vivant(e)

liven up ['laɪvn-] vt animer ♦ vi s'animer

liver ['lɪvər] n foie m

lives [laɪvz] npl of **life**

livestock ['laɪvstɔk] n bétail m, cheptel m

livid ['lɪvɪd] adj livide, blafard(e); (inf: furious) furieux(-euse), furibond(e)

living ['lɪvɪŋ] adj vivant(e), en vie ♦ n: **to earn** or **make a ~** gagner sa vie; **~ conditions** npl conditions fpl de vie; **~ room** n salle f de séjour; **~ standards** npl niveau m de vie; **~ wage** n salaire m permettant de vivre (décemment)

lizard ['lɪzəd] n lézard m

load [ləud] n (weight) poids m; (thing carried) chargement m, charge f ♦ vt (also: **~ up**): **to ~ (with)** charger (de); (gun, camera) charger (avec); (COMPUT) charger; **a ~ of, ~s of** (fig) un or des tas de, des masses de; **to talk a ~ of**

rubbish dire des bêtises; **~ed** adj (question) insidieux(-euse); (inf: rich) bourré(e) de fric

loaf [ləuf] (pl **loaves**) n pain m, miche f

loan [ləun] n prêt m ♦ vt prêter; **on ~** prêté(e), en prêt

loath [ləuθ] adj: **to be ~ to do** répugner à faire

loathe [ləuð] vt détester, avoir en horreur

loaves [ləuvz] npl of **loaf**

lobby ['lɔbɪ] n hall m, entrée f; (POL) groupe m de pression, lobby m ♦ vt faire pression sur

lobster ['lɔbstə*] n homard m

local ['ləukl] adj local(e) ♦ n (BRIT: pub) pub m or café m du coin; **the ~s** npl (inhabitants) les gens mpl du pays or du coin;
~ anaesthetic n anesthésie locale;
~ authority n collectivité locale, municipalité f; **~ call** n communication urbaine;
~ government n administration locale or municipale; **~ity** [ləu'kælɪtɪ] n région f, environs mpl; (position) lieu m

locate [ləu'keɪt] vt (find) trouver, repérer; (situate): **to be ~d in** être situé(e) à or en; **location** n emplacement m; **on location** (CINEMA) en extérieur

loch [lɔx] n lac m, loch m

lock [lɔk] n (of door, box) serrure f; (of canal) écluse f; (of hair) mèche f, boucle f ♦ vt (with key) fermer à clé ♦ vi (door etc) fermer à clé; (wheels) se bloquer; **~ in** vt enfermer; **~ out** vt enfermer dehors; (deliberately) mettre à la porte; **~ up** vt (criminal) enfermer; (house) fermer à clé ♦ vi tout fermer (à clé)

locker ['lɔkə*] n casier m; (in station) consigne f automatique

locket ['lɔkɪt] n médaillon m

locksmith ['lɔksmɪθ] n serrurier m

lockup ['lɔkʌp] n (prison) prison f

locum ['ləukəm] n (MED) suppléant(e) (de médecin)

lodge [lɔdʒ] n pavillon m (de gardien); (hunting ~) pavillon de chasse ♦ vi (person): **to ~ (with)** être logé(e) (chez), être en pension (chez); (bullet) se loger ♦ vt: **to ~ a complaint** porter plainte; **~r** n locataire m/f; (with meals) pensionnaire m/f; **lodgings** npl chambre f; meublé m

loft [lɔft] n grenier m

lofty ['lɔftɪ] adj (noble) noble, élevé(e); (haughty) hautain(e)

log [lɔg] n (of wood) bûche f; (book) = logbook ♦ vt (record) noter; **~book** n (NAUT) livre m or journal m de bord; (AVIAT) carnet m de vol; (of car) ≈ carte grise

loggerheads ['lɔgəhedz] npl: **at ~ (with)** à couteaux tirés (avec)

logic ['lɔdʒɪk] n logique f; **~al** adj logique

loin [lɔɪn] n (CULIN) filet m, longe f

loiter ['lɔɪtə*] vi traîner

loll [lɔl] vi (also: **~ about**) se prélasser,

fainéanter

lollipop ['lɔlɪpɔp] n sucette f; **~ man/lady** (BRIT: irreg) n contractuel qui fait traverser la rue aux enfants

lolly ['lɔlɪ] (inf) n (lollipop) sucette f; (money) fric m

London ['lʌndən] n Londres m; **~er** n Londonien(ne)

lone [ləun] adj solitaire

loneliness ['ləunlɪnɪs] n solitude f, isolement m

lonely ['ləunlɪ] adj seul(e); solitaire, isolé(e)

long [lɔŋ] adj long (longue) ♦ adv longtemps ♦ vi: **to ~ for sth** avoir très envie de qch; attendre qch avec impatience; **so or as ~ as** pourvu que; **don't be ~!** dépêchez-vous!; **how ~ is this river/course?** quelle est la longueur de ce fleuve/la durée de ce cours?; **6 metres ~** (long) de 6 mètres; **6 months ~** qui dure 6 mois, de 6 mois; **all night ~** toute la nuit; **he no ~er comes** il ne vient plus; **they're no ~er going out together** ils ne sortent plus ensemble; **I can't stand it any ~er** je ne peux plus le supporter; **~ before/after** longtemps avant/après; **before ~** (+future) avant peu, dans peu de temps; (+past) peu (de temps) après; **at ~ last** enfin; **~-distance** adj (call) interurbain(e); **~er** ['lɔŋgə*] adv see **long**; **~hand** n écriture normale or courante; **~ing** n désir m, envie f, nostalgie f

longitude ['lɔŋgɪtjuːd] n longitude f

long: ~ jump n saut m en longueur; **~-life** adj (batteries etc) longue durée inv; (milk) longue conservation; **~-lost** adj (person) perdu(e) de vue depuis longtemps; **~-range** adj à longue portée; **~-sighted** adj (MED) presbyte; **~-standing** adj de longue date; **~-suffering** adj empreint(e) d'une patience résignée; extrêmement patient(e); **~-term** adj à long terme; **~ wave** n grandes ondes; **~-winded** adj intarissable, interminable

loo [luː] (BRIT: inf) n W.-C. mpl, petit coin

look [luk] vi regarder; (seem) sembler, paraître, avoir l'air; (building etc): **to ~ south/(out) onto the sea** donner au sud/sur la mer ♦ n regard m; (appearance) air m, allure f, aspect m; **~s** npl (good ~s) physique m, beauté f; **to have a ~** regarder; **~! regardez!; ~ (here)!** (annoyance) écoutez!; **~ after** vt fus (care for, deal with) s'occuper de; **~ at** vt fus regarder; (problem etc) examiner; **~ back** vi: **to ~ back on** (event etc) évoquer, repenser à; **~ down on** vt fus (fig) regarder de haut, dédaigner; **~ for** vt fus chercher; **~ forward to** vt fus attendre avec impatience; **we ~ forward to hearing from you** (in letter) dans l'attente de vous lire; **~ into** vt fus examiner, étudier; **~ on** vi regarder (en spectateur); **~ out** vi (beware): **to ~ out (for)** prendre

garde (à), faire attention (à); **~ out for** vt
fus être à la recherche de; guetter; **~ round**
vi regarder derrière soi, se retourner; **~ to** vt
fus (rely on) compter sur; **~ up** vi lever les
yeux; (improve) s'améliorer ♦ vt (word, name)
chercher; **~ up to** vt fus avoir du respect
pour ♦ n poste m de guet; (person) guetteur
m; **to be on the ~ out (for)** guetter

loom [lu:m] vi (also: **~ up**) surgir; (approach:
event etc) être imminent(e); (threaten)
menacer ♦ n (for weaving) métier m à tisser

loony ['lu:nɪ] (inf) adj, n timbré(e), cinglé(e)

loop [lu:p] n boucle f; **~hole** n (fig) porte f
de sortie; échappatoire f

loose [lu:s] adj (knot, screw) desserré(e);
(clothes) ample, lâche; (hair) dénoué(e),
épars(e); (not firmly fixed) pas solide;
(morals, discipline) relâché(e) ♦ n: **on the ~** en
liberté; **~ change** n petite monnaie; **~ chippings** npl (on road) gravillons mpl; **~ end** n:
to be at a ~ end or (US) **at ~ ends** ne pas trop
savoir quoi faire; **~ly** adv sans serrer; (impre-
cisely) approximativement; **~n** vt desserrer

loot [lu:t] n (inf: money) pognon m, fric m
♦ vt piller

lopsided ['lɒp'saɪdɪd] adj de travers,
asymétrique

lord [lɔ:d] n seigneur m; **L~ Smith** lord Smith;
the L~ le Seigneur; **good L~!** mon Dieu!; **the
(House of) L~s** (BRIT) la Chambre des lords;
my L~ = your Lordship; **L~ship** n: **your
L~ship** Monsieur le comte/le baron/le juge;
(to bishop) Monseigneur

lore [lɔ:ʳ] n tradition(s) f(pl)

lorry ['lɒrɪ] (BRIT) n camion m; **~ driver** (BRIT)
n camionneur m, routier m

lose [lu:z] (pt, pp **lost**) vt, vi perdre; **to
~ (time)** (clock) retarder; **to get lost** ♦ vi se
perdre; **~r** n perdant(e)

loss [lɒs] n perte f; **to be at a ~** être perplexe
or embarrassé(e)

lost [lɒst] pt, pp of **lose** ♦ adj perdu(e); **~ and
found** (US), **~ property** n objets trouvés

lot [lɒt] n (at set) lot m; **the ~** le tout; **a ~ (of)**
beaucoup (de); **~s of** des tas de; **to draw ~s
(for sth)** tirer (qch) au sort

lotion ['ləʊʃən] n lotion f

lottery ['lɒtərɪ] n loterie f

loud [laʊd] adj bruyant(e), sonore; (voice)
fort(e); (support, condemnation) vigou-
reux(-euse); (gaudy) voyant(e), tapa-
geur(-euse) ♦ adv (speak etc) fort; **out ~** tout
haut; **~-hailer** (BRIT) n porte-voix m inv; **~ly**
adv fort, bruyamment; **~speaker** n haut-
parleur m

lounge [laʊndʒ] n salon m; (at airport) salle f;
(BRIT: also: **~ bar**) (salle de) café m or bar m
♦ vi (also: **~ about** or **around**) se prélasser,
paresser; **~ suit** (BRIT) n complet m; (on

invitation) "tenue de ville"

louse [laʊs] (pl **lice**) n pou m

lousy ['laʊzɪ] (inf) adj infect(e), moche; **I feel
~** je suis mal fichu(e)

lout [laʊt] n rustre m, butor m

lovable ['lʌvəbl] adj adorable; très
sympathique

love [lʌv] n amour m ♦ vt aimer; (caringly,
kindly) aimer beaucoup; **"~ (from) Anne"**
"affectueusement, Anne"; **I ~ chocolate**
j'adore le chocolat; **to be/fall in ~ with** être/
tomber amoureux(-euse) de; **to make ~** faire
l'amour; **"15 ~"** (TENNIS) "15 à rien or zéro";
~ affair n liaison (amoureuse); **~ life** n vie
sentimentale

lovely ['lʌvlɪ] adj (très) joli(e), ravissant(e);
(delightful: person) charmant(e); (holiday etc)
(très) agréable

lover ['lʌvəʳ] n amant m; (person in love)
amoureux(-euse); (amateur): **a ~ of** un
amateur de; un(e) amoureux(-euse) de

loving ['lʌvɪŋ] adj affectueux(-euse), tendre

low [ləʊ] adj bas (basse); (quality)
mauvais(e), inférieur(e); (person: depressed)
déprimé(e); (: ill) bas (basse), affaibli(e)
♦ adv bas ♦ n (METEOROLOGY) dépression f; **to
be ~ on** être à court de; **to feel ~** se sentir
déprimé(e); **to reach an all-time ~** être au
plus bas; **~-alcohol** adj peu alcoolisé(e); **~-
calorie** adj hypocalorique; **~-cut** adj (dress)
décolleté(e); **~er** adj inférieur(e) ♦ vt
abaisser, baisser; **~er sixth** (BRIT) n (SCOL)
première f; **~-fat** adj maigre; **~lands** npl
(GEO) plaines fpl; **~ly** adj humble, modeste

loyal ['lɔɪəl] adj loyal(e), fidèle; **~ty** n loyauté
f, fidélité f; **~ty card** n carte f de fidélité

lozenge ['lɒzɪndʒ] n (MED) pastille f

LP n abbr = **long-playing record**

L-plates ['elpleɪts] (BRIT) npl plaques fpl
d'apprenti conducteur

Ltd abbr (= limited) ≈ S.A.

lubricant ['lu:brɪkənt] n lubrifiant m

lubricate ['lu:brɪkeɪt] vt lubrifier, graisser

luck [lʌk] n chance f; **bad ~** malchance f,
malheur m; **bad or hard or tough ~!** pas de
chance!; **good ~!** bonne chance!; **~ily** adv
heureusement, par bonheur; **~y** adj (person)
qui a de la chance; (coincidence, event)
heureux(-euse); (object) porte-bonheur inv

ludicrous ['lu:dɪkrəs] adj ridicule, absurde

lug [lʌg] (inf) vt traîner, tirer

luggage ['lʌgɪdʒ] n bagages mpl; **~ rack** n
(on car) galerie f

lukewarm ['lu:kwɔ:m] adj tiède

lull [lʌl] n accalmie f; (in conversation) pause f
♦ vt: **to ~ sb to sleep** bercer qn pour qu'il
s'endorme; **to be ~ed into a false sense of
security** s'endormir dans une fausse sécurité

lullaby ['lʌləbaɪ] n berceuse f

lumbago [lʌmˈbeɪgəu] n lumbago m

lumber [ˈlʌmbəʳ] n (wood) bois m de charpente; (junk) bric-à-brac m inv; **~jack** n bûcheron m

luminous [ˈluːmɪnəs] adj lumineux(-euse)

lump [lʌmp] n morceau m; (swelling) grosseur f ♦ vt: **to ~ together** réunir, mettre en tas; **~ sum** n somme globale or forfaitaire; **~y** adj (sauce) avec des grumeaux; (bed) défoncé(e), peu confortable

lunar [ˈluːnəʳ] adj lunaire

lunatic [ˈluːnətɪk] adj fou (folle), cinglé(e) (inf)

lunch [lʌntʃ] n déjeuner m

luncheon [ˈlʌntʃən] n déjeuner m (chic); **~ meat** n sorte de mortadelle; **~ voucher** (BRIT) n chèque-repas m

lung [lʌŋ] n poumon m

lunge [lʌndʒ] vi (also: **~ forward**) faire un mouvement brusque en avant; **to ~ at** envoyer or assener un coup à

lurch [ləːtʃ] vi vaciller, tituber ♦ n écart m brusque: **to leave sb in the ~** laisser qn se débrouiller or se dépêtrer tout(e) seul(e)

lure [luəʳ] n (attraction) attrait m, charme m ♦ vt attirer or persuader par la ruse

lurid [ˈluərɪd] adj affreux(-euse), atroce; (pej: colour, dress) criard(e)

lurk [ləːk] vi se tapir, se cacher

luscious [ˈlʌʃəs] adj succulent(e); appétissant(e)

lush [lʌʃ] adj luxuriant(e)

lust [lʌst] n (sexual) désir m; (fig): **~ for** soif f de; **~y** adj vigoureux(-euse), robuste

Luxembourg [ˈlʌksəmbəːg] n Luxembourg m

luxurious [lʌgˈzjuərɪəs] adj luxueux(-euse)

luxury [ˈlʌkʃərɪ] n luxe m ♦ cpd de luxe

lying [ˈlaɪɪŋ] n mensonge(s) m(pl) ♦ vb see **lie**

lyrical [ˈlɪrɪkl] adj lyrique

lyrics [ˈlɪrɪks] npl (of song) paroles fpl

M, m

m. abbr = **metre**; **mile**; **million**

M.A. abbr = **Master of Arts**

mac [mæk] (BRIT) n imper(méable) m

macaroni [mækəˈrəunɪ] n macaroni mpl

machine [məˈʃiːn] n machine f ♦ vt (TECH) façonner à la machine; (dress etc) coudre à la machine; **~ gun** n mitrailleuse f; **~ language** n (COMPUT) langage-machine m; **~ry** n machinerie f, machines fpl; (fig) mécanisme(s) m(pl)

mackerel [ˈmækrl] n inv maquereau m

mackintosh [ˈmækɪntɔʃ] (BRIT) n imperméable m

mad [mæd] adj fou (folle); (foolish)

insensé(e); (angry) furieux(-euse); (keen): **to be ~ about** être fou (folle) de

madam [ˈmædəm] n madame f

madden [ˈmædn] vt exaspérer

made [meɪd] pt, pp of **make**

Madeira [məˈdɪərə] n (GEO) Madère f; (wine) madère m

made-to-measure [ˈmeɪdtəˈmeʒəʳ] (BRIT) adj fait(e) sur mesure

madly [ˈmædlɪ] adv follement; **~ in love** éperdument amoureux(-euse)

madman [ˈmædmən] (irreg) n fou m

madness [ˈmædnɪs] n folie f

magazine [mægəˈziːn] n (PRESS) magazine m, revue f; (RADIO, TV: also: **~ programme**) magazine

maggot [ˈmægət] n ver m, asticot m

magic [ˈmædʒɪk] n magie f ♦ adj magique; **~al** adj magique; (experience, evening) merveilleux(-euse); **~ian** [məˈdʒɪʃən] n magicien(ne); (conjurer) prestidigitateur m

magistrate [ˈmædʒɪstreɪt] n magistrat m; juge m

magnet [ˈmægnɪt] n aimant m; **~ic** [mægˈnetɪk] adj magnétique

magnificent [mægˈnɪfɪsnt] adj superbe, magnifique; (splendid: robe, building) somptueux(-euse), magnifique

magnify [ˈmægnɪfaɪ] vt grossir; (sound) amplifier; **~ing glass** n loupe f

magnitude [ˈmægnɪtjuːd] n ampleur f

magpie [ˈmægpaɪ] n pie f

mahogany [məˈhɔgənɪ] n acajou m

maid [meɪd] n bonne f; **old ~** (pej) vieille fille

maiden [ˈmeɪdn] n jeune fille f ♦ adj (aunt etc) non mariée; (speech, voyage) inaugural(e); **~ name** n nom m de jeune fille

mail [meɪl] n poste f; (letters) courrier m ♦ vt envoyer (par la poste); **~box** (US) n boîte f aux lettres; **~ing list** n liste f d'adresses; **~ order** n vente f or achat m par correspondance

maim [meɪm] vt mutiler

main [meɪn] adj principal(e) ♦ n: **the ~(s)** n(pl) (gas, water) conduite principale, canalisation f; **the ~s** npl (ELEC) le secteur; **the ~ thing** l'essentiel m; **in the ~** dans l'ensemble; **~frame** n (COMPUT) (gros) ordinateur, unité centrale; **~land** n continent m; **~ly** adv principalement, surtout; **~ road** n grand-route f; **~stay** n (fig) pilier m; **~stream** n courant principal

maintain [meɪnˈteɪn] vt entretenir; (continue) maintenir; (affirm) soutenir; **maintenance** [ˈmeɪntənəns] n entretien m; (alimony) pension f alimentaire

maize [meɪz] n maïs m

majestic [məˈdʒestɪk] adj majestueux(-euse)

majesty [ˈmædʒɪstɪ] n majesté f

major ['meɪdʒər] n (MIL) commandant m ♦ adj (important) important(e); (most important) principal(e); (MUS) majeur(e)

Majorca [məˈjɔːkə] n Majorque f

majority [məˈdʒɔrɪtɪ] n majorité f

make [meɪk] (pt, pp made) vt faire; (manufacture) faire, fabriquer; (earn) gagner; (cause to be): **to ~ sb sad** etc rendre qn triste etc; (force): **to ~ sb do sth** obliger qn à faire qch, faire faire qch à qn; (equal): **2 and 2 ~ 4** 2 et 2 font 4 ♦ n fabrication f; (brand) marque f; **to ~ a fool of sb** (ridicule) ridiculiser qn; (trick) avoir or duper qn; **to ~ a profit** faire un or des bénéfice(s); **to ~ a loss** essuyer une perte; **to ~ it** (arrive) arriver; (achieve sth) parvenir à qch, réussir; **what time do you ~ it?** quelle heure avez-vous?; **to ~ do with** se contenter de; se débrouiller avec; **~ for** vt fus (place) se diriger vers; **~ out** vt (write out: cheque) faire; (decipher) déchiffrer; (understand) comprendre; (see) distinguer; **~ up** vt (constitute) constituer; (invent) inventer, imaginer; (parcel, bed) faire ♦ vi se réconcilier; (with cosmetics) se maquiller; **~ up for** vt fus compenser; **~-believe** n: **it's just ~-believe** (game) c'est pour faire semblant; (invention) c'est de l'invention pure; **~r** n fabricant m, faiseur m; **~shift** adj provisoire, improvisé(e); **~-up** n maquillage m

making ['meɪkɪŋ] n (fig): **in the ~** en formation or gestation; **to have the ~s of** (actor, athlete etc) avoir l'étoffe de

malaria [məˈlɛərɪə] n malaria f

Malaysia [məˈleɪzɪə] n Malaisie f

male [meɪl] n (BIO) mâle m ♦ adj mâle; (sex, attitude) masculin(e); (child etc) du sexe masculin

malevolent [məˈlɛvələnt] adj malveillant(e)

malfunction [mælˈfʌŋkʃən] n fonctionnement défectueux

malice ['mælɪs] n méchanceté f, malveillance f; **malicious** [məˈlɪʃəs] adj méchant(e), malveillant(e)

malignant [məˈlɪgnənt] adj (MED) ma-lin(-igne)

mall [mɔːl] n (also: **shopping ~**) centre commercial

mallet ['mælɪt] n maillet m

malpractice [mælˈpræktɪs] n faute professionnelle; négligence f

malt [mɔːlt] n malt m ♦ cpd (also: **~ whisky**) pur malt

Malta ['mɔːltə] n Malte f

mammal ['mæml] n mammifère m

mammoth ['mæməθ] n mammouth m ♦ adj géant(e), monstre

man [mæn] (pl **men**) n homme m ♦ vt (NAUT: ship) garnir d'hommes; (MIL: gun) servir; (: post) être de service à; (machine) assurer le fonctionnement de; **an old ~** un vieillard; **~ and wife** mari et femme

manage ['mænɪdʒ] vi se débrouiller ♦ vt (be in charge of) s'occuper de; (: business etc) gérer; (control: ship) manier, manœuvrer; (: person) savoir s'y prendre avec; **to ~ to do** réussir à faire; **~able** adj (task) faisable; (number) raisonnable; **~ment** n gestion f, administration f, direction f; **~r** n directeur m; administrateur m; (SPORT) manager m; (of artist) impresario m; **~ress** [mænɪdʒəˈrɛs] n directrice f; gérante f; **~rial** [mænɪˈdʒɪərɪəl] adj directorial(e); (skills) de cadre, de gestion; **managing director** n directeur général

mandarin ['mændərɪn] n (also: **~ orange**) mandarine f; (person) mandarin m

mandatory ['mændətərɪ] adj obligatoire

mane [meɪn] n crinière f

maneuver [məˈnuːvər] (US) vt, vi, n = manoeuvre

manfully ['mænfəlɪ] adv vaillamment

mangle ['mæŋgl] vt déchiqueter; mutiler

mango ['mæŋgəu] (pl **~es**) n mangue f

mangy ['meɪndʒɪ] adj galeux(-euse)

man: ~handle vt malmener; **~hole** n trou m d'homme; **~hood** n âge m d'homme; virilité f; **~-hour** n heure f de main-d'œuvre; **~hunt** n (POLICE) chasse f à l'homme

mania ['meɪnɪə] n manie f; **~c** ['meɪnɪæk] n maniaque m/f; (fig) fou (folle) m/f; **manic** ['mænɪk] adj maniaque

manicure ['mænɪkjuər] n manucure f

manifest ['mænɪfɛst] vt manifester ♦ adj manifeste, évident(e); **~o** [mænɪˈfɛstəu] n manifeste m

manipulate [məˈnɪpjuleɪt] vt manipuler; (system, situation) exploiter

man: ~kind [mænˈkaɪnd] n humanité f, genre humain; **~ly** adj viril(e); **~-made** adj artificiel(le); (fibre) synthétique

manner ['mænər] n manière f, façon f; (behaviour) attitude f, comportement m; (sort): **all ~ of** toutes sortes de; **~s** npl (behaviour) manières f; **~ism** n particularité f de langage (or de comportement), tic m

manoeuvre [məˈnuːvər] (US **maneuver**) vt (move) manœuvrer; (manipulate: person) manipuler; (: situation) exploiter ♦ vi manœuvrer ♦ n manœuvre f

manor ['mænər] n (also: **~ house**) manoir m

manpower ['mænpauər] n main-d'œuvre f

mansion ['mænʃən] n château m, manoir m

manslaughter ['mænslɔːtər] n homicide m involontaire

mantelpiece ['mæntlpiːs] n cheminée f

manual ['mænjuəl] adj manuel(le) ♦ n manuel m

manufacture [mænjuˈfæktʃər] vt fabriquer

◆ n fabrication f; **~r** n fabricant m

manure [mə'njuəʳ] n fumier m

manuscript ['mænjuskrɪpt] n manuscrit m

many ['menɪ] adj beaucoup de, de nombreux(-euses) ◆ pron beaucoup, un grand nombre; **a great ~** un grand nombre (de); **~ a ...** bien des ..., plus d'un(e) ...

map [mæp] n carte f; (of town) plan m; **~ out** vt tracer; (task) planifier

maple ['meɪpl] n érable m

mar [mɑːʳ] vt gâcher, gâter

marathon ['mærəθən] n marathon m

marble ['mɑːbl] n marbre m; (toy) bille f

March [mɑːtʃ] n mars m

march [mɑːtʃ] vi marcher au pas; (fig: protesters) défiler ◆ n marche f; (demonstration) manifestation f

mare [meəʳ] n jument f

margarine [mɑːdʒə'riːn] n margarine f

margin ['mɑːdʒɪn] n marge f; **~al (seat)** n (POL) siège disputé

marigold ['mærɪɡəuld] n souci m

marijuana [mærɪ'wɑːnə] n marijuana f

marina [mə'riːnə] n (harbour) marina f

marine [mə'riːn] adj marin(e) ◆ n fusilier marin; (US) marine m

marital ['mærɪtl] adj matrimonial(e); **~ status** situation f de famille

marjoram ['mɑːdʒərəm] n marjolaine f

mark [mɑːk] n marque f; (of skid etc) trace f; (BRIT: SCOL) note f; (currency) mark m ◆ vt marquer; (stain) tacher; (BRIT: SCOL) noter; corriger; **to ~ time** marquer le pas; **~er** n (sign) jalon m; (bookmark) signet m

market ['mɑːkɪt] n marché m ◆ vt (COMM) commercialiser; **~ garden** (BRIT) n jardin maraîcher; **~ing** n marketing m; **~place** n place f du marché; (COMM) marché m; **~ research** n étude f de marché

marksman ['mɑːksmən] (irreg) n tireur m d'élite

marmalade ['mɑːməleɪd] n confiture f d'oranges

maroon [mə'ruːn] vt: **to be ~ed** être abandonné(e); (fig) être bloqué(e) ◆ adj bordeaux inv

marquee [mɑː'kiː] n chapiteau m

marriage ['mærɪdʒ] n mariage m; **~ certificate** n extrait m d'acte de mariage

married ['mærɪd] adj marié(e); (life, love) conjugal(e)

marrow ['mærəu] n moelle f; (vegetable) courge f

marry ['mærɪ] vt épouser, se marier avec; (subj: father, priest etc) marier ◆ vi (also: **get married**) se marier

Mars [mɑːz] n (planet) Mars f

marsh [mɑːʃ] n marais m, marécage m

marshal ['mɑːʃl] n maréchal m; (US: fire, police) ≈ capitaine m; (SPORT) membre m du service d'ordre ◆ vt rassembler

marshy ['mɑːʃɪ] adj marécageux(-euse)

martyr ['mɑːtəʳ] n martyr(e); **~dom** n martyre m

marvel ['mɑːvl] n merveille f ◆ vi: **to ~ (at)** s'émerveiller (de); **~lous** (US **marvelous**) adj merveilleux(-euse)

Marxist ['mɑːksɪst] adj marxiste ◆ n marxiste m/f

marzipan ['mɑːzɪpæn] n pâte f d'amandes

mascara [mæs'kɑːrə] n mascara m

masculine ['mæskjulɪn] adj masculin(e)

mash [mæʃ] vt écraser, réduire en purée; **~ed potatoes** npl purée f de pommes de terre

mask [mɑːsk] n masque m ◆ vt masquer

mason ['meɪsn] n (also: **stonemason**) maçon m; (also: **freemason**) franc-maçon m; **~ry** n maçonnerie f

masquerade [mæskə'reɪd] vi: **to ~ as** se faire passer pour

mass [mæs] n multitude f, masse f; (PHYSICS) masse; (REL) messe f ◆ cpd (communication) de masse; (unemployment) massif(-ive) ◆ vi se masser; **the ~es** les masses; **~es of** des tas de

massacre ['mæsəkəʳ] n massacre m

massage ['mæsɑːʒ] n massage m ◆ vt masser

massive ['mæsɪv] adj énorme, massif(-ive)

mass media n inv mass-media mpl

mass production n fabrication f en série

mast [mɑːst] n mât m; (RADIO) pylône m

master ['mɑːstəʳ] n maître m; (in secondary school) professeur m; (title for boys): **M~ X** Monsieur X ◆ vt maîtriser; (learn) apprendre à fond; **~ly** adj magistral(e); **~mind** n esprit supérieur ◆ vt diriger, être le cerveau de; **M~ of Arts/Science** n ≈ maîtrise f (en lettres/sciences); **~piece** n chef-d'œuvre m; **~plan** n stratégie f d'ensemble; **~y** n maîtrise f; connaissance parfaite

mat [mæt] n petit tapis; (also: **doormat**) paillasson m; (also: **tablemat**) napperon m ◆ adj = **matt**

match [mætʃ] n allumette f; (game) match m, partie f; (fig) égal(e) ◆ vt (also: **~ up**) assortir; (go well with) aller bien avec; s'assortir à; (equal) égaler, valoir ◆ vi être assorti(e); **to be a good ~** être bien assorti(e); **~box** n boîte f d'allumettes; **~ing** adj assorti(e)

mate [meɪt] n (inf) copain (copine); (animal) partenaire m/f, mâle/femelle; (in merchant navy) second m ◆ vi s'accoupler

material [mə'tɪərɪəl] n (substance) matière f, matériau m; (cloth) tissu m, étoffe f; (information, data) données fpl ◆ adj matériel(le); (relevant: evidence) pertinent(e); **~s** npl (equipment) matériaux mpl

maternal [məˈtəːnl] adj maternel(le)
maternity [məˈtəːnɪtɪ] n maternité f;
~ **dress** n robe f de grossesse; ~ **hospital** n
maternité f
mathematical [mæθəˈmætɪkl] adj
mathématique
mathematics [mæθəˈmætɪks] n
mathématiques fpl
maths [mæθs] (US **math**) n math(s) fpl
matinée [ˈmætɪneɪ] n matinée f
mating call n appel m du mâle
matrices [ˈmeɪtrɪsɪːz] npl of **matrix**
matriculation [mətrɪkjuˈleɪʃən] n inscription
f
matrimonial [mætrɪˈməunɪəl] adj
matrimonial(e), conjugal(e)
matrimony [ˈmætrɪmənɪ] n mariage m
matrix [ˈmeɪtrɪks] (pl **matrices**) n matrice f
matron [ˈmeɪtrən] n (in hospital) infirmière-
chef f; (in school) infirmière
mat(t) [mæt] adj mat(e)
matted [ˈmætɪd] adj emmêlé(e)
matter [ˈmætəʳ] n question f; (PHYSICS)
matière f; (content) contenu m, fond m;
(MED: pus) pus m ♦ vi importer; ~**s** npl
(affairs, situation) la situation; **it doesn't** ~ cela
n'a pas d'importance; (I don't mind) cela ne
fait rien; **what's the** ~? qu'est-ce qu'il y a?,
qu'est-ce qui ne va pas?; **no** ~ **what** quoiqu'il
arrive; **as a** ~ **of course** tout naturellement; **as
a** ~ **of fact** en fait; ~**-of-fact** adj terre à terre;
(voice) neutre
mattress [ˈmætrɪs] n matelas m
mature [məˈtjuəʳ] adj mûr(e); (cheese)
fait(e); (wine) arrivé(e) à maturité ♦ vi
(person) mûrir; (wine, cheese) se faire
maul [mɔːl] vt lacérer
mauve [məuv] adj mauve
maximum [ˈmæksɪməm] (pl **maxima**) adj
maximum ♦ n maximum m
May [meɪ] n mai m; ~ **Day** n le Premier Mai;
see also **mayday**
may [meɪ] (conditional **might**) vi (indicating
possibility): **he** ~ **come** il se peut qu'il vienne;
(be allowed to): ~ **I smoke?** puis-je fumer?;
(wishes): ~ **God bless you!** que) Dieu vous
bénisse!; **you** ~ **as well go** à votre place, je
partirais
maybe [ˈmeɪbiː] adv peut-être; ~ **he'll** ...
peut-être qu'il ...
mayday [ˈmeɪdeɪ] n SOS m
mayhem [ˈmeɪhem] n grabuge m
mayonnaise [meɪəˈneɪz] n mayonnaise f
mayor [mɛəʳ] n maire m; ~**ess** n épouse f du
maire
maze [meɪz] n labyrinthe m, dédale m
M.D. n abbr (= Doctor of Medicine) titre
universitaire; = **managing director**
me [miː] pron me, m' +vowel; (stressed, after

prep) moi; **he heard** ~ il m'a entendu(e); **give**
~ **a book** donnez-moi un livre; **after** ~ après
moi
meadow [ˈmedəu] n prairie f, pré m
meagre [ˈmiːɡəʳ] (US **meager**) adj maigre
meal [miːl] n repas m; (flour) farine f; ~**time**
n l'heure f du repas
mean [miːn] (pt, pp **meant**) adj (with money)
avare, radin(e); (unkind) méchant(e);
(shabby) misérable; (average) moyen(ne)
♦ vt signifier, vouloir dire; (refer to) faire
allusion à, parler de; (intend): **to** ~ **to do** avoir
l'intention de faire ♦ n moyenne f; ~**s** npl
(way, money) moyens mpl; **by** ~**s of** par
l'intermédiaire de; au moyen de; **by all** ~**s!** je
vous en prie!; **to be** ~**t for sb/sth** être
destiné(e) à qn/qch; **do you** ~ **it?** vous êtes
sérieux?; **what do you** ~? que voulez-vous
dire?
meander [mɪˈændəʳ] vi faire des méandres
meaning [ˈmiːnɪŋ] n signification f, sens m;
~**ful** adj significatif(-ive); (relationship,
occasion) important(e); ~**less** adj dénué(e)
de sens
meanness [ˈmiːnnɪs] n (with money) avarice
f; (unkindness) méchanceté f; (shabbiness)
médiocrité f
meant [ment] pt, pp of **mean**
meantime [ˈmiːntaɪm] adv (also: **in the** ~)
pendant ce temps
meanwhile [ˈmiːnwaɪl] adv = **meantime**
measles [ˈmiːzlz] n rougeole f
measure [ˈmeʒəʳ] vt, vi mesurer ♦ n mesure
f; (ruler) règle (graduée); ~**ments** npl
mesures fpl; **chest/hip** ~**ment(s)** tour m de
poitrine/hanches
meat [miːt] n viande f; ~**ball** n boulette f de
viande
Mecca [ˈmekə] n La Mecque
mechanic [mɪˈkænɪk] n mécanicien m; ~**al**
adj mécanique; ~**s** n (PHYSICS) mécanique f
♦ npl (of reading, government etc) mécanisme
m
mechanism [ˈmekənɪzəm] n mécanisme m
medal [ˈmedl] n médaille f; ~**lion** [mɪˈdælɪən]
n médaillon m; ~**list** (US **medalist**) n (SPORT)
médaillé(e)
meddle [ˈmedl] vi: **to** ~ **in** se mêler de,
s'occuper de; **to** ~ **with** toucher à
media [ˈmiːdɪə] npl media mpl
mediaeval [medɪˈiːvl] adj = **medieval**
median [ˈmiːdɪən] (US) n (also: ~ **strip**)
bande médiane
mediate [ˈmiːdɪeɪt] vi servir d'intermédiaire
Medicaid ® [ˈmedɪkeɪd] (US) n assistance
médicale aux indigents
medical [ˈmedɪkl] adj médical(e) ♦ n visite
médicale
Medicare ® [ˈmedɪkɛəʳ] (US) n assistance

médicale aux personnes âgées

medication [medɪ'keɪʃən] *n* (*drugs*) médicaments *mpl*

medicine ['medsɪn] *n* médecine *f*; (*drug*) médicament *m*

medieval [medɪ'iːvl] *adj* médiéval(e)

mediocre [miːdɪ'əukəʳ] *adj* médiocre

meditate ['medɪteɪt] *vi* méditer

Mediterranean [medɪtə'reɪnɪən] *adj* méditerranéen(ne); **the ~ (Sea)** la (mer) Méditerranée

medium ['miːdɪəm] (*pl* **media**) *adj* moyen(ne) ♦ *n* (*means*) moyen *m*; (*pl* ~*s: person*) médium *m*; **the happy ~** le juste milieu; **~-sized** *adj* de taille moyenne; **~ wave** *n* ondes moyennes

medley ['medlɪ] *n* mélange *m*; (*MUS*) pot-pourri *m*

meek [miːk] *adj* doux (douce), humble

meet [miːt] (*pt, pp* met) *vt* rencontrer; (*by arrangement*) retrouver, rejoindre; (*for the first time*) faire la connaissance de; (*go and fetch*): **I'll ~ you at the station** j'irai te chercher à la gare; (*opponent, danger*) faire face à; (*obligations*) satisfaire à ♦ *vi* (*friends*) se rencontrer, se retrouver; (*in session*) se réunir; (*join: lines, roads*) se rejoindre; **~ with** *vt fus* rencontrer; **~ing** *n* rencontre *f*; (*session: of club etc*) réunion *f*; (*POL*) meeting *m*; **she's at a ~ing** (*COMM*) elle est en conférence

mega ['megə] (*inf*) *adv*: **he's ~ rich** il est hyper-riche; **~byte** *n* (*COMPUT*) méga-octet *m*; **~phone** *n* porte-voix *m inv*

melancholy ['melənkəlɪ] *n* mélancolie *f* ♦ *adj* mélancolique

mellow ['meləu] *adj* velouté(e); doux (douce); (*sound*) mélodieux(-euse) ♦ *vi* (*person*) s'adoucir

melody ['melədɪ] *n* mélodie *f*

melon ['melən] *n* melon *m*

melt [melt] *vi* fondre ♦ *vt* faire fondre; (*metal*) fondre; **~ away** *vi* fondre complètement; **~ down** *vt* fondre; **~down** *n* fusion *f* (du cœur d'un réacteur nucléaire); **~ing pot** *n* (*fig*) creuset *m*

member ['membəʳ] *n* membre *m*; **M~ of Parliament** (*BRIT*) député *m*; **M~ of the European Parliament** Eurodéputé *m*; **~ship** *n* adhésion *f*; statut *m* de membre; (*members*) membres *mpl*, adhérents *mpl*; **~ship card** *n* carte *f* de membre

memento [mə'mentəu] *n* souvenir *m*

memo ['meməu] *n* note *f* (de service)

memoirs ['memwɑːz] *npl* mémoires *mpl*

memorandum [memə'rændəm] (*pl* **memoranda**) *n* note *f* (de service)

memorial [mɪ'mɔːrɪəl] *n* mémorial *m* ♦ *adj* commémoratif(-ive)

memorize ['meməraɪz] *vt* apprendre par

cœur; retenir

memory ['memərɪ] *n* mémoire *f*; (*recollection*) souvenir *m*

men [men] *npl of* **man**

menace ['menɪs] *n* menace *f*; (*nuisance*) plaie *f* ♦ *vt* menacer; **menacing** *adj* menaçant(e)

mend [mend] *vt* réparer; (*darn*) raccommoder, repriser ♦ *n*: **on the ~** en voie de guérison; **to ~ one's ways** s'amender; **~ing** *n* réparation *f*; (*clothes*) raccommodage *m*

menial ['miːnɪəl] *adj* subalterne

meningitis [menɪn'dʒaɪtɪs] *n* méningite *f*

menopause ['menəupɔːz] *n* ménopause *f*

menstruation [menstru'eɪʃən] *n* menstruation *f*

mental ['mentl] *adj* mental(e); **~ity** [men'tælɪtɪ] *n* mentalité *f*

mention ['menʃən] *n* mention *f* ♦ *vt* mentionner, faire mention de; **don't ~ it!** je vous en prie, il n'y a pas de quoi!

menu ['menjuː] *n* (*set ~, COMPUT*) menu *m*; (*list of dishes*) carte *f*

MEP *n abbr* = **Member of the European Parliament**

mercenary ['məːsɪnərɪ] *adj* intéressé(e), mercenaire ♦ *n* mercenaire *m*

merchandise ['məːtʃəndaɪz] *n* marchandises *fpl*

merchant ['məːtʃənt] *n* négociant *m*, marchand *m*; **~ bank** (*BRIT*) *n* banque *f* d'affaires; **~ navy** (*US* **merchant marine**) *n* marine marchande

merciful ['məːsɪful] *adj* miséricordieux(-euse), clément(e); **a ~ release** une délivrance

merciless ['məːsɪlɪs] *adj* impitoyable, sans pitié

mercury ['məːkjurɪ] *n* mercure *m*

mercy ['məːsɪ] *n* pitié *f*, indulgence *f*; (*REL*) miséricorde *f*; **at the ~ of** à la merci de

mere [mɪəʳ] *adj* simple; (*chance*) pur(e); **a ~ two hours** seulement deux heures; **~ly** *adv* simplement, purement

merge [məːdʒ] *vt* unir ♦ *vi* (*colours, shapes, sounds*) se mêler; (*roads*) se joindre; (*COMM*) fusionner; **~r** *n* (*COMM*) fusion *f*

meringue [mə'ræŋ] *n* meringue *f*

merit ['merɪt] *n* mérite *m*, valeur *f*

mermaid ['məːmeɪd] *n* sirène *f*

merry ['merɪ] *adj* gai(e); **M~ Christmas!** Joyeux Noël!; **~-go-round** *n* manège *m*

mesh [meʃ] *n* maille *f*

mesmerize ['mezməraɪz] *vt* hypnotiser; fasciner

mess [mes] *n* désordre *m*, fouillis *m*, pagaille *f*; (*muddle: of situation*) gâchis *m*; (*dirt*) saleté *f*; (*MIL*) mess *m*, cantine *f*; **~ about** (*inf*) *vi* perdre son temps; **~ about with** (*inf*) *vt fus* tripoter; **~ around** (*inf*) *vi* = **mess about**;

~ around with vt fus = mess about with;
~ up vt (dirty) salir; (spoil) gâcher
message ['mesɪdʒ] n message m;
messenger ['mesɪndʒə'] n messager m
Messrs ['mesəz] abbr (on letters) MM
messy ['mesɪ] adj sale; en désordre
met [met] pt, pp of meet
metal ['metl] n métal m; **~lic** [mɪ'tælɪk] adj
métallique
meteorology [miːtɪə'rɔlədʒɪ] n
météorologie f
meter ['miːtə'] n (instrument) compteur m;
(also: **parking ~**) parcomètre m; (US: unit)
= metre
method ['meθəd] n méthode f; **~ical**
[mɪ'θɔdɪkl] adj méthodique; **M~ist** n
méthodiste m/f
meths [meθs] (BRIT) n = **methylated spirit**
methylated spirit ['meθɪleɪtɪd-] (BRIT) n
alcool m à brûler
metre ['miːtə'] (US **meter**) n mètre m; **metric**
['metrɪk] adj métrique
metropolitan [metrə'pɔlɪtn] adj
métropolitain(e); **the M~ Police** (BRIT) la
police londonienne
mettle ['metl] n: **to be on one's ~** être
d'attaque
mew [mjuː] vi (cat) miauler
mews [mjuːz] (BRIT) n: **~ cottage** cottage
aménagé dans une ancienne écurie
Mexico ['meksɪkəʊ] n Mexique m
miaow [miː'aʊ] vi miauler
mice [maɪs] npl of mouse
micro ['maɪkrəʊ] n (also: **~computer**) micro-
ordinateur m; **~chip** n puce f; **~phone** n
microphone m; **~scope** n microscope m;
~wave n (also: **~wave oven**) four m à
micro-ondes
mid [mɪd] adj: **in ~ May** à la mi-mai;
~ afternoon le milieu de l'après-midi; **in ~ air**
en plein ciel; **~day** n midi m
middle ['mɪdl] n milieu m; (waist) taille f
♦ adj du milieu; (average) moyen(ne); **in the
~ of the night** au milieu de la nuit; **~-aged**
adj d'un certain âge; **M~ Ages** npl: **the
M~ Ages** le moyen âge; **~-class** adj ≈
bourgeois(e); **~ class(es)** n(pl): **the
~ class(es)** ≈ les classes moyennes; **M~ East**
n Proche-Orient m, Moyen-Orient m; **~man**
(irreg) n intermédiaire m; **~ name** n
deuxième nom m; **~-of-the-road** adj
(politician) modéré(e); (music) neutre;
~weight n (BOXING) poids moyen;
middling adj moyen(ne)
midge [mɪdʒ] n moucheron m
midget ['mɪdʒɪt] n nain(e)
Midlands ['mɪdləndz] npl comtés du centre de
l'Angleterre
midnight ['mɪdnaɪt] n minuit m

midriff ['mɪdrɪf] n estomac m, taille f
midst [mɪdst] n: **in the ~ of** au milieu de
mid [mɪd-]: **~summer** [mɪd'sʌmə'] n milieu
m de l'été; **~way** [mɪd'weɪ] adj, adv:
~ (between) à mi-chemin (entre); **~ through**
... au milieu de ..., en plein(e) ...; **~week**
[mɪd'wiːk] adj au milieu de la semaine
midwife ['mɪdwaɪf] (pl **midwives**) n sage-
femme f
might [maɪt] vb see may ♦ n puissance f,
force f; **~y** adj puissant(e)
migraine ['miːgreɪn] n migraine f
migrant ['maɪgrənt] adj (bird) migra-
teur(-trice); (worker) saisonnier(-ère)
migrate [maɪ'greɪt] vi émigrer
mike [maɪk] n abbr (= microphone) micro m
mild [maɪld] adj doux (douce); (reproach,
infection) léger(-ère); (illness) bénin(-igne);
(interest) modéré(e); (taste) peu relevé(e)
♦ n (beer) bière légère; **~ly** adv doucement;
légèrement; **to put it ~ly** c'est le moins qu'on
puisse dire
mile [maɪl] n mi(l)le m (= 1609 m); **~age** n
distance f en milles; ≈ kilométrage m;
~ometer [maɪ'lɔmɪtə'] n compteur m (kilométrique); **~stone** n borne f; (fig) jalon m
militant ['mɪlɪtnt] adj militant(e)
military ['mɪlɪtərɪ] adj militaire
militia [mɪ'lɪʃə] n milice(s) f(pl)
milk [mɪlk] n lait m ♦ vt (cow) traire; (fig:
person) dépouiller, plumer; (: situation)
exploiter à fond; **~ chocolate** n chocolat m
au lait; **~man** (irreg) n laitier m; **~ shake** n
milk-shake m; **~y** adj (drink) au lait; (colour)
laiteux(-euse); **M~y Way** n voie lactée
mill [mɪl] n moulin m; (steel ~) aciérie f;
(spinning ~) filature f; (flour ~) minoterie f
♦ vt moudre, broyer ♦ vi (also: **~ about**)
grouiller; **~er** n meunier m
millennium bug [mɪ'lenɪəm-] n bogue m
or bug m de l'an 2000
milligram(me) ['mɪlɪɡræm] n milligramme
m
millimetre ['mɪlɪmiːtə'] (US **millimeter**) n
millimètre m
million ['mɪljən] n million m; **~aire** n
millionnaire m
milometer [maɪ'lɔmɪtə'] n ≈ compteur m
kilométrique
mime [maɪm] n mime m ♦ vt, vi mimer;
mimic ['mɪmɪk] n imitateur(-trice) ♦ vt
imiter, contrefaire
min. abbr = minute(s); minimum
mince [mɪns] vt hacher ♦ n (BRIT: CULIN:)
viande hachée, hachis m; **~meat** n (fruit)
hachis de fruits secs utilisé en pâtisserie; (US:
meat) viande hachée, hachis; **~ pie** n (sweet)
sorte de tarte aux fruits secs; **~r** n hachoir m
mind [maɪnd] n esprit m ♦ vt (attend to, look

after) s'occuper de; (*be careful*) faire attention à; (*object to*): **I don't ~ the noise** le bruit ne me dérange pas; **I don't ~** cela ne me dérange pas; **it is on my ~** cela me préoccupe; **to my ~** à mon avis or sens; **to be out of one's ~** ne plus avoir toute sa raison; **to keep** or **bear sth in ~** tenir compte de qch; **to make up one's ~** se décider; **~ you, ...** remarquez ...; **never ~** ça ne fait rien; (*don't worry*) ne vous en faites pas; **"~ the step"** "attention à la marche"; **~er** n (*child-minder*) gardienne f; (*inf: bodyguard*) ange gardien (*fig*); **~ful** *adj*: **~ful of** attentif(-ive) à, soucieux(-euse) de; **~less** *adj* irréfléchi(e); (*boring, job*) idiot(e)

mine¹ [maɪn] *pron* le (la) mien(ne), les miens (miennes) ♦ *adj*: **this book is ~** ce livre est à moi

mine² [maɪn] *n* mine f ♦ *vt* (*coal*) extraire; (*ship, beach*) miner; **~field** *n* champ *m* de mines; (*fig*) situation (très délicate); **~r** n mineur *m*

mineral ['mɪnərəl] *adj* minéral(e) ♦ *n* minéral *m*; **~s** *npl* (*BRIT: soft drinks*) boissons gazeuses; **~ water** *n* eau minérale

mingle ['mɪŋgl] *vi*: **to ~ with** se mêler à

miniature ['mɪnətʃər] *adj* (en) miniature ♦ *n* miniature f

minibus ['mɪnɪbʌs] *n* minibus *m*

minimal ['mɪnɪml] *adj* minime

minimize ['mɪnɪmaɪz] *vt* (*reduce*) réduire au minimum; (*play down*) minimiser

minimum ['mɪnɪməm] (*pl* **minima**) *adj, n* minimum *m*

mining ['maɪnɪŋ] *n* exploitation minière

miniskirt ['mɪnɪskɜːt] *n* mini jupe f

minister ['mɪnɪstər] *n* (*BRIT: POL*) ministre *m*; (*REL*) pasteur *m* ♦ *vi*: **to ~ to sb('s needs)** pourvoir aux besoins de qn; **~ial** [mɪnɪs'tɪərɪəl] (*BRIT*) *adj* (*POL*) ministériel(le); **ministry** *n* (*BRIT: POL*) ministère *m*; (*REL*): **to go into the ministry** devenir pasteur

mink [mɪŋk] *n* vison *m*

minor ['maɪnər] *adj* petit(e), de peu d'importance; (*MUS, poet, problem*) mineur(e) ♦ *n* (*LAW*) mineur(e)

minority [maɪ'nɔrɪtɪ] *n* minorité f

mint [mɪnt] *n* (*plant*) menthe f; (*sweet*) bonbon *m* à la menthe ♦ *vt* (*coins*) battre; **the (Royal) M~,** (*US*) **the (US) M~** ≈ l'Hôtel *m* de la Monnaie; **in ~ condition** à l'état de neuf

minus ['maɪnəs] *n* (*also*: **~ sign**) signe *m* moins ♦ *prep* moins

minute¹ [maɪ'njuːt] *adj* minuscule; (*detail, search*) minutieux(-euse)

minute² ['mɪnɪt] *n* minute f; **~s** *npl* (*official record*) procès-verbal, compte rendu

miracle ['mɪrəkl] *n* miracle *m*

mirage ['mɪrɑːʒ] *n* mirage *m*

mirror ['mɪrər] *n* miroir *m*, glace f; (*in car*) rétroviseur *m*

mirth [mɜːθ] *n* gaieté f

misadventure [mɪsəd'ventʃər] *n* mésaventure f

misapprehension ['mɪsæprɪ'henʃən] *n* malentendu *m*, méprise f

misappropriate [mɪsə'prəuprɪeɪt] *vt* détourner

misbehave [mɪsbɪ'heɪv] *vi* mal se conduire

miscalculate [mɪs'kælkjuleɪt] *vt* mal calculer

miscarriage ['mɪskærɪdʒ] *n* (*MED*) fausse couche; **~ of justice** erreur f judiciaire

miscellaneous [mɪsɪ'leɪnɪəs] *adj* (*items*) divers(es); (*selection*) varié(e)

mischief ['mɪstʃɪf] *n* (*naughtiness*) sottises *fpl*; (*fun*) farce f; (*playfulness*) espièglerie f; (*maliciousness*) méchanceté f; **mischievous** ['mɪstʃɪvəs] *adj* (*playful, naughty*) coquin(e), espiègle

misconception ['mɪskən'sepʃən] *n* idée fausse

misconduct [mɪs'kɒndʌkt] *n* inconduite f, **professional ~** faute professionnelle

misdemeanour [mɪsdɪ'miːnər] (*US* **misdemeanor**) *n* écart *m* de conduite; infraction f

miser ['maɪzər] *n* avare *m/f*

miserable ['mɪzərəbl] *adj* (*person, expression*) malheureux(-euse); (*conditions*) misérable; (*weather*) maussade; (*offer, donation*) minable; (*failure*) pitoyable

miserly ['maɪzəlɪ] *adj* avare

misery ['mɪzərɪ] *n* (*unhappiness*) tristesse f; (*pain*) souffrances *fpl*; (*wretchedness*) misère f

misfire [mɪs'faɪər] *vi* rater

misfit ['mɪsfɪt] *n* (*person*) inadapté(e)

misfortune [mɪs'fɔːtʃən] *n* malchance f, malheur *m*

misgiving [mɪs'gɪvɪŋ] *n* (*apprehension*) craintes *fpl*; **to have ~s about** avoir des doutes quant à

misguided [mɪs'gaɪdɪd] *adj* malavisé(e)

mishandle [mɪs'hændl] *vt* (*mismanage*) mal s'y prendre pour faire or résoudre etc

mishap ['mɪshæp] *n* mésaventure f

misinform [mɪsɪn'fɔːm] *vt* mal renseigner

misinterpret [mɪsɪn'tɜːprɪt] *vt* mal interpréter

misjudge [mɪs'dʒʌdʒ] *vt* méjuger

mislay [mɪs'leɪ] (*irreg: like* **lay**) *vt* égarer

mislead [mɪs'liːd] (*irreg: like* **lead**) *vt* induire en erreur; **~ing** *adj* trompeur(-euse)

mismanage [mɪs'mænɪdʒ] *vt* mal gérer

misplace [mɪs'pleɪs] *vt* égarer

misprint ['mɪsprɪnt] *n* faute f d'impression

Miss [mɪs] *n* Mademoiselle

miss [mɪs] *vt* (*fail to get, attend or see*) manquer, rater; (*regret the absence of*): **I**

~ him/it il/cela me manque ♦ *vi* manquer ♦ *n* (*shot*) coup manqué; **~ out** (*BRIT*) *vt* oublier

misshapen [mɪsˈʃeɪpən] *adj* difforme

missile [ˈmɪsaɪl] *n* (*MIL*) missile *m*; (*object thrown*) projectile *m*

missing [ˈmɪsɪŋ] *adj* manquant(e); (*after escape, disaster: person*) disparu(e); **to go ~** disparaître; **to be ~** avoir disparu

mission [ˈmɪʃən] *n* mission *f*; **~ary** [ˈmɪʃənrɪ] *n* missionnaire *m/f*; **~ statement** *n* déclaration *f* d'intention

mist [mɪst] *n* brume *f* ♦ *vi* (*also:* **~ over:** *eyes*) s'embuer; **~ over** *vi* (*windows etc*) s'embuer; **~ up** *vi* = mist over

mistake [mɪsˈteɪk] (*irreg: like take*) *n* erreur *f*, faute *f* ♦ *vt* (*meaning, remark*) mal comprendre; se méprendre sur; **to make a ~** se tromper, faire une erreur; **by ~** par erreur, par inadvertance; **to ~ for** prendre pour; **~n** *pp of* **mistake** ♦ *adj* (*idea etc*) erroné(e); **to be ~n** faire erreur, se tromper

mister [ˈmɪstər] (*inf*) *n* Monsieur *m*; *see also* **Mr**

mistletoe [ˈmɪsltəu] *n* gui *m*

mistook [mɪsˈtuk] *pt of* **mistake**

mistress [ˈmɪstrɪs] *n* maîtresse *f*; (*BRIT: in primary school*) institutrice *f*; (: *in secondary school*) professeur *m*

mistrust [mɪsˈtrʌst] *vt* se méfier de

misty [ˈmɪstɪ] *adj* brumeux(-euse); (*glasses, window*) embué(e)

misunderstand [mɪsʌndəˈstænd] (*irreg*) *vt, vi* mal comprendre; **~ing** *n* méprise *f*, malentendu *m*

misuse [*n* mɪsˈjuːs, *vb* mɪsˈjuːz] *n* mauvais emploi *m*; (*of power*) abus *m* ♦ *vt* mal employer; abuser de; **~ of funds** détournement *m* de fonds

mitigate [ˈmɪtɪgeɪt] *vt* atténuer

mitt(en) [ˈmɪt(n)] *n* mitaine *f*; moufle *f*

mix [mɪks] *vt* mélanger; (*sauce, drink etc*) préparer ♦ *vi* se mélanger; (*socialize*): **he doesn't ~ well** il est peu sociable ♦ *n* mélange *m*; **to ~ with** (*people*) fréquenter; **~ up** *vt* mélanger; (*confuse*) confondre; **~ed** *adj* (*feelings, reactions*) contradictoire; (*salad*) mélangé(e); (*school, marriage*) mixte; **~ed grill** *n* assortiment *m* de grillades; **~ed-up** *adj* (*confused*) désorienté(e), embrouillé(e); **~er** *n* (*for food*) batteur *m*, mixer *m*; (*person*): **he is a good ~er** il est très liant; **~ture** *n* assortiment *m*, mélange *m*; (*MED*) préparation *f*; **~-up** *n* confusion *f*

mm *abbr* (= *millimetre*) mm

moan [məun] *n* gémissement *m* ♦ *vi* gémir; (*inf: complain*): **to ~ (about)** se plaindre (de)

moat [məut] *n* fossé *m*, douves *fpl*

mob [mɔb] *n* foule *f*; (*disorderly*) cohue *f* ♦ *vt* assaillir

mobile [ˈməubaɪl] *adj* mobile ♦ *n* mobile *m*; **~ home** *n* (grande) caravane; **~ phone** *n* téléphone portatif

mock [mɔk] *vt* ridiculiser; (*laugh at*) se moquer de ♦ *adj* faux (fausse); **~ exam** examen blanc; **~ery** *n* moquerie *f*, raillerie *f*; **to make a ~ery of** tourner en dérision; **~-up** *n* maquette *f*

mod [mɔd] *adj see* **convenience**

mode [məud] *n* mode *m*

model [ˈmɔdl] *n* modèle *m*; (*person: for fashion*) mannequin *m*; (: *for artist*) modèle ♦ *vt* (*with clay etc*) modeler ♦ *vi* travailler comme mannequin ♦ *adj* (*railway: toy*) modèle réduit *inv*; (*child, factory*) modèle; **to ~ clothes** présenter des vêtements; **to ~ o.s. on** imiter

modem [ˈməudɛm] (*COMPUT*) *n* modem *m*

moderate [*adj* ˈmɔdərət, *vb* ˈmɔdəreɪt] *adj* modéré(e); (*amount, change*) peu important(e) ♦ *vi* se calmer ♦ *vt* modérer

modern [ˈmɔdən] *adj* moderne; **~ize** *vt* moderniser

modest [ˈmɔdɪst] *adj* modeste; **~y** *n* modestie *f*

modify [ˈmɔdɪfaɪ] *vt* modifier

mogul [ˈməugl] *n* (*fig*) nabab *m*

mohair [ˈməuhɛər] *n* mohair *m*

moist [mɔɪst] *adj* humide, moite; **~en** *vt* humecter; mouiller légèrement; **~ure** *n* humidité *f*; **~urizer** *n* produit hydratant

molar [ˈməulər] *n* molaire *f*

molasses [məˈlæsɪz] *n* mélasse *f*

mold [məuld] (*US*) *n, vt* = **mould**

mole [məul] *n* (*animal, fig: spy*) taupe *f*; (*spot*) grain *m* de beauté

molest [məˈlɛst] *vt* (*harass*) molester; (*LAW: sexually*) attenter à la pudeur de

mollycoddle [ˈmɔlɪkɔdl] *vt* chouchouter, couver

molt [məult] (*US*) *vi* = **moult**

molten [ˈməultən] *adj* fondu(e); (*rock*) en fusion

mom [mɔm] (*US*) *n* = **mum**

moment [ˈməumənt] *n* moment *m*, instant *m*; **at the ~** en ce moment; **at that ~** à ce moment-là; **~ary** *adj* momentané(e), passager(-ère); **~ous** [məuˈmɛntəs] *adj* important(e), capital(e)

momentum [məuˈmɛntəm] *n* élan *m*, vitesse acquise; (*fig*) dynamique *f*; **to gather ~** prendre de la vitesse

mommy [ˈmɔmɪ] (*US*) *n* maman *f*

Monaco [ˈmɔnəkəu] *n* Monaco *m*

monarch [ˈmɔnək] *n* monarque *m*; **~y** *n* monarchie *f*

monastery [ˈmɔnəstərɪ] *n* monastère *m*

Monday [ˈmʌndɪ] *n* lundi *m*

monetary [ˈmʌnɪtərɪ] *adj* monétaire

money ['mʌnɪ] n argent m; **to make ~** gagner de l'argent; **~ belt** n ceinture-portefeuille f; **~ order** n mandat m; **~-spinner** (inf) n mine f d'or (fig)

mongrel ['mʌŋgrəl] n (dog) bâtard m

monitor ['mɔnɪtər] n (TV, COMPUT) moniteur m ♦ vt contrôler; (broadcast) être à l'écoute de; (progress) suivre (de près)

monk [mʌŋk] n moine m

monkey ['mʌŋkɪ] n singe m; **~ nut** (BRIT) n cacahuète f

monopoly [mə'nɔpəlɪ] n monopole m

monotone ['mɔnətəun] n ton m (or voix f) monocorde; **monotonous** [mə'nɔtənəs] adj monotone

monsoon [mɔn'suːn] n mousson f

monster ['mɔnstər] n monstre m; **monstrous** ['mɔnstrəs] adj monstrueux(-euse); (huge) gigantesque

month [mʌnθ] n mois m; **~ly** adj mensuel(le) ♦ adv mensuellement

monument ['mɔnjumənt] n monument m

moo [muː] vi meugler, beugler

mood [muːd] n humeur f, disposition f; **to be in a good/bad ~** être de bonne/mauvaise humeur; **~y** adj (variable) d'humeur changeante, lunatique; (sullen) morose, maussade

moon [muːn] n lune f; **~light** n clair m de lune; **~lighting** n travail m au noir; **~lit** adj: **a ~lit night** une nuit de lune

moor [muər] n lande f ♦ vt (ship) amarrer ♦ vi mouiller; **~land** n lande f

moose [muːs] n inv élan m

mop [mɔp] n balai m à laver; (for dishes) lavette f (à vaisselle) ♦ vt essuyer; **~ of hair** tignasse f; **~ up** vt éponger

mope [məup] vi avoir le cafard, se morfondre

moped ['məuped] n cyclomoteur m

moral ['mɔrl] adj moral(e) ♦ n morale f; **~s** npl (attitude, behaviour) moralité f

morale [mɔ'rɑːl] n moral m

morality [mə'rælɪtɪ] n moralité f

morass [mə'ræs] n marais m, marécage m

---

more [mɔːr] adj 1 (greater in number etc) plus (de), davantage; **more people/work (than)** plus de gens/de travail (que)
2 (additional) encore (de); **do you want (some) more tea?** voulez-vous encore du thé?; **I have no** or **I don't have any more money** je n'ai plus d'argent; **it'll take a few more weeks** ça prendra encore quelques semaines
♦ pron plus, davantage; **more than 10** plus de 10; **it cost more than we expected** cela a coûté plus que prévu; **I want more** j'en veux plus or davantage; **is there any more?** est-ce

qu'il en reste?; **there's no more** il n'y en a plus; **a little more** un peu plus; **many/much more** beaucoup plus, bien davantage
♦ adv: **more dangerous/easily (than)** plus dangereux/facilement (que); **more and more expensive** de plus en plus cher; **more or less** plus ou moins; **more than ever** plus que jamais

---

moreover [mɔː'rəuvər] adv de plus

morning ['mɔːnɪŋ] n matin m; matinée f ♦ cpd matinal(e); (paper) du matin; **in the ~** le matin; **7 o'clock in the ~** 7 heures du matin; **~ sickness** n nausées matinales

Morocco [mə'rɔkəu] n Maroc m

moron ['mɔːrɔn] (inf) n idiot(e)

Morse [mɔːs] n: **~ code** morse m

morsel ['mɔːsl] n bouchée f

mortar ['mɔːtər] n mortier m

mortgage ['mɔːgɪdʒ] n hypothèque f; (loan) prêt m (or crédit m) hypothécaire ♦ vt hypothéquer; **~ company** (US) n société f de crédit immobilier

mortuary ['mɔːtjuərɪ] n morgue f

mosaic [məu'zeɪɪk] n mosaïque f

Moscow ['mɔskəu] n Moscou

Moslem ['mɔzləm] adj, n = **Muslim**

mosque [mɔsk] n mosquée f

mosquito [mɔs'kiːtəu] (pl **~es**) n moustique m

moss [mɔs] n mousse f

most [məust] adj la plupart de; le plus de ♦ pron la plupart ♦ adv le plus; (very) très, extrêmement; **the ~** (also: + adjective) le plus; **~ of** la plus grande partie de; **~ of them** la plupart d'entre eux; **I saw (the) ~** j'en ai vu la plupart; c'est moi qui en ai vu le plus; **at the (very) ~** au plus; **to make the ~ of** profiter au maximum de; **~ly** adv (chiefly) surtout, (usually) généralement

MOT n abbr (BRIT: = Ministry of Transport): **the MOT (test)** la visite technique (annuelle) obligatoire des véhicules à moteur

motel [məu'tel] n motel m

moth [mɔθ] n papillon m de nuit; (in clothes) mite f

mother ['mʌðər] n mère f ♦ vt (act as ~ to) servir de mère à; (pamper, protect) materner; **~ country** mère patrie; **~hood** n maternité f; **~-in-law** n belle-mère f; **~ly** adj maternel(le); **~-of-pearl** n nacre f; **M~'s Day** n fête f des Mères; **~-to-be** n future maman; **~ tongue** n langue maternelle

motion ['məuʃən] n mouvement m; (gesture) geste m; (at meeting) motion f ♦ vt, vi: **to ~ (to) sb to do** faire signe à qn de faire; **~less** adj immobile, sans mouvement; **~ picture** n film m

motivated ['məutɪveɪtɪd] adj motivé(e);

motivation [məutɪ'veɪʃən] n motivation f
motive ['məutɪv] n motif m, mobile m
motley ['mɔtlɪ] adj hétéroclite
motor ['məutər] n moteur m; (BRIT: inf:
vehicle) auto f ♦ cpd (industry, vehicle)
automobile; **~bike** n moto f; **~boat** n
bateau m à moteur; **~car** (BRIT) n automobile
f; **~cycle** n vélomoteur m; **~cycle racing** n
course f de motos; **~cyclist** n motocycliste
m/f; **~ing** (BRIT) n tourisme m automobile;
~ist n automobiliste m/f; **~ mechanic** n
mécanicien m garagiste; **~ racing** (BRIT) n
course f automobile; **~ trade** n secteur m de
l'automobile; **~way** (BRIT) n autoroute f
mottled ['mɔtld] adj tacheté(e), marbré(e)
motto ['mɔtəu] (pl **~es**) n devise f
mould [məuld] (US **mold**) n moule m;
(mildew) moisissure f ♦ vt mouler, modeler;
(fig) façonner; **mo(u)ldy** adj moisi(e);
(smell) de moisi
moult [məult] (US **molt**) vi muer
mound [maund] n monticule m, tertre m;
(heap) monceau m, tas m
mount [maunt] n mont m, montagne f ♦ vt
monter ♦ vi (inflation, tension) augmenter;
(also: **~ up**: problems etc) s'accumuler; **~ up**
vi (bills, costs, savings) s'accumuler
mountain ['mauntɪn] n montagne f ♦ cpd
de montagne; **~ bike** n VTT m, vélo tout-
terrain; **~eer** [mauntɪ'nɪər] n alpiniste m/f;
~eering n alpinisme m; **~ous** adj
montagneux(-euse); **~ rescue team** n
équipe f de secours en montagne; **~side** n
flanc m or versant m de la montagne
mourn [mɔːn] vt pleurer ♦ vi: **to ~ (for)**
(person) pleurer (la mort de); **~er** n
parent(e) or ami(e) du défunt; personne f en
deuil; **~ing** n deuil m; **in ~ing** en deuil
mouse [maus] (pl **mice**) n (also COMPUT)
souris f; **~trap** n souricière f
mousse [muːs] n mousse f
moustache [məsˈtɑːʃ] (US **mustache**) n
moustache(s) f(pl)
mousy ['mausɪ] adj (hair) d'un châtain terne
mouth [mauθ] (pl **~s**) n bouche f; (of dog,
cat) gueule f; (of river) embouchure f; (of
hole, cave) ouverture f; **~ful** n bouchée f;
~ organ n harmonica m; **~piece** n (of
musical instrument) embouchure f;
(spokesman) porte-parole m inv; **~wash** n
eau f dentifrice; **~-watering** adj qui met
l'eau à la bouche
movable ['muːvəbl] adj mobile
move [muːv] n (~ment) mouvement m; (in
game) coup m; (: turn to play) tour m;
(~change: of house) déménagement m; (: of
job) changement m d'emploi ♦ vt déplacer,
bouger; (emotionally) émouvoir; (POL:
resolution etc) proposer; (in game) jouer ♦ vi

(gen) bouger, remuer; (traffic) circuler; (also:
~ house) déménager; (situation) progresser;
that was a good ~ bien joué!; **to get a ~ on** se
dépêcher, se remuer; **~ about** vi
(fidget) remuer; (travel) voyager, se déplacer;
(change residence, job) ne pas rester au même
endroit; **~ along** vi se pousser; **~ around** vi
= move about; **~ away** vi s'en aller; **~ back**
vi revenir, retourner; **~ forward** vi avancer;
~ in vi (to a house) emménager; (police,
soldiers) intervenir; **~ on** vi se remettre en
route; **~ out** vi (of house) déménager;
~ over vi se pousser, se déplacer; **~ up** vi
(pupil) passer dans la classe supérieure;
(employee) avoir de l'avancement; **~able** adj
= movable
movement ['muːvmənt] n mouvement m
movie ['muːvɪ] n film m; **the ~s** le cinéma
moving ['muːvɪŋ] adj en mouvement;
(emotional) émouvant(e)
mow [məu] (pt **mowed**, pp **mowed** or **mown**)
vt faucher; (lawn) tondre; **~ down** vt
faucher; **~er** n (also: **lawnmower**) tondeuse f
à gazon
MP n abbr = Member of Parliament
mph abbr = miles per hour
Mr ['mɪstər] n: **~ Smith** Monsieur Smith, M.
Smith
Mrs ['mɪsɪz] n: **~ Smith** Madame Smith, Mme
Smith
Ms [mɪz] n (= Miss or Mrs): **~ Smith** Madame
Smith, Mme Smith
MSc abbr = Master of Science
much [mʌtʃ] adj beaucoup de ♦ adv, n, pron
beaucoup; **how ~ is it?** combien est-ce que ça
coûte?; **too ~** trop (de); **as ~ as** autant de
muck [mʌk] n (dirt) saleté f; **~ about** or
around (inf) vi faire l'imbécile; **~ up** (inf) vt
(exam, interview) se planter à (fam); **~y** adj
(très) sale; (book, film) cochon(ne)
mud [mʌd] n boue f
muddle ['mʌdl] n (mess) pagaille f, désordre
m; (mix-up) confusion f ♦ vt (also: **~ up**)
embrouiller; **~ through** vi se débrouiller
muddy ['mʌdɪ] adj boueux(-euse)
mudguard ['mʌdgɑːd] n garde-boue m inv
muesli ['mjuːzlɪ] n muesli m
muffin ['mʌfɪn] n muffin m
muffle ['mʌfl] vt (sound) assourdir, étouffer;
(against cold) emmitoufler; **~d** adj (sound)
étouffé(e); (person) emmitouflé(e); **~r** (US) n
(AUT) silencieux m
mug [mʌg] n (cup) grande tasse (sans
soucoupe); (: for beer) chope f; (inf: face)
bouille f; (: fool) poire f ♦ vt (assault)
agresser; **~ger** n agresseur m; **~ging** n
agression f
muggy ['mʌgɪ] adj lourd(e), moite

mule [mjuːl] n mule f
multi-level ['mʌltɪlevl] (US) adj
= **multistorey**
multiple ['mʌltɪpl] adj multiple ♦ n multiple
m; ~ **sclerosis** [-sklɪ'rəusɪs] n sclérose f en
plaques
multiplex cinema ['mʌltɪpleks-] n cinéma
m multisalles
multiplication [mʌltɪplɪ'keɪʃən] n
multiplication f; **multiply** ['mʌltɪplaɪ] vt
multiplier ♦ vi se multiplier
multistorey ['mʌltɪ'stɔːrɪ] (BRIT) adj
(building) à étages; (car park) à étages or
niveaux multiples ♦ n (car park) parking m à
plusieurs étages
mum [mʌm] (BRIT: inf) n maman f ♦ adj: **to
keep** ~ ne pas souffler mot
mumble ['mʌmbl] vt, vi marmotter,
marmonner
mummy ['mʌmɪ] n (BRIT: mother) maman f;
(embalmed) momie f
mumps [mʌmps] n oreillons mpl
munch [mʌntʃ] vt, vi mâcher
mundane [mʌn'deɪn] adj banal(e), terre à
terre inv
municipal [mjuː'nɪsɪpl] adj municipal(e)
murder ['məːdər] n meurtre m, assassinat m
♦ vt assassiner; ~**er** n meurtrier m, assassin
m; ~**ous** ['məːdərəs] adj meurtrier(-ère)
murky ['məːkɪ] adj sombre, ténébreux(-euse);
(water) trouble
murmur ['məːmər] n murmure m ♦ vt, vi
murmurer
muscle ['mʌsl] n muscle m; (fig) force f; ~
in vi (on territory) envahir; (on success)
exploiter; **muscular** ['mʌskjulər] adj
musculaire; (person, arm) musclé(e)
muse [mjuːz] vi méditer, songer
museum [mjuː'zɪəm] n musée m
mushroom ['mʌʃrum] n champignon m ♦ vi
pousser comme un champignon
music ['mjuːzɪk] n musique f; ~**al** adj
musical(e); (person) musicien(ne) ♦ n (show)
comédie musicale; ~**al instrument** n
instrument m de musique; ~ **centre** n chaîne
compacte; ~**ian** [mjuː'zɪʃən] n musicien(ne)
Muslim ['mʌzlɪm] adj, n musulman(e)
muslin ['mʌzlɪn] n mousseline f
mussel ['mʌsl] n moule f
must [mʌst] aux vb (obligation): **I ~ do it** je
dois le faire, il faut que je le fasse;
(probability): **he ~ be there by now** il doit y
être maintenant, il y est probablement
maintenant; (suggestion, invitation): **you
~ come and see me** il faut que vous veniez me
voir; (indicating sth unwelcome): **why ~ he
behave so badly?** qu'est-ce qui le pousse à se
conduire si mal? ♦ n nécessité f, impératif m;
it's a ~ c'est indispensable

mustache ['mʌstæʃ] (US) n = **moustache**
mustard ['mʌstəd] n moutarde f
muster ['mʌstər] vt rassembler
mustn't ['mʌsnt] = **must not**
mute [mjuːt] adj muet(te); ~**d** adj (colour)
sourd(e); (reaction) voilé(e)
mutiny ['mjuːtɪnɪ] n mutinerie f ♦ vi se
mutiner
mutter ['mʌtər] vt, vi marmonner, marmotter
mutton ['mʌtn] n mouton m
mutual ['mjuːtʃuəl] adj mutuel(le),
réciproque; (benefit, interest) commun(e);
~**ly** adv mutuellement
muzzle ['mʌzl] n museau m, (protective
device) muselière f; (of gun) gueule f ♦ vt
museler
my [maɪ] adj mon (ma), mes pl; ~ **house/car/
gloves** ma maison/mon auto/mes gants; **I've
washed ~ hair/cut ~ finger** je me suis lavé les
cheveux/coupé le doigt; ~**self** [maɪ'sɛlf] pron
(reflexive) me; (emphatic) moi-même; (after
prep) moi; see also **oneself**
mysterious [mɪs'tɪərɪəs] adj mysté-
rieux(-euse)
mystery ['mɪstərɪ] n mystère m
mystify ['mɪstɪfaɪ] vt mystifier; (puzzle)
ébahir
myth [mɪθ] n mythe m; ~**ology** [mɪ'θɔlədʒɪ]
n mythologie f

N, n

n/a abbr = **not applicable**
naff [næf] (BRIT: inf) adj nul(le)
nag [næg] vt (scold) être toujours après,
reprendre sans arrêt; ~**ging** adj (doubt, pain)
persistant(e)
nail [neɪl] n (human) ongle m; (metal) clou m
♦ vt clouer; **to ~ sb down to a date/price**
contraindre qn à accepter or donner une
date/un prix; ~**brush** n brosse f à ongles;
~**file** n lime f à ongles; ~ **polish** n vernis m à
ongles; ~ **polish remover** n dissolvant m;
~ **scissors** npl ciseaux mpl à ongles;
~ **varnish** (BRIT) n = **nail polish**
naïve [naɪ'iːv] adj naïf(-ïve)
naked ['neɪkɪd] adj nu(e)
name [neɪm] n nom m; (reputation)
réputation f ♦ vt nommer; (identify:
accomplice etc) citer; (price, date) fixer,
donner; **by ~** par son nom; **in the ~ of** au
nom de; **what's your ~?** comment vous
appelez-vous?; ~**less** adj sans nom; (witness,
contributor) anonyme; ~**ly** adv à savoir;
~**sake** n homonyme m
nanny ['nænɪ] n bonne f d'enfants
nap [næp] n (sleep) (petit) somme ♦ vi: **to be
caught ~ping** être pris à l'improviste or en

défaut

nape [neɪp] n: ~ **of the neck** nuque f

napkin ['næpkɪn] n serviette f (de table)

nappy ['næpɪ] (BRIT) n couche f (gen pl);
~ **rash** n: **to have ~ rash** avoir les fesses
rouges

narcissus [nɑːˈsɪsəs] (pl **narcissi**) n narcisse
m

narcotic [nɑːˈkɒtɪk] n (drug) stupéfiant m;
(MED) narcotique m

narrative ['nærətɪv] n récit m

narrow ['nærəʊ] adj étroit(e); (fig)
restreint(e), limité(e) ♦ vi (road) devenir plus
étroit, se rétrécir; (gap, difference) se réduire;
to have a ~ escape l'échapper belle; **to ~ sth
down to** réduire qch à; ~**ly** adv: **he ~ly
missed injury/the tree** il a failli se blesser/
rentrer dans l'arbre; ~**minded** adj à l'esprit
étroit, borné(e); (attitude) borné

nasty ['nɑːstɪ] adj (person: malicious)
méchant(e); (: rude) très désagréable;
(smell) dégoûtant(e); (wound, situation,
disease) mauvais(e)

nation ['neɪʃən] n nation f

national ['næʃənl] adj national(e) ♦ n
(abroad) ressortissant(e); (when home)
national(e); ~ **anthem** n hymne national;
~ **dress** n costume national; **N~ Health
Service** (BRIT) n service national de santé;
≈ Sécurité Sociale; **N~ Insurance** (BRIT) n
≈ Sécurité Sociale; ~**ism** n nationalisme m;
~**ist** adj nationaliste ♦ n nationaliste m/f;
~**ity** [næʃəˈnælɪtɪ] n nationalité f; ~**ize** vt
nationaliser; ~**ly** adv (as a nation) du point
de vue national; (nationwide) dans le pays
entier; ~ **park** n parc national

nationwide ['neɪʃənwaɪd] adj s'étendant à
l'ensemble du pays; (problem) à l'échelle du
pays entier ♦ adv à travers or dans tout le
pays

native ['neɪtɪv] n autochtone m/f, habitant(e)
du pays ♦ adj du pays, indigène; (country)
natal(e); (ability) inné(e); **a ~ of Russia** une
personne originaire de Russie; **a ~ speaker of
French** une personne de langue maternelle
française; **N~ American** n Indien(ne)
d'Amérique; ~ **language** n langue
maternelle

NATO ['neɪtəʊ] n abbr (= North Atlantic Treaty
Organization) OTAN f

natural ['nætʃrəl] adj naturel(le); ~ **gas** n
gaz naturel; ~**ist** n naturaliste m/f; ~**ly** adv
naturellement

nature ['neɪtʃəʳ] n nature f; **by ~** par
tempérament, de nature

naught [nɔːt] n = **nought**

naughty ['nɔːtɪ] adj (child) vilain(e), pas sage

nausea ['nɔːsɪə] n nausée f

naval ['neɪvl] adj naval(e); ~ **officer** n officier

m de marine

nave [neɪv] n nef f

navel ['neɪvl] n nombril m

navigate ['nævɪgeɪt] vt (steer) diriger; (plot
course) naviguer ♦ vi naviguer; **navigation**
[nævɪˈgeɪʃən] n navigation f

navvy ['nævɪ] (BRIT) n terrassier m

navy ['neɪvɪ] n marine f; ~**(-blue)** adj bleu
marine inv

Nazi ['nɑːtsɪ] n Nazi(e)

NB abbr (= nota bene) NB

near [nɪəʳ] adj proche ♦ adv près ♦ prep (also:
~ **to**) près de ♦ vt approcher de; ~**by**
[nɪəˈbaɪ] adj proche ♦ adv tout près, à
proximité; ~**ly** adv presque; **I ~ly fell** j'ai failli
tomber; ~ **miss** n (AVIAT) quasi-collision f;
that was a ~ miss (gen) il s'en est fallu de
peu; (of shot) c'est passé très près; ~**side** n
(AUT: in Britain) côté m gauche; (: in US,
Europe etc) côté droit; ~**-sighted** adj myope

neat [niːt] adj (person, work) soigné(e); (room
etc) bien tenu(e) or rangé(e); (skilful) habile;
(spirits) pur(e); ~**ly** adv avec soin or ordre;
habilement

necessarily ['nesɪsrɪlɪ] adv nécessairement

necessary ['nesɪsrɪ] adj nécessaire;
necessity [nɪˈsesɪtɪ] n nécessité f; (thing
needed) chose nécessaire or essentielle;
necessities npl nécessaire m

neck [nek] n cou m; (of animal, garment)
encolure f; (of bottle) goulot m ♦ vi (inf) se
peloter; ~ **and** ~ à égalité; ~**lace** n collier m;
~**line** n encolure f; ~**tie** n cravate f

need [niːd] n besoin m ♦ vt avoir besoin de;
to ~ to do devoir faire; avoir besoin de faire;
you don't ~ to go vous n'avez pas besoin or
vous n'êtes pas obligé de partir

needle ['niːdl] n aiguille f ♦ vt asticoter,
tourmenter

needless ['niːdlɪs] adj inutile

needlework ['niːdlwəːk] n (activity) travaux
mpl d'aiguille; (object(s)) ouvrage m

needn't ['niːdnt] = need not

needy ['niːdɪ] adj nécessiteux(-euse)

negative ['negətɪv] n (PHOT, ELEC) négatif m;
(LING) terme m de négation ♦ adj néga-
tif(-ive); ~ **equity** situation dans laquelle la valeur d'une maison est inférieure à celle de
l'emprunt-logement contracté pour la payer

neglect [nɪˈglekt] vt négliger ♦ n le fait de
négliger; (state of ~) abandon m; ~**ed** adj
négligé(e), à l'abandon

negligee ['neglɪʒeɪ] n déshabillé m

negotiate [nɪˈgəʊʃɪeɪt] vi, vt négocier;
negotiation [nɪgəʊʃɪˈeɪʃən] n négociation f,
pourparlers mpl

neigh [neɪ] vi hennir

neighbour ['neɪbəʳ] (US **neighbor**) n
voisin(e); ~**hood** n (place) quartier m;

(*people*) voisinage *m*; ~**ing** *adj* voisin(e), avoisinant(e); ~**ly** *adj* obligeant(e); (*action etc*) amical(e)

neither [ˈnaɪðəʳ] *adj*, *pron* aucun(e) (des deux), ni l'un(e) ni l'autre ♦ *conj*: **I didn't move and ~ did Claude** je n'ai pas bougé, (et) Claude non plus ♦ *adv*: ~ **good nor bad ni bon ni mauvais**; ..., ~ **did I refuse** ..., (et or mais) je n'ai pas non plus refusé ...

neon [ˈniːɔn] *n* néon *m*; ~ **light** *n* lampe *f* au néon

nephew [ˈnevjuː] *n* neveu *m*

nerve [nəːv] *n* nerf *m*; (*fig*: *courage*) sang-froid *m*, courage *m*, (: *impudence*) aplomb *m*, toupet *m*; **to have a fit of ~s** avoir le trac; ~**racking** *adj* angoissant(e)

nervous [ˈnəːvəs] *adj* nerveux(-euse); (*anxious*) inquiet(-ète), plein(e) d'appréhension; (*timid*) intimidé(e); ~ **breakdown** *n* dépression nerveuse

nest [nɛst] *n* nid *m* ♦ *vi* (se) nicher, faire son nid; ~ **egg** *n* (*fig*) bas *m* de laine, magot *m*

nestle [ˈnɛsl] *vi* se blottir

net [nɛt] *n* filet *m*; **the N~** (*Internet*) le Net ♦ *adj* net(te) ♦ *vt* (*fish etc*) prendre au filet; (*profit*) rapporter; ~**ball** *n* netball *m*

Netherlands [ˈnɛðələndz] *npl*: **the ~** les Pays-Bas *mpl*

nett [nɛt] *adj* = **net**

netting [ˈnɛtɪŋ] *n* (*for fence etc*) treillis *m*, grillage *m*

nettle [ˈnɛtl] *n* ortie *f*

network [ˈnɛtwəːk] *n* réseau *m*

neurotic [njuəˈrɔtɪk] *adj* névrosé(e)

neuter [ˈnjuːtəʳ] *adj* neutre ♦ *vt* (*cat etc*) châtrer, couper

neutral [ˈnjuːtrəl] *adj* neutre ♦ *n* (*AUT*) point mort; ~**ize** *vt* neutraliser

never [ˈnɛvəʳ] *adv* (ne ...) jamais; ~ **again** plus jamais; ~ **in my life** jamais de ma vie; *see also* **mind**; ~**-ending** *adj* interminable; ~**theless** *adv* néanmoins, malgré tout

new [njuː] *adj* nouveau (nouvelle); (*brand ~*) neuf (neuve); **N~ Age** *n* New Age *m*; ~**born** *adj* nouveau-né(e); ~**comer** *n* nouveau venu/nouvelle venue; ~**-fangled** [ˈnjuːˈfæŋgld] (*pej*) *adj* ultramoderne (et farfelu(e)); ~**-found** *adj* (*enthusiasm*) de fraîche date; (*friend*) nouveau (nouvelle); ~**ly** *adv* nouvellement, récemment; ~**ly-weds** *npl* jeunes mariés *mpl*

news [njuːz] *n* nouvelle(s) *f(pl)*; (*RADIO, TV*) informations *fpl*, actualités *fpl*; **a piece of ~** une nouvelle; ~ **agency** *n* agence *f* de presse; ~**agent** (*BRIT*) *n* marchand *m* de journaux; ~**caster** *n* présentateur(-trice); ~ **flash** *n* flash *m* d'information; ~**letter** *n* bulletin *m*; ~**paper** *n* journal *m*; ~**print** *n* papier *m* (de) journal; ~**reader** *n*

= **newscaster**; ~**reel** *n* actualités (filmées); ~ **stand** *n* kiosque *m* à journaux

newt [njuːt] *n* triton *m*

New Year *n* Nouvel An; ~**'s Day** *n* le jour de l'An; ~**'s Eve** *n* la Saint-Sylvestre

New Zealand [-ˈziːlənd] *n* la Nouvelle-Zélande; ~**er** *n* Néo-zélandais(e)

next [nɛkst] *adj* (*seat, room*) voisin(e), d'à côté; (*meeting, bus stop*) suivant(e); (*in time*) prochain(e) ♦ *adv* (*place*) à côté; (*time*) la fois suivante, la prochaine fois; (*afterwards*) ensuite; **the ~ day** le lendemain, le jour suivant or d'après; ~ **year** l'année prochaine; ~ **time** la prochaine fois; ~ **to** à côté de; ~ **to nothing** presque rien; ~, **please!** (*at doctor's etc*) au suivant!; ~ **door** *adv* à côté ♦ *adj* d'à côté; ~**-of-kin** *n* parent *m* le plus proche

NHS *n abbr* = **National Health Service**

nib [nɪb] *n* (bec *m* de) plume *f*

nibble [ˈnɪbl] *vt* grignoter

nice [naɪs] *adj* (*pleasant, likeable*) agréable; (*pretty*) joli(e); (*kind*) gentil(le); ~**ly** *adv* agréablement; joliment; gentiment

niceties [ˈnaɪsɪtɪz] *npl* subtilités *fpl*

nick [nɪk] *n* (*indentation*) encoche *f*; (*wound*) entaille *f* ♦ *vt* (*BRIT*: *inf*) faucher, piquer; **in the ~ of time** juste à temps

nickel [ˈnɪkl] *n* nickel *m*; (*US*) pièce *f* de 5 cents

nickname [ˈnɪkneɪm] *n* surnom *m* ♦ *vt* surnommer

nicotine patch [ˈnɪkətiːn-] *n* timbre *m* anti-tabac, patch *m*

niece [niːs] *n* nièce *f*

Nigeria [naɪˈdʒɪərɪə] *n* Nigéria *m* or *f*

niggling [ˈnɪglɪŋ] *adj* (*person*) tatillon(ne); (*detail*) insignifiant(e); (*doubts, injury*) persistant(e)

night [naɪt] *n* nuit *f*; (*evening*) soir *m*; **at** ~ la nuit; **by** ~ de nuit; **the ~ before last** avant-hier soir; ~**cap** *n* boisson prise avant le coucher; ~ **club** *n* boîte *f* de nuit; ~**dress** *n* chemise *f* de nuit; ~**fall** *n* tombée *f* de la nuit; ~**gown** *n* chemise *f* de nuit; ~**ie** [ˈnaɪtɪ] *n* chemise *f* de nuit; ~**ingale** [ˈnaɪtɪŋgeɪl] *n* rossignol *m*; ~**life** *n* vie *f* nocturne; ~**ly** *adj* de chaque nuit or soir; (*by night*) nocturne ♦ *adv* chaque nuit or soir; ~**mare** *n* cauchemar *m*; ~ **porter** *n* gardien *m* de nuit, concierge *m* de service la nuit; ~ **school** *n* cours *mpl* du soir; ~ **shift** *n* équipe *f* de nuit; ~**-time** *n* nuit *f*; ~ **watchman** *n* veilleur *m* or gardien *m* de nuit

nil [nɪl] *n* rien *m*; (*BRIT*: *SPORT*) zéro *m*

Nile [naɪl] *n*: **the ~** le Nil

nimble [ˈnɪmbl] *adj* agile

nine [naɪn] *num* neuf; ~**teen** [ˈnaɪnˈtiːn] *num* dix-neuf; ~**ty** [ˈnaɪntɪ] *num* quatre-vingt-dix; **ninth** [naɪnθ] *num* neuvième

nip [nɪp] *vt* pincer
nipple ['nɪpl] *n* (ANAT) mamelon *m*, bout *m* du sein
nitrogen ['naɪtrədʒən] *n* azote *m*

KEYWORD
---

no [nəʊ] (*pl* noes) *adv* (*opposite of "yes"*) non; **are you coming? - no (I'm not)** est-ce que vous venez? - non; **would you like some more? - no thank you** vous en voulez encore? - non merci
♦ *adj* (*not any*) pas de, aucun(e) (*used with "ne"*); **I have no money/books** je n'ai pas d'argent/de livres; **no student would have done it** aucun étudiant ne l'aurait fait; **"no smoking"** "défense de fumer"; **"no dogs"** "les chiens ne sont pas admis"
♦ *n* non *m*

---

nobility [nəʊ'bɪlɪtɪ] *n* noblesse *f*
noble ['nəʊbl] *adj* noble
nobody ['nəʊbədɪ] *pron* personne
nod [nɒd] *vi* faire un signe de tête (*affirmatif ou amical*); (*sleep*) somnoler ♦ *vt*: **to ~ one's head** faire un signe de (la) tête; (*in agreement*) faire signe que oui ♦ *n* signe *m* de (la) tête; **~ off** *vi* s'assoupir
noise [nɔɪz] *n* bruit *m*; **noisy** *adj* bruyant(e)
nominal ['nɒmɪnl] *adj* symbolique
nominate ['nɒmɪneɪt] *vt* (*propose*) proposer; (*appoint*) nommer; **nominee** [nɒmɪ'niː] *n* candidat agréé; personne nommée
non... [nɒn] *prefix* non-; **~-alcoholic** *adj* non-alcoolisé(e); **~committal** *adj* évasif(-ive); **~descript** *adj* quelconque, indéfinissable
none [nʌn] *pron* aucun(e); **~ of you** aucun d'entre vous, personne parmi vous; **I've ~ left** je n'en ai plus; **he's ~ the worse for it** il ne s'en porte pas plus mal
nonentity [nɒ'nentɪtɪ] *n* personne insignifiante
nonetheless ['nʌnðə'les] *adv* néanmoins
non-existent [nɒnɪg'zɪstənt] *adj* inexistant(e)
non-fiction [nɒn'fɪkʃən] *n* littérature *f* non-romanesque
nonplussed [nɒn'plʌst] *adj* perplexe
nonsense ['nɒnsəns] *n* absurdités *fpl*, idioties *fpl*; **~!** ne dites pas d'idioties!
non-: **~-smoker** *n* non-fumeur *m*; **~-smoking** *adj* non-fumeur; **~-stick** *adj* qui n'attache pas; **~-stop** *adj* direct(e), sans arrêt (*or* escale) ♦ *adv* sans arrêt
noodles ['nuːdlz] *npl* nouilles *fpl*
nook [nʊk] *n*: **~s and crannies** recoins *mpl*
noon [nuːn] *n* midi *m*
no one ['nəʊwʌn] *pron* = **nobody**
noose [nuːs] *n* nœud coulant; (*hangman's*)

corde *f*
nor [nɔː] *conj* = **neither** ♦ *adv see* **neither**
norm [nɔːm] *n* norme *f*
normal *adj* normal(e); **~ly** ['nɔːməlɪ] *adv* normalement
Normandy ['nɔːməndɪ] *n* Normandie *f*
north [nɔːθ] *n* nord *m* ♦ *adj* du nord, nord *inv* ♦ *adv* au *or* vers le nord; **N~ America** *n* Amérique *f* du Nord; **~-east** *n* nord-est *m*; **~erly** ['nɔːðəlɪ] *adj* du nord; **~ern** ['nɔːðən] *adj* du nord, septentrional(e); **N~ern Ireland** *n* Irlande *f* du Nord; **N~ Pole** *n* pôle *m* Nord; **N~ Sea** *n* mer *f* du Nord; **~ward(s)** *adv* vers le nord; **~-west** *n* nord-ouest *m*
Norway ['nɔːweɪ] *n* Norvège *f*; **Norwegian** [nɔː'wiːdʒən] *adj* norvégien(ne) ♦ *n* Norvégien(ne); (LING) norvégien *m*
nose [nəʊz] *n* nez *m*; **~ about, around** *vi* fouiner *or* fureter (partout); **~bleed** *n* saignement *m* du nez; **~-dive** *n* (descente *f* en) piqué *m*; **~y** (*inf*) *adj* = **nosy**
nostalgia [nɒs'tældʒɪə] *n* nostalgie *f*
nostril ['nɒstrɪl] *n* narine *f*; (*of horse*) naseau *m*
nosy ['nəʊzɪ] (*inf*) *adj* curieux(-euse)
not [nɒt] *adv* (ne ...) pas; **he is ~** *or* **isn't here** il n'est pas ici; **you must ~** *or* **mustn't do that** tu ne dois pas faire ça; **it's too late, isn't it** *or* **is it ~?** c'est trop tard, n'est-ce pas?; **~ yet/now** pas encore/maintenant; **~ at all** pas du tout; *see also* **all**; **only**
notably ['nəʊtəblɪ] *adv* (*particularly*) en particulier; (*markedly*) spécialement
notary ['nəʊtərɪ] *n* notaire *m*
notch [nɒtʃ] *n* encoche *f*
note [nəʊt] *n* note *f*; (*letter*) mot *m*; (*banknote*) billet *m* ♦ *vt* (*also*: **~ down**) noter; (*observe*) constater; **~book** *n* carnet *m*; **~d** *adj* réputé(e); **~pad** *n* bloc-notes *m*; **~paper** *n* papier *m* à lettres
nothing ['nʌθɪŋ] *n* rien *m*; **he does ~** il ne fait rien; **~ new** rien de nouveau; **for ~** pour rien
notice ['nəʊtɪs] *n* (*announcement, warning*) avis *m*; (*period of time*) délai *m*; (*resignation*) démission *f*; (*dismissal*) congé *m* ♦ *vt* remarquer, s'apercevoir de; **to take ~ of** prêter attention à; **to bring sth to sb's ~** porter qch à la connaissance de qn; **at short ~** dans un délai très court; **until further ~** jusqu'à nouvel ordre; **to hand in one's ~** donner sa démission, démissionner; **~able** *adj* visible; **~ board** (BRIT) *n* panneau *m* d'affichage
notify ['nəʊtɪfaɪ] *vt*: **to ~ sth to sb** notifier qch à qn; **to ~ sb (of sth)** avertir qn (de qch)
notion ['nəʊʃən] *n* idée *f*; (*concept*) notion *f*
notorious [nəʊ'tɔːrɪəs] *adj* notoire (*souvent en mal*)

nought [nɔːt] n zéro m
noun [naun] n nom m
nourish ['nʌrɪʃ] vt nourrir; **~ing** adj
nourrissant(e); **~ment** n nourriture f
novel ['nɔvl] n roman m ♦ adj nouveau
(nouvelle), original(e); **~ist** n romancier m;
~ty n nouveauté f
November [nəu'vembər] n novembre m
now [nau] adv maintenant ♦ conj: ~ **(that)**
maintenant que; **right ~** tout de suite; **by ~** à
l'heure qu'il est; **just ~: that's the fashion just
~** c'est la mode en ce moment; **~ and then,
~ and again** de temps en temps; **from ~ on**
dorénavant, **~adays** adv de nos jours
nowhere ['nəuwɛər] adv nulle part
nozzle ['nɔzl] n (of hose etc) ajutage m; (of
vacuum cleaner) suceur m
nuclear ['njuːklɪər] adj nucléaire
nucleus ['njuːklɪəs] (pl nuclei) n noyau m
nude [njuːd] adj nu(e) ♦ n nu m; **in the ~**
(tout(e)) nu(e)
nudge [nʌdʒ] vt donner un (petit) coup de
coude à
nudist ['njuːdɪst] n nudiste m/f
nuisance ['njuːsns] n: **it's a ~** c'est (très)
embêtant; **he's a ~** il est assommant or casse-
pieds; **what a ~!** quelle barbe!
null [nʌl] adj: **~ and void** nul(le) et non
avenu(e)
numb [nʌm] adj engourdi(e); (with fear)
paralysé(e)
number ['nʌmbər] n nombre m; (numeral)
chiffre m; (of house, bank account etc)
numéro m ♦ vt numéroter; (amount to)
compter; **a ~ of** un certain nombre de; **they
were seven in ~** ils étaient (au nombre de)
sept; **to be ~ed among** compter parmi;
~ plate n (AUT) plaque f minéralogique or
d'immatriculation
numeral ['njuːmərəl] n chiffre m
numerate ['njuːmərɪt] (BRIT) adj: **to be ~**
avoir des notions d'arithmétique
numerical [njuː'merɪkl] adj numérique
numerous ['njuːmərəs] adj nombreux(-euse)
nun [nʌn] n religieuse f, sœur f
nurse [nɜːs] n infirmière f ♦ vt (patient, cold)
soigner
nursery ['nɜːsərɪ] n (room) nursery f;
(institution) crèche f; (for plants) pépinière f;
~ rhyme n comptine f, chansonnette f pour
enfants; **~ school** n école maternelle;
~ slope n (SKI) piste f pour débutants
nursing ['nɜːsɪŋ] n (profession) profession f
d'infirmière; (care) soins mpl; **~ home** n
clinique f; maison f de convalescence
nut [nʌt] n (of metal) écrou m; (fruit) noix f;
noisette f; cacahuète f; **~crackers** npl casse-
noix m inv, casse-noisette(s) m
nutmeg ['nʌtmeg] n (noix f) muscade f

nutritious [njuː'trɪʃəs] adj nutritif(-ive),
nourrissant(e)
nuts [nʌts] (inf) adj dingue
nutshell ['nʌtʃel] n: **in a ~** en un mot
nutter ['nʌtər] (BRIT: inf) n: **he's a complete ~**
il est complètement cinglé
nylon ['naɪlɔn] n nylon m ♦ adj de or en
nylon

O, o

oak [əuk] n chêne m ♦ adj de or en (bois de)
chêne
OAP (BRIT) n abbr = **old-age pensioner**
oar [ɔːr] n aviron m, rame f
oasis [əu'eɪsɪs] (pl oases) n oasis f
oath [əuθ] n serment m; (swear word) juron
m; **under ~**, (BRIT) **on ~** sous serment
oatmeal ['əutmiːl] n flocons mpl d'avoine
oats [əuts] n avoine f
obedience [ə'biːdɪəns] n obéissance f;
obedient adj obéissant(e)
obey [ə'beɪ] vt obéir à; (instructions) se
conformer à
obituary [ə'bɪtjuərɪ] n nécrologie f
object [n 'ɔbdʒɪkt, vb əb'dʒekt] n objet m;
(purpose) but m, objet; (LING) complément m
d'objet ♦ vi: **to ~ to** (attitude) désapprouver;
(proposal) protester contre; **expense is no ~**
l'argent n'est pas un problème; **he ~ed that ...**
il a fait valoir or a objecté que ...; **I ~!** je
proteste!; **~ion** [əb'dʒekʃən] n objection f;
~ionable adj très désagréable; (language)
choquant(e); **~ive** n objectif m ♦ adj
objectif(-ive)
obligation [ɔblɪ'geɪʃən] n obligation f, devoir
m; **without ~** sans engagement; **obligatory**
[ə'blɪgətərɪ] adj obligatoire
oblige [ə'blaɪdʒ] vt (force): **to ~ sb to do**
obliger or forcer qn à faire; (do a favour)
rendre service à, obliger; **to be ~d to sb for
sth** être obligé(e) à qn de qch; **obliging** adj
obligeant(e), serviable
oblique [ə'bliːk] adj oblique; (allusion)
indirect(e)
obliterate [ə'blɪtəreɪt] vt effacer
oblivion [ə'blɪvɪən] n oubli m; **oblivious**
adj: **oblivious of** oublieux(-euse) de
oblong ['ɔblɔŋ] adj oblong (oblongue) ♦ n
rectangle m
obnoxious [əb'nɔkʃəs] adj odieux(-euse);
(smell) nauséabond(e)
oboe ['əubəu] n hautbois m
obscene [əb'siːn] adj obscène
obscure [əb'skjuər] adj obscur(e) ♦ vt
obscurcir; (hide: sun) cacher
observant [əb'zɜːvənt] adj observa-
teur(-trice)

observation [ɔbzə'veɪʃən] n (remark) observation f; (watching) surveillance f
observatory [əb'zɔːvətrɪ] n observatoire m
observe [əb'zɔːv] vt observer; (remark) observer or remarquer; ~**r** n observateur(-trice)
obsess [əb'sɛs] vt obséder; ~**ive** adj obsédant(e)
obsolete ['ɔbsəliːt] adj dépassé(e); démodé(e)
obstacle ['ɔbstəkl] n obstacle m; ~ **race** n course f d'obstacles
obstinate ['ɔbstɪnɪt] adj obstiné(e)
obstruct [əb'strʌkt] vt (block) boucher, obstruer; (hinder) entraver
obtain [əb'teɪn] vt obtenir
obvious ['ɔbvɪəs] adj évident(e), manifeste; ~**ly** adv manifestement; ~**ly not!** bien sûr que non!
occasion [ə'keɪʒən] n occasion f; (event) événement m; ~**al** adj pris(e) or fait(e) etc de temps en temps; occasionnel(le); ~**ally** adv de temps en temps, quelquefois
occupation [ɔkju'peɪʃən] n occupation f; (job) métier m, profession f; ~**al hazard** n risque m du métier
occupier ['ɔkjupaɪər] n occupant(e)
occupy ['ɔkjupaɪ] vt occuper; **to ~ o.s. in** or **with doing** s'occuper à faire
occur [ə'kɔːr] vi (event) se produire; (phenomenon, error) se rencontrer; **to ~ to sb** venir à l'esprit de qn; ~**rence** n (existence) présence f, existence f; (event) cas m, fait m
ocean ['əuʃən] n océan m
o'clock [ə'klɔk] adv: **it is 5** ~ il est 5 heures
OCR n abbr = **optical character reader**; **optical character recognition**
October [ɔk'təubər] n octobre m
octopus ['ɔktəpəs] n pieuvre f
odd [ɔd] adj (strange) bizarre, curieux(-euse); (number) impair(e); (not of a set) dépareillé(e); **60-~** 60 et quelques; **at ~ times** de temps en temps; **the ~ one out** l'exception f; ~**ity** n (person) excentrique m/f; (thing) curiosité f; ~-**job man** n homme m à tout faire; ~ **jobs** npl petits travaux divers; ~**ly** adv bizarrement, curieusement; ~**ments** npl (COMM) fins fpl de série; ~**s** npl (in betting) cote f; **it makes no ~s** cela n'a pas d'importance; **at ~s** en désaccord; ~**s and ends** de petites choses
odour ['əudər] (US **odor**) n odeur f

of [ɔv, əv] prep **1** (gen) de; **a friend of ours** un de nos amis; **a boy of 10** un garçon de 10 ans; **that was kind of you** c'était gentil de votre part
2 (expressing quantity, amount, dates etc) de;

a kilo of flour un kilo de farine; **how much of this do you need?** combien vous en faut-il?; **there were 3 of them** (people) ils étaient 3; (objects) il y en avait 3; **3 of us went** 3 d'entre nous y sont allé(e)s; **the 5th of July** le 5 juillet
3 (from, out of) en, de; **a statue of marble** une statue de or en marbre; **made of wood** (fait) en bois

off [ɔf] adj, adv (engine) coupé(e); (tap) fermé(e); (BRIT: food: bad) mauvais(e); (: milk: bad) tourné(e); (absent) absent(e); (cancelled) annulé(e) ♦ prep de; sur; **to be ~** (to leave) partir, s'en aller; **to be ~ sick** être absent pour cause de maladie; **a day ~** un jour de congé; **to have an ~ day** n'être pas en forme; **he had his coat ~** il avait enlevé son manteau; **10% ~** (COMM) 10% de rabais; ~ **the coast** au large de la côte; **I'm ~ meat** je ne mange plus de viande, je n'aime plus la viande; **on the ~ chance** à tout hasard
offal ['ɔfl] n (CULIN) abats mpl
off-colour ['ɔf'kʌlər] (BRIT) adj (ill) malade, mal fichu(e)
offence [ə'fɛns] (US **offense**) n (crime) délit m, infraction f; **to take ~ at** se vexer de, s'offenser de
offend [ə'fɛnd] vt (person) offenser, blesser; ~**er** n délinquant(e)
offense [ə'fɛns] (US) n = **offence**
offensive [ə'fɛnsɪv] adj offensant(e), choquant(e); (smell etc) très déplaisant(e); (weapon) offensif(-ive) ♦ n (MIL) offensive f
offer ['ɔfər] n offre f, proposition f ♦ vt offrir, proposer; **"on ~"** (COMM) "en promotion"; ~**ing** n offrande f
offhand [ɔf'hænd] adj désinvolte ♦ adv spontanément
office ['ɔfɪs] n (place, room) bureau m; (position) charge f, fonction f; **doctor's ~** (US) cabinet (médical); **to take ~** entrer en fonctions; ~ **automation** n bureautique f; ~ **block** (US **office building**) n immeuble m de bureaux; ~ **hours** npl heures fpl de bureau; (US: MED) heures de consultation
officer ['ɔfɪsər] n (MIL etc) officier m; (also: **police ~**) agent m (de police); (of organization) membre m du bureau directeur
office worker n employé(e) de bureau
official [ə'fɪʃl] adj officiel(le) ♦ n officiel m; (civil servant) fonctionnaire m/f; employé(e)
officiate [ə'fɪʃɪeɪt] vi (REL) officier; **to ~ at a marriage** célébrer un mariage
officious [ə'fɪʃəs] adj trop empressé(e)
offing ['ɔfɪŋ] n: **in the ~** (fig) en perspective
off- ~**licence** (BRIT) n (shop) débit m de vins et de spiritueux; ~**line** adj, adv (COMPUT) (en mode) autonome; (: switched off) non

connecté(e); **~-peak** *adj* aux heures creuses; (*electricity, heating, ticket*) au tarif heures creuses; **~-putting** (*BRIT*) *adj* (*remark*) rébarbatif(-ive); (*person*) rebutant(e), peu engageant(e); **~-road vehicle** *n* véhicule *m* tout-terrain; **~-season** *adj, adv* hors-saison *inv*; **~-set** (*irreg*) *vt* (*counteract*) contrebalancer, compenser; **~-shoot** *n* (*fig*) ramification *f*, antenne *f*; **~-shore** *adj* (*breeze*) de terre; (*fishing*) côtier(-ère); **~-side** *adj* (*SPORT*) hors jeu; (*AUT: in Britain*) de droite; (*: in US, Europe*) de gauche; **~-spring** *n inv* progéniture *f*; **~-stage** *adv* dans les coulisses; **~-the-peg** (*US off-the-rack*) *adj* en prêt-à-porter; **~-white** *adj* blanc cassé *inv*

Oftel ['ɔftel] *n organisme qui supervise les télécommunications*

often ['ɔfn] *adv* souvent; **how ~ do you go?** vous y allez tous les combien?; **how ~ have you gone there?** vous y êtes allé combien de fois?

Ofwat ['ɔfwɔt] *n organisme qui surveille les activités des compagnies des eaux*

oh [əu] *excl* ô!, oh!, ah!

oil [ɔil] *n* huile *f*; (*petroleum*) pétrole *m*; (*for central heating*) mazout *m* ♦ *vt* (*machine*) graisser; **~can** *n* burette *f* de graissage; (*for storing*) bidon *m* à huile; **~field** *n* gisement *m* de pétrole; **~ filter** *n* (*AUT*) filtre *m* à huile; **~ painting** *n* peinture *f* à l'huile; **~ refinery** *n* raffinerie *f*; **~ rig** *n* derrick *m*; (*at sea*) plate-forme pétrolière; **~ slick** *n* nappe *f* de mazout; **~ tanker** *n* (*ship*) pétrolier *m*; (*truck*) camion-citerne *m*; **~ well** *n* puits *m* de pétrole; **~y** *adj* huileux(-euse); (*food*) gras(se)

ointment ['ɔintmənt] *n* onguent *m*

O.K., okay ['əu'kei] *excl* d'accord! ♦ *adj* (*average*) pas mal ♦ *vt* approuver, donner son accord à; **is it ~?, are you ~?** ça va?

old [əuld] *adj* vieux (vieille); (*person*) vieux, âgé(e); (*former*) ancien(ne), vieux; **how ~ are you?** quel âge avez-vous?; **he's 10 years ~** il a 10 ans, il est âgé de 10 ans; **~er brother/sister** frère/sœur aîné(e); **~ age** vieillesse *f*; **~ age pensioner** (*BRIT*) *n* retraité(e); **~-fashioned** *adj* démodé(e); (*person*) vieux jeu *inv*

olive ['ɔliv] *n* (*fruit*) olive *f*; (*tree*) olivier *m* ♦ *adj* (*also:* **~-green**) (vert) olive *inv*; **~ oil** *n* huile *f* d'olive

Olympic [əu'limpik] *adj* olympique; **the ~ Games, the ~s** les Jeux *mpl* olympiques

omelet(te) ['ɔmlit] *n* omelette *f*

omen ['əumən] *n* présage *m*

ominous ['ɔminəs] *adj* menaçant(e), inquiétant(e); (*event*) de mauvais augure

omit [əu'mit] *vt* omettre; **to ~ to do** omettre de faire

KEYWORD

on [ɔn] *prep* **1** (*indicating position*) sur; **on the table** sur la table; **on the wall** sur le *or* au mur; **on the left** à gauche

2 (*indicating means, method, condition etc*): **on foot** à pied; **on the train/plane** (*be*) dans le train/l'avion; (*go*) en train/avion; **on the telephone/radio/television** au téléphone/à la radio/à la télévision; **to be on drugs** se droguer; **on holiday** en vacances

3 (*referring to time*): **on Friday** vendredi; **on Fridays** le vendredi; **on June 20th** le 20 juin; **a week on Friday** vendredi en huit; **on arrival** à l'arrivée; **on seeing this** en voyant cela

4 (*about, concerning*) sur, de; **a book on Balzac/physics** un livre sur Balzac/de physique

♦ *adv* **1** (*referring to dress, covering*): **to have one's coat on** avoir (mis) son manteau; **to put one's coat on** mettre son manteau; **what's she got on?** qu'est-ce qu'elle porte?; **screw the lid on tightly** vissez bien le couvercle

2 (*further, continuously*): **to walk** etc **on** continuer à marcher *etc*; **on and off** de temps à autre

♦ *adj* **1** (*in operation: machine*) en marche; (*: radio, TV, light*) allumé(e); (*: tap, gas*) ouvert(e); (*: brakes*) mis(e); **is the meeting still on?** (*not cancelled*) est-ce que la réunion a bien lieu?; (*in progress*) la réunion dure-t-elle encore?; **when is this film on?** quand passe ce film?

2 (*inf*): **that's not on!** (*not acceptable*) cela ne se fait pas!; (*not possible*) pas question!

once [wʌns] *adv* une fois; (*formerly*) autrefois ♦ *conj* une fois que; **~ he had left/it was done** une fois qu'il fut parti/que ce fut terminé; **at ~** tout de suite, immédiatement; (*simultaneously*) à la fois; **~ a week** une fois par semaine; **~ more** encore une fois; **~ and for all** une fois pour toutes; **~ upon a time** il y avait une fois, il était une fois

oncoming ['ɔnkʌmiŋ] *adj* (*traffic*) venant en sens inverse

KEYWORD

one [wʌn] *num* un(e); **one hundred and fifty** cent cinquante; **one day** un jour

♦ *adj* **1** (*sole*) seul(e), unique; **the one book which** l'unique *or* le seul livre qui; **the one man who** le seul (homme) qui

2 (*same*) même; **they came in the one car** ils sont venus dans la même voiture

♦ *pron* **1**: **this one** celui-ci (celle-ci); **that one** celui-là (celle-là); **I've already got one/a red one** j'en ai déjà un(e)/un(e) rouge; **one by one** un(e) à *or* par un(e)

2: **one another** l'un(e) l'autre; **to look at one**

another se regarder

3 (*impersonal*) on; **one never knows** on ne sait jamais; **to cut one's finger** se couper le doigt

one: **~-day excursion** (*US*) *n* billet *m* d'aller-retour (valable pour la journée); **~-man** *adj* (*business*) dirigé(e) *etc* par un seul homme; **~-man band** *n* homme-orchestre *m*; **~-off** (*BRIT: inf*) *n* exemplaire *m* unique

oneself [wʌn'self] *pron* (*reflexive*) se; (*after prep*) soi(-même); (*emphatic*) soi-même; **to hurt ~** se faire mal; **to keep sth for ~** garder qch pour soi; **to talk to ~** se parler à soi-même

one: **~-sided** *adj* (*argument*) unilatéral; **~-to-~** *adj* (*relationship*) univoque; **~-way** *adj* (*street, traffic*) à sens unique

ongoing ['ɔngəuɪŋ] *adj* en cours; (*relationship*) suivi(e)

onion ['ʌnjən] *n* oignon *m*

on-line ['ɔnlaɪn] *adj, adv* (*COMPUT*) en ligne; (: *switched on*) connecté(e)

onlooker ['ɔnlukə] *n* spectateur(-trice)

only ['əunlɪ] *adv* seulement ♦ *adj* seul(e), unique ♦ *conj* seulement, mais; **an ~ child** un enfant unique; **not ~ ... but also** non seulement ... mais aussi

onset ['ɔnsɛt] *n* début *m*; (*of winter, old age*) approche *f*

onshore ['ɔnʃɔ:'] *adj* (*wind*) du large

onslaught ['ɔnslɔ:t] *n* attaque *f*, assaut *m*

onto ['ɔntu] *prep* = **on to**

onward(s) ['ɔnwəd(z)] *adv* (*move*) en avant; **from that time ~** à partir de ce moment

ooze [u:z] *vi* suinter

opaque [əu'peɪk] *adj* opaque

OPEC ['əupɛk] *n abbr* (= *Organization of Petroleum-Exporting Countries*) O.P.E.P. *f*

open ['əupn] *adj* ouvert(e); (*car*) découvert(e); (*road, view*) dégagé(e); (*meeting*) public(-ique); (*admiration*) manifeste ♦ *vt* ouvrir ♦ *vi* (*flower, eyes, door, debate*) s'ouvrir; (*shop, bank, museum*) ouvrir; (*book etc: commence*) commencer, débuter; **in the ~ (air)** en plein air; **~ on to** *vt fus* (*subj: room, door*) donner sur; **~ up** *vt* ouvrir; (*blocked road*) dégager ♦ *vi* s'ouvrir; **~ing** *n* ouverture *f*; (*opportunity*) occasion *f* ♦ *adj* (*remarks*) préliminaire; **~ing hours** *npl* heures *fpl* d'ouverture; **~ly** *adv* ouvertement; **~-minded** *adj* à l'esprit ouvert; **~-necked** *adj* à col ouvert; **~-plan** *adj* sans cloisons

opera ['ɔpərə] *n* opéra *m*; **~ singer** *n* chanteur(-euse) d'opéra

operate ['ɔpəreɪt] *vt* (*machine*) faire marcher, faire fonctionner ♦ *vi* fonctionner; (*MED*): **to ~ (on sb)** opérer (qn)

operatic [ɔpə'rætɪk] *adj* d'opéra

operating table ['ɔpəreɪtɪŋ-] *n* table *f* d'opération

operating theatre *n* salle *f* d'opération

operation [ɔpə'reɪʃən] *n* opération *f*; (*of machine*) fonctionnement *m*; **to be in ~** (*system, law*) être en vigueur; **to have an ~** (*MED*) se faire opérer

operative ['ɔpərətɪv] *adj* (*measure*) en vigueur

operator ['ɔpəreɪtə] *n* (*of machine*) opérateur(-trice); (*TEL*) téléphoniste *m/f*

opinion [ə'pɪnjən] *n* opinion *f*, avis *m*; **in my ~** à mon avis; **~ated** *adj* aux idées bien arrêtées; **~ poll** *n* sondage *m* d'opinion

opponent [ə'pəunənt] *n* adversaire *m/f*

opportunity [ɔpə'tju:nɪtɪ] *n* occasion *f*; **to take the ~ of doing** profiter de l'occasion pour faire; en profiter pour faire

oppose [ə'pəuz] *vt* s'opposer à; **~d to** opposé(e) à; **as ~d to** par opposition à; **opposing** *adj* (*side*) opposé(e)

opposite ['ɔpəzɪt] *adj* opposé(e); (*house etc*) d'en face ♦ *adv* en face ♦ *prep* en face de ♦ *n* opposé *m*, contraire *m*; **the ~ sex** l'autre sexe, le sexe opposé; **opposition** [ɔpə'zɪʃən] *n* opposition *f*

oppressive [ə'prɛsɪv] *adj* (*political regime*) oppressif(-ive); (*weather*) lourd(e); (*heat*) accablant(e)

opt [ɔpt] *vi*: **to ~ for** opter pour; **to ~ to do** choisir de faire; **~ out** *vi*: **to ~ out of** choisir de ne pas participer à *or* de ne pas faire

optical ['ɔptɪkl] *adj* optique; (*instrument*) d'optique; **~ character recognition/reader** *n* lecture *f*/lecteur *m* optique

optician [ɔp'tɪʃən] *n* opticien(ne)

optimist ['ɔptɪmɪst] *n* optimiste *m/f*; **~ic** [ɔptɪ'mɪstɪk] *adj* optimiste

option ['ɔpʃən] *n* choix *m*, option *f*; (*SCOL*) matière *f* à option; (*COMM*) option; **~al** *adj* facultatif(-ive); (*COMM*) en option

or [ɔ:'] *conj* ou; (*with negative*): **he hasn't seen ~ heard anything** il n'a rien vu ni entendu; **~ else** sinon; ou bien

oral ['ɔ:rəl] *adj* oral(e) ♦ *n* oral *m*

orange ['ɔrɪndʒ] *n* (*fruit*) orange *f* ♦ *adj* orange *inv*

orbit ['ɔ:bɪt] *n* orbite *f* ♦ *vt* graviter autour de; **~al** (*motorway*) *n* périphérique *m*

orchard ['ɔ:tʃəd] *n* verger *m*

orchestra ['ɔ:kɪstrə] *n* orchestre *m*; (*US: seating*) (fauteuils *mpl* d')orchestre

orchid ['ɔ:kɪd] *n* orchidée *f*

ordain [ɔ:'deɪn] *vt* (*REL*) ordonner

ordeal [ɔ:'di:l] *n* épreuve *f*

order ['ɔ:də'] *n* ordre *m*; (*COMM*) commande *f* ♦ *vt* ordonner; (*COMM*) commander; **in ~** en ordre; (*document*) en règle; **in (working) ~** en état de marche; **out of ~** (*not in correct ~*) en désordre; (*not working*) en dérangement; **in ~ to do/that** pour faire/que +*sub*; **on ~** (*COMM*) en commande; **to ~ sb to do** ordonner à qn de faire; **~ form** *n* bon *m* de commande; **~ly** *n* (*MIL*) ordonnance *f*; (*MED*) garçon *m* de salle ♦ *adj* (*room*) en ordre; (*person*) qui a de l'ordre

ordinary ['ɔ:dnrɪ] *adj* ordinaire, normal(e); (*pej*) ordinaire, quelconque; **out of the ~** exceptionnel(le)

Ordnance Survey map ['ɔ:dnəns-] *n* ≈ carte *f* d'Etat-Major

ore [ɔ:] *n* minerai *m*

organ ['ɔ:gən] *n* organe *m*, (*MUS*) orgue *m*, orgues *fpl*; **~ic** [ɔ:'gænɪk] *adj* organique; (*food*) biologique

organization [ɔ:gənaɪ'zeɪʃən] *n* organisation *f*

organize ['ɔ:gənaɪz] *vt* organiser; **~r** *n* organisateur(-trice)

orgasm ['ɔ:gæzəm] *n* orgasme *m*

Orient ['ɔ:rɪənt] *n*: **the ~** l'Orient *m*; **o~al** [ɔ:rɪ'ɛntl] *adj* oriental(e)

origin ['ɔrɪdʒɪn] *n* origine *f*

original [ə'rɪdʒɪnl] *adj* original(e); (*earliest*) originel(le) ♦ *n* original *m*; **~ly** *adv* (*at first*) à l'origine

originate [ə'rɪdʒɪneɪt] *vi*: **to ~ from** (*person*) être originaire de; (*suggestion*) provenir de; **to ~ in** prendre naissance dans; avoir son origine dans

Orkney ['ɔ:knɪ] *n* (*also*: **the ~ Islands**) les Orcades *fpl*

ornament ['ɔ:nəmənt] *n* ornement *m*; (*trinket*) bibelot *m*; **~al** [ɔ:nə'mɛntl] *adj* décoratif(-ive); (*garden*) d'agrément

ornate [ɔ:'neɪt] *adj* très orné(e)

orphan ['ɔ:fn] *n* orphelin(e)

orthopaedic [ɔ:θə'pi:dɪk] (*US* **orthopedic**) *adj* orthopédique

ostensibly [ɔs'tɛnsɪblɪ] *adv* en apparence

ostentatious [ɔstɛn'teɪʃəs] *adj* prétentieux(-euse)

ostracize ['ɔstrəsaɪz] *vt* frapper d'ostracisme

ostrich ['ɔstrɪtʃ] *n* autruche *f*

other ['ʌðə] *adj* autre ♦ *pron*: **the ~** (*one*) l'autre; **~s** (~ *people*) d'autres; **~ than** autrement que; à part; **~wise** *adv*, *conj* autrement

otter ['ɔtə] *n* loutre *f*

ouch [autʃ] *excl* aïe!

ought [ɔ:t] (*pt* **ought**) *aux vb*: **I ~ to do it** je devrais le faire, il faudrait que je le fasse; **this ~ to have been corrected** cela aurait dû être corrigé; **he ~ to win** il devrait gagner

ounce [auns] *n* once *f* (= 28.35g; 16 in a pound)

our ['auə] *adj* notre, nos *pl*; *see also* **my**; **~s** *pron* le (la) nôtre, les nôtres; *see also* **mine¹**;

~selves [auə'sɛlvz] *pron pl* (*reflexive, after preposition*) nous; (*emphatic*) nous-mêmes; *see also* **oneself**

oust [aust] *vt* évincer

out [aut] *adv* dehors; (*published, not at home etc*) sorti(e); (*light, fire*) éteint(e); **~ here** ici; **~ there** là-bas; **he's ~** (*absent*) il est sorti; (*unconscious*) il est sans connaissance; **to be ~ in one's calculations** s'être trompé dans ses calculs; **to run/back** *etc* **~** sortir en courant/en reculant *etc*; **~ loud** à haute voix; **~ of** (~*side*) en dehors de; (*because of: anger etc*) par; (*from among*): **~ of 10** sur 10; (*without*): **~ of petrol** sans essence, à court d'essence; **~ of order** (*machine*) en panne; (*TEL: line*) en dérangement; **~-and-~** *adj* (*liar, thief etc*) véritable; **~back** *n* (*in Australia*): **the ~back** l'intérieur *m*; **~board** *n* (*also*: **~board motor**) (*moteur m*) hors-bord *m*; **~break** *n* (*of war, disease*) début *m*; (*of violence*) éruption *f*; **~burst** *n* explosion *f*, accès *m*; **~cast** *n* exilé(e), (*socially*) paria *m*; **~come** *n* issue *f*, résultat *m*; **~crop** *n* (*of rock*) affleurement *m*; **~cry** *n* tollé (général); **~dated** *adj* démodé(e); **~do** (*irreg*) *vt* surpasser; **~door** *adj* de or en plein air; **~doors** *adv* dehors; au grand air

outer ['autə] *adj* extérieur(e); **~ space** *n* espace *m* cosmique

outfit ['autfɪt] *n* (*clothes*) tenue *f*

out: **~going** *adj* (*character*) ouvert(e), extraverti(e); (*departing*) sortant(e); **~goings** (*BRIT*) *npl* (*expenses*) dépenses *fpl*, **~grow** (*irreg*) *vt* (*clothes*) devenir trop grand(e) pour; **~house** *n* appentis *m*, remise *f*

outing ['autɪŋ] *n* sortie *f*, excursion *f*

out: **~law** *n* hors-la-loi *m inv* ♦ *vt* mettre hors-la-loi; **~lay** *n* dépenses *fpl*; (*investment*) mise *f* de fonds; **~let** *n* (*for liquid etc*) issue *f*, sortie *f*; (*US: ELEC*) prise *f* de courant; (*also*: **retail ~let**) point *m* de vente; **~line** *n* (*shape*) contour *m*; (*summary*) esquisse *f*, grandes lignes ♦ *vt* (*fig: theory, plan*) exposer à grands traits; **~live** *vt* survivre à; **~look** *n* perspective *f*; (*fig*) attitude *f*; **~lying** *adj* écarté(e); **~moded** *adj* démodé(e); dépassé(e); **~number** *vt* surpasser en nombre; **~-of-date** *adj* (*passport*) périmé(e); (*theory etc*) dépassé(e); (*clothes etc*) démodé(e); **~-of-the-way** *adj* (*place*) loin de tout; **~patient** *n* malade *m/f* en consultation externe; **~post** *n* avant-poste *m*; **~put** *n* rendement *m*, production *f*; (*COMPUT*) sortie *f*

outrage ['autreɪdʒ] *n* (*anger*) indignation *f*; (*violent act*) atrocité *f*; (*scandal*) scandale *m* ♦ *vt* outrager; **~ous** [aut'reɪdʒəs] *adj* atroce; scandaleux(-euse)

outright [*adv* aut'raɪt, *adj* 'autraɪt] *adv*

complètement; (*deny, refuse*)
catégoriquement; (*ask*) carrément; (*kill*) sur
le coup ♦ *adj* complet(-ète); catégorique
outset ['autset] *n* début *m*
outside [aut'saɪd] *n* extérieur *m* ♦ *adj*
extérieur(e) ♦ *adv* (au) dehors, à l'extérieur
♦ *prep* hors de, à l'extérieur de; **at the ~** (*fig*)
au plus *or* maximum; **~ lane** *n* (*AUT: in
Britain*) voie *f* de droite; (: *in US, Europe*) voie
de gauche; **~ line** *n* (*TEL*) ligne extérieure; **~r**
n (*stranger*) étranger(-ère)
out: ~size ['autsaɪz] *adj* énorme; (*clothes*)
grande taille *inv*; **~skirts** *npl* faubourgs *mpl*;
~spoken *adj* très franc (franche);
~standing *adj* remarquable,
exceptionnel(le); (*unfinished*) en suspens;
(*debt*) impayé(e); (*problem*) non réglé(e);
~stay *vt*: **to ~stay one's welcome** abuser de
l'hospitalité de son hôte; **~stretched**
[aut'strɛtʃt] *adj* (*hand*) tendu(e); **~strip**
[aut'strɪp] *vt* (*competitors, demand*) dépasser;
~ tray *n* courrier *m* "départ"
outward ['autwəd] *adj* (*sign, appearances*)
extérieur(e); (*journey*) (d')aller
outweigh [aut'weɪ] *vt* l'emporter sur
outwit [aut'wɪt] *vt* se montrer plus malin que
oval ['əuvl] *adj* ovale ♦ *n* ovale *m*
ovary ['əuvərɪ] *n* ovaire *m*
oven ['ʌvn] *n* four *m*; **~proof** *adj* allant au
four
over ['əuvəʳ] *adv* (par-)dessus ♦ *adj* (*finished*)
fini(e), terminé(e); (*too much*) en plus ♦ *prep*
sur; par-dessus; (*above*) au-dessus de; (*on the
other side of*) de l'autre côté de; (*more than*)
plus de; (*during*) pendant; **~ here** ici; **~ there**
là-bas; **all ~** (*everywhere*) partout, fini(e);
~ and ~ (again) à plusieurs reprises; **~ and
above** en plus de; **to ask sb ~** inviter qn (à
passer)
overall [*adj, n* 'əuvərɔːl, *adv* əuvər'ɔːl] *adj*
(*length, cost etc*) total(e); (*study*) d'ensemble
♦ *n* (*BRIT*) blouse *f* ♦ *adv* dans l'ensemble, en
général; **~s** *npl* bleus *mpl* (de travail)
over: ~awe *vt* impressionner; **~balance** *vi*
basculer; **~board** *adv* (*NAUT*) par-dessus
bord; **~book** *vt* faire du surbooking; **~cast**
adj couvert(e)
overcharge [əuvə'tʃɑːdʒ] *vt*: **to ~ sb for sth**
faire payer qch trop cher à qn
overcoat ['əuvəkəut] *n* pardessus *m*
overcome [əuvə'kʌm] (*irreg*) *vt* (*defeat*)
triompher de; (*difficulty*) surmonter
over: ~crowded *adj* bondé(e); **~do** (*irreg*)
vt exagérer; (*overcook*) trop cuire; **to ~do it**
(*work etc*) se surmener; **~dose** *n* dose
excessive; **~draft** *n* découvert *m*; **~drawn**
adj (*account*) à découvert; (*person*) dont le
compte est à découvert; **~due** *adj* en retard;
(*change, reform*) qui tarde; **~estimate** *vt*

surestimer
overflow [əuvə'fləu] *vi* déborder ♦ *n* (*also:
~ pipe*) tuyau *m* d'écoulement, trop-plein *m*
overgrown [əuvə'grəun] *adj* (*garden*)
envahi(e) par la végétation
overhaul [*vb* əuvə'hɔːl, *n* 'əuvəhɔːl] *vt* réviser
♦ *n* révision *f*
overhead [*adv* əuvə'hɛd, *adj, n* 'əuvəhɛd]
adv au-dessus ♦ *adj* aérien(ne); (*lighting*)
vertical(e) ♦ *n* (*US*) = **overheads**; **~s** *npl*
(*expenses*) frais généraux; **~ projector** *n*
rétroprojecteur *m*
over: ~hear (*irreg*) *vt* entendre (par hasard);
~heat *vi* (*engine*) chauffer; **~joyed** *adj*:
~joyed (at) ravi(e) (de), enchanté(e) (de)
overland ['əuvəlænd] *adj, adv* par voie de
terre
overlap [əuvə'læp] *vi* se chevaucher
over: ~leaf *adv* au verso; **~load** *vt*
surcharger; **~look** *vt* (*have view of*) donner
sur; (*miss: by mistake*) oublier; (*forgive*)
fermer les yeux sur
overnight [əuvə'naɪt, *adj* 'əuvənaɪt] *adv*
(*happen*) durant la nuit; (*fig*) soudain ♦ *adj*
d'une (*or* de) nuit; **he stayed there ~** il y a
passé la nuit
overpass ['əuvəpɑːs] *n* pont autoroutier
overpower [əuvə'pauəʳ] *vt* vaincre; (*fig*)
accabler; **~ing** *adj* (*heat, stench*) suffocant(e)
over: ~rate *vt* surestimer; **~ride** (*irreg: like
ride*) *vt* (*order, objection*) passer outre à;
~riding *adj* prépondérant(e); **~rule** *vt*
(*decision*) annuler; (*claim*) rejeter; (*person*)
rejeter l'avis de; **~run** (*irreg: like* run) *vt*
(*country*) occuper; (*time limit*) dépasser
overseas [əuvə'siːz] *adv* outre-mer; (*abroad*)
à l'étranger ♦ *adj* (*trade*) extérieur(e);
(*visitor*) étranger(-ère)
overshadow [əuvə'ʃædəu] *vt* (*fig*) éclipser
oversight ['əuvəsaɪt] *n* omission *f*, oubli *m*
oversleep [əuvə'sliːp] (*irreg*) *vi* se réveiller
(trop) tard
overstep [əuvə'stɛp] *vt*: **to ~ the mark**
dépasser la mesure
overt [au'vəːt] *adj* non dissimulé(e)
overtake [əuvə'teɪk] (*irreg*) *vt* (*AUT*) dépasser,
doubler
over: ~throw (*irreg*) *vt* (*government*)
renverser; **~time** *n* heures *fpl*
supplémentaires; **~tone** *n* (*also: ~tones*)
note *f*, sous-entendus *mpl*
overture ['əuvətʃuəʳ] *n* (*MUS, fig*) ouverture *f*
over: ~turn *vt* renverser ♦ *vi* se retourner;
~weight *adj* (*person*) trop gros(se);
~whelm *vt* (*subj: emotion*) accabler; (*enemy,
opponent*) écraser; **~whelming** *adj* (*victory,
defeat*) écrasant(e); (*desire*) irrésistible
overwrought [əuvə'rɔːt] *adj* excédé(e)
owe [əu] *vt*: **to ~ sb sth, to ~ sth to sb** devoir

qch à qn; **owing to** *prep* à cause de, en raison de

owl [aul] *n* hibou *m*

own [əun] *vt* posséder ♦ *adj* propre; **a room of my ~** une chambre à moi, ma propre chambre; **to get one's ~ back** prendre sa revanche; **on one's ~** tout(e) seul(e); **~ up** *vi* avouer; **~er** *n* propriétaire *m/f*; **~ership** *n* possession *f*

ox [ɔks] (*pl* **~en**) *n* bœuf *m*; **~tail** *n*: **~tail soup** soupe *f* à la queue de bœuf

oxygen ['ɔksɪdʒən] *n* oxygène *m*

oyster ['ɔɪstər] *n* huître *f*

oz. *abbr* = **ounce(s)**

ozone ['əuzəun]: **~-friendly** *adj* qui n'attaque pas *or* qui préserve la couche d'ozone; **~ hole** *n* trou *m* d'ozone; **~ layer** *n* couche *f* d'ozone

P, p

p *abbr* = **penny; pence**

PA *n abbr* = **personal assistant; public address system**

pa [pɑː] (*inf*) *n* papa *m*

p.a. *abbr* = **per annum**

pace [peɪs] *n* pas *m*; (*speed*) allure *f*; vitesse *f* ♦ *vi*: **to ~ up and down** faire les cent pas; **to keep ~ with** aller à la même vitesse que; **~maker** *n* (*MED*) stimulateur *m* cardiaque; (*SPORT: also:* **~setter**) meneur(-euse) de train

Pacific [pə'sɪfɪk] *n*: **the ~ (Ocean)** le Pacifique, l'océan *m* Pacifique

pack [pæk] *n* (*~et, US: of cigarettes*) paquet *m*; (*of hounds*) meute *f*; (*of thieves etc*) bande *f*, (*back ~*) sac *m* à dos; (*of cards*) jeu *m* ♦ *vt* (*goods*) empaqueter, emballer; (*box*) remplir; (*cram*) entasser; **to ~ one's suitcase** faire sa valise; **to ~ (one's bags)** faire ses bagages; **to ~ sb off** expédier qn à; **~ it in!** laisse tomber!, écrase!

package ['pækɪdʒ] *n* paquet *m*; (*also:* **~ deal**) forfait *m*; **~ tour** (*BRIT*) *n* voyage organisé

packed *adj* (*crowded*) bondé(e); **~ lunch** (*BRIT*) *n* repas froid

packet ['pækɪt] *n* paquet *m*

packing ['pækɪŋ] *n* emballage *m*; **~ case** *n* caisse *f* (d'emballage)

pact [pækt] *n* pacte *m*; traité *m*

pad [pæd] *n* bloc(-notes) *m*; (*to prevent friction*) tampon *m* ♦ *vt* (*inf: home*) piaule *f* ♦ *vt* rembourrer; **~ding** *n* rembourrage *m*

paddle ['pædl] *n* (*oar*) pagaie *f*; (*US: for table tennis*) raquette *f* de ping-pong ♦ *vt*: **to ~ a canoe etc** pagayer ♦ *vi* barboter, faire trempette; **paddling pool** (*BRIT*) *n* petit bassin

paddock ['pædək] *n* enclos *m*; (*RACING*)

paddock *m*

padlock ['pædlɔk] *n* cadenas *m*

paediatrics [piːdɪ'ætrɪks] (*US* **pediatrics**) *n* pédiatrie *f*

pagan ['peɪɡən] *adj, n* païen(ne)

page [peɪdʒ] *n* (*of book*) page *f*; (*also:* **~ boy**) groom *m*, chasseur *m*; (*at wedding*) garçon *m* d'honneur ♦ *vt* (*in hotel etc*) (faire) appeler

pageant ['pædʒənt] *n* spectacle *m* historique; **~ry** *n* apparat *m*, pompe *f*

pager ['peɪdʒər], **paging device** *n* (*TEL*) récepteur *m* d'appels

paid [peɪd] *pt, pp of* **pay** ♦ *adj* (*work, official*) rémunéré(e); (*holiday*) payé(e); **to put ~ to** (*BRIT*) mettre fin à, régler

pail [peɪl] *n* seau *m*

pain [peɪn] *n* douleur *f*; **to be in ~** souffrir, avoir mal; **to take ~s to do** se donner du mal pour faire; **~ed** *adj* peiné(e), chagrin(e); **~ful** *adj* douloureux(-euse); (*fig*) difficile, pénible; **~fully** *adv* (*fig: very*) terriblement; **~killer** *n* analgésique *m*; **~less** *adj* indolore; **~staking** ['peɪnzteɪkɪŋ] *adj* (*person*) soigneux(-euse); (*work*) soigné(e)

paint [peɪnt] *n* peinture *f* ♦ *vt* peindre; **to ~ the door blue** peindre la porte en bleu; **~brush** *n* pinceau *m*; **~er** *n* peintre *m*; **~ing** *n* peinture *f*; (*picture*) tableau *m*; **~work** *n* peinture *f*

pair [pɛər] *n* (*of shoes, gloves etc*) paire *f*; (*of people*) couple *m*; **~ of scissors** (paire de) ciseaux *mpl*; **~ of trousers** pantalon *m*

pajamas [pə'dʒɑːməz] (*US*) *npl* pyjama(s) *m(pl)*

Pakistan [pɑːkɪ'stɑːn] *n* Pakistan *m*; **~i** *adj* pakistanais(e) ♦ *n* Pakistanais(e)

pal [pæl] (*inf*) *n* copain (copine)

palace ['pæləs] *n* palais *m*

palatable ['pælɪtəbl] *adj* bon (bonne), agréable au goût

palate ['pælɪt] *n* palais *m* (*ANAT*)

pale [peɪl] *adj* pâle ♦ *n*: **beyond the ~** (*behaviour*) inacceptable; **to grow ~** pâlir

Palestine ['pælɪstaɪn] *n* Palestine *f*, **Palestinian** [pælɪs'tɪnɪən] *adj* palestinien(ne) ♦ *n* Palestinien(ne)

palette ['pælɪt] *n* palette *f*

pall [pɔːl] *n* (*of smoke*) voile *m* ♦ *vi* devenir lassant(e)

pallet ['pælɪt] *n* (*for goods*) palette *f*

pallid ['pælɪd] *adj* blême

palm [pɑːm] *n* (*of hand*) paume *f*; (*also:* **~ tree**) palmier *m* ♦ *vt*: **to ~ sth off on sb** (*inf*) refiler qch à qn; **P~ Sunday** *n* le dimanche des Rameaux

paltry ['pɔːltrɪ] *adj* dérisoire

pamper ['pæmpər] *vt* gâter, dorloter

pamphlet ['pæmflət] *n* brochure *f*

pan [pæn] *n* (*also:* **saucepan**) casserole *f*;

(*also:* frying ~) poêle f; **~cake** n crêpe f

panda ['pændə] n panda m

pandemonium [pændɪ'məunɪəm] n tohu-bohu m

pander ['pændəʳ] vi: **to ~ to** flatter bassement; obéir servilement à

pane [peɪn] n carreau m, vitre f

panel ['pænl] n (*of wood, cloth etc*) panneau m; (*RADIO, TV*) experts mpl; (*for interview, exams*) jury m; **~ling** (*US* **paneling**) n boiseries fpl

pang [pæŋ] n: **~s of remorse/jealousy** affres mpl du remords/de la jalousie; **~s of hunger/conscience** tiraillements mpl d'estomac/de la conscience

panic ['pænɪk] n panique f, affolement m ♦ vi s'affoler, paniquer; **~ky** adj (*person*) qui panique or s'affole facilement; **~-stricken** adj affolé(e)

pansy ['pænzɪ] n (*BOT*) pensée f; (*inf: pej*) tapette f, pédé m

pant [pænt] vi haleter

panther ['pænθəʳ] n panthère f

panties ['pæntɪz] npl slip m

pantomime ['pæntəmaɪm] (*BRIT*) n spectacle m de Noël

pantry ['pæntrɪ] n garde-manger m inv

pants [pænts] npl (*BRIT: woman's*) slip m; (: *man's*) slip, caleçon m; (*US: trousers*) pantalon m

pantyhose ['pæntɪhəuz] (*US*) npl collant m

paper ['peɪpəʳ] n papier m; (*also:* **wallpaper**) papier peint; (*also:* **newspaper**) journal m; (*academic essay*) article m; (*exam*) épreuve écrite ♦ adj en or de papier ♦ vt tapisser (de papier peint); **~s** npl (*also:* **identity ~s**) papiers (d'identité); **~back** n livre m de poche; livre broché or non relié; **~ bag** n sac m en papier; **~ clip** n trombone m; **~ hankie** n mouchoir m en papier; **~weight** n presse-papiers m inv; **~work** n papiers mpl; (*pej*) paperasserie f

par [pɑːʳ] n pair m; (*GOLF*) normale f du parcours; **on a ~ with** à égalité avec, au même niveau que

parachute ['pærəʃuːt] n parachute m

parade [pə'reɪd] n défilé m ♦ vt (*fig*) faire étalage de ♦ vi défiler

paradise ['pærədaɪs] n paradis m

paradox ['pærədɔks] n paradoxe m; **~ically** [pærə'dɔksɪklɪ] adv paradoxalement

paraffin ['pærəfɪn] (*BRIT*) n (*also:* **~ oil**) pétrole (lampant)

paragon ['pærəgən] n modèle m

paragraph ['pærəgrɑːf] n paragraphe m

parallel ['pærəlɛl] adj parallèle; (*fig*) semblable ♦ n (*line*) parallèle f; (*fig, GEO*) parallèle m

paralyse ['pærəlaɪz] (*BRIT*) vt paralyser;

paralysis [pə'rælɪsɪs] n paralysie f; **paralyze** (*US*) vt = **paralyse**

paramount ['pærəmaunt] adj: **of ~ importance** de la plus haute or grande importance

paranoid ['pærənɔɪd] adj (*PSYCH*) paranoïaque

paraphernalia [pærəfə'neɪlɪə] n attirail m

parasol ['pærəsɔl] n ombrelle f; (*over table*) parasol m

paratrooper ['pærətruːpəʳ] n parachutiste m (*soldat*)

parcel ['pɑːsl] n paquet m, colis m ♦ vt (*also:* **~ up**) empaqueter

parchment ['pɑːtʃmənt] n parchemin m

pardon ['pɑːdn] n pardon m; grâce f ♦ vt pardonner à; **~ me!, I beg your ~!** pardon!, je suis désolé!; **(I beg your) ~?, (*US*) ~ me?** pardon?

parent ['pɛərənt] n père m or mère f; **~s** npl parents mpl

Paris ['pærɪs] n Paris

parish ['pærɪʃ] n paroisse f; (*BRIT: civil*) ≈ commune f

Parisian [pə'rɪzɪən] adj parisien(ne) ♦ n Parisien(ne)

park [pɑːk] n parc m, jardin public ♦ vt garer ♦ vi se garer

parking ['pɑːkɪŋ] n stationnement m; **"no ~"** "stationnement interdit"; **~ lot** (*US*) n parking m, parc m de stationnement; **~ meter** n parcomètre m; **~ ticket** n P.V. m

parliament ['pɑːləmənt] n parlement m; **~ary** [pɑːlə'mɛntərɪ] adj parlementaire

parlour ['pɑːləʳ] (*US* **parlor**) n salon m

parochial [pə'rəukɪəl] (*pej*) adj à l'esprit de clocher

parole [pə'rəul] n: **on ~** en liberté conditionnelle

parrot ['pærət] n perroquet m

parry ['pærɪ] vt (*blow*) esquiver

parsley ['pɑːslɪ] n persil m

parsnip ['pɑːsnɪp] n panais m

parson ['pɑːsn] n ecclésiastique m; (*Church of England*) pasteur m

part [pɑːt] n partie f; (*of machine*) pièce f; (*THEATRE etc*) rôle m; (*of serial*) épisode m; (*US: in hair*) raie f ♦ adv = **partly** ♦ vt séparer ♦ vi (*people*) se séparer; (*crowd*) s'ouvrir; **to take ~ in** participer à, prendre part à; **to take sth in good ~** prendre qch du bon côté; **to take sb's ~** prendre le parti de qn, prendre parti pour qn; **for my ~** en ce qui me concerne; **for the most ~** dans la plupart des cas; **~ with** vt fus se séparer de; **~ exchange** (*BRIT*) n: **in ~ exchange** en reprise

partial ['pɑːʃl] adj (*not complete*) partiel(le); **to be ~ to** avoir un faible pour

participate [pɑ:'tɪsɪpeɪt] vi: **to ~ (in)** participer (à), prendre part (à); **participation** [pɑ:tɪsɪ'peɪʃən] n participation f

participle ['pɑ:tɪsɪpl] n participe m

particle ['pɑ:tɪkl] n particule f

particular [pə'tɪkjulə¹] adj particulier(-ère); (special) spécial(e); (fussy) difficile; méticuleux(-euse); **~s** npl (details) détails mpl; (personal) nom, adresse etc; **in ~** en particulier; **~ly** adv particulièrement

parting ['pɑ:tɪŋ] n séparation f; (BRIT: in hair) raie f ♦ adj d'adieu

partisan [pɑ:tɪ'zæn] n partisan(e) ♦ adj partisan(e); de parti

partition [pɑ:'tɪʃən] n (wall) cloison f; (POL) partition f, division f

partly ['pɑ:tlɪ] adv en partie, partiellement

partner ['pɑ:tnə¹] n partenaire m/f; (in marriage) conjoint(e); (boyfriend, girlfriend) ami(e); (COMM) associé(e); (at dance) cavalier(-ère); **~ship** n association f

partridge ['pɑ:trɪdʒ] n perdrix f

part-time ['pɑ:t'taɪm] adj, adv à mi-temps, à temps partiel

party ['pɑ:tɪ] n (POL) parti m; (group) groupe m; (LAW) partie f; (celebration) réception f; soirée f; fête f ♦ cpd (POL) de or du parti; **~ dress** n robe habillée

pass [pɑ:s] vt passer; (place) passer devant; (friend) croiser; (overtake) dépasser; (exam) être reçu(e) à, réussir; (approve) approuver, accepter ♦ vi passer; (SCOL) être reçu(e) or admis(e), réussir ♦ n (permit) laissez-passer m inv; carte f d'accès or d'abonnement; (in mountains) col m, (SPORT) passe f, (SCOL. also: **~ mark**): **to get a ~** être reçu(e) (sans mention); **to make a ~ at sb** (inf) faire des avances à qn; **~ away** vi mourir; **~ by** vi passer ♦ vt négliger; **~ on** vt (news, object) transmettre; (illness) passer; **~ out** vi s'évanouir; **~ up** vt (opportunity) laisser passer; **~able** adj (road) praticable; (work) acceptable

passage ['pæsɪdʒ] n (also: **~way**) couloir m; (gen, in book) passage m; (by boat) traversée f

passbook ['pɑ:sbuk] n livret m

passenger ['pæsɪndʒə¹] n passager(-ère)

passer-by [pɑ:sə'baɪ] (pl **~s-~**) n passant(e)

passing ['pɑ:sɪŋ] adj (fig) passager(-ère); **in ~** en passant; **~ place** n (AUT) aire f de croisement

passion ['pæʃən] n passion f; **~ate** adj passionné(e)

passive ['pæsɪv] adj (also LING) passif(-ive); **~ smoking** n tabagisme m passif

Passover ['pɑ:səuvə¹] n Pâque f (juive)

passport ['pɑ:spɔ:t] n passeport m;

~ control n contrôle m des passeports; **~ office** n bureau m de délivrance des passeports

password ['pɑ:swɜ:d] n mot m de passe

past [pɑ:st] prep (in front of) devant; (further than) au delà de, plus loin que; après; (later than) après ♦ adj passé(e); (president etc) ancien(ne) ♦ n passé m; **he's ~ forty** il a dépassé la quarantaine, il a plus de or passé quarante ans; **for the ~ few/3 days** depuis quelques/3 jours; ces derniers/3 derniers jours; **ten/quarter ~ eight** huit heures dix/un or et quart

pasta ['pæstə] n pâtes fpl

paste [peɪst] n pâte f; (meat ~) pâté m (à tartiner); (tomato ~) purée f, concentré m; (glue) colle f (de pâte) ♦ vt coller

pasteurized ['pæstʃəraɪzd] adj pasteurisé(e)

pastille ['pæstɪl] n pastille f

pastime ['pɑ:staɪm] n passe-temps m inv

pastry ['peɪstrɪ] n pâte f; (cake) pâtisserie f

pasture ['pɑ:stʃə¹] n pâturage m

pasty [n 'pæstɪ, adj 'peɪstɪ] n petit pâté (en croûte) ♦ adj (complexion) terreux(-euse)

pat [pæt] vt tapoter; (dog) caresser

patch [pætʃ] n (of material) pièce f; (eye ~) cache m; (spot) tache f; (on tyre) rustine f ♦ vt (clothes) rapiécer; **(to go through) a bad ~** (passer par) une période difficile; **~ up** vt réparer (grossièrement); **to ~ up a quarrel** se raccommoder; **~y** adj inégal(e); (incomplete) fragmentaire

pâté ['pæteɪ] n pâté m, terrine f

patent ['peɪtnt] n brevet m (d'invention) ♦ vt faire breveter ♦ adj patent(e), manifeste; **~ leather** n cuir verni

paternal [pə'tɜ:nl] adj paternel(le)

path [pɑ:θ] n chemin m, sentier m; (in garden) allée f; (trajectory) trajectoire f

pathetic [pə'θetɪk] adj (pitiful) pitoyable; (very bad) lamentable, minable

pathological [pæθə'lɔdʒɪkl] adj pathologique

pathway ['pɑ:θweɪ] n sentier m, passage m

patience ['peɪʃns] n patience f; (BRIT: CARDS) réussite f

patient ['peɪʃnt] n malade m/f; (of dentist etc) patient(e) ♦ adj patient(e)

patio ['pætɪəu] n patio m

patriotic [pætrɪ'ɔtɪk] adj patriotique; (person) patriote

patrol [pə'trəul] n patrouille f ♦ vt patrouiller dans; **~ car** n voiture f de police; **~man** (irreg) (US) n agent m de police

patron ['peɪtrən] n (in shop) client(e); (of charity) patron(ne); **~ of the arts** mécène m; **~ize** ['pætrənaɪz] vt (pej) traiter avec condescendance; (shop, club) être (un) client or un habitué de

patter ['pætə'] n crépitement m, tapotement m; (sales talk) boniment m

pattern ['pætən] n (design) motif m; (SEWING) patron m

pauper ['pɔːpə'] n indigent(e)

pause [pɔːz] n pause f, arrêt m ♦ vi faire une pause, s'arrêter

pave [peɪv] vt paver, daller; **to ~ the way for** ouvrir la voie à

pavement ['peɪvmənt] (BRIT) n trottoir m

pavilion [pə'vɪlɪən] n pavillon m; tente f

paving ['peɪvɪŋ] n (material) pavé m, dalle f; **~ stone** n pavé m

paw [pɔː] n patte f

pawn [pɔːn] n (CHESS, also fig) pion m ♦ vt mettre en gage; **~broker** n prêteur m sur gages; **~shop** n mont-de-piété m

pay [peɪ] (pt, pp **paid**) n salaire m; paie f ♦ vt payer ♦ vi payer; (be profitable) être rentable; **to ~ attention** (to) prêter attention (à); **to ~ sb a visit** rendre visite à qn; **to ~ one's respects to sb** présenter ses respects à qn; **~ back** vt rembourser; **~ for** vt fus payer; **~ in** vt verser; **~ off** vt régler, acquitter; (person) rembourser ♦ vi (scheme, decision) se révéler payant(e); **~ up** vt (money) payer; **~able** adj: **~able to sb** (cheque) à l'ordre de qn; **~ee** [peɪ'iː] n bénéficiaire m/f; **~ envelope** (US) n = **pay packet**; **~ment** n paiement m; règlement m; **monthly ~ment** mensualité f; **~ packet** (BRIT) n paie f; **~ phone** n cabine f téléphonique, téléphone public; **~roll** n registre m du personnel; **~ slip** (BRIT) n bulletin m de paie; **~ television** n chaînes fpl payantes

PC n abbr = **personal computer**

p.c. abbr = **per cent**

pea [piː] n (petit) pois

peace [piːs] n paix f; (calm) calme m, tranquillité f; **~ful** adj paisible, calme

peach [piːtʃ] n pêche f

peacock ['piːkɔk] n paon m

peak [piːk] n (mountain) pic m, cime f; (of cap) visière f; (fig: highest level) maximum m; (: of career, fame) apogée m; **~ hours** npl heures fpl de pointe

peal [piːl] n (of bells) carillon m; **~ of laughter** éclat m de rire

peanut ['piːnʌt] n arachide f, cacahuète f; **~ butter** n beurre m de cacahuète

pear [pɛə'] n poire f

pearl [pɔːl] n perle f

peasant ['pɛznt] n paysan(ne)

peat [piːt] n tourbe f

pebble ['pɛbl] n caillou m, galet m

peck [pɛk] vt (also: **~ at**) donner un coup de bec à ♦ n coup m de bec; (kiss) bise f; **~ing order** n ordre m des préséances; **~ish** (BRIT: inf) adj: **I feel ~ish** je mangerais bien quelque chose

peculiar [pɪ'kjuːlɪə'] adj étrange, bizarre, curieux(-euse); **~ to** particulier(-ère) à

pedal ['pɛdl] n pédale f ♦ vi pédaler

pedantic [pɪ'dæntɪk] adj pédant(e)

peddler ['pɛdlə'] n (of drugs) revendeur(-euse)

pedestal ['pɛdəstl] n piédestal m

pedestrian [pɪ'dɛstrɪən] n piéton m; **~ crossing** (BRIT) n passage clouté; **~ized** adj: **a ~ized street** une rue piétonne

pediatrics [piːdɪ'ætrɪks] (US) n = **paediatrics**

pedigree ['pɛdɪgriː] n ascendance f; (of animal) pedigree m ♦ cpd (animal) de race

pee [piː] (inf) vi faire pipi, pisser

peek [piːk] vi jeter un coup d'œil (furtif)

peel [piːl] n pelure f, épluchure f; (of orange, lemon) écorce f ♦ vt peler, éplucher ♦ vi (paint etc) s'écailler; (wallpaper) se décoller; (skin) peler

peep [piːp] n (BRIT: look) coup d'œil furtif; (sound) pépiement m ♦ vi (BRIT) jeter un coup d'œil (furtif); **~ out** (BRIT) vi se montrer (furtivement); **~hole** n judas m

peer [pɪə'] vi: **to ~ at** regarder attentivement, scruter ♦ n (noble) pair m; (equal) pair, égal(e); **~age** ['pɪərɪdʒ] n pairie f

peeved [piːvd] adj irrité(e), fâché(e)

peg [pɛg] n (for coat etc) patère f; (BRIT: also: **clothes ~**) pince f à linge

Pekin(g)ese [piːkɪ'niːz] n (dog) pékinois m

pelican ['pɛlɪkən] n pélican m; **~ crossing** (BRIT) n (AUT) feu m à commande manuelle

pellet ['pɛlɪt] n boulette f; (of lead) plomb m

pelt [pɛlt] vt: **to ~ sb (with)** bombarder qn (de) ♦ vi (rain) tomber à seaux; (inf: run) courir à toutes jambes ♦ n peau f

pelvis ['pɛlvɪs] n bassin m

pen [pɛn] n (for writing) stylo m; (for sheep) parc m

penal ['piːnl] adj pénal(e); (system, colony) pénitentiaire; **~ize** ['piːnəlaɪz] vt pénaliser

penalty ['pɛnltɪ] n pénalité f; sanction f; (fine) amende f; (SPORT) pénalisation f; (FOOTBALL) penalty m; (RUGBY) pénalité f

penance ['pɛnəns] n pénitence f

pence [pɛns] (BRIT) npl of **penny**

pencil ['pɛnsl] n crayon m; **~ case** n trousse f (d'écolier); **~ sharpener** n taille-crayon(s) m inv

pendant ['pɛndnt] n pendentif m

pending ['pɛndɪŋ] prep en attendant ♦ adj en suspens

pendulum ['pɛndjuləm] n (of clock) balancier m

penetrate ['pɛnɪtreɪt] vt pénétrer dans; pénétrer

penfriend ['pɛnfrɛnd] (BRIT) n correspondant(e)

penguin ['peŋgwɪn] n pingouin m
penicillin [penɪ'sɪlɪn] n pénicilline f
peninsula [pə'nɪnsjulə] n péninsule f
penis ['piːnɪs] n pénis m, verge f
penitentiary [penɪ'tenʃən] n prison f
penknife ['pennaɪf] n canif m
pen name n nom m de plume, pseudonyme m
penniless ['penɪlɪs] adj sans le sou
penny ['penɪ] (pl pennies or (BRIT) pence) n penny m
penpal ['penpæl] n correspondant(e)
pension ['penʃən] n pension f; (from company) retraite f; ~er (BRIT) n retraité(e); ~ fund n caisse f de pension; ~ plan n plan m de retraite
pentathlon [pen'tæθlɔn] n pentathlon m
Pentecost ['pentɪkɔst] n Pentecôte f
penthouse ['penthaus] n appartement m (de luxe) (en attique)
pent-up ['pentʌp] adj (feelings) refoulé(e)
penultimate [pe'nʌltɪmət] adj avant-dernier(-ère)
people ['piːpl] npl gens mpl; personnes fpl; (inhabitants) population f; (POL) peuple m ♦ n (nation, race) peuple m; **several ~ came** plusieurs personnes sont venues; **~ say that ...** on dit que ...
pep up ['pep-] (inf) vt remonter
pepper ['pepər] n poivre m; (vegetable) poivron m ♦ vt (fig): **to ~ with** bombarder de; **~ mill** n moulin m à poivre; **~mint** n (sweet) pastille f de menthe
peptalk ['peptɔːk] (inf) n (petit) discours d'encouragement
per [pəːr] prep par; **~ hour** (miles etc) à l'heure; (fee) (de) l'heure; **~ kilo** etc le kilo etc; **~ annum** par an; **~ capita** par personne, par habitant
perceive [pə'siːv] vt percevoir; (notice) remarquer, s'apercevoir de
per cent adv pour cent; **percentage** n pourcentage m
perception [pə'sepʃən] n perception f; (insight) perspicacité f
perceptive [pə'septɪv] adj pénétrant(e); (person) perspicace
perch [pəːtʃ] n (fish) perche f; (for bird) perchoir m ♦ vi: **to ~ on** se percher sur
percolator ['pəːkəleɪtər] n cafetière f (électrique)
percussion [pə'kʌʃən] n percussion f
perennial [pə'renɪəl] adj perpétuel(le); (BOT) vivace
perfect [adj, n 'pəːfɪkt, vb pə'fekt] adj parfait(e) ♦ n (also: ~ tense) parfait m ♦ vt parfaire; mettre au point; **~ly** adv parfaitement
perforate ['pəːfəreɪt] vt perforer, percer;

perforation [pəːfə'reɪʃən] n perforation f
perform [pə'fɔːm] vt (carry out) exécuter; (concert etc) jouer, donner ♦ vi jouer; **~ance** n représentation f, spectacle m; (of an artist) interprétation f; (SPORT) performance f; (of car, engine) fonctionnement m, (of company, economy) résultats mpl; **~er** n artiste m/f, interprète m/f
perfume ['pəːfjuːm] n parfum m
perhaps [pə'hæps] adv peut-être
peril ['perɪl] n péril m
perimeter [pə'rɪmɪtər] n périmètre m
period ['pɪərɪəd] n période f; (of history) époque f; (SCOL) cours m; (full stop) point m; (MED) règles fpl ♦ adj (costume, furniture) d'époque; **~ic(al)** [pɪərɪ'ɔdɪk(l)] adj périodique; **~ical** [pɪərɪ'ɔdɪkl] n périodique m
peripheral [pə'rɪfərəl] adj périphérique ♦ n (COMPUT) périphérique m
perish ['perɪʃ] vi périr; (decay) se détériorer; **~able** adj périssable
perjury ['pəːdʒərɪ] n parjure m, faux serment
perk [pəːk] n avantage m accessoire, à côté m; **~ up** vi (cheer up) se ragaillardir; **~y** adj (cheerful) guilleret(te)
perm [pəːm] n (for hair) permanente f
permanent ['pəːmənənt] adj permanent(e)
permeate ['pəːmɪeɪt] vi s'infiltrer ♦ vt s'infiltrer dans; pénétrer
permissible [pə'mɪsɪbl] adj permis(e), acceptable
permission [pə'mɪʃən] n permission f, autorisation f
permissive [pə'mɪsɪv] adj tolérant(e), permissif(-ive)
permit [n 'pəːmɪt, vb pə'mɪt] n permis m ♦ vt permettre
perpendicular [pəːpən'dɪkjulər] adj perpendiculaire
perplex [pə'pleks] vt (person) rendre perplexe
persecute ['pəːsɪkjuːt] vt persécuter
persevere [pəːsɪ'vɪər] vi persévérer
Persian ['pəːʃən] adj persan(e) ♦ n (LING) persan m; **the ~ Gulf** le golfe Persique
persist [pə'sɪst] vi: **to ~ (in doing)** persister or s'obstiner (à faire); **~ent** [pə'sɪstənt] adj persistant(e), tenace; **~ent vegetative state** état m végétatif persistant
person ['pəːsn] n personne f; **in ~** en personne; **~al** adj personnel(le); **~al assistant** n secrétaire privé(e); **~al column** n annonces personnelles; **~al computer** n ordinateur personnel; **~ality** [pəːsə'nælɪtɪ] n personnalité f; **~ally** adv personnellement; **to take sth ~ally** se sentir visé(e) (par qch); **~al organizer** n filofax m ®; **~al stereo** n Walkman ® m, baladeur m
personnel [pəːsə'nel] n personnel m
perspective [pə'spektɪv] n perspective f; **to**

get things into ~ faire la part des choses
Perspex ® ['pə:speks] n plexiglas ® m
perspiration [pə:spɪ'reɪʃən] n transpiration f
persuade [pə'sweɪd] vt: **to ~ sb to do sth** persuader qn de faire qch; **persuasion** [pə'sweɪʒən] n persuasion f; (creed) religion f
perverse [pə'və:s] adj pervers(e); (contrary) contrariant(e); **pervert** [n 'pə:və:t, vb pə'və:t] n perverti(e) ♦ vt pervertir; (words) déformer
pessimist ['pesɪmɪst] n pessimiste m/f; **~ic** [pesɪ'mɪstɪk] adj pessimiste
pest [pest] n animal m (or insecte m) nuisible; (fig) fléau m
pester ['pestər] vt importuner, harceler
pet [pet] n animal familier ♦ cpd (favourite) favori(te) ♦ vt (stroke) caresser, câliner; **teacher's ~** chouchou m du professeur; **~ hate** bête noire
petal ['petl] n pétale m
peter out ['pi:tə-] vi (stream, conversation) tarir; (meeting) tourner court; (road) se perdre
petite [pə'ti:t] adj menu(e)
petition [pə'tɪʃən] n pétition f
petrified ['petrɪfaɪd] adj (fig) mort(e) de peur
petrol ['petrəl] (BRIT) n essence f; **four-star ~** super m; **~ can** n bidon m à essence
petroleum [pə'trəʊlɪəm] n pétrole m
petrol: ~ pump (BRIT) n pompe f à essence; **~ station** (BRIT) n station-service f; **~ tank** (BRIT) n réservoir m d'essence
petticoat ['petɪkəʊt] n combinaison f
petty ['petɪ] adj (mean) mesquin(e); (unimportant) insignifiant(e), sans importance; **~ cash** n caisse f des dépenses courantes; **~ officer** n second-maître m
petulant ['petjʊlənt] adj boudeur(-euse), irritable
pew [pju:] n banc m (d'église)
pewter ['pju:tər] n étain m
phantom ['fæntəm] n fantôme m
pharmacy ['fɑ:məsɪ] n pharmacie f
phase [feɪz] n phase f ♦ vt: **to ~ sth in/out** introduire/supprimer qch progressivement
PhD abbr = Doctor of Philosophy ♦ n abbr (title) ≈ docteur m (en droit or lettres etc), ≈ doctorat m; (person) titulaire m/f d'un doctorat
pheasant ['feznt] n faisan m
phenomenon [fə'nɔmɪnən] (pl **phenomena**) n phénomène m
philosophical [fɪlə'sɔfɪkl] adj philosophique
philosophy [fɪ'lɔsəfɪ] n philosophie f
phobia ['fəʊbjə] n phobie f
phone [fəʊn] n téléphone m ♦ vt téléphoner; **to be on the ~** avoir le téléphone; (be calling) être au téléphone; **~ back** vt, vi rappeler; **~ up** vt téléphoner à ♦ vi téléphoner; **~ bill**

n facture f de téléphone; **~ book** n annuaire m; **~ booth, ~ box** (BRIT) n cabine f téléphonique; **~ call** n coup m de fil or de téléphone; **~card** n carte f de téléphone; **~-in** (BRIT) n (RADIO, TV) programme m à ligne ouverte; **~ number** n numéro m de téléphone
phonetics [fə'netɪks] n phonétique f
phoney ['fəʊnɪ] adj faux (fausse), factice; (person) pas franc (franche), poseur(-euse)
photo ['fəʊtəʊ] n photo f; **~copier** n photocopieuse f; **~copy** n photocopie f ♦ vt photocopier; **~graph** n photographie f ♦ vt photographier; **~grapher** [fə'tɔgrəfər] n photographe m/f; **~graphy** [fə'tɔgrəfɪ] n photographie f
phrase [freɪz] n expression f; (LING) locution f ♦ vt exprimer; **~ book** n recueil m d'expressions (pour touristes)
physical ['fɪzɪkl] adj physique; **~ education** n éducation f physique; **~ly** adv physiquement
physician [fɪ'zɪʃən] n médecin m
physicist ['fɪzɪsɪst] n physicien(ne)
physics ['fɪzɪks] n physique f
physiotherapist [fɪzɪəʊ'θerəpɪst] n kinésithérapeute m/f
physiotherapy [fɪzɪəʊ'θerəpɪ] n kinésithérapie f
physique [fɪ'zi:k] n physique m; constitution f
pianist ['pi:ənɪst] n pianiste m/f
piano [pɪ'ænəʊ] n piano m
pick [pɪk] n (tool: also: **~axe**) pic m, pioche f ♦ vt choisir; (fruit etc) cueillir; (remove) prendre; (lock) forcer; **take your ~** faites votre choix; **the ~ of** le (la) meilleur(e) de; **to ~ one's nose** se mettre les doigts dans le nez; **to ~ one's teeth** se curer les dents; **to ~ a quarrel with sb** chercher noise à qn; **~ at** vt fus: **to ~ at one's food** manger du bout des dents, chipoter; **~ on** vt fus (person) harceler; **~ out** vt choisir; (distinguish) distinguer; **~ up** vi (improve) s'améliorer ♦ vt ramasser; (collect) passer prendre; (AUT: give lift to) prendre, emmener; (learn) apprendre; (RADIO) capter; **to ~ up speed** prendre de la vitesse; **to ~ o.s. up** se relever
picket ['pɪkɪt] n (in strike) piquet m de grève ♦ vt mettre un piquet de grève devant
pickle ['pɪkl] n (also: **~s**: as condiment) pickles mpl; petits légumes macérés dans du vinaigre ♦ vt conserver dans du vinaigre or dans de la saumure; **to be in a ~** (mess) être dans le pétrin
pickpocket ['pɪkpɔkɪt] n pickpocket m
pick-up ['pɪkʌp] n (small truck) pick-up m inv
picnic ['pɪknɪk] n pique-nique m
picture ['pɪktʃər] n image f; (painting)

peinture f, tableau m; (etching) gravure f;
(photograph) photo(graphie) f; (drawing)
dessin m; (film) film m; (fig) description f;
tableau m ♦ vt se représenter; **the ~s** (BRIT:
inf) le cinéma; **~ book** n livre m d'images
picturesque [pɪktʃə'rɛsk] adj pittoresque
pie [paɪ] n tourte f; (of fruit) tarte f; (of meat)
pâté m en croûte
piece [pi:s] n morceau m; (item): **a ~ of
furniture/advice** un meuble/conseil ♦ vt: **to
~ together** rassembler; **to take to ~s**
démonter; **~meal** adv (irregularly) au coup
par coup; (bit by bit) par bouts; **~work** n
travail m aux pièces
pie chart n graphique m circulaire,
camembert m
pier [pɪəʳ] n jetée f
pierce [pɪəs] vt percer, transpercer; **~d** adj
(ears etc) percé(e)
pig [pɪg] n cochon m, porc m
pigeon ['pɪdʒən] n pigeon m; **~hole** n casier
m
piggy bank ['pɪgɪ-] n tirelire f
pig: ~headed adj entêté(e), têtu(e); **~let** n
porcelet m, petit cochon m; **~skin** n peau m de
porc; **~sty** n porcherie f; **~tail** n natte f,
tresse f
pike [paɪk] n (fish) brochet m
pilchard ['pɪltʃəd] n pilchard m (sorte de
sardine)
pile [paɪl] n (pillar, of books) pile f; (heap) tas
m; (of carpet) poils mpl ♦ vt (also: **~ up**)
empiler, entasser ♦ vi (also: **~ up**) s'entasser,
s'accumuler; **to ~ into** (car) s'entasser dans;
~s npl hémorroïdes fpl; **~-up** n (AUT)
télescopage m, collision f en série
pilfering ['pɪlfərɪŋ] n chapardage m
pilgrim ['pɪlgrɪm] n pèlerin m
pill [pɪl] n pilule f
pillage ['pɪlɪdʒ] vt piller
pillar ['pɪləʳ] n pilier m; **~ box** (BRIT) n boîte f
aux lettres (publique)
pillion ['pɪljən] n: **to ride ~** (on motorcycle)
monter derrière
pillow ['pɪləu] n oreiller m; **~case** n taie f
d'oreiller
pilot ['paɪlət] n pilote m ♦ cpd (scheme etc)
pilote, expérimental(e) ♦ vt piloter; **~ light** n
veilleuse f
pimp [pɪmp] n souteneur m, maquereau m
pimple ['pɪmpl] n bouton m
pin [pɪn] n épingle f; (TECH) cheville f ♦ vt
épingler; **~s and needles** fourmis fpl; **to ~ sb
down** (fig) obliger qn à répondre; **to ~ sth on
sb** (fig) mettre qch sur le dos de qn
PIN [pɪn] n abbr (= personal identification
number) numéro m d'identification personnel
pinafore ['pɪnəfɔːʳ] n tablier m
pinball ['pɪnbɔːl] n flipper m

pincers ['pɪnsəz] npl tenailles fpl; (of crab etc)
pinces fpl
pinch [pɪntʃ] n (of salt etc) pincée f ♦ vt
pincer; (inf: steal) piquer, chiper; **at a ~** à la
rigueur
pincushion ['pɪnkuʃən] n pelote f à épingles
pine [paɪn] n (also: **~ tree**) pin m ♦ vi: **to ~
for** s'ennuyer de, désirer ardemment; **~ away** vi
dépérir
pineapple ['paɪnæpl] n ananas m
ping [pɪŋ] n (noise) tintement m; **~-pong** ®
n ping-pong ® m
pink [pɪŋk] adj rose ♦ n (colour) rose m; (BOT)
œillet m, mignardise f
PIN (number) ['pɪn(-)] n code m
confidentiel
pinpoint ['pɪnpɔɪnt] vt indiquer or localiser
(avec précision); (problem) mettre le doigt
sur
pint [paɪnt] n pinte f (BRIT = 0.57l; US = 0.47l);
(BRIT: inf) ≈ demi m
pioneer [paɪə'nɪəʳ] n pionnier m
pious ['paɪəs] adj pieux(-euse)
pip [pɪp] n (seed) pépin m; **the ~s** npl (BRIT:
time signal on radio) le(s) top(s) sonore(s)
pipe [paɪp] n tuyau m, conduite f; (for
smoking) pipe f ♦ vt amener par tuyau; **~s** npl
(also: **bagpipes**) cornemuse f; **~ cleaner** n
cure-pipe m; **~ dream** n chimère f, château
m en Espagne; **~line** n pipe-line m; **~r** n
joueur(-euse) de cornemuse
piping ['paɪpɪŋ] adv: **~ hot** très chaud(e)
pique ['pi:k] n dépit m
pirate ['paɪərət] n pirate m; **~d** adj pirate
Pisces ['paɪsi:z] n les Poissons mpl
piss [pɪs] (inf!) vi pisser; **~ed** (inf!) adj (drunk)
bourré(e)
pistol ['pɪstl] n pistolet m
piston ['pɪstən] n piston m
pit [pɪt] n trou m, fosse f; (also: **coal ~**) puits m
de mine; (quarry) carrière f ♦ vt: **to ~ one's
wits against sb** se mesurer à qn; **~s** npl (AUT)
aire f de service
pitch [pɪtʃ] n (MUS) ton m; (BRIT: SPORT)
terrain m; (tar) poix f; (fig) degré m; point m
♦ vt (throw) lancer ♦ vi (fall) tomber; **to ~ a
tent** dresser une tente; **~-black** adj noir(e)
(comme du cirage); **~ed battle** n bataille
rangée
pitfall ['pɪtfɔːl] n piège m
pith [pɪθ] n (of orange etc) intérieur m de
l'écorce; **~y** adj piquant(e)
pitiful ['pɪtɪful] adj (touching) pitoyable
pitiless ['pɪtɪlɪs] adj impitoyable
pittance ['pɪtns] n salaire m de misère
pity ['pɪtɪ] n pitié f ♦ vt plaindre; **what a ~!**
quel dommage!
pizza ['pi:tsə] n pizza f
placard ['plækɑːd] n affiche f; (in march)

pancarte f

placate [pləˈkeɪt] vt apaiser, calmer

place [pleɪs] n endroit m, lieu m; (proper position, job, rank, seat) place f; (home): **at/to his ~** chez lui ♦ vt (object) placer, mettre; (identify) situer; reconnaître; **to take ~** avoir lieu; **out of ~** (not suitable) déplacé(e), inopportun(e); **to change ~s with sb** changer de place avec qn; **in the first ~** d'abord, en premier

plague [pleɪg] n fléau m; (MED) peste f ♦ vt (fig) tourmenter

plaice [pleɪs] n inv carrelet m

plaid [plæd] n tissu écossais

plain [pleɪn] adj (in one colour) uni(e); (simple) simple; (clear) clair(e), évident(e); (not handsome) quelconque, ordinaire ♦ adv franchement, carrément ♦ n plaine f; **~ chocolate** n chocolat m à croquer; **~ clothes** adj (police officer) en civil; **~ly** adv clairement; (frankly) carrément, sans détours

plaintiff [ˈpleɪntɪf] n plaignant(e)

plait [plæt] n tresse f, natte f

plan [plæn] n plan m; (scheme) projet m ♦ vt (think in advance) projeter; (prepare) organiser; (house) dresser les plans de, concevoir ♦ vi faire des projets; **to ~ to do** prévoir de faire

plane [pleɪn] n (AVIAT) avion m; (ART, MATH etc) plan m; (fig) niveau m, plan; (tool) rabot m; (also: **~ tree**) platane m ♦ vt raboter

planet [ˈplænɪt] n planète f

plank [plæŋk] n planche f

planner [ˈplænə^r] n planificateur(-trice); (town ~) urbaniste m/f

planning [ˈplænɪŋ] n planification f; **family ~** planning familial; **~ permission** n permis m de construire

plant [plɑːnt] n plante f; (machinery) matériel m; (factory) usine f ♦ vt planter; (bomb) poser; (microphone, incriminating evidence) cacher

plaster [ˈplɑːstə^r] n plâtre m; (also: **~ of Paris**) plâtre à mouler; (BRIT: also: **sticking ~**) pansement adhésif ♦ vt plâtrer; (cover): **to ~ with** couvrir de; **~ed** (inf) adj soûl(e)

plastic [ˈplæstɪk] n plastique m ♦ adj (made of ~) en plastique; **~ bag** n sac m en plastique

Plasticine ® [ˈplæstɪsiːn] n pâte f à modeler

plastic surgery n chirurgie f esthétique

plate [pleɪt] n (dish) assiette f; (in book) gravure f, planche f; (dental ~) dentier m

plateau [ˈplætəu] (pl **~s** or **~x**) n plateau m

plate glass n verre m (de vitrine)

platform [ˈplætfɔːm] n plate-forme f; (at meeting) tribune f; (stage) estrade f; (RAIL) quai m

platinum [ˈplætɪnəm] n platine m

platter [ˈplætə^r] n plat m

plausible [ˈplɔːzɪbl] adj plausible; (person) convaincant(e)

play [pleɪ] n (THEATRE) pièce f (de théâtre) ♦ vt (game) jouer à; (team, opponent) jouer contre; (instrument) jouer de; (part, piece of music, note) jouer; (record etc) passer ♦ vi jouer; **to ~ safe** ne prendre aucun risque; **~ down** vt minimiser; **~ up** vi (cause trouble) faire des siennes; **~boy** n playboy m; **~er** n joueur(-euse); (THEATRE) acteur(-trice); (MUS) musicien(ne); **~ful** adj enjoué(e); **~ground** n cour f de récréation; (in park) aire f de jeux; **~group** n garderie f; **~ing card** n carte f à jouer; **~ing field** n terrain m de sport; **~mate** n camarade m/f, copain (copine); **~-off** n (SPORT) belle f; **~pen** n parc m (pour bébé); **~thing** n jouet m; **~time** n récréation f; **~wright** n dramaturge m

plc abbr (= public limited company) SARL f

plea [pliː] n (request) appel m; (LAW) défense f

plead [pliːd] vt plaider; (give as excuse) invoquer ♦ vi (LAW) plaider; (beg): **to ~ with sb** implorer qn

pleasant [ˈplɛznt] adj agréable; **~ries** npl (polite remarks) civilités fpl

please [pliːz] excl s'il te (or vous) plaît ♦ vt plaire à ♦ vi plaire; (think fit): **do as you ~** faites comme il vous plaira; **~ yourself!** à ta (or votre) guise!; **~d** adj: **~d (with)** content(e) (de); **~d to meet you** enchanté (de faire votre connaissance); **pleasing** adj plaisant(e), qui fait plaisir

pleasure [ˈplɛʒə^r] n plaisir m; **"it's a ~"** "je vous en prie"

pleat [pliːt] n pli m

pledge [plɛdʒ] n (promise) promesse f ♦ vt engager; promettre

plentiful [ˈplɛntɪful] adj abondant(e), copieux(-euse)

plenty [ˈplɛntɪ] n: **~ of** beaucoup de; (bien) assez de

pliable [ˈplaɪəbl] adj flexible; (person) malléable

pliers [ˈplaɪəz] npl pinces fpl

plight [plaɪt] n situation f critique

plimsolls [ˈplɪmsəlz] (BRIT) npl chaussures fpl de tennis, tennis mpl

plinth [plɪnθ] n (of statue) socle m

P.L.O. n abbr (= Palestine Liberation Organization) OLP f

plod [plɔd] vi avancer péniblement; (fig) peiner

plonk [plɔŋk] (inf) n (BRIT: wine) pinard m, piquette f ♦ vt: **to ~ sth down** poser brusquement qch

plot [plɔt] n complot m, conspiration f; (of story, play) intrigue f; (of land) lot m de terrain, lopin m ♦ vt (sb's downfall)

comploter; (*mark out*) pointer; relever,
déterminer ♦ *vi* comploter
plough [plau] (*US* **plow**) *n* charrue *f* ♦ *vt*
(*earth*) labourer; **to ~ money into** investir
dans; **~ through** *vt fus* (*snow etc*) avancer
péniblement dans; **~man's lunch** (*BRIT*) *n*
assiette froide avec du pain, du fromage et des
pickles
ploy [plɔɪ] *n* stratagème *m*
pluck [plʌk] *vt* (*fruit*) cueillir; (*musical
instrument*) pincer; (*bird*) plumer; (*eyebrow*)
épiler ♦ *n* courage *m*, cran *m*; **to ~ up
courage** prendre son courage à deux mains
plug [plʌg] *n* (*ELEC*) prise *f* de courant;
(*stopper*) bouchon *m*, bonde *f*; (*AUT: also:*
spark(ing) ~) bougie *f* ♦ *vt* (*hole*) boucher;
(*inf: advertise*) faire du battage pour; **~ in** *vt*
(*ELEC*) brancher
plum [plʌm] *n* (*fruit*) prune *f* ♦ *cpd:* **~ job**
(*inf*) travail *m* en or
plumb [plʌm] *vt:* **to ~ the depths** (*fig*)
toucher le fond (du désespoir)
plumber ['plʌmər] *n* plombier *m*
plumbing ['plʌmɪŋ] *n* (*trade*) plomberie *f*;
(*piping*) tuyauterie *f*
plummet ['plʌmɪt] *vi:* **to ~ (down)** plonger,
dégringoler
plump [plʌmp] *adj* rondelet(te), dodu(e),
bien en chair ♦ *vi:* **to ~ for** (*inf: choose*) se
décider pour
plunder ['plʌndər] *n* pillage *m*; (*loot*) butin *m*
♦ *vt* piller
plunge [plʌndʒ] *n* plongeon *m*; (*fig*) chute *f*
♦ *vt* plonger ♦ *vi* (*dive*) plonger; (*fall*)
tomber, dégringoler; **to take the ~** se jeter à
l'eau; **plunging** ['plʌndʒɪŋ] *adj:* **plunging
neckline** décolleté plongeant
pluperfect [pluː'pəːfɪkt] *n* plus-que-parfait *m*
plural ['pluərl] *adj* pluriel(le) ♦ *n* pluriel *m*
plus [plʌs] *n* (*also:* **~ sign**) signe *m* plus
♦ *prep* plus; **ten/twenty ~** plus de dix/vingt
plush [plʌʃ] *adj* somptueux(-euse)
ply [plaɪ] *vt* (*a trade*) exercer ♦ *vi* (*ship*) faire
la navette ♦ *n* (*of wool, rope*) fil *m*, brin *m*; **to
~ sb with drink** donner continuellement à
boire à qn; **to ~ sb with questions** presser qn
de questions; **~wood** *n* contre-plaqué *m*
PM *n abbr* = **Prime Minister**
p.m. *adv abbr* (= *post meridiem*) de l'après-
midi
pneumatic drill [njuː'mætɪk-] *n* marteau-
piqueur *m*
pneumonia [njuː'məunɪə] *n* pneumonie *f*
poach [pəutʃ] *vt* (*cook*) pocher; (*steal*) pêcher (*or* chasser) sans permis ♦ *vi* braconner;
~ed egg *n* œuf poché, **~er** *n* braconnier *m*
P.O. box *n abbr* = **post office box**
pocket ['pɔkɪt] *n* poche *f* ♦ *vt* empocher; **to
be out of ~** (*BRIT*) en être de sa poche;

~book (*US*) *n* (*wallet*) portefeuille *m*;
~ calculator *n* calculette *f*; **~ knife** *n* canif
m; **~ money** *n* argent *m* de poche
pod [pɔd] *n* cosse *f*
podgy ['pɔdʒɪ] *adj* rondelet(te)
podiatrist [pɔ'diːətrɪst] (*US*) *n* pédicure *m/f*,
podologue *m/f*
poem ['pəuɪm] *n* poème *m*
poet ['pəuɪt] *n* poète *m*; **~ic** [pəu'ɛtɪk] *adj*
poétique; **~ry** ['pəuɪtrɪ] *n* poésie *f*
poignant ['pɔɪnjənt] *adj* poignant(e);
(*sharp*) vif (vive)
point [pɔɪnt] *n* point *m*; (*tip*) pointe *f*; (*in
time*) moment *m*; (*in space*) endroit *m*;
(*subject, idea*) point, sujet *m*; (*purpose*) sens
m; (*ELEC*) prise *f*; (*also:* **decimal ~**): **2 ~ 3 (2.3)**
2 virgule 3 (2,3) ♦ *vt* (*show*) indiquer; (*gun
etc*): **to ~ sth at** braquer *or* diriger qch sur
♦ *vi:* **to ~ at** montrer du doigt; **~s** *npl* (*AUT*)
vis platinées; (*RAIL*) aiguillage *m*; **to be on the
~ of doing sth** être sur le point de faire qch;
to make a ~ of faire; **to miss the ~** ne pas manquer de
faire; **to get the ~** comprendre, saisir; **to miss
the ~** ne pas comprendre; **to come to the ~**
en venir au fait; **there's no ~ (in doing)** cela
ne sert à rien (de faire); **~ out** *vt* faire
remarquer, souligner; **~ to** *vt fus* (*fig*)
indiquer; **~-blank** *adv* (*fig*) catégoriquement;
(*also:* **at ~-blank range**) à bout portant; **~ed**
adj (*shape*) pointu(e); (*remark*) plein(e) de
sous-entendus; **~er** *n* (*needle*) aiguille *f*;
(*piece of advice*) conseil *m*; (*clue*) indice *m*;
~less *adj* inutile, vain(e); **~ of view** *n* point
m de vue
poise [pɔɪz] *n* (*composure*) calme *m*
poison ['pɔɪzn] *n* poison *m* ♦ *vt*
empoisonner; **~ous** *adj* (*snake*) veni-
meux(-euse); (*plant*) vénéneux(-euse);
(*fumes etc*) toxique
poke [pəuk] *vt* (*fire*) tisonner; (*jab with finger,
stick etc*) piquer; pousser du doigt; (*put*): **to
~ sth in(to)** fourrer *or* enfoncer qch dans;
~ about *vi* fureter; **~r** *n* tisonnier *m*; (*CARDS*)
poker *m*
poky ['pəukɪ] *adj* exigu(ë)
Poland ['pəulənd] *n* Pologne *f*
polar ['pəulər] *adj* polaire; **~ bear** *n* ours
blanc
Pole [pəul] *n* Polonais(e)
pole [pəul] *n* poteau *m*; (*of wood*) mât *m*,
perche *f*; (*GEO*) pôle *m*; **~ bean** (*US*) *n*
haricot *m* (à rames); **~ vault** *n* saut *m* à la
perche
police [pə'liːs] *npl* police *f* ♦ *vt* maintenir
l'ordre dans; **~ car** *n* voiture *f* de police;
~man (*irreg*) *n* agent *m* de police, policier
m; **~ station** *n* commissariat *m* de police;
~woman (*irreg*) *n* femme-agent *f*
policy ['pɔlɪsɪ] *n* politique *f*; (*also:* **insurance**

~) police f (d'assurance)
polio ['pəʊlɪəʊ] n polio f
Polish ['pəʊlɪʃ] adj polonais(e) ♦ n (LING) polonais m
polish ['pɒlɪʃ] n (for shoes) cirage m; (for floor) cire f, encaustique f; (shine) éclat m, poli m; (fig: refinement) raffinement m ♦ vt (put ~ on shoes, wood) cirer; (make shiny) astiquer, faire briller; ~ **off** (inf) vt (food) liquider; ~**ed** adj (fig) raffiné(e)
polite [pə'laɪt] adj poli(e); **in ~ society** dans la bonne société; ~**ly** adv poliment; ~**ness** n politesse f
political [pə'lɪtɪkl] adj politique; ~**ly correct** adj politiquement correct(e)
politician [pɒlɪ'tɪʃən] n homme m/femme f politique
politics ['pɒlɪtɪks] npl politique f
poll [pəʊl] n scrutin m, vote m; (also: **opinion ~**) sondage m (d'opinion) ♦ vt obtenir
pollen ['pɒlən] n pollen m
polling day ['pəʊlɪŋ-] (BRIT) n jour m des élections
polling station (BRIT) n bureau m de vote
pollute [pə'lu:t] vt polluer; **pollution** n pollution f
polo ['pəʊləʊ] n polo m; ~-**necked** adj à col roulé; ~ **shirt** n polo m
polyester [pɒlɪ'estəʳ] n polyester m
polystyrene [pɒlɪ'staɪriːn] n polystyrène m
polythene ['pɒlɪθiːn] n polyéthylène m; ~ **bag** n sac m en plastique
pomegranate ['pɒmɪɡrænɪt] n grenade f
pomp [pɒmp] n pompe f, faste f, apparat m; ~**ous** adj pompeux(-euse)
pond [pɒnd] n étang m; mare f
ponder ['pɒndəʳ] vt considérer, peser; ~**ous** adj pesant(e), lourd(e)
pong [pɒŋ] (BRIT: inf) n puanteur f
pony ['pəʊnɪ] n poney m; ~**tail** n queue f de cheval; ~ **trekking** (BRIT) n randonnée f à cheval
poodle ['puːdl] n caniche m
pool [puːl] n (of rain) flaque f; (pond) mare f; (also: **swimming ~**) piscine f; (billiards) poule f ♦ vt mettre en commun; ~**s** npl (football ~s) ≈ loto sportif
poor [pʊəʳ] adj pauvre; (mediocre) médiocre, faible, mauvais(e) ♦ npl: **the ~** les pauvres mpl; ~**ly** adj souffrant(e), malade ♦ adv mal; médiocrement
pop [pɒp] n (MUS) musique f pop; (drink) boisson gazeuse; (US: inf: father) papa m; (noise) bruit sec ♦ vt (put) mettre (rapidement) ♦ vi éclater; (cork) sauter; ~ **in** vi entrer en passant; ~ **out** vi sortir (brièvement); ~ **up** vi apparaître, surgir; ~**corn** n pop-corn m
pope [pəʊp] n pape m

poplar ['pɒpləʳ] n peuplier m
popper ['pɒpəʳ] (BRIT: inf) n bouton-pression m
poppy ['pɒpɪ] n coquelicot m; pavot m
Popsicle ® ['pɒpsɪkl] (US) n esquimau m (glace)
popular ['pɒpjʊləʳ] adj populaire; (fashionable) à la mode
population [pɒpjʊ'leɪʃən] n population f
porcelain ['pɔːslɪn] n porcelaine f
porch [pɔːtʃ] n porche m; (US) véranda f
porcupine ['pɔːkjʊpaɪn] n porc-épic m
pore [pɔːʳ] n pore m ♦ vi: **to ~ over** s'absorber dans, être plongé(e) dans
pork [pɔːk] n porc m
porn [pɔːn] (inf) adj, n porno m
pornographic [pɔːnə'ɡræfɪk] adj pornographique
pornography [pɔː'nɒɡrəfɪ] n pornographie f
porpoise ['pɔːpəs] n marsouin m
porridge ['pɒrɪdʒ] n porridge m
port [pɔːt] n (harbour) port m; (NAUT: left side) bâbord m; (wine) porto m; ~ **of call** escale f
portable ['pɔːtəbl] adj portatif(-ive)
porter ['pɔːtəʳ] n (for luggage) porteur m; (doorkeeper) gardien(ne); portier m
portfolio [pɔːt'fəʊlɪəʊ] n portefeuille m; (of artist) portfolio m
porthole ['pɔːthəʊl] n hublot m
portion ['pɔːʃən] n portion f, part f
portrait ['pɔːtreɪt] n portrait m
portray [pɔː'treɪ] vt faire le portrait de; (in writing) dépeindre, représenter; (subj: actor) jouer
Portugal ['pɔːtjʊɡl] n Portugal m; **Portuguese** [pɔːtju'ɡiːz] adj portugais(e) ♦ n inv Portugais(e); (LING) portugais m
pose [pəʊz] n pose f ♦ vi (pretend): **to ~ as** se poser en ♦ vt poser; (problem) créer
posh [pɒʃ] (inf) adj chic inv
position [pə'zɪʃən] n position f; (job) situation f ♦ vt placer
positive ['pɒzɪtɪv] adj positif(-ive); (certain) sûr(e), certain(e); (definite) formel(le), catégorique
possess [pə'zɛs] vt posséder; ~**ion** n possession f
possibility [pɒsɪ'bɪlɪtɪ] n possibilité f; éventualité f
possible ['pɒsɪbl] adj possible; **as big as ~** aussi gros que possible; **possibly** adv (perhaps) peut-être; **if you possibly can** si cela vous est possible; **I cannot possibly come** il m'est impossible de venir
post [pəʊst] n poste f; (BRIT: letters, delivery) courrier m; (job, situation, MIL) poste m; (pole) poteau m ♦ vt (BRIT: send by ~) poster; (: appoint): **to ~ to** affecter à; ~**age** n tarifs mpl d'affranchissement; ~**al order** n mandat(-poste) m; ~**box** (BRIT) n boîte f aux

lettres; **~card** n carte postale; **~code** (BRIT) n code postal

poster ['pəustər] n affiche f

poste restante [pəust'restã:nt] (BRIT) n poste restante

postgraduate ['pəust'grædjuət] n ≈ étudiant(e) de troisième cycle

posthumous ['pɔstjuməs] adj posthume

postman ['pəustmən] (irreg) n facteur m

postmark ['pəustmɑːk] n cachet m (de la poste)

postmortem [pəust'mɔːtəm] n autopsie f

post office n (building) poste f; (organization): **the P~ O~** les Postes; **~ ~ box** n boîte postale

postpone [pəus'pəun] vt remettre (à plus tard)

posture ['pɔstʃər] n posture f; (fig) attitude f

postwar ['pəust'wɔːr] adj d'après-guerre

postwoman ['pəustwumən] n factrice f

posy ['pəuzɪ] n petit bouquet

pot [pɔt] n pot m; (for cooking) marmite f; casserole f; (teapot) théière f; (coffee pot) cafetière f; (inf: marijuana) herbe f ♦ vt (plant) mettre en pot; **to go to ~** (inf: work, performance) aller à vau-l'eau

potato [pə'teɪtəu] (pl **~es**) n pomme f de terre; **~ peeler** n épluche-légumes m inv

potent ['pəutnt] adj puissant(e); (drink) fort(e), très alcoolisé(e); (man) viril

potential [pə'tɛnʃl] adj potentiel(le) ♦ n potentiel m

pothole ['pɔthəul] n (in road) nid m de poule; (BRIT: underground) gouffre m, caverne f; **potholing** (BRIT) n: **to go potholing** faire de la spéléologie

potluck [pɔt'lʌk] n: **to take ~** tenter sa chance

pot plant n plante f d'appartement

potted ['pɔtɪd] adj (food) en conserve; (plant) en pot; (abbreviated) abrégé(e)

potter ['pɔtər] n potier m ♦ vi: **to ~ around, ~ about** (BRIT) bricoler; **~y** n poterie f

potty ['pɔtɪ] adj (inf: mad) dingue ♦ n (child's) pot m

pouch [pautʃ] n (ZOOL) poche f; (for tobacco) blague f; (for money) bourse f

poultry ['pəultrɪ] n volaille f

pounce [pauns] vi: **to ~ (on)** bondir (sur), sauter (sur)

pound [paund] n (unit of money) livre f; (unit of weight) livre ♦ vt (beat) bourrer de coups, marteler; (crush) piler, pulvériser ♦ vi (heart) battre violemment, taper

pour [pɔːr] vt verser ♦ vi couler à flots; **to ~ (with rain)** pleuvoir à verse; **to ~ sb a drink** verser or servir à boire à qn; **~ away** vt vider; **~ in** vi (people) affluer, se précipiter; (news, letters etc) arriver en masse; **~ off** vt = pour

away; **~ out** vi (people) sortir en masse ♦ vt vider; (fig) déverser; (serve: a drink) verser; **~ing** ['pɔːrɪŋ] adj: **~ing rain** pluie f torrentielle

pout [paut] vi faire la moue

poverty ['pɔvətɪ] n pauvreté f, misère f; **~-stricken** adj pauvre, déshérité(e)

powder ['paudər] n poudre f ♦ vt: **to ~ one's face** se poudrer; **~ compact** n poudrier m; **~ed milk** n lait m en poudre; **~ room** n toilettes fpl (pour dames)

power ['pauər] n (strength) puissance f, force f; (ability, authority) pouvoir m; (of speech, thought) faculté f; (ELEC) courant m; **to be in ~** (POL etc) être au pouvoir; **~ cut** (BRIT) n coupure f de courant; **~ed** adj: **~ed by** actionné(e) par, fonctionnant à; **~ failure** n panne f de courant; **~ful** adj puissant(e); **~less** adj impuissant(e); **~ point** (BRIT) n prise f de courant; **~ station** n centrale f électrique; **~ struggle** n lutte f pour le pouvoir

p.p. abbr (= per procurationem): **p.p. J. Smith** pour M. J. Smith

PR n abbr = **public relations**

practical ['præktɪkl] adj pratique; **~ity** [præktɪ'kælɪtɪ] (no pl) n (of person) sens m pratique; **~ities** npl (of situation) aspect m pratique; **~ joke** n farce f; **~ly** adv (almost) pratiquement

practice ['præktɪs] n pratique f; (of profession) exercice m; (at football etc) entraînement m; (business) cabinet m ♦ vt, vi (US) = **practise**; **in ~** (in reality) en pratique; **out of ~** rouillé(e)

practise ['præktɪs] (US **practice**) vt (musical instrument) travailler; (train for: sport) s'entraîner à; (a sport, religion) pratiquer; (profession) exercer ♦ vi s'exercer, travailler; (train) s'entraîner; (lawyer, doctor) exercer; **practising** adj (Christian etc) pratiquant(e); (lawyer) en exercice

practitioner [præk'tɪʃənər] n praticien(ne)

prairie ['prɛərɪ] n steppe f, prairie f

praise [preɪz] n éloge(s) m(pl), louange(s) f(pl) ♦ vt louer, faire l'éloge de; **~worthy** adj digne d'éloges

pram [præm] (BRIT) n landau m, voiture f d'enfant

prance [prɑːns] vi (also: **~ about**: person) se pavaner

prank [præŋk] n farce f

prawn [prɔːn] n crevette f (rose); **~ cocktail** n cocktail m de crevettes

pray [preɪ] vi prier; **~er** [prɛər] n prière f

preach [priːtʃ] vt, vi prêcher

precaution [prɪ'kɔːʃən] n précaution f

precede [prɪ'siːd] vt précéder

precedent ['prɛsɪdənt] n précédent m

preceding [prɪ'siːdɪŋ] adj qui précède/

précédait etc

precinct ['priːsɪŋkt] n (US) circonscription f, arrondissement m; **~s** npl (neighbourhood) alentours mpl, environs mpl; **pedestrian ~** (BRIT) zone piétonnière or piétonne; **shopping ~** (BRIT) centre commercial

precious ['prɛʃəs] adj précieux(-euse)

precipitate [prɪ'sɪpɪteɪt] vt précipiter

precise [prɪ'saɪs] adj précis(e); **~ly** adv précisément

precocious [prɪ'kəʊʃəs] adj précoce

precondition ['priːkən'dɪʃən] n condition f nécessaire

predecessor ['priːdɪsesəʳ] n prédécesseur m

predicament [prɪ'dɪkəmənt] n situation f difficile

predict [prɪ'dɪkt] vt prédire; **~able** adj prévisible

predominantly [prɪ'dɔmɪnəntlɪ] adv en majeure partie; surtout

pre-empt [priː'ɛmt] vt anticiper, devancer

preen [priːn] vt: **to ~ itself** (bird) se lisser les plumes; **to ~ o.s.** s'admirer

prefab ['priːfæb] n bâtiment préfabriqué

preface ['prɛfəs] n préface f

prefect ['priːfɛkt] (BRIT) n (in school) élève chargé(e) de certaines fonctions de discipline

prefer [prɪ'fɜːʳ] vt préférer; **~ably** ['prɛfrəblɪ] adv de préférence; **~ence** ['prɛfrəns] n préférence f; **~ential** [prɛfə'rɛnʃəl] adj: **~ential treatment** traitement m de faveur or préférentiel

prefix ['priːfɪks] n préfixe m

pregnancy ['prɛgnənsɪ] n grossesse f

pregnant ['prɛgnənt] adj enceinte; (animal) pleine

prehistoric ['priːhɪs'tɔrɪk] adj préhistorique

prejudice ['prɛdʒʊdɪs] n préjugé m; **~d** (person) plein(e) de préjugés; (in a matter) partial(e)

premarital ['priː'mærɪtl] adj avant le mariage

premature ['prɛmətʃʊəʳ] adj prématuré(e)

premenstrual syndrome [priː'mɛnstruəl-] n syndrome prémenstruel

premier ['prɛmɪəʳ] adj premier(-ère), principal(e) ♦ n (POL) Premier ministre

première ['prɛmɪəʳ] n première f

Premier League n première division

premise ['prɛmɪs] n prémisse f; **~s** npl (building) locaux mpl; **on the ~s** sur les lieux; sur place

premium ['priːmɪəm] n prime f; **to be at a ~** faire prime; **~ bond** (BRIT) n bon m à lot, obligation f à prime

premonition [prɛmə'nɪʃən] n prémonition f

preoccupied [priː'ɔkjupaɪd] adj préoccupé(e)

prep [prɛp] n (SCOL) étude f

prepaid [priː'peɪd] adj payé(e) d'avance

preparation [prɛpə'reɪʃən] n préparation f; **~s** npl (for trip, war) préparatifs mpl

preparatory [prɪ'pærətərɪ] adj préliminaire; **~ school** (BRIT) n école primaire privée

prepare [prɪ'pɛəʳ] vt préparer ♦ vi: **to ~ for** se préparer à; **~d to** prêt(e) à

preposition [prɛpə'zɪʃən] n préposition f

preposterous [prɪ'pɔstərəs] adj absurde

prep school n = **preparatory school**

prerequisite [priː'rɛkwɪzɪt] n condition f préalable

Presbyterian [prɛzbɪ'tɪərɪən] adj, n presbytérien(ne) m/f

prescribe [prɪ'skraɪb] vt prescrire; **prescription** [prɪ'skrɪpʃən] n (MED) ordonnance f; (: medicine) médicament (obtenu sur ordonnance)

presence ['prɛzns] n présence f; **~ of mind** présence d'esprit

present [adj, n 'prɛznt, vb prɪ'zɛnt] adj présent(e) ♦ n (gift) cadeau m; (actuality) présent m ♦ vt présenter; (prize, medal) remettre; (give): **to ~ sb with sth** or **sth to sb** offrir qch à qn; **to give sb a ~** offrir un cadeau à qn; **at ~** en ce moment; **~ation** [prɛzn'teɪʃən] n présentation f; (ceremony) remise f du cadeau (or de la médaille etc); **~-day** adj contemporain(e), actuel(le); **~er** n (RADIO, TV) présentateur(-trice); **~ly** adv (with verb in past) peu après; (soon) tout à l'heure, bientôt; (at present) en ce moment

preservative [prɪ'zɜːvətɪv] n agent m de conservation

preserve [prɪ'zɜːv] vt (keep safe) préserver, protéger; (maintain) conserver, garder; (food) mettre en conserve ♦ n (often pl: jam) confiture f

president ['prɛzɪdənt] n président(e); **~ial** [prɛzɪ'dɛnʃl] adj présidentiel(le)

press [prɛs] n presse f; (for wine) pressoir m ♦ vt (squeeze) presser, serrer; (push) appuyer sur; (clothes: iron) repasser; (put ~ure on) faire pression sur; (insist): **to ~ sth on sb** presser qn d'accepter qch ♦ vi appuyer, peser; **to ~ for sth** faire pression pour obtenir qch; **we are ~ed for time/money** le temps/l'argent nous manque; **~ on** vi continuer; **~ conference** n conférence f de presse; **~ing** adj urgent(e), pressant(e); **~ stud** (BRIT) n bouton-pression m; **~-up** (BRIT) n traction f

pressure ['prɛʃəʳ] n pression f; (stress) tension f; **to put ~ on sb** (to do) faire pression sur qn (pour qu'il/elle fasse); **~ cooker** n cocotte-minute f; **~ gauge** n manomètre m; **~ group** n groupe m de pression

prestige [prɛs'tiːʒ] n prestige m; **prestigious** [prɛs'tɪdʒəs] adj prestigieux(-euse)

presumably [prɪˈzjuːməblɪ] adv
vraisemblablement

presume [prɪˈzjuːm] vt présumer, supposer

pretence [prɪˈtens] (US **pretense**) n (claim)
prétention f; **under false ~s** sous des prétextes
fallacieux

pretend [prɪˈtend] vt (feign) feindre, simuler
♦ vi faire semblant

pretext [ˈpriːtekst] n prétexte m

pretty [ˈprɪtɪ] adj joli(e) ♦ adv assez

prevail [prɪˈveɪl] vi (be usual) avoir cours;
(win) l'emporter, prévaloir; **~ing** adj
dominant(e); **prevalent** [ˈprevələnt] adj
répandu(e), courant(e)

prevent [prɪˈvent] vt: **to ~ (from doing)**
empêcher (de faire); **~ative** [prɪˈventətɪv],
~ive [prɪˈventɪv] adj préventif(-ive)

preview [ˈpriːvjuː] n (of film etc) avant-
première f

previous [ˈpriːvɪəs] adj précédent(e);
antérieur(e); **~ly** adv précédemment,
auparavant

prewar [priːˈwɔːr] adj d'avant-guerre

prey [preɪ] n proie f ♦ vi: **to ~ on** s'attaquer à;
it was ~ing on his mind cela le travaillait

price [praɪs] n prix m ♦ vt (goods) fixer le prix
de; **~less** adj sans prix, inestimable; **~ list** n
liste f des prix, tarif m

prick [prɪk] n piqûre f ♦ vt piquer; **to ~ up
one's ears** dresser or tendre l'oreille

prickle [ˈprɪkl] n (of plant) épine f;
(sensation) picotement m; **prickly** adj
piquant(e), épineux(-euse); **prickly heat** n
fièvre f miliaire

pride [praɪd] n orgueil m; fierté f ♦ vt: **to
~ o.s. on** se flatter de; s'enorgueillir de

priest [priːst] n prêtre m; **~hood** n prêtrise f,
sacerdoce m

prim [prɪm] adj collet monté inv, guindé(e)

primarily [ˈpraɪmərɪlɪ] adv principalement,
essentiellement

primary [ˈpraɪmərɪ] adj (first in importance)
premier(-ère), primordial(e), principal(e) ♦ n
(US: election) (élection f) primaire f,
~ school (BRIT) n école primaire f

prime [praɪm] adj primordial(e),
fondamental(e); (excellent) excellent(e) ♦ n:
in the ~ of life dans la fleur de l'âge ♦ vt
(wood) apprêter; (fig) mettre au courant;
P~ Minister n Premier ministre m

primeval adj primitif(-ive); **~ forest** forêt f
vierge

primitive [ˈprɪmɪtɪv] adj primitif(-ive)

primrose [ˈprɪmrəʊz] n primevère f

primus (stove) ® [ˈpraɪməs-] (BRIT) n
réchaud m de camping

prince [prɪns] n prince m

princess [prɪnˈses] n princesse f

principal [ˈprɪnsɪpl] adj principal(e) ♦ n

(headmaster) directeur(-trice), principal m

principle [ˈprɪnsɪpl] n principe m; **in/on ~**
en/par principe

print [prɪnt] n (mark) empreinte f; (letters)
caractères mpl; (ART) gravure f, estampe f;
(: photograph) photo f ♦ vt imprimer; (publish) publier; (write in block letters) écrire en
caractères d'imprimerie; **out of ~** épuisé(e);
~ed matter n imprimé(s) m(pl); **~er** n
imprimeur m; (machine) imprimante f; **~ing**
n impression f; **~-out** n copie f papier

prior [ˈpraɪər] adj antérieur(e), précédent(e);
(more important) prioritaire ♦ adv: **~ to doing**
avant de faire; **~ity** [praɪˈɔrɪtɪ] n priorité f

prise [praɪz] vt: **to ~ open** forcer

prison [ˈprɪzn] n prison f ♦ cpd pénitentiaire;
~er n prisonnier(-ère)

pristine [ˈprɪstiːn] adj parfait(e)

privacy [ˈprɪvəsɪ] n intimité f, solitude f

private [ˈpraɪvɪt] adj privé(e); (personal)
personnel(le); (house, lesson) particu-
lier(-ère); (quiet: place) tranquille; (reserved:
person) secret(-ète) ♦ n soldat m de
deuxième classe; **"~"** (on envelope)
"personnelle"; **in ~** en privé; **~ detective** n
détective privé; **~ enterprise** n l'entreprise
privée; **~ property** n propriété privée;
privatize vt privatiser

privet [ˈprɪvɪt] n troène m

privilege [ˈprɪvɪlɪdʒ] n privilège m

privy [ˈprɪvɪ] adj: **to be ~ to** être au courant
de

prize [praɪz] n prix m ♦ adj (example, idiot)
parfait(e); (bull, novel) primé(e) ♦ vt priser,
faire grand cas de; **~-giving** n distribution f
des prix; **~winner** n gagnant(e)

pro [prəʊ] n (SPORT) professionnel(le); **the ~s
and cons** le pour et le contre

probability [prɔbəˈbɪlɪtɪ] n probabilité f

probable [ˈprɔbəbl] adj probable; **probably**
adv probablement

probation [prəˈbeɪʃən] n: **on ~** (LAW) en
liberté surveillée, en sursis; (employee) à
l'essai

probe [prəʊb] n (MED, SPACE) sonde f;
(enquiry) enquête f, investigation f ♦ vt
sonder, explorer

problem [ˈprɔbləm] n problème m

procedure [prəˈsiːdʒər] n (ADMIN, LAW)
procédure f; (method) marche f à suivre,
façon f de procéder

proceed [prəˈsiːd] vi continuer; (go forward)
avancer; **to ~ (with)** continuer, poursuivre; **to
~ to do** se mettre à faire; **~ings** npl (LAW)
poursuites fpl; (meeting) réunion f, séance f;
~s [ˈprəʊsiːdz] npl produit m, recette f

process [ˈprəʊses] n processus m; (method)
procédé m ♦ vt traiter; **~ing** n (PHOT)
développement m; **~ion** [prəˈseʃən] n défilé

m, cortège *m*; (*REL*) procession *f*; **funeral ~ion** (*on foot*) cortège *m* funèbre; (*in cars*) convoi *m* mortuaire

proclaim [prə'kleɪm] *vt* déclarer, proclamer

procrastinate [prəu'kræstɪneɪt] *vi* faire traîner les choses, vouloir tout remettre au lendemain

procure [prə'kjuər] *vt* obtenir

prod [prɒd] *vt* pousser

prodigal ['prɒdɪgl] *adj* prodigue

prodigy ['prɒdɪdʒɪ] *n* prodige *m*

produce [*n* 'prɒdjuːs, *vb* prə'djuːs] *n* (*AGR*) produits *mpl* ♦ *vt* produire; (*to show*) présenter; (*cause*) provoquer, causer; (*THEATRE*) monter, mettre en scène; **~r** *n* producteur *m*; (*THEATRE*) metteur *m* en scène

product ['prɒdʌkt] *n* produit *m*

production [prə'dʌkʃən] *n* production *f*; (*THEATRE*) mise *f* en scène; **~ line** *n* chaîne *f* (de fabrication)

productivity [prɒdʌk'tɪvɪtɪ] *n* productivité *f*

profession [prə'feʃən] *n* profession *f*; **~al** *n* professionnel(le) ♦ *adj* professionnel(le); (*work*) de professionnel; **~ally** *adv* professionnellement; (*SPORT: play*) en professionnel; **she sings ~ally** c'est une chanteuse professionnelle; **I only know him ~ally** je n'ai avec lui que des relations de travail

professor [prə'fesər] *n* professeur *m* (*titulaire d'une chaire*)

proficiency [prə'fɪʃənsɪ] *n* compétence *f*, aptitude *f*

profile ['prəufaɪl] *n* profil *m*

profit ['prɒfɪt] *n* bénéfice *m*; profit *m* ♦ *vi*: **to ~ (by or from)** profiter (de); **~able** *adj* lucratif(-ive), rentable

profound [prə'faund] *adj* profond(e)

profusely [prə'fjuːslɪ] *adv* abondamment; avec effusion

prognosis [prɒg'nəusɪs] (*pl* **prognoses**) *n* pronostic *m*

programme ['prəugræm] (*US* **program**) *n* programme *m*; (*RADIO, TV*) émission *f* ♦ *vt* programmer; **~r** (*US* **programer**) *n* programmeur(-euse); **programming** (*US* **programing**) *n* programmation *f*

progress [*n* 'prəugres, *vb* prə'gres] *n* progrès *m(pl)* ♦ *vi* progresser, avancer; **in ~** en cours; **~ive** [prə'gresɪv] *adj* progressif(-ive); (*person*) progressiste

prohibit [prə'hɪbɪt] *vt* interdire, défendre

project [*n* 'prɒdʒekt, *vb* prə'dʒekt] *n* (*plan*) projet *m*, plan *m*; (*venture*) opération *f*, entreprise *f*; (*research*) étude *f*, dossier *m* ♦ *vt* projeter ♦ *vi* faire saillie, s'avancer; **~ion** *n* projection *f*; (*overhang*) saillie *f*; **~or** *n* projecteur *m*

prolong [prə'lɒŋ] *vt* prolonger

prom [prɒm] *n abbr* = **promenade**; (*US: ball*) bal *m* d'étudiants

promenade [prɒmə'nɑːd] *n* (*by sea*) esplanade *f*, promenade *f*; **~ concert** (*BRIT*) *n* concert *m* populaire (de musique classique)

prominent ['prɒmɪnənt] *adj* (*standing out*) proéminent(e); (*important*) important(e)

promiscuous [prə'mɪskjuəs] *adj* (*sexually*) de mœurs légères

promise ['prɒmɪs] *n* promesse *f* ♦ *vt, vi* promettre; **promising** *adj* prometteur(-euse)

promote [prə'məut] *vt* promouvoir; (*new product*) faire la promotion de; **~r** *n* (*of event*) organisateur(-trice); (*of cause, idea*) promoteur(-trice); **promotion** *n* promotion *f*

prompt [prɒmpt] *adj* rapide ♦ *adv* (*punctually*) à l'heure ♦ *n* (*COMPUT*) message *m* (de guidage) ♦ *vt* provoquer; (*person*) inciter, pousser; (*THEATRE*) souffler (son rôle or ses répliques) à; **~ly** *adv* rapidement, sans délai; ponctuellement

prone [prəun] *adj* (*lying*) couché(e) (face contre terre); **~ to** enclin(e) à

prong [prɒŋ] *n* (*of fork*) dent *f*

pronoun ['prəunaun] *n* pronom *m*

pronounce [prə'nauns] *vt* prononcer; **pronunciation** [prənʌnsɪ'eɪʃən] *n* prononciation *f*

proof [pruːf] *n* preuve *f*; (*TYP*) épreuve *f* ♦ *adj*: **~ against** à l'épreuve de

prop [prɒp] *n* support *m*, étai *m*; (*fig*) soutien *m* ♦ *vt* (*also: ~ up*) étayer, soutenir; (*lean*): **to ~ sth against** appuyer qch contre or à

propaganda [prɒpə'gændə] *n* propagande *f*

propel [prə'pel] *vt* propulser, faire avancer; **~ler** *n* hélice *f*

propensity [prə'pensɪtɪ] *n*: **a ~ for** or **to/to do** une propension à/à faire

proper ['prɒpər] *adj* (*suited, right*) approprié(e), bon (bonne); (*seemly*) correct(e), convenable; (*authentic*) vrai(e), véritable; (*referring to place*): **the village ~** le village proprement dit; **~ly** *adv* correctement, convenablement; **~ noun** *n* nom *m* propre

property ['prɒpətɪ] *n* propriété *f*; (*things owned*) biens *mpl*; propriété(s) *f(pl)*; (*land*) terres *fpl*

prophecy ['prɒfɪsɪ] *n* prophétie *f*

prophesy ['prɒfɪsaɪ] *vt* prédire

prophet ['prɒfɪt] *n* prophète *m*

proportion [prə'pɔːʃən] *n* proportion *f*; (*share*) part *f*; partie *f*; **~al, ~ate** *adj* proportionnel(le)

proposal [prə'pəuzl] *n* proposition *f*, offre *f*; (*plan*) projet *m*; (*of marriage*) demande *f* en mariage

propose [prə'pəuz] *vt* proposer, suggérer ♦ *vi* faire sa demande en mariage; **to ~ to do** avoir l'intention de faire; **proposition** [prɒpə'-

zıʃən] n proposition f

proprietor [prə'praɪətə^r] n propriétaire m/f

propriety [prə'praɪətɪ] n (seemliness) bienséance f, convenance f

prose [prəuz] n (not poetry) prose f

prosecute ['prɔsɪkju:t] vt poursuivre; **prosecution** [prɔsɪ'kju:ʃən] n poursuites fpl judiciaires; (accusing side) partie plaignante; **prosecutor** n (US: plaintiff) plaignant(e); (also: **public prosecutor**) procureur m, ministère public

prospect [n 'prɔspekt, vb prə'spekt] n perspective f ♦ vt, vi prospecter; **~s** npl (for work etc) possibilités fpl d'avenir, débouchés mpl; **~ing** n (for gold, oil etc) prospection f; **~ive** adj (possible) éventuel(le); (future) futur(e)

prospectus [prə'spektəs] n prospectus m

prosperity [prɔ'spɛrɪtɪ] n prospérité f

prostitute ['prɔstɪtju:t] n prostitué(e)

protect [prə'tekt] vt protéger; **~ive** adj protecteur(-trice); (clothing) de protection

protein ['prəuti:n] n protéine f

protest [n 'prəutest, vb prə'test] n protestation f ♦ vi, vt: **to ~ (that)** protester (que)

Protestant ['prɔtɪstənt] adj, n protestant(e)

protester [prə'testə^r] n manifestant(e)

protracted [prə'træktɪd] adj prolongé(e)

protrude [prə'tru:d] vi avancer, dépasser

proud [praud] adj fier(ère); (pej) orgueilleux(-euse)

prove [pru:v] vt prouver, démontrer ♦ vi: **to ~ (to be) correct** etc s'avérer juste etc; **to ~ o.s.** montrer ce dont on est capable

proverb ['prɔvə:b] n proverbe m

provide [prə'vaɪd] vt fournir; **to ~ sb with sth** fournir qch à qn; **~ for** vt fus (person) subvenir aux besoins de; (future event) prévoir; **~d (that)** conj à condition que +sub; **providing** conj: **providing (that)** à condition que +sub

province ['prɔvɪns] n province f; (fig) domaine m; **provincial** [prə'vɪnʃəl] adj provincial(e)

provision [prə'vɪʒən] n (supplying) fourniture f; approvisionnement m; (stipulation) disposition f; **~s** npl (food) provisions fpl; **~al** adj provisoire

proviso [prə'vaɪzəu] n condition f

provocative [prə'vɔkətɪv] adj provocateur(-trice), provocant(e)

provoke [prə'vəuk] vt provoquer

prowess ['prauɪs] n prouesse f

prowl [praul] vi (also: **~ about**, **~ around**) rôder ♦ n: **on the ~** à l'affût; **~er** n rôdeur(-euse)

proxy ['prɔksɪ] n procuration f

prudent ['pru:dnt] adj prudent(e)

prune [pru:n] n pruneau m ♦ vt élaguer

pry [praɪ] vi: **to ~ into** fourrer son nez dans

PS n abbr (= postscript) p.s.

psalm [sɑ:m] n psaume m

pseudonym ['sju:dənɪm] n pseudonyme m

psyche ['saɪkɪ] n psychisme m

psychiatrist [saɪ'kaɪətrɪst] n psychiatre m/f

psychic ['saɪkɪk] adj (also: **~al**) (méta)psychique; (person) doué(e) d'un sixième sens

psychoanalyst [saɪkəu'ænəlɪst] n psychanalyste m/f

psychological [saɪkə'lɔdʒɪkl] adj psychologique

psychologist [saɪ'kɔlədʒɪst] n psychologue m/f

psychology [saɪ'kɔlədʒɪ] n psychologie f

PTO abbr (= please turn over) T.S.V.P.

pub [pʌb] n (public house) pub m

public ['pʌblɪk] adj public(-ique) ♦ n public m; **in ~** en public; **to make ~** rendre public; **~ address system** n (system m de) sonorisation f; hauts-parleurs mpl

publican ['pʌblɪkən] n patron m de pub

public: **~ company** n société f anonyme (cotée en Bourse); **~ convenience** (BRIT) n toilettes fpl; **~ holiday** n jour férié; **~ house** (BRIT) n pub m

publicity [pʌb'lɪsɪtɪ] n publicité f

publicize ['pʌblɪsaɪz] vt faire connaître, rendre public(-ique)

public: **~ opinion** n opinion publique; **~ relations** n relations publiques; **~ school** n (BRIT) école (secondaire) privée; (US) école publique; **~-spirited** adj qui fait preuve de civisme; **~ transport** n transports mpl en commun

publish ['pʌblɪʃ] vt publier; **~er** n éditeur m; **~ing** n édition f

pub lunch n repas m de bistrot

pucker ['pʌkə^r] vt plisser

pudding ['pudɪŋ] n pudding m; (BRIT: sweet) dessert m, entremets m, **black ~**, (US) **blood ~** boudin (noir)

puddle ['pʌdl] n flaque f (d'eau)

puff [pʌf] n bouffée f ♦ vt: **to ~ one's pipe** tirer sur sa pipe ♦ vi (pant) haleter; **~ out** vt (fill with air) gonfler; **~ pastry** (US **puff paste**) n pâte feuilletée; **~y** adj bouffi(e), boursouflé(e)

pull [pul] n (tug): **to give sth a ~** tirer sur qch ♦ vt tirer; (trigger) presser ♦ vi tirer; **to ~ to pieces** mettre en morceaux; **to ~ one's punches** ménager son adversaire; **to ~ one's weight** faire sa part (du travail); **to ~ o.s. together** se ressaisir; **to ~ sb's leg** (fig) faire marcher qn; **~ apart** vt (break) mettre en pièces, démantibuler; **~ down** vt (house) démolir; **~ in** vi (AUT) entrer; (RAIL) entrer en gare; **~ off** vt enlever, ôter; (deal etc) mener à bien, conclure; **~ out** vi démarrer, partir ♦ vt sortir; arracher; **~ over** vi (AUT) se ranger; **~ through** vi s'en sortir; **~ up** vi (stop) s'arrêter ♦ vt remonter; (uproot) déraciner, arracher

pulley ['puli] n poulie f

pullover ['puləuvəʳ] n pull(-over) m, tricot m

pulp [pʌlp] n (of fruit) pulpe f

pulpit ['pulpit] n chaire f

pulsate [pʌl'seit] vi battre, palpiter; (music) vibrer

pulse [pʌls] n (of blood) pouls m; (of heart) battement m; (of music, engine) vibrations fpl; (BOT, CULIN) légume sec

pump [pʌmp] n pompe f; (shoe) escarpin m ♦ vt pomper; **~ up** vt gonfler

pumpkin ['pʌmpkin] n potiron m, citrouille f

pun [pʌn] n jeu m de mots, calembour m

punch [pʌntʃ] n (blow) coup m de poing; (tool) poinçon m; (drink) punch m ♦ vt (hit): **to ~ sb/sth** donner un coup de poing à qn/ sur qch; **~line** n (of joke) conclusion f; **~-up** (BRIT: inf) n bagarre f

punctual ['pʌŋktjuəl] adj ponctuel(le)

punctuation [pʌŋktju'eiʃən] n ponctuation f

puncture ['pʌŋktʃəʳ] n crevaison f

pundit ['pʌndit] n individu m qui pontifie, pontife m

pungent ['pʌndʒənt] adj piquant(e), âcre

punish ['pʌniʃ] vt punir; **~ment** n punition f, châtiment m

punk [pʌŋk] n (also: ~ rocker) punk m/f; (also: ~ rock) le punk rock; (US: inf: hoodlum) voyou m

punt [pʌnt] n (boat) bachot m

punter ['pʌntəʳ] (BRIT) n (gambler) parieur(-euse); (inf): **the ~s** le public

puny ['pjuːni] adj chétif(-ive); (effort) piteux(-euse)

pup [pʌp] n chiot m

pupil ['pjuːpl] n (SCOL) élève m/f; (of eye) pupille f

puppet ['pʌpit] n marionnette f, pantin m

puppy ['pʌpi] n chiot m, jeune chien(ne)

purchase ['pəːtʃis] n achat m ♦ vt acheter; **~r** n acheteur(-euse)

pure [pjuəʳ] adj pur(e); **~ly** adv purement

purge [pəːdʒ] n purge f ♦ vt purger

purple ['pəːpl] adj violet(te); (face) cramoisi(e)

purpose ['pəːpəs] n intention f, but m; **on ~** exprès; **~ful** adj déterminé(e), résolu(e)

purr [pəːʳ] vi ronronner

purse [pəːs] n (BRIT: for money) porte-monnaie m inv; (US: handbag) sac m à main ♦ vt serrer, pincer

purser ['pəːsəʳ] n (NAUT) commissaire m du bord

pursue [pə'sjuː] vt poursuivre; **pursuit** [pə'sjuːt] n poursuite f; (occupation) occupation f, activité f

push [puʃ] n poussée f ♦ vt pousser; (button) appuyer sur; (product) faire de la publicité pour; (thrust): **to ~ sth (into)** enfoncer qch (dans) ♦ vi pousser; (demand): **to ~ for** exiger, demander avec insistance; **~ aside** vt écarter; **~ off** (inf) vi filer, ficher le camp; **~ on** vi (continue) continuer; **~ through** vi se frayer un chemin ♦ vt (measure) faire accepter; **~ up** vt (total, prices) faire monter; **~chair** (BRIT) n poussette f; **~er** n (drug pusher) revendeur(-euse) (de drogue), ravitailleur(-euse) (en drogue); **~over** (inf) n: **it's a ~over** c'est un jeu d'enfant; **~-up** (US) n traction f; **~y** (pej) adj arriviste

puss [pus], **pussy (cat)** ['pusi(kæt)] (inf) n minet m

put [put] (pt, pp put) vt mettre, poser, placer; (say) dire, exprimer; (a question) poser; (case, view) exposer, présenter; (estimate) estimer; **~ about** vt (rumour) faire courir; **~ across** vt (ideas etc) communiquer; **~ away** vt (store) ranger; **~ back** vt (replace) remettre, replacer; (postpone) remettre; (delay) retarder; **~ by** vt (money) mettre de côté, économiser; **~ down** vt (parcel etc) poser, déposer; (in writing) mettre par écrit, inscrire; (suppress: revolt etc) réprimer, faire cesser; (animal) abattre; (dog, cat) faire piquer; (attribute) attribuer; **~ forward** vt (ideas) avancer; **~ in** vt (gas, electricity) installer; (application, complaint) soumettre; (time, effort) consacrer; **~ off** vt (light etc) éteindre; (postpone) remettre à plus tard, ajourner; (discourage) dissuader; **~ on** vt (clothes, lipstick, record) mettre; (light etc) allumer; (play etc) monter; (food: cook) mettre à cuire ou à chauffer; (gain): **to ~ on weight** prendre du poids, grossir; **to ~ the brakes on** freiner; **to ~ the kettle on** mettre l'eau à chauffer; **~ out** vt (take out) mettre dehors; (one's hand) tendre; (light etc) éteindre; (person: inconvenience) déranger, gêner; **~ through** vt (TEL: call) passer; (: person) mettre en communication; (plan) faire accepter; **~ up** vt (raise) lever, relever, remonter; (pin up) afficher; (hang) accrocher; (build) construire, ériger; (tent) monter; (umbrella) ouvrir; (increase) augmenter; (accommodate) loger; **~ up with** vt fus supporter

putt [pʌt] n coup roulé; **~ing green** n green m

putty ['pʌti] n mastic m

put-up ['putʌp] (BRIT) adj: **~~ job** coup monté

puzzle ['pʌzl] n énigme f, mystère m; (jigsaw)

puzzle *m* ♦ *vt* intriguer, rendre perplexe ♦ *vi* se creuser la tête; **~d** *adj* perplexe; **puzzling** *adj* déconcertant(e)

pyjamas [pə'dʒɑːməz] (*BRIT*) *npl* pyjama(s) *m(pl)*

pylon ['paɪlən] *n* pylône *m*

pyramid ['pɪrəmɪd] *n* pyramide *f*

Pyrenees [pɪrə'niːz] *npl*: **the ~** les Pyrénées *fpl*

Q, q

quack [kwæk] *n* (*of duck*) coin-coin *m inv*; (*pej: doctor*) charlatan *m*

quad [kwɔd] *n abbr* = **quadrangle**; **quadruplet**

quadrangle ['kwɔdræŋgl] *n* (*courtyard*) cour *f*

quadruple [kwɔ'druːpl] *vt*, *vi* quadrupler; **~ts** *npl* quadruplés

quail [kweɪl] *n* (*ZOOL*) caille *f* ♦ *vi*: **to ~ at** or **before** reculer devant

quaint [kweɪnt] *adj* bizarre, (*house, village*) au charme vieillot, pittoresque

quake [kweɪk] *vi* trembler

qualification [kwɔlɪfɪ'keɪʃən] *n* (*often pl: degree etc*) diplôme *m*; (*training*) qualification(s) *f(pl)*, expérience *f*; (*ability*) compétence(s) *f(pl)*; (*limitation*) réserve *f*, restriction *f*

qualified ['kwɔlɪfaɪd] *adj* (*trained*) qualifié(e); (*professionally*) diplômé(e); (*fit, competent*) compétent(e), qualifié(e); (*limited*) conditionnel(le)

qualify ['kwɔlɪfaɪ] *vt* qualifier; (*modify*) atténuer, nuancer ♦ *vi*: **to ~ (as)** obtenir son diplôme (de); **to ~ (for)** remplir les conditions requises (pour); (*SPORT*) se qualifier (pour)

quality ['kwɔlɪtɪ] *n* qualité *f*, **~ time** *n* moments privilégiés

qualm [kwɑːm] *n* doute *m*; scrupule *m*

quandary ['kwɔndrɪ] *n*: **in a ~** devant un dilemme, dans l'embarras

quantity ['kwɔntɪtɪ] *n* quantité *f*; **~ surveyor** *n* métreur *m* vérificateur

quarantine ['kwɔrntiːn] *n* quarantaine *f*

quarrel ['kwɔrl] *n* querelle *f*, dispute *f* ♦ *vi* se disputer, se quereller

quarry ['kwɔrɪ] *n* (*for stone*) carrière *f*; (*animal*) proie *f*, gibier *m*

quart [kwɔːt] *n* ≈ litre *m*

quarter ['kwɔːtəʳ] *n* quart *m*; (*US: coin: 25 cents*) quart de dollar; (*of year*) trimestre *m*; (*district*) quartier *m* ♦ *vt* (*divide*) partager en quartiers or en quatre; **~s** *npl* (*living ~*) logement *m*; (*MIL*) quartiers *mpl*, cantonnement *m*; **a ~ of an hour** un quart d'heure; **~ final** *n* quart *m* de finale; **~ly** *adj* trimestriel(le) ♦ *adv* tous les trois mois

quartet(te) [kwɔː'tet] *n* quatuor *m*; (*jazz players*) quartette *m*

quartz [kwɔːts] *n* quartz *m*

quash [kwɔʃ] *vt* (*verdict*) annuler

quaver ['kweɪvəʳ] *vi* trembler

quay [kiː] *n* (*also*: **~side**) quai *m*

queasy ['kwiːzɪ] *adj*: **to feel ~** avoir mal au cœur

queen [kwiːn] *n* reine *f*; (*CARDS etc*) dame *f*; **~ mother** *n* reine mère *f*

queer [kwɪəʳ] *adj* étrange, curieux(-euse); (*suspicious*) louche ♦ *n* (*inf!*) homosexuel *m*

quell [kwel] *vt* réprimer, étouffer

quench [kwentʃ] *vt*: **to ~ one's thirst** se désaltérer

query ['kwɪərɪ] *n* question *f* ♦ *vt* remettre en question, mettre en doute

quest [kwest] *n* recherche *f*, quête *f*

question ['kwestʃən] *n* question *f* ♦ *vt* (*person*) interroger; (*plan, idea*) remettre en question, mettre en doute; **beyond ~** sans aucun doute; **out of the ~** hors de question; **~able** *adj* discutable; **~ mark** *n* point *m* d'interrogation; **~naire** [kwestʃə'neəʳ] *n* questionnaire *m*

queue [kjuː] (*BRIT*) *n* queue *f*, file *f* ♦ *vi* (*also*: **~ up**) faire la queue

quibble ['kwɪbl] *vi*: **~ (about)** or (**over**) or (**with sth**) ergoter (sur qch)

quick [kwɪk] *adj* rapide; (*agile*) agile, vif (vive) ♦ *n*: **cut to the ~** (*fig*) touché(e) au vif; **be ~!** dépêche-toi!; **~en** *vt* accélérer, presser ♦ *vi* s'accélérer, devenir plus rapide; **~ly** *adv* vite, rapidement; **~sand** *n* sables mouvants; **~-witted** *adj* à l'esprit vif

quid [kwɪd] (*BRIT: inf*) *n, pl inv* livre *f*

quiet ['kwaɪət] *adj* tranquille, calme; (*voice*) bas(se); (*ceremony, colour*) discret(-ète) ♦ *n* tranquillité *f*, calme *m*; (*silence*) silence *m* ♦ *vt*, *vi* (*US*) = **quieten**; **keep ~!** tais-toi!; **~en** *vi* (*also*: **~en down**) se calmer, s'apaiser ♦ *vt* calmer, apaiser; **~ly** *adv* tranquillement, calmement; (*silently*) silencieusement; **~ness** *n* tranquillité *f*, calme *m*; (*silence*) silence *m*

quilt [kwɪlt] *n* édredon *m*; (*continental ~*) couette *f*

quin [kwɪn] *n abbr* = **quintuplet**

quintuplets [kwɪn'tjuːplɪts] *npl* quintuplé(e)s

quip [kwɪp] *n* remarque piquante or spirituelle, pointe *f*

quirk [kwəːk] *n* bizarrerie *f*

quit [kwɪt] (*pt, pp* **quit** or **quitted**) *vt* quitter; (*smoking, grumbling*) arrêter de ♦ *vi* (*give up*) abandonner, renoncer; (*resign*) démissionner

quite [kwaɪt] *adv* (*rather*) assez, plutôt; (*entirely*) complètement, tout à fait; (*following a negative = almost*): **that's not ~ big enough** ce n'est pas tout à fait assez grand; **I**

~ **understand** je comprends très bien; ~ **a few of them** un assez grand nombre d'entre eux; ~ **(so)!** exactement!

quits [kwɪts] *adj:* ~ **(with)** quitte (envers); **let's call it** ~ restons-en là

quiver ['kwɪvəʳ] *vi* trembler, frémir

quiz [kwɪz] *n (game)* jeu-concours *m* ♦ *vt* interroger; ~**zical** *adj* narquois(e)

quota ['kwəʊtə] *n* quota *m*

quotation [kwəʊ'teɪʃən] *n* citation *f*; *(estimate)* devis *m*; ~ **marks** *npl* guillemets *mpl*

quote [kwəʊt] *n* citation *f*; *(estimate)* devis *m* ♦ *vt* citer; *(price)* indiquer; ~**s** *npl* guillemets *mpl*

R, r

rabbi ['ræbaɪ] *n* rabbin *m*

rabbit ['ræbɪt] *n* lapin *m*; ~ **hutch** *n* clapier *m*

rabble ['ræbl] *(pej) n* populace *f*

rabies ['reɪbiːz] *n* rage *f*

RAC *n abbr (BRIT) = Royal Automobile Club*

rac(c)oon [rə'kuːn] *n* raton laveur

race [reɪs] *n (species)* race *f*; *(competition, rush)* course *f* ♦ *vt (horse)* faire courir *vi (compete)* faire la course, courir; *(hurry)* aller à toute vitesse, courir; *(engine)* s'emballer; *(pulse)* augmenter; ~ **car** *(US) n* = **racing car**; ~ **car driver** *n (US)* = **racing driver**; ~**course** *n* champ *m* de courses; ~**horse** *n* cheval *m* de course; ~**r** *n (bike)* vélo *m* de course; ~**track** *n* piste *f*

racial ['reɪʃl] *adj* racial(e)

racing ['reɪsɪŋ] *n* courses *fpl*; ~ **car** *(BRIT) n* voiture *f* de course; ~ **driver** *(BRIT) n* pilote *m* de course

racism ['reɪsɪzəm] *n* racisme *m*; **racist** *adj* raciste *m/f*

rack [ræk] *n (for guns, tools)* râtelier *m*; *(also:* **luggage** ~) porte-bagages *m inv*, filet *m* à bagages; *(also:* **roof** ~) galerie *f*; *(dish* ~) égouttoir *m* ♦ *vt* tourmenter; **to** ~ **one's brains** se creuser la cervelle

racket ['rækɪt] *n (for tennis)* raquette *f*; *(noise)* tapage *m*; vacarme *m*; *(swindle)* escroquerie *f*

racquet ['rækɪt] *n* raquette *f*

racy ['reɪsɪ] *adj* plein(e) de verve; *(slightly indecent)* osé(e)

radar ['reɪdɑːʳ] *n* radar *m*

radial ['reɪdɪəl] *adj (also:* ~-**ply**) à carcasse radiale

radiant ['reɪdɪənt] *adj* rayonnant(e)

radiate ['reɪdɪeɪt] *vt (heat)* émettre, dégager; *(emotion)* rayonner de ♦ *vi (lines)* rayonner; **radiation** [reɪdɪ'eɪʃən] *n* rayonnement *m*;

(radioactive) radiation *f*; **radiator** ['reɪdɪeɪtəʳ] *n* radiateur *m*

radical ['rædɪkl] *adj* radical(e)

radii ['reɪdɪaɪ] *npl of* **radius**

radio ['reɪdɪəu] *n* radio *f* ♦ *vt* appeler par radio; **on the** ~ à la radio; ~**active** ['reɪ-dɪəu'æktɪv] *adj* radioactif(-ive); ~ **cass-ette** *n* radiocassette *m*; ~-**controlled** *adj* téléguidé(e); ~ **station** *n* station *f* de radio

radish ['rædɪʃ] *n* radis *m*

radius ['reɪdɪəs] *(pl* **radii**) *n* rayon *m*

RAF *n abbr = Royal Air Force*

raffle ['ræfl] *n* tombola *f*

raft [rɑːft] *n (craft; also: life* ~) radeau *m*

rafter ['rɑːftəʳ] *n* chevron *m*

rag [ræg] *n* chiffon *m*, *(pej: newspaper)* feuille *f* de chou, torchon *m*; *(student* ~) attractions organisées au profit d'œuvres de charité; ~**s** *npl (torn clothes etc)* haillons *mpl*; ~ **doll** *n* poupée *f* de chiffon

rage [reɪdʒ] *n (fury)* rage *f*, fureur *f* ♦ *vi (person)* être fou (folle) de rage; *(storm)* faire rage, être déchaîné(e); **it's all the** ~ cela fait fureur

ragged ['rægɪd] *adj (edge)* inégal(e); *(clothes)* en loques; *(appearance)* déguenillé(e)

raid [reɪd] *n (attack; also: MIL)* raid *m*; *(criminal)* hold-up *m inv*; *(by police)* descente *f*, rafle *f* ♦ *vt* faire un raid sur *ou* un hold-up *ou* une descente dans

rail [reɪl] *n (on stairs)* rampe *f*; *(on bridge, balcony)* balustrade *f*; *(of ship)* bastingage *m*; ~**s** *npl (track)* rails *mpl*, voie ferrée; **by** ~ par chemin de fer, en train; ~**ing(s)** *n(pl)* grille *f*; ~**road** *(US)*, ~**way** *(BRIT) n (track)* voie ferrée; *(company)* chemin *m* de fer; ~**way line** *(BRIT) n* ligne *f* de chemin de fer; ~**wayman** *(BRIT) (irreg) n* cheminot *m*; ~**way station** *(BRIT) n* gare *f*

rain [reɪn] *n* pluie *f* ♦ *vi* pleuvoir; **in the** ~ sous la pluie; **it's** ~**ing** il pleut; ~**bow** *n* arc-en-ciel *m*; ~**coat** *n* imperméable *m*; ~**drop** *n* goutte *f* de pluie; ~**fall** *n* chute *f* de pluie; *(measurement)* hauteur *f* des précipitations; ~**forest** *n* forêt *f* tropicale humide; ~**y** *adj* pluvieux(-euse)

raise [reɪz] *n* augmentation *f* ♦ *vt (lift)* lever; hausser; *(increase)* augmenter; *(morale)* remonter; *(standards)* améliorer; *(question, doubt)* provoquer, soulever; *(cattle, family)* élever; *(crop)* faire pousser; *(funds)* rassembler; *(loan)* obtenir; *(army)* lever; **to** ~ **one's voice** élever la voix

raisin ['reɪzn] *n* raisin sec

rake [reɪk] *n (tool)* râteau *m* ♦ *vt (garden, leaves)* ratisser

rally ['rælɪ] *n (POL etc)* meeting *m*, rassemblement *m*; *(AUT)* rallye *m*; *(TENNIS)* échange m ♦ vt (*support*) gagner ♦ vi (*sick person*) aller mieux; (*Stock Exchange*) reprendre; **~ round** vt fus venir en aide à

RAM [ræm] n abbr (= random access memory) mémoire vive

ram [ræm] n bélier m ♦ vt enfoncer; (*crash into*) emboutir; percuter

ramble ['ræmbl] n randonnée f ♦ vi (*walk*) se promener, faire une randonnée; (*talk: also:* **~ on**) discourir, pérorer; **~r** n promeneur(-euse), randonneur(-euse); (*BOT*) rosier grimpant; **rambling** adj (*speech*) décousu(e); (*house*) plein(e) de coins et de recoins; (*BOT*) grimpant(e)

ramp [ræmp] n (*incline*) rampe f; dénivellation f; **on ~, off ~** (*US: AUT*) bretelle f d'accès

rampage [ræm'peɪdʒ] n: **to be on the ~** se déchaîner

rampant ['ræmpənt] adj (*disease etc*) qui sévit

ram raiding [reɪdɪŋ] n pillage d'un magasin en enfonçant la vitrine avec une voiture

ramshackle ['ræmʃækl] adj (*house*) délabré(e); (*car etc*) déglingué(e)

ran [ræn] pt of **run**

ranch [rɑːntʃ] n ranch m; **~er** n propriétaire m de ranch

rancid ['rænsɪd] adj rance

rancour ['ræŋkəᶜ] (*US* **rancor**) n rancune f

random ['rændəm] adj fait(e) or établi(e) au hasard; (*MATH*) aléatoire ♦ n: **at ~** au hasard; **~ access** n (*COMPUT*) accès sélectif

randy ['rændɪ] (*BRIT: inf*) adj excité(e); lubrique

rang [ræŋ] pt of **ring**

range [reɪndʒ] n (*of mountains*) chaîne f; (*of missile, voice*) portée f; (*of products*) choix m, gamme f (*MIL: also:* **shooting ~**) champ m de tir; (*indoor*) stand m de tir; (*also:* **kitchen ~**) fourneau m (de cuisine) ♦ vt (*place in a line*) mettre en rang, ranger ♦ vi: **to ~ over** (*extend*) couvrir; **to ~ from ... to** aller de ... à; **a ~ of** (*series: of proposals etc*) divers(e)

ranger ['reɪndʒəᶜ] n garde forestier

rank [ræŋk] n rang m; (*MIL*) grade m; (*BRIT: also:* **taxi ~**) station f de taxis ♦ vi: **to ~ among** compter or se classer parmi ♦ adj (*stinking*) fétide, puant(e); **the ~ and file** (*fig*) la masse, la base

ransack ['rænsæk] vt fouiller (à fond); (*plunder*) piller

ransom ['rænsəm] n rançon f; **to hold to ~** (*fig*) exercer un chantage sur

rant [rænt] vi fulminer

rap [ræp] vt frapper sur or à; taper sur ♦ n; **~ music** rap m

rape [reɪp] n viol m; (*BOT*) colza m ♦ vt violer; **~(seed) oil** n huile f de colza

rapid ['ræpɪd] adj rapide; **~s** npl (*GEO*)

rapides mpl

rapist ['reɪpɪst] n violeur m

rapport [ræ'pɔːᶜ] n entente f

rapturous ['ræptʃərəs] adj enthousiaste, frénétique

rare [reəᶜ] adj rare; (*CULIN: steak*) saignant(e)

raring ['reərɪŋ] adj: **~ to go** (*inf*) très impatient(e) de commencer

rascal ['rɑːskl] n vaurien m

rash [ræʃ] adj imprudent(e), irréfléchi(e) ♦ n (*MED*) rougeur f, éruption f; (*spate: of events*) série (noire)

rasher ['ræʃəᶜ] n fine tranche (de lard)

raspberry ['rɑːzbərɪ] n framboise f; **~ bush** n framboisier m

rasping ['rɑːspɪŋ] adj: **~ noise** grincement m

rat [ræt] n rat m

rate [reɪt] n taux m; (*speed*) vitesse f, rythme m; (*price*) tarif m ♦ vt classer; évaluer; **~s** npl (*BRIT: tax*) impôts locaux; (*fees*) tarifs mpl; **to ~ sb/sth as** considérer qn/qch comme; **~able value** (*BRIT*) n valeur locative imposable; **~payer** ['reɪtpeɪəᶜ] (*BRIT*) n contribuable m/f (*payant les impôts locaux*)

rather ['rɑːðəᶜ] adv plutôt; **it's ~ expensive** c'est assez cher; (*too much*) c'est un peu cher; **there's ~ a lot** il y en a beaucoup; **I would** or **I'd ~ go** j'aimerais mieux or je préférerais partir

rating ['reɪtɪŋ] n (*assessment*) évaluation f; (*score*) classement m; **~s** npl (*RADIO, TV*) indice m d'écoute

ratio ['reɪʃɪəʊ] n proportion f

ration ['ræʃən] n (*gen pl*) ration(s) f(pl)

rational ['ræʃənl] adj raisonnable, sensé(e); (*solution, reasoning*) logique; **~e** [ræʃə'nɑːl] n raisonnement m; **~ize** vt rationaliser; (*conduct*) essayer d'expliquer or de motiver

rat race n foire f d'empoigne

rattle ['rætl] n (*of door, window*) battement m; (*of coins, chain*) cliquetis m; (*of train, engine*) bruit m de ferraille; (*object: for baby*) hochet m ♦ vi cliqueter; (*car, bus*): **to ~ along** rouler dans un bruit de ferraille ♦ vt agiter (*bruyamment*); (*unnerve*) déconcerter; **~snake** n serpent m à sonnettes

raucous ['rɔːkəs] adj rauque; (*noisy*) bruyant(e), tapageur(-euse)

rave [reɪv] vi (*in anger*) s'emporter; (*with enthusiasm*) s'extasier; (*MED*) délirer ♦ n (*BRIT: inf: party*) rave f, soirée f techno

raven ['reɪvən] n corbeau m

ravenous ['rævənəs] adj affamé(e)

ravine [rə'viːn] n ravin m

raving ['reɪvɪŋ] adj: **~ lunatic** ♦ n fou (folle) furieux(-euse)

ravishing ['rævɪʃɪŋ] adj enchanteur(-eresse)

raw [rɔː] adj (*uncooked*) cru(e); (*not processed*) brut(e); (*sore*) à vif, irrité(e);

(*inexperienced*) inexpérimenté(e); (*weather, day*) froid(e) et humide; ~ **deal** (*inf*) *n* sale coup *m*; ~ **material** *n* matière première

ray [reɪ] *n* rayon *m*; ~ **of hope** lueur *f* d'espoir

raze [reɪz] *vt* (*also*: ~ **to the ground**) raser, détruire

razor [ˈreɪzər] *n* rasoir *m*; ~ **blade** *n* lame *f* de rasoir

Rd *abbr* = **road**

RE *n abbr* = **religious education**

re [riː] *prep* concernant

reach [riːtʃ] *n* portée *f*, atteinte *f*; (*of river etc*) étendue *f* ♦ *vt* atteindre; (*conclusion, decision*) parvenir à ♦ *vi* s'étendre, étendre le bras; **out of/within** ~ hors de/à portée; **within** ~ **of the shops** pas trop loin des *or* à proximité des magasins; ~ **out** *vt* tendre ♦ *vi*: **to** ~ **out (for)** allonger le bras (pour prendre)

react [riːˈækt] *vi* réagir; ~**ion** *n* réaction *f*

reactor [riːˈæktər] *n* réacteur *m*

read [riːd, *pt, pp* red] (*pt, pp* **read**) *vi* lire ♦ *vt* lire; (*understand*) comprendre, interpréter; (*study*) étudier; (*meter*) relever; ~ **out** *vt* lire à haute voix; ~**able** *adj* facile or agréable à lire; (*writing*) lisible; ~**er** *n* lecteur (-trice); (*BRIT: at university*) chargé(e) d'enseignement; ~**ership** *n* (*of paper etc*) (nombre *m* de) lecteurs *mpl*

readily [ˈredɪlɪ] *adv* volontiers, avec empressement; (*easily*) facilement

readiness [ˈredɪnɪs] *n* empressement *m*; **in** ~ (*prepared*) prêt(e)

reading [ˈriːdɪŋ] *n* lecture *f*; (*understanding*) interprétation *f*; (*on instrument*) indications *fpl*

ready [ˈredɪ] *adj* prêt(e); (*willing*) prêt, disposé(e); (*available*) disponible ♦ *n*: **at the** ~ (*MIL*) prêt à faire feu; **to get** ~ se préparer ♦ *vt* préparer; ~-**made** *adj* tout(e) fait(e); ~-**to-wear** *adj* prêt(e) à porter

real [rɪəl] *adj* véritable, réel(le); **in** ~ **terms** dans la réalité; ~ **estate** *n* biens fonciers or immobiliers; ~**istic** [rɪəˈlɪstɪk] *adj* réaliste; ~**ity** [rɪˈælɪtɪ] *n* réalité *f*

realization [rɪəlaɪˈzeɪʃən] *n* (*awareness*) prise *f* de conscience; (*fulfilment; also: of asset*) réalisation *f*

realize [ˈrɪəlaɪz] *vt* (*understand*) se rendre compte de; (*a project, COMM: asset*) réaliser

really [ˈrɪəlɪ] *adv* vraiment; ~? vraiment?, c'est vrai?

realm [relm] *n* royaume *m*; (*fig*) domaine *m*

realtor ® [ˈrɪəltɔːr] (*US*) *n* agent immobilier

reap [riːp] *vt* moissonner; (*fig*) récolter

reappear [riːəˈpɪər] *vi* réapparaître, reparaître

rear [rɪər] *adj* de derrière, arrière *inv*; (*AUT: wheel etc*) arrière ♦ *n* arrière *m* ♦ *vt* (*cattle, family*) élever ♦ *vi* (*also*: ~ **up**: *animal*) se cabrer; ~**guard** *n* (*MIL*) arrière-garde *f*; ~-**view mirror** *n* (*AUT*) rétroviseur *m*

reason [ˈriːzn] *n* raison *f* ♦ *vi*: **to** ~ **with sb** raisonner qn, faire entendre raison à qn; **to have** ~ **to think** avoir lieu de penser; **it stands to** ~ **that** il va sans dire que; ~**able** *adj* raisonnable; (*not bad*) acceptable; ~**ably** *adv* raisonnablement; ~**ing** *n* raisonnement *m*

reassurance [riːəˈʃuərəns] *n* réconfort *m*; (*factual*) assurance *f*, garantie *f*

reassure [riːəˈʃuər] *vt* rassurer

rebate [ˈriːbeɪt] *n* (*on tax etc*) dégrèvement *m*

rebel [*n* ˈrebl, *vb* rɪˈbel] *n* rebelle *m/f* ♦ *vi* se rebeller, se révolter; ~**lious** [rɪˈbeljəs] *adj* rebelle

rebound [*vb* rɪˈbaund, *n* ˈriːbaund] *vi* (*ball*) rebondir ♦ *n* rebond *m*; **to marry on the** ~ se marier immédiatement après une déception amoureuse

rebuff [rɪˈbʌf] *n* rebuffade *f*

rebuke [rɪˈbjuːk] *vt* réprimander

rebut [rɪˈbʌt] *vt* réfuter

recall [*vb* rɪˈkɔːl, *n* ˈriːkɔl] *vt* rappeler; (*remember*) se rappeler, se souvenir de ♦ *n* rappel *m*; (*ability to remember*) mémoire *f*

recant [rɪˈkænt] *vi* se rétracter; (*REL*) abjurer

recap [ˈriːkæp], **recapitulate** [riːkəˈpɪtjuleɪt] *vt, vi* récapituler

rec'd *abbr* = **received**

recede [rɪˈsiːd] *vi* (*tide*) descendre; (*disappear*) disparaître peu à peu; (*memory, hope*) s'estomper; **receding** *adj* (*chin*) fuyant(e); **receding hairline** front dégarni

receipt [rɪˈsiːt] *n* (*document*) reçu *m*; (*for parcel etc*) accusé *m* de réception; (*act of receiving*) réception *f*; ~**s** *npl* (*COMM*) recettes *fpl*

receive [rɪˈsiːv] *vt* recevoir; ~**r** *n* (*TEL*) récepteur *m*, combiné *m*; (*RADIO*) récepteur *m*; (*of stolen goods*) receleur *m*; (*LAW*) administrateur *m* judiciaire

recent [ˈriːsnt] *adj* récent(e); ~**ly** *adv* récemment

receptacle [rɪˈseptɪkl] *n* récipient *m*

reception [rɪˈsepʃən] *n* réception *f*; (*welcome*) accueil *m*, réception; ~ **desk** *n* réception *f*; ~**ist** *n* réceptionniste *m/f*

recess [rɪˈses] *n* (*in room*) renfoncement *m*, alcôve *f*; (*secret place*) recoin *m*; (*POL etc: holiday*) vacances *fpl*

recession [rɪˈseʃən] *n* récession *f*

recipe [ˈresɪpɪ] *n* recette *f*

recipient [rɪˈsɪpɪənt] *n* (*of payment*) bénéficiaire *m/f*; (*of letter*) destinataire *m/f*

recital [rɪˈsaɪtl] *n* récital *m*

recite [rɪˈsaɪt] *vt* (*poem*) réciter

reckless [ˈrekləs] *adj* (*driver etc*) imprudent(e)

reckon [ˈrekən] *vt* (*count*) calculer, compter; (*think*): **I** ~ **that** ... je pense que ...; ~ **on** *vt fus* compter sur, s'attendre à; ~**ing** *n* compte *m*, calcul *m*; estimation *f*

reclaim [rɪ'kleɪm] vt (demand back) réclamer (le remboursement or la restitution de); (land: from sea) assécher; (waste materials) récupérer

recline [rɪ'klaɪn] vi être allongé(e) or étendu(e); **reclining** adj (seat) à dossier réglable

recluse [rɪ'kluːs] n reclus(e), ermite m

recognition [rekəg'nɪʃən] n reconnaissance f; **to gain ~** être reconnu(e); **transformed beyond ~** méconnaissable

recognizable ['rekəgnaɪzəbl] adj: **~ (by)** reconnaissable (à)

recognize ['rekəgnaɪz] vt: **to ~ (by/as)** reconnaître (à/comme étant)

recoil [vb rɪ'kɔɪl, n 'riːkɔɪl] vi (person): **to ~ (from sth/doing sth)** reculer (devant qch/ l'idée de faire qch) ♦ n (of gun) recul m

recollect [rekə'lekt] vt se rappeler, se souvenir de; **~ion** n souvenir m

recommend [rekə'mend] vt recommander

reconcile ['rekənsaɪl] vt (two people) réconcilier; (two facts) concilier, accorder; **to ~ o.s. to** se résigner à

recondition [riːkən'dɪʃən] vt remettre à neuf; réviser entièrement

reconnoitre [rekə'nɔɪtər] (US **reconnoiter**) vt (MIL) reconnaître

reconsider [riːkən'sɪdər] vt reconsidérer

reconstruct [riːkən'strʌkt] vt (building) reconstruire; (crime, policy, system) reconstituer

record [n 'rekɔːd, vb rɪ'kɔːd] n rapport m, récit m; (of meeting etc) procès-verbal m; (register) registre m; (file) dossier m; (also: **criminal ~**) casier m judiciaire; (MUS: disc) disque m; (SPORT) record m; (COMPUT) article m ♦ vt (set down) noter; (MUS: song etc) enregistrer; **in ~ time** en un temps record inv; **off the ~** ♦ adj officieux(-euse) ♦ adv officieusement; **~ card** n (in file) fiche f; **~ed delivery** n (BRIT: POST): **~ed delivery letter** etc lettre etc recommandée; **~er** n (MUS) flûte f à bec; **~ holder** n (SPORT) détenteur(-trice) du record; **~ing** n (MUS) enregistre- ment m; **~ player** n tourne- disque m

recount [rɪ'kaunt] vt raconter

re-count ['riːkaunt] n (POL: of votes) deuxième compte m

recoup [rɪ'kuːp] vt: **to ~ one's losses** récupérer ce qu'on a perdu, se refaire

recourse [rɪ'kɔːs] n: **to have ~ to** avoir recours à

recover [rɪ'kʌvər] vt récupérer ♦ vi: **to ~ (from)** (illness) se rétablir (de); (from shock) se remettre (de); **~y** n récupération f; rétablissement m; (ECON) redressement m

recreation [rekrɪ'eɪʃən] n récréation f,

détente f; **~al** adj pour la détente, récréa- tif(-ive)

recruit [rɪ'kruːt] n recrue f ♦ vt recruter

rectangle ['rektæŋgl] n rectangle m; **rectangular** [rek'tæŋgjulər] adj rectangulaire

rectify ['rektɪfaɪ] vt (error) rectifier, corriger

rector ['rektər] n (REL) pasteur m

recuperate [rɪ'kjuːpəreɪt] vi récupérer; (from illness) se rétablir

recur [rɪ'kəː] vi se reproduire; (symptoms) réapparaître; **~rence** n répétition f; réapparition f; **~rent** adj périodique, fréquent(e)

recycle [riː'saɪkl] vt recycler; **recycling** n recyclage m

red [red] n rouge m; (POL: pej) rouge m/f ♦ adj rouge; (hair) roux (rousse); **in the ~** (account) à découvert; (business) en déficit; **~ carpet treatment** n réception f en grande pompe; **R~ Cross** n Croix-Rouge f; **~currant** n groseille f (rouge); **~den** vt, vi rougir

redecorate [riː'dekəreɪt] vt (with wallpaper) retapisser; (with paint) refaire les peintures

redeem [rɪ'diːm] vt (debt) rembourser; (sth in pawn) dégager; (fig, also REL) racheter; **~ing** adj (feature) qui sauve, qui rachète (le reste)

redeploy [riːdɪ'plɔɪ] vt (resources) réorganiser

red: **~-haired** adj roux (rousse); **~-handed** adj: **to be caught ~-handed** être pris(e) en flagrant délit or la main dans le sac; **~head** n roux (rousse); **~ herring** n (fig) diversion f, fausse piste; **~-hot** adj chauffé(e) au rouge, brûlant(e)

redirect [riːdaɪ'rekt] vt (mail) faire suivre

red light n: **to go through a ~** (AUT) brûler un feu rouge; **red-light district** n quartier m des prostituées

redo [riː'duː] (irreg) vt refaire

redress [rɪ'dres] n réparation f ♦ vt redresser

red: **R~ Sea** n mer Rouge f; **~skin** n Peau- Rouge m/f; **~ tape** n (fig) paperasserie (administrative)

reduce [rɪ'djuːs] vt réduire; (lower) abaisser; **"~ speed now"** (AUT) "ralentir"; **reduction** [rɪ'dʌkʃən] n réduction f; (discount) rabais m

redundancy [rɪ'dʌndənsɪ] n (BRIT) licenciement m, mise f au chômage

redundant [rɪ'dʌndnt] adj (BRIT: worker) mis(e) au chômage, licencié(e); (detail, object) superflu(e); **to be made ~** être licencié(e), être mis(e) au chômage

reed [riːd] n (BOT) roseau m; (MUS: of clarinet etc) hanche f

reef [riːf] n (at sea) récif m, écueil m

reek [riːk] vi: **to ~ (of)** puer, empester

reel [riːl] n bobine f; (FISHING) moulinet m; (CINEMA) bande f; (dance) quadrille écossais

♦ *vi* (*sway*) chanceler; **~ in** *vt* (*fish, line*) ramener

ref [ref] (*inf*) *n abbr* (= *referee*) arbitre *m*

refectory [rɪˈfektərɪ] *n* réfectoire *m*

refer [rɪˈfəːr] *vt*: **to ~ sb to** (*inquirer: for information, patient: to specialist*) adresser qn à; (*reader: to text*) renvoyer qn à; (*dispute, decision*): **to ~ sth to** soumettre qch à ♦ *vi*: **~ to** (*allude to*) parler de, faire allusion à; (*consult*) se reporter à

referee [refəˈriː] *n* arbitre *m*; (*BRIT: for job application*) répondant(e)

reference [ˈrefrəns] *n* référence *f*, renvoi *m*; (*mention*) allusion *f*, mention *f*; (*for job application: letter*) références, lettre *f* de recommandation; **with ~ to** (*COMM: in letter*) me référant à, suite à; **~ book** *n* ouvrage *m* de référence

refill [*vb* riːˈfɪl, *n* ˈriːfɪl] *vt* remplir à nouveau; (*pen, lighter etc*) recharger ♦ *n* (*for pen etc*) recharge *f*

refine [rɪˈfaɪn] *vt* (*sugar, oil*) raffiner; (*taste*) affiner; (*theory, idea*) fignoler (*inf*); **~d** *adj* (*person, taste*) raffiné(e); **~ry** *n* raffinerie *f*

reflect [rɪˈflekt] *vt* (*light, image*) réfléchir, refléter; (*fig*) refléter ♦ *vi* (*think*) réfléchir, méditer; **it ~s badly on him** cela le discrédite; **it ~s well on him** c'est tout à son honneur; **~ion** *n* réflexion *f*; (*image*) reflet *m*; (*criticism*): **~ion on** critique *f* de; atteinte *f* à; **on ~ion** réflexion faite

reflex [ˈriːfleks] *adj* réflexe ♦ *n* réflexe *m*; **~ive** [rɪˈfleksɪv] *adj* (*LING*) réfléchi(e)

reform [rɪˈfɔːm] *n* réforme *f* ♦ *vt* réformer; **~atory** [rɪˈfɔːmətərɪ] (*US*) *n* ≈ centre *m* d'éducation surveillée

refrain [rɪˈfreɪn] *vi*: **to ~ from doing** s'abstenir de faire ♦ *n* refrain *m*

refresh [rɪˈfreʃ] *vt* rafraîchir; (*subj: sleep*) reposer; **~er course** (*BRIT*) *n* cours *m* de recyclage; **~ing** *adj* (*drink*) rafraîchissant(e); (*sleep*) réparateur(-trice); **~ments** *npl* rafraîchissements *mpl*

refrigerator [rɪˈfrɪdʒəreɪtər] *n* réfrigérateur *m*, frigidaire ® *m*

refuel [riːˈfjuəl] *vi* se ravitailler en carburant

refuge [ˈrefjuːdʒ] *n* refuge *m*; **to take ~ in** se réfugier dans; **~e** [refjuˈdʒiː] *n* réfugié(e)

refund [*n* ˈriːfʌnd, *vb* rɪˈfʌnd] *n* remboursement *m* ♦ *vt* rembourser

refurbish [riːˈfəːbɪʃ] *vt* remettre à neuf

refusal [rɪˈfjuːzəl] *n* refus *m*; **to have first ~ on** avoir droit de préemption sur

refuse¹ [rɪˈfjuːz] *vt, vi* refuser

refuse² [ˈrefjuːs] *n* ordures *fpl*, détritus *mpl*; **~ collection** *n* ramassage *m* d'ordures

regain [rɪˈgeɪn] *vt* regagner; retrouver

regal [ˈriːgl] *adj* royal(e)

regard [rɪˈgɑːd] *n* respect *m*, estime *f*, considération *f* ♦ *vt* considérer; **to give one's ~s to** faire ses amitiés à; **"with kindest ~s"** "bien amicalement"; **as ~s, with ~ to** = **regarding**; **~ing** *prep* en ce qui concerne; **~less** *adv* quand même; **~less of** sans se soucier de

régime [reɪˈʒiːm] *n* régime *m*

regiment [ˈredʒɪmənt] *n* régiment *m*; **~al** [redʒɪˈmentl] *adj* d'un ou du régiment

region [ˈriːdʒən] *n* région *f*; **in the ~ of** (*fig*) aux alentours de; **~al** *adj* régional(e)

register [ˈredʒɪstər] *n* registre *m*; (*also: electoral ~*) liste électorale ♦ *vt* enregistrer; (*birth, death*) déclarer; (*vehicle*) immatriculer; (*POST: letter*) envoyer en recommandé; (*subj: instrument*) marquer ♦ *vi* s'inscrire; (*at hotel*) signer le registre; (*make impression*) être (bien) compris(e); **~ed** *adj* (*letter, parcel*) recommandé(e); **~ed trademark** *n* marque déposée; **registrar** [ˈredʒɪstrɑːr] *n* officier *m* de l'état civil; **registration** [redʒɪsˈtreɪʃən] *n* enregistrement *m*; (*BRIT: AUT: also: registration number*) numéro *m* d'immatriculation

registry [ˈredʒɪstrɪ] *n* bureau *m* de l'enregistrement; **~ office** (*BRIT*) *n* bureau *m* de l'état civil; **to get married in a ~ office** ≈ se marier à la mairie

regret [rɪˈgret] *n* regret *m* ♦ *vt* regretter; **~fully** *adv* à ou avec regret

regular [ˈregjulər] *adj* régulier(-ère); (*usual*) habituel(le); (*soldier*) de métier ♦ *n* (*client etc*) habitué(e); **~ly** *adv* régulièrement

regulate [ˈregjuleɪt] *vt* régler; **regulation** [regjuˈleɪʃən] *n* (*rule*) règlement *m*; (*adjustment*) réglage *m*

rehabilitation [ˈriːəbɪlɪˈteɪʃən] *n* (*of offender*) réinsertion *f*; (*of addict*) réadaptation *f*

rehearsal [rɪˈhəːsəl] *n* répétition *f*

rehearse [rɪˈhəːs] *vt* répéter

reign [reɪn] *n* règne *m* ♦ *vi* régner

reimburse [riːɪmˈbəːs] *vt* rembourser

rein [reɪn] *n* (*for horse*) rêne *f*

reindeer [ˈreɪndɪər] *n, pl inv* renne *m*

reinforce [riːɪnˈfɔːs] *vt* renforcer; **~d concrete** *n* béton armé; **~ments** *npl* (*MIL*) renfort(s) *m(pl)*

reinstate [riːɪnˈsteɪt] *vt* rétablir, réintégrer

reject [*n* ˈriːdʒekt, *vb* rɪˈdʒekt] *n* (*COMM*) article *m* de rebut ♦ *vt* refuser; (*idea*) rejeter; **~ion** *n* rejet *m*, refus *m*

rejoice [rɪˈdʒɔɪs] *vi*: **to ~ (at or over)** se réjouir (de)

rejuvenate [rɪˈdʒuːvəneɪt] *vt* rajeunir

relapse [rɪˈlæps] *n* (*MED*) rechute *f*

relate [rɪˈleɪt] *vt* (*tell*) raconter; (*connect*) établir un rapport entre ♦ *vi*: **this ~s to** cela se rapporte à; **to ~ to sb** entretenir des rapports avec qn; **~d** *adj* apparenté(e); **relating to** *prep* concernant

relation [rɪ'leɪʃən] *n* (*person*) parent(e); (*link*) rapport *m*, lien *m*; **~ship** *n* rapport *m*, lien *m*; (*personal ties*) relations *fpl*, rapports; (*also: family ~ship*) lien de parenté

relative ['relətɪv] *n* parent(e) ♦ *adj* relatif(-ive); **all her ~s** toute sa famille; **~ly** *adv* relativement

relax [rɪ'læks] *vi* (*muscle*) se relâcher; (*person: unwind*) se détendre ♦ *vt* relâcher; (*mind, person*) détendre; **~ation** [ri:læk'seɪʃən] *n* relâchement *m*; (*of mind*) détente *f*, relaxation *f*; (*recreation*) détente, délassement *m*; **~ed** *adj* détendu(e); **~ing** *adj* délassant(e)

relay [*n* 'ri:leɪ, *vb* rɪ'leɪ] *n* (*SPORT*) course *f* de relais ♦ *vt* (*message*) retransmettre, relayer

release [rɪ'li:s] *n* (*from prison, obligation*) libération *f*; (*of gas etc*) émission *f*; (*of film etc*) sortie *f*; (*new recording*) disque *m* ♦ *vt* (*prisoner*) libérer; (*gas etc*) émettre, dégager; (*free: from wreckage etc*) dégager; (*TECH: catch, spring etc*) faire jouer; (*book, film*) sortir; (*report, news*) rendre public, publier

relegate ['relɪgeɪt] *vt* reléguer; (*BRIT: SPORT*): **to be ~d** descendre dans une division inférieure

relent [rɪ'lent] *vi* se laisser fléchir; **~less** *adj* implacable; (*unceasing*) continuel(le)

relevant ['reləvənt] *adj* (*question*) pertinent(e); (*fact*) significatif(-ive), (*information*) utile; **~ to** ayant rapport à, approprié à

reliable [rɪ'laɪəbl] *adj* (*person, firm*) sérieux(-euse), fiable; (*method, machine*) fiable; (*news, information*) sûr(e); **reliably** *adv*: **to be reliably informed** savoir de source sûre

reliance [rɪ'laɪəns] *n*: **~ (on)** (*person*) confiance *f* (en); (*drugs, promises*) besoin *m* (de), dépendance *f* (de)

relic ['relɪk] *n* (*REL*) relique *f*; (*of the past*) vestige *m*

relief [rɪ'li:f] *n* (*from pain, anxiety etc*) soulagement *m*; (*help, supplies*) secours *m(pl)*; (*ART, GEO*) relief *m*

relieve [rɪ'li:v] *vt* (*pain, patient*) soulager; (*fear, worry*) dissiper; (*bring help*) secourir; (*take over from: gen*) relayer; (: *guard*) relever; **to ~ sb of sth** débarrasser qn de qch; **to ~ o.s.** se soulager

religion [rɪ'lɪdʒən] *n* religion *f*; **religious** *adj* religieux(-euse); (*book*) de piété

relinquish [rɪ'lɪŋkwɪʃ] *vt* abandonner; (*plan, habit*) renoncer à

relish ['relɪʃ] *n* (*CULIN*) condiment *m*; (*enjoyment*) délectation *f* ♦ *vt* (*food etc*) savourer; **to ~ doing** se délecter à faire

relocate [ri:ləu'keɪt] *vt* installer ailleurs ♦ *vi* déménager, s'installer ailleurs

reluctance [rɪ'lʌktəns] *n* répugnance *f*

reluctant [rɪ'lʌktənt] *adj* peu disposé(e), qui hésite; **~ly** *adv* à contrecœur

rely on [rɪ'laɪ-] *vt fus* (*be dependent*) dépendre de; (*trust*) compter sur

remain [rɪ'meɪn] *vi* rester; **~der** *n* reste *m*; **~ing** *adj* qui reste; **~s** *npl* restes *mpl*

remake ['ri:meɪk] *n* (*CINEMA*) remake *m*

remand [rɪ'mɑ:nd] *n*: **on ~** en détention préventive ♦ *vt*: **to be ~ed in custody** être placé(e) en détention préventive

remark [rɪ'mɑ:k] *n* remarque *f*, observation *f* ♦ *vt* (*faire*) remarquer, dire; **~able** *adj* remarquable; **~ably** *adv* remarquablement

remarry [ri:'mærɪ] *vi* se remarier

remedial [rɪ'mi:dɪəl] *adj* (*tuition, classes*) de rattrapage; **~ exercises** gymnastique corrective

remedy ['remədɪ] *n*: **~ (for)** remède *m* (contre *or* à) ♦ *vt* remédier à

remember [rɪ'membə*] *vt* se rappeler, se souvenir de; (*send greetings*): **~ me to him** saluez-le de ma part; **remembrance** *n* souvenir *m*; mémoire *f*; **Remembrance Day** *n* le jour de l'Armistice

remind [rɪ'maɪnd] *vt*: **to ~ sb of** rappeler à qn; **to ~ sb to do** faire penser à qn à faire, rappeler à qn qu'il doit faire; **~er** *n* (*souvenir*) souvenir *m*; (*letter*) rappel *m*

reminisce [remɪ'nɪs] *vi*: **to ~ (about)** évoquer ses souvenirs (de); **~nt** *adj*: **to be ~nt of** rappeler, faire penser à

remiss [rɪ'mɪs] *adj* négligent(e); **~ion** *n* (*of illness, sins*) rémission *f*; (*of debt, prison sentence*) remise *f*

remit [rɪ'mɪt] *vt* (*send: money*) envoyer; **~tance** *n* paiement *m*

remnant ['remnənt] *n* reste *m*, restant *m*; (*of cloth*) coupon *m*; **~s** *npl* (*COMM*) fins *fpl* de série

remorse [rɪ'mɔ:s] *n* remords *m*; **~ful** *adj* plein(e) de remords; **~less** *adj* (*fig*) impitoyable

remote [rɪ'məut] *adj* éloigné(e), lointain(e); (*person*) distant(e); (*possibility*) vague; **~ control** *n* télécommande *f*; **~ly** *adv* au loin; (*slightly*) très vaguement

remould ['ri:məuld] (*BRIT*) *n* (*tyre*) pneu rechapé

removable [rɪ'mu:vəbl] *adj* (*detachable*) amovible

removal [rɪ'mu:vəl] *n* (*taking away*) enlèvement *m*; suppression *f*; (*BRIT: from house*) déménagement *m*; (*from office: dismissal*) renvoi *m*; (*of stain*) nettoyage *m*; (*MED*) ablation *f*; **~ van** (*BRIT*) *n* camion *m* de déménagement

remove [rɪ'muːv] vt enlever, retirer; (employee) renvoyer; (stain) faire partir; (abuse) supprimer; (doubt) chasser

render ['rɛndəʳ] vt rendre; ~ing n (MUS etc) interprétation f

rendezvous ['rɔndɪvuː] n rendez-vous m inv

renew [rɪ'njuː] vt renouveler; (negotiations) reprendre; (acquaintance) renouer; ~able adj (energy) renouvelable; ~al n renouvellement m; reprise f

renounce [rɪ'nauns] vt renoncer à

renovate ['rɛnəveɪt] vt rénover; (art work) restaurer

renown [rɪ'naun] n renommée f; ~ed adj renommé(e)

rent [rɛnt] n loyer m ♦ vt louer; ~al n (for television, car) (prix m de) location f

reorganize [riːˈɔːɡənaɪz] vt réorganiser

rep [rɛp] n abbr = **representative**; **repertory**

repair [rɪ'pɛəʳ] n réparation f ♦ vt réparer; in good/bad ~ en bon/mauvais état; ~ kit n trousse f de réparation

repatriate [riːˈpætrieɪt] vt rapatrier

repay [riːˈpeɪ] vt (irreg) vt (money, creditor) rembourser; (sb's efforts) récompenser; ~ment n remboursement m

repeal [rɪ'piːl] n (of law) abrogation f ♦ vt (law) abroger

repeat [rɪ'piːt] n (RADIO, TV) reprise f ♦ vt répéter; (COMM: order) renouveler; (SCOL: a class) redoubler ♦ vi répéter; ~edly adv souvent, à plusieurs reprises

repel [rɪ'pɛl] vt repousser; ~lent adj repoussant(e) ♦ n: insect ~lent insectifuge m

repent [rɪ'pɛnt] vi: to ~ (of) se repentir (de); ~ance n repentir m

repertory ['rɛpətərɪ] n (also: ~ theatre) théâtre m de répertoire

repetition [rɛpɪ'tɪʃən] n répétition f

repetitive [rɪ'pɛtɪtɪv] adj (movement, work) répétitif(-ive); (speech) plein(e) de redites

replace [rɪ'pleɪs] vt (put back) remettre, replacer; (take the place of) remplacer; ~ment n (substitution) remplacement m; (person) remplaçant(e)

replay ['riːpleɪ] n (of match) match rejoué; (of tape, film) répétition f

replenish [rɪ'plɛnɪʃ] vt (glass) remplir (de nouveau); (stock etc) réapprovisionner

replica ['rɛplɪkə] n réplique f, copie exacte

reply [rɪ'plaɪ] n réponse f ♦ vi répondre

report [rɪ'pɔːt] n rapport m; (PRESS etc) reportage m; (BRIT: also: **school** ~) bulletin m (scolaire); (of gun) détonation f ♦ vt rapporter, faire un compte rendu de; (PRESS etc) faire un reportage sur; (bring to notice: occurrence) signaler ♦ vi (make a ~) faire un rapport (or un reportage); (present o.s.): to ~ (to sb) se présenter (chez qn); (be responsible to): to ~ to sb être sous les ordres de qn; ~ card (US, SCOTTISH) n bulletin m scolaire; ~edly adv: she is ~edly living in ... elle habiterait ...; he ~edly told them to ... il leur aurait ordonné de ...; ~er n reporter m

repose [rɪ'pauz] n: in ~ en ou au repos

represent [rɛprɪ'zɛnt] vt représenter; (view, belief) présenter, expliquer; (describe): to ~ sth as présenter or décrire qch comme; ~ation [rɛprɪzɛn'teɪʃən] n représentation f; ~ations npl (protest) démarche f; ~ative [rɛprɪ'zɛntətɪv] n représentant(e); (US: POL) député m ♦ adj représentatif(-ive), caractéristique

repress [rɪ'prɛs] vt réprimer; ~ion n répression f

reprieve [rɪ'priːv] n (LAW) grâce f; (fig) sursis m, délai m

reprisal [rɪ'praɪzl] n: ~s npl représailles fpl

reproach [rɪ'prəutʃ] vt: to ~ sb with sth reprocher qch à qn; ~ful adj de reproche

reproduce [riːprə'djuːs] vt reproduire ♦ vi se reproduire; **reproduction** [riːprə'dʌkʃən] n reproduction f

reproof [rɪ'pruːf] n reproche m

reptile ['rɛptaɪl] n reptile m

republic [rɪ'pʌblɪk] n république f; ~an adj républicain(e)

repudiate [rɪ'pjuːdɪeɪt] vt répudier, rejeter

repulsive [rɪ'pʌlsɪv] adj repoussant(e), répulsif(-ive)

reputable ['rɛpjutəbl] adj de bonne réputation; (occupation) honorable

reputation [rɛpju'teɪʃən] n réputation f

reputed [rɪ'pjuːtɪd] adj (supposed) supposé(e); ~ly adv d'après ce qu'on dit

request [rɪ'kwɛst] n demande f; (formal) requête f ♦ vt: to ~ (of or from sb) demander (à qn); ~ **stop** (BRIT) n (for bus) arrêt m facultatif

require [rɪ'kwaɪəʳ] vt (need: subj: person) avoir besoin de; (: thing, situation) demander; (want) exiger; (order): to ~ sb to do sth/sth of sb exiger que qn fasse qch/qch de qn; ~ment n exigence f; besoin m; condition requise

requisition [rɛkwɪ'zɪʃən] n: ~ (for) demande f (de) ♦ vt (MIL) réquisitionner

rescue ['rɛskjuː] n (from accident) sauvetage m; (help) secours mpl ♦ vt sauver; ~ **party** n équipe f de sauvetage; ~r n sauveteur m

research [rɪ'səːtʃ] n recherche(s) f(pl) ♦ vt faire des recherches sur

resemblance [rɪ'zɛmbləns] n ressemblance f

resemble [rɪ'zɛmbl] vt ressembler à

resent [rɪ'zɛnt] vt être contrarié(e) par; ~ful adj irrité(e), plein(e) de ressentiment; ~ment n ressentiment m

reservation [rɛzə'veɪʃən] n (booking)

réservation f; (*doubt*) réserve f; (*for tribe*) réserve; **to make a ~ (in a hotel/a restaurant/on a plane)** réserver or retenir une chambre/une table/une place

reserve [rɪ'zɜːv] n réserve f; (*SPORT*) remplaçant(e) ♦ vt (*seats etc*) réserver, retenir; **~s** npl (*MIL*) réservistes mpl; **in ~** en réserve; **~d** adj réservé(e)s

reshuffle [riː'ʃʌfl] n: **Cabinet ~** (*POL*) remaniement ministériel

residence ['rezɪdəns] n résidence f; **~ permit** (*BRIT*) n permis m de séjour

resident ['rezɪdənt] n résident(e) ♦ adj résidant(e); **~ial** [rezɪ'denʃəl] adj résidentiel(le); (*course*) avec hébergement sur place; **~ial school** n internat m

residue ['rezɪdjuː] n reste m; (*CHEM, PHYSICS*) résidu m

resign [rɪ'zaɪn] vt (*one's post*) démissionner de ♦ vi démissionner; **to ~ o.s. to** se résigner à; **~ation** [rezɪg'neɪʃən] n (*of post*) démission f, (*state of mind*) résignation f; **~ed** adj résigné(e)

resilient [rɪ'zɪlɪənt] adj (*material*) élastique; (*person*) qui réagit, qui a du ressort

resist [rɪ'zɪst] vt résister à; **~ance** n résistance f

resit [riː'sɪt] vt (*exam*) repasser ♦ n deuxième session f (*d'un examen*)

resolution [rezə'luːʃən] n résolution f

resolve [rɪ'zɔlv] n résolution f ♦ vt (*problem*) résoudre ♦ vi: **to ~ to do** résoudre or décider de faire

resort [rɪ'zɔːt] n (*seaside town*) station f balnéaire; (*ski ~*) station de ski; (*recourse*) recours m ♦ vi: **to ~ to** avoir recours à; **in the last ~** en dernier ressort

resounding [rɪ'zaundɪŋ] adj retentissant(e)

resource [rɪ'sɔːs] n ressource f; **~s** npl (*supplies, wealth etc*) ressources f; **~ful** adj ingénieux(-euse), débrouillard(e)

respect [rɪs'pekt] n respect m ♦ vt respecter; **~s** npl (*compliments*) respects, hommages mpl; **with ~ to** en ce qui concerne; **in this ~** à cet égard; **~able** adj respectable; **~ful** adj respectueux(-euse); **~ively** adv respectivement

respite ['respaɪt] n répit m

respond [rɪs'pɔnd] vi répondre; (*react*) réagir; **response** n réponse f; réaction f

responsibility [rɪspɔnsɪ'bɪlɪtɪ] n responsabilité f

responsible [rɪs'pɔnsɪbl] adj (*liable*): **~ (for)** responsable (de); (*person*) digne de confiance; (*job*) qui comporte des responsabilités

responsive [rɪs'pɔnsɪv] adj qui réagit; (*person*) qui n'est pas réservé(e) or indifférent(e)

rest [rest] n repos m; (*stop*) arrêt m, pause f; (*MUS*) silence m; (*support*) support m, appui m; (*remainder*) reste m, restant m ♦ vi se reposer; (*be supported*): **to ~ on** appuyer or reposer sur; (*remain*) rester ♦ vt (*lean*): **to ~ sth on/against** appuyer qch sur/contre; **the ~ of them** les autres; **it ~s with him to ...** c'est à lui de ...

restaurant ['restərɔŋ] n restaurant m; **~ car** (*BRIT*) n wagon-restaurant m

restful ['restful] adj reposant(e)

restive ['restɪv] adj agité(e), impatient(e); (*horse*) rétif(-ive)

restless ['restlɪs] adj agité(e)

restoration [restə'reɪʃən] n restauration f; restitution f; rétablissement m

restore [rɪ'stɔː] vt (*building*) restaurer; (*sth stolen*) restituer; (*peace, health*) rétablir; **to ~ to** (*former state*) ramener à

restrain [rɪs'treɪn] vt contenir; (*person*): **to ~ (from doing)** retenir (de faire); **~ed** adj (*style*) sobre; (*manner*) mesuré(e); **~t** n (*restriction*) contrainte f; (*moderation*) retenue f

restrict [rɪs'trɪkt] vt restreindre, limiter; **~ion** n restriction f, limitation f

rest room (*US*) n toilettes fpl

result [rɪ'zʌlt] n résultat m ♦ vi: **to ~ in** aboutir à, se terminer par; **as a ~ of** à la suite de

resume [rɪ'zjuːm] vt, vi (*work, journey*) reprendre

résumé ['reɪzjuːmeɪ] n résumé m; (*US*) curriculum vitae m

resumption [rɪ'zʌmpʃən] n reprise f

resurgence [rɪ'sɜːdʒəns] n (*of energy, activity*) regain m

resurrection [rezə'rekʃən] n résurrection f

resuscitate [rɪ'sʌsɪteɪt] vt (*MED*) réanimer

retail ['riːteɪl] adj de or au détail ♦ adv au détail; **~er** n détaillant(e); **~ price** n prix m de détail

retain [rɪ'teɪn] vt (*keep*) garder, conserver; **~er** n (*fee*) acompte m, provision f

retaliate [rɪ'tælɪeɪt] vi: **to ~ (against)** se venger (de); **retaliation** [rɪtælɪ'eɪʃən] n représailles fpl, vengeance f

retarded [rɪ'tɑːdɪd] adj retardé(e)

retch [retʃ] vi avoir des haut-le-cœur

retentive [rɪ'tentɪv] adj: **~ memory** excellente mémoire

retina ['retɪnə] n rétine f

retire [rɪ'taɪə] vi (*give up work*) prendre sa retraite; (*withdraw*) se retirer, partir; (*go to bed*) (aller) se coucher; **~d** adj (*person*) retraité(e); **~ment** n retraite f; **retiring** adj (*shy*) réservé(e); (*leaving*) sortant(e)

retort [rɪ'tɔːt] vi riposter

retrace [riː'treɪs] vt: **to ~ one's steps** revenir

sur ses pas
retract [rɪ'trækt] vt (statement, claws) rétracter; (undercarriage, aerial) rentrer, escamoter
retrain [ri:'treɪn] vt (worker) recycler
retread ['ri:tred] n (tyre) pneu rechapé
retreat [rɪ'tri:t] n retraite f ♦ vi battre en retraite
retribution [retrɪ'bju:ʃən] n châtiment m
retrieval [rɪ'tri:vəl] n (see vb) récupération f; réparation f
retrieve [rɪ'tri:v] vt (sth lost) récupérer; (situation, honour) sauver; (error, loss) réparer; ~r n chien m d'arrêt
retrospect ['retrəspekt] n: in ~ rétrospectivement, après coup; ~ive [retrə'spektɪv] adj rétrospectif(-ive); (law) rétroactif(-ive)
return [rɪ'tɜ:n] n (going or coming back) retour m; (of sth stolen etc) restitution f; (FINANCE: from land, shares) rendement m, rapport m ♦ cpd (journey) de retour; (BRIT: ticket) aller et retour; (match) retour ♦ vi (come back) revenir; (go back) retourner ♦ vt rendre; (bring back) rapporter; (send back; also: ball) renvoyer; (put back) remettre; (POL: candidate) élire; ~s npl (COMM) recettes fpl; (FINANCE) bénéfices mpl; in ~ (for) en échange (de); by ~ (of post) par retour (du courrier); many happy ~s (of the day)! bon anniversaire!
reunion [ri:'ju:nɪən] n réunion f
reunite [ri:ju:'naɪt] vt réunir
reuse [ri:'ju:z] vt réutiliser
rev [rev] n abbr (AUT: = revolution) tour m ♦ vt (also: rev up) emballer
revamp [ri:'væmp] vt (firm, system etc) réorganiser
reveal [rɪ'vi:l] vt (make known) révéler; (display) laisser voir; ~ing adj révélateur(-trice); (dress) au décolleté généreux or suggestif
revel ['revl] vi: to ~ in sth/in doing se délecter de qch/à faire
revenge [rɪ'vendʒ] n vengeance f; to take ~ on (enemy) se venger sur
revenue ['revənju:] n revenu m
reverberate [rɪ'vɜ:bəreɪt] vi (sound) retentir, se répercuter; (fig: shock etc) se propager
reverence ['revərəns] n vénération f, révérence f
Reverend ['revərənd] adj (in titles): the ~ John Smith (Anglican) le révérend John Smith; (Catholic) l'abbé (John) Smith; (Protestant) le pasteur (John) Smith
reversal [rɪ'vɜ:sl] n (of opinion) revirement m; (of order) renversement m; (of direction) changement m
reverse [rɪ'vɜ:s] n contraire m, opposé m;

(back) dos m, envers m; (of paper) verso m; (of coin; also: setback) revers m; (AUT: also: ~ gear) marche f arrière ♦ adj (order, direction) opposé(e), inverse ♦ vt (order, position) changer, inverser; (direction, policy) changer complètement de; (decision) annuler; (roles) renverser; (car) faire marche arrière avec ♦ vi (BRIT: AUT) faire marche arrière; he ~d (the car) into a wall il a embouti un mur en marche arrière; ~d charge call (BRIT) n (TEL) communication f en PCV; reversing lights (BRIT) npl (AUT) feux mpl de marche arrière or de recul
revert [rɪ'vɜ:t] vi: to ~ to revenir à, retourner à
review [rɪ'vju:] n revue f; (of book, film) critique f, compte rendu; (of situation, policy) examen m, bilan m ♦ vt passer en revue; faire la critique de; examiner; ~er n critique m
revise [rɪ'vaɪz] vt réviser, modifier; (manuscript) revoir, corriger ♦ vi (study) réviser; **revision** [rɪ'vɪʒən] n révision f
revival [rɪ'vaɪvəl] n reprise f; (recovery) rétablissement m; (of faith) renouveau m
revive [rɪ'vaɪv] vt (person) ranimer; (custom) rétablir; (economy) relancer; (hope, courage) raviver, faire renaître; (play) reprendre ♦ vi (person) reprendre connaissance; (: from ill health) se rétablir; (hope etc) renaître; (activity) reprendre
revoke [rɪ'vəuk] vt révoquer; (law) abroger
revolt [rɪ'vəult] n révolte f ♦ vi se révolter, se rebeller ♦ vt révolter, dégoûter; ~ing adj dégoûtant(e)
revolution [revə'lu:ʃən] n révolution f; (of wheel etc) tour m; ~ary adj révolutionnaire ♦ n révolutionnaire m/f
revolve [rɪ'vɒlv] vi tourner
revolver [rɪ'vɒlvə'] n revolver m
revolving [rɪ'vɒlvɪŋ] adj tournant(e); (chair) pivotant(e); ~ door n (porte f à) tambour m
revulsion [rɪ'vʌlʃən] n dégoût m, répugnance f
reward [rɪ'wɔ:d] n récompense f ♦ vt: to ~ (for) récompenser (de); ~ing adj (fig) qui (en) vaut la peine, gratifiant(e)
rewind [ri:'waɪnd] (irreg) vt (tape) rembobiner
rewire [ri:'waɪə'] vt (house) refaire l'installation électrique de
rheumatism ['ru:mətɪzəm] n rhumatisme m
Rhine [raɪn] n Rhin m
rhinoceros [raɪ'nɒsərəs] n rhinocéros m
Rhone [rəun] n Rhône m
rhubarb ['ru:bɑ:b] n rhubarbe f
rhyme [raɪm] n rime f; (verse) vers mpl
rhythm ['rɪðm] n rythme m
rib [rɪb] n (ANAT) côte f
ribbon ['rɪbən] n ruban m; in ~s (torn) en lambeaux

rice [raɪs] n riz m; ~ **pudding** n riz au lait
rich [rɪtʃ] adj riche; (gift, clothes) somptueux(-euse) ♦ npl: **the ~** les riches mpl; **~es** npl richesses fpl; **~ly** adv richement; (deserved, earned) largement
rickets ['rɪkɪts] n rachitisme m
rid [rɪd] (pt, pp **rid**) vt: **to ~ sb of** débarrasser qn de; **to get ~ of** se débarrasser de
riddle ['rɪdl] n (puzzle) énigme f ♦ vt: **to be ~d with** être criblé(e) de; (fig: guilt, corruption, doubts) être en proie à
ride [raɪd] (pt **rode**, pp **ridden**) n promenade f, tour m; (distance covered) trajet m ♦ vi (as sport) monter (à cheval), faire du cheval; (go somewhere: on horse, bicycle) aller (à cheval or bicyclette etc); (journey: on bicycle, motorcycle, bus) rouler ♦ vt (a certain horse) monter; (distance) parcourir, faire; **to take sb for a ~** (fig) faire marcher qn; **to ~ a horse/ bicycle** monter à cheval/à bicyclette; **~r** n cavalier(ère); (in race) jockey m; (on bicycle) cycliste m/f; (on motorcycle) motocycliste m/f
ridge [rɪdʒ] n (of roof, mountain) arête f; (of hill) faîte m; (on object) strie f
ridicule ['rɪdɪkjuːl] n ridicule m, dérision f
ridiculous [rɪ'dɪkjuləs] adj ridicule
riding ['raɪdɪŋ] n équitation f; ~ **school** n manège m, école f d'équitation
rife [raɪf] adj répandu(e); ~ **with** abondant(e) en, plein(e) de
riffraff ['rɪfræf] n racaille f
rifle ['raɪfl] n fusil m (à canon rayé) ♦ vt vider, dévaliser; ~ **through** vt (belongings) fouiller; (papers) feuilleter; ~ **range** n champ m de tir; (at fair) stand m de tir
rift [rɪft] n fente f, fissure f; (fig: disagreement) désaccord m
rig [rɪg] n (also: **oil** ~: at sea) plate-forme pétrolière ♦ vt (election etc) truquer; ~ **out** (BRIT) vt: **to ~ out as/in** habiller en/de; ~ **up** vt arranger, faire avec des moyens de fortune; **~ging** n (NAUT) gréement m
right [raɪt] adj (correctly chosen: answer, road etc) bon (bonne); (true) juste, exact(e); (suitable) approprié(e), convenable; (just) juste, équitable; (morally good) bien inv; (not left) droit(e) ♦ n (what is morally ~) bien m; (title, claim) droit m; (not left) droite f ♦ adv (answer) correctement, juste; (treat) bien, comme il faut; (not on the left) à droite ♦ vt redresser ♦ excl bon!; **to be ~** (person) avoir raison; (answer) être juste or correct(e); (clock) à l'heure (juste); **by ~s** en toute justice; **on the ~** à droite; **to be in the ~** avoir raison; ~ **now** en ce moment même; tout de suite; ~ **in the middle** en plein milieu; ~ **away** immédiatement; ~ **angle** n (MATH) angle droit; **~eous** ['raɪtʃəs] adj droit(e), vertueux(-euse); (anger) justifié(e); **~ful** adj

légitime; **~-handed** adj (person) droitier(-ère); **~-hand man** n bras droit (fig); **~-hand side** n la droite; **~ly** adv (with reason) à juste titre; ~ **of way** n droit m de passage; (AUT) priorité f; **~-wing** adj (POL) de droite
rigid ['rɪdʒɪd] adj rigide; (principle, control) strict(e)
rigmarole ['rɪgmərəul] n comédie f
rigorous ['rɪgərəs] adj rigoureux(-euse)
rile [raɪl] vt agacer
rim [rɪm] n bord m; (of spectacles) monture f; (of wheel) jante f
rind [raɪnd] n (of bacon) couenne f; (of lemon etc) écorce f, zeste m; (of cheese) croûte f
ring [rɪŋ] (pt **rang**, pp **rung**) n anneau m; (on finger) bague f; (also: **wedding** ~) alliance f; (of people, objects) cercle m; (of spies) réseau m; (of smoke etc) rond m; (arena) piste f, arène f; (for boxing) ring m; (sound of bell) sonnerie f ♦ vi (telephone, bell) sonner; (person: by telephone) téléphoner; (also: ~ **out**: voice, words) retentir; (ears) bourdonner ♦ vt (BRIT: TEL: also: ~ **up**) téléphoner à, appeler; (bell) faire sonner; **to ~ the bell** sonner; **to give sb a ~** (BRIT: TEL) appeler qn; ~ **back** (BRIT) vt, vi (TEL) rappeler; ~ **off** (BRIT) vi (TEL) raccrocher; ~ **up** (BRIT) vt (TEL) appeler; **~binder** n classeur m à anneaux; **~ing** ['rɪŋɪŋ] n (of telephone) sonnerie f; (of bell) tintement m; (in ears) bourdonnement m; **~ing tone** (BRIT) n (TEL) sonnerie f; **~leader** n (of gang) chef m, meneur m, **~lets** npl anglaises fpl; ~ **road** (BRIT) n route f de ceinture; (motorway) périphérique m
rink [rɪŋk] n (also: **ice** ~) patinoire f
rinse [rɪns] vt rincer
riot ['raɪət] n émeute f; (of flowers, colour) profusion f ♦ vi faire une émeute, manifester avec violence; **to run ~** se déchaîner; **~ous** adj (mob, assembly) séditieux(-euse), déchaîné(e); (living, behaviour) débauché(e); (party) très animé(e); (welcome) délirant(e)
rip [rɪp] n déchirure f ♦ vt déchirer ♦ vi se déchirer; **~cord** n poignée f d'ouverture
ripe [raɪp] adj (fruit) mûr(e); (cheese) fait(e); **~n** vt mûrir ♦ vi mûrir
rip-off ['rɪpɔf] (inf) n: **it's a ~~!** c'est de l'arnaque!
ripple ['rɪpl] n ondulation f; (of applause, laughter) cascade f ♦ vi onduler
rise [raɪz] (pt **rose**, pp **risen**) n (slope) côte f, pente f; (hill) hauteur f; (increase: in wages: BRIT) augmentation f; (: in prices, temperature) hausse f, augmentation f; (fig: to power etc) ascension f ♦ vi s'élever, monter; (prices, numbers) augmenter; (waters) monter; (sun; person: from chair, bed) se lever; (also: ~ **up**: tower, building) s'élever; (:

rebel) se révolter; se rebeller; (*in rank*) s'élever; **to give ~ to** donner lieu à; **to ~ to the occasion** se montrer à la hauteur; **~r** *n*: **to be an early ~r** être matinal(e); **rising** *adj* (*number, prices*) en hausse; (*tide*) montant(e); (*sun, moon*) levant(e)

risk [rɪsk] *n* risque *m* ♦ *vt* risquer; **at** ~ en danger; **at one's own ~** à ses risques et périls; **~y** *adj* risqué(e)

rissole ['rɪsəul] *n* croquette *f*

rite [raɪt] *n* rite *m*; **last ~s** derniers sacrements

ritual ['rɪtjuəl] *adj* rituel(le) ♦ *n* rituel *m*

rival ['raɪvl] *adj, n* rival(e); (*in business*) concurrent(e) ♦ *vt* (*match*) égaler; **~ry** ['raɪvlrɪ] *n* rivalité *f*, concurrence *f*

river ['rɪvə'] *n* rivière *f*; (*major, also fig*) fleuve *m* ♦ *cpd* (*port, traffic*) fluvial(e); **up/down** ~ en amont/aval; **~bank** *n* rive *f*, berge *f*; **~bed** *n* lit *m* (de rivière or de fleuve)

rivet ['rɪvɪt] *n* rivet *m* ♦ *vt* (*fig*) river, fixer

Riviera [rɪvɪ'eərə] *n*: **the (French) ~** la Côte d'Azur; **the Italian ~** la Riviera (italienne)

road [rəud] *n* route *f*; (*in town*) rue *f*; (*fig*) chemin, voie *f*; **major/minor ~** route principale *or* à priorité/voie secondaire; **~ accident** *n* accident *m* de la circulation; **~block** *n* barrage routier; **~hog** *n* chauffard *m*; **~ map** *n* carte routière; **~ rage** *n* comportement très agressif de certains usagers de la route; **~ safety** *n* sécurité routière; **~side** *n* bord *m* de la route, bas-côté *m*; **~ sign** *n* panneau *m* de signalisation; **~way** *n* chaussée *f*; **~ works** *npl* travaux *mpl* (de réfection des routes); **~worthy** *adj* en bon état de marche

roam [rəum] *vi* errer, vagabonder

roar [rɔː'] *n* rugissement *m*; (*of crowd*) hurlements *mpl*; (*of vehicle, thunder, storm*) grondement *m* ♦ *vi* rugir; hurler; gronder; **to ~ with laughter** éclater de rire; **to do a ~ing trade** faire des affaires d'or

roast [rəust] *n* rôti *m* ♦ *vt* (faire) rôtir; (*coffee*) griller, torréfier; **~ beef** *n* rôti *m* de bœuf, rosbif *m*

rob [rɔb] *vt* (*person*) voler; (*bank*) dévaliser; **to ~ sb of sth** voler *or* dérober qch à qn; (*fig: deprive*) priver qn de qch; **~ber** *n* bandit *m*, voleur *m*; **~bery** *n* vol *m*

robe [rəub] *n* (*for ceremony etc*) robe *f*; (*also: bathrobe*) peignoir *m*; (*US*) couverture *f*

robin ['rɔbɪn] *n* rouge-gorge *m*

robot ['rəubɔt] *n* robot *m*

robust [rəu'bʌst] *adj* robuste; (*material, appetite*) solide

rock [rɔk] *n* (*substance*) roche *f*, roc *m*; (*boulder*) rocher *m*; (*US: small stone*) caillou *m*; (*BRIT: sweet*) ≈ sucre *m* d'orge ♦ *vt* (*swing gently: cradle*) balancer; (: *child*) bercer; (*shake*) ébranler, secouer ♦ *vi* (se) balancer; être ébranlé(e) *or* secoué(e); **on the ~s**

(*drink*) avec des glaçons; (*marriage etc*) en train de craquer; **~ and roll** *n* rock (and roll) *m*, rock'n'roll *m*; **~-bottom** *adj* (*fig: prices*) sacrifié(e); **~ery** *n* (jardin *m* de) rocaille *f*

rocket ['rɔkɪt] *n* fusée *f*; (*MIL*) fusée, roquette *f*

rocking chair ['rɔkɪŋ-] *n* fauteuil *m* à bascule

rocking horse *n* cheval *m* à bascule

rocky ['rɔkɪ] *adj* (*hill*) rocheux(-euse); (*path*) rocailleux(-euse)

rod [rɔd] *n* (*wooden*) baguette *f*; (*metallic*) tringle *f*; (*TECH*) tige *f*; (*also: fishing ~*) canne *f* à pêche

rode [rəud] *pt of* ride

rodent ['rəudnt] *n* rongeur *m*

rodeo ['rəudɪəu] *n* (*US*) *n* rodéo *m*

roe [rəu] *n* (*species: also: ~ deer*) chevreuil *m*; (*of fish: also: hard ~*) œufs *mpl* de poisson; **soft ~** laitance *f*

rogue [rəug] *n* coquin(e)

role [rəul] *n* rôle *m*; **~ play** *n* jeu *m* de rôle

roll [rəul] *n* rouleau *m*; (*of banknotes*) liasse *f*; (*also: bread ~*) petit pain; (*register*) liste *f*; (*sound: of drums etc*) roulement *m* ♦ *vt* rouler; (*also: ~ up*) enrouler; (: *sleeves*) retrousser; (*also: ~ out: pastry*) étendre au rouleau, abaisser ♦ *vi* rouler; **~ about** *vi* rouler ça et là; (*person*) se rouler par terre; **~ around** *vi* = roll about; **~ by** *vi* (*time*) s'écouler, passer; **~ over** *vi* se retourner; **~ up** *vi* (*inf: arrive*) arriver, s'amener ♦ *vt* rouler; **~ call** *n* appel *m*; **~er** *n* rouleau *m*; (*wheel*) roulette *f*; (*for road*) rouleau compresseur; **~er blade** *n* patin *m* en ligne; **~er coaster** *n* montagnes *fpl* russes; **~er skates** *npl* patins *mpl* à roulettes; **~er skating** *n* patin *m* à roulettes; **~ing** *adj* (*landscape*) onduleux(-euse); **~ing pin** *n* rouleau *m* à pâtisserie; **~ing stock** *n* (*RAIL*) matériel roulant

ROM [rɔm] *n abbr* (= read only memory) mémoire morte

Roman ['rəumən] *adj* romain(e); **~ Catholic** *adj, n* catholique *m/f*

romance [rə'mæns] *n* (*love affair*) idylle *f*; (*charm*) poésie *f*; (*novel*) roman *m* à l'eau de rose

Romania [rəu'meɪnɪə] *n* Roumanie *f*; **~n** *adj* roumain(e) ♦ *n* Roumain(e); (*LING*) roumain *m*

Roman numeral *n* chiffre romain

romantic [rə'mæntɪk] *adj* romantique; sentimental(e)

Rome [rəum] *n* Rome

romp [rɔmp] *n* jeux bruyants ♦ *vi* (*also: ~ about*) s'ébattre, jouer bruyamment; **~ers** *npl* barboteuse *f*

roof [ruːf] (*pl* **~s**) *n* toit *m* ♦ *vt* couvrir (d'un toit); **the ~ of the mouth** la voûte du palais;

~ing n toiture f; **~ rack** n (AUT) galerie f

rook [ruk] n (bird) freux m; (CHESS) tour f

room [ru:m] n (in house) pièce f; (also: bedroom) chambre f (à coucher); (in school etc) salle f; (space) place f; **~s** npl (lodging) meublé m; "**~s to let**" (BRIT) or "**~s for rent**" (US) "chambres à louer"; **single/double ~** chambre pour une personne/deux personnes; **there is ~ for improvement** cela laisse à désirer; **~ing house** n (US) maison f or immeuble m de rapport; **~mate** n camarade m/f de chambre; **~ service** n service m des chambres (dans un hôtel); **~y** adj spacieux(-euse); (garment) ample

roost [ru:st] vi se jucher

rooster ['ru:stə⁺] n (esp US) coq m

root [ru:t] n (BOT, MATH) racine f; (fig: of problem) origine f, fond m ♦ vi (plant) s'enraciner; **~ about** vi (fig) fouiller; **~ for** vt fus encourager, applaudir; **~ out** vt (find) dénicher

rope [rəup] n corde f; (NAUT) cordage m ♦ vt (tie up or together) attacher; (climbers: also: **~ together**) encorder; (area: also: **~ off**) interdire l'accès de; (: divide off) séparer; **to know the ~s** (fig) être au courant, connaître les ficelles; **~ in** vt (fig: person) embringuer

rosary ['rəuzəri] n chapelet m

rose [rəuz] pt of rise ♦ n rose f; (also: **~bush**) rosier m; (on watering can) pomme f

rosé ['rəuzei] n rosé m

rosebud ['rəuzbʌd] n bouton m de rose

rosemary ['rəuzməri] n romarin m

roster ['rɔstə⁺] n: **duty ~** tableau m de service

rostrum ['rɔstrəm] n tribune f (pour un orateur etc)

rosy ['rəuzi] adj rose: **a ~ future** un bel avenir

rot [rɔt] n (decay) pourriture f; (fig: pej) idioties fpl ♦ vt, vi pourrir

rota ['rəutə] n liste f, tableau m de service; **on a ~ basis** par roulement

rotary ['rəutəri] adj rotatif(-ive)

rotate [rəu'teit] vt (revolve) faire tourner; (change round: jobs) faire à tour de rôle ♦ vi (revolve) tourner; **rotating** adj (movement) tournant(e)

rotten ['rɔtn] adj (decayed) pourri(e); (dishonest) corrompu(e); (inf: bad) mauvais(e), moche; **to feel ~** (ill) être mal fichu(e)

rotund [rəu'tʌnd] adj (person) rondelet(te)

rough [rʌf] adj (cloth, skin) rêche, rugueux(-euse); (terrain) accidenté(e); (path) rocailleux(-euse); (voice) rauque, rude; (person, manner: coarse) rude, fruste; (: violent) brutal(e); (district, weather) mauvais(e); (sea) houleux(-euse); (plan etc) ébauché(e); (guess) approximatif(-ive) ♦ n (GOLF) rough m ♦ vt: **to ~ it** vivre à la dure;

to sleep ~ (BRIT) coucher à la dure; **~age** n fibres fpl alimentaires; **~-and-ready** adj rudimentaire; **~ copy**, **~ draft** n brouillon m; **~ly** adv (handle) rudement, brutalement; (speak) avec brusquerie; (make) grossièrement; (approximately) à peu près, en gros

roulette [ru:'let] n roulette f

Roumania [ru:'meiniə] n = Romania

round [raund] adj rond(e) ♦ n (BRIT: of toast) tranche f; (duty: of policeman, milkman etc) tournée f; (: of doctor) visites fpl; (game: of cards, in competition) partie f; (BOXING) round m; (of talks) série f ♦ vt (corner) tourner ♦ prep autour de ♦ adv: **all ~** tout autour; **the long way ~** (par) le chemin le plus long; **all the year ~** toute l'année; **it's just ~ the corner** (fig) c'est tout près; **~ the clock** 24 heures sur 24; **to go ~ to sb's (house)** aller chez qn; **go ~ the back** passez par derrière; **enough to go ~** assez pour tout le monde; **~ of ammunition** cartouche f; **~ of applause** ban m, applaudissements mpl; **~ of drinks** tournée f; **~ of sandwiches** sandwich m; **~ off** vt (speech etc) terminer; **~ up** vt rassembler; (criminals) effectuer une rafle de; (price, figure) arrondir (au chiffre supérieur); **~about** n (BRIT: AUT) rond-point m (à sens giratoire); (: at fair) manège m (de chevaux de bois) ♦ adj (route, means) détourné(e); **~ers** n (game) sorte de baseball; **~ly** adv (fig) tout net, carrément; **~ trip** n (voyage m) aller et retour m; **~up** n rassemblement m; (of criminals) rafle f

rouse [rauz] vt (wake up) réveiller; (stir up) susciter; provoquer; éveiller; **rousing** adj (welcome) enthousiaste

route [ru:t] n itinéraire m; (of bus) parcours m; (of trade, shipping) route f

routine [ru:'ti:n] adj (work) ordinaire, courant(e); (procedure) d'usage ♦ n (habits) habitudes fpl; (pej) train-train m; (THEATRE) numéro m

rove [rəuv] vt (area, streets) errer dans

row¹ [rəu] n (line) rangée f, (of people, seats, KNITTING) rang m; (behind one another: of cars, people) file f ♦ vi (in boat) ramer; (as sport) faire de l'aviron ♦ vt (boat) faire aller à la rame or à l'aviron; **in a ~** (fig) d'affilée

row² [rau] n (noise) vacarme m; (dispute) dispute f, querelle f; (scolding) réprimande f, savon m ♦ vi se disputer, se quereller

rowboat ['rəubəut] (US) n canot m (à rames)

rowdy ['raudi] adj chahuteur(-euse); (occasion) tapageur(-euse)

rowing ['rəuiŋ] n canotage m; (as sport) aviron m; **~ boat** (BRIT) n canot m (à rames)

royal ['rɔiəl] adj royal(e); **R~ Air Force** (BRIT) n armée de l'air britannique; **~ty** n (royal persons) (membres mpl de la) famille royale;

(*payment: to author*) droits *mpl* d'auteur; (*: to inventor*) royalties *fpl*

rpm *abbr* (AUT) (= *revolutions per minute*) tr/mn

RSVP *abbr* (= *répondez s'il vous plaît*) R.S.V.P.

Rt Hon. *abbr* (BRIT: = *Right Honourable*) titre donné aux députés de la Chambre des communes

rub [rʌb] *vt* frotter; frictionner; (*hands*) se frotter ♦ *n* (*with cloth*) coup *m* chiffon *or* de torchon; **to give sth a ~** donner un coup de chiffon *or* de torchon à; **to ~ sb up** (BRIT) *or* **to ~ sb** (US) **the wrong way** prendre qn à rebrousse-poil; **~ off** *vi* partir; **~ off on** *vt fus* déteindre sur; **~ out** *vt* effacer

rubber ['rʌbəʳ] *n* caoutchouc *m*; (BRIT: *eraser*) gomme *f* (à effacer); **~ band** *n* élastique *m*; **~ plant** *n* caoutchouc *m* (*plante verte*)

rubbish ['rʌbɪʃ] *n* (*from household*) ordures *fpl*; (*fig: pej*) camelote *f*; (*: nonsense*) bêtises *fpl*, idioties *fpl*; **~ bin** *n* poubelle *f*; **~ dump** *n* décharge publique, dépotoir *m*

rubble ['rʌbl] *n* décombres *mpl*; (*smaller*) gravats *mpl*; (CONSTR) blocage *m*

ruby ['ruːbɪ] *n* rubis *m*

rucksack ['rʌksæk] *n* sac *m* à dos

rudder ['rʌdəʳ] *n* gouvernail *m*

ruddy ['rʌdɪ] *adj* (*face*) coloré(e); (*inf: damned*) sacré(e), fichu(e)

rude [ruːd] *adj* (*impolite*) impoli(e); (*coarse*) grossier(-ère); (*shocking*) indécent(e), inconvenant(e)

ruffle ['rʌfl] *vt* (*hair*) ébouriffer; (*clothes*) chiffonner; (*fig: person*): **to get ~d** s'énerver

rug [rʌg] *n* petit tapis; (BRIT: *blanket*) couverture *f*

rugby ['rʌgbɪ] *n* (*also:* **~ football**) rugby *m*

rugged ['rʌgɪd] *adj* (*landscape*) accidenté(e); (*features, character*) rude

ruin ['ruːɪn] *n* ruine *f* ♦ *vt* ruiner; (*spoil, clothes*) abîmer; (*event*) gâcher; **~s** *npl* (*of building*) ruine(s)

rule [ruːl] *n* règle *f*; (*regulation*) règlement *m*; (*government*) autorité *f*, gouvernement *m* ♦ *vt* (*country*) gouverner; (*person*) dominer ♦ *vi* commander; (LAW) statuer; **as a ~** normalement, en règle générale; **~ out** *vt* exclure; **~d** *adj* (*paper*) réglé(e); **~r** *n* (*sovereign*) souverain(e); (*for measuring*) règle *f*; **ruling** *adj* (*party*) au pouvoir; (*class*) dirigeant(e) ♦ *n* (LAW) décision *f*

rum [rʌm] *n* rhum *m*

Rumania [ruːˈmeɪnɪə] *n* = **Romania**

rumble ['rʌmbl] *vi* gronder; (*stomach, pipe*) gargouiller

rummage ['rʌmɪdʒ] *vi* fouiller

rumour ['ruːməʳ] (US **rumor**) *n* rumeur *f*, bruit *m* (qui court) ♦ *vt*: **it is ~ed that** le bruit court que

rump [rʌmp] *n* (*of animal*) croupe *f*; (*inf: of person*) postérieur *m*; **~ steak** *n* rumsteck *m*

rumpus ['rʌmpəs] (*inf*) *n* tapage *m*, chahut *m*

run [rʌn] (*pt* **ran**, *pp* **run**) *n* (*fast pace*) (pas *m* de) course *f*; (*outing*) tour *m or* promenade *f* (en voiture); (*distance travelled*) parcours *m*, trajet *m*; (*series*) suite *f*, série *f*; (THEATRE) série de représentations; (SKI) piste *f*; (CRICKET, BASEBALL) point *m*; (*in tights, stockings*) maille filée, échelle *f* ♦ *vt* (*operate: business*) diriger; (*: competition, course*) organiser; (*: hotel, house*) tenir; (*race*) participer à; (COMPUT) exécuter; (*to pass: hand, finger*) passer; (*water, bath*) faire couler; (PRESS: *feature*) publier ♦ *vi* courir; (*flee*) s'enfuir; (*work: machine, factory*) marcher; (*bus, train*) circuler; (*continue: play*) se jouer; (*: contract*) être valide; (*flow: river, bath; nose*) couler; (*colours, washing*) déteindre; (*in election*) être candidat, se présenter; **to go for a ~** faire un peu de course à pied; **there was a ~ on ...** (*meat, tickets*) les gens se sont rués sur ...; **in the long ~** à longue échéance; à la longue; en fin de compte; **on the ~** en fuite; **I'll ~ you to the station** je vais vous emmener *or* conduire à la gare; **to ~ a risk** courir un risque; **~ about** *vi* (*children*) courir çà et là; **~ across** *vt fus* (*find*) trouver par hasard; **~ around** *vi* = **run about**; **~ away** *vi* s'enfuir; **~ down** *vt* (*production*) réduire progressivement; (*factory*) réduire progressivement la production de; (AUT) renverser; (*criticize*) critiquer, dénigrer; **to be ~ down** (*person: tired*) être fatigué(e) *or* à plat; **~ in** (BRIT) *vt* (*car*) roder; **~ into** *vt fus* (*meet: person*) rencontrer par hasard; (*trouble*) se heurter à; (*collide with*) heurter; **~ off** *vi* s'enfuir ♦ *vt* (*water*) laisser s'écouler; (*copies*) tirer; **~ out** *vi* (*person*) sortir en courant; (*liquid*) couler; (*lease*) expirer; (*money*) être épuisé(e); **~ out of** *vt fus* se trouver à court de; **~ over** *vt* (AUT) écraser ♦ *vt fus* (*revise*) revoir, reprendre; **~ through** *vt fus* (*recapitulate*) reprendre; (*play*) répéter; **~ up** *vt*: **to ~ up against** (*difficulties*) se heurter à; **to ~ up a debt** s'endetter; **~away** *adj* (*horse*) emballé(e); (*truck*) fou (folle); (*person*) fugitif(-ive); (*teenager*) fugueur(-euse)

rung [rʌŋ] *pp of* **ring** ♦ *n* (*of ladder*) barreau *m*

runner ['rʌnəʳ] *n* (*in race: person*) coureur(-euse); (*: horse*) partant *m*; (*on sledge*) patin *m*; (*for drawer etc*) coulisseau *m*; **~ bean** (BRIT) *n* haricot *m* (à rames); **~-up** *n* second(e)

running ['rʌnɪŋ] *n* course *f*; (*of business, organization*) gestion *f*, direction *f* ♦ *adj* (*water*) courant(e); **to be in/out of the ~ for sth** être/ne pas être sur les rangs pour qch; **6**

days ~ 6 jours de suite; **~ commentary** n commentaire détaillé; **~ costs** npl frais mpl d'exploitation

runny ['rʌnɪ] adj qui coule

run-of-the-mill ['rʌnəvðə'mɪl] adj ordinaire, banal(e)

runt [rʌnt] n avorton m

run-up ['rʌnʌp] n: **~~ to sth** (election etc) période f précédant qch

runway ['rʌnweɪ] n (AVIAT) piste f

rupture ['rʌptʃə'] n (MED) hernie f

rural ['ruərl] adj rural(e)

rush [rʌʃ] n (hurry) hâte f, précipitation f; (of crowd, COMM: sudden demand) ruée f; (current) flot m; (of emotion) vague f; (BOT) jonc m ♦ vt (hurry) transporter or envoyer d'urgence ♦ vi se précipiter; **~ hour** n heures fpl de pointe

rusk [rʌsk] n biscotte f

Russia ['rʌʃə] n Russie f; **~n** adj russe ♦ n Russe m/f; (LING) russe m

rust [rʌst] n rouille f ♦ vi rouiller

rustic ['rʌstɪk] adj rustique

rustle ['rʌsl] vi bruire, produire un bruissement ♦ vt froisser

rustproof ['rʌstpruːf] adj inoxydable

rusty ['rʌstɪ] adj rouillé(e)

rut [rʌt] n ornière f; (ZOOL) rut m; **to be in a ~** suivre l'ornière, s'encroûter

ruthless ['ruːθlɪs] adj sans pitié, impitoyable

rye [raɪ] n seigle m

S, s

Sabbath ['sæbəθ] n (Jewish) sabbat m; (Christian) dimanche m

sabotage ['sæbətɑːʒ] n sabotage m ♦ vt saboter

saccharin(e) ['sækərɪn] n saccharine f

sachet ['sæʃeɪ] n sachet m

sack [sæk] n (bag) sac m ♦ vt (dismiss) renvoyer, mettre à la porte; (plunder) piller, mettre à sac; **to get the ~** être renvoyé(e), être mis(e) à la porte; **~ing** n (material) toile f à sac; (dismissal) renvoi m

sacrament ['sækrəmənt] n sacrement m

sacred ['seɪkrɪd] adj sacré(e)

sacrifice ['sækrɪfaɪs] n sacrifice m ♦ vt sacrifier

sad [sæd] adj triste; (deplorable) triste, fâcheux(-euse)

saddle ['sædl] n selle f ♦ vt (horse) seller; **to be ~d with sth** (inf) avoir qch sur les bras; **~bag** n sacoche f

sadistic [sə'dɪstɪk] adj sadique

sadly ['sædlɪ] adv tristement; (unfortunately) malheureusement; (seriously) fort

sadness ['sædnɪs] n tristesse f

s.a.e. n abbr = **stamped addressed envelope**

safe [seɪf] adj (out of danger) hors de danger, en sécurité; (not dangerous) sans danger; (cautious) prudent(e); (sure: bet etc) assuré(e) ♦ n coffre-fort m; **~ from** à l'abri de; **~ and sound** sain(e) et sauf (sauve); **(just) to be on the ~ side** pour plus de sûreté, par précaution; **~ journey!** bon voyage!; **~-conduct** n sauf-conduit m; **~-deposit** n (vault) dépôt m de coffres-forts; (box) coffre-fort m; **~guard** n sauvegarde f, protection f ♦ vt sauvegarder, protéger; **~keeping** n bonne garde f; **~ly** adv (assume, say) sans risque d'erreur; (drive, arrive) sans accident; **~ sex** n rapports mpl sexuels sans risque

safety ['seɪftɪ] n sécurité f; **~ belt** n ceinture f de sécurité; **~ pin** n épingle f de sûreté or de nourrice; **~ valve** n soupape f de sûreté

sag [sæg] vi s'affaisser; (hem, breasts) pendre

sage [seɪdʒ] n (herb) sauge f; (person) sage m

Sagittarius [sædʒɪ'tɛərɪəs] n le Sagittaire

Sahara [sə'hɑːrə] n: **the ~ (Desert)** le (désert du) Sahara

said [sɛd] pt, pp of **say**

sail [seɪl] n (on boat) voile f; (trip): **to go for a ~** faire un tour en bateau ♦ vt (boat) manœuvrer, piloter ♦ vi (travel: ship) avancer, naviguer; (set off) partir, prendre la mer; (SPORT) faire de la voile; **they ~ed into Le Havre** ils sont entrés dans le port du Havre; **~ through** vi, vt fus (fig) réussir haut la main; **~boat** (US) n bateau m à voiles, voilier m; **~ing** n (SPORT) voile f; **to go ~ing** faire de la voile; **~ing boat** n bateau m à voiles, voilier m; **~ing ship** n grand voilier m; **~or** n marin m, matelot m

saint [seɪnt] n saint(e)

sake [seɪk] n: **for the ~ of** pour (l'amour de), dans l'intérêt de; par égard pour

salad ['sæləd] n salade f; **~ bowl** n saladier m; **~ cream** (BRIT) n (sorte f de) mayonnaise f; **~ dressing** n vinaigrette f

salami [sə'lɑːmɪ] n salami m

salary ['sælərɪ] n salaire m

sale [seɪl] n vente f; (at reduced prices) soldes mpl; "for ~" "à vendre"; **on ~** en vente; **on ~ or return** vendu(e) avec faculté de retour; **~room** n salle f des ventes; **~s assistant** (US **sales clerk**) n vendeur(-euse); **~sman** (irreg) n vendeur m; (representative) représentant m; **~s rep** n (COMM) représentant(e) m/f; **~swoman** (irreg) n vendeuse f; (representative) représentante f

salmon ['sæmən] n inv saumon m

salon ['sælɔn] n salon m

saloon [sə'luːn] n (US) bar m; (BRIT: AUT) berline f; (ship's lounge) salon m

salt [sɔːlt] n sel m ♦ vt saler; **~ cellar** n salière f; **~water** adj de mer; **~y** adj salé(e)

salute [sə'luːt] n salut m ♦ vt saluer

salvage ['sælvɪdʒ] n (saving) sauvetage m; (things saved) biens sauvés or récupérés ♦ vt sauver, récupérer

salvation [sæl'veɪʃən] n salut m; **S~ Army** n armée f du Salut

same [seɪm] adj même ♦ pron: **the ~** le (la) même, les mêmes; **the ~ book as** le même livre que; **at the ~ time** en même temps; **all** or **just the ~** tout de même, quand même; **to do the ~** faire de même, en faire autant; **to do the ~ as sb** faire comme qn; **the ~ to you!** à vous de même!; (after insult) toi-même!

sample ['sɑ:mpl] n échantillon m; (blood) prélèvement m ♦ vt (food, wine) goûter

sanction ['sæŋkʃən] n approbation f, sanction f

sanctity ['sæŋktɪtɪ] n sainteté f, caractère sacré

sanctuary ['sæŋktjuərɪ] n (holy place) sanctuaire m; (refuge) asile m; (for wild life) réserve f

sand [sænd] n sable m ♦ vt (furniture: also: ~ **down**) poncer

sandal ['sændl] n sandale f

sand: ~box n (US) n tas m de sable; **~castle** n château m de sable; **~paper** n papier m de verre; **~pit** n (BRIT) (for children) tas m de sable; **~stone** n grès m

sandwich ['sændwɪtʃ] n sandwich m; **cheese/ham ~** sandwich au fromage/jambon; **~ course** (BRIT) n cours m de formation professionnelle

sandy ['sændɪ] adj sablonneux(-euse), (colour) sable inv, blond roux inv

sane [seɪn] adj (person) sain(e) d'esprit; (outlook) sensé(e), sain(e)

sang [sæŋ] pt of **sing**

sanitary ['sænɪtərɪ] adj (system, arrangements) sanitaire; (clean) hygiénique; **~ towel** (US **sanitary napkin**) n serviette f hygiénique

sanitation [sænɪ'teɪʃən] n (in house) installations fpl sanitaires; (in town) système m sanitaire; **~ department** (US) n service m de voirie

sanity ['sænɪtɪ] n santé mentale; (common sense) bon sens

sank [sæŋk] pt of **sink**

Santa Claus [sæntə'klɔ:z] n le père Noël

sap [sæp] n (of plants) sève f ♦ vt (strength) saper, miner

sapling ['sæplɪŋ] n jeune arbre m

sapphire ['sæfaɪər] n saphir m

sarcasm ['sɑ:kæzm] n sarcasme m, raillerie f;
sarcastic [sɑ:'kæstɪk] adj sarcastique

sardine [sɑ:'di:n] n sardine f

Sardinia [sɑ:'dɪnɪə] n Sardaigne f

sash [sæʃ] n écharpe f

sat [sæt] pt, pp of **sit**

satchel ['sætʃl] n cartable m

satellite ['sætəlaɪt] n satellite m; **~ dish** n antenne f parabolique; **~ television** n télévision f par câble

satin ['sætɪn] n satin m ♦ adj en or de satin, satiné(e)

satire ['sætaɪər] n satire f

satisfaction [sætɪs'fækʃən] n satisfaction f

satisfactory [sætɪs'fæktərɪ] adj satisfaisant(e)

satisfied ['sætɪsfaɪd] adj satisfait(e)

satisfy ['sætɪsfaɪ] vt satisfaire, contenter; (convince) convaincre, persuader; **~ing** adj satisfaisant(e)

Saturday ['sætədɪ] n samedi m

sauce [sɔ:s] n sauce f; **~pan** n casserole f

saucer ['sɔ:sər] n soucoupe f

Saudi ['saudi-]: **~ Arabia** n Arabie Saoudite; **~ (Arabian)** adj saoudien(ne)

sauna ['sɔ:nə] n sauna m

saunter ['sɔ:ntər] vi: **to ~ along/in/out** etc marcher/entrer/sortir etc d'un pas nonchalant

sausage ['sɒsɪdʒ] n saucisse f; (cold meat) saucisson m; **~ roll** n ≈ friand m

savage ['sævɪdʒ] adj (cruel, fierce) brutal(e), féroce; (primitive) primitif(-ive), sauvage ♦ n sauvage m/f

save [seɪv] vt (person, belongings) sauver; (money) mettre de côté, économiser; (time) (faire) gagner; (keep) garder; (COMPUT) sauvegarder; (SPORT: stop) arrêter; (avoid: trouble) éviter ♦ vi (also: ~ **up**) mettre de l'argent de côté ♦ n (SPORT) arrêt m (du ballon) ♦ prep sauf, à l'exception de

saving ['seɪvɪŋ] n économie f ♦ adj: **the ~ grace of sth** ce qui rachète qch; **~s** npl (money saved) économies fpl; **~s account** n compte m d'épargne; **~s bank** n caisse f d'épargne

saviour ['seɪvjər] (US **savior**) n sauveur m

savour ['seɪvər] (US **savor**) vt savourer; **~y** (US **savory**) adj (dish: not sweet) salé(e)

saw [sɔ:] (pt sawed, pp sawed or sawn) vt scier ♦ n (tool) scie f ♦ pt of **see**; **~dust** n sciure f; **~mill** n scierie f; **~n-off** adj: **~n-off shotgun** carabine f à canon scié

sax [sæks] (inf) n saxo m

saxophone ['sæksəfəun] n saxophone m

say [seɪ] (pt, pp said) n: **to have one's ~** dire ce qu'on a à dire ♦ vt dire; **to have a** or **some ~ in sth** avoir voix au chapitre; **could you ~ that again?** pourriez-vous répéter ce que vous venez de dire?; **that goes without ~ing** cela va sans dire, cela va de soi; **~ing** n dicton m, proverbe m

scab [skæb] n croûte f; (pej) jaune m

scaffold ['skæfəld] n échafaud m; **~ing** n échafaudage m

scald [skɔ:ld] n brûlure f ♦ vt ébouillanter

scale [skeɪl] n (of fish) écaille f; (MUS) gamme

f; (of ruler, thermometer etc) graduation f, échelle (graduée); (of salaries, fees etc) barème m; (of map, also size, extent) échelle ♦ vt (mountain) escalader; ~s npl (for weighing) balance f; (also: **bathroom** ~) pèse-personne m inv; **on a large** ~ sur une grande échelle, en grand; ~ **of charges** tableau m des tarifs; ~ **down** vt réduire

scallop ['skɔləp] n coquille f Saint-Jacques; (SEWING) feston m

scalp [skælp] n cuir chevelu ♦ vt scalper

scampi ['skæmpɪ] npl langoustines (frites), scampi mpl

scan [skæn] vt scruter, examiner; (glance at quickly) parcourir; (TV, RADAR) balayer ♦ n (MED) scanographie f

scandal ['skændl] n scandale m; (gossip) ragots mpl

Scandinavia [skændɪ'neɪvɪə] n Scandinavie f; ~n adj scandinave

scant [skænt] adj insuffisant(e); ~y ['skæntɪ] adj peu abondant(e), insuffisant(e); (underwear) minuscule

scapegoat ['skeɪpgəʊt] n bouc m émissaire

scar [skɑː] n cicatrice f ♦ vt marquer (d'une cicatrice)

scarce [skɛəs] adj rare, peu abondant(e); **to make o.s.** ~ (inf) se sauver; ~**ly** adv à peine; **scarcity** n manque m, pénurie f

scare [skɛəʳ] n peur f, panique f ♦ vt effrayer, faire peur à; **to** ~ **sb stiff** faire une peur bleue à qn; **bomb** ~ alerte f à la bombe; ~ **away** vt faire fuir; ~ **off** vt = **scare away**; ~**crow** n épouvantail m; ~**d** adj: **to be** ~**d** avoir peur

scarf [skɑːf] (pl ~s or **scarves**) n (long) écharpe f; (square) foulard m

scarlet ['skɑːlɪt] adj écarlate; ~ **fever** n scarlatine f

scary ['skɛərɪ] (inf) adj effrayant(e)

scathing ['skeɪðɪŋ] adj cinglant(e), acerbe

scatter ['skætəʳ] vt éparpiller, répandre; (crowd) disperser ♦ vi se disperser; ~**brained** adj écervelé(e), étourdi(e)

scavenger ['skævəndʒəʳ] n (person: in bins etc) pilleur m de poubelles

scene [siːn] n scène f; (of crime, accident) lieu(x) m(pl); (sight, view) spectacle m, vue f; ~**ry** ['siːnərɪ] n (THEATRE) décor(s) m(pl); (landscape) paysage m; **scenic** adj (picturesque) offrant de beaux paysages or panoramas

scent [sɛnt] n parfum m, odeur f; (track) piste f

sceptical ['skɛptɪkl] (US **skeptical**) adj sceptique

schedule ['ʃɛdjuːl, (US) 'skɛdjuːl] n programme m, plan m; (of trains) horaire m; (of prices etc) barème m, tarif m ♦ vt prévoir; **on** ~ à l'heure (prévue); à la date prévue; **to**

be ahead of/behind ~ avoir de l'avance/du retard; ~**d flight** n vol régulier

scheme [skiːm] n plan m, projet m; (dishonest plan, plot) complot m, combine f; (arrangement) arrangement m, classification f; (pension ~ etc) régime m ♦ vi comploter, manigancer; **scheming** adj rusé(e), intrigant(e) ♦ n manigances fpl, intrigues fpl

scholar ['skɔləʳ] n érudit(e); (pupil) boursier(-ère); ~**ship** n (knowledge) érudition f; (grant) bourse f (d'études)

school [skuːl] n école f; (secondary ~) collège m, lycée m; (US: university) université f; (in university) faculté f ♦ cpd scolaire; ~**book** n livre m scolaire or de classe; ~**boy** n écolier m; collégien m, lycéen m; ~**children** npl écoliers mpl; collégiens mpl, lycéens mpl; ~**girl** n écolière f; collégienne f, lycéenne f; ~**ing** n instruction f, études fpl; ~**master** n (primary) instituteur m; (secondary) professeur m; ~**mistress** n institutrice f; professeur m; ~**teacher** n instituteur(-trice), professeur m

science ['saɪəns] n science f; ~ **fiction** n science-fiction f; **scientific** [saɪən'tɪfɪk] adj scientifique; **scientist** n scientifique m/f; (eminent) savant m

scissors ['sɪzəz] npl ciseaux mpl

scoff [skɔf] vt (BRIT: inf: eat) avaler, bouffer ♦ vi: **to** ~ **(at)** (mock) se moquer (de)

scold [skəʊld] vt gronder

scone [skɔn] n sorte de petit pain rond au lait

scoop [skuːp] n pelle f (à main); (for ice cream) boule f à glace; (PRESS) scoop m; ~ **out** vt évider, creuser; ~ **up** vt ramasser

scooter ['skuːtəʳ] n (also: **motor** ~) scooter m; (toy) trottinette f

scope [skəʊp] n (capacity: of plan, undertaking) portée f, envergure f; (: of person) compétence f, capacités fpl; (opportunity) possibilités fpl; **within the** ~ **of** dans les limites de

scorch [skɔːtʃ] vt (clothes) brûler (légèrement), roussir; (earth, grass) dessécher, brûler

score [skɔːʳ] n score m, décompte m des points; (MUS) partition f; (twenty) vingt ♦ vt (goal, point) marquer; (success) remporter ♦ vi marquer des points; (FOOTBALL) marquer un but; (keep ~) compter les points; ~**s of** (very many) beaucoup de, un tas de (fam); **on that** ~ sur ce chapitre, à cet égard; **to** ~ **6 out of 10** obtenir 6 sur 10; ~ **out** vt rayer, barrer, biffer; ~**board** n tableau m

scorn [skɔːn] n mépris m, dédain m

Scorpio ['skɔːpɪəʊ] n le Scorpion

Scot [skɔt] n Écossais(e)

Scotch [skɔtʃ] n whisky m, scotch m

scot-free ['skɔt'friː] adv: **to get off** ~~ s'en

tirer sans être puni(e)

Scotland ['skɔtlənd] n Écosse f; **Scots** adj écossais(e); **Scotsman** (irreg) n Écossais; **Scotswoman** (irreg) n Écossaise f; **Scottish** adj écossais(e)

scoundrel ['skaundrl] n vaurien m

scour ['skauər] vt (search) battre, parcourir

scout [skaut] n (MIL) éclaireur m; (also: **boy ~**) scout m; **girl ~** (US) guide f; **~ around** vi explorer, chercher

scowl [skaul] vi se renfrogner, avoir l'air maussade; **to ~ at** regarder de travers

scrabble ['skræbl] vi (also: **~ around**: search) chercher à tâtons; (claw): **to ~ (at)** gratter ♦ n: **S~** ® Scrabble ® m

scram [skræm] (inf) vi ficher le camp

scramble ['skræmbl] n (rush) bousculade f, ruée f ♦ vi: **to ~ up/down** grimper/descendre tant bien que mal; **to ~ out** sortir or descendre à toute vitesse; **to ~ through** se frayer un passage (à travers); **to ~ for** se bousculer or se disputer pour (avoir); **~d eggs** npl œufs brouillés

scrap [skræp] n bout m, morceau m; (fight) bagarre f; (also: **~ iron**) ferraille f ♦ vt jeter, mettre au rebut; (fig) abandonner, laisser tomber ♦ vi (fight) se bagarrer; **~s** npl (waste) déchets mpl; **~book** n album m; **~ dealer** n marchand m de ferraille

scrape [skreɪp] vt, vi gratter, racler ♦ n: **to get into a ~** s'attirer des ennuis; **to ~ through** réussir de justesse; **~ together** vt (money) racler ses fonds de tiroir pour réunir

scrap: **~ heap** n: **on the ~ heap** (fig) au rancart or rebut; **~ merchant** (BRIT) n marchand m de ferraille; **~ paper** n papier m brouillon

scratch [skrætʃ] n égratignure f, rayure f; éraflure f; (from claw) coup m de griffe ♦ cpd: **~ team** équipe de fortune or improvisée ♦ vt (rub) (se) gratter; (record) rayer; (paint etc) érafler; (with claw, nail) griffer ♦ vi (se) gratter; **to start from ~** partir de zéro; **to be up to ~** être à la hauteur

scrawl [skrɔːl] vi gribouiller

scrawny ['skrɔːnɪ] adj décharné(e)

scream [skriːm] n cri perçant, hurlement m ♦ vi crier, hurler

screech [skriːtʃ] vi hurler; (tyres) crisser; (brakes) grincer

screen [skriːn] n écran m; (in room) paravent m; (fig) écran, rideau m ♦ vt (conceal) masquer, cacher; (from the wind etc) abriter, protéger; (film) projeter; (candidates etc) filtrer; **~ing** n (MED) test m (or tests) de dépistage; **~play** n scénario m

screw [skruː] n vis f ♦ vt (also: **~ in**) visser; **~ up** vt (paper etc) froisser; **to ~ up one's eyes** plisser les yeux; **~driver** n tournevis m

scribble ['skrɪbl] vt, vi gribouiller, griffonner

script [skrɪpt] n (CINEMA etc) scénario m, texte m; (system of writing) écriture f script m

Scripture(s) ['skrɪptʃər(-əz)] n(pl) (Christian) Écriture sainte; (other religions) écritures saintes

scroll [skrəul] n rouleau m

scrounge [skraundʒ] (inf) vt: **to ~ sth off** or **from sb** taper qn de qch; **~r** (inf) n parasite m

scrub [skrʌb] n (land) broussailles fpl ♦ vt (floor) nettoyer à la brosse; (pan) récurer; (washing) frotter; (inf: cancel) annuler

scruff [skrʌf] n: **by the ~ of the neck** par la peau du cou

scruffy ['skrʌfɪ] adj débraillé(e)

scrum(mage) ['skrʌm(ɪdʒ)] n (RUGBY) mêlée f

scruple ['skruːpl] n scrupule m

scrutiny ['skruːtɪnɪ] n examen minutieux

scuff [skʌf] vt érafler

scuffle ['skʌfl] n échauffourée f, rixe f

sculptor ['skʌlptər] n sculpteur m

sculpture ['skʌlptʃər] n sculpture f

scum [skʌm] n écume f, mousse f; (pej: people) rebut m, lie f

scurry ['skʌrɪ] vi filer à toute allure; **to ~ off** détaler, se sauver

scuttle ['skʌtl] n (also: **coal ~**) seau m (à charbon) ♦ vt (ship) saborder ♦ vi (scamper): **to ~ away** or **off** détaler

scythe [saɪð] n faux f

SDP n abbr (= Social Democratic Party) parti m social-démocrate

sea [siː] n mer f ♦ cpd marin(e), de (la) mer; **by ~** (travel) par mer, en bateau; **on the ~** (boat) en mer; (town) au bord de la mer; **to be all at ~** (fig) nager complètement; **out to ~** au large; **(out) at ~** en mer; **~board** n côte f; **~food** n fruits mpl de mer; **~front** n bord m de mer; **~going** adj (ship) de mer; **~gull** n mouette f

seal [siːl] n (animal) phoque m; (stamp) sceau m, cachet m ♦ vt sceller; (envelope) coller; (: with ~) cacheter; **~ off** vt (forbid entry to) interdire l'accès à

sea level n niveau m de la mer

sea lion n otarie f

seam [siːm] n couture f; (of coal) veine f, filon m

seaman ['siːmən] (irreg) n marin m

seance ['seɪɔns] n séance f de spiritisme

seaplane ['siːpleɪn] n hydravion m

search [sɔːtʃ] n (for person, thing, COMPUT) recherche(s) f(pl); (LAW: at sb's home) perquisition f ♦ vt fouiller; (examine) examiner minutieusement; scruter ♦ vi: **to ~ for** chercher; **in ~ of** à la recherche de; **~ through** vt fus fouiller; **~ing** adj pénétrant(e); **~light** n projecteur m; **~ party**

n expédition *f* de secours; **~ warrant** *n* mandat *m* de perquisition

sea: **~shore** *n* rivage *m*, plage *f*, bord *m* de (la) mer; **~sick** *adj*: **to be ~sick** avoir le mal de mer; **~side** *n* bord *m* de la mer; **~side resort** *n* station *f* balnéaire

season ['si:zn] *n* saison *f* ♦ *vt* assaisonner, relever; **to be in/out of ~** être/ne pas être de saison; **~al** *adj* (*work*) saisonnier(-ère); **~ed** *adj* (*fig*) expérimenté(e); **~ ticket** *n* carte *f* d'abonnement

seat [si:t] *n* siège *m*; (*in bus, train: place*) place *f*; (*buttocks*) postérieur *m*; (*of trousers*) fond *m* ♦ *vt* faire asseoir, placer; (*have room for*) avoir des places assises pour, pouvoir accueillir; **~ belt** *n* ceinture *f* de sécurité

sea: **~ water** *n* eau *f* de mer; **~weed** *n* algues *fpl*; **~worthy** *adj* en état de naviguer

sec. *abbr* = **second(s)**

secluded [sɪ'klu:dɪd] *adj* retiré(e), à l'écart

seclusion [sɪ'klu:ʒən] *n* solitude *f*

second¹ ['sɛkənd] (*BRIT*) *vt* (*employee*) affecter provisoirement

second² ['sɛkənd] *adj* deuxième, second(e) ♦ *adv* (*in race etc*) en seconde position ♦ *n* (*unit of time*) seconde *f*; (*AUT: ~ gear*) seconde; (*COMM: imperfect*) article *m* de second choix; (*BRIT: UNIV*) licence *f* avec mention ♦ *vt* (*motion*) appuyer; **~ary** *adj* secondaire; **~ary school** *n* collège *m*, lycée *m*; **~-class** *adj* de deuxième classe; (*RAIL*) de seconde (classe); (*POST*) au tarif réduit; (*pej*) de qualité inférieure ♦ *adv* (*RAIL*) en seconde; (*POST*) au tarif réduit; **~hand** *adj* d'occasion; de seconde main; **~ hand** *n* (*on clock*) trotteuse *f*; **~ly** *adv* deuxièmement; **~ment** [sɪ'kɔndmənt] (*BRIT*) *n* détachement *m*; **~-rate** *adj* de deuxième ordre, de qualité inférieure; **~ thoughts** *npl* doutes *mpl*; **on ~ thoughts** *or* (*US*) **thought** à la réflexion

secrecy ['si:krəsɪ] *n* secret *m*

secret ['si:krɪt] *adj* secret(-ète) ♦ *n* secret *m*; **in ~** en secret, secrètement, en cachette

secretary ['sɛkrətərɪ] *n* secrétaire *m/f*; (*COMM*) secrétaire général; **S~ of State (for)** (*BRIT: POL*) ministre *m* (de)

secretive ['si:krətɪv] *adj* dissimulé(e)

secretly ['si:krɪtlɪ] *adv* en secret, secrètement

sectarian [sɛk'tɛərɪən] *adj* sectaire

section ['sɛkʃən] *n* section *f*; (*of document*) section, article *m*, paragraphe *m*; (*cut*) coupe *f*

sector ['sɛktəʳ] *n* secteur *m*

secular ['sɛkjulaʳ] *adj* profane; laïque; séculier(-ère)

secure [sɪ'kjuaʳ] *adj* (*free from anxiety*) sans inquiétude, sécurisé(e); (*firmly fixed*) solide, bien attaché(e) (*or* fermé(e) *etc*); (*in safe place*) en lieu sûr, en sûreté ♦ *vt* (*fix*) fixer,

attacher; (*get*) obtenir, se procurer

security [sɪ'kjuarɪtɪ] *n* sécurité *f*, mesures *fpl* de sécurité; (*for loan*) caution *f*, garantie *f*; **~ guard** *n* garde chargé de la sécurité; (*when transporting money*) convoyeur *m* de fonds

sedate [sɪ'deɪt] *adj* calme; posé(e) ♦ *vt* (*MED*) donner des sédatifs à

sedative ['sɛdɪtɪv] *n* calmant *m*, sédatif *m*

seduce [sɪ'dju:s] *vt* séduire; **seduction** [sɪ'dʌkʃən] *n* séduction *f*; **seductive** *adj* séduisant(e); (*smile*) séducteur(-trice); (*fig: offer*) alléchant(e)

see [si:] (*pt* saw, *pp* seen) *vt* voir; (*accompany*): **to ~ sb to the door** reconduire *or* raccompagner qn jusqu'à la porte ♦ *vi* voir ♦ *n* évêché *m*; **to ~ that** (*ensure*) veiller à ce que +*sub*, faire en sorte que +*sub*, s'assurer que; **~ you soon!** à bientôt!; **~ about** *vt fus* s'occuper de; **~ off** *vt* accompagner (à la gare *or* à l'aéroport *etc*); **~ through** *vt* mener à bonne fin ♦ *vt fus* voir clair dans; **~ to** *vt fus* s'occuper de, se charger de

seed [si:d] *n* graine *f*; (*sperm*) semence *f*; (*fig*) germe *m*; (*TENNIS etc*) tête *f* de série; **to go to ~** monter en graine; (*fig*) se laisser aller; **~ling** *n* jeune plant, semis *m*; **~y** *adj* (*shabby*) minable, miteux(-euse)

seeing ['si:ɪŋ] *conj*: **~ (that)** vu que, étant donné que

seek [si:k] (*pt, pp* sought) *vt* chercher, rechercher

seem [si:m] *vi* sembler, paraître; **there ~s to be ...** il semble qu'il y a ...; on dirait qu'il y a ...; **~ingly** *adv* apparemment

seen [si:n] *pp of* **see**

seep [si:p] *vi* suinter, filtrer

seesaw ['si:sɔ:] *n* (jeu *m* de) bascule *f*

seethe [si:ð] *vi* être en effervescence; **to ~ with anger** bouillir de colère

see-through ['si:θru:] *adj* transparent(e)

segment ['sɛgmənt] *n* segment *m*; (*of orange*) quartier *m*

segregate ['sɛgrɪgeɪt] *vt* séparer, isoler

seize [si:z] *vt* saisir, attraper; (*take possession of*) s'emparer de; (*opportunity*) saisir; **~ up** *vi* (*TECH*) se gripper; **~ (up)on** *vt fus* saisir, sauter sur

seizure ['si:ʒəʳ] *n* (*MED*) crise *f*, attaque *f*; (*of power*) prise *f*

seldom ['sɛldəm] *adv* rarement

select [sɪ'lɛkt] *adj* choisi(e), d'élite ♦ *vt* sélectionner, choisir; **~ion** *n* sélection *f*, choix *m*

self [sɛlf] (*pl* selves) *n*: **the ~** le moi *inv* ♦ *prefix* auto-; **~-assured** *adj* sûr(e) de soi; **~-catering** (*BRIT*) *adj* avec cuisine, où l'on peut faire sa cuisine; **~-centred** (*US* self-centered) *adj* égocentrique; **~-confidence** *n* confiance f en soi; **~-conscious** adj timide, qui manque d'assurance; **~-contained** (BRIT) adj (flat) avec entrée particulière, indépendant(e); **~-defence** (US self-defense) n autodéfense f; (LAW) légitime défense f; **~-discipline** n discipline personnelle; **~-employed** adj qui travaille à son compte; **~-evident** adj: to be **~-evident** être évident(e), aller de soi; **~-governing** adj autonome; **~-indulgent** adj qui ne se refuse rien; **~-interest** n intérêt personnel; **~ish** adj égoïste; **~ishness** n égoïsme m; **~less** adj désintéressé(e); **~-pity** n apitoiement m sur soi-même; **~-possessed** adj assuré(e); **~-preservation** n instinct m de conservation; **~-respect** n respect m de soi, amour-propre m; **~-righteous** adj suffisant(e); **~-sacrifice** n abnégation f; **~-satisfied** adj content(e) de soi, suffisant(e); **~-service** n libre-service, self-service; **~-sufficient** adj autosuffisant(e); (person: independent) indépendant(e); **~-taught** adj (artist, pianist) qui a appris par lui-même

sell [sɛl] (pt, pp **sold**) vt vendre ♦ vi se vendre; **to ~ at** or **for 10 F** se vendre 10 F; **~ off** vt liquider; **~ out** vi: **to ~ out (of sth)** (use up stock) vendre tout son stock (de qch); **the tickets are all sold out** il ne reste plus de billets; **~-by date** n date f limite de vente; **~er** n vendeur(-euse), marchand(e); **~ing price** n prix m de vente

Sellotape ® ['sɛləʊteɪp] (BRIT) n papier m collant, scotch ® m

selves [sɛlvz] npl of **self**

semblance ['sɛmblns] n semblant m

semen ['si:mən] n sperme m

semester [sɪ'mɛstər] (esp US) n semestre m

semi ['sɛmɪ] prefix semi-, demi-; à demi, à moitié; **~circle** n demi-cercle m; **~colon** n point-virgule m; **~detached (house)** (BRIT) n maison jumelée or jumelle; **~final** n demi-finale f

seminar ['sɛmɪnɑːr] n séminaire m; **~y** n (REL: for priests) séminaire m

semiskilled [sɛmɪ'skɪld] adj: **~ worker** ouvrier(-ère) spécialisé(e)

semi-skimmed milk [sɛmɪ'skɪmd-] n lait m demi-écrémé

senate ['sɛnɪt] n sénat m; **senator** n sénateur m

send [sɛnd] (pt, pp **sent**) vt envoyer; **~ away** vt (letter, goods) envoyer, expédier; (unwelcome visitor) renvoyer; **~ away for** vt fus commander par correspondance, se faire envoyer; **~ back** vt renvoyer; **~ for** vt fus envoyer chercher; faire venir; **~ off** vt (goods) envoyer, expédier; (BRIT: SPORT: player) expulser or renvoyer du terrain; **~ out** vt

(invitation) envoyer (par la poste); (light, heat, signal) émettre; **~ up** vt faire monter; (BRIT: parody) mettre en boîte, parodier; **~er** n expéditeur(-trice); **~-off** n: **a good ~-off** des adieux chaleureux

senior ['si:nɪər] adj (high-ranking) de haut niveau; (of higher rank): **to be ~ to sb** être supérieur de qn ♦ n (older): **she is 15 years his ~** elle est son aînée de 15 ans, elle est plus âgée que lui de 15 ans; **~ citizen** n personne âgée; **~ity** [si:nɪ'ɔrɪtɪ] n (in service) ancienneté f

sensation [sɛn'seɪʃən] n sensation f; **~al** adj qui fait sensation; (marvellous) sensationnel(le)

sense [sɛns] n sens m; (feeling) sentiment m; (meaning) sens, signification f; (wisdom) bon sens ♦ vt sentir, pressentir; **it makes ~** c'est logique; **~less** adj insensé(e), stupide; (unconscious) sans connaissance

sensible ['sɛnsɪbl] adj sensé(e), raisonnable; sage

sensitive ['sɛnsɪtɪv] adj sensible

sensual ['sɛnsjʊəl] adj sensuel(le)

sensuous ['sɛnsjʊəs] adj voluptueux(-euse), sensuel(le)

sent [sɛnt] pt, pp of **send**

sentence ['sɛntns] n (LING) phrase f; (LAW: judgment) condamnation f, sentence f; (: punishment) peine f ♦ vt: **to ~ sb to death/ to 5 years in prison** condamner qn à mort/à 5 ans de prison

sentiment ['sɛntɪmənt] n sentiment m; (opinion) opinion f, avis m; **~al** [sɛntɪ'mɛntl] adj sentimental(e)

sentry ['sɛntrɪ] n sentinelle f

separate [adj 'sɛprɪt, vb 'sɛpəreɪt] adj séparé(e), indépendant(e), différent(e) ♦ vt séparer; (make a distinction between) distinguer ♦ vi se séparer; **~ly** adv séparément; **~s** npl (clothes) coordonnés mpl; **separation** [sɛpə'reɪʃən] n séparation f

September [sɛp'tɛmbər] n septembre m

septic ['sɛptɪk] adj (wound) infecté(e); **~ tank** n fosse f septique

sequel ['si:kwl] n conséquence f; séquelles fpl; (of story) suite f

sequence ['si:kwəns] n ordre m, suite f; (film ~) séquence f; (dance ~) numéro m

sequin ['si:kwɪn] n paillette f

Serbia ['sɜ:bɪə] n Serbie f

serene [sɪ'ri:n] adj serein(e), calme, paisible

sergeant ['sɑ:dʒənt] n sergent m; (POLICE) brigadier m

serial ['sɪərɪəl] n feuilleton m; **~ killer** n meurtrier m tuant en série; **~ number** n numéro m de série

series ['sɪərɪz] n inv série f; (PUBLISHING) collection f

serious ['sɪərɪəs] adj sérieux(-euse); (illness) grave; **~ly** adv sérieusement; (hurt) gravement

sermon ['sɜːmən] n sermon m

serrated [sɪ'reɪtɪd] adj en dents de scie

servant ['sɜːvənt] n domestique m/f; (fig) serviteur/servante

serve [sɜːv] vt (employer etc) servir, être au service de; (purpose) servir à; (customer, food, meal) servir; (subj: train) desservir; (apprenticeship) faire, accomplir; (prison term) purger ♦ vi servir; (be useful): **to ~ as/for/to do** servir de/à/à faire ♦ n (TENNIS) service m; **it ~s him right** c'est bien fait pour lui; **~ out**, **~ up** vt (food) servir

service ['sɜːvɪs] n service m; (AUT: maintenance) révision f ♦ vt (car, washing machine) réviser; **the S~s** les forces armées; **to be of ~ to sb** rendre service à qn; **15% ~ included** service 15% compris; **~ not included** service non compris; **~able** adj pratique, commode; **~ area** n (on motorway) aire f de services; **~ charge** (BRIT) n service m; **~man** (irreg) n militaire m; **~ station** n station-service f

serviette [sɜːvɪ'et] (BRIT) n serviette f (de table)

session ['seʃən] n séance f

set [set] (pt, pp **set**) n série f, assortiment m; (of tools etc) jeu m; (RADIO, TV) poste m; (TENNIS) set m; (group of people) cercle m, milieu m; (THEATRE: stage) scène f; (: scenery) décor m; (MATH) ensemble m; (HAIRDRESSING) mise f en plis ♦ adj (fixed) fixe, déterminé(e); (ready) prêt(e) ♦ vt (place) poser, placer; (fix, establish) fixer; (: record) établir; (adjust) régler; (decide: rules etc) fixer, choisir; (task) donner; (exam) composer ♦ vi (sun) se coucher; (jam, jelly, concrete) prendre; (bone) se ressouder; **to be ~ on doing** être résolu à faire; **to ~ the table** mettre la table; **to ~** (to music) mettre en musique; **to ~ on fire** mettre le feu à; **to ~ free** libérer; **to ~ sth going** déclencher qch; **to ~ sail** prendre la mer; **~ about** vt fus (task) entreprendre, se mettre à; **~ aside** vt mettre de côté; (time) garder; **~ back** vt (in time): **to ~ back (by)** retarder (de); (cost): **to ~ sb back £5** coûter 5 livres à qn; **~ off** vi se mettre en route, partir ♦ vt (bomb) faire exploser; (cause to start) déclencher; (show up well) mettre en valeur, faire valoir; **~ out** vi se mettre en route, partir ♦ vt (arrange) disposer; (arguments) présenter, exposer; **to ~ out to do** entreprendre de faire, avoir pour but or intention de faire; **~ up** vt (organization) fonder, créer; **~back** n (hitch) revers m, contretemps m; **~ menu** n menu m

settee [se'tiː] n canapé m

setting ['setɪŋ] n cadre m; (of jewel) monture f; (position: of controls) réglage m

settle ['setl] vt (argument, matter, account) régler; (problem) résoudre; (MED: calm) calmer ♦ vi (bird, dust etc) se poser; (also: ~ down) s'installer, se fixer; (calm down) se calmer; **to ~ for sth** accepter qch, se contenter de qch; **to ~ on sth** opter or se décider pour qch; **~ in** vi s'installer; **~ up** vi: **to ~ up with sb** régler (ce que l'on doit à) qn; **~ment** n (payment) règlement m; (agreement) accord m; (village etc) établissement m; hameau m; **~r** n colon m

setup ['setʌp] n (arrangement) manière f dont les choses sont organisées; (situation) situation f

seven ['sevn] num sept; **~teen** num dix-sept; **~th** num septième; **~ty** num soixante-dix

sever ['sevər] vt couper, trancher; (relations) rompre

several ['sevərl] adj, pron plusieurs m/fpl; **~ of us** plusieurs d'entre nous

severance ['sevərəns] n (of relations) rupture f; **~ pay** n indemnité f de licenciement

severe [sɪ'vɪər] adj (stern) sévère, strict(e); (serious) grave, sérieux(-euse); (plain) sévère, austère; **severity** [sɪ'verɪtɪ] n sévérité f; gravité f; rigueur f

sew [səu] (pt sewed, pp sewn) vt, vi coudre; **~ up** vt (re)coudre

sewage ['suːɪdʒ] n vidange(s) f(pl)

sewer ['suːər] n égout m

sewing ['səuɪŋ] n couture f; (item(s)) ouvrage m; **~ machine** n machine f à coudre

sewn [səun] pp of **sew**

sex [seks] n sexe m; **to have ~ with** avoir des rapports (sexuels) avec; **~ism** n sexisme m; **~ist** adj sexiste; **~ual** ['seksjuəl] adj sexuel(le); **~uality** [seksju'ælɪtɪ] n sexualité f; **~y** adj sexy inv

shabby ['ʃæbɪ] adj miteux(-euse); (behaviour) mesquin(e), méprisable

shack [ʃæk] n cabane f, hutte f

shackles ['ʃæklz] npl chaînes fpl, entraves fpl

shade [ʃeɪd] n ombre f; (for lamp) abat-jour m inv; (of colour) nuance f, ton m ♦ vt abriter du soleil, ombrager; **in the ~** à l'ombre; **a ~ too large/more** un tout petit peu trop grand(e)/plus

shadow ['ʃædəu] n ombre f ♦ vt (follow) filer; **~ cabinet** (BRIT) n (POL) cabinet parallèle formé par l'Opposition; **~y** adj ombragé(e); (dim) vague, indistinct(e)

shady ['ʃeɪdɪ] adj ombragé(e); (fig: dishonest) louche, véreux(-euse)

shaft [ʃɑːft] n (of arrow, spear) hampe f; (AUT, TECH) arbre m; (of mine) puits m; (of lift) cage f; (of light) rayon m, trait m

shaggy ['ʃægɪ] adj hirsute; en broussaille

shake [ʃeɪk] (*pt* shook, *pp* shaken) *vt* secouer; (*bottle, cocktail*) agiter; (*house, confidence*) ébranler ♦ *vi* trembler; **to ~ one's head** (*in refusal*) dire or faire non de la tête; (*in dismay*) secouer la tête; **to ~ hands with sb** serrer la main à qn; **~ off** *vt* secouer; (*pursuer*) se débarrasser de; **~ up** *vt* secouer; **~n** *pp* of shake; **shaky** *adj* (*hand, voice*) tremblant(e); (*building*) branlant(e), peu solide

shall [ʃæl] *aux vb*: **I ~ go** j'irai; **~ I open the door?** j'ouvre la porte?; **I'll get the coffee, ~ I?** je vais chercher le café, d'accord?

shallow [ˈʃæləʊ] *adj* peu profond(e); (*fig*) superficiel(le)

sham [ʃæm] *n* frime *f* ♦ *vt* simuler

shambles [ˈʃæmblz] *n* (*muddle*) confusion *f*, pagaïe *f*, fouillis *m*

shame [ʃeɪm] *n* honte *f* ♦ *vt* faire honte à; **it is a ~ (that/to do)** c'est dommage (que +*sub*/de faire); **what a ~!** quel dommage!; **~ful** *adj* honteux(-euse), scandaleux(-euse); **~less** *adj* éhonté(e)

shampoo [ʃæmˈpuː] *n* shampooing *m* ♦ *vt* faire un shampooing à; **~ and set** *n* shampooing *m* (et) mise *f* en plis

shamrock [ˈʃæmrɒk] *n* trèfle *m* (*emblème de l'Irlande*)

shandy [ˈʃændɪ] *n* bière panachée

shan't [ʃɑːnt] = shall not

shanty town [ˈʃæntɪ-] *n* bidonville *m*

shape [ʃeɪp] *n* forme *f* ♦ *vt* façonner, modeler; (*sb's ideas*) former; (*sb's life*) déterminer ♦ *vi* (*also: ~ up: events*) prendre tournure; (*: person*) faire des progrès, s'en sortir; **to take ~** prendre forme or tournure; **~d** *suffix*: **heart-~d** en forme de cœur; **~less** *adj* informe, sans forme; **~ly** *adj* bien proportionné(e), beau (belle)

share [ʃɛəʳ] *n* part *f*; (*COMM*) action *f* ♦ *vt* partager; (*have in common*) avoir en commun; **~ out** *vi* partager; **~holder** *n* actionnaire *m/f*

shark [ʃɑːk] *n* requin *m*

sharp [ʃɑːp] *adj* (*razor, knife*) tranchant(e), bien aiguisé(e); (*point, voice*) aigu(-guë); (*nose, chin*) pointu(e); (*outline, increase*) net(te); (*cold, pain*) vif (vive); (*taste*) piquant(e), âcre; (*MUS*) dièse; (*person: quick-witted*) vif (vive), éveillé(e); (*: unscrupulous*) malhonnête ♦ *n* (*MUS*) dièse *m* ♦ *adv* (*precisely*): **at 2 o'clock ~** à 2 heures pile or précises; **~en** *vt* aiguiser; (*pencil*) tailler; **~ener** *n* (*also*: **pencil ~ener**) taille-crayon(s) *m inv*; **~-eyed** *adj* à qui rien n'échappe; **~ly** *adv* (*turn, stop*) brusquement; (*stand out*) nettement; (*criticize, retort*) sèchement, vertement

shatter [ˈʃætəʳ] *vt* briser; (*fig: upset*) bouleverser; (*: ruin*) briser, ruiner ♦ *vi* voler en éclats, se briser

shave [ʃeɪv] *vt* raser ♦ *vi* se raser ♦ *n*: **to have a ~** se raser; **~r** *n* (*also*: **electric ~r**) rasoir *m* électrique

shaving [ˈʃeɪvɪŋ] *n* (*action*) rasage *m*; **~s** *npl* (*of wood etc*) copeaux *mpl*; **~ brush** *n* blaireau *m*; **~ cream** *n* crème *f* à raser; **~ foam** *n* mousse *f* à raser

shawl [ʃɔːl] *n* châle *m*

she [ʃiː] *pron* elle ♦ *prefix*: **~-cat** chatte *f*; **~-elephant** éléphant *m* femelle

sheaf [ʃiːf] (*pl* sheaves) *n* gerbe *f*; (*of papers*) liasse *f*

shear [ʃɪəʳ] (*pt* sheared, *pp* shorn) *vt* (*sheep*) tondre; **~s** *npl* (*for hedge*) cisaille(s) *f(pl)*

sheath [ʃiːθ] *n* gaine *f*, fourreau *m*, étui *m*; (*contraceptive*) préservatif *m*

shed [ʃed] *n* (*pt*, *pp* shed) *n* remise *f*, resserre *f* ♦ *vt* perdre; (*tears*) verser, répandre; (*workers*) congédier

she'd [ʃiːd] = she had; she would

sheen [ʃiːn] *n* lustre *m*

sheep [ʃiːp] *n inv* mouton *m*; **~dog** *n* chien *m* de berger; **~skin** *n* peau *f* de mouton

sheer [ʃɪəʳ] *adj* (*utter*) pur(e), pur et simple; (*steep*) à pic, abrupt(e); (*almost transparent*) extrêmement fin(e) ♦ *adv* à pic, abruptement

sheet [ʃiːt] *n* (*on bed*) drap *m*; (*of paper*) feuille *f*; (*of glass, metal etc*) feuille, plaque *f*

sheik(h) [ʃeɪk] *n* cheik *m*

shelf [ʃelf] (*pl* shelves) *n* étagère *f*, rayon *m*

shell [ʃel] *n* (*on beach*) coquillage *m*; (*of egg, nut etc*) coquille *f*; (*explosive*) obus *m*; (*of building*) carcasse *f* ♦ *vt* (*peas*) écosser; (*MIL*) bombarder (d'obus)

she'll [ʃiːl] = she will; she shall

shellfish [ˈʃelfɪʃ] *n inv* (*crab etc*) crustacé *m*; (*scallop etc*) coquillage *m* ♦ *npl* (*as food*) fruits *mpl* de mer

shell suit *n* survêtement *m* (*en synthétique froissé*)

shelter [ˈʃeltəʳ] *n* abri *m*, refuge *m* ♦ *vt* abriter, protéger; (*give lodging to*) donner asile à ♦ *vi* s'abriter, se mettre à l'abri; **~ed housing** *n* foyers *mpl* (*pour personnes âgées ou handicapées*)

shelve [ʃelv] *vt* (*fig*) mettre en suspens or en sommeil; **~s** *npl* of shelf

shepherd [ˈʃepəd] *n* berger *m* ♦ *vt* (*guide*) guider, escorter; **~'s pie** (*BRIT*) *n* ≈ hachis *m* Parmentier

sheriff [ˈʃerɪf] (*US*) *n* shérif *m*

sherry [ˈʃerɪ] *n* xérès *m*, sherry *m*

she's [ʃiːz] = she is; she has

Shetland [ˈʃetlənd] *n* (*also: the ~ Islands*) les îles *fpl* Shetland

shield [ʃiːld] *n* bouclier *m*; (*protection*) écran *m* de protection ♦ *vt*: **to ~ (from)** protéger

(de or contre)

shift [ʃɪft] n (change) changement m; (work period) période f de travail; (of workers) équipe f, poste m ♦ vt déplacer, changer de place; (remove) enlever ♦ vi changer de place, bouger; ~ **work** n travail m en équipe or par relais or par roulement; ~**y** adj sournois(e); (eyes) fuyant(e)

shimmer ['ʃɪmə'] vi miroiter, chatoyer

shin [ʃɪn] n tibia m

shine [ʃaɪn] (pt, pp **shone**) n éclat m, brillant m ♦ vi briller ♦ vt (torch etc): **to ~ on** braquer sur; (polish: pt, pp ~d) faire briller or reluire

shingle ['ʃɪŋgl] n (on beach) galets mpl; ~**s** n (MED) zona m

shiny ['ʃaɪnɪ] adj brillant(e)

ship [ʃɪp] n bateau m; (large) navire m ♦ vt transporter (par mer); (send) expédier (par mer); ~**building** n construction navale; ~**ment** n cargaison f; ~**ping** n (ships) navires mpl; (the industry) industrie navale; (transport) transport m; ~**wreck** n (ship) épave f; (event) naufrage m ♦ vt: **to be ~wrecked** faire naufrage; ~**yard** n chantier naval

shire ['ʃaɪə'] (BRIT) n comté m

shirt [ʃə:t] n (man's) chemise f; (woman's) chemisier m; **in (one's) ~ sleeves** en bras de chemise

shit [ʃɪt] (infl) n, excl merde f (!)

shiver ['ʃɪvə'] n frisson m ♦ vi frissonner

shoal [ʃəʊl] n (of fish) banc m; (fig: also: ~**s**) masse f, foule f

shock [ʃɒk] n choc m; (ELEC) secousse f; (MED) commotion f, choc ♦ vt (offend) choquer, scandaliser; (upset) bouleverser; ~ **absorber** n amortisseur m; ~**ing** adj (scandalizing) choquant(e), scandaleux(-euse); (appalling) épouvantable

shoddy ['ʃɒdɪ] adj de mauvaise qualité, mal fait(e)

shoe [ʃu:] (pt, pp **shod**) n chaussure f, soulier m; (also: **horseshoe**) fer m à cheval ♦ vt (horse) ferrer; ~**lace** n lacet m (de soulier); ~ **polish** n cirage m; ~ **shop** n magasin m de chaussures; ~**string** n (fig): **on a ~string** avec un budget dérisoire

shone [ʃɒn] pt, pp of **shine**

shook [ʃʊk] pt of **shake**

shoot [ʃu:t] (pt, pp **shot**) n (on branch, seedling) pousse f ♦ vt (game) chasser; tirer; abattre; (person) blesser (or tuer) d'un coup de fusil (de or revolver); (execute) fusiller; (arrow) tirer; (gun) tirer un coup de; (film) tourner ♦ vi (with gun, bow): **to ~ (at)** tirer (sur); (FOOTBALL) shooter, tirer; ~ **down** vt (plane) abattre; ~ **in** vi entrer comme une flèche; ~ **out** vi sortir comme une flèche; ~ **up** vi (fig) monter en flèche; ~**ing** n

(shots) coups mpl de feu, fusillade f; (HUNTING) chasse f; ~**ing star** n étoile filante

shop [ʃɒp] n magasin m; (workshop) atelier m ♦ vi (also: **go ~ping**) faire ses courses or ses achats; ~ **assistant** n vendeur(-euse); ~ **floor** (BRIT) n (INDUSTRY: fig) ouvriers mpl; ~**keeper** n commerçant(e); ~**lifting** n vol m à l'étalage; ~**per** n personne f qui fait ses courses, acheteur(-euse); ~**ping** n (goods) achats mpl, provisions fpl; ~**ping bag** n sac m (à provisions); ~**ping centre** (US **shopping center**) n centre commercial; ~**-soiled** adj défraîchi(e), qui a fait la vitrine; ~ **steward** (BRIT) n (INDUSTRY) délégué(e) syndical(e); ~ **window** n vitrine f

shore [ʃɔ:'] n (of sea, lake) rivage m, rive f ♦ vt: **to ~ (up)** étayer; **on ~** à terre

shorn [ʃɔ:n] pp of **shear**

short [ʃɔ:t] adj (not long) court(e); (soon finished) court, bref (brève); (person, step) petit(e); (curt) brusque, sec (sèche); (insufficient) insuffisant(e); **to be/run ~ of sth** être à court de or manquer de qch; **in ~** bref; **~ of doing** ... à moins de faire ...; **everything ~ of** tout sauf; **it is ~ for** c'est l'abréviation or le diminutif de; **to cut ~** (speech, visit) abréger, écourter; **to fall ~ of** ne pas être à la hauteur de; **to run ~ of** arriver à court de, venir à manquer de; **to stop ~** s'arrêter net; **to stop ~ of** ne pas aller jusqu'à; ~**age** n manque m, pénurie f; ~**bread** n ≈ sablé m; ~**-change** vt ne pas rendre assez à; ~**circuit** n court circuit m; ~**coming** n défaut m; ~**(crust) pastry** (BRIT) n pâte brisée; ~**cut** n raccourci m; ~**en** vt raccourcir; (text, visit) abréger; ~**fall** n déficit m; ~**hand** (BRIT) n sténo(graphie) f; ~**hand typist** (BRIT) n sténodactylo m/f; ~**list** (BRIT) n (for job) liste f des candidats sélectionnés; ~**ly** adv bientôt, sous peu; ~ **notice** n: **at ~ notice** au dernier moment; ~**s** npl: **(a pair of) ~s** un short; ~**-sighted** adj (BRIT) myope; (fig) qui manque de clairvoyance; ~**-staffed** adj à court de personnel; ~ **stay** adj (car park) de courte durée; ~ **story** n nouvelle f; ~**-tempered** adj qui s'emporte facilement; ~**-term** adj (effect) à court terme; ~ **wave** n (RADIO) ondes courtes

shot [ʃɒt] pt, pp of **shoot** ♦ n coup m (de feu); (try) coup, essai m; (injection) piqûre f; (PHOT) photo f; **he's a good/poor ~** il tire bien/mal; **like a ~** comme une flèche; (very readily) sans hésiter; ~**gun** n fusil m de chasse

should [ʃʊd] aux vb: **I ~ go now** je devrais partir maintenant; **he ~ be there now** il devrait être arrivé maintenant; **I ~ go if I were you** si j'étais vous, j'irais; **I ~ like to** j'aimerais bien, volontiers

shoulder ['ʃəuldər] n épaule f ♦ vt (fig) endosser, se charger de; ~ **bag** n sac m à bandoulière; ~ **blade** n omoplate f

shouldn't ['ʃudnt] = should not

shout [ʃaut] n cri m ♦ vt crier ♦ vi (also: ~ **out**) crier, pousser des cris; ~ **down** vt huer; ~**ing** n cris mpl

shove [ʃʌv] vt pousser; (inf: put): **to** ~ **sth in** fourrer or ficher qch dans; ~ **off** (inf) vi ficher le camp

shovel ['ʃʌvl] n pelle f

show [ʃəu] (pt showed, pp shown) n (of emotion) manifestation f, démonstration f; (semblance) semblant m, apparence f; (exhibition) exposition f, salon m; (THEATRE, TV) spectacle m ♦ vt montrer; (film) donner; (courage etc) faire preuve de, manifester; (exhibit) exposer ♦ vi se voir, être visible; **for** ~ pour l'effet; **on** ~ (exhibits etc) exposé(e); ~ **in** vt (person) faire entrer; ~ **off** vi (pej) crâner ♦ vt (display) faire valoir; ~ **out** vt (person) reconduire (jusqu'à la porte); ~ **up** vi (stand out) ressortir; (inf: turn up) se montrer ♦ vt (flaw) faire ressortir; ~ **business** n le monde du spectacle; ~**down** n épreuve f de force

shower ['ʃauər] n (rain) averse f; (of stones etc) pluie f, grêle f; (~bath) douche f ♦ vi prendre une douche, se doucher ♦ vt: **to** ~ **sb with** (gifts etc) combler qn de; **to have** or **take a** ~ prendre une douche; ~**proof** adj imperméabilisé(e)

showing ['ʃəuɪŋ] n (of film) projection f

show jumping [-dʒʌmpɪŋ] n concours m hippique

shown [ʃəun] pp of show

show: ~**-off** (inf) n (person) crâneur(-euse), m'as-tu-vu(e); ~**piece** n (of exhibition) trésor m; ~**room** n magasin m or salle f d'exposition

shrank [ʃræŋk] pt of shrink

shrapnel ['ʃræpnl] n éclats mpl d'obus

shred [ʃred] n (gen pl) lambeau m, petit morceau ♦ vt mettre en lambeaux, déchirer; (CULIN: grate) râper; (: lettuce etc) couper en lanières; ~**der** n (for vegetables) râpeur m; (for documents) déchiqueteuse f

shrewd [ʃruːd] adj astucieux(-euse), perspicace; (businessman) habile

shriek [ʃriːk] vi hurler, crier

shrill [ʃrɪl] adj perçant(e), aigu(-guë), strident(e)

shrimp [ʃrɪmp] n crevette f

shrine [ʃraɪn] n (place) lieu m de pèlerinage

shrink [ʃrɪŋk] (pt shrank, pp shrunk) vi rétrécir; (fig) se réduire, diminuer; (move: also: ~ **away**) reculer ♦ vt (wool) faire rétrécir ♦ n (inf: pej) psychiatre m/f, psy m/f; **to** ~ **from (doing) sth** reculer devant (la

pensée de faire) qch; ~**wrap** vt emballer sous film plastique

shrivel ['ʃrɪvl] vt (also: ~ **up**) ratatiner, flétrir ♦ vi se ratatiner, se flétrir

shroud [ʃraud] n linceul m ♦ vt: ~**ed in mystery** enveloppé(e) de mystère

Shrove Tuesday ['ʃrəuv-] n (le) Mardi gras

shrub [ʃrʌb] n arbuste m; ~**bery** n massif m d'arbustes

shrug [ʃrʌg] vt, vi: **to** ~ **(one's shoulders)** hausser les épaules; ~ **off** vt faire fi de

shrunk [ʃrʌŋk] pp of shrink

shudder ['ʃʌdər] vi frissonner, frémir

shuffle ['ʃʌfl] vt (cards) battre; **to** ~ **(one's feet)** traîner les pieds

shun [ʃʌn] vt éviter, fuir

shunt [ʃʌnt] vt (RAIL) aiguiller

shut [ʃʌt] (pt, pp shut) vt fermer ♦ vi (se) fermer; ~ **down** vt, vi fermer définitivement; ~ **off** vt couper, arrêter; ~ **up** vi (inf: keep quiet) se taire ♦ vt (close) fermer; (silence) faire taire; ~**ter** n volet m; (PHOT) obturateur m

shuttle ['ʃʌtl] n navette f; (also: ~ **service**) (service m de) navette f; ~**cock** n volant m (de badminton); ~ **diplomacy** n navettes fpl diplomatiques

shy [ʃaɪ] adj timide

Siberia [saɪ'bɪərɪə] n Sibérie f

Sicily ['sɪsɪlɪ] n Sicile f

sick [sɪk] adj (ill) malade; (vomiting): **to be** ~ vomir; (humour) noir(e), macabre; **to feel** ~ avoir envie de vomir, avoir mal au cœur; **to be** ~ **of** (fig) en avoir assez de; ~ **bay** n infirmerie f; ~**en** vt écœurer; ~**ening** adj (fig) écœurant(e), dégoûtant(e)

sickle ['sɪkl] n faucille f

sick: ~ **leave** n congé m de maladie; ~**ly** adj maladif(-ive), souffreteux(-euse); (causing nausea) écœurant(e); ~**ness** n maladie f; (vomiting) vomissement(s) m(pl); ~ **note** n (from parents) mot m d'absence; (from doctor) certificat médical; ~ **pay** n indemnité f de maladie

side [saɪd] n côté m; (of lake, road) bord m; (team) camp m, équipe f ♦ adj (door, entrance) latéral(e) ♦ vi: **to** ~ **with sb** prendre le parti de qn, se ranger du côté de qn; **by the** ~ **of** au bord de; ~ **by** ~ côte à côte; **from** ~ **to** ~ d'un côté à l'autre; **to take** ~**s (with)** prendre parti (pour); ~**board** n buffet m; ~**boards** (BRIT), ~**burns** npl (whiskers) pattes fpl; ~ **drum** n tambour plat; ~ **effect** n effet m secondaire; ~**light** n (AUT) veilleuse f; ~**line** n (SPORT) ligne f de) touche f; (fig) travail m secondaire; ~**long** adj oblique; ~**show** n attraction f; ~**step** vt (fig) éluder; éviter; ~ **street** n (petite) rue transversale; ~**track** vt (fig) faire dévier de son sujet; ~**walk** (US) n trottoir m; ~**ways** adv de côté

siding ['saɪdɪŋ] n (RAIL) voie f de garage
siege [siːdʒ] n siège m
sieve [sɪv] n tamis m, passoire f
sift [sɪft] vt (fig: also: ~ **through**) passer en revue; (lit: flour etc) passer au tamis
sigh [saɪ] n soupir m ♦ vi soupirer, pousser un soupir
sight [saɪt] n (faculty) vue f; (spectacle) spectacle m; (on gun) mire f ♦ vt apercevoir; **in ~** visible; **out of ~** hors de vue; **~seeing** n tourisme m; **to go ~seeing** faire du tourisme
sign [saɪn] n signe m; (with hand etc) signe, geste m; (notice) panneau m, écriteau m ♦ vt signer; **~ on** vi (as unemployed) s'inscrire au chômage; (for course) s'inscrire ♦ vt (employee) embaucher; **~ over** vt: **to ~ sth over to sb** céder qch par écrit à qn; **~ up** vt engager ♦ vi (MIL) s'engager; (for course) s'inscrire
signal ['sɪɡnl] n signal m ♦ vi (AUT) mettre son clignotant ♦ vt (person) faire signe à; (message) communiquer par signaux; **~man** (irreg) n (RAIL) aiguilleur m
signature ['sɪɡnətʃər] n signature f; **~ tune** n indicatif musical
signet ring ['sɪɡnət-] n chevalière f
significance [sɪɡ'nɪfɪkəns] n signification f; importance f
significant [sɪɡ'nɪfɪkənt] adj significatif(-ive); (important) important(e), considérable
sign language n langage m per signes
signpost ['saɪnpəʊst] n poteau indicateur
silence ['saɪləns] n silence m ♦ vt faire taire, réduire au silence; **~r** n (on gun, BRIT: AUT) silencieux m
silent ['saɪlənt] adj silencieux(-euse); (film) muet(te); **to remain ~** garder le silence, ne rien dire; **~ partner** n (COMM) bailleur m de fonds, commanditaire m
silhouette [sɪlu:'et] n silhouette f
silicon chip ['sɪlɪkən-] n puce f électronique
silk [sɪlk] n soie f ♦ cpd de or en soie; **~y** adj soyeux(-euse)
silly ['sɪlɪ] adj stupide, sot(te), bête
silt [sɪlt] n vase f; limon m
silver ['sɪlvər] n argent m; (money) monnaie f (en pièces d'argent); (also: **~ware**) argenterie f ♦ adj d'argent, en argent; **~ paper** (BRIT) n papier m d'argent or d'étain; **~-plated** adj plaqué(e) argent inv; **~smith** n orfèvre m/f; **~y** adj argenté(e)
similar ['sɪmɪlər] adj: **~ (to)** semblable (à); **~ly** adv de la même façon, de même
simmer ['sɪmər] vi cuire à feu doux, mijoter
simple ['sɪmpl] adj simple; **simplicity** [sɪm'plɪsɪtɪ] n simplicité f; **simply** adv (without fuss) avec simplicité
simultaneous [sɪməl'teɪnɪəs] adj simultané(e)

sin [sɪn] n péché m ♦ vi pécher
since [sɪns] adv, prep depuis ♦ conj (time) depuis que; (because) puisque, étant donné que, comme; **~ then, ever ~** depuis ce moment-là
sincere [sɪn'sɪər] adj sincère; **~ly** adv see yours; **sincerity** [sɪn'serɪtɪ] n sincérité f
sinew ['sɪnjuː] n tendon m
sing [sɪŋ] (pt **sang**, pp **sung**) vt, vi chanter
Singapore [sɪŋɡə'pɔːr] n Singapour m
singe [sɪndʒ] vt brûler légèrement; (clothes) roussir
singer ['sɪŋər] n chanteur(-euse)
singing ['sɪŋɪŋ] n chant m
single ['sɪŋɡl] adj seul(e), unique; (unmarried) célibataire; (not double) simple ♦ n (BRIT: also: **~ ticket**) aller m (simple); (record) 45 tours m; **~ out** vt choisir; (distinguish) distinguer; **~ bed** n lit m d'une personne; **~-breasted** adj droit(e); **~ file** n: **in ~ file** en file indienne; **~-handed** adv tout(e) seul(e), sans (aucune) aide; **~-minded** adj résolu(e), tenace; **~ parent** n parent m unique; **~ room** n chambre f à un lit or pour une personne; **~s** n (TENNIS) simple m; **~-track road** n route f à voie unique; **singly** adv séparément
singular ['sɪŋɡjulər] adj singulier(-ère), étrange; (outstanding) remarquable, (LING) (au) singulier, du singulier ♦ n singulier m
sinister ['sɪnɪstər] adj sinistre
sink [sɪŋk] (pt **sank**, pp **sunk**) n évier m ♦ vt (ship) (faire) couler, faire sombrer; (foundations) creuser ♦ vi couler, sombrer; (ground etc) s'affaisser; (also: **~ back, ~ down**) s'affaisser, se laisser retomber; **to ~ sth into** enfoncer qch dans; **my heart sank** j'ai complètement perdu courage; **~ in** vi (fig) pénétrer, être compris(e)
sinner ['sɪnər] n pécheur(-eresse)
sinus ['saɪnəs] n sinus m inv
sip [sɪp] n gorgée f ♦ vt boire à petites gorgées
siphon ['saɪfən] n siphon m; **~ off** vt siphonner; (money: illegally) détourner
sir [sər] n monsieur m; **S~ John Smith** sir John Smith; **yes ~** oui, Monsieur
siren ['saɪərn] n sirène f
sirloin ['səːlɔɪn] n (also: **~ steak**) aloyau m
sissy ['sɪsɪ] (inf) n (coward) poule mouillée
sister ['sɪstər] n sœur f; (nun) religieuse f, sœur; (BRIT: nurse) infirmière f en chef; **~-in-law** n belle-sœur f
sit [sɪt] (pt, pp **sat**) vi s'asseoir; (be ~ting) être assis(e); (assembly) être en séance, siéger; (for painter) poser ♦ vt (exam) passer, se présenter à; **~ down** vi s'asseoir; **~ in on** vt fus assister à; **~ up** vi s'asseoir; (straight) se redresser; (not go to bed) rester debout, ne pas se coucher

sitcom ['sɪtkɔm] n abbr (= situation comedy) comédie f de situation

site [saɪt] n emplacement m, site m; (also: **building ~**) chantier m ♦ vt placer

sit-in ['sɪtɪn] n (demonstration) sit-in m inv, occupation f (de locaux)

sitting ['sɪtɪŋ] n (of assembly etc) séance f; (in canteen) service m; **~ room** n salon m

situated ['sɪtjueɪtɪd] adj situé(e)

situation [sɪtju'eɪʃən] n situation f; **"~s vacant"** (BRIT) "offres d'emploi"

six [sɪks] num six; **~teen** num seize; **~th** num sixième; **~ty** num soixante

size [saɪz] n taille f; dimensions fpl; (of clothing) taille; (of shoes) pointure f; (fig) ampleur f; (glue) colle f; **~ up** vt juger, jauger; **~able** adj assez grand(e); assez important(e)

sizzle ['sɪzl] vi grésiller

skate [skeɪt] n patin m; (fish: pl inv) raie f ♦ vi patiner; **~board** n skateboard m, planche f à roulettes; **~boarding** n skateboard m; **~r** n patineur(-euse); **skating** n patinage m; **skating rink** n patinoire f

skeleton ['skelɪtn] n squelette m; (outline) schéma m; **~ staff** n effectifs réduits

skeptical ['skeptɪkl] (US) adj = **sceptical**

sketch [sketʃ] n (drawing) croquis m, esquisse f; (THEATRE) sketch m, saynète f ♦ vt esquisser, faire un croquis or une esquisse de; **~ book** n carnet m à dessin; **~y** adj incomplet(-ète), fragmentaire

skewer ['skjuːər] n brochette f

ski [skiː] n ski m ♦ vi skier, faire du ski; **~ boot** n chaussure f de ski

skid [skɪd] vi déraper

ski: **~er** n skieur(-euse); **~ing** n ski m; **~ jump** n saut m à skis

skilful ['skɪlful] (US **skillful**) adj habile, adroit(e)

ski lift n remonte-pente m inv

skill [skɪl] n habileté f, adresse f, talent m; (requiring training: gen pl) compétences fpl; **~ed** adj habile, adroit(e); (worker) qualifié(e)

skim [skɪm] vt (milk) écrémer; (glide over) raser, effleurer ♦ vi: **to ~ through** (fig) parcourir; **~med milk** n lait écrémé

skimp [skɪmp] vt (also: **~ on**: work) bâcler, faire à la va-vite; (: cloth etc) lésiner sur; **~y** adj (skirt) étriqué(e)

skin [skɪn] n peau f ♦ vt (fruit etc) éplucher; (animal) écorcher; **~ cancer** n cancer m de la peau; **~-deep** adj superficiel(le); **~-diving** n plongée sous-marine; **~head** n skinhead m/f; **~ny** adj maigre, maigrichon(ne); **~tight** adj (jeans etc) moulant(e), ajusté(e)

skip [skɪp] n petit bond or saut; (BRIT: container) benne f ♦ vi gambader, sautiller; (with rope) sauter à la corde ♦ vt sauter

ski pass n forfait-skieur(s) m

ski pole n bâton m de ski

skipper ['skɪpər] n capitaine m; (in race) skipper m

skipping rope ['skɪpɪŋ-] (BRIT) n corde f à sauter

skirmish ['skɜːmɪʃ] n escarmouche f, accrochage m

skirt [skɜːt] n jupe f ♦ vt longer, contourner; **~ing board** (BRIT) n plinthe f

ski: **~ slope** n piste f de ski; **~ suit** n combinaison f (de ski); **~ tow** n remonte-pente m inv

skittle ['skɪtl] n quille f; **~s** n (game) (jeu m de) quilles fpl

skive [skaɪv] (BRIT: inf) vi tirer au flanc

skull [skʌl] n crâne m

skunk [skʌŋk] n mouffette f

sky [skaɪ] n ciel m; **~light** n lucarne f; **~scraper** n gratte-ciel m inv

slab [slæb] n (of stone) dalle f; (of food) grosse tranche

slack [slæk] adj (loose) lâche, desserré(e); (slow) stagnant(e); (careless) négligent(e), peu sérieux(-euse) or consciencieux(-euse); **~s** npl (trousers) pantalon m; **~en** vi ralentir, diminuer ♦ vt (speed) réduire; (grip) relâcher; (clothing) desserrer

slag heap [slæg-] n crassier m

slag off (BRIT: inf) vt dire du mal de

slam [slæm] vt (door) (faire) claquer; (throw) jeter violemment, flanquer (fam); (criticize) démolir ♦ vi claquer

slander ['slɑːndər] n calomnie f; diffamation f

slang [slæŋ] n argot m

slant [slɑːnt] n inclinaison f; (fig) angle m, point m de vue; **~ed** adj = **slanting**; **~ing** adj en pente, incliné(e); **~ing eyes** yeux bridés

slap [slæp] n claque f, gifle f; tape f ♦ vt donner une claque or une gifle or une tape à; (paint) appliquer rapidement ♦ adv (directly) tout droit, en plein; **~dash** adj fait(e) sans soin or à la va-vite; (person) insouciant(e), négligent(e); **~stick** n (comedy) grosse farce, style m tarte à la crème; **~-up** (BRIT) adj: **a ~-up meal** un repas extra or fameux

slash [slæʃ] vt entailler, taillader; (fig: prices) casser

slat [slæt] n latte f, lame f

slate [sleɪt] n ardoise f ♦ vt (fig: criticize) éreinter, démolir

slaughter ['slɔːtər] n carnage m, massacre m ♦ vt (animal) abattre; (people) massacrer; **~house** n abattoir m

slave [sleɪv] n esclave m/f ♦ vi (also: **~ away**) trimer, travailler comme un forçat; **~ry** n esclavage m

slay [sleɪ] (pt **slew**, pp **slain**) vt tuer

sleazy ['sliːzɪ] adj miteux(-euse), minable

sledge [slɛdʒ] n luge f ♦ vi: **to go sledging** faire de la luge

sledgehammer ['slɛdʒhæmər] n marteau m de forgeron

sleek [sliːk] adj (hair, fur etc) brillant(e), lisse; (car, boat etc) aux lignes pures or élégantes

sleep [sliːp] (pt, pp **slept**) n sommeil m ♦ vi dormir; (spend night) dormir, coucher; **to go to ~** s'endormir; **~ around** vi coucher à droite et à gauche; **~ in** vi (oversleep) se réveiller trop tard; **~er** (BRIT) n (RAIL: train) train-couchettes m; (: berth) couchette f; **~ing bag** n sac m de couchage; **~ing car** n (RAIL) wagon-lit m, voiture-lit f; **~ing partner** (BRIT) n = **silent partner**; **~ing pill** n somnifère m; **~less** adj: **a ~less night** une nuit blanche; **~walker** n somnambule m/f; **~y** adj qui a sommeil; (fig) endormi(e)

sleet [sliːt] n neige fondue

sleeve [sliːv] n manche f; (of record) pochette f

sleigh [sleɪ] n traîneau m

sleight [slaɪt] n: **~ of hand** tour m de passe-passe

slender ['slɛndər] adj svelte, mince; (fig) faible, ténu(e)

slept [slɛpt] pt, pp of **sleep**

slew [sluː] vi (also: **~ around**) virer, pivoter ♦ pt of **slay**

slice [slaɪs] n tranche f; (round) rondelle f; (utensil) spatule f, truelle f ♦ vt couper en tranches (or en rondelles)

slick [slɪk] adj (skilful) brillant(e) (en apparence); (salesman) qui a du bagout ♦ n (also: **oil ~**) nappe f de pétrole, marée noire

slide [slaɪd] (pt, pp **slid**) n (in playground) toboggan m; (PHOT) diapositive f; (BRIT: also: **hair ~**) barrette f; (in prices) chute f, baisse f ♦ vt (faire) glisser ♦ vi glisser; **sliding** adj (door) coulissant(e); **sliding scale** n échelle f mobile

slight [slaɪt] adj (slim) mince, menu(e); (frail) frêle; (trivial) faible, insignifiant(e); (small) petit(e), léger(-ère) (before n) ♦ n offense f, affront m; **not in the ~est** pas le moins du monde, pas du tout; **~ly** adv légèrement, un peu

slim [slɪm] adj mince ♦ vi maigrir; (diet) suivre un régime amaigrissant

slime [slaɪm] n (mud) vase f; (other substance) substance visqueuse

slimming ['slɪmɪŋ] adj (diet, pills) amaigrissant(e); (foodstuff) qui ne fait pas grossir

sling [slɪŋ] (pt, pp **slung**) n (MED) écharpe f; (for baby) porte-bébé m; (weapon) fronde f, lance-pierre m ♦ vt lancer, jeter

slip [slɪp] n faux pas; (mistake) erreur f; étourderie f; (underskirt) combinaison f; (of paper) petite feuille, fiche f ♦ vt (slide) glisser ♦ vi glisser; (decline) baisser; (move smoothly): **to ~ into/out of** se glisser or se faufiler dans/hors de; **to ~ sth on/off** enfiler/enlever qch; **to give sb the ~** fausser compagnie à qn; **a ~ of the tongue** un lapsus; **~ away** vi s'esquiver; **~ in** vt glisser ♦ vi (errors) s'y glisser; **~ out** vi sortir; **~ up** vi faire une erreur, gaffer; **~ped disc** n déplacement m de vertèbre

slipper ['slɪpər] n pantoufle f

slippery ['slɪpərɪ] adj glissant(e)

slip: **~ road** (BRIT) n (to motorway) bretelle f d'accès; **~-up** n bévue f; **~way** n cale f (de construction or de lancement)

slit [slɪt] (pt, pp **slit**) n fente f; (cut) incision f ♦ vt fendre; couper; inciser

slither ['slɪðər] vi glisser; (snake) onduler

sliver ['slɪvər] n (of glass, wood) éclat m; (of cheese etc) petit morceau, fine tranche

slob [slɔb] (inf) n rustaud(e)

slog [slɔg] (BRIT) vi travailler très dur ♦ n gros effort; tâche fastidieuse

slogan ['sləugən] n slogan m

slope [sləup] n pente f, côte f; (side of mountain) versant m; (slant) inclinaison f ♦ vi: **to ~ down** être or descendre en pente; **to ~ up** monter; **sloping** adj en pente; (writing) penché(e)

sloppy ['slɔpɪ] adj (work) peu soigné(e), bâclé(e); (appearance) négligé(e), débraillé(e)

slot [slɔt] n fente f ♦ vt: **to ~ sth into** encastrer or insérer qch dans

sloth [sləuθ] n (laziness) paresse f

slouch [slautʃ] vi avoir le dos rond, être voûté(e)

slovenly ['slʌvənlɪ] adj sale, débraillé(e); (work) négligé(e)

slow [sləu] adj lent(e); (watch): **to be ~** retarder ♦ adv lentement ♦ vt, vi (also: **~ down, ~ up**) ralentir; **"~"** (road sign) "ralentir"; **~ly** adv lentement; **~ motion** n: **in ~ motion** au ralenti

sludge [slʌdʒ] n boue f

slug [slʌg] n limace f; (bullet) balle f

sluggish ['slʌgɪʃ] adj (person) mou (molle), lent(e); (stream, engine, trading) lent

sluice [sluːs] n (also: **~ gate**) vanne f

slum [slʌm] n (house) taudis m

slump [slʌmp] n baisse soudaine, effondrement m; (ECON) crise f ♦ vi s'effondrer, s'affaisser

slung [slʌŋ] pt, pp of **sling**

slur [sləːr] n (fig: smear): **~ (on)** atteinte f (à); insinuation f (contre) ♦ vt mal articuler

slush [slʌʃ] n neige fondue

slut [slʌt] (pej) n souillon f

sly [slaɪ] adj (person) rusé(e); (smile, expression, remark) sournois(e)

smack [smæk] n (slap) tape f; (on face) gifle f
♦ vt donner une tape à; (on face) gifler; (on
bottom) donner la fessée à ♦ vi: **to ~ of** avoir
des relents de, sentir

small [smɔːl] adj petit(e); **~ ads** (BRIT) npl
petites annonces; **~ change** n petite or
menue monnaie; **~holder** (BRIT) n petit
cultivateur; **~ hours** npl: **in the ~ hours** au
petit matin; **~pox** n variole f; **~ talk** n
menus propos

smart [smɑːt] adj (neat, fashionable)
élégant(e), chic inv; (clever) intelligent(e),
astucieux(-euse), futé(e); (quick) rapide, vif
(vive), prompt(e) ♦ vi faire mal, brûler; (fig)
être piqué(e) au vif; **~ card** n carte f à puce;
~en up vi devenir plus élégant(e), se faire
beau (belle) ♦ vt rendre plus élégant(e)

smash [smæʃ] n (also: **~-up**) collision f,
accident m; (also: **~ hit**) succès foudroyant
♦ vt casser, briser, fracasser; (opponent)
écraser; (SPORT: record) pulvériser ♦ vi se
briser, se fracasser; s'écraser; **~ing** (inf) adj
formidable

smattering ['smætərɪŋ] n: **a ~ of** quelques
notions de

smear [smɪəʳ] n tache f, salissure f; trace f;
(MED) frottis m ♦ vt enduire; (make dirty)
salir; **~ campaign** n campagne f de
diffamation

smell [smɛl] (pt, pp **smelt** or **smelled**) n odeur
f; (sense) odorat m ♦ vt sentir ♦ vi (food etc):
to ~ (of) sentir (de); (pej) sentir mauvais; **~y**
adj qui sent mauvais, malodorant(e)

smile [smaɪl] n sourire m ♦ vi sourire

smirk [smɜːk] n petit sourire suffisant or
affecté

smock [smɔk] n blouse f

smog [smɔg] n brouillard mêlé de fumée,
smog m

smoke [sməuk] n fumée f ♦ vt, vi fumer; **~d**
adj (bacon, glass) fumé(e); **~r** n (person)
fumeur(-euse); (RAIL) wagon m fumeurs;
~ screen n rideau m or écran m de fumée;
(fig) paravent m; **smoking** n tabagisme m;
"no smoking" (sign) "défense de fumer"; **to
give up smoking** arrêter de fumer; **smoking
compartment** (US **smoking car**) n wagon m
fumeurs; **smoky** adj enfumé(e); (taste)
fumé(e)

smolder ['sməuldəʳ] (US) vi = **smoulder**

smooth [smuːð] adj lisse; (sauce) onctu-
eux(-euse), (flavour, whisky) moelleux(-euse);
(movement) régulier(-ère), sans à-coups or
heurts; (pej: person) doucereux(-euse),
mielleux(-euse) ♦ vt (also: **~ out**: skirt, paper)
lisser, défroisser; (: creases, difficulties) faire
disparaître

smother ['smʌðəʳ] vt étouffer

smoulder ['sməuldəʳ] (US **smolder**) vi couver

smudge [smʌdʒ] n tache f, bavure f ♦ vt
salir, maculer

smug [smʌg] adj suffisant(e)

smuggle ['smʌgl] vt passer en contrebande
or en fraude; **~r** n contrebandier(-ère);
smuggling n contrebande f

smutty ['smʌtɪ] adj (fig) grossier(-ère),
obscène

snack [snæk] n casse-croûte m inv; **~ bar** n
snack(-bar) m

snag [snæg] n inconvénient m, difficulté f

snail [sneɪl] n escargot m

snake [sneɪk] n serpent m

snap [snæp] n (sound) claquement m, bruit
sec; (photograph) photo f, instantané m ♦ adj
subit(e); fait(e) sans réfléchir ♦ vt (break)
casser net; (fingers) faire claquer ♦ vi se
casser net or avec un bruit sec; (speak
sharply) parler d'un ton brusque; **to ~ shut** se
refermer brusquement; **~ at** vt fus (subj: dog)
essayer de mordre; **~ off** vi (break) casser
net; **~ up** vt sauter sur, saisir; **~py** (inf) adj
prompt(e); (slogan) qui a du punch; **make it
~py!** grouille-toi, et que ça saute!; **~shot** n
photo f, instantané m

snare [snɛəʳ] n piège m

snarl [snɑːl] vi gronder

snatch [snætʃ] n (small amount): **~es of** des
fragments mpl or bribes fpl de ♦ vt saisir (d'un
geste vif); (steal) voler

sneak [sniːk] vi: **to ~ in/out** entrer/sortir
furtivement or à la dérobée ♦ n (inf: pej:
informer) faux jeton; **to ~ up on sb**
s'approcher de qn sans faire de bruit; **~ers**
npl tennis mpl, baskets mpl

sneer [snɪəʳ] vi ricaner; **to ~ at** traiter avec
mépris

sneeze [sniːz] vi éternuer

sniff [snɪf] vi renifler ♦ vt renifler, flairer; (glue,
drugs) sniffer, respirer

snigger ['snɪgəʳ] vi ricaner; pouffer de rire

snip [snɪp] n (cut) petit coup; (BRIT: inf:
bargain) (bonne) occasion or affaire f ♦ vt
couper

sniper ['snaɪpəʳ] n tireur embusqué

snippet ['snɪpɪt] n bribe(s) f(pl)

snob [snɔb] n snob m/f; **~bish** adj snob inv

snooker ['snuːkəʳ] n sorte de jeu de billard

snoop [snuːp] vi: **to ~ about** fureter

snooze [snuːz] n petit somme ♦ vi faire un
petit somme

snore [snɔːʳ] vi ronfler

snorkel ['snɔːkl] n (of swimmer) tuba m

snort [snɔːt] vi grogner; (horse) renâcler

snout [snaut] n museau m

snow [snəu] n neige f ♦ vi neiger; **~ball** n
boule f de neige; **~bound** adj enneigé(e),
bloqué(e) par la neige; **~drift** n congère f;
~drop n perce-neige m or f; **~fall** n chute f

de neige; **~flake** n flocon m de neige; **~man** (*irreg*) n bonhomme m de neige; **~plough** (*US* **snowplow**) n chasse-neige m inv; **~shoe** n raquette f (*pour la neige*); **~storm** n tempête f de neige

snub [snʌb] vt repousser, snober ♦ n rebuffade f; **~-nosed** adj au nez retroussé

snuff [snʌf] n tabac m à priser

snug [snʌg] adj douillet(te), confortable; (*person*) bien au chaud

snuggle [ˈsnʌgl] vi: **to ~ up to sb** se serrer or se blottir contre qn

---
KEYWORD
---

so [səu] adv 1 (*thus, likewise*) ainsi; **if so** oui; **so do** or **have I** moi aussi; **it's 5 o'clock – so it is!** il est 5 heures – en effet! or c'est vrai!; **I hope/think so** je l'espère/le crois; **so far** jusqu'ici, jusqu'à maintenant; (*in past*) jusque-là

2 (*in comparisons etc: to such a degree*) si, tellement; **so big (that)** si or tellement grand (que); **she's not so clever as her brother** elle n'est pas aussi intelligente que son frère

3: **so much** ♦ adj, adv tant (de); **I've got so much work** j'ai tant de travail; **I love you so much** je vous aime tant; **so many** tant (de)

4 (*phrases*): **10 or so** à peu près or environ 10; **so long!** (*inf*: *goodbye*) au revoir!, à un de ces jours!

♦ conj 1 (*expressing purpose*): **so as to do** pour faire, afin de faire; **so (that)** pour que or afin que +*sub*

2 (*expressing result*) donc, par conséquent; **so that** si bien que, de (telle) sorte que

soak [səuk] vt faire tremper; (*drench*) tremper ♦ vi tremper; **~ in** vi être absorbé(e); **~ up** vt absorber; **~ing** adj trempé(e)

soap [səup] n savon m; **~flakes** npl paillettes fpl de savon; **~ opera** n feuilleton télévisé; **~ powder** n lessive f; **~y** adj savonneux(-euse)

soar [sɔːr] vi monter (en flèche), s'élancer; (*building*) s'élancer

sob [sɔb] n sanglot m ♦ vi sangloter

sober [ˈsəubər] adj qui n'est pas (or plus) ivre; (*serious*) sérieux(-euse), sensé(e); (*colour, style*) sobre, discret(-ète); **~ up** vt dessoûler (*inf*) ♦ vi dessoûler (*inf*)

so-called [ˈsəuˈkɔːld] adj soi-disant inv

soccer [ˈsɔkər] n football m

social [ˈsəuʃl] adj social(e); (*sociable*) sociable ♦ n (*petite*) fête; **~ club** n amicale f, foyer m; **~ism** n socialisme m; **~ist** adj socialiste ♦ n socialiste m/f; **~ize** vi: **to ~ize (with)** lier connaissance (avec); parler (avec); **~ security** (*BRIT*) n aide sociale; **~ work** n

assistance sociale, travail social; **~ worker** n assistant(e) social(e)

society [səˈsaɪətɪ] n société f; (*club*) société, association f; (*also*: **high ~**) (haute) société, grand monde

sociology [səusɪˈɔlədʒɪ] n sociologie f

sock [sɔk] n chaussette f

socket [ˈsɔkɪt] n cavité f; (*BRIT: ELEC: also*: **wall ~**) prise f de courant

sod [sɔd] n (*of earth*) motte f; (*BRIT: inf!*) con m (!); salaud m (!)

soda [ˈsəudə] n (*CHEM*) soude f; (*also*: **~ water**) eau f de Seltz; (*US: also*: **~ pop**) soda m

sofa [ˈsəufə] n sofa m, canapé m

soft [sɔft] adj (*not rough*) doux (douce); (*not hard*) doux (mou (molle)); (*not loud*) doux, léger(-ère); (*kind*) doux, gentil(le); **~ drink** n boisson non alcoolisée; **~en** vt (r)amollir; (*fig*) adoucir; atténuer ♦ vi se ramollir; s'adoucir; s'atténuer; **~ly** adv doucement; gentiment; **~ness** n douceur f; **~ware** n (*COMPUT*) logiciel m, software m

soggy [ˈsɔgɪ] adj trempé(e), détrempé(e)

soil [sɔɪl] n (*earth*) sol m, terre f ♦ vt salir; (*fig*) souiller

solar [ˈsəulər] adj solaire; **~ panel** n panneau m solaire; **~ power** n énergie solaire

sold [səuld] pt, pp of **sell**

solder [ˈsəuldər] vt souder (*au fil à souder*) ♦ n soudure f

soldier [ˈsəuldʒər] n soldat m, militaire m

sole [səul] n (*of foot*) plante f; (*of shoe*) semelle f; (*fish: pl inv*) sole f ♦ adj seul(e), unique

solemn [ˈsɔləm] adj solennel(le); (*person*) sérieux(-euse), grave

sole trader n (*COMM*) chef m d'entreprise individuelle

solicit [səˈlɪsɪt] vt (*request*) solliciter ♦ vi (*prostitute*) racoler

solicitor [səˈlɪsɪtər] n (*for wills etc*) ≈ notaire m; (*in court*) ≈ avocat m

solid [ˈsɔlɪd] adj solide; (*not hollow*) plein(e), compact(e), massif(-ive); (*entire*): **3 ~ hours** 3 heures entières ♦ n solide m

solidarity [sɔlɪˈdærɪtɪ] n solidarité f

solitary [ˈsɔlɪtərɪ] adj solitaire; **~ confinement** n (*LAW*) isolement m

solo [ˈsəuləu] n solo m ♦ adv (*fly*) en solitaire; **~ist** n soliste m/f

soluble [ˈsɔljubl] adj soluble

solution [səˈluːʃən] n solution f

solve [sɔlv] vt résoudre

solvent [ˈsɔlvənt] adj (*COMM*) solvable ♦ n (*CHEM*) (dis)solvant m

---
KEYWORD
---

some [sʌm] adj 1 (*a certain amount or number of*): **some tea/water/ice cream** du

thé/de l'eau/de la glace; some **children/
apples** des enfants/pommes
2 (*certain: in contrasts*): **some people say that
...** il y a des gens qui disent que ...; **some
films were excellent, but most ...** certains films
étaient excellents, mais la plupart ...
3 (*unspecified*): **some woman was asking for
you** il y avait une dame qui vous demandait;
he was asking for some book (or other) il
demandait un livre quelconque; **some day** un
de ces jours; **some day next week** un jour la
semaine prochaine
♦ *pron* **1** (*a certain number*) quelques-un(e)s,
certain(e)s; **I've got some** (*books etc*) j'en ai
(quelques-uns); **some (of them) have been
sold** certains ont été vendus
2 (*a certain amount*) un peu; **I've got some**
(*money, milk*) j'en ai (un peu)
♦ *adv*: **some** 10 **people** quelque 10 personnes,
10 personnes environ

some: **~body** ['sʌmbədɪ] *pron* = **someone**;
~how *adv* d'une façon ou d'une autre; (*for
some reason*) pour une raison ou une autre;
~one *pron* quelqu'un; **~place** (*US*) *adv*
= **somewhere**
somersault ['sʌməsɔːlt] *n* culbute *f*, saut
périlleux ♦ *vi* faire la culbute *or* un saut
périlleux; (*car*) faire un tonneau
some: **~thing** *pron* quelque chose; **~thing
interesting** quelque chose d'intéressant;
~time *adv* (*in future*) un de ces jours, un
jour ou l'autre; (*in past*): **~time last month** au
cours du mois dernier; **~times** *adv*
quelquefois, parfois; **~what** *adv* quelque
peu, un peu; **~where** *adv* quelque part
son [sʌn] *n* fils *m*
song [sɒŋ] *n* chanson *f*; (*of bird*) chant *m*
son-in-law ['sʌnɪnlɔː] *n* gendre *m*, beau-fils
m
soon [suːn] *adv* bientôt; (*early*) tôt;
~ afterwards peu après; *see also as*; **~er** *adv*
(*time*) plus tôt; (*preference*): **I would ~er do**
j'aimerais autant *or* je préférerais faire; **~er or
later** tôt ou tard
soot [sut] *n* suie *f*
soothe [suːð] *vt* calmer, apaiser
sophisticated [sə'fɪstɪkeɪtɪd] *adj* raffiné(e);
sophistiqué(e); (*machinery*) hautement
perfectionné(e), très complexe
sophomore ['sɒfəmɔːʳ] (*US*) *n* étudiant(e)
de seconde année
sopping ['sɒpɪŋ] *adj* (*also:* **~ wet**)
complètement trempé(e)
soppy ['sɒpɪ] (*pej*) *adj* sentimental(e)
soprano [sə'prɑːnəʊ] *n* (*singer*) soprano
m/f
sorcerer ['sɔːsərəʳ] *n* sorcier *m*
sore [sɔːʳ] *adj* (*painful*) douloureux(-euse),

sensible ♦ *n* plaie *f*; **~ly** ['sɔːlɪ] *adv* (*tempted*)
fortement
sorrow ['sɒrəʊ] *n* peine *f*, chagrin *m*
sorry ['sɒrɪ] *adj* désolé(e); (*condition, excuse*)
triste, déplorable; **~!** pardon!, excusez-moi!;
~? pardon?; **to feel ~ for sb** plaindre qn
sort [sɔːt] *n* genre *m*, espèce *f*, sorte *f* ♦ *vt*
(*also:* **~ out**) trier; classer; ranger; (: *problems*) résoudre, régler; **~ing office** ['sɔːtɪŋ-]
n bureau *m* de tri
SOS *n* S.O.S. *m*
so-so ['səʊsəʊ] *adv* comme ci comme ça
sought [sɔːt] *pt, pp of* **seek**
soul [səʊl] *n* âme *f*; **~ful** ['səʊlful] *adj*
sentimental(e); (*eyes*) expressif(-ive)
sound [saʊnd] *adj* (*healthy*) en bonne santé,
sain(e); (*safe, not damaged*) solide, en bon
état; (*reliable, not superficial*) sérieux(-euse),
solide; (*sensible*) sensé(e) ♦ *adv*: **~ asleep**
profondément endormi(e) ♦ *n* son *m*; bruit
m; (*GEO*) détroit *m*, bras *m* de mer ♦ *vt*
(*alarm*) sonner ♦ *vi* sonner, retentir; (*fig:
seem*) sembler (être); **to ~ like** ressembler à;
~ out *vt* sonder; **~ barrier** *n* mur *m* du son;
~ bite *n* phrase *f* toute faite (*pour être citée
dans les médias*); **~ effects** *npl* bruitage *m*;
~ly *adv* (*sleep*) profondément; (*beat*)
complètement, à plate couture; **~proof** *adj*
insonorisé(e); **~track** *n* (*of film*) bande *f*
sonore
soup [suːp] *n* soupe *f*, potage *m*; **~ plate** *n*
assiette creuse *or* à soupe; **~spoon** *n* cuiller *f*
à soupe
sour ['saʊəʳ] *adj* aigre; **it's ~ grapes** (*fig*) c'est
du dépit
source [sɔːs] *n* source *f*
south [saʊθ] *n* sud *m* ♦ *adj* sud *inv*, du sud
♦ *adv* au sud, vers le sud; **S~ Africa** *n*
Afrique *f* du Sud; **S~ African** *adj* sud-
africain(e) ♦ *n* Sud-Africain(e); **S~ America**
n Amérique *f* du Sud; **S~ American** *adj*
sud-américain(e) ♦ *n* Sud-Américain(e); **~-
east** *n* sud-est *m*; **~erly** ['sʌðəlɪ] *adj* (*wind*)
au sud; **~ern** ['sʌðən] *adj* (du) sud; méridio-
nal(e); **S~ Pole** *n* Pôle *m* Sud; **S~ Wales** *n*
sud *m* du Pays de Galles; **~ward(s)** *adv* vers
le sud; **~-west** *n* sud-ouest *m*
souvenir [suːvə'nɪəʳ] *n* (*objet*) souvenir *m*
sovereign ['sɒvrɪn] *n* souverain(e)
soviet ['səʊvɪət] *adj* soviétique; **the S~ Union**
l'Union *f* soviétique
sow¹ [saʊ] *n* truie *f*
sow² [səʊ] (*pt* **sowed**, *pp* **sown**) *vt* semer
sown [səʊn] *pp of* **sow²**
soya ['sɔɪə] (*US* **soy**) *n*: **~ bean** graine *f* de soja;
soy(a) sauce sauce *f* au soja
spa [spɑː] *n* (*town*) station thermale; (*US: also:*
health ~) établissement *m* de cure de
rajeunissement *etc*

space [speɪs] n espace m; (room) place f; espace; (length of time) laps m de temps ♦ cpd spatial(e) ♦ vt (also: ~ out) espacer; **~craft** n engin spatial; **~man** (irreg) n astronaute m, cosmonaute m; **~ship** n = **spacecraft**; **spacing** n espacement m; **spacious** ['speɪʃəs] adj spacieux(-euse), grand(e)

spade [speɪd] n (tool) bêche f, pelle f; (child's) pelle; **~s** npl (CARDS) pique m

Spain [speɪn] n Espagne f

span [spæn] n (of bird, plane) envergure f; (of arch) portée f; (in time) espace m de temps, durée f ♦ vt enjamber, franchir; (fig) couvrir, embrasser

Spaniard ['spænjəd] n Espagnol(e)

spaniel ['spænjəl] n épagneul m

Spanish ['spænɪʃ] adj espagnol(e) ♦ n (LING) espagnol m; **the ~** npl les Espagnols mpl

spank [spæŋk] vt donner une fessée à

spanner ['spænər] n (BRIT) clé f (de mécanicien)

spare [spɛər] adj de réserve, de rechange; (surplus) de or en trop, de reste ♦ n (part) pièce f de rechange, pièce détachée ♦ vt (do without) se passer de; (afford to give) donner, accorder; (refrain from hurting) épargner; **to ~** (surplus) en surplus, de trop; **~ part** n pièce f de rechange, pièce détachée; **~ time** n moments mpl de loisir, temps m libre; **~ wheel** n (AUT) roue f de secours; **sparingly** adv avec modération

spark [spɑːk] n étincelle f; **~(ing) plug** n bougie f

sparkle ['spɑːkl] n scintillement m, éclat m ♦ vi étinceler, scintiller; **sparkling** adj (wine) mousseux(-euse), pétillant(e); (water) pétillant(e); (fig: conversation, performance) étincelant(e), pétillant(e)

sparrow ['spærəu] n moineau m

sparse [spɑːs] adj clairsemé(e)

spartan ['spɑːtən] adj (fig) spartiate

spasm ['spæzəm] n (MED) spasme m; **~odic** [spæz'mɔdɪk] adj (fig) intermittent(e)

spastic ['spæstɪk] n handicapé(e) moteur

spat [spæt] pt, pp of **spit**

spate [speɪt] n (fig): **a ~ of** une avalanche or un torrent de

spawn [spɔːn] vi frayer ♦ n frai m

speak [spiːk] (pt spoke, pp spoken) vt parler; (truth) dire ♦ vi parler; (make a speech) prendre la parole; **to ~ to sb/of or about sth** parler à qn/de qch; **~ up!** parle plus fort!; **~er** n (in public) orateur m; (also: loudspeaker) haut parleur m; **the S~er** (BRIT: POL) le président de la chambre des Communes; (US: POL) le président de la chambre des Représentants

spear [spɪər] n lance f ♦ vt transpercer;

~head vt (attack etc) mener

spec [spek] (inf) n: **on ~** à tout hasard

special ['speʃl] adj spécial(e); **~ist** n spécialiste m/f; **~ity** [speʃɪ'ælɪtɪ] n spécialité f; **~ize** vi: **to ~ize (in)** se spécialiser (dans); **~ly** adv spécialement, particulièrement; **~ty** (esp US) n = **speciality**

species ['spiːʃiːz] n inv espèce f

specific [spə'sɪfɪk] adj précis(e); particulier(-ère); (BOT, CHEM etc) spécifique; **~ally** adv expressément, explicitement; **~ation** [spesɪfɪ'keɪʃən] n (TECH) spécification f; (requirement) stipulation f

specimen ['spesɪmən] n spécimen m, échantillon m; (of blood) prélèvement m

speck [spek] n petite tache, petit point; (particle) grain m

speckled ['spekld] adj tacheté(e), moucheté(e)

specs [speks] (inf) npl lunettes fpl

spectacle ['spektəkl] n spectacle m; **~s** npl (glasses) lunettes fpl; **spectacular** [spek'tækjulər] adj spectaculaire

spectator [spek'teɪtər] n spectateur(-trice)

spectrum ['spektrəm] (pl spectra) n spectre m

speculation [spekju'leɪʃən] n spéculation f

speech [spiːtʃ] n (faculty) parole f; (talk) discours m, allocution f; (manner of speaking) façon f de parler, langage m; (enunciation) élocution f; **~less** adj muet(te)

speed [spiːd] n vitesse f; (promptness) rapidité f ♦ vi: **to ~ along/past** etc aller/passer etc à toute vitesse or allure; **at full** or **top ~** à toute vitesse or allure; **~ up** vi aller plus vite, accélérer ♦ vt accélérer; **~boat** n vedette f, hors-bord m inv; **~ily** adv rapidement, promptement; **~ing** n (AUT) excès m de vitesse; **~ limit** n limitation f de vitesse, vitesse maximale permise; **~ometer** [spɪ'dɔmɪtər] n compteur m (de vitesse); **~way** n (SPORT: also: **~way racing**) épreuve(s) f(pl) de vitesse de motos; **~y** adj rapide, prompt(e)

spell [spel] (pt, pp spelt or spelled) n (also: **magic ~**) sortilège m, charme m; (period of time) (courte) période f ♦ vt (in writing) écrire, orthographier; (aloud) épeler; (fig) signifier; **to cast a ~ on sb** jeter un sort à qn; **he can't ~** il fait des fautes d'orthographe; **~bound** adj envoûté(e), subjugué(e); **~ing** n orthographe f

spend [spend] (pt, pp spent) vt (money) dépenser; (time, life) passer; consacrer; **~thrift** n dépensier(-ère)

sperm [spəːm] n sperme m

sphere [sfɪər] n sphère f

spice [spaɪs] n épice f; **spicy** adj épicé(e), relevé(e); (fig) piquant(e)

spider ['spaɪdəʳ] n araignée f

spike [spaɪk] n pointe f; (BOT) épi m

spill [spɪl] (pt, pp spilt or spilled) vt renverser; répandre ♦ vi se répandre; ~ **over** vi déborder

spin [spɪn] (pt spun or span, pp spun) n (revolution of wheel) tour m; (AVIAT) (chute f en) vrille f; (trip in car) petit tour, balade f ♦ vt (wool etc) filer; (wheel) faire tourner ♦ vi filer; (turn) tourner, tournoyer

spinach ['spɪnɪtʃ] n épinard m; (as food) épinards

spinal ['spaɪnl] adj vertébral(e), spinal(e); ~ **cord** n moelle épinière

spin doctor n personne employée pour présenter un parti politique sous un jour favorable

spin-dryer [spɪn'draɪəʳ] (BRIT) n essoreuse f

spine [spaɪn] n colonne vertébrale; (thorn) épine f; **~less** adj (fig) mou (molle)

spinning ['spɪnɪŋ] n (of thread) filature f; ~ **top** n toupie f

spin-off ['spɪnɔf] n avantage inattendu; sous-produit m

spinster ['spɪnstəʳ] n célibataire f; vieille fille (péj)

spiral ['spaɪərl] n spirale f ♦ vi (fig) monter en flèche; ~ **staircase** n escalier m en colimaçon

spire ['spaɪəʳ] n flèche f, aiguille f

spirit ['spɪrɪt] n esprit m; (mood) état m d'esprit; (courage) courage m, énergie f; **~s** npl (drink) spiritueux mpl, alcool m; **in good ~s** de bonne humeur; **~ed** adj vif (vive), fougueux(-euse), plein(e) d'allant; **~ual** adj spirituel(le); (religious) religieux(-euse)

spit [spɪt] (pt, pp spat) n (for roasting) broche f; (saliva) salive f ♦ vi cracher; (sound) crépiter

spite [spaɪt] n rancune f, dépit m ♦ vt contrarier, vexer; **in ~ of** en dépit de, malgré; **~ful** adj méchant(e), malveillant(e)

spittle ['spɪtl] n salive f; (of animal) bave f; (spat out) crachat m

splash [splæʃ] n (sound) plouf m; (of colour) tache f ♦ vt éclabousser ♦ vi (also: ~ **about**) barboter, patauger

spleen [spliːn] n (ANAT) rate f

splendid ['splendɪd] adj splendide, superbe, magnifique

splint [splɪnt] n attelle f, éclisse f

splinter ['splɪntəʳ] n (in wood) écharde f; (glass) éclat m ♦ vi se briser, se fendre

split [splɪt] (pt, pp split) n fente f, déchirure f; (fig: POL) scission f ♦ vt diviser; (work, profits) partager, répartir ♦ vi (divide) se diviser; ~ **up** vi (couple) se séparer, rompre; (meeting) se disperser

spoil [spɔɪl] (pt, pp spoilt or spoiled) vt (damage) abîmer; (mar) gâcher; (child) gâter; **~s** npl butin m; (fig: profits) bénéfices npl; **~sport** n trouble-fête m, rabat-joie m

spoke [spəuk] pt of speak ♦ n (of wheel) rayon m

spoken ['spəukn] pp of speak

spokesman ['spəuksmən], **spokeswoman** ['spəukswumən] (irreg) n porte-parole m inv

sponge [spʌndʒ] n éponge f; (also: ~ **cake**) ≈ biscuit m de Savoie ♦ vt éponger ♦ vi: **to ~ off** or **on** vivre aux crochets de; ~ **bag** (BRIT) n trousse f de toilette

sponsor ['spɔnsəʳ] n (RADIO, TV, SPORT) sponsor m; (for application) parrain m, marraine f; (BRIT: for fund-raising event) donateur(-trice) ♦ vt sponsoriser; parrainer; faire un don à; **~ship** n sponsoring m; parrainage m; dons mpl

spontaneous [spɔn'teɪnɪəs] adj spontané(e)

spooky ['spuːkɪ] (inf) adj qui donne la chair de poule

spool [spuːl] n bobine f

spoon [spuːn] n cuiller f; **~-feed** vt nourrir à la cuiller; (fig) mâcher le travail à; **~ful** n cuillerée f

sport [spɔːt] n sport m; (person) chic type (fille) ♦ vt arborer; **~ing** adj sportif(-ive); **to give sb a ~ing chance** donner sa chance à qn; ~ **jacket** (US) n = **sports jacket**; **~s car** n voiture f de sport; **~s jacket** (BRIT) n veste f de sport; **~sman** (irreg) n sportif m; **~smanship** n esprit sportif, sportivité f; **~swear** n vêtements mpl de sport; **~swoman** (irreg) n sportive f; **~y** adj sportif(-ive)

spot [spɔt] n tache f; (dot: on pattern) pois m; (pimple) bouton m; (place) endroit m, coin m; (RADIO, TV: in programme: for person) numéro m; (: for activity) rubrique f; (small amount): **a ~ of** un peu de ♦ vt (notice) apercevoir, repérer; **on the ~** sur place, sur les lieux; (immediately) sur-le-champ; (in difficulty) dans l'embarras; ~ **check** n sondage m, vérification ponctuelle; **~less** adj immaculé(e); **~light** n projecteur m; **~ted** adj (fabric) à pois; **~ty** adj (face, person) boutonneux(-euse)

spouse [spaus] n époux (épouse)

spout [spaut] n (of jug) bec m; (of pipe) orifice m ♦ vi jaillir

sprain [spreɪn] n entorse f, foulure f ♦ vt: **to ~ one's ankle** etc se fouler or se tordre la cheville etc

sprang [spræŋ] pt of spring

sprawl [sprɔːl] vi s'étaler

spray [spreɪ] n jet m (en fines gouttelettes); (from sea) embruns mpl, vaporisateur m; (for garden) pulvérisateur m; (aerosol) bombe f; (of flowers) petit bouquet ♦ vt vaporiser,

pulvériser; (*crops*) traiter
spread [spred] (*pt, pp* **spread**) *n* (*distribution*)
répartition *f*; (*CULIN*) pâte *f* à tartiner; (*inf:
meal*) festin *m* ♦ *vt* étendre, étaler; répandre;
(*wealth, workload*) distribuer ♦ *vi* (*disease,
news*) se propager; (*also: ~ out: stain*)
s'étaler; ~ **out** *vi* (*people*) se disperser; **~-
eagled** *adj* étendu(e) bras et jambes écartés;
~sheet *n* (*COMPUT*) tableur *m*
spree [spri:] *n*: **to go on a ~** faire la fête
sprightly ['spraɪtlɪ] *adj* alerte
spring [sprɪŋ] (*pt* **sprang**, *pp* **sprung**) *n* (*leap*)
bond, saut *m*; (*coiled metal*) ressort *m*;
(*season*) printemps *m*; (*of water*) source *f* ♦
vi (*leap*) bondir, sauter; **in ~** au printemps; **to
~ from** provenir de; **~ up** *vi* (*problem*) se
présenter, surgir; (*plant, buildings*) surgir de
terre; **~board** *n* tremplin *m*; **~-clean(ing)** *n*
grand nettoyage de printemps; **~time** *n*
printemps *m*
sprinkle ['sprɪŋkl] *vt*: **to ~ water** etc **on**,
~ with water etc asperger d'eau etc; **to
~ sugar** etc **on**, **~ with sugar** etc saupoudrer
de sucre etc; **~r** *n* (*for lawn*) arroseur *m*; (*to
put out fire*) diffuseur *m* d'extincteur
automatique d'incendie
sprint [sprɪnt] *n* sprint *m* ♦ *vi* courir à toute
vitesse; (*SPORT*) sprinter; **~er** *n* sprin-
teur(-euse)
sprout [spraʊt] *vi* germer, pousser; **~s** *npl*
(*also:* **Brussels ~s**) choux *mpl* de Bruxelles
spruce [spru:s] *n inv* épicéa *m* ♦ *adj* net(te),
pimpant(e)
sprung [sprʌŋ] *pp of* **spring**
spun [spʌn] *pt, pp of* **spin**
spur [spə:] *n* éperon *m*; (*fig*) aiguillon *m* ♦ *vt*
(*also: ~ on*) éperonner; aiguillonner; **on the
~ of the moment** sous l'impulsion du moment
spurious ['spjʊərɪəs] *adj* faux (fausse)
spurn [spə:n] *vt* repousser avec mépris
spurt [spə:t] *n* (*of blood*) jaillissement *m*; (*of
energy*) regain *m*, sursaut *m* ♦ *vi* jaillir, gicler
spy [spaɪ] *n* espion(ne) ♦ *vi*: **to ~ on**
espionner, épier; (*see*) apercevoir; **~ing** *n*
espionnage *m*
sq. *abbr* = **square**
squabble ['skwɔbl] *vi* se chamailler
squad [skwɔd] *n* (*MIL, POLICE*) escouade *f*,
groupe *m*; (*FOOTBALL*) contingent *m*
squadron ['skwɔdrn] *n* (*MIL*) escadron *m*;
(*AVIAT, NAUT*) escadrille *f*
squalid ['skwɔlɪd] *adj* sordide
squall [skwɔ:l] *n* rafale *f*, bourrasque *f*
squalor ['skwɔlə] *n* conditions *fpl* sordides
squander ['skwɔndə] *vt* gaspiller, dilapider
square [skwɛə] *n* carré *m*; (*in town*) place *f*
♦ *adj* carré(e); (*inf: ideas, tastes*) vieux jeu *inv*
♦ *vt* (*arrange*) régler; arranger; (*MATH*) élever
au carré ♦ *vi* (*reconcile*) concilier; **all ~** quitte;

à égalité; **a ~ meal** un repas convenable; **2
metres ~** (de) 2 mètres sur 2; **2 ~ metres** 2
mètres carrés; **~ly** *adv* carrément
squash [skwɔʃ] *n* (*BRIT: drink*): **lemon/orange
~** citronnade *f*/orangeade *f*; (*US: marrow*)
courge *f*; (*SPORT*) squash *m* ♦ *vt* écraser
squat [skwɔt] *adj* petit(e) et épais(se),
ramassé(e) ♦ *vi* (*also: ~ down*) s'accroupir;
~ter *n* squatter *m*
squeak [skwi:k] *vi* grincer, crier; (*mouse*)
pousser un petit cri
squeal [skwi:l] *vi* pousser un *or* des cri(s)
aigu(s) *or* perçant(s); (*brakes*) grincer
squeamish ['skwi:mɪʃ] *adj* facilement
dégoûté(e)
squeeze [skwi:z] *n* pression *f*; (*ECON*)
restrictions *fpl* de crédit ♦ *vt* presser; (*hand,
arm*) serrer; **~ out** *vt* exprimer
squelch [skweltʃ] *vi* faire un bruit de succion
squid [skwɪd] *n* calmar *m*
squiggle ['skwɪgl] *n* gribouillis *m*
squint [skwɪnt] *vi* loucher ♦ *n*: **he has a ~** il
louche, il souffre de strabisme
squirm [skwə:m] *vi* se tortiller
squirrel ['skwɪrəl] *n* écureuil *m*
squirt [skwə:t] *vi* jaillir, gicler
Sr *abbr* = **senior**
St *abbr* = **saint; street**
stab [stæb] *n* (*with knife etc*) coup *m* (de
couteau etc); (*of pain*) lancée *f*; (*inf: try*): **to
have a ~ at (doing) sth** s'essayer à (faire) qch
♦ *vt* poignarder
stable ['steɪbl] *n* écurie *f* ♦ *adj* stable
stack [stæk] *n* tas *m*, pile *f* ♦ *vt* (*also: ~ up*)
empiler, entasser
stadium ['steɪdɪəm] (*pl* **stadia** *or* **~s**) *n* stade
m
staff [stɑ:f] *n* (*workforce*) personnel *m*; (*BRIT:
SCOL*) professeurs *mpl* ♦ *vt* pourvoir en
personnel
stag [stæg] *n* cerf *m*
stage [steɪdʒ] *n* scène *f*; (*platform*) estrade *f*
♦ *n* (*point*) étape *f*, stade *m*; (*profession*): **the
~** le théâtre ♦ *vt* (*play*) monter, mettre en
scène; (*demonstration*) organiser; **in ~s** par
étapes, par degrés; **~coach** *n* diligence *f*;
~ manager *n* régisseur *m*
stagger ['stægə] *vi* chanceler, tituber ♦ *vt*
(*person: amaze*) stupéfier; (*hours, holidays*)
étaler, échelonner; **~ing** *adj* (*amazing*)
stupéfiant(e), renversant(e)
stagnate [stæg'neɪt] *vi* stagner, croupir
stag party *n* enterrement *m* de vie de
garçon
staid [steɪd] *adj* posé(e), rassis(e)
stain [steɪn] *n* tache *f*; (*colouring*) colorant *m*
♦ *vt* tacher; (*wood*) teindre; **~ed glass
window** *n* vitrail *m*; **~less steel** *n* acier *m*
inoxydable, inox *m*; **~ remover** *n* détachant

m

stair [stɛəʳ] *n* (*step*) marche *f*; **~s** *npl* (*flight of steps*) escalier *m*; **~case**, **~way** *n* escalier *m*

stake [steɪk] *n* pieu *m*, poteau *m*; (*BETTING*) enjeu *m*; (*COMM: interest*) intérêts *mpl* ♦ *vt* risquer, jouer; **to be at ~** être en jeu; **to ~ one's claim (to)** revendiquer

stale [steɪl] *adj* (*bread*) rassis(e); (*food*) pas frais (fraîche); (*beer*) éventé(e); (*smell*) de renfermé; (*air*) confiné(e)

stalemate [ˈsteɪlmeɪt] *n* (*CHESS*) pat *m*; (*fig*) impasse *f*

stalk [stɔːk] *n* tige *f* ♦ *vt* traquer ♦ *vi*: **to ~ out/off** sortir/partir d'un air digne

stall [stɔːl] *n* (*BRIT: in street, market etc*) éventaire *m*, étal *m*; (*in stable*) stalle *f* ♦ *vt* (*AUT*) caler; (*delay*) retarder ♦ *vi* (*AUT*) caler; (*fig*) essayer de gagner du temps; **~s** *npl* (*BRIT: in cinema, theatre*) orchestre *m*

stallion [ˈstæljən] *n* étalon *m* (*cheval*)

stamina [ˈstæmɪnə] *n* résistance *f*, endurance *f*

stammer [ˈstæməʳ] *n* bégaiement *m* ♦ *vi* bégayer

stamp [stæmp] *n* timbre *m*; (*rubber ~*) tampon *m*; (*mark, also fig*) empreinte *f* ♦ *vi* (*also: ~ one's foot*) taper du pied ♦ *vt* (*letter*) timbrer; (*with rubber ~*) tamponner; **~ album** *n* album *m* de timbres(-poste); **~ collecting** *n* philatélie *f*

stampede [stæmˈpiːd] *n* ruée *f*

stance [stæns] *n* position *f*

stand [stænd] (*pt, pp stood*) *n* (*position*) position *f*; (*for taxis*) station *f* (de taxis); (*music ~*) pupitre *m* à musique; (*COMM*) étalage *m*, stand *m*; (*SPORT: also: ~s*) tribune *f* ♦ *vi* être ou se tenir (debout); (*rise*) se lever, se mettre debout; (*be placed*) se trouver; (*remain: offer etc*) rester valable; (*BRIT: in election*) être candidat(e), se présenter ♦ *vt* (*place*) mettre, poser; (*tolerate, withstand*) supporter; (*treat, invite to*) offrir, payer; **to make** *ou* **take a ~** prendre position; **to ~ at** (*score, value etc*) être de; **to ~ for parliament** (*BRIT*) se présenter aux élections législatives; **~ by** *vi* (*be ready*) se tenir prêt(e) ♦ *vt fus* (*opinion*) s'en tenir à; (*person*) ne pas abandonner, soutenir; **~ down** *vi* (*withdraw*) se retirer; **~ for** *vt fus* (*signify*) représenter, signifier; (*tolerate*) supporter, tolérer; **~ in for** *vt fus* remplacer; **~ out** *vi* (*be prominent*) ressortir; **~ up** *vi* (*rise*) se lever, se mettre debout; **~ up for** *vt fus* défendre; **~ up to** *vt fus* tenir tête à, résister à

standard [ˈstændəd] *n* (*level*) niveau (voulu); (*norm*) norme *f*, étalon *m*; (*criterion*) critère *m*; (*flag*) étendard *m* ♦ *adj* (*size etc*) ordinaire, normal(e); courant(e); (*text*) de base; **~s** *npl* (*morals*) morale *f*, principes *mpl*

~ lamp (*BRIT*) *n* lampadaire *m*; **~ of living** *n* niveau *m* de vie

stand-by [ˈstændbaɪ] *n* remplaçant(e); **to be on ~~** se tenir prêt(e) (à intervenir); être de garde; **~~ ticket** *n* (*AVIAT*) billet *m* stand-by

stand-in [ˈstændɪn] *n* remplaçant(e)

standing [ˈstændɪŋ] *adj* debout *inv*; (*permanent*) permanent(e) ♦ *n* réputation *f*, rang *m*, standing *m*; **of many years' ~** qui dure *ou* existe depuis longtemps; **~ joke** *n* vieux sujet de plaisanterie; **~ order** (*BRIT*) *n* (*at bank*) virement *m* automatique, prélèvement *m* bancaire; **~ room** *n* places *fpl* debout

standpoint [ˈstændpɔɪnt] *n* point *m* de vue

standstill [ˈstændstɪl] *n*: **at a ~** paralysé(e); **to come to a ~** s'immobiliser, s'arrêter

stank [stæŋk] *pt of* **stink**

staple [ˈsteɪpl] *n* (*for papers*) agrafe *f* ♦ *adj* (*food etc*) de base ♦ *vt* agrafer; **~r** *n* agrafeuse *f*

star [stɑːʳ] *n* étoile *f*; (*celebrity*) vedette *f* ♦ *vi*: **to ~ (in)** être la vedette (de) ♦ *vt* (*CINEMA etc*) avoir pour vedette; **the ~s** *npl* l'horoscope *m*

starboard [ˈstɑːbəd] *n* tribord *m*

starch [stɑːtʃ] *n* amidon *m*; (*in food*) fécule *f*

stardom [ˈstɑːdəm] *n* célébrité *f*

stare [stɛəʳ] *n* regard *m* fixe ♦ *vi*: **to ~ at** regarder fixement

starfish [ˈstɑːfɪʃ] *n* étoile *f* de mer

stark [stɑːk] *adj* (*bleak*) désolé(e), morne ♦ *adv*: **~ naked** complètement nu(e)

starling [ˈstɑːlɪŋ] *n* étourneau *m*

starry [ˈstɑːrɪ] *adj* étoilé(e); **~-eyed** *adj* (*innocent*) ingénu(e)

start [stɑːt] *n* commencement *m*, début *m*; (*of race*) départ *m*; (*sudden movement*) sursaut *m*; (*advantage*) avance *f*, avantage *m* ♦ *vt* commencer; (*found*) créer; (*engine*) mettre en marche ♦ *vi* partir, se mettre en route; (*jump*) sursauter; **to ~ doing** *ou* **to do sth** se mettre à faire qch; **~ off** *vi* commencer; (*leave*) partir; **~ up** *vi* commencer; (*car*) démarrer ♦ *vt* (*business*) créer; (*car*) mettre en marche; **~er** *n* (*AUT*) démarreur *m*; (*SPORT: official*) starter *m*; (*BRIT: CULIN*) entrée *f*; **~ing point** *n* point *m* de départ

startle [ˈstɑːtl] *vt* faire sursauter; donner un choc à; **startling** *adj* (*news*) surprenant(e)

starvation [stɑːˈveɪʃən] *n* faim *f*, famine *f*

starve [stɑːv] *vi* mourir de faim; être affamé(e) ♦ *vt* affamer

state [steɪt] *n* état *m*; (*POL*) État ♦ *vt* déclarer, affirmer; **the S~s** *npl* (*America*) les États-Unis *mpl*; **to be in a ~** être dans tous ses états; **~ly** *adj* majestueux(-euse), imposant(e); **~ly home** *n* château *m*; **~ment** *n* déclaration *f*; **~sman** (*irreg*) *n* homme *m* d'État

static ['stætik] n (RADIO, TV) parasites mpl
♦ adj statique
station ['steɪʃən] n gare f; (police ~) poste m
de police ♦ vt placer, poster
stationary ['steɪʃnərɪ] adj à l'arrêt, immobile
stationer ['steɪʃnə'] n papetier(-ère); ~'s
(**shop**) n papeterie f; ~**y** n papier m à
lettres, petit matériel de bureau
stationmaster ['steɪʃənmɑːstə'] n (RAIL)
chef m de gare
station wagon (US) n break m
statistic n statistique f; ~**s** [stə'tɪstɪks] n
(science) statistique f
statue ['stætjuː] n statue f
status ['steɪtəs] n position f, situation f;
(official) statut m; (prestige) prestige m;
~ **symbol** n signe extérieur de richesse
statute ['stætjuːt] n loi f, statut m; **statutory**
adj statutaire, prévu(e) par un article de loi
staunch [stɔːntʃ] adj sûr(e), loyal(e)
stay [steɪ] n (period of time) séjour m ♦ vi
rester; (reside) loger; (spend some time)
séjourner, to ~ **put** ne pas bouger; to ~ **with**
friends loger chez des amis; to ~ **the night**
passer la nuit; ~ **behind** vi rester en arrière;
~ **in** vi (at home) rester à la maison; ~ **on** vi
rester; ~ **out** vi (of house) ne pas rentrer;
~ **up** vi (at night) ne pas se coucher; ~**ing
power** n endurance f
stead [sted] n: in sb's ~ à la place de qn; to
stand sb in good ~ être très utile à qn
steadfast ['stedfɑːst] adj ferme, résolu(e)
steadily ['stedɪlɪ] adv (regularly)
progressivement; (firmly) fermement; (: walk)
d'un pas ferme; (fixedly: look) sans détourner
les yeux
steady ['stedɪ] adj stable, solide, ferme;
(regular) constant(e), régulier(-ère); (person)
calme, pondéré(e) ♦ vt stabiliser; (nerves)
calmer; a ~ **boyfriend** un petit ami
steak [steɪk] n (beef) bifteck m, steak m; (fish,
pork) tranche f
steal [stiːl] (pt **stole**, pp **stolen**) vt voler ♦ vi
voler; (move secretly) se faufiler, se déplacer
furtivement
stealth [stelθ] n: **by** ~ furtivement
steam [stiːm] n vapeur f ♦ vt (CULIN) cuire à
la vapeur ♦ vi fumer; ~ **engine** n locomotive
f à vapeur; ~**er** n (boat un m à) vapeur m;
~**ship** n = **steamer**; ~**y** adj embué(e),
humide
steel [stiːl] n acier m ♦ adj d'acier; ~**works** n
aciérie f
steep [stiːp] adj raide, escarpé(e); (price)
excessif(-ive)
steeple ['stiːpl] n clocher m
steer [stɪə'] vt diriger; (boat) gouverner;
(person) guider, conduire ♦ vi tenir le
gouvernail; ~**ing** n (AUT) conduite f; ~**ing**

wheel n volant m
stem [stem] n (of plant) tige f; (of glass) pied
m ♦ vt contenir, arrêter, juguler; ~ **from** vt
fus provenir de, découler de
stench [stentʃ] n puanteur f
stencil ['stensl] n stencil m; (pattern used)
pochoir m ♦ vt polycopier
stenographer [ste'nɔgrəfə'] (US) n
sténographe m/f
step [step] n pas m; (stair) marche f; (action)
mesure f, disposition f ♦ vi: to ~ **forward/back**
faire un pas en avant/arrière, avancer/reculer;
~**s** npl (BRIT) = **stepladder**; **to be in/out of
~** (**with**) (fig) aller dans le sens (de)/être
déphasé(e) (par rapport à); ~ **down** vi (fig)
se retirer, se désister; ~ **up** vt augmenter;
intensifier; ~**brother** n demi-frère m;
~**daughter** n belle-fille f; ~**father** n beau-
père m; ~**ladder** (BRIT) n escabeau m;
~**mother** n belle-mère f; ~**ping stone** n
pierre f de gué; (fig) tremplin m; ~**sister** n
demi-sœur f; ~**son** n beau-fils m
stereo ['stɪərɪəʊ] n (sound) stéréo f; (hi-fi)
chaîne f stéréo inv ♦ adj (also: ~**phonic**)
stéréo(phonique)
sterile ['sterail] adj stérile; **sterilize** ['sterɪlaɪz]
vt stériliser
sterling ['stɜːlɪŋ] adj (silver) de bon aloi,
fin(e) ♦ n (ECON) livres fpl sterling inv; a
pound ~ une livre sterling
stern [stɜːn] adj sévère ♦ n (NAUT) arrière m,
poupe f
stew [stjuː] n ragoût m ♦ vt, vi cuire (à la
casserole)
steward ['stjuːəd] n (on ship, plane, train)
steward m; ~**ess** n hôtesse f (de l')air)
stick [stɪk] (pt, pp **stuck**) n bâton m; (walking
~) canne f ♦ vt (glue) coller; (inf: put)
mettre, fourrer; (: tolerate) supporter;
(thrust): to ~ **sth into** planter or enfoncer qch
dans ♦ vi (become attached) rester collé(e) or
fixé(e); (be unmoveable: wheels etc) se
bloquer; (remain) rester; ~ **out** vi dépasser,
sortir; ~ **up** vi = **stick out**; ~ **up for** vt fus
défendre; ~**er** n auto-collant m; ~**ing
plaster** n sparadrap m, pansement adhésif
stick-up ['stɪkʌp] (inf) n braquage m, hold-
up m inv
sticky ['stɪkɪ] adj poisseux(-euse); (label)
adhésif(-ive); (situation) délicat(e)
stiff [stɪf] adj raide; rigide; dur(e); (difficult)
difficile, ardu(e); (cold) froid(e), distant(e);
(strong, high) fort(e), élevé(e) ♦ adv: to be
bored/scared/frozen ~ s'ennuyer à mort/être
mort(e) de peur/froid; ~**en** vi se raidir;
~ **neck** n torticolis m
stifle ['staɪfl] vt étouffer, réprimer
stigma ['stɪgmə] n stigmate m
stile [staɪl] n échalier m

stiletto [stɪˈlɛtəu] (BRIT) n (also: ~ **heel**) talon m aiguille

still [stɪl] adj immobile ♦ adv (up to this time) encore, toujours; (even) encore; (nonetheless) quand même, tout de même; **~born** adj mort-né(e); ~ **life** n nature morte

stilt [stɪlt] n (for walking on) échasse f; (pile) pilotis m

stilted [ˈstɪltɪd] adj guindé(e), emprunté(e)

stimulate [ˈstɪmjuleɪt] vt stimuler

stimuli [ˈstɪmjulaɪ] npl of **stimulus**

stimulus [ˈstɪmjuləs] (pl **stimuli**) n stimulant m; (BIOL, PSYCH) stimulus m

sting [stɪŋ] (pt, pp **stung**) n piqûre f; (organ) dard m ♦ vt, vi piquer

stingy [ˈstɪndʒɪ] adj avare, pingre

stink [stɪŋk] (pt **stank**, pp **stunk**) n puanteur f ♦ vi puer, empester; **~ing** (inf) adj (fig) infect(e), vache; a **~ing** ... un(e) foutu(e) ...

stint [stɪnt] n part f de travail ♦ vi: **to ~ on** lésiner sur, être chiche de

stir [stəːʳ] n agitation f, sensation f ♦ vt remuer ♦ vi remuer, bouger; **~ up** vt (trouble) fomenter, provoquer

stirrup [ˈstɪrəp] n étrier m

stitch [stɪtʃ] n (SEWING) point m; (KNITTING) maille f; (MED) point de suture; (pain) point de côté ♦ vt coudre, piquer; (MED) suturer

stoat [stəut] n hermine f (avec son pelage d'été)

stock [stɔk] n réserve f, provision f; (COMM) stock m; (AGR) cheptel m, bétail m; (CULIN) bouillon m; (descent, origin) souche f; (FINANCE) valeurs fpl, titres mpl ♦ adj (fig: reply etc) classique ♦ vt (have in ~) avoir, vendre; **~s and shares** valeurs (mobilières), titres; **in/out of ~** en stock ou en magasin/ épuisé(e); **to take ~ of** (fig) faire le point de; **~ up** vi: **to ~ up (with)** s'approvisionner (en); **~broker** n agent m de change; **~ cube** n bouillon-cube m; **~ exchange** n Bourse f

stocking [ˈstɔkɪŋ] n bas m

stock: **~ market** n Bourse f, marché financier; **~pile** n stock m, réserve f ♦ vt stocker, accumuler; **~taking** (BRIT) n (COMM) inventaire m

stocky [ˈstɔkɪ] adj trapu(e), râblé(e)

stodgy [ˈstɔdʒɪ] adj bourratif(-ive), lourd(e)

stoke [stəuk] vt (fire) garnir, entretenir; (boiler) chauffer

stole [stəul] pt of **steal** ♦ n étole f

stolen [ˈstəuln] pp of **steal**

stomach [ˈstʌmək] n estomac m; (abdomen) ventre m ♦ vt digérer, supporter; **~ache** n mal m à l'estomac ou au ventre

stone [stəun] n pierre f; (pebble) caillou m, galet m; (in fruit) noyau m; (MED) calcul m; (BRIT: weight) 6,348 kg ♦ adj de ou en pierre ♦ vt (person) lancer des pierres sur, lapider;

~cold adj complètement froid(e); **~deaf** adj sourd(e) comme un pot; **~work** n maçonnerie f

stood [stud] pt, pp of **stand**

stool [stuːl] n tabouret m

stoop [stuːp] vi (also: **have a ~**) être voûté(e); (also: ~ **down**: bend) se baisser

stop [stɔp] n arrêt m; halte f; (in punctuation: also: **full ~**) point m ♦ vt arrêter, bloquer; (break off) interrompre; (also: **put a ~ to**) mettre fin à ♦ vi s'arrêter; (rain, noise etc) cesser, s'arrêter; **to ~ doing sth** cesser ou arrêter de faire qch; **~ dead** vi s'arrêter net; **~ off** vi faire une courte halte; **~ up** vt (hole) boucher; **~gap** n (person) bouche-trou m; (measure) mesure f intérimaire; **~over** n halte f; (AVIAT) escale f; **~page** n (strike) arrêt de travail; (blockage) obstruction f; **~per** n bouchon m; **~ press** n nouvelles fpl de dernière heure; **~watch** n chronomètre m

storage [ˈstɔːrɪdʒ] n entreposage m; **~ heater** n radiateur m électrique par accumulation

store [stɔːʳ] n (stock) provision f, réserve f; (depot) entrepôt m; (BRIT: large shop) grand magasin; (US) magasin m ♦ vt emmagasiner; (information) enregistrer; **~s** npl (food) provisions; **in ~** en réserve; **~ up** vt mettre en réserve; accumuler; **~room** n réserve f, magasin m

storey [ˈstɔːrɪ] (US **story**) n étage m

stork [stɔːk] n cigogne f

storm [stɔːm] n tempête f; (thunderstorm) orage m ♦ vi (fig) fulminer ♦ vt prendre d'assaut; **~y** adj orageux(-euse)

story [ˈstɔːrɪ] n histoire f; récit m; (US) = **storey**; **~book** n livre m d'histoires ou de contes

stout [staut] adj solide; (fat) gros(se), corpulent(e) ♦ n bière brune

stove [stəuv] n (for cooking) fourneau m; (: small) réchaud m; (for heating) poêle m

stow [stəu] vt (also: ~ **away**) ranger; **~away** n passager(-ère) clandestin(e)

straddle [ˈstrædl] vt enjamber, être à cheval sur

straggle [ˈstrægl] vi être (or marcher) en désordre

straight [streɪt] adj droit(e); (hair) raide; (frank) honnête, franc (franche); (simple) simple ♦ adv (tout) droit; (drink) sec, sans eau; **to put or get ~** (fig) mettre au clair; **~ away**, **~ off** (at once) tout de suite; **~en** vt ajuster; (bed) arranger; **~en out** vt (fig) débrouiller; **~-faced** adj impassible; **~forward** adj simple; (honest) honnête, direct(e)

strain [streɪn] n tension f; pression f; (physical) effort m; (mental) tension (nerveuse); (*breed*) race f ♦ vt (*stretch: resources etc*) mettre à rude épreuve, grever; (*hurt: back etc*) se faire mal à; (*vegetables*) égoutter; ~s npl (*MUS*) accords mpl, accents mpl; **back** ~ tour m de rein; **~ed** adj (*muscle*) froissé(e); (*laugh etc*) forcé(e), contraint(e); (*relations*) tendu(e); **~er** n passoire f

strait [streɪt] n (*GEO*) détroit m; **~s** npl: **to be in dire ~s** avoir de sérieux ennuis (d'argent); **~jacket** n camisole f de force; **~-laced** [streɪt'leɪst] adj collet monté inv

strand [strænd] n (*of thread*) fil m, brin m; (*of rope*) toron m; (*of hair*) mèche f; **~ed** adj en rade, en plan

strange [streɪndʒ] adj (*not known*) inconnu(e); (*odd*) étrange, bizarre; **~ly** adv étrangement, bizarrement; *see also* enough; **~r** n inconnu(e); (*from another area*) étranger(-ère)

strangle ['stræŋgl] vt étrangler; **~hold** n (*fig*) emprise totale, mainmise f

strap [stræp] n lanière f, courroie f, sangle f; (*of slip, dress*) bretelle f

strategic [strə'tiːdʒɪk] adj stratégique; **strategy** ['strætɪdʒɪ] n stratégie f

straw [strɔː] n paille f; **that's the last ~!** ça, c'est le comble!

strawberry ['strɔːbərɪ] n fraise f

stray [streɪ] adj (*animal*) perdu(e), errant(e); (*scattered*) isolé(e) ♦ vi s'égarer; **~ bullet** n balle perdue

streak [striːk] n bande f, filet m; (*in hair*) raie f ♦ vt zébrer, strier ♦ vi: **to ~ past** passer à toute allure

stream [striːm] n (*brook*) ruisseau m; (*current*) courant m, flot m; (*of people*) défilé ininterrompu, flot ♦ vt (*SCOL*) répartir par niveau ♦ vi ruisseler; **to ~ in/out** entrer/sortir à flots

streamer ['striːmər] n serpentin m; (*banner*) banderole f

streamlined ['striːmlaɪnd] adj aérodynamique; (*fig*) rationalisé(e)

street [striːt] n rue f; **~car** n (*US*) tramway m; **~ lamp** n réverbère m; **~ plan** n plan m (des rues); **~wise** (*inf*) adj futé(e), réaliste

strength [strɛŋθ] n force f; (*of girder, knot etc*) solidité f; **~en** vt (*muscle etc*) fortifier; (*nation, case etc*) renforcer; (*building, ECON*) consolider

strenuous ['strɛnjuəs] adj vigoureux(-euse), énergique

stress [strɛs] n (*force, pressure*) pression f; (*mental strain*) tension (nerveuse), stress m; (*accent*) accent m ♦ vt insister sur, souligner

stretch [strɛtʃ] n (*of sand etc*) étendue f ♦ vi s'étirer; (*extend*): **to ~ to** or **as far as** s'étendre jusqu'à ♦ vt tendre, étirer; (*fig*) pousser (au maximum); **~ out** vi s'étendre

♦ vt (*arm etc*) allonger, tendre; (*spread*) étendre

stretcher ['strɛtʃər] n brancard m, civière f

stretchy ['strɛtʃɪ] adj élastique

strewn [struːn] adj: **~ with** jonché(e) de

stricken ['strɪkən] adj (*person*) très éprouvé(e); (*city, industry etc*) dévasté(e); **~ with** (*disease etc*) frappé(e) or atteint(e) de

strict [strɪkt] adj strict(e)

stride [straɪd] (*pt* strode, *pp* stridden) n grand pas, enjambée ♦ vi marcher à grands pas

strife [straɪf] n conflit m, dissensions fpl

strike [straɪk] (*pt*, *pp* struck) n grève f; (*of oil etc*) découverte f; (*attack*) raid m ♦ vt frapper; (*oil etc*) trouver, découvrir; (*deal*) conclure ♦ vi faire grève; (*attack*) attaquer; (*clock*) sonner; **on ~** (*workers*) en grève; **to ~ a match** frotter une allumette; **~ down** vt terrasser; **~ up** vt (*MUS*) se mettre à jouer; **to ~ up a friendship with** se lier d'amitié avec; **to ~ up a conversation (with)** engager une conversation (avec); **~r** n gréviste m/f; (*SPORT*) buteur m; **striking** adj frappant(e), saisissant(e); (*attractive*) éblouissant(e)

string [strɪŋ] (*pt*, *pp* strung) n ficelle f; (*row: of beads*) rang m; (*: of onions*) chapelet m; (*MUS*) corde f ♦ vt: **to ~ out** échelonner; **the ~s** npl (*MUS*) les instruments mpl à cordes; **to ~ together** enchaîner; **to pull ~s** (*fig*) faire jouer le piston; **~(ed) instrument** n (*MUS*) instrument m à cordes

stringent ['strɪndʒənt] adj rigoureux(-euse)

strip [strɪp] n bande f ♦ vt (*undress*) déshabiller; (*paint*) décaper; (*also: ~ down: machine*) démonter ♦ vi se déshabiller; **~ cartoon** n bande dessinée

stripe [straɪp] n raie f, rayure f, (*MIL*) galon m; **~d** adj rayé(e), à rayures

strip: **~ lighting** (*BRIT*) n éclairage m au néon or fluorescent; **~per** n strip-teaseur(-euse) f; **~ search** n fouille corporelle (*en faisant se déshabiller la personne*) ♦ vt: **he was ~ searched** on l'a fait se déshabiller et soumis à une fouille corporelle

stripy ['straɪpɪ] adj rayé(e)

strive [straɪv] (*pt* strove, *pp* striven) vi: **to ~ to do/for sth** s'efforcer de faire/d'obtenir qch

strode [strəud] pt of stride

stroke [strəuk] n coup m; (*SWIMMING*) nage f; (*MED*) attaque f ♦ vt caresser; **at a ~** d'un (seul) coup

stroll [strəul] n petite promenade ♦ vi flâner, se promener nonchalamment; **~er** n (*US*) n (*pushchair*) poussette f

strong [strɔŋ] adj fort(e); vigoureux(-euse); (*heart, nerves*) solide; **they are 50 ~** ils sont au nombre de 50; **~hold** n bastion m; **~ly** adv fortement, avec force; vigoureusement; solidement; ~room *n* chambre forte

strove [strəuv] *pt of* **strive**

struck [strʌk] *pt, pp of* **strike**

structural ['strʌktʃrəl] *adj* structural(e); (*CONSTR: defect*) de construction; (*damage*) affectant les parties portantes

structure ['strʌktʃər] *n* structure *f*; (*building*) construction *f*

struggle ['strʌgl] *n* lutte *f* ♦ *vi* lutter, se battre

strum [strʌm] *vt* (*guitar*) jouer (en sourdine) de

strung [strʌŋ] *pt, pp of* **string**

strut [strʌt] *n* étai *m*, support *m* ♦ *vi* se pavaner

stub [stʌb] *n* (*of cigarette*) bout *m*, mégot *m*; (*of cheque etc*) talon *m* ♦ *vt*: **to ~ one's toe** se cogner le doigt de pied; ~ **out** *vt* écraser

stubble ['stʌbl] *n* chaume *m*; (*on chin*) barbe *f* de plusieurs jours

stubborn ['stʌbən] *adj* têtu(e), obstiné(e), opiniâtre

stuck [stʌk] *pt, pp of* **stick** ♦ *adj* (*jammed*) bloqué(e), coincé(e); ~-**up** (*inf*) *adj* prétentieux(-euse)

stud [stʌd] *n* (*on boots etc*) clou *m*; (*on collar*) bouton *m* de col; (*earring*) petite boucle d'oreille; (*of horses: also:* ~ **farm**) écurie *f*, haras *m*; (*also:* ~ **horse**) étalon *m* ♦ *vt* (*fig*): ~**ded with** parsemé(e) or criblé(e) de

student ['stju:dənt] *n* étudiant(e) ♦ *adj* estudiantin(e); d'étudiant; ~ **driver** (*US*) *n* (*conducteur-trice*) débutant(e)

studio ['stju:dɪəu] *n* studio *m*, atelier *m*; (*TV etc*) studio

studious ['stju:dɪəs] *adj* studieux(-euse), appliqué(e); (*attention*) soutenu(e); ~**ly** *adv* (*carefully*) soigneusement

study ['stʌdɪ] *n* étude *f*; (*room*) bureau *m* ♦ *vt* étudier; (*examine*) examiner ♦ *vi* étudier, faire ses études

stuff [stʌf] *n* chose(s) *f(pl)*; affaires *fpl*, trucs *mpl*; (*substance*) substance *f* ♦ *vt* rembourrer; (*CULIN*) farcir; (*inf: push*) fourrer; ~**ing** *n* bourre *f*, rembourrage *m*; (*CULIN*) farce *f*; ~**y** *adj* (*room*) mal ventilé(e) or aéré(e); (*ideas*) vieux jeu *inv*

stumble ['stʌmbl] *vi* trébucher; **to ~ across** or **on** (*fig*) tomber sur; **stumbling block** *n* pierre *f* d'achoppement

stump [stʌmp] *n* souche *f*; (*of limb*) moignon *m* ♦ *vt*: **to be ~ed** sécher, ne pas savoir que répondre

stun [stʌn] *vt* étourdir; (*fig*) abasourdir

stung [stʌŋ] *pt, pp of* **sting**

stunk [stʌŋk] *pp of* **stink**

stunned [stʌnd] *adj* sidéré(e)

stunning ['stʌnɪŋ] *adj* (*news etc*)

stupéfiant(e); (*girl etc*) éblouissant(e)

stunt [stʌnt] *n* (*in film*) cascade *f*, acrobatie *f*; (*publicity ~*) truc *m* publicitaire ♦ *vt* retarder, arrêter; ~**man** ['stʌntmæn] (*irreg*) *n* cascadeur *m*

stupendous [stju:'pɛndəs] *adj* prodigieux(-euse), fantastique

stupid ['stju:pɪd] *adj* stupide, bête; ~**ity** [stju:'pɪdɪtɪ] *n* stupidité *f*, bêtise *f*

sturdy ['stə:dɪ] *adj* robuste; solide

stutter ['stʌtər] *vi* bégayer

sty [staɪ] *n* (*for pigs*) porcherie *f*

stye [staɪ] *n* (*MED*) orgelet *m*

style [staɪl] *n* style *m*; (*distinction*) allure *f*, cachet *m*, style; **stylish** *adj* élégant(e), chic *inv*

stylus ['staɪləs] (*pl* **styli** *or* -**es**) *n* (*of record player*) pointe *f* de lecture

suave [swɑ:v] *adj* doucereux(-euse), onctueux(-euse)

sub... [sʌb] *prefix* sub..., sous-; ~**conscious** *adj* subconscient(e); ~**contract** *vt* soustraiter

subdue [səb'dju:] *vt* subjuguer, soumettre; ~**d** *adj* (*light*) tamisé(e); (*person*) qui a perdu de son entrain

subject [*n* 'sʌbdʒɪkt, *vb* səb'dʒɛkt] *n* sujet *m*; (*SCOL*) matière *f* ♦ *vt*: **to ~ to** soumettre à; exposer à; **to be ~ to** (*law*) être soumis(e) à; (*disease*) être sujet(te) à; ~**ive** [səb'dʒɛktɪv] *adj* subjectif(-ive); ~ **matter** *n* (*content*) contenu *m*

sublet [sʌb'lɛt] *vt* sous-louer

submarine [sʌbmə'ri:n] *n* sous-marin *m*

submerge [səb'mə:dʒ] *vt* submerger ♦ *vi* plonger

submission [səb'mɪʃən] *n* soumission *f*; **submissive** *adj* soumis(e)

submit [səb'mɪt] *vt* soumettre ♦ *vi* se soumettre

subnormal [sʌb'nɔ:məl] *adj* au-dessous de la normale

subordinate [sə'bɔ:dɪnət] *adj* subalterne ♦ *n* subordonné(e)

subpoena [səb'pi:nə] *n* (*LAW*) citation *f*, assignation *f*

subscribe [səb'skraɪb] *vi* cotiser; **to ~ to** (*opinion, fund*) souscrire à; (*newspaper*) s'abonner à; être abonné(e) à; ~**r** *n* (*to periodical, telephone*) abonné(e); **subscription** [səb'skrɪpʃən] *n* (*to magazine etc*) abonnement *m*

subsequent ['sʌbsɪkwənt] *adj* ultérieur(e), suivant(e); consécutif(-ive); ~**ly** *adv* par la suite

subside [səb'saɪd] *vi* (*flood*) baisser; (*wind, feelings*) tomber; ~**nce** [səb'saɪdns] *n* affaissement *m*

subsidiary [səb'sɪdɪərɪ] *adj* subsidiaire;

accessoire ♦ n filiale f
subsidize ['sʌbsɪdaɪz] vt subventionner;
    subsidy ['sʌbsɪdɪ] n subvention f
substance ['sʌbstəns] n substance f
substantial [səb'stænʃl] adj substantiel(le);
    (fig) important(e); **~ly** adv consi-
    dérablement; (in essence) en grande
    partie
substantiate [səb'stænʃɪeɪt] vt étayer,
    fournir des preuves à l'appui de
substitute [səb'stækt] n (person)
    remplaçant(e); (thing) succédané m ♦ vt: to
    ~ sth/sb for substituer qch/qn à, remplacer
    par qch/qn
subterranean [sʌbtə'reɪnɪən] adj
    souterrain(e)
subtitle ['sʌbtaɪtl] n (CINEMA, TV) sous-titre m;
    ~d adj sous-titré(e)
subtle ['sʌtl] adj subtil(e)
subtotal [sʌb'təutl] n total partiel
subtract [səb'trækt] vt soustraire, retrancher;
    ~ion n soustraction f
suburb ['sʌbə:b] n faubourg m; **the ~s** npl la
    banlieue; **~an** [sə'bə:bən] adj de banlieue,
    suburbain(e); **~ia** [sə'bə:bɪə] n la banlieue
subway ['sʌbweɪ] n (US: railway) métro m;
    (BRIT: underpass) passage souterrain
succeed [sək'si:d] vi réussir ♦ vt succéder à;
    to ~ in doing réussir à faire; **~ing** adj
    (following) suivant(e)
success [sək'ses] n succès m; réussite f; **~ful**
    adj (venture) couronné(e) de succès; **to be
    ~ful (in doing)** réussir (à faire); **~fully** adv
    avec succès
succession [sək'seʃən] n succession f; **3
    days in ~** 3 jours de suite
successive [sək'sesɪv] adj successif(-ive);
    consécutif(-ive)
such [sʌtʃ] adj tel (telle); (of that kind): **~ a
    book** un livre de ce genre, un livre pareil, un
    tel livre; (so much): **~ courage** un tel courage
    ♦ adv si; **~ books** des livres de ce genre, des
    livres pareils, de tels livres; **~ a long trip** un si
    long voyage; **~ a lot of** tellement or tant de;
    ~ as (like) tel que, comme; **as ~** en tant que
    tel, à proprement parler; **~-and-~** adj tel ou
    tel
suck [sʌk] vt sucer; (breast, bottle) téter; **~er**
    n ventouse f; (inf) poire f
suction ['sʌkʃən] n succion f
sudden ['sʌdn] adj soudain(e), subit(e); **all
    of a ~** soudain, tout à coup; **~ly** adv
    brusquement, tout à coup, soudain
suds [sʌdz] npl eau savonneuse
sue [su:] vt poursuivre en justice, intenter un
    procès à
suede [sweɪd] n daim m
suet ['suɪt] n graisse f de rognon
suffer ['sʌfər] vt souffrir, subir; (bear) tolérer,

supporter ♦ vi souffrir; **~er** n (MED) malade
    m/f; **~ing** n souffrance(s) f(pl)
sufficient [sə'fɪʃənt] adj suffisant(e); **~ money**
    suffisamment d'argent; **~ly** adv suffisamment,
    assez
suffocate ['sʌfəkeɪt] vi suffoquer; étouffer
sugar ['ʃugər] n sucre m ♦ vt sucrer; **~ beet** n
    betterave sucrière; **~ cane** n canne f à sucre
suggest [sə'dʒest] vt suggérer, proposer;
    (indicate) dénoter; **~ion** n suggestion f
suicide ['suɪsaɪd] n suicide m; see also **commit**
suit [su:t] n (man's) costume m, complet m;
    (woman's) tailleur m, ensemble m; (LAW)
    poursuite(s) f(pl), procès m; (CARDS) couleur f
    ♦ vt aller à; convenir à; (adapt): **to ~ sth to**
    adapter ou approprier qch à; **well ~ed** (well
    matched) faits l'un pour l'autre, très bien
    assortis; **~able** adj qui convient;
    approprié(e); **~ably** adv comme il se doit (or
    se devait etc), convenablement
suitcase ['su:tkeɪs] n valise f
suite [swi:t] n (of rooms, also MUS) suite f;
    (furniture): **bedroom/dining room ~**
    (ensemble m de) chambre f à coucher/salle f
    à manger
suitor ['su:tər] n soupirant m, prétendant m
sulfur ['sʌlfər] (US) n = **sulphur**
sulk [sʌlk] vi bouder; **~y** adj boudeur(-euse),
    maussade
sullen ['sʌlən] adj renfrogné(e), maussade
sulphur ['sʌlfər] (US **sulfur**) n soufre m
sultana [sʌl'tɑ:nə] n (CULIN) raisin (sec) de
    Smyrne
sultry ['sʌltrɪ] adj étouffant(e)
sum [sʌm] n somme f; (SCOL etc) calcul m;
    ~ up vt, vi résumer
summarize ['sʌmərɑɪz] vt résumer
summary ['sʌmərɪ] n résumé m
summer ['sʌmər] n été m ♦ adj d'été,
    estival(e); **~house** n (in garden) pavillon m;
    ~time n été m; **~ time** n (by clock) heure f
    d'été
summit ['sʌmɪt] n sommet m
summon ['sʌmən] vt appeler, convoquer;
    ~ up vt rassembler, faire appel à; **~s** n
    citation f, assignation f
sun [sʌn] n soleil m; **in the ~** au soleil; **~bathe**
    vi prendre un bain de soleil; **~block** n écran
    m total; **~burn** n coup m de soleil;
    ~burned, ~burnt adj (tanned) bronzé(e)
Sunday ['sʌndɪ] n dimanche m; **~ school** n
    ≈ catéchisme m
sundial ['sʌndaɪəl] n cadran m solaire
sundown ['sʌndaun] n coucher m du (or de)
    soleil
sundries ['sʌndrɪz] npl articles divers
sundry ['sʌndrɪ] adj divers(e), différent(e)
    ♦ n: **all and ~** tout le monde, n'importe qui
sunflower ['sʌnflauər] n tournesol m

sung [sʌŋ] *pp of* **sing**

sunglasses ['sʌnglɑːsɪz] *npl* lunettes *fpl* de soleil

sunk [sʌŋk] *pp of* **sink**

sun: **~light** *n* (lumière *f* du) soleil *m*; **~lit** *adj* ensoleillé(e); **~ny** *adj* ensoleillé(e); **~rise** *n* lever *m* du (*or de*) soleil; **~ roof** *n* (*AUT*) toit ouvrant; **~screen** *n* crème *f* solaire; **~set** *n* coucher *m* du (*or de*) soleil; **~shade** *n* (*over table*) parasol *m*; **~shine** *n* (lumière *f* du) soleil *m*; **~stroke** *n* insolation *f*; **~tan** *n* bronzage *m*; **~tan lotion** *n* lotion *f or* lait *m* solaire; **~tan oil** *n* huile *f* solaire

super ['suːpə^r] (*inf*) *adj* formidable

superannuation [suːpərænjuˈeɪʃən] *n* (*contribution*) cotisations *fpl* pour la pension

superb [suːˈpəːb] *adj* superbe, magnifique

supercilious [suːpəˈsɪlɪəs] *adj* hautain(e), dédaigneux(-euse)

superficial [suːpəˈfɪʃəl] *adj* superficiel(le)

superimpose ['suːpərɪmˈpəʊz] *vt* superposer

superintendent [suːpərɪnˈtendənt] *n* directeur(-trice); (*POLICE*) ≈ commissaire *m*

superior [suˈpɪərɪə^r] *adj, n* supérieur(e); **~ity** [supɪərɪˈɒrɪtɪ] *n* supériorité *f*

superlative [suˈpəːlətɪv] *n* (*LING*) superlatif *m*

superman ['suːpəmæn] (*irreg*) *n* surhomme *m*

supermarket ['suːpəmɑːkɪt] *n* supermarché *m*

supernatural [suːpəˈnætʃərəl] *adj* surnaturel(le)

superpower ['suːpəpauə^r] *n* (*POL*) superpuissance *f*

supersede [suːpəˈsiːd] *vt* remplacer, supplanter

superstitious [suːpəˈstɪʃəs] *adj* superstitieux(-euse)

supervise ['suːpəvaɪz] *vt* surveiller, diriger; **supervision** [suːpəˈvɪʒən] *n* surveillance *f*; contrôle *m*; **supervisor** *n* surveillant(e); (*in shop*) chef *m* de rayon

supper ['sʌpə^r] *n* dîner *m*; (*late*) souper *m*

supple ['sʌpl] *adj* souple

supplement [*n* 'sʌplɪmənt, *vb* sʌplɪˈment] *n* supplément *m* ♦ *vt* compléter; **~ary** [sʌplɪˈmentərɪ] *adj* supplémentaire; **~ary benefit** (*BRIT*) *n* allocation *f* (supplémentaire) d'aide sociale

supplier [səˈplaɪə^r] *n* fournisseur *m*

supply [səˈplaɪ] *vt* (*provide*) fournir; (*equip*): **to ~ (with)** approvisionner *or* ravitailler (en); fournir (en) ♦ *n* provision *f*, réserve *f*; (*~ing*) approvisionnement *m*; **supplies** *npl* (*food*) vivres *mpl*; (*MIL*) subsistances *fpl*; **~ teacher** (*BRIT*) *n* suppléant(e)

support [səˈpɔːt] *n* (*moral, financial etc*) soutien *m*, appui *m*; (*TECH*) support *m*, soutien ♦ *vt* soutenir, supporter; (*financially*) subvenir aux besoins de; (*uphold*) être pour, être partisan de, appuyer; **~er** *n* (*POL etc*) partisan(e); (*SPORT*) supporter *m*

suppose [səˈpəʊz] *vt* supposer; imaginer; **to be ~d to do** être censé(e) faire; **~dly** [səˈpəʊzɪdlɪ] *adv* soi-disant; **supposing** *conj* si, à supposer que +*sub*

suppress [səˈpres] *vt* (*revolt*) réprimer; (*information*) supprimer; (*yawn*) étouffer; (*feelings*) refouler

supreme [suˈpriːm] *adj* suprême

surcharge ['səːtʃɑːdʒ] *n* surcharge *f*

sure [ʃuə^r] *adj* sûr(e); (*definite, convinced*) sûr, certain(e); **~!** (*of course*) bien sûr!; **~ enough** effectivement; **to make ~ of sth** s'assurer de *or* vérifier qch; **to make ~ that** s'assurer *or* vérifier que; **~ly** *adv* sûrement; certainement

surf [səːf] *n* (*waves*) ressac *m*

surface ['səːfɪs] *n* surface *f* ♦ *vt* (*road*) poser un revêtement sur ♦ *vi* remonter à la surface; faire surface; **~ mail** *n* courrier *m* par voie de terre (*or maritime*)

surfboard ['səːfbɔːd] *n* planche *f* de surf

surfeit ['səːfɪt] *n*: **a ~ of** un excès de; une indigestion de

surfing ['səːfɪŋ] *n* surf *m*

surge [səːdʒ] *n* vague *f*, montée *f* ♦ *vi* déferler

surgeon ['səːdʒən] *n* chirurgien *m*

surgery ['səːdʒərɪ] *n* chirurgie *f*; (*BRIT: room*) cabinet *m* (de consultation); (: *also*: **~ hours**) heures *fpl* de consultation

surgical ['səːdʒɪkl] *adj* chirurgical(e); **~ spirit** (*BRIT*) *n* alcool *m* à 90°

surname ['səːneɪm] *n* nom *m* de famille

surplus ['səːpləs] *n* surplus *m*, excédent *m* ♦ *adj* en surplus, de trop; (*COMM*) excédentaire

surprise [səˈpraɪz] *n* surprise *f*; (*astonishment*) étonnement *m* ♦ *vt* surprendre; (*astonish*) étonner; **surprising** *adj* surprenant(e), étonnant(e); **surprisingly** *adv* (*easy, helpful*) étonnamment

surrender [səˈrendə^r] *n* reddition *f*, capitulation *f* ♦ *vi* se rendre, capituler

surreptitious [sʌrəpˈtɪʃəs] *adj* subreptice, furtif(-ive)

surrogate ['sʌrəgɪt] *n* substitut *m*; **~ mother** *n* mère porteuse *or* de substitution

surround [səˈraʊnd] *vt* entourer; (*MIL etc*) encercler; **~ing** *adj* environnant(e); **~ings** *npl* environs *mpl*, alentours *mpl*

surveillance [səːˈveɪləns] *n* surveillance *f*

survey [*n* 'səːveɪ, *vb* səːˈveɪ] *n* enquête *f*, étude *f*; (*in housebuying etc*) inspection *f*, (rapport *m* d')expertise *f*; (*of land*) levé *m* ♦ *vt* enquêter sur; inspecter; (*look at*) embrasser du regard; **~or** *n* (*of house*) expert *m*; (*of land*) (arpenteur *m*) géomètre *m*

survival [səˈvaɪvl] *n* survie *f*; (*relic*) vestige *m*

survive [sə'vaɪv] vi survivre; (custom etc) subsister ♦ vt survivre à; **survivor** n survivant(e); (fig) battant(e)

susceptible [sə'sɛptəbl] adj: ~ **(to)** sensible (à); (disease) prédisposé(e) (à)

suspect [adj, n 'sʌspɛkt, vb səs'pɛkt] adj, n suspect(e) ♦ vt soupçonner, suspecter

suspend [səs'pɛnd] vt suspendre; **~ed sentence** n condamnation f avec sursis; **~er belt** n porte-jarretelles m inv; **~ers** npl (BRIT) jarretelles fpl; (US) bretelles fpl

suspense [səs'pɛns] n attente f, incertitude f; (in film etc) suspense m

suspension [səs'pɛnʃən] n suspension f; (of driving licence) retrait m provisoire; **~ bridge** n pont suspendu

suspicion [səs'pɪʃən] n soupçon(s) m(pl)

suspicious adj (suspecting) soupçon-neux(-euse), méfiant(e); (causing suspicion) suspect(e)

sustain [səs'teɪn] vt soutenir; (food etc) nourrir, donner des forces à; (suffer) subir; recevoir; (development, growth etc) viable; **~ed** adj (effort) soutenu(e), prolongé(e); **sustenance** ['sʌstɪnəns] n nourriture f; (money) moyens mpl de subsistance

swab [swɔb] n (MED) tampon m

swagger ['swægə'] vi plastronner

swallow ['swɔləu] n (bird) hirondelle f ♦ vt avaler; **~ up** vt engloutir

swam [swæm] pt of swim

swamp [swɔmp] n marais m, marécage m ♦ vt submerger

swan [swɔn] n cygne m

swap [swɔp] vt: **to ~ (for)** échanger (contre), troquer (contre)

swarm [swɔːm] n essaim m ♦ vi fourmiller, grouiller

swastika ['swɔstɪkə] n croix gammée

swat [swɔt] vt écraser

sway [sweɪ] vi se balancer, osciller ♦ vt (influence) influencer

swear [swɛə'] (pt swore, pp sworn) vt, vi jurer; **~word** n juron m, gros mot

sweat [swɛt] n sueur f, transpiration f ♦ vi suer

sweater ['swɛtə'] n tricot m, pull m

sweaty ['swɛtɪ] adj en sueur, moite or mouillé(e) de sueur

Swede [swiːd] n Suédois(e)

swede [swiːd] (BRIT) n rutabaga m

Sweden ['swiːdn] n Suède f; **Swedish** adj suédois(e) ♦ n (LING) suédois m

sweep [swiːp] (pt, pp swept) n (also: chimney ~) ramoneur m ♦ vt balayer; (subj: current) emporter; **~ away** vt balayer; entraîner; emporter; **~ past** vi passer majestueusement or rapidement; **~ up** vt, vi

balayer; **~ing** adj (gesture) large; circulaire; a **~ing statement** une généralisation hâtive

sweet [swiːt] n (candy) bonbon m; (BRIT: pudding) dessert m ♦ adj doux (douce); (not savoury) sucré(e); (fig: kind) gentil(le); (baby) mignon(ne); **~corn** ['swiːtkɔːn] n maïs m; **~en** vt adoucir; (with sugar) sucrer; **~heart** n amoureux(-euse); **~ness** n goût sucré; douceur f; **~ pea** n pois m de senteur

swell [swɛl] (pt swelled, pp swollen or swelled) n (of sea) houle f ♦ adj (US: inf: excellent) chouette ♦ vi grossir, augmenter; (sound) s'enfler; (MED) enfler; **~ing** n (MED) enflure f; (lump) grosseur f

sweltering ['swɛltərɪŋ] adj étouffant(e), oppressant(e)

swept [swɛpt] pt, pp of sweep

swerve [swəːv] vi faire une embardée or un écart; dévier

swift [swɪft] n (bird) martinet m ♦ adj rapide, prompt(e)

swig [swɪg] (inf) n (drink) lampée f

swill [swɪl] vt (also: ~ out, ~ down) laver à grande eau

swim [swɪm] (pt swam, pp swum) n: **to go for a ~** aller nager or se baigner ♦ vi nager; (SPORT) faire de la natation; (head, room) tourner ♦ vt traverser (à la nage); (a length) faire (à la nage); **~mer** n nageur(-euse); **~ming** n natation f; **~ming cap** n bonnet m de bain; **~ming costume** (BRIT) n maillot m (de bain); **~ming pool** n piscine f; **~ming trunks** npl caleçon m or slip m de bain; **~suit** n maillot m (de bain)

swindle ['swɪndl] n escroquerie f

swine [swaɪn] (inf!) n inv salaud m (!)

swing [swɪŋ] (pt, pp swung) n balançoire f; (movement) balancement m, oscillations fpl; (change: in opinion etc) revirement m ♦ vt balancer, faire osciller; (also: ~ round) tourner, faire virer ♦ vi se balancer, osciller; (also: ~ round) virer, tourner; **to be in full ~** battre son plein; **~ bridge** n pont tournant; **~ door** (US swinging door) n porte battante

swingeing ['swɪndʒɪŋ] (BRIT) adj écrasant(e); (cuts etc) considérable

swipe [swaɪp] (inf) vt (steal) piquer

swirl [swəːl] vi tourbillonner, tournoyer

Swiss [swɪs] adj suisse ♦ n inv Suisse m/f

switch [swɪtʃ] n (for light, radio etc) bouton m; (change) changement m, revirement m ♦ vt changer; **~ off** vt éteindre; (engine) arrêter; **~ on** vt allumer; (engine, machine) mettre en marche; **~board** n (TEL) standard m

Switzerland ['swɪtsələnd] n Suisse f

swivel ['swɪvl] vi (also: ~ round) pivoter, tourner

swollen ['swəulən] pp of swell

swoon [swu:n] vi se pâmer

swoop [swu:p] n (by police) descente f ♦ vi (also: ~ **down**) descendre en piqué, piquer

swop [swɔp] vt = **swap**

sword [sɔ:d] n épée f; **~fish** n espadon m

swore [swɔ:ʳ] pt of **swear**

sworn [swɔ:n] pp of **swear** ♦ adj (statement, evidence) donné(e) sous serment

swot [swɔt] vi bûcher, potasser

swum [swʌm] pp of **swim**

swung [swʌŋ] pt, pp of **swing**

syllable [ˈsɪləbl] n syllabe f

syllabus [ˈsɪləbəs] n programme m

symbol [ˈsɪmbl] n symbole m

symmetry [ˈsɪmɪtrɪ] n symétrie f

sympathetic [sɪmpəˈθetɪk] adj compatissant(e); bienveillant(e), compréhensif(-ive); (likeable) sympathique; **~ towards** bien disposé(e) envers

sympathize [ˈsɪmpəθaɪz] vi: **to ~ with sb** plaindre qn; (in grief) s'associer à la douleur de qn; **to ~ with sth** comprendre qch; **~r** n (POL) sympathisant(e)

sympathy [ˈsɪmpəθɪ] n (pity) compassion f; **sympathies** npl (support) soutien m; **left-wing etc sympathies** penchants mpl à gauche etc; **in ~ with** (strike) en or par solidarité avec; **with our deepest ~** en vous priant d'accepter nos sincères condoléances

symphony [ˈsɪmfənɪ] n symphonie f

symptom [ˈsɪmptəm] n symptôme m; indice m

syndicate [ˈsɪndɪkɪt] n syndicat m, coopérative f

synopsis [sɪˈnɔpsɪs] n (pl **synopses**) n résumé m

synthetic [sɪnˈθetɪk] adj synthétique

syphon [ˈsaɪfən] n, vb = **siphon**

Syria [ˈsɪrɪə] n Syrie f

syringe [sɪˈrɪndʒ] n seringue f

syrup [ˈsɪrəp] n sirop m; (also: **golden ~**) mélasse raffinée

system [ˈsɪstəm] n système m; (ANAT) organisme m; **~atic** [sɪstəˈmætɪk] adj systématique; méthodique; **~ disk** n (COMPUT) disque m système; **~s analyst** n analyste fonctionnel(le)

T, t

ta [tɑ:] (BRIT: inf) excl merci!

tab [tæb] n (label) étiquette f; (on drinks can etc) languette f; **to keep ~s on** (fig) surveiller

tabby [ˈtæbɪ] n (also: ~ **cat**) chat(te) tigré(e)

table [ˈteɪbl] n table f ♦ vt (BRIT: motion etc) présenter; **to lay** or **set the ~** mettre le couvert or la table; **~cloth** n nappe f; **~ d'hôte** [tɑ:blˈdəʊt] adj (meal) à prix fixe; **~ lamp** n

lampe f de table; **~mat** n (for plate) napperon m, set m; (for hot dish) dessous-de-plat m inv; **~ of contents** n table f des matières; **~spoon** n cuiller f de service; (also: **~spoonful**: as measurement) cuillerée f à soupe

tablet [ˈtæblɪt] n (MED) comprimé m

table tennis n ping-pong ® m, tennis m de table

table wine n vin m de table

tabloid [ˈtæblɔɪd] n quotidien m populaire

tack [tæk] n (nail) petit clou ♦ vt clouer; (fig) direction f; (BRIT: stitch) faufiler ♦ vi tirer un or des bord(s)

tackle [ˈtækl] n matériel m, équipement m; (for lifting) appareil m de levage; (RUGBY) plaquage m ♦ vt (difficulty, animal, burglar etc) s'attaquer à; (person: challenge) s'expliquer avec; (RUGBY) plaquer

tacky [ˈtækɪ] adj collant(e); (pej: of poor quality) miteux(-euse)

tact [tækt] n tact m; **~ful** adj plein(e) de tact

tactical [ˈtæktɪkl] adj tactique

tactics [ˈtæktɪks] npl tactique f

tactless [ˈtæktlɪs] adj qui manque de tact

tadpole [ˈtædpəʊl] n têtard m

tag [tæg] n étiquette f; **~ along** vi suivre

tail [teɪl] n queue f; (of shirt) pan m ♦ vt (follow) suivre, filer; **~s** npl habit m; **~ away**, **~ off** vi (in size, quality etc) baisser peu à peu; **~back** (BRIT) n (AUT) bouchon m; **~ end** n bout m, fin f; **~gate** n (AUT) hayon m arrière

tailor [ˈteɪləʳ] n tailleur m; (in cut) coupe f; **~-made** adj fait(e) sur mesure; (fig) conçu(e) spécialement

tailwind [ˈteɪlwɪnd] n vent m arrière inv

tainted [ˈteɪntɪd] adj (food) gâté(e); (water, air) infecté(e); (fig) souillé(e)

take [teɪk] (pt **took**, pp **taken**) vt prendre; (gain: prize) remporter; (require: effort, courage) demander; (tolerate) accepter, supporter; (hold: passengers etc) contenir; (accompany) emmener, accompagner; (bring, carry) apporter, emporter; (exam) passer, se présenter à; **to ~ sth from** (drawer etc) prendre qch dans; (person) prendre qch à; **I ~ it that** ... je suppose que ...; **~ after** vt fus ressembler à; **~ apart** vt démonter; **~ away** vt enlever; (carry off) emporter; **~ back** vt (return) rendre, rapporter; (one's words) retirer; **~ down** vt (building) démolir; (letter etc) prendre, écrire; **~ in** vt (deceive) tromper, rouler; (understand) comprendre, saisir; (include) comprendre, inclure; (lodger) prendre; **~ off** vi (AVIAT) décoller ♦ vt (go away) s'en aller; (remove) enlever; **~ on** vt (work) accepter, se charger de; (employee) prendre, embaucher; (opponent) accepter de se battre contre; **~ out** vt (invite) emmener, sortir; (*remove*) enlever; **to ~ sth out of sth** (*drawer, pocket etc*) prendre qch dans qch; **~ over** vt (*business*) reprendre ♦ vi: **to ~ over from sb** prendre la relève de qn; **~ to** vt fus (*person*) se prendre d'amitié pour; (*thing*) prendre goût à; **~ up** vt (*activity*) se mettre à; (*dress*) raccourcir; (*occupy: time, space*) prendre, occuper; **to ~ sb up on an offer** accepter la proposition de qn; **~away** (*BRIT*) adj (*food*) à emporter ♦ n (*shop, restaurant*) café m qui vend de plats à emporter; **~off** n (*AVIAT*) décollage m; **~over** n (*COMM*) rachat m; **takings** npl (*COMM*) recette f

talc [tælk] n (*also:* **~ powder**) talc m

tale [teɪl] n (*story*) conte m, histoire f; (*account*) récit m; **to tell ~s** (*fig*) rapporter

talent ['tælnt] n talent m, don m; **~ed** adj doué(e), plein(e) de talent

talk [tɔ:k] n (*a speech*) causerie f, exposé m; (*conversation*) discussion f, entretien m; (*gossip*) racontars mpl ♦ vi parler; **~s** npl (*POL etc*) entretiens mpl; **to ~ about** parler de; **to ~ sb into/out of doing** persuader qn de faire/ ne pas faire; **to ~ shop** parler métier or affaires; **~ over** vt discuter (de); **~ative** adj bavard(e); **~ show** n causerie (télévisée or radiodiffusée)

tall [tɔ:l] adj (*person*) grand(e); (*building, tree*) haut(e); **to be 6 feet ~** ≈ mesurer 1 mètre 80; **~ story** n histoire f invraisemblable

tally ['tælɪ] n compte m ♦ vi: **to ~ (with)** correspondre (à)

talon ['tælən] n griffe f; (*of eagle*) serre f

tame [teɪm] adj apprivoisé(e); (*fig: story, style*) insipide

tamper ['tæmpər] vi: **to ~ with** toucher à

tampon ['tæmpɔn] n tampon m (hygiénique or périodique)

tan [tæn] n (*also:* **suntan**) bronzage m ♦ vt, vi bronzer ♦ adj (*colour*) brun roux inv

tang [tæŋ] n odeur (*or saveur*) piquante

tangent ['tændʒənt] n (*MATH*) tangente f; **to go off at a ~** (*fig*) changer de sujet

tangerine [tændʒə'ri:n] n mandarine f

tangle ['tæŋgl] n enchevêtrement m; **to get in(to) a ~** s'embrouiller

tank [tæŋk] n (*water ~*) réservoir m; (*for fish*) aquarium m; (*MIL*) char m d'assaut, tank m

tanker ['tæŋkər] n (*ship*) pétrolier m, tanker m; (*truck*) camion-citerne m

tantalizing ['tæntəlaɪzɪŋ] adj (*smell*) extrêmement appétissant(e); (*offer*) terriblement tentant(e)

tantamount ['tæntəmaunt] adj: **~ to** qui équivaut à

tantrum ['tæntrəm] n accès m de colère

tap [tæp] n (*on sink etc*) robinet m; (*gentle blow*) petite tape ♦ vt frapper or taper légèrement; (*resources*) exploiter, utiliser;

(*telephone*) mettre sur écoute; **on ~** (*fig: resources*) disponible; **~-dancing** n claquettes fpl

tape [teɪp] n ruban m; (*also:* **magnetic ~**) bande f (magnétique); (*cassette*) cassette f; (*sticky*) scotch m ♦ vt (*record*) enregistrer; (*stick with ~*) coller avec du scotch; **~ deck** n platine f d'enregistrement; **~ measure** n mètre m à ruban

taper ['teɪpər] vi s'effiler

tape recorder n magnétophone m

tapestry ['tæpɪstrɪ] n tapisserie f

tar [tɑ:] n goudron m

target ['tɑ:gɪt] n cible f; (*fig*) objectif m

tariff ['tærɪf] n (*COMM*) tarif m; (*taxes*) tarif douanier

tarmac ['tɑ:mæk] n (*BRIT: on road*) macadam m; (*AVIAT*) piste f

tarnish ['tɑ:nɪʃ] vt ternir

tarpaulin [tɑ:'pɔ:lɪn] n bâche (goudronnée)

tarragon ['tærəgən] n estragon m

tart [tɑ:t] n (*CULIN*) tarte f; (*BRIT: inf: prostitute*) putain f ♦ adj (*flavour*) âpre, aigrelet(te); **~ up** (*BRIT: inf*) vt (*object*) retaper; **to ~ o.s. up** se faire beau (belle), s'attifer (*pej*)

tartan ['tɑ:tn] n tartan m ♦ adj écossais(e)

tartar ['tɑ:tər] n (*on teeth*) tartre m; **~(e) sauce** n sauce f tartare

task [tɑ:sk] n tâche f; **to take sb to ~** prendre qn à partie; **~ force** n (*MIL, POLICE*) détachement spécial

tassel ['tæsl] n gland m; pompon m

taste [teɪst] n goût m; (*fig: glimpse, idea*) idée f, aperçu m ♦ vt goûter ♦ vi: **to ~ of or like** (*fish etc*) avoir le or un goût de; **you can ~ the garlic (in it)** on sent bien l'ail; **can I have a ~ of this wine?** puis-je goûter un peu de ce vin?; **in good/bad ~** de bon/mauvais goût; **~ful** adj de bon goût; **~less** adj (*food*) fade; (*remark*) de mauvais goût; **tasty** adj savoureux(-euse), délicieux(-euse)

tatters ['tætəz] npl: **in ~** en lambeaux

tattoo [tə'tu:] n tatouage m; (*spectacle*) parade f militaire ♦ vt tatouer

tatty ['tætɪ] (*BRIT: inf*) adj (*clothes*) fripé(e); (*shop, area*) délabré(e)

taught [tɔ:t] pt, pp of **teach**

taunt [tɔ:nt] n raillerie f ♦ vt railler

Taurus ['tɔ:rəs] n le Taureau

taut [tɔ:t] adj tendu(e)

tax [tæks] n (*on goods etc*) taxe f; (*on income*) impôts mpl, contributions fpl ♦ vt taxer; imposer; (*fig: patience etc*) mettre à l'épreuve; **~able** adj (*income*) imposable; **~ation** [tæk'seɪʃən] n taxation f; impôts mpl, contributions fpl; **~ avoidance** n dégrèvement fiscal; **~ disc** (*BRIT*) n (*AUT*) vignette f (automobile); **~ evasion** n fraude fiscale; ~-**free** adj exempt(e) d'impôts

taxi ['tæksɪ] n taxi m ♦ vi (AVIAT) rouler (lentement) au sol; ~ **driver** n chauffeur m de taxi; ~ **rank** (BRIT) n station f de taxis; ~ **stand** n = taxi rank

tax: ~ **payer** n contribuable m/f; ~ **relief** n dégrèvement fiscal; ~ **return** n déclaration f d'impôts or de revenus

TB n abbr = **tuberculosis**

tea [tiː] n thé m; (BRIT: snack: for children) goûter m; **high** ~ collation combinant goûter et dîner; ~ **bag** n sachet m de thé; ~ **break** (BRIT) n pause-thé f

teach [tiːtʃ] (pt, pp taught) vt: **to** ~ **sb sth**, ~ **sth to sb** apprendre qch à qn; (in school etc) enseigner qch à qn ♦ vi enseigner; ~**er** n (in secondary school) professeur m; (in primary school) instituteur(-trice); ~**ing** n enseignement m

tea: ~ **cloth** n torchon m; ~ **cosy** n cloche f à thé; ~**cup** n tasse f à thé

teak [tiːk] n teck m

tea leaves npl feuilles fpl de thé

team [tiːm] n équipe f; (of animals) attelage m; ~**work** n travail m d'équipe

teapot ['tiːpɒt] n théière f

tear¹ [tɛəʳ] (pt tore, pp torn) n déchirure f ♦ vt déchirer ♦ vi se déchirer; ~ **along** vi (rush) aller à toute vitesse; ~ **up** vt (sheet of paper etc) déchirer, mettre en morceaux or pièces

tear² [tɪəʳ] n larme f; **in** ~**s** en larmes; ~**ful** adj larmoyant(e); ~ **gas** n gaz m lacrymogène

tearoom ['tiːruːm] n salon m de thé

tease [tiːz] vt taquiner; (unkindly) tourmenter

tea set n service m à thé

teaspoon ['tiːspuːn] n petite cuiller; (also: ~**ful**: as measurement) ≈ cuillerée f à café

teat [tiːt] n tétine f

teatime ['tiːtaɪm] n l'heure f du thé

tea towel (BRIT) n torchon m (à vaisselle)

technical ['tɛknɪkl] adj technique; ~**ity** [tɛknɪˈkælɪtɪ] n (detail) détail m technique; (point of law) vice m de forme; ~**ly** adv techniquement; (strictly speaking) en théorie

technician [tɛkˈnɪʃən] n technicien(ne)

technique [tɛkˈniːk] n technique f

techno ['tɛknəʊ] n (music) techno f

technological [tɛknəˈlɒdʒɪkl] adj technologique

technology [tɛkˈnɒlədʒɪ] n technologie f

teddy (bear) ['tɛdɪ(-)] n ours m en peluche

tedious ['tiːdɪəs] adj fastidieux(-euse)

tee [tiː] n (GOLF) tee m

teem [tiːm] vi: **to** ~ (**with**) grouiller (de); **it is** ~**ing (with rain)** il pleut à torrents

teenage ['tiːneɪdʒ] adj (fashions etc) pour jeunes, pour adolescents; (children) adolescent(e); ~**r** n adolescent(e)

teens [tiːnz] npl: **to be in one's** ~ être

adolescent(e)

tee-shirt ['tiːʃəːt] n = **T-shirt**

teeter ['tiːtəʳ] vi chanceler, vaciller

teeth [tiːθ] npl of **tooth**

teethe [tiːð] vi percer ses dents

teething troubles ['tiːðɪŋ-] npl (fig) difficultés initiales

teetotal ['tiːˈtəʊtl] adj (person) qui ne boit jamais d'alcool

tele ['tɛlɪ-]: ~**communications** npl télécommunications fpl; ~**conferencing** n téléconférence(s) f(pl); ~**gram** n télégramme m; ~**graph** n télégraphe m; ~**graph pole** n poteau m télégraphique

telephone ['tɛlɪfəʊn] n téléphone m ♦ vt (person) téléphoner à; (message) téléphoner; **on the** ~ au téléphone; **to be on the** ~ (BRIT: have a ~) avoir le téléphone; ~ **booth**, ~ **box** (BRIT) n cabine f téléphonique; ~ **call** n coup m de téléphone, appel m téléphonique; ~ **directory** n annuaire m (du téléphone); ~ **number** n numéro m de téléphone; **telephonist** [təˈlɛfənɪst] (BRIT) n téléphoniste m/f

telescope ['tɛlɪskəʊp] n télescope m

television ['tɛlɪvɪʒən] n télévision f; **on** ~ à la télévision; ~ **set** n (poste f de) télévision m

telex ['tɛlɛks] n télex m

tell [tɛl] (pt, pp told) vt dire; (relate: story) raconter; (distinguish): **to** ~ **sth from** distinguer qch de ♦ vi (talk): **to** ~ (**of**) parler (de); (have effect) se faire sentir, se voir; **to** ~ **sb to do** dire à qn de faire; ~ **off** vt réprimander, gronder; ~**er** n (in bank) caissier(-ère); ~**ing** adj (remark, detail) révélateur(-trice); ~**tale** adj (sign) éloquent(e), révélateur(-trice)

telly ['tɛlɪ] (BRIT: inf) n abbr (= television) télé f

temp [tɛmp] n abbr (= temporary) (secrétaire f) intérimaire f

temper ['tɛmpəʳ] n (nature) caractère m; (mood) humeur f; (fit of anger) colère f ♦ vt (moderate) tempérer, adoucir; **to be in a** ~ être en colère; **to lose one's** ~ se mettre en colère

temperament ['tɛmprəmənt] n (nature) tempérament m; ~**al** [tɛmprəˈmɛntl] adj capricieux(-euse)

temperate ['tɛmprət] adj (climate, country) tempéré(e)

temperature ['tɛmprətʃəʳ] n température f; **to have** or **run a** ~ avoir de la fièvre

temple ['tɛmpl] n (building) temple m; (ANAT) tempe f

temporary ['tɛmpərərɪ] adj temporaire, provisoire; (job, worker) temporaire

tempt [tɛmpt] vt tenter; **to** ~ **sb into doing** persuader qn de faire; ~**ation** [tɛmpˈteɪʃən] n tentation f; ~**ing** adj tentant(e)

ten [tɛn] *num* dix

tenacity [tə'næsɪtɪ] *n* ténacité *f*

tenancy ['tɛnənsɪ] *n* location *f*; état *m* de locataire

tenant ['tɛnənt] *n* locataire *m/f*

tend [tɛnd] *vt* s'occuper de ♦ *vi*: **to ~ to do** avoir tendance à faire; **~ency** ['tɛndənsɪ] *n* tendance *f*

tender ['tɛndər] *adj* tendre; (*delicate*) délicat(e); (*sore*) sensible ♦ *n* (*COMM: offer*) soumission *f* ♦ *vt* offrir

tenement ['tɛnəmənt] *n* immeuble *m*

tennis ['tɛnɪs] *n* tennis *m*; **~ ball** *n* balle *f* de tennis; **~ court** *n* (court *m* de) tennis; **~ player** *n* joueur(-euse) de tennis; **~ racket** *n* raquette *f* de tennis; **~ shoes** *npl* (chaussures *fpl* de) tennis *mpl*

tenor ['tɛnər] *n* (*MUS*) ténor *m*

tenpin bowling ['tɛnpɪn-] (*BRIT*) *n* bowling *m* (à dix quilles)

tense [tɛns] *adj* tendu(e) ♦ *n* (*LING*) temps *m*

tension ['tɛnʃən] *n* tension *f*

tent [tɛnt] *n* tente *f*

tentative ['tɛntətɪv] *adj* timide, hésitant(e); (*conclusion*) provisoire

tenterhooks ['tɛntəhuks] *npl*: **on ~** sur des charbons ardents

tenth [tɛnθ] *num* dixième

tent peg *n* piquet *m* de tente

tent pole *n* montant *m* de tente

tenuous ['tɛnjuəs] *adj* ténu(e)

tenure ['tɛnjuər] *n* (*of property*) bail *m*; (*of job*) période *f* de jouissance

tepid ['tɛpɪd] *adj* tiède

term [təːm] *n* terme *m*; (*SCOL*) trimestre *m* ♦ *vt* appeler; **~s** *npl* (*conditions*) conditions *fpl*, (*COMM*) tarif *m*; **in the short/long ~** à court/long terme; **to come to ~s with** (*problem*) faire face à

terminal ['təːmɪnl] *adj* (*disease*) dans sa phase terminale; (*patient*) incurable ♦ *n* (*ELEC*) borne *f*; (*for oil, ore etc, COMPUT*) terminal *m*; (*also: air ~*) aérogare *f*; (*BRIT: also: coach ~*) gare routière; **~ly** *adv*: **to be ~ly ill** être condamné(e)

terminate ['təːmɪneɪt] *vt* mettre fin à; (*pregnancy*) interrompre

termini ['təːmɪnaɪ] *npl of* **terminus**

terminus ['təːmɪnəs] (*pl* **termini**) *n* terminus *m inv*

terrace ['tɛrəs] *n* terrasse *f*; (*BRIT: row of houses*) rangée *f* de maisons (*attenantes*); **the ~s** *npl* (*BRIT: SPORT*) les gradins *mpl*; **~d** *adj* (*garden*) en terrasses

terracotta ['tɛrə'kɒtə] *n* terre cuite

terrain [tɛ'reɪn] *n* terrain *m* (*sol*)

terrible ['tɛrɪbl] *adj* terrible, atroce; (*weather, conditions*) affreux(-euse), épouvantable; **terribly** *adv* terriblement; (*very badly*)

affreusement mal

terrier ['tɛrɪər] *n* terrier *m* (*chien*)

terrific [tə'rɪfɪk] *adj* fantastique, incroyable, terrible; (*wonderful*) formidable, sensationnel(le)

terrify ['tɛrɪfaɪ] *vt* terrifier

territory ['tɛrɪtərɪ] *n* territoire *m*

terror ['tɛrər] *n* terreur *f*; **~ism** *n* terrorisme *m*; **~ist** *n* terroriste *m/f*

test [tɛst] *n* (*trial, check*) essai *m*; (*of courage etc*) épreuve *f*; (*MED*) examen *m*; (*CHEM*) analyse *f*; (*SCOL*) interrogation *f*; (*also: driving ~*) (examen du) permis *m* de conduire ♦ *vt* essayer; mettre à l'épreuve; examiner; analyser; faire subir une interrogation à

testament ['tɛstəmənt] *n* testament *m*; **the Old/New T~** l'Ancien/le Nouveau Testament

testicle ['tɛstɪkl] *n* testicule *m*

testify ['tɛstɪfaɪ] *vi* (*LAW*) témoigner, déposer; **to ~ to sth** attester qch

testimony ['tɛstɪmənɪ] *n* témoignage *m*; (*clear proof*): **to be (a) ~ to** être la preuve de

test match *n* (*CRICKET, RUGBY*) match international

test tube *n* éprouvette *f*

tetanus ['tɛtənəs] *n* tétanos *m*

tether ['tɛðər] *vt* attacher ♦ *n*: **at the end of one's ~** à bout (de patience)

text [tɛkst] *n* texte *m*; **~book** *n* manuel *m*

textile ['tɛkstaɪl] *n* textile *m*

texture ['tɛkstʃər] *n* texture *f*; (*of skin, paper etc*) grain *m*

Thailand ['taɪlænd] *n* Thaïlande *f*

Thames [tɛmz] *n*: **the ~** la Tamise

than [ðæn, ðən] *conj* que; (*with numerals*): **more ~ 10/once** plus de 10/d'une fois; **I have more/less ~ you** j'en ai plus/moins que toi; **she has more apples ~ pears** elle a plus de pommes que de poires

thank [θæŋk] *vt* remercier, dire merci à; **~s** *npl* (*gratitude*) remerciements *mpl* ♦ *excl* merci!; **~ you (very much)** merci (beaucoup); **~s to** grâce à; **~ God!** Dieu merci!; **~ful** *adj*: **~ful (for)** reconnaissant(e) (de); **~less** *adj* ingrat(e); **T~sgiving (Day)** *n* jour *m* d'action de grâce (*fête américaine*)

KEYWORD

---

that [ðæt] *adj* (*demonstrative: pl those*) ce, cet +*vowel or h mute*, cette *f*; **that man/woman/ book** cet homme/cette femme/ce livre; (*not "this"*) cet homme-là/cette femme-là/ce livre-là; **that one** celui-là (celle-là)

♦ *pron* **1** (*demonstrative: pl those*) ce; (*not "this one"*) cela, ça: **who's that?** qui est-ce?; **what's that?** qu'est-ce que c'est?; **is that you?** c'est toi?; **I prefer this to that** je préfère ceci à cela *or* ça; **that's what he said** c'est *or* voilà ce qu'il a dit; **that is (to say)** c'est-à-dire, à savoir

2 (*relative: subject*) qui; (: *object*) que; (: *indirect*) lequel (laquelle), lesquels (lesquelles) *pl*; **the book that I read** le livre que j'ai lu; **the books that are in the library** les livres qui sont dans la bibliothèque; **all that I have** tout ce que j'ai; **the box that I put it in** la boîte dans laquelle je l'ai mis; **the people that I spoke to** les gens auxquels or à qui j'ai parlé
3 (*relative: of time*) où; **the day that he came** le jour où il est venu
♦ *conj* que; **he thought that I was ill** il pensait que j'étais malade
♦ *adv* (*demonstrative*): **I can't work that much** je ne peux pas travailler autant que cela; **I didn't know it was that bad** je ne savais pas que c'était si or aussi mauvais; **it's about that high** c'est à peu près de cette hauteur

thatched [θætʃt] *adj* (*roof*) de chaume; **~ cottage** chaumière *f*

thaw [θɔː] *n* dégel *m* ♦ *vi* (*ice*) fondre; (*food*) dégeler ♦ *vt* (*food: also*: **~ out**) (faire) dégeler

KEYWORD

the [ðiː, ðə] *def art* 1 (*gen*) le, la *f*, l' +*vowel or h mute*, les *pl*; **the boy/girl/ink** le garçon/la fille/l'encre; **the children** les enfants; **the history of the world** l'histoire du monde; **give it to the postman** donne-le au facteur; **to play the piano/flute** jouer du piano/de la flûte; **the rich and the poor** les riches et les pauvres
2 (*in titles*): **Elizabeth the First** Elisabeth première; **Peter the Great** Pierre le Grand
3 (*in comparisons*): **the more he works, the more he earns** plus il travaille, plus il gagne de l'argent

theatre ['θɪətəʳ] *n* théâtre *m*; (*also: lecture ~*) amphi(théâtre) *m*; (*MED: also:* **operating ~**) salle *f* d'opération; **~-goer** *n* habitué(e) du théâtre; **theatrical** [θɪˈætrɪkl] *adj* théâtral(e)

theft [θeft] *n* vol *m* (*larcin*)

their [ðɛəʳ] *adj* leur; (*pl*) leurs; *see also* my; **~s** *pron* le (la) leur; (*pl*) les leurs; *see also* mine¹

them [ðɛm, ðəm] *pron* (*direct*) les; (*indirect*) leur; (*stressed, after prep*) eux (elles); *see also* me

theme [θiːm] *n* thème *m*; **~ park** *n* parc *m* (d'attraction) à thème; **~ song** *n* chanson principale

themselves [ðəmˈsɛlvz] *pl pron* (*reflexive*) se; (*emphatic, after prep*) eux-mêmes (elles-mêmes); *see also* oneself

then [ðɛn] *adv* (*at that time*) alors, à ce moment-là; (*next*) puis, ensuite; (*and also*) et puis ♦ *conj* (*therefore*) alors, dans ce cas ♦ *adj*: **the ~ president** le président d'alors or de l'époque; **by ~** (*past*) à ce moment-là; (*future*) d'ici là; **from ~ on** dès lors

theology [θɪˈɔlədʒɪ] *n* théologie *f*

theoretical [θɪəˈrɛtɪkl] *adj* théorique

theory ['θɪərɪ] *n* théorie *f*

therapy ['θɛrəpɪ] *n* thérapie *f*

KEYWORD

there [ðɛəʳ] *adv* 1: **there is, there are** il y a; **there are 3 of them** (*people, things*) il y en a 3; **there has been an accident** il y a eu un accident
2 (*referring to place*) là, là-bas; **it's there** c'est là(-bas); **in/on/up/down there** là-dedans/là-dessus/là-haut/en bas; **he went there on Friday** il y est allé vendredi; **I want that book there** je veux ce livre-là; **there he is!** le voilà!
3: **there, there** (*esp to child*) allons, allons!

there: **~abouts** *adv* (*place*) par là, près de là; (*amount*) environ, à peu près; **~after** *adv* par la suite; **~by** *adv* ainsi; **~fore** *adv* donc, par conséquent; **~'s = there is; there has**

thermal ['θəːml] *adj* (*springs*) thermal(e); (*underwear*) en thermolactyl ®; (*COMPUT: paper*) thermosensible; (: *printer*) thermique

thermometer [θəˈmɔmɪtəʳ] *n* thermomètre *m*

Thermos ® ['θəːməs] *n* (*also:* **~ flask**) thermos ® *m or f inv*

thermostat ['θəːməustæt] *n* thermostat *m*

thesaurus [θɪˈsɔːrəs] *n* dictionnaire *m* des synonymes

these [ðiːz] *pl adj* ces; (*not "those"*): **~ books** ces livres-ci ♦ *pl pron* ceux-ci (celles-ci)

thesis ['θiːsɪs] (*pl* **theses**) *n* thèse *f*

they [ðeɪ] *pl pron* ils (elles); (*stressed*) eux (elles); **~ say that ...** (*it is said that*) on dit que ...; **~'d = they had; they would; ~'ll = they shall; they will; ~'re = they are; ~'ve = they have**

thick [θɪk] *adj* épais(se); (*stupid*) bête, borné(e) ♦ *n*: **in the ~ of** au beau milieu de, en plein cœur de; **it's 20 cm ~** il/elle a 20 cm d'épaisseur; **~en** *vi* s'épaissir ♦ *vt* (*sauce etc*) épaissir; **~ness** *n* épaisseur *f*; **~set** *adj* trapu(e), costaud(e)

thief [θiːf] (*pl* **thieves**) *n* voleur(-euse)

thigh [θaɪ] *n* cuisse *f*

thimble ['θɪmbl] *n* dé *m* (à coudre)

thin [θɪn] *adj* mince; (*skinny*) maigre; (*soup, sauce*) peu épais(se), clair(e); (*hair, crowd*) clairsemé(e) ♦ *vt*: **to ~ (down)** (*sauce, paint*) délayer

thing [θɪŋ] *n* chose *f*; (*object*) objet *m*; (*contraption*) truc *m*; (*mania*): **to have a ~ about** être obsédé(e) par; **~s** *npl* (*belongings*) affaires *fpl*; **poor ~!** le (la) pauvre!; **the best ~ would be to** le mieux serait de; **how are ~s?** comment ça va?

think [θɪŋk] (*pt, pp* **thought**) *vi* penser,

réfléchir; (*believe*) penser ♦ vt (*imagine*) imaginer; **what did you ~ of them?** qu'avez-vous pensé d'eux?; **to ~ about sth/sb** penser à qch/qn; **I'll ~ about it** je vais y réfléchir; **to ~ of doing** avoir l'idée de faire; **I ~ so/not** je crois or pense que oui/non; **to ~ well of** avoir une haute opinion de; **~ over** vt bien réfléchir à; **~ up** vt inventer, trouver; **~ tank** n groupe m de réflexion

thinly ['θɪnlɪ] adv (*cut*) en fines tranches; (*spread*) en une couche mince

third [θə:d] num troisième ♦ n (*fraction*) tiers m; (*AUT*) troisième (vitesse) f; (*BRIT: SCOL: degree*) ≈ licence f sans mention; **~ly** adv troisièmement; **~ party insurance** (*BRIT*) n assurance f au tiers; **~-rate** adj de qualité médiocre; **the T~ World** n le tiers monde

thirst [θə:st] n soif f; **~y** adj (*person*) qui a soif, assoiffé(e); (*work*) qui donne soif; **to be ~y** avoir soif

thirteen [θə:'ti:n] num treize

thirty ['θə:tɪ] num trente

―――――――――――
KEYWORD
―――――――――――

this [ðɪs] adj (*demonstrative: pl these*) ce, cet +*vowel or h mute*, cette f; **this man/woman/book** cet homme/cette femme/ce livre; (*not "that"*) cet homme-ci/cette femme-ci/ce livre-ci; **this one** celui-ci (celle-ci)
♦ pron (*demonstrative: pl these*) ce; (*not "that one"*) celui-ci (celle-ci), ceci; **who's this?** qui est-ce?; **what's this?** qu'est-ce que c'est?, **I prefer this to that** je préfère ceci à cela; **this is what he said** voici ce qu'il a dit; **this is Mr Brown** (*in introductions*) je vous présente Mr Brown; (*in photo*) c'est Mr Brown; (*on telephone*) ici Mr Brown
♦ adv (*demonstrative*): **it was about this big** c'était à peu près de cette grandeur or grand comme ça; **I didn't know it was this bad** je ne savais pas que c'était si or aussi mauvais

thistle ['θɪsl] n chardon m

thorn [θɔ:n] n épine f

thorough ['θʌrə] adj (*search*) minutieux(-euse); (*knowledge, research*) approfondi(e); (*work, person*) consciencieux(-euse); (*cleaning*) à fond; **~bred** n (*horse*) pur-sang m inv; **~fare** n route f; **"no ~fare"** "passage interdit"; **~ly** adv minutieusement; en profondeur; à fond; (*very*) tout à fait

those [ðəuz] pl adj ces; (*not "these"*): **~ books** ces livres-là ♦ pl pron ceux-là (celles-là)

though [ðəu] conj bien que +sub, quoique +sub ♦ adv pourtant

thought [θɔ:t] pt, pp of **think** ♦ n pensée f; (*idea*) idée f; (*opinion*) avis m; **~ful** adj (*deep in thought*) pensif(-ive); (*serious*) réfléchi(e); (*considerate*) prévenant(e); **~less** adj

étourdi(e); qui manque de considération

thousand ['θauzənd] num mille; **two ~** deux mille; **~s of** des milliers de; **~th** num millième

thrash [θræʃ] vt rouer de coups; donner une correction à; (*defeat*) battre à plate couture; **~ about, ~ around** vi se débattre; **~ out** vt débattre de

thread [θred] n fil m; (*TECH*) pas m, filetage m ♦ vt (*needle*) enfiler; **~bare** adj râpé(e), élimé(e)

threat [θret] n menace f; **~en** vi menacer ♦ vt: **to ~en sb with sth/to do** menacer qn de qch/de faire

three [θri:] num trois; **~-dimensional** adj à trois dimensions; **~-piece suit** n complet m (avec gilet); **~-piece suite** n salon m comprenant un canapé et deux fauteuils assortis; **~-ply** adj (*wool*) trois fils inv

threshold ['θreʃhəuld] n seuil m

threw [θru:] pt of **throw**

thrifty ['θrɪftɪ] adj économe

thrill [θrɪl] n (*excitement*) émotion f, sensation forte; (*shudder*) frisson m ♦ vt (*audience*) électriser; **to be ~ed** (*with gift etc*) être ravi(e); **~er** n film m (or roman m or pièce f) à suspense; **~ing** adj saisissant(e), palpitant(e)

thrive [θraɪv] (*pt, pp thrived*) vi pousser, se développer; (*business*) prospérer; **he ~s on it** cela lui réussit; **thriving** adj (*business, community*) prospère

throat [θrəut] n gorge f; **to have a sore ~** avoir mal à la gorge

throb [θrɔb] vi (*heart*) palpiter; (*engine*) vibrer; **my head is ~bing** j'ai des élancements dans la tête

throes [θrəuz] npl: **in the ~ of** au beau milieu de

throne [θrəun] n trône m

throng ['θrɔŋ] n foule f ♦ vt se presser dans

throttle ['θrɔtl] n (*AUT*) accélérateur m ♦ vt étrangler

through [θru:] prep à travers; (*time*) pendant, durant; (*by means of*) par, par l'intermédiaire de; (*owing to*) à cause de ♦ adj (*ticket, train, passage*) direct(e) ♦ adv à travers; **to put sb ~ to sb** (*BRIT: TEL*) passer qn à qn; **to be ~** (*BRIT: TEL*) avoir la communication; (*esp US: have finished*) avoir fini; **to be ~ with sb** (*relationship*) avoir rompu avec qn; **"no ~ road"** (*BRIT*) "impasse"; **~out** prep (*place*) partout dans; (*time*) durant tout(e) le (la) ♦ adv partout

throw [θrəu] (*pt threw, pp thrown*) n jet m; (*SPORT*) lancer m ♦ vt lancer, jeter; (*SPORT*) lancer; (*rider*) désarçonner; (*fig*) décontenancer; **to ~ a party** donner une réception; **~ away** vt jeter; **~ off** vt se débarrasser de; **~ out** vt jeter; (*reject*) rejeter;

(*person*) mettre à la porte; **~ up** *vi* vomir; **~away** *vt* à jeter; (*remark*) fait(e) en passant; **~-in** *n* (*SPORT*) remise *f* en jeu

thru [θruː] (*US*) = **through**

thrush [θrʌʃ] *n* (*bird*) grive *f*

thrust [θrʌst] (*pt, pp* thrust) *n* (*TECH*) poussée *f* ♦ *vt* pousser brusquement; (*push in*) enfoncer

thud [θʌd] *n* bruit sourd

thug [θʌg] *n* voyou *m*

thumb [θʌm] *n* (*ANAT*) pouce *m* ♦ *vt*: **to ~ a lift** faire de l'auto-stop, arrêter une voiture; **~ through** *vt* (*book*) feuilleter; **~tack** (*US*) *n* punaise *f* (*clou*)

thump [θʌmp] *n* grand coup; (*sound*) bruit sourd ♦ *vt* cogner sur ♦ *vi* cogner, battre fort

thunder ['θʌndər] *n* tonnerre *m* ♦ *vi* tonner; (*train etc*): **to ~ past** passer dans un grondement *or* un bruit de tonnerre; **~bolt** *n* foudre *f*; **~clap** *n* coup *m* de tonnerre; **~storm** *n* orage *m*; **~y** *adj* orageux(-euse)

Thursday ['θɜːzdɪ] *n* jeudi *m*

thus [ðʌs] *adv* ainsi

thwart [θwɔːt] *vt* contrecarrer

thyme [taɪm] *n* thym *m*

tiara [tɪ'ɑːrə] *n* diadème *m*

tick [tɪk] *n* (*sound: of clock*) tic-tac *m*; (*mark*) coche *f*; (*ZOOL*) tique *f*; (*BRIT: inf*): **in a ~** dans une seconde ♦ *vi* faire tic-tac ♦ *vt* (*item on list*) cocher; **~ off** *vt* (*item on list*) cocher; (*person*) réprimander, attraper; **~ over** *vi* (*engine*) tourner au ralenti; (*fig*) aller *or* marcher doucettement

ticket ['tɪkɪt] *n* billet *m*; (*for bus, tube*) ticket *m*; (*in shop: on goods*) étiquette *f*; (*for library*) carte *f*; (*parking ~*) papillon *m*, p.-v. *m*; **~ collector**, **~ inspector** *n* contrôleur(-euse); **~ office** *n* guichet *m*, bureau *m* de vente des billets

tickle ['tɪkl] *vt, vi* chatouiller; **ticklish** *adj* (*person*) chatouilleux(-euse); (*problem*) épineux(-euse)

tidal ['taɪdl] *adj* (*force*) de la marée; (*estuary*) à marée; **~ wave** *n* raz-de-marée *m inv*

tidbit ['tɪdbɪt] (*US*) *n* = **titbit**

tiddlywinks ['tɪdlɪwɪŋks] *n* jeu *m* de puce

tide [taɪd] *n* marée *f*; (*fig: of events*) cours *m* ♦ *vt*: **to ~ sb over** dépanner qn; **high/low ~** marée haute/basse

tidy ['taɪdɪ] *adj* (*room*) bien rangé(e); (*dress, work*) net(te), soigné(e); (*person*) ordonné(e), qui a de l'ordre ♦ *vt* (*also: ~ up*) ranger

tie [taɪ] *n* (*string etc*) cordon *m*; (*BRIT: also: necktie*) cravate *f*; (*fig: link*) lien *m*; (*SPORT: draw*) égalité *f* de points; match nul ♦ *vt* (*parcel*) attacher; (*ribbon, shoelaces*) nouer ♦ *vi* (*SPORT*) faire match nul; finir à égalité de points; **to ~ sth in a bow** faire un nœud à *or*

avec qch; **to ~ a knot in sth** faire un nœud à qch; **~ down** *vt* (*fig*): **to ~ sb down (to)** contraindre qn (à accepter); **to be ~d down** (*by relationship*) se fixer; **~ up** *vt* (*parcel*) ficeler; (*dog, boat*) attacher; (*prisoner*) ligoter; (*arrangements*) conclure; **to be ~d up** (*busy*) être pris(e) *or* occupé(e)

tier [tɪər] *n* gradin *m*; (*of cake*) étage *m*

tiger ['taɪgər] *n* tigre *m*

tight [taɪt] *adj* (*rope*) tendu(e), raide; (*clothes*) étroit(e), très juste; (*budget, programme, bend*) serré(e); (*control*) strict(e), sévère; (*inf: drunk*) ivre, rond(e) ♦ *adv* (*squeeze*) très fort; (*shut*) hermétiquement, bien; **~en** *vt* (*rope*) tendre; (*screw*) resserrer; (*control*) renforcer ♦ *vi* se tendre, se resserrer; **~fisted** *adj* avare; **~ly** *adv* (*grasp*) bien, très fort; **~rope** *n* corde *f* raide; **~s** (*BRIT*) *npl* collant *m*

tile [taɪl] *n* (*on roof*) tuile *f*; (*on wall or floor*) carreau *m*; **~d** *adj* en tuiles; carrelé(e)

till [tɪl] *n* caisse (enregistreuse) ♦ *vt* (*land*) cultiver ♦ *prep, conj* = **until**

tiller ['tɪlər] *n* (*NAUT*) barre *f* (du gouvernail)

tilt [tɪlt] *vt* pencher, incliner ♦ *vi* pencher, être incliné(e)

timber ['tɪmbər] *n* (*material*) bois *m* (de construction); (*trees*) arbres *mpl*

time [taɪm] *n* temps *m*; (*epoch: often pl*) époque *f*, temps; (*by clock*) heure *f*; (*moment*) moment *m*; (*occasion, also MATH*) fois *f*; (*MUS*) mesure *f* ♦ *vt* (*race*) chronométrer; (*programme*) minuter; (*visit*) fixer; (*remark etc*) choisir le moment de; **a long ~** un long moment, longtemps; **for the ~ being** pour le moment; **4 at a ~** 4 à la fois; **from ~ to ~** de temps en temps; **at ~s** parfois; **in ~** (*soon enough*) à temps; (*after some ~*) avec le temps, à la longue; (*MUS*) en mesure; **in a week's ~** dans une semaine; **in no ~** en un rien de temps; **any ~** n'importe quand; **on ~** à l'heure; **5 ~s 5** 5 fois 5; **what ~ is it?** quelle heure est-il?; **to have a good ~** bien s'amuser; **~ bomb** *n* bombe *f* à retardement; **~ lag** (*BRIT*) *n* décalage *m*; (*in travel*) décalage horaire; **~less** *adj* éternel(le); **~ly** *adj* opportun(e); **~ off** *n* temps *m* libre; **~r** *n* (*TECH*) minuteur *m*; (*in kitchen*) compte-minutes *m inv*; **~scale** *n* délais *mpl*; **~share** *n* maison *f*/appartement *m* en multipropriété; **~ switch** (*BRIT*) *n* minuteur *m*; (*for lighting*) minuterie *f*; **~table** *n* (*RAIL*) (indicateur *m*) horaire *m*; (*SCOL*) emploi *m* du temps; **~ zone** *n* fuseau *m* horaire

timid ['tɪmɪd] *adj* timide; (*easily scared*) peureux(-euse)

timing ['taɪmɪŋ] *n* minutage *m*; chronométrage *m*; **the ~ of his resignation** le moment choisi pour sa démission

timpani ['tɪmpənɪ] npl timbales fpl

tin [tɪn] n étain m; (also: ~ **plate**) fer-blanc m; (BRIT: can) boîte f (de conserve); (for storage) boîte f; ~**foil** n papier m d'étain or aluminium

tinge [tɪndʒ] n nuance f ♦ vt: ~**d with** teinté(e) de

tingle ['tɪŋgl] vi picoter; (person) avoir des picotements

tinker ['tɪŋkə*] n (gipsy) romanichel m; ~ **with** vt fus bricoler, rafistoler

tinkle ['tɪŋkl] vi tinter

tinned [tɪnd] (BRIT) adj (food) en boîte, en conserve

tin opener [-'əupnə*] (BRIT) n ouvre-boîte(s) m

tinsel ['tɪnsl] n guirlandes fpl de Noël (argentées)

tint [tɪnt] n teinte f; (for hair) shampooing colorant; ~**ed** adj (hair) teint(e); (spectacles, glass) teinté(e)

tiny ['taɪnɪ] adj minuscule

tip [tɪp] n (end) bout m; (gratuity) pourboire m; (BRIT: for rubbish) décharge f; (advice) tuyau m ♦ vt (waiter) donner un pourboire à; (tilt) incliner; (overturn: also: ~ **over**) renverser; (empty: ~ **out**) déverser; ~**-off** n (hint) tuyau m; ~**ped** (BRIT) adj (cigarette) (à bout) filtre inv

tipsy ['tɪpsɪ] (inf) adj un peu ivre, éméché(e)

tiptoe ['tɪptəu] n: **on** ~ sur la pointe des pieds

tiptop ['tɪp'tɔp] adj: **in** ~ **condition** en excellent état

tire ['taɪə*] n (US) = **tyre** ♦ vt fatiguer ♦ vi se fatiguer; ~**d** adj fatigué(e); **to be** ~**d of** en avoir assez de, être las (lasse) de; ~**less** adj (person) infatigable; (efforts) inlassable; ~**some** adj ennuyeux(-euse); **tiring** adj fatigant(e)

tissue ['tɪʃu:] n tissu m; (paper handkerchief) mouchoir m en papier, kleenex ® m; ~ **paper** n papier m de soie

tit [tɪt] n (bird) mésange f; **to give** ~ **for tat** rendre la pareille

titbit ['tɪtbɪt] n (food) friandise f; (news) potin m

title ['taɪtl] n titre m; ~ **deed** n (LAW) titre (constitutif) de propriété; ~ **role** n rôle principal

TM abbr = **trademark**

to [tu:, tə] prep 1 (direction) à; **to go to France/Portugal/London/school** aller en France/au Portugal/à Londres/à l'école; **to go to Claude's/the doctor's** aller chez Claude/le docteur; **the road to Edinburgh** la route d'Édimbourg

2 (as far as) (jusqu')à; **to count to 10** compter jusqu'à 10; **from 40 to 50 people** de 40 à 50 personnes

3 (with expressions of time): **a quarter to 5** 5 heures moins le quart; **it's twenty to 3** il est 3 heures moins vingt

4 (for, of) de; **the key to the front door** la clé de la porte d'entrée; **a letter to his wife** une lettre (adressée) à sa femme

5 (expressing indirect object) à; **to give sth to sb** donner qch à qn; **to talk to sb** parler à qn

6 (in relation to) à; **3 goals to 2** 3 (buts) à 2; **30 miles to the gallon** 9,4 litres aux cent (km)

7 (purpose, result): **to come to sb's aid** venir au secours de qn, porter secours à qn; **to sentence sb to death** condamner qn à mort; **to my surprise** à ma grande surprise

♦ with vb 1 (simple infinitive): **to go/eat** aller/manger

2 (following another vb): **to want/try/start to do** vouloir/essayer de/commencer à faire

3 (with vb omitted): **I don't want to** je ne veux pas

4 (purpose, result) pour; **I did it to help you** je l'ai fait pour vous aider

5 (equivalent to relative clause): **I have things to do** j'ai des choses à faire; **the main thing is to try** l'important est d'essayer

6 (after adjective): **ready to go** prêt(e) à partir; **too old/young to ...** trop vieux/jeune pour ...

♦ adv: **push/pull the door to** tirez/poussez la porte

toad [təud] n crapaud m

toadstool ['təudstu:l] n champignon (vénéneux)

toast [təust] n (CULIN) pain grillé, toast m; (drink, speech) toast m ♦ vt (CULIN) faire griller; (drink to) porter un toast à; ~**er** n grille-pain m inv

tobacco [tə'bækəu] n tabac m; ~**nist** n marchand(e) de tabac; ~**nist's** (**shop**) n (bureau m de) tabac m

toboggan [tə'bɔgən] n toboggan m; (child's) luge f ♦ vi: **to go** ~**ing** faire de la luge

today [tə'deɪ] adv (also fig) aujourd'hui ♦ n aujourd'hui m

toddler ['tɔdlə*] n enfant m/f qui commence à marcher, bambin m

toe [təu] n doigt m de pied, orteil m; (of shoe) bout m ♦ vt: **to** ~ **the line** (fig) obéir, se conformer; ~**nail** n ongle m du pied

toffee ['tɔfɪ] n caramel m; ~ **apple** (BRIT) n pomme caramélisée

together [tə'geðə*] adv ensemble; (at same time) en même temps; ~ **with** avec

toil [tɔɪl] n dur travail, labeur m ♦ vi peiner

toilet ['tɔɪlət] n (BRIT: lavatory) toilettes fpl ♦ cpd (accessories etc) de toilette; ~ **bag** n nécessaire m de toilette; ~ **paper** n papier m hygiénique; ~**ries** npl articles mpl de toilette;

~ roll n rouleau m de papier hygiénique

token ['təukən] n (sign) marque f, témoignage m; (metal disc) jeton m ♦ adj (strike, payment etc) symbolique; **book/record ~** (BRIT) chèque-livre/-disque m; **gift ~** bon-cadeau m

told [təuld] pt, pp of **tell**

tolerable ['tɔlərəbl] adj (bearable) tolérable; (fairly good) passable

tolerant ['tɔlərnt] adj: **~ (of)** tolérant(e) (à l'égard de)

tolerate ['tɔləreɪt] vt supporter, tolérer

toll [təul] n (tax, charge) péage m ♦ vi (bell) sonner; **the accident ~ on the roads** le nombre des victimes de la route

tomato [tə'mɑːtəu] (pl **~es**) n tomate f

tomb [tuːm] n tombe f

tomboy ['tɔmbɔɪ] n garçon manqué

tombstone ['tuːmstəun] n pierre tombale

tomcat ['tɔmkæt] n matou m

tomorrow [tə'mɔrəu] adv (also fig) demain ♦ n demain m; **the day after ~** après-demain; **~ morning** demain matin

ton [tʌn] n tonne f (BRIT = 1016kg; US = 907kg); (metric) tonne (= 1000 kg); **~s of** (inf) des tas de

tone [təun] n ton m ♦ vi (also: **~ in**) s'harmoniser; **~ down** vt (colour, criticism) adoucir; (sound) baisser; **~ up** vt (muscles) tonifier; **~-deaf** adj qui n'a pas d'oreille

tongs [tɔŋz] npl (for coal) pincettes fpl; (for hair) fer m à friser

tongue [tʌŋ] n langue f; **~ in cheek** ironiquement; **~-tied** adj (fig) muet(te); **~ twister** n phrase f très difficile à prononcer

tonic ['tɔnɪk] n (MED) tonique m; (also: **~ water**) tonic m, Schweppes ® m

tonight [tə'naɪt] adv, n cette nuit; (this evening) ce soir

tonsil ['tɔnsl] n amygdale f; **~litis** [tɔnsɪ'laɪtɪs] n angine f

too [tuː] adv (excessively) trop; (also) aussi; **~ much** adv trop ♦ adj trop de; **~ many** trop de; **~ bad!** tant pis!

took [tuk] pt of **take**

tool [tuːl] n outil m; **~ box** n boîte f à outils

toot [tuːt] n (of car horn) coup m de klaxon; (of whistle) coup m de sifflet ♦ vi (with car horn) klaxonner

tooth [tuːθ] (pl **teeth**) n (ANAT, TECH) dent f; **~ache** n mal m de dents; **~brush** n brosse f à dents; **~paste** n (pâte f à) dentifrice m; **~pick** n cure-dent m

top [tɔp] n (of mountain, head) sommet m; (of page, ladder, garment) haut m; (of box, cupboard, table) dessus m; (lid: of box, jar) couvercle m; (: of bottle) bouchon m; (toy) toupie f ♦ adj du haut; (in rank) pre-mier(-ère); (best) meilleur(e) ♦ vt (exceed)

dépasser; (be first in) être en tête de; **on ~ of** sur; (in addition to) en plus de; **from ~ to bottom** de fond en comble; **~ up** (US **~ off**) vt (bottle) remplir; (salary) compléter; **~ floor** n dernier étage; **~ hat** n haut-de-forme m; **~-heavy** adj (object) trop lourd(e) du haut

topic ['tɔpɪk] n sujet m, thème m; **~al** adj d'actualité

top: ~less adj (bather etc) aux seins nus; **~-level** adj (talks) au plus haut niveau; **~most** adj le (la) plus haut(e)

topple ['tɔpl] vt renverser, faire tomber ♦ vi basculer; tomber

top-secret ['tɔp'siːkrɪt] adj top secret(-ète)

topsy-turvy ['tɔpsɪ'təːvɪ] adj, adv sens dessus dessous

torch [tɔːtʃ] n torche f; (BRIT: electric) lampe f de poche

tore [tɔːr] pt of **tear**[1]

torment [n 'tɔːmɛnt, vb tɔː'mɛnt] n tourment m ♦ vt tourmenter; (fig: annoy) harceler

torn [tɔːn] pp of **tear**[1]

tornado [tɔː'neɪdəu] (pl **~es**) n tornade f

torpedo [tɔː'piːdəu] (pl **~es**) n torpille f

torrent ['tɔrnt] n torrent m; **~ial** [tɔ'rɛnʃl] adj torrentiel(le)

tortoise ['tɔːtəs] n tortue f; **~shell** adj en écaille

torture ['tɔːtʃər] n torture f ♦ vt torturer

Tory ['tɔːrɪ] (BRIT: POL) adj, n tory (m/f), conservateur(-trice)

toss [tɔs] vt lancer, jeter; (pancake) faire sauter; (head) rejeter en arrière; **to ~ a coin** jouer à pile ou face; **to ~ up for sth** jouer qch à pile ou face; **to ~ and turn** (in bed) se tourner et se retourner

tot [tɔt] n (BRIT: drink) petit verre; (child) bambin m

total ['təutl] adj total(e) ♦ n total m ♦ vt (add up) faire le total de, additionner; (amount to) s'élever à; **~ly** adv totalement

totter ['tɔtər] vi chanceler

touch [tʌtʃ] n contact m, toucher m; (sense, also skill: of pianist etc) toucher ♦ vt (tamper with) toucher à; **a ~ of** (fig) un petit peu de; une touche de; **to get in ~ with** prendre contact avec; **to lose ~** (friends) se perdre de vue; **~ on** vt fus (topic) effleurer, aborder; **~ up** vt (paint) retoucher; **~-and-go** adj incertain(e); **~down** n atterrissage m; (on sea) amerrissage m; (US: FOOTBALL) touché-en-but m; **~ed** adj (moved) touché(e); **~ing** adj touchant(e), attendrissant(e); **~line** n (SPORT) (ligne f de) touche f; **~y** adj (person) susceptible

tough [tʌf] adj dur(e); (resistant) résistant(e), solide; (meat) dur, coriace; (firm) inflexible; (task) dur, pénible; **~en** vt (character) endurcir; (*glass etc*) renforcer

toupee ['tu:peɪ] *n* postiche *m*

tour ['tuəʳ] *n* voyage *m*; (*also:* **package ~**) voyage organisé; (*of town, museum*) tour *m*, visite *f*; (*by artist*) tournée *f* ♦ *vt* visiter; **~ guide** *n* (*person*) guide *m/f*

tourism ['tuərɪzm] *n* tourisme *m*

tourist ['tuərɪst] *n* touriste *m/f* ♦ *cpd* touristique; **~ office** *n* syndicat *m* d'initiative

tournament ['tuənəmənt] *n* tournoi *m*

tousled ['tauzld] *adj* (*hair*) ébouriffé(e)

tout [taut] *vi*: **to ~ for** essayer de raccrocher, racoler ♦ *n* (*also:* **ticket ~**) revendeur *m* de billets

tow [təu] *vt* remorquer; (*caravan, trailer*) tracter; **"on ~"** (*BRIT*) **or "in ~"** (*US*) (*AUT*) "véhicule en remorque"

toward(s) [tə'wɔːd(z)] *prep* vers; (*of attitude*) envers, à l'égard de; (*of purpose*) pour

towel ['tauəl] *n* serviette *f* (de toilette); **~ling** *n* (*fabric*) tissu éponge *m*; **~ rail** (*US* **towel rack**) *n* porte-serviettes *m inv*

tower ['tauəʳ] *n* tour *f*; **~ block** (*BRIT*) *n* tour *f* (d'habitation); **~ing** *adj* très haut(e), imposant(e)

town [taun] *n* ville *f*; **to go to ~** aller en ville; (*fig*) y mettre le paquet; **~ centre** *n* centre *m* de la ville, centre-ville *m*; **~ council** *n* conseil municipal; **~ hall** *n* ≈ mairie *f*; **~ plan** *n* plan *m* de ville; **~ planning** *n* urbanisme *m*

towrope ['təurəup] *n* (câble *m* de) remorque *f*

tow truck (*US*) *n* dépanneuse *f*

toy [tɔɪ] *n* jouet *m*; **~ with** *vt fus* jouer avec; (*idea*) caresser

trace [treɪs] *n* trace *f* ♦ *vt* (*draw*) tracer, dessiner; (*follow*) suivre la trace de; (*locate*) retrouver, **tracing paper** *n* papier-calque *m*

track [træk] *n* (*mark*) trace *f*, piste *f*; (*path: gen*) chemin *m*, piste *f*; (*: of bullet etc*) trajectoire *f*; (*: of suspect, animal*) piste *f*; (*RAIL*) voie ferrée, rails *mpl*; (*on tape, SPORT*) piste; (*on record*) plage *f* ♦ *vt* suivre la trace or la piste de; **to keep ~ of** suivre; **~ down** *vt* (*prey*) trouver et capturer; (*sth lost*) finir par retrouver; **~suit** *n* survêtement *m*

tract [trækt] *n* (*of land*) étendue *f*

traction ['trækʃən] *n* traction *f*; (*MED*): **in ~** en extension

tractor ['træktəʳ] *n* tracteur *m*

trade [treɪd] *n* commerce *m*; (*skill, job*) métier *m* ♦ *vi* faire du commerce ♦ *vt* (*exchange*): **to ~ sth (for sth)** échanger qch (contre qch); **~ in** *vt* (*old car etc*) faire reprendre; **~ fair** *n* foire(-exposition) commerciale; **~-in price** *n* prix à la reprise; **~mark** *n* marque *f* de fabrique; **~ name** *n* nom *m* de marque; **~r** *n* commerçant(e), négociant(e); **~sman** (*irreg*)

n (*shopkeeper*) commerçant; **~ union** *n* syndicat *m*; **~ unionist** *n* syndicaliste *m/f*

tradition [trə'dɪʃən] *n* tradition *f*; **~al** *adj* traditionnel(le)

traffic ['træfɪk] *n* trafic *m*; (*cars*) circulation *f* ♦ *vi*: **to ~ in** (*pej: liquor, drugs*) faire le trafic de; **~ calming** *n* ralentissement *m* de la circulation; **~ circle** (*US*) *n* rond-point *m*; **~ jam** *n* embouteillage *m*; **~ lights** *npl* feux *mpl* (de signalisation); **~ warden** *n* contractuel(le)

tragedy ['trædʒədɪ] *n* tragédie *f*

tragic ['trædʒɪk] *adj* tragique

trail [treɪl] *n* (*tracks*) trace *f*, piste *f*; (*path*) chemin *m*, piste; (*of smoke etc*) traînée *f* ♦ *vt* traîner, tirer; (*follow*) suivre ♦ *vi* traîner; (*in game, contest*) être en retard; **~ behind** *vi* traîner, être à la traîne; **~er** *n* (*AUT*) remorque *f*; (*US*) caravane *f*; (*CINEMA*) bande-annonce *f*; **~er truck** (*US*) *n* (camion *m*) semi-remorque *m*

train [treɪn] *n* train *m*; (*in underground*) rame *f*; (*of dress*) traîne *f* ♦ *vt* (*apprentice, doctor etc*) former; (*sportsman*) entraîner; (*dog*) dresser; (*memory*) exercer; (*point: gun etc*): **to ~ sth on** braquer qch sur ♦ *vi* suivre une formation; (*SPORT*) s'entraîner; **one's ~ of thought** le fil de sa pensée; **~ed** *adj* qualifié(e), qui a reçu une formation; (*animal*) dressé(e); **~ee** [treɪ'niː] *n* stagiaire *m/f*; (*in trade*) apprenti(e); **~er** *n* (*SPORT: coach*) entraîneur(-euse), (*: shoe*) chaussure *f* de sport; (*of dogs etc*) dresseur(-euse); **~ing** *n* formation *f*; entraînement *m*; **in ~ing** (*SPORT*) à l'entraînement; (*fit*) en forme; **~ing college** *n* école professionnelle; (*for teachers*) ≈ école normale; **~ing shoes** *npl* chaussures *fpl* de sport

trait [treɪt] *n* trait *m* (de caractère)

traitor ['treɪtəʳ] *n* traître *m*

tram [træm] (*BRIT*) *n* (*also:* **~car**) tram(way) *m*

tramp [træmp] *n* (*person*) vagabond(e), clochard(e); (*inf: pej: woman*): **to be a ~** être coureuse ♦ *vi* marcher d'un pas lourd

trample ['træmpl] *vt*: **to ~ (underfoot)** piétiner

trampoline ['træmpəliːn] *n* trampoline *m*

tranquil ['træŋkwɪl] *adj* tranquille; **~lizer** (*US* **tranquilizer**) *n* (*MED*) tranquillisant *m*

transact [træn'zækt] *vt* (*business*) traiter; **~ion** *n* transaction *f*

transatlantic ['trænzət'læntɪk] *adj* transatlantique

transfer [*n* 'trænsfəʳ, *vb* træns'fəːʳ] *n* (*gen, also SPORT*) transfert *m*; (*POL: of power*) passation *f*; (*picture, design*) décalcomanie *f*; (*: stick-on*) autocollant *m* ♦ *vt* transférer; passer; **to ~ the charges** (*BRIT: TEL*) téléphoner en P.C.V.; **~ desk** *n* (*AVIAT*) guichet *m* de transit

transform [trænsˈfɔːm] vt transformer

transfusion [trænsˈfjuːʒən] n transfusion f

transient [ˈtrænzɪənt] adj transitoire, éphémère

transistor [trænˈzɪstəʳ] n (~ radio) transistor m

transit [ˈtrænzɪt] n: **in ~** en transit

transitive [ˈtrænzɪtɪv] adj (LING) transitif(-ive)

transit lounge n salle f de transit

translate [trænzˈleɪt] vt traduire; **translation** n traduction f; **translator** n traducteur(-trice)

transmission [trænzˈmɪʃən] n transmission f

transmit [trænzˈmɪt] vt transmettre; (RADIO, TV) émettre

transparency [trænsˈpɛərnsɪ] n (of glass etc) transparence f; (BRIT: PHOT) diapositive f

transparent [trænsˈpærnt] adj transparent(e)

transpire [trænsˈpaɪəʳ] vi (turn out): **it ~d that ...** on a appris que ...; (happen) arriver

transplant [vb trænsˈplɑːnt, n ˈtrænsplɑːnt] vt transplanter; (seedlings) repiquer ♦ n (MED) transplantation f

transport [n ˈtrænspɔːt, vb trænsˈpɔːt] n transport m; (car) moyen m de transport, voiture f ♦ vt transporter; **~ation** [ˈtrænspɔːˈteɪʃən] n transport m; (means of transportation) moyen m de transport; **~ café** (BRIT) n ≈ restaurant m de routiers

trap [træp] n (snare, trick) piège m; (carriage) cabriolet m ♦ vt prendre au piège; (confine) coincer; **~ door** n trappe f

trapeze [trəˈpiːz] n trapèze m

trappings [ˈtræpɪŋz] npl ornements mpl, attributs mpl

trash [træʃ] (pej) n (goods) camelote f; (nonsense) sottises fpl; **~ can** (US) n poubelle f; **~y** (inf) adj de camelote; (novel) de quatre sous

trauma [ˈtrɔːmə] n traumatisme m; **~tic** [trɔːˈmætɪk] adj traumatisant(e)

travel [ˈtrævl] n voyage(s) m(pl) ♦ vi voyager; (news, sound) circuler, se propager ♦ vt (distance) parcourir; **~ agency** n agence f de voyages; **~ agent** n agent m de voyages; **~ler** (US **traveler**) n voyageur(-euse); **~ler's cheque** (US **traveler's check**) n chèque m de voyage; **~ling** (US **traveling**) n voyage(s) m(pl); **~ sickness** n mal m de la route (or de mer or de l'air)

trawler [ˈtrɔːləʳ] n chalutier m

tray [treɪ] n (for carrying) plateau m; (on desk) corbeille f

treacherous [ˈtrɛtʃərəs] adj (person, look) traître(-esse); (ground, tide) dont il faut se méfier

treacle [ˈtriːkl] n mélasse f

tread [trɛd] (pt **trod**, pp **trodden**) n pas m; (sound) bruit m de pas; (of tyre) chape f, bande f de roulement ♦ vi marcher; **~ on** vt fus marcher sur

treason [ˈtriːzn] n trahison f

treasure [ˈtrɛʒəʳ] n trésor m ♦ vt (value) tenir beaucoup à; **~r** n trésorier(-ère); **treasury** n: **the Treasury**, (US) **the Treasury Department** le ministère des Finances

treat [triːt] n petit cadeau, petite surprise ♦ vt traiter; **to ~ sb to sth** offrir qch à qn

treatment [ˈtriːtmənt] n traitement m

treaty [ˈtriːtɪ] n traité m

treble [ˈtrɛbl] adj triple ♦ vt, vi tripler; **~ clef** n (MUS) clé f de sol

tree [triː] n arbre m

trek [trɛk] n (long) voyage; (on foot) (longue) marche, tirée f

tremble [ˈtrɛmbl] vi trembler

tremendous [trɪˈmɛndəs] adj (enormous) énorme, fantastique; (excellent) formidable

tremor [ˈtrɛməʳ] n tremblement m; (also: **earth ~**) secousse f sismique

trench [trɛntʃ] n tranchée f

trend [trɛnd] n (tendency) tendance f; (of events) cours m; (fashion) mode f; **~y** adj (idea, person) dans le vent; (clothes) dernier cri inv

trespass [ˈtrɛspəs] vi: **to ~ on** s'introduire sans permission dans; **"no ~ing"** "propriété privée", "défense d'entrer"

trestle [ˈtrɛsl] n tréteau m

trial [ˈtraɪəl] n (LAW) procès m, jugement m; (test: of machine etc) essai m; **~s** npl (unpleasant experiences) épreuves fpl; **to be on ~** (LAW) passer en jugement; **by ~ and error** par tâtonnements; **~ period** n période f d'essai

triangle [ˈtraɪæŋgl] n (MATH, MUS) triangle m; **triangular** [traɪˈæŋgjuləʳ] adj triangulaire

tribe [traɪb] n tribu f; **~sman** (irreg) n membre m d'une tribu

tribunal [traɪˈbjuːnl] n tribunal m

tributary [ˈtrɪbjutərɪ] n (river) affluent m

tribute [ˈtrɪbjuːt] n tribut m, hommage m; **to pay ~ to** rendre hommage à

trick [trɪk] n (magic ~) tour m; (joke, prank) tour, farce f; (skill, knack) astuce f, truc m; (CARDS) levée f ♦ vt attraper, rouler; **to play a ~ on sb** jouer un tour à qn; **that should do the ~** ça devrait faire l'affaire; **~ery** n ruse f

trickle [ˈtrɪkl] n (of water etc) filet m ♦ vi couler en un filet ou goutte à goutte

tricky [ˈtrɪkɪ] adj difficile, délicat(e)

tricycle [ˈtraɪsɪkl] n tricycle m

trifle [ˈtraɪfl] n bagatelle f; (CULIN) ≈ diplomate m ♦ adv: **a ~ long** un peu long; **trifling** adj insignifiant(e)

trigger [ˈtrɪgəʳ] n (of gun) gâchette f; **~ off** vt

déclencher

trim [trɪm] adj (house, garden) bien tenu(e); (figure) svelte ♦ n (haircut etc) légère coupe; (on car) garnitures fpl ♦ vt (cut) couper légèrement; (NAUT: a sail) gréer; (decorate): **to ~ (with)** décorer (de); **~mings** npl (CULIN) garniture f

trinket ['trɪŋkɪt] n bibelot m; (piece of jewellery) colifichet m

trip [trɪp] n voyage m; (excursion) excursion f; (stumble) faux pas ♦ vi faire un faux pas, trébucher; **on a ~** en voyage; **~ up** vi trébucher ♦ vt faire un croc-en-jambe à

tripe [traɪp] n (CULIN) tripes fpl; (pej: rubbish) idioties fpl

triple ['trɪpl] adj triple; **~ts** npl triplés(-ées); **triplicate** ['trɪplɪkət] n: **in triplicate** en trois exemplaires

tripod ['traɪpɔd] n trépied m

trite [traɪt] (pej) adj banal(e)

triumph ['traɪəmf] n triomphe m ♦ vi: **to ~ (over)** triompher (de)

trivia ['trɪvɪə] (pej) npl futilités fpl; **~l** adj insignifiant(e); (commonplace) banal(e)

trod [trɔd] pt of **tread**; **~den** pp of **tread**

trolley ['trɔlɪ] n chariot m

trombone [trɔm'bəun] n trombone m

troop [tru:p] n bande f, groupe m ♦ vi: **to ~ in/ out** entrer/sortir en groupe; **~s** npl (MIL) troupes fpl; (: men) hommes mpl, soldats mpl; **~ing the colour** (BRIT) n (ceremony) le salut au drapeau

trophy ['trəufɪ] n trophée m

tropic ['trɔpɪk] n tropique m; **~al** adj tropical(e)

trot [trɔt] n trot m ♦ vi trotter; **on the ~** (BRIT: fig) d'affilée

trouble ['trʌbl] n difficulté(s) f(pl), problème(s) m(pl); (worry) ennuis mpl, soucis mpl; (bother, effort) peine f; (POL) troubles mpl; (MED): **stomach etc ~** troubles gastriques etc ♦ vt (disturb) déranger, gêner; (worry) inquiéter ♦ vi: **to ~ to do** prendre la peine de faire; **~s** npl (POL etc) troubles mpl; (personal) ennuis, soucis; **to be in ~** avoir des ennuis; (ship, climber etc) être en difficulté; **what's the ~?** qu'est-ce qui ne va pas?; **~d** adj (person) inquiet(-ète); (epoch, life) agité(e); **~maker** n élément perturbateur, fauteur m de troubles; **~shooter** n (in conflict) médiateur m; **~some** adj (child) fatigant(e), difficile; (cough etc) gênant(e)

trough [trɔf] n (also: **drinking ~**) abreuvoir m; (also: **feeding ~**) auge f; (depression) creux m

trousers ['trauzəz] npl pantalon m; **short ~** culottes courtes

trout [traut] n inv truite f

trowel ['trauəl] n truelle f; (garden tool) déplantoir m

truant ['truənt] (BRIT) n: **to play ~** faire l'école buissonnière

truce [tru:s] n trêve f

truck [trʌk] n camion m; (RAIL) wagon m à plate-forme; **~ driver** n camionneur m; **~ farm** (US) n jardin maraîcher

true [tru:] adj vrai(e); (accurate) exact(e); (genuine) vrai, véritable; (faithful) fidèle; **to come ~** se réaliser

truffle ['trʌfl] n truffe f

truly ['tru:lɪ] adv vraiment, réellement; (truthfully) sans mentir; see also **yours**

trump [trʌmp] n (also: **~ card**) atout m

trumpet ['trʌmpɪt] n trompette f

truncheon ['trʌntʃən] (BRIT) n bâton m (d'agent de police); matraque f

trundle ['trʌndl] vt, vi: **to ~ along** rouler lentement (et bruyamment)

trunk [trʌŋk] n (of tree, person) tronc m; (of elephant) trompe f; (case) malle f; (US: AUT) coffre m; **~s** npl (also: **swimming ~s**) maillot m or slip m de bain

truss [trʌs] vt: **to ~ (up)** ligoter

trust [trʌst] n confiance f; (responsibility) charge f; (LAW) fidéicommis m ♦ vt (rely on) avoir confiance en; (hope) espérer; (entrust): **to ~ sth to sb** confier qch à qn; **to take sth on ~** accepter qch les yeux fermés; **~ed** adj en qui l'on a confiance; **~ee** [trʌs'ti:] n (LAW) fidéicommissaire m/f; (of school etc) administrateur(-trice); **~ful, ~ing** adj confiant(e); **~worthy** adj digne de confiance

truth [tru:θ] n vérité f; **~ful** adj (person) qui dit la vérité; (answer) sincère

try [traɪ] n essai m, tentative f; (RUGBY) essai ♦ vt (attempt) essayer, tenter; (test: sth new; also: **~ out**) essayer, tester; (LAW: person) juger; (strain) éprouver ♦ vi essayer; **to have a ~** essayer; **to ~ to do** essayer de faire; (seek) chercher à faire; **~ on** vt (clothes) essayer; **~ing** adj pénible

T-shirt ['ti:ʃə:t] n tee-shirt m

T-square ['ti:skwɛə] n équerre f en T, té m

tub [tʌb] n cuve f; (for washing clothes) baquet m; (bath) baignoire f

tubby ['tʌbɪ] adj rondelet(te)

tube [tju:b] n tube m; (BRIT: underground) métro m; (for tyre) chambre f à air

tuberculosis [tjubə:kju'ləusɪs] n tuberculose f

TUC n abbr (BRIT: Trades Union Congress) confédération des syndicats britanniques

tuck [tʌk] vt (put) mettre; **~ away** vt cacher, ranger; **~ in** vt rentrer; (child) border ♦ vi (eat) manger (de bon appétit); **~ up** vt (child) border; **~ shop** (BRIT) n boutique f à provisions (dans une école)

Tuesday ['tju:zdɪ] n mardi m

tuft [tʌft] n touffe f

tug [tʌg] n (ship) remorqueur m ♦ vt tirer (sur); **~-of-war** n lutte f à la corde; (fig) lutte acharnée

tuition [tjuːˈɪʃən] n (BRIT) leçons fpl; (: private ~) cours particuliers; (US: school fees) frais mpl de scolarité

tulip [ˈtjuːlɪp] n tulipe f

tumble [ˈtʌmbl] n (fall) chute f, culbute f ♦ vi tomber, dégringoler; **to ~ to sth** (inf) réaliser qch; **~down** adj délabré(e); **~ dryer** (BRIT) n séchoir m à air chaud

tumbler [ˈtʌmbləʳ] n (glass) verre (droit), gobelet m

tummy [ˈtʌmɪ] (inf) n ventre m; **~ upset** n maux mpl de ventre

tumour [ˈtjuːməʳ] (US tumor) n tumeur f

tuna [ˈtjuːnə] n inv (also: ~ fish) thon m

tune [tjuːn] n (melody) air m ♦ vt (MUS) accorder; (RADIO, TV, AUT) régler; **to be in/out of ~** (instrument) être accordé/désaccordé; (singer) chanter juste/faux; **to be in/out of ~ with** (fig) être en accord/désaccord avec; **~ in** vi (RADIO, TV): **to ~ in (to)** se mettre à l'écoute (de); **~ up** vi (musician) accorder son instrument; **~ful** adj mélodieux(-euse); **~r** n: **piano ~r** accordeur m (de pianos)

tunic [ˈtjuːnɪk] n tunique f

Tunisia [tjuːˈnɪzɪə] n Tunisie f

tunnel [ˈtʌnl] n tunnel m; (in mine) galerie f ♦ vi percer un tunnel

turbulence [ˈtəːbjuləns] n (AVIAT) turbulence f

tureen [təˈriːn] n (for soup) soupière f; (for vegetables) légumier m

turf [təːf] n gazon m; (clod) motte f (de gazon) ♦ vt gazonner; **~ out** (inf) vt (person) jeter dehors

Turk [təːk] n Turc (Turque)

Turkey [ˈtəːkɪ] n Turquie f

turkey [ˈtəːkɪ] n dindon m, dinde f

Turkish [ˈtəːkɪʃ] adj turc (turque) ♦ n (LING) turc m

turmoil [ˈtəːmɔɪl] n trouble m, bouleversement m; **in ~** en émoi, en effervescence

turn [təːn] n tour m; (in road) tournant m; (of mind, events) tournure f; (performance) numéro m; (MED) crise f, attaque f ♦ vt tourner; (collar, steak) retourner; (change): **to ~ sth into** changer qch en ♦ vi (object, wind, milk) tourner; (person: look back) se (re)tourner; (reverse direction) faire demi-tour; (become) devenir; (age) atteindre; **to ~ into** se changer en; **a good ~** un service; **it gave me quite a ~** ça m'a fait un coup; "no left **~**" (AUT) "défense de tourner à gauche"; **it's your ~** c'est (à) votre tour; **in ~** à son tour; à tour de rôle; **to take ~s (at)** se relayer (pour or à); **~ away** vi se détourner ♦ vt

(applicants) refuser; **~ back** vi revenir, faire demi-tour ♦ vt (person, vehicle) faire faire demi-tour à; (clock) reculer; **~ down** vt (refuse) rejeter, refuser; (reduce) baisser; (fold) rabattre; **~ in** vi (inf: go to bed) aller se coucher ♦ vt (fold) rentrer; **~ off** vi (from road) tourner ♦ vt (light, radio etc) éteindre; (tap) fermer; (engine) arrêter; **~ on** vt (light, radio etc) allumer; (tap) ouvrir; (engine) mettre en marche; **~ out** vt (light, gas) éteindre; (produce) produire ♦ vi (voters, troops etc) se présenter; **to ~ out to be** ... s'avérer ..., se révéler ...; **~ over** vi (person) se retourner ♦ vt (object) retourner; (page) tourner; **~ round** vi faire demi-tour; (rotate) tourner; **~ up** vi (person) arriver, se pointer (inf); (lost object) être retrouvé(e) ♦ vt (collar) remonter; (radio, heater) mettre plus fort; **~ing** n (in road) tournant m; **~ing point** n (fig) tournant m, moment décisif

turnip [ˈtəːnɪp] n navet m

turn: **~out** n (of voters) taux m de participation; **~over** n (COMM: amount of money) chiffre m d'affaires; (: of goods) roulement m; (: of staff) renouvellement m, changement m; **~pike** (US) n autoroute f à péage; **~stile** n tourniquet m (d'entrée); **~table** n (on record player) platine f; **~-up** (BRIT) n (on trousers) revers m

turpentine [ˈtəːpəntaɪn] n (also: turps) (essence f de) térébenthine f

turquoise [ˈtəːkwɔɪz] n (stone) turquoise f ♦ adj turquoise inv

turret [ˈtʌrɪt] n tourelle f

turtle [ˈtəːtl] n tortue marine or d'eau douce; **~neck (sweater)** n (BRIT) pullover m à col montant; (US) pullover à col roulé

tusk [tʌsk] n défense f

tutor [ˈtjuːtəʳ] n (in college) directeur(-trice) d'études; (private teacher) précepteur(-trice), **~ial** [tjuːˈtɔːrɪəl] n (SCOL) (séance f de) travaux mpl pratiques

tuxedo [tʌkˈsiːdəu] (US) n smoking m

TV n abbr (= television) télé f

twang [twæŋ] n (of instrument) son vibrant; (of voice) ton nasillard

tweed [twiːd] n tweed m

tweezers [ˈtwiːzəz] npl pince f à épiler

twelfth [twelfθ] num douzième

twelve [twelv] num douze; **at ~ (o'clock)** à midi; (midnight) à minuit

twentieth [ˈtwentɪɪθ] num vingtième

twenty [ˈtwentɪ] num vingt

twice [twaɪs] adv deux fois; **~ as much** deux fois plus

twiddle [ˈtwɪdl] vt, vi: **to ~ (with) sth** tripoter qch; **to ~ one's thumbs** (fig) se tourner les pouces

twig [twɪg] n brindille f ♦ vi (inf) piger

twilight ['twaɪlaɪt] n crépuscule m

twin [twɪn] adj, n jumeau(-elle) ♦ vt jumeler; ~-**(bedded) room** n chambre f à deux lits; ~ **beds** npl lits jumeaux

twine [twaɪn] n ficelle f ♦ vi (plant) s'enrouler

twinge [twɪndʒ] n (of pain) élancement m; a ~ **of conscience** un certain remords; a ~ **of regret** un pincement au cœur

twinkle ['twɪŋkl] vi scintiller; (eyes) pétiller

twirl [twə:l] vt faire tournoyer ♦ vi tournoyer

twist [twɪst] n torsion f, tour m; (in road) virage m; (in wire, flex) tortillon m; (in story) coup m de théâtre ♦ vt tordre; (weave) entortiller; (roll around) enrouler; (fig) déformer ♦ vi (road, river) serpenter

twit [twɪt] (inf) n crétin(e)

twitch [twɪtʃ] n (pull) coup sec, saccade f; (nervous) tic m ♦ vi se convulser; avoir un tic

two [tu:] num deux; **to put ~ and ~ together** (fig) faire le rapprochement; ~-**door** adj (AUT) à deux portes; ~-**faced** (pej) adj (person) faux (fausse); ~-**fold** adv: **to increase ~fold** doubler; ~-**piece (suit)** n (man's) costume m (deux-pièces); (woman's) (tailleur m) deux-pièces m inv; ~-**piece (swimsuit)** n (maillot m de bain) deux-pièces m inv; ~-**some** n (people) couple m; ~-**way** adj (traffic) dans les deux sens

tycoon [taɪˈkuːn] n: (business) ~ gros homme d'affaires

type [taɪp] n (category) type m, genre m, espèce f; (model, example) type m, modèle m; (TYP) type, caractère m ♦ vt (letter etc) taper (à la machine); ~ **cast** adj (actor) condamné(e) à toujours jouer le même rôle; ~-**face** n (TYP) œil m de caractère; ~**script** n texte dactylographié; ~**writer** n machine f à écrire; ~**written** adj dactylographié(e)

typhoid ['taɪfɔɪd] n typhoïde f

typical ['tɪpɪkl] adj typique, caractéristique

typing ['taɪpɪŋ] n dactylo(graphie) f

typist ['taɪpɪst] n dactylo m/f

tyrant ['taɪərnt] n tyran m

tyre ['taɪər] (US **tire**) n pneu m; ~ **pressure** n pression f (de gonflage)

U, u

U-bend ['juːbend] n (in pipe) coude m

ubiquitous [juːˈbɪkwɪtəs] adj omniprésent(e)

udder ['ʌdər] n pis m, mamelle f

UFO ['juːfəu] n abbr (= unidentified flying object) OVNI m

Uganda [juːˈɡændə] n Ouganda m

ugh [əːh] excl pouah!

ugly ['ʌɡlɪ] adj laid(e), vilain(e); (situation) inquiétant(e)

UHT abbr (= ultra heat treated): **UHT milk** lait m UHT or longue conservation

UK n abbr = **United Kingdom**

ulcer ['ʌlsər] n ulcère m; (also: **mouth ~**) aphte f

Ulster ['ʌlstər] n Ulster m; (inf: Northern Ireland) Irlande f du Nord

ulterior [ʌlˈtɪərɪər] adj: ~ **motive** arrière-pensée f

ultimate ['ʌltɪmət] adj ultime, final(e); (authority) suprême; ~**ly** adv (at last) en fin de compte; (fundamentally) finalement

ultrasound ['ʌltrəsaund] n ultrason m

umbilical cord [ʌmˈbɪlɪkl-] n cordon ombilical

umbrella [ʌmˈbrelə] n parapluie m; (for sun) parasol m

umpire ['ʌmpaɪər] n arbitre m

umpteen [ʌmpˈtiːn] adj je ne sais combien de; ~**th** adj: **for the ~th time** pour la nième fois

UN n abbr = **United Nations**

unable [ʌnˈeɪbl] adj: **to be ~** ne pas pouvoir, être dans l'impossibilité de; (incapable) être incapable de

unacceptable [ʌnəkˈseptəbl] adj (behaviour) inadmissible; (price, proposal) inacceptable

unaccompanied [ʌnəˈkʌmpənɪd] adj (child, lady) non accompagné(e); (song) sans accompagnement

unaccustomed [ʌnəˈkʌstəmd] adj: **to be ~ to sth** ne pas avoir l'habitude de qch

unanimous [juːˈnænɪməs] adj unanime; ~**ly** adv à l'unanimité

unarmed [ʌnˈɑːmd] adj (without a weapon) non armé(e); (combat) sans armes

unattached [ʌnəˈtætʃt] adj libre, sans attaches; (part) non attaché(e), indépendant(e)

unattended [ʌnəˈtendɪd] adj (car, child, luggage) sans surveillance

unattractive [ʌnəˈtræktɪv] adj peu attrayant(e); (character) peu sympathique

unauthorized [ʌnˈɔːθəraɪzd] adj non autorisé(e), sans autorisation

unavoidable [ʌnəˈvɔɪdəbl] adj inévitable

unaware [ʌnəˈweər] adj: **to be ~ of** ignorer, être inconscient(e) de; ~**s** adv à l'improviste, au dépourvu

unbalanced [ʌnˈbælənst] adj déséquilibré(e); (report) peu objectif(-ive)

unbearable [ʌnˈbeərəbl] adj insupportable

unbeatable [ʌnˈbiːtəbl] adj imbattable

unbeknown(st) [ʌnbɪˈnaun(st)] adv: ~ **to me/Peter** à mon insu/l'insu de Peter

unbelievable [ʌnbɪˈliːvəbl] adj incroyable

unbend [ʌnˈbend] (irreg) vi se détendre ♦ vt (wire) redresser, détordre

unbiased [ʌnˈbaɪəst] adj impartial(e)

unborn [ʌnˈbɔːn] adj à naître, qui n'est pas

encore né(e)

unbreakable [ʌn'breɪkəbl] *adj* incassable

unbroken [ʌn'brəukən] *adj* intact(e); (*fig*)
continu(e), ininterrompu(e)

unbutton [ʌn'bʌtn] *vt* déboutonner

uncalled-for [ʌn'kɔːldfɔːʳ] *adj* déplacé(e),
injustifié(e)

uncanny [ʌn'kænɪ] *adj* étrange, troublant(e)

unceremonious [ʌnserɪ'məunɪəs] *adj*
(*abrupt, rude*) brusque

uncertain [ʌn'səːtn] *adj* incertain(e);
(*hesitant*) hésitant(e); **in no ~ terms** sans
équivoque possible; **~ty** *n* incertitude *f*,
doute(s) *m(pl)*

uncivilized [ʌn'sɪvɪlaɪzd] *adj* (*gen*) non
civilisé(e); (*fig: behaviour etc*) barbare, (*hour*)
indu(e)

uncle ['ʌŋkl] *n* oncle *m*

uncomfortable [ʌn'kʌmfətəbl] *adj*
inconfortable, peu confortable; (*uneasy*) mal
à l'aise, gêné(e); (*situation*) désagréable

uncommon [ʌn'kɔmən] *adj* rare, singu-
lier(-ère), peu commun(e)

uncompromising [ʌn'kɔmprəmaɪzɪŋ] *adj*
intransigeant(e), inflexible

unconcerned [ʌnkən'səːnd] *adj*: **to be
~ (about)** ne pas s'inquiéter (de)

unconditional [ʌnkən'dɪʃənl] *adj* sans
conditions

unconscious [ʌn'kɔnʃəs] *adj* sans
connaissance, évanoui(e); (*unaware*): **~ of**
inconscient(e) de ♦ *n*: **the ~** l'inconscient *m*;
~ly *adv* inconsciemment

uncontrollable [ʌnkən'trəuləbl] *adj*
indiscipliné(e); (*temper, laughter*) irrépressible

unconventional [ʌnkən'venʃənl] *adj* peu
conventionnel(le)

uncouth [ʌn'kuːθ] *adj* grossier(-ère), fruste

uncover [ʌn'kʌvəʳ] *vt* découvrir

undecided [ʌndɪ'saɪdɪd] *adj* indécis(e),
irrésolu(e)

under ['ʌndəʳ] *prep* sous; (*less than*) (de)
moins de; au-dessous de; (*according to*)
selon, en vertu de ♦ *adv* au-dessous; en
dessous; **~ there** là-dessous; **~ repair** en
(cours de) réparation; **~age** *adj* (*person*)
qui n'a pas l'âge réglementaire; **~carriage** *n*
(*AVIAT*) train *m* d'atterrissage; **~charge** *vt*
ne pas faire payer assez à; **~coat** *n* (*paint*)
couche *f* de fond; **~cover** *adj* secret(-ète),
clandestin(e); **~current** *n* courant *or*
sentiment sous-jacent; **~cut** (*irreg*) *vt*
vendre moins cher que; **~dog** *n* opprimé *m*;
~done *adj* (*CULIN*) saignant(e); (*pej*) pas
assez cuit(e); **~estimate** *vt* sous-estimer;
~fed *adj* sous-alimenté(e); **~foot** *adv* sous
les pieds; **~go** (*irreg*) *vt* subir; (*treatment*)
suivre; **~graduate** *n* étudiant(e) (qui
prépare la licence); **~ground** *n* (*BRIT*:

railway) métro *m*; (*POL*) clandestinité *f* ♦ *adj*
souterrain(e); (*fig*) clandestin(e) ♦ *adv* dans
la clandestinité, clandestinement; **~growth** *n*
broussailles *fpl*, sous-bois *m*; **~hand(ed)** *adj*
(*fig: behaviour, method etc*) en dessous; **~lie**
(*irreg*) *vt* être à la base de; **~line** *vt* souligner;
~mine *vt* saper, miner; **~neath** *adv* (en)
dessous ♦ *prep* sous, au-dessous de; **~paid**
adj sous-payé(e); **~pants** *npl* caleçon *m*, slip
m; **~pass** (*BRIT*) *n* passage souterrain; (*on
motorway*) passage inférieur; **~privileged** *adj*
défavorisé(e), économiquement faible; **~rate**
vt sous-estimer; **~shirt** (*US*) *n* tricot *m* de
corps; **~shorts** (*US*) *npl* caleçon *m*, slip *m*;
~side *n* dessous *m*; **~skirt** (*BRIT*) *n* jupon *m*

understand [ʌndə'stænd] (*irreg: like stand*)
vt, vi comprendre; **I ~ that ...** je me suis laissé
dire que ...; je crois comprendre que ...;
~able *adj* compréhensible; **~ing** *adj*
compréhensif(-ive) ♦ *n* compréhension *f*;
(*agreement*) accord *m*

understatement ['ʌndəsteɪtmənt] *n*: **that's
an ~** c'est (bien) peu dire, le terme est faible

understood [ʌndə'stud] *pt, pp* of
understand ♦ *adj* entendu(e); (*implied*) sous-
entendu(e)

understudy ['ʌndəstʌdɪ] *n* doublure *f*

undertake [ʌndə'teɪk] (*irreg*) *vt*
entreprendre; se charger de; **to ~ to do sth**
s'engager à faire qch

undertaker ['ʌndəteɪkəʳ] *n* entrepreneur *m*
des pompes funèbres, croque-mort *m*

undertaking ['ʌndəteɪkɪŋ] *n* entreprise *f*;
(*promise*) promesse *f*

under: **~tone** *n*: **in an ~tone** à mi-voix;
~water *adv* sous l'eau ♦ *adj* sous-marin(e);
~wear *n* sous-vêtements *mpl*; (*women's only*)
dessous *mpl*; **~world** *n* (*of crime*) milieu *m*,
pègre *f*; **~write** *n* (*INSURANCE*) assureur *m*

undies ['ʌndɪz] (*inf*) *npl* dessous *mpl*, lingerie
f

undiplomatic ['ʌndɪplə'mætɪk] *adj* peu
diplomatique

undo [ʌn'duː] (*irreg*) *vt* défaire; **~ing** *n* ruine
f, perte *f*

undoubted [ʌn'dautɪd] *adj* indubitable,
certain(e); **~ly** *adv* sans aucun doute

undress [ʌn'dres] *vi* se déshabiller

undue [ʌn'djuː] *adj* indu(e), excessif(-ive)

undulating ['ʌndjuleɪtɪŋ] *adj* ondoyant(e),
onduleux(-euse)

unduly [ʌn'djuːlɪ] *adv* trop, excessivement

unearth [ʌn'əːθ] *vt* déterrer; (*fig*) dénicher

unearthly [ʌn'əːθlɪ] *adj* (*hour*) indu(e),
impossible

uneasy [ʌn'iːzɪ] *adj* mal à l'aise, gêné(e);
(*worried*) inquiet(-ète); (*feeling*) désagréable;
(*peace, truce*) fragile

uneconomic(al) ['ʌniːkə'nɔmɪk(l)] *adj* peu

économique
uneducated [ʌnˈɛdjukeɪtɪd] adj (person) sans instruction
unemployed [ʌnɪmˈplɔɪd] adj sans travail, en or au chômage ♦ n: the ~ les chômeurs mpl; **unemployment** n chômage m
unending [ʌnˈɛndɪŋ] adj interminable, sans fin
unerring [ʌnˈəːrɪŋ] adj infaillible, sûr(e)
uneven [ʌnˈiːvn] adj inégal(e); (quality, work) irrégulier(-ère)
unexpected [ʌnɪksˈpɛktɪd] adj inattendu(e), imprévu(e); **~ly** [ʌnɪksˈpɛktɪdlɪ] adv (arrive) à l'improviste; (succeed) contre toute attente
unfailing [ʌnˈfeɪlɪŋ] adj (remedy) infaillible
unfair [ʌnˈfɛəʳ] adj: ~ **(to)** injuste (envers)
unfaithful [ʌnˈfeɪθful] adj infidèle
unfamiliar [ʌnfəˈmɪlɪəʳ] adj étrange, inconnu(e); **to be ~ with** mal connaître
unfashionable [ʌnˈfæʃnəbl] adj (clothes) démodé(e); (place) peu chic inv
unfasten [ʌnˈfaːsn] vt défaire; détacher; (open) ouvrir
unfavourable [ʌnˈfeɪvrəbl] (US **unfavorable**) adj défavorable
unfeeling [ʌnˈfiːlɪŋ] adj insensible, dur(e)
unfinished [ʌnˈfɪnɪʃt] adj inachevé(e)
unfit [ʌnˈfɪt] adj en mauvaise santé; pas en forme; (incompetent): ~ **(for)** impropre (à); (work, service) inapte (à)
unfold [ʌnˈfəuld] vt déplier ♦ vi se dérouler
unforeseen [ˈʌnfɔːˈsiːn] adj imprévu(e)
unforgettable [ʌnfəˈɡɛtəbl] adj inoubliable
unfortunate [ʌnˈfɔːtʃənət] adj malheureux(-euse); (event, remark) malencontreux(-euse); **~ly** adv malheureusement
unfounded [ʌnˈfaundɪd] adj sans fondement
unfriendly [ʌnˈfrɛndlɪ] adj inamical(e), peu aimable
ungainly [ʌnˈɡeɪnlɪ] adj gauche, dégingandé(e)
ungodly [ʌnˈɡɔdlɪ] adj (hour) indu(e)
ungrateful [ʌnˈɡreɪtful] adj ingrat(e)
unhappiness [ʌnˈhæpɪnɪs] n tristesse f, peine f
unhappy [ʌnˈhæpɪ] adj triste, malheureux(-euse); ~ **about** or **with** (arrangements etc) mécontent(e) de, peu satisfait(e) de
unharmed [ʌnˈhaːmd] adj indemne, sain(e) et sauf (sauve)
UNHCR n abbr (= United Nations High Commission for refugees) HCR m
unhealthy [ʌnˈhɛlθɪ] adj malsain(e); (person) maladif(-ive)
unheard-of [ʌnˈhɜːdɔv] adj inouï(e), sans précédent
unhurt [ʌnˈhɜːt] adj indemne
unidentified [ʌnaɪˈdɛntɪfaɪd] adj non identifié(e); see also **UFO**
uniform [ˈjuːnɪfɔːm] n uniforme m ♦ adj uniforme
uninhabited [ʌnɪnˈhæbɪtɪd] adj inhabité(e)
unintentional [ʌnɪnˈtɛnʃənəl] adj involontaire
union [ˈjuːnjən] n union f; (also: **trade ~**) syndicat m ♦ cpd du syndicat, syndical(e); **U~ Jack** n drapeau du Royaume-Uni
unique [juːˈniːk] adj unique
UNISON [ˈjuːnɪsn] n grand syndicat des services publics en Grande-Bretagne
unison [ˈjuːnɪsn] n: **in ~** (sing) à l'unisson; (say) en chœur
unit [ˈjuːnɪt] n unité f; (section: of furniture etc) élément m, bloc m; **kitchen ~** élément de cuisine
unite [juːˈnaɪt] vt unir ♦ vi s'unir; **~d** adj uni(e); unifié(e); (effort) conjugué(e); **U~d Kingdom** n Royaume-Uni m; **U~d Nations (Organization)** n (Organisation f des) Nations unies; **U~d States (of America)** n États-Unis mpl
unit trust (BRIT) n fonds commun de placement
unity [ˈjuːnɪtɪ] n unité f
universal [juːnɪˈvəːsl] adj universel(le)
universe [ˈjuːnɪvəːs] n univers m
university [juːnɪˈvəːsɪtɪ] n université f
unjust [ʌnˈdʒʌst] adj injuste
unkempt [ʌnˈkɛmpt] adj négligé(e), débraillé(e); (hair) mal peigné(e)
unkind [ʌnˈkaɪnd] adj peu gentil(le), méchant(e)
unknown [ʌnˈnəun] adj inconnu(e)
unlawful [ʌnˈlɔːful] adj illégal(e)
unleaded [ˈʌnˈlɛdɪd] adj (petrol, fuel) sans plomb
unleash [ʌnˈliːʃ] vt (fig) déchaîner, déclencher
unless [ʌnˈlɛs] conj: ~ **he leaves** à moins qu'il ne parte
unlike [ʌnˈlaɪk] adj dissemblable, différent(e) ♦ prep contrairement à
unlikely [ʌnˈlaɪklɪ] adj (happening) improbable; (explanation) invraisemblable
unlimited [ʌnˈlɪmɪtɪd] adj illimité(e)
unlisted [ˈʌnˈlɪstɪd] (US) adj (TEL) sur la liste rouge
unload [ʌnˈləud] vt décharger
unlock [ʌnˈlɔk] vt ouvrir
unlucky [ʌnˈlʌkɪ] adj (person) malchanceux(-euse); (object, number) qui porte malheur; **to be ~** (person) ne pas avoir de chance
unmarried [ʌnˈmærɪd] adj célibataire
unmistak(e)able [ʌnmɪsˈteɪkəbl] adj indubitable; qu'on ne peut pas ne pas reconnaître

unmitigated [ʌnˈmɪtɪgeɪtɪd] adj non mitigé(e), absolu(e), pur(e)

unnatural [ʌnˈnætʃrəl] adj non naturel(le); (habit) contre nature

unnecessary [ʌnˈnesəsərɪ] adj inutile, superflu(e)

unnoticed [ʌnˈnəʊtɪst] adj: (to go or pass) ~ (passer) inaperçu(e)

UNO n abbr = United Nations Organization

unobtainable [ʌnəbˈteɪnəbl] adj impossible à obtenir

unobtrusive [ʌnəbˈtruːsɪv] adj discret(-ète)

unofficial [ʌnəˈfɪʃl] adj (news) officieux(-euse); (strike) sauvage

unorthodox [ʌnˈɔːθədɔks] adj peu orthodoxe; (REL) hétérodoxe

unpack [ʌnˈpæk] vi défaire sa valise ♦ vt (suitcase) défaire; (belongings) déballer

unpalatable [ʌnˈpælətəbl] adj (meal) mauvais(e); (truth) désagréable (à entendre)

unparalleled [ʌnˈpærəleld] adj incomparable, sans égal

unpleasant [ʌnˈpleznt] adj déplaisant(e), désagréable

unplug [ʌnˈplʌg] vt débrancher

unpopular [ʌnˈpɔpjuləʳ] adj impopulaire

unprecedented [ʌnˈpresɪdəntɪd] adj sans précédent

unpredictable [ʌnprɪˈdɪktəbl] adj imprévisible

unprofessional [ʌnprəˈfeʃənl] adj: ~ conduct manquement m aux devoirs de la profession

UNPROFOR n abbr (= United Nations Protection Force) FORPRONU f

unqualified [ʌnˈkwɔlɪfaɪd] adj (teacher) non diplômé(e), sans titres; (success, disaster) sans réserve, total(e)

unquestionably [ʌnˈkwestʃənəblɪ] adv incontestablement

unravel [ʌnˈrævl] vt démêler

unreal [ʌnˈrɪəl] adj irréel(le); (extraordinary) incroyable

unrealistic [ʌnrɪəˈlɪstɪk] adj irréaliste; peu réaliste

unreasonable [ʌnˈriːznəbl] adj qui n'est pas raisonnable

unrelated [ʌnrɪˈleɪtɪd] adj sans rapport; sans lien de parenté

unreliable [ʌnrɪˈlaɪəbl] adj sur qui (or quoi) on ne peut pas compter, peu fiable

unremitting [ʌnrɪˈmɪtɪŋ] adj inlassable, infatigable, acharné(e)

unreservedly [ʌnrɪˈzɜːvɪdlɪ] adv sans réserve

unrest [ʌnˈrest] n agitation f, troubles mpl

unroll [ʌnˈrəʊl] vt dérouler

unruly [ʌnˈruːlɪ] adj indiscipliné(e)

unsafe [ʌnˈseɪf] adj (in danger) en danger; (journey, car) dangereux(-euse)

unsaid [ʌnˈsed] adj: to leave sth ~ passer qch sous silence

unsatisfactory [ˈʌnsætɪsˈfæktərɪ] adj peu satisfaisant(e)

unsavoury [ʌnˈseɪvərɪ] (US **unsavory**) adj (fig) peu recommandable

unscathed [ʌnˈskeɪðd] adj indemne

unscrew [ʌnˈskruː] vt dévisser

unscrupulous [ʌnˈskruːpjuləs] adj sans scrupules

unsettled [ʌnˈsetld] adj perturbé(e); instable

unshaven [ʌnˈʃeɪvn] adj non or mal rasé(e)

unsightly [ʌnˈsaɪtlɪ] adj disgracieux(-euse), laid(e)

unskilled [ʌnˈskɪld] adj: ~ worker manœuvre m

unspeakable [ʌnˈspiːkəbl] adj indicible; (awful) innommable

unstable [ʌnˈsteɪbl] adj instable

unsteady [ʌnˈstedɪ] adj mal assuré(e), chancelant(e), instable

unstuck [ʌnˈstʌk] adj: to come ~ se décoller; (plan) tomber à l'eau

unsuccessful [ʌnsəkˈsesful] adj (attempt) infructueux(-euse), vain(e); (writer, proposal) qui n'a pas de succès; to be ~ (in attempting sth) ne pas réussir; ne pas avoir de succès; (application) ne pas être retenu(e)

unsuitable [ʌnˈsuːtəbl] adj qui ne convient pas, peu approprié(e); inopportun(e)

unsure [ʌnˈʃuəʳ] adj pas sûr(e); to be ~ of o.s. manquer de confiance en soi

unsuspecting [ʌnsəsˈpektɪŋ] adj qui ne se doute de rien

unsympathetic [ˈʌnsɪmpəˈθetɪk] adj (person) antipathique; (attitude) peu compatissant(e)

untapped [ʌnˈtæpt] adj (resources) inexploité(e)

unthinkable [ʌnˈθɪŋkəbl] adj impensable, inconcevable

untidy [ʌnˈtaɪdɪ] adj (room) en désordre; (appearance, person) débraillé(e); (person: in character) sans ordre, désordonné

untie [ʌnˈtaɪ] vt (knot, parcel) défaire; (prisoner, dog) détacher

until [ənˈtɪl] prep jusqu'à; (after negative) avant ♦ conj jusqu'à ce que +sub; (in past, after negative) avant que +sub; ~ he comes jusqu'à ce qu'il vienne, jusqu'à son arrivée; ~ now jusqu'à présent, jusqu'ici; ~ then jusque-là

untimely [ʌnˈtaɪmlɪ] adj inopportun(e); (death) prématuré(e)

untold [ʌnˈtəʊld] adj (story) jamais raconté(e); (wealth) incalculable; (joy, suffering) indescriptible

untoward [ʌntəˈwɔːd] adj fâcheux(-euse), malencontreux(-euse)

unused¹ [ʌnˈjuːzd] adj (clothes) neuf (neuve)

unused² [ʌnˈjuːst] adj: **to be ~ to sth/to doing sth** ne pas avoir l'habitude de qch/de faire qch

unusual [ʌnˈjuːʒuəl] adj insolite, exceptionnel(le), rare

unveil [ʌnˈveɪl] vt dévoiler

unwanted [ʌnˈwɒntɪd] adj (child, pregnancy) non désiré(e); (clothes etc) à donner

unwelcome [ʌnˈwɛlkəm] adj importun(e); (news) fâcheux(-euse)

unwell [ʌnˈwɛl] adj souffrant(e); **to feel ~** ne pas se sentir bien

unwieldy [ʌnˈwiːldɪ] adj (object) difficile à manier; (system) lourd(e)

unwilling [ʌnˈwɪlɪŋ] adj: **to be ~ to do** ne pas vouloir faire; **~ly** adv à contrecœur, contre son gré

unwind [ʌnˈwaɪnd] (irreg) vt dérouler ♦ vi (relax) se détendre

unwise [ʌnˈwaɪz] adj irréfléchi(e), imprudent(e)

unwitting [ʌnˈwɪtɪŋ] adj involontaire

unworkable [ʌnˈwəːkəbl] adj (plan) impraticable

unworthy [ʌnˈwəːðɪ] adj indigne

unwrap [ʌnˈræp] vt défaire; ouvrir

unwritten [ʌnˈrɪtn] adj (agreement) tacite

KEYWORD

up [ʌp] prep: **he went up the stairs/the hill** il a monté l'escalier/la colline; **the cat was up a tree** le chat était dans un arbre; **they live further up the street** ils habitent plus haut dans la rue

♦ adv 1 (upwards, higher): **up in the sky/the mountains** (là-haut) dans le ciel/les montagnes; **put it a bit higher up** mettez-le un peu plus haut; **up there** là-haut; **up above** au-dessus

2: **to be up** (out of bed) être levé(e); (prices) avoir augmenté or monté

3: **up to** (as far as) jusqu'à; **up to now** jusqu'à présent

4: **to be up to** (depending on): **it's up to you** c'est à vous de décider; (equal to): **he's not up to it** (job, task etc) il n'en est pas capable; (inf: be doing): **what is he up to?** qu'est-ce qu'il peut bien faire?

♦ n: **ups and downs** hauts et bas mpl

---

up-and-coming [ʌpəndˈkʌmɪŋ] adj plein(e) d'avenir or de promesses

upbringing [ˈʌpbrɪŋɪŋ] n éducation f

update [ʌpˈdeɪt] vt mettre à jour

upgrade [ʌpˈɡreɪd] vt (house) moderniser; (job) revaloriser; (employee) promouvoir

upheaval [ʌpˈhiːvl] n bouleversement m; branle-bas m

uphill [ˈʌpˈhɪl] adj qui monte; (fig: task) difficile, pénible ♦ adv (face, look) en amont; **to go ~** monter

uphold [ʌpˈhəuld] (irreg) vt (law, decision) maintenir

upholstery [ʌpˈhəulstərɪ] n rembourrage m; (cover) tissu m d'ameublement; (of car) garniture f

upkeep [ˈʌpkiːp] n entretien m

upon [əˈpɒn] prep sur

upper [ˈʌpə] adj supérieur(e); du dessus ♦ n (of shoe) empeigne f; **~-class** adj de la haute société, aristocratique; **~ hand** n: **to have the ~ hand** avoir le dessus; **~most** adj le (la) plus haut(e); **what was ~most in my mind** ce à quoi je pensais surtout; **~ sixth** n terminale f

upright [ˈʌpraɪt] adj droit(e); vertical(e); (fig) droit, honnête

uprising [ˈʌpraɪzɪŋ] n soulèvement m, insurrection f

uproar [ˈʌprɔːr] n tumulte m; (protests) tempête f de protestations

uproot [ʌpˈruːt] vt déraciner

upset [n ˈʌpset, vb, adj ʌpˈset] (irreg: like set) n bouleversement m; (stomach ~) indigestion f ♦ vt (glass etc) renverser; (plan) déranger; (person: offend) contrarier; (: grieve) faire de la peine à; bouleverser ♦ adj contrarié(e); peiné(e); (stomach) dérangé(e)

upshot [ˈʌpʃɒt] n résultat m

upside-down [ʌpsaɪdˈdaun] adv à l'envers; **to turn ~ ~** mettre sens dessus dessous

upstairs [ʌpˈstɛəz] adv en haut ♦ adj (room) du dessus, d'en haut ♦ n: **the ~** l'étage m

upstart [ˈʌpstɑːt] (pej) n parvenu(e)

upstream [ʌpˈstriːm] adv en amont

uptake [ˈʌpteɪk] n: **to be quick/slow on the ~** comprendre vite/être lent à comprendre

uptight [ʌpˈtaɪt] (inf) adj très tendu(e), crispé(e)

up-to-date [ˈʌptəˈdeɪt] adj moderne; (information) très récent(e)

upturn [ˈʌptəːn] n (in luck) retournement m; (COMM: in market) hausse f

upward [ˈʌpwəd] adj ascendant(e); vers le haut; **~(s)** adv vers le haut; **~(s) of 200** 200 et plus

urban [ˈəːbən] adj urbain(e); **~ clearway** n rue f à stationnement interdit

urbane [əːˈbeɪn] adj urbain(e), courtois(e)

urchin [ˈəːtʃɪn] n polisson m

urge [əːdʒ] n besoin m; envie f; forte envie, désir m ♦ vt: **to ~ sb to do** exhorter qn à faire, pousser qn à faire; recommander vivement à qn de faire

urgency [ˈəːdʒənsɪ] n urgence f; (of tone) insistance f

urgent [ˈəːdʒənt] adj urgent(e); (tone) insistant(e), pressant(e)

urinal ['juərɪnl] n urinoir m

urine ['juərɪn] n urine f

urn [əːn] n urne f; (also: **tea ~**) fontaine f à thé

US n abbr = **United States**

us [ʌs] pron nous; see also **me**

USA n abbr = **United States of America**

use [n juːs, vb juːz] n emploi m, utilisation f; usage m; (~fulness) utilité f ♦ vt se servir de, utiliser, employer; **in ~** en usage; **out of ~** hors d'usage; **to be of ~** servir, être utile; **it's no ~** ça ne sert à rien; **she ~d to do it** elle le faisait (autrefois), elle avait coutume de le faire; **~d to: to be ~d to** avoir l'habitude de, être habitué(e) à; **~ up** vt finir, épuiser; consommer; **~d** [juːzd] adj (car) d'occasion; **~ful** ['juːsful] adj utile; **~fulness** n utilité f; **~less** ['juːslɪs] adj inutile; (person: hopeless) nul(le); **~r** ['juːzəʳ] n utilisateur(-trice), usager m; **~r-friendly** adj (computer) convivial(e), facile d'emploi

usher ['ʌʃəʳ] n (at wedding ceremony) placeur m; **~ette** [ʌʃə'rɛt] n (in cinema) ouvreuse f

usual ['juːʒuəl] adj habituel(le); **as ~** comme d'habitude; **~ly** ['juːʒuəlɪ] adv d'habitude, d'ordinaire

utensil [juː'tɛnsl] n ustensile m

uterus ['juːtərəs] n utérus m

utility [juː'tɪlɪtɪ] n utilité f; (also: **public ~**) service public; **~ room** n buanderie f

utmost ['ʌtməust] adj extrême, le (la) plus grand(e) ♦ n: **to do one's ~** faire tout son possible

utter ['ʌtəʳ] adj total(e), complet(-ète) ♦ vt (words) prononcer, proférer; (sounds) émettre; **~ance** n paroles fpl; **~ly** adv complètement, totalement

U-turn ['juː'təːn] n demi-tour m

V, v

v. abbr = **verse**; **versus**; **volt**; (= vide) voir

vacancy ['veɪkənsɪ] n (BRIT: job) poste vacant; (room) chambre f disponible; **"no vacancies"** "complet"

vacant ['veɪkənt] adj (seat etc) libre, disponible; (expression) distrait(e)

vacate [və'keɪt] vt quitter

vacation [və'keɪʃən] n vacances fpl

vaccinate ['væksɪneɪt] vt vacciner

vacuum ['vækjum] n vide m; **~ cleaner** n aspirateur m; **~-packed** adj emballé(e) sous vide

vagina [və'dʒaɪnə] n vagin m

vagrant ['veɪɡrənt] n vagabond(e)

vague [veɪɡ] adj vague, imprécis(e); (blurred: photo, outline) flou(e); **~ly** adv vaguement

vain [veɪn] adj (useless) vain(e); (conceited) vaniteux(-euse); **in ~** en vain

valentine ['væləntaɪn] n (also: **~ card**) carte f de la Saint-Valentin; (person) bien-aimé(e) (le jour de la Saint-Valentin); **V~'s day** n Saint-Valentin f

valiant ['vælɪənt] adj vaillant(e)

valid ['vælɪd] adj valable; (document) valable, valide

valley ['vælɪ] n vallée f

valour ['væləʳ] (US **valor**) n courage m

valuable ['væljuəbl] adj (jewel) de valeur; (time, help) précieux(-euse); **~s** npl objets mpl de valeur

valuation [vælju'eɪʃən] n (price) estimation f; (quality) appréciation f

value ['væljuː] n valeur f ♦ vt (fix price) évaluer, expertiser; (appreciate) apprécier; **~ added tax** (BRIT) n taxe f à la valeur ajoutée; **~d** adj (person) estimé(e); (advice) précieux(-euse)

valve [vælv] n (in machine) soupape f, valve f; (MED) valve, valvule f

van [væn] n (AUT) camionnette f

vandal ['vændl] n vandale m/f; **~ism** n vandalisme m; **~ize** vt saccager

vanguard ['vænɡɑːd] n (fig): **in the ~ of** à l'avant-garde de

vanilla [və'nɪlə] n vanille f

vanish ['vænɪʃ] vi disparaître

vanity ['vænɪtɪ] n vanité f

vantage point ['vɑːntɪdʒ-] n bonne position

vapour ['veɪpəʳ] (US **vapor**) n vapeur f; (on window) buée f

variable ['veərɪəbl] adj variable; (mood) changeant(e)

variance ['veərɪəns] n: **to be at ~ (with)** être en désaccord (avec); (facts) être en contradiction (avec)

varicose ['værɪkəus] adj: **~ veins** varices fpl

varied ['veərɪd] adj varié(e), divers(e)

variety [və'raɪətɪ] n variété f; (quantity) nombre m, quantité f; **~ show** n (spectacle m de) variétés fpl

various ['veərɪəs] adj divers(e), différent(e); (several) divers, plusieurs

varnish ['vɑːnɪʃ] n vernis m ♦ vt vernir

vary ['veərɪ] vt, vi varier, changer

vase [vɑːz] n vase m

Vaseline ® ['væsɪliːn] n vaseline f

vast [vɑːst] adj vaste, immense; (amount, success) énorme

VAT [væt] n abbr (= value added tax) TVA f

vat [væt] n cuve f

vault [vɔːlt] n (of roof) voûte f; (tomb) caveau m; (in bank) salle f des coffres; chambre forte ♦ vt (also: **~ over**) sauter (d'un bond)

vaunted ['vɔːntɪd] adj: **much-~** tant vanté(e)

VCR n abbr = **video cassette recorder**

VD n abbr = **venereal disease**

VDU n abbr = **visual display unit**

veal [viːl] n veau m
veer [vɪəʳ] vi tourner; virer
vegan ['viːgən] n végétalien(ne)
vegeburger ['vedʒɪbɜːgəʳ] n burger végétarien
vegetable ['vedʒtəbl] n légume m ♦ adj végétal(e)
vegetarian [vedʒɪ'teərɪən] adj, n végétarien(ne)
vehement ['viːɪmənt] adj violent(e), impétueux(-euse); (impassioned) ardent(e)
vehicle ['viːɪkl] n véhicule m
veil [veɪl] n voile m
vein [veɪn] n veine f; (on leaf) nervure f
velocity [vɪ'lɒsɪtɪ] n vitesse f
velvet ['velvɪt] n velours m
vending machine ['vendɪŋ-] n distributeur m automatique
veneer [və'nɪəʳ] n (on furniture) placage m; (fig) vernis m
venereal [vɪ'nɪərɪəl] adj: ~ **disease** maladie vénérienne
Venetian blind [vɪ'niːʃən-] n store vénitien
vengeance ['vendʒəns] n vengeance f; **with a ~** (fig) vraiment, pour de bon
venison ['venɪsn] n venaison f
venom ['venəm] n venin m
vent [vent] n conduit m d'aération; (in dress, jacket) fente f ♦ vt (fig: one's feelings) donner libre cours à
ventilator ['ventɪleɪtəʳ] n ventilateur m
ventriloquist [ven'trɪləkwɪst] n ventriloque m/f
venture ['ventʃəʳ] n entreprise f ♦ vt risquer, hasarder ♦ vi s'aventurer, se risquer
venue ['venjuː] n lieu m
verb [vɜːb] n verbe m; **~al** adj verbal(e); (translation) littéral(e)
verbatim [vɜː'beɪtɪm] adj, adv mot pour mot
verdict ['vɜːdɪkt] n verdict m
verge [vɜːdʒ] n (BRIT) bord m, bas-côté m; **"soft ~s"** (BRIT: AUT) "accotement non stabilisé"; **on the ~ of doing** sur le point de faire; ~ **on** vt fus approcher de
verify ['verɪfaɪ] vt vérifier; (confirm) confirmer
vermin ['vɜːmɪn] npl animaux mpl nuisibles; (insects) vermine f
vermouth ['vɜːməθ] n vermouth m
versatile ['vɜːsətaɪl] adj polyvalent(e)
verse [vɜːs] n (poetry) vers mpl; (stanza) strophe f; (in Bible) verset m
version ['vɜːʃən] n version f
versus ['vɜːsəs] prep contre
vertical ['vɜːtɪkl] adj vertical(e) ♦ n verticale f
vertigo ['vɜːtɪgəu] n vertige m
verve [vɜːv] n brio m, enthousiasme m
very ['verɪ] adv très ♦ adj: **the ~ book which** le livre même que; **the ~ last** le tout dernier; **at the ~ least** tout au moins; **~ much** beaucoup

vessel ['vesl] n (ANAT, NAUT) vaisseau m; (container) récipient m
vest [vest] n (BRIT) tricot m de corps; (US: waistcoat) gilet m
vested interest ['vestɪd-] n (COMM) droits acquis
vet [vet] n abbr (BRIT: veterinary surgeon) vétérinaire m/f ♦ vt examiner soigneusement
veteran ['vetərn] n vétéran m; (also: **war ~**) ancien combattant
veterinary surgeon ['vetrɪnərɪ-] (BRIT), **veterinarian** [vetrɪ'neərɪən] (US) n vétérinaire m/f
veto ['viːtəu] (pl **~es**) n veto m ♦ vt opposer son veto à
vex [veks] vt fâcher, contrarier; **~ed** adj (question) controversé(e)
via ['vaɪə] prep par, via
viable ['vaɪəbl] adj viable
vibrate [vaɪ'breɪt] vi vibrer
vicar ['vɪkəʳ] n pasteur m (de l'Église anglicane); **~age** n presbytère m
vicarious [vɪ'keərɪəs] adj indirect(e)
vice [vaɪs] n (evil) vice m; (TECH) étau m
vice- [vaɪs] prefix vice-
vice squad n ≈ brigade mondaine
vice versa ['vaɪsɪ'vɜːsə] adv vice versa
vicinity [vɪ'sɪnɪtɪ] n environs mpl, alentours mpl
vicious ['vɪʃəs] adj (remark) cruel(le), méchant(e); (blow) brutal(e); (dog) méchant(e), dangereux(-euse); (horse) vicieux(-euse); ~ **circle** n cercle vicieux
victim ['vɪktɪm] n victime f
victor ['vɪktəʳ] n vainqueur m
Victorian [vɪk'tɔːrɪən] adj victorien(ne)
victory ['vɪktərɪ] n victoire f
video ['vɪdɪəu] cpd vidéo inv ♦ n (~ **film**) vidéo f; (also: ~ **cassette**) vidéocassette f; (also: ~ **cassette recorder**) magnétoscope m; ~ **tape** n bande f vidéo inv; (cassette) vidéocassette f; ~ **wall** n mur m d'images vidéo
vie [vaɪ] vi: **to ~ with** rivaliser avec
Vienna [vɪ'enə] n Vienne
Vietnam ['vjet'næm] n Việt-Nam m, Vietnam m; **~ese** [vjetnə'miːz] adj vietnamien(ne) ♦ n inv Vietnamien(ne); (LING) vietnamien m
view [vjuː] n vue f; (opinion) avis m, vue ♦ vt voir, regarder; (situation) considérer; (house) visiter; **in full ~ of** sous les yeux de; **in ~ of the weather/the fact that** étant donné le temps/ que; **in my ~** à mon avis; **~er** n (TV) téléspectateur(-trice); **~finder** n viseur m; **~point** n point m de vue
vigorous ['vɪgərəs] adj vigoureux(-euse)
vile [vaɪl] adj (action) vil(e); (smell, food) abominable; (temper) massacrant(e)
villa ['vɪlə] n villa f
village ['vɪlɪdʒ] n village m; **~r** n villageois(e)

villain ['vɪlən] n (scoundrel) scélérat m; (BRIT: criminal) bandit m; (in novel etc) traître m

vindicate ['vɪndɪkeɪt] vt (person) innocenter; (action) justifier

vindictive [vɪn'dɪktɪv] adj vindicatif(-ive), rancunier(-ère)

vine [vaɪn] n vigne f; (climbing plant) plante grimpante

vinegar ['vɪnɪɡər] n vinaigre m

vineyard ['vɪnjɑːd] n vignoble m

vintage ['vɪntɪdʒ] n (year) année f, millésime m; ~ **car** n voiture f d'époque; ~ **wine** n vin m de grand cru

viola [vɪ'əulə] n (MUS) alto m

violate ['vaɪəleɪt] vt violer

violence ['vaɪələns] n violence f

violent ['vaɪələnt] adj violent(e)

violet ['vaɪələt] adj violet(te) ♦ n (colour) violet m; (plant) violette f

violin [vaɪə'lɪn] n violon m; ~**ist** [vaɪə'lɪnɪst] n violoniste m/f

VIP n abbr (= very important person) V.I.P. m

virgin ['vəːdʒɪn] n vierge f ♦ adj vierge

Virgo ['vəːɡəu] n la Vierge

virile ['vɪraɪl] adj viril(e)

virtually ['vəːtjuəlɪ] adv (almost) pratiquement

virtual reality ['vəːtjuəl-] n (COMPUT) réalité virtuelle

virtue ['vəːtjuː] n vertu f; (advantage) mérite m, avantage m; **by ~ of** en vertu or en raison de; **virtuous** adj vertueux(-euse)

virus ['vaɪərəs] n (COMPUT) virus m

visa ['viːzə] n visa m

visibility [vɪzɪ'bɪlɪtɪ] n visibilité f

visible ['vɪzəbl] adj visible

vision ['vɪʒən] n (sight) vue f, vision f; (foresight, in dream) vision

visit ['vɪzɪt] n visite f; (stay) séjour m ♦ vt (person) rendre visite à; (place) visiter; ~**ing hours** npl (in hospital etc) heures fpl de visite; ~**or** n visiteur(-euse); (to one's house) visite f, invité(e); ~**or centre** n hall m or centre m d'accueil

visor ['vaɪzər] n visière f

vista ['vɪstə] n vue f

visual ['vɪzjuəl] adj visuel(le); ~ **aid** n support visuel; ~ **display unit** n console f de visualisation, visuel m; ~**ize** vt se représenter, s'imaginer; ~**ly-impaired** adj malvoyant(e)

vital ['vaɪtl] adj vital(e); (person) plein(e) d'entrain; ~**ly** adv (important) absolument; ~ **statistics** npl (fig) mensurations fpl

vitamin ['vɪtəmɪn] n vitamine f

vivacious [vɪ'veɪʃəs] adj animé(e), qui a de la vivacité

vivid ['vɪvɪd] adj (account) vivant(e); (light, imagination) vif (vive); ~**ly** adv (describe) d'une manière vivante; (remember) de façon précise

V-neck ['viːnɛk] n décolleté m en V

vocabulary [vəu'kæbjulərɪ] n vocabulaire m

vocal ['vəukl] adj vocal(e); (articulate) qui sait s'exprimer; ~ **cords** npl cordes vocales

vocation [vəu'keɪʃən] n vocation f; ~**al** adj professionnel(le)

vociferous [və'sɪfərəs] adj bruyant(e)

vodka ['vɔdkə] n vodka f

vogue [vəuɡ] n: **in ~** en vogue f

voice [vɔɪs] n voix f ♦ vt (opinion) exprimer, formuler; ~**mail** n (system) messagerie f vocale; (device) boîte f vocale

void [vɔɪd] n vide m ♦ adj nul(le); ~ **of** vide de, dépourvu(e) de

volatile ['vɔlətaɪl] adj volatil(e); (person) versatile; (situation) explosif(-ive)

volcano [vɔl'keɪnəu] (pl ~**es**) n volcan m

volition [və'lɪʃən] n: **of one's own ~** de son propre gré

volley ['vɔlɪ] n (of gunfire) salve f; (of stones etc) grêle f, volée f; (of questions) multitude f, série f; (TENNIS etc) volée f; ~**ball** n vol-ley(-ball) m

volt [vəult] n volt m; ~**age** n tension f, voltage m

volume ['vɔljuːm] n volume m

voluntarily ['vɔləntrɪlɪ] adv volontairement

voluntary ['vɔləntərɪ] adj volontaire; (unpaid) bénévole

volunteer [vɔlən'tɪər] n volontaire m/f ♦ vi (MIL) s'engager comme volontaire; **to ~ to do** se proposer pour faire

vomit ['vɔmɪt] vt, vi vomir

vote [vəut] n vote m, suffrage m; (cast) voix f, vote; (franchise) droit m de vote ♦ vt (elect): **to be ~d chairman** etc être élu président etc; (propose): **to ~ that** proposer que ♦ vi voter; ~ **of thanks** discours m de remerciement; ~**r** n électeur(-trice); **voting** n scrutin m, vote m

voucher ['vautʃər] n (for meal, petrol, gift) bon m

vouch for ['vautʃ-] vt fus se porter garant de

vow [vau] n vœu m, serment m ♦ vi jurer

vowel ['vauəl] n voyelle f

voyage ['vɔɪɪdʒ] n voyage m par mer, traversée f; (by spacecraft) voyage

vulgar ['vʌlɡər] adj vulgaire

vulnerable ['vʌlnərəbl] adj vulnérable

vulture ['vʌltʃər] n vautour m

W, w

wad [wɔd] n (of cotton wool, paper) tampon m; (of banknotes etc) liasse f

waddle ['wɔdl] vi se dandiner

wade [weɪd] vi: **to ~ through** marcher dans, patauger dans; (fig: book) s'évertuer à lire

wafer ['weɪfər] n (CULIN) gaufrette f

waffle ['wɒfl] n (CULIN) gaufre f; (inf) verbiage m, remplissage m ♦ vi parler pour ne rien dire, faire du remplissage

waft [wɒft] vt porter ♦ vi flotter

wag [wæg] vt agiter, remuer ♦ vi remuer

wage [weɪdʒ] n (also: ~s) salaire m, paye f ♦ vt: to ~ war faire la guerre; **~ earner** n salarié(e); **~ packet** n (enveloppe f de) paye f

wager ['weɪdʒər] n pari m

wag(g)on ['wægən] n (horse-drawn) chariot m; (BRIT: RAIL) wagon m (de marchandises)

wail [weɪl] vi gémir; (siren) hurler

waist [weɪst] n taille f; **~coat** (BRIT) n gilet m; **~line** n (tour m de) taille f

wait [weɪt] n attente f ♦ vi attendre; **to keep sb ~ing** faire attendre qn; **to ~ for** attendre; I **can't ~ to ...** (fig) je meurs d'envie de ...; **~ behind** vi rester (à attendre); **~ on** vt fus servir; **~er** n garçon m (de café), serveur m; **~ing** n: "no **~ing**" (BRIT: AUT) "stationnement interdit"; **~ing list** n liste f d'attente, **~ing room** n salle f d'attente; **~ress** n serveuse f

waive [weɪv] vt renoncer à, abandonner

wake [weɪk] (pt woke, waked, pp woken, waked) vt (also: **~ up**) réveiller ♦ vi (also: **~ up**) se réveiller ♦ n (for dead person) veillée f mortuaire; (NAUT) sillage m

Wales [weɪlz] n pays m de Galles; **the Prince of ~** le prince de Galles

walk [wɔːk] n promenade f; (short) petit tour m; (gait) démarche f; (path) chemin m; (in park etc) allée f ♦ vi marcher; (for pleasure, exercise) se promener ♦ vt (distance) faire à pied; (dog) promener; **10 minutes' ~ from** à 10 minutes à pied de; **from all ~s of life** de toutes conditions sociales; **~ out** vi (audience) sortir, quitter la salle; (workers) se mettre en grève; **~ out on** (inf) vt fus quitter, plaquer; **~er** n (person) marcheur(-euse); **~ie-talkie** n talkie-walkie m; **~ing** n marche f à pied; **~ing shoes** npl chaussures fpl de marche; **~ing stick** n canne f; **W~man** ® n Walkman ® m; **~out** n (of workers) grève-surprise f; **~over** (inf) n victoire f or examen m etc facile; **~way** n promenade f

wall [wɔːl] n mur m; (of tunnel, cave etc) paroi m; **~ed** adj (city) fortifié(e); (garden) entouré(e) d'un mur, clos(e)

wallet ['wɒlɪt] n portefeuille m

wallflower ['wɔːlflaʊər] n giroflée f; **to be a ~** (fig) faire tapisserie

wallow ['wɒləʊ] vi se vautrer

wallpaper ['wɔːlpeɪpər] n papier peint ♦ vt tapisser

walnut ['wɔːlnʌt] n noix f; (tree, wood) noyer m

walrus ['wɔːlrəs] (pl ~ or ~es) n morse m

waltz [wɔːlts] n valse f ♦ vi valser

wand [wɒnd] n (also: **magic ~**) baguette f (magique)

wander ['wɒndər] vi (person) errer; (thoughts) vagabonder, errer ♦ vt errer dans

wane [weɪn] vi (moon) décroître; (reputation) décliner

wangle ['wæŋgl] (BRIT: inf) vt se débrouiller pour avoir; carotter

want [wɒnt] vt vouloir; (need) avoir besoin de ♦ n: **for ~ of** par manque de, faute de; **~s** npl (needs) besoins mpl; **to ~ to do** vouloir faire; **to ~ sb to do** vouloir que qn fasse; **~ed** adj (criminal) recherché(e) par la police; **"cook ~ed"** "on recherche un cuisinier"; **~ing** adj: **to be found ~ing** ne pas être à la hauteur

war [wɔːr] n guerre f; **to make ~ (on)** faire la guerre (à)

ward [wɔːd] n (in hospital) salle f; (POL) canton m; (LAW: child) pupille m/f; **~ off** vt (attack, enemy) repousser, éviter

warden ['wɔːdn] n gardien(ne), (BRIT: of institution) directeur(-trice); (: also: **traffic ~**) contractuel(le); (of youth hostel) père m or mère f aubergiste

warder ['wɔːdər] (BRIT) n gardien m de prison

wardrobe ['wɔːdrəʊb] n (cupboard) armoire f; (clothes) garde-robe f; (THEATRE) costumes mpl

warehouse ['wɛəhaʊs] n entrepôt m

wares [wɛəz] npl marchandises fpl

warfare ['wɔːfɛər] n guerre f

warhead ['wɔːhɛd] n (MIL) ogive f

warily ['wɛərɪlɪ] adv avec prudence

warm [wɔːm] adj chaud(e); (thanks, welcome, applause, person) chaleureux(-euse); **it's ~** il fait chaud; **I'm ~** j'ai chaud; **~ up** vi (person, room) se réchauffer; (water) chauffer; (athlete) s'échauffer ♦ vt (food) (faire) réchauffer, (faire) chauffer; (engine) faire chauffer; **~-hearted** adj affectueux(-euse); **~ly** adv chaudement; chaleureusement; **~th** n chaleur f

warn [wɔːn] vt avertir, prévenir; **to ~ sb (not) to do** conseiller à qn de (ne pas) faire; **~ing** n avertissement m; (notice) avis m; (signal) avertisseur m; **~ing light** n avertisseur lumineux; **~ing triangle** n (AUT) triangle m de présignalisation

warp [wɔːp] vi (wood) travailler, se déformer ♦ vt (fig: character) pervertir

warrant ['wɒrnt] n (guarantee) garantie f; (LAW: to arrest) mandat m d'arrêt; (: to search) mandat de perquisition; **~y** n garantie f

warren ['wɒrən] n (of rabbits) terrier m; (fig: of streets etc) dédale m

warrior ['wɒrɪər] n guerrier(-ère)

Warsaw ['wɔːsɔː] n Varsovie

warship ['wɔːʃɪp] n navire m de guerre

wart [wɔːt] n verrue f

wartime ['wɔːtaɪm] n: **in ~** en temps de guerre

wary ['wɛərɪ] adj prudent(e)

was [wɔz] pt of **be**

wash [wɔʃ] vt laver ♦ vi se laver; (sea): **to ~ over/against sth** inonder/baigner qch ♦ n (clothes) lessive f; (~ing programme) lavage m; (of ship) sillage m; **to have a ~** se laver, faire sa toilette; **to give sth a ~** laver qch; **~ away** vt (stain) enlever au lavage; (subj: river etc) emporter; **~ off** vi partir au lavage; **~ up** vi (BRIT) faire la vaisselle; (US) se débarbouiller; **~able** adj lavable; **~basin** (US **washbowl**) n lavabo m; **~cloth** (US) n gant de toilette; **~er** n (TECH) rondelle f, joint m; **~ing** n (dirty) linge m; (clean) lessive f; **~ing machine** n machine f à laver; **~ing powder** (BRIT) n lessive f (en poudre); **~ing-up** n vaisselle f; **~ing-up liquid** n produit m pour la vaisselle; **~-out** (inf) n désastre m; **~room** (US) n toilettes fpl

wasn't ['wɔznt] = **was not**

wasp [wɔsp] n guêpe f

wastage ['weɪstɪdʒ] n gaspillage m; (in manufacturing, transport etc) pertes fpl, déchets mpl; **natural ~** départs naturels

waste [weɪst] n gaspillage m; (of time) perte f; (rubbish) déchets mpl; (also: **household ~**) ordures fpl ♦ adj (land, ground: in city) à l'abandon; (leftover) de trop ♦ vt gaspiller; (time, opportunity) perdre; **~s** npl (area) étendue f désertique; **~ away** vi dépérir; **~ disposal unit** (BRIT) n broyeur m d'ordures; **~ful** adj gaspilleur(-euse); (process) peu économique; **~ ground** (BRIT) n terrain m vague; **~paper basket** n corbeille f à papier

watch [wɔtʃ] n montre f; (act of ~ing) surveillance f; guet m; (MIL: guards) garde f; (NAUT: guards, spell of duty) quart m ♦ vt (look at) observer; (: match, programme, TV) regarder; (spy on, guard) surveiller; (be careful of) faire attention à ♦ vi regarder; (keep guard) monter la garde; **~ out** vi faire attention; **~dog** n chien m de garde; (fig) gardien(ne); **~ful** adj attentif(-ive), vigilant(e); **~maker** n horloger(-ère); **~man** (irreg) n see **night**; **~strap** n bracelet m de montre

water ['wɔːtə'] n eau f ♦ vt (plant, garden) arroser ♦ vi (eyes) larmoyer; (mouth): **it makes my mouth ~** j'en ai l'eau à la bouche; **in British ~s** dans les eaux territoriales britanniques; **~ down** vt (milk) couper d'eau; (fig: story) édulcorer; **~colour** (US **watercolor**) n aquarelle f; **~cress** n cresson m (de fontaine); **~fall** n chute f d'eau; **~ heater** n chauffe-eau m; **~ing can** n arrosoir m; **~ lily** n nénuphar m; **~line** n (NAUT) ligne f de flottaison; **~logged** adj (ground) détrempé(e); **~ main** n canalisation f d'eau; **~melon** n pastèque f; **~proof** adj imperméable; **~shed** n (GEO) ligne f de partage des eaux; (fig) moment m critique, point décisif; **~-skiing** n ski m nautique; **~tight** adj étanche; **~way** n cours m d'eau navigable; **~works** n (building) station f hydraulique; **~y** adj (coffee, soup) trop faible; (eyes) humide, larmoyant(e)

watt [wɔt] n watt m

wave [weɪv] n vague f; (of hand) geste m, signe m; (RADIO) onde f; (in hair) ondulation f ♦ vi faire signe de la main; (flag) flotter au vent; (grass) ondoyer ♦ vt (handkerchief) agiter; (stick) brandir; **~length** n longueur f d'ondes

waver ['weɪvə'] vi vaciller; (voice) trembler; (person) hésiter

wavy ['weɪvɪ] adj (hair, surface) ondulé(e); (line) onduleux(-euse)

wax [wæks] n cire f; (for skis) fart m ♦ vt cirer; (car) lustrer; (skis) farter ♦ vi (moon) croître; **~works** npl personnages mpl de cire ♦ n musée m de cire

way [weɪ] n chemin m, voie f; (distance) distance f; (direction) chemin, direction f; (manner) façon f, manière f; (habit) habitude f, façon; **which ~? - this ~** par où? - par ici; **on the ~** (en route) en route; **to be on one's ~** être en route; **to go out of one's ~ to do** (fig) se donner du mal pour faire; **to be in the ~** bloquer le passage; (fig) gêner; **to lose one's ~** perdre son chemin; **under ~** en cours; **in a ~** dans un sens; **in some ~s** à certains égards; **no ~!** (inf) pas question!; **by the ~** ... à propos ...; **"~ in"** (BRIT) "entrée"; **"~ out"** (BRIT) "sortie"; **the ~ back** le chemin du retour; **"give ~"** (BRIT: AUT) "cédez le passage"; **~lay** (irreg) vt attaquer

wayward ['weɪwəd] adj capricieux(-euse), entêté(e)

W.C. n abbr w.c. mpl, waters mpl

we [wiː] pl pron nous

weak [wiːk] adj faible; (health) fragile; (beam etc) peu solide; **~en** vi faiblir, décliner ♦ vt affaiblir; **~ling** n (physically) gringalet m; (morally etc) faible m/f; **~ness** n faiblesse f; (fault) point m faible; **to have a ~ness for** avoir un faible pour

wealth [welθ] n (money, resources) richesse(s) f(pl); (of details) profusion f; **~y** adj riche

wean [wiːn] vt sevrer

weapon ['wepən] n arme f

wear [wɛə'] (pt **wore**, pp **worn**) n (use) usage m; (deterioration through use) usure f;

(*clothing*): **sports/babywear** vêtements *mpl* de sport/pour bébés ♦ *vt* (*clothes*) porter; (*put on*) mettre; (*damage: through use*) user ♦ *vi* (*last*) faire de l'usage; (*rub etc through*) s'user; **town/evening ~** tenue *f* de ville/soirée; **~ away** *vt* user, ronger ♦ *vi* (*inscription*) s'effacer; **~ down** *vt* user; (*strength, person*) épuiser; **~ off** *vi* disparaître; **~ out** *vt* user; (*person, strength*) épuiser; **~ and tear** *n* usure *f*

weary ['wɪərɪ] *adj* (*tired*) épuisé(e); (*dispirited*) las (lasse), abattu(e) ♦ *vi*: **to ~ of** se lasser de

weasel ['wi:zl] *n* (ZOOL) belette *f*

weather ['wɛðər] *n* temps *m* ♦ *vt* (*tempest, crisis*) essuyer, réchapper à, survivre à; **under the ~** (*fig: ill*) mal fichu(e); **~-beaten** *adj* (*person*) hâlé(e); (*building*) dégradé(e) par les intempéries; **~cock** *n* girouette *f*; **~ forecast** *n* prévisions *fpl* météorologiques, météo *f*; **~ man** (*irreg*) (*inf*) *n* météorologue *m*; **~ vane** *n* = **weathercock**

weave [wi:v] (*pt* **wove**, *pp* **woven**) *vt* (*cloth*) tisser; (*basket*) tresser; **~r** *n* tisserand(e)

web [wɛb] *n* (*of spider*) toile *f*; (*on foot*) palmure *f*; (*fabric, also fig*) tissu *m*; **the (World Wide) W~** le Web

website ['wɛbsaɪt] *n* (COMPUT) site *m* Web

wed [wɛd] (*pt, pp* **wedded**) *vt* épouser ♦ *vi* se marier

we'd [wi:d] = **we had; we would**

wedding [wɛdɪŋ] *n* mariage *m*; **silver/golden ~** (*anniversary*) noces *fpl* d'argent/d'or; **~ day** *n* jour *m* du mariage; **~ dress** *n* robe *f* de mariée; **~ ring** *n* alliance *f*

wedge [wɛdʒ] *n* (*of wood etc*) coin *m*, cale *f*; (*of cake*) part *f* ♦ *vt* (*fix*) caler; (*pack tightly*) enfoncer

Wednesday ['wɛnzdɪ] *n* mercredi *m*

wee [wi:] (SCOTTISH) *adj* (tout(e)) petit(e)

weed [wi:d] *n* mauvaise herbe *f* ♦ *vt* désherber; **~killer** *n* désherbant *m*; **~y** *adj* (*man*) gringalet

week [wi:k] *n* semaine *f*; **a ~ today/on Friday** aujourd'hui/vendredi en huit; **~day** *n* jour *m* de semaine; (COMM) jour ouvrable; **~end** *n* week-end *m*; **~ly** *adv* une fois par semaine, chaque semaine ♦ *adj* hebdomadaire

weep [wi:p] (*pt, pp* **wept**) *vi* (*person*) pleurer; **~ing willow** *n* saule pleureur

weigh [weɪ] *vt, vi* peser; **to ~ anchor** lever l'ancre; **~ down** *vt* (*person, animal*) écraser; (*fig: with worry*) accabler; **~ up** *vt* examiner

weight [weɪt] *n* poids *m*; **to lose/put on ~** maigrir/grossir; **~ing** *n* (*allowance*) indemnité *f*, allocation *f*; **~lifter** *n* haltérophile *m*; **~lifting** *n* haltérophilie *f*; **~y** *adj* lourd(e); (*important*) de poids, important(e)

weir [wɪər] *n* barrage *m*

weird [wɪəd] *adj* bizarre

welcome ['wɛlkəm] *adj* bienvenu(e) ♦ *n* accueil *m* ♦ *vt* accueillir; (*also: bid ~*) souhaiter la bienvenue à; (*be glad of*) se réjouir de; **thank you - you're ~!** merci - de rien *or* il n'y a pas de quoi!

welder ['wɛldər] *n* soudeur(-euse)

welfare ['wɛlfɛər] *n* (*wellbeing*) bien-être *m*; (*social aid*) assistance sociale; **~ state** *n* État-providence *m*

well [wɛl] *n* puits *m* ♦ *adv* bien ♦ *adj*: **to be ~** aller bien ♦ *excl* eh bien!; (*relief also*) bon!; (*resignation*) enfin!; **as ~** aussi, également; **as ~ as** en plus de; **~ done!** bravo!; **get ~ soon** remets-toi vite!; **to do ~** bien réussir; (*business*) prospérer; **~ up** *vi* monter

we'll [wi:l] = **we will; we shall**

well: **~-behaved** *adj* sage, obéissant(e); **~-being** *n* bien-être *m*; **~-built** *adj* (*person*) bien bâti(e); **~-deserved** *adj* (*bien*) mérité(e); **~-dressed** *adj* bien habillé(e); **~-heeled** (*inf*) *adj* (*wealthy*) nanti(e)

wellingtons ['wɛlɪŋtənz] *npl* (*also:* **wellington boots**) bottes *fpl* de caoutchouc

well: **~-known** *adj* (*person*) bien connu(e); **~-mannered** *adj* bien élevé(e); **~-meaning** *adj* bien intentionné(e); **~-off** *adj* aisé(e); **~-read** *adj* cultivé(e); **~-to-do** *adj* aisé(e); **~-wishers** *npl* amis *mpl* et admirateurs *mpl*; (*friends*) amis *mpl*

Welsh [wɛlʃ] *adj* gallois(e) ♦ *n* (LING) gallois *m*; **the ~** *npl* (*people*) les Gallois *mpl*; **~man** (*irreg*) *n* Gallois *m*; **~woman** (*irreg*) *n* Galloise *f*

went [wɛnt] *pt of* **go**

wept [wɛpt] *pt, pp of* **weep**

were [wə:r] *pt of* **be**

we're [wɪər] = **we are**

weren't [wə:nt] = **were not**

west [wɛst] *n* ouest *m* ♦ *adj* ouest *inv*, de *or* à l'ouest ♦ *adv* à *or* vers l'ouest; **the W~** l'Occident *m*, l'Ouest; **the W~ Country** (BRIT) ♦ *n* le sud-ouest de l'Angleterre; **~erly** *adj* (*wind*) d'ouest; (*point*) à l'ouest; **~ern** *adj* occidental(e), de *or* à l'ouest ♦ *n* (CINEMA) western *m*; **W~ Indian** *adj* antillais(e) ♦ *n* Antillais(e); **W~ Indies** *npl* Antilles *fpl*; **~ward(s)** *adv* vers l'ouest

wet [wɛt] *adj* mouillé(e); (*damp*) humide; (*soaked*) trempé(e); (*rainy*) pluvieux(-euse) ♦ *n* (BRIT: POL) modéré *m* du parti conservateur; **to get ~** se mouiller; **"~ paint"** "attention peinture fraîche"; **~ suit** *n* combinaison *f* de plongée

we've [wi:v] = **we have**

whack [wæk] *vt* donner un grand coup à

whale [weɪl] *n* (ZOOL) baleine *f*

wharf [wɔ:f] (*pl* **wharves**) *n* quai *m*

what [wɔt] *adj* quel(le); **what size is he?**
quelle taille fait-il?; **what colour is it?** de
quelle couleur est-ce?; **what books do you
need?** quels livres vous faut-il?; **what a mess!**
quel désordre!

♦ *pron* **1** (*interrogative*) que, *prep* +quoi;
what are you doing? que faites-vous?, qu'est-
ce que vous faites?; **what is happening?**
qu'est-ce qui se passe?, que se passe-t-il?;
what are you talking about? de quoi parlez-
vous?; **what is it called?** comment est-ce que
ça s'appelle?; **what about me?** et moi?; **what
about doing ...?** et si on faisait ...?
2 (*relative: subject*) ce qui; (: *direct object*) ce
que; (: *indirect object*) ce +*prep* +quoi, ce
dont; **I saw what you did/was on the table**
j'ai vu ce que vous avez fait/ce qui était sur la
table; **tell me what you remember** dites-moi
ce dont vous vous souvenez
♦ *excl* (*disbelieving*) quoi!, comment!

whatever [wɔt'evəʳ] *adj*: ~ **book** quel que
soit le livre que (*or* qui) +*sub*; n'importe quel
livre ♦ *pron*: **do ~ is necessary** faites (tout) ce
qui est nécessaire; ~ **happens** quoi qu'il
arrive; **no reason ~** pas la moindre raison;
nothing ~ rien du tout
whatsoever [wɔtsəu'evəʳ] *adj* = **whatever**
wheat [wi:t] *n* blé *m*, froment *m*
wheedle [ˈwi:dl] *vt*: **to ~ sb into doing sth**
cajoler *or* enjôler qn pour qu'il fasse qch; **to
~ sth out of sb** obtenir qch de qn par des
cajoleries
wheel [wi:l] *n* roue *f*; (*also:* **steering ~**) volant
m; (*NAUT*) gouvernail *m* ♦ *vt* (*pram etc*)
pousser ♦ *vi* (*birds*) tournoyer; (*also:* ~ **round:**
person) virevolter; **~barrow** *n* brouette *f*;
~chair *n* fauteuil roulant; ~ **clamp** *n* (*AUT*)
sabot *m* (de Denver)
wheeze [wi:z] *vi* respirer bruyamment

when [wɛn] *adv* quand; **when did he go?**
quand est-ce qu'il est parti?
♦ *conj* **1** (*at, during, after the time that*)
quand, lorsque; **she was reading when I came
in** elle lisait quand *or* lorsque je suis entré
2 (*on, at which*): **on the day when I met him**
le jour où je l'ai rencontré
3 (*whereas*) alors que; **I thought I was wrong
when in fact I was right** j'ai cru que j'avais
tort alors qu'en fait j'avais raison

whenever [wɛn'evəʳ] *adv* quand donc ♦ *conj*
quand; (*every time that*) chaque fois que
where [wɛəʳ] *adv, conj* où; **this is ~** c'est là
que; **~abouts** [ˈwɛərəbauts] *adv* où donc

♦ *n*: **nobody knows his ~abouts** personne ne
sait où il se trouve; **~as** [wɛərˈæz] *conj* alors
que; **~by** *adv* par lequel (*or* laquelle *etc*);
wherever [wɛərˈevəʳ] *adv* où donc ♦ *conj* où
que +*sub*; **~withal** [ˈwɛəwiðɔ:l] *n* moyens
mpl

whether [ˈwɛðəʳ] *conj* si; **I don't know ~ to
accept or not** je ne sais pas si je dois accepter
ou non; **it's doubtful ~** il est peu probable
que +*sub*; ~ **you go or not** que vous y alliez
ou non

which [wɪtʃ] *adj* (*interrogative: direct, indirect*)
quel(le); **which picture do you want?** quel
tableau voulez-vous?; **which one?** lequel
(laquelle)?; **in which case** auquel cas
♦ *pron* **1** (*interrogative*) lequel (laquelle),
lesquels (lesquelles) *pl*; **I don't mind which**
peu importe lequel; **which (of these) are
yours?** lesquels sont à vous?; **tell me which
you want** dites-moi lesquels *or* ceux que vous
voulez
2 (*relative: subject*) qui; (: *object*) que, *prep*
+lequel (laquelle); **the apple which you ate/
which is on the table** la pomme que vous
avez mangée/qui est sur la table; **the chair on
which you are sitting** la chaise sur laquelle
vous êtes assis; **the book of which you spoke**
le livre dont vous avez parlé; **he knew, which
is true/I feared** il le savait, ce qui est vrai/ce
que je craignais; **after which** après quoi

whichever [wɪtʃˈevəʳ] *adj*: **take ~ book you
prefer** prenez le livre que vous préférez, peu
importe lequel; ~ **book you take** quel que soit
le livre que vous preniez
while [waɪl] *n* moment *m* ♦ *conj* pendant
que; (*as long as*) tant que; (*whereas*) alors
que; bien que +*sub*; **for a ~** pendant quelque
temps; ~ **away** *vt* (*time*) (faire) passer
whim [wɪm] *n* caprice *m*
whimper [ˈwɪmpəʳ] *vi* geindre
whimsical [ˈwɪmzɪkəl] *adj* (*person*)
capricieux(-euse); (*look, story*) étrange
whine [waɪn] *vi* gémir, geindre
whip [wɪp] *n* fouet *m*; (*for riding*) cravache *f*;
(*POL: person*) chef de file assurant la discipline
dans son groupe parlementaire ♦ *vt* fouetter;
(*eggs*) battre; (*move quickly*) enlever/sortir
brusquement; **~ped cream** *n* crème
fouettée; **~-round** (*BRIT*) *n* collecte *f*
whirl [wə:l] *vi* tourbillonner; (*dancers*)
tournoyer ♦ *vt* faire tourbillonner; faire
tournoyer; **~pool** *n* tourbillon *m*; **~wind** *n*
tornade *f*
whirr [wə:ʳ] *vi* (*motor etc*) ronronner;
(: *louder*) vrombir
whisk [wɪsk] *n* (*CULIN*) fouet *m* ♦ *vt* fouetter;

(eggs) battre; **to ~ sb away** or **off** emmener qn rapidement

whiskers ['wɪskəz] *npl (of animal)* moustaches *fpl*; *(of man)* favoris *mpl*

whisky ['wɪskɪ] *(IRELAND, US* **whiskey***) n* whisky *m*

whisper ['wɪspə'] *vt, vi* chuchoter

whistle ['wɪsl] *n (sound)* sifflement *m*; *(object)* sifflet *m* ♦ *vi* siffler

white [waɪt] *adj* blanc (blanche); *(with fear)* blême ♦ *n* blanc *m*; *(person)* blanc (blanche); **~ coffee** *(BRIT)* n café *m* au lait, (café) crème *m*; **~-collar worker** *n* employé(e) de bureau; **~ elephant** *n (fig)* objet dispendieux et superflu; **~ lie** *n* pieux mensonge; **~ paper** *n (POL)* livre blanc; **~wash** *vt* blanchir à la chaux; *(fig)* blanchir ♦ *n (paint)* blanc *m* de chaux

whiting ['waɪtɪŋ] *n inv (fish)* merlan *m*

Whitsun ['wɪtsn] *n* la Pentecôte

whizz [wɪz] *vi*: **to ~ past** or **by** passer à toute vitesse; **~ kid** *(inf)* n petit prodige

who [huː] *pron* qui; **~ dunit** ['huːdʌnɪt] *(inf)* n roman policier

whoever [huː'evə'] *pron*: **~ finds it** celui (celle) qui le trouve; **ask ~ you like** demandez à qui vous voulez; **~ he marries** quelle que soit la personne qu'il épouse; **~ told you that?** qui a bien pu vous dire ça?

whole [həʊl] *adj (complete)* entier(-ère), tout(e); *(not broken)* intact(e), complet(-ète) ♦ *n (all)*: **the ~** la totalité de, tout(e) le (la); *(entire unit)* tout *m*; **the ~ of the town** la ville tout entière; **on the ~**, **as a ~** dans l'ensemble; **~food(s)** *n(pl)* aliments complets; **~-hearted** *adj* sans réserve(s); **~meal** *(BRIT)* adj *(bread, flour)* complet(-ète); **~sale** *n (vente f en)* gros *m* ♦ *adj (price)* de gros; *(destruction)* systématique ♦ *adj* en gros; **~saler** *n* grossiste *m/f*; **~some** *adj* sain(e); **~wheat** *adj* = **wholemeal**; **wholly** ['həʊlɪ] *adv* entièrement, tout à fait

KEYWORD

whom [huːm] *pron* **1** *(interrogative)* qui; **whom did you see?** qui avez-vous vu?; **to whom did you give it?** à qui l'avez-vous donné?

2 *(relative)* que, *prep* +qui; **the man whom I saw/to whom I spoke** l'homme que j'ai vu/à qui j'ai parlé

whooping cough ['huːpɪŋ-] *n* coqueluche *f*

whore [hɔː'] *(inf: pej)* n putain *f*

KEYWORD

whose [huːz] *adj* **1** *(possessive: interrogative)*: **whose book is this?** à qui est ce livre?; **whose**

pencil have you taken? à qui le crayon que vous avez pris?, c'est le crayon de qui que vous avez pris?; **whose daughter are you?** de qui êtes-vous la fille?

2 *(possessive: relative)*: **the man whose son you rescued** l'homme dont *or* de qui vous avez sauvé le fils; **the girl whose sister you were speaking to** la fille à la sœur de qui *or* de laquelle vous parliez; **the woman whose car was stolen** la femme dont la voiture a été volée

♦ *pron* à qui; **whose is this?** à qui est ceci?; **I know whose it is** je sais à qui c'est

why [waɪ] *adv* pourquoi ♦ *excl* eh bien!, tiens!; **the reason ~** la raison pour laquelle; **tell me ~** dites-moi pourquoi; **~ not?** pourquoi pas?

wicked ['wɪkɪd] *adj* mauvais(e), méchant(e); *(crime)* pervers(e); *(mischievous)* malicieux(-euse)

wicket ['wɪkɪt] *n (CRICKET)* guichet *m*; terrain *m (entre les deux guichets)*

wide [waɪd] *adj* large; *(area, knowledge)* vaste, très étendu(e); *(choice)* grand(e) ♦ *adv*: **to open ~** ouvrir tout grand; **to shoot ~** tirer à côté; **~-awake** *adj* bien éveillé(e); **~ly** *adv (differing)* radicalement; *(spaced)* sur une grande étendue; *(believed)* généralement; *(travel)* beaucoup; **~n** *vt* élargir ♦ *vi* s'élargir; **~ open** *adj* grand(e) ouvert(e); **~spread** *adj (belief etc)* très répandu(e)

widow ['wɪdəʊ] *n* veuve *f*; **~ed** *adj* veuf (veuve); **~er** *n* veuf *m*

width [wɪdθ] *n* largeur *f*

wield [wiːld] *vt (sword)* manier; *(power)* exercer

wife [waɪf] *(pl* **wives***) n* femme *f*, épouse *f*

wig [wɪg] *n* perruque *f*

wiggle ['wɪgl] *vt* agiter, remuer

wild [waɪld] *adj* sauvage; *(sea)* déchaîné(e); *(idea, life)* fou (folle); *(behaviour)* extravagant(e), déchaîné(e); **to make a ~ guess** émettre une hypothèse à tout hasard; **~erness** ['wɪldənɪs] *n* désert *m*, région *f* sauvage; **~life** *n (animals)* faune *f*; **~ly** *adv (behave)* de manière déchaînée; *(applaud)* frénétiquement; *(hit, guess)* au hasard; *(happy)* follement; **~s** *npl (remote area)* régions *fpl* sauvages

wilful ['wɪlful] *(US* **willful***) adj (person)* obstiné(e); *(action)* délibéré(e)

KEYWORD

will [wɪl] *(vt: pt, pp* **willed** *) aux vb* **1** *(forming future tense)*: **I will finish it tomorrow** je le finirai demain; **I will have finished it by tomorrow** je l'aurai fini d'ici demain; **will you do it? - yes I will/no I won't** le ferez-vous? -

oui/non

2 (*in conjectures, predictions*): **he will** or **he'll be there by now** il doit être arrivé à l'heure qu'il est; **that will be the postman** ça doit être le facteur

3 (*in commands, requests, offers*): **will you be quiet!** voulez-vous bien vous taire!; **will you help me?** est-ce que vous pouvez m'aider?; **will you have a cup of tea?** voulez-vous une tasse de thé?; **I won't put up with it!** je ne le tolérerai pas!

♦ *vt*: **to will sb to do** souhaiter ardemment que qn fasse; **he willed himself to go on** par un suprême effort de volonté, il continua ♦ *n* volonté *f*; testament *m*

willing ['wɪlɪŋ] *adj* de bonne volonté, serviable; **he's ~ to do it** il est disposé à le faire, il veut bien le faire; **~ly** *adv* volontiers; **~ness** *n* bonne volonté

willow ['wɪləu] *n* saule *m*

willpower ['wɪl'pauəʳ] *n* volonté *f*

willy-nilly ['wɪlɪ'nɪlɪ] *adv* bon gré mal gré

wilt [wɪlt] *vi* dépérir; (*flower*) se faner

win [wɪn] (*pt, pp* **won**) *n* (*in sports etc*) victoire *f* ♦ *vt* gagner; (*prize*) remporter; (*popularity*) acquérir ♦ *vi* gagner; **~ over** *vt* convaincre; **~ round** (*BRIT*) *vt* = **win over**

wince [wɪns] *vi* tressaillir

winch [wɪntʃ] *n* treuil *m*

wind[1] [wɪnd] *n* (*also MED*) vent *m*; (*breath*) souffle *m* ♦ *vt* (*take breath*) couper le souffle à

wind[2] [waɪnd] (*pt, pp* **wound**) *vt* enrouler; (*wrap*) envelopper; (*clock, toy*) remonter ♦ *vi* (*road, river*) serpenter; **~ up** *vt* (*clock*) remonter; (*debate*) terminer, clôturer

windfall ['wɪndfɔːl] *n* coup *m* de chance

winding ['waɪndɪŋ] *adj* (*road*) sinueux(-euse); (*staircase*) tournant(e)

wind instrument [wɪnd-] *n* (*MUS*) instrument *m* à vent

windmill ['wɪndmɪl] *n* moulin *m* à vent

window ['wɪndəu] *n* fenêtre *f*; (*in car, train, also: ~ pane*) vitre *f*; (*in shop etc*) vitrine *f*; **~ box** *n* jardinière *f*; **~ cleaner** *n* (*person*) laveur(-euse) de vitres; **~ ledge** *n* rebord *m* de la fenêtre; **~ pane** *n* vitre *f*, carreau *m*; **~-shopping** *n*: **to go ~-shopping** faire du lèche-vitrines; **~sill** ['wɪndəusɪl] *n* (*inside*) appui *m* de la fenêtre; (*outside*) rebord *m* de la fenêtre

windpipe ['wɪndpaɪp] *n* trachée *f*

wind power ['wɪnd-] *n* énergie éolienne

windscreen ['wɪndskriːn] *n* pare-brise *m inv*; **~ washer** *n* lave-glace *m inv*; **~ wiper** *n* essuie-glace *m inv*

windshield ['wɪndʃiːld] (*US*) *n* = **windscreen**

windswept ['wɪndswept] *adj* balayé(e) par

le vent; (*person*) ébouriffé(e)

windy ['wɪndɪ] *adj* venteux(-euse); **it's ~** il y a du vent

wine [waɪn] *n* vin *m*; **~ bar** *n* bar *m* à vin; **~ cellar** *n* cave *f* à vin; **~ glass** *n* verre *m* à vin; **~ list** *n* carte *f* des vins; **~ waiter** *n* sommelier *m*

wing [wɪŋ] *n* aile *f*; **~s** *npl* (*THEATRE*) coulisses *fpl*; **~er** *n* (*SPORT*) ailier *m*

wink [wɪŋk] *n* clin *m* d'œil ♦ *vi* faire un clin d'œil; (*blink*) cligner des yeux

winner ['wɪnəʳ] *n* gagnant(e)

winning ['wɪnɪŋ] *adj* (*team*) gagnant(e); (*goal*) décisif(-ive); **~s** *npl* gains *mpl*

winter ['wɪntəʳ] *n* hiver *m*; **in ~** en hiver; **~ sports** *npl* sports *mpl* d'hiver; **wintry** *adj* hivernal(e)

wipe [waɪp] *n*: **to give sth a ~** donner un coup de torchon/de chiffon/d'éponge à qch ♦ *vt* essuyer; (*erase: tape*) effacer; **~ off** *vt* enlever; **~ out** *vt* (*debt*) éteindre, amortir; (*memory*) effacer; (*destroy*) anéantir; **~ up** *vt* essuyer

wire ['waɪəʳ] *n* fil *m* (de fer); (*ELEC*) fil électrique; (*TEL*) télégramme *m* ♦ *vt* (*house*) faire l'installation électrique de; (*also: ~ up*) brancher; (*person: send telegram to*) télégraphier à; **~less** (*BRIT*) *n* poste *m* de radio; **wiring** *n* installation *f* électrique; **wiry** *adj* noueux(-euse), nerveux(-euse); (*hair*) dru(e)

wisdom ['wɪzdəm] *n* sagesse *f*; (*of action*) prudence *f*; **~ tooth** *n* dent *f* de sagesse

wise [waɪz] *adj* sage, prudent(e); (*remark*) judicieux(-euse) ♦ *suffix*: **...wise**: **timewise** *etc* en ce qui concerne le temps *etc*

wish [wɪʃ] *n* (*desire*) désir *m*; (*specific desire*) souhait *m*, vœu *m* ♦ *vt* souhaiter, désirer, vouloir; **best ~es** (*on birthday etc*) meilleurs vœux; **with best ~es** (*in letter*) bien amicalement; **to ~ sb goodbye** dire au revoir à qn; **he ~ed me well** il m'a souhaité bonne chance; **to ~ to do/sb to do** désirer or vouloir faire/que qn fasse; **to ~ for** souhaiter; **~ful** *adj*: **it's ~ful thinking** c'est prendre ses désirs pour des réalités

wistful ['wɪstful] *adj* mélancolique

wit [wɪt] *n* (*gen pl*) intelligence *f*, esprit *m*; (*presence of mind*) présence *f* d'esprit; (*wittiness*) esprit; (*person*) homme/femme d'esprit

witch [wɪtʃ] *n* sorcière *f*; **~craft** *n* sorcellerie *f*

KEYWORD

with [wɪð, wɪθ] *prep* **1** (*in the company of*) avec; (*at the home of*) chez; **we stayed with friends** nous avons logé chez des amis; **I'll be with you in a minute** je suis à vous dans un instant

2 (*descriptive*): **a room with a view** une chambre avec vue; **the man with the grey hat/blue eyes** l'homme au chapeau gris/aux yeux bleus

3 (*indicating manner, means, cause*): **with tears in her eyes** les larmes aux yeux; **to walk with a stick** marcher avec une canne; **red with anger** rouge de colère; **to shake with fear** trembler de peur; **to fill sth with water** remplir qch d'eau

4: I'm with you (*I understand*) je vous suis; **to be with it** (*inf: up-to-date*) être dans le vent

withdraw [wɪθˈdrɔː] (*irreg*) *vt* retirer ♦ *vi* se retirer; **~al** *n* retrait m; **~al symptoms** *npl* (*MED*): **to have ~al symptoms** être en état de manque; **~n** *adj* (*person*) renfermé(e)

wither [ˈwɪðəʳ] *vi* (*plant*) se faner

withhold [wɪθˈhəuld] (*irreg*) *vt* (*money*) retenir; **to ~ (from)** (*information*) cacher (à); (*permission*) refuser (à)

within [wɪðˈɪn] *prep* à l'intérieur de ♦ *adv* à l'intérieur, **~ his reach** à sa portée, **~ sight of** en vue de; **~ a kilometre of** à moins d'un kilomètre de; **~ the week** avant la fin de la semaine

without [wɪðˈaut] *prep* sans; **~ a coat** sans manteau; **~ speaking** sans parler; **to go ~ sth** se passer de qch

withstand [wɪθˈstænd] (*irreg*) *vt* résister à

witness [ˈwɪtnɪs] *n* (*person*) témoin m ♦ *vt* (*event*) être témoin de; (*document*) attester l'authenticité de; **to bear ~ (to)** (*fig*) attester; **~ box** (*US* **witness stand**) *n* barre f des témoins

witty [ˈwɪtɪ] *adj* spirituel(le), plein(e) d'esprit

wives [waɪvz] *npl of* **wife**

wizard [ˈwɪzəd] *n* magicien m

wk *abbr* = **week**

wobble [ˈwɔbl] *vi* trembler; (*chair*) branler

woe [wəu] *n* malheur m

woke [wəuk] *pt of* **wake**; **~n** *pp of* **wake**

wolf [wulf] (*pl* **wolves**) *n* loup m

woman [ˈwumən] (*pl* **women**) *n* femme f; **~ doctor** *n* femme f médecin; **~ly** *adj* féminin(e)

womb [wuːm] *n* (*ANAT*) utérus m

women [ˈwɪmɪn] *npl of* **woman**; **~'s lib** (*inf*) *n* MLF m; **W~'s (Liberation) Movement** *n* mouvement m de libération de la femme

won [wʌn] *pt, pp of* **win**

wonder [ˈwʌndəʳ] *n* merveille f, miracle m; (*feeling*) émerveillement m ♦ *vi*: **to ~ whether/why** se demander si/pourquoi; **to ~ at** (*marvel*) s'émerveiller de; **to ~ about** songer à; **it's no ~ (that)** il n'est pas étonnant (que +*sub*); **~ful** *adj* merveilleux(-euse)

won't [wəunt] = **will not**

wood [wud] *n* (*timber, forest*) bois m;

~ carving *n* sculpture f en or sur bois; **~ed** *adj* boisé(e); **~en** *adj* en bois; (*fig*) raide; inexpressif(-ive); **~pecker** *n* pic m (*oiseau*); **~wind** *n* (*MUS*): **the ~wind** les bois *mpl*; **~work** *n* menuiserie f; **~worm** *n* ver m du bois

wool [wul] *n* laine f; **to pull the ~ over sb's eyes** (*fig*) en faire accroire à qn; **~len** (*US* **woolen**) *adj* de or en laine; (*industry*) lainier(-ère); **~lens** *npl* (*clothes*) lainages *mpl*; **~ly** (*US* **wooly**) *adj* laineux(-euse); (*fig: ideas*) confus(e)

word [wəːd] *n* mot m; (*promise*) parole f; (*news*) nouvelles *fpl* ♦ *vt* rédiger, formuler; **in other ~s** en d'autres termes; **to break/keep one's ~** manquer à sa parole/tenir parole; **~ing** *n* termes *mpl*; libellé m; **~ processing** *n* traitement m de texte; **~ processor** *n* machine f de traitement de texte

wore [wɔːʳ] *pt of* **wear**

work [wəːk] *n* travail m; (*ART, LITERATURE*) œuvre f ♦ *vi* travailler; (*mechanism*) marcher, fonctionner; (*plan etc*) marcher; (*medicine*) agir ♦ *vt* (*clay, wood etc*) travailler; (*mine etc*) exploiter; (*machine*) faire marcher or fonctionner; (*miracles, wonders etc*) faire; **to be out of ~** être sans emploi; **to ~ loose** se défaire, se desserrer; **~able** *adj* (*solution*) réalisable; **~ on** *vt fus* travailler à; (*influence*) (essayer d')influencer; **~ out** *vi* (*plans etc*) marcher ♦ *vt* (*problem*) résoudre; (*plan*) élaborer; **it ~s out at £100** ça fait 100 livres; **~ up** *vt*: **to get ~ed up** se mettre dans tous ses états; **~aholic** [wəːkəˈhɔlɪk] *n* bourreau m de travail; **~er** *n* travailleur(-euse), ouvrier(-ère); **~ experience** *n* stage m; **~force** *n* main-d'œuvre f; **~ing class** *n* classe ouvrière; **~ing class** *adj* ouvrier(-ère); **~ing order** *n*: **in ~ing order** en état de marche; **~man** (*irreg*) *n* ouvrier m; **~manship** (*skill*) *n* métier m, habileté f; **~s** *n* (*BRIT: factory*) usine f ♦ *npl* (*of clock, machine*) mécanisme m; **~ sheet** *n* (*COMPUT*) feuille f de programmation; **~shop** *n* atelier m; **~ station** *n* poste m de travail; **~-to-rule** (*BRIT*) *n* grève f du zèle

world [wəːld] *n* monde m ♦ *cpd* (*champion*) du monde; (*power, war*) mondial(e); **to think the ~ of sb** (*fig*) avoir une haute opinion de qn; **~ly** *adj* de ce monde; (*knowledgeable*) qui a l'expérience du monde; **~wide** *adj* universel(le); **W~-Wide Web** *n* Web m

worm [wəːm] *n* ver m

worn [wɔːn] *pp of* **wear** ♦ *adj* usé(e); **~-out** *adj* (*object*) complètement usé(e); (*person*) épuisé(e)

worried [ˈwʌrɪd] *adj* inquiet(-ète)

worry [ˈwʌrɪ] *n* souci m ♦ *vt* inquiéter ♦ *vi* s'inquiéter, se faire du souci

worse [wə:s] adj pire, plus mauvais(e) ♦ adv plus mal ♦ n pire m; **a change for the ~** une détérioration; **~n** vt, vi empirer; **~ off** adj moins à l'aise financièrement; (fig): **you'll be ~ off this way** ça ira moins bien de cette façon

worship ['wə:ʃip] n culte m ♦ vt (God) rendre un culte à; (person) adorer; **Your W~** (BRIT: to mayor) Monsieur le maire; (: to judge) Monsieur le juge

worst [wə:st] adj le (la) pire, le (la) plus mauvais(e) ♦ adv le plus mal ♦ n pire m; **at ~** au pis aller

worth [wə:θ] n valeur f ♦ adj: **to be ~** valoir; **it's ~ it** cela en vaut la peine, ça vaut la peine; **it is ~ one's while (to do)** on gagne (à faire); **~less** adj qui ne vaut rien; **~while** adj (activity, cause) utile, louable

worthy ['wə:ði] adj (person) digne; (motive) louable; **~ of** digne de

┌─────────────┐
│ KEYWORD   │
└─────────────┘

would [wud] aux vb **1** (conditional tense): **if you asked him he would do it** si vous le lui demandiez, il le ferait; **if you had asked him he would have done it** si vous le lui aviez demandé, il l'aurait fait

2 (in offers, invitations, requests): **would you like a biscuit?** voulez-vous un biscuit?; **would you close the door please?** voulez-vous fermer la porte, s'il vous plaît?

3 (in indirect speech): **I said I would do it** j'ai dit que je le ferais

4 (emphatic): **it WOULD have to snow today!** naturellement il neige aujourd'hui! or il fallait qu'il neige aujourd'hui!

5 (insistence): **she wouldn't do it** elle n'a pas voulu or elle a refusé de le faire

6 (conjecture): **it would have been midnight** il devait être minuit

7 (indicating habit): **he would go there on Mondays** il y allait le lundi

would-be ['wudbi:] (pej) adj soi-disant
wouldn't ['wudnt] = **would not**
wound¹ [wu:nd] n blessure f ♦ vt blesser
wound² [waund] pt, pp of **wind²**
wove [wəuv] pt of **weave**; **~n** pp of **weave**
wrap [ræp] vt (also: **~ up**) envelopper, emballer; (wind) enrouler; **~per** n (BRIT: of book) couverture f; (on chocolate) emballage m, papier m; **~ping paper** n papier m d'emballage; (for gift) papier cadeau
wreak [ri:k] vt: **to ~ havoc (on)** avoir un effet désastreux (sur)
wreath [ri:θ] (pl **~s**) n couronne f
wreck [rɛk] n (ship) épave f; (vehicle) véhicule accidenté; (pej: person) loque humaine ♦ vt démolir; (fig) briser, ruiner;

~age n débris mpl; (of building) décombres mpl; (of ship) épave f
wren [rɛn] n (ZOOL) roitelet m
wrench [rɛntʃ] n (TECH) clé f (à écrous); (tug) violent mouvement de torsion; (fig) déchirement m ♦ vt tirer violemment sur, tordre; **to ~ sth from** arracher qch à or de
wrestle ['rɛsl] vi: **to ~ (with sb)** lutter (avec qn); **~r** n lutteur(-euse); **wrestling** n lutte f; (also: **all-in wrestling**) catch m, lutte f libre
wretched ['rɛtʃid] adj misérable; (inf) maudit(e)
wriggle ['rɪgl] vi (also: **~ about**) se tortiller
wring [rɪŋ] (pt, pp **wrung**) vt tordre; (wet clothes) essorer; (fig): **to ~ sth out of sb** arracher qch à qn
wrinkle ['rɪŋkl] n (on skin) ride f; (on paper etc) pli m ♦ vt plisser ♦ vi se plisser; **~d** adj (skin, face) ridé(e)
wrist [rɪst] n poignet m; **~watch** n montre-bracelet f
writ [rɪt] n acte m judiciaire
write [raɪt] (pt **wrote**, pp **written**) vt, vi écrire; (prescription) rédiger; **~ down** vt noter; (put in writing) mettre par écrit; **~ off** vt (debt) passer aux profits et pertes; (project) mettre une croix sur; **~ out** vt écrire; **~ up** vt rédiger; **~-off** n perte totale; **~r** n auteur m, écrivain m
writhe [raɪð] vi se tordre
writing ['raɪtɪŋ] n écriture f; (of author) œuvres fpl; **in ~** par écrit; **~ paper** n papier m à lettres
wrong [rɔŋ] adj (incorrect) faux (fausse); (morally) mauvais(e); (wicked) mal; (unfair) injuste ♦ adv mal ♦ n tort m ♦ vt faire du tort à, léser; **you are ~ to do it** tu as tort de le faire; **you are ~ about that, you've got it ~** tu te trompes; **what's ~?** qu'est-ce qui ne va pas?; **you've got the ~ number** vous vous êtes trompé de numéro; **to go ~** (person) se tromper; (plan) mal tourner; (machine) tomber en panne; **to be in the ~** avoir tort; **~ful** adj injustifié(e); **~ly** adv mal, incorrectement; **~ side** n (of material) envers m
wrote [rəut] pt of **write**
wrought iron [rɔ:t] n fer forgé
wrung [rʌŋ] pt, pp of **wring**
wt. abbr = **weight**
WWW n abbr (= World Wide Web): **the ~** le Web

X, x

Xmas ['ɛksməs] n abbr = **Christmas**
X-ray ['ɛksreɪ] n (ray) rayon m X; (photo) radio(graphie) f

xylophone ['zaɪləfəun] n xylophone m

Y, y

yacht [jɔt] n yacht m; voilier m; **~ing** n yachting m, navigation f de plaisance; **~sman** (irreg) n plaisancier m

Yank [jæŋk], **Yankee** ['jæŋkɪ] (pej) n Amerloque m/f

yap [jæp] vi (dog) japper

yard [jɑːd] n (of house etc) cour f; (measure) yard m (= 91,4 cm); **~stick** n (fig) mesure f, critères mpl

yarn [jɑːn] n fil m; (tale) longue histoire

yawn [jɔːn] n bâillement m ♦ vi bâiller; **~ing** adj (gap) béant(e)

yd. abbr = **yard(s)**

yeah [jɛə] (inf) adv ouais

year [jɪəʳ] n an m, année f; **to be 8 ~s old** avoir 8 ans; **an eight-~-old child** un enfant de huit ans; **~ly** adj annuel(le) ♦ adv annuellement

yearn [jəːn] vi: **to ~ for sth** aspirer à qch, languir après qch

yeast [jiːst] n levure f

yell [jɛl] vi hurler

yellow ['jɛləu] adj jaune

yelp [jɛlp] vi japper; glapir

yes [jɛs] adv oui; (answering negative question) si ♦ n oui m; **to say/answer ~** dire/répondre oui

yesterday ['jɛstədɪ] adv hier ♦ n hier m; **~ morning/evening** hier matin/soir; **all day ~** toute la journée d'hier

yet [jɛt] adv encore; déjà ♦ conj pourtant, néanmoins; **it is not finished ~** ce n'est pas encore fini or toujours pas fini; **the best ~** le meilleur jusqu'ici or jusque-là; **as ~** jusqu'ici, encore

yew [juː] n if m

yield [jiːld] n production f, rendement m; rapport m ♦ vt produire, rendre, rapporter; (surrender) céder ♦ vi céder; (US: AUT) céder la priorité

YMCA n abbr (= Young Men's Christian Association) YMCA m

yob [jɔb] (BRIT: inf) n loubar(d) m

yoghourt ['jəugət] n yaourt m

yog(h)urt ['jəugət] n = **yoghourt**

yoke [jəuk] n joug m

yolk [jəuk] n jaune m (d'œuf)

you [juː] pron **1** (subject) tu; (polite form) vous; (plural) vous; **you French enjoy your food** vous autres Français, vous aimez bien manger; **you and I will go** toi et moi or vous et moi, nous irons

2 (object: direct, indirect) te, t' +vowel; vous;

I know you je te or vous connais; **I gave it to you** je vous l'ai donné, je te l'ai donné

3 (stressed) toi; vous; **I told YOU to do it** c'est à toi or vous que j'ai dit de le faire

4 (after prep, in comparisons) toi; vous; **it's for you** c'est pour toi or vous; **she's younger than you** elle est plus jeune que toi or vous

5 (impersonal: one) on; **fresh air does you good** l'air frais fait du bien; **you never know** on ne sait jamais

you'd [juːd] = **you had; you would**

you'll [juːl] = **you will; you shall**

young [jʌŋ] adj jeune ♦ npl (of animal) petits mpl; (people): **the ~** les jeunes, la jeunesse; **~er** [jʌŋgəʳ] adj (brother etc) cadet(te); **~ster** n jeune m (garçon m); (child) enfant m/f

your [jɔːʳ] adj ton (ta), tes pl; (polite form, pl) votre, vos pl; see also **my**

you're [juəʳ] = **you are**

yours [jɔːz] pron le (la) tien(ne), les tiens (tiennes); (polite form, pl) le (la) vôtre, les vôtres; **~ sincerely/faithfully/truly** veuillez agréer l'expression de mes sentiments les meilleurs; see also **mine**[1]

yourself [jɔː'sɛlf] pron (reflexive) te; (: polite form) vous; (after prep) toi; vous; (emphatic) toi-même; vous-même; see also **oneself**

yourselves pl pron vous, (emphatic) vous-mêmes

youth [juːθ] n jeunesse f; (young man: pl ~s) jeune homme m; **~ club** n centre m de jeunes; **~ful** adj jeune, (enthusiasm) de jeunesse, juvénile; **~ hostel** n auberge f de jeunesse

you've [juːv] = **you have**

YTS n abbr (BRIT: Youth Training Scheme) ≈ TUC m

Yugoslav ['juːgəuslɑːv] adj yougoslave ♦ n Yougoslave m/f

Yugoslavia ['juːgəu'slɑːvɪə] n Yougoslavie f

yuppie ['jʌpɪ] (inf) n yuppie m/f

YWCA n abbr (= Young Women's Christian Association) YWCA m

Z, z

zany ['zeɪnɪ] adj farfelu(e), loufoque

zap [zæp] vt (COMPUT) effacer

zeal [ziːl] n zèle m, ferveur f; empressement m

zebra ['ziːbrə] n zèbre m; **~ crossing** (BRIT) n passage clouté or pour piétons

zero ['zɪərəu] n zéro m

zest [zɛst] n entrain m, élan m; (of orange) zeste m

zigzag ['zɪgzæg] n zigzag m

Zimbabwe [zɪm'bɑːbwɪ] n Zimbabwe m

Zimmer frame ['zɪmə-] *n* déambulateur *m*

zinc [zɪŋk] *n* zinc *m*

zip [zɪp] *n* fermeture *f* éclair ® ♦ *vt* (*also:* ~ **up**) fermer avec une fermeture éclair ®; ~ **code** (*US*) *n* code postal; **~per** (*US*) *n* = zip

zit [zɪt] (*inf*) *n* bouton *m*

zodiac ['zəudɪæk] *n* zodiaque *m*

zone [zəun] *n* zone *f*

zoo [zu:] *n* zoo *m*

zoom [zu:m] *vi*: **to ~ past** passer en trombe; ~ **lens** *n* zoom *m*

zucchini [zu:'ki:nɪ] (*US*) *n(pl)* courgette(s) *f(pl)*

VERB TABLES

1 Participe présent **2** Participe passé **3** Présent **4** Imparfait **5** Futur **6** Conditionnel **7** Subjonctif présent

acquérir 1 acquérant **2** acquis **3** acquiers, acquérons, acquièrent **4** acquérais **5** acquerrai **7** acquière

ALLER 1 allant **2** allé **3** vais, vas, va, allons, allez, vont **4** allais **5** irai **6** irais **7** aille

asseoir 1 asseyant **2** assis **3** assieds, asseyons, asseyez, asseyent **4** asseyais **5** assiérai **7** asseye

atteindre 1 atteignant **2** atteint **3** atteins, atteignons **4** atteignais **7** atteigne

AVOIR 1 ayant **2** eu **3** ai, as, a, avons, avez, ont **4** avais **5** aurai **6** aurais **7** aie, aies, ait, ayons, ayez, aient

battre 1 battant **2** battu **3** bats, bat, battons **4** battais **7** batte

boire 1 buvant **2** bu **3** bois, buvons, boivent **4** buvais **7** boive

bouillir 1 bouillant **2** bouilli **3** bous, bouillons **4** bouillais **7** bouille

conclure 1 concluant **2** conclu **3** conclus, concluons **4** concluais **7** conclue

conduire 1 conduisant **2** conduit **3** conduis, conduisons **4** conduisais **7** conduise

connaître 1 connaissant **2** connu **3** connais, connaît, connaissons **4** connaissais **7** connaisse

coudre 1 cousant **2** cousu **3** couds, cousons, cousez, cousent **4** cousais **7** couse

courir 1 courant **2** couru **3** cours, courons **4** courais **5** courrai **7** coure

couvrir 1 couvrant **2** couvert **3** couvre, couvrons **4** couvrais **7** couvre

craindre 1 craignant **2** craint **3** crains, craignons **4** craignais **7** craigne

croire 1 croyant **2** cru **3** crois, croyons, croient **4** croyais **7** croie

croître 1 croissant **2** crû, crue, crus, crues **3** croîs, croissons **4** croissais **7** croisse

cueillir 1 cueillant **2** cueilli **3** cueille, cueillons **4** cueillais **5** cueillerai **7** cueille

devoir 1 devant **2** dû, due, dus, dues **3** dois, devons, doivent **4** devais **5** devrai **7** doive

dire 1 disant **2** dit **3** dis, disons, dites, disent **4** disais **7** dise

dormir 1 dormant **2** dormi **3** dors, dormons **4** dormais **7** dorme

écrire 1 écrivant **2** écrit **3** écris, écrivons **4** écrivais **7** écrive

ÊTRE 1 étant **2** été **3** suis, es, est, sommes, êtes, sont **4** étais **5** serai **6** serais **7** sois, sois, soit, soyons, soyez, soient

FAIRE 1 faisant **2** fait **3** fais, fais, fait, faisons, faites, font **4** faisais **5** ferai **6** ferais **7** fasse

falloir 2 fallu **3** faut **4** fallait **5** faudra **7** faille

FINIR 1 finissant **2** fini **3** finis, finis, finit, finissons, finissez, finissent **4** finissais **5** finirai **6** finirais **7** finisse

fuir 1 fuyant **2** fui **3** fuis, fuyons, fuient **4** fuyais **7** fuie

joindre 1 joignant **2** joint **3** joins, joignons **4** joignais **7** joigne

lire 1 lisant **2** lu **3** lis, lisons **4** lisais **7** lise

luire 1 luisant **2** lui **3** luis, luisons **4** luisais **7** luise

maudire 1 maudissant **2** maudit **3** maudis, maudissons **4** maudissait **7** maudisse

mentir 1 mentant **2** menti **3** mens, mentons **4** mentais **7** mente

mettre 1 mettant **2** mis **3** mets, mettons **4** mettais **7** mette

mourir 1 mourant 2 mort 3 meurs, mourons, meurent 4 mourais 5 mourrai 7 meure

naître 1 naissant 2 né 3 nais, naît, naissons 4 naissais 7 naisse

offrir 1 offrant 2 offert 3 offre, offrons 4 offrais 7 offre

PARLER 1 parlant 2 parlé 3 parle, parles, parle, parlons, parlez, parlent 4 parlais, parlais, parlait, parlions, parliez, parlaient 5 parlerai, parleras, parlera, parlerons, parlerez, parleront 6 parlerais, parlerais, parlerait, parlerions, parleriez, parleraient 7 parle, parles, parle, parlions, parliez, parlent *impératif* parle! parlez!

partir 1 partant 2 parti 3 pars, partons 4 partais 7 parte

plaire 1 plaisant 2 plu 3 plais, plaît, plaisons 4 plaisais 7 plaise

pleuvoir 1 pleuvant 2 plu 3 pleut, pleuvent 4 pleuvait 5 pleuvra 7 pleuve

pourvoir 1 pourvoyant 2 pourvu 3 pourvois, pourvoyons, pourvoient 4 pourvoyais 7 pourvoie

pouvoir 1 pouvant 2 pu 3 peux, peut, pouvons, peuvent 4 pouvais 5 pourrai 7 puisse

prendre 1 prenant 2 pris 3 prends, prenons, prennent 4 prenais 7 prenne

prévoir *like voir* 5 prévoirai

RECEVOIR 1 recevant 2 reçu 3 reçois, reçois, reçoit, recevons, recevez, reçoivent 4 recevais 5 recevrai 6 recevrais 7 reçoive

RENDRE 1 rendant 2 rendu 3 rends, rends, rend, rendons, rendez, rendent 4 rendais 5 rendrai

6 rendrais 7 rende

résoudre 1 résolvant 2 résolu 3 résous, résolvons 4 résolvais 7 résolve

rire 1 riant 2 ri 3 ris, rions 4 riais 7 rie

savoir 1 sachant 2 su 3 sais, savons, savent 4 savais 5 saurai 7 sache *impératif* sache, sachons, sachez

servir 1 servant 2 servi 3 sers, servons 4 servais 7 serve

sortir 1 sortant 2 sorti 3 sors, sortons 4 sortais 7 sorte

souffrir 1 souffrant 2 souffert 3 souffre, souffrons 4 souffrais 7 souffre

suffire 1 suffisant 2 suffi 3 suffis, suffisons 4 suffisais 7 suffise

suivre 1 suivant 2 suivi 3 suis, suivons 4 suivais 7 suive

taire 1 taisant 2 tu 3 tais, taisons 4 taisais 7 taise

tenir 1 tenant 2 tenu 3 tiens, tenons, tiennent 4 tenais 5 tiendrai 7 tienne

vaincre 1 vainquant 2 vaincu 3 vaincs, vainc, vainquons 4 vainquais 7 vainque

valoir 1 valant 2 valu 3 vaux, vaut, valons 4 valais 5 vaudrai 7 vaille

venir 1 venant 2 venu 3 viens, venons, viennent 4 venais 5 viendrai 7 vienne

vivre 1 vivant 2 vécu 3 vis, vivons 4 vivais 7 vive

voir 1 voyant 2 vu 3 vois, voyons, voient 4 voyais 5 verrai 7 voie

vouloir 1 voulant 2 voulu 3 veux, veut, voulons, veulent 4 voulais 5 voudrai 7 veuille *impératif* veuillez

VERBES IRRÉGULIERS

present	pt	pp	present	pt	pp
arise	arose	arisen	draw	drew	drawn
awake	awoke	awaked	dream	dreamed, dreamt	dreamed, dreamt
be (am, is, are; being)	was, were	been	drink	drank	drunk
			drive	drove	driven
bear	bore	born(e)	dwell	dwelt	dwelt
beat	beat	beaten	eat	ate	eaten
become	became	become	fall	fell	fallen
begin	began	begun	feed	fed	fed
behold	beheld	beheld	feel	felt	felt
bend	bent	bent	fight	fought	fought
beset	beset	beset	find	found	found
bet	bet, betted	bet, betted	flee	fled	fled
			fling	flung	flung
bid	bid, bade	bid, bidden	fly (flies)	flew	flown
			forbid	forbade	forbidden
bind	bound	bound	forecast	forecast	forecast
bite	bit	bitten	forget	forgot	forgotten
bleed	bled	bled	forgive	forgave	forgiven
blow	blew	blown	forsake	forsook	forsaken
break	broke	broken	freeze	froze	frozen
breed	bred	bred	get	got	got, (US) gotten
bring	brought	brought			
build	built	built	give	gave	given
burn	burnt, burned	burnt, burned	go (goes)	went	gone
			grind	ground	ground
burst	burst	burst	grow	grew	grown
buy	bought	bought	hang	hung, hanged	hung, hanged
can	could	(been able)			
			have (has; having)	had	had
cast	cast	cast			
catch	caught	caught			
choose	chose	chosen	hear	heard	heard
cling	clung	clung	hide	hid	hidden
come	came	come	hit	hit	hit
cost	cost	cost	hold	held	held
creep	crept	crept	hurt	hurt	hurt
cut	cut	cut	keep	kept	kept
deal	dealt	dealt	kneel	knelt, kneeled	knelt, kneeled
dig	dug	dug			
do (3rd person; he/she/it/does)	did	done	know	knew	known
			lay	laid	laid
			lead	led	led
			lean	leant,	leant,

433

present	pt	pp	present	pt	pp
	leaned	leaned	shrink	shrank	shrunk
leap	leapt,	leapt,	shut	shut	shut
	leaped	leaped	sing	sang	sung
learn	learnt,	learnt,	sink	sank	sunk
	learned	learned	sit	sat	sat
leave	left	left	slay	slew	slain
lend	lent	lent	sleep	slept	slept
let	let	let	slide	slid	slid
lie (lying)	lay	lain	sling	slung	slung
light	lit,	lit,	slit	slit	slit
	lighted	lighted	smell	smelt,	smelt,
lose	lost	lost		smelled	smelled
make	made	made	sow	sowed	sown,
may	might	—			sowed
mean	meant	meant	speak	spoke	spoken
meet	met	met	speed	sped,	sped,
mistake	mistook	mistaken		speeded	speeded
mow	mowed	mown,	spell	spelt,	spelt,
		mowed		spelled	spelled
must	(had to)	(had to)	spend	spent	spent
pay	paid	paid	spill	spilt,	spilt,
put	put	put		spilled	spilled
quit	quit,	quit,	spin	spun	spun
	quitted	quitted	spit	spat	spat
read	read	read	split	split	split
rid	rid	rid	spoil	spoiled,	spoiled,
ride	rode	ridden		spoilt	spoilt
ring	rang	rung	spread	spread	spread
rise	rose	risen	spring	sprang	sprung
run	ran	run	stand	stood	stood
saw	sawed	sawn	steal	stole	stolen
say	said	said	stick	stuck	stuck
see	saw	seen	sting	stung	stung
seek	sought	sought	stink	stank	stunk
sell	sold	sold	stride	strode	stridden
send	sent	sent	strike	struck	struck,
set	set	set			stricken
shake	shook	shaken	strive	strove	striven
shall	should	—	swear	swore	sworn
shear	sheared	shorn,	sweep	swept	swept
		sheared	swell	swelled	swollen,
shed	shed	shed			swelled
shine	shone	shone	swim	swam	swum
shoot	shot	shot	swing	swung	swung
show	showed	shown	take	took	taken

present	pt	pp	present	pt	pp
teach	taught	taught	weave	wove,	woven,
tear	tore	torn		weaved	weaved
tell	told	told	wed	wedded,	wedded,
think	thought	thought		wed	wed
throw	threw	thrown	weep	wept	wept
thrust	thrust	thrust	win	won	won
tread	trod	trodden	wind	wound	wound
wake	woke,	woken,	wring	wrung	wrung
	waked	waked	write	wrote	written
wear	wore	worn			